Silverlight Recipes

A Problem Solution Approach

Jit Ghosh
Rob Cameron

Silverlight Recipes: A Problem Solution Approach

ISBN-13 (pbk): 978-1-4302-2435-8

ISBN-13 (electronic): 978-1-4302-2436-5

Printed and bound in the United States of America 9 8 7 6 5 4 3 2 1

Lead Editor: Jonathan Hassell
Technical Reviewer: Ashish Ghoda
Editorial Board: Clay Andres, Steve Anglin, Mark Beckner, Ewan Buckingham, Tony Campbell, Gary Cornell, Jonathan Gennick, Michelle Lowman, Matthew Moodie, Jeffrey Pepper, Frank Pohlmann, Ben Renow-Clarke, Dominic Shakeshaft, Matt Wade, Tom Welsh
Project Manager: Anita Castro
Copy Editor: Heather Lang and Tiffany Taylor
Compositor: Lynn L'Heureux
Indexer: Julie Grady
Artist: April Milne

Distributed to the book trade worldwide by Springer-Verlag New York, Inc., 233 Spring Street, 6th Floor, New York, NY 10013. Phone 1-800-SPRINGER, fax 201-348-4505, e-mail orders-ny@springer-sbm.com, or visit http://www.springeronline.com.

For information on translations, please e-mail info@apress.com, or visit http://www.apress.com.

Apress and friends of ED books may be purchased in bulk for academic, corporate, or promotional use. eBook versions and licenses are also available for most titles. For more information, reference our Special Bulk Sales–eBook Licensing web page at http://www.apress.com/info/bulksales.

The source code for this book is available to readers at http://www.apress.com. You will need to answer questions pertaining to this book in order to successfully download the code.

For Sumona, my wife, the love of my life and the source of all my inspiration; and Pixie, the greatest kid on this planet, and the best daughter one could ever have. You are the lights of my life.

—Jit

To my beautiful and loving wife, Ally, and daughters Amanda and Anna, who bring so much joy to my life.

—Rob

Contents at a Glance

■Forword xxiv

■About the Author xxvi

■About the Technical Reviewer xxvii

■Acknowledgments xxviii

■Introduction xxix

■Chapter 1: A Quick Tour of Silverlight 3 Development 1

■Chapter 2: Application Design and Programming Model 31

■Chapter 3: Developing User Experiences 117

■Chapter 4: Data Binding 275

■Chapter 5: Controls 359

■Chapter 6: Browser Integration 515

■Chapter 7: Networking and Web Service Integration 599

■Chapter 8: Integrating Rich Media 753

■Chapter 9: Building LOB Applications 893

■Index 937

iv

Contents

■Forword xxiv

■About the Author xxvi

■About the Technical Reviewer xxvii

■Acknowledgments xxviii

■Introduction xxix

■Chapter 1: A Quick Tour of Silverlight 3 Development 1

   Getting Up to Speed with Silverlight 3 1

      Major Media Enhancements 3

      Enhanced User Experience Rendering Capabilities 4

      Rich Internet Applications and Line-of-Business Enhancements 4

      Data Support Improvements 5

      Browser Support 5

      Out-of-Browser Capabilities 5

      Silverlight and WPF 6

   1-1. Setting Up the Silverlight 3 Environment 6

      Problem 6

      Solution 6

      How It Works 7

   1-2. Installing Additional Silverlight-Related Services and Controls 7

      Problem 7

      Solution 7

      How It Works 8

   1-3. Understanding the Structure of a Silverlight Solution 8

      Problem 8

      Solution 8

      How It Works 8

The Code...9

1-4. Understanding the Developer/Designer Workflow 17

    Problem 17

    Solution 17

    How It Works 17

The Tools 17

The Process 19

1-5. Understanding the Basics of Expression Blend 3..20

    Problem 20

    Solution 20

    How It Works 20

    The Code...23

1-6. Accessing Source Control 27

    Problem 27

    Solution 27

    How It Works 27

1-7. Running Silverlight 3 on a Mac 28

    Problem 28

    Solution 28

    How It Works 28

1-8. Running Silverlight on Linux 29

    Problem 29

    Solution 29

    How It Works 29

■Chapter 2: Application Design and Programming Model................................. 31

The Mechanics of Silverlight Applications...31

2-1. Adding a Custom Class 32

    Problem 32

    Solution 32

    How It Works 32

    The Code...33

2-2. Adding a Custom Control 39

    Problem 39

    Solution 39

    How It Works 39

The Code 39

2-3. Locating a Control 42

    Problem 42

    Solution 42

    How It Works 43

    The Code 43

2-4. Dynamically Loading XAML from JavaScript 47

    Problem 47

    Solution 47

    How It Works 47

    The Code 48

2-5. Dynamically Loading XAML from Managed Code 52

    Problem 52

    Solution 52

    How It Works 52

    The Code 52

2-6. Persisting Data on the Client 54

    Problem 54

    Solution 54

    How It Works 54

    The Code 56

2-7. Opening a Local File from a Silverlight Application 61

    Problem 61

    Solution 61

    How It Works 61

    The Code 62

2-8. Accessing XML Data with an XmlReader 66

    Problem 66

    Solution 66

    How It Works 66

    The Code 66

2-9. Accessing XML Data with LINQ 69

    Problem 69

    Solution 69

    How It Works 69

The Code 70

2-10. Managing Unhandled Exceptions 74

    Problem 74

    Solution 74

    How It Works 74

2-11. Executing Work on a Background Thread with Updates 75

    Problem 75

    Solution 75

    How It Works 75

    The Code 76

2-12. Updating the UI from a Background Thread 85

    Problem 85

    Solution 85

    How It Works 86

    The Code 87

2-13. Managing XAML Resources 90

    Problem 90

    Solution 90

    How It Works 90

    The Code 91

2-14. Managing Embedded Resources 96

    Problem 96

    Solution 96

    How It Works 96

    The Code 97

2-15. Creating Silverlight Using Ruby, Python, or JScript 101

    Problem 101

    Solution 101

    How It Works 101

    The Code 102

2-16. Creating Application Services 105

    Problem 105

    Solution 105

    How It Works 105

    The Code 106

2-17. Managing Resources in Large Projects..111

Problem 111

Solution 111

How It Works 111

The Code..112

2-18. Save a File Anywhere on the User's System...114

Problem 114

Solution 114

How It Works 114

The Code..115

■Chapter 3: Developing User Experiences 117

3-1. Importing Art from Expression Design 118

Problem 118

Solution 118

How It Works 118

3-2. Working with Color and Gradients in Blend 121

Problem 121

Solution 121

How It Works 121

The Code..124

3-3. Positioning UI Elements with a Canvas 132

Problem 132

Solution 132

How It Works 132

The Code..133

3-4. Positioning UI Elements with a StackPanel..136

Problem 136

Solution 136

How It Works 136

The Code..137

3-5. Positioning UI Elements with a Grid 140

Problem 140

Solution 140

How It Works 140

The Code..142

3-6. Using Shapes to Draw..146
    Problem..146
    Solution...146
    How It Works..146

3-7. Using Paths to Draw..152
    Problem..152
    Solution...152
    How It Works..152
    The Code..153

3-8. Using Geometries to Draw 159
    Problem..159
    Solution...159
    How It Works..159
    The Code..159

3-9. Providing Scrollable Content..165
    Problem..165
    Solution...165
    How It Works..165
    The Code..165

3-10. Applying a Border to Elements...167
    Problem..167
    Solution...167
    How It Works..168
    The Code..171

3-11. Using Simple Animations with Objects 173
    Problem..173
    Solution...173
    How It Works..173
    The Code..175

3-12. Animating UI Elements with Keyframes 181
    Problem..181
    Solution...181
    How It Works..181
    The Code..184

3-13. Transforming an Object..191

Problem 191

Solution 191

How It Works 192

The Code 193

3-14. Creating a Simple Cartoon Scene 197

Problem 197

Solution 197

How It Works 197

The Code 197

3-15. Handling Keyboard Input 209

Problem 209

Solution 209

How It Works 209

The Code 210

3-16. Working with Ink 216

Problem 216

Solution 216

How It Works 216

The Code 217

3-17. Adding 3-D Effects to UI Elements 223

Problem 223

Solution 223

How It Works 223

The Code 224

3-18. Dynamically Creating Bitmaps 235

Problem 235

Solution 235

How It Works 235

The Code 235

3-19. Improving Graphic Animation and Video Performance 243

Problem 243

Solution 243

How It Works 243

The Code 243

3-20. Improve Animation with Custom Easing Functions......................................247

Problem 247

Solution 247

How It Works 247

The Code 248

3-21. Adding Pixel Shader Visual Effects 254

Problem 254

Solution 254

How It Works 254

The Code 255

3-22. Create and Work with Design-Time Data in Expression Blend 259

Problem 259

Solution 259

How It Works 259

The Code 262

3-23. Reuse Application Interactivity with Behaviors 270

Problem 270

Solution 270

How It Works 270

The Code 270

3-24. Prototype Application Design 272

Problem 272

Solution 272

How It Works 272

The Code 272

■Chapter 4: Data Binding 275

4-1. Binding Application Data to the UI 275

Problem 275

Solution 275

How It Works 275

Binding Expression 276

Dependency Properties 276

Associating the Data Source 276

The Code 277

4-2. Binding Using a DataTemplate 283

Problem 283

Solution 283

How It Works 284

Declaring a DataTemplate 284

Using a DataTemplate 285

The Code 286

4-3. Receiving Change Notifications for Bound Data 291

Problem 291

Solution 291

How It Works 291

Change Notification for Noncollection Types 291

Change Notification for Collection Types..293

The Code 293

4-4. Converting Values During Data Binding 309

Problem 309

Solution 309

How It Works 309

Implementing Value Conversion 310

The Code 311

4-5. Binding Across Elements 323

Problem 323

Solution 323

How It Works 323

Binding to Another Element...323

Binding to Self 323

Binding to the TemplatedParent 324

The Code 324

4-6. Validating Input for Bound Data 331

Problem 331

Solution 331

How It Works 331

Validation Error Notification..331

Getting Error Information 331

Getting a Validation Error Summary 332

The Code 332

4-7. Controlling Updates...347

Problem 347

Solution 347

How It Works 347

The Code 348

■Chapter 5: Controls 359

A Word About the Samples 360

5-1. Customizing a Control's Basic Appearance 360

Problem 360

Solution 360

How It Works 360

Style Scoping 361

The Code 362

5-2. Replacing the Default UI of a Control 364

Problem 364

Solution 364

How It Works 364

Control Template Syntax 364

Setting the Template 364

Using Expression Blend to Design a Template 365

Template Bindings 367

Content Model and Presenter Controls 368

Visual State Management 370

The Code 375

5-3. Customizing the Default ListBoxItem UI 381

Problem 381

Solution 381

How It Works 381

The Code 381

5-4. Displaying Information in a Pop-up 390

Problem 390

Solution 390

How It Works 390

Creating and Initializing the Pop-up 390

Positioning the Pop-up 391

Creating Pop-up Content 392

The Code 392

5-5. Displaying Row Details in a DataGrid 402

    Problem 402

    Solution 402

    How It Works 402

    The Code 403

5-6. Applying Custom Templates to a DataGrid Cell 412

    Problem 412

    Solution 412

    How It Works 412

    The Code 412

5-7. Creating Custom Column Types for a DataGrid 418

    Problem 418

    Solution 418

    How It Works 419

The GenerateElement() Method 419

The GenerateEditingElement() Method 419

The PrepareCellForEdit() Method 420

The CancelCellEdit() Method 420

    The Code 420

5-8. Creating a Composite User Control 425

    Problem 425

    Solution 425

    How It Works 425

User Control Structure 426

XAML Loading 427

Dependency Properties 428

    The Code 430

5-9. Creating a Custom Layout Container 439

    Problem 439

    Solution 439

    How It Works 440

Motivation and Mechanics 440

The MeasureOverride() Method 440

The ArrangeOverride() Method 441

The Code 441

Using the WrapPanel 447

5-10. Creating a Custom Control 453

    Problem 453

    Solution 453

    How It Works 453

Custom Control Structure 453

TemplateBinding vs. RelativeSource Binding to TemplatedParent 456

    The Code 456

Using the Control 461

5-11. Defining a Custom Visual State 470

    Problem 470

    Solution 470

    How It Works 470

    The Code 471

5-12. Controlling ScrollViewer Scroll Behavior 482

    Problem 482

    Solution 482

    How It Works 482

The VisualTreeHelper class 483

    The Code 483

5-13. Customizing the Binding Validation User Interface 492

    Problem 492

    Solution 492

    How It Works 492

Validation Error Tooltip 493

The ValidationSummary Control 497

    The Code 498

5-14. Control Behavior in Expression Blend 507

    Problem 507

    Solution 507

    How It Works 508

Property Attributes 508

    CategoryAttribute 508

    DescriptionAttribute 509

EditorBrowsableAttribute 509
Designer-Unsafe Code..510
Including Sample Data..511
   The Code...512
■Chapter 6: Browser Integration 515
  6-1. Hosting Silverlight in HTML on Any Platform 515
   Problem 515
   Solution 515
   How It Works 516
   The Code...518
  6-2. Hosting Silverlight in ASP.NET 520
   Problem 520
   Solution 520
   How It Works 520
   The Code...521
  6-3. Setting Focus for Keyboard Input...521
   Problem 521
   Solution 521
   How It Works 521
   The Code...521
  6-4. Implementing a Full-Screen UI...528
   Problem 528
   Solution 528
   How It Works 528
   The Code...530
  6-5. Calling a JavaScript Method from Managed Code 537
   Problem 537
   Solution 537
   How It Works 537
   The Code...539
  6-6. Calling a Managed Code Method from JavaScript 546
   Problem 546
   Solution 546
   How It Works 546
   The Code...548

6-7. Exchanging Data Among Multiple Plug-ins 560
    Problem 560
    Solution 560
    How It Works 561
    The Code 561

6-8. Embedding Silverlight Within a Windows Gadget 567
    Problem 567
    Solution 567
    How It Works 567
    The Code 573

6-9. Embed Silverlight in an Internet Explorer 8 Web Slice 583
    Problem 583
    Solution 583
    How It Works 584
    The Code 584

6-10. Take Advantage of the Navigation Framework 588
    Problem 588
    Solution 588
    How It Works 589
    The Code 591

■Chapter 7: Networking and Web Service Integration 599

A Quick Word about the Samples 600

7-1. Consuming a WCF Service 601
    Problem 601
    Solution 601
    How It Works 601

Invoking a Service Operation 603

Configuring a WCF Service for Silverlight 604
    The Code 605

7-2. Exchanging XML Messages over HTTP 623
    Problem 623
    Solution 623
    How It Works 623

Using HttpWebRequest/HttpWebResponse in Silverlight 623
    Using GET 624

Using POST 624

Handling Asynchronous Invocation 624

Configuring WCF to Use Non-SOAP Endpoints...624

The Code 625

7-3. Using JSON Serialization over HTTP 635

Problem 635

Solution 635

How It Works 636

JSON...636

Using the DataContractJsonSerializer Type 637

Configuring WCF to Use JSON 637

The Code 637

7-4. Accessing Resources over HTTP...641

Problem 641

Solution 641

How It Works 641

Downloading/Uploading Resources...641

Reading/Writing Remote Streams 642

WebClient and HTTP Endpoints 642

Canceling Long-Running Operations 642

The Code 642

7-5. Using Sockets to Communicate over TCP 667

Problem 667

Solution 667

How It Works 667

The Sockets API in Silverlight..667

Cross-Domain Policy and Port Requirements..670

The Code 670

Running the Sample Code 670

The Client..671

The Chat Server 690

The Policy Server 697

7-6. Enabling Cross-Domain Access 700

Problem 700

Solution 700

How It Works 700

The Code 702

7-7. 704

Problem 704

Solution 704

How It Works 704

Preparing the Application 704

Installing the Application 707

Customizing the Installation Flow 708

Sensing Network Availability 710

Updating Locally Installed Applications 710

The Code 711

7-8. Exchanging Data Between Silverlight Applications 732

Problem 732

Solution 733

How It Works 733

Receiver Registration 733

Receiving Messages 734

Sending Messages 734

Request-Response 735

The Code 736

■Chapter 8: Integrating Rich Media 753

8-1. Adding Video to a Page 753

Problem 753

Solution 753

How It Works 754

Using MediaElement 754

VideoBrush 754

The Code 757

8-2. Creating a Complete Video Player 758

Problem 758

Solution 758

How It Works 758

Acquiring Media 759

Controlling Media Play 759

MediaElement States...760

Seeking Within the Media..760

Volume...761

    The Code..761

Installing the Sample Code..761

The Player Code..763

The MediaSlider Custom Control 775

The MediaButtonsPanel Custom Control 785

8-3. Adding Streaming Media Support..790

    Problem 790

    Solution 790

    How It Works 790

Network Considerations 790

Windows Media Services 791

Setting Up WMS 2008...791

Setting Up Publishing Points 793

    The Code..796

Changes to the Player...797

8-4. Using Playlists to Package Media 831

    Problem 831

    Solution 831

    How It Works 831

Server-Side Playlists 832

Client-Side Playlists..834

    The Code..835

8-5. Using Markers to Display Timed Content..837

    Problem 837

    Solution 837

    How It Works 837

Encoding Markers Using Expression Encoder 3 837

MediaElement and Markers...839

    The Code..839

8-6. Displaying and Seeking Using SMPTE Timecodes 854

    Problem 854

    Solution 854

How It Works 854

Frame Rate 854

Timecodes 855

Timecodes and Silverlight 855

The Code 856

8-7. Building a Managed Decoder for Silverlight 868

Problem 868

Solution 868

How It Works 868

Silverlight, Containers, and Codecs 869

MediaStreamSource 869

Initializing the Media Stream 870

Sampling 872

Stream Switching 873

Seeking 873

The Code 874

The Recorder 874

The Custom MediaStreamSource 882

■Chapter 9: Building LOB Applications 893

9-1. Creating a LOB Application Framework 894

Problem 894

Solution 894

How It Works 894

The Code 895

9-2. Adding Data to a LOB Application 906

Problem 906

Solution 906

How It Works 906

The Code 907

9-3. Adding Advanced LOB Data Access with Data-Form Support 915

Problem 915

Solution 915

How It Works 915

The Code 916

9-4. Adding Support for Data Validation 924

Problem 924

Solution 924

How It Works 924

The Code..925

9-5. Adding .NET RIA Services to an Existing Application 930

Problem 930

Solution 930

How It Works 930

The Code..931

9-6. Using the .NET RIA Services Class Library to Isolate Services........................933

Problem 933

Solution 933

How It Works 933

The Code..933

■Index 937

Foreword

Being asked to write a foreword for a book is like being asked to be the best man or maid of honor in a wedding. You participate with the intention to support and to represent the curators of a new entity (in this case, a book) with pride and integrity. You also have to be genuine or the "crowd" will see right through you.

For the past 10 years I have worked at Microsoft, helping build products, marketing new initiatives, and most important, evangelizing. During my tenure in Microsoft's Developer and Platform Evangelism team, I have had the great pleasure to work with some of the brightest, connected, realistic, and passionate technologists. Jit Ghosh and Rob Cameron are from this camp and they are what make this book unique.

Purchasing decisions are made for lots of reasons, but most of the time it comes down to true value and trust. In other words, do you trust the brand? Do you trust the builder? Do you trust the author? Can you find something else of greater value? How do you quantify the value? The last question is tricky when you are selecting a book on emerging technologies, in this case Silverlight. A book can be useless even before the ink dries, yet other books become classics, impervious to time. This is where authors play the most important role; they can bring immeasurable value to a subject because of their experience and perspective. Sure, Jit and Rob know Silverlight—they have it down cold—but what they really bring to the table is years of experience and perspective working directly with customers and helping them adopt Microsoft technologies.

The authors have peppered this text with links to Microsoft Knowledge Base articles, they bridge the chasm of Windows Presentation Foundation (WPF) to Silverlight, and they highlight the subtleties—after all, nine times out of ten, it's the edge case that catches us when tackling something new. Most important, they use a classic problem-solution pattern to educate the reader. For me, this is the best way to learn. The .NET Framework, WPF, and Silverlight each contain hundreds of APIs. The task of connecting the dots can be daunting—especially when you are pressed for time. The problem-solution pattern helps make learning more digestible. Jit and Rob use a "recipe" metaphor to tie the problem-solution concept together. The real value here is that they know exactly what to "serve." Another interesting aspect of this book is the style and tone of the writing. The book has an easy-to-read, cause-and-effect style that helps you move through content in an efficient manner.

I've had the opportunity to work with the authors on numerous occasions. They work "in the field"—they are the first contact points with our customers. Jit and Rob shoulder the responsibility every day to guide our customers in the right direction, to drive our product groups to make informed decisions, and to evangelize with pragmatism.

This book represents an extension of Jit and Rob's passion to spread the word, to share their experiences from the field, to pass along the lessons they have learned. At Microsoft we have many opportunities to connect with communities of developers and designers; blogs, events, whitepapers, partner conventions—communicating is part of our DNA, especially on the Evangelism team. A book, however, has a unique gravity that is hard to explain. Many people want to write books, but few follow through on their desires. A blog entry is one thing, but a book has a whole different dimension of responsibility. Those who are successful are motivated by seeing the value in a broader collection of ideas brought together in an actionable, valuable set of guidance.

Jit and Rob picked a terrific time to write a book on Silverlight. We are now at the forefront of a new era on interactivity on the Web. Silverlight is a galvanizer designed to bring together Microsoft's client platform technologies, services initiative, and web technologies to drive the next wave of media experiences and rich Internet applications. Silverlight 3 is ready for prime time, and this book represents the roadmap to help you build the right application. I hope you find this book helpful in your endeavors to reach your goals in the next web space. Go shape the future.

Sincerely,
Eric Schmidt
Director of Media and Monetization Evangelism
Microsoft Corporation

About the Author

Jit Ghosh is an Industry Architect with the Developer Platform Evangelism team at Microsoft, working on digital media solutions. Jit has over 16 years of solutions architecture and software engineering experience. In the last few years he has focused on broadcast, digital content publishing, and advertising space. You can read more about Jit's current work at `http://blogs.msdn.com/jitghosh`.

Employed by Microsoft since 2001, **Rob Cameron** is an Evangelist with Microsoft Corporation and is based out of Atlanta, Georgia. As part of Microsoft's Communication Sector Developer & Platform Evangelism team, Rob focuses on development tools and technologies, from the server to the mobile device for telecommunications, cable, media and entertainment, and hosting companies. Rob coauthored (along with Dale Michalk) *Building ASP.NET Server Controls* (Apress, 2003), wrote the operations chapter for *Pro BizTalk 2006*, (Apress, 2006) and recently completed another book with Dale Michalk titled *Pro ASP.NET 3.5 Server Controls and AJAX Components* (Apress, 2008). He has a master's degree in information technology management and a bachelor's degree in computer science. Visit Rob's blog at `http://blogs.msdn.com/RobCamer`.

About the Technical Reviewer

 Awarded with British Computer Society (BCS) Fellowship, **Ashish Ghoda** is a customer-focused and business values–driven senior IT executive with more than 12 years of IT leadership, technical and financial management, and enterprise architect experience.

He is founder and president of Technology Opinion LLC, a unique collaborative venture striving for strategic excellence by providing partnerships with different organizations and the IT community. He is also the associate director at a Big Four accounting firm.

He provides strategic advice to achieve IT goals and to define product and technology road maps of organizations. He also provides training in and speaks on IT leadership areas and Microsoft technologies, and architects and develops customer-centric software services.

As an accomplished author, Ashish authored *Accelerated Silverlight 3 (Apress, April 2009)* and *Pro Silveright for the Enterprise (Apress, June 2009)* books from Apress and several articles on Microsoft technologies and IT management areas for *MSDN Magazine, TechnologyOpinion.com*, and *advice.cio.com*. He also reviews research papers submitted for the Innovative and Collaborative Business and E-Business Tracks of the European Conference on Information System (ECIS).

Ashish has a Master's degree in Information Systems from New Jersey Institute of Technology (NJIT) and is Microsoft Certified Application Developer (MCAD).

Acknowledgments

Writing a book is a long and incredible journey that requires the support and care of a lot of individuals. The authors would like to acknowledge the help and support from some amazing people without whose direct or indirect involvement this book would never have come into being:

Scott Guthrie, Kevin Gallo, Joe Stegman, and members of the Silverlight product team for envisioning and creating an amazing technology that we have become thoroughly addicted to

Our manager, Harry Mower, and Carlos McKinley, Director Communications Sector DPE for supporting us during this effort and for always encouraging our passion for technology

Joe Stegman, Mike Harsh, Ashish Shetty, Dave Relyea, David Anson, Scott Boehmer, Ben Waggoner, Christian Schormann, Charles Finkelstein, and many other product team members who have been exceptionally patient and forthcoming in answering all of our technical questions

Christopher Carper and Eric Schmidt, for involving us in projects that have helped grow our expertise in Silverlight over the past couple of years

Apress is a great company to work for as an author, as evidenced by their care and feeding in getting this book into production. Thanks to Ewan Buckingham for having faith in this book. A heartfelt thanks to Anita Castro and Heather Lang for stewarding this book to completion and for being patient in light of the slipped schedules and author changes. Thanks to the editing and production folks from Apress—copy editor Liz Welch and production editor Janet Vail, and the others who we don't know by name but whose efforts helped make this book possible. We would also like to thank Ashish Ghoda, who reviewed the book and provided great feedback.

From Jit: I would also like to thank my family, especially my wonderful wife Sumona for being the force behind everything I have ever achieved and for making me believe in myself; and my beautiful daughter Pixie for being patient when Daddy could not make time and for never forgetting the daily dose of hugs and kisses. And lastly, a huge thanks to Rob Cameron for agreeing to work with me on this book, for sharing his insight on authoring, and for his technical acumen—without Rob, this book would have remained a dream.

From Rob: I would like to thank my family—especially my lovely wife Ally for her dedication to our family and for encouraging me to reach for new heights. I would also like to thank my mom and grandparents. Without their love and assistance, I may never have found my passion for computers and programming. I would also like to thank Jit Ghosh for being a fantastic coauthor on this gigantic effort.

Introduction

Silverlight Tools for Visual Studio 2008, Visual Studio 2008, and Microsoft Expression Blend 3 give you the power to design innovative and powerful Silverlight 3 user interfaces. They give you access to cutting-edge graphics, animation, rich controls, and data binding in the powerful XML Application Markup Language (XAML) declarative language. For application logic, you can continue to use all the usual Visual Studio 2008 features such as debugging and access to your favorite development language, like C# or VB, and dynamic languages such as IronPython, IronRuby, and Managed JScript. What is truly amazing is that the breadth of the .NET Framework 3.5, including functionality such as multithreading, generics, LINQ, and extension methods, is included in such a diminutively sized browser plug-in.

While rich Internet application (RIA) development tools have been around for a while, Silverlight 3 makes RIA development real for traditional developers letting them use their favorite tools and programming languages to create fabulous user experiences. This book builds on the previous version that covered Silverlight 2, with many recipes updated to reflect any chances or enhancements in Silverlight 3. In addition, 28 recipes were added to this edition to cover new features only available in Silverlight 3. There is also a new chapter on .NET RIA Services. Here is a quick summary:

Chapter 2
2.16 Creating Application Services
2.17 Managing Resources in Large Projects
2.18 Save a File Anywhere on the Users System

Chapter 3
3-17 Adding 3-D Effects to UE Elements
3-18 Dynamically Creating Bitmaps
3-19 Improving Graphic Animation and Video Performance
3-20 Improve Animation with Custom Easing Functions
3-21 Adding Pixel Shader Visual Effects
3-22 Create and Work with Design-Time Data in Expression Blend
3-23 Reuse Application Interactivity with Expression Blend Behaviors
3-24 Prototype Application Design with Sketchflow

Chapter 4
4-5. Binding Across Elements
4-6. Validating Input for Bound Data
4-7. Controlling Updates

Chapter 5
5-12. Controlling ScrollViewer Scroll Behavior
5-13. Customizing the Binding Validation User Interface
5-14. Control Behavior in Expression blend

Chapter 6
6-9 Embed Silverlight in an Internet Explorer 8 Web Slice
6-10 Take Advantage of the Navigation Framework

Chapter 7
7-7. Installing an application locally
7-8. Exchanging Data between Silverlight Applications

Chapter 8
8-6. Displaying and Seeking using SMPTE Timecodes
8-7. Building a managed decoder for Silverlight

Chapter 9
9-1 Create a LOB Application Framework
9-2 Add Data to a LOB Application
9-3 Add Advanced LOB Data Access with Data Form Support
9-4 Add Support for Data Validation
9-5 Add .NET RIA Services to an Existing Silverlight App

As you can see, this book is more than a minor update!

Who This Book Is For

If you are a web application developer looking for ways to create rich, interactive, and immersive browser-hosted applications using Microsoft Silverlight and .NET, then this book will give you the information you need on the core concepts and techniques fundamental to Silverlight-based development. Even if you did not have Silverlight in mind, the book will help you see the possibilities and understand what you can (and in some cases can't) achieve with the technology.

Having an understanding of the .NET Framework will help, but if you are an experienced developer new to the .NET Framework, you will still be able to learn Silverlight 3 using this book because much of the development is in the XAML markup language as well as in code.

■ Note   You still may want to grab a programming in C# text such as Christian Gross's *Beginning C# 2008: From Novice to Professional, Second Edition* (Apress, 2008) if you are not confident with C#.

If you are a Windows Presentation Foundation (WPF) developer, this book will help you understand how to work with Silverlight 3, which uses the same markup language but is a subset of WPF functionality packaged in a cross-browser and cross-platform plug-in.

The example code in this book is written in C#. However, much of the development is in the XAML, not in C#, so if you are a VB.NET developer, the markup is almost exactly the same. For the examples that do include C# code in the code-behind, the code translates pretty easily, as the .NET Framework 3.5 for Silverlight is language agnostic.

If you are a developer in need of learning a particular technique, this book is for you as it is task driven in Apress's recipe format. Each major facet of Silverlight 3 development is presented with a description of the topic in the form of a problem statement, a "How It Works" section, and a section that walks through the recipe sample code.

How This Book Is Structured

This book consists of chapters that focus on individual topic areas of Silverlight. Each chapter attempts to address core concepts and techniques as individual recipes in that topic area. Chapters 1, 2, and 3 are primarily intended to help you grasp the fundamental concepts of Silverlight, including a quick tour of the developer tools, the Silverlight programming model, and XAML-based UI development. Many of these concepts are critical to understanding the later chapters, so we advise you to start the book by reading these chapters first. Chapters 4 through 8 address the topics of data binding, control customization, and development; browser integration; networking and web services; and rich media integration.

Prerequisites

You will need a version of Visual Studio 2008, with Service Pack 1 of Visual Studio 2008 applied. You will also need to install Silverlight 3 Tools for Visual Studio 2008 Service Pack 1. You can use any version of Visual Studio 2008, and you can download the free version of Visual Studio 2008 Express edition here:

http://www.microsoft.com/express/vcsharp/Default.aspx

You can get the Silverlight tools from http://silverlight.net/GetStarted/, and you can download a trial version of Expression Blend 3 from http://www.microsoft.com/Expression. If you are an MSDN Subscriber, you can also download it from subscriber downloads. You will also need to apply Service Pack 1 to Expression Blend 3.

Some of the recipes in this book use a SQL Server Express 2008 database. You can download SQL Server Express 2008 for free from http://www.microsoft.com/express/sql/. For some of the recipes in Chapter 8, you may need a video encoder. You can download a trial version of Microsoft Expression Encoder from http://www.microsoft.com/Expression.

Downloading the Code

The code is available in zip file format in the Source Code/Download section of the Apress web site. Please review the readme.txt for setup instructions.

Contacting the Authors

To reach the authors, please go to their blogs and click the Email link to send them an email.

Jit Ghosh: http://blogs.msdn.com/jitghosh
Rob Cameron: http://blogs.msdn.com/RobCamer

CHAPTER 1

■ ■ ■

A Quick Tour of Silverlight 3 Development

This is a recipes book, which means it is prescriptive, targeting specific scenarios that developers are likely to encounter. You don't have to read the chapters in order, though we did put some thought into chapter organization for readers who want to proceed that way. Silverlight is now on its third version, adding amazing new features sure to please developers and designers alike. Still, some developers and designers may be relatively new to Silverlight, and if you're among those folks, this chapter may be essential to help you get started. Otherwise, it's likely to be a helpful review.

In our first recipe, we cover setting up the development and designer environment, and in the subsequent recipes, we expand on the capabilities each tool provides. The recipe format follows this outline:

- *Title*: Description of the recipe

- *Problem*: The challenge that the recipe solves

- *Solution*: A short description of the approach

- *How It Works*: Detailed explanation on the approach

- *The Code*: An implementation of the described approach to solve the problem

Getting Up to Speed with Silverlight 3

Silverlight is Microsoft's cross-browser, cross-platform, and cross-device plug-in for delivering the next generation of .NET Framework–based rich interactive applications for the Web. Silverlight runs on Windows in Internet Explorer 6 or higher, Mozilla Firefox, and Chrome build 1251 and higher. Silverlight also runs on the Apple Mac in both Safari and Firefox, as well as on Linux in Firefox as part of the Moonlight project (http://www.mono-project.com/Moonlight). Moonlight is a collaboration project between Novell and Microsoft to bring Silverlight to Linux.

Figure 1-1 shows a Silverlight application running in Firefox.

Figure 1-1. *Firefox running a Silverlight 3 application*

Because Silverlight is a browser plug-in, the user is prompted to install the plug-in if it is not already present, which is the same behavior as similar technologies like Adobe Flash. Once the plug-in is installed, which takes about ten seconds on most Internet connections, Silverlight content can be downloaded and run.

Because Silverlight is client-side technology, Silverlight content can be hosted on any backend system—just as any other web-based content such as HTML pages and JavaScript can be hosted from a Windows server, a Linux server, or any other web-serving technology.

Microsoft announced Silverlight for Windows Mobile at the MIX '08 conference. At the same time, Nokia announced plans to port Silverlight on Symbian as well, substantially extending the reach of Silverlight for mobile devices. No official dates have been announced for Silverlight for mobile.

You may be asking, "Did Microsoft port the .NET Framework to additional platforms?" The answer is both "yes" and "no." The full desktop and server versions of the .NET Framework runtime has not been ported to other platforms. However, the product team did encapsulate a tiny common language runtime (CLR) into the plug-in and made it cross-browser as well as cross-platform.

What makes Silverlight so compelling is that much of the power and programmability of the .NET Framework is available within a relatively small 4.7-MB plug-in on Windows. Here is a summary of some your favorite .NET Framework namespaces available in Silverlight 2 and Silverlight 3:

- `System`
- `System.Collections`
- `System.Collections.Generic`
- `System.Diagnostics`
- `System.Globalization`
- `System.IO`
- `System.Linq`
- `System.NET`
- `System.Reflection`
- `System.Runtime`
- `System.Security`
- `System.ServiceModel`
- `System.Text`
- `System.Windows`
- `System.XML`

As you can see, Silverlight 2 packed a powerful .NET Framework base class library that continues to be available in Silverlight 3. However, Silverlight 3 builds on top of it by introducing more than 50 new features, including support for running Silverlight applications out of the browser and dramatic video performance and quality improvements, as well as features that improve developer productivity. Some of the highlights are the following:

- Major media enhancements like H.264 video support
- Out-of-browser support, which allows web applications to run offline
- Significant graphics improvements including 3-D graphics support and graphics processing unit (GPU) acceleration
- Improved developer and designer tools including a full editable and interactive designer for Silverlight that will be available in Visual Studio 2010 when it ships

Major Media Enhancements

Media support has been dramatically enhanced, including improved streaming capabilities in the Internet Information Services (IIS) Media Services extension called Smooth Streaming with support for live and on-demand true HD (720p or better playback. Smooth Streaming dynamically detects and seamlessly switches the video quality media based on local bandwidth and CPU conditions. Silverlight 3 also includes true HD playback when viewing content in full-screen mode utilizing GPU acceleration at 720p+.

Silverlight 1 and 2 provided support for VC-1 and the WMA formats. Silverlight 3 offers native support for MPEG-4 based H.264/Advanced Audio Coding (AAC) audio, enabling content distributors to deliver HD content to all supported platforms. In addition, Silverlight 3 supports a new raw AV pipeline that can be extended to provide support for a wide variety of third-party codecs. This allows audio and video content to be decoded outside of the runtime environment.

Silverlight 3 includes built-in support for Digital Rights Management (DRM) powered by PlayReady Content Protection enabling in-browser DRM using Advanced Encryption Standard (AES) or Windows Media DRM.

Enhanced User Experience Rendering Capabilities

The product team has worked to enhance programmability for rich user experiences in Silverlight 3 including new 3-D graphics, animation features, hardware-accelerated effects, and text improvements.

With bitmap caching, Silverlight 3 greatly improves rendering performance by allowing users to cache vector content, text, and controls into bitmaps. This allows background content that needs to scale but does not change internally to be cached for better performance. There is also a new Bitmap API that allows developers to write pixels to a bitmap, allowing developers to edit scanned documents or photos in addition to creating special effects for cached bitmaps from elements displayed on the screen.

With support for perspective 3-D graphics, developers are no longer limited to simulated 3-D in a 2-D plane. You can now rotate or scale live content in space without having to author additional code.

Shaders are computer programs that execute on the GPU. Shaders have been an important part of game development for years. Windows Presentation Foundation (WPF) added support for Pixel Shader effects in .NET Framework 3.5. SP1. Shader support is added in Silverlight 3 and allows developers to incorporate amazing effects with relatively little effort.

Improved animation effects in Silverlight 3 help make animation more natural in appearance. Examples are spring and bounce, but you can also provide you own mathematical function to describe animation. Silverlight 3 also provides much more efficient support for font rendering and text animation, also taking advantage of local fonts.

Support for application themes and control skinning are also incorporated in Silverlight 3. Styles can be applied applicationwide and can build on each other or be combined; you also have the ability to dynamically change styles at runtime. Controls can be more easily skinned and maintained outside of an application for easy sharing between applications.

Rich Internet Applications and Line-of-Business Enhancements

Silverlight 3 adds an amazing range of new controls packaged with full source code, which in itself is a huge learning resource. Silverlight 3 includes over 60 fully skinnable, customizable, and ready-to-use controls in the following categories:

- Charting and media

- Layout containers such as DockPanel and Viewbox

- A dialog to easily write files for offline support

- Support for multipage applications with built in navigation

- New controls like AutoCompleteBox, TreeView, DataForm, and DataPager

The controls come with seven professionally designed themes available at the Expression Gallery at http://gallery.expression.microsoft.com/en-us/. The controls also ship with full source code for review and modification.

One of the most important additions to Silverlight for line-of-business (LOB) applications is the .NET RIA Services platform that provides near automatic support for *n*-tier data applications.

■**Note** RIA Services is in Community Technology Preview (CTP) when Silverlight 3 released. However, based on user feedback, Microsoft has removed production restrictions typical with a CTP. Therefore, you are free to use RIA Services in you applications, but this CTP does not have the typical official "go live" license with support. More information can be found at http://timheuer.com/blog/archive/2009/06/09/ria-services-roadmap-updated.aspx.

.NET RIA Services makes it very easy to load, sort, filter, page, and edit data loaded from a server-side data source in Silverlight 3.

Data Support Improvements

Beyond additional controls, Silverlight 3 improves data support with the ability to bind data between elements without having to write additional code. As an example, the zoom level for the new Bing Maps for Enterprise Silverlight control can databind to the value property of a Slider control without writing C# code.

The new DataForm control can databind to a record or object and automatically create nested controls databound to individual fields of a database record or object properties. For two-way datasources, the DataForm can provide automatically generated edit support.

Silverlight 3 adds support for data validation that will automatically catch incorrect values and warn the application user with the built-in validation controls.

Browser Support

Browser support is enhanced with the new navigation application model that allows book marking of pages within a Silverlight 3 application. Pages are created individually by inheriting from System.Windows.Controls.Page, instead of UserControl, but are hosted within a UserControl element.

Silverlight 3 solves search engine optimization (SEO) challenges by utilizing business objects on the server combined with ASP.NET and site maps to automatically mirror database-driven RIA content into HTML that is easily indexed by Internet search engines.

Out-of-Browser Capabilities

The new out-of-browser experience available in Silverlight 3 allows end users the ability to add Silverlight 3 applications to their local desktop without having to download an additional runtime or browser plug-in; the application can even be accessed when the user is not connected to the Internet. Internet connectivity is automatically detected, and applications can react intelligently to cache a user's data until the Internet connection is restored.

Out-of-browser support includes the ability to add a link to the application on the desktop or Start menu, enabling one-click access. Because offline Silverlight 3 applications are stored in the browser's local isolated cache and run within a sandbox, additional user privileges are not required to run the application.

Application maintenance is easy with the automatic update functionality built into the out-of-browser Silverlight support. When a user launches an out-of-browser Silverlight application, Silverlight automatically checks for new versions on the server and will update automatically if an update is found.

For a full list of new features in Silverlight, please check out this web site: `http://silverlight.net/GetStarted/overview.aspx`.

Silverlight and WPF

From an application user interface (UI) development perspective, Silverlight 3 is most similar to WPF. If you understand WPF, you pretty much will understand how to build UIs in Silverlight. In fact, Silverlight is a subset of WPF. Likewise, learning Silverlight also provides skills for creating WPF applications when needed, for example, in scenarios where full access to the underlying hardware or full 3-D programming support is required.

In case you are not familiar with WPF, it is the new desktop application framework introduced in the .NET Framework 3.0 that runs on top of DirectX, providing it with capabilities for building rich dynamic desktop applications. WPF can run inside a browser as an Extensible Application Markup Language (XAML) browser application. XAML browser applications (XBAPs) will run in Firefox or Internet Explorer but only on Windows because WPF requires the full desktop framework.

Both Silverlight 3 and WPF are coded in XAML with a code-behind file, which allows for interesting scenarios of sharing UI code between a desktop application and cross-platform browser application as long as you build to the Silverlight 3 programming model. Silverlight 3 is a rich subset of WPF, but not all capabilities in WPF are implemented in Silverlight 3.

Silverlight 3 can be coded with Notepad and the software development kit (SDK), but it might not be the most productive development effort. We don't see a big market for Silverlight 3 Notepad development, so we are going to spend most of our time with two tools: Visual Studio 2008 Service Pack 1 and Expression Blend 3.

Visual Studio 2008 provides XAML and source code editing with excellent IntelliSense and debugging support. Expression Blend 3 targets designers, though developers will find it useful as well; it provides a visual design surface for Silverlight 3 UI development.

■**Note** Silverlight 3 support will be enhanced in Visual Studio 2010 with a fully interactive and editable designer similar to what is available for WPF.

1-1. Setting Up the Silverlight 3 Environment

Problem

You need to set up a Silverlight 3 development and designer environment.

Solution

Uninstall any previous versions of Silverlight 1, Silverlight 2, Silverlight 3 beta tools, runtime, and Expression Blend 3 beta that are installed. Install Silverlight 3 Tools and SDK, Visual Studio 2008 SP1, and Expression Blend 3 following the latest installation guidance at http://Silverlight.net

How It Works

The steps listed at `http://Silverlight.net/GetStarted` cover the details, but the first step is to install a version of Visual Studio 2008 with Service Pack 1.

■**Note** Silverlight 3 is supported on Visual Studio 2008 Express SP1.

At `http://Silverlight.net/GetStarted`, you can obtain ilverlight Tools for Visual Studio 2008 SP1, which includes the runtime (if not already installed), the project templates, debugging support, the SDK, and documentation files.

Install the Silverlight Tools to enable development of Silverlight 3 in Visual Studio 2008. The installation will want you to close any conflicting application such as Internet Explorer; otherwise, a reboot may be required.

At the same URL, another tool is available called Deep Zoom Composer. This tool allows developers to prepare images for use with the Deep Zoom feature in Silverlight 3. Deep Zoom allows users to explore collections of super-high-resolution imagery, from a 2- or 3-megapixel shot from a digital camera to gigapixel scans of museum pieces, all without waiting for huge file downloads. The simple zooming interface allows users to explore entire collections down to specific details in extreme close-up, all with fantastic performance and smooth transitions. A great implementation of the Deep Zoom is the Hard Rock Café web site, where users can get up close to their huge collection of memorabilia. Here is the site's URL: `http://memorabilia.hardrock.com/`.

The next step is to install Expression Blend 3. This is an important tool in the application creation arsenal that is part of the Expression Studio product line. If you are a Microsoft Developer Network (MSDN) Premium subscriber, you can obtain Expression Blend from MSDN downloads. If you are not an MSDN Premier subscriber, you can download a trial version at `http://www.microsoft.com/expression/try-it/Default.aspx`. As noted earlier, Silverlight 3 and Expression Blend 3released to manufacturing (RTM)July 2009. Even as a developer, you will want to have Expression Blend 3 installed along with Visual Studio 2008. If developers keep their source code in Microsoft Team Foundation Server, the designer will be able to check out and check in code directly with the enhanced features of Expression Blend 3, which includes support for accessing source code control directly.

1-2. Installing Additional Silverlight-Related Services and Controls

Problem

You want to be able to take advantage of the additional services and controls available to Silverlight 3 developers such as .NET RIA Services, the Silverlight Toolkit, and Bing Maps for Enterprise Silverlight control.

Solution

Download and install .NET RIA Services, the Silverlight 3 Toolkit, and the Bing Maps for Enterprise Silverlight control.

How It Works

The Silverlight Toolkit is a collection of Silverlight controls, components, and utilities made available separate from the normal Silverlight release cycle. The toolkit adds new functionality for designers and developers. It includes full source code, unit tests, samples and documentation for many new controls covering charting, styling, layout, and user input. It also provides an opportunity for the community to provide feedback. The Silverlight Toolkit can be obtained at http://www.codeplex.com/Silverlight.

.NET RIA Services is a framework that provides a pattern for creating middle-tier and client-side classes to provide access to data. It takes a model-driven approach that starts with an ADO.NET Entity Framework model. A domain service is created based on the Entity Framework model that allows the developer to add custom operations and logic to interact with the model. .NET RIA Services then generates client-side access code that combined with custom controls allows you to easily create data-driven applications in Silverlight 3. Here is a link to download the Microsoft .NET RIA Services July CTP release: http://www.microsoft.com/downloads/details.aspx?FamilyID=76bb3a07-3846-4564-b0c3-27972bcaabce&displaylang=en.

■**Note** Please check to Microsoft's site for CTP updates as they become available.

The Bing Maps for Enterprise Silverlight control provides a native Silverlight control that provides very smooth panning and zooming functionality. It supports all the things you would expect from a Bing Maps control, such as street view, aerial view, layers, icons, and overlays, providing a very powerful way to display geospatially referenced data within the Silverlight rich presentation framework. The Bing Maps for Enterprise Silverlight control can be downloaded here (after registering): http://connect.microsoft.com/silverlightmapcontrolctp.

1-3. Understanding the Structure of a Silverlight Solution

Problem

You need to understand the structure of a Silverlight 3 solution and projects.

Solution

Create a new Silverlight application in Visual Studio, and review the solution and project files.

How It Works

Once the Silverlight Tools are installed and help is configured, open Visual Studio 2008, choose File ➤ New ➤ Project, and click the Silverlight folder to see the available project templates. Three templates are available: Silverlight Class Library, Silverlight Application, and Silverlight Navigation Application (which is new in Silverlight 3).

The Silverlight Class Library template generates a straightforward class library project that you can use to separate Silverlight 3 application assets into additional assemblies that can be shared by multiple applications.

The Silverlight Application template is what developers start with to create a Silverlight application, which begins with up to two projects: one containing the Silverlight application project and another optional project containing web pages to host the Silverlight application for testing. You can, of course, add more Silverlight applications to the solution; the Visual Studio Add Silverlight Application wizard will automatically create test pages and add them to the existing web project if desired.

You can also create a Silverlight application that has just the Silverlight application without a separate web project. In this case, Visual Studio will dynamically create a test page for the control. We recommend starting out with an actual web project, so you can see how to host Silverlight applications in web pages, but we cover both options in this recipe.

You can also add Silverlight applications to any Visual Studio solution and the project wizard will ask you whether you want to add test pages to the existing web project (if there is one), which makes it easy to add new applications to an existing Visual Studio web solution. If there isn't an existing web project in a Visual Studio solution, the project wizard will prompt you to create one.

The third application template available in Silverlight 3 is called Silverlight Navigation Application. When you create a new application with this template, it starts out with the same options as when creating a regular Silverlight Application and includes up to two projects as well. The difference is that the new Silverlight Navigation Application supports views to allow easy navigation between application forms. This template also provides support for the browser Back and Forward buttons, as well as support for allowing users bookmark individual application views in browser favorites. We'll cover this new application model in more detail in Chapter 6.

The Code

When you create a new Silverlight application project, type a name, select the project location, and then click OK. The New Silverlight Application dialog appears (see in Figure 1-2).

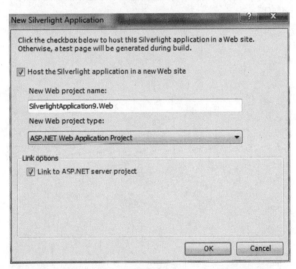

Figure 1-2. *The New Silverlight Application dialog*

The default option is to add a new web application to the solution for hosting the control. This option creates a web project for you with two pages, an ASPX page and an HTML page that are both automatically configured to host the Silverlight application. This is a great option to start out with when creating Silverlight applications.

When you opt for adding the web site, Silverlight defaults to a web project type of ASP.NET Web Application Project. If you instead select ASP.NET Web Site, you get a simple file-based web project. We prefer to stick with the default ASP.NET Web Application Project, because it allows more project configuration such as specifying a static port for the web site. This is handy when you're creating web services and want to keep the port number consistent. You can choose the name for the test web site as well. Also, the web site properties includes a Silverlight Applications tab that links the Silverlight project to the web site, copying the output to the default `ClientBin` folder, but you can customize the location in the web site.

After the project is created, if you go into the web site's properties dialog and click the Silverlight Applications tab, you will see the Change button, which allows you to specify that you would like to use configuration specific folders. This option allows you to specify if you want to copy the `.xap` file to a configuration-specific (debug, release, or custom configuration) subfolder of the build's target folder (`ClientBin`) or simply copy the chosen build configuration (debug or release) into `ClientBin` directly.

Just so you're aware, the XAP file is the output of the Silverlight application project. It contains the assemblies, manifest, and other output files that are loaded by the Silverlight 3 plug-in to execute the application. The XAP file is actually just a ZIP file renamed with the `.xap` extension, so you can crack one open to see what is inside by simply changing the extension to `.zip`.

If you uncheck the "Host the Silverlight application in a new Web site" option in the New Silverlight Application dialog, a web project is not created. This option results in a solution with a single project containing the Silverlight control. When you run the application, an HTML page is generated that hosts the application. Our preference is to create a separate web application project and not use the dynamically generated HTML test page option, but it is good to have options.

Once you've chosen the Silverlight Application option to have a separate project-based web site in the file system and you've updated the name for the web site project, click OK to create the initial solution. Figure 1-3 shows the initial project layout in Solution Explorer.

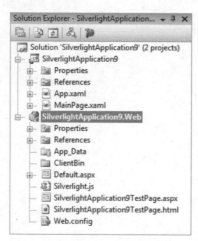

Figure 1-3. *The Silverlight 3 initial project layout*

The Silverlight application project named "1.3 Understand the Structure of a Silverlight Solution" consists of two files: `App.xaml` and `MainPage.xaml`. There are also corresponding code-behind files: `App.xaml.cs` and `MainPage.xaml.cs`. The class in the `App.xaml` file serves as the start-up object for the

Silverlight application. Listings 1-1 and 1-2 show the initial App.xaml file and its code-behind, App.xaml.cs, respectively.

Listing 1-1. *Recipe 1-3's App.xaml File*

```xml
<Application xmlns="http://schemas.microsoft.com/winfx/2006/xaml/presentation"
             xmlns:x="http://schemas.microsoft.com/winfx/2006/xaml"
             x:Class="Ch01_IntroToSilverlight.Recipe1_3.App"
             >
    <Application.Resources>

    </Application.Resources>
</Application>
```

Listing 1-2. *Recipe 1-3's Initial App.xaml.cs Class File*

```csharp
using System;
using System.Windows;

namespace Ch01_IntroToSilverlight.Recipe1_3
{
  public partial class App : Application
  {

    public App()
    {
      this.Startup += this.Application_Startup;
      this.Exit += this.Application_Exit;
      this.UnhandledException += this.Application_UnhandledException;

      InitializeComponent();
    }

    private void Application_Startup(object sender, StartupEventArgs e)
    {
      this.RootVisual = new MainPage();
    }

    private void Application_Exit(object sender, EventArgs e)
    {

    }
    private void Application_UnhandledException(object sender,
    ApplicationUnhandledExceptionEventArgs e)
    {
```

```
// If the app is running outside of the debugger then report the exception
//using the browser's exception mechanism. On IE this will display it a
//yellow alert icon in the status bar and Firefox will display a script error.
if (!System.Diagnostics.Debugger.IsAttached)
{

  // NOTE: This will allow the application to continue running after an
  //exception has been thrown but not handled.
  // For production applications this error handling should be replaced with
  //something that will report the error to the website and stop
  //the application.
  e.Handled = true;

  try
  {
    string errorMsg = e.ExceptionObject.Message + e.ExceptionObject.
        StackTrace;
    errorMsg = errorMsg.Replace('"', '\'').Replace("\r\n", @"\n");

    System.Windows.Browser.HtmlPage.Window.Eval("throw new Error(\
    "Unhandled Error in Silverlight Application " + errorMsg + "\");");
  }
  catch (Exception)
  {
  }
}
}
}
}
```

Both files contain partial classes for the Ch01_IntroToSilverlight.Recipe1_3.App class that inherits from the System.Windows.Application class. Notice at the top of App.xaml in the <Application> element two namespaces are declared that are required for Silverlight 3 development. Also, in the <Application> element tag is an x:Class attribute linking the App.xaml markup file to the App.xaml.cs code-behind file with the related partial class. The App.xaml file is a good place to store applicationwide resources such as styles and templates, which we cover in Chapters 4 and 5.

The App.xaml.cs class file implements methods of the Application class, such as the constructor where events are wired up and InitializeComponent() is called to process the XAML markup. The App_Startup event sets the visual root to the Page class defined in MainPage.xaml and MainPage.xaml.cs. Application_Exit is implemented as a placeholder for the developer to add logic needed to handle the exit process. Finally, Application_UnhandledException is implemented to provide a basic top-level exception handler event.

All of the UI and execution logic for the Silverlight 3 application exists in the MainPage class XAML and code-behind class file. Listings 1-3 and 1-4 show the MainMainPage.xaml file and its code-behind, MainMainPage.
xaml.cs.

There is a lot of code in these listings that we do cover in detail here, since this is an introductory chapter, but we wanted to demonstrate more than a simple "Hello World" application when you run the application. Most of the code was generated by Expression Blend 3 to produce the animation, which we cover in detail in Chapter 3. We also provide an overview of Expression Blend 3 in the next recipe.

Listing 1-3. *Recipe 1-3's MainMainPage.xaml File*

```
<UserControl x:Class="Ch01_IntroToSilverlight.Recipe1_3.MainPage"
    xmlns="http://schemas.microsoft.com/winfx/2006/xaml/presentation"
    xmlns:x="http://schemas.microsoft.com/winfx/2006/xaml" >
  <Grid x:Name="LayoutRoot">
    <TextBlock Text="Hello from Silverlight 3!!!" />
  </Grid>
</UserControl>
```

Listing 1-4. *Recipe 1-3's Main MainPage.xaml.cs Class File*

```
using System.Windows.Controls;

namespace Ch01_IntroToSilverlight.Recipe1_3
{
  public partial class MainPage : UserControl
  {
    public MainPage()
    {
      InitializeComponent();
    }
  }
}
```

Both files contain partial classes for the Ch01_IntroToSilverlight.Recipe1_3.MainPage class that inherits from the System.Windows.Controls.UserControl class. At the top of MainMainPage.xaml in the <UserControl> element, notice that two namespaces are declared; these are required for Silverlight 3 development. Also, in the <UserControl> element tag is an x:Class attribute linking the MainMainPage.xaml markup file to the MainMainPage.xaml.cs code-behind file with the related partial class. The MainMainPage.xaml file is a good place to store resources that apply to an entire page, such as styles and templates, which we cover in Chapter 2.

The project settings for the Silverlight application have a Silverlight tab, as shown in Figure 1-4.

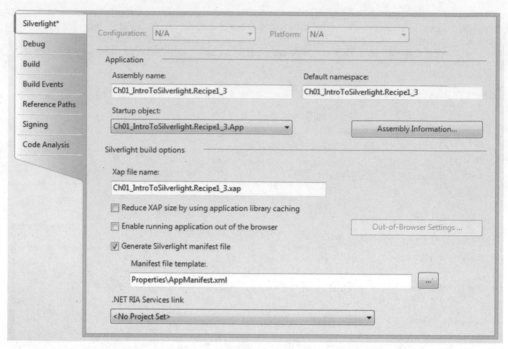

Figure 1-4. *The Silverlight application settings tab in the Silverlight project settings*

In addition to the properties typically available for a .NET application are the XAP file name and an option that lets you specify whether you want to generate a Silverlight manifest file. Silverlight 3 introduces two additional settings:

- *Reduce XAP size by using application library caching*: Caches framework assemblies on the client in order to improve performance

- *Enable running application out of browser*: Enables out-of-browser capabilities, which is covered in detail in Chapter 7

The other project in the solution is the TestWeb web project. The web project consists of two pages per Silverlight application. One file is an ASPX page, and the other is an HTML page. So the corresponding files for the Silverlight application we just covered are Recipe1.3TestPage.aspx and Recipe1.3TestPage.html. Both pages instantiate the Silverlight application. The ASPX page uses an instance of the ASP.NET server control System.Web.UI.SilverlightControls.Silverlight to create the application within the browser. Here is an example of the markup from the ASPX page:

```
<asp:Silverlight ID="Xaml1" runat="server"
Source="~/ClientBin/Ch01_IntroToSilverlight.Recipe1_3.xap"
MinimumVersion="3.0.40307.0 " Width="100%" Height="100%" />
```

You can see the reference to the XAP file in the ASP.NET markup. The HTML page manually creates the Silverlight application using an <object> tag. Here is an example of the HTML markup from the HTML page:

```
<object data="data:application/x-silverlight-2,"
   type="application/x-silverlight-2" width="100%" height="100%">
<param name="source" value="ClientBin/Ch06_BrowserIntegration.Recipe1_3.xap"/>
<param name="onError" value="onSilverlightError" />
<param name="background" value="white" />
<param name="minRuntimeVersion" value="3.0.40624.0" />
<param name="autoUpgrade" value="true" />
<a href="http://go.microsoft.com/fwlink/?LinkID=149156&v=3.0.40624.0"
   style="text-decoration:none">
  <img src="http://go.microsoft.com/fwlink/?LinkId=108181"
    alt="Get Microsoft Silverlight" style="border-style:none"/>
</a>
</object>
<iframe id="_sl_historyFrame" style="visibility:hidden;height:0px;
   width:0px;border:0px">
</iframe>
```

The `<object>` tag shown here is essentially what the ASP.NET server control renders at runtime. There is the reference to the XAP file as well as some client-side JavaScript events, such as onSilverlightError, wired in. Also notice the iframe named sl_historyFrame. This iframe is required to provide support for integration with browser navigation book marking and deep linking, which we cover in Chapter 6.

Figure 1-5 shows the project settings for the TestWeb web project.

The tab shown in Figure 1-5 lists the Silverlight projects available in the solution, where the XAP file should be copied to (the ClientBin folder), as well as whether there should be configuration specific folders under the ClientBin folder for debug or release versions of the Silverlight application.

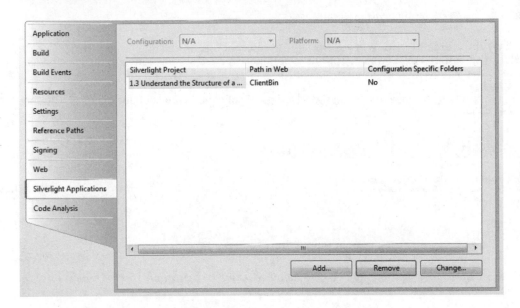

Figure 1-5. *The SilverlightApplications tab in the web project settings*

Notice also in Figure 1-5 the Add, Remove, and Change buttons. The Add button allows you to easily add a Silverlight application to a web project. Let's say you have an existing ASP.NET application, and you now want to add to a Silverlight application. Open the project settings for the web project, and click the Add button to display the Add Silverlight Application dialog shown in Figure 1-6.

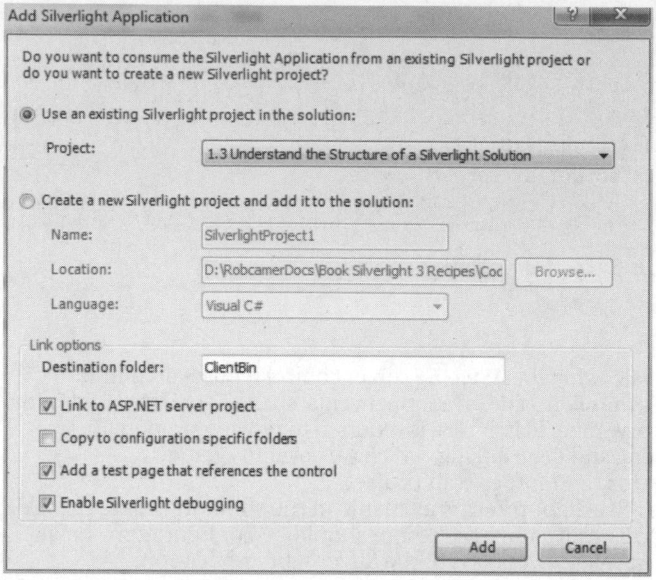

Figure 1-6. *The Add Silverlight Application dialog*

You have the option to create a new Silverlight 3 project or add an existing project form the prepopulated Project combo box, as well as options to configure related settings, such as the specifying the destination folder, including configuration specific folders, adding test pages, and enabling Silverlight debugging.

When you click the Change button on the Silverlight Applications tab, a dialog displays with the message shown in Figure 1-7.

Figure 1-7. *Clicking the Change button allows you to switch to using configuration-specific folders for debug/release versions.*

This dialog allows you to switch to using configuration files for debug, release or custom configuration versions. When you click the Remove button on the Silverlight Applications tab, you'll see the dialog shown in Figure 1-8.

Figure 1-8. *Clicking the Remove button opens this dialog, which lets you remove a Silverlight application from a web project.*

1-4. Understanding the Developer/Designer Workflow

Problem

You need to understand the developer and designer workflow for creating Silverlight applications.

Solution

Learn the capabilities of the Visual Studio 2008 and Expression Blend 3 environments. Depending on the type of application, determine whether a dedicated UI designer is required for the project or whether the developer will handle the UI development and the coding. If the application requires a dedicated designer due to UI requirements, introduce the designer to Expression Blend 3.

How It Works

With any application development effort, many roles, such as project manager, architect, developer, tester, and designer, are involved. Depending on the target application, the role of the designer can greatly vary in the amount of effort required. For an intranet LOB application, the designer may not have much more of a role than letting developers know where the required corporate application standard resources, such as Cascading Style Sheets (CSS) styles, and images, are located. In a public-facing rich media application, a designer may be heavily involved, from conception of the application all the way through development and user experience testing.

For Silverlight, the same generalizations apply. You can build powerful desktop-like applications within Silverlight that may not require a dedicated designer. Or, you can build RIAs that require dedicated designer skills from start to finish.

The Tools

Silverlight developers do not have to become full-fledged designers. Developers and designers can work independently in an integrated environment with full source code control access from both Visual

Studio and Expression Blend 3. However, from a practical standpoint, developers may want to become familiar with Expression Blend 3.

Visual Studio 2008 SP1 does not provide a designer surface. Visual Studio 2008 includes first-class IntelliSense support for editing XAML, but using it can be tedious for complex UI layout. Expression Blend 3 is a great tool for designing Silverlight 3 UIs.

■**Note** You can open a solution in Expression Blend 3 from within Visual Studio by right-clicking MainPage.xaml and selecting Open in Expression Blend from the context menu.

Visual Studio 2010 will include a fully interactive design surface for Silverlight 3 applications.

Expression Blend 3 provides rich designer support that includes drag-and-drop control editing, visual creation of animation timelines, and a rich properties window. Unlike Expression Blend 2 SP1, Expression Blend 3 includes full IntelliSense support as well.

Figure 1-9 shows the beginnings of a Silverlight media player rendered in Expression Blend 3. We don't have any code for this recipe; the screenshots are conceptual in nature.

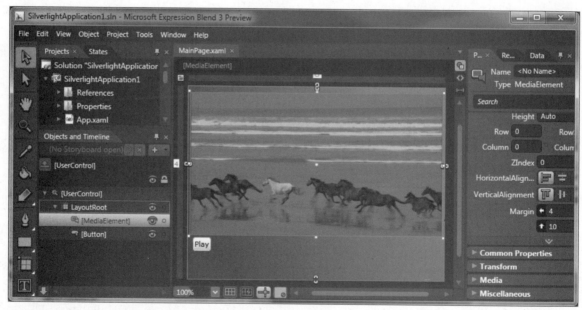

Figure 1-9. *A Silverlight 3 application in Expression Blend 3*

Notice that the media element and video render at design time in Expression Blend 3. Also, the Properties window on the right-side of the screenshot provides full access to an element's properties. As in Visual Studio 2008, there is a XAML tab that is available on the top right-side of the Artboard by clicking the button with this caption "< >" that lets you view the underlying markup in Expression Blend 3, but there is no IntelliSense support as with Visual Studio 2008.

The Process

After the above review in this recipe, the developer/designer workflow should start to take shape in your mind. UI development is primarily done in Expression Blend 3 and coding in Visual Studio. Both Expression Blend 3 and Visual Studio 2008 can create the initial Silverlight 3 project, but the UI design will most likely start out in wireframe diagrams realized in Adobe Creative Suite or Expression Design and then be exported to XAML. There are a few third-party converters available that will export from Adobe tools to XAML:

- http://www.mikeswanson.com/XAMLExport/

- http://www.infragistics.com/design/Fireworks_XAML_Exporter.aspx

Expression Blend 3 also has two new menu items under File that will import from Adobe Photoshop or Illustrator.

Figure 1-10 provides a visual representation of this iterative development and design process.

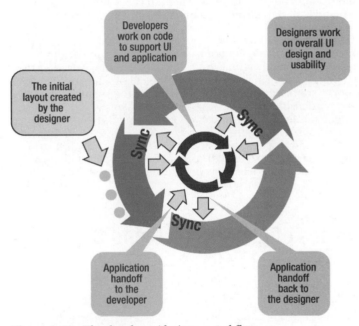

Figure 1-10. *The developer/designer workflow*

For a highly interactive, rich UI, the designer role may want to perform initial layout of the application, as shown in Figure 1-10, developing the initial UI concepts. Unlike when building mock-ups in an image-editing tool, what is great about Silverlight 3 and Expression Blend 3 is that the mock-up of a visually compelling UI can become the foundation of the actual UI. As Figure 1-10 shows, designers can focus on UI design and usability in the outer loop, while the developers focus on writing the code behind the UI as well as the rest of the application. Periodic synchronization points allow the application to be fully integrated between the developer and designer workflows with minimal overhead because of the common underlying markup.

■**Note** Expression Blend 3 includes new functionality called SketchFlow that allows designers and developers to build rich and dynamic prototypes very quickly.

As an alternative to starting the development process, a developer can start to build the basic UI with Visual Studio 2008 and then hand off the UI to a designer, who then refines the application's layout, adding animation and control templates. This workflow would make sense if you are migrating an existing .NET application to Silverlight—the developer must first get the code working within the Silverlight programming model, make adjustments, and lay out a basic UI.

Developers can also open a Silverlight application in Expression Blend 3 from Visual Studio 2008 by right-clicking the `MainMainPage.xaml` file and selecting Open in Expression Blend from the context menu. Doing so opens the entire solution in Expression Blend 3.

The synchronization illustrated in Figure 1-10 occurs either manually by sharing folders or via source-code integration available in both Visual Studio and in Expression Blend 3. With Expression Blend 2, designers had to use the stand-alone Team Foundation Server client to check files in and out of source code control. Now with Expression Blend 3, designers are even more integrated into the design/development process.

A point to emphasize is that, unlike with other technologies, the output from the rich design tool, XAML, is what actually is compiled into the application. For comparison purposes, in Windows Forms development, a designer cannot create a rich, highly visual control in the technology used by the developer directly. Instead, the designer might use a drawing tool such as Adobe Photoshop or Microsoft PowerPoint to create a mock-up. The developer starts from scratch using separate tools and technology and attempts to create a custom control that renders like the mock-up. This creates a developer/designer disconnect, or lag, between design changes and coding implementation, because the designer and developer work in separate toolsets.

XAML technology enables you to use a wide range of tools since it is well formed XML. The fact that XAML can be compiled directly permits the developer to take the output from the design team and directly utilize it in the application, completely removing the lag between the designer and the developer.

1-5. Understanding the Basics of Expression Blend 3

Problem

You need to understand how to create a UI in Expression Blend 3.

Solution

Learn the basics of the Expression Blend 3 environment.

How It Works

As mentioned previously, Expression Blend 3 is a visual design tool that generates XAML. It is a powerful tool that is worthy of a book dedicated to completely understanding the environment. While this book is not exclusively about Expression Blend 3, we will cover the basics of the environment to help communicate steps when performing tasks visually.

Visual Studio developers may find Expression Blend 3 to be a dramatic departure from what they are familiar with in Visual Studio. However, developers will want to know how to work in Expression Blend 3 for maximum productivity. Figure 1-11 shows the Expression Blend UI with major elements pointed out.

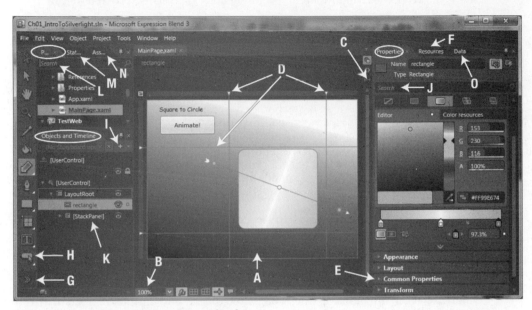

Figure 1-11. *Navigating Expression Blend 3*

Figure 1-11 shows Expression Blend 3 with a simple project opened. The project is contrived but suits our purpose of providing an overview of the tool's major features. When the button is clicked, an animation is kicked off that turns the square into a circle and then back into a square again. Table 1-1 provides a quick description of the annotated points.

Table 1-1. *Expression Blend 3 Features*

Annotation	Description
A	This is the designer surface, also known in the documentation as the Artboard, which supports drag-and-drop editing.
B	Use this to zoom in or out of the designer surface as needed. Zoom out to see the entire application, or zoom in close to perform precise visual editing.
C	Tabs allow you to switch between the design surface, the XAML markup, or split view to see both the design surface and XAML.
D	These represent grid lines for laying out controls in the UI. When you move the mouse over the edge of the Grid control, the UI provides a visual cue that you can add a grid line.

Table 1-1. *Continued*

Annotation	Description
E	This is the Properties window; here, several sections are collapsed so that they fit in the view.
F	This is the Resources window, which lists available resources such as styles and templates, We cover these resources throughout this book, particularly in Chapters 2, 4, and 5.
G	Clicking this chevron brings up the Asset Library, where you can search for a control if you are not sure what the icon is or whether it is visible. The Asset Library is similar to the Visual Studio toolbar area where controls are listed.
H	The little arrow in the lower-right corner under some of the controls shown in the Asset Library is a visual cue that related controls are available for quick access. Clicking and holding the arrow brings up a small window listing the related controls. Click a control, and it becomes the visual control for that section of the Asset Library.
I	Clicking this button creates a new Storyboard object. You use storyboards to design animations. We talk more about storyboards later in this chapter.
J	This is the extremely useful Search text box. Type a property name, and Expression Blend 3 will search the list of properties available for the control and bring the property into view for easy access. Be sure to clear the Search text box when you've finished. Otherwise, it can be confusing when you switch objects and the filter entered in the Search text box does not apply, resulting in a blank properties window.
K	The XAML visual tree is listed in this area of Expression Blend 3. The yellow frame around the LayoutRoot control indicates that the LayoutRoot control is the active element. This means that double-clicking a control in the Asset Library will insert that control as a child to the LayoutRoot control. Double-clicking another control, such as the StackPanel, would make that one the active element and the insertion point for child controls dragged on the visual design surface.
L	New in Expression Blend 3, this extremely useful Search text box allows you to find project files quickly.
M	Support for the Visual State Manager has been improved in Expression Blend 3 with an improved user interface. More states for controls are displayed with a warning indicator when a property has been changed in more than one state group.
N	New in Expression Blend 3, the Assets tab provides fast access to project, controls, styles, behaviors, and effects assets in a nicely organized list.
O	New in Expression Blend 3, the Data tab provides designers the ability to create either a sample or live data source that makes it easier to design a data binding UI.

The Code

At first glance, Expression Blend 3 looks a lot like Visual Studio with a Projects tab (circled in Figure 1-11) that lists the solution, project, and files as in Visual Studio (see Figure 1-12).

Figure 1-12. *Expression Blend 3's Projects tab*

In Figure 1-11, the "I" points to a button that lets you create a new Storyboard object. When you click that button, you are prompted to provide a name or key for the storyboard in the Create Storyboard Resource dialog. Click OK to put Expression Blend 3 into time line recording mode, which is shown in Figure 1-13.

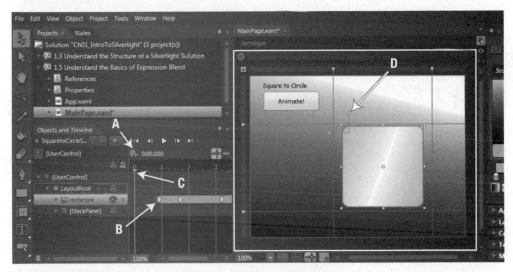

Figure 1-13. *Expression Blend 3 with time line recording on*

When Expression Blend 3 is in time line recording mode, you can visually create animations. We are now going to create an animation that has four keyframes. We animate a Rectangle object in the shape of a square that will transition from a square appearance to a circle appearance between the first and second keyframes. The animation will keep the circle appearance between the second and third keyframes and finally transition from the circle appearance to a square appearance between the third and fourth keyframes.

To create this animation, click the Record Keyframe button that the letter "A" points to in Figure 1-13. This creates a keyframe wherever the yellow vertical line in the time line is located. The letter B in Figure 1-13 points to the keyframe we created at the start time of 0 seconds on the time line. We then drag the yellow vertical time line pointed to by the letter C to 1 second. Clicking the Record Keyframe button creates a keyframe at that point in the time line where the yellow vertical line sits, as shown in Figure 1-14.

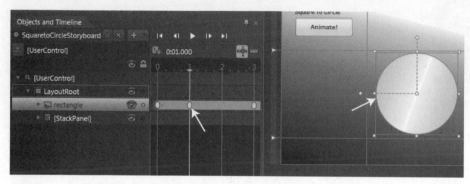

Figure 1-14. *Adding a keyframe to create an animation*

We then adjusted the square to make it look like a circle by dragging the handles pointed to in Figure 1-13 with the letter "D" to create the circle shown in Figure 1-14 at time of 1 second. This results in an animation transitioning from a square to a circle over a period of 1 second. We want the circle appearance to last for 2 seconds more, so we copy the keyframe at 1 second and paste it at a time of 3 seconds on the time line. This results in the appearance not changing from 1 second to 3 seconds; the shape remains a circle.

We now want the animation to transition back to a square. At a time of 4 seconds on the time line, we add a copy of the original keyframe at 0 seconds, which is a square. This results in an animation that transitions back to the square appearance between a time of 3 and 4 seconds on the time line.

A great technique to adopt when you need an animation to go back to its original look is the use of copy and paste. Notice in Figure 1-14 that there are four keyframes for the Rectangle object in the visual tree. The first keyframe is set at 0 seconds to represent the initial state. At 1 second, a keyframe is created, as shown in Figure 1-14, with the shape now looking like a circle. When this animation runs, the square will smoothly transition into a circle.

The third keyframe shown in Figure 1-14 is a copy of the second Keyframe, so that from 1 second to 3 seconds on the time line, the circle shape is maintained. To copy a Keyframe, simply right-click it, and select Copy from the context menu. When you paste the object, the paste location for the keyframe is wherever the yellow vertical line is located along the time line. So, to paste a copy at 3 seconds, move the yellow vertical time line to 3 seconds and press Ctrl+V to paste.

For the fourth Keyframe, copy the first Keyframe as before, move the yellow timeline to 4 seconds, and then press Ctrl+V to paste. Click the DVD Player-like play button at the top of the timeline window to test the animation and fine-tune as desired. We cover animations in more detail in Chapter 3, but we wanted to provide an introduction here as part of learning Expression Blend 3.

The last step is to add code that kicks off the storyboard to MainMainPage.xaml.cs. To do this, switch to the same solution opened in Visual Studio 2008. Locate the Button XAML, and type a space inside the first part of the <Button> element tag to invoke IntelliSense, as shown in Figure 1-15.

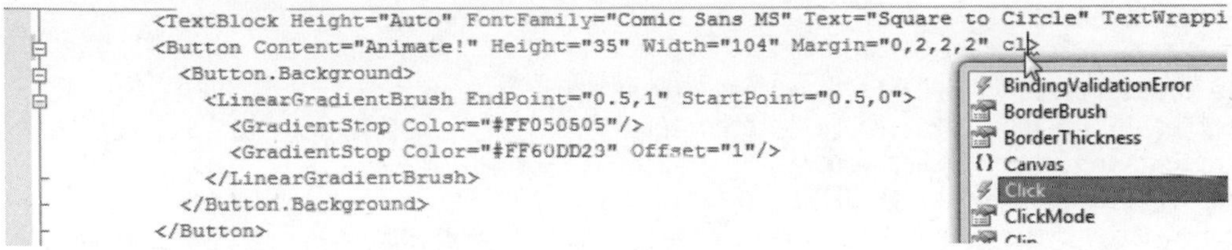

```
<TextBlock Height="Auto" FontFamily="Comic Sans MS" Text="Square to Circle" TextWrappi
<Button Content="Animate!" Height="35" Width="104" Margin="0,2,2,2" cl
  <Button.Background>
    <LinearGradientBrush EndPoint="0.5,1" StartPoint="0.5,0">
      <GradientStop Color="#FF050505"/>
      <GradientStop Color="#FF60DD23" Offset="1"/>
    </LinearGradientBrush>
  </Button.Background>
</Button>
```
BindingValidationError
BorderBrush
BorderThickness
{} Canvas
Click
ClickMode
Clip

Figure 1-15. *Adding an event in Visual Studio 2008*

It takes one line of code to launch the animation when the button is clicked:

```
SquaretoCircleStoryboard.Begin();
```

Listings 1-5 and 1-6 show the MainMainPage.xaml and MainMainPage.xaml.cs files, respectively.

Listing 1-5. *Recipe 1-5's MainPage.xaml File*

```xml
<UserControl x:Class="Ch01_IntroToSilverlight.Recipe1_5.MainPage"
    xmlns="http://schemas.microsoft.com/winfx/2006/xaml/presentation"
    xmlns:x="http://schemas.microsoft.com/winfx/2006/xaml"
    Width="400" Height="300" xmlns:d=
"http://schemas.microsoft.com/expression/blend/2008" xmlns:mc=
"http://schemas.openxmlformats.org/markup-compatibility/2006"
mc:Ignorable="d">
  <UserControl.Resources>
    <Storyboard x:Name="SquaretoCircleStoryboard">
      <DoubleAnimationUsingKeyframes BeginTime="00:00:00"
        Storyboard.TargetName="rectangle"
        Storyboard.TargetProperty="(Rectangle.RadiusX)">
        <SplineDoubleKeyFrame KeyTime="00:00:00" Value="12"/>
        <SplineDoubleKeyFrame KeyTime="00:00:01" Value="75"/>
        <SplineDoubleKeyFrame KeyTime="00:00:03" Value="75"/>
        <SplineDoubleKeyFrame KeyTime="00:00:04" Value="12"/>
      </DoubleAnimationUsingKeyframes>
      <DoubleAnimationUsingKeyframes BeginTime="00:00:00"
        Storyboard.TargetName="rectangle"
        Storyboard.TargetProperty="(Rectangle.RadiusY)">
        <SplineDoubleKeyFrame KeyTime="00:00:00" Value="12"/>
        <SplineDoubleKeyFrame KeyTime="00:00:01" Value="75"/>
        <SplineDoubleKeyFrame KeyTime="00:00:03" Value="75"/>
        <SplineDoubleKeyFrame KeyTime="00:00:04" Value="12"/>
      </DoubleAnimationUsingKeyframes>
    </Storyboard>
  </UserControl.Resources>
```

25

```xml
<Grid x:Name="LayoutRoot">
  <Grid.Background>
    <LinearGradientBrush EndPoint="0.810999989509583,0.18299999833107"
      StartPoint="0.630999982357025,1.15100002288818">
      <GradientStop Color="#FF000000"/>
      <GradientStop Color="#FFFFFFFF" Offset="1"/>
    </LinearGradientBrush>
  </Grid.Background>
  <Grid.RowDefinitions>
    <RowDefinition Height="0.3*"/>
    <RowDefinition Height="0.54*"/>
    <RowDefinition Height="0.16*"/>
  </Grid.RowDefinitions>
  <Grid.ColumnDefinitions>
    <ColumnDefinition Width="0.39*"/>
    <ColumnDefinition Width="0.461*"/>
    <ColumnDefinition Width="0.149*"/>
  </Grid.ColumnDefinitions>
  <Rectangle  Margin="17.2000007629395,4,17.2000007629395,8" Height="150"
    Width="150" Grid.Column="1" Grid.Row="1" RadiusX="12" RadiusY="12"
          x:Name="rectangle">
    <Rectangle.Fill>
      <LinearGradientBrush EndPoint="1.32400000095367,0.783999979496002"
        StartPoint="-0.310999989509583,0.172000005841255">
        <GradientStop Color="#FF99E674" Offset="0.004"/>
        <GradientStop Color="#FFFFFFFF" Offset="0.504"/>
        <GradientStop Color="#FF99E674" Offset="0.97299998998641968"/>
      </LinearGradientBrush>
    </Rectangle.Fill>
  </Rectangle>
  <StackPanel Margin="8,8,8,8" Grid.Column="0" Grid.Row="0">
    <TextBlock Height="Auto" FontFamily="Comic Sans MS" Text="Square to Circle"
      TextWrapping="Wrap" Width="150" Margin="15,2,2,2"/>
    <Button Content="Animate!" Height="35" Width="104" Margin="0,2,2,2"
      Click="Button_Click">
      <Button.Background>
        <LinearGradientBrush EndPoint="0.5,1" StartPoint="0.5,0">
          <GradientStop Color="#FF050505"/>
          <GradientStop Color="#FF60DD23" Offset="1"/>
        </LinearGradientBrush>
      </Button.Background>
    </Button>
  </StackPanel>

</Grid>
</UserControl>
```

Listing 1-6. *Recipe 1-5's MainPage.xaml.cs File*

```
using System.Windows;
using System.Windows.Controls;

namespace Ch01_IntroToSilverlight.Recipe1_5
{
  public partial class MainPage : UserControl
  {
    public Page()
    {
      InitializeComponent();
    }

    private void Button_Click(object sender, RoutedEventArgs e)
    {
      SquaretoCircleStoryboard.Begin();
    }
  }
}
```

This recipe covers the basics to help you get started. We cover Expression Blend 3 in Chapter 3 as well, but for the most up-to-date information, visit this web site for self-study tutorials, starter kits, training videos, virtual labs, and webcasts: http://expression.microsoft.com/en-us/cc136522.aspx.

1-6. Accessing Source Control

Problem

You need to understand how a non–Visual Studio user such as a designer can access a Silverlight 3 project from Team Foundation Server (TFS), Microsoft's Application Lifecycle Management (ALM) and source code control soluton

Solution

Use the new source code support built into Expression Blend 3. Otherwise, use the stand-alone Team Foundation Client Windows application or the TFS Web Access client to connect to TFS and check in and out source code.

How It Works

Given the highly iterative nature that Silverlight development can entail, designers will most likely access the application source code more frequently than before when designers generally simply provided an image and didn't interact with source directly throughout the development timeline, so it is important that source code integrity be maintained no matter who is working on the application.

Designers will generally spend their time in Expression Blend 3 designing and building Silverlight 3 applications. For most real Silverlight applications, developers will want to store source code within TFS or another source code application.

Most, if not all, source code control applications have stand-alone clients that do not require Visual Studio to access source code. Designers can use the stand-alone client access tools appropriate for their environments, and they should work with their development team counterparts to obtain the appropriate client for their systems.

If the source code is stored in Team Foundation Server, designers should use the integrated source code control support available in Expression Blend 3. To enable source code control in Expression Blend 3, download the Microsoft Visual Studio Team System 2008 Team Explorer available at `http://www.microsoft.com/downloads/details.aspx?FamilyID=0ed12659-3d41-4420-bbb0-a46e51bfca86&DisplayLang=en`.

The download s an ISO so you will have to first burn it to a CD or mount the ISO virtually using a third-party utility. Next, install Visual Studio 2008 SP1. The last step is to install a hotfix (KB967483) by selecting Downloads at `http://code.msdn.microsoft.com/KB967483`.

After installing the updates, contact your administrator for the project's Team Foundation Server to obtain the correct permissions. Once you have permissions, such as the Contributor role, that will allows you to add or modify files, use Team Explorer to create a workspace on your computer. This URL provides the steps to create a workspace: `http://msdn.microsoft.com/en-us/library/ms181384.aspx`.

The workspace is a local folder that is mapped to the source code repository. This URL explains how to download a solution or project to your computer:
`http://msdn.microsoft.com/en-us/library/ms181385.aspx`.

When you open the solution in Expression Blend 3 additional source code control menu items will be enabled when you right-click on the Solution, Project, and individual files that will allow you to check items in and out of source code control. If you are not familiar with how source code control works, please go to Help ➤ User Guide in Expression Blend and type **source control** in the index for more information.

1-7. Running Silverlight 3 on a Mac

Problem

You need to run Silverlight 3 on a Mac.

Solution

On your Mac, navigate to a web site running Silverlight 3 to automatically download the plug-in, or download it at `http://go.microsoft.com/fwlink/?LinkID=149156&v=3.0.40624.0`.

How It Works

Silverlight, versions 2 and 3, is a cross-platform, cross-browser plug-in designed to automatically install when the web browser accesses a site running Silverlight . Note that Silverlight 3 works on Intel-based Mac systems, not the PowerPC.

1-8. Running Silverlight on Linux

Problem

You need to run Silverlight applications on a Linux system.

Solution

Download the Moonlight plug-in from http://www.mono-project.com/Moonlight.

To access the Moonlight Getting Started page at the Mono project, go to http://www.mono-project.com/Moonlight#Getting_Started.

How It Works

In partnership with Microsoft, Novell is providing an implementation of Silverlight for Linux called Moonlight. Moonlight 2 betais available for the major Linux distributions, with support for Firefox, Konqueror, and Opera browsers.

The goal of the implementation is to allow Moonlight to run any Silverlight application without having to recompile that application. To view screenshots of Moonlight running existing Silverlight demonstrations, go to http://www.mono-project.com/Screenshots.

CHAPTER 2

■ ■ ■

Application Design and Programming Model

The Mechanics of Silverlight Applications

Silverlight is a UI or presentation layer programming model for rich interactive client-side user interaction. Silverlight also includes strong distributed application hooks coupled with rich data binding to facilitate a solid application architecture that will be familiar to traditional .NET or Java developers. This means that the same overall design principles that architects and developers live by today for web or n-tier applications can apply to Silverlight-based applications as well. Silverlight provides excellent support for calling services, whether those services are based on Simple Object Access Protocol SOAP, representational state transfer (REST), plain old XML (POX) or JavaScript Object Notation (JSON).

■**Note** Please refer to Chapter 1 for information on how to set up the environment and create a Silverlight 3 project. Chapter 7 covers networking and web services in detail. In Chapter 9, we cover .NET RIA services in detail.

The Silverlight platform consists of three major components: the presentation framework, the .NET Framework for Silverlight, and the installer/updater. The presentation framework contains of a rich set of XAML UI controls, media playback support, digital rights management, as well as support for user input, data binding, and presentation features like vector graphics, animation, and layout.

The .NET Framework for Silverlight is a subset of the full .NET Framework that contains a rich set of components and libraries. One of the features for Silverlight 3 is a closer alignment with WPF. The .NET Framework for Silverlight includes extensible UI controls and powerful networking capabilities, as well as base class libraries and the common language runtime. Some parts of the .NET Framework for Silverlight are deployed as part of the runtime encapsulated within the cross-platform browser plug-in. Other parts, such as some UI controls, Language Integrated Query LINQ to XML, and so forth, are packaged with your application and downloaded to the browser as a separate assembly as part of the .xap container.

■**Note** Take a moment to browse the topic Silverlight Reference by Namespace in the Silverlight SDK help file. You will see that the .NET Framework for Silverlight contains a rich subset of the full version of the .NET Framework, including support for generics, collections, diagnostics, reflection, cryptography, and LINQ, just to name a few components.

We provided detailed highlights in Chapter 1, but to quickly review, Silverlight 3 introduces more than 50 new features, including support for running Silverlight applications out of the browser, dramatic video performance and quality improvements, and features that improve developer productivity in the following areas:

- Media

- User experience rendering capabilities

- RIAs and LOB applications

- Data support

- Browser support

- Out-of-browser capabilities

The third major component of the Silverlight platform is the installation and update control that simplifies the process of installing the plug-in for first-time users of your application. As its name suggests, this control provides low-impact, automatic updates to the plug-in as they become available.

In this chapter, we will focus on the Silverlight application programming model in the .NET Framework. We'll cover topics like custom components, concurrency, resource management, and persistence, all of which facilitate integration into the overall application architecture.

2-1. Adding a Custom Class

Problem

You want to add a custom class to your application and access the class in the Extensible Application Markup Language (XAML), which is the markup similar to the ASPX page in ASP.NET.

Solution

Add an XML namespace to the <UserControl> tag in your Silverlight application to make the custom class available to the Silverlight application.

How It Works

Most of the time, applications consist of more than one class. You can add a class to project by right-clicking a Silverlight project and selecting Add ➤ Class. Classes can also be brought in through a separate project or assembly just as you would in any other .NET application. Also, you still add a using statement if the class is in a different namespace.

In general, for Silverlight applications much of the code is written in XAML, which is an XML markup language, so it takes an additional step to make the class available within the XAML markup. This step involves adding an xmlns namespace import statement to the <UserControl> tag.

The Code

In this recipe, we will work with a class named Organization that we will add to the Silverlight application. The Organization class is just a fictitious class example with a few example data items. The Organization class is in the same Ch02_ProgrammingModel.Recipe2_1 namespace as the MainPage.xaml.cs file (in Silverlight 2 it was Page.xaml), so we can access the Organization class directly without having to add a using statement. If the Organization class was in a separate assembly with a different namespace, you would need to add a reference to the other assembly and a using statement as you normally would to access a class within an application.

At the top of MainPage.xaml, you will notice namespace declarations within the <UserControl> tag:

```
xmlns="http://schemas.microsoft.com/winfx/2006/xaml/presentation"
xmlns:x="http://schemas.microsoft.com/winfx/2006/xaml"
```

The first statement imports the presentation framework namespace as the default namespace. The second declaration maps an additional XAML namespace, mapping it to the x: prefix. To access the Organization class within MainPage.xaml, we need to add an additional namespace declaration with a unique prefix by typing xmlns:data= in the <UserControl> tag. We use the prefix data because we want to data bind to the People collection in the Organization class. You can pick any prefix you want, but it helps to use something that makes sense for the application. Figure 2-1 shows the support in Visual Studio 2008 that lets us easily import the Ch02_ProgrammingModel.Recipe2_1 namespace.

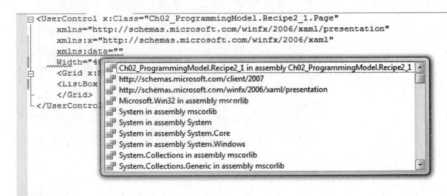

Figure 2-1. *The namespace import IntelliSense window*

Selecting the first line in the pop-up IntelliSense window imports the correct namespace that allows us to access the Organization class within the Silverlight XAML markup, resulting in this namespace statement:

```
xmlns:data="clr-namespace:Ch02_ProgrammingModel.Recipe2_1"
```

We add a ListBox control to the XAML to help test our ability to access the Organization class. Let's use Microsoft Expression Blend 3 to set the ItemSource property on the ListBox control. First, save the solution, and then open the solution in Blend so that it is open in both Expression Blend 3 and Visual Studio, as described in Recipe 1-5. Inside Expression Blend, open MainPage.xaml. Select the ListBox so that it is highlighted, and then enter Item in the Properties search box to bring the ItemSource to the top of the Properties window, as shown in Figure 2-2.

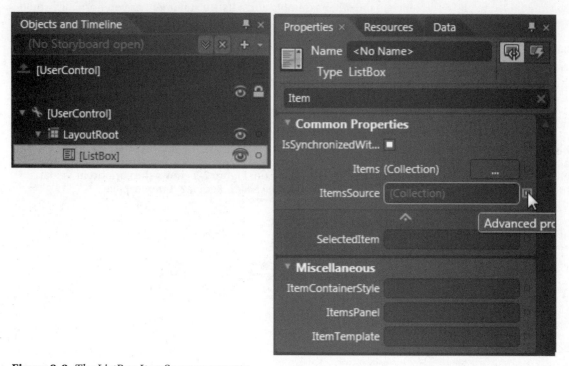

Figure 2-2. *The ListBox ItemSource property*

Notice in Figure 2-2 that there is a small button highlighted by the mouse pointer hovering over it. Clicking this button provides access to the "Advanced property options" menu, shown in Figure 2-3.

Figure 2-3. *The "Advanced property option"s menu*

Click the "Data binding" option to open the "Create Data binding" dialog shown in Figure 2-4. The astute reader will notice in Figure 2-4 that in addition to Data Field and Explicit Data Context, Element Property is no longer grayed out as it is in Silverlight 2 and Expression Blend 2 SP1. In Silverlight 3, it is possible for controls to data bind to values of other elements or controls. We cover data binding to elements in Chapter 4 in detail.

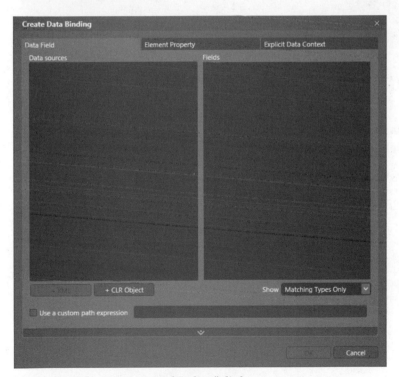

Figure 2-4. *The "Create Data binding" dialog*

For now, click the +CLR Object button to open the Define New Object Data Source dialog shown in Figure 2-5.

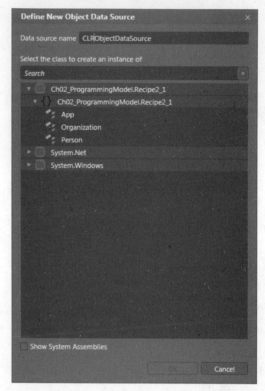

Figure 2-5. *The Define New Object Data Source dialog*

Select Organization, and then click OK to create the OrganizationDS object. Select the OrganizationDS object in the "Create Data binding" dialog and then expand the Organization object in the Fields pane on the right to display the People collection. Select the People collection, and click Finish to set the ItemSource for the ListBox to the People collection. Save the solution in Expression Blend 3 and switch back to Visual Studio to view the generated XAML.

When you run the sample, the ListBox displays three items that contain the text Ch02_ProgrammingModel.Recipe2_1.Person, which is the type that is stored in the People collection. In Chapter 4, we cover how to use data templates to render the values for the type's properties, such as FirstName and LastName, instead of the name of the type.

Listing 2-1 shows the Organization class file.

Listing 2-1. *Recipe 2-1's Organization Class File*

```
using System.Collections.Generic;

namespace Ch02_ProgrammingModel.Recipe2_1
{
  public class Organization
  {
    private List<Person> _people;
    public List<Person> People
    {
      get
      {
        if (null == _people)
          return Populate();
        else
          return _people;
      }
    }

    private List<Person> Populate()
    {
      _people = new List<Person>
          { //C# 3.0 Object Initializers
            new Person {FirstName="John",LastName="Smith", Age=20},
            new Person{FirstName="Sean",LastName="Jones", Age=25},
            new Person{FirstName="Kevin",LastName="Smith", Age=30}
          };
      return _people;
    }
  }

   public class Person
   {
    public string FirstName { get; set; }
    public string LastName { get; set; }
    public int Age { get; set; }
   }
}
```

Listing 2-2 shows the result of the work in Expression Blend 3.

Listing 2-2. *The MainPage.xaml File*

```
<UserControl x:Class="Ch02_ProgrammingModel.Recipe2_1.MainPage"
  xmlns="http://schemas.microsoft.com/winfx/2006/xaml/presentation"
  xmlns:x="http://schemas.microsoft.com/winfx/2006/xaml"
  xmlns:data="clr-namespace:Ch02_ProgrammingModel.Recipe2_1"
  Width="400" Height="300"
  xmlns:d="http://schemas.microsoft.com/expression/blend/2008"
  xmlns:mc=
"http://schemas.openxmlformats.org/markup-compatibility/2006" mc:Ignorable="d" >

  <UserControl.Resources>
    <data:Organization x:Key="OrganizationDS" d:IsDataSource="True"/>
  </UserControl.Resources>

  <Grid x:Name="LayoutRoot" Background="White">
    <ListBox ItemsSource="{Binding Mode=OneWay, Path=People,
      Source={StaticResource OrganizationDS}}" />
  </Grid>
</UserControl>
```

Expression Blend 3 added a couple of `xmlns` statements to the `<UserControl>` tag shown here:

```
xmlns:d="http://schemas.microsoft.com/expression/blend/2008"
xmlns:mc="http://schemas.openxmlformats.org/
markup-compatibility/2006" mc:Ignorable="d"
```

These namespaces are used by Expression Blend for code generation and can be removed if desired. However, you will need to edit the XAML in the code file as well if they use the `mc:` or `d:` namespace reference. Now, let's discuss the new resource added to the `UserControl` as part of configuring the data binding:

```
<UserControl.Resources>
  <data:Organization x:Key="OrganizationDS" d:IsDataSource="True"/>
</UserControl.Resources>
```

The resource uses the `data:` prefix we defined in Visual Studio to gain access to the `Organization` class and sets the `x:Key` property so that we can access the resource by name as `OrganizationDS`.

The other interesting markup change is the value configured on the `ListBox`'s `DataContext` property:

```
DataContext="{Binding Mode=OneWay, Path=People,
Source={StaticResource OrganizationDS}}"
```

You can see that the `DataContext` is set to the `People` collection via the `Path` property on the `Binding` object, which is available by setting the `Source` property to the static resource `OrganizationDS`. As a result, the `Listbox` will display the list of people in the UI. We cover data binding in detail in Chapter 4, so we do not dive into data binding here. The goal of the recipe has been fulfilled with gaining access to the custom class in the XAML file.

2-2. Adding a Custom Control

Problem

You want to add a custom control to your Silverlight application to enhance the user interface of an application.

Solution

Add a reference to the assembly containing the custom control, and add a `clr-namespace` reference via an `xmlns` attribute in the `<UserControl>` tag of `MainPage.xaml`.

How It Works

The steps to make a custom server control are similar to the steps to add a custom class in Recipe 2-1. First, we need a custom control. We'll use one from a separate solution titled `SimpleControl` that creates a simple control consisting of a `TextBlock` that displays the text `Full Name:` in front of the value set for the `FullName` property on the control. We don't go into detail on how to create the `SimpleControl` here, because we describe how to create custom controls in Chapter 5.

The Code

In the `\Code\Ch02_ProgrammingModel\Recipe2.2\SimpleControl` folder that is part of the source code download for this book, you'll fine the simple example control solution. To run the code for this recipe, you must first open the `SimpleControl` solution and build it to create the `SimpleControl.dll` assembly. Next, open the Chapter 2 solution that contains the sample code for this chapter, and make sure the reference is available in the Recipe 2-2 project. To make the custom control available, add a reference to the assembly in your project to the `SimpleControl` assembly, and then, add an `xmlns` import to the `<UserControl>` tag. After that, the `SimpleControl` assembly and namespace will be listed as shown in Figure 2-6.

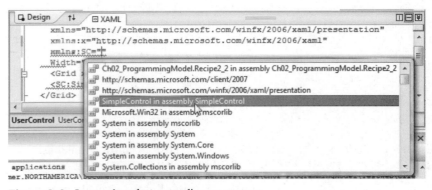

Figure 2-6. *Importing the control's namespace*

Once the control's namespace is imported, the control can be added to the XAML in Visual Studio using the SC: namespace.

```
<SC:SimpleControl FullName="Rob Cameron and Jit Ghosh" FontSize="18" />
```

Listing 2-3 shows the complete MainPage.xaml file for this recipe.

Listing 2-3. *Recipe 2-2's MainPage.xaml File*

```
<UserControl x:Class="Ch02_ProgrammingModel.Recipe2_2.MainPage"
    xmlns="http://schemas.microsoft.com/winfx/2006/xaml/presentation"
    xmlns:x="http://schemas.microsoft.com/winfx/2006/xaml"
    xmlns:SC="clr-namespace:SimpleControl;assembly=SimpleControl"
    Width="400" Height="300">
    <Grid x:Name="LayoutRoot" Background="White">
      <SC:SimpleControl FullName="Rob Cameron and Jit Ghosh"
    FontSize="18" f/>
    </Grid>
</UserControl>
```

You can see the xmlns namespace that imports the SimpleControl namespace and assembly as well as the XAML markup to add the control to the page. Figure 2-7 shows the control at runtime.

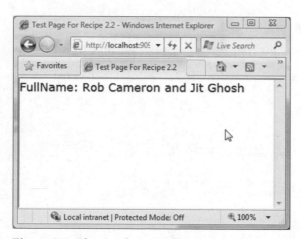

Figure 2-7. *The simple control in action*

While the purpose of this recipe is to understand how to make a custom control available in XAML, we list the source code for the SimpleControl object here for reference purposes. If you would like to learn how to build custom controls for Silverlight, please see Chapter 5. Listing 2-4 shows the contents of the generic.xaml file. generic.xaml is the default file name for a control's XAML file and is located in the Themes subdirectory for the project.

Listing 2-4. *Recipe 2-2's SimpleControl Generic.xaml File*

```
<ResourceDictionary
  xmlns="http://schemas.microsoft.com/client/2007"
  xmlns:x="http://schemas.microsoft.com/winfx/2006/xaml"
  xmlns:SimpleControl="clr-namespace:SimpleControl">
  <Style TargetType="SimpleControl:SimpleControl">
    <Setter Property="Template">
      <Setter.Value>
        <ControlTemplate TargetType="SimpleControl:SimpleControl">
          <Grid x:Name="Root">
            <TextBlock x:Name="fullNameTextBlock" Text="" />
          </Grid>
        </ControlTemplate>
      </Setter.Value>
    </Setter>
  </Style>
</ResourceDictionary>
```

Listing 2-5 shows the contents of the control's code-behind file.

Listing 2-5. *Recipe 2-2's SimpleControl Class File*

```
using System.Windows;
using System.Windows.Controls;

namespace SimpleControl
{
  public class SimpleControl : Control
  {
    protected TextBlock _fullNameTextBlock;

    public SimpleControl()
    {
      this.DefaultStyleKey = this.GetType();
    }

    public string FullName
    {
      get { return (string)GetValue(FullNameProperty); }
      set { SetValue(FullNameProperty, value); }
    }
```

```
public static readonly DependencyProperty FullNameProperty =
    DependencyProperty.Register("FullName", typeof(string),
    typeof(SimpleControl), new PropertyMetadata(OnFullNameChanged));

protected static void OnFullNameChanged(DependencyObject o,
  DependencyPropertyChangedEventArgs args)
{
  SimpleControl hc = o as SimpleControl;
  if (hc != null)
  {
    if (hc._fullNameTextBlock != null)
      hc._fullNameTextBlock.Text =
        controlLogic(args.NewValue.ToString());
  }
}

public override void OnApplyTemplate()
{
  base.OnApplyTemplate();
  _fullNameTextBlock =
    GetTemplateChild("fullNameTextBlock") as TextBlock;
  _fullNameTextBlock.Text =
    controlLogic((string)GetValue(FullNameProperty));
}

private static string controlLogic(string targetValue)
{
  return string.Format("FullName: {0}", targetValue);
}
  }
}
```

2-3. Locating a Control

Problem

You need to locate a control within the XAML visual tree at runtime.

Solution

Use FrameworkElement.FindName to locate a control at runtime.

How It Works

The abstract base class for controls in Silverlight is the DependencyObject class that represents objects participating in the Silverlight dependency property system. UIElement inherits from DependencyObject and represents objects that have visual appearance and that can perform basic input. FrameworkElement inherits from UIElement and provides common APIs for elements to participate in Silverlight layout, as well as APIs related to data binding, the object tree, and object lifetime.

One of the available members on FrameworkElement is FindName, which takes a string that contains the name of a control and returns either an object reference or null. The FindName method provides a convenient way of locating a control within the XAML visual tree without having to walk through the object tree.

In order for a control to be found, it must have its Name property set in code or via the x:Name property in XAML. XAML is hierarchical by nature, since it is an XML tree where there is a root element that contains child elements. After the XAML processor creates the object tree from markup, the x:Name attribute provides a reference to markup elements that is accessible in the code-behind file, such as in event handler code.

Names must be unique within an XAML namescope, which we cover in the next couple of paragraphs. The XAML <UserControl> by default defined in MainPage.xaml as the MainPage class is the most common namescope and is referred to as the root XAML namescope. Calling APIs that dynamically load XAML can define additional namescopes as well. Refer to Recipes 2-4 and 2-5 to learn more about how to dynamically load XAML.

When XAML is added dynamically to the visual tree, the tree remains unified, but a new namescope will be created at the point where the dynamic XAML is attached. Templates and resources define their own namescopes independently of the containing page where the style or template is applied.

The reason for the detailed discussion regarding namescopes is because FindName works within the constraint of namescopes. If you call FindName from the MainPage level to get a named object in the root XAML namescope, the call will succeed as usual. However, if you call FindName from the MainPage level, the method will not find the objects in the new discrete XAML namescope created by Load or within templates or resources. To find an element with FindName within newly created namescopes, retain a reference to an object or UIElement within the namescope, and call FindName from the element that is within the new namescope in the XAML visual tree.

Since FindName is part of the visual control base class FrameworkElement, it is accessible in all visual controls and can be called just about anywhere. What is convenient about FindName is that if the XAML element has child elements, they are all searched recursively for the requested named element. FindName will search the current XAML namescope in both the up (parent) and down (children) direction within the visual object tree defined in XAML.

The Code

The code for this recipe (Listing 2-6) has a bit more application logic than previous recipes so far in this book. It lays out a few controls and then provides a method for the user to enter a control name to find. It then provides feedback on whether or not it was successful in finding the control.

Listing 2-6. *Recipe 2-3's MainPage.xaml File*

```
<UserControl x:Class="Ch02_ProgrammingModel.Recipe2_3.MainPage"
    xmlns="http://schemas.microsoft.com/winfx/2006/xaml/presentation"
    xmlns:x="http://schemas.microsoft.com/winfx/2006/xaml"
    Width="400" Height="300">
```

```xml
<Grid x:Name="LayoutRoot" Background="White">
  <Grid.RowDefinitions>
    <RowDefinition Height="0.483*"/>
    <RowDefinition Height="0.517*"/>
  </Grid.RowDefinitions>
  <StackPanel Grid.RowSpan="2">
    <TextBlock x:Name="TextBlock1" Margin="4">TextBlock1</TextBlock>
    <TextBlock x:Name="TextBlock2" Margin="4">TextBlock2</TextBlock>
    <TextBlock x:Name="TextBlock3" Margin="4">TextBlock3</TextBlock>
    <TextBlock x:Name="TextBlock4" Margin="4">TextBlock4</TextBlock>
    <Rectangle Fill="Navy" Height="10" Margin="2"></Rectangle>
  </StackPanel>
  <StackPanel Grid.Row="1" Margin="2">
    <TextBlock Margin="2" TextWrapping="Wrap">
      Type the Name of a TextBlock from the above list.</TextBlock>
    <TextBox x:Name="ControlName" Height="24" KeyDown="ControlName_KeyDown"
      Margin="2" Grid.Row="1" TextWrapping="Wrap"/>
    <Button Content="Click To Find the Name Entered." Margin="2"
      Click="Button_Click"></Button>
  </StackPanel>
</Grid>
</UserControl>
```

The MainPage.xaml file shown in Listing 2-6 has a Grid split into two sections, each with a StackPanel control. The top StackPanel has four TextBlock controls with matching x:Name and Text values. There is also a blue Rectangle control to provide some UI separation. The bottom StackPanel has a TextBlock with some instructions, a TextBox to receive user input, and a Button to kick off the FindName call. Listing 2-7 shows the MainPage.xaml.cs class file.

Listing 2-7. *Recipe 2-3's MainPage.xaml.cs Class File*

```csharp
using System.Windows;
using System.Windows.Controls;
using System.Windows.Input;
using System.Windows.Media;

namespace Ch02_ProgrammingModel.Recipe2_3
{
  public partial class MainPage : UserControl
  {
    public Page()
    {
      InitializeComponent();
    }
```

```
private void Button_Click(object sender, RoutedEventArgs e)
{
  TextBlock tb = (TextBlock)LayoutRoot.FindName(ControlName.Text);
  if (tb != null)
    tb.FontSize = 20.0;
  else
  {
    ControlName.Foreground = new SolidColorBrush(
                           Color.FromArgb(255, 200, 124, 124));
    ControlName.Text = "Control not found! Please try again.";
  }
}

private void ControlName_KeyDown(object sender, KeyEventArgs e)
{
  ControlName.Foreground = new SolidColorBrush(Color.FromArgb(255, 0, 0, 0));
}
}
}
```

There are two events in the code-behind file: one for clicking the button and another for the KeyDown for the TextBox. The Button_Click event tries to find a control with the name entered in the TextBox. If the entered value is valid and the control can be found, the FontSize is changed to 20.0 for the found TextBlock.

If the entered value is not valid, a message is put into the TextBox stating that the control was not found based on the entered value, and the font color is changed to a reddish color. The KeyDown event simply resets the font color for the TextBox back to black. We purposely did not use any of the great new animation features available in Silverlight and instead chose to have Windows Forms–like simple animation in the UI. In Chapter 3, we'll go into detail on how to take advantage of the great animation features in Silverlight.

Figure 2-8 shows the initial layout of the UI.

Figure 2-9 shows the application when the correct value for the name of a TextBlock control is entered and the Button is clicked. TextBlock2 is entered for the value, and the font size is changed to 20, enlarging the text in TextBlock2.

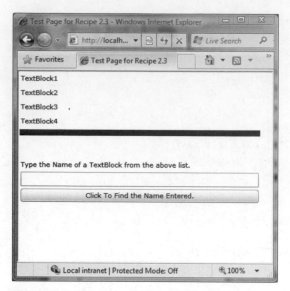

Figure 2-8. *The recipe's UI initial layout*

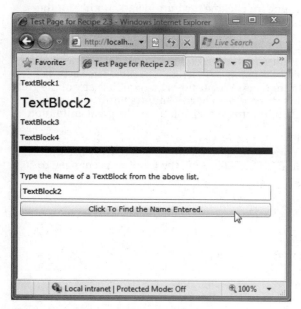

Figure 2-9. *Recipe 2-3's UI after entering a valid control name*

Figure 2-10 shows the UI when an incorrect value is entered. The font color is changed, and an error message is put into the TextBox control.

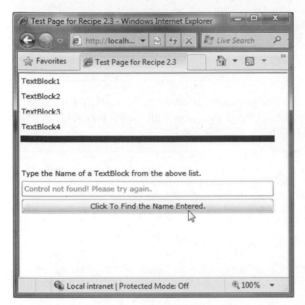

Figure 2-10. *Recipe 2-3's UI after entering an invalid control name*

2-4. Dynamically Loading XAML from JavaScript

Problem

You need to dynamically load XAML at runtime from JavaScript.

Solution

Use the CreateFromXaml method in JavaScript to dynamically load XAML markup at runtime into a Silverlight 3 application. Use FindName to locate the parent control where the XAML will be attached in the visual object tree. We covered FindName in Recipe 2-3.

How It Works

Silverlight 3 runs as an Internet browser plug-in that is created from within an HTML <object> tag in the browser. Even though Silverlight 3 has a managed code execution model, the Silverlight 3 plug-in is still accessible from and can interoperate with HTML using JavaScript, as in Silverlight 1.0. Chapter 6 covers browser integration in detail, so this recipe focuses only on how to dynamically load XAML from JavaScript using CreateFromXaml.

The Code

There are two ways to approach this recipe: using an HTML page or using an ASP.NET page. The plain-old HTML page can be used as a guide for configuring Silverlight for non-Microsoft platforms.

For the ASPX page, we'll use the default test page created by Visual Studio 2008. We'll also add a button to the ASPX test page and a script reference to a JavaScript file that will load the XAML (in this case one named Recipe2.4.js in the /js folder).

■**Note** Silverlight 2 developer tools included an ASP.NET Silverlight control to configure a Silverlight application. In Silverlight 3, the control has been removed. The techniques for hosting the Silverlight control covered here will work with any web technology, because it is simply HTML with the <object> tag.

For the ASPX page, the Silverlight 3 plug-in is configured directly in an <object> tag located inside a <div> tag. The default ASPX test page created by Visual Studio 2008 does not include an id value in the <object> declaration, so set the value for id to SilverlightPlugInID so that it can be accessed in JavaScript using the document.getElementById method:

```
var slControl = document.getElementById("SilverlightPlugInID");
```

After obtaining a reference to the Silverlight plug-in, we can create a new Silverlight control, using the CreateFromXaml method on the Content property of the plug-in, and hold a JavaScript reference to it:

```
slControl.Content.CreateFromXaml(
 '<Ellipse Height="200" Width="200" Fill="Navy" />');
```

We next call the FindName method on the Silverlight plug-in to access the XAML control tree in MainPage.xaml to obtain a reference to the default root <Grid> control with an x:Name of "LayoutRoot":

```
var layoutRoot = slControl.content.FindName("LayoutRoot");
```

Once we have a reference to the <Grid> control, we can add the control we created with the CreateFromXaml method to the Grid's Children collection using the Add method:

```
layoutRoot.Children.Add(e);
```

When you attach XAML to a visual tree, the added tree creates a new namescope for that XAML within the existing scope of the Page UserControl class. Calling FindName to locate a control within the newly added XAML from the Page level will not succeed, because the method will search inside the newly created namescope. The best way to manage this is to retain a reference to the newly added XAML and call FindName from the reference.

The only additional code we need to add to the ASPX test page is logic to enable the button after the Silverlight control is fully loaded. If you do not take this into account and call FindName before the Silverlight application is fully loaded, FindName will return null. The way to manage this is to put logic inside the OnLoad method for the Silverlight plug-in object that does not access or allow access to the control tree until the event fires:

```
function onSilverlightLoad(sender, args)
{
  var btn = document.getElementById("testButton");
  btn.disabled = false;
}
```

In the ASPX test page, the code in onSilverlightLoad simply enables the button. Otherwise, if the button was not disabled and the button is clicked before the control is fully loaded, a null reference exception occurs. To assign the OnLoad event to the Silverlight plug-in, set a <param> tag on the <object> tag:

```
<param name="onload" value="onSilverlightLoad" />
```

The MainPage.xaml is not modified for this recipe, so it is not listed here. All of the action occurs in the custom script file and the HTML and ASP.NET test pages shown in Listings 2-8 and 2-9.

In Listing 2-8, we use the HTML getElementById to obtain a reference to the Silverlight control. Next, we create an ellipse, and add it to the existing XAML content. The JavaScript file in Listing 2-8 is referenced by the HTML and ASP.NET page.

Listing 2-8. *The Recipe2.4.js JavaScript File*

```
function createEllipse()
{
    var slControl = document.getElementById("SilverlightPlugInID");
    var e =
        slControl.Content.CreateFromXaml(
            '<Ellipse Height="200" Width="200" Fill="Navy" />');
    var layoutRoot = slControl.content.FindName("LayoutRoot");
    layoutRoot.Children.Add(e);
}

function onSilverlightLoad(sender, args)
{
  var btn = document.getElementById("testButton");
  btn.disabled = false;
}
```

Listing 2-9 includes the script file in Listing 2-8. Also in Listing 2-9, the onSilverlightLoad event from Listing 2-8 is assigned to the Silverlight control's onload event, dynamically adding the XAML.

Listing 2-9. *Recipe 2-4's TestPage.aspx File*

```
<%@ Page Language="C#" AutoEventWireup="true" %>
<!DOCTYPE html PUBLIC "-//W3C//DTD XHTML 1.0 Transitional//EN"
  "http://www.w3.org/TR/xhtml1/DTD/xhtml1-transitional.dtd">
<script runat="server">
```

```
    protected void Page_Load(object sender, EventArgs e)
    {
      testButton.Attributes.Add("onclick", "createEllipse();");
    }
</script>

<html xmlns="http://www.w3.org/1999/xhtml">
<head id="Head1" runat="server">
    <title>Test Page For Recipe 2.4</title>

    <script src="js/Recipe2.4.js" type="text/javascript"></script>

    <style type="text/css">
    html, body {
        height: 100%;
        overflow: auto;
    }
    body {
        padding: 0;
        margin: 0;
    }
    #silverlightControlHost {
        height: 100%;
        text-align:center;
    }
    </style>
    <script type="text/javascript" src="Silverlight.js"></script>
    <script type="text/javascript">
      function onSilverlightError(sender, args) {
        var appSource = "";
        if (sender != null && sender != 0) {
          appSource = sender.getHost().Source;
        }

        var errorType = args.ErrorType;
        var iErrorCode = args.ErrorCode;

        if (errorType == "ImageError" || errorType == "MediaError") {
          return;
        }

        var errMsg = "Unhandled Error in Silverlight Application " +
                            appSource + "\n";
```

```
          errMsg += "Code: " + iErrorCode + "      \n";
          errMsg += "Category: " + errorType + "          \n";
          errMsg += "Message: " + args.ErrorMessage + "        \n";

          if (errorType == "ParserError") {
            errMsg += "File: " + args.xamlFile + "      \n";
            errMsg += "Line: " + args.lineNumber + "       \n";
            errMsg += "Position: " + args.charPosition + "       \n";
          }
          else if (errorType == "RuntimeError") {
            if (args.lineNumber != 0) {
              errMsg += "Line: " + args.lineNumber + "       \n";
              errMsg += "Position: " + args.charPosition + "        \n";
            }
            errMsg += "MethodName: " + args.methodName + "        \n";
          }

          throw new Error(errMsg);
        }
      </script>
  </head>

  <body>
    <form id="form1" runat="server" style="height:100%;">
        <asp:Button ID="testButton" runat="server" Enabled="false"
                  ext="Click Me!" UseSubmitBehavior="false" />
        <div id="silverlightControlHost">
        <object id="SilverlightPlugInID" data="data:application/x-silverlight-2,"
            type="application/x-silverlight-2" width="100%" height="100%">
          <param name="source" value="ClientBin/Ch02_ProgrammingModel.Recipe2_4.xap"/>
          <param name="onerror" value="onSilverlightError" />
          <param name="onload" value="onSilverlightLoad" />
          <param name="background" value="white" />
          <param name="minRuntimeVersion" value="3.0.40520.0" />
          <param name="autoUpgrade" value="true" />
          <a href="http://go.microsoft.com/fwlink/?LinkID=
                  149156&v=3.0.40520.0" style="text-decoration: none;">
              <img src="http://go.microsoft.com/fwlink/?LinkId=108181"
                  alt="Get Microsoft Silverlight" style="border-style: none"/>
          </a>
        </object><iframe id="_sl_historyFrame"
                    style='visibility:hidden;height:0;width:0;border:0px'></iframe></div>
    </form>
  </body>
</html>
```

2-5. Dynamically Loading XAML from Managed Code

Problem

You need to dynamically load XAML at runtime from managed code.

Solution

Use the XamlReader object to dynamically load XAML markup at runtime from managed code.

How It Works

The XamlReader object sits in the System.Windows.Markup namespace. The static Load method takes a string of XAML and converts the string to an object or object tree, depending on what is contained within the XAML string. The static Load method then returns a reference to root element created of type UIElement, which can be added to the UI visual tree. Since all XAML elements inherit from UIElement, it makes sense that the return type from Load would also be UIElement. The string must consist of valid markup with the addition of two namespaces on the top-level element in the XAML contained in the string:

```
xmlns="http://schemas.microsoft.com/client/2007"
xmlns:x="xmlns:x='http://schemas.microsoft.com/winfx/2006/xaml"
```

Once you have a valid string of XAML, pass it to the Load method, and a UIElement object reference is returned. The final step is to convert the object to a UIElement or descendant class and add it as a child to the desired parent element in the visual tree.

The Code

Using the XamlReader.Load method is pretty straightforward. We add a Button to the XAML markup and a Click event handler named Button_Click where the XamlReader.Load method is called. Listing 2-10 shows the code for MainPage.xaml.

For the sample code in Listing 2-11, the XAML that is dynamically created is already located in a string named xamlString in the Click event handler to keep things simple. In Chapter 6, we cover how to pass data via browser integration, and in Chapter 7, you'll learn how to obtain data via networking and web services.

Listing 2-10. *Recipe 2-5's MainPage.xaml File*

```xml
<UserControl x:Class="Ch02_ProgrammingModel.Recipe2_5.MainPage"
    xmlns="http://schemas.microsoft.com/winfx/2006/xaml/presentation"
    xmlns:x="http://schemas.microsoft.com/winfx/2006/xaml"
    Width="400" Height="300">
  <Grid x:Name="LayoutRoot" Background="White">
    <Grid.ColumnDefinitions>
      <ColumnDefinition Width="0.415*"/>
      <ColumnDefinition Width="0.585*"/>
    </Grid.ColumnDefinitions>
```

```
<Grid.RowDefinitions>
  <RowDefinition Height="0.15*"/>
  <RowDefinition Height="0.85*"/>
</Grid.RowDefinitions>
<Button Click="Button_Click" Margin="10" Content="Click To Load XAML" />

  </Grid>
</UserControl>
```

Listing 2-11. *Recipe 2-5's MainPage.xaml.cs Class File*

```csharp
using System.Windows;
using System.Windows.Controls;
using System.Windows.Markup;

namespace Ch02_ProgrammingModel.Recipe2_5
{
  public partial class MainPage : UserControl
  {
    public Page()
    {
      InitializeComponent();
    }

    private void Button_Click(object sender, RoutedEventArgs e)
    {
      string xamlString =
        "<Ellipse xmlns=\"http://schemas.microsoft.com/client/2007\"
            xmlns:x=\"xmlns:x='http://schemas.microsoft.com/winfx/2006/xaml\"
        Height=\"200\" Width=\"200\" Fill=\"Navy\" Grid.Column=\"1\"
        Grid.Row=\"1\" />";
      UIElement element = (UIElement)XamlReader.Load(xamlString);
      LayoutRoot.Children.Add(element);
    }
  }
}
```

So when the button on the test page is clicked, the XAML containing the Ellipse markup is loaded into the element and added to the Children of the root Grid control named LayoutRoot, adding the Ellipse to the visual tree so that it is displayed on the MainPage. Figure 2-11shows the final UI for the recipe.

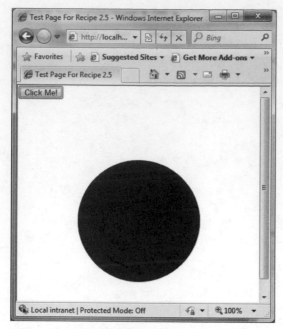

Figure 2-11. *Recipe 2-5s final UI*

2-6. Persisting Data on the Client

Problem

You need to persist data on the end user's machine.

Solution

Use isolated storage to store data on the client.

How It Works

In some situations, you may want to store data to the client's computer, such as user-specific settings or application state information. However, it is not possible to use the regular file system of the operating system from a web browser application, because native file system operations require full trust, but Web-based applications run in a partial-trust isolated sandbox.

Isolated storage provides a safe client-side storage area for partial-trust applications to persist information on a per-user basis. In Silverlight, all I/O operations are restricted to the isolated storage. Silverlight 3 includes the ability to run Silverlight applications out-of-browser when online or offline. Offline Silverlight applications can still access the same isolated storage area as they can when running in the browser, so users have seamless access to their data. We cover offline Silverlight 3 applications in Chapter 7.

Besides storing settings, isolated storage can be used to improve user experience as well as reduce bandwidth by storing partially filled-out forms, so that the form data can be reloaded when the user returns, even if, for example, the user stored the data using Internet Explorer but access the application later using Firefox.

The System.IO.IsolatedStorage namespace contains types for creating and using a virtual file system. Table 2-1 lists the classes available in this namespace.

Table 2-1. *Classes Related to IsolatedStorage*

Class	Description
IsolatedStorageException	Exception that is thrown when an isolated storage operation fails
IsolatedStorageFile	Represents an isolated storage area containing files and directories
IsolatedStorageFileStream	Represents a file within isolated storage
IsolatedStorageSettings	Provides a Dictionary object that stores key-value pairs within isolated storage

Isolated storage is not unlimited. Administrators can set user quota restrictions that limit the amount of data that can be stored in isolated storage, so it is not suited for large amounts of data. The default size of isolated storage for in browser Silverlight applications is 1MB. The default size of isolated storage for out-of-browser Silverlight applications at install time (called detach) is 25MB.

■**Note** Isolated storage is not encrypted, though developers can encrypt and decrypt files stored in local storage if desired. Developers can also sign and validate signatures using the SHA1 hash function. .

The quota can be increased further by the user through the UI thread, usually as a result of a UI event handler. Otherwise,the quota cannot be increased on a background thread or without user action. Isolated storage remains intact even if the browser cache is cleared, but isolated storage can be manually deleted by the user or application.

Applications can request more space by invoking the IsolatedStorageFile.IncreaseQuotaTo() method in response to a user-initiated event, such as a mouse click or key press, as noted previously.

To work with isolated storage, first obtain an isolated store for the application using the IsolatedStorageFile.
GetUserStoreForApplication method. This returns an IsolatedStorageFile object, which you can use to create directories using the CreateDirectory method and files using the CreateFile method. The CreateFile method returns an IsolatedStorageFileStream object. The IsolatedStorageFileStream class inherits from FileStream, so you can use the class with StreamReader and StreamWriter objects.

Another option is to use the IsolatedStorageSettings class, which is a Dictionary object that can be used to quickly store key/value pairs in isolated storage.

The Code

To test isolated storage, our sample does two things. It allows a user to store and update a setting using the IsolatedStorageSettings class and to save and reload form state between browser sessions. Figure 2-12 shows the UI with a mock form.

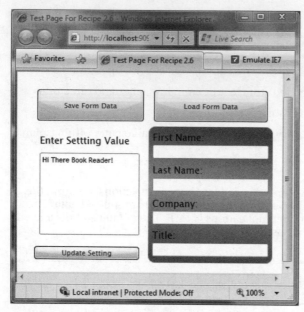

Figure 2-12. *Recipe 2-6's test application UI*

The Silverlight application shown in Figure 2-12 has a TextBox on the left with "Hi There Book Reader!" as a value. Any value entered in this TextBox is stored in the IsolatedStorageSettings dictionary object, which is a convenient place to store name/value pair settings or data. The UserControl.Loaded event handler pulls this setting out of the collection, and the ButtonUpdateSetting event handler stores the setting when the Button titled Update Setting is clicked.

The Save Form Data button and the Load Form Data button both work with the sample form fields located in the rounded green/silver area on the right side of the application. The Save Form Data button concatenates the text from the form data into a string, with each value separated by the pipe (|) symbol. The Load Form Data button reads in the data as a String and calls String.Split to separate the fields into an array of string values.

The SaveFormData_Click event stores the form data into isolated storage. In general, any data that is persisted into IsolatedStorage is persisted between browser sessions. The ReadFormData_Click event retrieves the data from the file created in isolated storage. Listings 2-12 and 2-13 show the code for the Silverlight application's MainPage class.

Listing 2-12. *Recipe 2-6's MainPage.xaml File*

```
<UserControl x:Class="Ch02_ProgrammingModel.Recipe2_6.MainPage"
    xmlns="http://schemas.microsoft.com/winfx/2006/xaml/presentation"
    xmlns:x="http://schemas.microsoft.com/winfx/2006/xaml"
    Width="400" Height="300" Loaded="UserControl_Loaded"  >
  <Grid x:Name="LayoutRoot" Background="#FFFFFFFF">
    <Grid.ColumnDefinitions>
      <ColumnDefinition Width="0.06*"/>
      <ColumnDefinition Width="0.455*"/>
      <ColumnDefinition Width="0.485*"/>
    </Grid.ColumnDefinitions>
    <Grid.RowDefinitions>
      <RowDefinition Height="0.08*"/>
      <RowDefinition Height="0.217*"/>
      <RowDefinition Height="0.61*"/>
      <RowDefinition Height="0.093*"/>
    </Grid.RowDefinitions>
    <Button HorizontalAlignment="Stretch" Margin="8 " VerticalAlignment="Stretch"
     Grid.Column="1" Grid.Row="1" Content="Save Form Data"
     Click="SaveFormData_Click"/>
    <StackPanel HorizontalAlignment="Stretch" Margin="8,8,10,8" Grid.Column="1"
        Grid.Row="2">
      <TextBlock Height="Auto" Width="Auto" Text="Enter Setting Value"
        TextWrapping="Wrap" Margin="4,4,4,4"/>
      <TextBox Height="126" Width="Auto" Text="" TextWrapping="Wrap"
        Margin="4,4,4,4" x:Name="settingTextData"/>
    </StackPanel>
    <Button HorizontalAlignment="Stretch" Margin="8" VerticalAlignment="Stretch"
       Grid.Column="2" Grid.Row="1" Content="Load Form Data"
       Click="ReadFormData_Click"/>
    <Button HorizontalAlignment="Stretch" Margin="4,4,14,4"
      VerticalAlignment="Stretch"
      Grid.Column="1" Grid.Row="3" Content="Update Setting"
      Click="ButtonUpdateSetting"/>
    <Border Grid.Column="2" Grid.Row="2" Grid.RowSpan="2"
    CornerRadius="10,10,10,10">
      <Border.Background>
        <LinearGradientBrush EndPoint="0.560000002384186,0.00300000002607703"
          StartPoint="0.439999997615814,0.996999979019165">
          <GradientStop Color="#FF586C57"/>
          <GradientStop Color="#FFA3BDA3" Offset="0.536"/>
          <GradientStop Color="#FF586C57" Offset="0.968999981880188"/>
        </LinearGradientBrush>
      </Border.Background>
    </Border.Background>
```

```xml
        <StackPanel Margin="4,4,4,4"  x:Name="FormData">
          <TextBlock Height="Auto" Width="Auto" Text="First Name:"
             TextWrapping="Wrap" Margin="2,2,2,0"/>
          <TextBox Height="Auto" Width="Auto" Text="" TextWrapping="Wrap" x:
             Name="Field1" Margin="2,0,2,4"/>
          <TextBlock Height="Auto" Width="Auto" Text="Last Name:"
             TextWrapping="Wrap" Margin="2,4,2,0"/>
          <TextBox Height="Auto" x:Name="Field2" Width="Auto" Text=""
            TextWrapping="Wrap" Margin="2,0,2,4"/>
          <TextBlock Height="Auto" Width="Auto" Text="Company:"
            TextWrapping="Wrap" Margin="2,4,2,0"/>
          <TextBox Height="Auto" x:Name="Field3" Width="Auto" Text=""
            TextWrapping="Wrap" Margin="2,0,2,2"/>
          <TextBlock Height="22.537" Width="182" Text="Title:"
             TextWrapping="Wrap" Margin="2,4,2,0"/>
          <TextBox Height="20.772" x:Name="Field4" Width="182" Text=""
             TextWrapping="Wrap" Margin="2,0,2,2"/>
        </StackPanel>
      </Border>
    </Grid>
</UserControl>
```

Listing 2-13 has the code-behind page for MainPage.xaml where the events are located. The code declares several class level variables such as settings that is used by the event handlers to load and save setting values to IsolatedStorage.

Listing 2-13. *Recipe 2-6's MainPage.xaml.cs Class File*

```csharp
using System.Linq;
using System.Windows;
using System.Windows.Controls;
using System.IO;
using System.IO.IsolatedStorage;
using System.Text;

namespace Ch02_ProgrammingModel.Recipe2_6
{
  public partial class MainPage : UserControl
  {
    private IsolatedStorageSettings settings =
                        IsolatedStorageSettings.ApplicationSettings;
    private string setting = "MySettings";
    private string FormDataFileName = "FormFields.data";
    private string FormDataDirectory = "FormData";
```

```
public Page()
{
  InitializeComponent();
}

private void UserControl_Loaded(object sender, RoutedEventArgs e)
{
  try
  {
    if (settings.Keys.Count != 0)
    {
      settingTextData.Text = settings[setting].ToString();
    }
  }
  catch (IsolatedStorageException ex)
  {
    settingTextData.Text = "Error saving setting: " + ex.Message;
  }
}

private void SaveFormData_Click(object sender, RoutedEventArgs e)
{
  try
  {
    using (var store = IsolatedStorageFile.GetUserStoreForApplication())
    {
      //Use to control loop for finding correct number of textboxes
      int TotalFields = 4;
      StringBuilder formData = new StringBuilder(50);
      for (int i = 1; i <= TotalFields; i++)
      {
        TextBox tb = FindName("Field" + i.ToString()) as TextBox;
        if (tb != null)
          formData.Append(th.Text);
        //If on last TextBox value, don't add "|" character to end of data
        if (i != TotalFields)
          formData.Append("|");
      }
      store.CreateDirectory(FormDataDirectory);
      IsolatedStorageFileStream fileHandle =
          store.CreateFile(System.IO.Path.Combine(
          FormDataDirectory, FormDataFileName));
```

```
      using (StreamWriter sw = new StreamWriter(fileHandle))
      {
        sw.WriteLine(formData);
        sw.Flush();
        sw.Close();
      }
    }
  }
  catch (IsolatedStorageException ex)
  {
    settingTextData.Text = "Error saving data: " + ex.Message;
  }
}

private void ReadFormData_Click(object sender, RoutedEventArgs e)
{
  using (var store = IsolatedStorageFile.GetUserStoreForApplication())
  {
    //Load form data using private string values for directory and filename
    string filePath =
      System.IO.Path.Combine(FormDataDirectory, FormDataFileName);
    //Check to see if file exists before proceeding
    if (store.FileExists(filePath))
    {
      using (StreamReader sr = new StreamReader(
          store.OpenFile(filePath, FileMode.Open, FileAccess.Read)))
      {
        string formData = sr.ReadLine();
        //Split string based on separator used in SaveFormData method
        string[] fieldValues = formData.Split('|');
        for (int i = 1; i <= fieldValues.Count(); i++)
        {
          //Use the FindName method to loop through TextBoxes
          TextBox tb = FindName("Field" + i.ToString()) as TextBox;
          if (tb != null)
            tb.Text = fieldValues[i - 1];
        }
        sr.Close();
      }
    }
  }
}
```

```
    private void ButtonUpdateSetting(object sender, RoutedEventArgs e)
    {
      try
      {
        settings[setting] = settingTextData.Text;
      }
      catch (IsolatedStorageException ex)
      {
        settingTextData.Text = "Error reading setting: " + ex.Message;
      }
    }
  }
}
```

2-7. Opening a Local File from a Silverlight Application

Problem

You need to select a local file on the client machine and upload it to the server.

Solution

Create an instance of the OpenFileDialog class, and display it to the user with the ShowDialog method. You can send the files to the server for processing, but we recommend that you let the user know anytime a file is sent to the server.

How It Works

The OpenFileDialog class displays a standard Windows, Mac, or Linux open file dialog depending on the platform that allows users to browse to files anywhere on their system. The OpenFileDialog class has Filter and FilterIndex properties, which allow you to set the file filter in much the same way a .NET developer would do in a WPF or Windows Forms application. You can specify the types of files you wish to open by specifying Filter like this:

```
fileDlg.Filter = "Tiff Files (*.tif)|*.tif|All Files (*.*)|*.*";
```

This value suggests that a TIFF file is expected, but the Filter value can be overridden by the user. The format is a description of the filter, such as Tiff Files (*.tif), followed by the filter pattern, such as *.tiff. Each filter option is separated by the pipe symbol. You can also have a more generic Filter, say for all image files, by separating the filter patterns with semicolons like this:

```
Image Files(*.BMP;*.JPG;*.GIF)|*.BMP;*.JPG;*.GIF|All files (*.*)|*.*
```

You can set the FileIndex property to a zero-based index to configure which filter is the default as well as allow the user to make multiple selections by setting the Multiselect property to true.

The OpenFileDialog class also has a Multiselect property, which defaults to false. When set to true, it allows the user to select multiple files. The ShowDialog method displays the dialog shown in Figure 2-13.

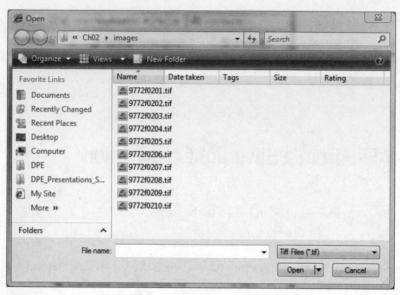

Figure 2-13. *The Open dialog in Windows*

The Code

The sample code for this recipe has a button that allows the user to select files in the local file system, including instances where Multiselect is set to true. The files that were selected are listed in a ListBox control.

When the user clicks the Select Files button in the test application, an Open dialog appears with a filter configured for TIFF files, as shown in Figure 2-13. Figure 2-14 shows the test application UI after the user selects several files and clicks the Open button in the dialog.

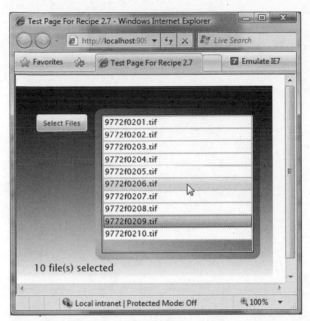

Figure 2-14. *Recipe 2-7's test application UI after selecting files using the Open dialog*

Clicking Open in the operating system's Open dialog causes the ShowDialog method to return true. Clicking Cancel causes the method to return false. When it returns true, you can use the Count() method on the OpenFileDialog.Files collection to determine the number of files returned.

To iterate over the selected files, you can use a foreach loop that steps through the Files collection. In the sample code, we simply add the filename to a ListBox object. However, the Files collection stores FileDialogFileInfo objects that contain two methods, OpenRead and OpenText. The OpenRead method returns a Stream object that allows a developer to read the file using a StreamReader class. The OpenText method returns a StreamReader with UTF-8 encoding that reads an existing text file. In Chapter 7, we'll cover Silverlight networking and web services that developers can use to upload a file to the server. Listings 2-14 and 2-15 show the code for the Recipe 2-7 test application.

Listing 2-14. *Recipe 2-7's MainPage.xaml File*

```
<UserControl x:Class="Ch02_ProgrammingModel.Recipe2_7.MainPage"
    xmlns="http://schemas.microsoft.com/winfx/2006/xaml/presentation"
    xmlns:x="http://schemas.microsoft.com/winfx/2006/xaml"
    Width="400" Height="300"
    xmlns:d="http://schemas.microsoft.com/expression/blend/2008"
    xmlns:mc="http://schemas.openxmlformats.org/markup-compatibility/2006"
    mc:Ignorable="d">
```

```xml
<Grid x:Name="LayoutRoot">
  <Grid.Background>
    <LinearGradientBrush EndPoint="0.5,1" StartPoint="0.5,0">
      <GradientStop Color="#FF000000"/>
      <GradientStop Color="#FFFFFFFF" Offset="1"/>
    </LinearGradientBrush>
  </Grid.Background>

  <Grid.RowDefinitions>
    <RowDefinition Height="0.117*"/>
    <RowDefinition Height="0.79*"/>
    <RowDefinition Height="0.093*"/>
  </Grid.RowDefinitions>
  <Grid.ColumnDefinitions>
    <ColumnDefinition Width="0.058*"/>
    <ColumnDefinition Width="0.252*"/>
    <ColumnDefinition Width="0.64*"/>
    <ColumnDefinition Width="0.05*"/>
  </Grid.ColumnDefinitions>
  <Button Height="28.9" HorizontalAlignment="Stretch" Margin="8,8,11,0"
   VerticalAlignment="Top" Width="81.8" Grid.Column="1" Grid.Row="1"
   Content="Select Files" d:LayoutOverrides="Height" x:Name="ButtonSelectFiles"
   Click="ButtonSelectFiles_Click"/>
  <TextBlock Margin="4,2,2,2" Grid.Column="1" Grid.Row="2" Text="Status"
    TextWrapping="Wrap" Grid.ColumnSpan="2" x:Name="StatusLabel"/>
  <Border Grid.Column="2" Grid.Row="1" Margin="0,0,0,0" CornerRadius="12">
    <Border.Background>
      <LinearGradientBrush EndPoint="0.916999995708466,0.0890000015497208"
        StartPoint="-0.0489999987185001,2.12400007247925">
        <GradientStop Color="#FF1D351E"/>
        <GradientStop Color="#FF1D351E" Offset="1"/>
        <GradientStop Color="#FFB7D8BA" Offset="0.50900000333786011"/>
      </LinearGradientBrush>
    </Border.Background>
    <ListBox x:Name="FileList" Foreground="#FF000000" Height="217"
      Width="236" Opacity="1"/>
  </Border>
  </Grid>
</UserControl>
```

Listing 2-15. *Recipe 2-7's MainPage.xaml.cs Class File*

```
using System.Linq;
using System.Windows;
using System.Windows.Controls;

namespace Ch02_ProgrammingModel.Recipe2_7
{
  public partial class MainPage : UserControl
  {
    public Page()
    {
      InitializeComponent();
    }

    private void ButtonSelectFiles_Click(object sender, RoutedEventArgs e)
    {
      //Create dialog
      OpenFileDialog fileDlg = new OpenFileDialog();
      //Set file filter as desired
      fileDlg.Filter = "Tiff Files (*.tif)|*.tif|All Files (*.*)|*.*";
      fileDlg.FilterIndex = 1;
      //Allow multiple files to be selected (false by default)
      fileDlg.Multiselect = true;
      //Show Open File Dialog
      if (true == fileDlg.ShowDialog())
      {
        StatusLabel.Text =
            fileDlg.Files.Count() + " file(s) selected";
        foreach (var file in fileDlg.Files)
        {
          FileList.Items.Add(file.Name);
        }
      }
    }
  }
}
```

2-8. Accessing XML Data with an XmlReader

Problem

You need to work with XML data in Silverlight using the XmlReader object.

Solution

Use the XmlReader object along with the necessary objects in the related System.Xml namespace to retrieve XML data.

How It Works

There are two ways to parse XML data in Silverlight: the XmlReader class and LINQ to XML, which is one of the new technologies that became available in .NET Framework 3.5. The XmlReader class is a fast-forward–only, noncaching XML parser. For processing large XML files, XmlReader is better suited than LINQ to XML for performance reasons.

The Silverlight XmlReader works in a similar manner as the XmlReader in the full version of the .NET Framework. Visit this site for details on the differences between the .NET Framework and the .NET Framework for Silverlight:

http://msdn.microsoft.com/en-us/library/cc189053(VS.95).aspx

The Code

The XmlReader class can be used to read XML data from the IsolatedStorage file system as well as from streams retrieved via the network just like in the full .NET Framework. One unique Silverlight ability that we take advantage of in this recipe is to use an XmlXapResolver to retrieve XML data embedded into the application's .xap file, which is the container for Silverlight applications (see Recipe 1-3). An XML resolver in .NET resolves, or evaluates, external XML resources. An XmlUrlResolver is used to resolve the Url location passed into XmlReader.Create. The XmalXapResolver looks for the name passed into XmlReader.Create within the .xap file for the application:

```
XmlReaderSettings XmlRdrSettings = new XmlReaderSettings();
XmlRdrSettings.XmlResolver = new XmlXapResolver();
XmlReader reader = XmlReader.Create("ApressBooks.xml",
XmlRdrSettings);
```

The resolver is configured for the XmlReaderSettings object that is passed into the Create method. For more information on the XmlReaderSettings class, refer to the MSDN documentation here:

http://msdn.microsoft.com/en-us/library/system.xml.xmlreadersettings(VS.95).aspx

The first step to create the test application for this recipe is to add the XML file to the Silverlight project and set its build action to Content. This puts the XML file into the assembly that is deployed to the web site so that the XmlReader can find it using the XmlXapResolver. Figure 2-15 shows the test application for this recipe.

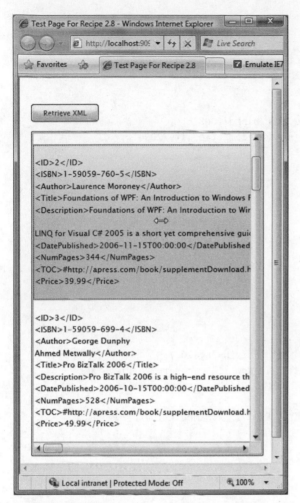

Figure 2-15. *Recipe 2-8's test application UI*

When you click the Button titled Retrieve XML, the event handler ButtonReadXML_Click uses the XmlReader and the XmlXapResolver to load the XML into a ListBox control using one line of code:

```
XmlData.Items.Add(reader.ReadInnerXml());
```

XmlData is the name of the ListBox control in the XAML for the recipe test application. The XML data is added to the Items collection for the ListBox. Listings 2-16 and 2-17 have the full code listings for this test application.

Listing 2-16. *Recipe 2-8's MainPage.xaml Class File*

```
<UserControl x:Class="Ch02_ProgrammingModel.Recipe2_8.MainPage"
    xmlns="http://schemas.microsoft.com/winfx/2006/xaml/presentation"
    xmlns:x="http://schemas.microsoft.com/winfx/2006/xaml"
    Width="400" Height="600"
    xmlns:d="http://schemas.microsoft.com/expression/blend/2008"
    xmlns:mc="http://schemas.openxmlformats.org/markup-compatibility/2006"
    mc:Ignorable="d">
  <Grid x:Name="LayoutRoot" Background="White">
    <Grid.RowDefinitions>
      <RowDefinition Height="0.027*"/>
      <RowDefinition Height="0.071*"/>
      <RowDefinition Height="0.869*"/>
      <RowDefinition Height="0.033*"/>
    </Grid.RowDefinitions>
    <Grid.ColumnDefinitions>
      <ColumnDefinition Width="0.025*"/>
      <ColumnDefinition Width="0.947*"/>
      <ColumnDefinition Width="0.028*"/>
    </Grid.ColumnDefinitions>
    <Button Height="27.1" HorizontalAlignment="Left" Margin="8,8,0,7.5"
     VerticalAlignment="Stretch" Grid.Column="1" Grid.Row="1" Content="Retrieve XML"
     d:LayoutOverrides="Height" x:Name="ButtonReadXML" Click="ButtonReadXML_Click"
     Width="106"/>
    <ListBox Margin="8,8,8,8" Grid.Column="1" Grid.Row="2" x:Name="XmlData"/>
  </Grid>
</UserControl>
```

Listing 2-17. *Recipe 2-8's MainPage.xaml.cs Class File*

```
using System.Windows;
using System.Windows.Controls;
using System.Xml;

namespace Ch02_ProgrammingModel.Recipe2_8
{
  public partial class MainPage : UserControl
  {
    public Page()
    {
      InitializeComponent();
    }
```

```
private void ButtonReadXML_Click(object sender, RoutedEventArgs e)
{

  XmlReaderSettings XmlRdrSettings = new XmlReaderSettings();
  XmlRdrSettings.XmlResolver = new XmlXapResolver();
  XmlReader reader = XmlReader.Create("ApressBooks.xml", XmlRdrSettings);

  // Moves the reader to the root element.
  reader.MoveToContent();

  while (!reader.EOF)
  {
    reader.ReadToFollowing("ApressBook");
    // Note that ReadInnerXml only returns the markup of the node's children
    // so the book's attributes are not returned.
    XmlData.Items.Add(reader.ReadInnerXml());
  }
  reader.Close();
  }
 }
}
```

2-9. Accessing XML Data with LINQ

Problem

You need to work with XML data in Silverlight using LINQ, because you would like to work with the XML data as a collection of objects.

Solution

Use the C# 3.0 language features and the System.Xml and System.Linq namespaces to query XML data.

How It Works

Again, what is great about Silverlight is that it is a rich subset of the full .NET Framework 3.5 and that it includes LINQ. There are many web sites, blogs, and books that cover LINQ, so we won't dive into all the details here.

■**Note** A great resource on LINQ is Joseph C. Rattz Jr.'s *Pro LINQ: Language Integrated Query in C#* 2008 (Apress, 2007).

The goal of this recipe is to show how to retrieve XML data using an XmlResolver—in this case the XmlXapResolver—and an XmlReader, and then load the XML data into an XDocument object.

We covered XmlResolver and XmlReader in the previous recipe. What's new in this recipe is calling XDocument.Load(XmlReader) to load the contents into an XDocument so that it can be queried using LINQ. The XDocument class, located in the System.Xml.Linq namespace, is the key object in LINQ to XML functionality.

The Code

Prior to LINQ to XML, developers worked with the XmlDocument class to create, modify, and read XML files. This wasn't the easiest thing to do, because you had to write a lot of code to walk the XML tree. LINQ to XML greatly simplifies any tasks when working with XML. In this example, we'll create a list of objects containing information on a few Apress books and display the data in a ListBox using a simple data template.

The relevant LINQ to XML functionality is located in the ApressBooks.cs class file. It contains an ApressBooks class that populates a List collection with another custom class called ApressBook, using the ApressBooks.RetrieveData method.

The code in Listing 2-18 can look a bit intimidating at first, but we will go through it line by line. The private member variable backing the public ApressBookList property is declared like this:

```
private List<ApressBook> _apressBookList;
```

This section of code is the actual LINQ query:

```
from b in xDoc.Descendants("ApressBook")
select….
```

The b variable is simply an anonymous type for retrieving a collection of objects from the XML file that are returned by the call to xDoc.Descendants("ApressBook"). The select keyword in the sample code creates an instance of the ApressBook class, but if we wanted to simply return a collection of strings containing the ISBN, we could use this code:

```
from b in xDoc.Descendants("ApressBook")
select b.Element("ISBN").Value
```

Instead, we take advantage of LINQ functionality to streamline creating a collection of ApressBook objects by using this code:

```
select new ApressBook()
{
    Author = b.Element("Author").Value,
    Title = b.Element("Title").Value,
    ISBN = b.Element("ISBN").Value,
    Description = b.Element("Description").Value,
    PublishedDate = Convert.ToDateTime(b.Element("DatePublished").Value),
    NumberOfPages = b.Element("NumPages").Value,
    Price = b.Element("Price").Value,
    ID = b.Element("ID").Value
}
```

The `select new` code is simply creating an instance of a collection containing `ApressBook` objects using C# 3.0 object initializer functionality. The value used to set each property for the `ApressBook` objects is data retrieved from the XML document, such as `b.Element("Author").Value`. Figure 2-16 shows the test application for this recipe.

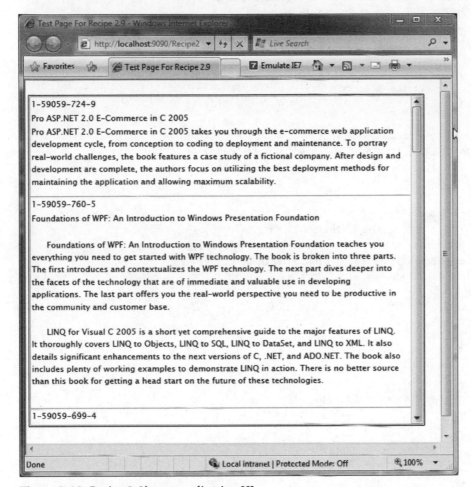

Figure 2-16. *Recipe 2-9's test application UI*

Unlike in Recipe 2-1, where we demonstrated how to add a class reference to an application but did not specify a data template, we do implement a simple data template for the `ListBox` control here, to show that the XML data is read in properly. We'll cover the details of data binding and data templates in Chapter 4. Listings 2-18 and 2-19 show the relevant code.

Listing 2-18. *Recipe 2-9's MainPage.xaml File*

```xml
<UserControl x:Class="Ch02_ProgrammingModel.Recipe2_9.MainPage"
    xmlns="http://schemas.microsoft.com/winfx/2006/xaml/presentation"
    xmlns:x="http://schemas.microsoft.com/winfx/2006/xaml"
    xmlns:data="clr-namespace:Ch02_ProgrammingModel.Recipe2_9"
    Width="600" Height="500" >

  <UserControl.Resources>
    <data:ApressBooks x:Key="ApressBooksDS" />
  </UserControl.Resources>

  <Grid x:Name="LayoutRoot" Background="White">
    <ListBox Margin="4,4,4,4" ItemsSource="{Binding Mode=OneWay,
      Path=ApressBookList, Source={StaticResource ApressBooksDS}}"  >
      <ListBox.ItemTemplate>
        <DataTemplate>
          <StackPanel Margin="2,2,2,2">
            <TextBlock Text="{Binding Path=ISBN}" Margin="0,0,0,2"/>
            <TextBlock Text="{Binding Path=Title}" Margin="0,0,0,2"/>
            <TextBlock Width="550" Text="{Binding Path=Description}"
                       TextWrapping="Wrap" Margin="0,0,0,10"/>
          </StackPanel>
        </DataTemplate>
      </ListBox.ItemTemplate>
    </ListBox>
  </Grid>
</UserControl>
```

Listing 2-19. *Recipe 2-9's ApressBooks.cs Class File*

```csharp
using System;
using System.Collections.Generic;
using System.Linq;
using System.Xml;
using System.Xml.Linq;
using System.Collections;

namespace Ch02_ProgrammingModel.Recipe2_9
{
  public class ApressBooks
  {
    private List<ApressBook> _apressBookList;
    public List<ApressBook> ApressBookList
    {
```

```csharp
    get
    {
      if (null == _apressBookList)
        RetrieveData();
      return _apressBookList;
    }
  }

  private void RetrieveData()
  {
    XmlReaderSettings XmlRdrSettings = new XmlReaderSettings();
    XmlRdrSettings.XmlResolver = new XmlXapResolver();
    XmlReader reader = XmlReader.Create("ApressBooks.xml", XmlRdrSettings);

    XDocument xDoc = XDocument.Load(reader);

    _apressBookList =
      (from b in xDoc.Descendants("ApressBook")
       select new ApressBook()
       {
         Author = b.Element("Author").Value,
         Title = b.Element("Title").Value,
         ISBN = b.Element("ISBN").Value,
         Description = b.Element("Description").Value,
         PublishedDate = Convert.ToDateTime(b.Element("DatePublished").Value),
         NumberOfPages = b.Element("NumPages").Value,
         Price = b.Element("Price").Value,
         ID = b.Element("ID").Value
       }).ToList();
  }
}

public class ApressBook
{
  public string Author { get; set; }
  public string Title { get; set; }
  public string ISBN { get; set; }
  public string Description { get; set; }
  public DateTime PublishedDate { get; set; }
  public string NumberOfPages { get; set; }
  public string Price { get; set; }
  public string ID { get; set; }
}
}
```

2-10. Managing Unhandled Exceptions

Problem

You need to manage unhandled exceptions in Silverlight.

Solution

Use the `Application.UnhandledException` event **Error! Bookmark not defined.**for your application.

How It Works

When you create a new Silverlight 3 application, the Visual Studio 2008 project template automatically implements a shell for the `Application.UnandledException` event with comments to help you get started in the `App.xaml.cs` file. This event handler can handle managed exceptions that originate from within your custom application code.

It is up to you, the developer, to decide whether or not an exception is fatal for the application. As an example, if you have a `Button` click event that retrieves data over the network but fails, the exception will be caught by the `Application.UnhandledException` event if there isn't a local exception handler in the `Button` click event. You can decide whether to prompt the user to retry or tell the user that the request cannot be performed and visually indicate that there is an unrecoverable error. The `Application.UnhandledException` event makes it convenient to implement centralized error handling and error reporting for a Silverlight application.

The `Application.UnhandledException` event cannot handle exceptions that originate from the Silverlight platform code (i.e., the plug-in itself). Platform code exceptions as well as exceptions that are not handled with the `UnhandledException` event are passed to the native/unmanaged error handler in the Silverlight plug-in. To handle exceptions at this level, implement a JavaScript `OnError` event handler in the Silverlight plug-in. To implement the `OnError` event handler, create a JavaScript event handler that follows this signature:

```
function onSLError(sender, args)
{
//error handling logic goes here
}
```

For an example of how to implement an `OnError` JavaScript handler, look no further than any one of the HTML or `.aspx` test pages that are automatically generated by the Visual Studio 2008 project template. Inside an HTML `<script>` tag is a function called `onSilverlightError` that implements basic error handling for the test page. Further down in the HTML or `.aspx` page, in the `<object>` tag for instantiating the Silverlight plug-in, the onerror parameter is passed a value of `onSilverlightError`:

```
<param name="onerror" value="onSilverlightError" />
```

There isn't any code for this recipe, since Visual Studio 2008 generates most of the sample code for you as part of the project template. Refer to the generated `.aspx` and HTML files for code examples on where to manage exceptions.

2-11. Executing Work on a Background Thread with Updates

Problem

You need to execute work in the background that provides updates on progress so that the UI can be responsive.

Solution

Use a background worker thread to execute work in the background.

How It Works

Silverlight 3 includes the System.Threading.Thread and System.Threading.ThreadPool classes as part of the .NET Framework for Silverlight. However, we recommend that you instead use the System.ComponentModel. BackgroundWorker class to execute work in the background of the UI. The BackgroundWorker class provides a nice abstraction layer over the gory details of safely synchronizing with the UI thread when using one of the lower-level classes like Thread and ThreadPool.

The BackgroundWorker class lets you indicate operation progress, completion, and cancellation in the Silverlight UI. For example, you can check whether the background operation is completed or canceled and display a message to the user.

To use a background worker thread, declare an instance of the BackgroundWorker class at the class level, not within an event handler:

```
BackgroundWorker bw = new BackgroundWorker();
```

You can specify whether you want to allow cancellation and progress reporting by setting one or both of the WorkerSupportsCancellation and WorkerReportsProgress properties on the BackgroundWorker object to true. The next step is to create an event handler for the BackgroundWorker. DoWork event. This is where you put the code for the time-consuming operation. Within the DoWork event, call the ReportProgress method to pass a percentage complete value that is between 0 and 100, which raises the ProgressChanged event on the BackgroundWorker object. The UI thread code can subscribe to the event and update the UI based on the progress. If you call the ReportProgress method when WorkerReportsProgress is set to false, an exception will occur.

Check the CancellationPending property of the BackgroundWorker object to determine if there is a pending request to cancel the background operation within the worker_DoWork member function. If CancellationPending is true, set BackgroundWorker.Cancel to true, and stop the operation. To pass data back to the calling process upon completion, set the Result property of the DoWorkerEventArgs object that is passed into the event handler to the object or collection containing the data. The DoWorkerEventArgs.Result is of type object and can therefore be assigned any object or collection of objects. The value of the Result property can be read when the RunWorkerCompleted event is raised upon completion of the operation.

The BackgroundWorker class tries to prevent deadlocks or cross-thread invocations that could be unsafe. There are some calls that are always assumed to be called on the UI thread, such as calling into the HTML Document Object Model (DOM) or a JavaScript function, so you are not allowed to call them from a BackgroundWorker class.

A deadlock occurs when two threads each hold on to a resource while requesting the resource that the other thread is holding. A deadlock will cause the browser to hang. It is easy to create a deadlock with two threads accessing the same resources in an application. Silverlight includes locking primitives, such as Montior or lock, as well as the ManualResetEvent class.

Exception must be caught within the background thread, because they will not be caught by the unhandled exception handler at the application level. If an exception occurs on the background thread, one option is to catch the exception and set Result to null as a signal that there was an error. Another option is to set a particular value to Result as a signal that a failure occurred.

The Code

In the sample code, we start with the code from Recipe 2-6, which includes a form that saves and loads data from isolated storage. We will save and load data from isolated storage while the background worker thread is executing to prove that the UI is not locked up by the long-running operation. We'll modify the UI to include a button to start the long-running operation as well as a bit of UI work to show what is going on. Figure 2-17 shows the UI.

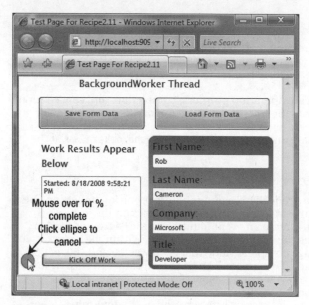

Figure 2-17. *Recipe 2-11's test UI*

To help keep things clean, the code that was copied from Recipe 2-6 is located in #region blocks so that it is not a distraction. There is a bit more code in this recipe, so we will walk through the major code sections. First, we declare a BackGroundWorker object named worker and initialize it in the constructor Page() for the Page class:

```
worker.WorkerReportsProgress = true;
worker.WorkerSupportsCancellation = true;
worker.DoWork += new DoWorkEventHandler(worker_DoWork);
worker.ProgressChanged +=
    new ProgressChangedEventHandler(worker_ProgressChanged);
worker.RunWorkerCompleted += new
RunWorkerCompletedEventHandler(worker_RunWorkerCompleted);
```

We configure the BackgroundWorker to support cancellation and progress reporting so that we can provide a simple UI to give status. Next, we wire up the DoWork, ProgressChanged, and RunWorkerCompleted events to handlers.

The DoWork event contains the code that the BackgroundWorker thread executes. This is where the long-running operation goes. ProgressChanged and RunWorkerCompleted are events where the UI thread can update status in the UI while the background work is safely executing.

In our DoWork event, we first check to see if there is a cancel request pending and break out of the loop if there is. Otherwise, we call Thread.Sleep to delay execution and ReportProgress to provide an updated percentage complete. The results of the background worker thread's effort are passed back to the main thread as the value of e.Result:

```
e.Result = Environment.NewLine + "Completed: " + DateTime.Now.ToString();
```

In our case, we simply pass back a string, but in a scenario with real background work, this could be a collection of data or objects received over the network. It is not safe to update the UI from DoWork, so that is why you must pass back results via the events.

To get the work started from the UI, we have a Kick Off Work button that has an event handler with the name DoWorkButton_Click. The code checks to see if the worker is already busy. If not, we set the status by adding text to the WorkResultsTextData TextBox to indicate that work has started, and we call worker.RunWorkerAsync to kick off the work.

To display a dynamic status in the UI, we have a simple ellipse with a Storyboard named AnimateStatusEllipse. We cover storyboards and animation in Chapter 3 In the button event handler, we call Begin on this object and set it to run continuously. The animation changes the color from green to yellow and then back to green, over and over, to indicate that work is in progress.

In the worker_ProgressChanged event handler, the UI thread receives the latest status from the background worker, available in the e.ProgressPercentage value. It is safe to update the UI in this method, so we set the tooltip on the status ellipse with the latest value.

The worker_RunWorkerCompleted event fires when the work successfully completes as well as when the background worker is cancelled by the UI thread, so we first check to see if e.Cancelled is not true. If the work successfully completes, we set the ellipse to green, update the tooltip to indicate that it is complete, and take the value passed in as e.Result and add it to the TextBox.Text value.

When the user clicks the ellipse, a dialog is displayed with two buttons so that the user can click Yes to cancel or decide not to cancel, as shown in Figure 2-18.

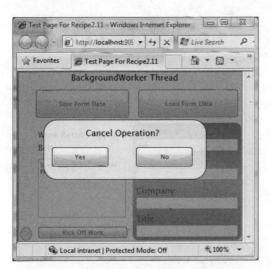

Figure 2-18. *The user can decide whether or not to cancel dialog.*

The StatusEllipse_MouseLeftButtonDown event checks to see if the background worker thread is actually running and then sets PromptCancelCanvas.Visibility to Visibility.Visible. That displays the dialog that simply consists of a large rectangle with a transparent look and a rounded white rectangle with the two buttons. Clicking Yes fires the ButtonConfirmCancelYes_Click event handler that calls the worker.CancelAsync method.

That completes our walkthrough of the code. Most of the other UI code is generated using Expression Blend, which we cover in Chapter 3. We recommend playing with the UI a bit to understand what it does and then reviewing the corresponding code. Listings 2-20 and 2-21 list the code for this recipe's test application.

Listing 2-20. *Recipe 2-11's MainPage.xaml File*

```
<UserControl x:Class="Ch02_ProgrammingModel.Recipe2_11.MainPage"
    xmlns="http://schemas.microsoft.com/winfx/2006/xaml/presentation"
    xmlns:x="http://schemas.microsoft.com/winfx/2006/xaml"
    Width="400" Height="300" xmlns:d=
    "http://schemas.microsoft.com/expression/blend/2008" xmlns:mc=
"http://schemas.openxmlformats.org/markup-compatibility/2006"
mc:Ignorable="d">
  <UserControl.Resources>
    <Storyboard x:Name="AnimateStatusEllipse">
      <ColorAnimationUsingKeyFrames BeginTime="00:00:00"
        Storyboard.TargetName="StatusEllipse"
        Storyboard.TargetProperty="(Shape.Fill).(SolidColorBrush.Color)">
        <SplineColorKeyFrame KeyTime="00:00:00" Value="#FF008000"/>
        <SplineColorKeyFrame KeyTime="00:00:01.5000000" Value="#FFFFFF00"/>
        <SplineColorKeyFrame KeyTime="00:00:03" Value="#FF008000"/>
        <SplineColorKeyFrame KeyTime="00:00:04.5000000" Value="#FF008000"/>
        <SplineColorKeyFrame KeyTime="00:00:06" Value="#FFFFFF00"/>
        <SplineColorKeyFrame KeyTime="00:00:07.5000000" Value="#FF008000"/>
      </ColorAnimationUsingKeyFrames>
      <DoubleAnimationUsingKeyFrames BeginTime="00:00:00" Storyboard.TargetName=
      "StatusEllipse" Storyboard.TargetProperty="(UIElement.Opacity)">
        <SplineDoubleKeyFrame KeyTime="00:00:00" Value="0.7"/>
        <SplineDoubleKeyFrame KeyTime="00:00:01.5000000" Value="0.5"/>
        <SplineDoubleKeyFrame KeyTime="00:00:03" Value="0.5"/>
        <SplineDoubleKeyFrame KeyTime="00:00:04.5000000" Value="0.7"/>
        <SplineDoubleKeyFrame KeyTime="00:00:06" Value="0.5"/>
        <SplineDoubleKeyFrame KeyTime="00:00:07.5000000" Value="0.5"/>
      </DoubleAnimationUsingKeyFrames>
      <DoubleAnimationUsingKeyFrames BeginTime="00:00:00"
        Storyboard.TargetName="StatusEllipse" Storyboard.TargetProperty=
        "(UIElement.RenderTransform).
            (TransformGroup.Children)[1].(SkewTransform.AngleX)">
        <SplineDoubleKeyFrame KeyTime="00:00:00" Value="0"/>
        <SplineDoubleKeyFrame KeyTime="00:00:01.5000000" Value="0"/>
```

```xml
        <SplineDoubleKeyFrame KeyTime="00:00:03" Value="0"/>
        <SplineDoubleKeyFrame KeyTime="00:00:04.5000000" Value="0"/>
        <SplineDoubleKeyFrame KeyTime="00:00:06" Value="0"/>
        <SplineDoubleKeyFrame KeyTime="00:00:07.5000000" Value="0"/>
      </DoubleAnimationUsingKeyFrames>
      <DoubleAnimationUsingKeyFrames BeginTime="00:00:00"
        Storyboard.TargetName="StatusEllipse" Storyboard.TargetProperty=
        "(UIElement.RenderTransform).
        (TransformGroup.Children)[1].(SkewTransform.AngleY)">
        <SplineDoubleKeyFrame KeyTime="00:00:00" Value="0"/>
        <SplineDoubleKeyFrame KeyTime="00:00:01.5000000" Value="0"/>
        <SplineDoubleKeyFrame KeyTime="00:00:03" Value="0"/>
        <SplineDoubleKeyFrame KeyTime="00:00:04.5000000" Value="0"/>
        <SplineDoubleKeyFrame KeyTime="00:00:06" Value="0"/>
        <SplineDoubleKeyFrame KeyTime="00:00:07.5000000" Value="0"/>
      </DoubleAnimationUsingKeyFrames>
    </Storyboard>
  </UserControl.Resources>
  <Grid x:Name="LayoutRoot" Background="#FFFFFFFF">
    <Grid.ColumnDefinitions>
      <ColumnDefinition Width="0.068*"/>
      <ColumnDefinition Width="0.438*"/>
      <ColumnDefinition Width="0.495*"/>
    </Grid.ColumnDefinitions>
    <Grid.RowDefinitions>
      <RowDefinition Height="0.08*"/>
      <RowDefinition Height="0.217*"/>
      <RowDefinition Height="0.61*"/>
      <RowDefinition Height="0.093*"/>
    </Grid.RowDefinitions>
    <Button HorizontalAlignment="Stretch" Margin="5,8,5,8"
     VerticalAlignment="Stretch" Grid.Column="1" Grid.Row="1"
      Content="Save Form Data" Click="SaveFormData_Click"/>
    <StackPanel HorizontalAlignment="Stretch"
    Margin="5,8,6,8" Grid.Column="1" Grid.Row="2">
      <TextBlock Height="Auto" Width="Auto" Text="Work Results Appear Below"
      TextWrapping="Wrap" Margin="4,4,4,4"/>
      <TextBox Height="103" Width="Auto" Text="" TextWrapping="Wrap"
      Margin="4,4,4,4" x:Name="WorkResultsTextData"/>
    </StackPanel>
    <Button HorizontalAlignment="Stretch" Margin="12,8,8,8"
      VerticalAlignment="Stretch"
     Grid.Column="2" Grid.Row="1" Content="Load Form Data"
     Click="ReadFormData_Click"/>
```

```xml
<Button HorizontalAlignment="Stretch" Margin="10,2,8,6"
  VerticalAlignment="Stretch"
   Grid.Column="1" Grid.Row="3" Content="Kick Off Work" x:Name="DoWorkButton"
   Click="DoWorkButton_Click"/>
<Border Grid.Column="2" Grid.Row="2" Grid.RowSpan="2" CornerRadius="10,10,10,10"
   Margin="1.80200004577637,2,2,2">
  <Border.Background>
    <LinearGradientBrush EndPoint="0.560000002384186,0.00300000002607703"
       StartPoint="0.439999997615814,0.996999979019165">
    <GradientStop Color="#FF586C57"/>
    <GradientStop Color="#FFA3BDA3" Offset="0.536"/>
    <GradientStop Color="#FF586C57" Offset="0.968999981880188"/>
    </LinearGradientBrush>
  </Border.Background>
  <StackPanel Margin="4,4,4,4"  x:Name="FormData">
    <TextBlock Height="Auto" Width="Auto" Text="First Name:" TextWrapping="Wrap"
    Margin="2,2,2,0"/>
    <TextBox Height="Auto" Width="Auto" Text="" TextWrapping="Wrap" x:
      Name="Field1" Margin="2,0,2,4"/>
    <TextBlock Height="Auto" Width="Auto" Text="Last Name:"
       TextWrapping="Wrap" Margin="2,4,2,0"/>
    <TextBox Height="Auto" x:Name="Field2" Width="Auto" Text=""
      TextWrapping="Wrap" Margin="2,0,2,4"/>
    <TextBlock Height="Auto" Width="Auto" Text="Company:"
      TextWrapping="Wrap" Margin="2,4,2,0"/>
    <TextBox Height="Auto" x:Name="Field3" Width="Auto" Text=""
      TextWrapping="Wrap" Margin="2,0,2,2"/>
    <TextBlock Height="22.537" Width="182" Text="Title:"
      TextWrapping="Wrap" Margin="2,4,2,0"/>
    <TextBox Height="20.772" x:Name="Field4" Width="182" Text=""
      TextWrapping="Wrap" Margin="2,0,2,2"/>
  </StackPanel>
</Border>
<Ellipse x:Name="StatusEllipse" Margin="4,2,2,2" Grid.Row="3" Stroke="#FF000000"
  Fill="#FF2D4DE0" MouseLeftButtonDown="StatusEllipse_MouseLeftButtonDown"
  RenderTransformOrigin="0.5,0.5" >
  <Ellipse.RenderTransform>
    <TransformGroup>
      <ScaleTransform/>
      <SkewTransform/>
      <RotateTransform/>
      <TranslateTransform/>
    </TransformGroup>
  </Ellipse.RenderTransform>
```

```xml
      <ToolTipService.ToolTip>
        <ToolTip Content="Click button to start work." />
      </ToolTipService.ToolTip>
    </Ellipse>
    <Canvas HorizontalAlignment="Stretch" Margin="0,0,2,8" Grid.RowSpan="4"
      Grid.ColumnSpan="3" x:Name="PromptCancelCanvas" Visibility="Collapsed">
      <Rectangle Height="300" Width="400" Fill="#FF808080" Stroke="#FF000000"
        Stretch="Fill" Opacity="0.6"/>
      <Canvas Height="106" Width="289" Canvas.Left="46" Canvas.Top="85">
        <Rectangle Height="106" Width="289" Fill="#FFFFFFFF" Stroke="#FF000000"
          RadiusX="23" RadiusY="23" Opacity="0.85"/>
        <Button Height="34" x:Name="ButtonConfirmCancelYes" Width="100"
          Canvas.Left="15" Canvas.Top="49" Content="Yes"
          Click="ButtonConfirmCancelYes_Click"/>
        <Button Height="34" x:Name="ButtonConfirmCancelNo" Width="100"
          Canvas.Left="164" Canvas.Top="49" Content="No" Click=
          "ButtonConfirmCancelNo_Click"/>
        <TextBlock Width="134.835" Canvas.Left="75" Canvas.Top="12.463"
          Text="Cancel Operation?" TextWrapping="Wrap"/>
      </Canvas>
    </Canvas>
    <TextBlock Margin="67.8270034790039,0,-88.802001953125,0" Grid.Column="1"
      Grid.ColumnSpan="1" Text="BackgroundWorker Thread" TextWrapping="Wrap"/>
  </Grid>
</UserControl>
```

Listing 2-21. *Recipe 2-11's Page.xam.cs File*

```csharp
using System;
using System.ComponentModel;
using System.IO;
using System.IO.IsolatedStorage;
using System.Linq;
using System.Text;
using System.Windows;
using System.Windows.Controls;
using System.Windows.Input;
using System.Windows.Media;
using System.Windows.Media.Animation;

namespace Ch02_ProgrammingModel.Recipe2_11
{
  public partial class MainPage : UserControl
  {
    private int WorkLoops=30;
```

```csharp
private BackgroundWorker worker = new BackgroundWorker();
#region Recipe 2-6 Declarations
private IsolatedStorageSettings settings =
        IsolatedStorageSettings.ApplicationSettings;
private string FormDataFileName = "FormFields.data";
private string FormDataDirectory = "FormData";
#endregion
public Page()
{
  InitializeComponent();

  //Configure BackgroundWorker thread
  worker.WorkerReportsProgress = true;
  worker.WorkerSupportsCancellation = true;
  worker.DoWork += new DoWorkEventHandler(worker_DoWork);
  worker.ProgressChanged +=
      new ProgressChangedEventHandler(worker_ProgressChanged);
  worker.RunWorkerCompleted += new
  RunWorkerCompletedEventHandler(worker_RunWorkerCompleted);
}

void worker_DoWork(object sender, DoWorkEventArgs e)
{
  for (int i = 1; i <= WorkLoops; i++)
  {
    //Check to see if the work has been canceled
    if ((worker.CancellationPending == true))
    {
      e.Cancel = true;
      break;
    }
    else
    {
      // Perform a time consuming operation and report progress.
      System.Threading.Thread.Sleep(1000);
      worker.ReportProgress((int)
          System.Math.Floor((double)i / (double)WorkLoops * 100.0));
    }
  }
  e.Result = Environment.NewLine + "Completed: " + DateTime.Now.ToString();
}

void worker_RunWorkerCompleted(object sender, RunWorkerCompletedEventArgs e)
{
  AnimateStatusEllipse.Stop();
```

```
  if (!e.Cancelled)
  {
    StatusEllipse.Fill = new SolidColorBrush(Color.FromArgb(255, 0, 255, 0));
    WorkResultsTextData.Text = WorkResultsTextData.Text + e.Result.ToString();
    ToolTipService.SetToolTip(StatusEllipse, "Work Complete.");
  }
  else
  {
    StatusEllipse.Fill = new SolidColorBrush(Color.FromArgb(255, 255, 255, 0));
    WorkResultsTextData.Text = WorkResultsTextData.Text +
      Environment.NewLine + "Canceled @: " + DateTime.Now.ToString();
    ToolTipService.SetToolTip(StatusEllipse, "Operation canceled by user.");
  }

}

void worker_ProgressChanged(object sender, ProgressChangedEventArgs e)
{
  if (PromptCancelCanvas.Visibility == Visibility.Collapsed)
    ToolTipService.SetToolTip(StatusEllipse, e.ProgressPercentage.ToString() +
      "% Complete.  Click to cancel...");
}

private void DoWorkButton_Click(object sender, RoutedEventArgs e)
{
  if (worker.IsBusy != true)
  {
    WorkResultsTextData.Text = "Started: "+DateTime.Now.ToString();
    worker.RunWorkerAsync(WorkResultsTextData.Text);
    AnimateStatusEllipse.RepeatBehavior = RepeatBehavior.Forever;
    AnimateStatusEllipse.Begin();
  }
}

private void StatusEllipse_MouseLeftButtonDown
    (object sender, MouseButtonEventArgs e)
{
  if (worker.IsBusy)
    PromptCancelCanvas.Visibility = Visibility.Visible;
}

private void ButtonConfirmCancelYes_Click(object sender, RoutedEventArgs e)
{
  worker.CancelAsync();
  PromptCancelCanvas.Visibility = Visibility.Collapsed;
}
```

```csharp
private void ButtonConfirmCancelNo_Click(object sender, RoutedEventArgs e)
{
  PromptCancelCanvas.Visibility = Visibility.Collapsed;
}
#region Recipe 2-6 Event Handlers
private void SaveFormData_Click(object sender, RoutedEventArgs e)
{
  try
  {
    using (var store = IsolatedStorageFile.GetUserStoreForApplication())
    {
      //Use to control loop for finding correct number of textboxes
      int TotalFields = 4;
      StringBuilder formData = new StringBuilder(50);
      for (int i = 1; i <= TotalFields; i++)
      {
        TextBox tb = FindName("Field" + i.ToString()) as TextBox;
        if (tb != null)
          formData.Append(tb.Text);
        //If on last TextBox value, don't add "|" character to end of data
        if (i != TotalFields)
          formData.Append("|");
      }
      store.CreateDirectory(FormDataDirectory);
      IsolatedStorageFileStream fileHandle = store.CreateFile(System.IO.Path.
      Combine(FormDataDirectory, FormDataFileName));

      using (StreamWriter sw = new StreamWriter(fileHandle))
      {
        sw.WriteLine(formData);
        sw.Flush();
        sw.Close();
      }
    }
  }
  catch (IsolatedStorageException ex)
  {
    WorkResultsTextData.Text = "Error saving data: " + ex.Message;
  }
}
```

```
private void ReadFormData_Click(object sender, RoutedEventArgs e)
{
  using (var store = IsolatedStorageFile.GetUserStoreForApplication())
  {
    //Load form data using private string values for directory and filename
    string filePath =
        System.IO.Path.Combine(FormDataDirectory, FormDataFileName);
    //Check to see if file exists before proceeding
    if (store.FileExists(filePath))
    {
      using (StreamReader sr = new StreamReader(
          store.OpenFile(filePath, FileMode.Open, FileAccess.Read)))
      {
        string formData = sr.ReadLine();
        //Split string based on separator used in SaveFormData method
        string[] fieldValues = formData.Split('|');
        for (int i = 1; i <= fieldValues.Count(); i++)
        {
          //Use the FindName method to loop through TextBoxes
          TextBox tb = FindName("Field" + i.ToString()) as TextBox;
          if (tb != null)
            tb.Text = fieldValues[i - 1];
        }
        sr.Close();
      }
    }
  }
}
#endregion
}
}
```

2-12. Updating the UI from a Background Thread

Problem

You need to update the UI from a background thread so that the UI can be responsive.

Solution

The Dispatcher class offers a safe way to call a method that updates the UI asynchronously from a background thread by providing services for managing the queue of work items for a thread. Both the Dispatcher and the BackgroundWorker classes can perform work on a separate thread. The

BackgroundWorker class supports progress reporting and cancellation. The Dispatcher class is useful when you need a simple way to queue up background work without progress reporting or cancellation.

How It Works

The .NET Framework for Silverlight includes the System.Threading namespace, which contains classes needed to manage a thread pool, launch threads, and synchronize threads, just like the full version of the .NET Framework.

As with most UI programming models such as Visual Basic 6, .NET Windows Forms, or WPF, it is not safe to access UI objects from a background thread. UI objects, such as Button, TextBox, and TextBlock objects, can only be safely accessed on the UI thread.

The role of the Dispatcher is to provide a way for a background thread to invoke a method that runs on the main thread so that it can safely update the UI. This approach is useful when you're retrieving data from the server using the asynchronous WebRequest class, as we demonstrate in this recipe. Figure 2-19 shows the UI for the application after the data is downloaded.

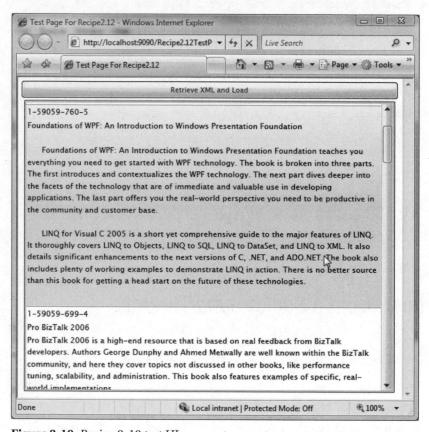

Figure 2-19. *Recipe 2-12 test UI*

The Code

The sample application for this recipe contains a button titled Retrieve XML and Load that when clicked fires the event RetrieveXMLandLoad_Click. This event creates an HttpWebRequest object that points to the location where Recipe 2-9's ApressBooks.xml file was copied.

```
Uri location =
    new Uri("http://localhost:9090/xml/ApressBooks.xml",UriKind.Absolute);
WebRequest request = HttpWebRequest.Create(location);
request.BeginGetResponse(
    new AsyncCallback(this.RetrieveXmlCompleted), request);
```

When the asynchronous web request completes, the code in the callback method RetrieveXmlCompleted executes. The following code retrieves the XML document from the response stream and stores it in an XDocument object:

```
HttpWebRequest request = ar.AsyncState as HttpWebRequest;
WebResponse response = request.EndGetResponse(ar);
Stream responseStream = response.GetResponseStream();
using (StreamReader streamreader = new StreamReader(responseStream))
{
  XDocument xDoc = XDocument.Load(streamreader);
...
```

The rest of the code in the callback method RetrieveXmlCompleted executes the same LINQ to XML as in Recipe 2-9 to obtain a List of ApressBook objects. The last line of code calls the Dispatcher object to queue UI work by calling BeginInvoke and passing in the method DataBindListBox on the UI thread passing in the List of ApressBook objects:

```
Dispatcher.BeginInvoke(() => DataBindListBox(_apressBookList));
```

The syntax looks a bit strange if you are not familiar with C# lambda expressions. The syntax is shorthand for creating a delegate object and mashing the parameters into the call. The method DataBindListBox has a single line of code to assign the ItemsSource property on the BooksListBox object:

```
BooksListBox.ItemsSource = list;
```

If we skip using the Dispatcher in the callback method RetrieveXmlCompleted for the HttpWebRequest and instead put the line of code to assign the ItemsSource property in the callback method directly, the UI will not be updated because the callback method returns on the background thread of the HttpWebRequest, not the UI thread. By calling Dispatcher.BeginInvoke to update the UI from the HttpWebRequest callback background thread, we queue the work to assign the List object to the ItemsSource so that it safely executes when the main UI thread literally has cycles available. Listings 2-22 and 2-23 show the source code for this recipe's test application.

Listing 2-22. *Recipe 2-12's MainPage.xaml File*

```
<UserControl x:Class="Ch02_ProgrammingModel.Recipe2_12.MainPage"
    xmlns="http://schemas.microsoft.com/winfx/2006/xaml/presentation"
    xmlns:x="http://schemas.microsoft.com/winfx/2006/xaml"
    Width="600" Height="500" >
  <Grid x:Name="LayoutRoot" Background="White" Margin="6,6,6,6">
```

```xml
    <StackPanel>
      <Button Content="Retrieve XML and Load"
           Click="RetrieveXMLandLoad_Click"></Button>
      <ListBox x:Name="BooksListBox" Margin="4,4,4,4" Height="452"  >
        <ListBox.ItemTemplate>
          <DataTemplate>
            <StackPanel Margin="2,2,2,2">
              <TextBlock Text="{Binding Path=ISBN}" Margin="0,0,0,2"/>
              <TextBlock Text="{Binding Path=Title}" Margin="0,0,0,2"/>
              <TextBlock Width="550" Text="{Binding Path=Description}"
                      TextWrapping="Wrap" Margin="0,0,0,10"/>
            </StackPanel>
          </DataTemplate>
        </ListBox.ItemTemplate>
      </ListBox>
    </StackPanel>
  </Grid>
</UserControl>
```

Listing 2-23. *Recipe 2-12's MainPage.xaml.cs File*

```csharp
using System;
using System.Collections.Generic;
using System.IO;
using System.Linq;
using System.Net;
using System.Windows;
using System.Windows.Controls;
using System.Xml.Linq;

namespace Ch02_ProgrammingModel.Recipe2_12
{
  public partial class MainPage : UserControl
  {
    public Page()
    {
      InitializeComponent();
    }
```

```csharp
private void RetrieveXMLandLoad_Click(object sender, RoutedEventArgs e)
{
  Uri location =
      new Uri("http://localhost:9090/xml/ApressBooks.xml", UriKind.Absolute);
  WebRequest request = HttpWebRequest.Create(location);
  request.BeginGetResponse(
      new AsyncCallback(this.RetrieveXmlCompleted), request);
}

void RetrieveXmlCompleted(IAsyncResult ar)
{
  List<ApressBook> _apressBookList;
  HttpWebRequest request = ar.AsyncState as HttpWebRequest;
  WebResponse response = request.EndGetResponse(ar);
  Stream responseStream = response.GetResponseStream();
  using (StreamReader streamreader = new StreamReader(responseStream))
  {
    XDocument xDoc = XDocument.Load(streamreader);
    _apressBookList =
    (from b in xDoc.Descendants("ApressBook")
     select new ApressBook()
     {
       Author = b.Element("Author").Value,
       Title = b.Element("Title").Value,
       ISBN = b.Element("ISBN").Value,
       Description = b.Element("Description").Value,
       PublishedDate = Convert.ToDateTime(b.Element("DatePublished").Value),
       NumberOfPages = b.Element("NumPages").Value,
       Price = b.Element("Price").Value,
       ID = b.Element("ID").Value
     }).ToList();
  }
  //Could use Anonymous delegate (does same as below line of code)
  //Dispatcher.BeginInvoke(
  //  delegate()
  //  {
  //    DataBindListBox(_apressBookList);
  //  }
  //  );
  //Use C# 3.0 Lambda
  Dispatcher.BeginInvoke(() => DataBindListBox(_apressBookList));
}
```

```
  void DataBindListBox(List<ApressBook> list)
  {
    BooksListBox.ItemsSource = list;
  }
}

public class ApressBook
{
  public string Author { get; set; }
  public string Title { get; set; }
  public string ISBN { get; set; }
  public string Description { get; set; }
  public DateTime PublishedDate { get; set; }
  public string NumberOfPages { get; set; }
  public string Price { get; set; }
  public string ID { get; set; }
}
}
```

2-13. Managing XAML Resources

Problem

You want to create a consistent UI without having to replicate styles, colors, templates, and so forth on individual elements, much in the same way that CSS resources are shared in a web application.

Solution

Take advantage of ResourceDictionary objects to store resources that can be accessed using the StaticResource markup extension. The Resources member introduced in the FrameworkElement class is of type ResourceDictionary, which is a Dictionary collection accessible via name/value pairs. The Resources member can be used to organize common styles, brushes, and colors for use across an application.

How It Works

A markup extension provides additional evaluation for a value set on an attribute in XAML. For example, a value can be configured for Background equal to the string "Green", which is evaluated by a TypeConverter that takes the string value and converts it to the Colors.Green enumerations value. You can also set Background equal to the hexadecimal value, such as #FF008000, which also equals the color Green.

Type converters are great for single string values converted to a particular type, which we cover in Chapter 5. A markup extension, such as StaticResource, allows more complex string values that consist of multiple types to be evaluated or substituted for the placeholder value of an attribute. A StaticResource value can be configured for any XAML property attribute except for event attributes. All markup extensions have the following syntax:

```
<element attribute="{MarkupExtensionName Value}"  />
```

When you first see this syntax, it looks a bit confusing, but once you understand it, you see the power that markup extensions provide. For the StaticResource markup extension, Value represents an x:ey name for a resource located in a Resources collection in the application. Usually resources are located at the Application or UserControl (page) level, but they can be located on any element that inherits from FrameworkElement, such as Grid or StackPanel objects.

Silverlight 3dds the ability to have a merged resource dictionary, which means you can place the contents of a resource dictionary in a separate file but have the resources treated as a logical part of the main XAML file. Resources stored in a merged resource dictionary are accesses only after all resources in the main XAML code file are checked for a match. The MergedDictionaries is a collection the UIElement.ResourceDictionary object. Here is an example:

```
<ResourceDictionary>
    <SolidColorBrush Color="#FFFFFFFF" x:Key="darkBrush"/>
    <ResourceDictionary.MergedDictionaries>
      <ResourceDictionary Source="/GradientsResourceDictionary.xaml">
      <ResourceDictionary Source="/StylesResourceDictionary.xaml">
    </ResourceDictionary.MergedDictionaries>
  </ResourceDictionary>
```

The separate resource dictionary files contain a <ResourceDictionary> declaration as the root element with the resources identified as if part of the MainPage.ResourceDictionary directly.

The Code

The sample application for this recipe includes a number of resources defined in the Page class. Here is an example resource defined at the <UserControl> level:

```
<UserControl.Resources>
  <Color x:Kcy="Pumpkin">#FFD5901F</Color>
  <Color x:Key="Lime">#FF75E564</Color>
  <LinearGradientBrush x:Key="PumpkinLimeBrush"
          EndPoint="0.5,1" StartPoint="0.5,0">
    <GradientStop Color="{StaticResource Lime}"/>
    <GradientStop Color="{StaticResource Pumpkin}" Offset="1"/>
  </LinearGradientBrush>
</UserControl.Resources>
```

Three resources are defined with two color resources and a brush resource. The brush is a `LinearGradientBrush` that references the color resources for the `GradientStop Color` value using the syntax discussed earlier:

```
{StaticResource Lime}
```

■**Note** For performance reasons, if a resource consists of other resources, define the resources in order of dependency as shown in the preceding example so that forward references can be avoided.

Notice that every resource has a name defined by the `x:Key` attribute, which is different than the `x:Name` attribute used to name XAML elements. This is the value used to reference a resource with the XAML on the page. For example, we add a `StackPanel` to `Grid.Row="0"` and `Grid.Column="0"` and configure the `Background` attribute to this value:

```
Background="{StaticResource PumpkinLimeBrush}"
```

Figure 2-20 shows the result.

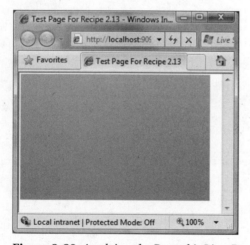

Figure 2-20. *Applying the PumpkinLimeBrush resource to a StackPanel*

Expression Blend 3 provides great support to create and manage resources. There is a Resources tab next to the Project and Properties tabs in the UI. You can expand the tree in the Resources tab to view resources created as part of the available objects, such as the `Application`, `Page`, and `StackPanel` levels, as shown in Figure 2-21.

Figure 2-21. *The Resources tab in Expression Blend 3*

Expression Blend 3 provides a drop-down editor for modifying resources right on the Resources tab, as shown in Figure 2-22.

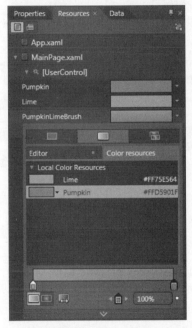

Figure 2-22. *In-place editing in the Resources tab*

Resources can be defined deeper in the XAML tree, such as on a Grid or StackPanel control, or even on a Rectangle directly. Any object that inherits from FrameworkElement has the Resources collection. Click the Advanced Properties Option button next to Background, and select Convert to New Resource in the pop-up menu in Expression Blend 3, as shown in Figure 2-23. The Create Brush Resource dialog limits your options to locating a resource either at the application or page level, as shown in Figure 2-23 (in the Define In section).

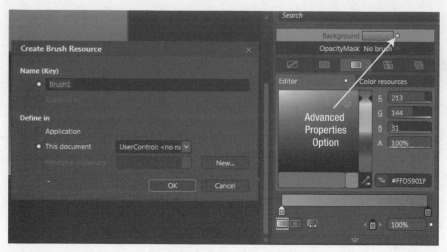

Figure 2-23. *Converting a brush to a resource*

If you want to define a resource at a different level, you can use Expression Blend 3 to create a resource at the document or UserControl level and then copy it to the location where you want it. As an example, let's define a new brush called FallBrush at the UserControl level and then move it to a new location, in this case a StackPanel, using the following code:

```
<StackPanel Grid.Column="0" Grid.Row="1"  Margin="2,2,2,2">
  <StackPanel.Resources>
    <LinearGradientBrush x:Key="FallBrush" EndPoint="0.5,1" StartPoint="0.5,0">
      <GradientStop Color="#FF000000"/>
      <GradientStop Color="#FFFFA500" Offset="1"/>
    </LinearGradientBrush>
  </StackPanel.Resources><Rectangle Margin="2,2,2,2" Stroke="#FF000000"
    Fill="{StaticResource FallBrush}" Height="193"/>
</StackPanel>
```

We've moved the FallBrush resource from the UserControl.Resources to StackPanel.Resources and applied it to a Rectangle, resulting in the UI shown in Figure 2-24. This limits use of the resource within the StackPanel only. For resources that need to be shared across the application, locate the resource at the page or application level.

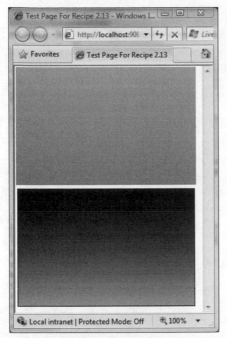

Figure 2-24. *Resource defined at StackPanel level applied to a rectangle (bottom)*

For this recipe, all of the modifications are in the XAML, shown in Listing 2-24.

Listing 2-24. *Recipe 2-13's MainPage.xaml File*

```
<UserControl x:Class="Ch02_ProgrammingModel.Recipe2_13.MainPage"
    xmlns="http://schemas.microsoft.com/winfx/2006/xaml/presentation"
    xmlns:x="http://schemas.microsoft.com/winfx/2006/xaml"
    Width="600" Height="400">
  <UserControl.Resources>
    <Color x:Key="Pumpkin">#FFD5901F</Color>
    <Color x:Key="Lime">#FF75E564</Color>
    <LinearGradientBrush x:Key="PumpkinLimeBrush"
      EndPoint="0.5,1" StartPoint="0.5,0">
      <GradientStop Color="{StaticResource Lime}"/>
      <GradientStop Color="{StaticResource Pumpkin}" Offset="1"/>
    </LinearGradientBrush>
  </UserControl.Resources>
  <Grid x:Name="LayoutRoot">
    <Grid.RowDefinitions>
      <RowDefinition Height="0.5*"/>
      <RowDefinition Height="0.5*"/>
    </Grid.RowDefinitions>
```

```
      <Grid.ColumnDefinitions>
        <ColumnDefinition Width="0.5*"/>
        <ColumnDefinition Width="0.5*"/>
      </Grid.ColumnDefinitions>
      <StackPanel Grid.Column="0" Grid.Row="0" Background=
      "{StaticResource PumpkinLimeBrush}" Margin="2,2,2,2">
      </StackPanel>
      <StackPanel Grid.Column="0" Grid.Row="1"  Margin="2,2,2,2">
        <StackPanel.Resources>
          <LinearGradientBrush x:Key="FallBrush" EndPoint="0.5,1" StartPoint="0.5,0">
            <GradientStop Color="#FF000000"/>
            <GradientStop Color="#FFFFA500" Offset="1"/>
          </LinearGradientBrush>
        </StackPanel.Resources>
        <Rectangle Margin="2,2,2,2" Stroke="#FF000000" Fill=
          "{StaticResource FallBrush}" Height="193"/>
      </StackPanel>
    </Grid>
</UserControl>
```

2-14. Managing Embedded Resources

Problem

You want to store resources inside of the Silverlight application container (the `.xap` file) and retrieve them at runtime, as opposed to simply putting the resources, such as images, in the file system and referencing as a URL.

Solution

Use the `Assembly.GetManifestResourceNames` and `Assembly.GetManifestResourceStream` methods to enumerate and retrieve resources embedded in a Silverlight application.

How It Works

To read embedded resources, you have to first embed them into the application. To embed resources such as images, video, and XML data, add the resources to the Silverlight application project, and set the build action for each resource to Embedded Resource. The next time you build the project, the resources will be embedded into the application.

To obtain a list of resources available in the application, you can call `Assembly.GetManifestResourceNames` to obtain the names as a string array:

```
Assembly app = Assembly.GetExecutingAssembly();
string[] resources = app.GetManifestResourceNames();
```

Once you have the name of the desired resource, you can call Assembly.GetManifestResourceStream to obtain the resource as a byte array and then convert it to the appropriate type.

The Code

The sample application for this recipe includes three images that have been configured to be an embedded resource in the assembly. The UI for the recipe has a simple gradient for the root Grid Background, a Button named RetrieveResourceNames to retrieve the resource names of embedded resources that are available, and a ListBox control named ResourceNames to display the names.

The application also has a Border control to provide a color outline for a nested Image control, which is where the embedded resources are displayed. We apply a simple 5 percent skew transformation to the Border to have more visual appeal. We cover transformations in Chapter 3.

When the application runs, the user can click the button to obtain a list of available resources, which includes the three images. Selecting an image name in the ListBox displays the image within the Border control. Figure 2-25 shows the application UI with an image selected.

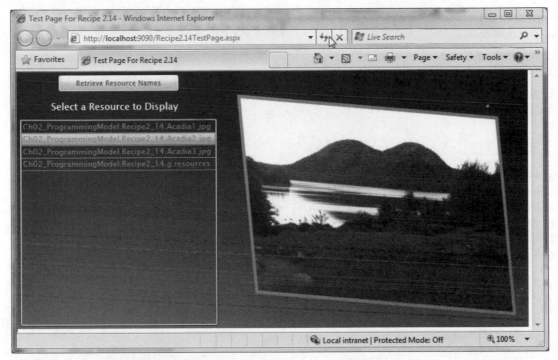

Figure 2-25. *Recipe 2-14 UI with an image selected*

The images are named Acadia1, Acadia2, and Acadia3 in the project file system. However, when they are embedded into the application binary, the namespace is added to the filename. Keep this in mind when loading resources if you're not first getting their names using the GetManifestResourceNames.

Notice the fourth resource listed in Figure 2-26. This resource is automatically generated as part of compiling and generating the application. This ListBox is transparent, and the foreground color for the items is orange. The ListBox's Foreground property is configured with a SolidColorBrush to provide the orange text. The ListBox's Background property is set to Transparent, which results in the transparency. The ListBox's ItemContainerStyle defaults to a white background, which we modified with this XAML for the style:

```
<ListBox.ItemContainerStyle>
  <Style TargetType="ListBoxItem">
    <Setter Property="Background" Value="Transparent"/>
  </Style>
</ListBox.ItemContainerStyle>
```

We cover styling controls in Chapter 5; this XAML is just a simple example of applying a style. Styles can also be resources that are loaded using the StaticResource markup extension.

The code file has two events: one to retrieve the list of resource names for the button click event and another that loads the resource into the Image object. We mentioned earlier that GetManifestResourceNames returns a string array of resource names, so that is easy enough to do. The somewhat more complex code is actually retrieving the resource as a byte array and converting it to an image.

We use a stream object to obtain the array of bytes that represents the binary resource data. We create a new System.Windows.Media.Imaging.BitMapImage object and call the SetSource method, passing in the stream of bytes:

```
BitmapImage bImage = new BitmapImage();
bImage.SetSource(stream);
```

This code loads the bytes into a BitmapImage object, which is then set as the Source for the Image control named ImageDisplay that renders the image to the screen. Listings 2-25 and 2-26 have the full code listing.

Listing 2-25. *Recipe 2-14's MainPage.xaml File*

```
<UserControl x:Class="Ch02_ProgrammingModel.Recipe2_14.MainPage"
    xmlns="http://schemas.microsoft.com/winfx/2006/xaml/presentation"
    xmlns:x="http://schemas.microsoft.com/winfx/2006/xaml"
    Width="800"
Height="400" xmlns:d="http://schemas.microsoft.com/expression/blend/2008"
xmlns:mc="http://schemas.openxmlformats.org/markup-compatibility/2006"
mc:Ignorable="d">
  <Grid x:Name="LayoutRoot">
    <Grid.ColumnDefinitions>
      <ColumnDefinition Width="0.41*"/>
      <ColumnDefinition Width="0.59*"/>
    </Grid.ColumnDefinitions>
    <Grid.RowDefinitions>
      <RowDefinition Height="0.172*"/>
      <RowDefinition Height="0.828*"/>
    </Grid.RowDefinitions>
```

```xml
<Grid.Background>
  <LinearGradientBrush EndPoint="0.5,1" StartPoint="0.5,0">
    <GradientStop Color="#FF000000"/>
    <GradientStop Color="#FF696767" Offset="1"/>
  </LinearGradientBrush>
</Grid.Background>
<ListBox x:Name="ResourceNames" Background="Transparent"
 HorizontalAlignment="Stretch" Margin="4,4,15,4" Grid.Row="1"
 SelectionChanged="ResourceNames_SelectionChanged">
  <ListBox.Foreground>
    <SolidColorBrush Color="#FFD18726"/>
  </ListBox.Foreground>
  <ListBox.ItemContainerStyle>
    <Style TargetType="ListBoxItem">
      <Setter Property="Background" Value="Transparent"/>
    </Style>
  </ListBox.ItemContainerStyle>
</ListBox>
<Button Height="26.4" HorizontalAlignment="Stretch"
 Margin="64,4,74,0" x:Name="RetrieveResourceNames"
 VerticalAlignment="Top" Content="Retrieve Resource Names"
 d:LayoutOverrides="VerticalAlignment, Height"
 Click="RetrieveResourceNames_Click"/>
<TextBlock HorizontalAlignment="Stretch" Margin="53,0,74,4"
 VerticalAlignment="Bottom" Text="Select a Resource to Display"
 TextWrapping="Wrap" Foreground="#FFFFFFFF" Height="22"/>
<Border Margin="29.2129993438721,
 -15.206000328064,32.7869987487793,35.6059989929199"
HorizontalAlignment="Stretch" BorderBrush="#FF000000"
x:Name="ImageBorder" RenderTransformOrigin="0.5,0.5"
Visibility="Collapsed" Height="310.8" VerticalAlignment="Stretch"
Grid.Column="1" Grid.ColumnSpan="1" Grid.Row="1" Grid.RowSpan="1"
d:LayoutOverrides="Height">
  <Border.Background>
    <SolidColorBrush Color="#FFD28826"/>
  </Border.Background>
  <Border.RenderTransform>
    <TransformGroup>
      <ScaleTransform/>
      <SkewTransform AngleX="5" AngleY="5"/>
      <RotateTransform/>
      <TranslateTransform/>
    </TransformGroup>
  </Border.RenderTransform>
</Border.RenderTransform>
```

```xaml
      <Image x:Name="ImageDisplay" Margin="5,5,5,5" Width="400"
        Height="300" OpacityMask="#FF000000" />
    </Border>
  </Grid>
</UserControl>
```

Listing 2-26. *Recipe 2-14's MainPage.xaml.cs File*

```csharp
using System.IO;
using System.Reflection;
using System.Windows;
using System.Windows.Controls;
using System.Windows.Media.Imaging;

namespace ChO2_ProgrammingModel.Recipe2_14
{
  public partial class MainPage : UserControl
  {
    public Page()
    {
      InitializeComponent();
    }

    private void RetrieveResourceNames_Click(object sender, RoutedEventArgs e)
    {
      Assembly app = Assembly.GetExecutingAssembly();
      string[] resources = app.GetManifestResourceNames();
      ResourceNames.Items.Clear();
      foreach (string s in resources)
      {
        ResourceNames.Items.Add(s);
      }
    }

    private void ResourceNames_SelectionChanged(object sender,
    SelectionChangedEventArgs e)
    {
      if ((ResourceNames.SelectedIndex != -1) && (ResourceNames.SelectedIndex != 3))
      {
        Assembly app = Assembly.GetExecutingAssembly();
        using (Stream stream = app.GetManifestResourceStream
        (ResourceNames.SelectedItem.ToString()))
```

```
            {
                BitmapImage bImage = new BitmapImage();
                bImage.SetSource(stream);
                ImageDisplay.Source = bImage;
                ImageBorder.Visibility = Visibility.Visible;
            }
        }
    }
  }
}
```

2-15. Creating Silverlight Using Ruby, Python, or JScript

Problem

You want to program Silverlight using either the IronRuby, IronPython, or Managed JScript dynamic languages.

Solution

Download and install the Dynamic Language Runtime SDK for Silverlight on Windows or on a Mac OS X system.

How It Works

The first step is to download the latest Silverlight Dynamic Languages SDK from CodePlex at http://sdlsdk.codeplex.com/Release/ProjectReleases.aspx?ReleaseId=25120. This URL takes you to the most recent version available (version 0.5.0) at the time of this writing, so be sure to check the Releases section to see if a more up-to-date version is available.

■**Note** While this book targets Silverlight 3 RTW we performed these steps with the Silverlight 3 Beta version of the Dynamic Languages SDK, because it was the most recent version available when this book was written. You will have to download the latest version of Silverlight Dynamic Languages SDK that works with Silverlight 3 RTM.

We downloaded the agdlr-version# (Everything) package and unzipped the contents to the Code\Ch02_ProgrammingModel\DLR_Download\ folder. We then copied the contents over to a directory named c:\SagDLR. The package includes the IronRuby and IronPython languages as part of the "everything" download.

■**Note** To program in IronRuby, download Ruby from `http://rubyforge.org/frs/?group_id=167` and install using the OneClick Installer for Windows. It will install Ruby at `c:\Ruby` on your hard drive.

After installing the Silverlight Dynamic Languages SDK and Ruby, you can build applications using the IronRuby, IronPython, or Managed JScript dynamic languages. At the time of this writing, there are no Visual Studio 2008 templates for dynamic languages, but the Silverlight Dynamic Languages SDK includes a tool named Chiron (`Chiron.exe`) that allows you to work with Silverlight and the dynamic languages.

■**Note** According to the Readme file that is included with the Silverlight Dynamic Languages SDK, these steps can be performed on a Mac OS X computer, but only if Mono is first installed on that computer. Mono can be obtained from `http://www.go-mono.com/mono-downloads/download.html`.

The Code

The simplest Silverlight application that uses a dynamic language consists of an HTML or ASPX file to host the application just as in a compiled Silverlight application, and an `app.xaml` file that defines the Silverlight UI, much as `MainPage.xaml` does for a compiled Silverlight application. The code-behind for `app.xaml` in a dynamic language application can be one of the following, depending on the language:

- `app.py`: The IronPython code-behind file

- `app.rb`: The IronRuby code-behind file

- `app.jsx`: The Managed JScript code-behind file

The ReadMe file that ships with the Silverlight Dynamic Languages SDK provides some instructions on how to create a new Silverlight application like the one that we describe here.

To create a new application, open a command prompt, and navigate to the script directory, which in our configuration is `c:\SLDLR\script`. To create a dynamic language Silverlight application, run the following command, but replace `language` with `ruby`, `python`, or `jscript`:

```
sl.bat language <application_name>
```

In our case, we create an application named `SilverlightDynamicApp` with the IronPython language using this command:

```
Sl.bat python SilverlightPythonApp
```

This code creates an application directory in the `c:\SLDLR\script\` directory named `SilverlightPythonApp`. In the `SilverlightPythonApp` directory, it creates three folders named `javascripts`, `python`, and `stylesheets`, as well as an HTML file named `index.html`.

The `javascripts` folder contains an `error.js` file with the typical `onSilverlightError` handler in it. The `stylesheets` directory contains two CSS files named `error.css` and `screen.css`: `screen.css` provides basic styling for the HTML page, and `error.css` provides highlighting for any errors that occur.

■**Note** The SilverlightPythonApp directory can be found in the Code\Ch02_ProgrammingModel\DLR_Download\ script\ directory of the accompanying source code for this book.

Since we created a Python-based application, the python directory contains app.xaml and app.py. As we mentioned earlier, in a dynamic language application, app.xaml contains the UI code. app.py is the code-behind written in IronPython. Listings 2-27 and 2-28 show the contents of these files.

Listing 2-27. *Recipe 2-15's app.xaml File*

```
<UserControl x:Class="System.Windows.Controls.UserControl"
             xmlns="http://schemas.microsoft.com/client/2007"
             xmlns:x="http://schemas.microsoft.com/winfx/2006/xaml">

  <Grid x:Name="layout_root" Background="White">
    <TextBlock x:Name="Message" FontSize="30" />
  </Grid>
</UserControl>
```

Listing 2-28. *Recipe 2-15 app.py Code File*

```
from System.Windows import Application
from System.Windows.Controls import UserControl

class App:
  def __init__(self):
    root = Application.Current.LoadRootVisual(UserControl(), "app.xaml")
    root.Message.Text = "Welcome to Python and Silverlight!"

App()
```

Listing 2-27 contains the UI XAML file, which looks similar to the typical MainPage.xaml file created as part of a compiled Silverlight application. If you are not familiar with the Python language, Listing 2-28 may look a bit strange, but you can generally understand that it imports a couple of namespaces with this code:

```
from System.Windows import Application
from System.Windows.Controls import UserControl
```

The class declaration is

```
class App:
  def __init__(self):
    root =
      Application.Current.LoadRootVisual(UserControl(), "app.xaml")
    root.Message.Text = "Welcome to Python and Silverlight!"
```

This last bit of code creates an instance of the App class:

```
App()
```

To compile and run this application, we execute this command in the C:\SLDLR\script\ SilverlightPythonApp directory:

```
C:\SLDLR\script\server.bat /b
```

The server.bat batch command launches Chiron.exe, which is a command-line utility that creates Silverlight XAP files as well as enables packageless development of dynamic Silverlight applications. Chiron creates the output from our simple dynamic language Silverlight application.

The server.bat batch command also opens the default web browser to http://localhost:2060 and maps the root directory to the directory where the batch command executes, which in this example is C:\SLDLR\script\SilverlightPythonApp, as shown in Figure 2-26.

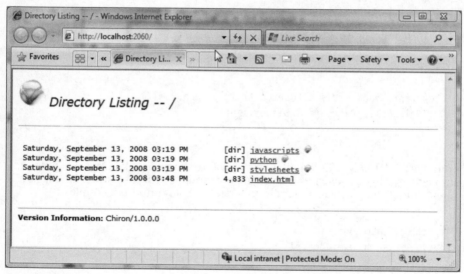

Figure 2-26. *Recipe 2-15's application running the SilverlightPythonApp*

Figure 2-27 displays the UI when we click index.html.

Figure 2-27. *Recipe 2-15's SilverlightPythonApp UI*

2-16. Creating Application Services

Problem

You want to package application functionality into reusable services and make those services available within a Silverlight project so that they are available for the lifetime of the application.

Solution

Create a class that implements the IApplicationService interface and possibly the IApplicationLifetimeAware interface. Add the class to the Application.ApplicationLifetimeObjects collection for the Silverlight application.

How It Works

Silverlight 3 includes support for services that are created by the Application object and added to the ApplicationLifetimeObjects collection on the Application object. The services are created before the MainPage UserControl and can hook into various events associated with application lifetime.

A class that implements IApplicationService interface implements the following methods:

IApplicationService.StartService(ApplicationServiceContext context)

IApplicationService.StopService()

The StartService method fires before UserControl_Loaded to allow the application service to initialize itself. Likewise, StopService fires after the MainPage UserControl is unloaded. This allows for service setup and teardown as necessary, though we had to take extra steps to ensure setup completes that we detail below in the code section.

Notice on the StartService method, there is a parameter passed in named context. The context parameter provides access to the initialization parameters via its ApplicationInitParams property that can be configured on an HTML <param> tag within the <object> tag that creates the Silverlight plug-in. Developers can provide information to the application service via the configured parameters on the plug-in. We cover initialization parameters in detail in Chapter 6.

Implementing the IApplicationService interface is the minimum requirement to create an application service. For more fine-grained control or interaction between the service and the application, developers can also implement the IApplicationLifetimeAware interface, which adds these additional methods to the application service:

- IApplicationLifetimeAware.Exited()

- IApplicationLifetimeAware.Exiting()

- IApplicationLifetimeAware.Started()

- IApplicationLifetimeAware.Starting()

The above events fire on the application service with respect to state of the application. For example, the Starting event fires before the Application_Startup event, while the Started event fires after the Application_Startup event. Likewise, the Exiting event fires before the Application_Exit event, while the Exited event fires after the Application_Exit event.

All of the IApplicationLifetimeAware interface events are bracketed by the two IApplicationService events, meaning that IApplicationService.StartService fires before IApplicationLifetimeAware.Starting and IApplicationService.StopService fires after IApplicationLifetimeAware.Exited event.

The Code

The example for this recipe performs to application functions related to configuration. The first function is that it stores a copy of plug-in initialization parameters as a public property on the application service instance. The second function is that the service retrieves an XML file from the server to obtain configuration settings.

The application service is implemented in a code file named ConfigurationSettingsService.cs, which implements both the IApplicationService and IApplicationLifetimeAware interfaces. We modified the default Application_Startup event in the App.xaml.cs class file so that it handles initialization correctly.

We also modify the MainPage_Loaded event in MainPage.xaml.cs file so that it data binds to the ConfigSettings Dictionary object on the service. Finally, we added a TextBlock and ListBox to MainPage.xaml to display the configuration settings. Listings 2-29 through 2-32 show the contents of these files. Listing 2-33 shows App.xaml for the recipe, which is where the application service is declared.

Listing 2-29. *Recipe 2-16's ConfigurationSettingsService.cs File*

```
using System;
using System.Collections.Generic;
using System.IO;
using System.Linq;
using System.Net;
using System.Windows;
using System.Xml.Linq;
```

```csharp
namespace Ch02_ProgrammingModel.Recipe2_16.Services
{
  public class ConfigurationSettingsService : IApplicationService,
  IApplicationLifetimeAware
  {
    //Event to allow the Application object know it is safe
    //to create the MainPage UI
    //i.e. the ConfigurationSettingsService is fully populated
    public event EventHandler ConfigurationSettingsLoaded;

    #region IApplicationService Members
    void IApplicationService.StartService(ApplicationServiceContext context)
    {
      InitParams = context.ApplicationInitParams;
      LoadConfigSettings();
    }

    private void LoadConfigSettings()
    {
      if (InitParams["configUrl"] != "")
      {
        WebClient wc = new WebClient();
        wc.OpenReadCompleted += wc_OpenReadCompleted;
        wc.OpenReadAsync(new Uri(InitParams["configUrl"]));
      }
    }

    void IApplicationService.StopService()
    {
    }
    #endregion

    #region IApplicationLifetimeAware Members
    public void Exited()
    {
    }

    public void Exiting()
    {
    }

    public void Started()
    {
    }
```

```csharp
    public void Starting()
    {
    }
    #endregion

    private void wc_OpenReadCompleted(object sender, OpenReadCompletedEventArgs e)
    {
      if (e.Error != null)
      {
        return;
      }
      using (Stream s = e.Result)
      {
        XDocument xDoc = XDocument.Load(s);
        ConfigSettings =
        (from setting in xDoc.Descendants("setting")
         select setting).ToDictionary(n => n.Element("key").Value, n =>
           n.Element("value").Value);

        //Check to see if the event has any handler's attached
        //Fire event if that is the case
        if (ConfigurationSettingsLoaded != null)
          ConfigurationSettingsLoaded(this, EventArgs.Empty);
      }
    }

    //Store initialization parameters from <object> tag
    public Dictionary<string, string> InitParams { get; set; }
    //Stores configuraiton settings retrieved from web server
    public Dictionary<string, string> ConfigSettings { get; set; }
  }
}
```

Listing 2-30. *Recipe 2-16's App.xaml.cs (partial) File*

```csharp
private void Application_Startup(object sender, StartupEventArgs e)
{
  ConfigurationSettingsService service =
App.Current.ApplicationLifetimeObjects[0]
    as ConfigurationSettingsService;

  //Wire up an anonymouse event handler that is fired when the
  //ConfigurationService is fully populated
```

```
//This ensures that we can access the ConfigSettings properties
//in MainPage_Loaded
service.ConfigurationSettingsLoaded +=
                        new EventHandler((s, args) =>
{
  this.RootVisual = new MainPage();
});
}
```

Listing 2-31. *Recipe 2-16's MainPage.xaml.cs (partial) File*

```
void MainPage_Loaded(object sender, RoutedEventArgs e)
{
  ConfigurationSettingsService service =
App.Current.ApplicationLifetimeObjects[0]
    as ConfigurationSettingsService;

  //Simple data bind to the ConfigSettings Dictionary
  SettingsList.ItemsSource = service.ConfigSettings;
}
```

Listing 2-32. *Recipe 2-16's MainPage.xaml (partial) File*

```xml
<UserControl x:Class="Ch02_ProgrammingModel.Recipe2_16.MainPage"
    xmlns="http://schemas.microsoft.com/winfx/2006/xaml/presentation"
    xmlns:x="http://schemas.microsoft.com/winfx/2006/xaml"
    xmlns:d="http://schemas.microsoft.com/expression/blend/2008"
    xmlns:mc="http://schemas.openxmlformats.org/markup-compatibility/2006"
    mc:Ignorable="d" d:DesignWidth="640" d:DesignHeight="480">
  <Grid x:Name="LayoutRoot">
   <StackPanel>
     <TextBlock HorizontalAlignment="Left" VerticalAlignment="Top"
                Text="Configuration Settings" TextWrapping="Wrap" Margin="6"/>
     <ListBox x:Name="SettingsList" Height="100" Margin="6,6,0,6"/>
   </StackPanel>
  </Grid>
</UserControl>
```

Listing 2-33. *Recipe 2-16's App.xaml File*

```xml
<Application xmlns="http://schemas.microsoft.com/winfx/2006/xaml/presentation"
             xmlns:x="http://schemas.microsoft.com/winfx/2006/xaml"
             x:Class="Ch02_ProgrammingModel.Recipe2_16.App"
             xmlns:MyServices="clr-namespace:
             Ch02_ProgrammingModel.Recipe2_16.Services">
    <Application.Resources>

    </Application.Resources>
  <Application.ApplicationLifetimeObjects>
    <MyServices:ConfigurationSettingsService x:Name="ConfigService"/>
  </Application.ApplicationLifetimeObjects>
</Application>
```

The URL used to retrieve the configuration file is configured on the plug-in control via initialization parameters so that it is not hard-coded into the Silverlight application itself.

In the "How it works" section for this recipe, we describe in detail the order in which the various events fire. We also mentioned that the MainPage_Loaded event on the UserControl fires after the IApplicationService.StartService event. However, in testing the application, the ConfigSettings collection was not populated in MainPage_Loaded as expected. If you think about it, this makes sense, because we need to make an asynchronous web request to retrieve settings from a URL. In this example, the webClient.OpenReadCompleted event was firing after MainPage_Loaded executed, making it impossible to access configuration settings at load time within the application itself.

The application pattern we utilize to maintain the proper event ordering is to add an event to the application service class, which in our example is declared like this in ConfigurationSettingsService.cs:

```
public event EventHandler ConfigurationSettingsLoaded;
```

In the WebClient.OpenReadCompleted event handler that fires after the web request call succeeds, we fire the event as long as there is an event subscriber:

```
if (ConfigurationSettingsLoaded != null)
  ConfigurationSettingsLoaded(this, EventArgs.Empty);
```

In this application pattern, there an event subscriber created as shown in Listing 2-31. It is an anonymous event handler show here:

```
service.ConfigurationSettingsLoaded += new EventHandler((s, args) =>
{
  this.RootVisual = new MainPage();
});
```

Using this pattern ensures that the application service is fully configured before the MainPage is instantiated, permitting the application to function as expected. Figure 2-28 shows the settings displayed in the basic UI.

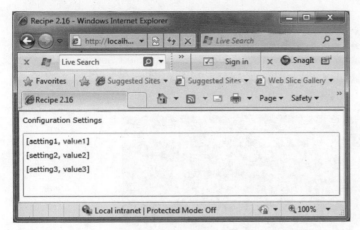

Figure 2-28. *Recipe 2-16 The Configuration Settings UI*

2-17. Managing Resources in Large Projects

Problem

You have a large project with many custom controls, templates, styles, etc. that exist in
ResourceDictionary objects. You would like to be able to store these ResourceDictionary objects in
separate XAML files or assemblies to keep source code more manageable, while also allowing updating
assemblies to be updated separately from the main application code.

Solution

Use a merged resource dictionary to reference external XAML files and assemblies to better organize
code.

How It Works

WPF has supported merged resource dictionaries as a way to improve organization for large
applications. Merged resource dictionaries make it possible to share resources across applications and
are also more conveniently isolated for localization than with Silverlight 2 where merged resource
dictionaries where not available.

Resources in a merged dictionary occupy a location in the resource lookup scope just after the
scope of the main resource dictionary they are merged into. Although a resource key must be unique
within any individual dictionary, a key can exist multiple times in a set of merged dictionaries, because
they are separate namescopes. We cover namescopes in Recipe 2-3.

Silverlight 3 adds support for merged resource dictionaries, making it more like WPF .
Silverlight 3 leverages the packed URI format for referencing resources available in WPF except that you
do not have to specify the pack:// protocol reference. We cover the details of how to reference merged
resource dictionaries in this recipe's "The Code" section.

The Code

Expression Blend 3 makes it easy to create a resource dictionary for your application that is merged with resources within the application itself. In Expression Blend 3, clicking the Create New Resource Dictionary button indicated by the arrow in Figure 2-29 opens the New Item dialog also shown in the figure.

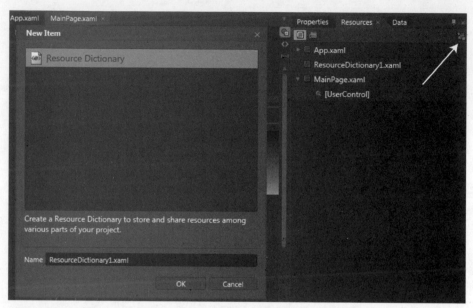

Figure 2-29. *Clicking the Create New Resource Dictionary*

When you click OK, Expression Blend 3 creates a new file in your project with the name specified. It also modifies the app.xaml file by adding the following ResourceDictionary.MergedDictionaries XAMP element to the Application.ResourceDictionary element:

```
<Application.Resources>
        <ResourceDictionary>
                <ResourceDictionary.MergedDictionaries>
                        <ResourceDictionary Source="ResourceDictionary1.xaml"/>
                </ResourceDictionary.MergedDictionaries>
        </ResourceDictionary>
</Application.Resources>
```

To place a style resource into a merged resource dictionary, select the element in Expression Blend 3, and click the Object ➤ Edit Style ➤ Create Empty menu item. To place a control template resource into a merged resource dictionary, follow the same steps but instead of clicking Edit Style, select Edit Template. In Figure 2-30, we selected the Rectangle and chose to edit its Style. Notice we selected "Resource dictionary" as the location where we want to define our new style.

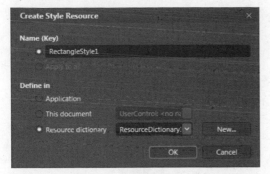

Figure 2-30. *The Create Style Resource dialog*

Clicking OK brings up the style editor in Expression Blend 3. Next, edit the style, and save it. We cover creating styles in Chapters 3 and 5, but for now, we are focusing on the merged resource dictionary functionality.

When we view the `Rectangle` in the designer, it now has the style applied to it that we just created. We cover how to apply styles in Recipe 2-13. Listing 2-34 has the source code for the `Rectangle` where the style is applied.

Listing 2-34. *Recipe 2-17's MainPage.xaml File*

```
<UserControl x:Class="Ch02_ProgrammingModel.Recipe2_17.MainPage"
    xmlns="http://schemas.microsoft.com/winfx/2006/xaml/presentation"
    xmlns:x="http://schemas.microsoft.com/winfx/2006/xaml"
    xmlns:d="http://schemas.microsoft.com/expression/blend/2008"
    xmlns:mc="http://schemas.openxmlformats.org/
        markup-compatibility/2006"
    mc:Ignorable="d" d:DesignWidth="640" d:DesignHeight="480">
  <Grid x:Name="LayoutRoot">
    <Grid.ColumnDefinitions>
      <ColumnDefinition Width="0.047*"/>
      <ColumnDefinition Width="0.953*"/>
    </Grid.ColumnDefinitions>
    <Grid.RowDefinitions>
      <RowDefinition Height="0.052*"/>
      <RowDefinition Height="0.948*"/>
    </Grid.RowDefinitions>
    <StackPanel Margin="8" Grid.Column="1" Grid.Row="1">
      <Rectangle Stroke="Black" Height="100"
              Style="{StaticResource RectangleStyle1}">
      </Rectangle>
      <TextBlock Text="I'm a TextBlock" TextWrapping="Wrap" Margin="4"/>
      <TextBlock Text="I'm another TextBlock" TextWrapping="Wrap" Margin="4"/>
      <Button Content="Button" Margin="4"/>
    </StackPanel>
  </Grid>
</UserControl>
```

You can see that the style RectangleStyl1 is applied to the Rectangle. We showed in this recipe how the merged resource dictionary is referenced in the App.xaml file. Listing 2-25 has the source code for the merged resource dictionary.

Listing 2-35. *Recipe 2-17's ResourceDictionary1.xaml File*

```
<ResourceDictionary
  xmlns="http://schemas.microsoft.com/winfx/2006/xaml/presentation"
  xmlns:x="http://schemas.microsoft.com/winfx/2006/xaml">e,.
  <Style x:Key="RectangleStyle1" TargetType="Rectangle">
    <Setter Property="Margin" Value="4"/>
    <Setter Property="Fill">
      <Setter.Value>
        <LinearGradientBrush EndPoint="0.5,1" StartPoint="0.5,0">
          <GradientStop Color="#FF243300"/>
          <GradientStop Color="#FFDEF3AB" Offset="1"/>
        </LinearGradientBrush>
      </Setter.Value>
    </Setter>
  </Style>
  <!-- Resource dictionary entries should be defined here. -->
</ResourceDictionary>
```

In Listing 2-35, you can see the style named RectangleStyle1 is defined. You can also define merged resource dictionaries in other assemblies as well. Please refer to the Silverlight 3 documentation for more information.

2-18. Save a File Anywhere on the User's System

Problem

You want to allow the user to save a file anywhere on their system without the constraints of isolated storage.

Solution

Use the SaveFileDialog object to persist a file to the user's file system from within a user-initiated event handler, such as a button click or key press.

How It Works

Silverlight 3 includes the new SaveFileDialog object, which allows the user to select a file location that the Silverlight application can save a file outside of isolated storage. In Recipe 2-7, we cover the OpenFileDialog object. Like the OpenFileDialog, the SaveFileDialog must be raised in an event handler resulting from user interaction such as a key press or button click. Once that's accomplished, using the SaveFileDialog is very straightforward, as we demonstrate in this recipe's "The Code" section.

The Code

The code presents a simple UI with a button that the user can click to bring up the SaveFileDialog object (see Figure 2-31).

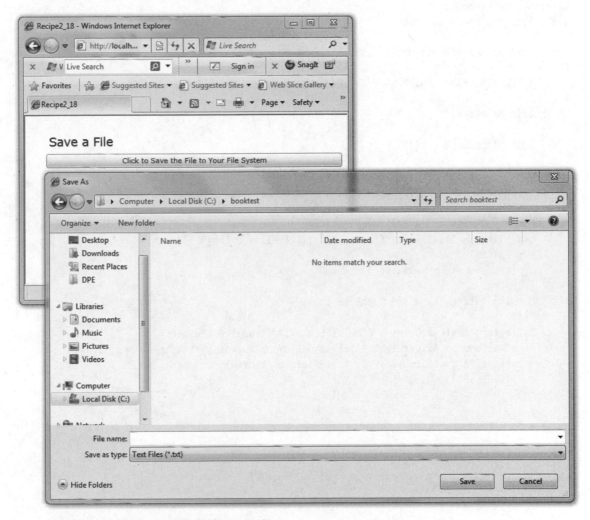

Figure 2-31. *Recipe 2-18's SaveFileDialog In Action*

Just as with most any file-related dialog box, developers can configure the filter (e.g., .txt or .tiff) as well as the default file type. We chose to write out a simple text file, so we went with Text Files (*.txt) as the default filter as shown in Figure 2-31. Listing 2-36 has the source code that displays the SaveFileDialog object and writes out the file to the returned stream by calling the OpenFile() method.

Listing 2-36. *Recipe 2-18's MainPage.xaml.cs File*

```csharp
using System.IO;
using System.Text;
using System.Windows;
using System.Windows.Controls;

namespace Ch02_ProgrammingModel.Recipe2_18
{
  public partial class MainPage : UserControl
  {
    public MainPage()
    {
      InitializeComponent();
    }

    private void btnSaveFile_Click(object sender, RoutedEventArgs e)
    {
      SaveFileDialog sfd = new SaveFileDialog();
      sfd.Filter = "Text Files (*.txt)|*.txt|All Files (*.*)|*.*";
      sfd.FilterIndex = 1;
      if (true == sfd.ShowDialog())
      {
        using (Stream fs = sfd.OpenFile())
        {
          byte[] textFileBytes = (new UTF8Encoding(true)).GetBytes(
          "Welcome to Silverlight 3!!!! \r\n\r\nYour Authors,\r\n\r\nRob and Jit");
          fs.Write(textFileBytes, 0, textFileBytes.Length);
          fs.Close();
        }
      }
    }
  }
}
```

CHAPTER 3

■ ■ ■

Developing User Experiences

This chapter outlines recipes involving the graphics subsystem. We will cover graphics fundamentals, animations, layout, image handling, keyboard handling, document features, and ink, just to name a few. Also covered will be the corresponding Expression Studio features.

In the previous two chapters, we provided an introduction to the Silverlight project model, the developer and designer tools, as well as an overview of the programming model, without getting too deep into the object model. In this chapter, we focus on the graphic primitive classes. In Chapter 5, we cover the controls; however, in this chapter we offer an overview of the base classes that provide layout support as well as other functionality for both the graphic primitive and control classes.

As with all of .NET, the root base class is Object. Next in line from Object is DependencyObject, which you will find in Windows Presentation Foundation (WPF) and Silverlight. DependencyObject provides dependency property system services to derived classes. The property system's primary function is to compute the values of properties and to provide system notification about values that have changed. We cover dependency properties in Chapter 5.

UIElement inherits from DependencyObject and serves as the base class for most objects that have visual appearance and that can process basic input. Example properties and events are Visibility, Opacity, Clip, GotFocus, KeyDown, and MouseLeftButtonDown.

FrameworkElement is common to System.Windows.Shapes namespace classes like Shape, Ellipse, and Rectangle and System.Windows.Controls namespace classes like Control, Button, and TextBox. The FrameworkElement base class implements layout, data binding, and the visual object tree functionality. Properties and events implemented in FrameworkElement include Margin, Padding, Height, Width, SizeChanged, and LayoutUpdated. This chapter primarily focuses on classes in the Shapes namespace, but we include a few classes in the Controls namespace to help demonstrate layout and UI concepts. As we mentioned, Chapter 5 covers controls in detail.

This chapter won't make you a designer, but it should help you understand how you can use the graphic primitives as well as how to use the layout features of Silverlight 3. If you are a designer, this chapter provides a high-level overview of the tools and user interface (UI) elements available for designing Silverlight applications.

In this chapter, we describe the graphic primitive basics in the first couple of recipes but do not go through every single object available, detailing properties and methods. We recommend that you read a Silverlight 3 book such as Robert Lair's *Beginning Silverlight 3: From Novice to Professional* (Apress, 2008) or check out the documentation on MSDN located here:

http://msdn.microsoft.com/en-us/library/cc838158(VS.95).aspx

After we cover the basics, we move on to more advanced animation control using keyframes, transformations, and keyboard input, and we discuss how to work with ink. For this chapter, we add eight new recipes covering additional topics available in Silverlight 3:

- 3-17 Adding 3-D Effects to UI Elements
- 3-18 Dynamically Creating Bitmaps
- 3-19 Improving Graphic Animation and Video Performance
- 3-20 Improve Animation with Custom Easing Functions
- 3-21 Adding Pixel Shader Visual Effects
- 3-22 Create and Work with Design-Time Data in Expression Blend
- 3-23 Reuse Application Interactivity with Expression Blend Behaviors
- 3-24 Prototype Application Design with SketchFlow

3-1. Importing Art from Expression Design

Problem

You need to use assets in a Silverlight application created by a designer in a design tool such as Expression Design. Or, you are a designer and need to share assets with Silverlight developers.

Solution

Take advantage of the built-in export capabilities in the design tool or add-ins available for the designer's favorite tool.

How It Works

As we mentioned in Chapter 1, Silverlight 3 UI elements are created using a declarative markup language know as Extensible Application Markup Language (XAML). XAML is a vector-based markup language that uses XML syntax, making it easy to input and export XAML in tools such as Expression Design and Expression Blend.

Expression Blend is a design tool geared toward technical designers and developers. Expression Design is a design tool geared toward pure designers. You can download a 60-day trial of Expression Studio 3 here:

```
http://www.microsoft.com/downloads/details.aspx?FamilyID=7e2f033b-c6b5-4565-93a5-
a6048246ce28&displaylang=en
```

The underlying markup is not viewable in Expression Design. It is a pure GUI design tool, to make it friendlier for designers to use. It can generate content usable in Expression Blend as well as web-design tools such as Expression Web. Figure 3-1 shows the Expression Design UI with our attempt at creating an ice cream cone using the built-in textures available in the Expression Design color palette drop-down.

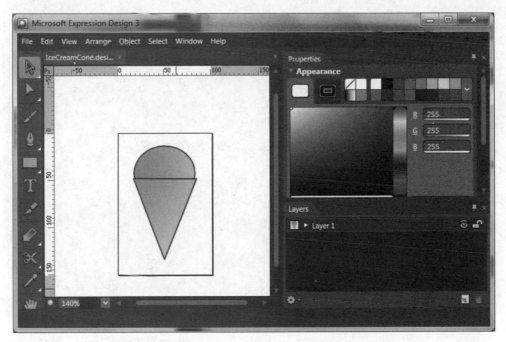

Figure 3-1. *Expression Design UI*

We don't cover all of the features available in Expression Design. To learn more, visit this site for self-study tutorials, starter kits, training videos, virtual labs, and webcasts:

http://expression.microsoft.com/en-us/cc136522.aspx

The one feature we do want to cover is how to make assets created in Expression Design available in Expression Blend and to developers. After the design is completed, choose File ➤ Export to open the Export dialog box, shown in Figure 3-2.

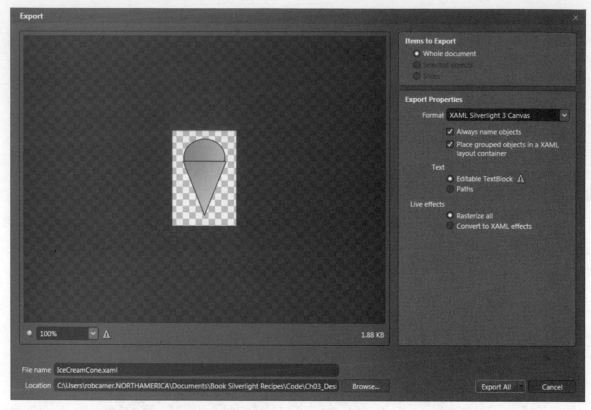

Figure 3-2. *Expression Design Export dialog box*

In the dialog box, select XAML Silverlight 3 Canvas as the format, and browse to the desired location to save the `.xaml` file. Then, click Export All to generate the `IceCreamCone.xaml` file (we put the file into the `Recipe3.1` directory). Next, add the exported file to the Recipe 3-1 Visual Studio project to make it available in Visual Studio, and copy the desired XAML from the `IceCreamCone.xaml` file into `MainPage.Xaml`. In this case, the XAML is essentially just the ice cream cone, which is contained in the third nested `<canvas>` object with the `x:Name` of `Group`. Now that the object is part of the project, open the solution in Expression Blend to fine-tune the object and placement as needed. You can also add the exported `IceCreamCone.xaml` file to the Recipe 3-1 project directly within Expression Blend without going through the steps in Visual Studio, which may be best for non-developers working in the Expression tools.

■**Note** XAML can be created with any text editor, among other tools such as Aurora, Electric Rain Xam3D, Windows Flip 3D, and Telestream, to name a few. In addition, Expression Design 3 and Expression Blend 3 can import files from a variety of tools, including Adobe Illustrator and Adobe Photoshop. Finally, if you search the Internet, a plug-in for Adobe Illustrator allows direct export to XAML.

Figure 3-3 shows the ice cream cone in the web browser.

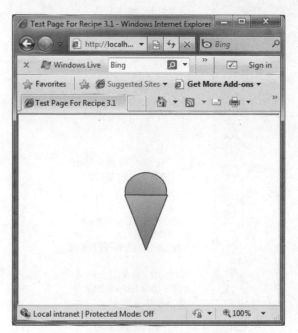

Figure 3-3. *The ice cream cone in the browser*

3-2. Working with Color and Gradients in Blend

Problem

You need to create and manipulate colors and gradients in Silverlight 3.

Solution

Use Expression Blend to create and manipulate classes that inherit from `System.Windows.Media.Brush`, such as `SolidColorBrush` and `GradientBrush`, to create colors and gradients.

How It Works

When you are working with brushes such as `SolidColorBrush` or `GradientBrush` objects, Expression Blend is useful. It has a dedicated section titled Brushes in the properties window, as shown in Figure 3-4, with a descendent of the `Shape` class selected in the Visual Tree.

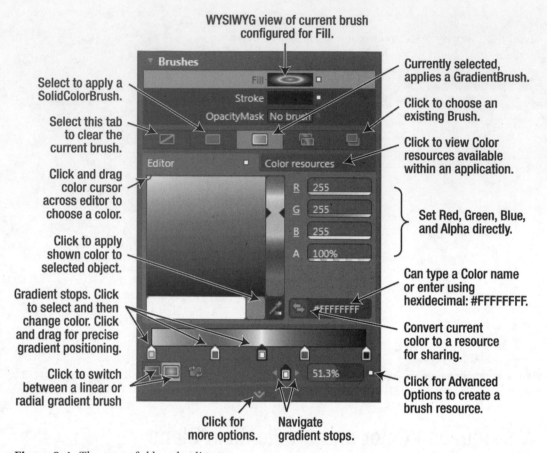

Figure 3-4. *The powerful brush editor*

Take a close look at Figure 3-4, and you will see that Expression Blend provides extensive visual editing tools for colors and gradients, as well as powerful support to create color resources and brush resources. Color resources help ensure consistency and reduce typing errors when you are entering the same color values over and over. Brush resources also help ensure consistency and promote reuse throughout an application.

In Silverlight 3, Expression Blend 3 adds additional options. Click the More Options button shown in Figure 3-4 to bring up the brush-editing options shown in Figure 3-5.

Figure 3-5. *Additional brush-editing options for radial gradients*

Figure 3-5 shows the additional options available when you are editing a gradient brush. When you edit a solid color brush, the only option available is opacity.

Notice in Figure 3-4 that after you select a Shape object such as an Ellipse, the top portion of the brush editor allows you to choose the Fill, Stroke, or OpacityMask. When you pick one of those three, you then decide whether to apply No Brush, a SolidColorBrush, a GradientBrush, or an existing brush resource by clicking one of the four tabs just below Fill, Stroke, and OpacityMask.

■**Note** We won't dive any further into OpacityMask, which applies varying levels of opacity to different parts of the object. You can find a thorough article about OpacityMask at http://msdn.microsoft.com/en-us/library/bb979637(VS.95).aspx.

Notice that the options shown in the Brushes section of the properties window depend on the type of object selected. For example, selecting a TextBox gives the options shown in Figure 3-6.

In Figure 3-6, you see a different set of brushes available for the TextBox control. In this case, the SelectionBackground option is configured with a gradient that renders when text is selected at runtime, as shown in the right portion of Figure 3-6. Silverlight 3 with Expression Blend 3 adds the option to visually edit the CaretBrush as well.

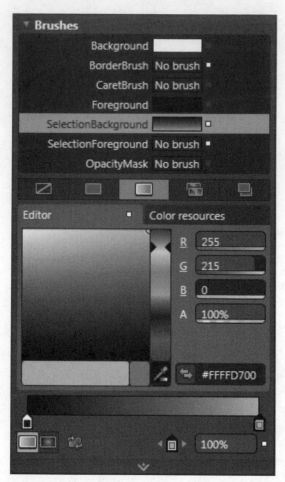

Figure 3-6. *The Brushes section when a* TextBox *control is selected*

The Code

For the code example in this recipe, we use the tools in Expression Blend to create various colors and gradients and apply them to objects. Listing 3-1 (which you'll see in a moment) has the full XAML, but let's walk through the code first.

Gradient brushes can produce interesting effects, create impressions of light and shadow, and give your UI elements a three-dimensional feel. Figure 3-7 compares a linear and a radial version of a gradient brush.

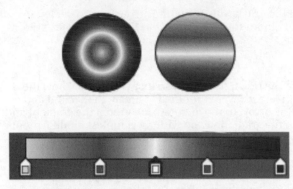

Figure 3-7. *Same gradient in radial (left) and linear (right) applied to an ellipse*

Both brushes in Figure 3-7 use the same gradient stops but with a different spread. Below the two ellipses in Figure 3-7 is a screen capture of the gradient stops with a faint off-white color on the left and black on the right. These correspond to the colors shown in the ellipses. For the radial spread on the left, the black gradient stop corresponds to the outer edge in a circular fashion. For the linear spread, the black gradient stop corresponds to the bottom of the right ellipse. The colors applied in the respective spread correspond to the gradient stops.

Earlier, Figure 3-4 showed the complete Expression Blend brush editor. As the instructions in the figure say, to create a gradient stop, you click the Gradient bar after selecting a gradient brush at the top of the editor. To remove a gradient stop, you drag it off of the Gradient bar.

Let's now introduce an additional tool to help customize a gradient's appearance: the Brush Transform tool, located in the Asset Manager on the left side of Expression Blend. The Brush Transform tool allows you to change the orientation of, stretch, and move a gradient applied to an element visually on the Artboard or design surface in Expression Blend, resulting in a new gradient value in the XAML. From an XAML perspective, when you use the Brush Transform tool, you are visually modifying the StartPoint and EndPoint of the gradient object.

Figure 3-8 shows four circles on the Artboard: at left, one with the default linear gradient; two with the same gradient as the first but with a different orientation and position applied using the Brush Transform tool; and a circle with a Green SolidColorBrush applied. The gradient for the first circle has the following StartPoint and EndPoint:

EndPoint="0.5,1" StartPoint="0.5,0"

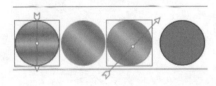

Figure 3-8. *Modifying a gradient with a brush transform*

We show a copy of the modified circle with the brush transform (the arrow from lower left to upper right) in the third circle from the left. The gradient for the third circle has the following StartPoint and EndPoint after we used the Brush Transform tool:

EndPoint="1.1,0.0" StartPoint="0.05,1.12"

The first circle shows the default position of the brush transform so that you can see how the orientation, position, and size of the brush transform (arrow) were modified to create the second and third circles. To use the Brush Transform tool, grab the arrow to move, rotate, or stretch the gradient and thus visually modify the StartPoint and EndPoint for the gradient. Even with the simplest modifications, gradients can provide a far more interesting interface than a SolidColorBrush in many scenarios.

The previous example demonstrated a linear gradient. We now turn to a radial gradient. In this case, use Expression Blend to create a donut, which we demonstrate in Recipe 3-7, using two Ellipses. Then, choose Combine ➤ Subtract to create a Path that is transparent in the middle, thus letting the background color show through. Apply a solid color brush to the left donut, as shown in Figure 3-9. Apply a linear gradient as before to the middle donut, which does not do much for its appearance. However, by switching the gradient from a linear to a radial gradient in the donut on the right, you make the appearance more appealing, as shown in Figure 3-9.

Figure 3-9. *From SolidColorBrush to radial gradient*

We next demonstrate how to apply an image brush to an object. Drag a Rectangle onto the design surface or Artboard in Expression Blend, name it RectImageBrush, apply rounded corners by modifying the RadiusX and RadiusY properties, and then set the Fill property to No Brush in the Brush Editor. Next, add an ImageBrush to the Rectangle in XAML:

```
<Rectangle HorizontalAlignment="Stretch" Margin="86,4,118,4"
VerticalAlignment="Stretch" Grid.Row="2" Stroke="#FF000000" RadiusY="38"
RadiusX="38" x:Name="RectImageBrush">
  <Rectangle.Fill>
    <ImageBrush ImageSource="/img/Landscape2.jpg"  Stretch="Fill" />
  </Rectangle.Fill>
</Rectangle>
```

```
<Rectangle.RenderTransform>
  <SkewTransform AngleX="20" AngleY="10"/>
</Rectangle.RenderTransform>
```

Figure 3-10 shows the results.

Figure 3-10. *Rectangle with ImageBrush applied*

The results in Figure 3-10 are similar to applying a Border object to an Image object, as shown in Recipe 3-10 later in this chapter, but with the addition of a SkewTransform, which we cover in Recipe 3-13.

Although an ImageBrush can create a static but compelling UI, a VideoBrush takes it one step further. You can apply a VideoBrush to the Foreground color of a TextBlock to create an interesting effect. Here is a snippet from MainPage.xaml for Recipe 3-2:

```
<TextBlock Margin="214,38.2000007629395,24,61"
           Grid.Row="3" TextWrapping="Wrap" Text="TextBlock" FontSize="72"
           FontFamily="Comic Sans MS" FontWeight="Bold">
  <TextBlock.Foreground>
    <VideoBrush SourceName="mElement" Stretch="UniformToFill" />
  </TextBlock.Foreground>
</TextBlock>
```

We had to hand-edit the Xaml in order to apply the VideoBrush. Notice the SourceName attribute on the VideoBrush object. This value must refer to the name of a MediaElement object, also in the XAML markup:

```
<MediaElement x:Name="mElement" AutoPlay="True" HorizontalAlignment="Stretch"
              Margin="4,4,421,0" Grid.Row="3" Width="175" Height="90"
              d:LayoutOverrides="Height" VerticalAlignment="Top"
              Source="/video/video.wmv"/>
```

You can set the opacity to 0 on the MediaElement object if you don't want it visible—it won't affect the video output for the VideoBrush object. In this example, we left the opacity of the MediaElement at 100% so that you can see how the TextBlock's Foreground color corresponds with the output in the MediaElement. The video is not included in the source code download at the Apress website, but you can copy a video from the sample videos on your computer to the TestWeb/ClientBin/Video/ folder and name the file video.wmv. Figure 3-11 shows the video playing as the Foreground color of the Text.

 **TextBlock**

Figure 3-11. *Foreground property as a VideoBrush*

Listing 3-1 contains the XAML markup from the previous code walkthrough.

Listing 3-1. *Recipe 3.2 MainPage.Xaml File*

```
<UserControl x:Class="Ch03_DevelopingUX.Recipe3_2.MainPage"
    xmlns="http://schemas.microsoft.com/winfx/2006/xaml/presentation"
    xmlns:x="http://schemas.microsoft.com/winfx/2006/xaml"
    Width="600" Height="800" mc:Ignorable="d"
    xmlns:d="http://schemas.microsoft.com/expression/blend/2008"
    xmlns:mc="http://schemas.openxmlformats.org/markup-compatibility/2006">
  <UserControl.Resources>
    <Color x:Key="MyGreen">#FF008000</Color>
    <RadialGradientBrush x:Key="GreenRadialBrush">
      <GradientStop Color="#FFE2EEE2"/>
      <GradientStop Color="#FF000000" Offset="1"/>
      <GradientStop Color="#FF178217" Offset="0.29499998688697815"/>
      <GradientStop Color="#FF008000" Offset="0.71399998664855957"/>
      <GradientStop Color="#FFFFFFFF" Offset="0.5130000114440918"/>
    </RadialGradientBrush>
  </UserControl.Resources>
  <Grid x:Name="LayoutRoot" Background="#FFFFFFFF">
    <Grid.RowDefinitions>
      <RowDefinition Height="0.121*"/>
      <RowDefinition Height="0.244*"/>
      <RowDefinition Height="0.391*"/>
      <RowDefinition Height="0.244*"/>
    </Grid.RowDefinitions>
```

```
<Ellipse HorizontalAlignment="Left" Margin="4,21,0,5.4"
  VerticalAlignment="Stretch" Width="70" Stroke="#FF000000">
  <Ellipse.Fill>
    <RadialGradientBrush>
      <GradientStop Color="#FFE2EEE2"/>
      <GradientStop Color="#FF000000" Offset="1"/>
      <GradientStop Color="#FF178217" Offset="0.29499998688697815"/>
      <GradientStop Color="#FF008000" Offset="0.71399998664855957"/>
      <GradientStop Color="#FFFFFFFF" Offset="0.5130000114440918"/>
    </RadialGradientBrush>
  </Ellipse.Fill>
</Ellipse>
<TextBox HorizontalAlignment="Right" Margin="0,44,24,29.7999992370605"
 VerticalAlignment="Stretch" Text="TextBox" TextWrapping="Wrap"
 FontSize="14" x:Name="txtFancySelection" Width="103">
  <TextBox.SelectionBackground>
    <LinearGradientBrush EndPoint="0.5,1" StartPoint="0.5,0">
      <GradientStop Color="#FF000080"/>
      <GradientStop Color="#FFFFD700" Offset="1"/>
    </LinearGradientBrush>
  </TextBox.SelectionBackground>
</TextBox>
<Ellipse HorizontalAlignment="Left" Margin="86,21,0,5.40000009536743"
  VerticalAlignment="Stretch" Width="70" Stroke="#FF000000">
  <Ellipse.Fill>
    <LinearGradientBrush EndPoint="0.5,1" StartPoint="0.5,0">
      <GradientStop Color="#FFE2EEE2"/>
      <GradientStop Color="#FF000000" Offset="1"/>
      <GradientStop Color="#FF178217" Offset="0.29499998688697815"/>
      <GradientStop Color="#FF008000" Offset="0.71399998664855957"/>
      <GradientStop Color="#FFFFFFFF" Offset="0.5130000114440918"/>
    </LinearGradientBrush>
  </Ellipse.Fill>
</Ellipse>
<Ellipse HorizontalAlignment="Left" Margin="168,21,0,5.40000009536743"
  VerticalAlignment="Stretch" Width="70" Stroke="#FF000000">
  <Ellipse.Fill>
    <LinearGradientBrush EndPoint="0.5,1" StartPoint="0.5,0">
      <GradientStop Color="#FFC6E4C6"/>
      <GradientStop Color="#FFC6E4C6" Offset="1"/>
      <GradientStop Color="#FF66B366" Offset="0.29499998688697815"/>
      <GradientStop Color="#FF66B366" Offset="0.71399998664855957"/>
      <GradientStop Color="#FFB6DCB6" Offset="0.5130000114440918"/>
    </LinearGradientBrush>
  </Ellipse.Fill>
</Ellipse>
```

```
<Ellipse HorizontalAlignment="Right" Margin="0,21,136,5.40000009536743"
  VerticalAlignment="Stretch" Width="70" Stroke="#FF000000"
  Fill="#FF66B366"/>
<Ellipse HorizontalAlignment="Stretch" Margin="240,21,290,5.40000009536743"
  VerticalAlignment="Stretch">
  <Ellipse.Fill>
    <LinearGradientBrush EndPoint="1.10000002384186,0.0280000008642673"
    StartPoint="0.0570000000298023,1.12199997901917">
      <GradientStop Color="#FFC6E4C6"/>
      <GradientStop Color="#FFC6E4C6" Offset="1"/>
      <GradientStop Color="#FF66B366" Offset="0.29499998688697815"/>
      <GradientStop Color="#FF66B366" Offset="0.71399998664855957"/>
      <GradientStop Color="#FFB6DCB6" Offset="0.5130000114440918"/>
    </LinearGradientBrush>
  </Ellipse.Fill>
</Ellipse>
<Ellipse HorizontalAlignment="Right" Margin="0,21,218,5.40000009536743"
  VerticalAlignment="Stretch" Width="70">
  <Ellipse.Fill>
    <LinearGradientBrush EndPoint="1.1,0.0" StartPoint="0.05,1.12">
      <GradientStop Color="#FFC6E4C6"/>
      <GradientStop Color="#FFC6E4C6" Offset="1"/>
      <GradientStop Color="#FF66B366" Offset="0.29499998688697815"/>
      <GradientStop Color="#FF66B366" Offset="0.71399998664855957"/>
      <GradientStop Color="#FFB6DCB6" Offset="0.5130000114440918"/>
    </LinearGradientBrush>
  </Ellipse.Fill>
</Ellipse>

<Path Stroke="#FFCEC2C2" HorizontalAlignment="Right" Margin="0,21.25,53,4"
 x:Name="GradientDonut" VerticalAlignment="Stretch" Stretch="Fill"
 Data="M169.68619,84.975204 C169.68619,131.62958 131.81258,169.4504
 85.093094,169.45041 C38.373619,169.45041 0.5,131.62958 0.5,84.975204
 C0.5,38.320839 38.373619,0.5 85.093094,0.5 C131.81258,0.5 169.68619,38.320839
 169.68619,84.975204 z M145.68619,84.975204 C145.68619,118.37474
 118.55774,145.45041 85.093094,145.45041 C51.628452,145.45041 24.5,118.37474
 24.5,84.975204 C24.5,51.575672 51.628452,24.5 85.093094,24.5 C118.55774,24.5
 145.68619,51.575672 145.68619,84.975204 z" Width="170.186" Grid.Row="1"
 Grid.RowSpan="1" d:LayoutOverrides="Width">
```

```
    <Path.Fill>
      <RadialGradientBrush>
        <GradientStop Color="#FF044506"/>
        <GradientStop Color="#FF044506" Offset="1"/>
        <GradientStop Color="#FF9BA999" Offset="0.281"/>
        <GradientStop Color="#FF044506" Offset="0.52700001001358032"/>
        <GradientStop Color="#FF9BA999" Offset="0.7279999852180481"/>
      </RadialGradientBrush>
    </Path.Fill>
  </Path>
<Path Stroke="#FFCEC2C2" HorizontalAlignment="Left" Margin="19,21.25,0,4"
 x:Name="SolidColorBrushDonut" VerticalAlignment="Stretch" Stretch="Fill"
 Data="M169.68619,84.975204 C169.68619,131.62958 131.81258,169.45041
 85.093094,169.45041 C38.373619,169.45041 0.5,131.62958 0.5,
 84.975204 C0.5,38.320839 38.373619,0.5 85.093094,0.5 C131.81258,
 0.5 169.68619,38.320839 169.68619,84.975204 z
M145.68619,84.975204 C145.68619,118.37474 118.55774,145.45041 85.093094,145.45041
C51.628452,145.45041 24.5,118.37474 24.5,84.975204 C24.5,51.575672 51.628452,24.5
85.093094,24.5 C118.55774,24.5 145.68619,51.575672 145.68619,84.975204 z"
Width="170.186" Fill="#FF3A8E3A" Grid.Row="1" d:LayoutOverrides="Width"/>
<Path Stroke="#FFCEC2C2" HorizontalAlignment="Stretch"
 Margin="198.406997680664,21.25,231.406997680664,4" x:Name="GradientDonut_Copy"
 VerticalAlignment="Stretch" Stretch="Fill" Data="M169.68619,84.975204
 C169.68619,131.62958 131.81258,169.45041 85.093094,169.45041
C38.373619,169.45041
0.5,131.62958 0.5,84.975204 C0.5,38.320839 38.373619,0.5 85.093094,0.5
C131.81258,0.5
169.68619,38.320839 169.68619,84.975204 z M145.68619,84.975204
C145.68619,118.37474 118.55774,145.45041 85.093094,145.45041
C51.628452,145.45041
24.5,118.37474 24.5,84.975204 C24.5,51.575672 51.628452,24.5 85.093094,24.5
C118.55774,24.5 145.68619,51.575672 145.68619,84.975204 z" Width="170.186"
Grid.Row="1" d:LayoutOverrides="Width">
  <Path.Fill>
    <LinearGradientBrush EndPoint="0.5,1" StartPoint="0.5,0">
      <GradientStop Color="#FF044506"/>
      <GradientStop Color="#FF044506" Offset="1"/>
      <GradientStop Color="#FF9BA999" Offset="0.28099998831748962"/>
      <GradientStop Color="#FF044506" Offset="0.52700001001358032"/>
      <GradientStop Color="#FF9BA999" Offset="0.7279999852180481"/>
    </LinearGradientBrush>
  </Path.Fill>
</Path>
```

```
    <Rectangle Margin="100,34,104,34" VerticalAlignment="Stretch"
      HorizontalAlignment="Stretch" Grid.Row="2" Stroke="#FF000000"
      RadiusY="38" RadiusX="38" x:Name="RectImageBrush"
      RenderTransformOrigin="0.5,0.5">
      <Rectangle.RenderTransform>
        <SkewTransform AngleX="20" AngleY="10"/>
      </Rectangle.RenderTransform>
      <Rectangle.Fill>
        <ImageBrush ImageSource="/img/Landscape2.jpg"  Stretch="Fill" />
      </Rectangle.Fill>
    </Rectangle>
<MediaElement x:Name="mElement" AutoPlay="True" HorizontalAlignment="Stretch"
              Margin="4,4,421,0" Grid.Row="3" Width="175" Height="90"
              d:LayoutOverrides="Height" VerticalAlignment="Top"
              Source="/video/video.wmv"/>
    <TextBlock Margin="214,38.2000007629395,24,61"
              Grid.Row="3" TextWrapping="Wrap" Text="TextBlock" FontSize="72"
              FontFamily="Comic Sans MS" FontWeight="Bold">
      <TextBlock.Foreground>
        <VideoBrush SourceName="mElement" Stretch="UniformToFill" />
      </TextBlock.Foreground>
    </TextBlock>

  </Grid>
</UserControl>
```

3-3. Positioning UI Elements with a Canvas

Problem

You need to understand how to position UI elements using coordinates for the left and top location for controls.

Solution

Learn how to work with the Canvas layout control that allows child controls to be placed using coordinates for the left and top values.

How It Works

Before we dive in with the Canvas object, we first provide a frame of reference for object positioning in a Windows Forms application. In a Windows Forms application, the fundamental UI container is the Form class. Another container would be a Panel class located within a Form object. For both the Form and Panel containers in Windows Forms applications, you position objects by specifying a Left and Top property for controls like the TextBox object. Hard-coding the Left and Top properties for controls does not provide dynamic UI layout in terms of resizing for different dots per inch (dpi) settings or screen resolutions, let alone provide a flexible UI when displaying data in a DataGrid with many columns of data.

Docking was introduced into Windows Forms to help provide a more dynamic UI by putting controls into panels and having them stick to one side or the other, leaving a dynamically resizing client area for a panel containing a DataGrid or similar control. Other tricks let you build a homegrown layout system in Windows that dynamically scales by recalculating object positions for dpi settings, screen resolutions, or the size of data displayed. All in all, these efforts have resulted in limited UI flexibility.

One of the most important features in Windows Presentation Foundation (WPF) that made it into Silverlight 3 is the layout system. The Silverlight 3 layout system enables dynamic positioning of vector-based UI elements using device-independent units or pixels that defaults to 96 units per inch, regardless of display resolution.

For example, if you set a rectangle to be 96 units high and 96 units wide in Expression Blend, the rectangle will be one inch square by default in Windows because the Windows default is 96 dpi. If you switch Windows to, say, 120 dpi, the rectangle in Expression Blend will still report as 96 units wide and tall, but the actual number in Windows will be 120 pixels wide and tall.

The Silverlight 3 layout system, which we cover in Recipe 3-4 in the "How It Works" section, includes containers that manage the size and position of controls placed within the container. UI elements are placed into one of three primary containers that inherit from the Panel base class:

- Canvas: Defines an area within which you can explicitly position child elements by coordinates relative to the Canvas area, which we cover in this recipe.

- StackPanel: Arranges child elements into a single line that can be oriented horizontally or vertically. We cover the StackPanel in Recipe 3-4.

- Grid: Defines an area containing rows and columns where elements can be placed. We cover the Grid in Recipe 3-5.

■**Note** Silverlight 3 introduces the TabPanel, DockPanel, and WrapPanel as well.

The Canvas object may feel most comfortable to developers who are not familiar with WPF or Silverlight and have built UIs in technologies similar to .NET Windows Forms. The Canvas container allows absolute positioning of UI elements, very similar to Windows Forms.

The Code

To try out the Canvas object, create a new Silverlight 3 project in Visual Studio, change the default root element from a Grid to a Canvas object, and add a TextBlock:

```
<Canvas x:Name="LayoutRoot" Background="White">
  <TextBlock>Hi There</TextBlock>
</Canvas>
```

This results in the text "Hi There" appearing in the upper-right corner of the Canvas object. To position the TextBlock 20 pixels in and 20 pixels down, you might be tempted to try to use a Left or Top attribute for the TextBlock as you would if you were using absolute positioning in ASP.NET or Windows Forms; but you won't find such an attribute. To position the TextBlock, use the following markup to set Left and Top for the control using attached-property syntax:

```
<TextBlock Canvas.Left="20" Canvas.Top="20">Hi There
</TextBlock>
```

Attached properties are a special form of dependency properties that can be added to a child UI element. Dependency properties are a new type of property used extensively in WPF and Silverlight 3 to enable styling, animation, automatic data binding through change notification, and other capabilities. For more information about dependency properties, refer to Chapters 4 and 5 as well as the MSDN documentation for Silverlight:

```
http://msdn.microsoft.com/en-us/library/cc221408(VS.95).aspx
```

When you invoke IntelliSense for the TextBlock, you see a list similar to the one shown in Figure 3-12.

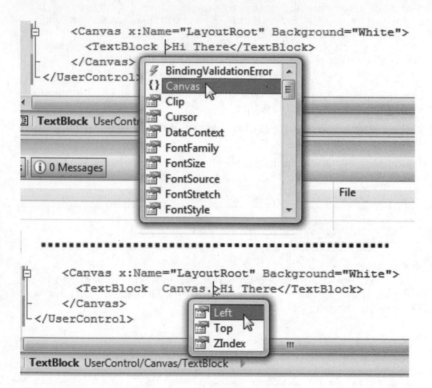

Figure 3-12. *Attached properties in IntelliSense*

The Canvas namespace appears in the IntelliSense list along with the other properties for the child control, in this case a TextBlock. When you select Canvas in the list, Canvas is added as an attribute to the TextBlock and the list of available attached properties displays as shown in Figure 3-12, resulting in this syntax for the TextBlock:

```
<TextBlock Canvas.Left="20" Canvas.Top="20">Hi There</TextBlock>
```

You can make copies of the TextBlock and adjust the text and position to have them display across the Canvas object. Listing 3-2 has multiple TextBlock objects positioned using the attached-property syntax.

Listing 3-2. *Recipe 3.3 MainPage.Xaml File*

```
<UserControl x:Class="Ch03_DevelopingUX.Recipe3_3.MainPage"
    xmlns="http://schemas.microsoft.com/winfx/2006/xaml/presentation"
    xmlns:x="http://schemas.microsoft.com/winfx/2006/xaml"
    Width="200" Height="200">
  <Canvas x:Name="LayoutRoot" Background="White">
    <TextBlock>Hi There Reader</TextBlock>
    <TextBlock Canvas.Left="20" Canvas.Top="20">Hi There</TextBlock>
    <TextBlock Canvas.Left="40"
     Canvas.Top="40">Silverlight</TextBlock>
    <TextBlock Canvas.Left="60" Canvas.Top="60">
     Silverlight</TextBlock>
    <TextBlock Canvas.Left="80" Canvas.Top="80">
     Silverlight</TextBlock>
    <TextBlock Canvas.Left="100" Canvas.Top="100">
     Silverlight</TextBlock>
  </Canvas>
</UserControl>
```

The UI for Recipe 3-3 looks like Figure 3-13.

Figure 3-13. *A* Canvas *with* TextBlock *objects positioned using attached-property syntax*

The Canvas is an improvement over traditional layout available in Windows Forms or similar technology, because it allows positioning in device-independent pixels. But the Canvas generally is not used for general application UI layout because it does not account for browser or window resizing like the StackPanel and Grid, which we cover in Recipes 3-4 and 3-5. A Canvas can be useful when you are building parts of a general application layout that require precise positioning that must not change, such as when you are building online games in Silverlight.

3-4. Positioning UI Elements with a StackPanel

Problem

You want to position elements in order (either horizontally or vertically) in an area of the application, using a flexible technique so that the controls automatically size and position themselves using the layout system.

Solution

Use a StackPanel control with either Horizontal or Vertical alignment as a container for the UI elements. Also use Margin and Padding to add space around elements that the layout system uses to position elements within the StackPanel container.

How It Works

In Recipe 3-3, we covered how to absolutely position elements using a Canvas panel within an application using coordinates for the Canvas.Top and Canvas.Left attached properties. However, the Canvas container does not fully integrate with the layout system in Silverlight because the positions of elements are fixed.

The layout system is a recursive operation that first sizes, then positions, and finally draws elements onscreen. It is a two-pass system that is applied starting at the top of the visual XAML tree and that works its way through the Children collection of each control. During the Measure pass, the desired size of each child element is determined. In the Arrange pass, each child element's size and position are finalized.

Two additional topics related to layout are Margin and Padding. Whereas all FrameworkElements have the Margin property, only objects that inherit from Control and the Border FrameworkElement have a Padding property. The difference is that Margin defines the extra space placed around the outside edges of the element, and Padding defines the extra spaced placed around the inside edges of the control.

You can use Margin and Padding to force mandatory separation between controls; it is applied by the layout system as the UI is resized, either programmatically or as the user resizes the browser. Values for Margin and Padding can be specified using three notations: a unique value for each edge, such as "1,2,3,4"; two numbers, such as "3,5", which applies 3 for the left and right and 5 for the top and bottom; or a single value such as "4". If you set the property to a single value, that Margin or Padding will be applied to the left, top, right, and bottom edges of the control. If you set each edge explicitly to "1,2,3,4", the order applied is left, top, right, bottom.

The StackPanel is a great way to lay out controls either vertically or horizontally within a general UI design that fully integrates with the sizing and positioning functionality of the layout system.

The Code

For this recipe, you create a new project in Visual Studio, replace the root Grid object with a StackPanel object in MainPage.Xaml, and change the Height for the UserControl to 440 and the Width to 440. Switch to Expression Blend, and add a few Rectangles by double-clicking the Rectangle tool in the Asset Library toolbar to fill the StackPanel, as shown in Figure 3-14.

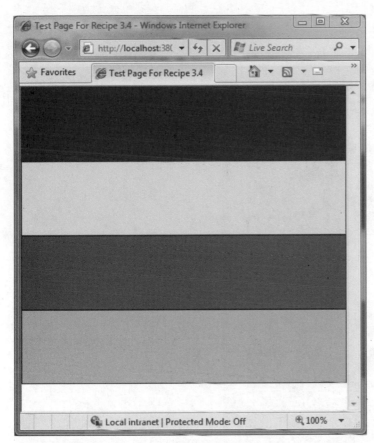

Figure 3-14. *A StackPanel with four Rectangle objects*

Unlike the Canvas, the StackPanel does not have any attached properties. You cannot specify a Top or Left property to position the elements. When you add elements by double-clicking the element in the Expression Blend Asset Library toolbar, the element is added to the current container (the element with the yellow box around it in the Objects and Timeline Visual Tree tool window) on the Artboard. The order of the elements displayed in the StackPanel is the order in which they are listed in the XAML Visual Tree.

By default, Rectangle elements are added with a Height of 100. The Width is not set, which means it has a default value of Auto. For the StackPanel, the Auto value causes the Rectangle to stretch to fill the width. Here is an example of the markup for the first Rectangle:

```
<Rectangle Height="100" Fill="#FF000080" Stroke="#FF000000"/>
```

The only value that is not a default is Fill, which you configure so that the Rectangles can be distinguished. The Rectangles are pushed up against the edge of the browser plug-in's edges as well as next to each other. Let's set a value for Margin on each Rectangle to see the effect. Apply these values for Margin to the Rectangles from top to bottom:

```
Margin="4"
Margin="0,0,4,0"
Margin="4,5"
Margin="4,0"
```

This results in the UI shown in Figure 3-15.

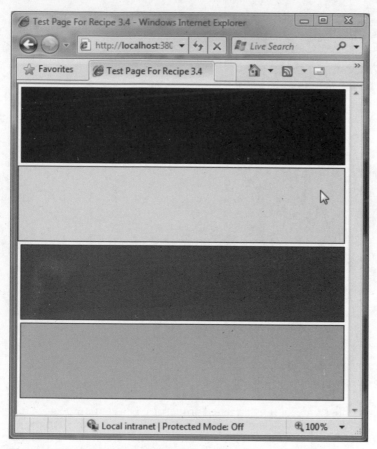

Figure 3-15. *A StackPanel with four Rectangles and Margin set*

Setting Margin="4" applies a 4-pixel margin to all four sides. Setting individual values such as Margin="1,2,3,4" applies a 1-pixel margin to the left side, 2 pixels to the top, 3 pixels to the right side, and 4 pixels to the bottom. Setting Margin="4,5" applies a 4-pixel margin to the left and right sides and a 5-pixel margin to the top and bottom.

In addition to the normal customization options such as Background HorizontalAlignment, the StackPanel has an Orientation property, with a default of Vertical.

Switching the Orientation property to Horizontal renders a blank screen. This is because the Rectangle objects are configured with a Width of Auto, and the Rectangle does not have any content such as text to force a value for Width. This results in a blank screen because Width is automatically set to 0. To fix this, you set the value of MinWidth to 100, resulting in the UI shown in Figure 3-16. Listing 3-3 shows the final source code for this recipe.

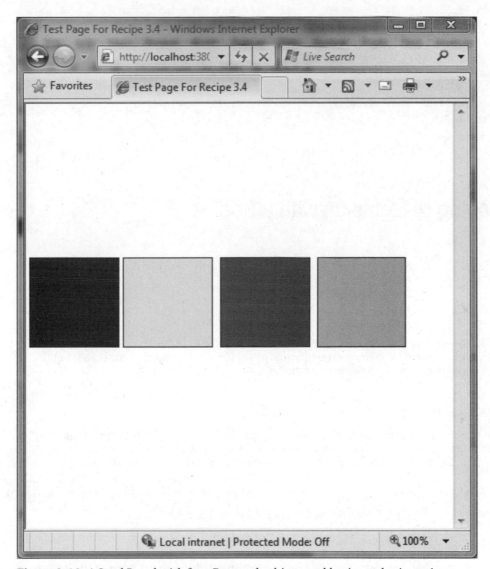

Figure 3-16. *A StackPanel with four Rectangle objects and horizontal orientation*

Listing 3-3. *Recipe 3.4 MainPage.Xaml File*

```xml
<UserControl x:Class="Ch03_DevelopingUX.Recipe3_4.MainPage"
    xmlns="http://schemas.microsoft.com/winfx/2006/xaml/presentation"
    xmlns:x="http://schemas.microsoft.com/winfx/2006/xaml"
    Width="440" Height="440">
  <StackPanel x:Name="LayoutRoot" Background="White" Orientation="Horizontal">
    <Rectangle Height="100" Fill="#FF000080" Stroke="#FF000000" Margin="4"
               MinWidth="100"/>
    <Rectangle Height="100" Fill="#FFFFFF00" Stroke="#FF000000"
               Margin="0,0,4,0" MinWidth="100"/>
    <Rectangle Height="100" Fill="#FF008000" Stroke="#FF000000" Margin="4,4"
               MinWidth="100"/>
    <Rectangle Height="100" Fill="#FF00FFFF" Stroke="#FF000000" Margin="4,0"
               MinWidth="100"/>

  </StackPanel>
</UserControl>
```

3-5. Positioning UI Elements with a Grid

Problem

You want to position multiple groups of elements and controls in a flexible way so that the controls automatically size and position themselves using the layout system.

Solution

Use the Grid panel to create Columns and Rows to separate UI areas. Use Grid.RowSpan and Grid.ColumnSpan to force content to span rows or columns as necessary. Finally, nest StackPanel and Canvas layout controls as necessary to create a powerful UI.

How It Works

The Grid control is the most powerful and flexible layout control available in the Silverlight layout system. In most scenarios, an application is a combination of Grid and StackPanel controls to lay out resizable UIs, using Canvas panels to create absolutely positioned content where needed.

■**Note**   We covered the StackPanel in Recipe 3-4 and Canvas in Recipe 3-3.

In Recipe 3-4, when we discussed the StackPanel, we also provided an overview of the layout system and examined Margin and Padding. Margin and Padding also apply to the Grid object, and we demonstrate how to combine Margin and Padding in the code section.

The Grid control is similar to an HTML table in laying out controls. It supports multiple rows and columns in the RowDefinitions and ColumnDefinitions collections. By default, if a control is nested inside a Grid without any rows or columns defined, the control renders in the upper-left corner, which represents row zero and column zero.

When you define columns and rows on a Grid, you can specify the Width in the ColumnDefinition object for a column and the Height in the RowDefinitions object for a row in pixels. You can also leave Width and Height set at their default value of Auto or specify Auto explicitly.

Leaving Width and Height set to Auto causes the Grid to size rows and columns equally as much as possible; however, the ultimate size is determined by the layout system, which takes into account the size of the content. For example, if a Grid has two rows defined with the default of Auto, but the content in the first row has a minimum size that is twice that of the content in the second row, the layout system causes the first row to be twice the width of the second.

The Grid supports a much more powerful method of sizing columns and rows: *star sizing*. When you specify a star (*) as the Width or Height of a column or row, the column or row receives a proportional amount of space. This XAML has the same effect as setting Width and Height to the default of Auto:

```
<Grid.ColumnDefinitions>
  <ColumnDefinition Width="*"/>
  <ColumnDefinition Width="*"/>
</Grid.ColumnDefinitions>
<Grid.RowDefinitions>
  <RowDefinition Height="*"/>
  <RowDefinition Height="*"/>
</Grid.RowDefinitions>
```

It gets interesting when you prepend an integer to * for Width or Height. For example, to give up to twice the amount of available space to the second column and second row, specify 2* for both the Width and Height, like this:

```
<Grid.ColumnDefinitions>
  <ColumnDefinition Width="*"/>
  <ColumnDefinition Width="2*"/>
</Grid.ColumnDefinitions>
<Grid.RowDefinitions>
  <RowDefinition Height="*"/>
  <RowDefinition Height="2*"/>
</Grid.RowDefinitions>
```

Note that we said "up to twice the amount"; that is because the layout system takes into account the minimum size required for content. If the second column wants twice as much space as the first column, the content in the first column may prevent the second column from getting all the requested space, depending on the minimum width values configured on the content in the first column.

■**Note** The GridSplitter control allows the user to resize the Grid at runtime. Refer to this site for more information: http://msdn.microsoft.com/en-us/library/system.windows.controls.gridsplitter(VS.95).aspx.

Like the Canvas object, the Grid also has attached properties for specifying where nested controls should be located. As we explained in Recipe 3-3, you use Canvas.Left and Canvas.Top to absolutely position nested content. For a Grid object, you specify the row and column for nested content; the Silverlight layout system positions the nested content, taking into account Margin, Padding, Alignment, and so forth.

To position a StackPanel in the second column and second row, you use a zero-based value like this:

```
<StackPanel Grid.Column="1" Grid.Row="1" >
```

To have a StackPanel positioned in row three, column two but span two columns and two rows, the XAML looks like this:

```
<StackPanel Grid.Column="1" Grid.ColumnSpan="2"
  Grid.Row="2" Grid.RowSpan="2">
```

The Code

By default, when you create a new project in Silverlight, it sets the root element to a Grid. For this application, you define two columns and two rows, giving up to twice the available space to the second column and second row using this XAML:

```
<Grid.ColumnDefinitions>
  <ColumnDefinition Width="*"/>
  <ColumnDefinition Width="2*"/>
</Grid.ColumnDefinitions>
<Grid.RowDefinitions>
  <RowDefinition Height="*"/>
  <RowDefinition Height="2*"/>
</Grid.RowDefinitions>
```

The Grid object has many additional configuration options, such as setting the minimum and maximum size on rows and columns as well as various ways to specify the size of rows and columns. For more information, refer to the MSDN documentation here:

```
http://msdn.microsoft.com/en-us/library/system.windows.controls.grid(VS.95).aspx
```

■Note When you are building a UI, set the height and width of the user control to the desired size before laying out controls. Silverlight 3 UIs are vector based and infinitely scalable, but it helps to have the right relationship between controls if they are laid out at the desired resolution. Otherwise, adjusting the desired size of the user control after building the UI will scale up or down the entire layout, which may not achieve the desired perspective without additional modification.

Within each quadrant, define a StackPanel that contains either four TextBlocks or four Rectangles, as shown in Figure 3-17.

In Figure 3-17, as the browser window expands, the StackPanel objects dynamically reposition, spreading out equally on the page. If you make the browser window smaller, eventually the MinWidth and MinHeight values on the Rectangle objects prevent the UI from proportionally reducing in size.

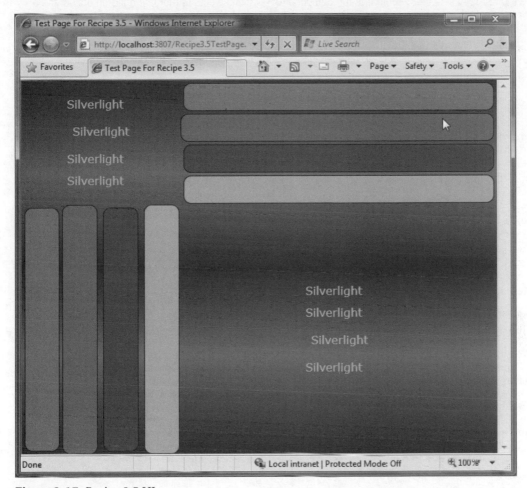

Figure 3-17. *Recipe 3.5 UI*

In general, you may be tempted to set Width and Height properties on controls without thinking; but doing so can alter how layout occurs for controls, usually to the detriment of the developer. And sometimes, when you lay out controls in Expression Blend, the program automatically sets Height and Width values for you even though the default is Auto. Our recommendation is to leave sizing values to the default value of Auto and then decide whether to specify a size or minimum size for a control. If you don't set a value for Height or Width, the default value is Auto.

■**Note** When you are building a UI with nested containers like Grid and StackPanel in Expression Blend, you may find that you cannot directly select a nested UI element like a TextBox with the default Selection tool. The black arrow at the top of the Asset Library toolbar is the Selection tool, which selects immediate children only of the control that has the yellow box around it in the Objects and Timeline window. You can move the yellow box to any nested container control by double-clicking a container control in the Objects and Timeline windows; another option is to use the Direct Selection tool (hotkey A), which is the white arrow just below the Selection tool in the Asset Library toolbar. The Direct Selection tool allows deep selection of an object on the design surface or Artboard.

Apply a gradient to the root Grid's Background property. For each StackPanel, clear the Background property so that it is transparent. You also create a custom Style for all the TextBlock objects using this XAML:

```
<UserControl.Resources>
  <Style TargetType="TextBlock" x:Key="TextBlockStyle">
    <Setter Property="Foreground" Value="#FFCBCBDF"/>
    <Setter Property="FontSize" Value="16"/>
    <Setter Property="VerticalAlignment" Value="Bottom"/>
  </Style>
</UserControl.Resources>
```

Here is an example of how to apply the style:

```
<TextBlock Margin="4,4,4,4" Style="{StaticResource TextBlockStyle}"
 Text="Silverlight" />
```

We cover the StaticResource markup extension in Recipe 2-13. We explore control styles in Chapter 5. Notice in Figure 3-16 that the TextBlock objects and Rectangle objects all have Margin applied to provide spacing around the controls. We also provide Padding="8,8" to the second TextBlock in the northwest quadrant and to the third TextBlock in the southeast quadrant. We cover padding in Recipe 3-4.

To demonstrate the automatic layout and resizing capabilities of the Grid and StackPanel, remove the Height and Width values from the UserControl tag. This allows the Silverlight 3 layout system to determine the size of objects based on the size of the overall browser window as well as any minimum size values for controls. Listing 3-4 has the complete source code for this recipe.

Listing 3-4. *Recipe 3.5 MainPage.Xaml File*

```
<UserControl x:Class="Ch03_DevelopingUX.Recipe3_5.MainPage"
    xmlns="http://schemas.microsoft.com/winfx/2006/xaml/presentation"
    xmlns:x="http://schemas.microsoft.com/winfx/2006/xaml">
  <UserControl.Resources>
    <Style TargetType="TextBlock" x:Key="TextBlockStyle">
      <Setter Property="Foreground" Value="#FFCBCBDF"/>
      <Setter Property="FontSize" Value="16"/>
      <Setter Property="VerticalAlignment" Value="Bottom"/>
    </Style>
  </UserControl.Resources>
```

```
<Grid x:Name="LayoutRoot" MinHeight="400"  MinWidth="600">
  <Grid.Background>
    <LinearGradientBrush EndPoint="0.5,1" StartPoint="0.5,0">
      <GradientStop Color="#FF26302B"/>
      <GradientStop Color="#FF26302B" Offset="1"/>
      <GradientStop Color="#FF26302B" Offset="0.50400000810623169"/>
      <GradientStop Color="#FF748A7F" Offset="0.25"/>
      <GradientStop Color="#FF748A7F" Offset="0.7369999885559082"/>
    </LinearGradientBrush>
  </Grid.Background>
  <Grid.ColumnDefinitions>
    <ColumnDefinition Width="*"/>
    <ColumnDefinition Width="2*"/>
  </Grid.ColumnDefinitions>
  <Grid.RowDefinitions>
    <RowDefinition Height="*"/>
    <RowDefinition Height="2*"/>
  </Grid.RowDefinitions>
  <StackPanel Grid.Row="0" Grid.Column="0"
   HorizontalAlignment="Center" VerticalAlignment="Center">
    <TextBlock Margin="4,4,4,4" Style="{StaticResource
     TextBlockStyle}" Text="Silverlight" />
    <TextBlock Margin="4,4,4,4" Padding="8,8"
     Style="{StaticResource TextBlockStyle}" Text="Silverlight" />
    <TextBlock Margin="4,4,4,4" Style="{StaticResource
     TextBlockStyle}" Text="Silverlight" />
    <TextBlock Margin="4,4,4,4" Style="{StaticResource
     TextBlockStyle}" Text="Silverlight" />
  </StackPanel>
  <StackPanel  Grid.Row="0" Grid.Column="1" >
    <Rectangle MinHeight="40" Fill="#FFBB8C27" Stroke="#FF000000"
     Margin="4" MinWidth="50" RadiusX="10" RadiusY="10" />
    <Rectangle MinHeight="40"  Fill="#FF6E6EEA" Stroke="#FF000000"
     Margin="0,0,4,0" MinWidth="50" RadiusX="10" RadiusY="10"/>
    <Rectangle MinHeight="40" Fill="#FF008000" Stroke="#FF000000"
     Margin="4,4" MinWidth="50" RadiusX="10" RadiusY="10"/>
    <Rectangle MinHeight="40" Fill="#FF00FFFF" Stroke="#FF000000"
     Margin="4,0" MinWidth="50" RadiusX="10" RadiusY="10"/>
  </StackPanel>
  <StackPanel Grid.Row="1" Grid.Column="0" Orientation=
   "Horizontal" >
    <Rectangle MinHeight="40" Fill="#FFBB8C27" Stroke="#FF000000"
     Margin="4"MinWidth="50" RadiusX="10" RadiusY="10"/>
```

```
        <Rectangle MinHeight="40"  Fill="#FF6E6EEA" Stroke="#FF000000"
         Margin="0,0,4,0" MinWidth="50" RadiusX="10" RadiusY="10"/>
        <Rectangle MinHeight="40" Fill="#FF008000" Stroke="#FF000000"
         Margin="4,4" MinWidth="50" RadiusX="10" RadiusY="10"/>
        <Rectangle MinHeight="40" Fill="#FF00FFFF" Stroke="#FF000000"
         Margin="4,0" MinWidth="50" RadiusX="10" RadiusY="10"/>
      </StackPanel>
      <StackPanel Grid.Row="1" Grid.Column="1"
       HorizontalAlignment="Center" VerticalAlignment="Center">
        <TextBlock Margin="4,4,4,4" Style="{StaticResource TextBlockStyle}"
         Text="Silverlight" />
        <TextBlock Margin="4,4,4,4" Style="{StaticResource TextBlockStyle}"
         Text="Silverlight" />
        <TextBlock Margin="4,4,4,4" Padding="8,8"
         Style="{StaticResource TextBlockStyle}" Text="Silverlight" />
        <TextBlock Margin="4,4,4,4" Style="{StaticResource TextBlockStyle}"
         Text="Silverlight" />
      </StackPanel>

    </Grid>
</UserControl>
```

3-6. Using Shapes to Draw

Problem

You need to use shapes to draw when building a Silverlight UI in Expression Blend.

Solution

Learn how to work with the drawing shapes such as the `Rectangle` and `Ellipse` in Expression Blend.

How It Works

Silverlight 3 includes vector graphic primitives that are infinitely scalable and easy to manipulate. The basic shapes include `Ellipse` and `Rectangle`, which are often converted to `Path` objects, which we cover in Recipe 3-6.

The `Ellipse` and `Rectangle` objects are predefined shapes that can be combined to create pretty much any other shape. They are less flexible than `Path` objects, but they can be easier to work with because they provide structure that is malleable.

For example, it is easy to visually create a perfect circle with an `Ellipse` by drawing an `Ellipse` on the surface and then adjusting the drawing by grabbing a corner and sliding the selection frame left, right, up, or down so that the bounding rectangle around the `Ellipse` has the same width and height. You can also set the `Width` and `Height` properties directly in the Expression Blend properties window. Figure 3-18 shows the mouse adjusting an `Ellipse` so that it is 102 by 102 pixels, forming a perfect circle.

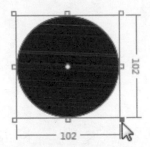

Figure 3-18. *Adjusting an Ellipse to create a perfect circle in Expression Blend*

You can also create a circle with a `Rectangle` shape. The first step is to drag a `Rectangle` onto the design surface or Artboard in Expression Blend and size it as when working with the `Ellipse`, to 100 × 100 pixels. Next, with the mouse, grab the handle in the upper-left corner of the `Rectangle`, and drag it as far as it will go down and to the right. Doing so yields a circle, as shown in Figure 3-19.

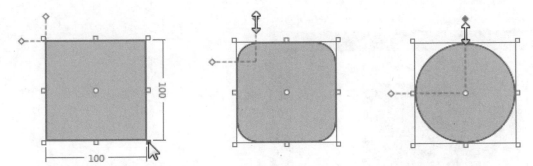

Figure 3-19. *Adjusting a Rectangle to create a perfect circle in Expression Blend*

What is accomplished visually can also be accomplished programmatically by setting the `RadiusX` and `RadiusY` value to half the length or width, assuming the length and width are the same on the `Rectangle`. If the length and width are not equal in value, you will create a circular shape, but it won't be a perfectly round circle.

As mentioned earlier, you can create drawings with shapes by combining them in Expression Blend. As an example, let's say you want to create a puffy cloud shape. Draw a circle using an `Ellipse` shape object that is 100×100 pixels. Make two copies, fill them with gray for a storm-cloud appearance, and arrange them as shown in Figure 3-20.

Figure 3-20. *Drawing a cloud with three Ellipses*

To create more of a cloud-like experience, you can use Expression Blend to combine the three shapes into a Path. First, select all three Ellipse objects by either Shift-clicking in the Objects and Timeline window or pressing Ctrl and left-clicking each Ellipse until all three are selected. Then, right-click either the objects listed in the Objects and Timeline window or the Artboard to bring up the Combine menu, as shown in Figure 3-21.

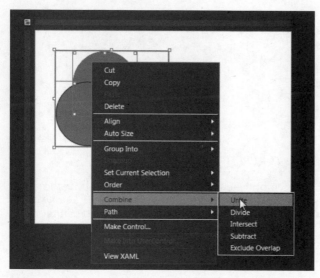

Figure 3-21. *Combine three Ellipses using Unite*

Select the Unite option, and Expression Blend combines the three shapes into a Path object, as shown in Figure 3-22.

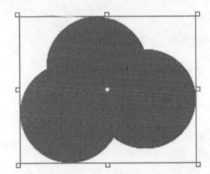

Figure 3-22. *Results of combining with Unite*

The three Ellipse shapes are now a single object that you can manipulate by resizing it or by applying a transform to rotate or skew it. To see what happened, here is the XAML before combining the Ellipses:

```
<Grid x:Name="LayoutRoot" Background="White">
  <Ellipse Height="100" HorizontalAlignment="Left" Margin="60,32,0,0"
    VerticalAlignment="Top" Width="100" Fill="#FF808080" Stroke="#FF000000"/>
  <Ellipse HorizontalAlignment="Stretch" Margin="108,65,192,135"
    VerticalAlignment="Stretch" Fill="#FF808080" Stroke="#FF000000"/>
  <Ellipse HorizontalAlignment="Left" Margin="33,79,0,121"
    VerticalAlignment="Stretch" Fill="#FF808080" Stroke="#FF000000" Width="100"/>
</Grid>
```

Here is the XAML after combining the Ellipses with Unite into a Path object:

```
<Grid x:Name="LayoutRoot" Background="White">
  <Path HorizontalAlignment="Stretch" Margin="33,32,192,121"
   VerticalAlignment="Stretch" Fill="#FF808080" Stretch="Fill" Stroke="#FF000000"
   Data="M77,0.5 C78.708633,0.49999899 80.397............77,0.5 z"/>
</Grid>
```

We didn't copy the exact resulting XAML (see the book's code for the full XAML) because it is almost a page of nothing but floating-point values for the Data property on the Path object; but you can see that the three Ellipses are now a single Path object. Let's explore the remaining options on the Combine menu:

- Subtract is interesting because parts of shapes under the first shape selected are removed or subtracted. Suppose you have three shapes, as shown at left in Figure 3-23, and you select the topmost Ellipse and then select Subtract. The results of the operation are shown in Figure 3-24 with the title "Subtract."

- Intersect does what you would expect: it removes all parts of the shapes except the interception of the shapes.

- Exclude Overlap excludes areas that are overlapped by some but not all shapes.

- Divide preserves all strokes but uses the fill of the topmost shape as the fill of all selected shapes, as shown at right in Figure 3-23.

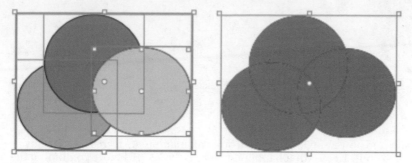

Figure 3-23. *The Divide option, before (left) and after*

Figure 3-24 shows the results of all of the Combine options.

By performing these types of combination options, you can create just about any shape required. As an example, let's say you need to create a ring. You could stick with an `Ellipse` and apply a relatively large number for the stroke, but that approach is limited because you cannot see clear inner and outer borders for the ring. Instead, let's use Combine ➤ Subtract.

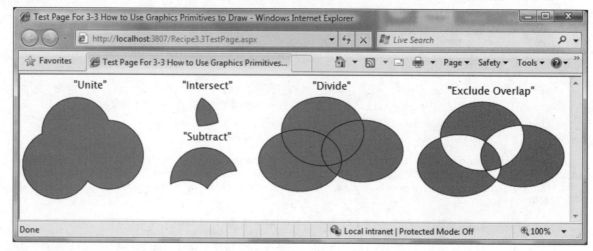

Figure 3-24. *The results of all the Combine options*

First, create an Ellipse that is 100 × 100 pixels in its rectangle bounding box when selected. Fill it with gray. Next, drag another Ellipse that is 70 × 70 pixels in size. Select both Ellipses. Then, in the Object menu, select Align ➤ Horizontal Centers and Vertical Centers so that the smaller Ellipse is perfectly aligned with the larger Ellipse. The order of selection matters, so first select the smaller Ellipse that you want to subtract from the larger Ellipse. While both Ellipses are selected, right-click, and select Combine ➤ Subtract. The result is a Path object that is a ring or donut with a transparent center, as shown in Figure 3-25.

Figure 3-25. *Path shaped as a ring via Combine ➤ Subtract*

Exclude Overlap could also generate Figure 3-25. Combine operations are not limited to shapes. You can include Path objects as well, as we cover in the next recipe. However, we first discuss the other available menu options that help designers quickly create complex drawings and reusable drawings.

Other menu options available in Expression Blend when you right-click an object (shape and/or Path) or selected objects are Group Into, Make Control, and the Path menu. Group Into allows you to quickly put an object or selected objects into a Grid, StackPanel, Canvas, ScrollViewer, or Border control; all of these inherit from Panel and are container controls. We covered Grid in Recipe 3-5, StackPanel in Recipe 3-4, and Canvas in Recipe 3-3. We cover ScrollViewer in Recipe 3-9 and Border in Recipe 3-10.

Make Control lets you quickly create a simple control out of the selected objects. For example, say you first select the StackPanel that contains the TextBox with the title "Exclude Overlap" and the Path where the Exclude Overlap operation was performed, as shown in Figure 3-23 earlier. Right-click and select Make Into UserControl to display the Make Into UserControl dialog, shown in Figure 3-26.

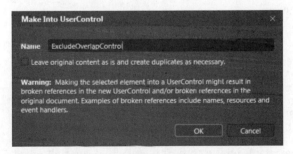

Figure 3-26. *The Make Into UserControl dialog*

As shown in Figure 3-26, name the control ExcludeOverlapControl, and leave the check box unchecked. If you check the check box, Expression Blend leaves the original content in place but puts a copy into a separate .xaml file. This is useful if you want to use the content as a separate control later. However, if you leave the check box unchecked, the content is removed from the MainPage.Xaml file, put into a separate .xaml file as a custom control, and then added back to the MainPage.Xaml file as a control reference. This custom control is available for use in other pages as well.

An `.xaml` file named `ExcludeOverlapControl.xaml` that contains the control is added to the project. To make the control more useful, remove the `White Background` color from the `LayoutRoot` object in the new control's Visual Tree in the Objects and Timeline window. This makes the object's background transparent, which may be desirable when you use the newly created control.

In the original `MainPage.Xaml` file, a new namespace is added to the `UserControl` root object:

```
xmlns:Shapes="clr-namespace:Shapes"
```

The original XAML markup for the `StackPanel` containing the `TextBox` and `Path` object is converted to this XAML, which references the new control:

```
<Shapes:ExcludeOverlapControl Margin="8,8,8,8" Grid.Column="3"/>
```

Although we don't cover the details of building controls in this chapter, we discuss them in Chapter 5. We show this functionality here for a scenario such as creating a drawing with controls, shapes, and path objects that represent something like a game piece in a computer game, when you want to be able to treat the result as a stand-alone control. At this point, a developer can add properties, methods, and events to the composite control by editing the code-behind file that is automatically created.

3-7. Using Paths to Draw

Problem

You need to understand how to create complex drawings that do not easily conform to a `Rectangle` or an `Ellipse`.

Solution

Learn how to work with the `Path` objects in Expression Blend using the Line, Pen, Pencil, and Direct Selection tools.

How It Works

Silverlight 3 includes several vector-graphic primitives that are infinitely scalable and easy to manipulate. The drawing tools include the Pen, Line, and Pencil, which are located on the Asset Library toolbar in Expression Blend. `Ellipse` and `Rectangle` are predefined shapes that you can combine to create pretty much any other shape, as we covered in Recipe 3-6.

The other tools create `Path` objects or lines that can be straight, curved, or free-form. Closing a `Path` causes the drawing to look like a shape. You can use the Pen tool to create paths containing straight lines and curves. The Line tool creates straight lines. You use the Pencil tool to create free-form `Paths`.

In Expression Blend, a Path menu option is available on the context menu when you right-click an object or selected objects. The Path menu has the submenu items listed in Table 3-1.

Table 3-1. *Path Context Menu Suboptions*

Option	Description
Convert to Path	Converts the selected object or objects on the Artboard into a Path object or multiple Path objects. It does not combine the objects into a single Path object if multiple objects are selected.
Make Clipping Path	Requires two objects, one located in front of the other. The shape or Path in front clips the shape or Path behind it, meaning that portions of the shape or Path behind the clipping\shape or Path are no longer visible. When you apply a clipping Path to an object, a Clip attribute is added to the object.
Release Clipping Path	Removes the Clip attribute from the object, making it a separate Path object on the Artboard, undoing the Make Clipping Path option.
Make Compound Path	Converts the selected objects on the Artboard into a single Path object. This is similar to the Combine ➤ Exclude Overlap option discussed earlier in that individual strokes are preserved and areas where not all of the objects overlap are clipped.
Release Compound Path	Reverses the Make Compound Path option, except that it converts the individual objects to Path objects. For example, if you select three Ellipse objects and then select Make Compound Path, the three Ellipse objects are converted into a single Path object. If you then select Release Compound Path, the single Path object is converted to three individual Path objects. Each Path object looks like the original Ellipse, but they are still Path objects under the covers.

As we mentioned earlier, the Path object represents a line that can be drawn directly with three different tools in Expression Blend: Line, Pen, and Pencil. As we noted when discussing the features of Expression Blend in Recipe 3-6 and this recipe, the output of various menu options is usually a Path object with a fairly large string of values for the Data attribute on the Path object. The Data attribute defines the shape of the line, which is essentially a series of points.

The Code

This recipe starts with the code from Recipe 3-6 where you drop three Ellipse objects on the Expression Blend Artboard and use the various Combine menu options to create complex Path objects.

If you use the Direct Selection tool to click the shape that results from choosing Combine ➤ Unite for the three Ellipses in Recipe 3-6, you see all the points that resulted from the Unite operation (see Figure 3-27).

153

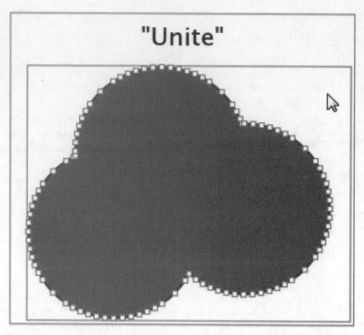

Figure 3-27. *The points of a Path resulting from combining three Ellipses with Unite*

The *Path Mini-Language* is the syntax used to define geometric paths. The value set for the Data attribute of a Path object as well as the Clip attribute for a shape is defined in the Path Mini-Language. As an example, draw a Rectangle that is 50 pixels square, and then convert it to a Path object. Here's the value for the Path's Data attribute after the Rectangle is converted to a Path:

```
Data=" M0.5,0.5 L49.5,0.5 L49.5,49.5 L0.5,49.5 z"
```

M specifies the start point. The three L commands specify drawing a line. The z command closes the current figure. This is a simple example, and the Path Mini-Language is capable of describing how to draw very complex objects. For more information, see the Silverlight 3 documentation on MSDN for a full description of the Path Mini-Language syntax:

```
http://msdn.microsoft.com/en-us/library/cc189041(VS.95).aspx
```

Although you can learn the full syntax of the Path Mini-Language, another option is to start drawing Path objects with the Line, Pen, or Pencil tool in conjunction with shapes such as Rectangle and Ellipse objects to create complex drawings. We covered shapes in the previous recipe, so we begin here with the Line tool.

The Line tool is located with Ellipse and Rectangle on the Asset Library toolbar. It draws straight Path objects by default. You can create a smooth curve with a Path drawn using the Line tool by selecting the Path with the Direct Selection or Pen tool, holding down the Alt key (which changes the mouse pointer to an angle shape), and then dragging the line to the desired curve, as shown in Figure 3-28.

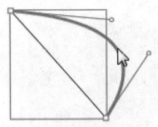

Figure 3-28. *Using the Direct Selection tool with the Alt key to curve a Path*

At first, this type of operation may not seem interesting. But if you draw a few Path objects with the Line tool and then apply a curve following the steps just explained, you can create a simple three-dimensional wireframe (see Figure 3-29).

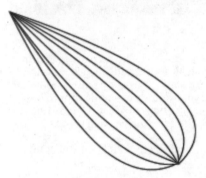

Figure 3-29. *Creating curves with the Line tool*

You don't want eight Path objects sitting in the Visual Tree. Multiselect all the Path objects, right-click one, and select the Group Into ➤ Canvas command, as shown in Figure 3-30, to combine everything into a single object in the Visual Tree.

Drawing with the Pen tool is similar to using the Line tool, but the Pen tool makes it easier to draw additional connected segments. With the Pen tool, you click where you want to start and then click where you want to add a connected point. Expression Blend draws the line for you between clicks or points.

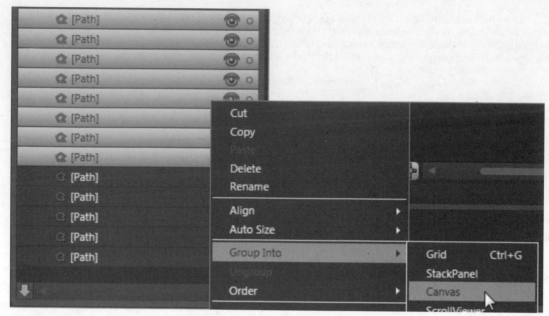

Figure 3-30. *Group Into menu in Expression Blend*

To close a drawing with the Pen tool, click back on a previous node on the line. To avoid adding another segment and also close a drawing, click back on the just previously added node, which adds the Path Mini-Language z to the value in the Data attribute. For example, if you want to create a two-node line, first click the Artboard to start the line, again click the Artboard where you want the second point to be located, and finally click back on the first node to close out the line. Clicking back on the first node does not add another segment; it results in the Path Mini-Language z being appended to the value in the Data attribute on the Path object.

You don't have to close a drawing with the Pen tool. You can draw a crooked line by clicking numerous points at odd angles, as in Figure 3-31.

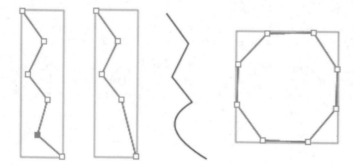

Figure 3-31. *Drawing with the Pen (left) and modifying with Alt (third from left)*

In Figure 3-31, we used the Pen tool to draw a line by clicking in a zigzag pattern down the Artboard. Notice that the second-from-the-bottom point is shaded a darker color in the drawing on the left, which indicates that the point is selected with either the Pen or Direct Selection tool. Clicking the Delete key results in the drawing that's second from the left. Finally, holding down Alt with the mouse over the bottom segment and applying a curve yields the drawing that's third from the left. It is also possible to draw shapes and close them out so that the start point and end point are the same, as in the drawing at far right.

Another way to draw with the Pen tool is to use the control handles. Select the Pen tool, and then left-click once where you want one end of the curve to be. Next, left-click the Artboard, but do not release the mouse button. Instead, drag, and you see a control handle appear that is tangent to the curve. Drag the control handle until you create the desired curve. If you click and drag again, another point is added, and a control handle appears for the new segment. When you are done drawing, you can click a point on a Path with the Direct Selection or Pen tool, and the control handles appear.

Control handles are a great way to smooth out the curve between connection points by lining up the tangents for each control handle on either side of a point. You can manipulate control handles with the mouse even after drawing the Path by clicking a point and then selecting the circle at the end of the control handle, as shown in Figure 3-32.

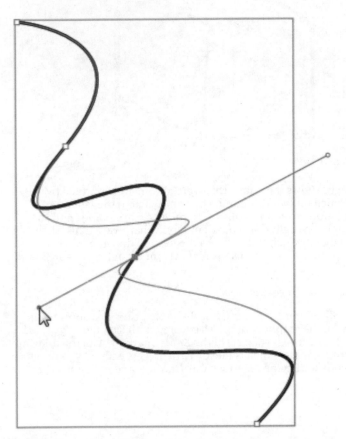

Figure 3-32. *Using a control handle to change the curve (dark color) to a new curve (lighter color)*

157

To add a node to an existing Path, select the Path with the Direct Selection tool, and then switch to the Pen tool. Move the mouse cursor over the desired location of the existing Path; the Pen tool displays a small plus sign at lower right. Click when the plus sign appears to add a node to the Path.

To add a node at the end of a Path, click the end point of a Path with the Pen tool, and then click on the Artboard where you want the new end point to be located. Expression Blend adds another node to the existing Path. If you miss clicking the end point and create a new Path object by mistake, click Undo (or press Ctrl+Z), and then try zooming in before clicking the end point.

To close a Path so that it is a fully enclosed shape, click one end of the Path, and then move the cursor over the other end of the Path. Click when the symbol at the Pen's lower right changes to a circle.

So far, we have covered the Line and Pen tools. Next, we cover the Pencil tool, which provides freehand drawing capabilities. Select the Pencil tool, and then begin drawing by left-clicking and holding down the mouse button. As you draw with the mouse, Expression Blend decides where to add points along the way. Figure 3-33 shows an attempt at drawing a box.

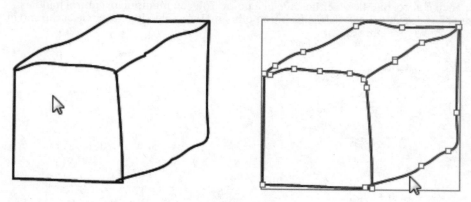

Figure 3-33. *Freehand drawing with the Pencil tool*

In Figure 3-33, the image on the right shows the points that were automatically added by Expression Blend when we draw with the Pencil tool. At this point, you can switch to the Pen tool and manipulate the points on the Path just like before, to smooth out areas, remove extra points, and so forth. The Pencil tool is very useful for a graphic designer with the right type of hardware tools, such as a stylus, to freehand-sketch a layout that can then be manipulated into the desired drawing.

If you want to learn more about how to use these tools to create vector art in Expression Blend, check out this screencast on Silverlight.net:

`http://silverlight.net/Learn/learnvideo.aspx?video=129`

The screencast series starts with a Silverlight 1.0 project, but the same principles apply when you are building vector art in Silverlight 3 with the graphic primitives covered in this recipe.

We don't list the code for this recipe because it consists of the XAML markup of all the drawing activities in Expression Blend that we describe earlier, which is mostly Path objects with very long values for the Data attribute. Refer to the sample code for Recipe 3-3 to see the drawings and try some of your own.

3-8. Using Geometries to Draw

Problem

You want to draw with lightweight graphics using a segment type or Ellipse, Rectangle, Line, or Path objects encapsulated in geometries.

Solution

Learn how to work with geometries like EllipseGeometry, PathGeometry, and LineGeometry, and segments like ArcSegment and GeometryGroup.

How It Works

Geometry objects such as EllipseGeometry, PathGeometry, and GeometryGroup are not visual objects like Ellipse, Path, and Rectangle. Shapes like Rectangle and Ellipse are UIElement objects and can render themselves. Geometries inherit directly from DependencyObject. As we described in Recipe 3-6 and Recipe 3-7, Shape and Path objects are readily usable for drawing and are powerful.

Geometries, on the other hand, do not inherit from UIElement and cannot render themselves. Geometries describe how to draw two-dimensional shapes. Both the Path object and objects that inherit from UIElement can take a geometry as a property and then draw it. For Path, it is the Data property; for UIElement, it is the Clip property.

You saw in the previous recipe that when you draw a Path using the Pen tool, the Data property is set to a value that follows the syntax of the Path Mini-Language. For example, you can draw a Path that describes a straight line to generate this XAML:

```
<Path Stroke="Black" StrokeThickness="1" Margin="2,2,2,2"
Data="M0,0 100,114 100,114"/>
```

In the test code for this recipe, here is the XAML for the same line drawn with the Data property, using a geometry to define how to draw the Path object:

```
<Path Stroke="Black" StrokeThickness="1" Margin="2,2,2,2" >
  <Path.Data>
    <LineGeometry StartPoint="0,0" EndPoint="100,114" />
  </Path.Data>
</Path>
```

The Code

In order to cover a few geometries, we have one application with several geometries drawn in it. We walk through each geometry to explain what we are trying to demonstrate.

As long as you define the Fill or Stroke property, you can render a geometry with a Path object. Here are a few examples that draw a Rectangle and an Ellipse, from the sample code for this recipe:

```
<Path Grid.Column="1" Fill="AliceBlue" Grid.Row="0" Stroke="Black"
StrokeThickness="1" Margin="2,2,2,2" >
  <Path.Data>
    <RectangleGeometry  Rect="20,20,70,40" />
  </Path.Data>
</Path>

<Path Grid.Column="2" Fill="AliceBlue" Grid.Row="0" Stroke="Black"
 StrokeThickness="1" Margin="2,2,2,2" >
  <Path.Data>
    <EllipseGeometry Center="50,50" RadiusX="30" RadiusY="30" />
  </Path.Data>
</Path>

<Path Grid.Column="2" Fill="AliceBlue" Grid.Row="1" Stroke="Black"
 StrokeThickness="1" Margin="2,2,2,2" >
  <Path.Data>
    <GeometryGroup>
      <LineGeometry StartPoint="0,50" EndPoint="140,50" />
      <RectangleGeometry  Rect="10,30,70,40" />
      <EllipseGeometry Center="100,50" RadiusX="30" RadiusY="30" />
    </GeometryGroup>
  </Path.Data>
</Path>
```

The last Path object in the sample code uses a GeometryGroup to combine multiple geometries (see Figure 3-34).

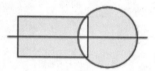

Figure 3-34. *Path object with a GeometryGroup containing multiple geometries*

We mentioned earlier that you can set the Clip property of objects that inherit from UIElement to a geometry value. The Image control inherits from UIElement, so you can set its Clip property to a geometry to yield a nice effect. First, set the background to a light blue color so that the clipping effect is more obvious than it would be with a white background.

Add two Image objects that point to the same image, which is 100 × 75 pixels in size. For the second Image object, apply a simple RectangleGeometry that has rounded corners to clip the image:

```
<Image.Clip>
   <RectangleGeometry Rect="0,0,100,75" RadiusX="25"  RadiusY="25"/>
</Image.Clip>
```

The results of setting the Clip property are shown in Figure 3-35, which compares the two images.

■Note   The image used in this recipe's sample code is located at the TestWeb web site in a folder named img under ClientBin.

Figure 3-35. *The results of setting the Clip property*

You can see that the bottom image has rounded corners for a smoother look. In the same manner, you can apply a geometry to a `MediaElement` so that the video appears to be playing on an old glass television set with rounded corners.

The last geometry we cover from the recipe's sample code is the `PathGeometry` object. The `PathGeometry` object can contain multiple segment objects such as `LineSegment`, `ArcSegment`, `BezierSegment`, `QuadraticBezierSegment`, and `PolyQuadraticBezierSegment`. These can be applied in unison as part of a `PathFigure` element collection in `PathGeometry`. Here is an example from Listing 3-5 that uses an `ArcSegment` and a `BezierSegment`:

```
<Path Stroke="Black" Grid.Row="2" Grid.Column="2" Margin="4,4,4,4">
  <Path.Data>
    <PathGeometry>
      <PathFigure StartPoint="20,20">
        <BezierSegment Point1="10,40" Point2="200,70" />
        <ArcSegment Point="100,10" Size="200,150" RotationAngle="25"
          IsLargeArc="False"  SweepDirection="Counterclockwise"/>
      </PathFigure>
    </PathGeometry>
  </Path.Data>
</Path>
```

Figure 3-36 shows the output for the `BezierSegment` and `ArcSegment`.

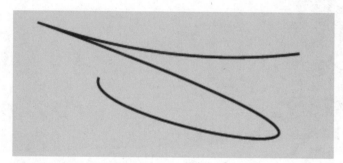

Figure 3-36. *The Bezier curve*

We don't get into the details of all the different segment objects available for drawing. Refer to the Silverlight 3 MSDN documentation for more information:

```
http://msdn.microsoft.com/en-us/library/cc189068(VS.95).aspx
```

■**Note** If you are building complex drawings in code, you must use geometry objects. The Path Mini-Language is available only in markup.

One last item to note is that when you work with Path objects in Expression Blend, it defaults to using the Path Mini-Language syntax for the Data value (or for the Clip property on UIElement objects). Keep this in mind if you wish to use geometries, because if you attempt to modify the appearance of a Path that uses geometries in Expression Blend, Blend converts the Path's Data value from a geometry declaration to a string containing Path Mini-Language. This may not be a concern, and we highly recommend using Expression Blend for the productivity that it provides; but we thought we should mention it just in case. Listing 3-5 shows this recipe's code.

Listing 3-5. *Recipe 3.8 MainPage.Xaml File*

```xaml
<UserControl x:Class="Ch03_DevelopingUX.Recipe3_8.MainPage"
    xmlns="http://schemas.microsoft.com/winfx/2006/xaml/presentation"
    xmlns:x="http://schemas.microsoft.com/winfx/2006/xaml"
    Width="400" Height="300">
  <Grid x:Name="LayoutRoot" Background="#FFDCDDE1">
    <Grid.RowDefinitions>
      <RowDefinition Height="0.396*"/>
      <RowDefinition Height="0.381*"/>
      <RowDefinition Height="0.223*"/>
    </Grid.RowDefinitions>
    <Grid.ColumnDefinitions>
      <ColumnDefinition Width="0.261*"/>
      <ColumnDefinition Width="0.284*"/>
      <ColumnDefinition Width="0.455*"/>
    </Grid.ColumnDefinitions>
    <Path Grid.Row="0" Grid.Column="0" Stroke="Black"
     StrokeThickness="1" Margin="2,2,2,2"
     Data="M0,0 100,114 100,114" />
    <Path Grid.Column="0" Grid.Row="1" Stroke="Black"
     StrokeThickness="1" Margin="2,2,2,2" >
      <Path.Data>
        <LineGeometry StartPoint="0,0" EndPoint="100,114" />
      </Path.Data>
    </Path>
    <Path Grid.Column="1" Fill="AliceBlue" Grid.Row="0" Stroke="Black"
        StrokeThickness="1" Margin="2,2,2,2" >
      <Path.Data>
        <RectangleGeometry  Rect="20,20,70,40" RadiusX="15"
        RadiusY="15"/>
      </Path.Data>
    </Path>
```

```xml
<Path Grid.Column="2" Fill="AliceBlue" Grid.Row="0" Stroke="Black"
    StrokeThickness="1" Margin="2,2,2,2" >
  <Path.Data>
    <EllipseGeometry Center="50,50" RadiusX="30" RadiusY="30" />
  </Path.Data>
</Path>
<Path Grid.Column="2" Fill="AliceBlue" Grid.Row="1" Stroke="Black"
    StrokeThickness="1" Margin="2,2,2,2" >
  <Path.Data>
    <GeometryGroup>
      <LineGeometry StartPoint="0,50" EndPoint="140,50" />
      <RectangleGeometry Rect="10,30,70,40" />
      <EllipseGeometry Center="100,50" RadiusX="30"
       RadiusY="30" />
    </GeometryGroup>
  </Path.Data>
</Path>
<StackPanel Grid.Column="1" Grid.Row="1" Grid.RowSpan="2"
 Margin="2,2,2,2">
  <Image Source="img/Landscape.jpg"  Width="100" Height="75"
        Margin="2,2,2,8"/>
  <Image Source="img/Landscape.jpg"  Width="100" Height="75"
   Margin="2,8,2,2">
    <Image.Clip>
      <RectangleGeometry Rect="0,0,100,75" RadiusX="25"
       RadiusY="25"/>
    </Image.Clip>
  </Image>
</StackPanel>
<Path Stroke="Black" Grid.Row="2" Margin="4,4,4,4">
  <Path.Data>
    <PathGeometry>
      <PathFigure>
        <ArcSegment Point="50,20" Size="50,150" RotationAngle="20"
         IsLargeArc="False" SweepDirection="Counterclockwise"/>
      </PathFigure>
    </PathGeometry>
  </Path.Data>
</Path>
```

```
  <Path Stroke="Black" Grid.Row="2" Grid.Column="2"
   Margin="28.046,8,-20.046,0">
    <Path.Data>
      <PathGeometry>
        <PathFigure StartPoint="20,20">
          <BezierSegment Point1="10,40" Point2="200,70" />
          <ArcSegment Point="100,10" Size="200,150"
           RotationAngle="25"
       IsLargeArc="False" SweepDirection="Counterclockwise"/>
        </PathFigure>
      </PathGeometry>
    </Path.Data>
  </Path>
 </Grid>
</UserControl>
```

3-9. Providing Scrollable Content

Problem

You need to provide scrollable content for layout purposes, or you need to apply a border to a control.

Solution

To provide scrollable content, use ScrollViewer as a container for the content. ScrollViewer can have exactly one child control, which is usually a layout panel such as a Grid, StackPanel, or Canvas object that contains additional content as desired.

How It Works

ScrollViewer is a control that has scrollbars so that you can scroll its contents vertically as well as horizontally. ScrollViewer can contain exactly one control. A StackPanel or a Grid is the best candidate; you can place multiple controls in the scrolling view by containing the controls within the StackPanel or Grid.

The ScrollViewer control has properties to control whether the scrollbars are visible, disabled, or automatically visible as needed: HorizontalScrollBarVisibility and VerticalScrollBarVisibility. If you set both to Auto, the horizontal and vertical scrollbars appear only when needed, based on the size and amount of content in the control. Other options are Disabled, Hidden, and Visible.

The Code

The sample code includes a TextBox, a Button, and a ScrollViewer control that initially contains a StackPanel. Type text into the TextBox, and click the Click to Add Text button. When the Button event fires, it dynamically adds a TextBlock to the StackPanel in the ScrollViewer. Perform this step a few times; when the StackPanel fills with TextBlock controls, the vertical scrollbar appears. If the entered text is long enough, the horizontal scrollbar appears. Figure 3-37 shows the results.

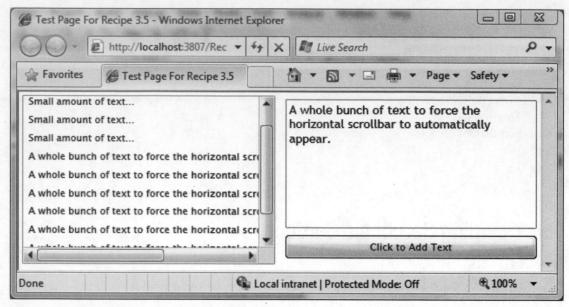

Figure 3-37. *The ScrollViewer in action*

Built-in controls like ListBox encapsulate a ScrollViewer as part of their default internal Visual Tree. It is handy that this functionality is readily available to developers when they need to display a large amount of data as part of the layout. Listings 3-6 and 3-7 show the code for this recipe.

Listing 3-6. *Recipe 3.9 MainPage.Xaml File*

```xml
<UserControl x:Class="Ch03_DevelopingUX.Recipe3_9.MainPage"
    xmlns="http://schemas.microsoft.com/winfx/2006/xaml/presentation"
    xmlns:x="http://schemas.microsoft.com/winfx/2006/xaml"
    Width="600" Height="261">
  <Grid x:Name="LayoutRoot" Background="White">
    <Grid.RowDefinitions>
      <RowDefinition Height="*"/>
    </Grid.RowDefinitions>
    <Grid.ColumnDefinitions>
      <ColumnDefinition Width="0.495*"/>
      <ColumnDefinition Width="0.505*"/>
    </Grid.ColumnDefinitions>
    <ScrollViewer Margin="4,4.135,4,4" HorizontalScrollBarVisibility="Auto"
     VerticalScrollBarVisibility="Auto">
      <StackPanel x:Name="spText" Margin="4,4,4,4"></StackPanel>
    </ScrollViewer>
```

```
  <StackPanel Margin="4,4.135,4,114.865" Grid.Column="1">
    <TextBox x:Name="typedText" Height="96" Text="TextBox"
    TextWrapping="Wrap" FontSize="14" Margin="4,4,4,4" BorderThickness="0"/>
    <Button x:Name="AddText" Content="Click to Add Text" Margin="4,4,4,4"
     Click="AddText_Click"/>
  </StackPanel>
 </Grid>
</UserControl>
```

Listing 3-7. *Recipe 3.9 MainPage.Xaml.cs Class File*

```
using System.Windows;
using System.Windows.Controls;

namespace Ch03_DesigningUX.Recipe3_5
{
  public partial class MainPage : UserControl
  {
    public MainPage()
    {
      InitializeComponent();
    }

    private void AddText_Click(object sender, RoutedEventArgs e)
    {
      TextBlock text = new TextBlock();
      text.Text = typedText.Text;
      text.Margin = new Thickness(2, 2, 2, 2);
      spText.Children.Add(text);
    }
  }
}
```

3-10. Applying a Border to Elements

Problem

You want to apply rounded corners to controls like the Image control that normally don't support them as well as provide a border and background to elements, to enhance visual appeal.

Solution

Put content in the Border control, and configure properties such as Background and CornerRadius to enhance visual appeal.

How It Works

The Border control inherits from FrameworkElement and is a container control. It can contain exactly one child element. However, the child element can be a Panel such as a Grid, StackPanel, or Canvas, which can contain additional controls.

When you add a Border to an application, the Background property is Transparent by default. You can apply a solid color or gradient brush to provide a background for the Border. You can also set the CornerRadius property to provide rounded corners, as shown in Figure 3-38, which has a CornerRadius of 20 for all four corners.

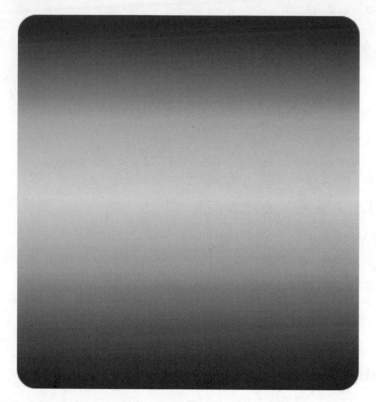

Figure 3-38. *Laying out a Border control*

Many controls, such as Image, TextBox, TextBlock, and so on, do not contain a CornerRadius property and have square corners. The Border property can apply rounded corners to contained objects. In Figure 3-38, the Border contains a Grid and applies rounded corners to its layout.

If you drop a TextBox onto the Border containing the Grid shown in Figure 3-38, the background of the TextBox is White by default. If you set it to Transparent, the Border's Background shows through.

You next want to apply a Border to a Textbox. Figure 3-39 shows how a plain TextBox appears on the gradient.

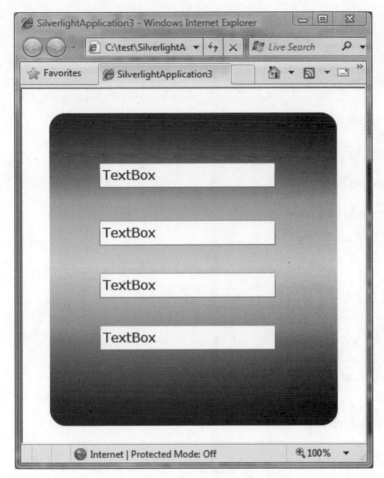

Figure 3-39. *Plain TextBoxes in the UI*

The TextBox controls are each placed in the Border. To make the Border control wrap the TextBox, clear the Height and Width properties of the Border and the TextBox controls so that they default to Auto; this shrinks the Border around the TextBox.

The size for the TextBox/Border combination is determined by the size of the font for the text in the TextBox as well as the Alignment and Margin settings of the Border and TextBox controls. Figure 3-40 shows the finished product for this recipe.

Figure 3-40. *Rounded corners for a TextBox control*

Here is the XAML markup for one of the Border/TextBox combinations:

```
<Border VerticalAlignment="Top" Margin="21,119,19,0"
 CornerRadius="12,12,12,12">
   <Border.Background>
      <RadialGradientBrush>
         <GradientStop Color="#FF003A74"/>
         <GradientStop Color="#FF636E95" Offset="1"/>
      </RadialGradientBrush>
   </Border.Background>
   <TextBox Background="{x:Null}" Text="TextBox" TextWrapping="Wrap"
    BorderBrush="{x:Null}" FontSize="16" Margin="5,5,5,5"/>
</Border>
```

You want the TextBox to "disappear" into the Border while retaining all of its functionality. Notice in Figure 3-40 that you cannot see the outline of the TextBox. This is because you set the Background and BorderBrush to Transparent or Null. Also, setting Border Background to a RadialGradient highlights the rounding effect of the CornerRadius of 12 all around.

To place the TextBox inside the Border so that it appears to be fully encapsulated, set a Margin of 5 all around the TextBox. This ensures nice spacing between the content and the Border edge.

The Code

The code in this recipe takes everything covered earlier and applies it to TextBox controls to provide a rounded appearance. You also use a Border to highlight an editing region with plain TextBox controls. Figure 3-41 shows the output.

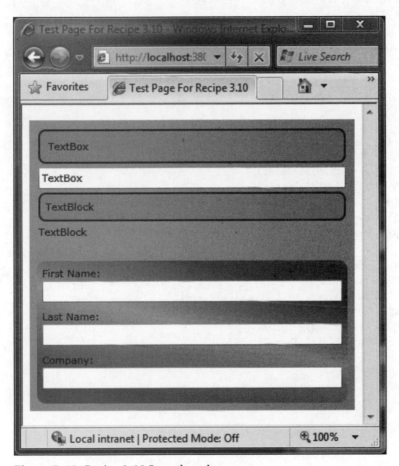

Figure 3-41. *Recipe 3-10 Sample code output*

Figure 3-41 shows two TextBox controls and two TextBlock controls, one inside a Border control and a plain version of each control. The bottom portion of the UI uses a Border control to highlight an area of the application. Listing 3-8 has the full XAML for the source code.

Listing 3-8. *Recipe 3.10 MainPage.Xaml File*

```xaml
<UserControl x:Class="Ch03_DevelopingUX.Recipe3_10.MainPage"
    xmlns="http://schemas.microsoft.com/winfx/2006/xaml/presentation"
    xmlns:x="http://schemas.microsoft.com/winfx/2006/xaml"
    xmlns:d=http://schemas.microsoft.com/expression/blend/2008
    xmlns:mc=http://schemas.openxmlformats.org/markup-compatibility/2006
    mc:Ignorable="d" >
  <Grid x:Name="LayoutRoot" MinWidth="350"  Background="#FFA9A9A9"
    Height="322" Margin="8,8,8,8">
    <Grid.RowDefinitions>
      <RowDefinition Height="0.46*"/>
      <RowDefinition Height="0.54*"/>
    </Grid.RowDefinitions>
    <Grid.ColumnDefinitions>
      <ColumnDefinition Width="*"/>
    </Grid.ColumnDefinitions>
    <StackPanel Margin="8,8,8,4">
      <Border Padding="4,4,4,4"  BorderThickness="2" Margin="2,2,2,2"
       Height="Auto" Width="Auto" CornerRadius="7,7,7,7"
       BorderBrush="#FF000080" Background="#726CB167">
        <TextBox Height="Auto" Width="Auto" Text="TextBox" TextWrapping="Wrap"
         Foreground="#FF000000" Background="#00FFFFFF" BorderBrush="{x:Null}"
         BorderThickness="2,2,2,2"/>
      </Border>
      <TextBox Height="Auto" Width="Auto" Text="TextBox" TextWrapping="Wrap"
       Margin="2,2,2,2" Opacity="1"/>
      <Border Padding="4,4,4,4" BorderThickness="2" Margin="2,2,2,2"
       Height="Auto" Width="Auto" CornerRadius="7,7,7,7"
       BorderBrush="#FF000080" Background="#726CB167">
        <TextBlock Height="Auto" Width="Auto" Text="TextBlock"
         TextWrapping="Wrap" Foreground="#FF000000" Margin="2,2,2,2"/>
      </Border>
      <TextBlock Height="Auto" Width="Auto" Text="TextBlock"
       TextWrapping="Wrap" Margin="2,2,2,2"/>
    </StackPanel>
```

```
<Border Grid.Column="0" CornerRadius="10,10,10,10"
  Margin="8,8,8,8" Grid.Row="1">
  <Border.Background>
    <LinearGradientBrush EndPoint="0.560000002384186,0.00300000002607703"
     StartPoint="0.439999997615814,0.996999979019165">
      <GradientStop Color="#FF586C57"/>
      <GradientStop Color="#FFA3BDA3" Offset="0.536"/>
      <GradientStop Color="#FF586C57" Offset="0.968999981880188"/>
    </LinearGradientBrush>
  </Border.Background>
  <StackPanel Margin="4,4,4,4"  x:Name="FormData">
    <TextBlock Height="Auto" Width="Auto" Text="First Name:"
     TextWrapping="Wrap" Margin="2,2,2,0"/>
    <TextBox Height="Auto" Width="Auto" Text="" TextWrapping="Wrap"
     x:Name="Field1" Margin="2,0,2,4"/>
    <TextBlock Height="Auto" Width="Auto" Text="Last Name:"
     TextWrapping="Wrap" Margin="2,4,2,0"/>
    <TextBox Height="Auto" x:Name="Field2" Width="Auto"
     TextWrapping="Wrap" Margin="2,0,2,4"/>
    <TextBlock Height="Auto" Width="Auto" Text="Company:"
     TextWrapping="Wrap" Margin="2,4,2,0"/>
    <TextBox Height="Auto" x:Name="Field3" Width="Auto"
     TextWrapping="Wrap" Margin="2,0,2,2"/>
  </StackPanel>
  </Border>
  </Grid>
</UserControl>
```

3-11. Using Simple Animations with Objects

Problem

You need to create dynamic UIs in Silverlight 3 with animation.

Solution

Take advantage of the built-in animation features available in Silverlight 3.

How It Works

Silverlight 3 has powerful animation capabilities that allow the designer or developer to animate any property value of type Double, Color, or Point. Animation lets you vary a property between two values over a specified period of time, thus providing the illusion of motion or transformation.

In Silverlight 3, the animation engine is left to interpret how to change the value over the specified period of time between the configured values for the property that is being animated.

To apply an animation to a UI element, create a `Storyboard`, and set `TargetName` and `TargetProperty` to specify the element and the property of the element to animate. Nest the animation within the `Storyboard` element in XAML like this:

```
<Storyboard x:Name="Rect1MouseMove">
  <DoubleAnimation BeginTime="00:00:00.5" From="1" To="7"
  AutoReverse="True" Duration="00:00:00.5"
  Storyboard.TargetName="Rect1"
  Storyboard.TargetProperty="(Shape.StrokeThickness)"/>
</Storyboard>
```

The `TargetName` and `TargetProperty` attributes are attached properties for the `Storyboard` class. `Storyboard` objects are usually created as resources within either the `Application.Resources` or `UserControl.Resources` element, making it easy to interact with the `Storyboard` by referencing it by the `x:Name` value. Also, a `Storyboard` can contain more than one animation, allowing one `Storyboard` to animate multiple objects and properties.

The `Storyboard` class provides `Begin`, `Pause`, `Stop`, and `Resume` methods you can use to control the `Storyboard` programmatically. For a `Button Click` event, the following code starts the animation:

```
private void Rect1_MouseEnter(object sender, MouseEventArgs e)
{
  Rect1MouseMove.Begin();
}
```

Triggers provide an elegant way of firing an animation. Silverlight 3 supports `Triggers` like WPF, where an animation is kicked off via XAML code only; but currently, the only supported event that can be associated with a trigger is `Loaded`. Here is an example:

```
<Rectangle.Triggers>
  <EventTrigger RoutedEvent="Rectangle.Loaded">
    <BeginStoryboard>
      <Storyboard>
        <DoubleAnimation Storyboard.TargetName="Rect1"
                         BeginTime="00:00:00.1"
        Storyboard.TargetProperty="(UIElement.Opacity)"
        From="0.0" To="1.0" Duration="0:0:1" />
      </Storyboard>
    </BeginStoryboard>
  </EventTrigger>
</Rectangle.Triggers>
```

■**Note** Keyframe animations provide greater control over animations, as we cover in Recipe 3-12.

The Code

The sample code uses a Rectangle, an Ellipse, and a copy of the StackPanel from Recipe 3-10 with a few TextBoxes with a Border. The goal is to liven up the interface. The first property you animate is the Opacity for all three objects in the Load event, which will make them fade in when the application starts. You first declare a DoubleAnimation (that is, animate a value of type Double) for the Rectangle named Rect1:

```
<DoubleAnimation Storyboard.TargetName="Rect1"
  BeginTime="00:00:00.1"
  Storyboard.TargetProperty="(UIElement.Opacity)"
  From="0.0" To="1.0" Duration="0:0:1" />
```

To make the objects appear at different times after the application loads for a more dramatic effect, configure BeginTime to 0.1 seconds for the Rectangle, 0.4 seconds for the Ellipse, and 0.8 seconds for the StackPanel. Set the TargetProperty to the common base class UIElement.Opacity to simplify the copying and pasting when you duplicate the animation for all three objects. Animate the Opacity property from 0 to 1 for all three objects so that they magically appear in sequence upon load.

The Loaded event is the only RoutedEvent supported in a Trigger for Silverlight 3. You can read more about RoutedEvents in the Silverlight documentation:

```
http://msdn.microsoft.com/en-us/library/system.windows.routedevent(VS.95).aspx
```

Silverlight lets you configure a Trigger in XAML for the Loaded event so that when the event fires, you play a Storyboard that animates the Opacity for each object without having to write any code:

```
<Rectangle.Triggers>
  <EventTrigger RoutedEvent="Rectangle.Loaded">
    <BeginStoryboard>
      <Storyboard>
        <DoubleAnimation Storyboard.TargetName="Rect1"
                         BeginTime="00:00:00.1"
                         Storyboard.TargetProperty="(UIElement.Opacity)"
                         From="0.0" To="1.0" Duration="0:0:1" />
      </Storyboard>
    </BeginStoryboard>
  </EventTrigger>
</Rectangle.Triggers>
```

You may wonder why the Storyboard is embedded in the Rectangle declaration and not configured as a Resource on the UserControl. The reason is that Silverlight 3 does not support loading a value for Storyboard using the StaticResource markup extension, which we covered in Recipe 2-13. Similar XAML configures a trigger for the Ellipse and StackPanel as well. A screenshot doesn't make a lot of sense for an animation, so just run the code to see how the three objects appear sequentially in the browser.

Next, add MouseEnter and MouseLeave animations for the Rectangle and Ellipse. You create one animation for the Rectangle and use it for both MouseEnter and MouseLeave, but you create two separate animations for MouseEnter and MouseLeave for the Ellipse.

Because MouseEnter and MouseLeave are not RoutedEvents, create the three Storyboard objects as resources on the UserControl; doing so keeps things tidy and provides a unique name for the x:key attribute so that you can reference the Storyboard objects by name. The Rectangle Storyboard changes

StrokeThickness from 1 to 7 over 0.5 seconds. Set AutoReverse to True so that it automatically reverts back to 1, which lets you avoid creating a separate animation for MouseEnter and MouseLeave. If you wanted the StrokeThickness to stay at 7 until the MouseLeave event fires, you would have two separate animations and leave AutoReverse at the default value of False.

To cause the animation to take place for the desired event, add MouseEnter and MouseLeave event handlers that call this single line of code:

```
Rect1MouseMove.Begin();
```

For the Ellipse, you animate using a ColorAnimation, but it is just as easy to create as the DoubleAnimation:

```
<ColorAnimation BeginTime="00:00:00" Duration="00:00:00.3"
                From="#FFC18125" To="#FF2DBD43"
                Storyboard.TargetName="Ellipse1"
                Storyboard.TargetProperty=
                "(Shape.Fill).(SolidColorBrush.Color)"/>
```

Instead of the From and To values being a Double value, they are a SolidColorBrush.Color value configured on the Shape.Fill property. We cover Brush objects in Recipe 3-9.

The last item to discuss is the PointAnimation used to animate a PathGeometry consisting of an ArcSegment object. PointAnimation is no more difficult than the previous two types of animation. Here is the code:

```
<Storyboard x:Name="PathClick">
  <PointAnimation AutoReverse="True"
    Storyboard.TargetProperty="Point"
    Storyboard.TargetName="animatedArcSegment"
    Duration="0:0:2" To="200,200"/>
</Storyboard>
```

This code animates the Point property on the ArcSegment to provide an interesting effect.

To see the animations, run the Recipe 3-11 test page, and the load animations fire. Move the mouse over the Rectangle and then move the mouse outside it, to see the DoubleAnimation alter the StrokeThickness. Move the mouse into the Ellipse and then move the mouse outside it, to see how the shorter duration changes the effect for the Ellipse's Fill animation. Finally, click the blue ArcSegment to see the PointAnimation take effect and then autoreverse. The code appears in Listings 3-9 and 3-10.

Listing 3-9. *Recipe 3.11 MainPage.Xaml File*

```
<UserControl x:Class="Ch03_DevelopingUX.Recipe3_11.MainPage"
    xmlns="http://schemas.microsoft.com/winfx/2006/xaml/presentation"
    xmlns:x="http://schemas.microsoft.com/winfx/2006/xaml"
    Width="600" Height="400"
    xmlns:d="http://schemas.microsoft.com/expression/blend/2008"
    xmlns:mc="http://schemas.openxmlformats.org/markup-compatibility/2006"
    mc:Ignorable="d">
```

```xml
<UserControl.Resources>
  <Storyboard x:Name="Rect1MouseMove">
    <DoubleAnimation BeginTime="00:00:00.5" From="1" To="7"
                     AutoReverse="True" Storyboard.TargetName="Rect1"
                     Storyboard.TargetProperty="(Shape.StrokeThickness)"
                     Duration="00:00:00.5"/>
  </Storyboard>
  <Storyboard x:Name="EllipseMouseEnter">
    <ColorAnimation BeginTime="00:00:00" Duration="00:00:00.3"
                    From="#FFC18125" To="#FF2DBD43"
                    Storyboard.TargetName="Ellipse1"
                    Storyboard.TargetProperty=
                    "(Shape.Fill).(SolidColorBrush.Color)"/>
  </Storyboard>
  <Storyboard x:Name="EllipseMouseLeave">
    <ColorAnimation BeginTime="00:00:00" Duration="00:00:00.3" To="#FFC18125"
                    Storyboard.TargetName="Ellipse1"
                    Storyboard.TargetProperty="(Shape.Fill).(SolidColorBrush.Color)"/>
  </Storyboard>
  <Storyboard x:Name="PathClick">
    <PointAnimation AutoReverse="True"
      Storyboard.TargetProperty="Point"
      Storyboard.TargetName="animatedArcSegment"
      Duration="0:0:2" To="200,200"/>
  </Storyboard>

</UserControl.Resources>

<Grid x:Name="LayoutRoot" Background="White">
  <Grid.RowDefinitions>
    <RowDefinition Height="0.432*"/>
    <RowDefinition Height="0.568*"/>
  </Grid.RowDefinitions>
  <Grid.ColumnDefinitions>
    <ColumnDefinition Width="0.467*"/>
    <ColumnDefinition Width="0.533*"/>
  </Grid.ColumnDefinitions>
  <Rectangle x:Name="Rect1" RadiusX="12" RadiusY="8" Opacity="0"
             HorizontalAlignment="Stretch" Margin="66,30,85,49"
             VerticalAlignment="Stretch" Width="129.2" Fill="#FF4863AF"
             Stroke="#FF000000" d:LayoutOverrides="Width"
             MouseEnter="Rect1_MouseEnter" MouseLeave="Rect1_MouseLeave">
    <Rectangle.Triggers>
      <EventTrigger RoutedEvent="Rectangle.Loaded">
        <BeginStoryboard>
```

```xml
            <Storyboard>
              <DoubleAnimation Storyboard.TargetName="Rect1"
                               BeginTime="00:00:00.1"
                               Storyboard.TargetProperty="(UIElement.Opacity)"
                               From="0.0" To="1.0" Duration="0:0:1" />
            </Storyboard>
          </BeginStoryboard>
        </EventTrigger>
      </Rectangle.Triggers>
    </Rectangle>
    <Ellipse x:Name="Ellipse1" HorizontalAlignment="Stretch"
             Margin="81,30,125,40" Opacity="0" VerticalAlignment="Stretch"
             Grid.Column="1" Fill="#FFC18125" Stroke="#FF000000"
             MouseEnter="Ellipse1_MouseEnter" MouseLeave="Ellipse1_MouseLeave">
      <Ellipse.Triggers>
        <EventTrigger RoutedEvent="Ellipse.Loaded">
          <BeginStoryboard>
            <Storyboard>
              <DoubleAnimation Storyboard.TargetName="Ellipse1"
                               BeginTime="00:00:00.4"
                               Storyboard.TargetProperty="(UIElement.Opacity)"
                               From="0.0" To="1.0" Duration="0:0:1" />
            </Storyboard>
          </BeginStoryboard>
        </EventTrigger>
      </Ellipse.Triggers>
    </Ellipse>
    <StackPanel Margin="4,4,4,4" Grid.Row="1" Grid.Column="0"
                x:Name="stackPanel" Opacity="0">
      <StackPanel.Triggers>
        <EventTrigger RoutedEvent="StackPanel.Loaded" >
          <BeginStoryboard>
            <Storyboard>
              <DoubleAnimation Storyboard.TargetName="stackPanel"
                  BeginTime="00:00:00.8" From="0.0" To="1.0" Duration="0:0:1"
                  Storyboard.TargetProperty="(UIElement.Opacity)"/>
            </Storyboard>
          </BeginStoryboard>
        </EventTrigger>
      </StackPanel.Triggers>
```

```xml
      <Border Padding="4,4,4,4"  BorderThickness="2" Margin="2,2,2,2"
            Height="Auto" Width="Auto" CornerRadius="7,7,7,7"
            BorderBrush="#FF000080" Background="#726CB167">
        <TextBox Height="Auto" Width="Auto" Text="TextBox"
              TextWrapping="Wrap" Foreground="#FF000000"
          Background="#00FFFFFF" BorderBrush="{x:Null}"/>
      </Border>
      <Border Padding="4,4,4,4"  BorderThickness="2" Margin="2,2,2,2"
            Height="Auto" Width="Auto" CornerRadius="7,7,7,7"
            BorderBrush="#FF000080" Background="#726CB167">
        <TextBox Height="Auto" Width="Auto" Text="TextBox"
              TextWrapping="Wrap" Foreground="#FF000000"
          Background="#00FFFFFF" BorderBrush="{x:Null}"/>
      </Border>
      <Border Padding="4,4,4,4"  BorderThickness="2" Margin="2,2,2,2"
            Height="Auto" Width="Auto" CornerRadius="7,7,7,7"
            BorderBrush="#FF000080" Background="#726CB167">
        <TextBox Height="Auto" Width="Auto" Text="TextBox"
              TextWrapping="Wrap" Foreground="#FF000000"
          Background="#00FFFFFF" BorderBrush="{x:Null}"/>
      </Border>
      <Border Padding="4,4,4,4"  BorderThickness="2" Margin="2,2,2,2"
            Height="Auto" Width="Auto" CornerRadius="7,7,7,7"
            BorderBrush="#FF000080" Background="#726CB167">
        <TextBox Height="Auto" Width="Auto" Text="TextBox"
              TextWrapping="Wrap" Foreground="#FF000000"
          Background="#00FFFFFF" BorderBrush="{x:Null}"/>
      </Border>
    </StackPanel>
    <Path Fill="Blue" Grid.Column="2" Grid.Row="2" Margin="10,10,10,10"
      MouseLeftButtonDown="Path_MouseLeftButtonDown">
      <Path.Data>
        <PathGeometry>
          <PathFigure>
            <ArcSegment x:Name="animatedArcSegment" Point="50,50" Size="50,150"
            RotationAngle="-20" IsLargeArc="False"
                  SweepDirection="Clockwise"/>
          </PathFigure>
        </PathGeometry>
      </Path.Data>
    </Path>
  </Grid>
</UserControl>
```

Listing 3-10. *Recipe 3.11 MainPage.Xaml.cs Class File*

```csharp
using System.Windows.Controls;
using System.Windows.Input;

namespace Ch03_DevelopingUX.Recipe3_11
{
  public partial class MainPage : UserControl
  {
    public MainPage()
    {
      InitializeComponent();
    }

    private void Rect1_MouseEnter(object sender, MouseEventArgs e)
    {
      Rect1MouseMove.Begin();
    }

    private void Rect1_MouseLeave(object sender, MouseEventArgs e)
    {
      Rect1MouseMove.Begin();
    }

    private void Ellipse1_MouseEnter(object sender, MouseEventArgs e)
    {
      EllipseMouseEnter.Begin();
    }

    private void Ellipse1_MouseLeave(object sender, MouseEventArgs e)
    {
      EllipseMouseLeave.Begin();
    }

    private void Path_MouseLeftButtonDown(object sender, MouseButtonEventArgs e)
    {
      PathClick.Begin();
    }
  }
}
```

3-12. Animating UI Elements with Keyframes

Problem

You need to animate UI objects using techniques to control how an animation interpolates over time, so that you can achieve more realistic effects like acceleration and deceleration.

Solution

Use the animation objects that support keyframes—such as the `ColorAnimationUsingKeyFrames`, `DoubleAnimationUsingKeyFrames`, `PointAnimationUsingKeyFrames`, and `ObjectAnimationUsingKeyFrames` classes—to create more realistic effects.

How It Works

We covered the basics of animation in Recipe 3-11. In Chapter 1, Recipe 1-5, we explained how to create keyframe animations as part of the Expression Blend walkthrough. In this recipe, we dive deeper into keyframe animations and explore animating multiple controls and properties in the same `Storyboard`, configuring the interpolation type for the animation, and easing in, easing out, or accelerating portions of the overall animation for fine-tuned control.

Just as in Recipe 3-11, keyframe animations work on certain types, including `Color`, `Double`, `Point`, and `Object` with the corresponding keyframe class of `ColorAnimationUsingKeyFrames`, `DoubleAnimationUsingKeyFrames`, `PointAnimationUsingKeyFrames`, and `ObjectAnimationUsingKeyFrames`.

Each of these classes includes a `KeyFrames` collection containing keyframe objects that correspond to the type being animated, with an additional wrinkle of the algorithm used to interpolate between keyframes.

The available interpolation options are linear, discrete, and splined. Linear interpolation animates at a constant rate for the duration of the segment. Discrete interpolation animates at discrete intervals without interpolation over time.

Splined interpolation is more similar to linear than discrete but provides the ability to accelerate or decelerate the animation within the duration of a segment. The spline-interpolation method has an additional property called `KeySpline` that defines a Bezier curve to create more realistic effects. The `KeySpline` property defines a Bezier curve with two control points that go from (0,0) to (1,1). The first control point defines the curve factor of the first half of the curve, and the second control point defines the curve factor for the second half of the curve; the curve factor defines the rate of change or acceleration for the spline keyframe.

When you create an animation as demonstrated in Recipe 1-5, each keyframe in the time line has a Common Properties section, which lists the values that are animated, as well as an Easing section, which shows the Bezier curve for the `KeySpline`. Figure 3-42 shows Expression Blend animating a ball falling to the ground and then bouncing.

When you play the animation, the ball falls with a linear speed and then bounces up and down a few times. The bouncing action is simulated by a bunch of keyframes toward the end of the animation time line; the keyframes move the ball up and down in smaller segments until it comes to rest. The linear speed is a result of the default `KeySpline` Bezier curve (shown in the Easing Configuration section of the properties window) that is applied to the second keyframe highlighted in the Objects and Timeline window shown in Figure 3-42.

Figure 3-42. *Animating a ball falling to the ground and bouncing*

In general, the segment of the animation where the easing applies corresponds to the time line before the currently selected keyframe point in the Objects and Timeline window. In this case, any easing that is applied to the properties of the highlighted keyframe (the second keyframe in Figure 3-42) is for the segment between the first and second keyframe, or between 0 and 1 seconds in the animation time line shown in the Objects and Timeline window. Figure 3-43 shows a zoomed-in view of the easing configuration section for this animation.

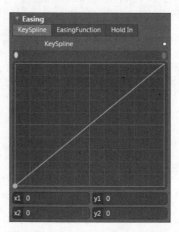

Figure 3-43. *Default KeySpline Bezier curve*

Notice the values set to 0 for x1, x2 and y1, y2, which corresponds to the value for the Bezier curve control points. Valid values are `Double` values between 0 and 1. The x1 and y1 values represent the beginning of the segment, or earlier in the time line. The x2 and y2 values represent the end of the segment, or later in the time line, bounded by the selected keyframe on the right and the previous keyframe (if there is one) on the left in the Objects and Timeline window. We cover custom easing functions available in Silverlight 3 in Recipe 3-20.

We mentioned earlier that the ball falls at a linear speed from top to bottom over a period of 1 second between the first and second keyframe. Thinking of the chart as time along the X axis and speed along the Y axis with an origin at the lower-left corner can help you understand how to change the values. To simulate acceleration as the ball moves from top to bottom, increase the value of x2 to the maximum value of 1, yielding the curve shown in Figure 3-44.

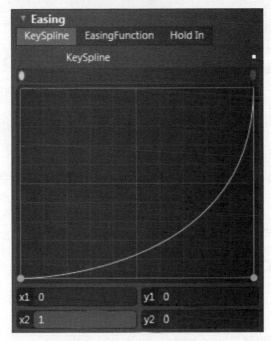

Figure 3-44. *Modified KeySpline Bezier curve with acceleration toward the end*

Keeping in mind that time is along the X axis and speed is along the Y axis, changing x2 to 1 pulls the curve down or slows the speed, gently increasing the speed until about two thirds of the way through, at which point the speed increases toward infinity at the end. Increasing speed over time is the definition of acceleration, and with this curve the falling ball looks more real. After the initial fall, you leave the default curve for the bounce up but use the curve shown in Figure 3-44 for the remaining shorter falls until the ball comes to rest. As you can see, splined interpolation is the most flexible algorithm and can provide the closest approximation of complex movement in the real world.

The Code

To test the falling ball, run the Recipe 3-12 application shown in Figure 3-45 and click the button above the blue Ellipse to drop it.

Figure 3-45. *Falling ball UI*

In addition to fine-tuning the animation, keyframes allow you to animate multiple values for multiple objects for the same Storyboard. To demonstrate, add a Rectangle and two Ellipses to the Artboard, as shown in Figure 3-46.

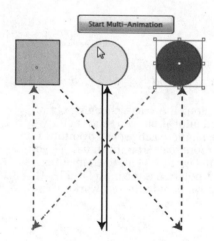

Figure 3-46. *Multianimation UI*

Next, create a `Storyboard` named `MultipleAnimations` following the steps in Recipe 1-5. Include an initial keyframe for each object. You want the two objects on the end to switch spots while the yellow `Ellipse` in the middle drops to the bottom and then returns to the top. The `Rectangle` and `Ellipse` on the ends move diagonally, switching locations back at the top, as shown by the arrows in Figure 3-46.

When the `Storyboard` is in recording mode, it is a matter of creating keyframes for each object either by selecting the object in the Visual Tree and clicking the New Keyframe button or by changing a setting on an object either via the properties window or by repositioning the object. The new keyframe is created wherever the vertical yellow cursor is located in the Objects and Timeline window. Figure 3-47 shows the `Storyboard` in edit mode with the yellow time line cursor at 0 seconds, when all three objects are animated.

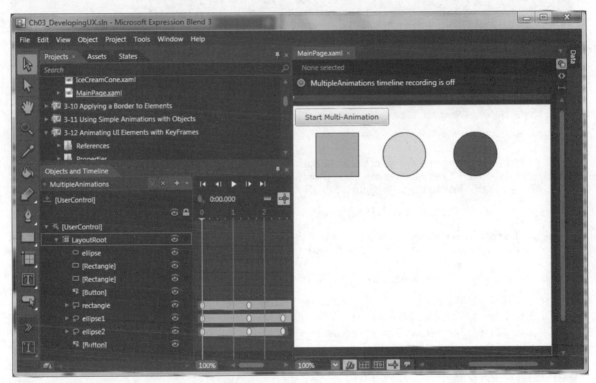

Figure 3-47. *Creating the multi-animation Storyboard*

You can grab individual keyframes and drag left or right in the time line for an object to fine-tune positioning in the time line. You can see the time line by changing or dragging the zoom percentage at lower left in the time line editor. You can also multiselect keyframes and drag them left or right in unison. Finally, if you are in Timeline recording mode and make a mistake, Edit ➤ Undo and Ctrl+Z are your best friends and have a deep undo queue.

Run the code, and click the Start Multi-Animation button. Play with the time line keyframes, dragging them left or right to test things out. Just remember to enter Timeline recording by clicking Timeline Recording Is Off on the Artboard to turn on recording. If you are finished editing a `Storyboard` and do not want to make any changes, you can close the `Storyboard` by clicking the Close Timeline button, as shown in Figure 3-48.

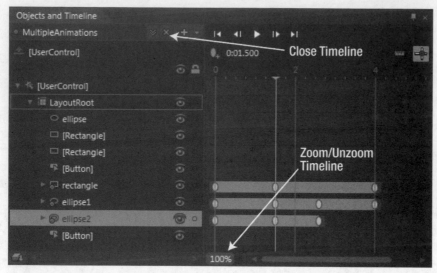

Figure 3-48. *Closing and zooming a Storyboard*

Although you generally work with animations in XAML, the animation classes are fully programmable in .NET managed code. For a walkthrough on how to work with animation classes in code, check out this link in the Silverlight 3 MSDN documentation:

http://msdn.microsoft.com/en-us/library/cc189069(VS.95).aspx

The entire XAML markup was generated using Expression Blend, as shown in Listing 3-11. The only custom code is in the code-behind file where the Storyboards are started, as shown in Listing 3-12.

Listing 3-11. *Recipe 3.12 MainPage.Xaml File*

```
<UserControl x:Class="Ch03_DevelopingUX.Recipe3_12.MainPage"
    xmlns="http://schemas.microsoft.com/winfx/2006/xaml/presentation"
    xmlns:x="http://schemas.microsoft.com/winfx/2006/xaml"
    Width="600" Height="400"
xmlns:d="http://schemas.microsoft.com/expression/blend/2008"
xmlns:mc=http://schemas.openxmlformats.org/markup-compatibility/2006
 mc:Ignorable="d">
  <UserControl.Resources>
    <Storyboard x:Name="BouncingBallStoryboard">
      <DoubleAnimationUsingKeyFrames BeginTime="00:00:00"
Storyboard.TargetName="ellipse"
```

```xml
Storyboard.TargetProperty="(UIElement.RenderTransform).
(TransformGroup.Children)[3].(TranslateTransform.Y)">
        <SplineDoubleKeyFrame KeyTime="00:00:00" Value="0"/>
        <SplineDoubleKeyFrame KeyTime="00:00:01" Value="272">
          <SplineDoubleKeyFrame.KeySpline>
            <KeySpline ControlPoint1="0,0" ControlPoint2="1,0"/>
          </SplineDoubleKeyFrame.KeySpline>
        </SplineDoubleKeyFrame>
        <SplineDoubleKeyFrame KeyTime="00:00:01.2000000" Value="200">
          <SplineDoubleKeyFrame.KeySpline>
            <KeySpline ControlPoint1="0,0" ControlPoint2="0,0"/>
          </SplineDoubleKeyFrame.KeySpline>
        </SplineDoubleKeyFrame>
        <SplineDoubleKeyFrame KeyTime="00:00:01.3000000" Value="272">
          <SplineDoubleKeyFrame.KeySpline>
            <KeySpline ControlPoint1="0,0" ControlPoint2="1,0"/>
          </SplineDoubleKeyFrame.KeySpline>
        </SplineDoubleKeyFrame>
        <SplineDoubleKeyFrame KeyTime="00:00:01.4000000" Value="240">
          <SplineDoubleKeyFrame.KeySpline>
            <KeySpline ControlPoint1="0,0" ControlPoint2="0,0"/>
          </SplineDoubleKeyFrame.KeySpline>
        </SplineDoubleKeyFrame>
        <SplineDoubleKeyFrame KeyTime="00:00:01.5000000" Value="272">
          <SplineDoubleKeyFrame.KeySpline>
            <KeySpline ControlPoint1="0,0" ControlPoint2="1,0"/>
          </SplineDoubleKeyFrame.KeySpline>
        </SplineDoubleKeyFrame>
        <SplineDoubleKeyFrame KeyTime="00:00:01.6000000" Value="260">
          <SplineDoubleKeyFrame.KeySpline>
            <KeySpline ControlPoint1="0,0" ControlPoint2="0,0"/>
          </SplineDoubleKeyFrame.KeySpline>
        </SplineDoubleKeyFrame>
        <SplineDoubleKeyFrame KeyTime="00:00:01.7000000" Value="272">
          <SplineDoubleKeyFrame.KeySpline>
            <KeySpline ControlPoint1="0,0" ControlPoint2="1,0"/>
          </SplineDoubleKeyFrame.KeySpline>
        </SplineDoubleKeyFrame>
      </DoubleAnimationUsingKeyFrames>
    </Storyboard>
```

```xml
<Storyboard x:Name="MultipleAnimations">
    <DoubleAnimationUsingKeyFrames BeginTime="00:00:00"
Storyboard.TargetName="ellipse2"
Storyboard.TargetProperty="(UIElement.RenderTransform).
 (TransformGroup.Children)[3].(TranslateTransform.Y)">
        <SplineDoubleKeyFrame KeyTime="00:00:00" Value="0"/>
        <SplineDoubleKeyFrame KeyTime="00:00:01.5000000" Value="258"/>
        <SplineDoubleKeyFrame KeyTime="00:00:02.6000000" Value="8"/>
    </DoubleAnimationUsingKeyFrames>
    <DoubleAnimationUsingKeyFrames BeginTime="00:00:00"
Storyboard.TargetName="ellipse2"
Storyboard.TargetProperty="(UIElement.RenderTransform).
(TransformGroup.Children)[3].(TranslateTransform.X)">
        <SplineDoubleKeyFrame KeyTime="00:00:00" Value="0"/>
        <SplineDoubleKeyFrame KeyTime="00:00:01.5000000" Value="-229"/>
        <SplineDoubleKeyFrame KeyTime="00:00:02.6000000" Value="-224"/>
    </DoubleAnimationUsingKeyFrames>
    <DoubleAnimationUsingKeyFrames BeginTime="00:00:00"
Storyboard.TargetName="ellipse1"
Storyboard.TargetProperty="(UIElement.RenderTransform).
(TransformGroup.Children)[3].(TranslateTransform.Y)">
        <SplineDoubleKeyFrame KeyTime="00:00:00" Value="0"/>
        <SplineDoubleKeyFrame KeyTime="00:00:01.5000000" Value="110"/>
        <SplineDoubleKeyFrame KeyTime="00:00:02.6000000" Value="255"/>
        <SplineDoubleKeyFrame KeyTime="00:00:04" Value="5"/>
    </DoubleAnimationUsingKeyFrames>
    <DoubleAnimationUsingKeyFrames BeginTime="00:00:00" Storyboard.TargetName="ellipse1"
Storyboard.TargetProperty="(UIElement.RenderTransform).
(TransformGroup.Children)[3].(TranslateTransform.X)">
        <SplineDoubleKeyFrame KeyTime="00:00:00" Value="0"/>
        <SplineDoubleKeyFrame KeyTime="00:00:01.5000000" Value="-2"/>
        <SplineDoubleKeyFrame KeyTime="00:00:02.6000000" Value="-2"/>
        <SplineDoubleKeyFrame KeyTime="00:00:04" Value="4"/>
    </DoubleAnimationUsingKeyFrames>
    <DoubleAnimationUsingKeyFrames BeginTime="00:00:00"
Storyboard.TargetName="rectangle"
Storyboard.TargetProperty="(UIElement.RenderTransform).
(TransformGroup.Children)[3].(TranslateTransform.X)">
        <SplineDoubleKeyFrame KeyTime="00:00:00" Value="0"/>
        <SplineDoubleKeyFrame KeyTime="00:00:01.5000000" Value="245"/>
        <SplineDoubleKeyFrame KeyTime="00:00:04" Value="250"/>
    </DoubleAnimationUsingKeyFrames>
    <DoubleAnimationUsingKeyFrames BeginTime="00:00:00"
```

```xml
Storyboard.TargetName="rectangle"
Storyboard.TargetProperty="(UIElement.RenderTransform).
(TransformGroup.Children)[3].(TranslateTransform.Y)">
        <SplineDoubleKeyFrame KeyTime="00:00:00" Value="0"/>
        <SplineDoubleKeyFrame KeyTime="00:00:01.5000000" Value="257"/>
        <SplineDoubleKeyFrame KeyTime="00:00:04" Value="10"/>
      </DoubleAnimationUsingKeyFrames>
      <ColorAnimationUsingKeyFrames BeginTime="00:00:00"
Storyboard.TargetName="ellipse2"
Storyboard.TargetProperty="(Shape.Fill).(SolidColorBrush.Color)">
        <SplineColorKeyFrame KeyTime="00:00:00" Value="#FFFF0000"/>
        <SplineColorKeyFrame KeyTime="00:00:01.5000000" Value="#3F00FDFD"/>
        <SplineColorKeyFrame KeyTime="00:00:02.6000000" Value="#FFFF0000"/>
      </ColorAnimationUsingKeyFrames>
      <ColorAnimationUsingKeyFrames BeginTime="00:00:00"
Storyboard.TargetName="ellipse1"
Storyboard.TargetProperty="(Shape.Fill).(SolidColorBrush.Color)">
        <SplineColorKeyFrame KeyTime="00:00:00" Value="#FFFFFF00"/>
        <SplineColorKeyFrame KeyTime="00:00:01.5000000" Value="#FFFFA500"/>
        <SplineColorKeyFrame KeyTime="00:00:02.6000000" Value="#FFFFA500"/>
        <SplineColorKeyFrame KeyTime="00:00:04" Value="#FF000080"/>
      </ColorAnimationUsingKeyFrames>
    </Storyboard>
  </UserControl.Resources>
  <Grid x:Name="LayoutRoot" Background="White">
    <Grid.ColumnDefinitions>
      <ColumnDefinition Width="0.31*"/>
      <ColumnDefinition Width="0.69*"/>
    </Grid.ColumnDefinitions>
    <Ellipse Height="70" HorizontalAlignment="Stretch"
Margin="49.560001373291,43.3120002746582,66.4400024414063,0"
VerticalAlignment="Top" Fill="#FF0000FF" Stroke="#FF000000"
x:Name="ellipse" RenderTransformOrigin="0.5,0.5">
      <Ellipse.RenderTransform>
        <TransformGroup>
          <ScaleTransform/>
          <SkewTransform/>
          <RotateTransform/>
          <TranslateTransform/>
        </TransformGroup>
      </Ellipse.RenderTransform>
    </Ellipse>

    <Rectangle Height="15.23" HorizontalAlignment="Stretch" Margin="0,0,0,0"
      VerticalAlignment="Bottom" Grid.ColumnSpan="2" Fill="#FF3A3A3F"
```

```
    d:LayoutOverrides="Height"/>
<Rectangle Height="14.508" HorizontalAlignment="Left"
  Margin="0,113.311996459961,0,0" VerticalAlignment="Top" Width="49.56"
  Fill="#FF352424" d:LayoutOverrides="Width, Height"/>
<Button Height="28" HorizontalAlignment="Stretch"
  Margin="4,4,4,0" VerticalAlignment="Top" Content="Click to Drop the Ball"
  Click="Button_Click"/>
<Rectangle Height="70" HorizontalAlignment="Left"
  Margin="37,43.3120002746582,0,0" VerticalAlignment="Top" Width="70"
  Grid.Column="1" Fill="#FF00FFFF" Stroke="#FF000000" x:Name="rectangle"
  RenderTransformOrigin="0.5,0.5">
  <Rectangle.RenderTransform>
    <TransformGroup>
      <ScaleTransform/>
      <SkewTransform/>
      <RotateTransform/>
      <TranslateTransform/>
    </TransformGroup>
  </Rectangle.RenderTransform>
</Rectangle>
<Ellipse Height="70" HorizontalAlignment="Stretch"
  Margin="145,43.3120002746582,199,0" VerticalAlignment="Top"
  Grid.Column="1" Fill="#FFFFFF00" Stroke="#FF000000" Width="70"
  x:Name="ellipse1" RenderTransformOrigin="0.5,0.5">
  <Ellipse.RenderTransform>
    <TransformGroup>
      <ScaleTransform/>
      <SkewTransform/>
      <RotateTransform/>
      <TranslateTransform/>
    </TransformGroup>
  </Ellipse.RenderTransform>
</Ellipse>
<Ellipse HorizontalAlignment="Right" Margin="0,43.3120002746582,85,0"
  VerticalAlignment="Top" Fill="#FFFF0000" Stroke="#FF000000" Grid.Column="1"
  Width="70" Height="70" x:Name="ellipse2" RenderTransformOrigin="0.5,0.5">
  <Ellipse.RenderTransform>
    <TransformGroup>
      <ScaleTransform/>
      <SkewTransform/>
      <RotateTransform/>
      <TranslateTransform/>
    </TransformGroup>
  </Ellipse.RenderTransform>
</Ellipse>
```

```
    <Button Height="28" HorizontalAlignment="Left" Margin="4,4,0,0"
        VerticalAlignment="Top" Width="151" Grid.Column="1"
        Content="Start Multi-Animation" Click="Button_Click_1"/>
  </Grid>
</UserControl>
```

Listing 3-12. *Recipe 3.12 MainPage.Xaml.cs Class File*

```
using System.Windows;
using System.Windows.Controls;

namespace Ch03_DesigningUX.Recipe3_12
{
  public partial class MainPage : UserControl
  {
    public MainPage()
    {
      InitializeComponent();
    }

    private void Button_Click(object sender, RoutedEventArgs e)
    {
      BouncingBallStoryboard.Begin();
    }

    private void Button_Click_1(object sender, RoutedEventArgs e)
    {
      MultipleAnimations.Begin();
    }
  }
}
```

3-13. Transforming an Object

Problem

You need to rotate, move, scale, or skew UI elements to produce a visual effect.

Solution

Apply a RotateTransform, ScaleTransform, SkewTransform, or TranslateTransform to alter a UI element's appearance.

How It Works

Silverlight supports two-dimensional Transform classes to rotate, scale, skew, and move objects. All transformations are performed by multiplying the coordinate space of an object by a transformation matrix. The matrix is made up of nine values in a three-by-three grid; the third column is constant, making it an affine transformation, which in the simplest terms means that anything that was a straight line continues to be straight after the transformation. For more information about the format of the transformation matrix in Silverlight, see

http://msdn.microsoft.com/en-us/library/cc189037(VS.95).aspx

Silverlight provides several high-level classes to make it easy to apply the most common types of transforms to an object. These classes are listed in Table 3-2.

Table 3-2. *Available Transforms in Silverlight 3*

Class Name	Description
MatrixTransform	Allows the designer or developer to create custom transformations that are not available through the other classes in this table. The transformation matrix is modified directly.
RotateTransform	Rotates an object by the configured Angle.
ScaleTransform	Scales an object by the configured amounts in the X and Y direction.
SkewTransform	Skews an object by the configured angles in the X and Y direction.
TranslateTransform	Moves an object by the configured amount in the X and Y direction.
TransformGroup	Lets the designer or developer apply multiple Transform operations to a single object. Note that the order of transforms listed in the group matters. Changing the order can alter the effect.

For RotateTransform, ScaleTransform, and SkewTransform, the effect is applied in reference to the upper-left corner or coordinate (0,0) for the object by default. You can alter the reference point by providing values for CenterX and CenterY.

We cover MatrixTransform because it provides the greatest flexibility to aid in understanding how transforms work. MatrixTransform explicitly sets the matrix described earlier to transform the object. Here is a MatrixTransform with the default values for the matrix:

```
<TextBox Height="Auto" Text="TextBox" TextWrapping="Wrap">
  <TextBox.RenderTransform>
    <MatrixTransform>
      <MatrixTransform.Matrix>
        <Matrix  M11="1" M12="0" M21="0" M22="1" OffsetX="0" OffsetY="0"  />
      </MatrixTransform.Matrix>
    </MatrixTransform>
  </TextBox.RenderTransform>
</TextBox>
```

The M11, M12, M21, and M22 values represent the locations in the matrix described at the URL listed earlier. OffsetX and OffsetY change the position of the object by the specified number of pixels in either the X (right) and/or Y (down) direction.

■**Note** Positive and negative floating-point values are valid for M11, M12, M21, M22, OffsetX, and OffsetY. Start by setting individual values with small numbers when you test it, to get a feel for how the matrix affects the object.

A shorthand notation for the preceding format is available on the MatrixTransform markup in the form M11,M12,M21,M22,OffsetX,OffsetY, which means the previous value can also be written

```
<MatrixTransform Matrix="1,0,0,1,0,0"/>
```

The sample code creates a MatrixTransform test bench that demonstrates how altering the values for M11, M12, M21, M22, OffsetX, and OffsetY alter the appearance of the object. When you run the sample, enter small values (between 0 and 2 for the M values) as well as positive and negative values to see the generated effect. If you enter a value that seems to make the TextBox disappear, click the Reset button.

As you alter values for M11, M12, M21, M22, OffsetX, and OffsetY, you can see how the changes affect the rendering for the TextBox, which indicates how the RotateTransform, ScaleTransform, SkewTransform, and TranslateTransform classes perform their work under the covers. These four classes provide a valuable service: they make the matrix math easier to work with by configuring the various properties available on those classes to perform the desired transformation.

Just as you can apply multiple effects with MatrixTransform by changing multiple values in the Matrix value, you can apply multiple effects with the RotateTransform, ScaleTransform, SkewTransform, and TranslateTransform classes by grouping them within a TransformGroup object.

In addition, these four classes are much easier to animate than MatrixTransform. With MatrixTransform, you have to do the math yourself to perform the animation, which may be nontrivial if you're applying multiple effects. On the other hand, the four transform classes have specific double properties like Angle, ScaleX, and ScaleY, depending on the transform applied, that can be animated with a DoubleAnimation or DoubleKeyframeAnimation. Recipe 3-14 covers how to animate these transform classes.

The Code

In general, MatrixTransform should be your choice of last resort for the reasons we've listed. Essentially, if you are unable to achieve the desired effect with a combination of the four higher-level transforms, then that is the time to use MatrixTransform.

However, this sample code creates a UI that lets you exercise MatrixTransform to understand how modifying the transform affects the UI element. Figure 3-49 shows the UI.

Enter numbers that are small, such as 0.2, to see the effect; otherwise, the transform may move the TextBox off the visible screen. As you change different values, you skew, rotate, and otherwise move the object, providing insight into how the RotateTransform, ScaleTransform, SkewTransform, and TranslateTransform classes work. Listing 3-13 contains the XAML for the UI, and Listing 3-14 shows the MainPage.Xaml.cs class file.

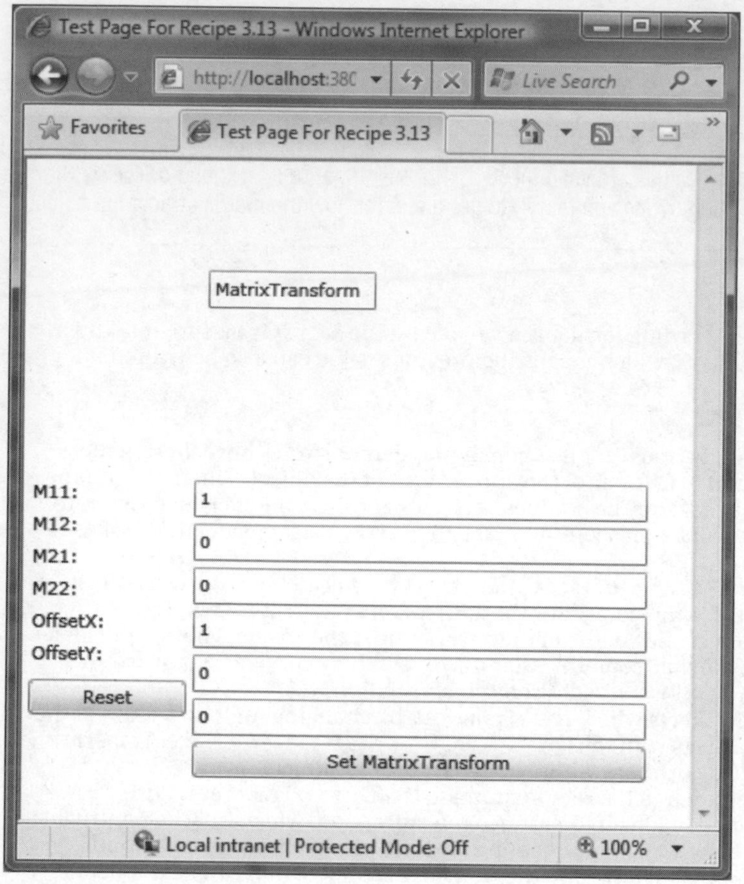

Figure 3-49. *Fun with a matrix*

Listing 3-13. *Recipe 3.13 MainPage.Xaml*

```xml
<UserControl x:Class="Ch03_DesigningUX.Recipe3_13.MainPage"
    xmlns="http://schemas.microsoft.com/winfx/2006/xaml/presentation"
    xmlns:x="http://schemas.microsoft.com/winfx/2006/xaml"
    xmlns:d="http://schemas.microsoft.com/expression/blend/2008"
    xmlns:mc="http://schemas.openxmlformats.org/markup-compatibility/2006"
    Width="400" Height="400" mc:Ignorable="d">
  <Grid x:Name="LayoutRoot" Background="White">
    <Grid.RowDefinitions>
      <RowDefinition Height="0.49*"/>
      <RowDefinition Height="0.51*"/>
    </Grid.RowDefinitions>
```

```xml
      <Grid.ColumnDefinitions>
        <ColumnDefinition Width="*"/>
      </Grid.ColumnDefinitions>
      <TextBox x:Name="txtMatrixTransform" Height="Auto" Margin="115,70,187,0"
          VerticalAlignment="Top" Text="MatrixTransform" TextWrapping="Wrap"
          HorizontalAlignment="Stretch" d:LayoutOverrides="Height">
        <TextBox.RenderTransform>
          <MatrixTransform>
            <MatrixTransform.Matrix>
              <Matrix  M11="1" M12="0" M21="0" M22="1" OffsetX="0" OffsetY="0"/>
            </MatrixTransform.Matrix>
          </MatrixTransform>
        </TextBox.RenderTransform>
      </TextBox>
      <StackPanel Margin="4,4,0,4" HorizontalAlignment="Left"
          VerticalAlignment="Stretch" Width="99.4" Grid.Row="1">
        <TextBlock Text="M11:" TextWrapping="Wrap" Margin="2,2,2,2"/>
        <TextBlock Text="M12:" TextWrapping="Wrap" Margin="2,2,2,2"/>
        <TextBlock Text="M21:" TextWrapping="Wrap" Margin="2,2,2,2"/>
        <TextBlock Text="M22:" TextWrapping="Wrap" Margin="2,2,2,2"/>
        <TextBlock Text="OffsetX:" TextWrapping="Wrap" Margin="2,2,2,2"/>
        <TextBlock Text="OffsetY:" TextWrapping="Wrap" Margin="2,2,2,2"/>
        <Button Height="Auto" Width="Auto" Content="Reset" Margin="0,6,0,0"
        Click="ResetMatrix"/>
      </StackPanel>
      <StackPanel Grid.Row="1" Margin="0,4,8,4" HorizontalAlignment="Right"
          VerticalAlignment="Stretch" Width="286.6" d:LayoutOverrides="Width">
        <TextBox x:Name="txtM11" Text="1" TextWrapping="Wrap" Margin="2,2,2,2"
                FontSize="10" FontFamily="Portable User Interface"/>
        <TextBox x:Name="txtM12" Text="0" TextWrapping="Wrap" Margin="2,2,2,2"
                FontSize="10" FontFamily="Portable User Interface"/>
        <TextBox x:Name="txtM21" Text="0" TextWrapping="Wrap" Margin="2,2,2,2"
                FontSize="10" FontFamily="Portable User Interface"/>
        <TextBox x:Name="txtM22" Text="1" TextWrapping="Wrap" Margin="2,2,2,2"
                FontSize="10" FontFamily="Portable User Interface"/>
        <TextBox x:Name="txtOffsetX" Text="0" TextWrapping="Wrap" Margin="2,2,2,2"
                FontSize="10" FontFamily="Portable User Interface"/>
        <TextBox x:Name="txtOffsetY" Text="0" TextWrapping="Wrap" Margin="2,2,2,2"
                FontSize="10" FontFamily="Portable User Interface"/>
        <Button Height="Auto" Width="Auto" Content="Set MatrixTransform"
                Margin="2,2,2,2" Click="ApplyMatrix"/>
      </StackPanel>
    </Grid>
  </UserControl>
```

Listing 3-14. *Recipe 3.13 MainPage.Xaml.cs Class File*

```csharp
using System;
using System.Windows;
using System.Windows.Controls;
using System.Windows.Media;

namespace Ch03_DesigningUX.Recipe3_13
{
  public partial class MainPage : UserControl
  {
    public MainPage()
    {
      InitializeComponent();
    }

    private void ApplyMatrix(object sender, RoutedEventArgs e)
    {
      MatrixTransform mt = (MatrixTransform)txtMatrixTransform.RenderTransform;
      try
      {
        Matrix m = new Matrix(Convert.ToDouble(txtM11.Text),
          Convert.ToDouble(txtM12.Text), Convert.ToDouble(txtM21.Text),
          Convert.ToDouble(txtM22.Text), Convert.ToDouble(txtOffsetX.Text),
          Convert.ToDouble(txtOffsetY.Text));
        mt.Matrix = m;
      }
      catch
      {
        txtMatrixTransform.Text = "Invalid-retry:-)";
        ResetMatrix(sender, e);
      }
    }

private void ResetMatrix(object sender, RoutedEventArgs e)
    {
      txtM11.Text = "1";
      txtM12.Text = "0";
      txtM21.Text = "0";
      txtM22.Text = "1";
      txtOffsetX.Text = "0";
      txtOffsetY.Text = "0";
      MatrixTransform mt = (MatrixTransform)txtMatrixTransform.RenderTransform;
      Matrix m = new Matrix(1, 0, 0, 1, 0, 0);
      mt.Matrix = m;
    }
  }
}
```

3-14. Creating a Simple Cartoon Scene

Problem

You need to create an animated scene for a cartoon or game in Silverlight 3.

Solution

First, create a static display of the cartoon scene. Next, create an animation Storyboard that alters the appropriate values for the RotateTransform, ScaleTransform, and SkewTransform classes over a period of time using the Objects and Timeline editing tool in Expression Blend.

How It Works

When you apply a transform in Expression Blend or create a transform via code, it is static in nature after it is applied. For example, here is a transform applied to a Rectangle:

```
<Rectangle Width="50" Height="50" Fill="Navy">
  <Rectangle.RenderTransform>
    <RotateTransform x:Name="RotateTransform" Angle="30"
    CenterX="25" CenterY="25" />
  </Rectangle.RenderTransform>
</Rectangle>
```

Figure 3-50 shows the Rectangle tilted 30 degrees.

Figure 3-50. *Rectangle with transform at design time*

The transform is static in that when the code runs, the Rectangle appears exactly the same.

The Code

Recall from Recipes 3-12 and 3-13 that the animation classes can animate the types Double, Color, and Point. Animating a transform is a matter of creating a Storyboard object, picking animation class like DoubleAnimation to animate a type of Double, and setting the key properties:

- TargetName
- TargetProperty
- From
- To
- Duration

As an example, create a `Storyboard` that continuously rotates a `Rectangle` as shown in Figure 3-50, animating a `RotateTransform` to perform a full 360-degree rotation every 5 seconds with this `Storyboard`:

```
<Storyboard x:Name="RotateStoryboard">
  <DoubleAnimation
   Storyboard.TargetName="RotateTransform"
   Storyboard.TargetProperty="Angle"
   From="0" To="360" Duration="0:0:5"
   RepeatBehavior="Forever" />
</Storyboard>
```

As you can see, it is straightforward to combine transforms with animation by editing XAML code. However, with the Objects and Timeline editor in Expression Blend, you can record a dynamic `Storyboard` to create a simple cartoon. For example, you can animate the `Angle` property for the `RotateTransform` to simulate a rolling boulder.

The application for this recipe is a cartoon-like boulder that rolls off an edge and tumbles down a hill with a couple of rocky bumps. First, draw the static scene in Figure 3-51.

Figure 3-51. *The static cartoon scene*

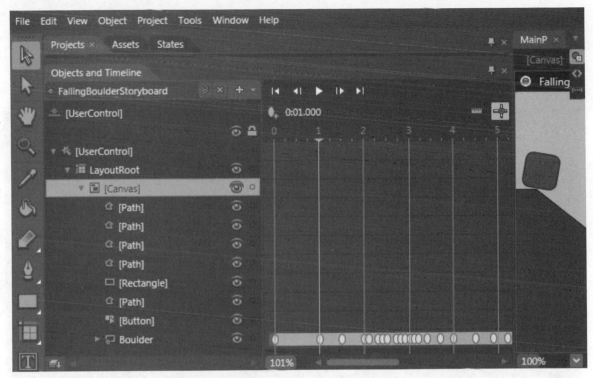

Figure 3-52. *The boulder rolling over the edge*

You next add two keyframes to simulate the boulder sliding down the side of the cliff. At the point at which the boulder hits the first bump, apply a scale transform of 1.1 to simulate the boulder hitting the edge. About 0.1 seconds later, scale it back to 1.0 so that the boulder appears to have a violent collision. Figure 3-53 shows the sequence; you can see that the boulder is slightly larger in the middle scene.

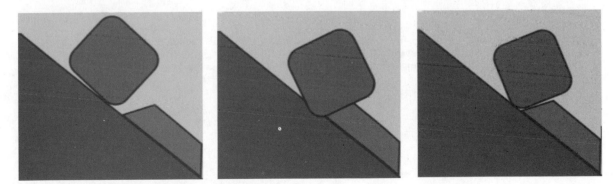

Figure 3-53. *The boulder striking the bump*

Continue to add keyframes by visualizing the spinning and falling action with a few smudges on the LCD screen; this helps line up the next point to animate, which includes another bump into a rock on the slope.

An important aid in visualizing the action of the animation is the trail left by the keyframes: bright bluish spots with smaller bluish spots in between, marking the animation flow. Change the Canvas Background color from sky blue to black to help highlight the animation path, as shown in Figure 3-54.

Figure 3-54. *The animation trail*

Change the canvas back to a sky blue color, and continue with the animation. After bouncing off the second bump, the boulder goes through a long spinning fall and finally comes to rest after colliding with the bump at the bottom of the slope. The final cartoon scene is shown in Figure 3-55.

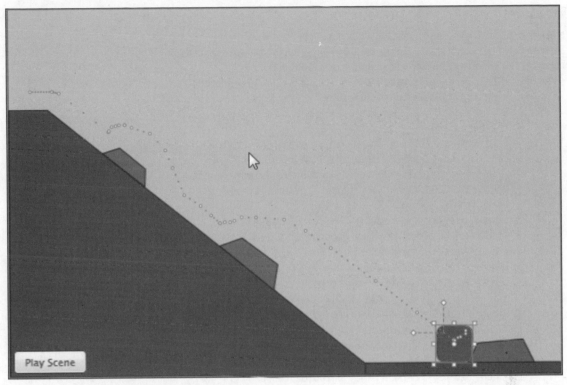

Figure 3-55. *The final cartoon scene*

The FallingBoulderStoryboard object includes a total of 41 keyframes. It would be extremely tedious and take up many pages to go through each change in every keyframe. Instead, we encourage you to open the project from the book's download, open the FallingBoulderStoryboard animation in the Objects and Timeline tool window, and step through the animation visually.

Keep an eye on the rotation transform throughout the animation to see what changes are made in addition to the location transform. The other transform that comes into play is the scale transform, which expands and then contracts the boulder when it gets close to the bumps on the slope.

Try sliding keyframes later or earlier in the time line, either individually or as a group, to see the effect on the cartoon scene. Also, be sure to zoom in and out for both the time line and the Artboard to get a good view of what is happening as you slide the yellow cursor back and forth in the time line.

The cartoon probably runs a bit slowly, but this helps you see what is going on with the animation. One area to improve would be to smooth out the rotation for the boulder. You could, for example, calculate a rotation velocity in degrees per second and try to maintain that speed between keyframes.

All the code is automatically generated by Expression Blend (except the button-click event attached to the button added at the end to let you kick off the animation). Listings 3-15 and 3-16 show the full code to give you an idea of how much is generated.

Listing 3-15. *Recipe 3.14 MainPage.Xaml File*

```xml
<UserControl x:Class="Ch03_DesigningUX.Recipe3_14.MainPage"
    xmlns="http://schemas.microsoft.com/winfx/2006/xaml/presentation"
    xmlns:x="http://schemas.microsoft.com/winfx/2006/xaml"
    xmlns:d="http://schemas.microsoft.com/expression/blend/2008"
    xmlns:mc="http://schemas.openxmlformats.org/markup-compatibility/2006"
    Width="600" Height="400"  mc:Ignorable="d">
  <UserControl.Resources>
    <Storyboard x:Name="FallingBoulderStoryboard">
      <DoubleAnimationUsingKeyFrames BeginTime="00:00:00"
        Storyboard.TargetName="Boulder" Storyboard.TargetProperty=
         "(UIElement.RenderTransform).(TransformGroup.Children)[3].
         (TranslateTransform.X)">
      <SplineDoubleKeyFrame KeyTime="00:00:00" Value="0"/>
      <SplineDoubleKeyFrame KeyTime="00:00:01" Value="24.057"/>
      <SplineDoubleKeyFrame KeyTime="00:00:01.5000000" Value="31.604"/>
      <SplineDoubleKeyFrame KeyTime="00:00:02" Value="85.378"/>
      <SplineDoubleKeyFrame KeyTime="00:00:02.1000000"
                            Value="86.14459228515625"/>
      <SplineDoubleKeyFrame KeyTime="00:00:02.3000000" Value="89.152"/>
      <SplineDoubleKeyFrame KeyTime="00:00:02.4000000" Value="93.346"/>
      <SplineDoubleKeyFrame KeyTime="00:00:02.5000000" Value="97.119"/>
      <SplineDoubleKeyFrame KeyTime="00:00:02.7000000" Value="103.251"/>
      <SplineDoubleKeyFrame KeyTime="00:00:02.8000000"
                            Value="103.25099945068359"/>
      <SplineDoubleKeyFrame KeyTime="00:00:03" Value="110.798"/>
      <SplineDoubleKeyFrame KeyTime="00:00:03.4000000" Value="130.609"/>
      <SplineDoubleKeyFrame KeyTime="00:00:03.7000000" Value="147.118"/>
      <SplineDoubleKeyFrame KeyTime="00:00:04" Value="154.665"/>
      <SplineDoubleKeyFrame KeyTime="00:00:04.5000000" Value="166.929"/>
      <SplineDoubleKeyFrame KeyTime="00:00:04.9000000" Value="184.382"/>
      <SplineDoubleKeyFrame KeyTime="00:00:05.2000000" Value="195.703"/>
      <SplineDoubleKeyFrame KeyTime="00:00:05.6000000" Value="205.099"/>
      <SplineDoubleKeyFrame KeyTime="00:00:05.7000000"
                            Value="205.0989990234375"/>
      <SplineDoubleKeyFrame KeyTime="00:00:05.8000000" Value="210.288"/>
      <SplineDoubleKeyFrame KeyTime="00:00:06" Value="215.948"/>
      <SplineDoubleKeyFrame KeyTime="00:00:06.2000000" Value="220.665"/>
      <SplineDoubleKeyFrame KeyTime="00:00:06.4000000" Value="228.684"/>
      <SplineDoubleKeyFrame KeyTime="00:00:06.7000000" Value="244.25"/>
      <SplineDoubleKeyFrame KeyTime="00:00:07.1000000" Value="274.911"/>
      <SplineDoubleKeyFrame KeyTime="00:00:07.4000000" Value="298.496"/>
      <SplineDoubleKeyFrame KeyTime="00:00:08" Value="326.326"/>
```

```
<SplineDoubleKeyFrame KeyTime="00:00:09" Value="374.911"/>
<SplineDoubleKeyFrame KeyTime="00:00:10" Value="420.666"/>
<SplineDoubleKeyFrame KeyTime="00:00:11" Value="459.817"/>
<SplineDoubleKeyFrame KeyTime="00:00:11.1000000" Value="461.232"/>
<SplineDoubleKeyFrame KeyTime="00:00:11.2000000" Value="464.534"/>
<SplineDoubleKeyFrame KeyTime="00:00:11.3000000" Value="467.305"/>
<SplineDoubleKeyFrame KeyTime="00:00:11.4000000" Value="472.965"/>
<SplineDoubleKeyFrame KeyTime="00:00:11.5000000" Value="472.965"/>
<SplineDoubleKeyFrame KeyTime="00:00:11.6000000" Value="460.229"/>
<SplineDoubleKeyFrame KeyTime="00:00:11.7000000"
                      Value="460.22900390625"/>
<SplineDoubleKeyFrame KeyTime="00:00:11.8000000"
                      Value="460.22900390625"/>
<SplineDoubleKeyFrame KeyTime="00:00:11.9000000"
                      Value="460.22900390625"/>
</DoubleAnimationUsingKeyFrames>
<DoubleAnimationUsingKeyFrames BeginTime="00:00:00"
  Storyboard.TargetName="Boulder" Storyboard.TargetProperty=
  "(UIElement.RenderTransform).(TransformGroup.Children)[2].
  (RotateTransform.Angle)">
<SplineDoubleKeyFrame KeyTime="00:00:00" Value="0"/>
<SplineDoubleKeyFrame KeyTime="00:00:01" Value="190"/>
<SplineDoubleKeyFrame KeyTime="00:00:01.5000000" Value="228.948"/>
<SplineDoubleKeyFrame KeyTime="00:00:02" Value="334.694"/>
<SplineDoubleKeyFrame KeyTime="00:00:02.1000000"
                      Value="338.22189331054688"/>
<SplineDoubleKeyFrame KeyTime="00:00:02.3000000" Value="352.062"/>
<SplineDoubleKeyFrame KeyTime="00:00:02.4000000" Value="355.422"/>
<SplineDoubleKeyFrame KeyTime="00:00:02.5000000" Value="370.738"/>
<SplineDoubleKeyFrame KeyTime="00:00:02.7000000" Value="406.588"/>
<SplineDoubleKeyFrame KeyTime="00:00:02.8000000" Value="417.056"/>
<SplineDoubleKeyFrame KeyTime="00:00:02.9000000" Value="435.254"/>
<SplineDoubleKeyFrame KeyTime="00:00:03" Value="451.662"/>
<SplineDoubleKeyFrame KeyTime="00:00:03.1000000" Value="465.047"/>
<SplineDoubleKeyFrame KeyTime="00:00:03.2000000" Value="493.733"/>
<SplineDoubleKeyFrame KeyTime="00:00:03.4000000" Value="555.096"/>
<SplineDoubleKeyFrame KeyTime="00:00:03.7000000" Value="599.291"/>
<SplineDoubleKeyFrame KeyTime="00:00:04" Value="632.511"/>
<SplineDoubleKeyFrame KeyTime="00:00:04.5000000" Value="668.156"/>
<SplineDoubleKeyFrame KeyTime="00:00:04.9000000" Value="679.123"/>
<SplineDoubleKeyFrame KeyTime="00:00:05.2000000" Value="669.482"/>
<SplineDoubleKeyFrame KeyTime="00:00:05.6000000"
                      Value="669.48199462890625"/>
```

```
        <SplineDoubleKeyFrame KeyTime="00:00:05.7000000"
                              Value="669.48199462890625"/>
        <SplineDoubleKeyFrame KeyTime="00:00:05.8000000" Value="679.084"/>
        <SplineDoubleKeyFrame KeyTime="00:00:06" Value="696.576"/>
        <SplineDoubleKeyFrame KeyTime="00:00:06.2000000" Value="716.48"/>
        <SplineDoubleKeyFrame KeyTime="00:00:06.4000000" Value="738.707"/>
        <SplineDoubleKeyFrame KeyTime="00:00:06.7000000" Value="771.96"/>
        <SplineDoubleKeyFrame KeyTime="00:00:07.1000000" Value="799.29"/>
        <SplineDoubleKeyFrame KeyTime="00:00:07.4000000" Value="839.167"/>
        <SplineDoubleKeyFrame KeyTime="00:00:08" Value="916.032"/>
        <SplineDoubleKeyFrame KeyTime="00:00:09" Value="1057.057"/>
        <SplineDoubleKeyFrame KeyTime="00:00:10" Value="1243.919"/>
        <SplineDoubleKeyFrame KeyTime="00:00:11" Value="1404.016"/>
        <SplineDoubleKeyFrame KeyTime="00:00:11.1000000" Value="1434.832"/>
        <SplineDoubleKeyFrame KeyTime="00:00:11.2000000" Value="1445.008"/>
        <SplineDoubleKeyFrame KeyTime="00:00:11.3000000" Value="1460.831"/>
        <SplineDoubleKeyFrame KeyTime="00:00:11.4000000" Value="1472.871"/>
        <SplineDoubleKeyFrame KeyTime="00:00:11.5000000" Value="1482.02"/>
        <SplineDoubleKeyFrame KeyTime="00:00:11.6000000" Value="1446.205"/>
        <SplineDoubleKeyFrame KeyTime="00:00:11.7000000" Value="1439.087"/>
        <SplineDoubleKeyFrame KeyTime="00:00:11.8000000" Value="1434.578"/>
        <SplineDoubleKeyFrame KeyTime="00:00:11.9000000" Value="1440.64"/>
    </DoubleAnimationUsingKeyFrames>
    <DoubleAnimationUsingKeyFrames BeginTime="00:00:00" Storyboard.TargetName=
      "Boulder" Storyboard.TargetProperty="(UIElement.RenderTransform).
      (TransformGroup.Children)[3].(TranslateTransform.Y)">
        <SplineDoubleKeyFrame KeyTime="00:00:00" Value="0"/>
        <SplineDoubleKeyFrame KeyTime="00:00:01" Value="0"/>
        <SplineDoubleKeyFrame KeyTime="00:00:01.5000000" Value="1.887"/>
        <SplineDoubleKeyFrame KeyTime="00:00:02" Value="44.811"/>
        <SplineDoubleKeyFrame KeyTime="00:00:02.1000000" Value="43.661109924316406"/>
        <SplineDoubleKeyFrame KeyTime="00:00:02.3000000" Value="39.15"/>
        <SplineDoubleKeyFrame KeyTime="00:00:02.4000000" Value="38.155"/>
        <SplineDoubleKeyFrame KeyTime="00:00:02.5000000" Value="37.212"/>
        <SplineDoubleKeyFrame KeyTime="00:00:02.7000000" Value="37.21"/>
        <SplineDoubleKeyFrame KeyTime="00:00:02.8000000" Value="37.212"/>
        <SplineDoubleKeyFrame KeyTime="00:00:03" Value="40.042"/>
        <SplineDoubleKeyFrame KeyTime="00:00:03.4000000" Value="46.646"/>
        <SplineDoubleKeyFrame KeyTime="00:00:03.7000000" Value="65.042"/>
        <SplineDoubleKeyFrame KeyTime="00:00:04" Value="84.382"/>
        <SplineDoubleKeyFrame KeyTime="00:00:04.5000000" Value="114.099"/>
        <SplineDoubleKeyFrame KeyTime="00:00:04.9000000" Value="125.891"/>
        <SplineDoubleKeyFrame KeyTime="00:00:05.2000000" Value="136.268"/>
```

```
<SplineDoubleKeyFrame KeyTime="00:00:05.6000000" Value="144.723"/>
<SplineDoubleKeyFrame KeyTime="00:00:05.7000000" Value="144.72300720214844"/>
<SplineDoubleKeyFrame KeyTime="00:00:05.8000000" Value="143.78"/>
<SplineDoubleKeyFrame KeyTime="00:00:06" Value="143.78"/>
<SplineDoubleKeyFrame KeyTime="00:00:06.2000000" Value="142.365"/>
<SplineDoubleKeyFrame KeyTime="00:00:06.4000000" Value="138.591"/>
<SplineDoubleKeyFrame KeyTime="00:00:06.7000000" Value="139.063"/>
<SplineDoubleKeyFrame KeyTime="00:00:07.1000000" Value="141.421"/>
<SplineDoubleKeyFrame KeyTime="00:00:07.4000000" Value="153.685"/>
<SplineDoubleKeyFrame KeyTime="00:00:08" Value="172.553"/>
<SplineDoubleKeyFrame KeyTime="00:00:09" Value="208.402"/>
<SplineDoubleKeyFrame KeyTime="00:00:10" Value="242.836"/>
<SplineDoubleKeyFrame KeyTime="00:00:11" Value="272.553"/>
<SplineDoubleKeyFrame KeyTime="00:00:11.1000000" Value="273.025"/>
<SplineDoubleKeyFrame KeyTime="00:00:11.2000000" Value="270.195"/>
<SplineDoubleKeyFrame KeyTime="00:00:11.3000000" Value="269.237"/>
<SplineDoubleKeyFrame KeyTime="00:00:11.4000000" Value="265.935"/>
<SplineDoubleKeyFrame KeyTime="00:00:11.5000000" Value="262.633"/>
<SplineDoubleKeyFrame KeyTime="00:00:11.6000000" Value="277.256"/>
<SplineDoubleKeyFrame KeyTime="00:00:11.7000000"
Value="277.25601196289062"/>
<SplineDoubleKeyFrame KeyTime="00:00:11.8000000"
Value="277.25601196289062"/>
<SplineDoubleKeyFrame KeyTime="00:00:11.9000000"
Value="277.25601196289062"/>
</DoubleAnimationUsingKeyFrames>
<DoubleAnimationUsingKeyFrames BeginTime="00:00:00"
    Storyboard.TargetName="Boulder" Storyboard.TargetProperty="(UIElement.
    RenderTransform).(TransformGroup.Children)[0].(ScaleTransform.ScaleX)">
<SplineDoubleKeyFrame KeyTime="00:00:01.5000000" Value="1"/>
<SplineDoubleKeyFrame KeyTime="00:00:02" Value="1.1"/>
<SplineDoubleKeyFrame KeyTime="00:00:02.1000000" Value="1"/>
<SplineDoubleKeyFrame KeyTime="00:00:02.3000000" Value="1"/>
<SplineDoubleKeyFrame KeyTime="00:00:02.4000000" Value="1"/>
<SplineDoubleKeyFrame KeyTime="00:00:02.5000000" Value="1"/>
<SplineDoubleKeyFrame KeyTime="00:00:02.7000000" Value="1"/>
<SplineDoubleKeyFrame KeyTime="00:00:02.8000000" Value="1"/>
<SplineDoubleKeyFrame KeyTime="00:00:03" Value="1"/>
<SplineDoubleKeyFrame KeyTime="00:00:03.4000000" Value="1"/>
<SplineDoubleKeyFrame KeyTime="00:00:03.7000000" Value="1"/>
<SplineDoubleKeyFrame KeyTime="00:00:04" Value="1"/>
<SplineDoubleKeyFrame KeyTime="00:00:04.5000000" Value="1"/>
<SplineDoubleKeyFrame KeyTime="00:00:04.9000000" Value="1"/>
<SplineDoubleKeyFrame KeyTime="00:00:05.2000000" Value="1"/>
```

```
        <SplineDoubleKeyFrame KeyTime="00:00:05.6000000" Value="1.1"/>
        <SplineDoubleKeyFrame KeyTime="00:00:05.7000000" Value="1"/>
        <SplineDoubleKeyFrame KeyTime="00:00:05.8000000" Value="1"/>
        <SplineDoubleKeyFrame KeyTime="00:00:06" Value="1"/>
        <SplineDoubleKeyFrame KeyTime="00:00:06.2000000" Value="1"/>
        <SplineDoubleKeyFrame KeyTime="00:00:06.4000000" Value="1"/>
        <SplineDoubleKeyFrame KeyTime="00:00:06.7000000" Value="1"/>
        <SplineDoubleKeyFrame KeyTime="00:00:07.1000000" Value="1"/>
        <SplineDoubleKeyFrame KeyTime="00:00:07.4000000" Value="1"/>
        <SplineDoubleKeyFrame KeyTime="00:00:08" Value="1"/>
        <SplineDoubleKeyFrame KeyTime="00:00:09" Value="1"/>
        <SplineDoubleKeyFrame KeyTime="00:00:10" Value="1"/>
        <SplineDoubleKeyFrame KeyTime="00:00:11" Value="1"/>
        <SplineDoubleKeyFrame KeyTime="00:00:11.1000000" Value="1"/>
        <SplineDoubleKeyFrame KeyTime="00:00:11.2000000" Value="1.1"/>
        <SplineDoubleKeyFrame KeyTime="00:00:11.3000000" Value="1"/>
        <SplineDoubleKeyFrame KeyTime="00:00:11.4000000" Value="1"/>
        <SplineDoubleKeyFrame KeyTime="00:00:11.5000000" Value="1"/>
        <SplineDoubleKeyFrame KeyTime="00:00:11.6000000" Value="1"/>
        <SplineDoubleKeyFrame KeyTime="00:00:11.7000000" Value="1"/>
        <SplineDoubleKeyFrame KeyTime="00:00:11.8000000" Value="1"/>
        <SplineDoubleKeyFrame KeyTime="00:00:11.9000000" Value="1"/>
    </DoubleAnimationUsingKeyFrames>
    <DoubleAnimationUsingKeyFrames BeginTime="00:00:00"
      Storyboard.TargetName="Boulder" Storyboard.TargetProperty=
      "(UIElement.RenderTransform).(TransformGroup.Children)[0].
      (ScaleTransform.ScaleY)">
        <SplineDoubleKeyFrame KeyTime="00:00:01.5000000" Value="1"/>
        <SplineDoubleKeyFrame KeyTime="00:00:02" Value="1.1"/>
        <SplineDoubleKeyFrame KeyTime="00:00:02.1000000" Value="1"/>
        <SplineDoubleKeyFrame KeyTime="00:00:02.3000000" Value="1"/>
        <SplineDoubleKeyFrame KeyTime="00:00:02.4000000" Value="1"/>
        <SplineDoubleKeyFrame KeyTime="00:00:02.5000000" Value="1"/>
        <SplineDoubleKeyFrame KeyTime="00:00:02.7000000" Value="1"/>
        <SplineDoubleKeyFrame KeyTime="00:00:02.8000000" Value="1"/>
        <SplineDoubleKeyFrame KeyTime="00:00:03" Value="1"/>
        <SplineDoubleKeyFrame KeyTime="00:00:03.4000000" Value="1"/>
        <SplineDoubleKeyFrame KeyTime="00:00:03.7000000" Value="1"/>
        <SplineDoubleKeyFrame KeyTime="00:00:04" Value="1"/>
        <SplineDoubleKeyFrame KeyTime="00:00:04.5000000" Value="1"/>
        <SplineDoubleKeyFrame KeyTime="00:00:04.9000000" Value="1"/>
        <SplineDoubleKeyFrame KeyTime="00:00:05.2000000" Value="1"/>
        <SplineDoubleKeyFrame KeyTime="00:00:05.6000000" Value="1.1"/>
        <SplineDoubleKeyFrame KeyTime="00:00:05.7000000" Value="1"/>
```

```xml
          <SplineDoubleKeyFrame KeyTime="00:00:05.8000000" Value="1"/>
          <SplineDoubleKeyFrame KeyTime="00:00:06" Value="1"/>
          <SplineDoubleKeyFrame KeyTime="00:00:06.2000000" Value="1"/>
          <SplineDoubleKeyFrame KeyTime="00:00:06.4000000" Value="1"/>
          <SplineDoubleKeyFrame KeyTime="00:00:06.7000000" Value="1"/>
          <SplineDoubleKeyFrame KeyTime="00:00:07.1000000" Value="1"/>
          <SplineDoubleKeyFrame KeyTime="00:00:07.4000000" Value="1"/>
          <SplineDoubleKeyFrame KeyTime="00:00:08" Value="1"/>
          <SplineDoubleKeyFrame KeyTime="00:00:09" Value="1"/>
          <SplineDoubleKeyFrame KeyTime="00:00:10" Value="1"/>
          <SplineDoubleKeyFrame KeyTime="00:00:11" Value="1"/>
          <SplineDoubleKeyFrame KeyTime="00:00:11.1000000" Value="1"/>
          <SplineDoubleKeyFrame KeyTime="00:00:11.2000000" Value="1.1"/>
          <SplineDoubleKeyFrame KeyTime="00:00:11.3000000" Value="1"/>
          <SplineDoubleKeyFrame KeyTime="00:00:11.4000000" Value="1"/>
          <SplineDoubleKeyFrame KeyTime="00:00:11.5000000" Value="1"/>
          <SplineDoubleKeyFrame KeyTime="00:00:11.6000000" Value="1"/>
          <SplineDoubleKeyFrame KeyTime="00:00:11.7000000" Value="1"/>
          <SplineDoubleKeyFrame KeyTime="00:00:11.8000000" Value="1"/>
          <SplineDoubleKeyFrame KeyTime="00:00:11.9000000" Value="1"/>
        </DoubleAnimationUsingKeyFrames>
      </Storyboard>
  </UserControl.Resources>
  <Grid x:Name="LayoutRoot" Background="White">
    <Canvas HorizontalAlignment="Stretch" VerticalAlignment="Stretch"
            Background="#FFADD8E6">
      <Path Height="290.503" Width="402.71" Canvas.Top="109.997"
            Fill="#FF006400" Stretch="Fill" Stroke="#FF000000"
            Data="M42.409161,0.5 L42.412846,0.50299871 ......... 61,0.5 z"/>
      <Path Height="43.308" Width="47.154" Canvas.Left="102.559"
            Canvas.Top="152.064" Fill="#FF935252" Stretch="Fill"
            Stroke="#FF000000" Data="M125,152.5641 ..........33339 z"/>
      <Path Height="57.41" Width="63.821" Canvas.Left="228.127"
            Canvas.Top="250.782" Fill="#FF935252" Stretch="Fill"
            Stroke="#FF000000" Data="M231.41026,259.61539 ....,.69498 z"/>
      <Path Height="30" Margin="0,0,0,0" Width="76" Canvas.Left="497"
            Canvas.Top="361.902" Fill="#FF935252" Stretch="Fill"
            Stroke="#FF000000" Data="M519,386 L531,361 L580,357 L594,385 z"/>
      <Rectangle Height="13.381" Width="213.443" Canvas.Left="386.557"
            Canvas.Top="386.902" Fill="#FF006400" Stroke="#FF000000"
            RadiusX="0" RadiusY="0"/>
      <Path Height="1" Width="1" Canvas.Left="43" Canvas.Top="-46"
            Fill="#FFFFFFFF" Stretch="Fill" Stroke="#FF000000"
            Data="M43,-46"/>
```

```
    <Button Height="25" Width="79.713" Canvas.Left="4" Canvas.Top="371"
            Content="Play Scene" Background="#FF00FF00" Click="Button_Click"/>

    <Rectangle Height="40" Margin="0,0,0,0" x:Name="Boulder" Width="39"
        RenderTransformOrigin="0.5,0.5" Canvas.Left="5" Canvas.Top="69.997"
        Fill="#FFA52A2A" Stroke="#FF000000" RadiusX="8" RadiusY="8">
      <Rectangle.RenderTransform>
        <TransformGroup>
          <ScaleTransform/>
          <SkewTransform/>
          <RotateTransform/>
          <TranslateTransform/>
        </TransformGroup>
      </Rectangle.RenderTransform>
    </Rectangle>
  </Canvas>
 </Grid>
</UserControl>
```

Listing 3-16. *Recipe 3.14 MainPage.Xaml.cs Class File*

```
using System.Windows;
using System.Windows.Controls;

namespace Ch03_DesigningUX.Recipe3_9
{
  public partial class MainPage : UserControl
  {
    public MainPage()
    {
      InitializeComponent();
    }

    private void Button_Click(object sender, RoutedEventArgs e)
    {
      FallingBoulderStoryboard.Begin();
    }
  }
}
```

3-15. Handling Keyboard Input

Problem

You need to capture keyboard input as part of an application UI, such as detecting when an arrow key is pressed in an online game.

Solution

Hook into the KeyDown and KeyUp event handlers so that code can detect when a key is pressed as well as released.

How It Works

Keyboard event-handler functions can be attached to any Silverlight 3 object that inherits either directly or indirectly from the UIElement class. The events that are available are KeyDown and KeyUp. KeyDown fires when a key is pressed *and* the Silverlight plug-in has focus in the web browser. KeyUp fires when a pressed key is released *and* the Silverlight plug-in has focus in the web browser.

■**Note**   Refer to Chapter 6 to learn how to set focus on the Silverlight control from JavaScript in the browser.

Event handlers for KeyUp and KeyDown include the ubiquitous sender parameter as well as an instance of KeyEventArgs, like this:

```
void OnKeyUp(object sender, KeyEventArgs e)
```

The object KeyEventArgs contains the following:

- Key: Returns an instance of an enumerations type of Key so that you can check for Key.Up, KeyDown, and so on. Key represents portable key codes common across platforms.

- PlatformKeyCode: For Key values that equal Key.Unknown, represents an integer that corresponds to the platform-specific key code.

- Handled: Set to true to stop the event from bubbling up to parent objects up the Visual Tree.

- Source: Indicates which object in the UI originally had focus when a key was pressed.

For Windows-specific platform key codes, see

```
http://msdn.microsoft.com/en-us/library/ms645540(VS.85).aspx
```

For Macintosh-specific key codes, refer to

```
http://go.microsoft.com/fwlink/?LinkId=97928
```

You can press modifier keys, such as Ctrl and Alt, together with other keys and generate their own keyboard events.

■**Note** Shift and Ctrl are common to Windows and Macintosh, but others are unique.

You check modifier keys by accessing the Keyboard.Modifiers property using bitwise operations, because multiple modifiers can be pressed simultaneously. This code checks to see if the modifier key Ctrl was pushed:

```
if ((Keyboard.Modifiers & ModifierKeys.Control) == ModifierKeys.Control)
```

The keyboard events KeyDown and KeyUp are routed events that bubble up from child to parent via the ownership chain in the Visual Tree. This means you can have a single handler for each event at the top of the ownership chain if you intend to handle keyboard events globally.

If a specific object in the UI needs to respond to a keyboard event, the object should implement its own KeyDown and KeyUp events. Within the events, the object should set the value of e.Handled to True for the instance of KeyEventArgs that is passed into the handler. This stops the bubbling of the event because it is not necessary to do so in this case.

■**Note** Keyboard events are prevented from being passed to keyboard event handlers in the application as a security feature. This prevents a Silverlight application from impersonating another application (or the entire desktop) and collecting keyboard-entered personal or private data.

The Code

The code starts by changing the root element from a Grid to a Canvas object because you do not need layout and you want to use coordinate positioning. Lay out a simple game UI using gradients and Path objects to create an ice cave.

The idea of the game is to have a radioactive ball bouncing around in the cave; you try to control the ball using the arrow keys. If the ball sits on a wall for too long, it melts the ice, and the cave collapses. This recipe doesn't implement the entire game, but you lay out the basic UI and set up the beginnings of the game to receive keyboard input.

You have two options to use with the KeyDown and KeyUp events. Which one to use depends on the type of game you are creating. The focus is using the arrow keys to provide input. If you are building a game where the player is in complete control of the movement—say, a flying game—you may want to use KeyDown to kick off a Storyboard or thread to keep the object moving while the key is held down. You can use the KeyUp event to signal that the movement should end by stopping the Storyboard or background thread.

For games where an object moves independently via some sort of artificial intelligence, if you want to provide input to counteract the movement (in this case, to keep the radioactive ball from touching a wall), it may be better game play to use the KeyUp event to apply discrete amounts of movement so that the user has to click faster or slower to maintain control. This game uses this approach first to see how it plays.

As mentioned earlier, you build a game board using gradients and Path objects to create an ice cave environment, as shown in Figure 3-56.

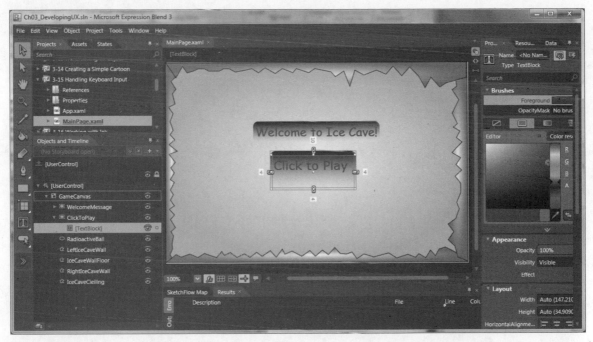

Figure 3-56. *Ice cave static UI*

Figure 3-56 is at design time in Expression Blend. Also create a simple `Storyboard` that animates a rotate transform to make the `RadioactiveBall` object more dynamic. In addition, set the `RadioactiveBall.Visibility` to `Visibility.Collapsed` so that it doesn't show up when the game is initially run.

Put a couple of messages in `TextBlocks`, including Click to Play; this receives a `Click` event to ensure the Silverlight control has focus before kicking off the game. The `Click` event sets `Visibility` to `Visibility.Collapsed` for the two `TextBlocks` and sets `Visibility` to `Visibility.Visible` for the `RadioactiveBall` object. You also kick off the rotation `Storyboard` named `SpinGameBallStoryboard`. Here is the `Click` event, and Figure 3-57 shows the application at runtime:

```
private void TextBlock_MouseLeftButtonDown(object sender, MouseButtonEventArgs e)
{
  ClickToPlay.Visibility = Visibility.Collapsed ;
  WelcomeMessage.Visibility = Visibility.Collapsed ;
  RadioactiveBall.Visibility = Visibility.Visible;
  SpinGameBallStoryboard.Begin();
}
```

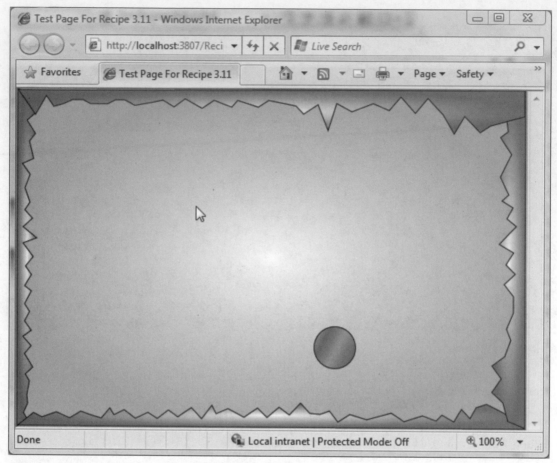

Figure 3-57. *Ice cave running in the browser*

When you run the game, it seems tedious and time consuming to move the radioactive ball around the scene, but that's because the radioactive ball does not have any artificial intelligence and doesn't move on its own. Imagine the ball flying around at different speeds while you push the arrow keys faster or slower to redirect the ball, keeping it off the walls for an ever-increasing period of time as you advance through levels. Each level could have a smaller cave through the use of a scale transform to make the four sides smaller.

Control over the RadioactiveBall object is broken into two separate handlers. One is the GameCanvas_KeyUp event handler that receives the KeyUp event, evaluates the Key, and performs some basic collision detection with the edges:

```
private void GameCanvas_KeyUp(object sender, KeyEventArgs e)
{
  switch (e.Key)
  {
    case Key.Right: if ((leftPosition) <= (this.Width -
    (RadioactiveBall.Width*1.25)))
                        leftPosition += moveSpeed;
                    break;
    case Key.Left: if (leftPosition >= (RadioactiveBall.Width * .25))
                        leftPosition -= moveSpeed;
                    break;
    case Key.Up: if (topPosition >= (RadioactiveBall.Height * .25))
                        topPosition -= moveSpeed;
                    break;
    case Key.Down: if (topPosition <= (this.Height - (RadioactiveBall.Height*1.25)))
                        topPosition += moveSpeed;
                    break;
  }
  Draw();
}
```

The other method, Draw, repositions the RadioactiveBall object to the new positions, which may be the current position due to collision detection. The only other interesting code is in the Page constructor; it wires up the KeyUp event handler and gets the initial position of the RadioactiveBall object:

```
this.KeyUp += new KeyEventHandler(GameCanvas_KeyUp);
leftPosition = (double)RadioactiveBall.GetValue(Canvas.LeftProperty);
topPosition = (double)RadioactiveBall.GetValue(Canvas.TopProperty);
```

That's it for the code in the code-behind file. The rest of the application is the resulting markup, as shown in Listing 3-17.

Listing 3-17. *Recipe 3.15 MainPage.Xaml File*

```
<UserControl x:Class="Ch03_DesigningUX.Recipe3_15.MainPage"
    xmlns="http://schemas.microsoft.com/winfx/2006/xaml/presentation"
    xmlns:x="http://schemas.microsoft.com/winfx/2006/xaml"
    Width="600" Height="400">
  <UserControl.Resources>
    <RadialGradientBrush x:Key="IceBrush">
      <GradientStop Color="#FFFFFFFF"/>
      <GradientStop Color="#FF6F74AB" Offset="1"/>
    </RadialGradientBrush>
```

```xml
            <LinearGradientBrush x:Key="MessageBorderBrush" EndPoint="0.501999974250793,1"
                        StartPoint="0.497999995946884,0">
          <GradientStop Color="#FF000000"/>
          <GradientStop Color="#33FFFFFF" Offset="1"/>
        </LinearGradientBrush>
        <Storyboard x:Name="SpinGameBallStoryboard" RepeatBehavior="Forever">
          <DoubleAnimationUsingKeyFrames BeginTime="00:00:00"
            Storyboard.TargetName="RadioactiveBall"
            Storyboard.TargetProperty="(UIElement.RenderTransform).(
            TransformGroup.Children)[2].(RotateTransform.Angle)">
          <SplineDoubleKeyFrame KeyTime="00:00:00" Value="0"/>
          <SplineDoubleKeyFrame KeyTime="00:00:02" Value="360">
            <SplineDoubleKeyFrame.KeySpline>
              <KeySpline ControlPoint1="0,0" ControlPoint2="1,1"/>
            </SplineDoubleKeyFrame.KeySpline>
          </SplineDoubleKeyFrame>
          </DoubleAnimationUsingKeyFrames>
        </Storyboard>
      </UserControl.Resources>
      <Canvas x:Name="GameCanvas" >
        <Canvas.Background>
          <RadialGradientBrush>
            <GradientStop Color="#FFFFFFFF"/>
            <GradientStop Color="#FFB3BBE8" Offset="1"/>
          </RadialGradientBrush>
        </Canvas.Background>
        <Border Background="{StaticResource MessageBorderBrush}" Height="Auto"
          x:Name="WelcomeMessage" Width="Auto" Canvas.Left="173" Canvas.Top="119"
          CornerRadius="10,10,10,10">
          <TextBlock Height="Auto" Width="Auto" FontFamily="Comic Sans MS"
           FontSize="24" Text="Welcome to Ice Cave!" TextWrapping="Wrap"
           Padding="2,2,2,2" Foreground="#FF044FB5"/>
        </Border>
        <Border x:Name="ClickToPlay" Height="Auto" Width="Auto" Canvas.Top="178"
          Canvas.Left="211" CornerRadius="10,10,10,10" Background=
          "{StaticResource MessageBorderBrush}" Margin="0,0,0,0" >
          <TextBlock Height="Auto" Width="150" FontSize="24" Text="Click to Play"
          TextWrapping="Wrap" MouseLeftButtonDown="TextBlock_MouseLeftButtonDown"
          Margin="4,4,4,4" Padding="2,2,2,2" Foreground="#FF044FB5" />
        </Border>
```

```xml
<Ellipse Height="50" Width="50" Canvas.Left="259" Canvas.Top="168.879"
  Stroke="#FF000000" Visibility="Collapsed" x:Name="RadioactiveBall"
  RenderTransformOrigin="0.5,0.5">
  <Ellipse.RenderTransform>
    <TransformGroup>
      <ScaleTransform/>
      <SkewTransform/>
      <RotateTransform/>
      <TranslateTransform/>
    </TransformGroup>
  </Ellipse.RenderTransform>
  <Ellipse.Fill>
    <LinearGradientBrush EndPoint="0.959999978542328,0.0219999998807907"
      StartPoint="0.0199999995529652,1.06200003623962">
      <GradientStop Color="#FFAED4B2"/>
      <GradientStop Color="#FFAED4B2" Offset="1"/>
      <GradientStop Color="#FF4A9B53" Offset="0.179"/>
      <GradientStop Color="#FF4A9B53" Offset="0.75"/>
      <GradientStop Color="#FF98BD9D" Offset="0.4869999885559082"/>
    </LinearGradientBrush>
  </Ellipse.Fill>
</Ellipse>
<Path Height="399" Width="25" Stretch="Fill" Stroke="#FF000000"
 Data="M0,0 L24……L0,398 z"
Canvas.Top="-0.5" Canvas.Left="-0.5"
Fill="{StaticResource IceBrush}" x:Name="LeftIceCaveWall"/>
<Path Height="30" Width="598" Canvas.Left="0.5" Canvas.Top="368.5"
 Fill="{StaticResource IceBrush}" Stretch="Fill" Stroke="#FF000000"
 Data="M1,397 L20… L598,398 z" x:Name="IceCaveWallFloor"/>
<Path Height="398" Width="40" Canvas.Left="558.5" Canvas.Top="-0.5"
 Fill="{StaticResource IceBrush}" Stretch="Fill" Stroke="#FF000000"
 Data="M598,397 L578….. L584,12 L597,0 z" x:Name="RightIceCaveWall"/>
<Path Height="53" Width="596" Canvas.Left="0.5" Canvas.Top="-0.5"
 Fill="{StaticResource IceBrush}" Stretch="Fill" Stroke="#FF000000"
 Data="M1,1 L21,19 L34,5….,19 L596,0 z" x:Name="IceCaveCeiling"/>
  </Canvas>
</UserControl>
```

3-16. Working with Ink

Problem

You want to let users draw directly on your Silverlight application in the web browser to allow image or video markup and handwriting recognition.

Solution

Use the InkPresenter control and associated events in your Silverlight 3 application to collect and process strokes. For handwriting recognition, use a Windows Communication Foundation (WCF) service to perform the handwriting recognition on the server side of the application and return the results to a Silverlight application.

How It Works

The term *stroke* when talking about ink refers to the process of putting a pen or stylus to a touch screen, moving it across the screen by either writing or making annotations, and then lifting it off the screen. Each stylus-down, move-across-the-screen, stylus-up cycle is an ink stroke. For computers that do not have a touch screen, clicking the mouse button, holding the mouse button down, moving across the screen, and then releasing the mouse button creates an ink stroke.

■**Note** Note that using a stylus on a tablet computer or digitizer results in much higher resolution than what a user achieves using a mouse, allowing for additional detail. Be sure to test your applications on a tablet PC as well as with a mouse on a desktop computer.

The InkPresenter object makes inking possible in an application. Ink strokes are stored as a collection that is part of the InkPresenter. If you drop an InkPresenter onto an application, run it, and try inking, nothing happens, because strokes are collected via the InkPresenter's events and methods.

Since .NET Framework 3.0, WPF provides great support for ink in desktop applications. Silverlight is a cross-browser, cross-platform programmatic subset of WPF, but one thing that WPF has that Silverlight does not is handwriting recognition. This is not a major limitation, because Silverlight is a web technology. Strokes can be sent back to the server for processing within a WCF service that makes the appropriate calls into the .NET Framework WPF assemblies to perform recognition and return the text to the Silverlight 3 application. This MSDN article provides an example of sending strokes to a server for handwriting-recognition processing:

http://msdn.microsoft.com/en-us/magazine/cc721604.aspx

InkPresenter is based on a Canvas object, but it is transparent by default and does not have a configurable Fill property. Therefore, InkPresenter is used in conjunction with other objects like Image, MediaElement, Canvas, and Border to provide a visible UI.

The Code

This recipe's sample code starts by expanding the size of the default Silverlight application to 800 × 600 and dividing the Grid into two rows and two columns. In Grid.Column 0 and Grid.Row 0, you place a Border with a simple gradient; place an InkPresenter inside the Border to provide an appearance of a drawing or writing surface.

As we mentioned earlier, you must use the events and methods of InkPresenter to process and collect strokes. The important events are MouseLeftButtonDown, MouseMove, and MouseLeftButtonUp. Here are the steps:

1. In MouseLeftButtonDown, create a new stroke, and add it to the InkPresenter's StrokeCollection.

2. In MouseMove, add StylusPoints to the newly added stroke as the mouse moves around.

3. In MouseLeftButtonUp, complete the newly added stroke.

Name the InkPresenter object InkEssentials and wire up handlers for the three events to the XAML in Visual Studio 2008:

```
<InkPresenter x:Name="InkEssentials" Background="Transparent"
  MouseLeftButtonDown="InkEssentials_MouseLeftButtonDown"
  MouseMove="InkEssentials_MouseMove" Height="Auto" Width="Auto"
  MouseLeftButtonUp="InkEssentials_MouseLeftButtonUp" />
```

■**Note** You *must* set the Background property on the InkPresenter to a value, any value, for the InkPresenter to receive mouse events and the ink functionality to work.

In the MainPage.Xaml.cs file, you implement the code to perform the three steps. In the MouseLeftButtonDown event, the sender is passed in as well as an event argument object of type MouseButtonEventArgs. The MouseButtonEventArgs object provides access to a copy of the stylus or mouse points generated as the mouse or stylus is moved across the screen via the e.StylusDevice.GetStylusPoints method.

The first step is to have the InkPresenter attempt to capture the mouse by calling CaptureMouse. That lets you respond to the MouseMove event and capture the generated stylus or mouse points as the mouse or stylus is moved across the screen:

```
private void InkEssentials_MouseLeftButtonDown(object sender,

MouseButtonEventArgs e)
{
  InkEssentials.CaptureMouse();
  _currentStroke = new System.Windows.Ink.Stroke();
  //Change color of the stroke and stroke outline
  _currentStroke.DrawingAttributes.Color = Colors.Orange;
  _currentStroke.DrawingAttributes.OutlineColor = Colors.Black;
  _currentStroke.StylusPoints.Add(
      e.StylusDevice.GetStylusPoints(InkEssentials));
  InkEssentials.Strokes.Add(_currentStroke);
}
```

In the MouseLeftButtonDown event, you copy the collected mouse or stylus points and add them to the current Stroke so that the Stroke can be drawn at the same points where the mouse or stylus moves, creating the effect of inking. As the mouse moves, you collect additional points in the MouseMove event:

```
private void InkEssentials_MouseMove(object sender, MouseEventArgs e)
{
  if (null != _currentStroke)
  {
    _currentStroke.StylusPoints.Add(
      e.StylusDevice.GetStylusPoints(InkEssentials));
  }
}

private void InkEssentials_MouseLeftButtonUp(object sender, MouseButtonEventArgs e)
{
  _currentStroke = null;
  InkEssentials.ReleaseMouseCapture();
}
```

When the user has finished inking or writing on the screen, they release the left mouse button, causing the MouseLeftButtonUp event to fire. When this event fires, you set the currentStroke variable to null because you have finished with that stroke. Because you are finished, you call ReleaseMouseCapture to stop collecting mouse or stylus point locations.

When you run the application, you can ink on the browser surface, as shown in Figure 3-58.

Figure 3-58. *Basic ink functionality in Silverlight 3*

Notice the orange ink with the black outline. The default is black ink, but when you create the stroke, you modify the DrawingAttributes in this code:

```
_currentStroke.DrawingAttributes.Color = Colors.Orange;
_currentStroke.DrawingAttributes.OutlineColor = Colors.Black;
```

Next, add another InkPresenter with an Image object behind it to provide a background. Write similar code to handle the MouseLeftButtonDown, MouseMove, and MouseLeftButtonUp events. Listings 3-18 and 3-19 show the code, and Figure 3-59 shows the output.

Figure 3-59. *InkPresenter with Image background*

Listing 3-18. *Recipe 3.16 MainPage.Xaml File*

```
<UserControl x:Class="Ch03_DesigningUX.Recipe3_16.MainPage"
    xmlns="http://schemas.microsoft.com/winfx/2006/xaml/presentation"
    xmlns:x="http://schemas.microsoft.com/winfx/2006/xaml"
    xmlns:d="http://schemas.microsoft.com/expression/blend/2008"
    xmlns:mc="http://schemas.openxmlformats.org/markup-compatibility/2006"
    Width="600" Height="800" mc:Ignorable="d">
    <Grid x:Name="LayoutRoot" Background="White">
      <Grid.RowDefinitions>
        <RowDefinition Height="0.502*"/>
        <RowDefinition Height="0.498*"/>
      </Grid.RowDefinitions>
      <Grid.ColumnDefinitions>
        <ColumnDefinition Width="0.5*"/>
        <ColumnDefinition Width="0.5*"/>
      </Grid.ColumnDefinitions>
```

```xml
      <Border Margin="4,4,4,4" CornerRadius="10,10,10,10" Padding="0,0,0,0" >
        <Border.Background>
          <LinearGradientBrush EndPoint="0.5,1" StartPoint="0.5,0">
            <GradientStop Color="#FF767373" Offset="0.004"/>
            <GradientStop Color="#FF1A1818" Offset="1"/>
            <GradientStop Color="#FF888686" Offset="0.473"/>
          </LinearGradientBrush>
        </Border.Background>
        <InkPresenter x:Name="InkEssentials" Background="Transparent"
          MouseLeftButtonDown="InkEssentials_MouseLeftButtonDown"
          MouseMove="InkEssentials_MouseMove" Height="Auto" Width="Auto"
          MouseLeftButtonUp="InkEssentials_MouseLeftButtonUp" />
      </Border>
      <Image Margin="4,4,4,4" Grid.Column="1" x:Name="Picture"
       Source="/img/VerticalLandscape.jpg"/>
      <InkPresenter Margin="4,4,4,4" Grid.Column="1" x:Name="InkPicture"
          MouseLeftButtonDown="InkPicture_MouseLeftButtonDown"
          MouseMove="InkPicture_MouseMove" Background="Transparent"
          MouseLeftButtonUp="InkPicture_MouseLeftButtonUp"/>
    </Grid>
</UserControl>
```

Listing 3-19. *Recipe 3.16 MainPage.Xaml.cs Class File*

```csharp
using System.IO.IsolatedStorage;
using System.Windows.Controls;
using System.Windows.Input;
using System.Windows.Media;
namespace Ch03_DesigningUX.Recipe3_16
{
  public partial class MainPage : UserControl
  {
    private System.Windows.Ink.Stroke _currentStroke;
    private System.Windows.Ink.Stroke _currentImageStroke;

    private IsolatedStorageSettings settings =
            IsolatedStorageSettings.ApplicationSettings;
    private string setting = "Ink";
    private string FormDataFileName = "ImageInk.data";
    private string FormDataDirectory = "InkData";
```

```csharp
public MainPage()
{
  InitializeComponent();
}
private void InkEssentials_MouseLeftButtonDown(object sender,
MouseButtonEventArgs e)
{
  InkEssentials.CaptureMouse();
  _currentStroke = new System.Windows.Ink.Stroke();
  //Change color of the stroke and stroke outline
  _currentStroke.DrawingAttributes.Color = Colors.Orange;
  _currentStroke.DrawingAttributes.OutlineColor = Colors.Black;
  _currentStroke.StylusPoints.Add(
      e.StylusDevice.GetStylusPoints(InkEssentials));
  InkEssentials.Strokes.Add(_currentStroke);
}

private void InkEssentials_MouseMove(object sender, MouseEventArgs e)
{
  if (null != _currentStroke)
  {
    _currentStroke.StylusPoints.Add(
        e.StylusDevice.GetStylusPoints(InkEssentials));
  }
}

private void InkEssentials_MouseLeftButtonUp(object sender,
MouseButtonEventArgs e)
{
  _currentStroke = null;
  InkEssentials.ReleaseMouseCapture();
}

private void InkPicture_MouseLeftButtonDown(object sender,
MouseButtonEventArgs e)
{
  InkPicture.CaptureMouse();
  _currentImageStroke = new System.Windows.Ink.Stroke();
  _currentImageStroke.StylusPoints.Add(
      e.StylusDevice.GetStylusPoints(InkPicture));
  InkPicture.Strokes.Add(_currentImageStroke);
}
```

```
    private void InkPicture_MouseMove(object sender, MouseEventArgs e)
    {
      if (null != _currentImageStroke)
      {
        _currentImageStroke.StylusPoints.Add(
          e.StylusDevice.GetStylusPoints(InkPicture));
      }
    }

    private void InkPicture_MouseLeftButtonUp(object sender, MouseButtonEventArgs e)
    {
      _currentImageStroke = null;
      InkPicture.ReleaseMouseCapture();
    }
  }
}
```

3-17. Adding 3-D Effects to UI Elements

Problem

You want to add three-dimensional effects to UI elements in your Silverlight application.

Solution

Use the new perspective transforms feature in Silverlight 3 to simulate displaying and moving UI elements in 3-D space.

How It Works

WPF has full support for 3-D graphics as well as perspective transforms to simulate 3-D effects. Silverlight 3 adds support for perspective transforms, which more easily let Silverlight developers simulate moving objects in 3-D effects.

■**Note** Silverlight 3 does not support true 3-D graphics like WPF or DirectX. However, with perspective transforms, you can achieve some very interesting effects.

The UIElement base class adds a property named Projection that is of type System.Windows. Media.Projection, which is an abstract base class. This property sets the perspective projection to apply when rendering the UIElement or descendent object. The Projection base class has two descendents that can be assigned to the UIElement.Projection property: Matrix3DProjection and PlaneProjection.

Matrix3DProjection is a wrapper class around a Matrix3D class. The Matrix3D class represents a 4 x 4 matrix. It can be used to create a standard Translate, Scale, Rotate, or Perspective matrix for transformations in 3-D space and should be familiar to game developers or anyone who programs software in 3-D space.

For more information about creating and working with 3-D matrixes, please refer to the DirectX documentation or a book that covers 3-D development:

http://msdn.microsoft.com/en-us/directx/default.aspx

The Matrix3DProjection class provides a way to apply an arbitrary 3-D matrix to a UIElement, allowing you to create highly customized transformations. The Matrix3DProjection has a minimal API, so you must write the code that correctly creates the necessary 3D transforms to achieve the desired affect.

If you do not need to support customized 3-D matrices, you can still easily apply 3-D effects via the PlaneProjection class. With the PlaneProjection class, you can create the illusion that an object is rotating toward or away from the user. The PlaneProjection object can be used to apply a static transformation to skew an object in 3-D. You can use this method to create a UI where objects appear to be stacked in 3-D space by applying unique PlaneProjection values. Combining the PlaneProjection class with Storyboard object lets you animate properties of the PlaneProjection class to create the illusion that a UIElement is moving through 3-D space.

The Code

In this recipe, you take advantage of the new Silverlight 3 Navigation Application template to create a couple of examples to help you better understand how to work with projections and perspective transforms.

The first example, shown in Figure 3-60, allows the user to apply rotation to the picture with a slider for the X, Y, and Z planes.

Notice that the values displayed for the amount of rotation in the X, Y, and Z planes are three-digit integers. Originally, the values were a one, two, or three-digit number on the left side of the decimal and a large number of digits to the right of the decimal point. Because the decimal values are not important, we wrote a simple value converter to truncate the decimal values and force it to display a three-digit integer. Listing 3-20 has the value converter source code.

Listing 3-20. *Recipe 3.17 DecimalFormatConverter.cs Code File*

```
using System;
using System.Windows.Data;

namespace Ch03_DevelopingUX.Recipe3_17.Converters
{
  public class DecimalFormatConverter : IValueConverter
  {
    public object Convert(object value, Type targetType,
      object parameter,System.Globalization.CultureInfo culture)
    {
      return String.Format(culture, "{0:000}", value);
    }
```

```
    public object ConvertBack(object value, Type targetType,
      object parameter, System.Globalization.CultureInfo culture)
    {
      throw new NotImplementedException();
    }
  }
}
```

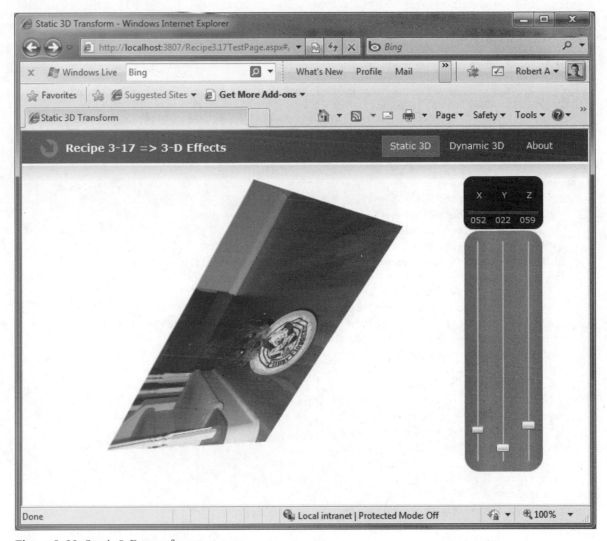

Figure 3-60. *Static 3-D transform test page*

To apply the value converter, specify it in the TextBlock element binding:

```
<TextBlock Margin="5,0,5,0" Text="{Binding Value,
ElementName=XaxisSlider,
Converter={StaticResource DecimalFormatConverter}}">
```

It is made available in the page as a StaticResource:

```
<FormatDecimal:DecimalFormatConverter
 x:Key="DecimalFormatConverter"/>
```

The FormatDecimal namespace is brought in here:

```
xmlns:FormatDecimal="clr-namespace:
Ch03_DevelopingUX.Recipe3_17.Converters"
```

You apply the slider values programmatically in the code-behind file because it is not possible to databind elements directly with the PlaneProjection's RotationX, RotationY, and RotationZ properties. The reason is that these are not DependencyProperties but are instead simple .NET properties. Listing 3-21 shows the Static3DTransform XAML file.

Listing 3-21. *Recipe 3.17 Static3DTransform.Xaml File*

```
<navigation:Page
x:Class="Ch03_DevelopingUX.Recipe3_17.Static3DTransform"
    xmlns="http://schemas.microsoft.com/winfx/2006/xaml/presentation"
    xmlns:x="http://schemas.microsoft.com/winfx/2006/xaml"
    xmlns:d="http://schemas.microsoft.com/expression/blend/2008"
    xmlns:mc="http://schemas.openxmlformats.org/markup-compatibility/2006"
    xmlns:navigation=
      "clr-namespace:System.Windows.Controls;assembly=
          System.Windows.Controls.Navigation"
    xmlns:FormatDecimal="clr-namespace:Ch03_DevelopingUX.Recipe3_17.Converters"
    mc:Ignorable="d" d:DesignWidth="640" d:DesignHeight="480"
    Title="Static 3D Transform"
    Style="{StaticResource PageStyle}">
  <navigation:Page.Resources>
    <Color x:Key="CustomGreen">#FFADFA97</Color>
    <FormatDecimal:DecimalFormatConverter
       x:Key="DecimalFormatConverter"/>
  </navigation:Page.Resources>

  <Grid x:Name="LayoutRoot">
    <Grid.ColumnDefinitions>
      <ColumnDefinition Width="0.831*"/>
      <ColumnDefinition Width="0.169*"/>
    </Grid.ColumnDefinitions>
```

```xml
        <Image HorizontalAlignment="Left"
          VerticalAlignment="Top" Margin="60"
          Source="/Ch03_DevelopingUX.Recipe3_17;Component/Assets/image.jpg"
          MaxWidth="452" MaxHeight="339" Width="400">
          <Image.Projection>
            <PlaneProjection x:Name="ImageRotation"/>
          </Image.Projection>
        </Image>
    <StackPanel Grid.Column="1"  Orientation="Vertical">
      <Border Background="#FF1A1A1A" CornerRadius="12" Width="106">
        <StackPanel Margin="4" >
        <StackPanel Orientation="Horizontal">
        <TextBlock Text="X" Margin="13">
          <TextBlock.Foreground>
            <SolidColorBrush Color=
                      "{StaticResource CustomGreen}"/>
          </TextBlock.Foreground>
        </TextBlock>
        <TextBlock Text="Y" Margin="13">
          <TextBlock.Foreground>
            <SolidColorBrush Color="
                      {StaticResource CustomGreen}"/>
          </TextBlock.Foreground>
        </TextBlock>
        <TextBlock Text="Z" Margin="13">
          <TextBlock.Foreground>
            <SolidColorBrush Color=
                      "{StaticResource CustomGreen}"/>
          </TextBlock.Foreground>
        </TextBlock>
      </StackPanel>
      <Rectangle Height="4" Fill="#FFD21416" Margin="2,0"></Rectangle>
      <StackPanel Orientation="Horizontal">
          <TextBlock Margin="5,0,5,0" Text=
               "{Binding Value, ElementName=XaxisSlider,
               Converter={StaticResource DecimalFormatConverter}}">
            <TextBlock.Foreground>
              <SolidColorBrush Color=
                        "{StaticResource CustomGreen}"/>
            </TextBlock.Foreground>
          </TextBlock>
```

```xml
    <TextBlock Margin="7,0,5,0" Text=
           "{Binding Value, ElementName=YaxisSlider,
           Converter={StaticResource DecimalFormatConverter}}">
        <TextBlock.Foreground>
          <SolidColorBrush Color=
                       "{StaticResource CustomGreen}"/>
        </TextBlock.Foreground>
      </TextBlock>
    <TextBlock Margin="7,0,5,0" Text=
           "{Binding Value, ElementName=ZaxisSlider, Converter=
           {StaticResource DecimalFormatConverter}}">
      <TextBlock.Foreground>
        <SolidColorBrush Color=
                       "{StaticResource CustomGreen}"/>
      </TextBlock.Foreground>
    </TextBlock>
    </StackPanel>
    </StackPanel>
    </Border>
<Border CornerRadius="20" Margin="2" MinHeight="320" Width="104">
<Border.Background>
      <LinearGradientBrush EndPoint="-1.038,0.5"
           StartPoint="2.038,0.5">
        <GradientStop Color="#FF7AC367" Offset="0.403"/>
        <GradientStop Color="#FF7AC367" Offset="0.562"/>
        <GradientStop Color="#FF44B324" Offset="0.313"/>
        <GradientStop Offset="0.665" Color="#FF44B324">
        </GradientStop>
        <GradientStop Color="#FF73B962" Offset="0.472"/>
      </LinearGradientBrush>
    </Border.Background>
    <StackPanel Orientation="Horizontal" >
      <Slider x:Name="XaxisSlider" HorizontalAlignment="Left"
       Margin="8"
       Orientation="Vertical" Maximum="360" LargeChange="18"
     ValueChanged="XaxisSlider_ValueChanged" SmallChange="1" />
      <Slider x:Name="YaxisSlider" HorizontalAlignment="Left"
       Margin="8"
      Orientation="Vertical" Maximum="360" LargeChange="18"
      ValueChanged="YaxisSlider_ValueChanged" SmallChange="1"/>
      <Slider x:Name="ZaxisSlider" HorizontalAlignment="Left"
       Margin="8"
```

```
          Orientation="Vertical" Maximum="360" LargeChange="18"
          ValueChanged="ZaxisSlider_ValueChanged" SmallChange="1"/>
        </StackPanel>
      </Border>
      </StackPanel>
    </Grid>
</navigation:Page>
```

Listing 3-22 contains the Static3DTransform XAML code file.

Listing 3-22. *Recipe 3.17 Static3DTransform.Xaml.cs Code File*

```csharp
using System.Windows;
using System.Windows.Controls;
using System.Windows.Navigation;

namespace Ch03_DevelopingUX.Recipe3_17
{
  public partial class Static3DTransform : Page
  {
    public Static3DTransform()
    {
      InitializeComponent();
    }
    // Executes when the user navigates to this page.
    protected override void OnNavigatedTo(NavigationEventArgs e)
    {
    }
    private void XaxisSlider_ValueChanged(object sender,
      RoutedPropertyChangedEventArgs<double> e)
    {
      ImageRotation.RotationX = e.NewValue;
    }
    private void YaxisSlider_ValueChanged(object sender,
      RoutedPropertyChangedEventArgs<double> e)
    {
      ImageRotation.RotationY = e.NewValue;
    }
    private void ZaxisSlider_ValueChanged(object sender,
      RoutedPropertyChangedEventArgs<double> e)
    {
      ImageRotation.RotationZ = e.NewValue;
    }
  }
}
```

The other example in this recipe demonstrates dynamic 3-D transformations using a Storyboard that projects two images rotating in 3-D space. Figure 3-61 shows the UI that lets you start an animation that rotates two images in 3-D space.

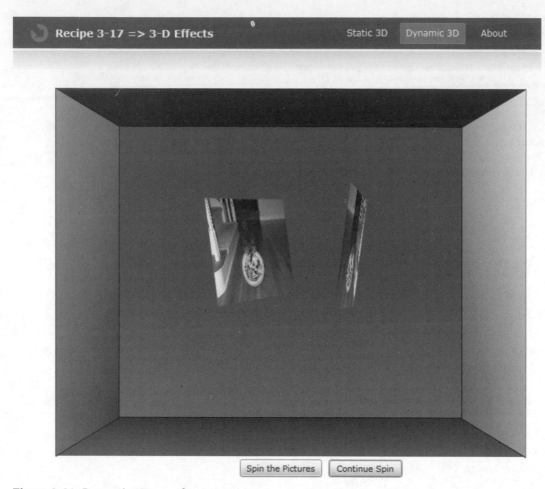

Figure 3-61. *Dynamic 3D transform test page*

The only code is for the buttons to control the storyboard. All the movement is contained in a Storyboard that animates over the RotationY, RotationZ, and Global Offset X and Y values.

The first example demonstrated how RotationY and RotationZ parameters. The Global Offset X and Y values control how the object appears as it is offset along the X, Y, and Z axes in 3-D space.

■**Note**   X values increase from left to right. Y values increase from top to bottom. Z axis values increase toward the user and decrease as an object moves further away.

To create the Storyboard in Expression Blend, orient the pictures opposite each other with a slight decline, using the RotationY and RotationZ properties to make the objects appear to face each other. The objects are not visible initially because they have a (+/-) 90-degree RotationY value, depending on the object.

Create the Storyboard time line with four keyframes 1 second apart, for a total of 4 seconds of rotation. The first and last keyframes have the same values to force the picture back to its original position. The other three keyframes change RotationY in 90-degree increments to give the appearance of revolving around a center point but always facing the center. RotationZ changes from 10 to 0 to emphasize the object either being closer or further away on the Z axis.

The other properties animated are the Global Offset X and Z values, because you want the pictures to move along a constant Y value (rotate left and right) while appearing closer when at the front and further away when at the back. You wrap the whole animation in a 3-D–looking room and use gradients to simulate depth. Listing 3-23 shows the Dynamic3DTransform XAML file. We do not show the code file because it is simple Storyboard start and stop code.

Listing 3-22. *Recipe 3.17 Dynamic3DTransform.Xaml File*

```
<navigation:Page
x:Class="Ch03_DevelopingUX.Recipe3_17.Dynamic3DTransform"
    xmlns="http://schemas.microsoft.com/winfx/2006/xaml/presentation"
    xmlns:x="http://schemas.microsoft.com/winfx/2006/xaml"
    xmlns:d="http://schemas.microsoft.com/expression/blend/2008"
    xmlns:mc="http://schemas.openxmlformats.org/markup-compatibility/2006"
    xmlns:navigation="clr-
namespace:System.Windows.Controls;assembly=System.Windows.Controls.Navigation"
    mc:Ignorable="d" d:DesignWidth="640" d:DesignHeight="550"
    Title="Dynamic 3D Transform"
    Style="{StaticResource PageStyle}">
  <navigation:Page.Resources>
    <Storyboard x:Name="Spin3DStoryboard">
      <DoubleAnimationUsingKeyFrames BeginTime="00:00:00"
        Storyboard.TargetName="image"
        Storyboard.TargetProperty=
        "(UIElement.Projection).(PlaneProjection.RotationZ)">
        <EasingDoubleKeyFrame KeyTime="00:00:00" Value="10"/>
        <EasingDoubleKeyFrame KeyTime="00:00:01" Value="0"/>
        <EasingDoubleKeyFrame KeyTime="00:00:02" Value="-10"/>
        <EasingDoubleKeyFrame KeyTime="00:00:03" Value="0"/>
        <EasingDoubleKeyFrame KeyTime="00:00:04" Value="10"/>
      </DoubleAnimationUsingKeyFrames>
      <DoubleAnimationUsingKeyFrames BeginTime="00:00:00"
        Storyboard.TargetName="image"
        Storyboard.TargetProperty=
        "(UIElement.Projection).(PlaneProjection.RotationY)">
        <EasingDoubleKeyFrame KeyTime="00:00:00" Value="-90"/>
        <EasingDoubleKeyFrame KeyTime="00:00:01" Value="-180"/>
```

```
    <EasingDoubleKeyFrame KeyTime="00:00:02" Value="-270"/>
    <EasingDoubleKeyFrame KeyTime="00:00:03" Value="-360"/>
    <EasingDoubleKeyFrame KeyTime="00:00:04" Value="-270"/>
</DoubleAnimationUsingKeyFrames>
<DoubleAnimationUsingKeyFrames BeginTime="00:00:00"
  Storyboard.TargetName="image"
  Storyboard.TargetProperty=
  "(UIElement.Projection).(PlaneProjection.GlobalOffsetX)">
    <EasingDoubleKeyFrame KeyTime="00:00:00" Value="0"/>
    <EasingDoubleKeyFrame KeyTime="00:00:01" Value="150"/>
    <EasingDoubleKeyFrame KeyTime="00:00:02" Value="300"/>
    <EasingDoubleKeyFrame KeyTime="00:00:03" Value="150"/>
    <EasingDoubleKeyFrame KeyTime="00:00:04" Value="0"/>
</DoubleAnimationUsingKeyFrames>
<DoubleAnimationUsingKeyFrames BeginTime="00:00:00"
  Storyboard.TargetName="image"
  Storyboard.TargetProperty=
  "(UIElement.Projection).(PlaneProjection.GlobalOffsetZ)">
    <EasingDoubleKeyFrame KeyTime="00:00:00" Value="0"/>
    <EasingDoubleKeyFrame KeyTime="00:00:01" Value="300"/>
    <EasingDoubleKeyFrame KeyTime="00:00:02" Value="0"/>
    <EasingDoubleKeyFrame KeyTime="00:00:03" Value="-300"/>
    <EasingDoubleKeyFrame KeyTime="00:00:04" Value="0"/>
</DoubleAnimationUsingKeyFrames>
<DoubleAnimationUsingKeyFrames BeginTime="00:00:00"
  Storyboard.TargetName="image1"
  Storyboard.TargetProperty=
  "(UIElement.Projection).(PlaneProjection.RotationZ)">
    <EasingDoubleKeyFrame KeyTime="00:00:02" Value="10"/>
    <EasingDoubleKeyFrame KeyTime="00:00:03" Value="0"/>
    <EasingDoubleKeyFrame KeyTime="00:00:04" Value="-10"/>
</DoubleAnimationUsingKeyFrames>
<DoubleAnimationUsingKeyFrames BeginTime="00:00:00"
  Storyboard.TargetName="image1"
  Storyboard.TargetProperty=
  "(UIElement.Projection).(PlaneProjection.RotationY)">
    <EasingDoubleKeyFrame KeyTime="00:00:00" Value="90"/>
    <EasingDoubleKeyFrame KeyTime="00:00:01" Value="0"/>
    <EasingDoubleKeyFrame KeyTime="00:00:02" Value="-90"/>
    <EasingDoubleKeyFrame KeyTime="00:00:03" Value="-180"/>
    <EasingDoubleKeyFrame KeyTime="00:00:04" Value="-270"/>
</DoubleAnimationUsingKeyFrames>
```

```xml
        <DoubleAnimationUsingKeyFrames BeginTime="00:00:00"
          Storyboard.TargetName="image1"
          Storyboard.TargetProperty=
          "(UIElement.Projection).(PlaneProjection.GlobalOffsetX)">
          <EasingDoubleKeyFrame KeyTime="00:00:02" Value="-300"/>
          <EasingDoubleKeyFrame KeyTime="00:00:03" Value="-150"/>
          <EasingDoubleKeyFrame KeyTime="00:00:04" Value="0"/>
        </DoubleAnimationUsingKeyFrames>
        <DoubleAnimationUsingKeyFrames BeginTime="00:00:00"
          Storyboard.TargetName="image1"
          Storyboard.TargetProperty=
          "(UIElement.Projection).(PlaneProjection.GlobalOffsetZ)">
          <EasingDoubleKeyFrame KeyTime="00:00:00" Value="0"/>
          <EasingDoubleKeyFrame KeyTime="00:00:01" Value="-300"/>
          <EasingDoubleKeyFrame KeyTime="00:00:02" Value="0"/>
          <EasingDoubleKeyFrame KeyTime="00:00:03" Value="300"/>
          <EasingDoubleKeyFrame KeyTime="00:00:04" Value="0"/>
        </DoubleAnimationUsingKeyFrames>
      </Storyboard>
    </navigation:Page.Resources>
    <Grid x:Name="LayoutRoot">
      <Canvas Width="640" Height="480">
        <Canvas.Background>
          <LinearGradientBrush EndPoint="0.505,-0.257" StartPoint="0.509,1.345">
            <GradientStop Color="Black" Offset="0.352"/>
            <GradientStop Color="#FF575555" Offset="1"/>
            <GradientStop Color="White" Offset="0"/>
            <GradientStop Color="#FF161515" Offset="0.79"/>
          </LinearGradientBrush>
        </Canvas.Background>
        <Rectangle Stroke="Black" Height="425" Width="250"
         Canvas.Left="-76" Canvas.Top="28">
          <Rectangle.Projection>
            <PlaneProjection RotationY="-70"/>
          </Rectangle.Projection>
          <Rectangle.Fill>
            <LinearGradientBrush EndPoint="-0.25,0.263" StartPoint="1.25,0.737">
              <GradientStop Color="#FF066100" Offset="0"/>
              <GradientStop Color="#FF89B886" Offset="1"/>
              <GradientStop Color="#FF33992C" Offset="0.494"/>
            </LinearGradientBrush>
          </Rectangle.Fill>
        </Rectangle>
```

```xml
    <Rectangle Stroke="Black" Height="380" Width="467"
     Canvas.Left="87" Canvas.Top="50">
      <Rectangle.Fill>
        <LinearGradientBrush EndPoint="0.5,1" StartPoint="0.5,0">
          <GradientStop Color="#F2805300" Offset="0"/>
          <GradientStop Color="#FF9D701E" Offset="1"/>
          <GradientStop Color="#F2805300" Offset="0.464"/>
        </LinearGradientBrush>
      </Rectangle.Fill>
    </Rectangle>
    <Rectangle Stroke="Black" Height="425" Width="250"
     Canvas.Left="467" Canvas.Top="28">
      <Rectangle.Projection>
        <PlaneProjection RotationY="70"/>
      </Rectangle.Projection>
      <Rectangle.Fill>
        <LinearGradientBrush EndPoint="1.243,0.257" StartPoint="-0.243,0.743">
          <GradientStop Color="#E5FF4700" Offset="0"/>
          <GradientStop Color="#FFF6EDEA" Offset="1"/>
        </LinearGradientBrush>
      </Rectangle.Fill>
    </Rectangle>
    <Image x:Name="image" HorizontalAlignment="Left" VerticalAlignment="Top"
     Margin="26,141,0,0" Height="140" Width="187"
     Source="/Ch03_DevelopingUX.Recipe3_17;Component/Assets/image.jpg"
     d:LayoutOverrides="HorizontalAlignment">
      <Image.Projection>
        <PlaneProjection x:Name="ImageRotation" RotationY="-90" RotationZ="10"/>
      </Image.Projection>
    </Image>
    <Image x:Name="image1" HorizontalAlignment="Left"
      Source="../Assets/image.jpg" Width="187" Margin="420,140,0,0" Height="140">
      <Image.Projection>
        <PlaneProjection x:Name="ImageRotation1" RotationY="90" RotationZ="-10"/>
      </Image.Projection>
    </Image>
  </Canvas>
  <Button x:Name="btnSpinPictures" Height="23" Margin="251,0,0,6"
   VerticalAlignment="Bottom" Content="Spin the Pictures"
   Click="btnSpinPictures_Click" Width="112" HorizontalAlignment="Left"/>
  <Button x:Name="btnPauseContinuePictures" Height="23" Margin="0,0,130,6"
   VerticalAlignment="Bottom" Content="Pause Spin" HorizontalAlignment="Right"
   Click="btnPauseContinuePictures_Click" Visibility="Collapsed" Width="100"/>
  </Grid>
</navigation:Page>
```

We do not cover `MainPage.xaml` or `MainPage.xaml.cs` because they wire up the navigation application template, which we cover in Chapter 6.

3-18. Dynamically Creating Bitmaps

Problem

You need to create bitmap images directly at runtime in your Silverlight application.

Solution

Use the new `WriteableBitmap` object in Silverlight 3 to create bitmap images at runtime.

How It Works

Silverlight 2 does not have the ability to create bitmaps at runtime. With Silverlight 3, you can use the `WriteableBitmap` class to create a new bitmap image in custom code or from other elements in the UI. To use the `WriteableBitmap` class, include the `System.Windows.Media.Imaging` namespace.

To create a custom bitmap from an element in the UI, you can use this constructor:

```
WriteableBitmap bmp = new WriteableBitmap(LayoutRoot, null);
```

`LayoutRoot` is the default name of the root `Grid` control in a new Silverlight application, so any UI elements contained in `LayoutRoot` are included in the created bitmap image. You specify `null` for the `Transform` to be applied to the image; however, you can specify a `Transform` that is applied as the last part of the operation, meaning the bitmap is created and then the `Transform` is applied. As an example, you can apply a transform that creates a reflection of the UI element from which the bitmap is created.

The other constructors available for `WriteableBitmap` take either a `BitmapSource` object or height and width values as a place holder for content that is created. The `BitmapSource` class is an abstract class, so the object to work with is the `BitmapImage` class. You can load a JPEG or PNG image into a `BitmapImage` by URI or using a stream.

The other `WriteableBitmap` constructor takes a height and width, which are used to generate the appropriate-sized `Pixels` property that points to an array of integers representing the image. With this constructor, you have a blank slate of pixels on which you can set values to create an image for more direct image control.

Initially in the Silverlight 3 beta, you could not directly set values on `Pixels`. Instead, you had to generate animations in UI elements and then create a `WriteableBitmap` from the UI elements. Because a few examples on the Web demonstrate how to use UI Elements, we focus on creating bitmaps by updating the `Pixels` property.

The Code

The example for this recipe imports a PNG or JPEG image into the application. It gives the user an option to add a watermark to the image and then save the image in a custom format. The user can clear the image and then reload the saved image with the watermark. Figure 3-62 shows the UI after importing an image.

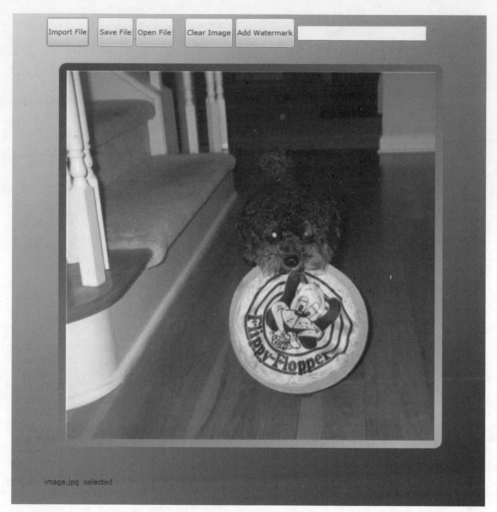

Figure 3-62. *The sample UI after importing an image*

Figure 3-63 shows the UI after adding a watermark to the image; it says, "Silverlight 3 is Great!!!"

Figure 3-63. *The sample UI after importing an image*

Listing 3-23 shows the XAML file.

Listing 3-23. *Recipe 3.18 MainPage.Xaml File*

```
<UserControl x:Class="Ch03_DevelopingUX.Recipe3_18.MainPage"
    xmlns="http://schemas.microsoft.com/winfx/2006/xaml/presentation"
    xmlns:x="http://schemas.microsoft.com/winfx/2006/xaml"
    xmlns:d="http://schemas.microsoft.com/expression/blend/2008"
    xmlns:mc="http://schemas.openxmlformats.org/
      markup-compatibility/2006" mc:Ignorable="d"
    >
```

```
<Grid x:Name="LayoutRoot">
  <Grid.Background>
    <LinearGradientBrush EndPoint="-0.131,-0.123" StartPoint="1.215,1.232">
      <GradientStop Color="#FF000000"/>
      <GradientStop Color="#FFFFFFFF" Offset="1"/>
    </LinearGradientBrush>
  </Grid.Background>
  <Grid.RowDefinitions>
    <RowDefinition Height="0.075*"/>
    <RowDefinition Height="0.832*"/>
    <RowDefinition Height="0.093*"/>
  </Grid.RowDefinitions>
  <Grid.ColumnDefinitions>
    <ColumnDefinition Width="0.059*"/>
    <ColumnDefinition Width="0.890*"/>
    <ColumnDefinition Width="0.051*"/>
  </Grid.ColumnDefinitions>
  <TextBlock Margin="8,4" Grid.Column="1" Grid.Row="2" Text="Status"
   TextWrapping="Wrap" x:Name="StatusLabel" VerticalAlignment="Center"/>
  <Border Grid.Column="1" Grid.Row="1" Margin="8" CornerRadius="12"
   x:Name="ImageContainer" Width="600" Height="600">
    <Border.Background>
      <LinearGradientBrush EndPoint="0.035,-0.031" StartPoint="1.649,2.131">
        <GradientStop Color="#FF1D351E"/>
        <GradientStop Color="#FF1D351E" Offset="1"/>
        <GradientStop Color="#FFB7D8BA" Offset="0.50900000333786011"/>
      </LinearGradientBrush>
    </Border.Background>
    <Grid>
      <Image x:Name="ImageContent" Stretch="UniformToFill"  Margin="12"/>
      <TextBlock TextWrapping="Wrap" Margin="8" RenderTransformOrigin="0.5,0.5"
       FontSize="16" FontWeight="Bold" Foreground="#FF000BFF"
       x:Name="txtBlockWatermark" Text="Silverlight 3 Rocks!!!!"
       TextAlignment="Center" d:LayoutOverrides="GridBox"
       VerticalAlignment="Bottom" Visibility="Collapsed"/>
    </Grid>
  </Border>
  <StackPanel Margin="8,4" Grid.Column="1" Orientation="Horizontal">
    <Button Margin="2,2,6,2" Content="Import File" x:Name="ButtonImportFiles"
     Click="ButtonImportFile_Click"/>
    <Button x:Name="btnSaveCustomFile"  Click="btnSaveCustomFile_Click"
      Content="Save File" Margin="8,2,2,2"/>
    <Button x:Name="btnOpenCustomFile"  Click="btnOpenCustomFile_Click"
      Content="Open File" Margin="2"/>
```

```
    <Button x:Name="btnClearImage"
      Content="Clear Image" Margin="16,2,2,2" Click="btnClearImage_Click"/>
    <Button x:Name="btnAddWatermark"
      Content="Add Watermark" Margin="2" Click="btnAddWatermark_Click"/>
    <TextBox x:Name="textWatermark" Margin="2" Width="202"
     HorizontalContentAlignment="Left" Height="24"/>
  </StackPanel>
 </Grid>
</UserControl>
```

Listing 3-24 shows the code-behind, which we cover next.

Listing 3-24. *Recipe 3.18 MainPage.Xaml.cs File*

```
using System;
using System.IO;
using System.Linq;
using System.Windows;
using System.Windows.Controls;
using System.Windows.Media;
using System.Windows.Media.Imaging;

namespace Ch03_DevelopingUX.Recipe3_18
{
  public partial class MainPage : UserControl
  {
    public MainPage()
    {
      InitializeComponent();
    }

    private void ButtonImportFile_Click(object sender, RoutedEventArgs e)
    {
      txtBlockWatermark.Visibility = Visibility.Collapsed;
      //Create dialog
      OpenFileDialog fileDlg = new OpenFileDialog();
      //Set file filter as desired
      fileDlg.Filter = "Png Files (*.png)|*.png|Jpeg Files (*.jpg)|*.jpg";
      fileDlg.FilterIndex = 1;
      //Allow multiple files to be selected (false by default)
      fileDlg.Multiselect = false;
```

```
//Show Open File Dialog
    BitmapImage img = new BitmapImage();
    if (true == fileDlg.ShowDialog())
    {
      StatusLabel.Text =
          fileDlg.File.Name + "  selected";
      using (FileStream reader = fileDlg.File.OpenRead())
      {
        img.SetSource(reader);
      }
      ImageContent.Source = img;
    }
  }

  private void btnSaveCustomFile_Click(object sender, RoutedEventArgs e)
  {
    SaveFileDialog sfd = new SaveFileDialog();
    sfd.Filter = "sl3 Files (*.sl3)|*.sl3";
    sfd.FilterIndex = 1;

    WriteableBitmap bmp = new WriteableBitmap(ImageContainer, null);

    if (true == sfd.ShowDialog())
    {
      byte[] flattend = null;
      flattend = bmp.Pixels.SelectMany((p)=>BitConverter.GetBytes(p)).ToArray();
      using (Stream fs = sfd.OpenFile())
      {
        fs.Write(flattend, 0, flattend.Length);
        fs.Flush();
        fs.Close();
      }
    }
  }

  private void btnOpenCustomFile_Click(object sender, RoutedEventArgs e)
  {
    txtBlockWatermark.Visibility = Visibility.Collapsed;
    OpenFileDialog fileDlg = new OpenFileDialog();
    fileDlg.Filter = "sl3 Files (*.sl3)|*.sl3";
    fileDlg.FilterIndex = 1;
    fileDlg.Multiselect = false;
```

```
      if (true == fileDlg.ShowDialog())
      {
        StatusLabel.Text =
            fileDlg.File.Name + "  selected";
        using (FileStream reader = fileDlg.File.OpenRead())
        {
          WriteableBitmap wrtBmp = null;
          wrtBmp = new WriteableBitmap(ImageContainer, null);
          byte[] fourBytes = new byte[4];

          int byteCounter = 0;
          int intCounter = 0;

          while (byteCounter < reader.Length - 1)
          {
            reader.Read(fourBytes,0, 4);
            wrtBmp.Pixels[intCounter] = BitConverter.ToInt32(fourBytes, 0);
            intCounter++;
            byteCounter += 4;
          }
          ImageContent.Source = wrtBmp;
        }
      }
    }
    private void btnClearImage_Click(object sender, RoutedEventArgs e)
    {
      txtBlockWatermark.Visibility = Visibility.Collapsed;
      txtBlockWatermark.Text = "";
      ImageContent.Source = null;
    }

    private void btnAddWatermark_Click(object sender, RoutedEventArgs e)
    {
      txtBlockWatermark.Visibility = Visibility.Visible;
      txtBlockWatermark.Text = textWatermark.Text;
    }
  }
}
```

The ButtonImportFile_Click event handler that imports an image uses the OpenFileDialog to let a user browse to a file. After a file is chosen, it is loaded into an image using a FileStream object with this code:

```
img.SetSource(reader);
```

The btnSaveCustomFile_Click event handler uses the new SaveFileDialog to allow the user to save the file outside of isolated storage in their file system. We cover the SaveFileDialog in Recipe 2-18. When you have a location to save the file, you can use a stream to save the bitmap bits stored in the WritableBitmap.Pixels property. The Pixels property is an array of integers, so you convert the int array to a byte array using the BitConverter with LINQ:

```
flattend = bmp.Pixels.SelectMany(
(p)=>BitConverter.GetBytes(p)).ToArray();
```

The btnOpenCustomFile_Click event handler does the opposite by reading bytes four at a time and using the BitConverter to convert the four bytes to an int. Each int is then set in order in the Pixels int array:

```
using (FileStream reader = fileDlg.File.OpenRead())
{
  WriteableBitmap wrtBmp = null;
  wrtBmp = new WriteableBitmap(ImageContainer, new TranslateTransform());
  byte[] fourBytes = new byte[4];

  int byteCounter = 0;
  int intCounter = 0;

  while (byteCounter < reader.Length - 1)
  {
    reader.Read(fourBytes,0, 4);
    wrtBmp.Pixels[intCounter] = BitConverter.ToInt32(fourBytes, 0);
    intCounter++;
    byteCounter += 4;
  }
}
```

When all of the bytes have been processed, the WriteableBitmap is set as the Source on the Image element. Note that the file format is not compatible with any of the standardized file formats. This can be remedied by implementing an encoder/decoder for a standard file format and obtaining raw bitmap data from the WriteableBitmap.Pixels property.

For simplicity, the code assumes a fixed size for the image based on the ImageContainer UI element. For a resizable UI, you also have to save the height and width of the image when saving and then use those values to instantiate a WriteableBitmap object with the correct dimensions in its constructor. You can add the dimensions to the stream as the first two bytes; with a little additional coding, you can have a more flexible custom format for internal use in an application.

3-19. Improving Graphic Animation and Video Performance

Problem

You want to maximize performance for graphic animations and video streaming.

Solution

Take advantage of the support for hardware acceleration and bitmap caching available in Silverlight 3.

How It Works

Silverlight 2 did not take advantage of hardware acceleration available in today's video display adapters. Silverlight 3 lets you take advantage of the available display hardware, processor, and video memory, to improve performance of Silverlight applications.

To enable GPU acceleration, configure the Silverlight 3 plug-in by adding this parameter to the standard <OBJECT> declaration:

```
<param name="enableGPUAcceleration" value="true" />
```

To take advantage of GPU acceleration, configure the UIElement.CacheMode property by configuring it to BitmapCache, which is the only valid option:

```
CacheMode="BitmapCache"
```

This setting caches visual elements as bitmaps after the first time they render. After an object is cached as a bitmap, it no longer goes through the rendering phase; the cached version on the GPU is displayed instead, potentially yielding significant performance improvements.

A related option that you can configure on the Silverlight plug-in is the enableCacheVisualation parameter. When set to True, it tints non-accelerated parts of the UI red.

The Code

To demonstrate how to configure an application as well as the potential performance improvements, you create a simple application that animates some sample XAML from Expression Design 3. Figure 3-64 shows the UI.

When you run the application without enabling GPU acceleration, a check in Windows Task Manager shows CPU utilization between 20% and 40%, mostly hovering around 25% to 30%.

Figure 3-64. *The sample UI*

Configure enableGPUAcceleration to True, and test again. The results are the same, as expected. Next, set CacheMode="BitmapCache" on LayoutRoot (the root Grid control) to try enabling bitmap caching for the entire application, which consists of a gradient configured on LayoutRoot and a Canvas that contains the pineapple. Also enable the visualization parameter to observe what parts of the UI are accelerated:

```
<param name="enableCacheVisualization" value="true" />
```

When you run the UI, it looks exactly like Figure 3-64 without any red tint, because the entire UI is accelerated; however, you do not see any noticeable performance improvement. Next, move the CacheMode="BitmapCache" attribute to the Canvas object that contains the XAML for the pineapple. Figure 3-65 shows the UI with the background tinted red because it is not accelerated—only the pineapple is accelerated.

Figure 3-65. *The GPU accelerated pineapple*

In this test run, you see a very noticeable performance improvement: CPU utilization drops to just a few percentage points, trending between 0% and 2%, which is much improved over the non-accelerated test. This goes to show that you should not apply the `BitmapCache` without validating the resulting performance improvements using the visualization parameter. Be sure to set the visualization parameter to `false` to remove the red tint for non-accelerated UI elements.

Note that if you run the same test by applying the `BitmapCache` attribute to a `MediaElement` when playing video, you will also see a fairly large reduction in CPU utilization.

The XAML code is straight forward, with much of the XAML in the `Storyboard` for the animation and the pineapple. Listing 3-25 shows the abbreviated XAML.

Listing 3-25. *Recipe 3.19 Abbreviated MainPage.Xaml File*

```xml
<UserControl x:Class="Ch03_DevelopingUX.Recipe3_19.MainPage"
    xmlns="http://schemas.microsoft.com/winfx/2006/xaml/presentation"
    xmlns:x="http://schemas.microsoft.com/winfx/2006/xaml"
    xmlns:d="http://schemas.microsoft.com/expression/blend/2008"
xmlns:mc="http://schemas.openxmlformats.org/markup-compatibility/2006"
    mc:Ignorable="d" d:DesignWidth="800" d:DesignHeight="600">
  <UserControl.Resources>
    <Storyboard x:Name="AnimatePineappleStoryboard"
            AutoReverse="true" RepeatBehavior="Forever" >
      <DoubleAnimationUsingKeyFrames
            BeginTime="00:00:00" Storyboard.TargetName="Pineapple"
        Storyboard.TargetProperty=
        "(UIElement.RenderTransform).(TransformGroup.Children)[3].
        (TranslateTransform.X)">
<!--- Removed storyboard code--->
</Storyboard>
  </UserControl.Resources>
  <Grid x:Name="LayoutRoot">
    <Grid.Background>
      <LinearGradientBrush EndPoint="0.5,1" StartPoint="0.5,0">
        <GradientStop Color="Black" Offset="0"/>
        <GradientStop Color="White" Offset="1"/>
      </LinearGradientBrush>
    </Grid.Background>
    <Canvas x:Name="Pineapple" Opacity="0.5" Margin="-81,-162,0,0" CacheMode="BitmapCache"
HorizontalAlignment="Left" Width="201" RenderTransformOrigin="0.5,0.5" Height="378"
VerticalAlignment="Top">
      <Canvas.RenderTransform>
        <TransformGroup>
          <ScaleTransform ScaleX="0.1" ScaleY="0.1"/>
          <SkewTransform/>
          <RotateTransform/>
          <TranslateTransform/>
        </TransformGroup>
      </Canvas.RenderTransform>
<!--- removed markup for pineapple --->    </Canvas>
  </Grid>
</UserControl>
```

The code-behind has a single line of code in Initialize():

```
AnimatePineappleStoryboard.Begin();
```

3-20. Improve Animation with Custom Easing Functions

Problem

You want to customize how animations appear so that they look more realistic.

Solution

Take advantage of one or more of the 11 new built-in easing functions, or create a custom easing function that implements the IEasingFunction interface or inherits from EasingFunctionBase.

How It Works

In Silverlight 2, you could visually create an animation that appeared more realistic by increasing distance over time in a time line—you could add an acceleration and adjust the KeySpline values as covered in Recipe 3-14. Although this approach worked for many scenarios, developers sometimes hand-coded animations to achieve a desired affect.

Silverlight 3 tries to make this much easier by adding support for custom easing functions as well as providing 11 built-in easing functions that can go a long way toward helping animations appear more realistic. Table 3-3 lists these functions.

Table 3-3. *Built-in Easing Functions*

Function Name	Description
BackEase	Adds inertia before an animation begins by retracting slightly in the opposite direction of the intended motion
BounceEase	Adds a bouncing effect to an animation
CircleEase	Adds acceleration or deceleration based on a circular function
CubicEase	Adds acceleration or deceleration using the formula $f(t)=t^3$
ElasticEase	Creates an animation that simulates an oscillating spring that eventually comes to rest
ExponentialEase	Adds acceleration or deceleration using an exponential formula
PowerEase	Adds acceleration or deceleration using the formula $f(t)=t^p$ where p is equal to the Power property
QuadraticEase	Adds acceleration or deceleration using the formula $f(t)=t^2$
QuarticEase	Adds acceleration or deceleration using the formula $f(t)=t^4$
QuinticEase	Adds acceleration or deceleration using the formula $f(t)=t^5$
SineEase	Adds acceleration or deceleration using a sine formula

You can apply a custom easing function or one of the built-in easing functions to an individual keyframe visually in Expression Blend by selecting the EasingFunction tab in the Easing section, as shown in Figure 3-66.

Figure 3-66. *Select an easing function to apply to a keyframe*

Notice at the bottom in Figure 3-66 that you can select a custom easing function that resides in the chapter's namespace or one of the built-in easing functions. You can also choose whether the easing function applies on the way in to the keyframe, on the way out, or to both.

Of course, it is possible to create an instance of an easing function class and apply it programmatically as well. But Expression Blend 3 provides a very visual way of applying easing functions and lets you see the results immediately by playing the animation at design-time.

The Code

For this recipe, you build a teeter-totter that rolls a ball back and forth at an even pace by default. Figure 3-67 shows an image from Expression Blend.

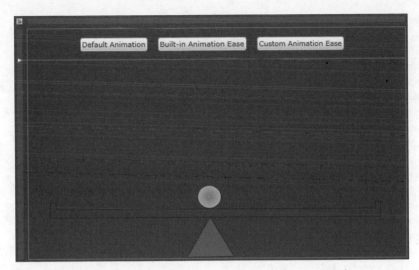

Figure 3-67. *The teeter-totter*

In Expression Blend, you select keyframes in the time line and apply one of the built-in easing functions to experiment with different appearances. Use a SineEase for both in and out when the ball is at the far right or far left. Also add a PowerEase with a Power of 2 for both in and out.

Now that you have visually designed which built-in ease functions you want to apply when the second button is clicked in the UI, assign names to the keyframes in Visual Studio so that you can programmatically apply the ease. Also remove the easing functions from the XAML so that when the Default Animation button in the UI is clicked, no easing is applied.

Listing 3-26 and 3-27 show the .Xaml and .Xaml.cs files, respectively.

Listing 3-26. *Recipe 3.20 MainPage.Xaml File*

```
<UserControl x:Class="Ch03_DevelopingUX.Recipe3_20.MainPage"
    xmlns="http://schemas.microsoft.com/winfx/2006/xaml/presentation"
    xmlns:x="http://schemas.microsoft.com/winfx/2006/xaml"
    xmlns:d="http://schemas.microsoft.com/expression/blend/2008"
    xmlns:mc="http://schemas.openxmlformats.org/markup-compatibility/2006"
    Width="590" Height="362" mc:Ignorable="d">
  <UserControl.Resources>
    <Storyboard x:Name="RollingBallStoryboard" RepeatBehavior="Forever">
      <DoubleAnimationUsingKeyFrames BeginTime="00:00:00"
        Storyboard.TargetName="rectangle" Storyboard.TargetProperty=
        "(UIElement.RenderTransform).(TransformGroup.Children)[2].(RotateTransform.Angle)">
        <EasingDoubleKeyFrame KeyTime="00:00:00" Value="0"/>
        <EasingDoubleKeyFrame KeyTime="00:00:01" Value="-12.655"/>
        <SplineDoubleKeyFrame KeyTime="00:00:02" Value="0"/>
        <EasingDoubleKeyFrame KeyTime="00:00:03" Value="13.557"/>
        <EasingDoubleKeyFrame KeyTime="00:00:04" Value="0"/>
      </DoubleAnimationUsingKeyFrames>
```

```xml
            <DoubleAnimationUsingKeyFrames BeginTime="00:00:00"
             Storyboard.TargetName="ball" Storyboard.TargetProperty=
             "(UIElement.RenderTransform).(TransformGroup.Children)[3].(TranslateTransform.X)">
              <EasingDoubleKeyFrame x:Name="PowerEase1" KeyTime="00:00:00" Value="0">
              </EasingDoubleKeyFrame>
              <EasingDoubleKeyFrame x:Name="SineEase1" KeyTime="00:00:01" Value="-223">
              </EasingDoubleKeyFrame>
              <EasingDoubleKeyFrame KeyTime="00:00:01.5000000" Value="-112.5"/>
              <EasingDoubleKeyFrame x:Name="PowerEase2" KeyTime="00:00:02" Value="0">
              </EasingDoubleKeyFrame>
              <EasingDoubleKeyFrame x:Name="SineEase2" KeyTime="00:00:03" Value="244">
              </EasingDoubleKeyFrame>
              <EasingDoubleKeyFrame KeyTime="00:00:03.5000000" Value="123"/>
              <EasingDoubleKeyFrame x:Name="PowerEase3" KeyTime="00:00:04" Value="0">
              </EasingDoubleKeyFrame>
            </DoubleAnimationUsingKeyFrames>
            <DoubleAnimationUsingKeyFrames BeginTime="00:00:00"
             Storyboard.TargetName="ball" Storyboard.TargetProperty=
             "(UIElement.RenderTransform).(TransformGroup.Children)[3].(TranslateTransform.Y)">
              <EasingDoubleKeyFrame x:Name="PowerEase4" KeyTime="00:00:00" Value="0">
              </EasingDoubleKeyFrame>
              <EasingDoubleKeyFrame KeyTime="00:00:00.5000000" Value="14.5"/>
              <EasingDoubleKeyFrame x:Name="SineEase3" KeyTime="00:00:01" Value="51">
              </EasingDoubleKeyFrame>
              <EasingDoubleKeyFrame KeyTime="00:00:01.5000000" Value="14.5"/>
              <EasingDoubleKeyFrame x:Name="PowerEase5" KeyTime="00:00:02" Value="0">
              </EasingDoubleKeyFrame>
              <EasingDoubleKeyFrame KeyTime="00:00:02.5000000" Value="14.5"/>
              <EasingDoubleKeyFrame x:Name="SineEase4" KeyTime="00:00:03" Value="55">
              </EasingDoubleKeyFrame>
              <EasingDoubleKeyFrame KeyTime="00:00:03.5000000" Value="13.5"/>
              <EasingDoubleKeyFrame x:Name="PowerEase6" KeyTime="00:00:04" Value="0">
              </EasingDoubleKeyFrame>
            </DoubleAnimationUsingKeyFrames>
          </Storyboard>
        </UserControl.Resources>
        <Grid x:Name="LayoutRoot">
          <Grid.RowDefinitions>
            <RowDefinition Height="0.135*"/>
            <RowDefinition Height="0.865*"/>
          </Grid.RowDefinitions>
      <StackPanel Orientation="Horizontal" Margin="2">
            <Button x:Name="btnDefaultAnimation" HorizontalAlignment="Center"
             Margin="80,8,8,8" Content="Default Animation"
             Click="btnDefaultAnimation_Click" VerticalAlignment="Center"/>
```

```xml
        <Button x:Name="btnBuiltInAnimation" HorizontalAlignment="Center" Margin="8"
          Content="Built-in Animation Ease" Click="btnBuiltInAnimation_Click"
          VerticalAlignment="Center"/>
        <Button x:Name="btnCustomAnimation" HorizontalAlignment="Center" Margin="8"
          Content="Custom Animation Ease" Click="btnCustomAnimation_Click"
          VerticalAlignment="Center"/>
      </StackPanel>
      <Path x:Name="rectangle" Fill="#FF002E7E" Stretch="Fill" Stroke="Black"
        Height="25" Margin="33,0,38.909,63" VerticalAlignment="Bottom"
        RenderTransformOrigin="0.499912530183792,0.719995724607971" Grid.Row="1"
        UseLayoutRounding="False" Data="M0.5,0.5 L9.5000019,0.5 L9.5000019,11.499801
L508.53659,11.499801 L508.59113,0.76702565 L517.591,0.81274098 L517.50037,18.655201
L517.50037,24.500023 L0.5,24.500023 L0.5,22.499994 L0.5,11.499801 z" >
        <Path.RenderTransform>
          <TransformGroup>
            <ScaleTransform/>
            <SkewTransform/>
            <RotateTransform/>
            <TranslateTransform/>
          </TransformGroup>
        </Path.RenderTransform>
      </Path>
      <Path x:Name="path" Fill="#FF267E00" Stretch="Fill" Stroke="Black" Height="63.5"
        Margin="246.5,0,271.5,1" VerticalAlignment="Bottom" UseLayoutRounding="False"
        Data="M390,537 L355,594 L425,593 z" Grid.Row="1"/>
      <Ellipse x:Name="ball" Stroke="Black" Height="37" Margin="263,0,290,77"
        VerticalAlignment="Bottom" RenderTransformOrigin="0.5,0.5" Grid.Row="1">
        <Ellipse.RenderTransform>
          <TransformGroup>
            <ScaleTransform/>
            <SkewTransform/>
            <RotateTransform/>
            <TranslateTransform/>
          </TransformGroup>
        </Ellipse.RenderTransform>
        <Ellipse.Fill>
          <RadialGradientBrush RadiusX="0.539" RadiusY="0.539"
            GradientOrigin="0.28,0.287">
            <GradientStop Color="#FFA5A3A3" Offset="0.991"/>
            <GradientStop Color="#FFC9C5C5"/>
            <GradientStop Color="#FF969292" Offset="0.905"/>
          </RadialGradientBrush>
        </Ellipse.Fill>
      </Ellipse>
    </Grid>
</UserControl>
```

Listing 3-27. *Recipe 3.20 MainPage.Xaml.cs File*

```
using System.Windows;
using System.Windows.Controls;
using System.Windows.Media.Animation;

namespace Ch03_DevelopingUX.Recipe3_20
{
  public partial class MainPage : UserControl
  {
    public MainPage()
    {
      InitializeComponent();
    }

    private void btnDefaultAnimation_Click(object sender, RoutedEventArgs e)
    {
      EasingDoubleKeyFrame EasingKF = null;

      for (int i = 1; i < 7; i++)
      {
        EasingKF = LayoutRoot.FindName("PowerEase" + i.ToString())
          as EasingDoubleKeyFrame;
        EasingKF.EasingFunction = null;
      }

      for (int i = 1; i < 5; i++)
      {
        EasingKF = LayoutRoot.FindName("SineEase" + i.ToString())
          as EasingDoubleKeyFrame;
        EasingKF.EasingFunction = null;
      }
      RollingBallStoryboard.Begin();
    }

    private void btnBuiltInAnimation_Click(object sender, RoutedEventArgs e)
    {
      PowerEase pe = new PowerEase();
      pe.Power = 2;
      pe.EasingMode = EasingMode.EaseInOut;
      SineEase se = new SineEase();
      se.EasingMode = EasingMode.EaseInOut;
      EasingDoubleKeyFrame EasingKF = null ;
```

```
    for (int i = 1; i < 7; i++)
    {
      EasingKF = LayoutRoot.FindName("PowerEase" + i.ToString())
        as EasingDoubleKeyFrame;
      EasingKF.EasingFunction = pe;
    }

    for (int i = 1; i < 5; i++)
    {
      EasingKF = LayoutRoot.FindName("SineEase" + i.ToString())
        as EasingDoubleKeyFrame;
      EasingKF.EasingFunction = se;
    }
    RollingBallStoryboard.Begin();
  }

  private void btnCustomAnimation_Click(object sender, RoutedEventArgs e)
  {
    PowerEase pe = new PowerEase();
    pe.Power = 2;
    pe.EasingMode = EasingMode.EaseInOut;
    SineEase se = new SineEase();
    se.EasingMode = EasingMode.EaseInOut;
    EasingDoubleKeyFrame EasingKF = null;

    MyCustomEasingFunction mce = new MyCustomEasingFunction();

    for (int i = 1; i < 7; i++)
    {
      EasingKF = LayoutRoot.FindName("PowerEase" + i.ToString())
        as EasingDoubleKeyFrame;
      EasingKF.EasingFunction = null ,
    }

    for (int i = 1; i < 5; i++)
    {
      EasingKF = LayoutRoot.FindName("SineEase" + i.ToString())
        as EasingDoubleKeyFrame;
      EasingKF.EasingFunction = mce;
    }
    RollingBallStoryboard.Begin();
  }
 }
}
```

The last button in the UI enables a custom easing function for the animation that uses the Math.Sqrt function to apply easing. When this button is clicked, you apply the custom ease when the ball rolls to either the left or right side. It gives the effect of accelerating into the stop and decelerating out of the stop. You can try whatever math function makes sense for your scenario with little effort. Listing 3-28 shows the code for the custom easing function.

Listing 3-28. *Recipe 3.20 MyCustomEasingFunction.cs File*

```
using System;
using System.Windows.Media.Animation;

namespace Ch03_DevelopingUX.Recipe3_20
{
  public class MyCustomEasingFunction : EasingFunctionBase
  {
    public MyCustomEasingFunction()
      : base()
    {

    }
    protected override double EaseInCore(double normalizedTime)
    {
      return Math.Sqrt(normalizedTime);
    }
  }
}
```

We do not show additional screenshots because static images do not represent the animations well. Check out the sample to see the differences and try some other variations.

3-21. Adding Pixel Shader Visual Effects

Problem

You want to add visual special effects to your Silverlight application, such as making a photo black and white or applying a distortion to an image.

Solution

Take advantage of the support for both built-in and custom pixel shaders in Silverlight 3.

How It Works

Pixel shaders have long been used in game development to provide the spectacular visual effects available in major console and computer game video game releases. Silverlight 3 introduces support for pixel shaders, including two built-in effects: drop shadows and motion blur. It also includes support for incorporating custom pixel shaders for even more compelling content.

Pixel-shader effects in Silverlight are rendered in software—they are not GPU accelerated. Applying effects to large portions of a UI or animating properties of effects can affect performance. Therefore, you need to thoroughly test applied effects to ensure good performance.

To apply an effect, you configure the Effect property on descendents of the UIElement base class. To manipulate effects programmatically, add this namespace to your code-behind:

```
System.Windows.Media.Effects
```

Only one effect can be applied at a time directly on a UIElement. One way to apply multiple effects is to apply one effect directly on the UIElement and other effect on a parent object. Effects applied to parent UIElements are also applied to child UIElements. Note that applying multiple pixel-shader effects can affect performance.

Pixel-shader effects are written in High Level Shading Language (HLSL) for DirectX. This link has more information about HLSL:

```
http://msdn.microsoft.com/en-us/library/bb509561(VS.85).aspx
```

Many books cover HLSL development, as does the documentation for the DirectX SDK. In addition, the DirectX Sample Browser has links to training on pixel-shader authoring.

HLSL pixel shaders are compiled using the DirectX SDK into a format that can be used programmatically in WPF and Silverlight. Tools in the WPF Futures CodePlex project can help you integrate pixel-shader compilation in a WPF solution. The tools have been modified to work with Silverlight projects as well, now that Silverlight 3 supports pixel shaders. You can download the tool and instructions here:

```
http://www.codeplex.com/wpf/Release/ProjectReleases.aspx?ReleaseId=14962
```

■**Note** You need to install the DirectX SDK to access compile-time support, in order to build the .ps files. It is available at downloads.microsoft.com. The SDK is updated frequently so please use the search functionality to obtain the latest version.

For a collection of sample pixel-shader effects, download the WPF library, which also works with Silverlight 3:

```
http://wpffx.codeplex.com/
```

You use these samples as part of the custom pixel effect example. You apply custom pixel-shader effects the same way you apply the built-in pixel shader effects.

The Code

This recipe uses the Silverlight Navigation Application with two view pages: one view to demonstrate the built-in pixel-shader effects, and the other view to demonstrate applying custom pixel-shader effects. We do not cover MainPage.xaml and MainPage.xaml.cs because they wire up the application. The first application page is shown in Figure 3-68.

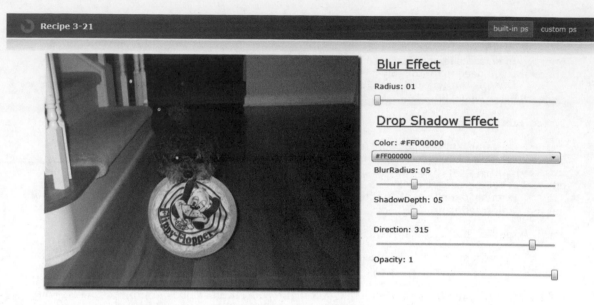

Figure 3-68. *The built-in pixel-shader demo page*

Two built-in pixel shaders are available in Silverlight 3: `BlurEffect` and `DropShadowEffect`. You can build a quick sample application that applies both affects to an `Image` object. You apply the `DropShadowEffect` directly to the `Image`, because only one pixel-shader effect can be applied to a `UIElement`. To apply the `BlurEffect`, you wrap the `Image` in a `Grid` object and apply the effect there. You can manipulate the sliders to see the effect of the various parameters available on the two effects. Here is the XAML for applying an effect to the `Grid` and `Image` objects:

```
<Grid x:Name="DogImageGrid" Margin="0,0,8,0">
  <Grid.Effect>
    <BlurEffect Radius="1" />
  </Grid.Effect>
  <Image x:Name="DogImage" Margin="8"
Source="/Ch03_DevelopingUX.Recipe3_21;Component/Assets/image.jpg"
    HorizontalAlignment="Center" VerticalAlignment="Top">
    <Image.Effect>
      <DropShadowEffect/>
    </Image.Effect>
  </Image>
</Grid>
```

You configure the `Radius` property to 1 for the `BlurEffect` applied to the `Grid` so that it doesn't alter the settings on the `DropShadowEffect` effect applied to the `Image`. Leave the default settings applied to the `DropShadowEffect`; the effect controls are also configured with the defaults.

The other application page in the UI demonstrates custom pixel-shader effects. Be sure to follow the steps in the "How Do I" section of this recipe to configure your development environment as well as download and install the necessary tools. You should also download the sample Pixel Shader Effects library available here, because it provides many useful sample effects:

http://wpffx.codeplex.com/

Demonstration videos are also available at this link. Extract the WPFSLFx folder to a directory of your choice. You can find the HLSL source code (.fx) files for the compiled pixel shaders in the WPF version of the ShaderEffectLibrary project. When you open the WPF project and select a .fx file, you see that its Build Action is set to Effect, taking advantage of the Visual Studio tools to integrate compiling the effect. To use it in Silverlight, copy the .ps output and add it to a Silverlight project.

Under the WPFSLFx folder in the SL folder are three projects. The SLShaderEffectLibrary and SLTransitionEffects projects contain the sample pixel-shader effects. Open the SLShaderEffectLibrary to find 23 compiled pixel-shader effects (.ps) in the ShaderSource folder; they were compiled using the DirectX SDK from .fx files. The .ps files are configured as a resource in the Silverlight project in the ShaderSource folder.

Each .ps file has a corresponding .cs class file in the EffectFiles folder. Look at the BandedSwirlEffect.cs file to see how to integrate the .ps compiled pixel shader. The class BandedSwirlEffect inherits from the ShaderEffect base class. In the constructor's code region, a static constructor creates an instance of the PixelShader class, setting the UriSource to the .ps file stored as a resource in the assembly.

The WPF project includes a nonstatic constructor to instantiate the effect as well as dependency properties that represent the properties declared in the BandedSwirl.fx HLSL source code file:

```
float2 center : register(C0);
float spiralStrength : register(C1);
float distanceThreshold : register(C2);
```

In the Silverlight project, the BandedSwirlEffect.cs code file contains three dependency properties that are linked to the corresponding pixel-shader registry like this:

```
public static readonly DependencyProperty CenterProperty =
  DependencyProperty.Register("Center", typeof(Point),
  typeof(BandedSwirlEffect),
  new UIPropertyMetadata(new Point(0.5, 0.5),
  PixelShaderConstantCallback(0)));
```

The method PixelShaderConstantCallback is a helper function available in Silverlight. It associates a dependency property value with a pixel shader's float constant register. Now that we have provided an overview of the process to integrate pixel shaders in Silverlight, you can copy the compiled output from the SLShaderEffectLibrary included with the WPF pixel-shader library provided by Microsoft on CodePlex to the sample code and apply custom effects to the same photograph used in the first example.

Drop a copy of SLShaderEffectLibrary.dll into the Recipe3.21 folder, and add a reference to it in the Recipe 3-21 project. Next, copy the UI from the first example; but remove the blur and drop shadow effects in Expression Blend by clicking the Advanced Options button for the Effect property and clicking Reset as well as the related controls for manipulating the pixel-shader settings.

Build the project, and switch to Expression Blend to apply a custom pixel-shader effect. Select the DogImage Image control, and click New next to the Effect property. Figure 3-69 shows that the SLShaderEffectLibrary is now available in the visual tools; you can see all the newly available pixel shaders you can test, including the BandedSwirlEffect we covered earlier.

Select BandedSwirlEffect as the test custom effect, and click OK. Figure 3-70 shows the immediate effect of the pixel shader on the image in the Expression Blend design surface.

Figure 3-69. *The newly available pixel-shader effects in Expression Blend*

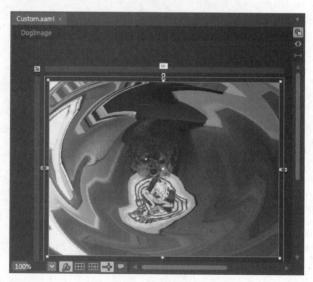

Figure 3-70. *The BandedSwirlEffect applied in Expression Blend*

The effect has a fish-eye appearance that would be interesting to animate as a way to bring a picture into view. To demonstrate animating the effect, first set the image to an Opacity of 0 as the starting point.

Next, create a new Storyboard in Expression Blend, and call it DogImageStoryboard. Create a keyframe at the starting point, and move the yellow time line to 1.5 seconds; set Opacity back to 100%, because you want the image to take 1.5 seconds to come into view. Expand DogImage in the Objects and Timeline window, and select the BandedSwirl property.

Here you can create keyframes between 0 and 1.5 seconds in the time line to animate the banded swirl. Add a couple of keyframes and adjust the SwirlStrength property on the BandedSwirlEffect, eventually setting it to 0 at 1.5 seconds so the image looks normal. Create a few more keyframes, experimenting with various settings and playing the animation in Expression Blend to see the results.

Finally, add a button to the UI to kick off the Storyboard. Run the sample code to see the results. We do not show the sample code for this recipe because most of the code is generated in Expression Blend from the earlier steps, and the code-behind contains minimal code. We recommend opening the Custom.xaml page in Expression Blend and playing around with the time line to see how you can improve the animation, or select a different pixel shader in the SLShaderEffectLibrary for a different approach.

3-22. Create and Work with Design-Time Data in Expression Blend

Problem

You want to create a data-driven UI without having to run the application in order to see the results.

Solution

Take advantage of the support in Expression Blend 3 for design-time datasources.

How It Works

When building a data-driven UI in Expression Blend 2, designers and developers are flying blind while creating data and item templates. You have to run the application and connect to live data in order to see the UI display the data. You must then fix any issues back in design-time and check them by running the application again.

With Expression Blend 3, you have access to the Data panel shown in Figure 3-71. Its features are listed in Table 3-4.

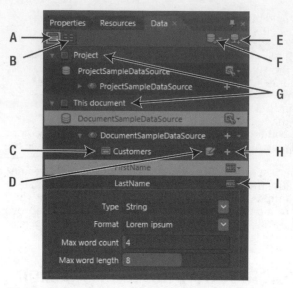

Figure 3-71. *The Data panel in Expression Blend 3*

Table 3-4. *Expression Blend 3 Data Panel Features*

Annotation	Description
A	Selected by default, list mode for the Data panel lets you drag the Customers collection shown in Figure 3-71 onto the Artboard and generates a ListBox data-bound to the Customers design-time datasource.
B	Details mode lets you drag a collection item like FirstName to the Artboard to create a control data-bound to the collection item. This action also configures the DataContext property of the parent container to the collection, in this case Customers.
C	This is a document-level datasource collection named Customers. In addition, a datasource named ProjectSampleDataSource is defined at the Project level.
D	Click this button to edit and further customize the collection. You can specify the type of value (String, Number, Boolean, or Image) as well as the format (for String, how many words; for Number, how many digits; and for Image, a folder location).
E	The "Add live data source" button allows you to add a live or real datasource to the application to display at runtime.
F	The "Add sample data source" button allows you to create a design-time datasource to help working with UI elements that display data.
G	You can define datasources at the document and project levels of an application.

Annotation	Description
H	Click the plus sign to add a simple property to a datasource collection, or click the down-arrow next to the plus sign to choose whether to add a simple property, a complex property, or a collection property to the design-time datasource.
I	Click the down-arrow for an individual property to edit the attributes for the property, such as its type and format, depending on the type of the property.

When you click the "Add sample data source" button shown as item F in Figure 3-71, it displays the dialog shown in Figure 3-72. You have the option of enabling the sample datasource at runtime as well, which is great for demonstrating the data-driven UI.

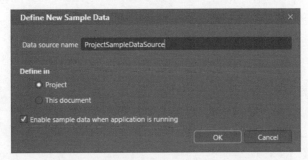

Figure 3-72. *The Define New Sample Data Dialog*

This allows you to work with the design-time data in Expression Blend while also displaying the design-time data at runtime for testing and demonstration purposes. You can also add a live datasource to the UI that pulls data from a live datasource for display at runtime, by clicking item E in Figure 3-71. As long as your schema is compatible between the design-time datasource and the live datasource, you can use both in an application. Let's say you start working with a design-time datasource to build your application. You add a live datasource to the Data panel in Expression Blend to make it available. Drag items from the live datasource, and drop them onto the control displaying the corresponding sample data.

■**Note** Clear the Enable When Running Application check box in the datasource properties to allow the live datasource to display data at runtime.

As long as the data schemas match, the sample data displays on the Artboard in Expression Blend and the live data displays when the application executes. This is because the sample datasource bindings are still available in the design-time properties.

The Code

This recipe borrows the ApressBooks class from Recipe 2-9 to serve as the live datasource. This class reads an XML file called ApressBooks.xml that is included as content within the project and that has the following structure:

```
<ApressBooks>
  <ApressBook>
    <ID/>
    <ISBN/>
    <Author/>
    <Title/>
    <Description/>
    <DatePublished/>
    <NumPages/>
    <Price/>
  </ApressBook>
  ...
</ApressBooks>
```

Listing 3-29 shows the ApressBooks.cs class file that reads the XML file to produce a C# List object of type ApressBooks.

Listing 3-29. *Recipe 3.22 ApressBooks Class File*

```csharp
using System;
using System.Collections.Generic;
using System.Linq;
using System.Xml;
using System.Xml.Linq;

namespace Ch03_DevelopingUX.Recipe3_22
{
  public class ApressBooks
  {
    private List<ApressBook> _apressBookList;
    public List<ApressBook> ApressBookList
    {
      get
      {
        if (null == _apressBookList)
          RetrieveData();
        return _apressBookList;
      }
    }
```

```
private void RetrieveData()
{
  XmlReaderSettings XmlRdrSettings = new XmlReaderSettings();
  XmlRdrSettings.XmlResolver = new XmlXapResolver();
  XmlReader reader = XmlReader.Create("ApressBooks.xml", XmlRdrSettings);

  XDocument xDoc = XDocument.Load(reader);

  _apressBookList =
    (from b in xDoc.Descendants("ApressBook")
     select new ApressBook()
     {
       Author = b.Element("Author").Value,
       Title = b.Element("Title").Value,
       ISBN = b.Element("ISBN").Value,
       Description = b.Element("Description").Value,
       PublishedDate = Convert.ToDateTime(b.Element("DatePublished").Value),
       NumberOfPages = b.Element("NumPages").Value,
       Price = b.Element("Price").Value,
       ID = b.Element("ID").Value
     }).ToList();
  }
}

public class ApressBook
{
  public string Author { get; set; }
  public string Title { get; set; }
  public string ISBN { get; set; }
  public string Description { get; set; }
  public DateTime PublishedDate { get; set; }
  public string NumberOfPages { get; set; }
  public string Price { get; set; }
  public string ID { get; set; }
  }
}
```

After adding a reference to System.Xml.Linq, everything compiles, and you are ready to experiment with the new Data panel features.

Start by clicking the "Add sample data source" button on the Expression Blend 3 Data panel to bring up the dialog shown in Figure 3-72. Name the datasource `ApressBooksSampleData`, and click `OK`. Also enable sample data when the application is running. Doing so sets the `DataContext` for the parent `Grid` named `LayoutRoot` to the sample datasource. If you unselect the option to display sample data at runtime, the sample datasource is configured on `d:DataContext`, not to the `DataContext` attribute. The `d:` namespace specifies that the property is valid only at design-time in Expression Blend 3 and is ignored at runtime.

This generates a new project-level sample datasource with two properties named `Property1` and `Property2`. Double-click the property names to edit then: change `Property1` to `ISBN` and `Property2` to `Title`, and change the default generated type for `Property2` to `String` instead of `Boolean`. Add a new property of type `String`, and name it `Description`. Also change the maximum word count to 20 from the default of 4 for the `Description` property, because it may contain many words. Finally, change the default name of `Collection` to `ApressBookCollection`.

Drag the `ApressBookCollection` item located under the `ApressBooksSampleData` item in the Data panel to the Artboard, to generate a `ListBox` control data bound to the sample data. Resize the `ListBox` to fill the available area. Figure 3-73 shows the sample data displayed in Expression Blend 3 at design-time.

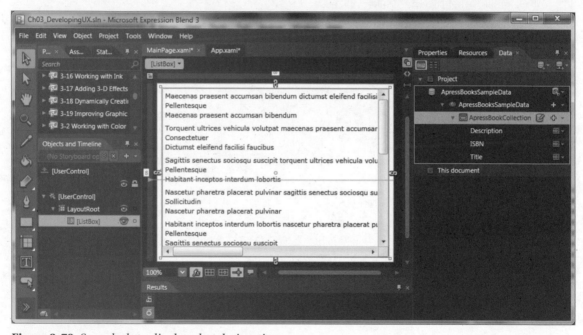

Figure 3-73. *Sample data displayed at design-time*

You can now edit the template by selecting the `ListBox`'s `ItemTemplate` property and selecting Edit Resource from the advanced property menu. Rearrange the generated `ItemTemplate` so that `ISBN` is at the top followed by `Title` and then `Description`.

The text generated by the sample data is the generic Latin you may have seen in PowerPoint or elsewhere. You can edit the sample data manually by clicking the Edit Sample Values button for the collection, which results in the dialog shown in Figure 3-74.

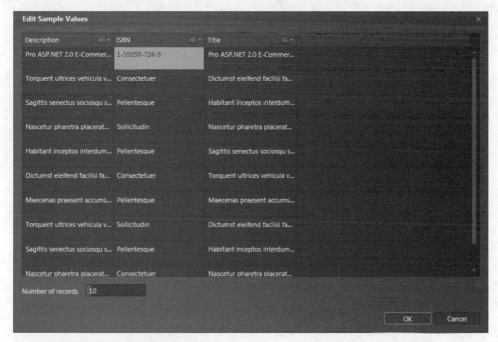

Figure 3-74. *Edit Sample Values dialog*

Manually editing a small amount of data for a simple UI may be acceptable, but it can get old for a large, complex datasource. This is when the Import Sample Data from XML menu option comes in handy. Select this option and point it to the ApressBooks.xml file, generating the datasource shown in Figure 3-75.

All the fields are added by default when you import sample data from an XML file. Next, modify the fields to just the three you are currently working with as part of the manually created sample data: ISBN, Title, and Description. As before, you can drag the new XML datasource onto the ListBox to update the design-time datasource so that real data is displayed; see Figure 3-76.

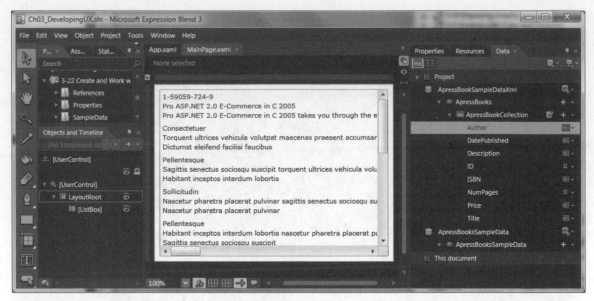

Figure 3-75. *XML-based sample datasource in the Data panel*

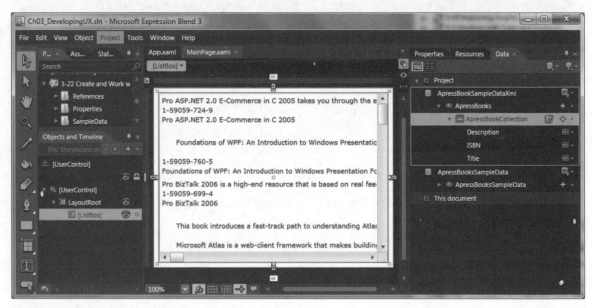

Figure 3-76. *Real data imported via XML*

To display live data at runtime, click the "Add live data source" button in the Data panel to display the dialog box shown in Figure 3-77. Choose the ApressBooks object.

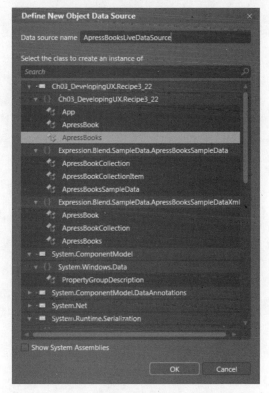

Figure 3-77. *Displaying real data imported via XML*

Switch the design-time datasource back to the manually created datasource by dragging it onto the ListBox in Expression Blend 3. Doing so demonstrates that the different datasources are automatically displayed depending on whether you are at design-time or runtime: the live datasource is displayed at runtime.

When you run the application with the manually created datasource, the first record is the edited record with the manually typed-in data, but the rest of the items are generated Latin data. At design-time, uncheck the Enable When Running the Application option for the manually created datasource. When you run the recipe sample in this state, no data is displayed at runtime.

To enable the live datasource on the ListBox, drag the ApressBook item (under the ApressBooksLiveDataSource item in the hierarchy) to the UI, dropping it onto LayoutRoot so that the mouse cursor says Bind LayoutRoot.DataContext to ApressBooksLiveDataSource. This action assigns the live datasource you just created to the DataContext property. Listing 3-30 shows the MainPage.xaml file.

Listing 3-30. *Recipe 3.22 MainPage.xaml File*

```xml
<UserControl
    xmlns="http://schemas.microsoft.com/winfx/2006/xaml/presentation"
    xmlns:x="http://schemas.microsoft.com/winfx/2006/xaml"
    xmlns:d="http://schemas.microsoft.com/expression/blend/2008"
    xmlns:mc="http://schemas.openxmlformats.org/markup-compatibility/2006"
    x:Class="Ch03_DevelopingUX.Recipe3_22.MainPage"
    Width="400" Height="300"  mc:Ignorable="d"  >
  <UserControl.Resources>

    <DataTemplate x:Key="ApressBookCollectionItemTemplate">
      <StackPanel>
        <TextBlock Text="{Binding Description}"/>
        <TextBlock Text="{Binding ISBN}"/>
        <TextBlock Text="{Binding Title}"/>
      </StackPanel>
    </DataTemplate>

  </UserControl.Resources>
    <Grid x:Name="LayoutRoot" Background="White"
     d:DataContext="{Binding Source={StaticResource ApressBooksSampleData}}"
      DataContext="{Binding Source={StaticResource ApressBooksLiveDataSource}}">
      <ListBox Margin="8"
      ItemTemplate="{StaticResource ApressBookCollectionItemTemplate}"
      ItemsSource="{Binding ApressBookList}" />
    </Grid>
</UserControl>
```

You can see in Listing 3-30 the DataContext and d:DataContext properties configured on the LayoutRoot Grid control to the design-time and runtime datasources. Initially, when you run the code, no data is displayed, because the design-time datasource collection name is ApressBookCollection. However, on the live datasource, the name is ApressBookList. In order to have the design-time and runtime datasources work properly, the collection names must be the same. When this is corrected, the datasources work as expected.

We do not show any of the code-behind files because there is no custom code to discuss. The only other code we show here in Listing 3-31 is App.xaml, where the three project-level datasources are created.

Listing 3-31. *Recipe 3.22 App.xaml File*

```xml
<Application xmlns="http://schemas.microsoft.com/winfx/2006/xaml/presentation"
 xmlns:x="http://schemas.microsoft.com/winfx/2006/xaml"
 xmlns:d="http://schemas.microsoft.com/expression/blend/2008"
 xmlns:mc="http://schemas.openxmlformats.org/markup-compatibility/2006"
 xmlns:SampleData1="clr-namespace:Expression.Blend.SampleData.ApressBooksSampleData"
 mc:Ignorable="d" xmlns:local="clr-namespace:Ch03_DevelopingUX.Recipe3_22"
 xmlns:SampleData="clr-namespace:Expression.Blend.SampleData.ApressBooksSampleDataXml"
 x:Class="Ch03_DevelopingUX.Recipe3_22.App">
  <Application.Resources>
    <local:ApressBooks x:Key="ApressBooksLiveDataSource" d:IsDataSource="True"/>
    <SampleData:ApressBooks x:Key="ApressBooksSampleDataXml"
                            d:IsDataSource="True"/>
    <SampleData1:ApressBooksSampleData x:Key="ApressBooksSampleData"
                            d:IsDataSource="True"/>
  </Application.Resources>
</Application>
```

Design-time datasources exist in generated classes created in a project folder named SampleData, which is added by Expression Blend when the datasources are created. In this folder is a subfolder that corresponds to each design-time datasource. Figure 3-78 shows the generated folders and code files.

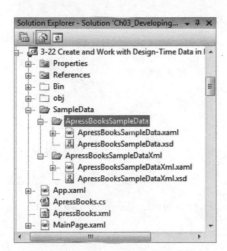

Figure 3-78. *The sample data's generated classes and schema*

3-23. Reuse Application Interactivity with Behaviors

Problem

You want to reuse designed interactivity across UI elements and applications.

Solution

Take advantage of the support for Expression Blend 3 behaviors and triggers that is available via the Expression Blend SDK, in the samples that ship with Expression Blend 3, and in examples available online.

How It Works

An Expression Blend 3 *behavior* is a reusable piece of interactivity that can be applied directly to UI elements in Expression Blend. Using the Expression Blend 3 SDK, you can create reusable libraries of behaviors that can be shared within a team, allowing interactivity to be applied in a consistent manner across a project.

Behaviors can be as simple as playing and stopping an animation; or they can be more complex, such as applying a realistic physics effect to an object. Figure 3-79 shows the Assets library filtered on Behaviors in Expression Blend 3.

Figure 3-79. *Behaviors that ship with Expression Blend 3*

To apply a behavior, drag it onto an element and configure its properties. We go through this process in the next section.

The Code

To try using a behavior, add a Rectangle element to the Artboard. You want to play one sound when the user moves the mouse over the Rectangle and then play another sound when the user moves the mouse outside of the Rectangle element.

In Silverlight 2, you would have had to write code to play the sound in the MouseEnter and MouseLeave event handlers, which seems like overkill when you consider that for a complex UI, many event handlers perform relatively simple tasks. That is the beauty of behaviors and triggers: they encapsulate simple to complex actions into markup, allowing for reuse.

For these example, drag a PlaySoundAction behavior from the Assets panel, drop it onto the Rectangle, and name it EnterSound. Do this step a second time, but name the second PlaySoundAction behavior LeaveSound. The PlaySoundAction behavior is added as a child object in the object tree, as shown in Figure 3-80.

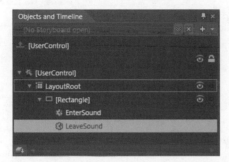

Figure 3-80. *Newly added behaviors nested under a target element*

The next step is to configure the properties for the behaviors to play a sound on the appropriate event. We recorded two sounds called Enter Rectangle and Leave Rectangle so you have some copyright-free (albeit cheesy) sounds to work with. Add both .wma files to the project with Build Action set to Content in Visual Studio 2008.

Moving back to Expression Blend 3, select the EnterSound behavior, and configure its properties by dragging the target symbol next to the SourceName property and dropping it on the Rectangle UI element. This step adds a default name of rectangle to the element and configures it as the SourceName element. Change EventName to MouseEnter as the trigger, and configure the Source property by browsing to the sound file in the project folder. Expression Blend is smart enough to change the file path to a relative path because the sound files are part of the project. Figure 3-81 shows the configuration for the EnterSound PlaySoundAction behavior.

Figure 3-81. EnterSound PlaySoundAction *configuration*

When you run the sample, there is a slight delay between the action and the sound, which is a result of us pausing about a second when we edited the sound—the sound plays immediately, but the recording includes about a second of dead space.

With respect to creating your own behaviors, many example behaviors are available for review online. The Expression Blend 3 Community Site has several behaviors available for download:

```
http://gallery.expression.microsoft.com/en-
us/site/search?f%5B0%5D.Type=RootCategory&f%5B0%5D.
Value=behaviors
```

Several additional example Expression Blend behaviors and triggers are available for download at `http://expressionblend.codeplex.com/`. The examples from CodePlex install into this directory: `C:\Program Files (x86)\Microsoft Expression\Blend 3 Samples`.

3-24. Prototype Application Design

Problem

You want to prototype an application design in a flexible, dynamic way using tools that support the designer/developer process.

Solution

Take advantage of Expression Blend 3 and SketchFlow to create rich, dynamic design prototypes that let designers manage the design process while providing solid integration with developers.

How It Works

In the early stages of the creative process, designers often start with pen and paper along with a stack of sticky pads and use arrows to simulate interactivity. SketchFlow provides a designer-focused toolset that supports the creative process while attempting to stay out of the way of free-flowing creativity.

SketchFlow lets designers sketch out ideas and then turn those ideas into working prototypes that are as rough or as real as the designer wants. When a designer is satisfied, the prototype can be demonstrated for review and comment using the SketchFlow player. An entire book could be dedicated to just Expression Blend 3 and SketchFlow; we provide just a quick overview to cover the highlights so that you are sufficiently aware of the capabilities to get started.

The Code

In Expression Blend 3+SketchFlow, choose File ➤ New to open the New Project dialog shown in Figure 3-82.

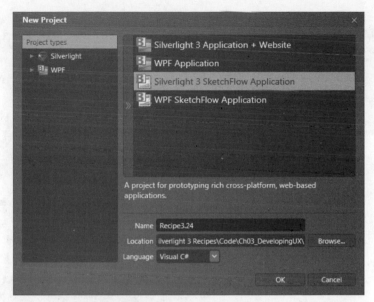

Figure 3-82. *Expression Blend 3+SketchFlow New Project dialog*

Clicking OK in Figure 3-82 generates two projects: one for the application and the other for the prototype screens that are stored in a resource dictionary. In this case, we made the project names and namespaces match the naming standards for the book's source code, resulting in two projects:

- 3-24 Prototype Application Design (the prototype application)

- 3-24 Prototype Application Design – Screens (the resource dictionary project)

Sketch a quick UI for a scuba shop named Scuba Adventures, creating a Welcome pane and a Confirm and Pay pane as shown in Figure 3-83.

Expression Blend 3+SketchFlow includes custom SketchFlow styles that are more visually conducive to the design process, providing a sketchy appearance. The controls are available in the Assets panel under Styles, as shown in Figure 3-83. Under the hood, the controls are the same ones you normally use, but with a custom look.

A more streamlined but similar animation tool is located above the Artboard in Figure 3-83. It is easy to create additional screens in the SketchFlow Map shown below the Artboard in Figure 3-83.

Under the File menu is the Package SketchFlow Project menu item, which you can use to package up the SketchFlow application for deployment on a web server for demonstration purposes. You can also build and run the project in Expression Blend to display the prototype in the SketchFlow player.

This recipe provides a quick overview of the capabilities in SketchFlow. For more information, check out the SketchFlow site:

```
http://expression.microsoft.com/en-us/ee215229.aspx
```

Figure 3-83. *Expression Blend 3+SketchFlow in action*

CHAPTER 4

■ ■ ■

Data Binding

All applications deal with information in some form or another. A slick user interface (UI) powered by a rich drawing and control framework can be pretty useless if there is no meaningful data to be displayed through it.

Application developers using UI frameworks like Silverlight need a powerful yet easy way of tying the application data to the UI they design. Data binding is a feature that enables just that.

Through data binding, developers can associate properties of application-level data classes to properties of UI elements. This association is evaluated at runtime, and data is automatically transferred back and forth between the UI and the business logic layer of the application (subject to additional parameters stipulated by the specific association). Such an association, called a *binding*, is implemented through the System.Windows.Data.Binding type.

Let's look at the recipes now, to see Binding and its associated properties in action.

4-1. Binding Application Data to the UI

Problem

You need to bind various properties on UI objects in Silverlight to application data available in managed code.

Solution

Use the Binding markup extension to specify the appropriate data bindings in XAML or use the FrameworkElement.SetBinding() method to do the same in the code-behind.

How It Works

The Binding markup extension or the FrameworkElement.SetBinding() method can be used to bind properties on instances of application data types to dependency properties defined on any type inheriting from FrameworkElement. The application data type properties are called the *source* properties for the binding, and the dependency properties are called the *target* properties.

Binding Expression

XAML exposes several markup extensions, one of which is Binding. A markup extension provides an extension to the default XAML namespaces and is used as a keyword within a set of curly braces in your XAML document. The syntax for using the Binding extension to bind some data to a property is as follows:

```
<object targetPropertyname =
  "{Binding sourcePropertyPath, oneOrMoreBindingProperties}" .../>
```

The entire Binding statement within the curly braces, including all the property settings, is collectively called a binding expression.

The targetPropertyName points to a dependency property on the XAML element. The sourcePropertyPath is the complete, qualified path to a property in the data source object hierarchy. The dot notation can be used to indicate properties belonging to type instances that are nested within other instances. The Binding extension also exposes several properties that can be set to impact various behaviors of the binding, such as the direction of the data flow, input validation behavior, or conversion of values. We will discuss most of the properties in subsequent recipes.

Dependency Properties

Dependency properties are unique to the Silverlight runtime and have some differences compared with standard .NET properties. One of the major differences is that a target property needs to be a dependency property to allow data binding. We introduce dependency properties in Chapter 2 and provide additional background on the Silverlight dependency property system in Chapter 5. You can also read about dependency properties in the Silverlight SDK documentation.

Associating the Data Source

The data source is a CLR object, and the source properties are public properties with at least public get accessors defined. The data source can be set as the DataContext on the element at the level where the binding is being set or on a containing element, thus making it automatically available as the DataContext to all children elements. The following is an example of using the DataContext, where a CLR type declared as a resource named CLRDS_Company is being used as the data source on the Grid, and the Text property on a contained TextBlock is being bound to the Street property on the data source object:

```
<Grid x:Name="LayoutRoot" Background="White"
    DataContext="{StaticResource CLRDS_Company}">
  <TextBlock Text="{Binding Street}"/>
</Grid>
```

The data source can also be set as the Source property on the binding itself. This may be necessary if the data for the elements in your UI came from different data sources and just providing a higher-level DataContext was not enough. A sample of the syntax for that would look like the following, where the Source can be set to a different data source than the one defined in the data context:

```
<TextBlock Text="{Binding Name,Source={StaticResource SomeOtherDS}}"/>
```

In either case, you can define the data source by referencing a CLR type as a resource in your XAML as shown here:

```
<UserControl.Resources>
  <local:Company x:Key="CLRDS_Company" />
</UserControl.Resources>
```

The local: prefix is a custom namespace defined to bring in the Company type. Both custom namespace mapping and the StaticResource extension used to reference such resources in XAML are covered in more detail in Chapter 2.

The Code

The CLR object model shown in Listing 4-1 has been used as the application data source for this sample.

Listing 4-1. *Application Data Classes*

```
using System.Collections.Generic;

namespace Ch04_DataBinding.Recipe4_1
{
  public class Employee
  {
    public string FirstName { get; set; }
    public string LastName { get; set; }
    public long PhoneNum { get; set; }
  }
  public class Company
  {
    public string Name { get; set; }
    public string Street { get; set; }
    public string City { get; set; }
    public string State { get; set; }
    public int ZipCode { get; set; }
    public List<Employee> Employees { get; set; }

    public Company()
    {
      this.Name = "Woodgrove Bank";
      this.Street = "555 Wall Street";
      this.City = "New York";
      this.State = "NY";
      this.ZipCode = 10005;
```

```
        this.Employees = new List<Employee>();

        this.Employees.Add(
            new Employee
            {
              FirstName = "Joe",
              LastName = "Duffin",
              PhoneNum = 2125551212
            });
        this.Employees.Add(
            new Employee
            {
              FirstName = "Alex",
              LastName = "Bleeker",
              PhoneNum = 7185551212
            });

        //rest of the initialization code omitted for brevity
        this.Employees.Add(new Employee
        {
          FirstName = "Nelly",
          LastName = "Myers",
          PhoneNum = 7325551212
        });
        this.Employees.Add(new Employee
        {
          FirstName = "Marcus",
          LastName = "Bernard",
          PhoneNum = 7325551414
        });
        this.Employees.Add(new Employee
        {
          FirstName = "Juliette",
          LastName = "Bernard",
          PhoneNum = 7325551414
        });
        this.Employees.Add(new Employee
        {
          FirstName = "Cory",
          LastName = "Winston",
          PhoneNum = 9085551414
        });
```

```
this.Employees.Add(new Employee
{
    FirstName = "Randall",
    LastName = "Valetta",
    PhoneNum = 2015551414
});

this.Employees.Add(new Employee
{
    FirstName = "Maurice",
    LastName = "Dutronc",
    PhoneNum = 3635551414
});
this.Employees.Add(new Employee
{
    FirstName = "Nathan",
    LastName = "Adams",
    PhoneNum = 3635551414
});
this.Employees.Add(new Employee
{
    FirstName = "Harold",
    LastName = "Anthony",
    PhoneNum = 3745551414
});
this.Employees.Add(new Employee
{
    FirstName = "Paul",
    LastName = "Gomez",
    PhoneNum = 3415551414
});

this.Employees.Add(new Employee
{
    FirstName = "Martha",
    LastName = "Willard",
    PhoneNum = 4795551414
});
this.Employees.Add(new Employee
{
    FirstName = "Barry",
    LastName = "Driver",
    PhoneNum = 4165551414
});
```

CHAPTER 4 ■ DATA BINDING

```
      this.Employees.Add(new Employee
      {
        FirstName = "Peter",
        LastName = "Martinson",
        PhoneNum = 4165551414
      });
      this.Employees.Add(new Employee
      {
        FirstName = "Mike",
        LastName = "Dempsey",
        PhoneNum = 4165551656
      });
    }
  }
}
```

The XAML page shown in Listing 4-2 declares an instance of the Company class to use as a data source.

Listing 4-2. *XAML for the Page*

```
<UserControl x:Class="Ch04_DataBinding.Recipe4_1.MainPage"
  xmlns="http://schemas.microsoft.com/winfx/2006/xaml/presentation"
  xmlns:x="http://schemas.microsoft.com/winfx/2006/xaml"
  xmlns:d="http://schemas.microsoft.com/expression/blend/2008"
  xmlns:mc="http://schemas.openxmlformats.org/markup-compatibility/2006"
  mc:Ignorable="d"
  xmlns:local="clr-namespace:Ch04_DataBinding.Recipe4_1"
  Width="400" Height="300" >

<UserControl.Resources>
  <local:Company x:Key="CLRDS_Company" />
</UserControl.Resources>

<Grid x:Name="LayoutRoot" Background="White"
      DataContext="{StaticResource CLRDS_Company}" Margin="8,8,8,8">

  <Grid.ColumnDefinitions>
    <ColumnDefinition Width="0.38*"/>
    <ColumnDefinition Width="0.032*"/>
    <ColumnDefinition Width="0.238*"/>
    <ColumnDefinition Width="0.028*"/>
    <ColumnDefinition Width="0.322*"/>
  </Grid.ColumnDefinitions>
```

```xml
    <Grid.RowDefinitions>
      <RowDefinition Height="0.103*"/>
      <RowDefinition Height="0.114*"/>
      <RowDefinition Height="0.783*"/>
    </Grid.RowDefinitions>
    <TextBlock  Grid.ColumnSpan="5" x:Name="tbxCompanyName"/>
    <TextBlock Text="{Binding Street}" Grid.ColumnSpan="1" Grid.Row="1" />
    <TextBlock Text="," Grid.Column="1" Grid.Row="1"  />
    <TextBlock Text="{Binding City}" Grid.Column="2"
               Grid.ColumnSpan="1" Grid.Row="1" />
    <TextBlock Text="," Grid.Column="3" Grid.ColumnSpan="1"
               Grid.Row="1" Grid.RowSpan="1"/>
    <StackPanel Margin="0,0,0,8" Orientation="Horizontal"
                Grid.Column="4" Grid.ColumnSpan="1"
            Grid.Row="1" Grid.RowSpan="1">
      <TextBlock Margin="0,0,5,0" Text="{Binding State}" />
      <TextBlock Text="{Binding Zip}"/>
    </StackPanel>
    <ListBox x:Name="lbxEmployees" Grid.RowSpan="1" Grid.Row="2"
             Grid.ColumnSpan="5" ItemsSource="{Binding Employees}">
      <ListBox.ItemTemplate>
        <DataTemplate>
          <Grid>
            <Grid.ColumnDefinitions>
              <ColumnDefinition Width="Auto"/>
              <ColumnDefinition Width="Auto"/>
              <ColumnDefinition Width="Auto"/>
            </Grid.ColumnDefinitions>
            <TextBlock Grid.Column="0" Text="{Binding FirstName}"
                       Margin="0,0,5,0" />
            <TextBlock Grid.Column="1" Text="{Binding LastName}"
                       Margin="0,0,5,0"/>
            <TextBlock Grid.Column="2" Text="{Binding PhoneNum}"/>
          </Grid>
        </DataTemplate>
      </ListBox.ItemTemplate>
    </ListBox>
  </Grid>

</UserControl>
```

To bind the data to the UI, we set the DataContext property on the top-level grid named LayoutRoot. As discussed earlier, the DataContext is made available to all contained controls inside the grid so that any binding expression automatically uses it as the binding source, thus negating the need to specify the source explicitly in the binding statement. So for each of the binding expressions in the UI for the controls contained immediately within the grid, we simply specify the name of the property in the Company type to which we want to bind the control's property.

We use a ListBox to display the Employees collection in the Company instance. We set the ItemTemplate for the ListBox to a DataTemplate that defines how each item in the ListBox is displayed. We will discuss the DataTemplate in greater detail later in this chapter, but for now, think of it as a way to package the UI representation of a specific data type. By binding the ItemsSource property of the ListBox to the Employees property on the Company instance, we effectively provide an instance of the Employee class as the data source for each item in the ListBox. In the DataTemplate, we can then bind properties of individual elements to properties on the Employee class to display employee data. The page output for the application is shown in Figure 4-1.

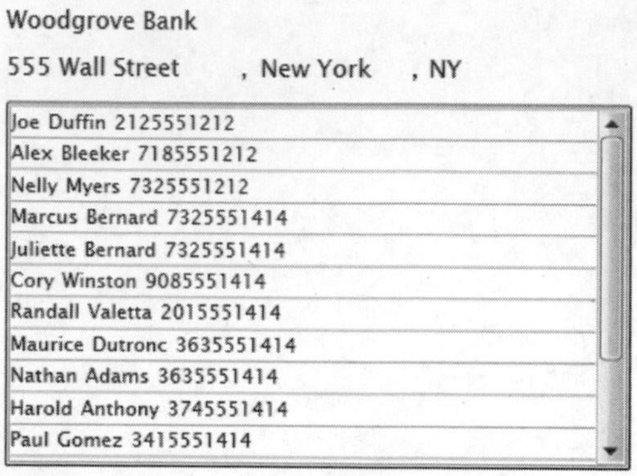

Woodgrove Bank

555 Wall Street   , New York   , NY

Joe Duffin 2125551212
Alex Bleeker 7185551212
Nelly Myers 7325551212
Marcus Bernard 7325551414
Juliette Bernard 7325551414
Cory Winston 9085551414
Randall Valetta 2015551414
Maurice Dutronc 3635551414
Nathan Adams 3635551414
Harold Anthony 3745551414
Paul Gomez 3415551414

Figure 4-1. *The data-bound page*

Note that the Company type being referenced as the CLRDS_Company resource will also need to have a default constructor defined to be referenced in XAML this way. If you do not have a default constructor, you can instantiate the type and set the DataContext in code like so:

```
LayoutRoot.DataContext = new Company(SomeParameter);
```

You can also create and set bindings in code if you need to. To do so, create and initialize an instance of the Binding type, and then use the SetBinding() method on the FrameworkElement type to associate it with a specific DependencyProperty, as shown in Listing 4-3.

Listing 4-3. *Creating a Binding in Code*

```
using System.Windows.Controls;
using System.Windows.Data;

namespace Ch04_DataBinding.Recipe4_1
{
  public partial class MainPage : UserControl
  {
    public MainPage()
    {
      InitializeComponent();
```

```
//In case you want to set the datacontext in code...
//LayoutRoot.DataContext = new Company();
//create a new Binding
Binding CompanyNameBinding = new Binding("Name");
//set properties on the Binding as needed
CompanyNameBinding.Mode = BindingMode.OneWay;
//apply the Binding to the DependencyProperty of
//choice on the appropriate object
tbxCompanyName.SetBinding(TextBlock.TextProperty,
  CompanyNameBinding);


    }
  }
}
```

Before you apply the Binding, you can also set various properties on the Binding to control its behavior. The BindingMode setting in Listing 4-3 is one such property. BindingMode controls the direction of data flow in the Binding, and the OneWay setting stipulates that data only flow from the source to the target in this case. We will discuss BindingMode in greater detail in recipe 4-3 later in the chapter.

To utilize the code in Listing 4-3, you will need to name the element that is targeted by the binding in XAML appropriately so that it becomes accessible to you in code. In the following snippet, we show how you can name the TextBlock tbxCompanyName in Listing 4-2 so that we can refer to it in code.

```
<Grid x:Name="LayoutRoot" Background="White"
DataContext="{StaticResource CLRDS_Company}">
  <!-- markup omitted for brevity -->
  <TextBlock  Grid.ColumnSpan="5" x:Name="tbxCompanyName"/>
</Grid>
```

4-2. Binding Using a DataTemplate

Problem

You need to apply a custom UI to data and specify how various parts of a complex data structure are bound to various parts of your complex UI. You also need this representation encapsulated so that it can be reused across your application wherever the related data structure is employed.

Solution

Define a DataTemplate and specify appropriate bindings to bind parts of the backing data structure to elements of the data template. Apply the DataTemplate where possible to apply a consistent UI to the bound data.

How It Works

A DataTemplate offers a way to provide a repeatable and consistent visual representation for a portion or all of a specific application data source within your UI. It encapsulates a portion of your UI and can be defined in terms of any of the standard drawing primitives and controls available, as well any custom controls you might write. Appropriate bindings applied to various properties of the constituent elements ties the DataTemplate to the backend application data source that it aims to provide the UI for.

Declaring a DataTemplate

Listing 4-4 shows a simple DataTemplate that binds the Text properties of several TextBlock controls to properties in a CLR type.

Listing 4-4. *A Simple DataTemplate*

```
<DataTemplate x:Key="dtAddress">
  <Grid >
    <Grid.RowDefinitions>
      <RowDefinition Height="Auto"/>
      <RowDefinition Height="Auto"/>
    </Grid.RowDefinitions>
    <Grid.ColumnDefinitions>
      <ColumnDefinition Width="Auto" />
    </Grid.ColumnDefinitions>
    <TextBlock x:Name="tblkStreet" HorizontalAlignment="Stretch"
               VerticalAlignment="Stretch" Text="{Binding Street}"
               TextWrapping="Wrap" Foreground="White" FontSize="12"
               FontWeight="Bold"/>
    <StackPanel  Grid.RowSpan="1" Orientation="Horizontal" Grid.Row="1"
                 VerticalAlignment="Stretch">
      <TextBlock  x:Name="tblkCity" Text="{Binding City}"
                  TextWrapping="Wrap" FontSize="12"
                  FontWeight="Bold" Foreground="White"/>
      <TextBlock  x:Name="tblkComma" Text="," TextWrapping="Wrap"
                  Margin="2,0,2,0" FontSize="12" FontWeight="Bold"
                  Foreground="White"/>
      <TextBlock  x:Name="tblkState" Text="{Binding State}"
                  TextWrapping="Wrap" FontSize="12"
                  FontWeight="Bold" Foreground="White"/>
      <TextBlock  x:Name="tblkZip" Text="{Binding ZipCode}"
                  TextWrapping="Wrap" Margin="3,0,0,0" FontSize="12"
                  FontWeight="Bold" Foreground="White"/>
    </StackPanel>
  </Grid>
</DataTemplate>
```

Note that a DataTemplate can be declared either as a resource that can be referenced using its x:Key value, as shown in Listing 4-4, or in place, as Listing 4-5 shows.

Listing 4-5. *A DataTemplate Declared and Used in Place*

```
<ContentControl x:Name="cntctrlEmployee" HorizontalAlignment="Stretch"
                VerticalAlignment="Stretch"
                Grid.Column="0" Background="Yellow" Margin="5,5,5,5"
                Height="200">
  <ContentControl.ContentTemplate>
    <DataTemplate>
      <TextBlock x:Name="tblkFirstName" Text="{Binding FirstName}"
                 TextWrapping="Wrap" FontSize="14" FontWeight="Bold"
                 Foreground="White" Margin="3,0,0,0"/>
    </DataTemplate>
  </ContentControl.ContentTemplate>
</ContentControl>
```

In Listing 4-5 we define and associate a DataTemplate to the ContentControl.ContentTemplate property in place. For in-place use, the DataTemplate is scoped to the containing element (in this case the ContentControl.ContentTemplate) and is not available for use outside that scope.

We can also define a DataTemplate as a resource either in the resource section of the page or that of the application. In the former case, the DataTemplate is control scoped—that is, it is available for use anywhere on the MainPage (which is a UserControl). In the latter case, it is available for use anywhere in the entire application. In keeping with the rules for anything stored as a resource in ResourceDictionaries, such a DataTemplate needs an x:Key defined so that it can be referenced for use via the StaticResource extension. Resource usage and ResourceDictionaries are covered in more detail in Chapter 2.

Using a DataTemplate

So how do you use a DataTemplate? You can apply one to either a ContentControl (or a derived control, like Button), or an ItemsControl (or a derived control, like ListBox). To apply the DataTemplate, you set the ContentControl.ContentTemplate property or the ItemsControl.ItemTemplate property to the DataTemplate, as shown here:

```
<ContentControl  ContentTemplate="{StaticResource dtAddress}" />
<ListBox  ItemTemplate="{StaticResource dtAddress}" />
```

At runtime, the data bound to the ContentControl.Content property, or each data item in the data collection bound to the ItemsControl.ItemsSource property, is used to provide data for the bound properties in the DataTemplate.

■**Note** In recipes in Chapter 5, we will show how you can write custom controls so that DataTemplates can be used to customize the look and feel of data bound to your control.

The Code

Listing 4-6 shows code for the classes that provide the data for this sample.

Listing 4-6. *Data Classes*

```
namespace Ch04_DataBinding.Recipe4_2
{
  public class Employee
  {
    public string FirstName { get; set; }
    public string LastName { get; set; }
    public long PhoneNum { get; set; }
    public string ImageUri
    {
      get
      {
        return "/" + FirstName + ".png";
      }
    }
    public Address Address { get; set; }
  }

  public class Address
  {
    public string Street { get; set; }
    public string City { get; set; }
    public string State { get; set; }
    public int ZipCode { get; set; }
  }
}
```

Listing 4-7 shows the code to initialize the data, defined in the constructor of the `MainPage` class, in the code-behind file for the `MainPage`.

Listing 4-7. *Data Initialization*

```
using System.Collections.Generic;
using System.Windows.Controls;

namespace Ch04_DataBinding.Recipe4_2
{
  public partial class MainPage : UserControl
  {
    public MainPage()
    {
```

```
InitializeComponent();

List<Employee> EmployeeList = new List<Employee>();

EmployeeList.Add(new Employee
    {
        FirstName = "Joe",
        LastName = "Duffin",
        PhoneNum = 2125551212,
        Address = new Address { Street = "2000 Mott Street",
            City = "New York", State = "NY", ZipCode = 10006 }
    });

EmployeeList.Add(new Employee
    {
        FirstName = "Alex",
        LastName = "Bleeker",
        PhoneNum = 7185551212,
        Address = new Address { Street = "11000 Clover Street",
            City = "New York", State = "NY", ZipCode = 10007 }
    });

EmployeeList.Add(new Employee
    {
        FirstName = "Nelly",
        LastName = "Myers",
        PhoneNum = 7325551212,
        Address = new Address { Street = "12000 Fay Road",
            City = "New York", State = "NY", ZipCode = 10016 }
    });

    cntctrlEmployee.Content = EmployeeList[0];
    itmctrlEmployees.ItemsSource = EmployeeList;
    }
  }
}
```

We define two data templates, one each for the Address type and the Employee type in the MainPage.xaml file, as shown in Listing 4-8.

Listing 4-8. *DataTemplates for the Address and Employee Data Types*

```
<UserControl.Resources>
  <DataTemplate x:Key="dtAddress">
    <Grid >
      <Grid.RowDefinitions>
        <RowDefinition Height="Auto"/>
        <RowDefinition Height="Auto"/>
      </Grid.RowDefinitions>
      <Grid.ColumnDefinitions>
        <ColumnDefinition Width="Auto" />
      </Grid.ColumnDefinitions>
      <TextBlock x:Name="tblkStreet" HorizontalAlignment="Stretch"
                 VerticalAlignment="Stretch" Text="{Binding Street}"
                 TextWrapping="Wrap" Foreground="White" FontSize="12"
                 FontWeight="Bold"/>
      <StackPanel  Grid.RowSpan="1" Orientation="Horizontal" Grid.Row="1"
                   VerticalAlignment="Stretch">
        <TextBlock  x:Name="tblkCity" Text="{Binding City}"
                    TextWrapping="Wrap" FontSize="12"
                    FontWeight="Bold" Foreground="White"/>
        <TextBlock  x:Name="tblkComma" Text="," TextWrapping="Wrap"
                    Margin="2,0,2,0" FontSize="12" FontWeight="Bold"
                    Foreground="White"/>
        <TextBlock  x:Name="tblkState" Text="{Binding State}"
                    TextWrapping="Wrap" FontSize="12"
                    FontWeight="Bold" Foreground="White"/>

        <TextBlock  x:Name="tblkZip" Text="{Binding ZipCode}"
                    TextWrapping="Wrap" Margin="3,0,0,0" FontSize="12"
                    FontWeight="Bold" Foreground="White"/>
      </StackPanel>
    </Grid>
  </DataTemplate>
  <DataTemplate x:Key="dtEmployee">
    <Grid Height="Auto" Width="300" Margin="5,5,5,5">
      <Grid.ColumnDefinitions>
        <ColumnDefinition Width="0.508*"/>
        <ColumnDefinition Width="0.492*"/>
      </Grid.ColumnDefinitions>
```

```xml
      <Grid.RowDefinitions>
        <RowDefinition Height="0.801*" />
        <RowDefinition Height="0.199*"/>
      </Grid.RowDefinitions>
      <Rectangle HorizontalAlignment="Stretch" Margin="0,-74.9660034179688,0,0"
                 Stroke="#FF000000" Grid.Row="1" Grid.RowSpan="1" RadiusX="3"
                 RadiusY="3" StrokeThickness="0" Fill="#FF9FA8E4"/>
      <Rectangle HorizontalAlignment="Stretch" Margin="0,0,0,0"
                 Grid.ColumnSpan="2" Grid.RowSpan="1" RadiusX="3"
                 RadiusY="3" Stroke="#FF686868" StrokeThickness="0"
                 Width="Auto">
        <Rectangle.Fill>
          <LinearGradientBrush EndPoint="0.5,1" StartPoint="0.5,0">
            <GradientStop Color="#FF000000"/>
            <GradientStop Color="#FF9FA8E4" Offset="1"/>
          </LinearGradientBrush>
        </Rectangle.Fill>
      </Rectangle>
      <Rectangle HorizontalAlignment="Stretch" Margin="3,3,3,3"
                 Stroke="#FF0A28EE" Grid.RowSpan="1"
                 StrokeThickness="5" VerticalAlignment="Stretch"/>
      <Image Margin="8,8,8,8" x:Name="imgEmployee"
             Source="{Binding ImageUri}"
             Stretch="Fill"
             HorizontalAlignment="Stretch" VerticalAlignment="Stretch"
             Grid.RowSpan="1"/>
      <StackPanel Margin="0,-0.114000000059605,0,0" Orientation="Horizontal"
                  Grid.Row="1" Grid.ColumnSpan="1" VerticalAlignment="Stretch"
                  Grid.RowSpan="1">
        <TextBlock x:Name="tblkFirstName" Text="{Binding FirstName}"
                   TextWrapping="Wrap" FontSize="14" FontWeight="Bold"
                   Foreground="White" Margin="3,0,0,0"/>
        <TextBlock x:Name="tblkLastName" Text="{Binding LastName}"
                   TextWrapping="Wrap" FontSize="14" FontWeight="Bold"
                   Margin="3,0,0,0" Foreground="White"/>
      </StackPanel>
      <StackPanel Margin="0,0,0,0" Grid.Column="1">
        <ContentControl ContentTemplate="{StaticResource dtAddress}"
                        Content="{Binding Address}" Foreground="#FF0A28EE" />
        <TextBlock x:Name="tblkPhoneNum" Text="{Binding PhoneNum}"
                   TextWrapping="Wrap" FontSize="12" FontWeight="Bold"
                   Margin="0,5,0,0" Foreground="White"/>
      </StackPanel>
    </Grid>
  </DataTemplate>
</UserControl.Resources>
```

You can see that a `DataTemplate` can in turn use another `DataTemplate` in a nested fashion. In dtEmployee earlier, we use a `ContentControl` to display an employee's address, and we reuse `dtAddress` as the `ContentTemplate`. This kind of reuse helps facilitate the consistency in UI representation of data, keeping in line with the promise of `DataTemplates`.

Applying the `DataTemplate` is simple. Let's apply it to a `ContentControl` like so

```
<ContentControl x:Name="cntctrlEmployee" HorizontalAlignment="Stretch"
            VerticalAlignment="Stretch"
            Grid.Column="0" Background="Yellow" Margin="5,5,5,5"
            ContentTemplate="{StaticResource dtEmployee}" Height="200"/>
```

and bind it to the first `Employee` in the `EmployeeList` collection, as shown in the `MainPage`'s constructor code in Listing 4-7:

```
cntctrlEmployee.Content = EmployeeList[0];
```

Figure 4-2 shows the `DataTemplate` in action.

Figure 4-2. *DataTemplate in action in a ContentControl*

Let's also apply the same `DataTemplate` to a `ListBox`:

```
<ListBox x:Name="itmctrlEmployees"
        HorizontalAlignment="Stretch" VerticalAlignment="Stretch"
        Grid.Column="1"
        Width="325"
        ItemTemplate="{StaticResource dtEmployee}"
        Height="400"/>
```

and bind it to the entire `EmployeeList` collection, as shown in the `MainPage`'s constructor code in Listing 4-7:

```
itmctrlEmployees.ItemsSource = EmployeeList;
```

This time, you see the `DataTemplate` being applied to each item in the `ListBox` but producing a consistent UI, as shown in Figure 4-3.

Figure 4-3. *DataTemplate applied to ItemTemplate of a ListBox*

4-3. Receiving Change Notifications for Bound Data

Problem

You have data-bound elements in your UI, and you want to enable change notifications and automatic refresh of the UI when the bound application data changes.

Solution

You implement the `System.ComponentModel.INotifyPropertyChanged` interface in your data types and the `System.Collections.Specialized.INotifyCollectionChanged` interface in your collection types. You then raise the events defined in these interfaces from the implementing types to provide change notifications. You also ensure that the `Mode` property for each data binding is set to either `BindingMode.OneWay` or `BindingMode.TwoWay` to enable automatic UI refresh.

How It Works

The Silverlight binding infrastructure is aware of these two special interfaces and automatically subscribes to change notification events defined in the interfaces when implemented by the data source types.

Change Notification for Noncollection Types

The `INotifyPropertyChanged` interface has a single event named `PropertyChanged`. The event parameter is of type `PropertyChangedEventArgs`, which accepts the name of the changing property as a string parameter to the constructor and exposes it through the `PropertyName` property. The `PropertyChangedEvntArgs` class is shown here:

```
public class PropertyChangedEventArgs : EventArgs
{
    // Fields
    private readonly string propertyName;

    // Methods
    public PropertyChangedEventArgs(string propertyName);

    // Properties
    public string PropertyName { get; }
}
```

Once you implement the INotifyPropertyChanged interface in your data source type, you raise PropertyChanged whenever you need to raise change notifications for any of the bound source properties. You pass in the name of the property being changed through an instance of PropertyChangedEventArgs. Listing 4-9 shows a small but pretty standard sample implementation.

Listing 4-9. *Sample Implementation of INotifyPropertyChanged*

```
public class Notifier : INotifyPropertyChanged
{
  //implementing INotifyPropertyChanged
  public event PropertyChangedEventHandler PropertyChanged;
  //utility method to raise PropertyChanged
  private void RaisePropertyChanged(PropertyChangedEventArgs e)
  {
    if (PropertyChanged != null)
      PropertyChanged(this, e);
  }

  private string _SomeBoundProperty;
  public string SomeBoundProperty
  {
    get { return _SomeBoundProperty; }
    set
    {
      //save old value
      string OldVal = _SomeBoundProperty;
      //compare with new value
      if (OldVal != value)
      {
        //if different, set property
        _SomeBoundProperty = value;
```

```
      //and raise PropertyChanged
      RaisePropertyChanged(new
        PropertyChangedEventArgs("SomeBoundProperty"));
    }

  }
 }
}
```

Change Notification for Collection Types

The INotifyCollectionChanged interface also has a single event, named CollectionChanged, which can be raised by implementing collection types to provide change notifications. The change information that can be gained for collections is richer in comparison to INotifyPropertyChanged, as you can see in the NotifyCollectionChangedEventArgs type listed here:

```
public sealed class NotifyCollectionChangedEventArgs : EventArgs
{
  // Other members omitted for brevity

  public NotifyCollectionChangedEventArgs(NotifyCollectionChangedAction action,
  object newItem, object oldItem, int index);

  public NotifyCollectionChangedAction Action { get; }

  public IList NewItems { get; }

  public int NewStartingIndex { get; }

  public IList OldItems { get; }

  public int OldStartingIndex { get; }
}
```

The code sample in the next section shows a custom collection that implements INotifyCollectionChanged.

The Code

The sample code for this recipe builds a simple data entry form over the data structures in Listing 4-10.

Listing 4-10. *Application Data Classes*

```
using System.Collections.Generic;
using System.Collections.Specialized;
using System.ComponentModel;

namespace Ch04_DataBinding.Recipe4_3
{
  public class Employee : INotifyPropertyChanged
  {

    public event PropertyChangedEventHandler PropertyChanged;
    private void RaisePropertyChanged(PropertyChangedEventArgs e)
    {
      if (PropertyChanged != null)
        PropertyChanged(this, e);
    }

    public Employee()
    {
    }

    private string _FirstName;
    public string FirstName
    {
      get { return _FirstName; }
      set
      {
        string OldVal = _FirstName;
        if (OldVal != value)
        {
          _FirstName = value;
          RaisePropertyChanged(new PropertyChangedEventArgs("FirstName"));
        }
      }
    }
```

```csharp
private string _LastName;
public string LastName
{
  get { return _LastName; }
  set
  {
    string OldVal = _LastName;
    if (OldVal != value)
    {
      _LastName = value;
      RaisePropertyChanged(new PropertyChangedEventArgs("LastName"));
    }
  }
}

private long _PhoneNum;
public long PhoneNum
{
  get { return _PhoneNum; }
  set
  {
    long OldVal = _PhoneNum;
    if (OldVal != value)
    {
      _PhoneNum = value;
      RaisePropertyChanged(new PropertyChangedEventArgs("PhoneNum"));
    }
  }
}

private Address _Address;
public Address Address
{
  get { return _Address; }
  set
  {
    Address OldVal = _Address;
    if (OldVal != value)
    {
      _Address = value;
      RaisePropertyChanged(new PropertyChangedEventArgs("Address"));
    }
  }
}
```

```
public class Address : INotifyPropertyChanged
{
  public event PropertyChangedEventHandler PropertyChanged;
  private void RaisePropertyChanged(PropertyChangedEventArgs e)
  {
    if (PropertyChanged != null)
      PropertyChanged(this, e);
  }

  private string _Street;
  public string Street
  {
    get { return _Street; }
    set
    {
      string OldVal = _Street;
      if (OldVal != value)
      {
        _Street = value;
        RaisePropertyChanged(new PropertyChangedEventArgs("Street"));
      }
    }
  }

  private string _City;
  public string City
  {
    get { return _City; }
    set
    {
      string OldVal = _City;
      if (OldVal != value)
      {
        _City = value;
        RaisePropertyChanged(new PropertyChangedEventArgs("City"));
      }
    }
  }

  private string _State;
  public string State
  {
    get { return _State; }
    set
```

```
  {
    string OldVal = _State;
    if (OldVal != value)
    {
      _State = value;
      RaisePropertyChanged(new PropertyChangedEventArgs("State"));
    }
  }
}

private int _ZipCode;
public int ZipCode
{
  get { return _ZipCode; }
  set
  {
    int OldVal = _ZipCode;
    if (OldVal != value)
    {
      _ZipCode = value;
      RaisePropertyChanged(new PropertyChangedEventArgs("ZipCode"));
    }
  }
}
}

public class EmployeeCollection : ICollection<Employee>,
  IList<Employee>,
  INotifyCollectionChanged
{
  private List<Employee> _internalList;

  public EmployeeCollection()
  {
    _internalList = new List<Employee>();
  }

  public event NotifyCollectionChangedEventHandler CollectionChanged;

  private void RaiseCollectionChanged(NotifyCollectionChangedEventArgs e)
  {
    if (CollectionChanged != null)
    {
      CollectionChanged(this, e);
    }
  }
```

```
//Methods/Properties that would possibly change the collection and its content
//need to raise the CollectionChanged event
public void Add(Employee item)
{
  _internalList.Add(item);
  RaiseCollectionChanged(
    new NotifyCollectionChangedEventArgs(NotifyCollectionChangedAction.Add,
      item, _internalList.Count - 1));
}
public void Clear()
{
  _internalList.Clear();
  RaiseCollectionChanged(
    new NotifyCollectionChangedEventArgs(NotifyCollectionChangedAction.Reset));
}
public bool Remove(Employee item)
{
  int idx = _internalList.IndexOf(item);
  bool RetVal = _internalList.Remove(item);
  if (RetVal)
    RaiseCollectionChanged(
      new NotifyCollectionChangedEventArgs(
        NotifyCollectionChangedAction.Remove, item, idx));
  return RetVal;
}
public void RemoveAt(int index)
{
  Employee item = null;
  if (index < _internalList.Count)
    item = _internalList[index];
  _internalList.RemoveAt(index);
  if (index < _internalList.Count)
    RaiseCollectionChanged(
      new NotifyCollectionChangedEventArgs(
        NotifyCollectionChangedAction.Remove, item, index));

}
public void Insert(int index, Employee item)
{
  _internalList.Insert(index, item);
  RaiseCollectionChanged(
    new NotifyCollectionChangedEventArgs(
      NotifyCollectionChangedAction.Add, item, index));
}
```

```csharp
    public Employee this[int index]
    {
      get { return _internalList[index]; }
      set
      {
        _internalList[index] = value;
        RaiseCollectionChanged(
          new NotifyCollectionChangedEventArgs(
            NotifyCollectionChangedAction.Replace, value, index));


      }
    }

    public bool Contains(Employee item)
    {
      return _internalList.Contains(item);
    }
    public void CopyTo(Employee[] array, int arrayIndex)
    {
      _internalList.CopyTo(array, arrayIndex);
    }
    public int Count
    {
      get { return _internalList.Count; }
    }
    public bool IsReadOnly
    {
      get { return ((IList<Employee>)_internalList).IsReadOnly; }
    }
    public IEnumerator<Employee> GetEnumerator()
    {
      return _internalList.GetEnumerator();
    }
    System.Collections.IEnumerator System.Collections.IEnumerable.GetEnumerator()
    {
      return (System.Collections.IEnumerator)_internalList.GetEnumerator();
    }
    public int IndexOf(Employee item)
    {
      return _internalList.IndexOf(item);
    }
  }

}
```

As shown in Listing 4-10, both the Employee and the Address types implement INotifyPropertyChanged to provide change notification. We also define a custom collection named EmployeeCollection for Employee instances and implement INotifyCollectionChanged on the collection type.

You can see the additional change information that can be accessed through the NotifyCollectionChangedEventArgs. Using the NotifyCollectionChangedAction enumeration, you can specify the type of change (Add, Remove, Replace, or Reset). You can also specify the item that changed and its index in the collection. This detail allows the binding infrastructure to optimize the binding so that the entire UI bound to the collection need not be refreshed for each change in the collection.

Also note that the System.Collections.ObjectModel contains a generic type named ObservableCollection<T> that already implements INotifyCollectionChanged. For all data binding scenarios, unless you have a specific reason to implement your own collection type, ObservableCollection<T> should meet your needs, as it does ours in the rest of this book.

However, ObservableCollection<T> simply extends Collection<T>, which is a base collection class in the framework. If you choose to have change notification enabled for some of the other, more advanced, collections in the framework, such as List<T> or LinkedList<T>, or if you have implemented your own custom collection types with custom business logic, implementing INotifyCollectionChanged is the way to go.

Another scenario where you might choose to implement a custom collection is if you want to declare the collection as a resource in your XAML. This would necessitate creating a nongeneric collection class, with a default constructor, and you would possibly want to initialize such a collection in the constructor. You can, however, extend ObservableCollection directly in such cases and do away with the need to implement any of the collection manipulation methods shown in the previous sample.

Listing 4-11 shows the simple data entry UI that we build on top of this collection.

Listing 4-11. *Data Entry UI XAML*

```
<UserControl x:Class="Ch04_DataBinding.Recipe4_3.MainPage"
            xmlns="http://schemas.microsoft.com/winfx/2006/xaml/presentation"
            xmlns:x="http://schemas.microsoft.com/winfx/2006/xaml"
            xmlns:local="clr-namespace:Ch04_DataBinding.Recipe4_3"
            xmlns:d="http://schemas.microsoft.com/expression/blend/2008"
            xmlns:mc="http://schemas.openxmlformats.org/markup-compatibility/2006"
            Width="400"
            Height="441">

    <UserControl.Resources>
        <!-- Employee collection Data source -->
        <local:EmployeeCollection x:Key="REF_EmployeeCollection" />
        <!-- Data template to be used for the Employee type -->
        <DataTemplate x:Key="dtEmployee">
            <StackPanel Orientation="Horizontal">
                <TextBlock Text="{Binding FirstName}" />
                <TextBlock Text="{Binding LastName}"
                           Margin="5,0,0,0" />
            </StackPanel>
        </DataTemplate>
    </UserControl.Resources>
```

```xml
<Grid x:Name="LayoutRoot"
      Background="White"
      Margin="10,10,10,10">
    <Grid.RowDefinitions>
        <RowDefinition Height="*" />
        <RowDefinition Height="Auto" />
        <RowDefinition Height="Auto" />
        <RowDefinition Height="Auto" />
    </Grid.RowDefinitions>
    <ListBox Grid.Row="0"
             x:Name="lbx_Employees"
             ItemsSource="{StaticResource REF_EmployeeCollection}"
             ItemTemplate="{StaticResource dtEmployee}"
             SelectionChanged="lbx_Employees_SelectionChanged" />
    <Grid x:Name="grid_NewButton"
          Margin="0,2,0,0"
          Grid.Row="1"
          HorizontalAlignment="Right">
        <Button  x:Name="btn_New"
                 Click="btn_New_Click"
                 Content="New Employee" />
    </Grid>
    <Border Grid.Row="2"
            Visibility="Collapsed"
            x:Name="border_EmployeeForm"
            Margin="0,2,0,0"
            BorderBrush="Black"
            BorderThickness="1"
            Padding="1,1,1,1">
        <Grid x:Name="grid_EmployeeForm">
            <Grid.ColumnDefinitions>
                <ColumnDefinition Width="0.142*" />
                <ColumnDefinition Width="0.379*" />
                <ColumnDefinition Width="0.1*" />
                <ColumnDefinition Width="0.097*" />
                <ColumnDefinition Width="0.082*" />
                <ColumnDefinition Width="0.2*" />
            </Grid.ColumnDefinitions>
            <Grid.RowDefinitions>
                <RowDefinition Height="0.10*" />
                <RowDefinition Height="0.15*" />
                <RowDefinition Height="0.15*" />
                <RowDefinition Height="0.15*" />
                <RowDefinition Height="0.45*" />
            </Grid.RowDefinitions>
```

```
<TextBox HorizontalAlignment="Stretch"
        Margin="1,1,1,1"
        x:Name="tbxFName"
        VerticalAlignment="Stretch"
        Text="{Binding FirstName, Mode=TwoWay}"
        Grid.Row="1"
        Width="Auto"
        Grid.RowSpan="1"
        Grid.ColumnSpan="2"
        Grid.Column="1" />
<TextBox HorizontalAlignment="Stretch"
        Margin="1,1,1,1"
        x:Name="tbxLName"
        VerticalAlignment="Stretch"
        Text="{Binding LastName, Mode=TwoWay}"
        Grid.Row="1"
        Grid.Column="3"
        Width="Auto"
        Grid.RowSpan="1"
        Grid.ColumnSpan="3" />
<TextBlock HorizontalAlignment="Stretch"
          Margin="1,1,1,1"
          VerticalAlignment="Stretch"
          Text="Last"
          TextWrapping="Wrap"
          Grid.RowSpan="1"
          Grid.Column="4"
          Grid.ColumnSpan="2"
          Height="Auto"
          Width="Auto" />
<TextBlock HorizontalAlignment="Center"
          Margin="1,1,1,1"
          VerticalAlignment="Center"
          Text="First"
          TextWrapping="Wrap"
          Grid.RowSpan="1"
          Grid.Column="1"
          Width="Auto"
          Height="Auto" />
```

```xml
<TextBlock HorizontalAlignment="Center"
           Margin="1,1,1,1"
           VerticalAlignment="Stretch"
           Text="Name"
           TextWrapping="Wrap"
           Grid.RowSpan="1"
           Grid.Row="1"
           Height="Auto"
           Width="Auto" />
<TextBlock HorizontalAlignment="Center"
           Margin="1,1,1,1"
           VerticalAlignment="Stretch"
           Text="Street"
           TextWrapping="Wrap"
           Grid.Row="2"
           Width="Auto" />
<TextBox HorizontalAlignment="Stretch"
         x:Name="tbxStreet"
         VerticalAlignment="Stretch"
         Text="{Binding Address.Street, Mode=TwoWay}"
         Grid.Row="2"
         Margin="1,1,1,1"
         Grid.Column="1"
         Grid.ColumnSpan="5"
         Width="Auto" />
<TextBlock HorizontalAlignment="Center"
           VerticalAlignment="Stretch"
           Text="City"
           TextWrapping="Wrap"
           Margin="1,1,1,1"
           Grid.Row="3" />
<TextBlock Text="State"
           Margin="1,1,1,1"
           TextWrapping="Wrap"
           Grid.Column="2"
           Grid.Row="3"
           HorizontalAlignment="Center" />
<TextBlock Text="Zip"
           Margin="1,1,1,1"
           TextWrapping="Wrap"
           Grid.Column="4"
           Grid.Row="3"
           HorizontalAlignment="Center" />
```

```xml
                    <TextBox HorizontalAlignment="Stretch"
                            x:Name="tbxCity"
                            Margin="1,1,1,1"
                            VerticalAlignment="Stretch"
                            Text="{Binding Address.City, Mode=TwoWay}"
                            Grid.Row="3"
                            Grid.Column="1" />
                    <TextBox Background="Transparent"
                            Grid.Column="3"
                            Margin="1,1,1,1"
                            Grid.Row="3"
                            Text="{Binding Address.State, Mode=TwoWay }"
                            x:Name="tbxState">
                    </TextBox>
                    <TextBox Background="Transparent"
                            Grid.Column="5"
                            Grid.Row="3"
                            Margin="1,1,1,1"
                            Text="{Binding Address.ZipCode, Mode=TwoWay }"
                            x:Name="tbxZipCode" />
                    <TextBlock HorizontalAlignment="Center"
                            VerticalAlignment="Stretch"
                            Text="Phone"
                            Margin="1,1,1,1"
                            TextWrapping="Wrap"
                            Grid.Row="4" />
                    <TextBox Grid.Column="1"
                            Grid.Row="4"
                            Margin="1,1,1,1"
                            Text="{Binding PhoneNum, Mode=TwoWay }"
                            x:Name="tbxPhoneNum" />
                    <Button  Grid.Column="5"
                            Margin="1,1,1,1"
                            Grid.Row="4"
                            Height="30.911"
                            VerticalAlignment="Top"
                            Content="Close"
                            x:Name="btnClose"
                            Click="btnClose_Click" />

            </Grid>
        </Border>
    </Grid>
</UserControl>
```

You can see that, for the editable controls, we set the Mode property of the binding to BindingMode.TwoWay. The Mode property can be set to one of three values:

- BindingMode.OneTime binds the value coming from the data source only once, when the element is initially displayed, and never again during the lifetime of the application. This is useful for static data that does not change for the lifetime of the application.

- BindingMode.OneWay refreshes the bound value with any changes that happens to the data source but does not propagate changes made in the UI to the bound data source. This is useful for data that is read only to the user but that can change through other means in the application. This is the default setting for Binding.Mode if you do not specify any setting in your XAML or code.

- BindingMode.TwoWay enables bidirectional propagation of changes and is the suitable mode for data-editing scenarios.

Running the sample produces the output shown in Figure 4-4.

Figure 4-4. *Initial output from the application*

Listing 4-12 shows the code-behind for the MainPage. As shown in the constructor, we initialize the bound EmployeeCollection instance with some initial Employee data. If you selected one of the records, you would see the output in Figure 4-5.

Listing 4-12. *Code-Behind for the Page*

```
using System.Windows;
using System.Windows.Controls;
using System.Collections.ObjectModel;

namespace Ch04_DataBinding.Recipe4_3
{
  public partial class MainPage : UserControl
  {
    public MainPage()
    {
      InitializeComponent();

      //initialize the employee collection with some sample data
      EmployeeCollection empColl = (EmployeeCollection)lbx_Employees.ItemsSource;

      empColl.Add(new Employee
      {
        FirstName = "Joe",
        LastName = "Duffin",
        PhoneNum = 2125551212,
        Address = new Address
        {
          Street = "2000 Mott Street",
          City = "New York",
          State = "NY",
          ZipCode = 10006
        }
      });

      empColl.Add(new Employee
      {
        FirstName = "Alex",
        LastName = "Bleeker",
        PhoneNum = 7185551212,
        Address = new Address
        {
          Street = "11000 Clover Street",
          City = "New York",
          State = "NY",
          ZipCode = 10007
        }
      });
```

```csharp
  empColl.Add(new Employee
  {
    FirstName = "Nelly",
    LastName = "Myers",
    PhoneNum = 7325551212,
    Address = new Address
    {
      Street = "12000 Fay Road",
      City = "New York",
      State = "NY",
      ZipCode = 10016
    }
  });
}

private void btn_New_Click(object sender, RoutedEventArgs e)
{
  //get the bound collection
  EmployeeCollection empColl = (EmployeeCollection)lbx_Employees.ItemsSource;
  //create and initialize a new Employee
  Employee newEmp = new Employee();
  newEmp.Address = new Address();
  //add it to the collection
  empColl.Add(newEmp);
  //set the current selection to the newly added employee.
  //This will cause selection change to fire, and set
  //the datacontext for the form appropriately
  lbx_Employees.SelectedItem = newEmp;

}

private void lbx_Employees_SelectionChanged(object sender,
  SelectionChangedEventArgs e)
{
  //set the datacontext of the form to the selected Employee
  grid_EmployeeForm.DataContext = (Employee)lbx_Employees.SelectedItem;
  //show the form
  border_EmployeeForm.Visibility = Visibility.Visible;
  grid_NewButton.Visibility = Visibility.Collapsed;
}
```

```
    private void btnClose_Click(object sender, RoutedEventArgs e)
    {
      //hide the form
      border_EmployeeForm.Visibility = Visibility.Collapsed;
      grid_NewButton.Visibility = Visibility.Visible;
    }
  }
}
```

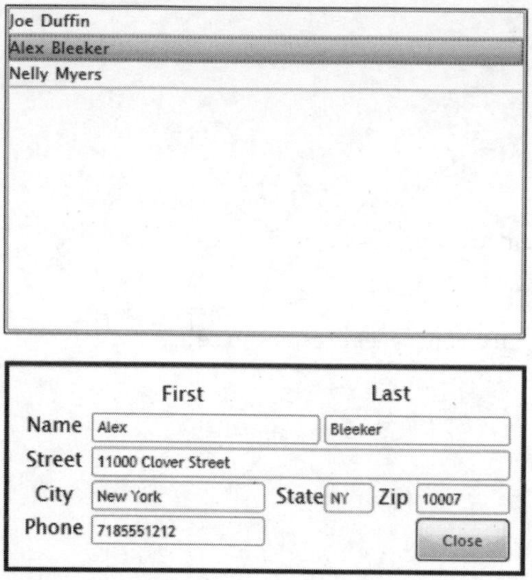

Figure 4-5. *Edit form for an existing employee*

In the SelectionChanged handler for lbxEmployees, named lbx_Employees_SelectionChanged() in Listing 4-12, we set the DataContext of the containing Grid named grid_EmployeeForm to the selected Employee data item. This populates the contained fields with various properties of the Employee instance based on the bindings defined in Listing 4-11. We then make the Grid visible.

If you try editing the First Name field, you should see it changing in the selected item in the ListBox once you tab out of the field after the edit. As the data entry form propagates the change back to the appropriate Employee item in the collection as a result of the TwoWay binding, this action in turn causes the ListBox's binding to the collection to refresh the selected item.

If you click the New Employee button, you should get a blank data entry form, as shown in Figure 4-6, and see a blank item added to the ListBox. To achieve this, we handle the Click event of the button in btn_New_Click (), again shown in Listing 4-12. We create a new instance of the Employee type, initialize it, and add it to the collection. This takes care of displaying the blank item in the ListBox through the change notification mechanism of INotifyCollectionChanged. We also programmatically make that item the selected item in the ListBox, which in turns fires the SelectionChanged handler of the ListBox, and the data entry form is displayed again, as described in the previous paragraph.

Filling the fields in the data entry form should again cause change notifications to be propagated to the ListBox, as you tab out of fields.

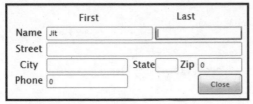

Figure 4-6. *Entering a new employee*

4-4. Converting Values During Data Binding

Problem

You are trying to bind to a data source and need to convert the source value to either a different type or a different value suitable for display in the UI.

Solution

Implement System.Windows.Data.IValueConverter to create a value converter type, and associate it to the binding to appropriately convert the value.

How It Works

Often, you will come across scenarios where the source value that you are trying to bind to is either of a data type that needs to be converted before it can be bound, or has the same data type as the target but needs some logical or contextual transformation before it can be meaningful to the UI.

As an example, imagine the Visibility property of a control. It is natural to think of Visibility as a Boolean, and thus express it in code as a bool. However, trying to bind a bool to the Visibility property of a Silverlight control will pose a challenge: in Silverlight, Visibility is expressed in terms of the Visibility enumeration, which has two values, Visible and Collapsed. In this case, you will need to convert from a source type (bool) to a target type (Visibility).

Imagine another scenario where you have the monthly spending of a family broken into categories as a data source, and you need to visually represent each expenditure as a percentage of the total. In this case, the data types of both the source and the target can be the same (say a double), but there is a logical transformation required between them—from an absolute value to a percentage.

Implementing Value Conversion

To use value conversion, you implement the System.Windows.Data.IValueConverter interface. The IValueConverter interface accommodates both source-to-target conversion (through the Convert() method) and target-to-source conversion (through the ConvertBack() method).

Listing 4-13 shows a sample converter implementation that converts bool to Visibility and back.

Listing 4-13. *Value Converter That Converts from bool to Visibility*

```
public class BoolToVisibilityConverter : IValueConverter
{
  public object Convert(object value, Type targetType,
    object parameter, System.Globalization.CultureInfo culture)
  {
    //check to see that the parameter types are conformant
    if (value.GetType() != typeof(bool) || targetType != typeof(Visibility))
      return null;
    bool src = (bool)value;
    //translate
    return (src == true) ? Visibility.Visible : Visibility.Collapsed;
  }

  public object ConvertBack(object value, Type targetType,
    object parameter, System.Globalization.CultureInfo culture)
  {
    //check to see that the parameter types are conformant
    if (value.GetType() != typeof(Visibility) || targetType != typeof(bool))
      return null;
    Visibility src = (Visibility)value;
    //translate
    return (src == Visibility.Visible) ? true : false;
  }
}
```

In both methods, the first parameter named value is the source value, and the second parameter named targetType is the data type of the target to which the value needs to be converted. The ConvertBack() method will need to be fully implemented if you have a two-way binding, where an edit on the UI would require the change to be sent back to the source. If you do not update the data through your UI, you can simply either return null or throw a suitable exception from the ConvertBack() method.

Also note that each method accepts a parameter, aptly named parameter, where you can pass additional information as may be required by the conversion logic, as well as the target culture as the last parameter, in case you need to take into account a difference in the culture between source and target.

To use the value converter, you first declare it as a resource in your XAML, with an appropriate custom namespace mapping to bring in the assembly, in this case local:

```
<local:BoolToVisibilityConverter x:Name="REF_BoolToVisibilityConverter" />
```

After the converter resource has been declared as shown here, you can associate it to a `Binding` by using its `Converter` property. Once the converter is associated, every piece of data flowing through the `Binding` either way is passed through the converter methods—`Convert()` if the data is flowing from the source to the target property, and `ConvertBack()` if it is the other way. A sample usage is shown here:

```
<ContentControl Visibility="{Binding IsControlVisible,
  Converter={StaticResource REF_BoolToVisibilityConverter}}"/>
```

where `IsControlVisible` is a Boolean property on a data source CLR type bound to the control.

The Code

The code sample builds a simple spending analysis application for a family, where the expenditure for different categories are maintained in a `DataGrid` and also graphed in a bar graph as a percentage of the total. The application allows you to change the spending in each category to different values and watch the graph change accordingly. It also allows you to drag any bar in the graph using your mouse and watch the corresponding value change in the `DataGrid`, maintaining the same total. Figure 4-7 shows the application output.

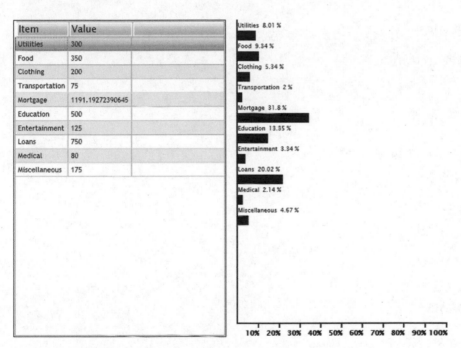

Figure 4-7. *Family spending chart*

Listing 4-14 shows the data classes used for this sample. The `Spending` class represents a specific expenditure, while the `SpendingCollection` extends `ObservableCollection<Spending>` to add some initialization code in a default constructor.

Listing 4-14. *Application Data Classes*

```
using System.Collections.ObjectModel;
using System.ComponentModel;
using System.Linq;

namespace Ch04_DataBinding.Recipe4_4
{
  public class SpendingCollection : ObservableCollection<Spending>,
    INotifyPropertyChanged
  {
    public SpendingCollection()
    {
      this.Add(new Spending
      {
        ParentCollection = this,
        Item = "Utilities",
        Amount = 300
      });
      this.Add(new Spending
      {
        ParentCollection = this,
        Item = "Food",
        Amount = 350
      });
      this.Add(new Spending
      {
        ParentCollection = this,
        Item = "Clothing",
        Amount = 200
      });
      this.Add(new Spending
      {
        ParentCollection = this,
        Item = "Transportation",
        Amount = 75
      });
      this.Add(new Spending
      {
        ParentCollection = this,
        Item = "Mortgage",
        Amount = 3000
      });
```

```
      this.Add(new Spending
      {
        ParentCollection = this,
        Item = "Education",
        Amount = 500
      });
      this.Add(new Spending
      {
        ParentCollection = this,
        Item = "Entertainment",
        Amount = 125
      });
      this.Add(new Spending
      {
        ParentCollection = this,
        Item = "Loans",
        Amount = 750
      });
      this.Add(new Spending
      {
        ParentCollection = this,
        Item = "Medical",
        Amount = 80
      });
      this.Add(new Spending
      {
        ParentCollection = this,
        Item = "Miscellaneous",
        Amount = 175
      });
    }

    public double Total
    {
      get
      {
        return this.Sum(spending => spending.Amount);
      }
    }
  }
```

```csharp
public class Spending : INotifyPropertyChanged
{

  public event PropertyChangedEventHandler PropertyChanged;
  internal void RaisePropertyChanged(PropertyChangedEventArgs e)
  {
    if (PropertyChanged != null)
    {
      PropertyChanged(this, e);
    }
  }


  SpendingCollection _ParentCollection = null;

  public SpendingCollection ParentCollection
  {
    get { return _ParentCollection; }
    set { _ParentCollection = value; }
  }

  private string _Item;
  public string Item
  {
    get { return _Item; }
    set
    {
      string OldVal = _Item;
      if (OldVal != value)
      {
        _Item = value;
        RaisePropertyChanged(new PropertyChangedEventArgs("Item"));

      }
    }
  }
}
```

```
    private double _Amount;
    public double Amount
    {
      get { return _Amount; }
      set
      {
        double OldVal = _Amount;
        if (OldVal != value)
        {
          _Amount = value;


          foreach (Spending sp in ParentCollection)
            sp.RaisePropertyChanged(new PropertyChangedEventArgs("Amount"));

        }
      }
    }
  }
}
```

Listing 4-15 shows the XAML for the page. If you look at the resources section, you will notice that we reference two value converters. SpendingToBarWidthConverter converts a double value representing Spending to another double value representing a corresponding bar width, and vice versa. SpendingToPercentageStringConverter converts a Spending value to a percentage of the total spending, and vice versa. We will discuss the converter implementations in more detail momentarily.

Listing 4-15. *XAML for the Page*

```
<UserControl x:Class="Ch04_DataBinding.Recipe4_4.MainPage"
    xmlns="http://schemas.microsoft.com/winfx/2006/xaml/presentation"
    xmlns:x="http://schemas.microsoft.com/winfx/2006/xaml"
    xmlns:data=
    "clr-namespace:System.Windows.Controls;assembly=System.Windows.Controls.Data"
    xmlns:local="clr-namespace:Ch04_DataBinding.Recipe4_4"
    Width="800" Height="510">

  <UserControl.Resources>
    <local:SpendingCollection x:Key="REF_SpendingList" />
    <local:SpendingToBarWidthConverter x:Key="REF_SpendingToBarWidthConverter" />
    <local:SpendingToPercentageStringConverter
      x:Key="REF_SpendingToPercentageStringConverter" />
```

```xml
        <DataTemplate x:Key="dtBarTemplate">
          <Grid HorizontalAlignment="Left" VerticalAlignment="Stretch"
                Height="30"  Margin="0,2,0,0" >
            <Grid.RowDefinitions>
              <RowDefinition Height="0.5*" />
              <RowDefinition Height="0.5*" />
            </Grid.RowDefinitions>
            <Rectangle Grid.Row="1" VerticalAlignment="Stretch"
                       Fill="Black" HorizontalAlignment="Left"
                       Width="{Binding Amount,Mode=TwoWay,
                        Converter={StaticResource REF_SpendingToBarWidthConverter},
                        ConverterParameter={StaticResource REF_SpendingList}}"
                       MouseMove="Rectangle_MouseMove"
                       MouseLeftButtonDown="Rectangle_MouseLeftButtonDown"
                       MouseLeftButtonUp="Rectangle_MouseLeftButtonUp"/>
            <StackPanel Orientation="Horizontal" Grid.Row="0">
              <TextBlock Text="{Binding Item}" FontSize="9" />
              <TextBlock Text="{Binding Amount,
                 Converter={StaticResource REF_SpendingToPercentageStringConverter},
                 ConverterParameter={StaticResource REF_SpendingList}}"
                       Margin="5,0,0,0"
                       FontSize="9"/>
            </StackPanel>
          </Grid>
        </DataTemplate>
    </UserControl.Resources>

    <Grid x:Name="LayoutRoot" Background="White" Width="694">
      <Grid.ColumnDefinitions>
        <ColumnDefinition Width="*"/>
        <ColumnDefinition Width="*"/>
      </Grid.ColumnDefinitions>
      <data:DataGrid HorizontalAlignment="Stretch" Margin="8,8,8,8"
                     VerticalAlignment="Stretch"
                     HeadersVisibility="Column" x:Name="dgSpending"
                     ItemsSource="{StaticResource REF_SpendingList}"
                     AutoGenerateColumns="False">
        <data:DataGrid.Columns>
          <data:DataGridTextColumn Header="Item"
                            Binding="{Binding Item,Mode=TwoWay}"/>
          <data:DataGridTextColumn Header="Value" Width="100"
                            Binding="{Binding Amount,Mode=TwoWay}"/>
        </data:DataGrid.Columns>
      </data:DataGrid>
```

```xml
<Grid HorizontalAlignment="Stretch" VerticalAlignment="Stretch"
      Grid.Column="1" Margin="8,8,8,8" x:Name="GraphRoot"
      DataContext="{StaticResource REF_SpendingList}">
  <Grid.RowDefinitions>
    <RowDefinition Height="*"/>
    <RowDefinition Height="20"/>
  </Grid.RowDefinitions>
  <Rectangle Height="Auto" HorizontalAlignment="Left"
             VerticalAlignment="Stretch" Width="2"
             Stroke="#FF000000" StrokeThickness="0"
             Fill="#FF000000" x:Name="rectYAxis" Margin="0,0,0,0"/>
  <Rectangle Height="2" HorizontalAlignment="Stretch"
             VerticalAlignment="Bottom" Fill="#FF000000"
             Stroke="#FF000000" StrokeThickness="0"
             Stretch="Fill" x:Name="rectXAxis" Margin="0,0,0,0"
             Width="350" />
  <Grid HorizontalAlignment="Stretch" VerticalAlignment="Stretch"
        Width="Auto" Grid.Row="1" Margin="2,0,0,0"
        x:Name="gridMarkers">
    <Grid.ColumnDefinitions>
      <ColumnDefinition Width="0.1*" />
      <ColumnDefinition Width="0.1*" />
      <ColumnDefinition Width="0.1*" />
      <ColumnDefinition Width="0.1*" />
      <ColumnDefinition Width="0.1*" />
      <ColumnDefinition Width="0.1*" />
      <ColumnDefinition Width="0.1*" />
      <ColumnDefinition Width="0.1*" />
      <ColumnDefinition Width="0.1*" />
      <ColumnDefinition Width="0.1*" />
    </Grid.ColumnDefinitions>
    <Grid.RowDefinitions>
      <RowDefinition Height="0.3*" />
      <RowDefinition Height="0.7*" />
    </Grid.RowDefinitions>
    <Rectangle Width="2" Fill="Black" VerticalAlignment="Stretch"
               HorizontalAlignment="Right" Grid.Column="0" />
    <Rectangle Width="2" Fill="Black" VerticalAlignment="Stretch"
               HorizontalAlignment="Right" Grid.Column="1" />
    <Rectangle Width="2" Fill="Black" VerticalAlignment="Stretch"
               HorizontalAlignment="Right" Grid.Column="2" />
    <Rectangle Width="2" Fill="Black" VerticalAlignment="Stretch"
               HorizontalAlignment="Right" Grid.Column="3" />
    <Rectangle Width="2" Fill="Black" VerticalAlignment="Stretch"
               HorizontalAlignment="Right" Grid.Column="4" />
```

```xml
        <Rectangle Width="2" Fill="Black" VerticalAlignment="Stretch"
                HorizontalAlignment="Right" Grid.Column="5" />
        <Rectangle Width="2" Fill="Black" VerticalAlignment="Stretch"
                HorizontalAlignment="Right" Grid.Column="6" />
        <Rectangle Width="2" Fill="Black" VerticalAlignment="Stretch"
                HorizontalAlignment="Right" Grid.Column="7" />
        <Rectangle Width="2" Fill="Black" VerticalAlignment="Stretch"
                HorizontalAlignment="Right" Grid.Column="8" />
        <Rectangle Width="2" Fill="Black" VerticalAlignment="Stretch"
                HorizontalAlignment="Right" Grid.Column="9" />
        <TextBlock HorizontalAlignment="Right" VerticalAlignment="Stretch"
                Grid.Row="1" Grid.Column="0" Text="10%" FontSize="11"
                FontWeight="Bold" />
        <TextBlock HorizontalAlignment="Right" VerticalAlignment="Stretch"
                Grid.Row="1" Grid.Column="1" Text="20%" FontSize="11"
                FontWeight="Bold" />
        <TextBlock HorizontalAlignment="Right" VerticalAlignment="Stretch"
                Grid.Row="1" Grid.Column="2" Text="30%" FontSize="11"
                FontWeight="Bold" />
        <TextBlock HorizontalAlignment="Right" VerticalAlignment="Stretch"
                Grid.Row="1" Grid.Column="3" Text="40%" FontSize="11"
                FontWeight="Bold" />
        <TextBlock HorizontalAlignment="Right" VerticalAlignment="Stretch"
                Grid.Row="1" Grid.Column="4" Text="50%" FontSize="11"
                FontWeight="Bold" />
        <TextBlock HorizontalAlignment="Right" VerticalAlignment="Stretch"
                Grid.Row="1" Grid.Column="5" Text="60%" FontSize="11"
                FontWeight="Bold" />
        <TextBlock HorizontalAlignment="Right" VerticalAlignment="Stretch"
                Grid.Row="1" Grid.Column="6" Text="70%" FontSize="11"
                FontWeight="Bold" />
        <TextBlock HorizontalAlignment="Right" VerticalAlignment="Stretch"
                Grid.Row="1" Grid.Column="7" Text="80%" FontSize="11"
                FontWeight="Bold" />
        <TextBlock HorizontalAlignment="Right" VerticalAlignment="Stretch"
                Grid.Row="1" Grid.Column="8" Text="90%" FontSize="11"
                FontWeight="Bold" />
        <TextBlock HorizontalAlignment="Right" VerticalAlignment="Stretch"
                Grid.Row="1" Grid.Column="9" Text="100%" FontSize="11"
                FontWeight="Bold" />
    </Grid>
```

```
        <Grid Height="Auto" HorizontalAlignment="Stretch" Margin="2,0,0,2"
            VerticalAlignment="Stretch" Width="Auto" x:Name="gridBars"
            ShowGridLines="True">
          <ItemsControl ItemsSource="{StaticResource REF_SpendingList}"
                        ItemTemplate="{StaticResource dtBarTemplate}" />
        </Grid>
      </Grid>
    </Grid>
</UserControl>
```

The rest of the XAML is pretty simple. The SpendingCollection, through a resource reference named REF_SpendingList, is bound to a DataGrid named dgMarkers. The bar graph is implemented as an ItemsControl, once again bound to the same SpendingCollection instance, using a DataTemplate named dtBarTemplate for each bar.

Note how we use the converters inside dtBarTemplate. We bind the Width of a Rectangle directly to the Amount property on the bound Spending instance, and then use the Converter property of the Binding to associate the SpendingToBarWidthConverter. We also bind the Text property of a TextBlock similarly, using the SpendingToPercentageStringConverter instead. On both occasions, we also pass in the entire SpendingCollection instance through the ConverterParameter property of the Binding. The ConverterParameter property value maps to the method parameter named parameter in both the Convert() and ConvertBack() methods on the value converter. This makes the collection available to us inside the converter code.

SpendingToBarWidthConverter, shown in Listing 4-16, is used to convert a spending value to the length of the corresponding bar in the bar graph; both data types are double.

Listing 4-16. *Value Converter Converting Spending to Bar Width*

```
using System;
using System.Windows;
using System.Windows.Data;
using System.Windows.Shapes;

namespace Ch04_DataBinding.Recipe4_4
{
  public class SpendingToBarWidthConverter : IValueConverter
  {
    public object Convert(object value, Type targetType,
      object parameter, System.Globalization.CultureInfo culture)
    {
      //verify validity of all the parameters
      if (value.GetType() != typeof(double) || targetType != typeof(double)
        || parameter == null
        || parameter.GetType() != typeof(SpendingCollection))
        return null;
      //cast appropriately
      double Spending = (double)value;
      double Total = ((SpendingCollection)parameter).Total;
```

```
    //find the xAxis
    Rectangle rectXAxis = (Rectangle)((MainPage)Application.Current.RootVisual)
      .FindName("rectXAxis");
    //calculate bar width in proportion to the xAxis width
    return (Spending / Total) * rectXAxis.Width;
  }

  public object ConvertBack(object value, Type targetType,
    object parameter, System.Globalization.CultureInfo culture)
  {
    //verify validity of all the parameters
    if (value.GetType() != typeof(double) || targetType != typeof(double)
      || parameter == null
      || parameter.GetType() != typeof(SpendingCollection))
      return null;
    //cast appropriately
    double BarWidth = (double)value;
    double Total = ((SpendingCollection)parameter).Total;
    //find the xAxis
    Rectangle rectXAxis = (Rectangle)((MainPage)Application.Current.RootVisual)
      .FindName("rectXAxis");
    //calculate new spending keeping total spending constant based on
    //new bar width to xAxis width ratio
    return (BarWidth / rectXAxis.Width) * Total;
  }
 }
}
```

To convert the spending value into bar width in SpendingToBarWidthConverter .Convert(), we calculate the ratio of the spending value in question to the total spending evaluated from the SpendingCollection passed in as parameter. We then calculate the bar width as the same ratio applied to the total width of the X axis of the graph, also defined as a Rectangle named rectXAxis in XAML. In SpendingToBarWidthConverter.
ConvertBack(), we reverse that calculation.

Listing 4-17 shows the SpendingToPercentageStringConverter code. The calculation of the percentage value in Convert() is again based off the spending total derived from the SpendingCollection instance, and then formatted appropriately to a string. Since we never do the reverse conversion, we do not implement ConvertBack() in this case.

Listing 4-17. *Value Converter Converting Spending to a Percentage String*

```
using System;
using System.Windows.Data;

namespace Ch04_DataBinding.Recipe4_4
{
  public class SpendingToPercentageStringConverter : IValueConverter
  {
```

```
public object Convert(object value, Type targetType,
  object parameter, System.Globalization.CultureInfo culture)
{
  //verify validity of all the parameters
  if (value.GetType() != typeof(double) || targetType != typeof(string)
    || parameter == null
    || parameter.GetType() != typeof(SpendingCollection))
    return null;
  //cast appropriately
  double Spending = (double)value;
  double Total = ((SpendingCollection)parameter).Total;
  //calculate the spending percentage and format as string
  return ((Spending / Total) * 100).ToString("###.##") + " %";
}

public object ConvertBack(object value, Type targetType,
  object parameter, System.Globalization.CultureInfo culture)
{
  throw new NotImplementedException();
}
  }
}
```

■**Note** There is no requirement that a value converter also perform a type conversion. In the code sample for SpendingToBarWidthConverter for example, we convert values of the same data type double, where the conversion is one of context—that is, from one kind of measure (Spending) to another (Width). Therefore, it is called a value conversion. There is another concept known as a TypeConverter, which we will discuss in more detail in Chapter 5.

Listing 4-18 shows the code-behind for the MainPage. Of note is the MouseMove handler Rectangle_MouseMove() for each Rectangle representing a bar in the ItemsControl. In the handler, we calculate the distance moved as the difference of the current mouse position and its previous position, and change the Width of the bar accordingly. We then store the current position as the previous position for the next move.

Listing 4-18. *Code-Behind for the Page*

```
using System.Windows;
using System.Windows.Controls;
using System.Windows.Input;
using System.Windows.Shapes;
```

```csharp
namespace Ch04_DataBinding.Recipe4_4
{
  public partial class MainPage : UserControl
  {
    private bool MouseLeftBtnDown = false;
    Point PreviousPos;
    public MainPage()
    {
      InitializeComponent();
    }

    private void Rectangle_MouseMove(object sender, MouseEventArgs e)
    {
      if (MouseLeftBtnDown)
      {
        Rectangle rect = (Rectangle)sender;
        Point CurrentPos = e.GetPosition(sender as Rectangle);
        double Moved = CurrentPos.X - PreviousPos.X;
        if (rect.Width + Moved >= 0)
        {
          rect.Width += Moved;
        }
        PreviousPos = CurrentPos;
      }
    }

    private void Rectangle_MouseLeftButtonDown(object sender,
      MouseButtonEventArgs e)
    {
      MouseLeftBtnDown = true;
      PreviousPos = e.GetPosition(sender as Rectangle);
    }

    private void Rectangle_MouseLeftButtonUp(object sender,
      MouseButtonEventArgs e)
    {
      MouseLeftBtnDown = false;
    }
  }
}
```

4-5. Binding Across Elements

Problem

You would like to data bind some property of a XAML element to a property on another element on the page, or to a different property on the source element itself.

Solution

To bind to a property on another element, name the source element, and then use the `ElementName` property on the binding. To bind to a property on the same element, use the `RelativeSource` property on the binding.

How It Works

In earlier recipes in this chapter, we have walked through binding a property (target) of a XAML element, to a property (source) on a CLR object. This is one possible scenario, and often you may encounter situations, where the binding scenarios are slightly different in terms of the binding source.

Binding to Another Element

In this scenario a property on an element on a page is data bound to a property on another element on the same page. You can achieve this by setting the `Binding.ElementName` property on the binding declaration to the name of the source element, and the `Binding.Path` property to the name of the property on the element. Note that this feature was introduced in Silverlight 3.

For an example consider a `Slider` control on a page, with a `TextBox` on the same page displaying the current value of the `Slider`. The snippet below illustrates such a binding arrangement.

```
<TextBox Text="{Binding Path=Value,ElementName=sliderSource, Mode=OneWay}" />
<Slider x:Name="sliderSource"
        Minimum="0"
        Maximum="100" />
```

Note in the snippet above, that the `Binding.ElementName` on the `TextBox.Text` property points to the `Slider` on the page. The rest of the binding declaration follows the usual binding rules – so for instance if we were to set the `Binding.Mode` value to TwoWay, editing the `TextBox.Text` to a permissible value within the `Slider`'s range would actually reset the `Slider` thumb to that value.

Binding to Self

In this scenario, a property on an element is data bound to another property on the same element. This is made possible by using the `Binding.RelativeSource` property. The `Binding.RelativeSource` property can be set of one of the two values specified in the `System.Windows.Data.RelativeSourceMode` enumeration: `Self` and `TemplatedParent`. Using the `RelativeSourceMode.Self` value allows the binding to use the element itself as a source for the binding.

In the following code snippet, we bind the ForeGround property of a TextBox to the Text property of the same TextBox. The intent is that if the user types in a valid color name in the TextBox, we display the edited text in that color. Since there is no conversion from string to a brush, we rely on a value converter to do the conversion for us.

```
<TextBox
  Foreground="{Binding Path=Text,RelativeSource={RelativeSource Self},
  Converter={StaticResource REF_ColorStringToBrushConverter}" />
```

Note the syntax of the RelativeSource attribute setting in the preceding binding expression. The format RelativeSource={RelativeSource <RelativeSourceMode>} is the required syntax.

Binding to the TemplatedParent

An instance of a control to which a control template is applied is the TemplatedParent to any element within the control template definition. The following snippet shows a possible binding, where a TextBox within a control template is binding its Foreground property to the TemplatedParent's Foreground property.

```
<ControlTemplate TargetType="MyControl">
  …
  <TextBox
     Foreground=
   "{Binding Path=Foreground,RelativeSource={RelativeSource TemplatedParent}}" />
  …

</ControlTemplate>
```

This will cause the TextBox to inherit the same Foreground brush that the developer decides to set on any particular instance of the control named MyControl.

This scenario is only useful within the context of control templating. We discuss controls and control templates in Chapter 5, and we will cover this scenario in more details there. This recipe does not elaborate on this scenario anymore.

The Code

The code sample for this recipe illustrates the element binding and self binding techniques discussed above. The sample uses the new 3-D capabilities in Silverlight to rotate a simple visual along the X, Y, and Z axes of a 3-D plane. The visual contains a Grid with the current angle values for each rotation axis displayed within a Border, and three separate Sliders are used to control the rotation angles. For more on the Silverlight 3-D capabilities please refer to Chapter 3 in this book.

Figure 4-8 shows the sample in action.

Figure 4-8. *Element and Self Binding sample*

The majority of the code is encapsulated in a user control named RotatorDemoControl. Listing 4-22 shows the complete XAML for RotatorDemoControl.

Listing 4-22. *XAML for RotatorDemoControl*

```
<UserControl x:Class="Ch04_DataBinding.Recipe4_5.RotatorDemoControl"
             xmlns="http://schemas.microsoft.com/winfx/2006/xaml/presentation"
             xmlns:x="http://schemas.microsoft.com/winfx/2006/xaml"
             xmlns:d="http://schemas.microsoft.com/expression/blend/2008"
             xmlns:mc="http://schemas.openxmlformats.org/markup-compatibility/2006"
             mc:Ignorable="d"
             xmlns:local="clr-namespace:Ch04_DataBinding.Recipe4_5"
             >

  <Grid x:Name="LayoutRoot">
    <Grid.RowDefinitions>
      <RowDefinition Height="0.75*" />
      <RowDefinition Height="0.25*" />
    </Grid.RowDefinitions>
    <Grid x:Name="target"
          Width="275"
          Height="100">
      <Grid.ColumnDefinitions>
        <ColumnDefinition />
        <ColumnDefinition />
        <ColumnDefinition />
      </Grid.ColumnDefinitions>
```

```xml
<Grid.RowDefinitions>
  <RowDefinition />
  <RowDefinition />
  <RowDefinition />
</Grid.RowDefinitions>
<Border BorderThickness="2"
        Grid.RowSpan="3"
        Grid.ColumnSpan="3"
        BorderBrush="Red"
        Background="AliceBlue"></Border>
<TextBlock Text="Rotation X"
        Margin="3,0,0,0" />
<TextBlock Text=":"
        Grid.Column="1" />
<TextBlock Text="{Binding Xangle}"
        Grid.Column="2"
        Margin="0,0,0,3" />
<TextBlock Text="Rotation Y"
        Grid.Row="1"
        Margin="3,0,0,0" />
<TextBlock Text=":"
        Grid.Column="1"
        Grid.Row="1" />
<TextBlock Text="{Binding Yangle}"
        Grid.Column="2"
        Grid.Row="1"
        Margin="0,0,0,3" />
<TextBlock Text="Rotation Z"
        Grid.Row="2"
        Margin="3,0,0,0" />
<TextBlock Text=":"
        Grid.Column="1"
        Grid.Row="2" />
<TextBlock Text="{Binding Zangle}"
        Grid.Column="2"
        Grid.Row="2"
        Margin="0,0,0,3" />
<Grid.Projection>
  <PlaneProjection x:Name="gridProjection" />
</Grid.Projection>
</Grid>
```

```
    <StackPanel Orientation="Vertical" HorizontalAlignment="Center"
                Grid.Row="1">
      <StackPanel Orientation="Horizontal"
                  Margin="0,10,0,10">
        <TextBlock Text="Rotate on X Axis: " />
        <Slider Minimum="0"
                Maximum="360"
                x:Name="sliderX"
                Value=
            "{Binding ElementName=gridProjection, Mode=TwoWay, Path=RotationX}"
                Width="125" />
      </StackPanel>
      <StackPanel Orientation="Horizontal"
                  Margin="0,10,0,10">
        <TextBlock Text="Rotate on Y Axis: " />
        <Slider Minimum="0"
                Maximum="360"
                x:Name="sliderY"
                Value=
            "{Binding ElementName=gridProjection, Mode=TwoWay, Path=RotationY}"
                Width="125" />
      </StackPanel>
      <StackPanel Orientation="Horizontal"
                  Margin="0,10,0,10">
        <TextBlock Text="Rotate on Z Axis: " />
        <Slider Minimum="0"
                Maximum="360"
                x:Name="sliderZ"
                Value=
            "{Binding ElementName=gridProjection, Mode=TwoWay, Path=RotationZ}"
                Width="125" />
      </StackPanel>
    </StackPanel>
  </Grid>
</UserControl>
```

As shown in Listing 4-22, the PlaneProjection named gridProjection projects the Grid to a 3-D plane. The PlaneProjection type exposes three properties, namely RotationX, RotationY and RotationZ, each of which can be independently set to an angle value between 0 and 360 degrees to rotate the Grid along that axis.

If you note the binding expression for the Value property of the Slider named sliderX, you will see that it is bound directly in a TwoWay mode to the RotationX property of gridProjection, utilizing the ElementName binding attribute. The range for sliderX is set to vary between 0 and 360, and changing this value will cause gridProjection to rotate along the X axis by that amount. The other two Sliders, sliderY and sliderZ, follow a similar arrangement to affect the RotationY and RotationZ properties of the gridProjection element.

Listing 4-23 shows the code behind for the RotatorDemoControl.

Listing 4-23. *Codebehind for RotatorDemoControl*

```
using System.ComponentModel;
using System.Windows;
using System.Windows.Controls;

namespace Ch04_DataBinding.Recipe4_5
{
  public partial class RotatorDemoControl : UserControl, InotifyPropertyChanged
  {
    public event PropertyChangedEventHandler PropertyChanged;

    public RotatorDemoControl()
    {
      InitializeComponent();

      sliderX.ValueChanged +=
        new RoutedPropertyChangedEventHandler<double>((s, e) =>
        {
        Xangle = sliderX.Value;
      });
      sliderY.ValueChanged +=
        new RoutedPropertyChangedEventHandler<double>((s, e) =>
        {
        Yangle = sliderY.Value;
      });
      sliderZ.ValueChanged +=
        new RoutedPropertyChangedEventHandler<double>((s, e) =>
        {
        Zangle = sliderZ.Value;
      });
    }

    private double _Xangle = default(double);

    public double Xangle
    {
      get
      {
        return _Xangle;
      }
```

```
    set
    {
      if (value != _Xangle)
      {
        _Xangle = value;
        if (PropertyChanged != null)
          PropertyChanged(this, new PropertyChangedEventArgs("Xangle"));
      }

    }
}

private double _Yangle = default(double);

public double Yangle
{
  get
  {
    return _Yangle;
  }

  set
  {
    if (value != _Yangle)
    {
      _Yangle = value;
      if (PropertyChanged != null)
        PropertyChanged(this, new PropertyChangedEventArgs("Yangle"));
    }

  }
}

private double _Zangle = default(double);
public double Zangle
{
  get
  {
    return _Zangle;
  }
```

```
    set
    {
      if (value != _Zangle)
      {
        _Zangle = value;
        if (PropertyChanged != null)
          PropertyChanged(this, new PropertyChangedEventArgs("Zangle"));
      }

    }
  }
}

}
```

As Listing 4-23 shows, the RotatorDemoControl control class exposes three properties named Xangle, Yangle, and Zangle with property change notification enabled. These values are updated when the corresponding slider values are changed, as shown in the event handlers of the ValueChanged events of the Sliders, in the constructor of the RotatorDemoControl class.

If you refer to the RotatorDemoControl XAML in Listing 4-22, you will note that there are three TextBlocks inside the rotated Grid that are respectively bound to these properties. The intention is to display the angle values as the Grid is rotated. Looking at the binding statements for these TextBlocks, you will note that they simply provide the Binding.Path values pointing to the properties on RotatorDemoControl. But how do the bindings know to use the control class as its data source? Take a look at Listing 4-24 that shows the XAML for the MainPage, which actually declares the RotatorDemoControl user control.

Listing 4-24. *XAML for MainPage*

```xml
<UserControl x:Class="Ch04_DataBinding.Recipe4_5.MainPage"
             xmlns="http://schemas.microsoft.com/winfx/2006/xaml/presentation"
             xmlns:x="http://schemas.microsoft.com/winfx/2006/xaml"
             xmlns:local="clr-namespace:Ch04_DataBinding.Recipe4_5"
             Width="640"
             Height="480">
  <Grid x:Name="LayoutRoot"
        Background="White">
    <local:RotatorDemoControl
        DataContext="{Binding RelativeSource={RelativeSource Self}}" />
  </Grid>
</UserControl>
```

Listing 4-24 shows that the DataContext for the RotatorDemoControl is bound to itself because the RelativeSource attribute is set to Self. This then sets the RotatorDemoControl instance as the data source for the TextBlock bindings that we were referring to earlier, and help display the angle values as notified through the corresponding properties on the RotatorDemoControl class.

4-6. Validating Input for Bound Data

Problem

You need to capture data validation errors in your application code and provide visual indications of such errors if needed.

Solution

Attach handlers to the `BindingValidationError` event of the control in question, and ensure that the binding is set to raise the event on validation exceptions.

How It Works

As you create Uis that are data bound to various controls in a `TwoWay` binding so that users of your application can edit the data, you often have the need for those edits to pass validation checks. And in the event one or more of those validations fail, you may want to capture the errors and display them to your users in a meaningful way.

Validation Error Notification

There is built-in support for notification of validation errors in the data binding subsystem within Silverlight. To enable this support, the `Binding.ValidatesOnExceptions` property needs to be set to `true` on the binding. This allows the framework to capture any exceptions raised during the setting of a property on a data source or during a type conversion and propagate them to your code as validation errors. This prevents the otherwise normal flow of your application suffering a crash from the exception being unhandled.

Most of the controls in the base class library that may typically be used in two-way bindings provide a built-in user interface to display the binding validation error to the user. The built-in user interface usually provides a small error icon overlaid on the control, hovering on which displays a tooltip beside the control to display the error message. The error message displayed is the `Exception.Message` property value of the raised exception. Once the error is corrected, the control logic automatically removes the error user interface.

Figure 4-9 shows a `TextBox` control displaying a validation error with the default error user interface.

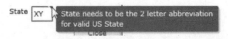

Figure 4-9. *TextBox control displaying validation error using default error UI*

Getting Error Information

In some cases, it may not be enough to simply display the error message. You may want programmatic access to the error information, for additional reasons like logging or some other custom handling of the error beyond the display of the standard error user interface.

To enable this, the `FrameworkElement` class (and by inheritance every control) can raise the `BindingValidationError` event whenever an exception gets propagated as a validation error, or an existing validation error is removed. To instruct the binding subsystem to raise this event, you need to set the Binding.NotifyOnValidationError property to true on the binding.

If you handle the BindingValidationError event, you can access detailed error information through the event argument of type ValidationErrorEventArgs. The ValidationErrorEventArgs.Action property, of type ValidationErrorEventAction has two possible values – ValidationErrorEventAction. Added indicating that a validation error has occurred, and ValidationErrorEventAction.Removed indicating that an error was corrected. The ValidationErrorEventArgs.Exception property gives you access to the actual exception that caused the validation error.

Getting a Validation Error Summary

In many applications it is common to show a summary of all the errors that a user might have made in performing the necessary data input. Typically, a summary display such as that will point out the fields where the errors were made, the nature of the error, and in some cases, will also include automatic navigation (click the entry in the summary to navigate to the field). This feature is also built into the Silverlight binding validation mechanism now and is enabled through the System.Windows.Controls. ValidationSummary control and its related classes, in the System.Windows.Controls.Data.Input assembly.

Once you place a ValidationSummary control in your page the binding subsystem automatically knows to populate it with the error entries, and binding errors occur. There is no additional wiring up that you have to perform. The following snippet shows a sample declaration:

```
<input:ValidationSummary />
```

Also note that validation errors are bubbled up the visual tree by the binding subsystem. This means that the ValidationSummary control can be placed anywhere in your page, as long as it is higher in the visual tree than the control(s) whose validation errors it is supposed to display.

Note that the default error and validation summary user interfaces can be customized using control templating. Please see Chapter 5 for more information on this.

Let's take a look at how all of this might work.

The Code

We'll modify recipe 4-3 to add input validation. We remove the custom collection class in favor of using a simple ObservableCollection. To add the validation on the data source, we adjust some of the property setters to throw exceptions if certain validation rules are not met. We also change the types of Employee.PhoneNum and Address.ZipCode properties to string to simply the validation logic. The application data classes with some of these modified property setters are shown in Listing 4-19.

Listing 4-19. *Application Data Classes*

```
using System;
using System.Collections.Generic;
using System.Collections.Specialized;
using System.ComponentModel;
using System.Linq;
```

```
namespace Ch04_DataBinding.Recipe4_6
{
  public class Employee : InotifyPropertyChanged
  {
    //InotifyPropertyChanged implementation
    public event PropertyChangedEventHandler PropertyChanged;
    private void RaisePropertyChanged(PropertyChangedEventArgs e)
    {
      if (PropertyChanged != null)
        PropertyChanged(this, e);
    }

    public Employee()
    {
    }

    private string _FirstName;
    public string FirstName
    {
      get { return _FirstName; }
      set
      {
        string OldVal = _FirstName;
        if (OldVal != value)
        {
          _FirstName = value;
          RaisePropertyChanged(new PropertyChangedEventArgs("FirstName"));
        }
      }
    }
    private string _LastName;
    public string LastName
    {
      get { return _LastName; }
      set
      {
        string OldVal = _LastName;
        if (OldVal != value)
        {
          _LastName = value;
          RaisePropertyChanged(new PropertyChangedEventArgs("LastName"));
        }
      }
    }
```

```
private string _PhoneNum;
public string PhoneNum
{
  get { return _PhoneNum; }
  set
  {
    string OldVal = _PhoneNum;

    if (value.Length != 10)
      throw new Exception("Phone Number has to be exactly 10 digits");
    try
    {
      Convert.ToInt64(value);
    }
    catch
    {
      throw new Exception("Phone Number has to be exactly 10 digits");
    }

    if (OldVal != value)
    {
      _PhoneNum = value;
      RaisePropertyChanged(new PropertyChangedEventArgs("PhoneNum"));
    }
  }
}
private Address _Address;
public Address Address
{
  get { return _Address; }
  set
  {
    Address OldVal = _Address;
    if (OldVal != value)
    {
      _Address = value;
      RaisePropertyChanged(new PropertyChangedEventArgs("Address"));
    }
  }
}
```

```csharp
    private bool _InError = default(bool);

    public bool InError
    {
      get
      {
        return _InError;
      }

      set
      {
        if (value != _InError)
        {
          _InError = value;
          if (PropertyChanged != null)
            PropertyChanged(this, new PropertyChangedEventArgs("InError"));
        }

      }
    }
  }

  public class Address : InotifyPropertyChanged
  {

    private static List<string> StateList =
      new List<string>(){ "AL","AK","AS","AZ","AR","CA","CO","CT","DE","DC","FM",
        "FL","GA","GU","HI","ID","IL","IN","IA","KS","KY","LA","ME","MH","MD","MA",
        "MI","MN","MS","MO","MT","NE","NV","NH","NJ","NM","NY","NC","ND","MP","OH",
« OK », »OR », »PW », »PA », »PR », »RI », »SC », »SD », »TN », »TX », »UT », »VT », »VI »,
»VA », »WA »,
        "WV","WI","WY" };

    public event PropertyChangedEventHandler PropertyChanged;
    private void RaisePropertyChanged(PropertyChangedEventArgs e)
    {
      if (PropertyChanged != null)
        PropertyChanged(this, e);
    }
```

335

```csharp
private string _Street;
public string Street
{
  get { return _Street; }
  set
  {
    string OldVal = _Street;
    if (OldVal != value)
    {
      _Street = value;
      RaisePropertyChanged(new PropertyChangedEventArgs("Street"));
    }
  }
}
private string _City;
public string City
{
  get { return _City; }
  set
  {
    string OldVal = _City;

    if (OldVal != value)
    {
      _City = value;
      RaisePropertyChanged(new PropertyChangedEventArgs("City"));
    }
  }
}
private string _State;
public string State
{
  get { return _State; }
  set
  {
    string OldVal = _State;
    //length needs to be 2 characters
    if (StateList.Contains(value) == false)
      throw new Exception(
        "State needs to be the 2 letter abbreviation for valid US State"
        );
```

```
      if (OldVal != value)
      {
        _State = value;
        RaisePropertyChanged(new PropertyChangedEventArgs("State"));
      }
    }
  }
}
private string _ZipCode;
public string ZipCode
{
  get { return _ZipCode; }
  set
  {
    string OldVal = _ZipCode;
    //length needs to be 5 characters
    if (value.Length != 5)
      throw new Exception("Zipcode needs to be exactly 5 digits");
    try
    {
      Convert.ToInt32(value);
    }
    catch
    {
      throw new Exception("Zipcode needs to be exactly 5 digits");
    }

    if (OldVal != value)
    {
      _ZipCode = value;
      RaisePropertyChanged(new PropertyChangedEventArgs("ZipCode"));
    }
  }
}
}

}
```

As Listing 4-19 shows, Employee.PhoneNum validates a phone number if it has exactly ten digits in its setter and raises an Exception otherwise. Similarly, Address.State and Address.ZipCode check for a two-letter state abbreviation and a five-digit ZIP code and raise Exceptions if those criteria are not met. Also note the new InError property on the Employee class; we will address its use in a little bit.

Listing 4-20 shows the complete XAML for the page.

Listing 4-20. *XAML for the Page*

```xml
<UserControl x:Class="Ch04_DataBinding.Recipe4_6.MainPage"
            xmlns="http://schemas.microsoft.com/winfx/2006/xaml/presentation"
            xmlns:x="http://schemas.microsoft.com/winfx/2006/xaml"
            xmlns:local="clr-namespace:Ch04_DataBinding.Recipe4_6"
            xmlns:d="http://schemas.microsoft.com/expression/blend/2008"
            xmlns:mc="http://schemas.openxmlformats.org/markup-compatibility/2006"
            xmlns:input=
"clr-namespace:System.Windows.Controls;assembly=System.Windows.Controls.Data.Input"
            mc:Ignorable="d"
            Width="400"
            Height="450">

  <UserControl.Resources>

    <local:BoolToVisibilityConverter x:Key="REF_BoolToVisibilityConverter" />

    <DataTemplate x:Key="dtEmployee">
      <Grid>
        <Grid.ColumnDefinitions>
          <ColumnDefinition Width="Auto" />
          <ColumnDefinition Width="Auto" />
          <ColumnDefinition Width="Auto" />
        </Grid.ColumnDefinitions>
        <TextBlock Text="{Binding FirstName}"/>
        <TextBlock Text="{Binding LastName}"
                   Grid.Column="1"
                   Grid.Row="0"
                   Margin="5,0,0,0" />
        <TextBlock Text=" -> Error!!" Foreground="Red"
                   Visibility=
      "{Binding InError, Converter={StaticResource REF_BoolToVisibilityConverter}}"
                   Grid.Column="2" />

      </Grid>
    </DataTemplate>
  </UserControl.Resources>
```

```xml
<Grid x:Name="LayoutRoot"
      Background="White"
      Margin="10,10,10,10">
  <Grid.RowDefinitions>
    <RowDefinition Height="*" />
    <RowDefinition Height="Auto" />
    <RowDefinition Height="Auto" />
    <RowDefinition Height="Auto" />
  </Grid.RowDefinitions>

  <ListBox Grid.Row="0"
           x:Name="lbx_Employees"
           ItemTemplate="{StaticResource dtEmployee}"
           SelectionChanged="lbx_Employees_SelectionChanged" />

  <Grid x:Name="grid_NewButton"
        Margin="0,2,0,0"
        Grid.Row="1"
        HorizontalAlignment="Right">
    <Button  x:Name="btn_New"
             Click="btn_New_Click"
             Content="New Employee" />
  </Grid>

  <input:ValidationSummary Grid.Row="2" Margin="0,10,0,5"/>
  <Border Grid.Row="3"
          Visibility="Collapsed"
          x:Name="border_EmployeeForm"
          Margin="0,2,0,0"
          BorderBrush="Black"
          BorderThickness="1"
          Padding="1,1,1,1">
    <Grid x:Name="grid_EmployeeForm">

      <Grid.ColumnDefinitions>
        <ColumnDefinition Width="0.142*" />
        <ColumnDefinition Width="0.379*" />
        <ColumnDefinition Width="0.1*" />
        <ColumnDefinition Width="0.097*" />
        <ColumnDefinition Width="0.082*" />
        <ColumnDefinition Width="0.2*" />
      </Grid.ColumnDefinitions>
      <Grid.RowDefinitions>
        <RowDefinition Height="0.10*" />
        <RowDefinition Height="0.15*" />
```

339

```xml
          <RowDefinition Height="0.15*" />
          <RowDefinition Height="0.15*" />
          <RowDefinition Height="0.45*" />
      </Grid.RowDefinitions>

      <TextBox HorizontalAlignment="Stretch"
              Margin="1,1,1,1"
              x:Name="tbxFName"
              VerticalAlignment="Stretch"
              Text="{Binding FirstName, Mode=TwoWay}"
              Grid.Row="1"
              Width="Auto"
              Grid.RowSpan="1"
              Grid.ColumnSpan="2"
              Grid.Column="1" />
      <TextBox HorizontalAlignment="Stretch"
              Margin="1,1,1,1"
              x:Name="tbxLName"
              VerticalAlignment="Stretch"
              Text="{Binding LastName, Mode=TwoWay}"
              Grid.Row="1"
              Grid.Column="3"
              Width="Auto"
              Grid.RowSpan="1"
              Grid.ColumnSpan="3" />
      <TextBlock HorizontalAlignment="Stretch"
              Margin="1,1,1,1"
              VerticalAlignment="Stretch"
              Text="Last"
              TextWrapping="Wrap"
              Grid.RowSpan="1"
              Grid.Column="4"
              Grid.ColumnSpan="2"
              Height="Auto"
              Width="Auto" />
      <TextBlock HorizontalAlignment="Center"
              Margin="1,1,1,1"
              VerticalAlignment="Center"
              Text="First"
              TextWrapping="Wrap"
              Grid.RowSpan="1"
              Grid.Column="1"
              Width="Auto"
              Height="Auto" />
```

```
<TextBlock HorizontalAlignment="Center"
           Margin="1,1,1,1"
           VerticalAlignment="Stretch"
           Text="Name"
           TextWrapping="Wrap"
           Grid.RowSpan="1"
           Grid.Row="1"
           Height="Auto"
           Width="Auto" />
<TextBlock HorizontalAlignment="Center"
           Margin="1,1,1,1"
           VerticalAlignment="Stretch"
           Text="Street"
           TextWrapping="Wrap"
           Grid.Row="2"
           Width="Auto" />
<TextBox HorizontalAlignment="Stretch"
         x:Name="tbxStreet"
         VerticalAlignment="Stretch"
         Text="{Binding Address.Street, Mode=TwoWay}"
         Grid.Row="2"
         Margin="1,1,1,1"
         Grid.Column="1"
         Grid.ColumnSpan="5"
         Width="Auto" />
<TextBlock HorizontalAlignment="Center"
           VerticalAlignment="Stretch"
           Text="City"
           TextWrapping="Wrap"
           Margin="1,1,1,1"
           Grid.Row="3" />
<TextBlock Text="State"
           Margin="1,1,1,1"
           TextWrapping="Wrap"
           Grid.Column="2"
           Grid.Row="3"
           HorizontalAlignment="Center" />
<TextBlock Text="Zip"
           Margin="1,1,1,1"
           TextWrapping="Wrap"
           Grid.Column="4"
           Grid.Row="3"
           HorizontalAlignment="Center" />
<TextBox HorizontalAlignment="Stretch"
         x:Name="tbxCity"
         Margin="1,1,1,1"
```

```
                    VerticalAlignment="Stretch"
                    Text="{Binding Address.City, Mode=TwoWay}"
                    Grid.Row="3"
                    Grid.Column="1" />
        <TextBox Background="Transparent"
                    Grid.Column="3"
                    Margin="1,1,1,1"
                    Grid.Row="3"
                    Text="{Binding Address.State, Mode=TwoWay,
                ValidatesOnExceptions=True,NotifyOnValidationError=True}"
                    x:Name="tbxState">
        </TextBox>
        <TextBox Background="Transparent"
                    Grid.Column="5"
                    Grid.Row="3"
                    Margin="1,1,1,1"
                    Text="{Binding Address.ZipCode, Mode=TwoWay ,
                     ValidatesOnExceptions=True,NotifyOnValidationError=True}"
                    x:Name="tbxZipCode" />

        <TextBlock HorizontalAlignment="Center"
                    VerticalAlignment="Stretch"
                    Text="Phone"
                    Margin="1,1,1,1"
                    TextWrapping="Wrap"
                    Grid.Row="4" />
        <TextBox Grid.Column="1"
                    Grid.Row="4"
                    Margin="1,1,1,1"
                    Text="{Binding PhoneNum, Mode=TwoWay ,
             ValidatesOnExceptions=True,NotifyOnValidationError=True}"
                    x:Name="tbxPhoneNum" />
        <Button   Grid.Column="5"
                    Margin="1,1,1,1"
                    Grid.Row="4"
                    Height="30.911"
                    VerticalAlignment="Top"
                    Content="Close"
                    x:Name="btnClose"
                    Click="btnClose_Click" />
        </Grid>
      </Border>
    </Grid>
</UserControl>
```

Note the binding expression for the TextBox. Text for displaying and editing a state, a ZIP code, and a phone number sets both ValidatesOnExceptions and NotifyOnValidationError to true. Also note that the dtEmployee data template now includes an extra TextBlock with its Visibility property bound to the InError property of the bound Employee instance. This TextBlock then displays an error string in red beside the Employee name when Employee.InError is set to true for the currently selected Employee instance in the lbx_Employees and hides it when not. Since the InError property is Boolean in type, we use a value converter to convert it to type Visibility for the binding to work. We cover value converters in more detail in recipe 4-4. For the source code of the converter used here, you can look at the BoolToVisibilityConverter class in the sample code for this recipe.

And last, note the ValidationSummary control in the second row of the top level Grid. As validation errors are made, the ValidationSummary control gets populated with entries describing the error, and clicking one of the items positions you in the control in error.

Listing 4-21 shows the complete code behind for the page.

Listing 4-21. *MainPage Code-Behind*

```
using System.Windows;
using System.Windows.Controls;
using System.Windows.Media;
using System.Collections.ObjectModel;
using System.Collections.Generic;

namespace Ch04_DataBinding.Recipe4_6
{
  public partial class MainPage : UserControl
  {
    public MainPage()
    {
      InitializeComponent();

      //initialize the employee collection with some sample data
      ObservableCollection<Employee> empColl = new ObservableCollection<Employee>();

      empColl.Add(new Employee
      {
        FirstName = "Joe",
        LastName = "Duffin",
        PhoneNum = "2125551212",
        Address = new Address
        {
          Street = "2000 Mott Street",
          City = "New York",
          State = "NY",
          ZipCode = "10006"
        }
      });
```

```
        empColl.Add(new Employee
        {
          FirstName = "Alex",
          LastName = "Bleeker",
          PhoneNum = "7185551212",
          Address = new Address
          {
            Street = "11000 Clover Street",
            City = "New York",
            State = "NY",
            ZipCode = "10007"
          }
        });

        empColl.Add(new Employee
        {
          FirstName = "Nelly",
          LastName = "Myers",
          PhoneNum = "7325551212",
          Address = new Address
          {
            Street = "12000 Fay Road",
            City = "New York",
            State = "NY",
            ZipCode = "10016"
          }
        });

        lbx_Employees.ItemsSource = empColl;

        this.BindingValidationError +=
          new System.EventHandler<ValidationErrorEventArgs>((s, e) =>
        {

          if (lbx_Employees.SelectedItem == null) return;
          //change the InError property of the currently selected Employee
          if(e.Action == ValidationErrorEventAction.Added)
            (lbx_Employees.SelectedItem as Employee).InError = true;
          else
            (lbx_Employees.SelectedItem as Employee).InError = false;

        });

    }
```

```csharp
private void btn_New_Click(object sender, RoutedEventArgs e)
{
  //get the bound collection
  ObservableCollection<Employee> empColl =
    (ObservableCollection<Employee>)lbx_Employees.ItemsSource;
  //create and initialize a new Employee
  Employee newEmp = new Employee();
  newEmp.Address = new Address();
  //add it to the collection
  empColl.Add(newEmp);
  //set the current selection to the newly added employee.
  //This will cause selection change to fire, and set the
  //datacontext for the form appropriately
  lbx_Employees.SelectedItem = newEmp;

}

private void lbx_Employees_SelectionChanged(object sender,
  SelectionChangedEventArgs e)
{
  //set the datacontext of the form to the selected Employee
  grid_EmployeeForm.DataContext = (Employee)lbx_Employees.SelectedItem;
  //show the form
  border_EmployeeForm.Visibility = Visibility.Visible;
  grid_NewButton.Visibility = Visibility.Collapsed;
}

private void btnClose_Click(object sender, RoutedEventArgs e)
{
  //hide the form
  if (lbx_Employees.SelectedItem != null)
    (lbx_Employees.SelectedItem as Employee).InError = false;
  border_EmployeeForm.Visibility = Visibility.Collapsed;
  grid_NewButton.Visibility = Visibility.Visible;
  }
  }
}
```

As you can see in the C# code-behind, we don't need to do anything special for the binding subsystem to display validation errors. If you refer to the BindingValidationError event handler on the page, you will see that we handle the event to update the InError property of the currently selected Employee in the lbx_Employees. If a validation error has occurred, we set it to true, and to false otherwise. If you refer to the XAML in Listing 4-20, this is the property change that notifies the data template dtEmployee to change the visibility of the error indicator TextBlock.

Also note that we are able to handle the BindingValidationError event on the page, even though the validation error happens at controls that are contained further down in the visual tree. As mentioned before, BindingValidationError events are bubbled all the way up to the highest level container in the XAML, so you are free to handle them anywhere in the visual tree, including in and higher than the control where it happened.

■**Note** If you are in debug mode in Visual Studio, the debugger will break at the exceptions raised in the property setters for the data classes. This is normal, and if you continue with processing, you will see the application behave the way it should. The Silverlight runtime absorbs the unhandled exceptions because of the error handling property settings on the Binding and translates them to notifications. However, the Visual Studio debugger has no notion of this, so it breaks on the exception if you are in debug mode.

Figure 4-10 illustrates the UI used to display a binding validation error, errors displayed in the ValidationSummary, a summary item selected, and the tooltip UI displaying the actual error message in the focused control that's in error.

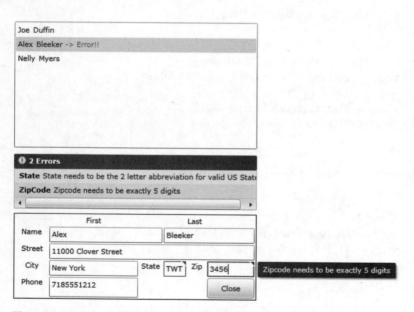

Figure 4-10. *Input validation error display with validation summary*

4-7. Controlling Updates

Problem

You would like to have explicit programmatic control on when property updates happen in a TwoWay data binding scenario.

Solution

Set the UpdateSourceTrigger attribute to Explicit in the binding declaration, and programmatically invoke BindingExpression.UpdateSource().

How It Works

The default behavior of most Silverlight controls is to send the updates occurring as a result of user edits directly to the bound property as soon as it occurs. For instance, when you change the text in a TextBox, whose Text property is data bound in a TwoWay mode, the bound property is updated as soon as the user tabs out or focus is shifted somewhere else through some other means.

Often, it may be desirable to hold the updates and batch them at the end of an edit session through some explicit user-driven mechanism like a Save button. A multitude of reasons could drive a decision like that: computed fields that can only be calculated when multiple other fields are populated, validation logic that involves dependencies across multiple fields, some preprocessing of the edited data before updates are applied, and so on.

Silverlight offers you this control through the Binding.UpdateSourceTrigger property. Setting this property to UpdateSourceTrigger.Explicit causes the runtime to hold all property updates, in the anticipation that you will perform the updates explicitly in code. The following code snippet shows a binding declaration for the Text property on a TextBox with the UpdateSourceTrigger attribute set to Explicit.

```
<TextBox HorizontalAlignment="Stretch"
 Margin="1,1,1,1"
 x:Name="tbxLName"
 VerticalAlignment="Stretch"
 Text=
"{Binding LastName, Mode=TwoWay,UpdateSourceTrigger=Explicit}"
 Grid.Row="1"
 Grid.Column="3"
 Width="Auto"
 Grid.RowSpan="1"
 Grid.ColumnSpan="3" />
```

To actually perform the updates, you need to access the `BindingExpression` instance supporting the binding in question and invoke the `BindingExpression.UpdateSource()` method on it. You can acquire the `BindingExpression` instance in question by using the `FrameworkElement.GetBindingExpression()` method and passing in the property whose related `BindingExpression` you may need. The code snippet below shows an example.

```
BindingExpression beLastName = tbxLName.GetBindingExpression(TextBox.TextProperty);
beLastName.UpdateSource();
```

Note that any validation logic that you have built into the property setters will execute only when `UpdateSource()` is invoked for that specific binding. So if you are batching the calls to `UpdateSource()`, it will cause all validation logic to be batched as well.

The Code

The code sample for this recipe extends the sample from recipe 4.6 to add explicit update support. A Save button is added to the employee edit user interface and any updates made are propagated back, when that button is clicked.

Figure 4-11 shows the state of the edit user interface before and after the Save button is clicked. Note that while we have potentially incorrect data in the `state`, `zipcode` and `phone` number fields, the validation check results only show up once the updates are attempted.

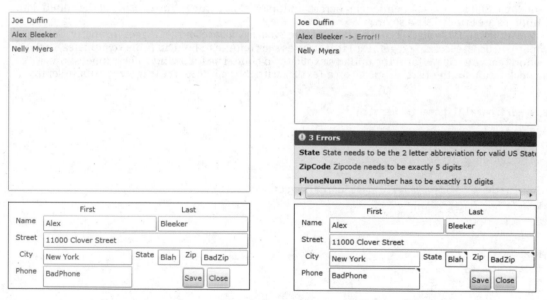

Figure 4-11. *Employee edit user interface before and after batched update attempt*

Listing 4-22 shows the XAML for the main page.

Listing 4-22. *XAML for MainPage*

```
<UserControl x:Class="Ch04_DataBinding.Recipe4_7.MainPage"
             xmlns="http://schemas.microsoft.com/winfx/2006/xaml/presentation"
             xmlns:x="http://schemas.microsoft.com/winfx/2006/xaml"
             xmlns:d="http://schemas.microsoft.com/expression/blend/2008"
             xmlns:local="clr-namespace:Ch04_DataBinding.Recipe4_7"
             xmlns:mc="http://schemas.openxmlformats.org/markup-compatibility/2006"
             xmlns:input=
"clr-namespace:System.Windows.Controls;assembly=System.Windows.Controls.Data.Input"
             Width="400"
             Height="450">
    <UserControl.Resources>

    <local:BoolToVisibilityConverter x:Key="REF_BoolToVisibilityConverter" />

    <DataTemplate x:Key="dtEmployee">
      <Grid>
        <Grid.ColumnDefinitions>
          <ColumnDefinition Width="Auto" />
          <ColumnDefinition Width="Auto" />
          <ColumnDefinition Width="Auto" />
        </Grid.ColumnDefinitions>
        <TextBlock Text="{Binding FirstName}" />
        <TextBlock Text="{Binding LastName}"
                   Grid.Column="1"
                   Grid.Row="0"
                   Margin="5,0,0,0" />
        <TextBlock Text=" -> Error!!"
                   Foreground="Red"
                   Visibility=
      "{Binding InError, Converter={StaticResource REF_BoolToVisibilityConverter}}"
                   Grid.Column="2" />

      </Grid>
    </DataTemplate>

  </UserControl.Resources>
    <Grid x:Name="LayoutRoot"
          Background="White"
          Margin="10,10,10,10">
```

```
    <Grid.RowDefinitions>
        <RowDefinition Height="*" />
        <RowDefinition Height="Auto" />
        <RowDefinition Height="Auto" />
        <RowDefinition Height="Auto" />
    </Grid.RowDefinitions>
    <ListBox Grid.Row="0"
            x:Name="lbx_Employees"
            ItemTemplate="{StaticResource dtEmployee}"
            SelectionChanged="lbx_Employees_SelectionChanged" />
    <Grid x:Name="grid_NewButton"
        Margin="0,2,0,0"
        Grid.Row="1"
        HorizontalAlignment="Right">
        <Button  x:Name="btn_New"
                Click="btn_New_Click"
                Content="New Employee" />
    </Grid>
<input:ValidationSummary Grid.Row="2"
                            Margin="0,10,0,5" />
<Border Grid.Row="3"
            Visibility="Collapsed"
            x:Name="border_EmployeeForm"
            Margin="0,2,0,0"
            BorderBrush="Black"
            BorderThickness="1"
            Padding="1,1,1,1">
        <Grid x:Name="grid_EmployeeForm">

            <Grid.ColumnDefinitions>
                <ColumnDefinition Width="0.142*" />
                <ColumnDefinition Width="0.379*" />
                <ColumnDefinition Width="0.1*" />
                <ColumnDefinition Width="0.097*" />
                <ColumnDefinition Width="0.082*" />
                <ColumnDefinition Width="0.2*" />
            </Grid.ColumnDefinitions>
            <Grid.RowDefinitions>
                <RowDefinition Height="0.10*" />
                <RowDefinition Height="0.15*" />
                <RowDefinition Height="0.15*" />
                <RowDefinition Height="0.15*" />
                <RowDefinition Height="0.45*" />
            </Grid.RowDefinitions>
```

```
<TextBox HorizontalAlignment="Stretch"
         Margin="1,1,1,1"
         x:Name="tbxFName"
         VerticalAlignment="Stretch"
         Text=
  "{Binding FirstName, Mode=TwoWay, UpdateSourceTrigger=Explicit}"
         Grid.Row="1"
         Width="Auto"
         Grid.RowSpan="1"
         Grid.ColumnSpan="2"
         Grid.Column="1" />
<TextBox HorizontalAlignment="Stretch"
         Margin="1,1,1,1"
         x:Name="tbxLName"
         VerticalAlignment="Stretch"
         Text=
    "{Binding LastName, Mode=TwoWay,UpdateSourceTrigger=Explicit}"
         Grid.Row="1"
         Grid.Column="3"
         Width="Auto"
         Grid.RowSpan="1"
         Grid.ColumnSpan="3" />
<TextBlock HorizontalAlignment="Stretch"
           Margin="1,1,1,1"
           VerticalAlignment="Stretch"
           Text="Last"
           TextWrapping="Wrap"
           Grid.RowSpan="1"
           Grid.Column="4"
           Grid.ColumnSpan="2"
           Height="Auto"
           Width="Auto" />
<TextBlock HorizontalAlignment="Center"
           Margin="1,1,1,1"
           VerticalAlignment="Center"
           Text="First"
           TextWrapping="Wrap"
           Grid.RowSpan="1"
           Grid.Column="1"
           Width="Auto"
           Height="Auto" />
```

```
            <TextBlock HorizontalAlignment="Center"
                       Margin="1,1,1,1"
                       VerticalAlignment="Stretch"
                       Text="Name"
                       TextWrapping="Wrap"
                       Grid.RowSpan="1"
                       Grid.Row="1"
                       Height="Auto"
                       Width="Auto" />
            <TextBlock HorizontalAlignment="Center"
                       Margin="1,1,1,1"
                       VerticalAlignment="Stretch"
                       Text="Street"
                       TextWrapping="Wrap"
                       Grid.Row="2"
                       Width="Auto" />
          <TextBox HorizontalAlignment="Stretch"
                   x:Name="tbxStreet"
                   VerticalAlignment="Stretch"
                   Text=
    "{Binding Address.Street, Mode=TwoWay, UpdateSourceTrigger=Explicit}"
                   Grid.Row="2"
                   Margin="1,1,1,1"
                   Grid.Column="1"
                   Grid.ColumnSpan="5"
                   Width="Auto" />
            <TextBlock HorizontalAlignment="Center"
                       VerticalAlignment="Stretch"
                       Text="City"
                       TextWrapping="Wrap"
                       Margin="1,1,1,1"
                       Grid.Row="3" />
            <TextBlock Text="State"
                       Margin="1,1,1,1"
                       TextWrapping="Wrap"
                       Grid.Column="2"
                       Grid.Row="3"
                       HorizontalAlignment="Center" />
```

```
            <TextBlock Text="Zip"
                    Margin="1,1,1,1"
                    TextWrapping="Wrap"
                    Grid.Column="4"
                    Grid.Row="3"
                    HorizontalAlignment="Center" />
            <TextBox HorizontalAlignment="Stretch"
                    x:Name="tbxCity"
                    Margin="1,1,1,1"
                    VerticalAlignment="Stretch"
                    Text-
        "{Binding Address.City, Mode=TwoWay, UpdateSourceTrigger=Explicit}"
                    Grid.Row="3"
                    Grid.Column="1" />


            <TextBox Background="Transparent"
                    Grid.Column="3"
                    Margin="1,1,1,1"
                    Grid.Row="3"
                    Text=
        "{Binding Address.State, Mode=TwoWay,UpdateSourceTrigger=Explicit,
        ValidatesOnExceptions=True,NotifyOnValidationError=True}"
                    x:Name="tbxState">
            </TextBox>


            <TextBox Background="Transparent"
                    Grid.Column="5"
                    Grid.Row="3"
                    Margin="1,1,1,1"
                    Text=
        "{Binding Address.ZipCode, Mode=TwoWay, UpdateSourceTrigger=Explicit,
            ValidatesOnExceptions-True,NotifyOnValidationError-True}"
                    x:Name="tbxZipCode" />


            <TextBlock HorizontalAlignment="Center"
                    VerticalAlignment="Stretch"
                    Text="Phone"
                    Margin="1,1,1,1"
                    TextWrapping="Wrap"
                    Grid.Row="4" />
```

```xml
            <TextBox Grid.Column="1"
                     Grid.Row="4"
                     Margin="1,1,1,1"
                     Text=
                "{Binding PhoneNum, Mode=TwoWay, UpdateSourceTrigger=Explicit,
        ValidatesOnExceptions=True,NotifyOnValidationError=True}"
                     x:Name="tbxPhoneNum" />
            <StackPanel Orientation="Horizontal"
                        Grid.Column="4"
                        Margin="1,1,1,1"
                        Grid.ColumnSpan="2"
                        Grid.Row="4">
                <Button Height="30.911"
                        Margin="2,2,2,0"
                        VerticalAlignment="Top"
                        Content="Save"
                        x:Name="btnSave"
                        Click="btnSave_Click" />
                <Button Height="30.911"
                        Margin="2,2,2,0"
                        VerticalAlignment="Top"
                        Content="Close"
                        x:Name="btnClose"
                        Click="btnClose_Click" />
            </StackPanel>

        </Grid>
      </Border>
    </Grid>
</UserControl>
```

Note the changes in XAML to the Binding declarations to set the UpdateSourceTrigger to Explicit. Listing 4-23 shows the code behind.

Listing 4-23. *Code behind to MainPage*

```
using System.Collections.ObjectModel;
using System.Linq;
using System.Windows;
using System.Windows.Controls;
using System.Windows.Data;
```

```csharp
namespace Ch04_DataBinding.Recipe4_7
{
  public partial class MainPage : UserControl
  {
    public MainPage()
    {
      InitializeComponent();

      //initialize the employee collection with some sample data
      ObservableCollection<Employee> empColl =
        new ObservableCollection<Employee>();

      empColl.Add(new Employee
      {
        FirstName = "Joe",
        LastName = "Duffin",
        PhoneNum = "2125551212",
        Address = new Address
        {
          Street = "2000 Mott Street",
          City = "New York",
          State = "NY",
          ZipCode = "10006"
        }
      });

      empColl.Add(new Employee
      {
        FirstName = "Alex",
        LastName = "Bleeker",
        PhoneNum = "7185551212",
        Address = new Address
        {
          Street = "11000 Clover Street",
          City = "New York",
          State = "NY",
          ZipCode = "10007"
        }
      });
```

```csharp
      empColl.Add(new Employee
      {
        FirstName = "Nelly",
        LastName = "Myers",
        PhoneNum = "7325551212",
        Address = new Address
        {
          Street = "12000 Fay Road",
          City = "New York",
          State = "NY",
          ZipCode = "10016"
        }
      });

      lbx_Employees.ItemsSource = empColl;

      this.BindingValidationError +=
        new System.EventHandler<ValidationErrorEventArgs>((s, e) =>
        {

          if (lbx_Employees.SelectedItem == null) return;
          //change the InError property of the currently selected Employee
          if (e.Action == ValidationErrorEventAction.Added)
            (lbx_Employees.SelectedItem as Employee).InError = true;
          else
            (lbx_Employees.SelectedItem as Employee).InError = false;

        });
    }

    private void btn_New_Click(object sender, RoutedEventArgs e)
    {
      //get the bound collection
      ObservableCollection<Employee> empColl =
        (ObservableCollection<Employee>)lbx_Employees.ItemsSource;
      //create and initialize a new Employee
      Employee newEmp = new Employee();
      newEmp.Address = new Address();
      //add it to the collection
      empColl.Add(newEmp);
```

```
        //set the current selection to the newly added employee.
        //This will cause selection change to fire, and set the
        //datacontext for the form appropriately
        lbx_Employees.SelectedItem = newEmp;

    }

    private void lbx_Employees_SelectionChanged(object sender,
      SelectionChangedEventArgs e)
    {
        //set the datacontext of the form to the selected Employee
        grid_EmployeeForm.DataContext = (Employee)lbx_Employees.SelectedItem;
        //show the form
        border_EmployeeForm.Visibility = Visibility.Visible;
        grid_NewButton.Visibility = Visibility.Collapsed;
    }

    private void btnClose_Click(object sender, RoutedEventArgs e)
    {
        //hide the form
        border_EmployeeForm.Visibility = Visibility.Collapsed;
        grid_NewButton.Visibility = Visibility.Visible;
    }

    private void btnSave_Click(object sender, RoutedEventArgs e)
    {

        var bindingExpressions =
          grid_EmployeeForm.Children.OfType<TextBox>().
          Select((tbx)=>tbx.GetBindingExpression(TextBox.TextProperty));
        foreach (BindingExpression be in bindingExpressions) be.UpdateSource();
    }
  }
}
```

Note the code in the Click event handler for btnSave. We perform a quick LINQ query on grid_EmployeeForm.Children collection, to get access to the BindingExpressions for the Text property of all the children of type TextBox. We then proceed to iterate through the collection of BindingExpressions and call UpdateSource() on each of them.

CHAPTER 5

■ ■ ■

Controls

If you are a presentation layer developer or designer, we probably do not need to tell you how important controls can be in building good-quality user interfaces efficiently and using a modular approach. To that end, any good-quality UI development framework comes with a comprehensive library of controls, and Silverlight is no exception. From basic controls like Button, RadioButton, and CheckBox to more advanced controls like Calendar and DataGrid, Silverlight offers a fairly wide set to choose from. Most of the Silverlight controls distributed as a part of the core runtime are found in the System.Windows.Controls and System.Windows.Controls.Primitives namespaces in the System.Windows assembly. Additional controls are distributed as a part of the Silverlight SDK and are found in the System.Windows.Controls.dll and System.Windows.Controls.Data.dll assemblies. The core runtime control assembly is added to all Silverlight projects created using Visual Studio, but references to the other two assemblies and appropriate namespace mappings for XAML usage will need to be added as needed.

Controls do not always meet the developer's needs right out of the box. More often than not, their default UI needs to be adapted for a specific application's needs. All Silverlight controls expose rich APIs consisting of various properties and methods that can be used to further customize the control's UI. Silverlight also incorporates the concept of styles. Styles allow you to collect specific settings for a control type and reapply them across many control instances, helping you achieve reuse as well UI standardization. And lastly, for those scenarios where the control developer's intent simply does not satisfy your needs for UI, Silverlight also incorporates control templates, a feature that allows you to completely replace a control's default UI with your own, while leaving the control's behavior intact.

Silverlight also allows you to write your own controls. You can write user controls (alternatively called composite controls) that are more application or domain specific and are usually crafted by composing a UI out of other existing controls. Or you can write custom controls, a more advanced control implementation strategy resulting in more general-purpose usage and allowing you to benefit from features like control templates.

While this chapter is on controls, our goal is not to cover in detail the usage and API for each control that Silverlight comes with. For one thing, that would take quite a lot of space, and for another, that information is easily found in the Silverlight documentation at http://msdn.microsoft.com/en-us/library/cc189048(VS.95).aspx and, to a large extent, in other books on Silverlight like Matthew MacDonald's *Pro Silverlight 3 in C#* (Apress, 2009). Instead we focus more on the following:

- Various extensibility mechanisms in the Silverlight control framework

- Common control customization scenarios

- Control authoring

Our hope is that once you get familiar with using the controls with help from the sources we've mentioned, these recipes will give you that additional knowledge to make you truly productive in using and authoring controls.

A Word About the Samples

Most of the control recipes in this chapter need to use some form of application data. To make it easier to structure the sample code, and to avoid having to repetitively explain the data source logic, we include a common Windows Communication Foundation(WCF) web service and use it as the data source for the recipes wherever applicable. The WCF service defines a set of service operations that expose various data elements from the `Production` schema in the `AdventureWorks` Online Transaction Processing (OLTP) sample database. LINQ to SQL is used to generate the data model and corresponding data classes for the tables in the schema that we have decided to use in the various samples. Once you download the sample code, the WCF service is in the `AdventureWorksDataService` project in the `Ch05_Controls` Visual Studio solution.

     For our example, we use SQL Server 2008 Express version, which you can download for free from `http://www.microsoft.com/express/sql/download/default.aspx`. When you install the product, take care to name the server `SQLEXPRESS`. This is the server name that our code samples expect. If you must change it, visit the `web.config` files for the web service project, and change the database connection strings to reflect your chosen server name.

     You will also need to install the `AdventureWorks` OLTP database sample for SQL Server 2008, which you can download at `http://www.codeplex.com/MSFTDBProdSamples/Release/ProjectReleases.aspx?ReleaseId=16040`. Note that you can get this database in two flavors: one that uses the new SQL Server 2008 data types and schema, and one that continues to use the SQL Server 2005 versions. We chose to use the 2005 schema version to attain a larger reach for those who might already have `AdventureWorks` installed, so keep that in mind while downloading. The installer packages will most likely be named `AdventureWorksDB.msi` or `AdventureWorksDB_x64.msi`, depending on your choice of the 32-bit or 64-bit architecture.

     We do not discuss the WCF service code in this chapter, and we hope you will navigate to the sample code to take a look as needed. To learn more about using a WCF service with Silverlight, check out Chapter 7. Recipe 7-4 uses LINQ to SQL in a similar approach as used here in the `AdventureWorks` service and will provide you with a good background for the related techniques.

5-1. Customizing a Control's Basic Appearance

Problem

You want to customize the look and feel of a control by setting various properties. Furthermore, you want to create an artifact that can be used repeatedly to apply these property values to multiple controls of the same type.

Solution

Create a style in XAML containing the necessary property settings. Then, apply the style to all controls of that type to get a consistent look and feel.

How It Works

A style is a collection of property value settings targeted to a control of a specific type. Styles are typically defined in XAML as a resource in a `ResourceDictionary`. The `TargetType` property for a style determines what control type the `Style` can be applied to. Once defined, the style can be accessed in XAML using the `StaticResource` markup extension.

Property settings in style definitions are defined using the `<Setter>` element, where `Setter.Property` is set to the name of the property on the target that you want the style to influence, and `Setter.Value` contains the value that you want to apply. The following code snippet shows a simple style definition for a `Button`, where the `Foreground` and the `FontSize` properties of the `Button` will be set to the values specified in the style definition:

```
<Style TargetType="Button"
       x:Key="STYLE_Button">
  <Setter Property="Foreground"
          Value="#FFF41414" />
  <Setter Property="FontSize"
          Value="18" />
</Style>
```

The `FrameworkElement` base class, and as such every control in the Silverlight Control Framework, exposes a `Style` dependency property. This property can be set on any control on a page, either in XAML or in the code-behind, to apply a style to that control. The following snippet shows the application of a style to a `Button` control:

```
<Button Style="{StaticResource STYLE_Button}" />
```

Starting with Silverlight 3, styles also support inheritance (i.e., you can define a new style based on an existing style). In the new style definition, you can choose to redefine existing property settings to new values, as well as add new property settings. The `BasedOn` attribute on a style definition needs to be set to the base style from which you are inheriting the current style. The snippet below shows an inherited style definition.

```
<Style TargetType="Button"
       x:Key="STYLE_InheritedButton"
       BasedOn="{StaticResource STYLE_Button}">
  <Setter Property="Width"
          Value="225" />
  <Setter Property="FontFamily"
          Value="Trebuchet" />
</Style>
```

Style Scoping

Also recall that styles are declared as resources. Consequently, in XAML markup, styles are scoped by the resource dictionary to which they belong. For example, a style defined in the `Resources` section of a page can be applied to any element in that page at any level of the hierarchy, whereas a style defined in the `Resources` section of a `Grid` can only be applied to elements within that `Grid`. To have a style be universally available to an application you can define the style in the `Application.Resources` section in your `App.xaml` file. You can also use a `MergedResourceDictionary` to bring in styles defined in external resource dictionaries. For more on `ResourceDictionary` and `MergedResourceDictionary`, please refer to related recipes in Chapter 2.

The Code

The code sample in Listing 5-1 demonstrates how to define styles and apply them to controls. The XAML page contains three instances each of a Button. Two of the Button instances have styles applied to it to illustrate the resulting changes in look and feel.

Listing 5-1. *A Sample Style Targeting a Button(MainPage.xaml)*

```
<UserControl x:Class="Ch05_Controls.Recipe5_1.MainPage"
             xmlns="http://schemas.microsoft.com/winfx/2006/xaml/presentation"
             xmlns:x="http://schemas.microsoft.com/winfx/2006/xaml"
             Width="400"
             Height="300">
  <UserControl.Resources>
    <Style TargetType="Button"
           x:Key="STYLE_Button">
      <Setter Property="Width"
              Value="100" />
      <Setter Property="Height"
              Value="30" />
      <Setter Property="Foreground"
              Value="#FFE41414" />
      <Setter Property="Background">
        <Setter.Value>
          <LinearGradientBrush EndPoint="0.5,1"
                               StartPoint="0.5,0">
            <GradientStop Color="#FFE26F56" />
            <GradientStop Color="#FFDA390B"
                          Offset="1" />
          </LinearGradientBrush>
        </Setter.Value>
      </Setter>
      <Setter Property="FontSize"
              Value="18" />
      <Setter Property="FontFamily"
              Value="Georgia" />
    </Style>

    <Style TargetType="Button"
           x:Key="STYLE_InheritedButton" BasedOn="{StaticResource STYLE_Button}">
      <Setter Property="Width"
              Value="225" />
      <Setter Property="FontFamily"
              Value="Trebuchet" />
      <Setter Property="Cursor"
              Value="Hand" />
```

```
    <Setter Property="Margin"
            Value="0,10,0,10" />
  </Style>

</UserControl.Resources>

<StackPanel x:Name="LayoutRoot"
            Background="White">
  <Button Content="Not Styled"
          Margin="0,0,0,20" />

  <Button Content="Styled" x:Name="Styled"
          Style="{StaticResource STYLE_Button}" />
  <Button Content="Inherited Style" x:Name="Inherited"
          Style="{StaticResource STYLE_InheritedButton}" />
</StackPanel>

</UserControl>
```

The style named STYLE_Button is being applied to the Button named Styled. STYLE_Button is being used to set several properties of the Button control, including its Height, Width, Foreground, and Background brushes, as well as some of the font-related properties.

The style named STYLE_InheritedButton inherits from STYLE_Button. You can see how we override the Width property to change its value to 225 from the original 100, and we override the FontFamily property to change it to the Trebuchet font. We also add two new property settings in the inherited style: a Margin property value setting and a Cursor property value setting. STYLE_InheritedButton is then applied to the Button named Inherited.

■**Note** Note the property element syntax for defining the Background property. The property element syntax allows setting the property value as a child element to the <Setter> element, instead of the inline string literal using the Value attribute. This can be used where the values being set are complex enough that they cannot be represented as a simple string literal.

Figure 5-1 shows the result of applying the style.

Figure 5-1. *Styled buttons versus the default look and feel*

Also note the Content property setting of the Button in Listing 5-1. A control's content model is discussed more in Recipe 5-2. For now it is sufficient to think of it as a way of placing additional content such as a text label inside the control.

5-2. Replacing the Default UI of a Control

Problem

Every control has an out-of-the-box user interface. You want to replace this default UI with a custom one in your application without having to write a new control.

Solution

Design a custom control template to express the new UI for the control, and apply it to the control using the Template property or through a Style in your application's XAML.

How It Works

Every Silverlight control that renders itself visually at runtime needs its UI defined as a part of the control writing process. The preferred mode of defining this UI is by designing a self-contained block of XAML and associating it with the control so that it can be loaded and rendered by the control code. This block of XAML is what forms the default control template for that control. In Recipe 5-10, we are going to show you how to specify the default control template while writing a custom control. In the next few sections, we focus on the mechanics of the control template itself and explore things you need to be aware of in modifying or replacing the control template for an existing control.

Control Template Syntax

A control template always starts with the XAML element <ControlTemplate>. The TargetType attribute must supply the CLR type of the control to which the template can be applied. Here is a sample declaration:

```
<UserControl.Resources>
  <ControlTemplate x:Key="ctCustomRadioButton" TargetType="RadioButton">
  <!--Template Definition Here -->
  </ControlTemplate>
</UserControl.Resources>
```

Inside the <ControlTemplate> tag, you can have any XAML as long as it is syntactically correct to be renderable. The template is typically defined as a stand-alone resource in a resource dictionary, where the x:Key attribute specifies the unique key for the template by which it can be referenced when applied to the control. For more on declaring resources, refer to Chapter 2.

Setting the Template

The Control base class exposes a Template property that can be set on any control to replace its template, as shown here:

```
<RadioButton Template="{StaticResource ctCustomRadioButton}"/>
```

You can also use a style to apply a template to a control:

```
<Style TargetType="RadioButton" x:Name="styleGelRadioButton">
  <Setter Property="Template" Value="{StaticResource ctCustomRadioButton}"/>
  <!--Other setters here -->
</Style>
<!--apply the Style and hence the template-->
<RadioButton Style="{StaticResource styleGelRadioButton}"/>
```

In the previous examples, we define the control templates as stand-alone resources; then, we reference them in a style or apply them using the Template property. Note that control templates can also be defined in line without having to declare them as a separate resource. The following XAML snippet demonstrates this:

```
<!-- defined in place in a Style -->
<Style TargetType="RadioButton" x:Name="styleGelRadioButton">
  <Setter Property="Template">
      <Setter.Value>
          <ControlTemplate TargetType="RadioButton">
              <!-- rest of the template -->
          </ControlTemplate>
      </Setter.Value>
  </Setter>
  <!-- rest of the setters -->
</Style>

<!-- defined in place in a control declaration -->
<RadioButton>
  <RadioButton.Template>
      <ControlTemplate TargetType="RadioButton">
          <!-- rest of the template -->
      </ControlTemplate>
  </RadioButton.Template>
</RadioButton>
```

Using Expression Blend to Design a Template

Expression Blend 3 offers excellent support for designing Silverlight user interfaces, including designing custom templates for controls. For a general introduction to Expression Blend usage and for UI design, refer to Chapters 1 and 3, respectively. In this recipe, we discuss Expression Blend 3 features that apply to control template design.

Once you have the control added to your scene in the Expression Blend designer window, you can right-click the control to bring up its context menu, as shown in Figure 5-2.

Figure 5-2. *Control context menu in Expression Blend 3*

You have the option of either creating an empty control template or having Expression Blend generate a copy of the default template. If the modifications you want to make are minor, it is often helpful to start with a copy. A copy also gives you a good look into the intentions of the original designers of the control. Note that when you choose to edit a copy, Expression Blend actually creates a style with the control template defined within that style using a setter for the Template property.

Once you specify a key for the new control template as shown in Figure 5-3, or the encapsulating style in the event you decide to edit a copy, Expression Blend switches the designer over to the control template (for the RadioButton in Figure 5-2). If you chose to create an empty template, Expression Blend creates a mostly empty visual tree for the control contained in a Grid for layout. If you chose to edit a copy, Expression Blend creates a style that contains a copy of the entire visual tree as supplied by the default template, which you can then modify. Figure 5-4 shows the differences.

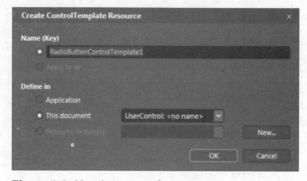

Figure 5-3. *Naming a template*

Figure 5-4. *Empty control template versus editing a copy*

From here on, designing the template is mostly like designing any other XAML-based UI in Expression Blend, with some additional features discussed next.

Template Bindings

When you are designing a control template, you have the option of setting values for the properties of the various elements that make up that template. In many cases, it may make sense to derive those values from the corresponding property settings on the control at the point of its use in an application. For example, you may want the Background property of an element inside the control template of a control assume whatever value is set on the Background property on the control itself when it is being used. However, while you are designing the control template, you have no way of knowing what those values might be. Therefore, you need a mechanism to indicate that a certain property value on an element in the template will be bound to a matching property value of the control at the point of use. The TemplateBinding construct allows you just that:

```
<ControlTemplate x:Key="ctGelRadioButton" TargetType="RadioButton">
  <Grid MaxHeight="{TemplateBinding MaxHeight}"
        MaxWidth="{TemplateBinding MaxWidth}"
        Background="{TemplateBinding Background}">
      <Ellipse Margin="0,0,0,0" x:Name="OuterRing"
      Stroke="{TemplateBinding Foreground}" StrokeThickness="2">
      </Ellipse>
  </Grid>
</ControlTemplate>
```

For the RadioButton control template shown here, we have the MaxHeight, MaxWidth, and Background properties of the top-level Grid and the Foreground property of the Ellipse template bound. These template bindings will cause whatever values are supplied to these properties in a RadioButton declaration using this template to be applied to these elements in the template, as specified by the template bindings. Template bindings are useful when you need the control consumer to be able to affect properties of the parts of the control template without having direct access to the parts themselves. However, it is not mandatory that template bindings be used in every control template definition.

If you are designing the template in Expression Blend 3, the context menu for each property (made available by clicking the little rectangle on the right of the property editor) offers you the choices of parent properties that you can bind to (see Figure 5-5).

Figure 5-5. *Binding a property within a template using Expression Blend 3*

Content Model and Presenter Controls

Controls often present content to their users in addition to the interactivity and event functionality they provide. For example, in Figure 5-6, the text "Option 1" is the content being displayed by the radio button. The part of the control design that specifies how it displays content is called the content model of the control.

Figure 5-6. *Radio button with content set to "Option 1"*

CHAPTER 5 ■ CONTROLS

To better understand this, let's consider the System.Windows.Controls.ContentControl type. The ContentControl has a dependency property called Content that can be set or bound to any content, which the ContentControl instance then displays. In case there is no built-in knowledge of how to display this content, you can also associate a data template through the ContentTemplate property to facilitate the display of the content. More than being useful in and of itself, the ContentControl serves as a base class for many other controls in Silverlight, such as Label, Button, or the RadioButton shown earlier.

The following snippet shows the XAML declaration for the RadioButton in Figure 5-6:

```
<RadioButton Content="Option 1" />
```

Figure 5-7 shows a radio button with slightly more complex content, including a text caption and an image displayed with the help of a data template.

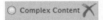

Figure 5-7. *Radio button with complex content*

This XAML snippet shows the RadioButton declaration:

```
<RadioButton Content="{Binding}" x:Name="rbtn">
  <RadioButton.ContentTemplate>
    <DataTemplate>
      <Grid>
        <Grid.ColumnDefinitions>
          <ColumnDefinition Width="Auto"/>
          <ColumnDefinition Width="Auto"/>
        </Grid.ColumnDefinitions>
        <TextBlock Text="{Binding Caption}" Grid.Column="0"
TextAlignment="Center" HorizontalAlignment="Center" VerticalAlignment="Center"/>
        <Image Source="{Binding Icon}" Grid.Column="1" Stretch="Fill"
idth="24" Height="24" Margin="3,0,0,0"/>
      </Grid>
    </DataTemplate>
  </RadioButton.ContentTemplate>
</RadioButton>
```

The content for the RadioButton can be set by setting its DataContext property to some instance of a CLR type that exposes two properties: Caption and Icon.

When you modify the control template for a control, you should be aware of the intended content model for that control, and to be fair to the control author's intentions, try to retain the same content model in your custom template. To facilitate this, the Silverlight control framework provides a specific category of controls called presenters. A presenter's purpose is to create a placeholder for content inside a control template. Through appropriate template bindings, content gets passed on to the presenter, which then displays the content in the rest of the visual tree of the template. You can also associate a data template (again preferably through a template binding), which is then used by the presenter to display the content.

369

Several types of content models and corresponding presenters are supplied in the framework, and we will look at many of them in various recipes in this chapter. For this sample, we need to understand the most fundamental of them all: the ContentPresenter control.

This XAML shows a ContentPresenter in action in a template for a RadioButton:

```
<ControlTemplate x:Key="ctCustomRadioButton"
                 TargetType="RadioButton">
  <Grid>
   <!-- rest of the template -->
    <ContentPresenter HorizontalAlignment="Center"
                      VerticalAlignment="Center"
                      Grid.Column="1" Margin="2,0,0,2"
          Content="{TemplateBinding Content}"
          ContentTemplate="{TemplateBinding ContentTemplate}"/>
  </Grid>
</ControlTemplate>
```

Notice the template bindings for the Content and the ContentTemplate properties of the ContentPresenter, which allow the values set for these properties on any instance of the RadioButton to be passed into the ContentPresenter for display. If those template bindings were absent, or if you did not have a ContentPresenter as shown earlier, setting the Content property on the RadioButton would have no effect, since there would be no placeholder inside the control's template to display that content.

Visual State Management

Controls often change their visual state as users interact with them. A check mark that appears in a Checkbox or a Button when it is clicked is an example of a visual state change. The Silverlight control framework includes a Visual State Manager (VSM) component that can be used to manage these state transitions.

The various possible visual states for a control are defined by the control author and further logically grouped into state groups. Each state managed by the VSM is implemented as a StoryBoard that can contain one or more animations that define the visual representation of moving from another state to this state. When designing a control template using Expression Blend, you can see the various state groups and the states in them in the States editor, as shown in Figure 5-8.

As you select a specific state, Expression Blend transitions into a storyboard recording mode for that state, as shown in Figure 5-9.

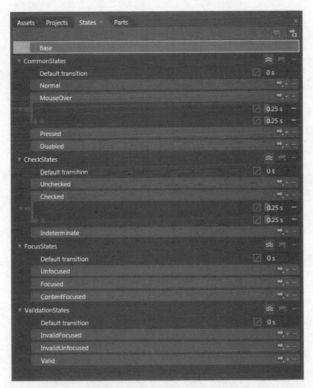

Figure 5-8. *The control template's States editor in Expression Blend 3*

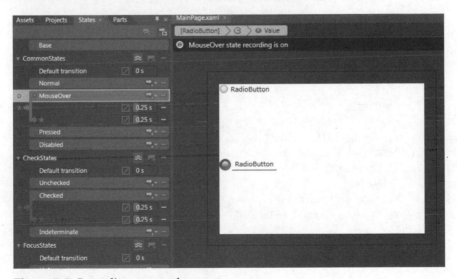

Figure 5-9. *Recording a state change*

The recording of a state change works just like recording a regular storyboard in Expression Blend, including the use of the storyboard time line editor to define a timeline for a specific keyframe animation in the state storyboard. For more on animation and storyboards, refer to recipes in Chapter 3.

In addition to defining each individual state as a storyboard, you can also optionally define the time duration of the transition from one state to another. Clicking the state transition icon for a state displays all the possible state transitions involving that state. Figure 5-10 shows the possible transitions to and from the MouseOver state for a control template, with * indicating any state.

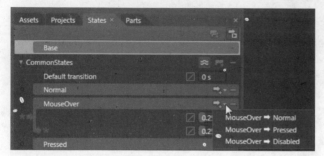

Figure 5-10. *State transitions for the MouseOver state*

In Figure 5-10, we have already defined the transition duration from any other state to the MouseOver state to be a quarter of a second. The following XAML shows a sample set of states and some of the possible transitions defined:

```
<vsm:VisualStateManager.VisualStateGroups>
  <vsm:VisualStateGroup x:Name="CommonStates">
    <vsm:VisualStateGroup.Transitions>
      <vsm:VisualTransition  GeneratedDuration="00:00:00.2500000" To="MouseOver"/>
      <vsm:VisualTransition GeneratedDuration="00:00:00.2500000" From="MouseOver"/>
    </vsm:VisualStateGroup.Transitions>
    <vsm:VisualState x:Name="Disabled"/>
    <vsm:VisualState x:Name="Normal">
      <Storyboard/>
    </vsm:VisualState>
    <vsm:VisualState x:Name="MouseOver">
      <Storyboard>
        <ColorAnimationUsingKeyFrames BeginTime="00:00:00"
          Duration="00:00:00.0010000"
          Storyboard.TargetName="OuterRing"
          Storyboard.TargetProperty=
              "(Shape.Stroke).(SolidColorBrush.Color)">
          <SplineColorKeyFrame KeyTime="00:00:00" Value="#FF144EEA"/>
        </ColorAnimationUsingKeyFrames>
```

```xml
      <ColorAnimationUsingKeyFrames BeginTime="00:00:00"
        Duration="00:00:00.0010000"
        Storyboard.TargetName="InnerCore"
        Storyboard.TargetProperty=
  "(Shape.Fill).(GradientBrush.GradientStops)[1].(GradientStop.Color)">
        <SplineColorKeyFrame KeyTime="00:00:00" Value="#FF144EEA"/>
      </ColorAnimationUsingKeyFrames>
    </Storyboard>
  </vsm:VisualState>
  <vsm:VisualState x:Name="Pressed"/>
</vsm:VisualStateGroup>
<vsm:VisualStateGroup x:Name="FocusStates">
  <vsm:VisualState x:Name="Unfocused">
    <Storyboard>
      <ObjectAnimationUsingKeyFrames
        Storyboard.TargetName="FocusIndicator"
        Storyboard.TargetProperty="Visibility"
        Duration="0">
        <DiscreteObjectKeyFrame KeyTime="0">
          <DiscreteObjectKeyFrame.Value>
            <Visibility>Collapsed</Visibility>
          </DiscreteObjectKeyFrame.Value>
        </DiscreteObjectKeyFrame>
      </ObjectAnimationUsingKeyFrames>
    </Storyboard>
  </vsm:VisualState>
  <vsm:VisualState x:Name="Focused">
    <Storyboard>
      <ObjectAnimationUsingKeyFrames
        Storyboard.TargetName="FocusIndicator"
        Storyboard.TargetProperty="Visibility"
        Duration="0">
        <DiscreteObjectKeyFrame KeyTime="0">
          <DiscreteObjectKeyFrame.Value>
            <Visibility>Visible</Visibility>
          </DiscreteObjectKeyFrame.Value>
        </DiscreteObjectKeyFrame>
      </ObjectAnimationUsingKeyFrames>
    </Storyboard>
  </vsm:VisualState>
  <vsm:VisualState x:Name="ContentFocused">
    <Storyboard>
      <ObjectAnimationUsingKeyFrames
        Storyboard.TargetName="FocusIndicator"
        Storyboard.TargetProperty="Visibility"
        Duration="0">
```

```
          <DiscreteObjectKeyFrame KeyTime="0">
            <DiscreteObjectKeyFrame.Value>
              <Visibility>Visible</Visibility>
            </DiscreteObjectKeyFrame.Value>
          </DiscreteObjectKeyFrame>
        </ObjectAnimationUsingKeyFrames>
      </Storyboard>
    </vsm:VisualState>
  </vsm:VisualStateGroup>
  <vsm:VisualStateGroup x:Name="CheckStates">
    <vsm:VisualStateGroup.Transitions>
      <vsm:VisualTransition GeneratedDuration="00:00:00.2500000" To="Checked"/>
      <vsm:VisualTransition GeneratedDuration="00:00:00.2500000" From="Checked"/>
    </vsm:VisualStateGroup.Transitions>
    <vsm:VisualState x:Name="Unchecked">
      <Storyboard/>
    </vsm:VisualState>
    <vsm:VisualState x:Name="Checked">
      <Storyboard>
        <ColorAnimationUsingKeyFrames
          BeginTime="00:00:00"
          Duration="00:00:00.0010000"
          Storyboard.TargetName="InnerCore"
          Storyboard.TargetProperty=
    "(Shape.Fill).(GradientBrush.GradientStops)[0].(GradientStop.Color)">
          <SplineColorKeyFrame KeyTime="00:00:00" Value="#FF144EEA"/>
        </ColorAnimationUsingKeyFrames>
      </Storyboard>
    </vsm:VisualState>
    <vsm:VisualState x:Name="Indeterminate"/>
  </vsm:VisualStateGroup>
</vsm:VisualStateManager.VisualStateGroups>
```

As you can see in the previous snippet, each visual state for the control is declared as a <vsm:VisualState> element. Each state has an associated storyboard, which can include one or more animations that all get executed by the runtime when that visual state is reached. These animations typically animate various properties of different parts of the control template to give the necessary visual cue indicating the state change. As an example, in the MouseOver state storyboard in the previous snippet, we have two animations defined within the storyboard. The first one animates the Stroke property on an element named OuterRing to a different solid color. The second one animates the Fill property of another element named InnerCore to a different gradient. You can also have an empty storyboard if you do not want to define any particular visual change for the control on reaching that state. The control's code determines when a specific visual state is reached, and we will see exactly how that is done in recipe 5-11 when we discuss a custom control implementing custom visual states.

You should also note the <vsm:VisualStateGroup> declarations that group visual states together. The VisualStateManager mandates that each state be contained in a group (even if that is the only state in it) and that each state be defined in exactly one group. In the previous snippet, you can also see

<vsm:VisualTransition> elements declared inside a state group. Each defined visual transition is a way to specify a time duration over which a transition from one state to another in a group should happen. In the previous example, transition from any state to the MouseOver state or the reverse is specified to happen over a quarter of a second.

You are not required to define an explicit storyboard for each state. For example, it is common to not define anything explicit for the Normal state, as shown in the previous XAML, since the default visual representation of the control template can be considered its normal state. However, that does not necessarily mean that you can leave out the state definition completely. In the case of the Normal state, for example, the empty storyboard causes the RadioButton to revert to its default look when none of the other defined visual states are applicable and, consequently, the Normal state is reached. If you left out that state definition, the control would never revert to the default look and feel once it transitions out of another state. We will take another look at visual states from a control author's perspective in recipe 5-11.

The Code

The code sample in this recipe replaces the default control template of a RadioButton with a custom template. Listing 5-2 shows the full XAML for the page.

Listing 5-2. *Defining and Applying a Custom RadioButton Control Template*

```xml
<UserControl x:Class="Ch05_Controls.Recipe5_2.MainPage"
    xmlns="http://schemas.microsoft.com/winfx/2006/xaml/presentation"
    xmlns:x="http://schemas.microsoft.com/winfx/2006/xaml"
    Width="400" Height="300"
    xmlns:vsm="clr-namespace:System.Windows;assembly=System.Windows">
  <UserControl.Resources>
    <!-- The Custom Control Template targeting a RadioButton -->
    <ControlTemplate x:Key="ctCustomRadioButton"
                     TargetType="RadioButton">
      <Grid Background="{TemplateBinding Background}"
                MinHeight="{TemplateBinding MinHeight}"
                MinWidth="{TemplateBinding MinWidth}"
                MaxWidth="{TemplateBinding MaxWidth}"
                MaxHeight="{TemplateBinding MaxHeight}">
        <vsm:VisualStateManager.VisualStateGroups>
          <vsm:VisualStateGroup x:Name="CommonStates">
            <vsm:VisualStateGroup.Transitions>
              <vsm:VisualTransition  GeneratedDuration="00:00:00.2500000"
 To="MouseOver"/>
              <vsm:VisualTransition GeneratedDuration="00:00:00.2500000"
 From="MouseOver"/>
            </vsm:VisualStateGroup.Transitions>
            <vsm:VisualState x:Name="Disabled"/>
            <vsm:VisualState x:Name="Normal">
              <Storyboard/>
            </vsm:VisualState>
```

```xml
<vsm:VisualState x:Name="MouseOver">
  <Storyboard>
    <ColorAnimationUsingKeyFrames BeginTime="00:00:00"
      Duration="00:00:00.0010000"
      Storyboard.TargetName="OuterRing"
      Storyboard.TargetProperty=
          "(Shape.Stroke).(SolidColorBrush.Color)">
      <SplineColorKeyFrame KeyTime="00:00:00" Value="#FF144EEA"/>
    </ColorAnimationUsingKeyFrames>
    <ColorAnimationUsingKeyFrames BeginTime="00:00:00"
      Duration="00:00:00.0010000"
      Storyboard.TargetName="InnerCore"
      Storyboard.TargetProperty=
"(Shape.Fill).(GradientBrush.GradientStops)[1].(GradientStop.Color)">
      <SplineColorKeyFrame KeyTime="00:00:00" Value="#FF144EEA"/>
    </ColorAnimationUsingKeyFrames>
  </Storyboard>
</vsm:VisualState>
<vsm:VisualState x:Name="Pressed"/>
</vsm:VisualStateGroup>
<vsm:VisualStateGroup x:Name="FocusStates">
  <vsm:VisualState x:Name="Unfocused">
    <Storyboard>
      <ObjectAnimationUsingKeyFrames
        Storyboard.TargetName="FocusIndicator"
        Storyboard.TargetProperty="Visibility"
        Duration="0">
        <DiscreteObjectKeyFrame KeyTime="0">
          <DiscreteObjectKeyFrame.Value>
            <Visibility>Collapsed</Visibility>
          </DiscreteObjectKeyFrame.Value>
        </DiscreteObjectKeyFrame>
      </ObjectAnimationUsingKeyFrames>
    </Storyboard>
  </vsm:VisualState>
  <vsm:VisualState x:Name="Focused">
    <Storyboard>
      <ObjectAnimationUsingKeyFrames
        Storyboard.TargetName="FocusIndicator"
        Storyboard.TargetProperty="Visibility"
        Duration="0">
```

```xml
            <DiscreteObjectKeyFrame KeyTime="0">
              <DiscreteObjectKeyFrame.Value>
                <Visibility>Visible</Visibility>
              </DiscreteObjectKeyFrame.Value>
            </DiscreteObjectKeyFrame>
          </ObjectAnimationUsingKeyFrames>
        </Storyboard>
      </vsm:VisualState>
      <vsm:VisualState x:Name="ContentFocused">
        <Storyboard>
          <ObjectAnimationUsingKeyFrames
            Storyboard.TargetName="FocusIndicator"
            Storyboard.TargetProperty="Visibility"
            Duration="0">
            <DiscreteObjectKeyFrame KeyTime="0">
              <DiscreteObjectKeyFrame.Value>
                <Visibility>Visible</Visibility>
              </DiscreteObjectKeyFrame.Value>
            </DiscreteObjectKeyFrame>
          </ObjectAnimationUsingKeyFrames>
        </Storyboard>
      </vsm:VisualState>
    </vsm:VisualStateGroup>
    <vsm:VisualStateGroup x:Name="CheckStates">
      <vsm:VisualStateGroup.Transitions>
        <vsm:VisualTransition GeneratedDuration="00:00:00.2500000"
To="Checked"/>
        <vsm:VisualTransition GeneratedDuration="00:00:00.2500000"
From="Checked"/>
      </vsm:VisualStateGroup.Transitions>
      <vsm:VisualState x:Name="Unchecked">
        <Storyboard/>
      </vsm:VisualState>
      <vsm:VisualState x:Name="Checked">
        <Storyboard>
          <ColorAnimationUsingKeyFrames
            BeginTime="00:00:00"
            Duration="00:00:00.0010000"
            Storyboard.TargetName="InnerCore"
            Storyboard.TargetProperty=
        "(Shape.Fill).(GradientBrush.GradientStops)[0].(GradientStop.Color)">
            <SplineColorKeyFrame KeyTime="00:00:00" Value="#FF144EEA"/>
          </ColorAnimationUsingKeyFrames>
        </Storyboard>
      </vsm:VisualState>
```

```xml
        <vsm:VisualState x:Name="Indeterminate"/>
      </vsm:VisualStateGroup>
</vsm:VisualStateManager.VisualStateGroups>
<Grid.ColumnDefinitions>
  <ColumnDefinition Width="0.20*"/>
  <ColumnDefinition Width="0.80*"/>
</Grid.ColumnDefinitions>
<Ellipse Margin="0,0,0,0" x:Name="OuterRing"
         Stroke="#00000000" StrokeThickness="2">
  <Ellipse.Fill>
    <LinearGradientBrush
      EndPoint="1.13300001621246,1.13999998569489"
      StartPoint="-0.0640000030398369,-0.0560000017285347">
      <GradientStop Color="#FF000000"/>
      <GradientStop Color="#FFADADAD" Offset="1"/>
    </LinearGradientBrush>
  </Ellipse.Fill>
</Ellipse>
<Grid Margin="0,0,0,0">
  <Grid.ColumnDefinitions>
    <ColumnDefinition Width="0.2*"/>
    <ColumnDefinition Width="0.6*"/>
    <ColumnDefinition Width="0.2*"/>
  </Grid.ColumnDefinitions>
  <Grid.RowDefinitions>
    <RowDefinition Height="0.2*"/>
    <RowDefinition Height="0.6*"/>
    <RowDefinition Height="0.2*"/>
  </Grid.RowDefinitions>

  <Ellipse x:Name="InnerRing"
           Fill="#FF000000"
           Grid.Column="1" Grid.Row="1"/>
  <Ellipse Grid.Row="1" Grid.Column="1"
           x:Name="InnerCore" Margin="0,0,0,0">
    <Ellipse.Fill>
      <LinearGradientBrush EndPoint="0.5,1" StartPoint="0.5,0">
        <GradientStop Color="#FFFFFFFF"/>
        <GradientStop Color="#FF000000" Offset="1"/>
      </LinearGradientBrush>
    </Ellipse.Fill>
  </Ellipse>
</Grid>
```

```
        <ContentPresenter HorizontalAlignment="Center"
                        VerticalAlignment="Center"
                        Grid.Column="1" Margin="2,0,0,2"
            Content="{TemplateBinding Content}"
            ContentTemplate="{TemplateBinding ContentTemplate}"/>
        <Rectangle Stroke="Black" x:Name="FocusIndicator" Grid.Column="1"
                StrokeThickness="0.5" Height="1"
                HorizontalAlignment="Stretch" VerticalAlignment="Bottom"
                Margin="2,0,0,0" />
    </Grid>
  </ControlTemplate>

  <!-- A style targeting the RadioButton referencing the control template -->
  <Style TargetType="RadioButton" x:Name="styleGelRadioButton">
    <Setter Property="Template" Value="{StaticResource ctCustomRadioButton}"/>
    <Setter Property="Height" Value="20" />
    <Setter Property="Width" Value="100" />
    <Setter Property="Background" Value="Transparent" />
  </Style>
</UserControl.Resources>

<Grid x:Name="LayoutRoot" Background="White" Margin="20,20,20,20">
  <Grid.RowDefinitions>
    <RowDefinition Height="0.5*"/>
    <RowDefinition Height="0.5*"/>
  </Grid.RowDefinitions>
  <!-- A RadioButton with default look & feel -->
  <RadioButton  HorizontalAlignment="Left" VerticalAlignment="Top"
                Content="RadioButton" GroupName="Test" Grid.Row="0"/>
  <!-- A RadioButton with the style (and hence the custom template) applied -->
  <RadioButton  HorizontalAlignment="Left" VerticalAlignment="Top"
                Content="RadioButton"
                Style="{StaticResource styleGelRadioButton}"
                GroupName="Test" Grid.Row="1"/>

</Grid>
</UserControl>
```

In Listing 5.2, our RadioButton control template, named ctCustomRadioButton, is primarily made up of three Ellipses, with the two Ellipses named InnerRing and InnerCore, situated in a Grid within the outer Ellipse named OuterRing. There is also a ContentPresenter to display any bound content, as well as a Rectangle (with Height set to 1 so that it appears as an underscore below the content) serving as a focus indicator, which has its Visibility initially set to Collapsed.

Figure 5-11 shows the `Normal` state comparisons between the custom template `RadioButton` with the default template.

Figure 5-11. *RadioButton Normal state with (left) and without (right) the custom template*

The `MouseOver` state is defined using a storyboard that changes the `Stroke` color of `OuterRing` and the `Fill` color of `InnerRing`. The result in comparison to the default `RadioButton` template is shown in Figure 5-12.

Figure 5-12. *RadioButton MouseOver state with (left) and without (right) the custom template*

The `Focused` and `ContentFocused` state storyboards make the `FocusIndicator` rectangle visible, while the `Unfocused` state storyboard hides it. The `Checked` state storyboard modifies the `Fill` color of the ellipse `InnerCore`. Figure 5-13 shows the `Checked` state of the `RadioButton` with focus on it.

Figure 5-13. *RadioButton Checked and Focused states with (left) and without (right) the custom template*

We also declare a style named `styleGelRadioButton`. We reference `ctCustomRadioButton` using a setter for the `Template` property, as well as set a few other defaults for some of the other properties in the control template. And last, for the page's UI, we declare two `RadioButtons`—one with the style `styleGelRadioButton` applied to it so that the custom template gets applied to it as well, and the other using just the default look and feel defined by the framework—to help you compare them visually.

Another important thing to note is the presence of specific elements in the control template definition with predetermined names. We will discuss this more in recipe 5-10 when we show how to write custom controls, but it is worth mentioning here in context of template customization. When the original control author designs the control, there may be dependencies in the control's code or in the definition of the default state change storyboards that would require specific names for different parts of the control template. If you decide to leave those elements out of your new control template, or name them differently, certain parts of the control's feature set or its visual representation may be rendered unavailable.

An example in Listing 5-2 is the `Rectangle` named `FocusIndicator`. The `RadioButton`'s default implementation includes state definitions for the `Focused`, `Unfocused`, and `ContentFocused` states that toggles the visibility of this `Rectangle` appropriately based on whether focus is on the control at any point in time. Should you decide to leave out or rename this `Rectangle` in your new template, you need to reauthor the state storyboards appropriately as well for the focus visual cue to function.

Control authors are advised to write controls defensively, so that a name dependency does not crash an application, and so that the control just silently shuts down the dependent feature. However, depending on the importance of the named element in the control's overall functionality, leaving or renaming certain elements may render the control useless. It is always worthwhile to look at the definition of the default control template in help documentation such as MSDN, where the named parts of the template and the related functionalities are mentioned, and doing so can aid you in making an informed decision about intended modifications.

However, if the dependency is in XAML through some state storyboard reference, you have the ability to modify the storyboard if you modify the element.

5-3. Customizing the Default ListBoxItem UI

Problem

You want to customize the default look and feel of an item inside a data-bound ListBox beyond what can be done using data templates.

Solution

Define and apply a custom control template to the ListBoxItem using the ItemContainerStyle on the ListBox.

How It Works

In data-bound ListBox scenarios, you typically do not explicitly add each individual item that the ListBox displays. When you bind the ItemsSource property on the ListBox to a collection (or set it in code), an entry is added to the ListBox automatically for each data item in the collection, optionally formatted based on a data template bound to the ItemTemplate property.

■**Note** 0For more on data binding and data templates, refer to Chapter 4.

Often, you might desire to change the look and feel of the items added beyond what the data template feature affords you. For example, you might want to change the selection behavior from the default display of a light blue selection bar on the item selected, to some other mode of selection display. Or you may notice that no matter what your data template specifies, the each item is finally displayed within a rectangular boundary, and you may want to change that.

Each such generated item is of type ListBoxItem, in turn derived from ContentControl. The default template applied to this ListBoxItem specifies some of the UI behavior of these items, including the ones we just mentioned as examples.

To customize that behavior, you need to design a custom template for the ListBoxItem control and apply it to each ListBoxItem in the ListBox. The ListBox control exposes a property named ItemContainerStyle, which can be bound to a style that gets applied to each ListBoxItem as they are generated. You can use this style to associate your custom template to the ListBoxItems in the ListBox.

The Code

This code sample demonstrates a custom template for a ListBoxItem. For the data source in this sample, we use the AdventureWorks WCF service discussed in the introduction to this chapter. Listing 5-3 shows the XAML for the page, with the control template defined in the resources section.

Listing 5-3. *XAML for the MainPage Showing ListBoxItem Control Template*

```xaml
<UserControl x:Class="Ch05_Controls.Recipe5_3.MainPage"
    xmlns="http://schemas.microsoft.com/winfx/2006/xaml/presentation"
    xmlns:x="http://schemas.microsoft.com/winfx/2006/xaml"
    Width="700" Height="800"
    xmlns:vsm="clr-namespace:System.Windows;assembly=System.Windows">
  <UserControl.Resources>
    <DataTemplate x:Key="dtProductInfo">
      <Grid>
        <Grid.RowDefinitions>
          <RowDefinition Height="Auto" />
          <RowDefinition Height="Auto" />
          <RowDefinition Height="Auto" />
        </Grid.RowDefinitions>
        <TextBlock Grid.Row="0" VerticalAlignment="Center"
                   HorizontalAlignment="Left" Text="{Binding Name}"
                   Margin="3,3,3,3"/>
        <StackPanel HorizontalAlignment="Left" Grid.Row="1"
                    Orientation="Horizontal" Margin="3,3,3,3">
          <TextBlock Text="$" Margin="0,0,2,0" />
          <TextBlock Grid.Row="1" Text="{Binding ListPrice}"/>
        </StackPanel>

        <StackPanel HorizontalAlignment="Left" Grid.Row="2"
                    Orientation="Horizontal" Margin="3,3,3,3">
          <Ellipse Height="15" Width="15"
                   Fill="{Binding InventoryLevelBrush}" Margin="0,0,2,0" />
          <TextBlock Text="{Binding InventoryLevelMessage}"  />
        </StackPanel>
      </Grid>
    </DataTemplate>
    <!-- custom ListBoxItem control template -->
    <ControlTemplate x:Key="ctCustomListBoxItem" TargetType="ListBoxItem">
      <Grid Background="{TemplateBinding Background}"
            Margin="{TemplateBinding Margin}">
        <Grid.RowDefinitions>
          <RowDefinition Height="0.225*" MinHeight="20"/>
          <RowDefinition Height="0.775*"/>
        </Grid.RowDefinitions>
        <vsm:VisualStateManager.VisualStateGroups>
          <vsm:VisualStateGroup x:Name="CommonStates">
            <vsm:VisualStateGroup.Transitions>
              <vsm:VisualTransition
                GeneratedDuration="00:00:00.0500000" To="MouseOver"/>
```

```xml
      <vsm:VisualTransition
        GeneratedDuration="00:00:00.0500000" From="MouseOver"/>
    </vsm:VisualStateGroup.Transitions>
    <vsm:VisualState x:Name="Normal">
      <Storyboard/>
    </vsm:VisualState>
    <vsm:VisualState x:Name="MouseOver">
      <Storyboard>
        <ColorAnimationUsingKeyFrames
          BeginTime="00:00:00"
          Duration="00:00:00.0010000"
          Storyboard.TargetName="BottomBorder"
          Storyboard.TargetProperty=
          "(Border.Background).(SolidColorBrush.Color)">
          <SplineColorKeyFrame KeyTime="00:00:00" Value="#FF68A3DE"/>
        </ColorAnimationUsingKeyFrames>
      </Storyboard>
    </vsm:VisualState>
  </vsm:VisualStateGroup>
  <vsm:VisualStateGroup x:Name="SelectionStates">
    <vsm:VisualState x:Name="Unselected">
      <Storyboard/>
    </vsm:VisualState>
    <vsm:VisualState x:Name="Selected">
      <Storyboard>
        <ColorAnimationUsingKeyFrames
        BeginTime="00:00:00"
        Duration="00:00:00.0010000"
        Storyboard.TargetName="TopBorder"
        Storyboard.TargetProperty=
          "(Border.Background).(SolidColorBrush.Color)">
          <SplineColorKeyFrame KeyTime="00:00:00" Value="#FFFF2D00"/>
        </ColorAnimationUsingKeyFrames>
        <ObjectAnimationUsingKeyFrames
        BeginTime="00:00:00"
        Duration="00:00:00.0010000"
        Storyboard.TargetName="SelectionIndicator"
        Storyboard.TargetProperty="(UIElement.Visibility)">
          <DiscreteObjectKeyFrame KeyTime="00:00:00">
            <DiscreteObjectKeyFrame.Value>
              <vsm:Visibility>Visible</vsm:Visibility>
            </DiscreteObjectKeyFrame.Value>
          </DiscreteObjectKeyFrame>
        </ObjectAnimationUsingKeyFrames>
      </Storyboard>
    </vsm:VisualState>
```

```xml
        <vsm:VisualState x:Name="SelectedUnfocused">
          <Storyboard>
            <ColorAnimationUsingKeyFrames
            BeginTime="00:00:00"
            Duration="00:00:00.0010000"
            Storyboard.TargetName="TopBorder"
            Storyboard.TargetProperty=
              "(Border.Background).(SolidColorBrush.Color)">
              <SplineColorKeyFrame KeyTime="00:00:00" Value="#FFFF2D00"/>
            </ColorAnimationUsingKeyFrames>
            <ObjectAnimationUsingKeyFrames
            BeginTime="00:00:00"
            Duration="00:00:00.0010000"
            Storyboard.TargetName="SelectionIndicator"
            Storyboard.TargetProperty="(UIElement.Visibility)">
              <DiscreteObjectKeyFrame KeyTime="00:00:00">
                <DiscreteObjectKeyFrame.Value>
                  <vsm:Visibility>Visible</vsm:Visibility>
                </DiscreteObjectKeyFrame.Value>
              </DiscreteObjectKeyFrame>
            </ObjectAnimationUsingKeyFrames>
          </Storyboard>
        </vsm:VisualState>
      </vsm:VisualStateGroup>
      <vsm:VisualStateGroup x:Name="FocusStates">
        <vsm:VisualState x:Name="Unfocused">
          <Storyboard/>
        </vsm:VisualState>
        <vsm:VisualState x:Name="Focused">
          <Storyboard>
            <ObjectAnimationUsingKeyFrames
            BeginTime="00:00:00"
            Duration="00:00:00.0010000"
            Storyboard.TargetName="FocusRect"
            Storyboard.TargetProperty="(UIElement.Visibility)">
              <DiscreteObjectKeyFrame KeyTime="00:00:00">
                <DiscreteObjectKeyFrame.Value>
                  <vsm:Visibility>Visible</vsm:Visibility>
                </DiscreteObjectKeyFrame.Value>
              </DiscreteObjectKeyFrame>
            </ObjectAnimationUsingKeyFrames>
          </Storyboard>
        </vsm:VisualState>
      </vsm:VisualStateGroup>
    </vsm:VisualStateManager.VisualStateGroups>
```

```
    <Border HorizontalAlignment="Stretch"
            Margin="0,0,0,0"
            VerticalAlignment="Stretch"
            CornerRadius="5,5,0,0"
            BorderBrush="#FF000000"
            BorderThickness="2,2,2,0"
            Background="#00000000"
            x:Name="TopBorder">
      <Grid x:Name="SelectionIndicator" Visibility="Collapsed"
            Width="18" Height="18"
            HorizontalAlignment="Left"
            VerticalAlignment="Center" Margin="2,2,2,2">
        <Path x:Name="Path" Stretch="Fill"
              StrokeThickness="1.99975" StrokeLineJoin="Round"
              Stroke="#FF000000" Fill="#FF27BC0F"
              Data="F1 M 0.999876,18.0503C 2.60366,
              16.4731 4.23013,14.9006 5.86216,13.3491L 12.6694,
              18.7519C 14.239,10.2011 20.9487,3.27808 29.8744,
              0.999878L 31.4453,2.68387C 23.1443,
              9.95105 17.8681,19.7496 16.5592,
              30.3293L 16.5592,30.2592L 0.999876,18.0503 Z "/>
      </Grid>
    </Border>
    <Border Margin="0,0,0,0" CornerRadius="0,0,5,5"
            BorderBrush="#FF000000" BorderThickness="2,2,2,2"
            Grid.Row="1" Padding="3,3,3,3" x:Name="BottomBorder"
            Background="#00000000">
      <Grid>
        <ContentPresenter  HorizontalAlignment="Left"
          Margin="3,3,3,3"
          Content="{TemplateBinding Content}"
          ContentTemplate="{TemplateBinding ContentTemplate}"/>
        <Rectangle HorizontalAlignment="Stretch" Margin="0,0,0,0" Width="Auto"
                   Stroke="#FF000000"
                   StrokeDashArray="0.75 0.15 0.25 0.5 0.25"
                   x:Name="FocusRect" Visibility="Collapsed"/>
      </Grid>
    </Border>
  </Grid>
</ControlTemplate>
```

```
  <!-- style using the custom ListBoxItem control template -->
  <Style x:Key="styleCustomListBoxItem" TargetType="ListBoxItem">
    <Setter Property="Template"
            Value="{StaticResource ctCustomListBoxItem}"/>
    <Setter Property="Margin" Value="3,5,3,5" />
  </Style>
</UserControl.Resources>
<Grid x:Name="LayoutRoot" Background="White" Height="Auto" Margin="20,20">
  <StackPanel Orientation="Horizontal" VerticalAlignment="Stretch"
              HorizontalAlignment="Stretch">
    <ListBox x:Name="lbxStandard" HorizontalAlignment="Stretch"
             VerticalAlignment="Stretch" Margin="0,0,25,0"
             ItemTemplate="{StaticResource dtProductInfo}" />

    <!-- applying a custom ListBoxItemTemplate using the ItemContainerStyle -->
    <ListBox x:Name="lbxCustom"
             HorizontalAlignment="Stretch"
             VerticalAlignment="Stretch"
             ItemTemplate="{StaticResource dtProductInfo}"
             ItemContainerStyle="{StaticResource styleCustomListBoxItem}"/>
  </StackPanel>

</Grid>
</UserControl>
```

Our control template named ctCustomListBoxItem is defined as two Border elements placed in two Rows of a top-level Grid. The Border element named TopBorder further contains a Grid SelectionIndicator, encapsulating a Path that represents a check mark. The BottomBorder element contains a ContentPresenter with appropriate TemplateBindings defined for several properties, including the Content and the ContentTemplate properties so that, once data bound, the data for each ListBoxItem gets displayed through this ContentPresenter inside BottomBorder. We also include a Rectangle named FocusRect with a dotted border; this Rectangle is overlaid on the ContentPresenter but is initially kept hidden, because we set the Visibility property to Visibility.Collapsed.

Figure 5-14 compares the Normal state of a ListBoxItem using this template to that of the default look and feel, with both ListBoxes bound to the same data source and using the same data template, defined as dtProductInfo in Listing 5-3 as well. For more on data templates, refer to Chapter 4.

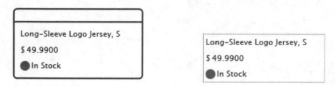

Figure 5-14. *Normal ListBoxItem state with (left) and without (right) the custom template*

If you refer to the storyboard for the MouseOver visual state in Listing 5-3, you will see that we change the background color of BottomBorder to indicate the state change. Figure 5-15 shows the result.

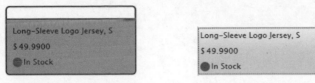

Figure 5-15. *MouseOver state with (left) and without (right) the custom template*

On a transition to the Selected state, we change the background color of TopBorder and make visible the SelectionIndicator Grid that contains the check mark. This gives the selected item a colored top bar with a check mark in it. For the Focused state, we make visible the focus indicator Rectangle FocusRect. Note that we also define a storyboard for the SelectedUnfocused state. The purpose of this state is to indicate a scenario when an item may be selected but the current focus is elsewhere, whereby we continue to show the colored top border and check mark but hide the focus rectangle. Figure 5-16 shows the results in comparison.

Figure 5-16. *Selected state with focus with (left) and without (right) the custom template*

We also define a style resource, styleCustomListBoxItem, in Listing 5-3 that associates the control template to a ListBoxItem. To show the control template in action, we have added two ListBoxes, named lbxStandard and lbxCustom, to our page, each using the same data template, dtProductInfo, as the ItemTemplate, but the one named lbxCustom has its style set to styleCustomListBoxItem.

Listing 5-4 shows the code-behind for the page.

Listing 5-4. *Code-Behind for the MainPage Containing the ListBox*

```
using System;
using System.Windows.Controls;
using System.Windows.Media;
using Ch05_Controls.Recipe5_3.AdvWorks;

namespace Ch05_Controls.Recipe5_3
{
  public partial class MainPage : UserControl
  {
    //WCF service client
    AdvWorksDataServiceClient client =
      new AdvWorksDataServiceClient();
```

```csharp
    public MainPage()
    {
      InitializeComponent();
      GetData();
    }

    private void GetData()
    {
      client.GetInventoryCompleted +=
        new EventHandler<GetInventoryCompletedEventArgs>(
          delegate(object sender, GetInventoryCompletedEventArgs e)
          {
            Product product = e.UserState as Product;
            product.ProductInventories = e.Result;
            product.InventoryLevelBrush = null;
            product.InventoryLevelMessage = null;

          });
      client.GetProductsCompleted +=
        new EventHandler<GetProductsCompletedEventArgs>(
          delegate(object sender, GetProductsCompletedEventArgs e)
          {

            lbxStandard.ItemsSource = e.Result;
            lbxCustom.ItemsSource = e.Result;

            foreach (Product p in e.Result)
            {
              client.GetInventoryAsync(p, p);
            }
          });

      client.GetProductsAsync();
    }
  }
}


namespace Ch05_Controls.Recipe5_3.AdvWorks
{

  public partial class Product
  {
    private SolidColorBrush _InventoryLevelBrush;
```

```csharp
public SolidColorBrush InventoryLevelBrush
    {
      get
      {
        return (this.ProductInventories == null
          || this.ProductInventories.Count == 0) ?
          new SolidColorBrush(Colors.Gray) :
          (this.ProductInventories[0].Quantity > this.SafetyStockLevel ?
          new SolidColorBrush(Colors.Green) :
          (this.ProductInventories[0].Quantity > this.ReorderPoint ?
          new SolidColorBrush(Colors.Yellow) : new SolidColorBrush(Colors.Red)));
      }
      set
      {
        //no actual value set here - just property change raised
        //can be set to null in code to cause rebinding, when
        //ProductInventories changes
        RaisePropertyChanged("InventoryLevelBrush");
      }

    }
    private string _InventoryLevelMessage;

    public string InventoryLevelMessage
    {
      get
      {
        return (this.ProductInventories == null
          || this.ProductInventories.Count == 0) ? "Stock Level Unknown"
          : (this.ProductInventories[0].Quantity > this.SafetyStockLevel
          ? "In Stock" :
          (this.ProductInventories[0].Quantity > this.ReorderPoint ?
          "Low Stock" : "Reorder Now"));
      }
      set
      {
        //no actual value set here - just property change raised
        //can be set to null in code to cause rebinding,
        //when ProductInventories changes
        RaisePropertyChanged("InventoryLevelMessage");
      }
    }
  }
}
```

We set the ItemsSource properties for both lbxStandard and lbxCustom to a list of Product data items obtained from the AdventureWorks WCF service, as shown in the GetData() method in Listing 5-4. We also populate inventory information for each Product instance from the same service as a collection of ProductInventory instances.

In the declaration of dtProductInfo in Listing 5-3, note the Ellipse with its Fill property bound to InventoryLevelBrush, and the TextBlock with its Text property bound to InventoryLevelMessage. These are both calculated values, exposed as properties on the Product class extended using the partial class facility, as shown in Listing 5-4. The InventoryLevelBrush property returns a SolidcolorBrush of different colors based on whether the total inventory is above or below certain levels, indicated by the SafetyStockLevel and ReorderPoint properties of the Product data class. The InventoryLevelMessage property applies the same logic to return differently formatted text messages instead.

5-4. Displaying Information in a Pop-up

Problem

You want to display a portion of the UI in a pop-up in response to an input event such as a mouse click.

Solution

Use the Popup element to contain and display the necessary UI.

How It Works

Popups are frequently used in UI design to display on-the-fly information in response to input events. Typical examples of where they can be useful are cascading menus, context menus, the drop-down portion of a combo box, and tooltips. Silverlight includes a type named Popup in the System.Windows.Controls.Primitives namespace. The Popup type is used by several other controls in the framework, such as the DatePicker, the Tooltip, and the DataGrid. However, you can directly use it in your own code as well.

Creating and Initializing the Pop-up

The Popup type is not a control—it derives directly from the FrameworkElement type. It is meant to be a container for a tree of elements and, therefore, has no visual representation of its own. While you can indeed include a Popup in XAML, because of positioning requirements that we will talk about momentarily, it is much more common to create an instance of the Popup in code and set its Child property to the root of the element tree representing the content you want to display inside the Popup. This code snippet shows setting a ContentControl as the Popup.Child:

```
Popup popupProducts = new Popup();
ListBox popupContent = new ListBox();
popupProducts.Child = popupContent;
```

Once you have prepared the Popup, you can toggle the Popup.IsOpen property to show or hide it.

Positioning the Pop-up

In most cases, you would want to display the Popup at a dynamically determined position on the page, relative to coordinates of an input event, such as a mouse click, or to that of some other element on the form. This explains why a Popup is typically not included by a designer in the XAML for the page but rather created in code—it does not make sense to subject it to the constraints of the layout system and determine its position up front unless you are using absolute positioning and a container like the Canvas.

To assist in the process of determining its position, the Popup type exposes two properties of type double: VerticalOffset and HorizontalOffset. These properties respectively define offsets from the top and left corners of the root element of the Page and are both set to zero by default, causing the Popup to display at the top-left corner of the Page root. To determine the appropriate page-based offsets for a Popup relative to some other element on the page, you typically need to perform some coordinate transforms. To understand this problem a little better, take a look at Figure 5-17.

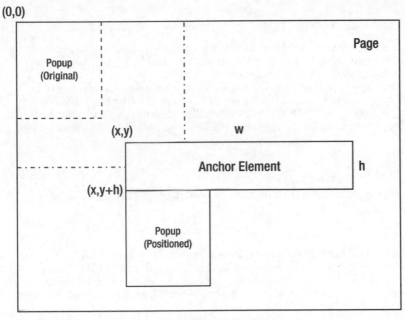

Figure 5-17. *Coordinate transformation for a Popup*

When you initially create a Popup instance, it is located at the top-left corner of the Page at coordinates (0,0), as shown by the dotted outline of the Popup in Figure 5-17.

Let's assume we need to align the Popup to the bottom-left corner of an element in the Page named AnchorElement. AnchorElement has Width set to w and Height set to h; its top-left coordinates are (x,y) relative to the Page, as shown in Figure 5-17. If we defined the Popup's desired coordinates with respect to the AnchorElement's coordinate space alone, they would be (0,h).

However, since we are going to position the Popup within the Page, we need to translate (0,h) in AnchorElement's coordinate space (the source coordinate space) to a suitable set of coordinates in the Page's coordinate space (the target coordinate space). Those would be (x,y + h) for it to be positioned at the desired spot, which means that the Popup needs to be offset by x horizontally, and by $y + h$ vertically from its original position of (0,0) within the Page to reach its new position.

The following code snippet shows how to achieve this:

```
GeneralTransform coordTnsfrm = this.TransformToVisual(AnchorElement);
Point pt = coordTnsfrm.Transform(new Point(0.0, AnchorElement.ActualHeight));
popupProducts.HorizontalOffset = pt.X;
popupProducts.VerticalOffset = pt.Y;
```

In the preceding snippet, we invoke TransformToVisual() on an UIElement that owns the target coordinate space and pass in another UIElement whose coordinate space acts as the source. The GeneralTransform that is returned from the call to TransformToVisual() can then be used to transform a Point defined in the source space to one in the target space.

We also transform a Point in AnchorElement's coordinate space, with X set to 0 and Y set to the height of AnchorElement (i.e., the bottom-left corner of AnchorElement) to the appropriate equivalent in the Page's coordinate space. We then use the X,Y values of the resulting Point to set the HorizontalOffset and the VerticalOffset values on the Popup to position it as we intended on the page.

Creating Pop-up Content

In initializing a Popup in code with content—that is, setting its Child property—you should avoid creating and initializing the entire content in code, especially if the content represents a fairly complex UI. You almost always want to take advantage of tools like Expression Blend to do that.

In the recipe code sample that we are about to discuss, we simply need a single ListBox to be the only child of the Popup, as you will see soon. Therefore, we are not burdened with creating an overtly complex UI in code. However, in the event you are faced with this challenge elsewhere and want to avoid the need to code an UI tree, one approach you can take is to use the ContentControl and data templates shown here:

```
Popup popupProducts = new Popup();
ContentControl popupContent = new ContentControl();
popupContent.ContentTemplate = this.Resources["dtPopupData"] as DataTemplate;
popupProducts.Child = popupContent;
popupContent.DataContext = ProdList;
```

We set the ContentTemplate of the ContentControl to a data template resource, initialize Popup.Child with the ContentControl, and then bind the ContentControl to appropriate data. This affords you the opportunity to host a fairly complex UI in a Popup but design it as a data template using a tool like Expression Blend, thus expressing it as XAML and keeping your code free of significant element creation and initialization logic.

The Code

The code sample for this recipe uses the Popup type to build a cascading menu that looks similar to the ones in Visual Studio.

Figure 5-18 shows the resulting menu look and feel. Keep in mind that the sample does not aim to illustrate a full-scale menu framework but rather just a usage pattern for the Popup type. However, if you do undertake the building of a menu system using Silverlight, we anticipate you will be using the Popup type, and the code in this sample will most likely come in handy.

Figure 5-18. *A cascading menu built using the Popup*

Listing 5-5 shows the `MenuItemData` class used to hold the data for a single menu item in our sample.

Listing 5-5. *Data Type for a Single Menu Item*

```
using System.Collections.Generic;
using System.Windows;
using System.Windows.Media.Imaging;

namespace Ch05_Controls.Recipe5_4
{
  //data for a single menu item
  public class MenuItemData
  {
    //image URI string used to load the image
    internal string ImageUri
    {
      set
      {
        MenuItemImage = new BitmapImage();
        MenuItemImage.SetSource(this.GetType().Assembly.
          GetManifestResourceStream(this.GetType().Namespace + "." + value));
      }
    }
    //menu item image
    public BitmapImage MenuItemImage { get; set; }
    //menu item caption
    public string MenuItemCaption { get; set; }
    //children items for submenus
    public List<MenuItemData> Children { get; set; }
    //parent menu item
    public MenuItemData Parent { get; set; }
```

```
      //toggle submenu arrow visibility based on presence of children items
      public Visibility SubMenuArrow
      {
        get
        {
          return (Children == null
            || Children.Count == 0 ?
            Visibility.Collapsed : Visibility.Visible);
        }
      }
    }
  }
}
```

The ImageUri property setter is used to load an image bitmap that can be accessed through the MenuItemImage property. You can learn more about loading assembly-embedded resources using GetManifestResourceStream() in Chapter 2. A submenu is defined by having entries in the Children collection. For an item in a submenu, the parent MenuItemData instance is contained in the Parent property. The SubMenuArrow property will be bound appropriately in XAML to control the visibility of the right arrow mark that indicates the presence of a submenu.

Listing 5-6 shows the code-behind for the page.

Listing 5-6. *Code-Behind for the MainPage Used to Display the Pop-up Menu*

```
using System.Collections.Generic;
using System.Windows;
using System.Windows.Controls;
using System.Windows.Controls.Primitives;
using System.Windows.Input;
using System.Windows.Media;

namespace Ch05_Controls.Recipe5_4
{
  public partial class MainPage : UserControl
  {
    //data for the top level menu
    internal List<MenuItemData> TopMenuData = null;
    //popups for the topmenu and the submenu
    Popup TopMenu, SubMenu;
    //Listboxes for the menu content
    ListBox lbxTopMenu, lbxSubMenu;

    public MainPage()
    {
      InitializeComponent();
      //initialize the menu data
      TopMenuData = new List<MenuItemData>
```

```
    {
      new MenuItemData{MenuItemCaption="Camera", ImageUri="Camera.png"},
      new MenuItemData{MenuItemCaption="CD Drive",ImageUri="CD_Drive.png"},
      new MenuItemData{MenuItemCaption="Computer",ImageUri="Computer.png"},
      new MenuItemData{MenuItemCaption="Dialup",ImageUri="Dialup.png"},
      new MenuItemData{MenuItemCaption="My Network",ImageUri="mynet.png"},
      new MenuItemData{MenuItemCaption="Mouse",ImageUri="Mouse.png"}
    };

    TopMenuData[4].Children = new List<MenuItemData>
      {
          new MenuItemData{MenuItemCaption="Network Folder",
            ImageUri="Network_Folder.png",Parent = TopMenuData[4]},
          new MenuItemData{MenuItemCaption="Network Center",
            ImageUri="Network_Center.png",Parent = TopMenuData[4]},
          new MenuItemData{MenuItemCaption="Connect To",
            ImageUri="Network_ConnectTo.png",Parent = TopMenuData[4]},
          new MenuItemData{MenuItemCaption="Internet",
            ImageUri="Network_Internet.png",Parent = TopMenuData[4]}
          };

    //create and initialize the top menu popup
    TopMenu = new Popup();
    lbxTopMenu = new ListBox();
    //set the listbox style to apply the menu look templating
    lbxTopMenu.Style = this.Resources["styleMenu"] as Style;
    //bind the topmenu data
    lbxTopMenu.ItemsSource = TopMenuData;
    TopMenu.Child = lbxTopMenu;

    //create and initialize the submenu
    SubMenu = new Popup();
    lbxSubMenu = new ListBox();
    lbxSubMenu.MouseLeave += new MouseEventHandler(lbxSubMenu_MouseLeave);
    lbxSubMenu.Style = this.Resources["styleMenu"] as Style;
    SubMenu.Child = lbxSubMenu;
}

//set the top menu position
private void SetTopMenuPosition(Popup Target,
  FrameworkElement CoordSpaceSource)
{
  //get the transform to use
  GeneralTransform transform = this.TransformToVisual(CoordSpaceSource);
```

```
      //transform the left-bottom corner
      Point pt = transform.Transform(new Point(0.0,
        CoordSpaceSource.ActualHeight));
      //set offsets accordingly
      Target.HorizontalOffset = pt.X;
      Target.VerticalOffset = pt.Y;
    }
    //set the submenu position
    private void SetSubMenuPosition(Popup Target,
      FrameworkElement CoordSpaceSource, int ItemIndex,
      FrameworkElement ParentMenuItem)
    {

      //get the transform to use
      GeneralTransform transform = this.TransformToVisual(CoordSpaceSource);
      //transform the right-top corner
      Point pt = transform.Transform(
        new Point(ParentMenuItem.ActualWidth,
          CoordSpaceSource.ActualHeight +
          (ParentMenuItem.ActualHeight * ItemIndex)));
      //set offsets accordingly
      Target.HorizontalOffset = pt.X;
      Target.VerticalOffset = pt.Y;
    }

    private void btnDropDown_Click(object sender, RoutedEventArgs e)
    {
      //position the top menu
      SetTopMenuPosition(TopMenu, LayoutRoot);
      //show or hide
      TopMenu.IsOpen = !TopMenu.IsOpen;
    }

    private void LbxItemRoot_MouseEnter(object sender, MouseEventArgs e)
    {
      //get the listboxitem for the selected top menu item
      ListBoxItem lbxItem = (sender as Grid).Parent as ListBoxItem;
      //get the bound MenuItemData
      MenuItemData midTop = (sender as Grid).DataContext as MenuItemData;
      //do we have children and are we on the top menu?
      if (midTop.Parent == null &&
        (midTop.Children == null || midTop.Children.Count == 0))
      {
        //do not show the submenu
        SubMenu.IsOpen = false;
      }
```

```
      else if (midTop.Children != null && midTop.Children.Count > 0)
      {
        //yes - position sub menu
        SetSubMenuPosition(SubMenu, LayoutRoot, TopMenuData.IndexOf(midTop),
          (sender as Grid));
        //bind to children MenuItemData collection
        lbxSubMenu.ItemsSource = midTop.Children;
        //show  submenu
        SubMenu.IsOpen = true;
      }


    }
    //leaving submenu - close it
    void lbxSubMenu_MouseLeave(object sender, MouseEventArgs e)
    {
      SubMenu.IsOpen = false;
    }
  }
}
```

In the constructor, we populate the data structures needed to create and initialize two Popups: TopMenu for the top-level menu, and SubMenu for a cascading submenu. ListBoxes lbxTopMenu and lbxSubMenu are used to provide the content inside the Popups, with a style named styleMenu customizing them to look like a menu. The data for the menus is stored as MenuItemData instances in the TopMenuData collection, with the Children property of the MenuItemData captioned My Network further filled with items for a submenu.

The top menu is displayed in the click handler btnDropDown_Click() of the menu drop-down button. We first call SetTopMenuPosition() to position the Popup, and then toggle its IsOpen property so that the menu either displays or is removed if it is already on display. The cascading submenu is displayed in the MouseEnter handler LbxItemRoot_MouseEnter() of an item in the top-level menu. We check to see if the top-level menu item has children, and if it does, we invoke SetSubMenuPosition() to position the submenu, set its data source Children collection, and toggle its display. In the MouseLeave event handler of the ListBox lbxSubMenu representing the submenu, we turn off the submenu.

Let's look at the SetTopMenuPosition() and SetSubMenuPosition() methods used to position the Popups. In both methods, the second parameter named CoordSpaceSource represents the source element whose coordinate space we need to transform from. If you refer to Listing 5-6, you will see that in case of SetTopMenuPosition(), this parameter is LayoutRoot, which is the Grid containing the menu drop-down button. The top menu Popup is then positioned along the Grid's bottom-left corner. In SetSubMenuPosition(), we again use LayoutRoot. But SetSubMenuPosition() accepts two additional parameters. The third parameter, named ItemIndex, represents the index of the selected item in lbxTopMenu, and the fourth parameter, named ParentMenuItem, is the containing Grid for the ListBoxItem on the top menu that has been just selected. To position the submenu pop-up aligned to the top-right corner of the ListBoxItem, we acquire the coordinate space transform as before. But then we transform the point using ParentMenuItem.ActualWidth as the x parameter to the Point instance, and the total height of all menu items up to but not including the one identified by ItemIndex as the y parameter. This causes the submenu to be positioned along the right edge of the top menu, with its top edge horizontally aligned with the parent menu item currently selected in the top menu.

Listing 5-7 shows the XAML for the page.

Listing 5-7. *XAML for the Page Hosting the Pop-up Menu*

```xaml
<UserControl x:Class="Ch05_Controls.Recipe5_4.MainPage"
    xmlns="http://schemas.microsoft.com/winfx/2006/xaml/presentation"
    xmlns:x="http://schemas.microsoft.com/winfx/2006/xaml"
    Width="400" Height="300"
    xmlns:vsm="clr-namespace:System.Windows;assembly=System.Windows">
  <UserControl.Resources>

    <ControlTemplate x:Key="ctMenuItem" TargetType="ListBoxItem">
      <Grid x:Name="LbxItemRoot" Height="20"
            MouseEnter="LbxItemRoot_MouseEnter"
        DataContext="{TemplateBinding Content}" >
        <Grid.ColumnDefinitions>
          <ColumnDefinition Width="24.0" MaxWidth="24.0"/>
          <ColumnDefinition Width="*"/>
        </Grid.ColumnDefinitions>
        <vsm:VisualStateManager.VisualStateGroups>
          <vsm:VisualStateGroup x:Name="CommonStates">
            <vsm:VisualState x:Name="Normal">
              <Storyboard/>
            </vsm:VisualState>
            <vsm:VisualState x:Name="MouseOver">
              <Storyboard>
                <ObjectAnimationUsingKeyFrames
                  BeginTime="00:00:00"
                  Duration="00:00:00.0010000"
                  Storyboard.TargetName="SelectionIndicator"
                  Storyboard.TargetProperty="(UIElement.Visibility)">
                <DiscreteObjectKeyFrame KeyTime="00:00:00">
                  <DiscreteObjectKeyFrame.Value>
                    <vsm:Visibility>Visible</vsm:Visibility>
                  </DiscreteObjectKeyFrame.Value>
                </DiscreteObjectKeyFrame>
                </ObjectAnimationUsingKeyFrames>
              </Storyboard>
            </vsm:VisualState>
          </vsm:VisualStateGroup>
          <vsm:VisualStateGroup x:Name="SelectionStates">
            <vsm:VisualState x:Name="Unselected"/>
            <vsm:VisualState x:Name="Selected"/>
            <vsm:VisualState x:Name="SelectedUnfocused"/>
          </vsm:VisualStateGroup>
```

```xml
    <vsm:VisualStateGroup x:Name="FocusStates">
      <vsm:VisualState x:Name="Unfocused"/>
      <vsm:VisualState x:Name="Focused"/>
    </vsm:VisualStateGroup>
  </vsm:VisualStateManager.VisualStateGroups>
  <Border Margin="0,0,0,0" Grid.Column="0" BorderThickness="0,0,2,0">
    <Border.Background>
      <LinearGradientBrush
        EndPoint="0.912000000476837,0.509999990463257"
        StartPoint="0,0.514999985694885">
        <GradientStop Color="#FFDDE9F4"/>
        <GradientStop Color="#FFADD5F5" Offset="1"/>
      </LinearGradientBrush>
    </Border.Background>
    <Border.BorderBrush>
      <LinearGradientBrush
        EndPoint="1.37399995326996,0.485000014305115"
        StartPoint="0.275000005960464,0.485000014305115">
        <GradientStop Color="#FF000000" Offset="0.5"/>
        <GradientStop Color="#FFFFFFFF" Offset="1"/>
      </LinearGradientBrush>
    </Border.BorderBrush>
  </Border>
  <Border Grid.Column="1" Background="White" />
  <Border HorizontalAlignment="Stretch"
          Margin="2,2,2,2" Width="Auto"
          Grid.Column="0" Grid.ColumnSpan="2"
          CornerRadius="3,3,3,3"
          BorderBrush="#FF1E7CDA"
          BorderThickness="1,1,1,1" x:Name="SelectionIndicator"
          Visibility="Collapsed">
    <Border.Background>
      <LinearGradientBrush EndPoint="0.5,1" StartPoint="0.5,0">
        <GradientStop Color="#FFFFFFFF" Offset="0.009"/>
        <GradientStop Color="#FF7AC5F0" Offset="1"/>
      </LinearGradientBrush>
    </Border.Background>
  </Border>
  <Grid Margin="2,2,2,2" Grid.ColumnSpan="2" HorizontalAlignment="Stretch"
        VerticalAlignment="Stretch" Background="Transparent">
    <Grid.ColumnDefinitions>
      <ColumnDefinition Width="22px"/>
      <ColumnDefinition Width="auto"/>
      <ColumnDefinition Width="auto"/>
    </Grid.ColumnDefinitions>
```

```xml
            <Image
                Source="{Binding MenuItemImage}"
                Width="16" Height="16" Stretch="Fill"
                Margin="3,0,3,0" Grid.Column="0"/>
            <TextBlock
                    Text="{Binding MenuItemCaption}" Margin="3,0,3,0"
                    Grid.Column="1"/>
            <Path x:Name="SubMenuArrow" Width="8" Height="8" Stretch="Fill"
                Fill="#FF000000"
                Data="F1 M 8.25,4.76315L 0,0L 0,9.52628L 8.25,4.76315 Z "
                Grid.Column="2" Visibility="{Binding SubMenuArrowVisibility}"
                Margin="3,0,5,0"/>
        </Grid>
      </Grid>
    </ControlTemplate>


    <Style TargetType="ListBoxItem" x:Key="styleMenuItem">
      <Setter Property="Template" Value="{StaticResource ctMenuItem}" />
    </Style>


    <ControlTemplate x:Key="ctMenuList" TargetType="ListBox">
      <Grid>
        <Border HorizontalAlignment="Stretch" VerticalAlignment="Stretch"
                Background="Black"  Margin="2.5,2.5,-2.5,-2.5" Opacity="0.35"/>
        <Border BorderBrush="#FFA7A7A7" BorderThickness="1"
                HorizontalAlignment="Left" VerticalAlignment="Top" >
          <ItemsPresenter/>
        </Border>
      </Grid>
    </ControlTemplate>


    <Style x:Key="styleMenu" TargetType="ListBox">
      <Setter Property="Template" Value="{StaticResource ctMenuList}" />
      <Setter Property="ItemContainerStyle"
              Value="{StaticResource styleMenuItem}" />
    </Style>


    <ControlTemplate TargetType="Button" x:Key="ctButton">
      <ContentPresenter HorizontalAlignment="Center" VerticalAlignment="Center"
        Content="{TemplateBinding Content}"
        ContentTemplate="{TemplateBinding ContentTemplate}"
        />
    </ControlTemplate>

</UserControl.Resources>
```

```
<Grid x:Name="LayoutRoot" HorizontalAlignment="Left" VerticalAlignment="Top">
  <StackPanel Orientation="Horizontal">
    <Border  BorderThickness="1,1,0,1" BorderBrush="#FF4169B1"
             HorizontalAlignment="Left" x:Name="border">
      <Border.Background>
        <LinearGradientBrush EndPoint="0.5,1" StartPoint="0.5,0">
          <GradientStop Color="#FFD9E9FB"/>
          <GradientStop Color="#FF88BCF9" Offset="1"/>
        </LinearGradientBrush>
      </Border.Background>
      <Image Width="16" Height="16" Source="Menu.png" Margin="5,5,5,5"/>
    </Border>
    <Border BorderThickness="0,1,1,1" BorderBrush="#FF4169B1"
            HorizontalAlignment="Left" x:Name="border1">
      <Border.Background>
        <LinearGradientBrush EndPoint="0.5,1" StartPoint="0.5,0">
          <GradientStop Color="#FFD9E9FB"/>
          <GradientStop Color="#FF88BCF9" Offset="1"/>
        </LinearGradientBrush>
      </Border.Background>
      <Button Height="16" Template="{StaticResource ctButton}"
              x:Name="btnDropDown" Margin="0,5,5,5" HorizontalAlignment="Stretch"
              VerticalAlignment="Stretch" Click="btnDropDown_Click"
Padding="5,5,5,5">
        <Button.Content>
          <Path x:Name="Path" Width="11.2578" Height="9.80142"  Stretch="Fill"
            Fill="#FF000000"
            Data="F1 M 12.3926,10.3748L 18.1113,0.677055L 6.85348,
                0.573364L 12.3926,10.3748 Z "/>
        </Button.Content>
      </Button>
    </Border>
  </StackPanel>
</Grid>
</UserControl>
```

The UI itself contains only the representation of the initial menu drop-down button that shows up when you run the page. This consists of everything that is inside the Grid named LayoutRoot, primarily a Button with its content set to a Path that displays the down arrow and an Image that is bound to a resource in the assembly named Menu.png, both contained inside some Borders.

The control template ctMenuItem is what gives each item the look and feel when it is applied to a ListBoxItem. Each ListBoxItem is bound to an instance of MenuItemData and is implemented using an Image bound to MenuItemImage, a TextBlock bound to MenuItemCaption, and a Path displaying a right arrow with its Visibility property bound to SubMenuArrow. The selection indicator is implemented as a Border with initial Visibility set to Collapsed. The visual state for MouseOver is used to make the selection indicator visible as you move your mouse among items in the menu. We also customize the

ListBox that represents an entire drop-down by applying another control template named ctMenuList to it. This simply puts an ItemsPresenter control inside a couple of Borders and gets rid of the usual scroll bars and other elements that are a part of a ListBox default template.

You apply the control templates to the Popups when you create the code, via the Style named styleMenu, as you have already seen in Listing 5-6.

5-5. Displaying Row Details in a DataGrid

Problem

You need to display additional detail information about a bound row in a DataGrid on demand so that the details portion is displayed in place within the DataGrid.

Solution

Use the RowDetailsTemplate property of the DataGrid to associate a data template that can be used to display additional data on demand.

How It Works

The DataGrid.RowDetailsTemplate property accepts a data template (covered in Chapter 4) that can be used to display additional data in place, associated with a bound row. This feature comes handy in many scenarios—to provide master-detail data where multiple detail records need to be displayed for a top-level row, or where additional information, not otherwise bound to top-level columns, needs to be displayed adjacent to a row.

The DataGrid.RowDetailsVisibilityMode property controls the visibility of the row details information at DataGrid scope. That is, setting it to Visible keeps it always visible for every bound row, whereas setting it to VisibleWhenSelected makes the details portion of a row visible when it is selected and collapsed back when selection moves off to another row. To control row details' visibility in code, set this property to Collapsed, which hides row details for every row, and instead use the DataGridRow.DetailsVisibility property on the individual row.

The DataGrid also exposes two useful events: LoadingRowDetails and UnloadingRowDetails. LoadingRowDetails is raised when the DataGrid initially applies the RowDetailsTemplate to the row. This is especially useful if you want to load the data for the row details in a delayed fashion—placing the code to load the data in the handler for LoadingRowDetails ensures that the data is only loaded when the user first expands the row details and is never executed again, unless the row details are explicitly unloaded. UnloadingRowDetails is raised when the rows are unloaded, such as when a method like DataGrid.ClearRows() is invoked.

The DataGrid also raises another event called RowDetailsVisibilityChanged every time a row detail is either made visible or is collapsed.

■**Note** The DataGrid control is found in the System.Windows.Controls.Data assembly, in the System. Windows.Controls namespace.

The Code

For this code sample, we bind a DataGrid to product data sourced from the AdventureWorks WCF service. Each row, in addition to the bound columns, also displays some row details data, including an image of the product, some inventory information, a product description, and another DataGrid displaying the cost history records of the product demonstrating a master-detail arrangement. Figure 5-19 shows the DataGrid with the row details of a row expanded.

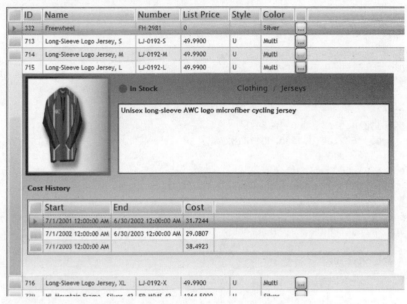

Figure 5-19. *Bound DataGrid using a RowDetailsTemplate*

Listing 5-8 shows the XAML for the page.

Listing 5-8. *XAML for the Page Hosting the DataGrid with Row Details*

```
<UserControl x:Class="Ch05_Controls.Recipe5_5.MainPage"
  xmlns="http://schemas.microsoft.com/winfx/2006/xaml/presentation"
  xmlns:x="http://schemas.microsoft.com/winfx/2006/xaml"
  xmlns:data=
  "clr-namespace:System.Windows.Controls;assembly=System.Windows.Controls.Data"
  Width="900" Height="600" >
  <UserControl.Resources>
    <DataTemplate x:Key="dtProductRowDetails">
      <Grid Height="350" Width="646">
        <Grid.RowDefinitions>
          <RowDefinition Height="0.127*"/>
          <RowDefinition Height="0.391*"/>
          <RowDefinition Height="0.482*"/>
        </Grid.RowDefinitions>
```

```
<Grid.Background>
  <LinearGradientBrush EndPoint="0.5,1" StartPoint="0.5,0">
    <GradientStop Color="#FF7D7A7A"/>
    <GradientStop Color="#FFFFFFFF" Offset="1"/>
  </LinearGradientBrush>
</Grid.Background>
<Grid.ColumnDefinitions>
  <ColumnDefinition Width="0.245*"/>
  <ColumnDefinition Width="0.755*"/>
</Grid.ColumnDefinitions>
<Border HorizontalAlignment="Stretch" Margin="5,5,5,5"
    VerticalAlignment="Stretch" Grid.RowSpan="2"
    BorderThickness="4,4,4,4">
  <Border.BorderBrush>
    <LinearGradientBrush
    EndPoint="1.02499997615814,0.448000013828278"
    StartPoint="-0.0130000002682209,0.448000013828278">
      <GradientStop Color="#FF000000"/>
      <GradientStop Color="#FF6C6C6C" Offset="1"/>
    </LinearGradientBrush>
  </Border.BorderBrush>
  <Image  MinHeight="50" MinWidth="50"
      Source="{Binding ProductPhoto.LargePhotoPNG}"
      Stretch="Fill"
      VerticalAlignment="Stretch"
      HorizontalAlignment="Stretch"/>
</Border>
<Grid HorizontalAlignment="Stretch" Margin="8,8,8,0"
    VerticalAlignment="Stretch"
    Grid.Column="1" Grid.RowSpan="1">
  <Grid.ColumnDefinitions>
    <ColumnDefinition Width="0.25*"/>
    <ColumnDefinition Width="0.3*"/>
    <ColumnDefinition Width="0.05*"/>
    <ColumnDefinition Width="0.4*"/>
  </Grid.ColumnDefinitions>
  <StackPanel HorizontalAlignment="Stretch" Grid.Column="0"
            Orientation="Horizontal" Margin="1,0,1,0">
    <Ellipse Height="15" Width="15"
            Fill="{Binding InventoryLevelBrush}" Margin="0,0,2,0" />
    <TextBlock Text="{Binding InventoryLevelMessage}" FontSize="12"
            FontWeight="Bold"
            VerticalAlignment="Center" Margin="2,0,0,0"/>
  </StackPanel>
```

```
    <TextBlock HorizontalAlignment="Stretch"
            VerticalAlignment="Center"
            Grid.ColumnSpan="1"
            Text="{Binding ProductCategory.Name}"
            TextAlignment="Right" TextWrapping="Wrap"
            Grid.Column="1" FontSize="13"/>
    <TextBlock HorizontalAlignment="Stretch"
            VerticalAlignment="Center"
            Grid.Column="2" Text="/"
            TextWrapping="Wrap" TextAlignment="Center"
            FontSize="13" />
    <TextBlock HorizontalAlignment="Stretch"
            VerticalAlignment="Center"
            Grid.Column="3" Grid.ColumnSpan="1"
            Text="{Binding ProductSubCategory.Name}"
            TextWrapping="Wrap" TextAlignment="Left"
            FontSize="13"/>
</Grid>
<StackPanel Orientation="Vertical"
            HorizontalAlignment="Stretch"
            VerticalAlignment="Stretch"
            Margin="8,8,8,8"
            Grid.ColumnSpan="2"
            Grid.Row="2" Grid.RowSpan="1" >
    <TextBlock Height="Auto" Width="Auto"
            FontSize="12" FontWeight="Bold"
            Text="Cost History" Margin="0,0,0,10"/>
    <data:DataGrid AutoGenerateColumns="False"
                ItemsSource="{Binding ProductCostHistories}">
        <data:DataGrid.Columns>
            <data:DataGridTextColumn Binding="{Binding StartDate}"
                                Header="Start"/>
            <data:DataGridTextColumn Binding="{Binding EndDate}"
                                Header="End"/>
            <data:DataGridTextColumn
                Binding="{Binding StandardCost}"
                Header="Cost"/>
        </data:DataGrid.Columns>
    </data:DataGrid>
</StackPanel>
<Border HorizontalAlignment="Stretch"
        Margin="8,8,8,8"
        VerticalAlignment="Stretch"
        Grid.Column="1"
        Grid.Row="1"
```

```
                Grid.RowSpan="1"
                BorderBrush="#FF000000"
                BorderThickness="1,1,1,1">
            <TextBox Height="Auto" Width="Auto"
                    FontSize="12"
                    FontWeight="Bold"
                    Text="{Binding ProductDescription.Description,Mode=TwoWay}"
                    TextWrapping="Wrap"/>
        </Border>
      </Grid>
    </DataTemplate>
  </UserControl.Resources>

  <Grid x:Name="LayoutRoot" Background="White">
    <data:DataGrid x:Name="dgProducts" AutoGenerateColumns="False"
            RowDetailsTemplate="{StaticResource dtProductRowDetails}"
            RowDetailsVisibilityMode="Collapsed">
      <data:DataGrid.Columns>
        <data:DataGridTextColumn
          Binding="{Binding ProductID}" Header="ID" />
        <data:DataGridTextColumn
          Binding="{Binding Name}" Header="Name" />
        <data:DataGridTextColumn
          Binding="{Binding ProductNumber}" Header="Number"/>
        <data:DataGridTextColumn
          Binding="{Binding ListPrice}" Header="List Price"/>
        <data:DataGridTextColumn
          Binding="{Binding Style}" Header="Style"/>
        <data:DataGridTextColumn
          Binding="{Binding Color}" Header="Color"/>
        <data:DataGridTemplateColumn>
          <data:DataGridTemplateColumn.CellTemplate>
            <DataTemplate x:Key="dtShowDetailTemplate">
              <Button Content="..." x:Name="ShowDetails"
                      Click="ShowDetails_Click" />
            </DataTemplate>
          </data:DataGridTemplateColumn.CellTemplate>
        </data:DataGridTemplateColumn>
      </data:DataGrid.Columns>
    </data:DataGrid>
  </Grid>
</UserControl>
```

The data template used for the RowDetailsTemplate is named dtProductRowDetails and contains fields bound to several properties in the Product data class, as well as some nested classes. It displays an image of the product, some category information, and some inventory information.

To use the data template in the DataGrid named dgProducts in our page, we set the DataGrid. RowDetailsVisibilityMode to Collapsed so that all rows have their detail information hidden to start with. To allow users to display row details on demand, an extra column of type DataGridTemplateColumn is added to the DataGrid, with a specific CellTemplate containing a Button. (You will learn more about column templates in the next recipe.) The CellTemplate causes a Button to be displayed in the last column of each bound row, and we use the Button's click handler ShowDetails_Click() to allow the user to toggle the Visibility of the row detail information, as shown the code-behind for the page in Listing 5-9.

Listing 5-9. *Code-Behind for the MainPage Hosting the DataGrid*

```
using System;
using System.IO;
using System.Windows;
using System.Windows.Controls;
using System.Windows.Media;
using System.Windows.Media.Imaging;
using Ch05_Controls.Recipe5_5.AdvWorks;

namespace Ch05_Controls.Recipe5_5
{
  public partial class MainPage : UserControl
  {
    AdvWorksDataServiceClient client =
      new AdvWorksDataServiceClient();


    public MainPage()
    {
      InitializeComponent();
      //async completion callbacks for the web service calls to get data
      client.GetPhotosCompleted +=
        new EventHandler<GetPhotosCompletedEventArgs>(
          delegate(object s1, GetPhotosCompletedEventArgs e1)
          {
            (e1.UserState as Product).ProductPhoto = e1.Result;
          });
      client.GetInventoryCompleted +=
        new EventHandler<GetInventoryCompletedEventArgs>(
          delegate(object s2, GetInventoryCompletedEventArgs e2)
          {
            (e2.UserState as Product).ProductInventories = e2.Result;
            (e2.UserState as Product).InventoryLevelBrush = null;
            (e2.UserState as Product).InventoryLevelMessage = null;
          });
```

```
client.GetCategoryCompleted +=
  new EventHandler<GetCategoryCompletedEventArgs>(
   delegate(object s3, GetCategoryCompletedEventArgs e3)
   {
     (e3.UserState as Product).ProductCategory = e3.Result;
   });
client.GetSubcategoryCompleted +=
  new EventHandler<GetSubcategoryCompletedEventArgs>(
    delegate(object s4, GetSubcategoryCompletedEventArgs e4)
    {
      (e4.UserState as Product).ProductSubCategory = e4.Result;
    });
client.GetDescriptionCompleted +=
  new EventHandler<GetDescriptionCompletedEventArgs>(
    delegate(object s5, GetDescriptionCompletedEventArgs e5)
    {
      (e5.UserState as Product).ProductDescription = e5.Result;
    });
client.GetProductCostHistoryCompleted +=
  new EventHandler<GetProductCostHistoryCompletedEventArgs>(
    delegate(object s6, GetProductCostHistoryCompletedEventArgs e6)
    {
      (e6.UserState as Product).ProductCostHistories = e6.Result;
    });

//LoadingRowDetails handler - here we make the calls to load
//row details data on demand
dgProducts.LoadingRowDetails +=
  new EventHandler<DataGridRowDetailsEventArgs>(
    delegate(object sender, DataGridRowDetailsEventArgs e)
    {
      Product prod = e.Row.DataContext as Product;
      if (prod.ProductInventories == null)
        client.GetInventoryAsync(prod, prod);
      if (prod.ProductCategory == null && prod.ProductSubcategoryID != null)
        client.GetCategoryAsync(prod, prod);
      if (prod.ProductSubCategory == null &&
        prod.ProductSubcategoryID != null)
        client.GetSubcategoryAsync(prod, prod);
      if (prod.ProductDescription == null)
        client.GetDescriptionAsync(prod, prod);
      if (prod.ProductPhoto == null)
        client.GetPhotosAsync(prod, prod);
```

```
          if (prod.ProductCostHistories == null)
            client.GetProductCostHistoryAsync(prod, prod);
        });
      GetData();
    }

    private void GetData()
    {
      //get the top level product data
      client.GetProductsCompleted +=
        new EventHandler<GetProductsCompletedEventArgs>(
          delegate(object sender, GetProductsCompletedEventArgs e)
          {
            dgProducts.ItemsSource = e.Result;
          });
      client.GetProductsAsync();
    }


    private void ShowDetails_Click(object sender, RoutedEventArgs e)
    {
      DataGridRow row = DataGridRow.GetRowContainingElement(sender as Button);
      row.DetailsVisibility =
        (row.DetailsVisibility == Visibility.Collapsed ?
        Visibility.Visible : Visibility.Collapsed);
    }
  }
}

namespace Ch05_Controls.Recipe5_5.AdvWorks
{
  public partial class ProductPhoto
  {
    private BitmapImage _LargePhotoPNG;

    public BitmapImage LargePhotoPNG
    {
      get
      {
        BitmapImage bim = new BitmapImage();
        MemoryStream ms = new MemoryStream(this.LargePhoto.Bytes);
        bim.SetSource(ms);
        ms.Close();
        return bim;
      }
```

```csharp
        set
        {
          RaisePropertyChanged("LargePhotoPNG");
        }
      }
    }


public partial class Product
  {
     private SolidColorBrush _InventoryLevelBrush;
     public SolidColorBrush InventoryLevelBrush
     {
       get
       {
         return (this.ProductInventories == null
           || this.ProductInventories.Count == 0) ?
           new SolidColorBrush(Colors.Gray) :
             (this.ProductInventories[0].Quantity > this.SafetyStockLevel ?
               new SolidColorBrush(Colors.Green) :
                 (this.ProductInventories[0].Quantity > this.ReorderPoint ?
                   new SolidColorBrush(Colors.Yellow) :
                   new SolidColorBrush(Colors.Red)));
       }
       set
       {
         //no actual value set here - just property change raised
         RaisePropertyChanged("InventoryLevelBrush");
       }


     }
     private string _InventoryLevelMessage;
     public string InventoryLevelMessage
     {
       get
       {
         return (this.ProductInventories == null
           || this.ProductInventories.Count == 0) ?
           "Stock Level Unknown" :
             (this.ProductInventories[0].Quantity > this.SafetyStockLevel ?
             "In Stock" :
               (this.ProductInventories[0].Quantity > this.ReorderPoint ?
                 "Low Stock" : "Reorder Now"));
       }
```

```
    set
    {
      //no actual value set here - just property change raised
      RaisePropertyChanged("InventoryLevelMessage");
    }
  }
  private ProductSubcategory _productSubCategory;
  public ProductSubcategory ProductSubCategory
  {
    get { return _productSubCategory; }
    set
    {
      _productSubCategory = value;
      RaisePropertyChanged("ProductSubCategory");
    }
  }
  private ProductCategory _productCategory;
  public ProductCategory ProductCategory
  {
    get { return _productCategory; }
    set { _productCategory = value; RaisePropertyChanged("ProductCategory"); }
  }
  private ProductDescription _productDescription;
  public ProductDescription ProductDescription
  {
    get { return _productDescription; }
    set
    {
      _productDescription = value;
      RaisePropertyChanged("ProductDescription");
    }
  }
  private ProductReview _productReview;
  public ProductReview ProductReview
  {
    get { return _productReview; }
    set { _productReview = value; RaisePropertyChanged("ProductReview"); }
  }
  private ProductPhoto _productPhoto;
  public ProductPhoto ProductPhoto
  {
    get { return _productPhoto; }
    set { _productPhoto = value; RaisePropertyChanged("ProductPhoto"); }
  }
  }
}
```

As shown in Listing 5-9, the data is acquired by calling the AdventureWorks WCF service, mentioned in the introduction to this chapter. The GetData() method loads the initial product data into the rows to which the DataGrid is bound. We set the DataGrid's ItemsSource in the completion handler for the GetProductsAsync() web service call. When the user toggles the visibility of a row's details for the first time, the LoadingRowDetails event is raised, and we fetch the row detail data from the web service in that handler, defined using an anonymous delegate in Listing 5-9.

The row detail data, once fetched, is bound to various parts of the UI by setting appropriate properties in the already bound Product instance, which in turn uses property change notification to update the UI. Just as we did in some of the previous recipes, we extend the Product partial class, as generated by the WCF service proxy, to include the additional property definitions.

5-6. Applying Custom Templates to a DataGrid Cell

Problem

You need a customized way of viewing and editing data that is not supported out of the box by any of the typed DataGridColumns like DataGridTextColumn or DataGridCheckBoxColumn. An example of such a customization could be viewing a color value rendered as a color stripe, as opposed to the color name string literal.

Solution

Use the CellTemplate and the CellEditingTemplate properties of the DataGridTemplateColumn to apply custom viewing and editing templates.

How It Works

The various DataGridColumn types like DataGridTextColumn and DataGridCheckBoxColumn are designed to support binding to specific CLR data types, such as String and Boolean, or to types that can be automatically converted to these types. The way that the data is viewed and edited in cells of these specific column types is predetermined by the framework. However, the need for you to be able to supply your own custom UI to view and edit data was well anticipated, and the DataGridTemplateColumn is supplied for exactly that purpose.

The DataGridTemplateColumn exposes two properties, CellTemplate and CellEditingTemplate, both of which accept data templates. Data templates are covered in greater detail in Chapter 4. When the column is data bound, the DataGrid binds the cell data item to the data template specified in CellTemplate to display the data in view mode. When the cell enters edit mode, the DataGrid switches to the CellEditingTemplate.

The Code

In this sample, we use a DataGrid bound to product data fetched from the AdventureWorks WCF service. The Product class exposes a Color property, which is defined as a String on the class. We bind the Color property to one of the DataGrid columns and show how to expose a more intuitive interface where the user can actually view the color itself for both viewing and editing the Color value, as compared to the default string editing experience exposed by the DataGridTextColumn.

Listing 5-10 shows the XAML.

Listing 5-10. *XAML for the MainPage Used to Demonstrate Custom DataGrid Column Templates*

```xaml
<UserControl x:Class="Ch05_Controls.Recipe5_6.MainPage"
 xmlns="http://schemas.microsoft.com/winfx/2006/xaml/presentation"
 xmlns:x="hLtp://schemas.microsoft.com/winfx/2006/xaml"
 xmlns:data=
 "clr-namespace:System.Windows.Controls;assembly=System.Windows.Controls.Data"
 xmlns:local="clr-namespace:Ch05_Controls.Recipe5_6"
 Width="800" Height="400"

>
  <UserControl.Resources>
    <local:ColorNameToBrushConverter x:Key="REF_ColorNameToBrushConverter"/>
    <DataTemplate x:Key="dtColorViewTemplate">
      <Border CornerRadius="5,5,5,5" BorderBrush="Black"
              BorderThickness="1,1,1,1" VerticalAlignment="Stretch"
              HorizontalAlignment="Stretch" Margin="1,1,1,1"
              Background="{Binding Color,
                Converter={StaticResource REF_ColorNameToBrushConverter}}"/>
    </DataTemplate>
    <DataTemplate x:Key="dtColorEditingTemplate">
      <Grid>
        <Grid.RowDefinitions>
          <RowDefinition Height="Auto" />
          <RowDefinition Height="Auto" />
        </Grid.RowDefinitions>
        <ListBox Grid.Row="0" VerticalAlignment="Stretch"
                 HorizontalAlignment="Stretch"
                 ItemsSource="{Binding ColorList}"
                 SelectedItem="{Binding Color, Mode=TwoWay}"
                 Height="200">
          <ListBox.ItemTemplate>
            <DataTemplate>
              <Border CornerRadius="5,5,5,5" BorderBrush="Black"
                      BorderThickness="1,1,1,1" Height="25" Width="70"
                      Margin="2,5,2,5"
                      Background=
                      "{Binding Converter=
                          {StaticResource REF_ColorNameToBrushConverter}}"/>
            </DataTemplate>
          </ListBox.ItemTemplate>
        </ListBox>
      </Grid>
    </DataTemplate>
  </UserControl.Resources>
```

413

```
<Grid x:Name="LayoutRoot" Background="White">
  <data:DataGrid x:Name="dgProducts" AutoGenerateColumns="False">
    <data:DataGrid.Columns>
      <data:DataGridTextColumn Binding="{Binding ProductID}"
                               Header="ID" />
      <data:DataGridTextColumn Binding="{Binding Name}"
                               Header="Name" />
      <data:DataGridTemplateColumn
        CellTemplate="{StaticResource dtColorViewTemplate}"
        CellEditingTemplate="{StaticResource dtColorEditingTemplate}"
        Header="Color" Width="100"/>
    </data:DataGrid.Columns>
  </data:DataGrid>
</Grid>
</UserControl>
```

In the DataGrid declaration named dgProducts, we use a DataGridTemplateColumn to bind to Product.Color. To get the custom UI for viewing and editing the Color property, we define two data templates, dtColorTemplate and dtColorEditingTemplate, and use them to set the CellTemplate and the CellEditingTemplate properties.

In view mode, where the bound DataGridTemplateColumn uses the CellTemplate to bind the data, we bind the Color value to the Background property of a Border, as shown in the data dtColorViewTemplate. In edit mode, where CellEditingTemplate is used, dtColorEditingTemplate uses a ListBox to display the list of available colors. The ListBox.SelectedItem is bound to Product.Color to represent the currently selected color. The binding mode is set to TwoWay so that any changes made by the user updates the Product instance and is reflected in the DataGrid when the cell moves out of edit mode.

Listing 5-11 shows the code-behind for the page.

Listing 5-11. *Code-Behind for the MainPage Demonstrating Custom DataGrid Column Templates*

```
using System;
using System.Collections.Generic;
using System.Collections.ObjectModel;
using System.Linq;
using System.Reflection;
using System.Windows.Controls;
using System.Windows.Data;
using System.Windows.Media;
using Ch05_Controls.Recipe5_6.AdvWorks;

namespace Ch05_Controls.Recipe5_6
{
  public partial class MainPage : UserControl
  {
    AdvWorksDataServiceClient client =
      new AdvWorksDataServiceClient();
    bool EditingColor = false;
```

```csharp
public MainPage()
{
  InitializeComponent();
  GetData();
}

private void GetData()
{
  client.GetProductsCompleted +=
    new EventHandler<GetProductsCompletedEventArgs>(
      delegate(object sender, GetProductsCompletedEventArgs e)
      {
        dgProducts.ItemsSource = e.Result;
      });

  client.GetProductsAsync();
}
}


public class ColorNameToBrushConverter : IValueConverter
{
  //convert from a string Color name to a SolidColorBrush
  public object Convert(object value, Type targetType,
    object parameter, System.Globalization.CultureInfo culture)
  {
    //substitute a null with Transparent
    if (value == null)
      value = "Transparent";
    //make sure the right types are being converted
    if (targetType != typeof(Brush) || value.GetType() != typeof(string))
      throw new NotSupportedException(
        string.Format("{0} to {1} is not supported by {2}",
        value.GetType().Name,
        targetType.Name,
        this.GetType().Name));

    SolidColorBrush scb = null;
    try
    {
      //get all the static Color properties defined in
      //System.Windows.Media.Colors
      List<PropertyInfo> ColorProps = typeof(Colors).
        GetProperties(BindingFlags.Public | BindingFlags.Static).ToList();
      //use LINQ to find the property whose name equates
      //to the string literal we are trying to convert
```

```
    List<PropertyInfo> piTarget = (from pi in ColorProps
                                     where pi.Name == (string)value
                                     select pi).ToList();
    //create a SolidColorBrush using the found Color property.
    //If none was found i.e. the string literal being converted
    //did not match any of the defined Color properties in Colors
    //use Transparent
    scb = new SolidColorBrush(piTarget.Count == 0 ?
      Colors.Transparent : (Color)(piTarget[0].GetValue(null, null)));
  }
  catch
  {
    //on exception, use Transparent
    scb = new SolidColorBrush(Colors.Transparent);
  }
  return scb;


}
//convert from a SolidColorBrush to a string Color name
public object ConvertBack(object value, Type targetType,
  object parameter, System.Globalization.CultureInfo culture)
{
  //make sure the right types are being converted
  if (targetType != typeof(string) || value.GetType() != typeof(Brush))
    throw new NotSupportedException(
      string.Format("{0} to {1} is not supported by {2}",
      value.GetType().Name,
      targetType.Name,
      this.GetType().Name));

  string ColorName = null;
  try
  {
    //get all the static Color properties defined
    //in System.Windows.Media.Colors
    List<PropertyInfo> ColorProps = typeof(Colors).
      GetProperties(BindingFlags.Public | BindingFlags.Static).ToList();
    //use LINQ to find the property whose value equates to the
    //Color on the Brush we are trying to convert
    List<PropertyInfo> piTarget = (from pi in ColorProps
                                     where (Color)pi.GetValue(null, null)
                                     == ((SolidColorBrush)value).Color
                                     select pi).ToList();
```

```
            //If a match is found get the Property name, if not use "Transparent"
            ColorName = (piTarget.Count == 0 ? "Transparent" : piTarget[0].Name);
        }
        catch
        {
            //on exception use Transparent
            ColorName = "Transparent";
        }
        return ColorName;
    }
  }
}

namespace Ch05_Controls.Recipe5_6.AdvWorks
{
  public partial class Product
  {
    private ObservableCollection<string> _ColorList;
    //color literals defined in System.Windows.Media.Colors
    public ObservableCollection<string> ColorList
    {
      get
      {
        return new ObservableCollection<string> {
        "Black",
        "Blue",
        "Brown",
        "Cyan",
        "DarkGray",
        "Gray",
        "Green",
        "LightGray",
        "Magenta",
        "Orange",
        "Purple",
        "Red",
        "Transparent",
        "White",
        "Yellow" };
      }
    }
  }
}
```

CHAPTER 5 ■ CONTROLS

The `ListBox.ItemsSource` is bound to the `Product.ColorList` property, defined in a partial extension of the `Product` proxy data type, which returns a collection of string literals representing names of the `Color` properties, as defined in the `System.Windows.Media.Colors` type. To display each item, an `ItemTemplate` similar to that in the view mode is used, where a `Border` is used to display the color choice, by binding the `Color` value to `Border.Background`.

Figure 5-20 shows the `DataGrid` `Color` column in view mode and edit mode side by side.

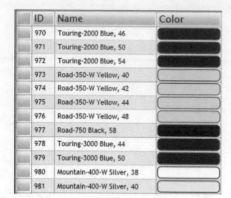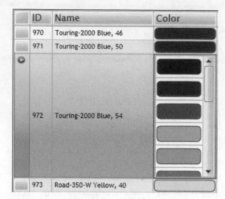

Figure 5-20. *The Color column in view mode (left) and edit mode (right)*

Also note in Listing 5-10 the use of a value converter of type `ColorNameToBrushConverter`. Since the `Border.Background` property is of type `SolidColorBrush` and `Product.Color` is a string literal, we need to facilitate an appropriate value conversion. Listing 5-11 shows the value converter code as well in the `ColorNameToBrushConverter` class. For more details on a value converter, refer to Chapter 4.

In both the conversion functions in the value converter implementation, we use reflection to enumerate the list of static properties of type `Color` defined on the type `System.Windows.Media.Colors`, each of which are named for the `Color` they represent. In `Convert()`, while trying to convert a `Color` name string to a `SolidColorBrush`, we find the matching `Color` property in the enumerated list of properties and use that to create and return the brush. In `ConvertBack()`, while trying to convert a `SolidColorBrush` to a color name string, we find the property with a `Color` value matching the `SolidColorBrush.Color` and use the property name as the color name string. If no matches are found, or we encounter exceptions, we fall back to `Colors.Transparent` as the default value.

5-7. Creating Custom Column Types for a DataGrid

Problem

You want to create a custom column type for a `DataGrid` to enable specific functionality to handle a particular data type or data item.

Solution

Extend the `DataGridBoundColumn` class, and add functionality to handle the view and edit modes for the intended data type or data item.

How It Works

The framework ships with a few prebuilt `DataGrid` column types for handling some of the standard data types. `DataGridTextColumn` is one of the most useful ones and can be used to view and edit any data that can be converted to a meaningful text representation. `DataGridCheckBoxColumn` is another one that can be used to view and edit a `Boolean` value as a `CheckBox` and with the current value mapped to its checked state.

In some situations, you want to implement custom logic to handle a specific data type or a program data item bound to a `DataGrid` column. One way to achieve that is through the use of the `DataGridTemplateColumn` column type and the use of `CellTemplate` and `CellEditingTemplate`, as shown in recipe 5-6 earlier. Yet another way is to create a new column type that encapsulates the custom logic, much like the ones that the framework ships with. The logic encapsulation in creating this custom column offers you the advantage of not having to rely on the consumers (UI layer developers) of your data to supply appropriate data templates, as well as the effect of standardizing and locking down how a specific data type or item gets treated inside a `DataGrid`.

In this second approach, you start by creating a new class extending the `System.Windows.Controls.DataGridBoundColumn` class in the `System.Windows.Controls.Data` assembly, which is also the base class for the framework-provided column types mentioned earlier. The `DataGridBoundColumn` exposes an API of abstract methods that, when overridden, allows you to easily control the UI and data-binding logic of cells in the custom column as they are switched between view and edit modes. The methods in this API that you will override most often are `GenerateElement()`, `GenerateEditingElement()`, `PrepareCellForEdit()`, and `CancelCellEdit()`. All of these methods, except `CancelCellEdit()`, are abstract methods, and therefore it is mandatory that you provide an appropriate implementation in your custom column code.

We discuss this API briefly next.

The GenerateElement() Method

This method is expected to create the UI that would be used by the `DataGrid` to display the bound value in every cell of that column. The created UI is returned in the form of a `FrameworkElement` from `GenerateElement()`. By overriding this method and supplying your custom logic, you can change the UI a bound cell uses to display its content. You are also expected to create and set appropriate data bindings for your newly created UI in this method so that data items are appropriately displayed in every cell. To do that, you can obtain the data binding set by the user in the XAML for the column through the `DataGridBoundColumn.Binding` property. You can then use the `SetBinding()` method to apply that binding to the appropriate parts of the UI you create before returning the UI as a `FrameworkElement`.

Also note that this method accepts two parameters passed in by the containing `DataGrid`: a cell of type `DataGridCell` and a data item of type `object`. The first parameter contains a reference to the instance of the `DataGridCell` that is currently being generated, and the second parameter refers to the data item bound to the current row. You don't have to use these parameters to successfully implement this method. One interesting use of these parameters is in a computed column scenario. Since the `dataItem` parameter contains the entire item bound to that row, you can easily compute a value based on parts of the data item and use that as the cell value bound to the UI you return from this method. We leave it to you to experiment further with these parameters.

The GenerateEditingElement() Method

This method is somewhat similar to `GenerateElement()` in purpose but is used for edit mode rather than view mode. When the user switches a cell to edit mode—for example, by clicking it—the `DataGrid` calls this method on the column type to generate the UI for the editing experience. The generated UI is again returned as a `FrameworkElement`. You can override this method in your custom column type to create a custom edit UI for your data type or item. The same requirements for applying the appropriate data bindings before you return the generated UI, as discussed for GenerateElement() earlier, apply here as well.

Also note that this method accepts the same parameter set as GenerateElement().

The PrepareCellForEdit() Method

This method is called by the DataGrid to obtain the unedited value from the bound cell before entering edit mode. The unedited value is retained by the DataGrid and made available to you in CancelCellEdit() so that edits made to the cell can be undone should a user choose to cancel an edit operation. The FrameworkElement type you created for the edit mode UI in GenerateEditingElement() is made available to you as the editingElement parameter. You can use that to obtain the current unedited value for the cell. The second parameter to this method, named editingEventArgs, is of type RoutedEventArgs. It contains information about the user gesture that caused the cell to move to edit mode. For keyboard-based input, it can be cast to KeyEventArgs, and for mouse input gestures, it can be cast to MouseButtonEventArgs. You should check the result of your cast to verify that it is non-null before using the parameter. This parameter can be used to implement additional logic, such as different editing behaviors if a specific key is pressed.

The CancelCellEdit() Method

This method is called if a user cancels an edit operation. The unedited value bound to the cell, prior to any changes made by the user in edit mode, is made available to you via the uneditedValue parameter, as is the FrameworkElement representing the edit UI through the editingElement parameter. You can undo the changes made by resetting the editingElement using the uneditedValue. The uneditedValue parameter is of type object, and consequently you will need to cast it to the appropriate type based on the bound data before you use it to reset the edit changes.

The Code

The code sample in this recipe creates a custom column type named DataGridDateColumn for editing DateTime types using the DatePicker control.

Listing 5-12 shows the code for DataGridDateColumn.

Listing 5-12. *DataGridDateColumn Class*

```
using System;
using System.ComponentModel;
using System.Windows;
using System.Windows.Controls;
using System.Windows.Data;
using System.Windows.Media;

namespace Ch05_Controls.Recipe5_7
{
  public class DataGridDateColumn : DataGridBoundColumn
  {
    [TypeConverter(typeof(DataGridDateTimeConverter))]
    public DateTime DisplayDateStart { get; set; }
```

```
    public Binding DisplayDateEndBinding { get; set; }

    protected override void CancelCellEdit(FrameworkElement editingElement,
      object uneditedValue)
    {
      //get the DatePicker
      DatePicker datepicker = (editingElement as Border).Child as DatePicker;
      if (datepicker != null)
      {
        //rest the relevant properties on the DatePicker to the original value
        //to reflect cancellation and undo changes made
        datepicker.SelectedDate = (DateTime)uneditedValue;
        datepicker.DisplayDate = (DateTime)uneditedValue;
      }
    }
    //edit mode
    protected override FrameworkElement GenerateEditingElement(
DataGridCell cell, object dataItem)
    {
      //create an outside Border
      Border border = new Border();
      border.BorderBrush = new SolidColorBrush(Colors.Blue);
      border.BorderThickness = new Thickness(1);
      border.HorizontalAlignment = HorizontalAlignment.Stretch;
      border.VerticalAlignment = VerticalAlignment.Stretch;
      //create the new DatePicker
      DatePicker datepicker = new DatePicker();
      //bind the DisplayDate to the bound data item
      datepicker.SetBinding(DatePicker.DisplayDateProperty,
        base.Binding);
      //bind the SelectedDate to the same
      datepicker.SetBinding(DatePicker.SelectedDateProperty,
        base.Binding);
      //bind the DisplayDate range
      //start value is provided directly through a property
      datepicker.DisplayDateStart = this.DisplayDateStart;
      //end value is another binding allowing developer to bind
      datepicker.SetBinding(DatePicker.DisplayDateEndProperty,
        this.DisplayDateEndBinding);
      border.Child = datepicker;
      //return the new control
      return border;
    }

    //view mode
```

```
      protected override FrameworkElement GenerateElement(DataGridCell cell,
object dataItem)
      {
        //create a TextBlock
        TextBlock block = new TextBlock();
        //bind the displayed text to the bound data item
        block.SetBinding(TextBlock.TextProperty, base.Binding);
        //return the new control
        return block;
      }
      protected override object PrepareCellForEdit(FrameworkElement editingElement,
        RoutedEventArgs editingEventArgs)
      {
        //get the datepicker
        DatePicker datepicker = (editingElement as Border).Child as DatePicker;
        //return the initially displayed date, which is the
        //same as the unchanged data item value
        return datepicker.DisplayDate;
      }
    }
  }
}
```

In `GenerateElement()`, we create a `TextBlock` as our control of choice to display the bound data. We then set the binding on the `TextBlock.Text` property to the `Binding` property on the column so that the date is displayed inside the `TextBlock`. In `GenerateEditingElement()`, we instead create a `Border` and nest a `DatePicker` control in it for date editing. Once the `DatePicker` control is created, we set both the `DisplayDate` (the date displayed in the editable text portion of the `DatePicker`) and the `SelectedDate` (the date value selected in the drop-down portion of the `DatePicker`) initially to the `Binding` property on the column. We also set a couple of other bindings that we will explain later in the recipe before we return the `Border`. In `PrepareCellForEdit()`, we return the currently displayed date to the `DataGrid` for retention in case of a cancellation, and in `CancelCellEdit()`, we reset the appropriate values on the `DatePicker` instance to the unedited value saved earlier through `PrepareCellForEdit()`.

Listing 5-13 shows the XAML declaration of a `DataGrid` using the `DataGridDateColumn` type. We once again use the `AdventureWorks` WCF service as a data source.

Listing 5-13. *XAML for the MainPage Demonstrating Custom DataGrid Column*

```
<UserControl x:Class="Ch05_Controls.Recipe5_7.MainPage"
  xmlns="http://schemas.microsoft.com/winfx/2006/xaml/presentation"
  xmlns:x="http://schemas.microsoft.com/winfx/2006/xaml"
  xmlns:data=
  "clr-namespace:System.Windows.Controls;assembly=System.Windows.Controls.Data"
  xmlns:local="clr-namespace:Ch05_Controls.Recipe5_7"
  Width="800" Height="400"
  xmlns:d="http://schemas.microsoft.com/expression/blend/2008"
  xmlns:mc="http://schemas.openxmlformats.org/markup-compatibility/2006"
  mc:Ignorable="d">
```

```
<UserControl.Resources>

</UserControl.Resources>
<Grid x:Name="LayoutRoot" Background="White">
<data:DataGrid x:Name="dgProducts" AutoGenerateColumns="False">
  <data:DataGrid.Columns>
    <data:DataGridTextColumn
      Binding="{Binding ProductID}" Header="ID" />
    <data:DataGridTextColumn
      Binding="{Binding Name}" Header="Name" />
    <local:DataGridDateColumn
      Binding="{Binding SellStartDate}"
      DisplayDateStart="01/01/2000"
      DisplayDateEndBinding="{Binding DisplayDateEnd}"
      Header="Available From" />
  </data:DataGrid.Columns>
</data:DataGrid>
</Grid>
</UserControl>
```

One of the challenges of this approach is that it may be desirable for the developer using the DataGridDateColumn to control some behavior of the internal DatePicker instance. For example, the DatePicker control exposes DisplayDateStart and DisplayDateEnd properties that determine the date range the DatePicker drop-down is limited to, and it may be desirable for the developer to specify this range when using the DataGridDateColumn. But since the DatePicker control instance is not visible outside the DataGridDateColumn code, there is no direct way for the developer to do so.

One way to allow developers to directly control these properties is to create corresponding properties on DataGridDateColumn so that they can be set in XAML, and those values can be used in your code to set the DatePicker properties. Referring to the DataGridDateColumn class in Listing 5-12, you can see the DisplayDateStart property of type DateTime, and you can also note it being set to a date string in the XAML in Listing 5-13. The value of this property is then used inside GenerateEditingElement() to set the similarly named property on the DatePicker instance.

Since the date string set in XAML needs to be converted to a DateTime type for the code to work correctly, we need a type conversion mechanism. The framework contains the TypeConverter class, which you can extend to create a type converter of your own. Listing 5-14 shows a type converter that converts from String to DateTime.

Listing 5-14. *DataGridDateTimeConverter Class*

```
using System;
using System.ComponentModel;
using System.Globalization;

namespace Ch05_Controls.Recipe5_7
{
  public class DataGridDateTimeConverter : TypeConverter
  {
    public override bool CanConvertFrom(ITypeDescriptorContext context,
```

```
      Type sourceType)
    {
      return (typeof(string) == sourceType);
    }
    public override bool CanConvertTo(ITypeDescriptorContext context,
      Type destinationType)
    {
      return (typeof(DateTime) == destinationType);
    }
    public override object ConvertFrom(ITypeDescriptorContext context,
      CultureInfo culture, object value)
    {
      DateTime target;
      target = DateTime.ParseExact(value as string, "d",
        CultureInfo.CurrentUICulture);
      return target;
    }
  }
}
```

The TypeConverterAttribute can be used to attach this type converter to our DataGridDateColumn. DisplayDateStart property, as shown in Listing 5-12. Note that in overriding the ConvertFrom() method in the TypeConverter implementation, the system passes in a CultureInfo instance as the second parameter. The CltureInfo parameter allows you to inspect the current culture. If you need to implement any additional conversion logic based on the locale, you can check this parameter and take the needed action in your code. In our case, we do not use the value, but just pass in CultureInfo.CurrentUICulture in our call to Datetime.ParseExact() to allow the DateTime value type to handle the rest of the conversion logic.

You might want to have such a property be set as a binding instead of a direct value setting, much like the Binding property on any DataGrid column. This allows the developer to associate a data binding with the property, and lets its value be derived at runtime from the source it is bound to, as opposed to being hard-coded.

As an example, let's say you want to expose a property named DisplayDateEndBinding on the DataGridDateColumn and use that to drive the value of the DisplayDateEnd property of the DatePicker instance. You can see the declaration of this property in Listing 5-12, and it is bound to a property named DisplayDateEnd on the data source in the XAML in Listing 5-13. This can then be used to attach the same binding to the DatePicker.DisplayDateEnd property, as shown in the GenerateEditingElement() method in Listing 5-12. Also shown in Listing 5-12 is an extension to the Product partial class that determines the value to be a year from the current date.

The code-behind for the MainPage in this sample there is not much code to discuss, beyond a call to the AdventureWorks WCF service discussed in the introduction to the chapter to populate the DataGrid. We leave it out and encourage the user to refer to the sample code for the book.

Figure 5-21 shows the DataGridDateColumn in action.

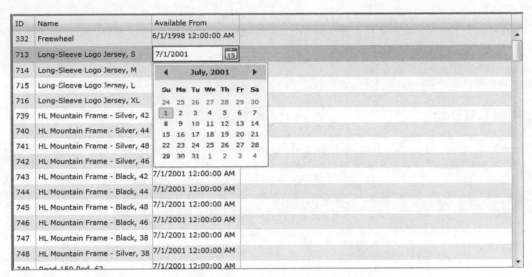

Figure 5-21. *DataGridDateColumn in edit mode*

5-8. Creating a Composite User Control

Problem

You need to compose a UI using existing controls and package it in a reusable format.

Solution

Use the Visual Studio 2008 Silverlight user control template to create a new class deriving from `UserControl`, and then add additional controls to `UserControl` to compose an UI.

How It Works

Silverlight offers two kinds of controls: user controls and custom controls. User controls are an effective way to package UI and related client-side processing logic tied to a specific business or application domain into a reusable unit that can then be consumed as a tag in XAML just as any other built-in primitive shape like `Ellipse` or `Rectangle` or another control can. There is excellent tool support for designing and implementing user controls both in Visual Studio and Expression Blend, making it the default choice for creating reusable user interface components with reasonable ease.

User controls allow you to create composite UIs by combining other custom or user controls. This ability makes them especially suitable for writing composite controls—in fact, most user controls that you will end up writing will be composite controls as well.

Custom controls, on the other hand, are the more powerful controls in Silverlight. All the controls in the `System.Windows.Controls` namespace that come with the framework are built as custom controls, and using them is typically the preferred way of implementing more general-purpose UI components that often are not limited to one particular application or business domain. Custom

425

controls also enable powerful features, such as control templates that allow radical customization of the control user interface. Recipes later in this chapter will cover custom control development in greater detail.

In the following sections, we are going to review a few concepts critical to understanding how a control works. This information will apply to your understanding of a user control as well as in later recipes when we discuss custom controls.

User Control Structure

Creating a user control is fairly easy if you are using Visual Studio 2008. With the Silverlight tools installed, Visual Studio offers you a template to add a new user control to a Silverlight project, through the Add New Item dialog box (see Figure 5-22).

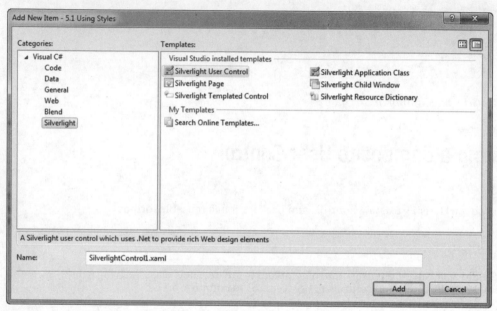

Figure 5-22. *Adding a new Silverlight user control to your project*

Once you add a user control, you should see an XAML document coupled with a code-behind file defining the user control. User controls are defined as partial classes deriving from the UserControl type in the System.Windows.Controls namespace. Visual Studio generates one such class when you add a new user control. The following is such a class for a user control named PagedProductsGrid:

```
namespace CompositeControlLib
{
  public partial class PagedProductsGrid : UserControl
  {

    public PagedProductsGrid()
    {
```

```
        InitializeComponent();
    }

  }
}
```

In the generated XAML document for the user control, you should see some skeletal XAML initially generated by Visual Studio, as shown here:

```
<UserControl x:Class="CompositeControlLib.PagedProductsGrid"
    xmlns="http://schemas.microsoft.com/winfx/2006/xaml/presentation"
    xmlns:x="http://schemas.microsoft.com/winfx/2006/xaml"
    Width="400" Height="300">
    <Grid x:Name="LayoutRoot" Background=="White" >
    </Grid>
</UserControl>
```

You will notice that the Visual Studio template adds a top-level Grid (conventionally named LayoutRoot) in the XAML. You can define the rest of the UI for the user control inside this Grid, or should you choose to, you can rename the Grid or even replace the Grid with some other container.

Note the x:Class attribute in the UserControl declaration in XAML. The value set here needs to be the namespace-qualified name of the partial class defined in the code-behind file. This mechanism allows the XAML declaration of the user control to be associated with the user control class at compile time.

XAML Loading

So how does the XAML for the user control get loaded at runtime? When you compile the user control project, a XAML parser generates some additional code to extend the user control partial class. This code is usually found in a file named <controlname>.g.cs inside the \obj\debug folder below your project's root folder. This generated code adds some startup functionality, which is encapsulated in a method named InitializeComponent(). You will find that the Visual Studio template already adds a call to InitializeComponent() to the constructor of your user control class. Listing 5-15 shows the generated code for a user control.

Listing 5-15. *Visual Studio–Generated Startup Code for a UserControl*

```
namespace CompositeControlLib
{
  public partial class PagedProductsGrid : System.Windows.Controls.UserControl
  {
    internal System.Windows.Controls.Grid LayoutRoot;
    internal System.Windows.Controls.DataGrid dgProductPage;
    internal System.Windows.Controls.ListBox lbxPageNum;
    private bool _contentLoaded;
```

```
/// <summary>
/// InitializeComponent
/// </summary>
[System.Diagnostics.DebuggerNonUserCodeAttribute()]
public void InitializeComponent()
{
  if (_contentLoaded)
  {
    return;
  }
  _contentLoaded = true;
  System.Windows.Application.LoadComponent(
    this,
    new System.Uri("/CompositeControlLib;component/PagedProductsGrid.xaml",
      System.UriKind.Relative));
  this.LayoutRoot =
    ((System.Windows.Controls.Grid)(this.FindName("LayoutRoot")));
  this.dgProductPage =
    ((System.Windows.Controls.DataGrid)(this.FindName("dgProductPage")));
  this.lbxPageNum =
    ((System.Windows.Controls.ListBox)(this.FindName("lbxPageNum")));
  }
 }
}
```

At the crux of this code is the `LoadComponent()` method, used at runtime to load the XAML included as a resource in the compiled assembly. Once the element tree defined in the XAML is formed, the `FrameworkElement.FindName()` is used to locate and store the instances for every named control in your XAML definition so that you can refer to them in your code. To learn more about resources and resource loading, refer to recipes in Chapter 2 of this book.

Dependency Properties

Control types expose properties as a means to allow the control consumer (a developer or a designer) to get or set various attributes of a control instance. Since controls in Silverlight are also .NET classes, properties can be implemented using the standard CLR property syntax.

Silverlight provides an extension to the standard CLR property system by introducing a new concept called a dependency property. A dependency property provides additional functionality that cannot be implemented using standard CLR properties. Among other features, the extended functionality includes the following:

- *Data binding*: Dependency properties can be data bound using either the XAML `{Binding. . .}` markup extension or the `Binding` class in code, thus allowing evaluation of its value at runtime. For more on data binding, see Chapter 4.

- *Styles*: Dependency properties can be set using setters in a style. For more on using styles, see recipe 5-1. Note that only dependency properties can be set this way using styles.

- *Resource referencing*: A dependency property can be set to refer to a predefined resource defined in a resource dictionary using the {StaticResource. . .} markup extension in XAML. For more on resources, refer to Chapter 2.

- *Animations*: For a property to be animated, it needs to be a dependency property. For more on animations, see Chapter 3.

A dependency property is implemented in code as a public static member of type DependencyProperty, where the implementing type needs to derive from DependencyObject. Listing 5-16 shows a sample declaration of a dependency property named MaximumProperty, representing a double valued maximum for some range.

Listing 5-16. *Sample Dependency Property Declaration*

```
public static DependencyProperty MaximumProperty =
  DependencyProperty.Register("Maximum",
  typeof(double?),
  typeof(NumericUpdown),
  new PropertyMetadata(100,new PropertyChangedCallback(MaximumChangedCallback)));

public double? Maximum
{
  get
  {
    return (double?)GetValue(MaximumProperty);
  }
  set
  {
    SetValue(MaximumProperty, value);
  }
}

internal static void MaximumChangedCallback(DependencyObject Target,
DependencyPropertyChangedEventArgs e)
{
  NumericUpdown target = Target as NumericUpdown;
  //other code to respond to the property change
}
```

The static method DependencyProperty.Register() is used to register the property with the Silverlight property system. The parameters to the method are a name for the property, the property data type, the containing type, and a PropertyMetadata instance. In our snippet above you can note the string "Maximum" as the property name, double? as the data type for the property, and the property owner to be a type named NumericUpDown. The PropertyMetadata parameter is constructed by passing in a default value for the property and a delegate to a static callback method that is invoked when the property value changes. Note that the defaultValue parameter is of type object. Also note that the callback method is only required if you intend to take some action when the value of the dependency property changes. If the value change has no impact on your control's logic, PropertyMetadata has another constructor that only accepts the defaultValue parameter.

A conventional way of naming the dependency property is by concatenating the string "Property" to the property name. You are free to change that convention; however, it is to your benefit to stick with it. The framework and the Silverlight SDK follow the same convention, and developers around the world will soon get used to this convention to determine whether or not a property is a dependency property.

Although the dependency property is declared static, the Silverlight property system maintains and provides access to values of the property on a per-instance basis. The DependencyObject.GetValue() method accepts a dependency property and returns the value of the property for the instance of the declaring type within which GetValue() is invoked. SetValue() accepts a dependency property and a value and sets that value for the instance within which SetValue() is invoked. A CLR property wrapper of the same name, minus the "Property" extension, as shown in Listing 5-16, is typically provided as shorthand to using the GetValue()/SetValue() pair for manipulating the property in code.

The instance on which the property change happened is passed in as the first parameter to the static property change callback handler. This allows you to cast it appropriately, as shown in MaximumChangedCallback() in Listing 5-16 earlier, and then take action on that instance in response to the property value change. The second parameter of type DependencyPropertyChangedEventArgs exposes two useful properties: the OldValue property exposes the value of the property before the change, and the NewValue property exposes the changed value.

The Code

The code sample for this recipe builds a user control named PagedProductsGrid that displays Product data in a grid form, coupled with paging logic, where the consumer of the control gets to specify how many records to display per page, and the control automatically adds a pager at the bottom that allows the user to navigate through pages.

Figure 5-23 shows the control in action. Also shown is the pager at the bottom, with the selected page in a solid blue rectangle, and the rectangular selection indicator on another page.

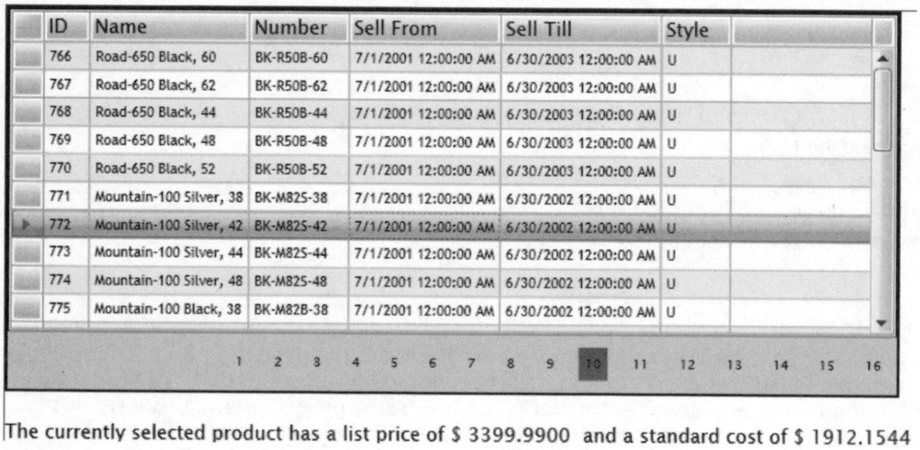

Figure 5-23. *Paged product data composite control*

Listing 5-17 shows the XAML for the PagedProductsGrid user control.

Listing 5-17. *XAML for PagedProductsGrid User Control*

```
<UserControl
  x:Class="Ch05_Controls.Recipe5_8.PagedProductsGrid"
  xmlns="http://schemas.microsoft.com/winfx/2006/xaml/presentation"
  xmlns:x="http://schemas.microsoft.com/winfx/2006/xaml"
  xmlns:vsm="clr-namespace:System.Windows;assembly=System.Windows"
  xmlns:data=
  "clr-namespace:System.Windows.Controls;assembly=System.Windows.Controls.Data"
  Width="700" Height="300">
  <UserControl.Resources>
    <!-- control template for Pager ListBoxItem -->
    <ControlTemplate TargetType="ListBoxItem" x:Key="ctLbxItemPageNum">
      <Grid>
        <vsm:VisualStateManager.VisualStateGroups>
          <vsm:VisualStateGroup x:Name="CommonStates">
            <vsm:VisualState x:Name="Normal">
              <Storyboard/>
            </vsm:VisualState>
            <vsm:VisualState x:Name="MouseOver">
              <Storyboard>
                <ColorAnimationUsingKeyFrames
                  BeginTime="00:00:00"
                  Duration="00:00:00.0010000"
                  Storyboard.TargetName="ContentBorder"
                  Storyboard.TargetProperty=
                  "(Border.BorderBrush).(SolidColorBrush.Color)">
                  <SplineColorKeyFrame KeyTime="00:00:00" Value="#FF091F88"/>
                </ColorAnimationUsingKeyFrames>
              </Storyboard>
            </vsm:VisualState>
          </vsm:VisualStateGroup>
          <vsm:VisualStateGroup x:Name="SelectionStates">
            <vsm:VisualState x:Name="Unselected">
              <Storyboard/>
            </vsm:VisualState>
            <vsm:VisualState x:Name="Selected">
              <Storyboard>
                <ColorAnimationUsingKeyFrames
                  BeginTime="00:00:00"
                  Duration="00:00:00.0010000"
                  Storyboard.TargetName="ContentBorder"
```

431

```xml
                            Storyboard.TargetProperty=
                            "(Border.Background).(SolidColorBrush.Color)">
                            <SplineColorKeyFrame KeyTime="00:00:00" Value="#FF1279F5"/>
                          </ColorAnimationUsingKeyFrames>
                        </Storyboard>
                      </vsm:VisualState>
                      <vsm:VisualState x:Name="SelectedUnfocused">
                        <Storyboard>
                          <ColorAnimationUsingKeyFrames
                            BeginTime="00:00:00"
                            Duration="00:00:00.0010000"
                            Storyboard.TargetName="ContentBorder"
                            Storyboard.TargetProperty=
                            "(Border.Background).(SolidColorBrush.Color)">
                            <SplineColorKeyFrame KeyTime="00:00:00" Value="#FF1279F5"/>
                          </ColorAnimationUsingKeyFrames>
                        </Storyboard>
                      </vsm:VisualState>
                    </vsm:VisualStateGroup>
                    <vsm:VisualStateGroup x:Name="FocusStates">
                      <vsm:VisualState x:Name="Unfocused">
                        <Storyboard/>
                      </vsm:VisualState>
                      <vsm:VisualState x:Name="Focused">
                        <Storyboard/>
                      </vsm:VisualState>
                    </vsm:VisualStateGroup>
                  </vsm:VisualStateManager.VisualStateGroups>

                  <Border HorizontalAlignment="Left"
                          VerticalAlignment="Top"
                          Margin="5,5,5,5"
                          Padding="5,5,5,5"
                          BorderBrush="#00091F88"
                          BorderThickness="2,2,2,2"
                          Background="#001279F5"
                          x:Name="ContentBorder">
                    <ContentPresenter
                      Content="{TemplateBinding Content}"
                      ContentTemplate="{TemplateBinding ContentTemplate}"/>
                  </Border>
                </Grid>
              </ControlTemplate>
```

```xml
<!-- style applying the Pager ListBoxItem control template -->
<Style x:Key="stylePageNum" TargetType="ListBoxItem">
  <Setter Property="Template" Value="{StaticResource ctlbxItemPageNum}" />
</Style>
<!-- Horizontal panel for the Pager ListBox -->
<ItemsPanelTemplate x:Key="iptHorizontalPanel">
  <StackPanel Orientation="Horizontal"/>
</ItemsPanelTemplate>

<!--Control template for Pager ListBox-->
<ControlTemplate x:Key="ctlbxPager" TargetType="ListBox">
  <Grid>
    <ItemsPresenter HorizontalAlignment="Left" VerticalAlignment="Top" />
  </Grid>
</ControlTemplate>
</UserControl.Resources>

<Border Background="LightGray" BorderBrush="Black" BorderThickness="2,2,2,2">
  <Grid x:Name="LayoutRoot">
    <Grid.RowDefinitions>
      <RowDefinition Height="85*" />
      <RowDefinition Height="15*" />
    </Grid.RowDefinitions>
    <!-- data grid to display Products data -->
    <data:DataGrid x:Name="dgProductPage" AutoGenerateColumns="False"
                   Grid.Row="0"
                   SelectionChanged="dgProductPage_SelectionChanged">
      <data:DataGrid.Columns>
        <data:DataGridTextColumn Binding="{Binding ProductID}"
                                 Header="ID" />
        <data:DataGridTextColumn Binding="{Binding Name}"
                                 Header="Name"/>
        <data:DataGridTextColumn Binding="{Binding ProductNumber}"
                                 Header="Number"/>
        <data:DataGridTextColumn Binding="{Binding SellStartDate}"
                                 Header="Sell From"/>
        <data:DataGridTextColumn Binding="{Binding SellEndDate}"
                                 Header="Sell Till"/>
        <data:DataGridTextColumn Binding="{Binding Style}"
                                 Header="Style"/>
      </data:DataGrid.Columns>
    </data:DataGrid>
```

```
    <!-- Pager Listbox-->
    <ListBox x:Name="lbxPager" Grid.Row="1"
            HorizontalAlignment="Right" VerticalAlignment="Center"
            SelectionChanged="lbxPager_SelectionChanged"
            ItemsPanel="{StaticResource iptHorizontalPanel}"
            ItemContainerStyle="{StaticResource stylePageNum}"
            Template="{StaticResource ctlbxPager}">
    </ListBox>
  </Grid>
 </Border>
</UserControl>
```

The user control has two primary parts: a DataGrid named dgProductPage with columns bound to the Product data type, and a ListBox acting as a pager.

The first thing to note about the pager ListBox is that we replace its default ItemsPanel with a horizontal StackPanel so that the page numbers appear horizontally moving from left to right. This is done by defining a custom ItemsPanelTemplate, named iptHorizontalPanel, and associating that with the ItemsPanel property on the ListBox. We will discuss panel customization in greater detail in later recipes.

We apply a custom control template, named ctlbxPager, to the ListBox. It simplifies the ListBox significantly, just leaving an ItemsPresenter for displaying the items inside a Grid.

We also customize each ListBoxItem by applying a custom control template, named ctLbxItemPageNum, to the ListBoxItem. The template defines the ListBoxItem as a ContentPresenter within a Border, and adds storyboards for the MouseOver, Selected, and SelectedUnfocused visual states, which cause a solid blue rectangle around the page number to indicate the selected page, and a blue border to indicate the one on which the mouse is hovering. A style named StylePagenum is used to associate this with the ListBox through its ItemContainerStyle property.

The AdventureWorks WCF service mentioned in the introduction is again used to deliver the data to the control. The following code shows the implementation of the AdventureWorks WCF service operation GetProductPage(), which returns a page of product data.

```
public List<Product> GetProductPage(int SkipCount, int TakeCount)
{
  ProductsDataContext dc = new ProductsDataContext();

  return (from Prod in dc.Products select Prod).Skip(SkipCount).
Take(TakeCount).ToList();
}
```

The SkipCount parameter to GetProductPage() indicates the number of rows to skip, and the TakeCount parameter indicates the number of rows to return after the skipping is done. LINQ exposes two handy operators, Skip and Take, that allow you to do just that on a collection of items.

Listing 5-18 shows the control code-behind.

Listing 5-18. *Code-Behind for the PagedProductsGrid Control*

```csharp
using System;
using System.Collections.Generic;
using System.Linq;
using System.Windows;
using System.Windows.Controls;
using Ch05_Controls.Recipe5_8.AdvWorks;

namespace Ch05_Controls.Recipe5_8
{
  public partial class PagedProductsGrid : UserControl
  {
    //WCF service proxy
    AdvWorksDataServiceClient client = new AdvWorksDataServiceClient();
    //raise an event when current record selection changes
    public event EventHandler<DataItemSelectionChangedEventArgs>
      DataItemSelectionChanged;
    //RecordsPerPage DP
    DependencyProperty RecordsPerPageProperty =
      DependencyProperty.Register("RecordsPerPage",
      typeof(int),
      typeof(PagedProductsGrid),
      new PropertyMetadata(20,
        new PropertyChangedCallback(
          PagedProductsGrid.RecordsPerPageChangedHandler)
        ));
    //CLR DP Wrapper
    public int RecordsPerPage
    {
      get
      {
        return (int)GetValue(RecordsPerPageProperty);
      }

      set
      {
        SetValue(RecordsPerPageProperty, value);
      }
    }
    //RecordPerPage DP value changed
    internal static void RecordsPerPageChangedHandler(DependencyObject sender,
      DependencyPropertyChangedEventArgs e)
    {
```

```
    PagedProductsGrid dg = sender as PagedProductsGrid;
    //call init data
    dg.InitData();
}

public PagedProductsGrid()
{
    InitializeComponent();
}

internal void InitData()
{
    //got data
    client.GetProductPageCompleted +=
        new EventHandler<GetProductPageCompletedEventArgs>(
            delegate(object Sender, GetProductPageCompletedEventArgs e)
            {
                //bind grid
                dgProductPage.ItemsSource = e.Result;
            });

    //got the count
    client.GetProductsCountCompleted +=
        new EventHandler<GetProductsCountCompletedEventArgs>(
            delegate(object Sender, GetProductsCountCompletedEventArgs e)
            {
                //set the pager control
                lbxPager.ItemsSource = new List<int>(Enumerable.Range(1,
                    (int)Math.Ceiling(e.Result / RecordsPerPage)));
                //get the first page of data
                client.GetProductPageAsync(0, RecordsPerPage);
            });
    //get the product count
    client.GetProductsCountAsync();
}
//page selection changed
private void lbxPager_SelectionChanged(object sender,
    SelectionChangedEventArgs e)
{
    //get page number
    int PageNum = (int)(lbxPager.SelectedItem);
    //fetch that page - handler defined in InitData()
    client.GetProductPageAsync(RecordsPerPage * (PageNum - 1), RecordsPerPage);

}
```

```
    //record selection changed
    private void dgProductPage_SelectionChanged(object sender, EventArgs e)
    {
      if (this.DataItemSelectionChanged != null)
      {
        //raise DataItemSelectionChanged
        this.DataItemSelectionChanged(this,
          new DataItemSelectionChangedEventArgs {
            CurrentItem = dgProductPage.SelectedItem as Product
          });
      }
    }
  }

  public class DataItemSelectionChangedEventArgs : EventArgs
  {
    public Product CurrentItem { get; internal set; }
  }
}
```

The InitData() function is used to load the data into the DataGrid. To facilitate paging, we first record the total number of Products available by calling the GetProductsCountAsync() service operation. In the callback handler for GetProductsCountAsync(), we set the lbxPager ListBox data to be a range of numbers, starting with 1 and ending at the maximum number of pages expected based on the record count we retrieved earlier. We set the value of the RecordsPerPage property that the developer has set.

We then call the service operation GetProductPageAsync() with SkipCount set to 0 and TakeCount set to the value of RecordsPerPage. The retrieved Product data gets bound to the DataGrid dgProductPage as the first page of data.

If the value of RecordsPerPage changes at runtime, we reinitialize the grid by calling InitData() again in RecordsPerPageChangedHandler(). We also handle the navigation to a different page by handling the SelectionChanged event in lbxPager, where we retrieve the page requested and call GetProductsDataAsync() again, with SkipCount set to the product of RecordsPerPage times the number of pages before the current one selected and TakeCount again set to RecordsPerPage.

To demonstrate events from a user control, we also define and raise an event named DataItemSelectionChanged whenever the current row selection in a DataGrid changes. We handle a change in row selection in the internal DataGrid dgProductPage, and in that handler, we raise the event. A custom event argument type of DataItemSelectionChangedEventArgs, also shown in Listing 5-18, is used to pass the actual Product instance bound to the current row to the event consumer.

To consume the user control in a page, we add a reference to the assembly containing the user control to our project. We then add a custom namespace declaration to dereference the types within the assembly in the page's XAML. Finally, we declare an instance of the control prefixed with the custom namespace in the XAML. Listing 5-19 shows the XAML for our consuming page.

■**Note** There is no strict requirement to implement your user control in a separate assembly from the application consuming it. We simply find it to be a best practice to follow, one that makes the control a lot more distributable and reusable.

Listing 5-19. *XAML for the Test Page Hosting the User Control*

```xaml
<UserControl x:Class="Ch05_Controls.Recipe5_8.MainPage"
    xmlns="http://schemas.microsoft.com/winfx/2006/xaml/presentation"
    xmlns:x="http://schemas.microsoft.com/winfx/2006/xaml"
    xmlns:composite=
"clr-namespace:Ch05_Controls.Recipe5_8;assembly=Ch05_Controls.Recipe5_8.ControlLib"
    >
  <Grid x:Name="LayoutRoot">
    <Grid.RowDefinitions>
      <RowDefinition Height="Auto"/>
      <RowDefinition Height="Auto" />
    </Grid.RowDefinitions>
    <!-- user control declaration -->
    <composite:PagedProductsGrid x:Name="PagedGrid"
            RecordsPerPage="30"
            DataItemSelectionChanged="PagedGrid_DataItemSelectionChanged"
            Grid.Row="0"  HorizontalAlignment="Left"/>
    <!-- content control with a data template that gets bound to
    selected data passed through user control raised event -->
    <ContentControl x:Name="ProductCostInfo" Grid.Row="1" Margin="0,20,0,0">
      <ContentControl.ContentTemplate>
        <DataTemplate>
          <StackPanel Orientation="Horizontal">
            <TextBlock
              Text="The currently selected product has a list price of $ "/>
            <TextBlock Text="{Binding ListPrice}"
                       Margin="0,0,10,0"
                       Foreground="Blue"/>
            <TextBlock Text="and a standard cost of $ "/>
            <TextBlock Text="{Binding StandardCost}"
                       Foreground="Blue"/>
          </StackPanel>
        </DataTemplate>
      </ContentControl.ContentTemplate>
    </ContentControl>
  </Grid>
</UserControl>
```

The custom namespace composite brings in the actual .NET namespace and the assembly reference into the XAML so that control can be referenced. We can then declare the control by prefixing its opening and closing tags with the namespace prefix. In Listing 5-19, we set the RecordsPerPage property to a value of 30 so that the control displays 30 records per page. If you refer to Listing 5-18, you will note that we provide a default value of 20 to RecordsPerPage in the PropertyMetadata constructor while registering the DependencyProperty.In the event you do not bind the RecordsPerPage property to some value in XAML, 20 will be the value applied to as a default. To illustrate consuming the

DataItemChanged event that we equipped the user control to raise, we also add a ContentControl named ProductCostInfo in our page with a data template that binds a couple of TextBlocks to the ListPrice and the StandardCost properties of a Product instance. We handle the DataItemChanged event, and in the handler, we bind the Product received through the event arguments to the ContentControl, as shown in the code-behind for the page in Listing 5-20.

Listing 5-20. *Code-Behind for the Test Page Hosting the User Control*

```
using System.Windows.Controls;

namespace Ch05_Controls.Recipe5_8
{
  public partial class MainPage : UserControl
  {
    public MainPage()
    {
      InitializeComponent();
    }

    private void PagedGrid_DataItemSelectionChanged(object sender,
      DataItemSelectionChangedEventArgs e)
    {
      if (e.CurrentItem != null)
        ProductCostInfo.Content = e.CurrentItem;
    }
  }
}
```

If you refer to Figure 5-23, you will see the resulting text on the page, right below the user control, showing the ListPrice and the StandardCost of the currently selected Product.

5-9. Creating a Custom Layout Container

Problem

You need to implement custom layout logic for child controls inside a parent container.

Solution

Implement a custom Panel to encapsulate the custom layout logic.

How It Works

Laying out your controls and other visual elements is an important part of crafting a compelling user interface. However, it always helps if the framework you are using provides some assistance in achieving that layout. There are some common layout scenarios, such as arranging your elements in a stack either vertically or horizontally, or specifying their position in terms of rows and columns in a table-like arrangement. And then of course there is absolute positioning, where you provide the exact X and Y coordinates for your element.

The Silverlight libraries include several layout containers that help in that process. Layout containers are elements that can contain other elements as children and implement a specific layout logic that arranges the children accordingly. `Canvas`, `StackPanel`, and `Grid` found in `System.Windows.Controls` are a few of these layout containers, with their layout logic consisting of absolute positioning, ordered stacking, and table style positioning, respectively. For more on these layout containers, and design-time support, refer to Chapter 3.

Motivation and Mechanics

The challenge for the framework designers is that it is hard to foresee all possible layout scenarios and implement a container for each in the framework. Consequently, there needs to be a way in which you can easily implement your own layout logic and plug it in so that it functions seamlessly with the rest of the framework types, just the way the built-in containers do.

The `System.Windows.Controls.Panel` abstract class was designed for exactly that purpose. The set of standard built-in layout containers like `Grid` and `StackPanel` extend the `Panel` class to implement their layout logic, and so can you.

To create your custom layout logic, you need to provide implementations of two virtual methods: `MeasureOverride()` and `ArrangeOverride()`. At runtime, these two methods are called on any custom panel implementation you build to give you an opportunity to appropriately lay out any contained children. Note that these two methods are defined in the `FrameworkElement` type, from which `Panel` itself derives. However, `FrameworkElement` has no built-in notion of child items, whereas the `Panel` class does by exposing a `Children` collection. Therefore, we use the `Panel` class as the root for all custom layout containers.

Now, let's look at the `MeasureOverride()` and `ArrangeOverride()` methods.

The MeasureOverride() Method

Layout essentially happens in two passes. In the first pass, the runtime provides an opportunity to the container to evaluate the size requirements of all its children and return a computed total size that the container desires from the layout system to position all the children according to its layout logic.

This first pass is implemented in `MeasureOverride()`. The parameter passed in to `MeasureOverride()` by the runtime is the total `availableSize` for all children of that container to be laid out. The goal of the `MeasureOverride()` method is to look at each child individually, calculate the size requirements of each, and compute a total size requirement, which is then returned from `MeasureOverride()` to the runtime. It is in computing this calculated total that you apply your layout logic. However, there is a standard way for measuring the desired size of each child that goes into that calculation. You need to call the `Measure()` method on each child, passing in the `availableSize` parameter, and the child returns its desired size. `Measure()` is a method implemented in `UIElement`, and it is a requirement to call `Measure()` on each child to guarantee accurate size measurement and placement in your layout.

This computed total may be greater than the `availableSize` parameter passed in, to indicate that more room than originally granted by the runtime's layout system is required for ideal layout of all the children for this container. However, what is finally granted is up to the runtime, based on the overall UI and the room available within the plug-in to display all content inside and outside this container.

The ArrangeOverride() Method

In the second pass of the layout process, the layout system calculates the most space it can allocate to a container based on the rest of the UI, and then calls ArrangeOverride(), passing that value in as the finalSize parameter. Keep in mind that the finalSize value may be less than the desired size that your MeasureOverride() implementation had calculated.

It is now up to your implementation of ArrangeOverride() to figure out a strategy of laying out the child elements within the finalSize determined by the layout system. The actual process of laying each individual child is done by calling the Arrange() method on the child itself. The Arrange() method accepts a Rectangle that determines the final area within which the child should be positioned. The return value from ArrangeOverride() is the finalSize required by the container, and unless your implementation can lay everything out within a space smaller than the finalSize value passed in, this in most cases is the unchanged value contained in the finalSize parameter.

Note that it is mandatory to call the Measure() and Arrange() methods on all children elements to have them laid out and rendered by the layout system. And since that is what we do inside MeasureOverride() and ArrangeOverride(), implementing overrides for both of these methods is also a requirement when implementing a layout container like a custom panel.

The Code

In this code sample, we will build a layout container extending the Panel type that can arrange its children in either a horizontal orientation (in rows) or a vertical one (in columns). It also automatically wraps all its children into successive rows or columns based on available space. We have named the implementing type WrapPanel, and Listing 5-21 shows the code.

Listing 5-21. *WrapPanel Implementation*

```
using System;
using System.Windows;
using System.Windows.Controls;

namespace Ch05_Controls.Recipe5_9
{
  public class WrapPanel : Panel
  {
    //Orientation dependency property
    DependencyProperty OrientationProperty =
      DependencyProperty.Register("Orientation", typeof(Orientation),
      typeof(WrapPanel),
      new PropertyMetadata(
        new PropertyChangedCallback(OrientationPropertyChangedCallback)));

    public Orientation Orientation
    {
      get
      {
        return (Orientation)GetValue(OrientationProperty);
      }
```

```
    set
    {
      SetValue(OrientationProperty, value);
    }
  }
  private static void OrientationPropertyChangedCallback(
    DependencyObject target, DependencyPropertyChangedEventArgs e)
  {
    //cause the layout to be redone on change of Orientation
    if (e.OldValue != e.NewValue)
      (target as WrapPanel).InvalidateMeasure();
  }

  public WrapPanel()
  {
    //initialize the orientation
    Orientation = Orientation.Horizontal;
  }
  protected override Size MeasureOverride(Size availableSize)
  {
    double DesiredWidth = 0;
    double DesiredHeight = 0;
    double RowHeight = 0;
    double RowWidth = 0;
    double ColHeight = 0;
    double ColWidth = 0;

    //call Measure() on each child - this is mandatory.
    //get the true measure of things by passing in infinite sizing
    foreach (UIElement uie in this.Children)
      uie.Measure(availableSize);
    //for horizontal orientation - children laid out in rows
    if (Orientation == Orientation.Horizontal)
    {
      //iterate over children
      for (int idx = 0; idx < this.Children.Count; idx++)
      {

        //if we are at a point where adding the next child would
        //put us at greater than the available width
        if (RowWidth + Children[idx].DesiredSize.Width
          >= availableSize.Width)
        {
          //set the desired width to the max of row width so far
          DesiredWidth = Math.Max(RowWidth, DesiredWidth);
```

```
      //accumulate the row height in preparation to move on to the next row
      DesiredHeight += RowHeight;
      //initialize the row height and row width for the next row iteration
      RowWidth = 0;
      RowHeight = 0;
    }
    //if on the other hand we are within width bounds
    if (RowWidth + Children[idx].DesiredSize.Width
      < availableSize.Width)
    {
      //increment the width of the current row by the child's width
      RowWidth += Children[idx].DesiredSize.Width;
      //set the row height if this child is taller
      //than the others in the row so far
      RowHeight = Math.Max(RowHeight,
        Children[idx].DesiredSize.Height);

    }
    //this means we ran out of children in the middle or exactly at the end
    //of a row
    if (RowWidth != 0 && RowHeight != 0)
    {
      //account for the last row
      DesiredWidth = Math.Max(RowWidth, DesiredWidth);
      DesiredHeight += RowHeight;
    }


  }
}
else //vertical orientation - children laid out in columns
{
  //iterate over children
  for (int idx = 0; idx < this.Children.Count; idx++)
  {
    //if we are at a point where adding the next child would
    //put us at greater than the available height
    if (ColHeight + Children[idx].DesiredSize.Height
      >= availableSize.Height)
    {
      //set the desired height to max of column height so far
      DesiredHeight = Math.Max(ColHeight, DesiredHeight);
      //accumulate the column width in preparation to
      //move on to the next column
      DesiredWidth += ColWidth;
```

```
            //initialize the column height and column width for the
            //next column iteration
            ColHeight = 0;
            ColWidth = 0;
          }
          //if on the other hand we are within height bounds
          if (ColHeight + Children[idx].DesiredSize.Height
            < availableSize.Height)
          {
            //increment the height of the current column by the child's height
            ColHeight += Children[idx].DesiredSize.Height;
            //set the column width if this child is wider
            //than the others in the column so far
            ColWidth = Math.Max(ColWidth,
              Children[idx].DesiredSize.Width);
          }
        }
        //this means we ran out of children in the middle or exactly at the end
        //of a column
        if (RowWidth != 0 && RowHeight != 0)
        {
          //account for the last row
          DesiredHeight = Math.Max(ColHeight, DesiredHeight);
          DesiredWidth += ColWidth;
        }
      }
      //return the desired size
      return new Size(DesiredWidth, DesiredHeight);
    }

    protected override Size ArrangeOverride(Size finalSize)
    {
      double ChildX = 0;
      double ChildY = 0;
      double FinalHeight = 0;
      double FinalWidth = 0;
      //horizontal orientation - children in rows
      if (Orientation == Orientation.Horizontal)
      {
        double RowHeight = 0;
        //iterate over children
        for (int idx = 0; idx < this.Children.Count; idx++)
        {
```

```
      //if we are about to go beyond width bounds with the next child
      if (ChildX + Children[idx].DesiredSize.Width
        >= finalSize.Width)
      {
        //move to next row
        ChildY += RowHeight;
        FinalHeight += RowHeight;
        FinalWidth = Math.Max(FinalWidth, ChildX);
        //shift to the left edge to start next row
        ChildX = 0;
      }
      //if we are within width bounds
      if (ChildX + Children[idx].DesiredSize.Width
        < finalSize.Width)
      {
        //lay out child at the current X,Y coords with
        //the desired width and height
        Children[idx].Arrange(new Rect(ChildX, ChildY,
          Children[idx].DesiredSize.Width,
          Children[idx].DesiredSize.Height));
        //increment X value to position next child horizontally right after the
        //currently laid out child
        ChildX += Children[idx].DesiredSize.Width;
        //set the row height if this child is taller
        //than the others in the row so far
        RowHeight = Math.Max(RowHeight,
          Children[idx].DesiredSize.Height);
      }
    }
  }
}
else //vertical orientation - children in columns
{
  double ColWidth = 0;
  //iterate over children
  for (int idx = 0; idx < this.Children.Count; idx++)
  {
    //if we are about to go beyond height bounds with the next child
    if (ChildY + Children[idx].DesiredSize.Height
      >= finalSize.Height)
    {
      //move to next column
      ChildX += ColWidth;
      FinalWidth += ColWidth;
      FinalHeight = Math.Max(FinalHeight, ChildY);
      //shift to the top edge to start next column
```

```
            ChildY = 0;
        }
        //if we are within height bounds
        if (ChildY + Children[idx].DesiredSize.Height
          < finalSize.Height)
        {
            //lay out child at the current X,Y coords with
            //the desired width and height
            Children[idx].Arrange(new Rect(ChildX, ChildY,
              Children[idx].DesiredSize.Width,
              Children[idx].DesiredSize.Height));
            //increment Y value to position next child vertically right below the
            //currently laid out child
            ChildY += Children[idx].DesiredSize.Height;
            //set the column width if this child is wider
            //than the others in the column so far
            ColWidth = Math.Max(ColWidth,
              Children[idx].DesiredSize.Width);
        }
    }
}
//return the original final size
return finalSize;
    }
  }
}
```

Let's first look at the measure pass. As we noted before, in MeasureOverride(), we are given the available size to work with, and we return the total desired size of the container in question with all its children. You can see in Listing 5-21 that we start off by calling Measure() on every child in the Children collection.

It is worth noting here that the measuring and arranging tasks are both recursive in nature. When you call Measure() on every child, the runtime ultimately calls MeasureOverride() on that child, which in turn calls Measure() on any children that child might have, and so on until MeasureOverride() gets called on every leaf element (i.e., an element without any more children). The desired size returned by MeasureOverride() at every level of recursion travels back to its parent and is available through the DesiredSize property on the child.

Once we call Measure() on each of the children in our code, and consequently populate the DesiredSize property on each of them, we then need to calculate the desired size of the entire WrapPanel based on the individual desired sizes of each child. To do that, we iterate over the Children collection and try to arrange them along rows or columns, based on the Orientation value of Horizontal or Vertical, respectively. Note that we do not actually create any rows or columns; rather, we simply try to calculate the size of such rows or columns.

So for example, in a Horizontal orientation, as we iterate over each child we add its width to a counter named RowWidth, indicating the current row's width. We also keep a track of the row's height by constantly evaluating the maximum height among the children added to that row up to that point. Once we reach a point where the addition of the next child would cause the row to go beyond the Width component of the DesiredSize parameter, we consider the row complete.

At this point, we track the maximum width of any such row calculated so far in a counter named DesiredWidth. The assumption is that the children could all have different sizes. In case they are all similarly sized, all those rows would be equal width as well, since the rows would break off at the exact same point every time. We also keep a measure of how much we are consuming on the Y axis with each row, using a counter named DesiredHeight, by adding up each row's height.

If the orientation was vertical, a similar logic is followed, with height and width interchanged in that context. Once we have iterated over each child, we have our desired size in the combination of the DesiredWidth and DesiredHeight counters, and we pass that out of MeasureOverride().

The arrange pass is similar in logic. We get the finalSize as the parameter to ArrangeOverride(). We break up our logic based on the Orientation setting as before. But this time, we actually lay each child out by calling the Arrange() method on the child. The UIElement.Arrange() method accepts a Rectangle and lays the element inside that Rectangle. As we iterate through each element, we increment placement coordinates (either the *x* value or the *y* value based on whether we are laying out in rows or columns) to position child elements one after the other, and when we reach bounds where we have to break into the next row or column, we move by either the row height or the column width calculated in a similar fashion, as we did in the MeasureOverride() implementation.

The Orientation property is implemented as a dependency property of type System.Windows. Controls.Orientation that can be used to specify a horizontal or vertical layout. In OrientationPropertyChangedCallback(), we call InvalidateMeasure() on the WrapPanel instance, if the property value is being changed. InvalidateMeasure() causes the layout system to redo the layout, starting again with the measure pass.

Using the WrapPanel

Let's consider using the WrapPanel in a user interface. One straightforward option is to use it in similar fashion to a StackPanel:

```
<wrappanellib:WrapPanel Orientation="Horizontal">
  <TextBlock Text="Child 1"/>
  <TextBlock Text="Child 2"/>
  <TextBlock Text="Child 3"/>
  <TextBlock Text="Child 4"/>
  <TextBlock Text="Child 5"/>
  <TextBlock Text="Child 6"/>
  <TextBlock Text="Child 7"/>
  <TextBlock Text="Child 8"/>
  <Button Content="Child 9" Width="60" Height="30"/>
  <Button Content="Child 10" Width="70" Height="30"/>
  <Button Content="Child 11" Width="60" Height="30"/>
  <RadioButton Content="Child 12" Width="90" Height="30"/>
  <RadioButton Content="Child 13" Width="60" Height="30"/>
  <Button Content="Child 14" Width="80" Height="30"/>
  <Button Content="Child 15" Width="60" Height="30"/>
</wrappanellib:WrapPanel>
```

This code snippet shows the standard XAML usage pattern where all children, a mixed bag of controls in this case, are listed within the WrapPanel declaration, much in the fashion of any other layout container. You should be able to cut and paste this code in your own sample application and use it as is. Just remember to reference the assembly from the sample code, and create a namespace mapping (we have mapped the wrappanellib namespace here).

Let's consider a slightly more interesting use of a custom panel. One of the interesting usages of a panel is to assist in the layout process of an `ItemsControl`. `ItemsControl` is the primary base control for visually representing a collection of many items. `ItemsControl` exposes a property named `ItemsPanel` of type `ItemsPanelTemplate` that can be defined in terms of any type that extends `Panel`. While you may or may not have used `ItemsControl` directly, a better used control is the `ListBox`, which extends the `ItemsControl` and, by virtue of that, uses a panel internally for layout. Let's see how we would replace the layout panel for a `ListBox` and control some of the panel's properties as well.

Listing 5-22 shows the XAML for a page with a `ListBox` in it, with its default panel replaced with our own `WrapPanel` from this recipe.

Listing 5-22. *XAML for a ListBox Using the WrapPanel for Layout*

```
<UserControl x:Class="Ch05_Controls.Recipe5_9.MainPage"
  xmlns="http://schemas.microsoft.com/winfx/2006/xaml/presentation"
  xmlns:x="http://schemas.microsoft.com/winfx/2006/xaml"
  xmlns:local="clr-namespace:Ch05_Controls.Recipe5_9"
  xmlns:wrappanellib=
"clr-namespace:Ch05_Controls.Recipe5_9;assembly=Ch05_Controls.Recipe5_9.WrapPanel"
  Width="585" Height="440">
  <UserControl.Resources>

    <local:ImagesCollection x:Key="dsImages" />

    <DataTemplate x:Key="dtImageItem">
      <Grid Background="#007A7575" Margin="10,10,10,10" >
        <Grid.RowDefinitions>
          <RowDefinition Height="0.5*"/>
          <RowDefinition Height="0.5*"/>
        </Grid.RowDefinitions>
        <Rectangle  Fill="#FF7A7575" Stroke="#FF000000"
                    RadiusX="5" RadiusY="5"/>
        <Image Margin="10,10,10,10" Width="50" Height="50"
               VerticalAlignment="Center"
               HorizontalAlignment="Center"
               Source="{Binding ImageFromResource}"/>

      </Grid>
    </DataTemplate>
```

```xml
    <Style TargetType="ListBox" x:Key="STYLE_WrapPanelListBox">
      <Setter Property="ItemsPanel">
        <Setter.Value>
          <ItemsPanelTemplate>
            <wrappanellib:WrapPanel Orientation="{Binding CurrentOrientation}"
                                    Width="600" Height="600"/>
          </ItemsPanelTemplate>
        </Setter.Value>
      </Setter>
    </Style>

</UserControl.Resources>

<Grid x:Name="LayoutRoot" Background="White">
  <Grid.RowDefinitions>
    <RowDefinition Height="*" />
    <RowDefinition Height="Auto" />
  </Grid.RowDefinitions>
  <ListBox x:Name="lbxWrapPanelTest"  Grid.Row="0"
           ItemTemplate="{StaticResource dtImageItem}"
           ItemsSource="{StaticResource dsImages}"
           Style="{StaticResource STYLE_WrapPanelListBox}">
  </ListBox>
  <StackPanel Orientation="Horizontal" Grid.Row="1">
    <RadioButton Content="Horizontal Arrangement" Margin="0,0,20,0"
                 GroupName="OrientationChoice" x:Name="rbtnHorizontal"
                 Checked="rbtnHorizontal_Checked" IsChecked="True"/>
    <RadioButton Content="Vertical Arrangement" Margin="0,0,0,0"
                 GroupName="OrientationChoice" x:Name="rbtnVertical"
                 Checked="rbtnVertical_Checked"/>
  </StackPanel>
</Grid>

</UserControl>
```

The first thing to note in Listing 5-22 is the ItemsPanelTemplate definition for the ListBox. The internal implementation of the ListBox in the framework uses a StackPanel as the panel, but we redefine it to use our own WrapPanel and set it as the value of the ItemsPanel property in a style targeting a ListBox. We then apply the style to the ListBox lbxWrapPanelTest. We will come back to more on this definition in a moment.

Also notice that lbxWrapPanelTest gets its data from a data source named dsImages pointing to a collection named ImagesCollection. The ItemTemplate is set to a data template dtImageItem that displays some images contained in dsImages; each image is encapsulated in a type named CustomImageSource.

Listing 5-23 shows the code CustomImageSource and ImagesCollection.

Listing 5-23. *Code for CustomImageSource and ImagesCollection Types*

```csharp
using System.Windows.Media.Imaging;
using System.Reflection;
using System.Collections.Generic;

namespace Ch05_Controls.Recipe5_9
{
  public class CustomImageSource
  {
    public string ImageName { get; set; }
    private BitmapImage _bitmapImage;
    public BitmapImage ImageFromResource
    {
      get
      {
        if (_bitmapImage == null)
        {
          _bitmapImage = new BitmapImage();
          _bitmapImage.SetSource(
            this.GetType().Assembly.GetManifestResourceStream(ImageName));
        }

        return _bitmapImage;
      }
    }
  }
  public class ImagesCollection : List<CustomImageSource>
  {
    public ImagesCollection()
    {
      Assembly thisAssembly = this.GetType().Assembly;
      List<string> ImageNames =
        new List<string>(thisAssembly.GetManifestResourceNames());

      foreach (string Name in ImageNames)
      {
        if (Name.Contains(".png"))
          this.Add(new CustomImageSource { ImageName = Name });
      }
    }
  }
}
```

The images used in this sample are embedded as resources in the project assembly. `ImagesCollection` uses `GetManifestResourceNames()` to get a collection of the string names of all the embedded resources. It then iterates over the collection of resource names, and uses `GetManifestResourceStream()` to acquire each resource as a stream. It creates a new `CustomImageSource` for each one ending with the `.png` extension indicating an image resource, and the `CustomImageSource` type constructor loads the image.

Let's take another look at that `ItemsPanelTemplate` definition. Once the `ItemsPanel` property is set on the `ListBoxItem`, the panel instance that is created internally by the `ListBox` is not made available to your application code in any way. However, there may be a need to access properties on the underlying panel from application code. An example could be the need to change our `WrapPanel`'s `Orientation` property to influence the `ListBox`'s layout. However, since the panel is not directly exposed, we need to take a slightly indirect approach to this.

Inside the `ItemsPanelTemplate` declaration, the `WrapPanel` has full access to the `DataContext` of its parent `ListBox` `lbxWrapPanelTest`. So this gives us a way to bind a property exposed by the panel to application data, as long as that data is made available through the `ListBox`'s `DataContext`. If you refer back to Listing 5-21, you will note that we bind the `WrapPanel.Orientation` property to the `CurrentOrientation` property of some data item. We further have two `RadioButtons` on the page with `Checked` event handlers defined in the code-behind. Listing 5-24 shows the code-behind for the page.

Listing 5-24. *Code-Behind for the MainPage Hosting the ListBox*

```
using System.Windows.Controls;
using System.ComponentModel;

namespace Ch05_Controls.Recipe5_9
{
  public partial class MainPage : UserControl
  {
    ListBoxPanelOrientation CurrentLbxOrientation =
      new ListBoxPanelOrientation { CurrentOrientation = Orientation.Horizontal };
    public MainPage()
    {
      InitializeComponent();
      lbxWrapPanelTest.DataContext = CurrentLbxOrientation;
    }

    private void rbtnHorizontal_Checked(object sender,
      System.Windows.RoutedEventArgs e)
    {
      CurrentLbxOrientation.CurrentOrientation = Orientation.Horizontal;
    }

    private void rbtnVertical_Checked(object sender,
      System.Windows.RoutedEventArgs e)
    {
      CurrentLbxOrientation.CurrentOrientation = Orientation.Vertical;
    }
  }
}
```

```
public class ListBoxPanelOrientation : INotifyPropertyChanged
{
  public event PropertyChangedEventHandler PropertyChanged;

  private Orientation _Current;
  public Orientation CurrentOrientation
  {
    get { return _Current; }
    set
    {
      _Current = value;
      if (PropertyChanged != null)
        PropertyChanged(this,
          new PropertyChangedEventArgs("CurrentOrientation"));
    }
  }
}
```

The ListBoxPanelOrientation type exposes the CurrentOrientation property enabled with property change notification as shown in Listing 5-24. We construct and initialize an instance of ListBoxPanelOrientation, and set it to the ListBox's DataContext. This causes the internal WrapPanel instance to adopt this orientation through the binding we discussed earlier. In the Checked event handlers of the RadioButtons, we change the CurrentOrientation value, which causes the ListBox to change its orientation dynamically, again because of the property change notification flowing back to the WrapPanel through the binding.

Figure 5-24 shows the ListBox and the contained WrapPanel in action.

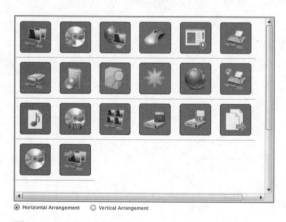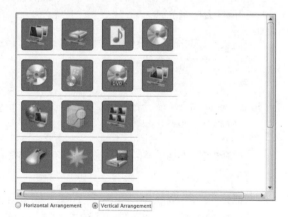

Figure 5-24. *A ListBox using the WrapPanel with different orientations*

452

5-10. Creating a Custom Control

Problem

You need to create a control structured in the same way as the controls in the framework, offering some of the same facilities like control templating.

Solution

Create a class that derives from either control or another type control derived type, provide a default control template in XAML, and implement control behavior by adding code to the derived class.

How It Works

For a general introduction to controls, dependency properties, and events, check out recipe 5-8 in this chapter. You can also look at recipe 5-1 for background information on styles, and recipe 5-2 for information on control templates. In this recipe, we will assume that you understand those topics.

Custom Control Structure

Custom controls are types that extend the Control, ContentControl, or ItemsControl class. The first thing to note is how a custom control defines its user interface.

Every assembly containing a custom control needs to contain an XAML file named generic.xaml as an assembly resource embedded in a folder named Themes. This naming standard is mandatory, as this resource is where the runtime looks for the default control UI. Visual Studio 2008 does not automatically generate a generic.xaml for you. You will have to explicitly create and add the file to your project. To do this, first add a blank project folder named Themes to your control project. Then, add a blank text file named generic.xaml to the Themes folder.

The generic.xaml file has to contain a ResourceDictionary, which in turn contains styles that define the default UI for each custom control contained in that assembly. This code snippet shows a sample:

```
<ResourceDictionary
xmlns="http://schemas.microsoft.com/winfx/2006/xaml/presentation"
xmlns:x="http://schemas.microsoft.com/winfx/2006/xaml"
xmlns:local="clr-namespace:Ch05_Controls.Recipe5_10">
  <!-- BEGIN: Progress Bar -->
  <ControlTemplate TargetType="local:ProgressBar" x:Key="ctProgressBar">
    <Grid>
      <!-- template definition -->
  </ControlTemplate>
  <Style TargetType="local:ProgressBar">
    <Setter Property="Template" Value="{StaticResource ctProgressBar}"/>
    <!-- other setters -->
  </Style>
  <!-- END: Progress Bar -->
</ResourceDictionary>
```

■**Note** We use a `ProgressBar` control sample in the snippet below. This does not reflect the template for the `ProgressBar` control that is shipped with the Silverlight libraries but is purely an example that we chose to illustrate our concept here.

You can copy the `ResourceDictionary` snippet without the content in between to your `generic.xaml`, and you have the basic structure ready to start adding templates to it.

As you can see, the UI of the control is defined as a control template, and then, a style targeted toward the control's type associates the control template with the `Template` property. In the constructor of the custom control, you need to instruct the runtime to apply this style to your custom control by setting the `DefaultStyleKey` property defined on the `Control` base class to the type of the control itself. As such, as you may have noted in the earlier code snippet, the style in this case does not need an `x:Key` attribute. This association is mandatory as well, since without this your custom control will not have a default UI.

The following code snippet shows an example:

```
public ProgressBar()
{
  base.DefaultStyleKey = typeof(ProgressBar);
}
```

With the `DefaultStyleKey` properly set, the runtime calls the `OnApplyTemplate()` virtual method on the control class. `OnApplyTemplate()` is an interception of the template-loading process, where your control code is given an opportunity to access the constituent parts of the template, store them for future references in your control code elsewhere, and initialize any of these parts as needed. To take advantage of this, you provide an override of `OnApplyTemplate()` in your code. To acquire references to any of the parts of the template, you can use the `GetTemplateChild()` method in that override. The following code snippet shows how to acquire an element named `elemPBar` in an `OnApplyTemplate()` override, store it in a local variable, and initialize its `Width` to 10:

```
internal FrameworkElement elemPBar { get; set; }

public override void OnApplyTemplate()
{
  base.OnApplyTemplate();
  elemPBar = this.GetTemplateChild("elemPBar") as FrameworkElement;
  if(elemPBar != null)
    elemPBar.Width = 10;
}
```

Note that providing an override to `OnApplyTemplate()` is not mandatory. However, in real situations, very rarely will you author a control that does not need to manipulate some part of its UI, and `OnApplyTemplate()` is the only place where you can get access to those elements.

You may also have observed that a hard dependency is created on the expected template structure in this process, because `GetTemplateChild()` looks for a part by its name (provided through the `x:Name` attribute in the template definition). Keep the following in mind:

- In your implementation of `OnApplyTemplate()`, always remember to call `OnApplyTemplate()` on the base class. This is especially important, since you might be extending another custom control (and not `Control` or `ContentControl` directly) and calling `OnApplyTemplate()` on the base type gives it the opportunity to do its own initialization properly.

- Code defensively by being prepared to encounter situations where a certain named template part you are looking for using `GetTemplatechild()` may not exist. This could happen if a developer was applying his or her own custom control template to your control and that template was designed without this named part in it. Checking for a `null` value before referencing the part anywhere else in your code is a good practice, since `GetTemplateChild()` would return `null` if the part was not found.

- Try to use a highest base class approach in assuming the part's CLR type in your code. For example, in the previous code snippet, where we demonstrated `OnApplyTemplate()`, we were casting the part to a `FrameworkElement` and then accessing its `Width` property. If the properties and methods exposed by a `FrameworkElement` provided us enough functionality to manipulate the part to the desired level everywhere in our code, using it as a `FrameworkElement` is sufficient for our needs. This allows a developer applying a custom template to your code to specify a different type for the same named part, as long as both the original and the replacement both inherit from the same base class, in our case `FrameworkElement`. For instance, the default template may have a part as a `Rectangle`. Since you only use its `Width` and `Height` properties in your control code, a developer can easily substitute that with a `Border` with the same name in his or her custom template.

Even with all of these safeguards, it never hurts to let other developers know your original intent for the template, which parts of the template are named, and what its type is. To assist in this, the framework defines an attribute named `TemplatePartAttribute` in `System.Windows` with two properties: `Name`, which contains the string name of a part, and `Type`, which contains the CLR type of the part element. Applying this attribute to your control class allows other code and design tools to use reflection on your control type and discover your template part name and type requirements. You can apply it multiple times, once for each named part required. This code snippet shows an application:

```
[TemplatePart(Name="elemPBar",Type=typeof(FrameworkElement))]
public class ProgressBar : ContentControl
{
}
```

One other thing to consider while implementing a custom control from scratch (that is, if you are not extending an existing control) is the choice of using the `Control`, `ContentControl`, or `ItemsControl` type as the base class. The general guideline is that if your control needs to display additional content beyond what is specified in the control's template, and if you need to allow developers to specify where that content comes from and how it is displayed, you should extend `ContentControl`. The `Content` property defined on `ContentControl` allows your control to take advantage of data binding for the content, and the `ContentTemplate` property lets you use a data template to display the content. If your control is expected to display a collection of data items, with the ability to bind to a source for those items, as well as specify a data template for displaying each item, you should extend `ItemsControl`. The `ItemsSource` and `ItemTemplate` properties on the `ItemsControl` facilitate those features. If none of the above is a requirement, you are free to directly extend the `Control` class.

TemplateBinding vs. RelativeSource Binding to TemplatedParent

In recipe 5-2, while discussing control templating, we pointed out the TemplateBinding declaration that allows you to bind the value of an element's property to another property on the template parent (i.e., an instance of the control whose control template the element is situated in). There is an alternative to the TemplateBinding syntax that we wanted to point out as well.

In recipe 4-5, we discussed the RelativeSource property on the Binding type, but we only discussed the effect of setting RelativeSource to RelativeSource.Self. Setting the property of an element within a control template to use a binding with RelativeSource set to RelativeSource.TemplatedParent has the same effect as using a TemplateBinding. So in effect the two syntaxes in the following snippet achieve similar results.

```
PropertyFoo="{TemplateBinding SomeParentProperty}"

PropertyFoo=
    "{Binding SomeParentProperty, RelativeSource={RelativeSource TemplatedParent}}"
```

There are some significant advantages in using the latter syntax based on a regular Binding, because you can take advantage of all the usual Binding niceties, like value conversion if the values of the source and the destination are incompatible, and binding direction settings to control the flow of data between the two.

You may be wondering at this point which to use in control templating scenarios and when. Our general guidance is to use the regular Binding syntax with RelativeSource set to TemplatedParent whenever possible, as this gives you a much richer programming model and better control on the binding as mentioned above. There is a supposed minimal performance gain in using TemplateBinding over a regular Binding, but we have not seen any noticeable difference in a decent-sized control template (one with 10 to 30 template bindings) versus a similar number of regular bindings with RelativeSource.TemplatedParent.

The rest of the functionality of the custom control can be implemented using familiar concepts such as dependency properties, events, methods, and control template design. The only other concept that is of paramount importance in custom control authoring is that of visual states. For more on visual states from a control consumer's perspective, refer to recipe 5-2 in this chapter. We are going to discuss visual state management in more detail from a control author's perspective in the next recipe. In the code sample for this recipe, we deliberately do not deal with visual states in an effort to simplify the example.

The Code

The code sample for this recipe illustrates the basic custom control concepts by implementing a ProgressBar control.

■**Note** The Silverlight control framework includes a ProgressBar control, and we in no way claim that you should use this implementation over the framework-supplied one. We chose this purely as a way to show you how to write a custom control, and we hope that purpose will be served here.

Listing 5-25 shows the generic.xaml for the ProgressBar control default UI.

Listing 5-25. *generic.xaml for ProgressBar*

```xml
<ResourceDictionary
xmlns="http://schemas.microsoft.com/winfx/2006/xaml/presentation"
xmlns:x="http://schemas.microsoft.com/winfx/2006/xaml"
xmlns:local="clr-namespace:Ch05_Controls.Recipe5_10">

  <local:OrientationToTransformConverter
    x:Key="REF_OrientationToTransformConverter" />

  <ControlTemplate TargetType="local:ProgressBar" x:Key="ctProgressBar">
    <Grid RenderTransformOrigin="0.5,0.5"
          x:Name="LayoutRoot"
          RenderTransform="{Binding Orientation,
            RelativeSource={RelativeSource TemplatedParent},
            Converter={StaticResource REF_OrientationToTransformConverter}}">
      <Rectangle Fill="{TemplateBinding Background}"
                 Stroke="Transparent" HorizontalAlignment="Stretch"
                 VerticalAlignment="Stretch" x:Name="rectBackground"/>
      <Rectangle x:Name="elemPBar"
                 Fill="{TemplateBinding Foreground}"
                 Stroke="Transparent"
                 VerticalAlignment="Stretch"
                 Width="0" HorizontalAlignment="Left"/>
      <ContentPresenter
        ContentTemplate="{TemplateBinding ContentTemplate}"
        Content="{TemplateBinding Content}"
        HorizontalAlignment="{TemplateBinding HorizontalContentAlignment}"
        VerticalAlignment="{TemplateBinding VerticalContentAlignment}"/>
    </Grid>
  </ControlTemplate>

  <Style TargetType="local:ProgressBar">
    <Setter Property="Template" Value="{StaticResource ctProgressBar}"/>
    <Setter Property="Height" Value="30" />
    <Setter Property="Width" Value="200" />
    <Setter Property="MaximumValue" Value="100" />
    <Setter Property="MinimumValue" Value="0" />
    <Setter Property="Orientation"
            Value="Horizontal" />
    <Setter Property="Foreground" >
      <Setter.Value>
        <LinearGradientBrush EndPoint="0.5,1" StartPoint="0.5,0">
          <GradientStop Color="#FF0040FF"/>
```

```
            <GradientStop Color="#FF8FA8F5" Offset="1"/>
          </LinearGradientBrush>
        </Setter.Value>
      </Setter>
      <Setter Property="Background" Value="White" />
    </Style>

</ResourceDictionary>
```

The control template ctProgressBar is made up of two Rectangles, one acting as a background for the control, and the other, named elemPBar, acting as the progress meter with its initial Width set to 0. This is the named template part that we acquire in our code later, and we'll change the Width based on CurrentValue.

We would like the user to have the ability to place content such as the current progress amount inside the control. We would also like users to be able to associate a data template with the control, and thus to define how any content should be formatted. So as you will see when we discuss the control code, our control class will extend ContentControl, and we include a ContentPresenter with the appropriate TemplateBindings in place. For some background on the control content model and TemplateBinding, refer to recipe 5-2.

Also note the resource declaration of a type named OrientationToTransformConverter and a binding setting on the RenderTransform property of the Grid LayoutRoot. We will revisit these in a little bit.

The style targeted to the ProgressBar control is what allows us to associate this template with the DefaultStyleKey property in code.

Listing 5-26 shows the control code.

Listing 5-26. *ProgressBar Control Code*

```
using System.Windows;
using System.Windows.Controls;
using System.Windows.Shapes;
using System.ComponentModel;

namespace Ch05_Controls.Recipe5_10
{
  [TemplatePart(Name="elemPBar",Type=typeof(FrameworkElement))]
  public class ProgressBar : ContentControl
  {
    public static DependencyProperty CurrentValueProperty =
      DependencyProperty.Register("CurrentValue",
      typeof(double), typeof(ProgressBar),
      new PropertyMetadata(0.0,
        new PropertyChangedCallback(ProgressBar.OnCurrentValueChanged)));
    public double CurrentValue
    {
      get { return (double)GetValue(CurrentValueProperty); }
      set { SetValue(CurrentValueProperty, value); }
    }
```

```
public static DependencyProperty MaximumValueProperty =
  DependencyProperty.Register("MaximumValue",
  typeof(double), typeof(ProgressBar), new PropertyMetadata(100.0));
public double MaximumValue
{
  get { return (double)GetValue(MaximumValueProperty); }
  set { SetValue(MaximumValueProperty, value); }
}
public static DependencyProperty MinimumValueProperty =
  DependencyProperty.Register("MinimumValue",
  typeof(double), typeof(ProgressBar), new PropertyMetadata(0.0));
public double MinimumValue
{
  get { return (double)GetValue(MinimumValueProperty); }
  set { SetValue(MinimumValueProperty, value); }    }


public Orientation Orientation
{
  get { return (Orientation)GetValue(OrientationProperty); }
  set { SetValue(OrientationProperty, value); }
}

public static readonly DependencyProperty OrientationProperty =
    DependencyProperty.Register("Orientation",
    typeof(Orientation), typeof(ProgressBar),
    new PropertyMetadata(Orientation.Horizontal));


internal FrameworkElement elemPBar { get; set; }

public ProgressBar()
{
  base.DefaultStyleKey = typeof(ProgressBar);
}

public override void OnApplyTemplate()
{
  base.OnApplyTemplate();
  elemPBar = this.GetTemplateChild("elemPBar") as FrameworkElement;
}
```

```
    internal static void OnCurrentValueChanged(DependencyObject Target,
      DependencyPropertyChangedEventArgs e)
    {
      ProgressBar pBar = Target as ProgressBar;
      if (pBar.elemPBar != null)
      {
        pBar.elemPBar.Width = (pBar.ActualWidth * (double)e.NewValue)
          / (pBar.MaximumValue - pBar.MinimumValue);
      }


    }


  }
}
```

As Listing 5-26 shows, our ProgressBar control exposes three dependency properties all of type double: MaximumValue and MinimumValue, which indicate the range of progress, and CurrentValue, which indicates the current progress at any instant. As you can see in the constructor, we load the default UI by setting the DefaultStyleKey property to the type of the ProgressBar control itself, which, as we discussed earlier, will load the style targeted to this control type from generic.xaml defined in Listing 5-25. In OnApplyTemplate(), we try to acquire a reference to a template part named elemPBar as a FrameworkElement and store it. Note that, in the template in Listing 5-25, the template part is defined as a Rectangle, but we expect it to be any derivative of FrameworkElement in our code, since all we need is the Width property.

Accordingly, we also decorate the ProgressBar class with a TemplatePartAttribute appropriately initialized.

In the property change callback for the CurrentValue dependency property, we check to see if we indeed have access to a template named elemPBar. If we do, we set the Width property of that FrameworkElement to a ratio of the CurrentValue, available through the NewValue property of the DependencyPropertyChangedEventArgs parameter, to the range of the ProgressBar instance.

Also note the Orientation DependencyProperty defined on the control. We want the ProgressBar to be displayed either horizontally or vertically depending on the Orientation setting. An easy way of doing this would be to apply a RotateTransform of –90 degrees to the entire ProgressBar whenever the Orientation changes to Vertical. To facilitate that, we first define a value converter that accepts an Orientation and returns a Transform. Listing 5-27 shows the code for this value converter.

Listing 5-27. *Value Converter to Convert Orientation to a RotateTransform*

```
using System;
using System.Windows.Controls;
using System.Windows.Data;
using System.Windows.Media;
```

```
namespace Ch05_Controls.Recipe5_10
{
  public class OrientationToTransformConverter : IValueConverter
  {
    public object Convert(object value, Type targetType,
      object parameter, System.Globalization.CultureInfo culture)
    {
      //check to see that the parameter types are conformant
      if (value == null || !(value is Orientation) ||
        targetType != typeof(Transform))
        return null;
      if ((Orientation)value == Orientation.Horizontal)
      {
        return new RotateTransform() { Angle = 0 };
      }
      else
      {
        return new RotateTransform() { Angle = -90 };
      }

    }


    public object ConvertBack(object value, Type targetType,
      object parameter, System.Globalization.CultureInfo culture)
    {
      throw new NotImplementedException();
    }
  }
}
```

If you refer to the control template XAML in Listing 5-25, you will see that the RenderTransform property on the outermost Grid named LayoutRoot is now bound to the Orientation property on the control using a regular binding with RelativeSource set to TemplatedParent, and using the OrientationToTransformConveter from Listing 5-27. Had we used a TemplateBinding instead, we would not have the ability to use the value converter the way we did here.

Using the Control

To use our code, we build a small application that downloads all the photos in the ProductPhotos table through the AdventureWorks WCF service discussed at the beginning of this chapter. We use the WebClient type to download the photos. For more on the WebClient, see recipe 7-4.

We display the photos in a ListBox and use the WrapPanel we created in recipe 5-10 to lay out the photos. We use ProgressBar controls to display the individual download progress of each photo, and another one for overall progress.

Listing 5-28 shows the XAML for our test page.

Listing 5-28. *XAML for the MainPage Hosting the Photo ListBox*

```xml
<UserControl x:Class="Ch05_Controls.Recipe5_10.MainPage"
    xmlns="http://schemas.microsoft.com/winfx/2006/xaml/presentation"
    xmlns:x="http://schemas.microsoft.com/winfx/2006/xaml"
    xmlns:custom=
"clr-namespace:Ch05_Controls.Recipe5_10;assembly=Ch05_Controls.Recipe5_10.PBarLib"
    xmlns:wrap=
"clr-namespace:Ch05_Controls.Recipe5_9;assembly=Ch05_Controls.Recipe5_9.WrapPanel"
    Width="700" Height="500">
  <UserControl.Resources>
    <DataTemplate x:Key="dtImageDisplay">
      <Border BorderBrush="Black" Padding="3,3,3,3"
            BorderThickness="2,2,2,2" CornerRadius="2,2,2,2">
        <Grid>
          <Image Source="{Binding PngImage}" Height="75"
                Width="75" Stretch="Uniform"
                Visibility="{Binding ImageVisible}"/>
          <custom:ProgressBar Height="25" Width="70" Margin="2,0,2,0"
                        CurrentValue="{Binding DownloadProgress}"
                        Content="{Binding DownloadProgress}"
                        Visibility="{Binding ProgBarVisible}"
                        MaximumValue="100" MinimumValue="0"
                        HorizontalAlignment="Center"
                        VerticalAlignment="Center"
                        HorizontalContentAlignment="Left"
                        VerticalContentAlignment="Center">
            <custom:ProgressBar.ContentTemplate>
              <DataTemplate>
                <StackPanel Orientation="Horizontal">
                  <TextBlock FontSize="10" Text="Downloaded" Margin="0,0,2,0"/>
                  <TextBlock FontSize="10" Text="{Binding}" Margin="0,0,2,0"/>
                  <TextBlock FontSize="10" Text="%" />
                </StackPanel>
              </DataTemplate>
            </custom:ProgressBar.ContentTemplate>
          </custom:ProgressBar>
        </Grid>
      </Border>
    </DataTemplate>
```

```xml
<ControlTemplate TargetType="custom:ProgressBar" x:Key="ctCustomProgressBar">
  <Grid>
    <Border Background="{TemplateBinding Background}"
            BorderBrush="Black"
            HorizontalAlignment="Stretch" CornerRadius="5,5,5,5"
            VerticalAlignment="Stretch"/>
    <Border x:Name="elemPBar"
            Background="{TemplateBinding Foreground}"
            BorderBrush="Transparent"
            VerticalAlignment="Stretch" CornerRadius="5,5,5,5"
            Width="0" HorizontalAlignment="Left"/>
    <ContentPresenter
    ContentTemplate="{TemplateBinding ContentTemplate}"
    Content="{TemplateBinding Content}"
    HorizontalAlignment="{TemplateBinding HorizontalContentAlignment}"
    VerticalAlignment="{TemplateBinding VerticalContentAlignment}"
    HorizontalContentAlignment="{TemplateBinding HorizontalContentAlignment}"
    VerticalContentAlignment="{TemplateBinding VerticalContentAlignment}"
    Foreground="Black"/>
  </Grid>
</ControlTemplate>

<Style TargetType="custom:ProgressBar" x:Key="STYLE_CustomProgressBar" >
  <Setter Property="Template" Value="{StaticResource ctCustomProgressBar}"/>
  <Setter Property="Foreground" >
    <Setter.Value>
      <LinearGradientBrush EndPoint="0.5,1" StartPoint="0.5,0">
        <GradientStop Color="#FF0040FF"/>
        <GradientStop Color="#FF8FA8F5" Offset="1"/>
      </LinearGradientBrush>
    </Setter.Value>
  </Setter>
  <Setter Property="Background" Value="White" />
</Style>

</UserControl.Resources>
<Grid x:Name="LayoutRoot" Background="White">
  <Grid.RowDefinitions>
    <RowDefinition Height="*"/>
    <RowDefinition Height="Auto"/>

  </Grid.RowDefinitions>
```

```xml
<ListBox ItemTemplate="{StaticResource dtImageDisplay}" x:Name="lbxImages" >
  <ListBox.ItemsPanel>
    <ItemsPanelTemplate>
      <wrap:WrapPanel Orientation="Horizontal" Height="1300" Width="700"/>
    </ItemsPanelTemplate>
  </ListBox.ItemsPanel>
</ListBox>
<custom:ProgressBar x:Name="pbarOverallProgress " Height="40" Width="600"
                    CurrentValue="{Binding ImageCount}"
                    Grid.Row="1" Margin="0,10,0,0"
                    MaximumValue="{Binding TotalImages}"
                    MinimumValue="0"
                    Content="{Binding}"
                    Style="{StaticResource STYLE_CustomProgressBar}"
                    HorizontalAlignment="Center" VerticalAlignment="Center"
                    HorizontalContentAlignment="Center"
                    VerticalContentAlignment="Center">
  <custom:ProgressBar.ContentTemplate>
    <DataTemplate>
      <StackPanel Orientation="Horizontal">
        <TextBlock FontSize="13" Text="Downloaded" Margin="0,0,2,0"/>
        <TextBlock FontSize="13" Text="{Binding ImageCount}"
                   Margin="0,0,2,0"/>
        <TextBlock FontSize="13" Text="of" Margin="0,0,2,0"/>
        <TextBlock FontSize="13" Text="{Binding TotalImages}"
                   Margin="0,0,2,0"/>
        <TextBlock FontSize="13" Text="images" />
      </StackPanel>
    </DataTemplate>
  </custom:ProgressBar.ContentTemplate>
</custom:ProgressBar>


  </Grid>
</UserControl>
```

As you can see, we use a data template named dtImageDisplay to display the images as items in our ListBox lbxImages. dtImageDisplay includes an Image control and a ProgressBar control. Image.Source is bound to the PngImage property of the current data item. The MinimumValue and MaximumValue properties on ProgressBar are set to a range of 0 to 100 to indicate a percentage value of progress, and the CurrentValue is bound to the DownloadProgress property of the current data item. The Content property on the ProgressBar is also bound to the DownloadProgress value, and a ContentTemplate is defined for the ProgressBar so that the DownloadProgress is displayed in a TextBlock within the ContentTemplate. The Visibility properties of both the Image and the ProgressBar controls are bound to two properties on the current data item as well.

The pbarOverallProgress Progressbar is set with its CurrentValue bound to the ImageCount property and its MaximumValue bound to the TotalImages property of the DataContext of the LayoutRoot

Grid. We again define an appropriate ContentTemplate to display the overall progress of our download in terms of the number of images downloaded.

Also note that we define a custom control template for the ProgressBar control and associate it with pbarOverallProgress through a style. In this template, we use Borders with rounded corners to replace the Rectangles used in the default template. Since we satisfy the named template part requirement, and both Border and Rectangle extend FrameworkElement (which is what we expect in our control code), our control continues to work fine with this new control template.

Listing 5-29 shows the code-behind for the page.

Listing 5-29. *Code-Behind for the Page Populating the Photo ListBox*

```
using System;
using System.Collections.ObjectModel;
using System.ComponentModel;
using System.IO;
using System.Net;
using System.Threading;
using System.Windows;
using System.Windows.Controls;
using System.Windows.Media.Imaging;
using System.Xml.Linq;
using Ch05_Controls.Recipe5_10.AdvWorks;

namespace Ch05_Controls.Recipe5_10
{
  public partial class MainPage : UserControl
  {
    AdvWorksDataServiceClient client =
      new AdvWorksDataServiceClient();

    private const string DownloadSvcUri =
      "http://localhost:9191/AdvWorksPhotoService.svc/Photos?Id={0}";

    internal TotalDownloadCounter TotalDownloadData = null;

    internal ObservableCollection<ImageData> listImages =
      new ObservableCollection<ImageData>();

    public MainPage()
    {
      InitializeComponent();
      GetPhotos();
    }
```

```
private void GetPhotos()
{
  listImages.Clear();
  lbxImages.ItemsSource = listImages;

  client.GetPhotoIdsCompleted +=
    new EventHandler<GetPhotoIdsCompletedEventArgs>(
      delegate(object sender, GetPhotoIdsCompletedEventArgs e)
      {
        TotalDownloadData =
          new TotalDownloadCounter
          {
            ImageCount = 0,
            TotalImages = e.Result.Count
          };
        LayoutRoot.DataContext = TotalDownloadData;
        foreach (int PhotoId in e.Result)
        {
          ImageData TempImageData =
            new ImageData
            {
              DownloadProgress = 0,
              ImageVisible = Visibility.Collapsed,
              ProgBarVisible = Visibility.Visible,
              PngImage = new BitmapImage()
            };

          listImages.Add(TempImageData);
          DownloadPhoto(PhotoId, TempImageData);
        }
      });
  client.GetPhotoIdsAsync();
}
private void DownloadPhoto(int PhotoId, ImageData TempImageData)
{
  WebClient wc = new WebClient();
  wc.DownloadProgressChanged +=
    new DownloadProgressChangedEventHandler(
      delegate(object sender, DownloadProgressChangedEventArgs e)
      {
        (e.UserState as ImageData).DownloadProgress = e.ProgressPercentage;
        Thread.Sleep(5);
      });
```

466

```csharp
      wc.DownloadStringCompleted +=
        new DownloadStringCompletedEventHandler(
          delegate(object sender, DownloadStringCompletedEventArgs e)
          {
            ImageData ImgSource = e.UserState as ImageData;
            //parse XML formatted response string into an XDocument
            XDocument xDoc = XDocument.Parse(e.Result);
            //grab the root, and decode the default base64
            //representation into the image bytes
            byte[] Buff = Convert.FromBase64String((string)xDoc.Root);
            //wrap in a memory stream, and
            MemoryStream ms = new MemoryStream(Buff);
            ImgSource.PngImage.SetSource(ms);
            ms.Close();
            (e.UserState as ImageData).ProgBarVisible = Visibility.Collapsed;
            (e.UserState as ImageData).ImageVisible = Visibility.Visible;
            ++TotalDownloadData.ImageCount;
          });

      wc.DownloadStringAsync(new Uri(
        string.Format(DownloadSvcUri, PhotoId)), TempImageData);
    }
  }

public class TotalDownloadCounter : INotifyPropertyChanged
{
  public event PropertyChangedEventHandler PropertyChanged;
  private double _TotalImages;
  public double TotalImages
  {
    get { return _TotalImages; }
    set
    {
      _TotalImages = value;
      if (PropertyChanged != null)
        PropertyChanged(this, new PropertyChangedEventArgs("TotalImages"));
    }
  }
```

```csharp
    private double _ImageCount;
    public double ImageCount
    {
      get { return _ImageCount; }
      set
      {
        _ImageCount = value;
        if (PropertyChanged != null)
          PropertyChanged(this, new PropertyChangedEventArgs("ImageCount"));
      }
    }
}

public class ImageData : INotifyPropertyChanged
{
  public event PropertyChangedEventHandler PropertyChanged;
  private double _DownloadProgress;
  public double DownloadProgress
  {
    get { return _DownloadProgress; }
    set
    {
      _DownloadProgress = value;
      if (PropertyChanged != null)
        PropertyChanged(this, new PropertyChangedEventArgs("DownloadProgress"));
    }
  }
  private Visibility _ImageVisible;
  public Visibility ImageVisible
  {
    get { return _ImageVisible; }
    set
    {
      _ImageVisible = value;
      if (PropertyChanged != null)
        PropertyChanged(this, new PropertyChangedEventArgs("ImageVisible"));
    }
  }
```

```
      private Visibility _ProgBarVisible;
      public Visibility ProgBarVisible
      {
        get { return _ProgBarVisible; }
        set
        {
          _ProgBarVisible = value;
          if (PropertyChanged != null)
            PropertyChanged(this, new PropertyChangedEventArgs("ProgBarVisible"));
        }
      }
      private BitmapImage _PngImage;
      public BitmapImage PngImage
      {
        get { return _PngImage; }
        set
        {
          _PngImage = value;
          if (PropertyChanged != null)
            PropertyChanged(this, new PropertyChangedEventArgs("PngImage"));
        }
      }
    }
  }
}
```

Instances of the TotalDownloadCounter and the ImageData types serve as the data sources for various bindings in our XAML in Listing 5-28.

In the GetData() method, we first get all the photo IDs through the GetPhotoIds() service operation. On completion. we initialize a new instance of TotalDownloadCounter and set the DataContext on LayoutRoot. We then iterate over the photo IDs and use the DownloadPhoto() method to download the photo. We create and initialize an ImageData instance so that the individual ProgressBar in the photo data template is visible, add it to the collection data source bound to the ListBox, and pass it to DownloadPhoto().

In DownloadPhoto(), we handle the DownloadProgressChanged event on the WebClient and update the DownloadProgress property of the ImageData instance, which causes each individual ProgressBar to report the download progress of that photo. Once the download is completed, we handle DownloadStringCompleted, where we convert the downloaded Base64 encoded string into an image and set the PngImage property to display the image. We also hide the individual ProgressBar and display the Image by setting the appropriately bound Visibility properties. Finally, we increment the TotalDownloadData.ImageCount so the pbarOverallProgress reports the number of full images downloaded so far.

To test the Orientation property of the ProgressBar control that we discussed earlier, simply set the Orientation property on the individual ProgressBar controls in the dtImageDisplay data template shown in Listing 5-28 to Vertical.

Figure 5-25 shows the user interface for the sample.

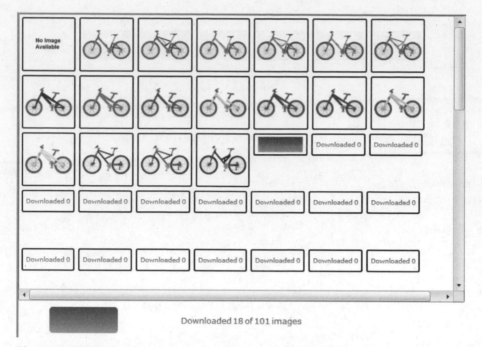

Figure 5-25. *Displaying a progress bar when downloading photos*

5-11. Defining a Custom Visual State

Problem

You want to define a custom visual state in a custom control that you are creating.

Solution

Use the `TemplateVisualStateAttribute` to declare the custom visual state on the control, define storyboards for the states in the control template, and then use `VisualStateManager.GoToState()` to navigate to the state when appropriate.

How It Works

As we mentioned in recipe 5-2, a visual state is identified by its `x:Name` attribute value and its membership is specified in a named group of states. And you also saw that a visual state is implemented in terms of a storyboard inside the control template for the control. For detailed background information on how you might be able to use them while consuming a control, see recipe 5-2. In this recipe, we discuss how to add your own visual state definition to a custom control.

The TemplateVisualStateAttribute type is the mechanism you use to add a visual state to your custom control implementation, where you specify the name and group membership of the state. This code snippet shows an example of adding two visual states to a custom control type named Expander:

```
[TemplateVisualState(Name = "Expanded", GroupName = "ExpanderStates")]
[TemplateVisualState(Name = "Normal", GroupName = "CommonStates")]
public class Expander : ContentControl
{

}
```

Note that the TemplateVisualState attribute declarations are purely suggestive in nature and are not required in order for visual states to work correctly. They help in providing information to the developer and to tools like Expression Blend (through .NET reflection) as to what visual states and state groups are expected by the control in its control template.

The System.Windows.VisualStateManager type is central to how visual states work. You use the VisualStateManager.GoToState() static method in appropriate places in your code where you might want to navigate the control to that state. The following code snippet shows an example where we are navigating to the Expanded state on a specific event handler inside a control's implementation:

```
void btnToggler_Checked(object sender, RoutedEventArgs e)
{
  VisualStateManager.GoToState(this, "Expanded", true);
}
```

The first parameter to GoToState() is the control instance itself, and the last parameter, if set to true, instructs the VisualStateManager to use any transitions defined in the control template; if it's set to false, transitions are ignored.

The Code

The code sample implements an Expander custom control with a header and body area, each with their own content and content template options. The default template also defines a Systems.Windows. Controls.Primitives.ToggleButton used to expand and contract the body of the Expander. The ToggleButton type is the base class for multistate buttons like CheckBox and RadioButton and exposes Checked and Unchecked states.

Listing 5-30 shows the control implementation for Expander.

Listing 5-30. *Expander Control Code*

```
using System.Windows;
using System.Windows.Controls;
using System.Windows.Controls.Primitives;

namespace Ch05_Controls.Recipe5_11
{
  [TemplateVisualState(Name = "Expanded", GroupName = "ExpanderStates")]
  [TemplateVisualState(Name = "Normal", GroupName = "CommonStates")]
  public class Expander : ContentControl
```

```
{

  public static DependencyProperty HeaderContentProperty =
    DependencyProperty.Register("HeaderContent", typeof(object),
    typeof(Expander),
    new PropertyMetadata(null));
  public object HeaderContent
  {
    get
    {
      return GetValue(HeaderContentProperty);
    }
    set
    {
      SetValue(HeaderContentProperty, value);
    }
  }

  public static DependencyProperty HeaderContentTemplateProperty =
    DependencyProperty.Register("HeaderContentTemplate", typeof(DataTemplate),
    typeof(Expander),
    new PropertyMetadata(null));
  public object HeaderContentTemplate
  {
    get
    {
      return (DataTemplate)GetValue(HeaderContentTemplateProperty);
    }
    set
    {
      SetValue(HeaderContentTemplateProperty, value);
    }
  }

  private ToggleButton btnToggler;

  public Expander()
  {
    base.DefaultStyleKey = typeof(Expander);
  }
  public override void OnApplyTemplate()
  {
    base.OnApplyTemplate();
    btnToggler = GetTemplateChild("toggler") as ToggleButton;
    if (btnToggler != null)
```

```
    {
      btnToggler.Checked += new RoutedEventHandler(btnToggler_Checked);
      btnToggler.Unchecked += new RoutedEventHandler(btnToggler_Unchecked);
    }
  }

  void btnToggler_Unchecked(object sender, RoutedEventArgs e)
  {
    VisualStateManager.GoToState(this, "Normal", true);
  }

  void btnToggler_Checked(object sender, RoutedEventArgs e)
  {
    VisualStateManager.GoToState(this, "Expanded", true);
  }

  }
}
```

You can see the definitions for the two visual states Expanded and Normal in Listing 5-30. In OnApplyTemplate(), we try to acquire the ToggleButton that we expect to be in the template. If we do, we attach handlers to the Checked and Unchecked events. In the btnToggler_Checked() handler, we navigate to the Expanded visual state, and in the btnToggler_Unchecked() handler, we navigate back to the Normal visual state.

As far as the control implementation goes, this is all we need to do to enable the visual states. The rest of the control's code is to support the Expander functionality. The two dependency properties HeaderContent and HeaderContentTemplate are defined to give the user an opportunity to provide content and define a data template for the Header part of the control. The Content and the ContentTemplate properties that the control inherits from ContentControl serve the same purpose for Expander body.

Listing 5-31 shows generic.xaml for the Expander.

Listing 5-31. *generic.xaml for the Expander Control*

```xml
<ResourceDictionary
  xmlns="http://schemas.microsoft.com/winfx/2006/xaml/presentation"
  xmlns:x="http://schemas.microsoft.com/winfx/2006/xaml"
  xmlns:local="clr-namespace:Ch05_Controls.Recipe5_11"
 xmlns:vsm="clr-namespace:System.Windows;assembly=System.Windows"
  >
  <ControlTemplate TargetType="ToggleButton" x:Key="ctExpanderToggle">
    <Grid>
      <Grid.RowDefinitions>
        <RowDefinition Height="0.3*" />
        <RowDefinition Height="0.4*" />
        <RowDefinition Height="0.3*" />
      </Grid.RowDefinitions>
```

```xml
        <Grid.ColumnDefinitions>
          <ColumnDefinition Width="0.3*" />
          <ColumnDefinition Width="0.4*" />
          <ColumnDefinition Width="0.3*" />
        </Grid.ColumnDefinitions>
        <vsm:VisualStateManager.VisualStateGroups>
          <vsm:VisualStateGroup x:Name="CommonStates">
            <vsm:VisualStateGroup.Transitions>
              <vsm:VisualTransition GeneratedDuration="00:00:00.2000000"
                                    To="MouseOver"/>
              <vsm:VisualTransition GeneratedDuration="00:00:00" From="MouseOver"/>
            </vsm:VisualStateGroup.Transitions>
            <vsm:VisualState x:Name="Normal">
              <Storyboard/>
            </vsm:VisualState>
            <vsm:VisualState x:Name="MouseOver">
              <Storyboard>
                <ColorAnimationUsingKeyFrames BeginTime="00:00:00"
                Duration="00:00:00.0010000"
                Storyboard.TargetName="Path"
                Storyboard.TargetProperty="(Shape.Fill).(SolidColorBrush.Color)">
                  <SplineColorKeyFrame KeyTime="00:00:00" Value="#FF000000"/>
                </ColorAnimationUsingKeyFrames>
              </Storyboard>
            </vsm:VisualState>

          </vsm:VisualStateGroup>

        </vsm:VisualStateManager.VisualStateGroups>
        <Path x:Name="Path" Stretch="Fill" Fill="#FF054B4A"
          Data="F1 M 15.1257,30.0726L 30.1081,0L 0,0.0718536L 15.1257,30.0726 Z "
          RenderTransformOrigin="0.5,0.5" Grid.Row="1" Grid.Column="1"/>
      </Grid>
    </ControlTemplate>

    <Style x:Key="styleExpanderToggle" TargetType="ToggleButton">
      <Setter Property="Template" Value="{StaticResource ctExpanderToggle}"/>
    </Style>
```

```xml
<ControlTemplate x:Key="ctExpander" TargetType="local:Expander">
  <Grid HorizontalAlignment="{TemplateBinding HorizontalAlignment}"
        VerticalAlignment="{TemplateBinding VerticalAlignment}">
    <vsm:VisualStateManager.VisualStateGroups>
      <vsm:VisualStateGroup x:Name="ExpanderStates">
        <vsm:VisualStateGroup.Transitions>
          <vsm:VisualTransition GeneratedDuration="00:00:00.2000000"
                                To="Expanded"/>
          <vsm:VisualTransition GeneratedDuration="00:00:00.2000000"
                                From="Expanded"/>
        </vsm:VisualStateGroup.Transitions>
        <vsm:VisualState x:Name="Normal">
          <Storyboard/>
        </vsm:VisualState>
        <vsm:VisualState x:Name="Expanded">
          <Storyboard>
            <ObjectAnimationUsingKeyFrames BeginTime="00:00:00"
                                Duration="00:00:00.0010000"
                                Storyboard.TargetName="Body"
                                Storyboard.TargetProperty="Visibility">
              <DiscreteObjectKeyFrame KeyTime="0">
                <DiscreteObjectKeyFrame.Value>
                  <Visibility>Visible</Visibility>
                </DiscreteObjectKeyFrame.Value>
              </DiscreteObjectKeyFrame>
            </ObjectAnimationUsingKeyFrames>
          </Storyboard>
        </vsm:VisualState>
      </vsm:VisualStateGroup>
    </vsm:VisualStateManager.VisualStateGroups>
    <Grid.RowDefinitions>
      <RowDefinition Height="0.2*"/>
      <RowDefinition Height="0.8*"/>
    </Grid.RowDefinitions>
    <Border Height="Auto" Margin="0,0,0,0" VerticalAlignment="Stretch"
            Grid.Row="0" BorderThickness="2,2,2,2" BorderBrush="#FF000000"
            x:Name="Header">
      <Border.Background>
        <LinearGradientBrush EndPoint="0.5,1" StartPoint="0.5,0">
          <GradientStop Color="#FF0BC4C3"/>
          <GradientStop Color="#FF055352" Offset="1"/>
        </LinearGradientBrush>
      </Border.Background>
```

```xml
      <Grid>
        <Grid.ColumnDefinitions>
          <ColumnDefinition Width="0.80*"/>
          <ColumnDefinition Width="0.20*"/>
        </Grid.ColumnDefinitions>
        <ToggleButton HorizontalAlignment="Center" VerticalAlignment="Center"
                      Content="ToggleButton" Margin="2,2,2,2" Grid.Column="1"
                      Style="{StaticResource styleExpanderToggle}"
                      x:Name="toggler" >
        </ToggleButton>
        <ContentPresenter HorizontalAlignment="Center"
                          VerticalAlignment="Center"
        Content="{TemplateBinding HeaderContent}"
        ContentTemplate="{TemplateBinding HeaderContentTemplate}"
        x:Name="cpHdr"/>
      </Grid>
    </Border>
    <Border Height="Auto" Margin="0,0,0,0" VerticalAlignment="Stretch"
            Grid.Row="1" Background="#FFFFFFFF"
            BorderThickness="2,0,2,2" BorderBrush="#FF000000"
            x:Name="Body"
            Visibility="Collapsed">
      <ContentPresenter HorizontalAlignment="Stretch"
                        VerticalAlignment="Stretch"
                        Content="{TemplateBinding Content}"
                        ContentTemplate="{TemplateBinding ContentTemplate}"
                        x:Name="cpBody"/>
    </Border>
  </Grid>

</ControlTemplate>
<Style TargetType="local:Expander">
  <Setter Property="HeaderContent" Value="Header here" />
  <Setter Property="HeaderContentTemplate">
    <Setter.Value>
      <DataTemplate>
        <TextBlock Text="{Binding}" />
      </DataTemplate>
    </Setter.Value>
  </Setter>
```

```xml
    <Setter Property="Content" Value="Body here" />
    <Setter Property="ContentTemplate">
      <Setter.Value>
        <DataTemplate>
          <TextBlock Text="{Binding}" />
        </DataTemplate>
      </Setter.Value>
    </Setter>
    <Setter Property="Template" Value="{StaticResource ctExpander}" />
  </Style>
</ResourceDictionary>
```

The ctExpander control template is made up of two primary parts: the header and the body. The header portion contains a Border named Header, a ContentPresenter named cpHdr, and a ToggleButton named toggler. cpHdr has its Content and ContentTemplate properties bound to the HeaderContent and the HeaderContentTemplate dependency properties, respectively, on the control. The body contains a Border named Body, within which is another ContentPresenter cpBody with its Content and ContentTemplate properties bound to the identical properties on the Expander control itself. The Border named Body has its initial visibility set to Collapsed. We also apply a custom template to the ToggleButton to fix its content to a Path representing a directional arrow pointing downward and include a specific MouseOver state to vary the color.

In ctExpander, you can also see the Expanded visual state defined as a storyboard, in which we use an ObjectAnimation to transition Body to a Visible state. Note that this is the default implementation of the state storyboard as defined by the original control author in the default template.

If we were to use the Expander control as defined here on a page, we would see the output as shown in Figure 5-26, which shows the Expander both in its Normal and Expanded states.

Figure 5-26. *Expander control using default UI in Normal and Expanded states*

Now, let's say we want to rotate the ToggleButton directional arrow to point upward when the body is expanded, to provide a visual cue to the user that the body will be Collapsed again on the next click of the ToggleButton. We want to do this without changing the control, but by providing a custom template when we use the control. Listing 5-32 shows an XAML page where we create a copy of the Expander control template and add an additional animation to the Expanded visual state to achieve this.

Listing 5-32. *Addition to the Expanded Visual State Through a Custom Template*

```xml
<UserControl x:Class="Ch05_Controls.Recipe5_11.MainPage"
    xmlns="http://schemas.microsoft.com/winfx/2006/xaml/presentation"
    xmlns:x="http://schemas.microsoft.com/winfx/2006/xaml"
    xmlns:exp=
"clr-namespace:Ch05_Controls.Recipe5_11;assembly=Ch05_Controls.Recipe5_11.ExpLib"
    xmlns:vsm="clr-namespace:System.Windows;assembly=System.Windows"
    Width="400" Height="300">
  <UserControl.Resources>
    <ControlTemplate TargetType="ToggleButton" x:Key="ctExpanderToggle">
      <Grid>
        <Grid.RowDefinitions>
          <RowDefinition Height="0.3*" />
          <RowDefinition Height="0.4*" />
          <RowDefinition Height="0.3*" />
        </Grid.RowDefinitions>
        <Grid.ColumnDefinitions>
          <ColumnDefinition Width="0.3*" />
          <ColumnDefinition Width="0.4*" />
          <ColumnDefinition Width="0.3*" />
        </Grid.ColumnDefinitions>
        <vsm:VisualStateManager.VisualStateGroups>
          <vsm:VisualStateGroup x:Name="CommonStates">
            <vsm:VisualStateGroup.Transitions>
              <vsm:VisualTransition GeneratedDuration="00:00:00.2000000"
                                    To="MouseOver"/>
              <vsm:VisualTransition GeneratedDuration="00:00:00" From="MouseOver"/>
            </vsm:VisualStateGroup.Transitions>
            <vsm:VisualState x:Name="Normal">
              <Storyboard/>
            </vsm:VisualState>
            <vsm:VisualState x:Name="MouseOver">
              <Storyboard>
                <ColorAnimationUsingKeyFrames BeginTime="00:00:00"
              Duration="00:00:00.0010000"
              Storyboard.TargetName="Path"
              Storyboard.TargetProperty="(Shape.Fill).(SolidColorBrush.Color)">
                  <SplineColorKeyFrame KeyTime="00:00:00" Value="#FF000000"/>
                </ColorAnimationUsingKeyFrames>
              </Storyboard>
            </vsm:VisualState>
          </vsm:VisualStateGroup>
        </vsm:VisualStateManager.VisualStateGroups>
```

```
        <Path x:Name="Path" Stretch="Fill" Fill="#FF054B4A"
        Data="F1 M 15.1257,30.0726L 30.1081,0L 0,0.0718536L 15.1257,30.0726 Z "
        RenderTransformOrigin="0.5,0.5" Grid.Row="1" Grid.Column="1"/>
     </Grid>
  </ControlTemplate>

  <Style x:Key="styleExpanderToggle" TargetType="ToggleButton">
     <Setter Property="Template" Value="{StaticResource ctExpanderToggle}"/>
  </Style>
  <ControlTemplate x:Key="ctCustomExpander" TargetType="exp:Expander">
     <Grid HorizontalAlignment="{TemplateBinding HorizontalAlignment}"
         VerticalAlignment="{TemplateBinding VerticalAlignment}">
       <vsm:VisualStateManager.VisualStateGroups>
         <vsm:VisualStateGroup x:Name="ExpanderStates">
           <vsm:VisualStateGroup.Transitions>
             <vsm:VisualTransition GeneratedDuration="00:00:00.2000000"
                                 To="Expanded"/>
             <vsm:VisualTransition GeneratedDuration="00:00:00.2000000"
                                 From="Expanded"/>
           </vsm:VisualStateGroup.Transitions>
           <vsm:VisualState x:Name="Normal">
             <Storyboard/>
           </vsm:VisualState>
           <vsm:VisualState x:Name="Expanded">
             <Storyboard>
                <DoubleAnimationUsingKeyFrames BeginTime="00:00:00"
                Duration="00:00:00.0010000"
                Storyboard.TargetName="toggler"
                Storyboard.TargetProperty=
"(UIElement.RenderTransform).(TransformGroup.Children)[2].(RotateTransform.Angle)">
                   <SplineDoubleKeyFrame KeyTime="00:00:00" Value="-180"/>
                </DoubleAnimationUsingKeyFrames>
                <ObjectAnimationUsingKeyFrames BeginTime="00:00:00"
                                Duration="00:00:00.0010000"
                                Storyboard.TargetName="Body"
                                Storyboard.TargetProperty="Visibility">
               <DiscreteObjectKeyFrame KeyTime="0">
                 <DiscreteObjectKeyFrame.Value>
                   <Visibility>Visible</Visibility>
                 </DiscreteObjectKeyFrame.Value>
               </DiscreteObjectKeyFrame>
              </ObjectAnimationUsingKeyFrames>
             </Storyboard>
           </vsm:VisualState>
         </vsm:VisualStateGroup>
       </vsm:VisualStateManager.VisualStateGroups>
```

```xml
<Grid.RowDefinitions>
  <RowDefinition Height="0.2*"/>
  <RowDefinition Height="0.8*"/>
</Grid.RowDefinitions>
<Border Height="Auto" Margin="0,0,0,0" VerticalAlignment="Stretch"
        Grid.Row="0" BorderThickness="2,2,2,2" BorderBrush="#FF000000"
        x:Name="Header">
  <Border.Background>
    <LinearGradientBrush EndPoint="0.5,1" StartPoint="0.5,0">
      <GradientStop Color="#FF0BC4C3"/>
      <GradientStop Color="#FF055352" Offset="1"/>
    </LinearGradientBrush>
  </Border.Background>
  <Grid>
    <Grid.ColumnDefinitions>
      <ColumnDefinition Width="0.80*"/>
      <ColumnDefinition Width="0.20*"/>
    </Grid.ColumnDefinitions>
    <ToggleButton HorizontalAlignment="Center" VerticalAlignment="Center"
                Content="ToggleButton" Margin="2,2,2,2" Grid.Column="1"
                Style="{StaticResource styleExpanderToggle}"
                x:Name="toggler" RenderTransformOrigin="0.5,0.5">
      <ToggleButton.RenderTransform>
        <TransformGroup>
          <ScaleTransform/>
          <SkewTransform/>
          <RotateTransform/>
          <TranslateTransform/>
        </TransformGroup>
      </ToggleButton.RenderTransform>
    </ToggleButton>
    <ContentPresenter HorizontalAlignment="Center"
                      VerticalAlignment="Center"
  Content="{TemplateBinding HeaderContent}"
  ContentTemplate="{TemplateBinding HeaderContentTemplate}"
  x:Name="cpHdr"/>
  </Grid>
</Border>
```

```
    <Border Height="Auto" Margin="0,0,0,0" VerticalAlignment="Stretch"
            Grid.Row="1" Background="#FFFFFFFF"
            BorderThickness="2,0,2,2" BorderBrush="#FF000000"
            x:Name="Body"
            Visibility="Collapsed">
        <ContentPresenter HorizontalAlignment="Stretch"
                    VerticalAlignment="Stretch"
                    Content="{TemplateBinding Content}"
                    ContentTemplate="{TemplateBinding ContentTemplate}"
                    x:Name="cpBody"/>
    </Border>
  </Grid>
</ControlTemplate>
<Style TargetType="exp:Expander" x:Key="STYLE_Expander">
  <Setter Property="Template" Value="{StaticResource ctCustomExpander}" />
</Style>

</UserControl.Resources>
  <Grid x:Name="LayoutRoot" Background="White">
  <exp:Expander Height="300" Width="200" Content="My Body"
              HeaderContent="My Header"
              Style="{StaticResource STYLE_Expander}" />
</Grid>
</UserControl>
```

As we mentioned before, in Listing 5-32, ctCustomExpander is a copy of the default control template for the Expander control. You can use Expression Blend to create a copy of a control template for a control. More on using Expression Blend for control templates is provided in recipe 5-2 in this chapter. The addition to note here is in the definition of the Expanded visual state in the ctCustomExpander control template, as well as in the Togglebutton named toggler. We add a TransformGroup to toggler and set its RenderTransformOrigin to (0.5,0.5). We then add an animation targeting toggler to the Expanded state storyboard to animate the angle of a RotateTransform on toggler to –180 degrees. This has the desired effect that we were seeking. Since the normal state defines no modifications to the template parts, the Togglebutton returns to its original downward-pointing state, once we move off of the Expanded state, by clicking it again to collapse the body. You can find more on animations in Chapter 3.

Also note that in both the default control template definition for the Expander in Listing 5-31 and in the custom control template definition for the same in Listing 5-32, we have left out several of the common state storyboard definitions for the ToggleButton, such as those for the Checked and Unchecked visual states. This is because, in our example, we do not need any specific visual cues to be provided to the user when these states occur. However, that does not mean that these states are not occurring at all. The ToggleButton control's code implementation does navigate to these states, but because of the lack of a storyboard definition in the templates, no corresponding visual state change occurs. Also note that we have defined the Normal visual state for the ToggleButton in both cases as an empty storyboard. We need this definition to allow visual state navigation to the initial normal visual state of the ToggleButton from any of our other visual states, like Expanded. Without this definition, once a visual state change took place, the Togglebutton control would never be able to return to its normal visual state.

Figure 5-27 shows the Expander control with the additions made to the Expanded visual state.

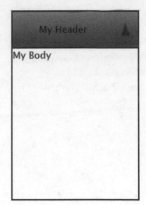

Figure 5-27. *Expander control with Expanded visual state additions through a custom template*

5-12. Controlling ScrollViewer Scroll Behavior

Problem

You want to programmatically control the scroll behavior of elements placed within a ScrollViewer control.

Solution

Traverse the visual tree to access the ScrollBars in the ScrollViewer, and handle ScrollBar.ValueChanged events to determine element positioning within the ScrollViewer.

How It Works

The System.Windows.Controls.ScrollViewer is a container control that can host content whose dimensions are much larger than the dimensions of the ScrollViewer itself. When the hosted content dimensions become larger in either Width or Height or both than the containing ScrollViewer, horizontal and vertical Scrollbars can be automatically displayed by the ScrollViewer to allow the user to view the content by scrolling within the ScrollViewer. In fact, many of the built-in controls like ListBox and DataGrid utilize a ScrollViewer internally to host content that has dimensions much greater than the container itself.

In scenarios where a ScrollViewer is used, you may also encounter the need to have some of the elements in the contained content follow a different scroll behavior than the default behavior imposed by the containing ScrollViewer. For instance, you may want a portion of the content to be constantly visible no matter in which direction and by how much the ScrollViewer is scrolled.

An appropriate attempt would be to figure out the amount of scroll and then apply an appropriate margin to the element that you want to keep visible (i.e., move the element in the direction of the scroll to keep it from disappearing beyond the visible bounds of the ScrollViewer).

The challenge with this is that the ScrollViewer does not raise any events as users scroll through the content. However, if you could access the ScrollBar controls contained in the ScrollViewer, you could attach handlers to the ValueChanged events of the ScrollBar and implement the necessary logic. But given that the ScrollViewer does not provide direct access to the internal ScrollBar control instances how do we go about doing that?

The VisualTreeHelper class

The System.Windows.Media.VisualTreeHelper class can help in traversing a visual tree and accessing elements in the tree that you do not have access to. The VisualTreeHelper class has several static utility methods that can be used to access the visual tree in several ways. The FindElementsInHostCoordinates() method has two overloads that accept a Rect or a Point defined in host coordinates (that is the coordinate system of the application's root visual) and find all the elements in the visual tree that intersect with that Point or fall within that Rect. Each overload also accepts a UIElement as a second parameter to denote the root of the search in the visual tree. If this parameter is set to null, the search covers the entire tree starting from the root. The VisualTreeHelper has other interesting methods like GetParent() to get the visual parent of an element or GetChild() to retrieve a child of an element at a specific index, and we encourage the reader to look up VisualTreeHelper documentation in MSDN at http://msdn.microsoft.com/en-us/library/system.windows.media.visualtreehelper(VS.95).aspx. This class can come very handy often.

For this recipe, we can use FindElementsInHostCoordinates() to locate the ScrollBars internal to the ScrollViewer's template definition and then respond to their events to control our scrolling behavior.

Let's now look at the code sample to see exactly how all of this ties together.

The Code

The code sample for this recipe hosts a ListBox within a ScrollViewer. The ListBox uses the WrapPanel we developed and used in recipe 5-9 as its ItemsPanel. Within the ScrollViewer is also a separate menu area that contains a ComboBox populated by product category data retrieved from the AdventureWorks WCF service discussed at the beginning of this chapter. Also, a Button in the menu area fetches all the products for that product category and populates the ListBox. Once the ListBox is populated, you will notice that scrolling the ScrollViewer scrolls the ListBox, but the menu area remains constantly in its position no matter the amount or the direction of the scroll.

Figure 5-28 shows the user interface of the application with the ScrollViewer scrolled partially both downward and to the right.

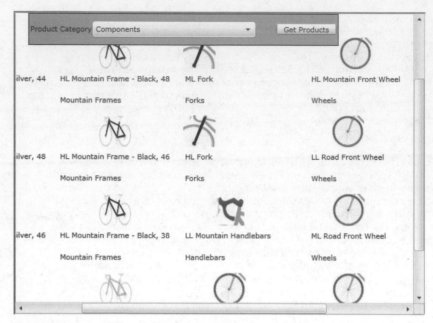

Figure 5-28. *ScrollViewer in a partially scrolled state with scroll invariant content*

Listing 5-33 shows the XAML for the page.

Listing 5-33. *XAML for MainPage*

```
<UserControl x:Class="Ch05_Controls.Recipe5_12.MainPage"
             xmlns="http://schemas.microsoft.com/winfx/2006/xaml/presentation"
             xmlns:x="http://schemas.microsoft.com/winfx/2006/xaml"
             xmlns:d="http://schemas.microsoft.com/expression/blend/2008"
             xmlns:mc="http://schemas.openxmlformats.org/markup-compatibility/2006"
             xmlns:Panel=
"clr-namespace:Ch05_Controls.Recipe5_9;assembly=Ch05_Controls.Recipe5_9.WrapPanel"
             Width="640"
             Height="474">
  <UserControl.Resources>

    <DataTemplate x:Key="dtProductItem">
      <Grid>
        <Grid.RowDefinitions>
          <RowDefinition Height="0.694*" />
          <RowDefinition Height="0.153*" />
          <RowDefinition Height="0.153*" />
        </Grid.RowDefinitions>
```

```
        <Image   MaxHeight="50"
                 MaxWidth="50"
                 Source="{Binding ProductPhoto.LargePhotoPNG}"
                 Stretch="Fill"
                 VerticalAlignment="Stretch"
                 HorizontalAlignment="Stretch" />
        <TextBlock Text="{Binding Name}"
                 TextWrapping="Wrap"
                 Margin="8,8,8,10"
                 Grid.Row="1" />
        <TextBlock Text="{Binding ProductSubCategory.Name}"
                 TextWrapping="Wrap"
                 Margin="8,8,8,10"
                 Grid.Row="2" />
      </Grid>
    </DataTemplate>


    <DataTemplate x:Key="dtCategory">
      <TextBlock Text="{Binding Name}" />
    </DataTemplate>
  </UserControl.Resources>

<ScrollViewer VerticalScrollBarVisibility="Auto"
              x:Name="scrollViewer"
              Padding="0"
              HorizontalScrollBarVisibility="Auto">
    <Grid x:Name="LayoutRoot">

      <Grid x:Name="ProductsData"
            Margin="0,50,0,0">
        <ListBox x:Name="lbxProducts"
                 ItemTemplate="{StaticResource dtProductItem}"
                 SelectionMode="Single">
          <ListBox.ItemsPanel>
            <ItemsPanelTemplate>
              <Panel:WrapPanel Orientation="Vertical"
                               Width="950"
                               Height="650" />
            </ItemsPanelTemplate>
          </ListBox.ItemsPanel>
        </ListBox>
      </Grid>
```

```xml
        <Border x:Name="brdrTopMenu"
                Height="50"
                VerticalAlignment="Top"
                HorizontalAlignment="Left"
                Margin="20,0,0,0"
                BorderBrush="Black"
                BorderThickness="1"
                Background="#FFA8A3A3"
                Padding="2,2,2,2">
            <Grid>
              <Grid.ColumnDefinitions>
                <ColumnDefinition Width="0.194*" />
                <ColumnDefinition Width="0.414*" />
                <ColumnDefinition Width="0.392*" />
              </Grid.ColumnDefinitions>
              <ComboBox x:Name="cbxCategories"
                        ItemTemplate="{StaticResource dtCategory}"
                        HorizontalAlignment="Right"
                        VerticalAlignment="Center"
                        Width="256"
                        Height="26"
                        Grid.Column="1" />
              <TextBlock HorizontalAlignment="Center"
                         VerticalAlignment="Center"
                         Text="Product Category"
                         TextWrapping="Wrap" />
              <Button x:Name="btnGetProducts"
                      Margin="31,11,0,14"
                      Content="Get Products"
                      HorizontalAlignment="Left"
                      Width="95"
                      Grid.Column="2"
                      VerticalAlignment="Center"
                      Click="btnGetProducts_Click" />
            </Grid>
        </Border>

    </Grid>
  </ScrollViewer>

</UserControl>
```

As you can see in Listing 5-33, the Grid named productsData contains the ListBox that displays the product items. The Border named brdrTopMenu contains the ComboBox displaying the product category information and the Button that causes the product items for that category to be fetched and displayed.

Both productsData and brdrTopMeny are further contained within a Grid named LayoutRoot, which in turn sits within a ScrollViewer named scrollViewer. The goal is to have scrollViewer be scrolled in any direction and have productsData (and hence the contained ListBox) be scrolled accordingly, but brdrTopMenu (and everything within) be always visible at the same position.

Listing 5-34 shows the code-behind implementing the necessary logic.

Listing 5-34. *Code-Behind for MainPage*

```
using System;
using System.Collections.Generic;
using System.IO;
using System.Linq;
using System.Windows;
using System.Windows.Controls;
using System.Windows.Controls.Primitives;
using System.Windows.Media;
using System.Windows.Media.Imaging;
using Ch05_Controls.Recipe5_12.AdvWorks;

namespace Ch05_Controls.Recipe5_12
{
  public partial class MainPage : UserControl
  {
    internal ScrollBar HScollBar = null;
    internal ScrollBar VScollBar = null;

    public MainPage()
    {
      InitializeComponent();

      AdvWorksDataServiceClient client = new AdvWorksDataServiceClient();
      client.GetAllCategoriesCompleted +=
        new EventHandler<GetAllCategoriesCompletedEventArgs>((s, e) =>
        {
          cbxCategories.ItemsSource = e.Result;
        });
      client.GetAllCategoriesAsync();

      scrollViewer.LayoutUpdated += new EventHandler((s, e) =>
      {
        if (HScollBar == null || VScollBar == null)
        {
          List<ScrollBar> scbars =
            VisualTreeHelper.FindElementsInHostCoordinates(
            scrollViewer.TransformToVisual(
            Application.Current.RootVisual).TransformBounds(
```

487

```
                new Rect(0, 0, scrollViewer.ActualWidth, scrollViewer.ActualHeight)),
                    scrollViewer).
                        Where((uie) => uie is ScrollBar).Cast<ScrollBar>().ToList();

            foreach (ScrollBar sc in scbars)
            {
                if (sc.Orientation == Orientation.Horizontal && HScollBar == null)
                {
                    HScollBar = sc;
                    sc.ValueChanged +=
                new RoutedPropertyChangedEventHandler<double>(OnHScrollValueChanged);
                }
                else if (sc.Orientation == Orientation.Vertical && VScollBar == null)
                {
                    VScollBar = sc;
                    sc.ValueChanged +=
                new RoutedPropertyChangedEventHandler<double>(OnVScrollValueChanged);
                }
            }
        }
    });
}

void OnHScrollValueChanged(object sender,
    RoutedPropertyChangedEventArgs<double> e)
{

    brdrTopMenu.Margin = new Thickness
    {
        Left = brdrTopMenu.Margin.Left + (e.NewValue - e.OldValue),
        Top = brdrTopMenu.Margin.Top,
        Right = brdrTopMenu.Margin.Right,
        Bottom = brdrTopMenu.Margin.Bottom
    };

}

void OnVScrollValueChanged(object sender,
    RoutedPropertyChangedEventArgs<double> e)
{
    brdrTopMenu.Margin = new Thickness
    {
        Left = brdrTopMenu.Margin.Left,
        Top = brdrTopMenu.Margin.Top + (e.NewValue - e.OldValue),
```

```
      Right = brdrTopMenu.Margin.Right,
      Bottom = brdrTopMenu.Margin.Bottom
    };
  }

  private void btnGetProducts_Click(object sender, RoutedEventArgs e)
  {
    AdvWorksDataServiceClient client = new AdvWorksDataServiceClient();
    client.GetProductsForCategoryCompleted +=
      new EventHandler<GetProductsForCategoryCompletedEventArgs>((s, args) =>
      {
        lbxProducts.ItemsSource = args.Result;
        client.GetSubcategoryCompleted +=
          new EventHandler<GetSubcategoryCompletedEventArgs>((s1, e1) =>
          {
            (e1.UserState as Product).ProductSubCategory = e1.Result;
          });
        client.GetPhotosCompleted +=
          new EventHandler<GetPhotosCompletedEventArgs>((s2, e2) =>
          {
            (e2.UserState as Product).ProductPhoto = e2.Result;
          });
        client.GetInventoryCompleted +=
          new EventHandler<GetInventoryCompletedEventArgs>((s3, e3) =>
          {
            Product p = (e3.UserState as Product);
            p.ProductInventories = e3.Result;
            p.InventoryLevelBrush = null;
            p.InventoryLevelMessage = null;
          });
        foreach (Product prod in args.Result)
        {
          client.GetPhotosAsync(prod, prod);
          client.GetSubcategoryAsync(prod, prod);
          client.GetInventoryAsync(prod, prod);
        }

      });
    if (cbxCategories.SelectedItem != null)
      client.
        GetProductsForCategoryAsync(
        cbxCategories.SelectedItem as ProductCategory);
  }

}
}
```

```
namespace Ch05_Controls.Recipe5_12.AdvWorks
{
  public partial class ProductPhoto
  {
    private BitmapImage _LargePhotoPNG;

    public BitmapImage LargePhotoPNG
    {
      get
      {
        BitmapImage bim = new BitmapImage();
        MemoryStream ms = new MemoryStream(this.LargePhoto.Bytes);
        bim.SetSource(ms);
        ms.Close();
        return bim;
      }
      set
      {
        RaisePropertyChanged("LargePhotoPNG");
      }
    }
  }

  public partial class Product
  {
    private SolidColorBrush _InventoryLevelBrush;
    public SolidColorBrush InventoryLevelBrush
    {
      get
      {
        return (this.ProductInventories == null
          || this.ProductInventories.Count == 0) ?
          new SolidColorBrush(Colors.Gray) :
            (this.ProductInventories[0].Quantity > this.SafetyStockLevel ?
              new SolidColorBrush(Colors.Green) :
                (this.ProductInventories[0].Quantity > this.ReorderPoint ?
                  new SolidColorBrush(Colors.Yellow) :
                  new SolidColorBrush(Colors.Red)));
      }
      set
      {
        //no actual value set here - just property change raised
        RaisePropertyChanged("InventoryLevelBrush");
      }
    }
```

```
    private string _InventoryLevelMessage;
    public string InventoryLevelMessage
    {
      get
      {
        return (this.ProductInventories == null
          || this.ProductInventories.Count == 0) ?
          "Stock Level Unknown" :
            (this.ProductInventories[0].Quantity > this.SafetyStockLevel ?
            "In Stock" :
              (this.ProductInventories[0].Quantity > this.ReorderPoint ?
                "Low Stock" : "Reorder Now"));
      }
      set
      {
        //no actual value set here - just property change raised
        RaisePropertyChanged("InventoryLevelMessage");
      }
    }
    private ProductSubcategory _productSubCategory;
    public ProductSubcategory ProductSubCategory
    {
      get { return _productSubCategory; }
      set
      {
        _productSubCategory = value;
        RaisePropertyChanged("ProductSubCategory");
      }
    }
    private ProductCategory _productCategory;
    public ProductCategory ProductCategory
    {
      get { return _productCategory; }
      set { _productCategory = value; RaisePropertyChanged("ProductCategory"); }
    }

    private ProductPhoto _productPhoto;
    public ProductPhoto ProductPhoto
    {
      get { return _productPhoto; }
      set { _productPhoto = value; RaisePropertyChanged("ProductPhoto"); }
    }
  }
}
```

We are going to discuss only the portions of the code that pertain to our immediate problem here. For an explanation of the rest of the code, most of which deals with WCF service calls to the AdventureWorks service to fetch data, you can refer to recipe 5-3.

In Listing 5-34, note the handler for the LayoutUpdated event for the ScrollViewer. We use the VisualTreeHelper.FindElementsInHostCoordinates() method to try to locate the two ScrollBars in the ScrollViewer. We pass in a Rect instance that contains a rectangle defining the bounds of the ScrollViewer transformed to host coordinates. For an explanation of coordinate system transformation using the TransformToVisual() method, you can refer to recipe 5-4. We also pass in the ScrollViewer as the second parameter to start the search of the visual tree at the ScrollViewer moving down. Finally, we filter the resulting collection using LINQ to extract just the ScrollBar typed instances.

Once that is done, we wire up handler to the ValueChanged events of each ScrollBar, and store them in two member variables named HScrollBar and VScrollBar, respectively. This needs a little bit more explanation. The ScrollViewer can be configured to display its ScrollBars automatically as needed (i.e., when the content dimensions grow beyond the visible bounds). Thus, depending on the current dimensions of the content and the ScrollViewer settings, either or neither ScrollBar may show up initially. Since the LayoutUpdated event gets raised by the ScrollViewer each time such a layout change occurs, we are guaranteed to eventually locate both ScrollBars, even if they are not available on the first occurrence of that event. To avoid attaching event handlers multiple times to the ValueChanged events, we store them in local variables, and we check for null to ensure this is the first time we are locating them.

If you look at the handlers for the ValueChanged events, named OnHScrollValueChanged and OnVScrollValueChanged, we simply set the appropriate Margin dimension on the brdrTopMenu element to the amount covered in the last scroll event. The Margin dimension used is either Margin.Left or Margin.Top depending on whether the scroll was a horizontal or a vertical one. This shift of Margin works both ways—depending on the direction of the scroll, the difference of e.NewValue and e.OldValue may be a positive or a negative value, thus moving the brdrTopMenu further away from or closer to the edge in question. This causes the brdrTopMenu to always seem to stay visible at the same position with respect to the visible portion of the content within the ScrollViewer.

5-13. Customizing the Binding Validation User Interface
Problem
You want to customize the default user interface built into Silverlight for displaying binding validation errors and validation summary.

Solution
To modify the validation error displayed at the control that is in error, customize the control template, and change the ValidationTooltipTemplate. To customize the ValidationSummary user interface, modify the ValidationSummary control template, which is a new addition in Silverlight 3.

How It Works
This recipe discusses the mechanisms to modify that default user interface. For more details on how the default user interface for displaying binding validation errors are utilized, please refer to recipe 4-6.

Validation Error Tooltip

The default user interface of a validation error involves a red border and a corner glyph on the control concerned and a ToolTip containing the error message that appears alongside the control when the user hovers on the glyph. Figure 4-9 shows this user interface.

This user interface is built into the template of the control with which the error display is associated. Unfortunately, there is no straightforward way to replace this user interface other than modifying the control template of the control in question. Let's use a TextBox control as an example, with its default control template shown in Listing 5-34. For the sake of brevity, we have listed only the portions pertinent to validation error display.

Listing 5-34. *Partial Control Template of a TextBox control*

```
<Style x:Key="styleTextBoxDefault" TargetType="TextBox">
  <Setter Property="BorderThickness" Value="1"/>
  <Setter Property="Background" Value="#FFFFFFFF"/>
  <Setter Property="Foreground" Value="#FF000000"/>
  <Setter Property="Padding" Value="2"/>
  <Setter Property="BorderBrush">
    <Setter.Value>
      <LinearGradientBrush EndPoint="0.5,1" StartPoint="0.5,0">
        <GradientStop Color="#FFA3AEB9" Offset="0"/>
        <GradientStop Color="#FF8399A9" Offset="0.375"/>
        <GradientStop Color="#FF718597" Offset="0.375"/>
        <GradientStop Color="#FF617584" Offset="1"/>
      </LinearGradientBrush>
    </Setter.Value>
  </Setter>
  <Setter Property="Template">
    <Setter.Value>
      <ControlTemplate TargetType="TextBox">
        <Grid x:Name="RootElement">
          <VisualStateManager.VisualStateGroups>
            ...
            <VisualStateGroup x:Name="ValidationStates">
              <VisualState x:Name="Valid"/>
              <VisualState x:Name="InvalidUnfocused">
                <Storyboard>
                  <ObjectAnimationUsingKeyFrames
                    Storyboard.TargetName="ValidationErrorElement"
                    Storyboard.TargetProperty="Visibility">
```

```xml
                    <DiscreteObjectKeyFrame KeyTime="0">
                      <DiscreteObjectKeyFrame.Value>
                        <Visibility>Visible</Visibility>
                      </DiscreteObjectKeyFrame.Value>
                    </DiscreteObjectKeyFrame>
                  </ObjectAnimationUsingKeyFrames>
              </Storyboard>
            </VisualState>
            <VisualState x:Name="InvalidFocused">
              <Storyboard>
                <ObjectAnimationUsingKeyFrames
                  Storyboard.TargetName="ValidationErrorElement"
                  Storyboard.TargetProperty="Visibility">
                  <DiscreteObjectKeyFrame KeyTime="0">
                    <DiscreteObjectKeyFrame.Value>
                      <Visibility>Visible</Visibility>
                    </DiscreteObjectKeyFrame.Value>
                  </DiscreteObjectKeyFrame>
                </ObjectAnimationUsingKeyFrames>
                <ObjectAnimationUsingKeyFrames
                  Storyboard.TargetName="validationTooltip"
                  Storyboard.TargetProperty="IsOpen">
                  <DiscreteObjectKeyFrame KeyTime="0">
                    <DiscreteObjectKeyFrame.Value>
                      <System:Boolean>True</System:Boolean>
                    </DiscreteObjectKeyFrame.Value>
                  </DiscreteObjectKeyFrame>
                </ObjectAnimationUsingKeyFrames>
              </Storyboard>
            </VisualState>
          </VisualStateGroup>
        </VisualStateManager.VisualStateGroups>

        ...
```

```
        <Border x:Name="ValidationErrorElement" Visibility="Collapsed"
               BorderBrush="#FFDB000C" BorderThickness="1" CornerRadius="1">
            <ToolTipService.ToolTip>
                <ToolTip x:Name="validationTooltip"
         DataContext="{Binding RelativeSource={RelativeSource TemplatedParent}}"
                    Template="{StaticResource ValidationToolTipTemplate}"
                    Placement="Right"
                    PlacementTarget=
                "{Binding RelativeSource={RelativeSource TemplatedParent}}">
                    <ToolTip.Triggers>
                        <EventTrigger RoutedEvent="Canvas.Loaded">
                            <BeginStoryboard>
                                <Storyboard>
                                    <ObjectAnimationUsingKeyFrames
                                        Storyboard.TargetName="validationTooltip"
                                        Storyboard.TargetProperty="IsHitTestVisible">
                                        <DiscreteObjectKeyFrame KeyTime="0">
                                            <DiscreteObjectKeyFrame.Value>
                                                <System:Boolean>true</System:Boolean>
                                            </DiscreteObjectKeyFrame.Value>
                                        </DiscreteObjectKeyFrame>
                                    </ObjectAnimationUsingKeyFrames>
                                </Storyboard>
                            </BeginStoryboard>
                        </EventTrigger>
                    </ToolTip.Triggers>
                </ToolTip>
            </ToolTipService.ToolTip>
            <Grid Height="12" HorizontalAlignment="Right" Margin="1,-4,-4,0"
                   VerticalAlignment="Top" Width="12" Background="Transparent">
                <Path Fill="#FFDC000C" Margin="1,3,0,0"
                    Data="M 1,0 L6,0 A 2,2 90 0 1 8,2 L8,7 z"/>
                <Path Fill="#ffffff" Margin="1,3,0,0"
                    Data="M 0,0 L2,0 L 8,6 L8,8"/>
            </Grid>
        </Border>
      </Grid>
    </ControlTemplate>
  </Setter.Value>
 </Setter>
</Style>
```

The first thing to notice in Listing 5-34 is the Border element named validationErrorElement, which has additional elements in it that constitute the red border and glyph displayed on a validation error. If you look at the visual states define don the TextBox control, you will see that the InvalidFocused and InvalidUnfocused states actually make the validatinoErrorElement visible, and as you may have correctly surmised, those states are navigated to from within the TextBox code when a validation error happens.

You should also note the ToolTip named validationToolTip associated with validationErrorElement. This is what causes the ToolTip error display when the user hovers on the glyph. As Listing 5-3 shows, tooltipErrorDisplay has its control template bound to a control template name ValidationToolTipTemplate. This control template is also automatically created whenever you create a custom template for the TextBox (or any other control that supports validation) in Expression Blend 3, and the default version is listed in Listing 5-35.

Listing 5-35. *Default ValidationTooltipTemplate definition*

```
<ControlTemplate x:Key="ValidationToolTipTemplate">
  <Grid x:Name="Root" Margin="5,0" Opacity="0" RenderTransformOrigin="0,0">
    <VisualStateManager.VisualStateGroups>
      <VisualStateGroup x:Name="OpenStates">
        <VisualStateGroup.Transitions>
          <VisualTransition GeneratedDuration="0"/>
          <VisualTransition GeneratedDuration="0:0:0.2" To="Open">
            <Storyboard>
              <DoubleAnimationUsingKeyFrames Storyboard.TargetName="xform"
                                              Storyboard.TargetProperty="X">
                <SplineDoubleKeyFrame KeyTime="0:0:0.2" Value="0"/>
              </DoubleAnimationUsingKeyFrames>
              <DoubleAnimationUsingKeyFrames Storyboard.TargetName="Root"
                                              Storyboard.TargetProperty="Opacity">
                <SplineDoubleKeyFrame KeyTime="0:0:0.2" Value="1"/>
              </DoubleAnimationUsingKeyFrames>
            </Storyboard>
          </VisualTransition>
        </VisualStateGroup.Transitions>
        <VisualState x:Name="Closed">
          <Storyboard>
            <DoubleAnimationUsingKeyFrames Storyboard.TargetName="Root"
                                            Storyboard.TargetProperty="Opacity">
              <SplineDoubleKeyFrame KeyTime="0" Value="0"/>
            </DoubleAnimationUsingKeyFrames>
          </Storyboard>
        </VisualState>
        <VisualState x:Name="Open">
          <Storyboard>
            <DoubleAnimationUsingKeyFrames Storyboard.TargetName="xform"
                                            Storyboard.TargetProperty="X">
              <SplineDoubleKeyFrame KeyTime="0" Value="0"/>
            </DoubleAnimationUsingKeyFrames>
```

```
    <DoubleAnimationUsingKeyFrames Storyboard.TargetName="Root"
                                    Storyboard.TargetProperty="Opacity">
        <SplineDoubleKeyFrame KeyTime="0" Value="1"/>
      </DoubleAnimationUsingKeyFrames>
    </Storyboard>
  </VisualState>
 </VisualStateGroup>
</VisualStateManager.VisualStateGroups>
<Grid.RenderTransform>
  <TranslateTransform x:Name="xform" X="-25"/>
</Grid.RenderTransform>
<Border Margin="4,4,-4,-4" Background="#052A2E31" CornerRadius="5"/>
<Border Margin="3,3,-3,-3" Background="#152A2E31" CornerRadius="4"/>
<Border Margin="2,2,-2,-2" Background="#252A2E31" CornerRadius="3"/>
<Border Margin="1,1,-1,-1" Background="#352A2E31" CornerRadius="2"/>
<Border Background="#FFDC000C" CornerRadius="2"/>
<Border CornerRadius="2">
  <TextBlock Margin="8,4,8,4" MaxWidth="250" UseLayoutRounding="false"
             Foreground="White"
             Text="{Binding (Validation.Errors)[0].ErrorContent}"
             TextWrapping="Wrap"/>
</Border>
</Grid>
</ControlTemplate>
```

The easiest place to start modifying the default appearance of the validation error display is to start by modifying the ValidationTooltipTemplate. We will show a small example of this in the code sample to follow.

Also note the binding declaration for the Text property of the TextBlock displaying the error message. The System.Windows.Controls.Validation class is static and exposes a dependency property named Errors, defined as a collection of ValidationError types. The ValidationError type, in turn, exposes an ErrorContent property of type Object and an Exception property of type Exception to define the actual error that it represents. Binding the Text property, as shown in Listing 5-35, to the ErrorContent property of the ValidationError type causes the error to be displayed within the ToolTip.

The ValidationSummary Control

The ValidationSummary control is used to display a collection of all validation errors on a form at any time during the edit process, and its default use is described in recipe 4-6, where as Figure 4-11 shows an example of the default user interface.

To enable customizing the header area of the ValidationSummary control, a HeaderTemplate property of type DataTemplate is available on the ValidationSummary control, which, in turn, uses the value set in the ValidationSummary.Header property as its data source. We will also show an example of this later on in the code sample.

The ValidationSummary control internally uses a ListBox to display the list of errors. Each item in the ListBox gets bound to an instance of a System.Windows.Controls.ValidationSummaryItem type. The ValidationSummaryItem instance is created automatically by the runtime for each validation error and exposes a MessageHeader and Message property that gets bound to each item in the ListBox using the ItemTemplate property setting on the internal ListBox.

The data template used for the `ListBox.ItemTemplate` inside the `ValidationSummary` is unfortunately defined within the default control template and not exposed externally through the `ValidationSummary` control. So to replace that data template and change how the `ValidationSummaryItem` properties get bound and displayed you would need to provide a custom template for the entire `ValidationSummary` control. We will show a simple example of this in the code sample.

If however you want to change the UI for each `ListBoxItem` that represents an error item, you can set `ValidationSummary.ErrorStyle` to a custom style containing your custom control template for a `ListBoxItem`, without having to modify the entire `ValidationSummary` control template. The style applied here gets bound to the `ItemContainerStyle` property of the `ListBox` that `ValidationSummary` uses internally, and hence impacts the look and feel of the `ListBoxItem` for each individual error item. We will look at an example of this as well.

The Code

To illustrate the ideas discussed in the preceding "How It Works" section, we extend the code sample from recipe 4-7. Since there are no changes to the code-behind for this, we only focus on the XAML, and instead of listing the entire XAML again, we list only pertinent parts. We encourage you to use the download files available for this book for the complete code listings. We start with a customization to the `ValidationToolTipTemplate` control template as shown in Listing 5-36.

Listing 5-36. *Customized ValidationToolTipTemplate*

```
<ControlTemplate x:Key="CustomValidationToolTipTemplate">
  <Grid x:Name="Root"
        Margin="5,0"
        Opacity="0"
        RenderTransformOrigin="0,0">
    <VisualStateManager.VisualStateGroups>
      <VisualStateGroup x:Name="OpenStates">
        <VisualStateGroup.Transitions>
          <VisualTransition GeneratedDuration="0" />
          <VisualTransition GeneratedDuration="0:0:0.2"
                            To="Open">
            <Storyboard>
              <DoubleAnimationUsingKeyFrames Storyboard.TargetName="xform"
                                             Storyboard.TargetProperty="X">
                <SplineDoubleKeyFrame KeyTime="0:0:0.2"
                                      Value="0" />
              </DoubleAnimationUsingKeyFrames>
              <DoubleAnimationUsingKeyFrames Storyboard.TargetName="Root"
                                             Storyboard.TargetProperty="Opacity">
                <SplineDoubleKeyFrame KeyTime="0:0:0.2"
                                      Value="1" />
              </DoubleAnimationUsingKeyFrames>
            </Storyboard>
          </VisualTransition>
        </VisualStateGroup.Transitions>
```

```
    <VisualState x:Name="Closed">
      <Storyboard>
        <DoubleAnimationUsingKeyFrames Storyboard.TargetName="Root"
                                       Storyboard.TargetProperty="Opacity">
          <SplineDoubleKeyFrame KeyTime="0"
                                Value="0" />
        </DoubleAnimationUsingKeyFrames>
      </Storyboard>
    </VisualState>
    <VisualState x:Name="Open">
      <Storyboard>
        <DoubleAnimationUsingKeyFrames Storyboard.TargetName="xform"
                                       Storyboard.TargetProperty="X">
          <SplineDoubleKeyFrame KeyTime="0"
                                Value="0" />
        </DoubleAnimationUsingKeyFrames>
        <DoubleAnimationUsingKeyFrames Storyboard.TargetName="Root"
                                       Storyboard.TargetProperty="Opacity">
          <SplineDoubleKeyFrame KeyTime="0"
                                Value="1" />
        </DoubleAnimationUsingKeyFrames>
      </Storyboard>
    </VisualState>
  </VisualStateGroup>
</VisualStateManager.VisualStateGroups>
<Grid.RenderTransform>
  <TranslateTransform x:Name="xform"
                      X="-25" />
</Grid.RenderTransform>
<Border Margin="4,4,-4,-4"
        Background="#052A2E31"
        CornerRadius="5" />
<Border Margin="3,3,-3,-3"
        Background="#152A2E31"
        CornerRadius="4" />
<Border Margin="2,2,-2,-2"
        Background="#252A2E31"
        CornerRadius="3" />
<Border Margin="1,1,-1,-1"
        Background="#352A2E31"
        CornerRadius="2" />
<Border Background="#FFDC000C"
        CornerRadius="2" />
<Border CornerRadius="2">
```

```xml
      <Grid>
        <Grid.RowDefinitions>
          <RowDefinition Height="Auto" />
          <RowDefinition Height="Auto" />
        </Grid.RowDefinitions>
        <TextBlock Margin="8,4,8,4"
                   MaxWidth="250"
                   UseLayoutRounding="false"
                   Foreground="White"
                   Text="{Binding (Validation.Errors)[0].ErrorContent}"
                   TextWrapping="Wrap" />
        <Border Background="White"
                Margin="6,2,6,2"
                BorderThickness="1"
                BorderBrush="Black"
                Grid.Row="1">
          <TextBlock UseLayoutRounding="false"
                     MaxWidth="250"
                     Margin="2"
                     Foreground="Black"
                     Text="{Binding (Validation.Errors)[0].Exception.StackTrace}"
                     TextWrapping="Wrap" />
        </Border>
      </Grid>
    </Border>
  </Grid>
</ControlTemplate>
```

If you compare this with the default implementation in Listing 5-34, you will note that we have added an extra TextBlock contained with a Border to the template with the TextBlock.Text property bound to the ValidationError.Exception.StackTrace property for the error being displayed.

Listing 5-37 shows the binding of the CustomValidationTooltipTemplate control template to the ToolTip.Template property for the validationToolTip within the TextBox control template and the containing TextBox style being applied to a TextBox.

Listing 5-37. *Applying CustomValidationToolTipTemplate to a TextBox*

```xml
<Style x:Key="styleTextBox"
       TargetType="TextBox">
  ...
  <Setter Property="Template">
    <Setter.Value>
      <ControlTemplate TargetType="TextBox">
        <Grid x:Name="RootElement">
          ...
```

```
        <Border x:Name="ValidationErrorElement"
                Visibility="Collapsed"
                BorderBrush="#FFDB000C"
                BorderThickness="1"
                CornerRadius="1">
          <ToolTipService.ToolTip>
            <ToolTip x:Name="validationTooltip"
                    DataContext=
                    "{Binding RelativeSource={RelativeSource TemplatedParent}}"
                    Template="{StaticResource CustomValidationToolTipTemplate}"
                    Placement="Right"
                    PlacementTarget="
                    {Binding RelativeSource={RelativeSource TemplatedParent}}">
              ...
            </ToolTip>
          </ToolTipService.ToolTip>
          ...
      </Grid>
    </ControlTemplate>
  </Setter.Value>
 </Setter>
</Style>

...
...


<TextBox Background="Transparent"
        Grid.Column="3"
        Margin="1,1,1,1"
        Grid.Row="3"
        Text="{Binding Address.State, Mode=TwoWay,
  NotifyOnValidationError=True, UpdateSourceTrigger=Explicit,
  ValidatesOnExceptions=True}"
        x:Name="tbxState"
        Style="{StaticResource styleTextBox}" />
```

This causes the stack trace to be displayed right below the error message as shown in Figure 5-29.

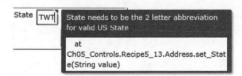

Figure 5-29. *Customized ValidationToolTipTemplate with a stack trace display*

Let's look at the `ValidationSummary` control customization now. We start by creating a custom control template for each individual `ListBoxItem` within the `ValidationSummaryItem`, as shown in Listing 5-38. Recall that this template can be applied through the `ValidationSummary.ErrorStyle` property to change the look and feel of each individual error item.

Listing 5-38. *Control Template for the ListBoxItem Used to Display Individual Error Items in a Validation Summary*

```
<Style x:Key="styleValidationSummaryErrorItem" TargetType="ListBoxItem">
  <Setter Property="Padding" Value="3"/>
  <Setter Property="HorizontalContentAlignment" Value="Left"/>
  <Setter Property="VerticalContentAlignment" Value="Top"/>
  <Setter Property="Background" Value="Transparent"/>
  <Setter Property="BorderThickness" Value="1"/>
  <Setter Property="TabNavigation" Value="Local"/>
  <Setter Property="Template">
    <Setter.Value>
      <ControlTemplate TargetType="ListBoxItem">
        <Grid x:Name="grid" Background="{TemplateBinding Background}">
          <VisualStateManager.VisualStateGroups>
            <VisualStateGroup x:Name="CommonStates">
              <VisualState x:Name="Normal"/>
              <VisualState x:Name="MouseOver">
                <Storyboard>
                  <DoubleAnimationUsingKeyFrames
        Storyboard.TargetName="fillColor" Storyboard.TargetProperty="Opacity">
                    <SplineDoubleKeyFrame KeyTime="0" Value=".35"/>
                  </DoubleAnimationUsingKeyFrames>
                </Storyboard>
              </VisualState>
              <VisualState x:Name="Disabled">
                <Storyboard>
                  <DoubleAnimationUsingKeyFrames
  Storyboard.TargetName="contentPresenter" Storyboard.TargetProperty="Opacity">
                    <SplineDoubleKeyFrame KeyTime="0" Value=".55"/>
                  </DoubleAnimationUsingKeyFrames>
                </Storyboard>
              </VisualState>
            </VisualStateGroup>
```

```xml
<VisualStateGroup x:Name="SelectionStates">
  <VisualState x:Name="Unselected"/>
  <VisualState x:Name="Selected">
    <Storyboard>
      <DoubleAnimationUsingKeyFrames

Storyboard.TargetName="fillColor2"
        Storyboard.TargetProperty="Opacity">
        <SplineDoubleKeyFrame KeyTime="0" Value=".75"/>
      </DoubleAnimationUsingKeyFrames>
      <DoubleAnimationUsingKeyFrames
        BeginTime="00:00:00"
        Duration="00:00:00.0010000"
        Storyboard.TargetName="contentPresenter"
Storyboard.TargetProperty="(UIElement.Effect).(DropShadowEffect.ShadowDepth)">
        <EasingDoubleKeyFrame KeyTime="00:00:00" Value="8"/>
      </DoubleAnimationUsingKeyFrames>
      <DoubleAnimationUsingKeyFrames BeginTime="00:00:00"
                                     Duration="00:00:00.0010000"
    Storyboard.TargetName="contentPresenter"
    Storyboard.TargetProperty="(UIElement.Effect).(DropShadowEffect.Opacity)">
        <EasingDoubleKeyFrame KeyTime="00:00:00" Value="1"/>
      </DoubleAnimationUsingKeyFrames>
    </Storyboard>
  </VisualState>
  <VisualState x:Name="SelectedUnfocused">
    <Storyboard>
      <DoubleAnimationUsingKeyFrames BeginTime="00:00:00"
                                     Duration="00:00:00.0010000"
Storyboard.TargetName="contentPresenter"
Storyboard.TargetProperty="(UIElement.Effect).(DropShadowEffect.ShadowDepth)">
        <EasingDoubleKeyFrame KeyTime="00:00:00" Value="5"/>
      </DoubleAnimationUsingKeyFrames>
      <DoubleAnimationUsingKeyFrames BeginTime="00:00:00"
                                     Duration="00:00:00.0010000"
    Storyboard.TargetName="contentPresenter"
    Storyboard.TargetProperty="(UIElement.Effect).(DropShadowEffect.Opacity)">
        <EasingDoubleKeyFrame KeyTime="00:00:00" Value="0.6"/>
      </DoubleAnimationUsingKeyFrames>
    </Storyboard>
  </VisualState>
</VisualStateGroup>
```

```xml
        <VisualStateGroup x:Name="FocusStates">
          <VisualState x:Name="Focused">
            <Storyboard>
              <ObjectAnimationUsingKeyFrames Duration="0"
Storyboard.TargetName="FocusVisualElement" Storyboard.TargetProperty="Visibility">
                <DiscreteObjectKeyFrame KeyTime="0">
                  <DiscreteObjectKeyFrame.Value>
                    <Visibility>Visible</Visibility>
                  </DiscreteObjectKeyFrame.Value>
                </DiscreteObjectKeyFrame>
              </ObjectAnimationUsingKeyFrames>
            </Storyboard>
          </VisualState>
          <VisualState x:Name="Unfocused"/>
        </VisualStateGroup>
      </VisualStateManager.VisualStateGroups>
      <Rectangle x:Name="fillColor" Fill="#FFBADDE9" RadiusX="1" RadiusY="1"
                 IsHitTestVisible="False" Opacity="0"/>
      <Rectangle x:Name="fillColor2" Fill="#FFBADDE9" RadiusX="1"
                 RadiusY="1" IsHitTestVisible="False" Opacity="0"/>
      <ContentPresenter x:Name="contentPresenter"
                        HorizontalAlignment=
                        "{TemplateBinding HorizontalContentAlignment}"
                        Margin="{TemplateBinding Padding}"
                        Content="{TemplateBinding Content}"
                        ContentTemplate=
                        "{TemplateBinding ContentTemplate}">
        <ContentPresenter.Effect>
          <DropShadowEffect Opacity="0"/>
        </ContentPresenter.Effect>
      </ContentPresenter>
      <Rectangle x:Name="FocusVisualElement" Stroke="#FF6DBDD1"
                 StrokeThickness="1" RadiusX="1" RadiusY="1"
                 Visibility="Collapsed"/>
    </Grid>
  </ControlTemplate>
  </Setter.Value>
  </Setter>
</Style>
```

We have kept this control template pretty much identical to the original as generated through Expression Blend. The only change we have made is the addition of a DropShadowEffect to the ContentPresenter in the template, and some animated changes to some of the DropShadowEffect properties as the various selection state changes happen on the ListBoxItem. You can, however, change this template as much as you want to as long as it targets a ListBoxItem.

Listing 5-39 also shows a custom template for the entire ValidationSummary control that changes the ItemTemplate data template for the internal ListBox. We only show the pertinent portions to keep the listing brief.

Listing 5-39. *Partial Implementation of a ValidationSummary Control Template*

```
<Style x:Key="styleValidationSummary"
       TargetType="input:ValidationSummary">
  ...
  <Setter Property="Template">
    <Setter.Value>
      <ControlTemplate TargetType="input:ValidationSummary">
        <Grid x:Name="ValidationSummary">

          ...

              <ListBox x:Name="SummaryListBox"
                       Height="Auto"
                       Style="{TemplateBinding SummaryListBoxStyle}"
                       Background="{x:Null}"
                       BorderThickness="0"
                       Foreground="{TemplateBinding Foreground}"
                       Padding="{TemplateBinding Padding}"
                       Grid.Row="1"
                       ItemContainerStyle="{TemplateBinding ErrorStyle}">
                <ListBox.ItemTemplate>
                  <DataTemplate>
                    <StackPanel Orientation="Horizontal">
                      <TextBlock Margin="4,0,0,0"
                                 FontWeight="Bold"
                                 Foreground="Red"
                                 Text="{Binding MessageHeader}" />
                      <TextBlock Margin="4,0,0,0"
                                 Text="{Binding Message}" />
                    </StackPanel>
                  </DataTemplate>
                </ListBox.ItemTemplate>
              </ListBox>
            ...

        </Grid>
      </Border>
    </Grid>
      </ControlTemplate>
    </Setter.Value>
  </Setter>
</Style>
```

The only change we make here is change the `DataTemplate` definition to turn the `ForeGround` color of the message header `TextBlock` to red. Listing 5-40 shows how all of this can be applied to a `ValidationSummary` control.

Listing 5-40. *ValidationSummary Control with a Custom Template and Custom Header and Item Styles*

```
<input:ValidationSummary Grid.Row="2"
            Header="{Binding ElementName=lbx_Employees, Path=SelectedItem}"
                        Margin="0,10,0,5"
                        ErrorStyle=
                        "{StaticResource styleValidationSummaryErrorItem}"
                        Style="{StaticResource styleValidationSummary}" >
  <input:ValidationSummary.HeaderTemplate>
    <DataTemplate>
      <Grid Background="Blue">
        <Grid.ColumnDefinitions>
          <ColumnDefinition Width="Auto" />
          <ColumnDefinition Width="Auto" />
        </Grid.ColumnDefinitions>
        <TextBlock UseLayoutRounding="False"
                   Foreground="White"
                   Text="Editing Errors:" />
        <TextBlock UseLayoutRounding="False"
                   Foreground="White"
                   FontWeight="Bold"
                   Text="{Binding FullName}"
                   Grid.Column="1" />
      </Grid>
    </DataTemplate>
  </input:ValidationSummary.HeaderTemplate>
</input:ValidationSummary>
```

Note in Listing 5-40 that we apply the `ListBoxItem` template by applying the containing style to the `ValidationSummary.ErrorStyle` property and apply the custom `ValidationSummary` template by applying the containing style to the `ValidationSummary` control itself. Note also that we define a new `HeaderTemplate` data template. We display the full name of the employee whose information has suffered the edit errors by binding a `TextBlock` in the `HeaderTemplate` to the `FullName` property of the currently selected `Employee`. And the current employee selection is passed in by binding the `ValidationSummary.Header` property to the `SelectedItem` property of `lbx_Employees` `ListBox` using the `ElementName` attribute on the binding.

Figure 5-30 shows the `ValidationSummary` customizations applied.

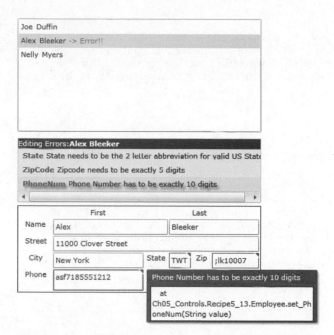

Figure 5-30. *ValidationSummary Control Customizations*

■**Note** As a final note on this recipe, we would also like to mention that we have deliberately kept the amount of modifications made to the validation UI templates here to a minimum. Our intention with this recipe was to show you the "where" and "how" of the validation UI customization mechanism. Once you know the right hooks, your creativity is the only limiting factor to how much customization you can make.

5-14. Control Behavior in Expression Blend

Problem

You want to author custom controls that integrate well with the Expression Blend 3 design environment.

Solution

Use the various designer targeted attributes to decorate your control properties and take appropriate care to not execute control code in design mode that can cause problems within a designer environment.

How It Works

If you intend to develop custom Silverlight controls, there is always a chance that your controls will be used by designers from within Expression Blend to design application user interfaces. There are steps you can take as a control author to ensure that your controls are well behaved when used with the Expression Blend environment.

Property Attributes

There are several attributes in the `System.ComponentModel` namespace in the `System` assembly that you can use to make sure that the control properties are well integrated with the Expression Blend property editor.

CategoryAttribute

As you may have noticed control properties are grouped into categories within the Expression Blend property editor. Some of the common property categories you may have already noticed within Expression Blend are `Layout` and `Appearance`. To make sure your control property is displayed in the appropriate category, you can decorate your property declaration with the `CategoryAttribute`, passing in a category name string. The following snippet shows a sample attribution for a dependency property named `CurrentValue` to a category named `ProgressBar Values`:

```
[Category("ProgressBar Values")]
    public double CurrentValue
    {
      get { return (double)GetValue(CurrentValueProperty); }
      set { SetValue(CurrentValueProperty, value); }
    }
}
```

This will cause a new category pane with the title ProgressBar Values to be introduced in the Blend property editor, and this property will show up in that category pane, as shown in Figure 5-31.

Figure 5-31. *A custom property category in Expression Blend*

Note that you can also add a custom control property to a pre-existing category, using the same attribute—just use the preexisting category name as the parameter to the `CategoryAttribute` application. Figure 5-32 shows a custom property named `Orientation` showing up in the Layout category in Blend, along with several other properties that the control inherited.

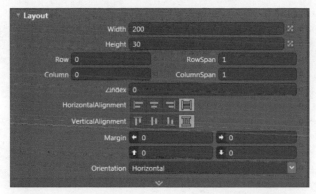

Figure 5-32. *A property added to an existing category in Expression Blend*

Also note that if you do not supply a `CategoryAttribute` to a custom property, it is displayed in the Miscellaneous category within Blend. It is always a good idea to supply a `CategoryAttribute` to help the designer intuitively find the property in an aptly named category.

DescriptionAttribute

The `DescriptionAttribute` allows you to add a short description to your property. When the designer hovers over the property label in the Expression Blend property editor, Blend displays this description in a tooltip. If applied well, these descriptions can be immensely helpful to the designer in deciphering the purpose of the property. The following code snippet shows the `description` attribute applied to a custom property:

```
[Description("The current value as indicated by the Progress Bar.")]
    public double CurrentValue
    {
      get { return (double)GetValue(CurrentValueProperty); }
      set { SetValue(CurrentValueProperty, value); }
}
```

Figure 5-33 shows this description being displayed within the Expression Blend property tooltip.

Figure 5-33. *DescriptionAttribute applied to a property.*

EditorBrowsableAttribute

The `EditorBrowsableAttribute` controls whether a property can be made visible in the property editor in Expression Blend, and if so in what capacity. You can pass in one of three possible enumerated values in

509

constructing the attribute instance. `EditorBrowsableState.Always` causes the property to be displayed in the default manner, whereas `EditorBrowsableState.Never` hides the property from being visible in the property editor. If you have a property that you intend to set only programmatically and not by a designer, this option might be a good one to use. And last, `EditorBrowsableState.Advanced` shows the property in the advanced section of the property pane for that category. The advanced section is collapsed by default and can be expanded by clicking the small arrow icon at the bottom-center of the property pane. This expanded section allows you to potentially mark certain properties for only advanced use. The following code snippet applies the `EditorBrowsableAttribute` to a property, using the `EditorBrowsableState.Advanced` enumerated value. Also note in the snippet that more than one of these of these attributes can be applied to a property as needed.

```
[Category("ProgressBar Values")]
    [Description("The maximum value that can be measured by the Progress Bar")]
    [EditorBrowsable(EditorBrowsableState.Advanced)]
    public double MaximumValue
    {
      get { return (double)GetValue(MaximumValueProperty); }
      set { SetValue(MaximumValueProperty, value); }
    }
}
```

Figure 5-34 shows this property in the advanced portion of the property pane.

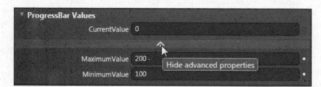

Figure 5-34. *EditorBrowsableAttribute setting on a property*

Designer-Unsafe Code

Although a custom control should be as general purpose as it can, we have seen custom controls in which control logic involves execution of code that relies on other aspects of the consuming application. An example of this could be parts of the control code calling out to a web service or being reliant on the presence of another application object in memory.

The important thing to keep in mind is that, when your control is loaded by Expression Blend, it is not running within the context of an application, and application-dependent logic may actually cause exceptions that will result in Expression Blend failing to loading your control at design time. If you cannot avoid having that kind of logic in your control, you need to guard it so that it does not execute when the control is loaded in a designer.

The best way to protect your application-dependent logic is to use the `System.ComponentModel.DesignerProperties` static class. The `DesignerProperties.IsInDesignTool` property returns `true` when the control is in design mode, and `false` otherwise. So when you want to execute control logic only if the control is being used outside the designer environment, you can conditionally execute that code only when `DesignerProperties.IsInDesignTool` is `false`.

When Expression Blend loads your custom control to the design surface, it will execute the control constructor and your override for the `OnApplyTemplate()` method, if you have one. It will also execute any `DependencyProperty` change handlers that you may have associated with your `DependencyProperty` definitions, when these properties are set for the first time (the default settings applied through the `PropertyMetadata`) or as they are set at design time through the property editor. These areas in your control code are ones where you should be especially careful to apply the practice explained in this section and guard any code that might not execute successfully outside the context of an application.

Including Sample Data

Controls often get the data they display from runtime data bindings. `ContentControl` and `ItemsControl` types (and their derivatives) are great examples of this. However, at design time, for a user to visualize the changes some of their property settings might make on the control's look and feel, it is often beneficial to have the control show some sample data within the designer. You can easily supply this data in your code, but you need to make sure that this code executes only when the control is being used within a designer—in effect exactly the opposite behavior from the one discussed in the previous section. The `DesignerProperties.IsInDesignTool` property can help here as well. With it, you can execute the code that adds sample data to your control at design time, only when the `IsInDesignTool` property is set to True. The following code snippet shows the `Content` property of a custom `ProgressBar` control to being set to some mock content at design time—in both the `OnApplyTemplate()` override as the initial value and the `DependencyProperty` change handler for the `CurrentValue` property. In both cases, we guard the code to ensure that this code only executes within the designer:

```
public override void OnApplyTemplate()
{
  base.OnApplyTemplate();
  //other code
  if (DesignerProperties.IsInDesignTool)
  {
    this.Content = string.Format("Progress {0}%", this.CurrentValue);
  }

}
internal static void OnCurrentValueChanged(DependencyObject Target,
  DependencyPropertyChangedEventArgs e)
{
  ProgressBar pBar = Target as ProgressBar;
  //other code
  if (DesignerProperties.IsInDesignTool)
  {
    pBar.Content = string.Format("Progress {0}%", (double)e.NewValue);
  }

}
```

Figure 5-35 shows the state of the `ProgressBar` control with the sample data in the designer when the `CurrentValue` property is changed to 30.

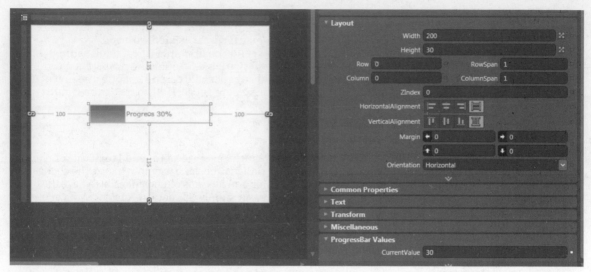

Figure 5-35. *Custom Control with sample content*

The Code

To illustrate the ideas discussed in this recipe, we show the application of the attributes and practices discussed on the sample `ProgressBar` control we built in recipe 5-10. Listing 5-41 shows the code for the control. Since there are no changes made to the control template for the control to illustrate these ideas, the XAML is not listed here anymore. To see the effects of this code, all you will need to do is place this control on a XAML page within Expression Blend and play with the various custom properties in the property editor.

Listing 5-41. *ProgressBar Control Sample with Designer-Related Attribution and Practices*

```
using System.Windows;
using System.Windows.Controls;
using System.Windows.Shapes;
using System.ComponentModel;

namespace Ch05_Controls.Recipe5_14
{
  [TemplatePart(Name="elemPBar",Type=typeof(FrameworkElement))]
  public class ProgressBar : ContentControl
  {

    public static DependencyProperty CurrentValueProperty =
      DependencyProperty.Register("CurrentValue",
      typeof(double), typeof(ProgressBar),
      new PropertyMetadata(0.0,
        new PropertyChangedCallback(ProgressBar.OnCurrentValueChanged)));
```

```
[Category("ProgressBar Values")]
[Description("The current value indicated by the Progress Bar")]
public double CurrentValue
{
  get { return (double)GetValue(CurrentValueProperty); }
  set { SetValue(CurrentValueProperty, value); }
}

public static DependencyProperty MaximumValueProperty =
  DependencyProperty.Register("MaximumValue",
  typeof(double), typeof(ProgressBar), new PropertyMetadata(100.0));
[Category("ProgressBar Values")]
[Description("The maximum value that can be measured by the Progress Bar")]
[EditorBrowsable(EditorBrowsableState.Advanced)]
public double MaximumValue
{
  get { return (double)GetValue(MaximumValueProperty); }
  set { SetValue(MaximumValueProperty, value); }
}

public static DependencyProperty MinimumValueProperty =
  DependencyProperty.Register("MinimumValue",
  typeof(double), typeof(ProgressBar), new PropertyMetadata(0.0));
[Category("ProgressBar Values")]
[EditorBrowsable(EditorBrowsableState.Advanced)]
[Description("The minimum value that can be measured by the Progress Bar")]
public double MinimumValue
{
  get { return (double)GetValue(MinimumValueProperty); }
  set { SetValue(MinimumValueProperty, value); }    }

[Category("Layout")]
public Orientation Orientation
{
  get { return (Orientation)GetValue(OrientationProperty); }
  set { SetValue(OrientationProperty, value); }
}

public static readonly DependencyProperty OrientationProperty =
    DependencyProperty.Register("Orientation",
    typeof(Orientation), typeof(ProgressBar),
    new PropertyMetadata(Orientation.Horizontal));
```

```
    internal FrameworkElement elemPBar { get; set; }

    public ProgressBar()
    {
      base.DefaultStyleKey = typeof(ProgressBar);
    }

    public override void OnApplyTemplate()
    {
      base.OnApplyTemplate();
      elemPBar = this.GetTemplateChild("elemPBar") as FrameworkElement;

      if (DesignerProperties.IsInDesignTool)
      {
        this.Content = string.Format("Progress {0}%",this.CurrentValue);
      }

    }


    internal static void OnCurrentValueChanged(DependencyObject Target,
      DependencyPropertyChangedEventArgs e)
    {
      ProgressBar pBar = Target as ProgressBar;
      if (pBar.elemPBar != null)
      {
        pBar.elemPBar.Width = (pBar.ActualWidth * (double)e.NewValue)
          / (pBar.MaximumValue - pBar.MinimumValue);
      }
      if (DesignerProperties.IsInDesignTool)
      {
        pBar.Content = string.Format("Progress {0}%", (double)e.NewValue);
      }

    }

  }
}
```

CHAPTER 6

■ ■ ■

Browser Integration

Silverlight 3 is a web browser–hosted control that runs in Internet Explorer and Firefox 2, as well as Safari or Firefox on the Macintosh. As such, there will be scenarios where developers need to customize how the control is configured. There will also be cases where developers need to modify the web browser Document Object Model (DOM) from Silverlight as well as situations where developers need to modify the Silverlight application from the DOM.

■**Note** Any performance or functionality differences that appear among Firefox, Safari, and Internet Explorer are considered bugs by Microsoft.

In Chapter 2, which focuses on the basics of the Silverlight programming model, we included recipes related to interacting with the browser:

- Recipe 2-3, "Using the FindName Method," demonstrates how to use FindName from JavaScript to locate and manipulate XAML elements from JavaScript.

- Recipe 2-4, "Dynamically Loading XAML from JavaScript," implements JavaScript that creates a piece of XAML and attaches it to the Silverlight control Visual Tree.

In this chapter, we cover how to customize the Silverlight 3 control within the browser. We also explain how to interact with the web browser DOM to provide a fully integrated web browsing experience.

6-1. Hosting Silverlight in HTML on Any Platform

Problem

You need to host the Silverlight 3 content in any technology that renders HTML.

Solution

Configure the Silverlight 3 browser control directly in HTML using the <object> tag. Modify or create JavaScript functions for error handling, loading, resizing, and so forth.

How It Works

The Silverlight 3 browser control is configurable with any web server-side technology such as ASP.NET, ASP classic, Java Server Pages (JSP), Ruby, or PHP because it is configured using the standard HTML <object> tag.

When you create a new Silverlight application, you have the option of having the project wizard create two test pages for the new Silverlight application, an .aspx test page and an .html test page. These pages serve as a starting point for configuring the Silverlight control. Here is a sample <object> tag from the HTML page:

```
<object data="data:application/x-silverlight-2," type="application/x-silverlight-2"
width="100%" height="100%">
  <param name="source" value="ClientBin/Ch06_BrowserIntegration.Recipe6_1.xap"/>
  <param name="onerror" value="onSilverlightError" />
  <param name="background" value="white" />
  <param name="minRuntimeVersion" value="3.0.40613.0" />
  <param name="autoUpgrade" value="true" />
  <a href="http://go.microsoft.com/fwlink/?LinkID=124807"
    style="text-decoration: none;">
      <img src="http://go.microsoft.com/fwlink/?LinkId=108181"
        alt="Get Microsoft Silverlight" style="border-style: none"/>
  </a>
</object>
```

The typical page includes a few CSS styles and a JavaScript function named onSilverlightError as well as a script include for Silverlight.js. The onSilverlightError function provides reporting for errors that are not handled within the Silverlight application. Some errors that cannot be handled in the Silverlight application, such as problems downloading the application .xap file.

Unhandled errors in the Silverlight application will bubble up to the Silverlight browser control and be reported to the user via the onSilverlightError function or any custom JavaScript function you write. By default, the onSilverlightError function is wired to the Silverlight control in the following line of code:

```
<param name="onerror" value="onSilverlightError" />
```

You do not have to use the onSilverlightError function as is. You can customize it or tap into any existing JavaScript error-handling routines that are part of an existing application.

■**Caution** Any errors bubbled up to the onSilverlightError function will cause the Silverlight application to stop working. Try to handle all errors that can be handled within the Silverlight application. Only catastrophic errors should be allowed to bubble up.

The <object> tag includes several configurable attributes; a key attribute is type, which determines the version of Silverlight that is needed by the application. For the final release version of Silverlight 3, type is set to "application/x-silverlight-3", but for the Silverlight 3 Beta the type is set to "application/x-silverlight-2 " to maintain compatibility with existing Silverlight 2 sites. Changing this value is part of the steps required to migrate from one version of Silverlight to the next.

Within the `<object>` tag are `<param>` tags that define parameters configured for the Silverlight browser plug-in. The one mandatory parameter is `source`, which defines the location of the application `.xap` file, or optionally, points to inline XAML if you're using the Silverlight unmanaged JavaScript programming model.

Recommended events are `onError` and `onResize`. As we mentioned earlier, by default, the `onError` parameter is set to the `onSilverlightError` function to report unhandled exceptions as well as runtime errors that occur at the plug-in level in the HTML page. We cover the `onResize` event in recipe 6-4. Table 6-1 lists other interesting parameters.

Table 6-1. *Additional Optional Parameters*

Parameter	Description
AutoUpgrade	Allows the developer to control whether an end user's Silverlight plug-in should be upgraded. The end user can still opt out even if the option is set to `true`.
Background	Sets the background color for the Silverlight 3 plug-in behind any Silverlight application content that renders to the content area but in front of HTML. This property defaults to `null`.
enableFramerateCounter	Displays the current frame rate in the browser's status bar in Internet Explorer on Windows. The default is `false`.
enableHtmlAccess	Enables or disables access to the web browser DOM. The default value is `false`. Set it to `true` if you want to access the web page from Silverlight. See recipe 6-5 for more information.
initParams	Comma-delimited string of initialization information in the form of `key1=value1,key2=value2`, and so on that can be accessed within Silverlight using managed code. Recipes 6-7 and 6-8 show you how to process parameters.
minRuntimeVersion	Specifies the minimum Silverlight 3 runtime version required by the Silverlight application.
maxFramerate	Specifies the upper limit on the frame rate for rendering content, with a default value of 60 frames per second.
onLoad	Set to a JavaScript function that fires after the Silverlight plug-in is instantiated and the XAML Visual Tree is loaded. See recipe 2-4 for an example that uses onLoad.
splashScreenSource	Set to the value of an `.xaml` file that is displayed as a splash screen while the application pointed to in the Source parameter is downloaded. See the MSDN documentation at http://msdn.microsoft.com/en-us/library/system.web.ui.silverlightcontrols.silverlight.splashscreensource(VS.95).aspx.

For more information on the other available parameters and instantiation objects, refer to the MSDN Silverlight documentation here:

http://msdn.microsoft.com/en-us/library/cc189089(VS.95).aspx#silverlight_plug_in

Within the `<object>` tag is an `<a>` HTML tag that displays the "Get Silverlight" image when the browser plug-in is not installed. Clicking the image will download the browser plug-in required by the Silverlight application.

Since this recipe is about the HTML page, we don't do anything relevant within the Silverlight application.

The Code

We generally do not show the source code for the hosting the HTML page or ASPX page in our recipes, because most of the work is done in the `MainPage.xaml` and `MainPage.xaml.cs` files that are in the Silverlight 3 application project. In this recipe, we will walk through the source for the HTML test page, which can be used with any web serving technology. Listing 6-1 serves as a starting point for hosting the Silverlight browser control generated by Visual Studio, but you can use it as a starting point for hosting Silverlight 3 in any web technology.

The HTML page in Listing 6-1 consists of a few CSS styles to layout the page, an error handling JavaScript script, and the HTML to host the control. The script reports runtime errors or unhandled exceptions by passing the error message to the browser in this line of code:

```
throw new Error(errMsg);
```

You can modify the JavaScript event as needed. For example, at the end of the `onSilverlightError` function you could instead assign errMessage to a `<div>` tag added to the page, and the message will be displayed in the `<div>` tag to the user with a message to restart.

Listing 6-1. *Typical Recipe HTML Test Page File*

```
<!DOCTYPE html PUBLIC "-//W3C//DTD XHTML 1.0 Transitional//EN"
  "http://www.w3.org/TR/xhtml1/DTD/xhtml1-transitional.dtd">
<html xmlns="http://www.w3.org/1999/xhtml">
<head>
  <title>SilverlightApplication1</title>
  <style type="text/css">
    html, body
    {
      height: 100%;
      overflow: auto;
    }
    body
    {
      padding: 0;
      margin: 0;
    }
    #silverlightControlHost
    {
      height: 100%;
      text-align: center;
    }
  </style>
```

```javascript
<script type="text/javascript" src="Silverlight.js"></script>

<script type="text/javascript">
  function onSilverlightError(sender, args) {
    var appSource = "";
    if (sender != null && sender != 0) {
      appSource = sender.getHost().Source;
    }

    var errorType = args.ErrorType;
    var iErrorCode = args.ErrorCode;

    if (errorType == "ImageError" || errorType == "MediaError") {
      return;
    }

    var errMsg = "Unhandled Error in Silverlight Application " +
        appSource + "\n";

    errMsg += "Code: " + iErrorCode + "    \n";
    errMsg += "Category: " + errorType + "        \n";
    errMsg += "Message: " + args.ErrorMessage + "      \n";

    if (errorType == "ParserError") {
      errMsg += "File: " + args.xamlFile + "      \n";
      errMsg += "Line: " + args.lineNumber + "      \n";
      errMsg += "Position: " + args.charPosition + "       \n";
    }
    else if (errorType == "RuntimeError") {
      if (args.lineNumber != 0) {
        errMsg += "Line: " + args.lineNumber + "       \n";
        errMsg += "Position: " + args.charPosition + "      \n";
      }
      errMsg += "MethodName: " + args.methodName + "       \n";
    }

    throw new Error(errMsg);
  }
</script>

</head>
```

```
<body>
  <form id="form1" runat="server" style="height: 100%">
  <div id="silverlightControlHost">
    <object data="data:application/x-silverlight-3," type="application/x-silverlight-3"
      width="100%" height="100%">
      <param name="source" value="ClientBin/
                                  Ch06_BrowserIntegration.Recipe6_1.xap" />
      <param name="onError" value="onSilverlightError" />
      <param name="background" value="white" />
      <param name="minRuntimeVersion" value="3.0.40613.0" />
      <param name="autoUpgrade" value="true" />
      <a href="http://go.microsoft.com/fwlink/?LinkID=149156&v=3.0.40613.0"
            style="text-decoration: none">
        <img src="http://go.microsoft.com/fwlink/?LinkId=108181" alt="Get Microsoft
Silverlight"
          style="border-style: none" />
      </a>
    </object>
    <iframe id="_sl_historyFrame" style="visibility: hidden;
       height: 0px; width: 0px;
      border: 0px"></iframe>
  </div>
  </form>
</body>
</html>
```

6-2. Hosting Silverlight in ASP.NET

Problem

You need to host Silverlight 3 content in ASP.NET.

Solution

Refer to Recipe 6-2 for information on hosing Silverlight in ASP.NET as well as any other technology.

How It Works

In Silverlight 2, an ASP.NET server control could be used to host Silverlight within the ASP.NET framework. This control is not shipped in Silverlight 3.

Developers could add the System.Web.Silverlight assembly from Silverligt 2 manually and use the server controls in an ASP.NET web page to host a Silverlight 3 application. However, the server control will not provide the latest installation logic, nor will it render the required iframe tag for Silverlight history support for example. See recipe 6-10 for more information on the new Silverlight Navigation Application project template.

The Code

There is no code for this recipe. The purpose of this recipe is simply to identify that the ASP.NET server control is no longer available in Silverlight 3.

6-3. Setting Focus for Keyboard Input

Problem

You want to ensure that the Silverlight control in a web page has focus when the page initially loads.

Solution

Create a JavaScript event handler and assign it to the Silverlight browser control's onload event handler.

How It Works

There are two levels of focus within a Silverlight application: at the browser level and within the Silverlight control itself. The Silverlight control cannot receive keyboard input unless it has focus within the web browser.

One way to ensure that the Silverlight application is completely downloaded and fully loaded is to create an onload JavaScript event handler sets the focus to the Silverlight control. Attach the onload event handler . to the Silverlight browser control, and then set the focus on the control.

The Code

First, create a simple Silverlight application that has a TextBlock with a title for the screen and two TextBox controls for first name and last name. We apply a little bit of color via a gradient brush to the application.

Besides the layout and gradient modifications, we also set TabIndex to 0 for the Enter First Name TextBox, set TabIndex to 1 for the Enter Last Name TextBox, and set TabIndex to 2 for the Enter Favorite Color TextBox. At this point, when we run the application, the cursor is not blinking in the TextFirstName TextBox, because the Silverlight application does not have focus on initial web page load. If you click anywhere on the Silverlight application, focus is sent to the TextFirstName TextBox because it has a tab index of 0.

The next bit of code for this recipe sets focus on the Silverlight browser control using JavaScript on the web page. We first modify the HTML page by assigning an ID of Silverlight1 to the <object> element that defines the Silverlight browser control. After that, we add a simple JavaScript event handler to a <script> block that sets focus on the <object> element for the Silverlight browser control:

```
function onSilverlightLoad(sender, args)
{
  var ctrl = document.getElementById("Silverlight1");
  ctrl.focus();
}
```

The final step is to wire the `onSilverlightLoad` event handler into the Silverlight browser control's onload event with this line of code within the `<object>` tag:

```
<param name="onload" value="onSilverlightLoad" />
```

When you run the page, you can see that focus is set on the first TextBox on loading the web page. To verify the behavior, remove the `<param>` tag for setting onload, and run the page again to see that focus is not moved to the Silverlight control without the onload event handler. Figure 6-1 shows the page as initially loaded without clicking the web page or the Silverlight browser control.

Appearance			Behavior	
BackColor			AutoUpgrade	True
BorderColor			Enabled	True
BorderStyle	NotSet		EnableTheming	True
BorderWidth			EnableViewState	True
CssClass			HtmlAccess	SameDomain
EnableFrameRateCounter	False		InitParameters	
EnableRedrawRegions	False		MaxFrameRate	0
Font			MinimumVersion	2.0.30911.0
ForeColor			OnPluginError	
PluginBackground			OnPluginFullScreenChang	
ScaleMode	None		OnPluginLoaded	
Source	~/ClientBin/Ch06_BrowserIntegration.Recipe6_1...		OnPluginResized	
SplashScreenSource			OnPluginSourceDownload	
Windowless	False		OnPluginSourceDownload	
Layout			ScriptType	
Height	**100%**		SkinID	
Width	**100%**		ToolTip	
			Visible	True

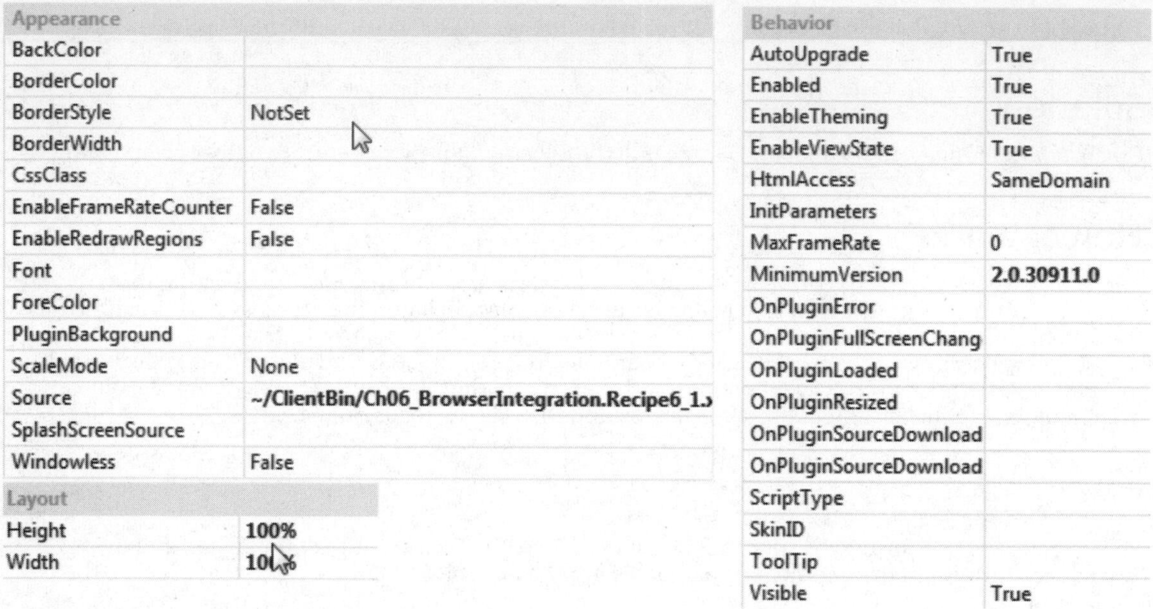

Figure 6-1. *Focus set on TextBox with TabIndex of 0*

Listing 6-2 shows the source code for the Silverlight application.

Listing 6-2. *Recipe 6-3's MainPage.xaml File*

```
<UserControl x:Class="Ch06_BrowserIntegration.Recipe6_3.MainPage"
    xmlns="http://schemas.microsoft.com/winfx/2006/xaml/presentation"
    xmlns:x="http://schemas.microsoft.com/winfx/2006/xaml"
    xmlns:d="http://schemas.microsoft.com/expression/blend/2008"
    xmlns:mc="http://schemas.openxmlformats.org/markup-compatibility/2006"
    Width="200" Height="200" mc:Ignorable="d">
```

```xml
<Border CornerRadius="20,20,20,20">
  <Border.Background>
    <RadialGradientBrush>
      <GradientStop Color="#FFFA6607" Offset="0.0040000001899898052"/>
      <GradientStop Color="#FFD4A282" Offset="1"/>
    </RadialGradientBrush>
  </Border.Background>
  <Grid x:Name="LayoutRoot" Margin="4,4,4,4">
    <Grid.ColumnDefinitions>
      <ColumnDefinition Width="0.078*"/>
      <ColumnDefinition Width="0.844*"/>
      <ColumnDefinition Width="0.078*"/>
    </Grid.ColumnDefinitions>
    <Grid.RowDefinitions>
      <RowDefinition Height="0.26*"/>
      <RowDefinition Height="0.74*"/>
    </Grid.RowDefinitions>
    <TextBlock Margin="4,4,6,23" FontSize="16" TextAlignment="Center"
     TextWrapping="Wrap" Grid.Column="1" d:LayoutOverrides="Height">
     <Run Foreground="#FF000080" Text="Collect Data"/></TextBlock>
    <StackPanel Margin="4,4,4,4" Grid.Row="1" Grid.Column="1">
      <Border Height="Auto" Width="Auto" CornerRadius="10,10,10,10"
          Margin="4,4,4,4">
        <Border.Background>
          <RadialGradientBrush SpreadMethod="Pad">
            <GradientStop Color="#FFD0CDAF"/>
            <GradientStop Color="#FF69E247" Offset="1"/>
          </RadialGradientBrush>
        </Border.Background>
        <TextBox Background="{x:Null}" Height="Auto" x:Name="TextFirstName"
         Width="Auto" Foreground="#FF0000FF" Text="Enter First Name"
         TextWrapping="Wrap" TabIndex="0"/>
      </Border>
      <Border Height="Auto" CornerRadius="10,10,10,10" Width="Auto"
        Margin="4,4,4,4">
        <Border.Background>
          <RadialGradientBrush SpreadMethod="Pad">
            <GradientStop Color="#FFD0CDAF"/>
            <GradientStop Color="#FF94E247" Offset="1"/>
          </RadialGradientBrush>
        </Border.Background>
        <TextBox Background="{x:Null}" Height="Auto" x:Name="TextLastName"
         Width="Auto" Foreground="#FF0000FF" Text="Enter Last Name"
         TextWrapping="Wrap" TabIndex="1"/>
      </Border>
```

```
      <Border Height="Auto" CornerRadius="10,10,10,10" Width="Auto"
       Margin="4,4,4,4">
        <Border.Background>
          <RadialGradientBrush SpreadMethod="Pad">
            <GradientStop Color="#FFD0CDAF"/>
            <GradientStop Color="#FF94E247" Offset="1"/>
          </RadialGradientBrush>
        </Border.Background>
        <TextBox Background="{x:Null}" Height="Auto" x:Name="TextFavoriteColor"
         Width="Auto" Foreground="#FF0000FF" Text="Enter Favorite Color"
         TextWrapping="Wrap" TabIndex="2"/>
      </Border>
    </StackPanel>
  </Grid>
 </Border>
</UserControl>
```

Listings 6-3 and 6-4 contain the source code for the HTML and .aspx files.

Listing 6-3. *Recipe 6-3's TestPage.html File*

```html
<!DOCTYPE html PUBLIC "-//W3C//DTD XHTML 1.0 Transitional//EN"
 "http://www.w3.org/TR/xhtml1/DTD/xhtml1-transitional.dtd">
<html xmlns="http://www.w3.org/1999/xhtml">
<head>
  <title>Test Page for Recipe 6.3</title>
  <style type="text/css">
    html, body
    {
      height: 100%;
      overflow: auto;
    }
    body
    {
      padding: 0;
      margin: 0;
    }
    #silverlightControlHost
    {
      height: 100%;
      text-align: center;
    }
  </style>
```

```
<script type="text/javascript" src="Silverlight.js"></script>

<script type="text/javascript">
  function onSilverlightLoad(sender, args) {
    var ctrl = document.getElementById("Silverlight1");
    ctrl.focus();
  }

  function onSilverlightError(sender, args) {
    var appSource = "";
    if (sender != null && sender != 0) {
      appSource = sender.getHost().Source;
    }

    var errorType = args.ErrorType;
    var iErrorCode = args.ErrorCode;

    if (errorType == "ImageError" || errorType == "MediaError") {
      return;
    }

    var errMsg = "Unhandled Error in Silverlight Application " +
          appSource + "\n";

    errMsg += "Code: " + iErrorCode + "    \n";
    errMsg += "Category: " + errorType + "      \n";
    errMsg += "Message: " + args.ErrorMessage + "     \n";

    if (errorType == "ParserError") {
      errMsg += "File: " + args.xamlFile + "     \n";
      errMsg += "Line: " + args.lineNumber + "     \n";
      errMsg += "Position: " + args.charPosition + "      \n";
    }
    else if (errorType == "RuntimeError") {
      if (args.lineNumber != 0) {
        errMsg += "Line: " + args.lineNumber + "      \n";
        errMsg += "Position: " + args.charPosition + "       \n";
      }
      errMsg += "MethodName: " + args.methodName + "      \n";
    }

    throw new Error(errMsg);
  }
</script>

</head>
```

```
<body>
  <form id="form1" runat="server" style="height: 100%">
  <div id="silverlightControlHost">
    <object id="Silverlight1" data="data:application/x-silverlight-2,"
      type="application/x-silverlight-2"
      width="100%" height="100%">
      <param name="source" value="ClientBin/Ch06_BrowserIntegration.Recipe6_3.xap" />
      <param name="onerror" value="onSilverlightError" />
      <param name="onload" value="onSilverlightLoad" />
      <param name="background" value="white" />
      <param name="minRuntimeVersion" value="3.0.40613.0" />
      <param name="autoUpgrade" value="true" />
      <a href="http://go.microsoft.com/fwlink/?LinkID=149156&v=3.0.40613.0"
        style="text-decoration: none">
        <img src="http://go.microsoft.com/fwlink/?LinkId=108181"
          alt="Get Microsoft Silverlight"
          style="border-style: none" />
      </a>
    </object>
    <iframe id="_sl_historyFrame" style="visibility: hidden; height: 0px;
      width: 0px; border: 0px"></iframe>
  </div>
  </form>
</body>
</html>
```

Listing 6-4. *Recipe 6-3's TestPage.aspx File*

```
<%@ Page Language="C#" AutoEventWireup="true" %>
<!DOCTYPE html PUBLIC "-//W3C//DTD XHTML 1.0 Transitional//EN"
  "http://www.w3.org/TR/xhtml1/DTD/xhtml1-transitional.dtd">
<html xmlns="http://www.w3.org/1999/xhtml">
<head runat="server">
  <title>Test Page for Recipe 6.3</title>
  <style type="text/css">
    html, body
    {
      height: 100%;
      overflow: auto;
    }
    body
    {
      padding: 0;
      margin: 0;
    }
```

```
   #silverlightControlHost
   {
     height: 100%;
     text-align: center;
   }
 </style>

 <script type="text/javascript" src="Silverlight.js"></script>

 <script type="text/javascript">
      function onSilverlightError(sender, args) {
          var appSource = "";
          if (sender != null && sender != 0) {
            appSource = sender.getHost().Source;
          }

          var errorType = args.ErrorType;
          var iErrorCode = args.ErrorCode;

          if (errorType == "ImageError" || errorType == "MediaError") {
            return;
          }

          var errMsg = "Unhandled Error in Silverlight Application " +
              appSource + "\n" ;

          errMsg += "Code: "+ iErrorCode + "     \n";
          errMsg += "Category: " + errorType + "        \n";
          errMsg += "Message: " + args.ErrorMessage + "      \n";

          if (errorType == "ParserError") {
              errMsg += "File: " + args.xamlFile + "      \n";
              errMsg += "Line: " + args.lineNumber + "      \n";
              errMsg += "Position: " + args.charPosition + "       \n";
          }
          else if (errorType == "RuntimeError") {
              if (args.lineNumber != 0) {
                  errMsg += "Line: " + args.lineNumber + "      \n";
                  errMsg += "Position: " + args.charPosition + "       \n";
              }
              errMsg += "MethodName: " + args.methodName + "      \n";
          }

          throw new Error(errMsg);
      }
 </script>

</head>
```

```
<body>
  <form id="form1" runat="server" style="height: 100%">
  <div id="silverlightControlHost">
    <object data="data:application/x-silverlight-2,"
      type="application/x-silverlight-2" width="100%" height="100%">
      <param name="source" value=
                             "ClientBin/Ch06_BrowserIntegration.Recipe6_3.xap" />
      <param name="onError" value="onSilverlightError" />
      <param name="onload" value="onSilverlightLoad" />
      <param name="background" value="white" />
      <param name="minRuntimeVersion" value="3.0.40613.0" />
      <param name="autoUpgrade" value="true" />
      <a href="http://go.microsoft.com/fwlink/?LinkID=149156&v=3.0.40613.0"
        style="text-decoration: none">
        <img src="http://go.microsoft.com/fwlink/?LinkId=108181"
        alt="Get Microsoft Silverlight" style="border-style: none" />
      </a>
    </object>
    <iframe id="_sl_historyFrame" style="visibility: hidden; height: 0px;
      width: 0px; border: 0px"></iframe>
  </div>
  </form>
</body>
</html>
```

6-4. Implementing a Full-Screen UI

Problem

You want your Silverlight application to run in full-screen mode as well as embedded mode.

Solution

To support full-screen mode, create an input mechanism such as a button or key combination to initiate full-screen mode. In the event handler for the button or key press, set IsFullScreen on the plug-in to true, and resize the UI elements to take up the entire screen.

How It Works

All of the examples in the previous chapters run Silverlight in embedded mode within the boundaries of the browser window. In full-screen mode, the Silverlight plug-in displays over the entire screen contents, rendering at the current resolution of the operating system. To set full-screen mode, call this line of code:

```
Application.Current.Host.Content.IsFullScreen =
  !Application.Current.Host.Content.IsFullScreen;
```

This line of code toggles full-screen mode, switching to full-screen mode if the plug-in is currently in embedded mode. This line of code will work only if it is in either a button or key press event handler. This is for security reasons to ensure that user input has switched the plug-in to full-screen mode—in other words, the application user initiated the action and knows that the plug-in is running in full-screen mode.

■**Note** If you try to switch to full-screen mode in the Load event, it will be ignored for security reasons. Full-screen mode requires that the user initiate full screen via a button click or key press event handler.

Once in full-screen mode, the UI elements do not automatically resize. Figure 6-2 shows what a 320×180-pixel UI looks like when IsFullScreen is set to true on a monitor that is set to a 1680×1050-pixel screen resolution.

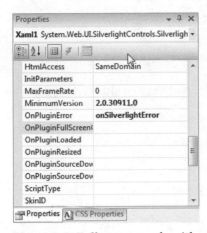

Figure 6-2. *Full-screen mode without resizing content*

The embedded UI renders in full screen with the same size as when in embedded mode unless the developer takes steps to resize the content in the Application.Current.Host.Content. FullScreenChanged event. There are generally two ways to handle resizing the UI:

- Automatically resize using a ScaleTransform.

- Manually resize by scaling pieces of the UI and repositioning elements as necessary to achieve the desired appearance.

Using a ScaleTransform is the quickest way to implement full screen because it takes advantage of the scalable vector graphics to maintain a crisp appearance upon resize. The downside is that applying a ScaleTransform to the entire UI may scale up parts of the UI that shouldn't be scaled, such as text or buttons.

Manually resizing pieces of the UI and manually repositioning elements provides precise control but takes more work. The advantage is that you can achieve the exact desired appearance for the entire UI by only scaling and repositioning as needed when done manually.

The Code

For this recipe, we demonstrate using the ScaleTransform with a twist. We employ an overall ScaleTransform to scale up the UI when in full-screen mode, but we also apply another ScaleTransform to limit how large the buttons grow when in full-screen mode.

Figure 6-4 shows the UI for the application before implementing full-screen mode. The application includes a Border, a MediaElement, and a few Button controls to control the content playback. We set a RectangleGeometry on the MediaElement.Clip property to give it rounded corners.

We copy a video from the sample videos included with Windows into the ClientBin/Video folder in the TestWeb web application project and rename the video to video.wmv.

■**Note** We cover how to integrate rich media in detail in Chapter 8.

We configure /Video/video.wmv for the MediaElement.Source property so that video plays when the UI is run. We also implement the events for the Play/Pause Button, the Stop Button, and the FullScreen Button to create the UI in Figure 6-4; the latter's event handler is shown here:

```
private void FullScreenButton_Click(object sender, RoutedEventArgs e)
{
  Application.Current.Host.Content.IsFullScreen =
    !Application.Current.Host.Content.IsFullScreen;
  if (Application.Current.Host.Content.IsFullScreen)
  {
    FullScreenButton.Content = "Emb";
  }
  else
  {
    FullScreenButton.Content = "Full";
  }
}
```

Next, we implement resizing functionality when the browser plug-in switches between full-screen and embedded mode. First, we create a ScaleTransform for the entire UI with this XAML:

```
<UserControl.RenderTransform>
  <ScaleTransform ScaleX="1" ScaleY="1" x:Name="ScaleToFullScreen" />
</UserControl.RenderTransform>
```

Then, we implement the FullScreenChanged event on the browser plug-in by adding this code to the constructor for the Page class:

```
Application.Current.Host.Content.FullScreenChanged +=
  new EventHandler(Content_FullScreenChanged);
```

Here is the Content_FullScreenChanged event handler:

```
void Content_FullScreenChanged(object sender, EventArgs e)
{
  if (!Application.Current.Host.Content.IsFullScreen)
  {
    ScaleToFullScreen.ScaleX = 1.0d;
    ScaleToFullScreen.ScaleY = 1.0d;
  }
  else
  {
    double pluginWidth = Application.Current.Host.Content.ActualWidth;
    double pluginHeight = Application.Current.Host.Content.ActualHeight;
    double scaleX = pluginWidth / _embeddedWidth;
    double scaleY = pluginHeight / _embeddedHeight;

    ScaleToFullScreen.ScaleX = scaleX;
    ScaleToFullScreen.ScaleY = scaleY;
  }
}
```

This code first checks to see if the browser plug-in is not in full-screen mode and sets the ScaleToFullScreen ScaleTransform's ScaleX and ScaleY attributes to 1 or to the original size for embedded mode. To calculate the scaling factors, we use the ActualWidth and ActualHeight values to determine the scaling factor. ActualWidth and ActualHeight reflect the actual rendering size of the Silverlight plug-in. When the ActualWidth or ActualHeight changes, it causes the onResize event to fire when the plug-in is in embedded mode. If the browser plug-in is in full-screen mode, the code first obtains the screen width and height from the ActualWidth and ActualHeight properties. Next, we calculate a scale factor to apply to the ScaleToFullScreen transform for the entire content, immediately resulting in scaling the UI to full the screen. Figure 6-3 shows the results.

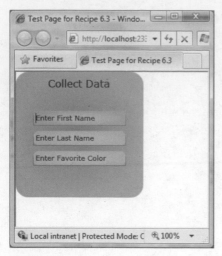

Figure 6-3. *Full-screen mode with uniform scale applied*

There may be scenarios where you don't want all of the content to be scaled uniformly. In this example, when viewed on a monitor in full-screen mode with the uniform scale applied, the `Button` elements appear a bit large even though they were evenly scaled.

In this case, we can apply a different scale to the `Button` elements so that they are scaled up to a lesser degree in full-screen mode. We also reposition the buttons to the lower-right corner when in full-screen mode. We first create a `ScaleTransform` resource on the `UserControl` element so that we could apply it to multiple parts of the UI if desired:

```
<UserControl.Resources>
  <ScaleTransform ScaleX="1" ScaleY="1" x:Key="ReduceScaleTransform" />
</UserControl.Resources>
```

We apply the `ReduceScaleTransform` to the `StackPanel` element containing the `Buttons` by setting the `RenderTransform` attribute on the `StackPanel` like this:

```
RenderTransform="{StaticResource ReduceScaleTransform}"
```

We alter the `FullScreenChanged` event so that it applies a reduced scale for this transform by adding this code when in full-screen mode:

```
((ScaleTransform)this.Resources["ReduceScaleTransform"]).ScaleX = scaleX * .10d;
((ScaleTransform)this.Resources["ReduceScaleTransform"]).ScaleY = scaleY * .10d;
ButtonPanel.HorizontalAlignment = HorizontalAlignment.Right;
```

We reduce the scale by taking the calculated uniform scale in the local variable `scaleX` and multiplying it by 0.1, which we determined by trial and error to look good on the screen. We also align the `StackPanel` to the right in full-screen mode and return to the center when in embedded mode. Figure 6-4 has the final UI.

Figure 6-4. *Recipe 6-4's final UI*

In Figure 6-4, the buttons are a little smaller and don't have giant text, which would detract from the video. As you can see, it is possible to use multiple ScaleTransform objects to achieve a reasonable user interface. Listings 6-5 and 6-6 contain the XAML and code for this recipe.

Listing 6-5. *Recipe 6-4's MainPage.xaml File*

```
<UserControl x:Class="Ch06_BrowserIntegration.Recipe6_4.MainPage"
    xmlns="http://schemas.microsoft.com/winfx/2006/xaml/presentation"
    xmlns:x="http://schemas.microsoft.com/winfx/2006/xaml"
    xmlns:System="clr-namespace:System;assembly=mscorlib"
    Height="216" Width="334">
  <UserControl.Resources>
    <ScaleTransform ScaleX="1" ScaleY="1" x:Key="ReduceScaleTransform" />
  </UserControl.Resources>
  <UserControl.RenderTransform>
    <ScaleTransform ScaleX="1" ScaleY="1" x:Name="ScaleToFullScreen" />
  </UserControl.RenderTransform>
```

```xml
        <Border CornerRadius="13,13,13,13" Margin="4"
                x:Name="MediaPlayerFrame">
          <Border.Background>
            <RadialGradientBrush SpreadMethod="Reflect">
              <GradientStop Color="#FF28D7A4" Offset="0.5"/>
              <GradientStop Color="#FF70E1BF" Offset="1"/>
              <GradientStop Color="#FF70E1BF" Offset="0.0040000001899898052"/>
            </RadialGradientBrush>
          </Border.Background>
          <Grid x:Name="MediaPlayerPanel" Height="210" Width="328">
            <Grid.RowDefinitions>
              <RowDefinition Height="0.848*"/>
              <RowDefinition Height="0.152*"/>
            </Grid.RowDefinitions>
            <MediaElement x:Name="mediaElement" Source="/Video/Video.wmv"
                Margin="4,2,4,2" MediaEnded="mediaElement_MediaEnded">
              <MediaElement.Clip>
                <RectangleGeometry  Rect="0,0,260,170" RadiusX="20"  RadiusY="20"/>
              </MediaElement.Clip>
            </MediaElement>
            <StackPanel x:Name="ButtonPanel" Grid.Column="0" Grid.Row="1"
             Orientation="Horizontal"  Margin="2" HorizontalAlignment="Center"
             RenderTransform="{StaticResource ReduceScaleTransform}" Height="26">
              <Button x:Name="PlayPauseButton" Content="Pause" Margin="2"
                    Click="PlayPauseButton_Click" MaxWidth="57" MaxHeight="34.5" />
              <Button Content="Stop" x:Name="StopButton" Margin="2"
                    Click="StopButton_Click" MaxWidth="47" MaxHeight="35" />
              <Button Content="Full" x:Name="FullScreenButton" Margin="2"
                    Click="FullScreenButton_Click" MaxWidth="47" MaxHeight="38" />
            </StackPanel>
          </Grid>
        </Border>
      </UserControl>
```

Listing 6-6. *Recipe 6-4's MainPage.xaml.cs File*

```csharp
using System;
using System.Windows;
using System.Windows.Controls;
using System.Windows.Media;
```

```
namespace Ch06_BrowserIntegration.Recipe6_4
{
  public partial class MainPage : UserControl
  {
    private double _embeddedWidth;
    private double _embeddedHeight;

    public MainPage()
    {
      InitializeComponent();
      Application.Current.Host.Content.FullScreenChanged += new
    EventHandler(Content_FullScreenChanged);
      this.Loaded += new RoutedEventHandler(Page_Loaded);
    }

    void Page_Loaded(object sender, RoutedEventArgs e)
    {
      //Store the embedded with and height so that we can
      //calculate the proper scale factor
      _embeddedWidth = this.Width;
      _embeddedHeight = this.Height;
    }

    void Content_FullScreenChanged(object sender, EventArgs e)
    {
      if (!Application.Current.Host.Content.IsFullScreen)
      {
        ScaleToFullScreen.ScaleX = 1.0d;
        ScaleToFullScreen.ScaleY = 1.0d;
        ((ScaleTransform)this.Resources["ReduceScaleTransform"]).ScaleX = 1.0d;
        ((ScaleTransform)this.Resources["ReduceScaleTransform"]).ScaleY = 1.0d;
        ButtonPanel.HorizontalAlignment = HorizontalAlignment.Center;
      }
      else
      {
        double pluginWidth = Application.Current.Host.Content.ActualWidth;
        double pluginHeight = Application.Current.Host.Content.ActualHeight;
        double scaleX = pluginWidth / _embeddedWidth;
        double scaleY = pluginHeight / _embeddedHeight;

        ScaleToFullScreen.ScaleX = scaleX;
        ScaleToFullScreen.ScaleY = scaleY;
```

```
    ((ScaleTransform)this.Resources["ReduceScaleTransform"]).ScaleX =
    scaleX * .10d;
    ((ScaleTransform)this.Resources["ReduceScaleTransform"]).ScaleY =
    scaleY * .10d;
    ButtonPanel.HorizontalAlignment = HorizontalAlignment.Right;
  }
}

private void FullScreenButton_Click(object sender, RoutedEventArgs e)
{
  Application.Current.Host.Content.IsFullScreen =
    !Application.Current.Host.Content.IsFullScreen;
  if (Application.Current.Host.Content.IsFullScreen)
  {
    FullScreenButton.Content = "Emb";
  }
  else
  {
    FullScreenButton.Content = "Full";
  }
}

private void PlayPauseButton_Click(object sender, RoutedEventArgs e)
{
  if ((mediaElement.CurrentState == MediaElementState.Stopped) ||
    (mediaElement.CurrentState == MediaElementState.Paused))
  {
    mediaElement.Play();
    PlayPauseButton.Content = "Pause";
  }
  else if (mediaElement.CurrentState == MediaElementState.Playing)
  {
    mediaElement.Pause();
    PlayPauseButton.Content = "Play";
  }
}

private void StopButton_Click(object sender, RoutedEventArgs e)
{
  mediaElement.Stop();
  PlayPauseButton.Content = "Play";
}
```

```
    private void mediaElement_MediaEnded(object sender, RoutedEventArgs e)
    {
      mediaElement.Position = new TimeSpan(0);
      PlayPauseButton.Content = "Play";
    }
  }
}
```

6-5. Calling a JavaScript Method from Managed Code

Problem

You have existing JavaScript code in a web application that you want to integrate into your Silverlight application without converting it to managed code.

Solution

Take advantage of the HTML Bridge to access JavaScript elements via the System.Windows.Browser namespace. Use the HtmlDocument object to obtain a reference to the HTML page's DOM. Use the HtmlPage object to invoke JavaScript methods.

How It Works

Silverlight 3 has technology for interacting between the Silverlight 3 managed code and the hosting browser's HTML DOM called the HTML Bridge. The HTML Bridge enables developers to call JavaScript from Silverlight managed code and expose entire managed code types to JavaScript. We'll cover the latter in recipe 6-6.

Developers can enable or disable HTML Bridge functionality by setting the enableHtmlAccess parameter on the Silverlight browser plug-in to true; the default as false, or disabled, as a security best practice.

For the default test page, add the following <param> to the <object> tag that instantiates the Silverlight plug-in:

```
<param name="enableHtmlAccess" value="true" />
```

Once this step is complete, it is possible to interact between managed code and the HTML DOM. For more information on the HTML Bridge security settings, go to

http://msdn.microsoft.com/en-us/library/cc645023(VS.95).aspx

Managed types can be passed as parameters to JavaScript functions and objects, and managed types can be returned from JavaScript functions. You can also assign managed types as event handlers for JavaScript as well as call JavaScript event handlers from managed types. Visit this site for more information on how to map types between the technologies:

http://msdn.microsoft.com/en-us/library/cc645079(VS.95).aspx

When writing JavaScript, you access HTML DOM objects using the `document.getElementById` method to obtain a reference to a named object within the HTML web page. Silverlight has similar functionality using this code:

```
HtmlDocument doc = HtmlPage.Document;
HtmlElement element = doc.GetElementById("Button1");
```

This code obtains a reference to `Button1` on the HTML page as an `HtmlElement` object in managed code. With the `HtmlElement` reference, developers can manipulate properties, attach events, and invoke methods, among other abilities listed in the MSDN Silverlight documentation:

```
http://msdn.microsoft.com/en-us/library/
    system.windows.browser.htmlelement(VS.95).aspx
```

The `System.Windows.Browser` namespace has other useful classes when interacting with JavaScript and the browser; these are listed in Table 6-2.

Table 6-2. *Key Classes in System.Windows.Browser Namespace*

Class	Description
BrowserInformation	Obtains the name, version, and operating system of the web browser hosting Silverlight
HtmlDocument	Used to access the HTML DOM from managed code
HtmlElement	Represents an HTML element in the DOM
HtmlPage	Grants access to the browser's DOM via the Document property, which can be assigned to and accessed via an instance of HtmlDocument
HtmlWindow	Represents a JavaScript window object in managed code
HtmlUtility	Provides useful methods to encode and decode HTML and URL strings

Additional classes related to making managed code are available in JavaScript, which we cover in the recipe 6-6. In this recipe, we focus on accessing JavaScript elements and methods from managed code.

To call JavaScript from managed code, you have to first enable browser interaction as described earlier by setting `enableHtmlAccess` to true.Next, you can invoke the JavaScript method from Silverlight by using the following line of code:

```
HtmlPage.Window.Invoke("fooGetData", args);
```

This line of code calls a JavaScript method named `fooGetData`, passing in arguments in an object array named `args`. The `Invoke()` method returns an object so if the JavaScript function `fooGetData` returns data, it can be received directly in Silverlight per the guidance at the following web site regarding rules on mapping data types between Silverlight and JavaScript:

```
http://msdn.microsoft.com/en-us/library/cc645079(VS.95).aspx
```

The code for this recipe takes advantage of the HTML Bridge functionality to manipulate elements in the browser DOM as well as invoke a JavaScript AJAX call from managed code and then have the JavaScript Ajax method call back into the Silverlight application with the returned data.

■**Note** In recipe, 6-6 you will learn how to call managed code from JavaScript.

The Code

We first create a simple user interface based on recipe 2-9, where we pull in XML data embedded into the .xap file. In this recipe, we call a JavaScript method that uses the Microsoft AJAX Library to make a web request to retrieve the XML data from the server. Before we cover how we retrieve the XML data via JavaScript, let's look at some additional points on the Silverlight and web page user interface.

In the Silverlight application UI for this recipe, we add a button called Update Data that, when clicked, makes the JavaScript call to retrieve the data. We also apply a little bit of styling by wrapping the Grid named LayoutRoot within a Border control named LayoutRootBorder. Then, on the outside, we apply another Grid with a Background SolidColorBrush that matches the second gradient stop on the GradientBrush applied to the LayoutRootBorder object.

We use the same brush for the outer Grid so that it blends with the background color set on the hosting web page. In Page_Loaded for the Silverlight application, we apply a bit of styling to the web page:

```
doc = HtmlPage.Document;
doc.SetProperty("bgColor", GetColor());
doc.GetElementById("silverlightControlHost").
        SetStyleAttribute("width",this.Width.ToString());
doc.GetElementById("silverlightControlHost").
        SetStyleAttribute("height", this.Height.ToString());
```

We obtain a reference to the DOM and set the background color (bgColor) of the web page to match the second gradient stop SolidColorBrush value on the Border control, which we obtain in the GetColor() method shown here:

```
private string GetColor()
{
  GradientBrush gb = layoutRootBorder.Background as GradientBrush;
  //Set background color to second gradient stop
  GradientStop gs = gb.GradientStops[1];
  return gs.Color.R.ToString("X2") + gs.Color.G.ToString("X2") +
                            gs.Color.B.ToString("X2");
}
```

In the default test pages, we remove all of the styling (setting Width and Height to 100%, etc.) and replace with a single style located in the Recipe6.5.css file shown here:

```
.PositionControl {
  top: 100px;
  left: 100px;
  float:right;
}
```

The style is applied to the <div> tag containing the Silverlight plug-in control using this code in both the .aspx and .html test pages:

```
<div id="silverlightControlHost" class="PositionControl" >
```

This style repositions the Silverlight plug-in along the right side of the browser window with some space from the right edge. There is some random chapter text at the top of the page just to fill in the page a bit (see Figure 6-5).

Figure 6-5. *Recipe 6-5's initial UI*

Listing 6-7 has the XAML for this recipe. Listing 6-9 has the code-behind for this recipe.

Listing 6-7. *Recipe 6-5's MainPage.xuml File*

```
<UserControl x:Class="Ch06_BrowserIntegration.Recipe6_5.MainPage"
    xmlns="http://schemas.microsoft.com/winfx/2006/xaml/presentation"
    xmlns:x="http://schemas.microsoft.com/winfx/2006/xaml"
    Width="600" Height="600" Background="{x:Null}">
  <Grid Background="#FFAFC6FE">
    <Border x:Name="LayoutRootBorder" CornerRadius="20,20,20,20" >
      <Border.Background>
        <LinearGradientBrush EndPoint="0.5,1" StartPoint="0.5,0">
          <GradientStop Color="#FF443EE1" Offset="0.0040000001899898052"/>
          <GradientStop Color="#FFAFC6FE" Offset="1"/>
        </LinearGradientBrush>
      </Border.Background>
      <Grid x:Name="LayoutRoot" Margin="12,12,12,12" Background="{x:Null}">
        <Grid.ColumnDefinitions>
          <ColumnDefinition Width="0.058*"/>
          <ColumnDefinition Width="0.878*"/>
          <ColumnDefinition Width="0.065*"/>
        </Grid.ColumnDefinitions>
        <Grid.RowDefinitions>
          <RowDefinition Height="0.097*"/>
          <RowDefinition Height="0.83*"/>
          <RowDefinition Height="0.073*"/>
        </Grid.RowDefinitions>
        <Button Height="Auto" HorizontalAlignment="Left" Margin="4,0,0,4"
      VerticalAlignment="Bottom" Width="Auto" Grid.Column="1" Content="Update Data"
      x:Name="UpdateDataButton" Click="UpdateDataButton_Click"/>
        <Border Grid.Column="1" Grid.Row="1" CornerRadius="13,13,13,13"
          Margin="10,10,10,10" >
          <Border.Background>
            <LinearGradientBrush EndPoint="0.5,1" StartPoint="0.5,0">
              <GradientStop Color="#FF4B4897"/>
              <GradientStop Color="#FF2F2AAA" Offset="1"/>
            </LinearGradientBrush>
          </Border.Background>
          <ListBox  x:Name="BookListBox" Margin="8,8,8,8" Background="{x:Null}"
      BorderBrush="{x:Null}"
      Foreground="#FF4EBA61" >
```

```xml
        <ListBox.ItemTemplate>
          <DataTemplate>
            <StackPanel Margin="2,2,2,2">
              <TextBlock Text="{Binding Path=ISBN}" Margin="0,0,0,2"/>
              <TextBlock Text="{Binding Path=Title}" Margin="0,0,0,2"/>
              <TextBlock Width="550" Text="{Binding Path=Description}"
                    TextWrapping="Wrap" Margin="0,0,0,10"/>
            </StackPanel>
          </DataTemplate>
        </ListBox.ItemTemplate>
      </ListBox>
    </Border>
  </Grid>
  </Border>
  </Grid>
</UserControl>
```

Listing 6-8. *Recipe 6-5's MainPage.xaml File*

```csharp
using System.Windows;
using System.Windows.Browser;
using System.Windows.Controls;
using System.Windows.Data;
using System.Windows.Media;

namespace Ch06_BrowserIntegration.Recipe6_5
{
  public partial class MainPage : UserControl
  {
    HtmlDocument doc;
    public MainPage()
    {
      InitializeComponent();
      Loaded += new RoutedEventHandler(Page_Loaded);
    }

    void Page_Loaded(object sender, RoutedEventArgs e)
    {
      doc = HtmlPage.Document;
      doc.SetProperty("bgColor", GetColor());
```

```
doc.GetElementById("silverlightControlHost").
            SetStyleAttribute("width", this.Width.ToString());
doc.GetElementById("silverlightControlHost").
            SetStyleAttribute("height", this.Height.ToString());

//Make scriptable type available to JavaScript
HtmlPage.RegisterScriptableObject("MainPage", this);
}

private string GetColor()
{
  GradientBrush gb = LayoutRootBorder.Background as GradientBrush;
  //Set background color to second gradient stop
  GradientStop gs = gb.GradientStops[1];
  //Remove alpha component from brush since it doesn't work for html
  //elements when setting background color.  ToString("X2") formats the
  //byte value as a hexidecimal value forcing 2 digits each if there are
  // not two digits for each component, it will cause an  error.
  return gs.Color.R.ToString("X2") + gs.Color.G.ToString("X2") +
                              gs.Color.B.ToString("X2");

}

private void UpdateDataButton_Click(object sender, RoutedEventArgs e)
{
  HtmlPage.Window.Invoke("getDataUsingJavaScriptAjaxAsync");
}

[ScriptableMember]
public void SetBookXMLData(string data)
{
  ApressBooks books = new ApressBooks(data);
  Binding b = new Binding("ApressBookList");
  b.Source = books.ApressBookList;
  BookListBox.ItemsSource = books.ApressBookList;
 }
 }
}
```

Now, let's see the JavaScript method created for this recipe that we call from Silverlight. We put all of our scripts into a js folder in the TestWeb web application. For the default test pages, download the Microsoft AJAX Library, and add a script reference to bring it into the web page:

```
<script type="text/javascript"
        src="js/System.Web.Extensions/1.0.61025.0/MicrosoftAjax.js"/>
```

■**Note** Download the Microsoft AJAX Library here: http://www.asp.net/ajax/downloads/library/.

We use the Microsoft AJAX Library as a convenient way to make a web request call that is abstracted from the browser, whether it's Internet Explorer, Firefox, or Safari. Listing 6-9 has the source code for the asynchronous Java web request call.

Listing 6-9. *Recipe6.5.js File*

```
///<reference name="MicrosoftAjax.js">
function getDataUsingJavaScriptAjaxAsync() {
    ///<summary>This method makes a web request to obtain an XML file</summary>
    ///<returns type="String" />
    var req = new Sys.Net.WebRequest();
    req.set_url("http://localhost:9090/xml/ApressBooks.xml");
    req.set_httpVerb("GET");
    req.set_userContext("user's context");
    req.add_completed(OnWebRequestCompleted);
    req.invoke();
}

function OnWebRequestCompleted(executor, eventArgs) {
    if (executor.get_responseAvailable()) {
        var xmlString = executor.get_responseData();
        //Call Managed Code method to pass back data - Covered in Recipe 6.6
        document.getElementById("Xaml1").Content.MainPage.SetBookXMLData(xmlString);
    }
}
```

Although this book does not focus on ASP.NET AJAX, we will cover the highlights of Listing 6-9. The first line (with the <reference name..> element commented out with three slashes) is the equivalent of a using in C#, and it brings in the Microsoft AJAX Library script file. We use the Sys.Net.WebRequest JavaScript class to make the web request asynchronously. When getDataUsingJavaScriptAjaxAsync is invoked in the Silverlight application's UpdateDataButton_Click event handler, the data is not immediately returned to the Silverlight application when this event handler executes:

```
private void UpdateDataButton_Click(object sender, RoutedEventArgs e)
{
    HtmlPage.Window.Invoke("getDataUsingJavaScriptAjaxAsync");
}
```

Instead, the web request asynchronously retrieves the data, which is returned via the OnWebRequestCompleted JavaScript method. The OnWebRequestCompleted JavaScript method shown in Listing 6-10 invokes a scriptable method called SetBookXMLData() located in the Silverlight application in order to return the data. A scriptable method is a managed code method that is made available in JavaScript. We cover how to call managed code in recipe 6-6 in detail.

To summarize, when the Silverlight Update Data Button is clicked, the event handler invokes the JavaScript method getDataUsingJavaScriptAjaxAsync to initiate the asynchronous call and immediately returns— that is, the UI thread is not blocking. When the ApressBooks.xml data is returned to the browser, the OnWebRequestCompleted JavaScript method passes the data back to Silverlight, where it is parsed by the class named ApressBooks using LINQ to XML. We cover this LINQ to XML functionality in recipe 2-9, so we don't show the listing here. The only difference is that the data binding that happens in XAML without any C# code in recipe 2-9 is now handled via this method in the Page class code-behind file:

```
[ScriptableMember]
public void SetBookXMLData(string data)
{
  ApressBooks books = new ApressBooks(data);
  Binding b = new Binding("ApressBookList");
  b.Source = books.ApressBookList;
  BookListBox.ItemsSource = books.ApressBookList;
}
```

Figure 6-6 shows the final UI when the button is clicked.

Figure 6-6. *Recipe 6-5's final UI with data-bound Apress book information*

6-6. Calling a Managed Code Method from JavaScript

Problem

You prefer to write complex operations in managed code but need to call the method from JavaScript as part of integrating Silverlight with a web site.

Solution

To make a managed code operation available in the browser, mark member functions with the `ScriptableMember` attribute. Next, make the scriptable type available on the HTML DOM by registering an instance of the scriptable object by calling `HtmlPage.RegisterScriptableObject`.

How It Works

There will be scenarios where a Silverlight application needs to be tightly integrated with web content such as when you have a robust existing web application where you are introducing Silverlight into the user experience. Cases where a web application needs to perform complex client-side calculations that would be better handled by managed code are great scenarios where the integration capabilities can prove valuable.

Developers can enable or disable HTML Bridge functionality by setting the `enableHtmlAccess` parameter on the Silverlight browser plug-in to a Boolean value, with the default `false`, or disabled.

For the default test page, add the following `<param>` to the `<object>` tag that instantiates the Silverlight plug-in:

```
<param name="enableHtmlAccess" value="true" />
```

Once this step is complete, it is possible to interact between managed code and the HTML DOM. For more information on the HTML Bridge security settings, see

```
http://msdn.microsoft.com/en-us/library/cc645023(VS.95).aspx
```

Managed types can be passed as parameters to JavaScript functions and objects and managed types can be returned from JavaScript functions. You can also assign managed types as event handlers for JavaScript as well as call JavaScript event handlers from managed types. Refer to this site for more information on how to map types between the technologies:

```
http://msdn.microsoft.com/en-us/library/cc645079(VS.95).aspx
```

To make an entire type available for scripting, mark it with the `ScriptableType` attribute. To mark individual methods as scriptable, apply the `ScriptableMember` to the individual methods. Both attributes reside in the `System.Windows.Browser` namespace.

To call a managed code method from JavaScript, you first declare the method and then decorate it with the `ScriptableMember` attribute as shown here:

```
[ScriptableMember]
public string MyMethod()
{
}
```

The next step is to make the object and its scriptable method available to JavaScript via the HTML Bridge by making this call in either `App.Startup` or `Page.Load` events.

```
HtmlPage.RegisterScriptableObject("foo", RootVisual); //App_Startup
HtmlPage.RegisterScriptableObject("foo", this); //Page_Load
```

If you need to pass a parameter to the managed scriptable method, you obtain a reference to an instance of the managed type with this JavaScript code:

```
var MyList =
  slPlugin.Content.BarObject.createManagedObject("List<string>");
```

You can then populate the variable reference in JavaScript using the corresponding JavaScript type's methods.

The final step is to call the scriptable method from JavaScript. The JavaScript code can be anywhere in the test page such as `document.load`, `Silverlight.onLoad`, or an event handler such as a button click. The HTML Bridge provides access to the managed code events via the Silverlight plug-in's `Content` property to make the call. Based on the example `RegisterScriptableObject()` and our scriptable method `MyMethod`, this line of JavaScript code shows how to make the call:

```
strVariable = document.getElementById("Xaml1").Content.foo.MyMethod();
```

When you register the object that has the scriptable methods, the first parameter passed into `RegisterScriptableObject()` is called the `scriptKey`. The value passed in as the `scriptKey`, in this case `foo`, is appended to `Content` after using `getElementById()` to find the Silverlight plug-in in the DOM.

You can also wire up a managed code event handler directly to a JavaScript event such as an HTML Button click. First create an event handler in the Silverlight application that follows this method signature:

```
private void MyJavaScriptEventHandler(object o, EventArgs e)
{
  // Code goes here…
}
```

The next step is to find the HTML element where the managed code event handler should be attached and attach the event handler to the desired JavaScript event:

```
doc.GetElementById("Button1").AttachEvent("click",
  new EventHandler(this. MyJavaScriptEventHandler));
```

When the HTML button `Button1` is clicked on the web page, the managed code event `MyJavaScriptEventHandler()` will execute.

The Code

For this recipe, we implement the concepts to show the rich integration possible between Silverlight and the HTML DOM. The first step is to set the enableHtmlAccess parameter to true so that the HTML Bridge is available in both the test page following the steps listed earlier. For the HTML page, we have only one way to build it: with plain old HTML and JavaScript. by adding a <script> tag to bring in a separate JavaScript file in the js folder named Recipe6.6.js containing the script.

For the sample code, we first demonstrate how to call a managed scriptable method with parameters. As mentioned in the previous section, you create a reference to a managed object that can then be populated using JavaScript code:

```
var MyList =
slPlugin.Content.BarObject.createManagedObject("List<string>");
MyList.push("Rob","Jit","Harry");
slPlugin.Content.BarObject.Foo(MyList);
```

The preceding code in onSilverlightLoaded creates a list object, populates it with some values and then passes it in to the Foo method. If you set a breakpoint in the Foo method, you will see that the method is successfully called and the values passed in. One other item to note is that we use this line of code in Page_Loaded to make the Bar class available in JavaScript:

```
HtmlPage.RegisterScriptableObject("BarObject", new Bar());
```

Next in the sample code, we want to grab the background color of the Silverlight control's main Grid control and apply it to the HTML page and a text input HTML element. For the HTML page, after enabling the HTML Bridge, we create an onSilverlightLoaded JavaScript event that we wire to the Silverlight plug-in's OnLoad event handler. We also remove the following line of code from the Silverlight plug-in parameter list because we want the application to configure the background at runtime.

```
<param name="background" value="white" />
```

The next step is to create the Silverlight managed code method on the Page class that we want to call from JavaScript. We name the method GetMyBackGroundColor() because it determines the color of the LayoutRoot Grid control and returns the color value as a red, green, blue (RGB) hexadecimal value. If the Grid.Background points to a GradientBrush, we grab the color value of the first GradientStop and pass that color back as the return value on the GetMyBackgroundColor method. Here is the line of code from Page_Load to make the GetMyBackGroundColor method available in JavaScript:

```
HtmlPage.RegisterScriptableObject("MainPage", this);
```

In the onSilverlightLoaded JavaScript event, we access the GetMyBackgroundColor() method with the following line of code:

```
colorRGB = document.getElementById("Xaml1").Content.MainPage.
GetMyBackgroundColor();
```

Once we have the color, we use the following to assign it to the text input control's backgroundColor property and to the document.bgColor property as well:

```
txt1 = document.getElementById("Text1");
txt1.value = colorRGB;
txt1.style.backgroundColor = colorRGB;
document.bgColor = colorRGB;
```

We set the width style attribute on the <div> containing Silverlight to equal the width of the Silverlight content from managed code in the Page.SizeChanged event. If we didn't do this, the document.bgColor value would not be visible. Otherwise, the default setting for the <div> in the generated test pages is to take over the entire browser screen height, and the background color set on the HTML page is not visible for most of the page.

To set the Width from managed code, we configure an ID on the HTML <div> tag in the ASP.NET page to silverlightControlHost, which matches the name automatically generated in the HTML test page. In managed code, we attach an event handler to the Page's SizeChanged event and execute the following code:

```
HtmlDocument doc = HtmlPage.Document;
doc.GetElementById("silverlightControlHost").
SetStyleAttribute("width", this.Width.ToString());
```

This code calls SetStyleAttribute() for the width attribute on the <div> and configures it with the Width configured on the managed code Page object. Figure 6-7 shows the results.

The Silverlight control is on the left side in Figure 6-7 just below the HTML Button, the "Color from Silverlight" text, and the text input HTML control with the RGB value returned by the GetMyBackgroundColor() method.

The Silverlight control in Figure 6-7 has a gradient that runs from top to bottom; the first gradient stop at the top matches the background color for the rest of the web page. Because we set the <div> width to match the Silverlight content Width, the light blue appears to wrap around the Silverlight plug-in. The light blue does not appear below the Silverlight plug-in because the height attribute remains set at 100% for the <div> containing the Silverlight plug-in.

The other custom code that we implement maps a managed code event handler to an HTML button Click event on the web page. The managed code method name is InvokedFromHtmlButtonClick() with this code:

```
private void InvokedFromHtmlButtonClick(object o, EventArgs e)
{
  MessageTextBlock.Text = "HTML button clicked at " + DateTime.Now.ToString();
}
```

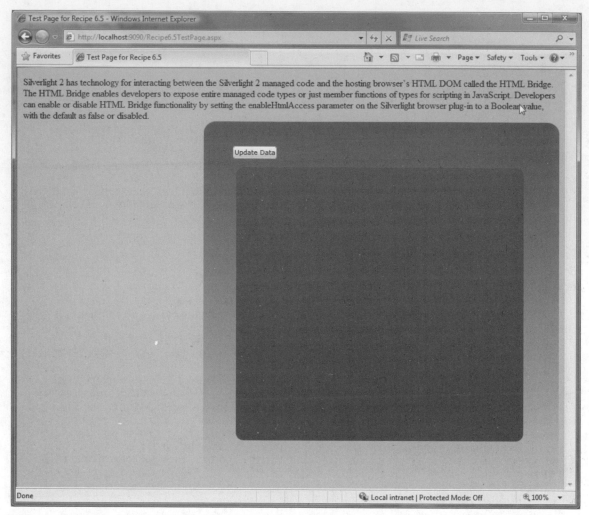

Figure 6-7. *Setting the web page background color from managed code*

We attach the managed code to the HTML button with this code in the Page_Load event handler:

```
HtmlDocument doc = HtmlPage.Document;
doc.GetElementById("Button1").AttachEvent("click",
 new EventHandler(this.InvokedFromHtmlButtonClick));
```

When you click the `Button` in the UI shown in Figure 6-7, Figure 6-8 is the resulting UI.

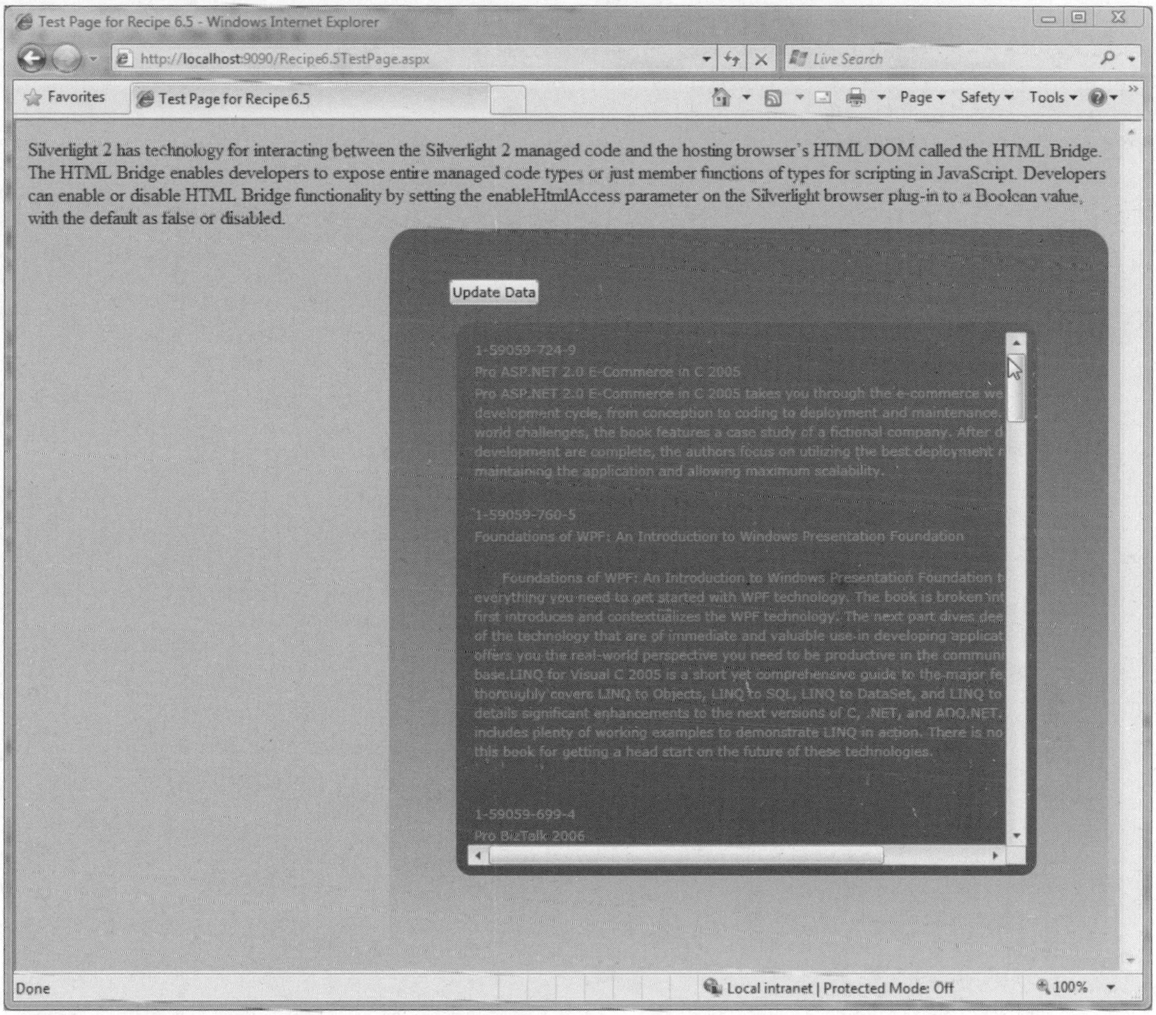

Figure 6-8. *Updated text with date/time displayed*

Since an ASP.NET `Button` server control always performs postback by default, we use an HTML input button on the `.aspx` page. It is possible to prevent the postback using client-side JavaScript; however, we want to call a Silverlight managed code method instead. Listing 6-10 shows the `MainPage.xaml` file, and Listing 6-11 shows the `MainPage.xaml.cs` file.

Listing 6-10. *Recipe 6-6's MainPage.xaml File*

```xml
<UserControl x:Class="Ch06_BrowserIntegration.Recipe6_6.MainPage"
    xmlns="http://schemas.microsoft.com/winfx/2006/xaml/presentation"
    xmlns:x="http://schemas.microsoft.com/winfx/2006/xaml"
    Width="400" Height="300" mc:Ignorable="d"
    xmlns:d="http://schemas.microsoft.com/expression/blend/2008"
    xmlns:mc="http://schemas.openxmlformats.org/markup-compatibility/2006" >
  <Grid x:Name="LayoutRoot">
    <Grid.Background>
      <LinearGradientBrush EndPoint="0.5,1" StartPoint="0.5,0">
        <GradientStop Color="#FF75C6E8"/>
        <GradientStop Color="#FF2828AA" Offset="1"/>
      </LinearGradientBrush>
    </Grid.Background>

    <Grid.RowDefinitions>
      <RowDefinition Height="0.043*"/>
      <RowDefinition Height="0.46*"/>
      <RowDefinition Height="0.497*"/>
    </Grid.RowDefinitions>
    <Grid.ColumnDefinitions>
      <ColumnDefinition Width="0.035*"/>
      <ColumnDefinition Width="0.91*"/>
      <ColumnDefinition Width="0.055*"/>
    </Grid.ColumnDefinitions>
    <TextBlock x:Name="MessageTextBlock" HorizontalAlignment="Left"
      Margin="4,4,0,0" VerticalAlignment="Top" Grid.Column="1" Grid.Row="1"
      Text="Your text goes here..." TextWrapping="Wrap"
      d:LayoutOverrides="HorizontalAlignment, VerticalAlignment, GridBox"
      FontSize="14" Width="194.999"/>
    <StackPanel Margin="4" Grid.Row="2" Grid.Column="1" >
      <Border Height="Auto" Width="Auto" CornerRadius="10,10,10,10"
          Margin="4">
        <Border.Background>
          <RadialGradientBrush SpreadMethod="Pad">
            <GradientStop Color="#FFD0CDAF"/>
            <GradientStop Color="#FF69E247" Offset="1"/>
          </RadialGradientBrush>
        </Border.Background>
        <TextBox Background="{x:Null}" Height="Auto" x:Name="TextFirstName"
            Width="Auto" Foreground="#FF0000FF" Text="Enter First Name"
            TextWrapping="Wrap" TabIndex="0" BorderBrush="{x:Null}" Margin="2"/>
      </Border>
```

```xml
            <Border Height="Auto" CornerRadius="10,10,10,10" Width="Auto"
                Margin="4">
              <Border.Background>
                <RadialGradientBrush SpreadMethod="Pad">
                  <GradientStop Color="#FFD0CDAF"/>
                  <GradientStop Color="#FF94E247" Offset="1"/>
                </RadialGradientBrush>
              </Border.Background>
              <TextBox Background="{x:Null}" Height="Auto" x:Name="TextLastName"
                  Width="Auto" Foreground="#FF0000FF" Text="Enter Last Name"
                  TextWrapping="Wrap" TabIndex="1" BorderBrush="{x:Null}" Margin="2"/>
            </Border>
            <Border Height="Auto" CornerRadius="10,10,10,10" Width="Auto"
                Margin="4">
              <Border.Background>
                <RadialGradientBrush SpreadMethod="Pad">
                  <GradientStop Color="#FFD0CDAF"/>
                  <GradientStop Color="#FF94E247" Offset="1"/>
                </RadialGradientBrush>
              </Border.Background>
              <TextBox Background="{x:Null}" x:Name="TextFavoriteColor"
                  Width="Auto" Foreground="#FF0000FF" Text="Enter Favorite Color"
                  TextWrapping="Wrap" TabIndex="2" BorderBrush="{x:Null}" Margin="2"/>
            </Border>
          </StackPanel>
        </Grid>
      </UserControl>
```

Listing 6-11. *Recipe 6-6's MainPage.xaml.cs File*

```csharp
using System;
using System.Windows;
using System.Windows.Browser;
using System.Windows.Controls;
using System.Windows.Media;

namespace Ch06_BrowserIntegration.Recipe6_6
{
  public partial class MainPage : UserControl
  {
    public MainPage()
    {
      InitializeComponent();
      Loaded += new RoutedEventHandler(Page_Loaded);
      SizeChanged += new SizeChangedEventHandler(Page_SizeChanged);
    }
```

```
void Page_Loaded(object sender, RoutedEventArgs e)
{
  //Make scriptable type available to JavaScript
  HtmlPage.RegisterScriptableObject("MainPage", this);
  HtmlPage.RegisterScriptableObject("BarObject", new Bar());

  HtmlDocument doc = HtmlPage.Document;
  doc.GetElementById("Button1").AttachEvent("click",
    new EventHandler(this.InvokedFromHtmlButtonClick));


}

void Page_SizeChanged(object sender, SizeChangedEventArgs e)
{
  //Set width of Div containing the SilverlightControl to width
  //of Silverlight content so that the HTML background displays
  //along side of the Silverlight control.  Otherwise the Silverlight
  //control will take up the entire page based on the html in the
  //default test pages that are created.
  HtmlDocument doc = HtmlPage.Document;
  doc.GetElementById("silverlightControlHost").SetStyleAttribute("width",
                                                 this.Width.ToString());

}

[ScriptableMember]
public string GetMyBackgroundColor()
{
  Brush b = LayoutRoot.Background;
  if (b is SolidColorBrush)
  {
    SolidColorBrush scb = b as SolidColorBrush;
    //Remove alpha component from brush since it doesn't work for
    //html elements when setting background color.
    //ToString("X2") formats the byte value as a hexidecimal value forcing
    //2 digits each if there are not two digits for each component, it will
    //cause a JavaScript error.
    return scb.Color.R.ToString("X2") + scb.Color.G.ToString("X2") +
           scb.Color.B.ToString("X2");
  }
  else if (b is GradientBrush)
  {
    GradientBrush gb = b as GradientBrush;
    //Arbitrarily pick the color of first gradient stop as the color
    //to pass back as the returned value.
    GradientStop gs = gb.GradientStops[0];
```

```
      //Remove alpha component from brush since it doesn't work for html
      //elements when setting background color.  ToString("X2") formats the
      //byte value as a hexidecimal value forcing 2 digits each if there are
      // not two digits for each component, it will cause a JavaScript error.
      return gs.Color.R.ToString("X2") + gs.Color.G.ToString("X2") +
                                      gs.Color.B.ToString("X2");
    }
    else
      return "#FFFFFF";
  }

  private void InvokedFromHtmlButtonClick(object o, EventArgs e)
  {
    MessageTextBlock.Text = "HTML button clicked at " +
      DateTime.Now.ToString();
  }
}
[ScriptableType]
public class Bar
{
  [ScriptableMember]
  public void Foo(List<string> param)
  { //Set a breakpoint
  }
}
}
```

Listings 6-12 and 6-13 show the .html and .aspx test files, respectively.

Listing 6-12. *Recipe 6-6's TestPage.html File*

```
<!DOCTYPE html PUBLIC "-//W3C//DTD XHTML 1.0 Transitional//EN"
 "http://www.w3.org/TR/xhtml1/DTD/xhtml1-transitional.dtd">
<html xmlns="http://www.w3.org/1999/xhtml">
<!-- saved from url=(0014)about:internet -->
<head>
  <title>Test Page for Recipe 6.6</title>
  <style type="text/css">
    html, body
    {
      height: 100%;
      overflow: auto;
    }
```

```
  body
  {
    padding: 0;
    margin: 0;
  }
  #silverlightControlHost
  {
    height: 100%;
    text-align: center;
  }
</style>

<script type="text/javascript" src="Silverlight.js"></script>

<script type="text/javascript" src="/js/Recipe6.6.js"></script>

<script type="text/javascript">
  function onSilverlightError(sender, args) {
    var appSource = "";
    if (sender != null && sender != 0) {
      appSource = sender.getHost().Source;
    }

    var errorType = args.ErrorType;
    var iErrorCode = args.ErrorCode;

    if (errorType == "ImageError" || errorType == "MediaError") {
      return;
    }

    var errMsg = "Unhandled Error in Silverlight Application " +
        appSource + "\n";

    errMsg += "Code: " + iErrorCode + "    \n";
    errMsg += "Category: " + errorType + "      \n";
    errMsg += "Message: " + args.ErrorMessage + "     \n";

    if (errorType == "ParserError") {
      errMsg += "File: " + args.xamlFile + "     \n";
      errMsg += "Line: " + args.lineNumber + "     \n";
      errMsg += "Position: " + args.charPosition + "      \n";
    }
```

```
      else if (errorType == "RuntimeError") {
        if (args.lineNumber != 0) {
          errMsg += "Line: " + args.lineNumber + "     \n";
          errMsg += "Position: " + args.charPosition + "     \n";
        }
        errMsg += "MethodName: " + args.methodName + "     \n";
      }

      throw new Error(errMsg);
    }
  </script>

</head>
<body>
  <form id="form1" runat="server" style="height: 100%">
  <div>
    <br />
    Value from Silverlight:
    <input id="Text1" type="text" /><br />
    <input id="Button1" type="button" value="button" /><br />
  </div>
  <div id="silverlightControlHost">
    <object id="Xaml1" data="data:application/x-silverlight-2,"
      type="application/x-silverlight-2"
      width="100%" height="100%">
      <param name="source" value="ClientBin/Ch06_BrowserIntegration.Recipe6_6.xap"/>
      <param name="onerror" value="onSilverlightError" />
      <param name="minRuntimeVersion" value="3.0.40613.0" />
      <param name="autoUpgrade" value="true" />
      <param name="enableHtmlAccess" value="true" />
      <param name="onload" value="onSilverlightLoaded" />
      <a href="http://go.microsoft.com/fwlink/?LinkID=141205"
       style="text-decoration: none;">
        <img src="http://go.microsoft.com/fwlink/?LinkId=108181"
         alt="Get Microsoft Silverlight" style="border-style: none" />
      </a>
    </object>
    <iframe id="_sl_historyFrame" style="visibility: hidden; height: 0px;
      width: 0px; border: 0px"></iframe>
  </div>
  </form>
</body>
</html>
```

Listing 6-13. *Recipe 6-6's TestPage.aspx File*

```
<%@ Page Language="C#" AutoEventWireup="true" %>

<!DOCTYPE html PUBLIC "-//W3C//DTD XHTML 1.0 Transitional//EN"
"http://www.w3.org/TR/xhtml1/DTD/xhtml1-transitional.dtd">
<html xmlns="http://www.w3.org/1999/xhtml">
<head runat="server">
  <title>Test Page for Recipe 6.6</title>
  <style type="text/css">
    html, body
    {
      height: 100%;
      overflow: auto;
    }
    body
    {
      padding: 0;
      margin: 0;
    }
    #silverlightControlHost
    {
      height: 100%;
      text-align: center;
    }
  </style>

  <script type="text/javascript" src="Silverlight.js"></script>

  <script type="text/javascript" src="/js/Recipe6.6.js"></script>

  <script type="text/javascript">
      function onSilverlightError(sender, args) {
          var appSource = "";
          if (sender != null && sender != 0) {
            appSource = sender.getHost().Source;
          }

          var errorType = args.ErrorType;
          var iErrorCode = args.ErrorCode;

          if (errorType == "ImageError" || errorType == "MediaError") {
            return;
          }
```

```
                var errMsg = "Unhandled Error in Silverlight Application " +
                appSource + "\n" ;

                errMsg += "Code: "+ iErrorCode + "      \n";
                errMsg += "Category: " + errorType + "        \n";
                errMsg += "Message: " + args.ErrorMessage + "       \n";

                if (errorType == "ParserError") {
                    errMsg += "File: " + args.xamlFile + "      \n";
                    errMsg += "Line: " + args.lineNumber + "      \n";
                    errMsg += "Position: " + args.charPosition + "       \n";
                }
                else if (errorType == "RuntimeError") {
                    if (args.lineNumber != 0) {
                        errMsg += "Line: " + args.lineNumber + "       \n";
                        errMsg += "Position: " +  args.charPosition + "        \n";
                    }
                    errMsg += "MethodName: " + args.methodName + "       \n";
                }

                throw new Error(errMsg);
        }
    </script>

</head>
<body>
  <form id="form1" runat="server" style="height: 100%">
  <div>
    <br />
    <asp:Label ID="Label1" runat="server" Text="Color from Silverlight:" />
    <asp:TextBox ID="Text1" runat="server"></asp:TextBox><br />
    <input id="Button1" type="button" value="button" />
  </div>
  <div id="silverlightControlHost">
    <object id="Xaml1" data="data:application/x-silverlight-2,"
     type="application/x-silverlight-2"
      width="100%" height="100%">
      <param name="source" value="ClientBin/Ch06_BrowserIntegration.Recipe6_6.xap"/>
      <param name="onerror" value="onSilverlightError" />
      <param name="minRuntimeVersion" value="3.0.40613.0" />
      <param name="autoUpgrade" value="true" />
      <param name="enableHtmlAccess" value="true" />
      <param name="onload" value="onSilverlightLoaded" />
```

```
        <a href="http://go.microsoft.com/fwlink/?LinkID=141205"
         style="text-decoration: none;">
          <img src="http://go.microsoft.com/fwlink/?LinkId=108181"
           alt="Get Microsoft Silverlight"
            style="border-style: none" />
        </a>
      </object>
      <iframe id="_sl_historyFrame" style="visibility: hidden; height: 0px;
                        width: 0px;
        border: 0px"></iframe>
    </div>
    </form>
</body>
</html>
```

Listing 6-14 contains the JavaScript called in this recipe to set the background color for the web page.

Listing 6-14. *Recipe 6-6's JavaScript File*

```
function onSilverlightLoaded(sender, args) {
    //Get Color from Page.GetMyColor
    colorRGB = document.getElementById("Xaml1").
                        Content.MainPage.GetMyBackgroundColor();
    //Obtain a reference to the html input textbox
    txt1 = document.getElementById("Text1");
    txt1.value = colorRGB;
    txt1.style.backgroundColor = colorRGB;
    //Set background of entire page to same color
    document.bgColor = colorRGB;
}
```

6-7. Exchanging Data Among Multiple Plug-ins
Problem
You have more than one Silverlight plug-in in your web page hosting content and you need to exchange data among the plug-ins.

Solution
Use the HTML Bridge covered in recipes 6-5 and 6-6 to expose methods from Silverlight to JavaScript using the ScriptableMethodAttribute. Call the methods as JavaScript methods using HtmlPage.Window. Invoke().

How It Works

We cover the details on working with the HTML Bridge in recipes 6-5 and 6-6. In this recipe, we focus on using the HTML Bridge to implement communication between multiple instances of the same Silverlight application.

This recipe implements communication via the HTML Bridge, which means that the data passed via the HTML Bridge must be JavaScript compatible. Refer to this site for more information on how to map types between the technologies:

http://msdn.microsoft.com/en-us/library/cc645079(VS.95).aspx

In this example, we implement pushing data as well as requesting data between two instances of the same Silverlight application. We establish a convention of naming the JavaScript methods with the name of the Silverlight plug-in ID as a prefix to the method name.

The Silverlight plug-in supports initialization parameters in the form of key/value pairs in a string like "Key1=Value1;Key2=Value2;Key3=Value3", providing support for multiple initialization parameters. In our case, we have one parameter that we pass in on the <object> tag in the .html page; this parameter is the other Silverlight plug-in we want to work with:

```
<param name ="initParams" value="PartnerControl=Xaml2" />
```

This code parses the initParams in Page_Loaded:

```
//Get passed parameter for partner control
 string initParams = HtmlPage.Plugin.GetProperty("initParams").ToString();
 string[] paramsArray = initParams.Split(';');
 string[] KeyValue = paramsArray[0].Split('=');
  _partnerControlID = KeyValue[1];
```

We pass in the parameter so that we know which control to talk to. The correct control is chosen by calling JavaScript methods that are prefixed with the partner control's name. So when sending data to the partner control, we make this call:

```
HtmlPage.Window.Invoke(_partnerControlID + "DoReceive",args);
```

In the DoReceive JavaScript functions, we pass in data from the control from a button click initiated by the user, calling the managed code function ReceiveData() from JavaScript, and passing in the data. When requesting data, we make this call:

```
string str = (string)HtmlPage.Window.Invoke(_partnerControlID + "RequestData");
```

In the RequestData JavaScript functions, we invoke the managed code RequestData() method via the JavaScript method. The managed code RequestData() method returns the data, which is then returned to the calling application via the HTML Bridge.

This simple convention provides an easy means of communicating between multiple Silverlight plug-ins within the same web page.

The Code

In this recipe's sample code, we modify the default test web pages, adding an additional instance of the Silverlight plug-in of the same Silverlight application, so both plug-in instances point to the

Ch06_BrowserIntegration.Recipe6_7.xap file. In both the .aspx and .html pages, we ensure that both Silverlight plug-in controls as well as their parent <div> containers have unique IDs in the page.

We also modify the test pages so that the height and width on all of the controls isn't set to 100% to keep the two plug-in instances visible and near each other to facilitate testing. We set the <object> tags hosting the Silverlight plug-in to 100% for Width. We create the four JavaScript functions to implement data-push and data-request in Recipe6.7.js located in the js folder. Listing 6-15 has the four JavaScript functions.

Listing 6-15. *Recipe 6-7's JavaScript File*

```
function Xaml1DoReceive(data)
{
    document.getElementById("Xaml1").Content.MainPage.ReceiveData(data);
}


function Xaml1RequestData()
{
    return document.getElementById("Xaml1").Content.MainPage.RequestData();
}


function Xaml2DoReceive(data)
{
    document.getElementById("Xaml2").Content.MainPage.ReceiveData(data);
}


function Xaml2RequestData(data)
{
    return document.getElementById("Xaml2").Content.MainPage.RequestData();
}
```

The XAML markup has a TextBlock at the top of the UI where the ID of the control instance is displayed. The ID is retrieved and set to the Text value of the TextBlock using this code:

```
ControlID.Text = HtmlPage.Plugin.Id;
```

The UI also has two buttons that make the calls to the appropriate JavaScript method with the Send Data button making the following call to push data to the other application hosted in a separate Silverlight plug-in on the same page:

```
HtmlPage.Window.Invoke(_partnerControlID + "DoReceive",args);
```

The other button, Request Data, makes this call to pull data from the other Silverlight application hosted on the page:

```
string str = (string)HtmlPage.Window.
Invoke(_partnerControlID + "RequestData");
```

There is a TextBox control so that the user can type data to send at the upper-right part of the UI. There are two TextBox controls on the lower-right part of the UI where pushed data is received and requested data is loaded, as shown in Figure 6-9.

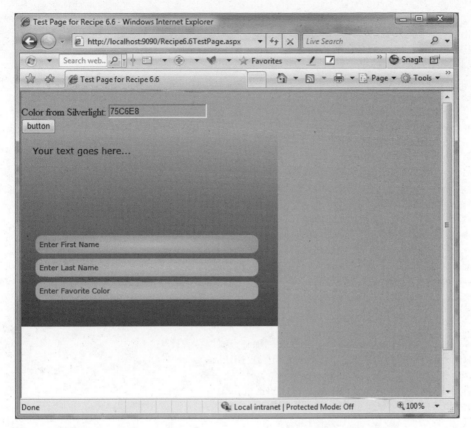

Figure 6-9. *Recipe 6-7's user interface*

Listings 6-16 and 6-17 have the XAML and code-behind file this recipe.

Listing 6-16. *Recipe 6-7's MainPage.xaml File*

```
<UserControl x:Class="Ch06_BrowserIntegration.Recipe6_7.MainPage"
    xmlns="http://schemas.microsoft.com/winfx/2006/xaml/presentation"
    xmlns:x="http://schemas.microsoft.com/winfx/2006/xaml"
    Width="400" Height="250" mc:Ignorable="d"
    xmlns:d="http://schemas.microsoft.com/expression/blend/2008"
    xmlns:mc="http://schemas.openxmlformats.org/markup-compatibility/2006">
    <Grid x:Name="LayoutRoot">
      <Grid.Background>
        <RadialGradientBrush>
          <GradientStop Color="#FFFFFFFF"/>
          <GradientStop Color="#FFB98585" Offset="1"/>
        </RadialGradientBrush>
      </Grid.Background>
```

```xml
      <Grid.RowDefinitions>
        <RowDefinition Height="0.067*"/>
        <RowDefinition Height="0.433*"/>
        <RowDefinition Height="0.43*"/>
        <RowDefinition Height="0.07*"/>
      </Grid.RowDefinitions>
      <Grid.ColumnDefinitions>
        <ColumnDefinition Width="0.055*"/>
        <ColumnDefinition Width="0.442*"/>
        <ColumnDefinition Width="0.45*"/>
        <ColumnDefinition Width="0.052*"/>
      </Grid.ColumnDefinitions>
      <Button x:Name="SendDataButton" Height="Auto" Margin="4,4,4,0"
       Click="SendDataButton_Click" Grid.Column="1" Grid.Row="1"
       VerticalAlignment="Top" Content="Send Data"/>
      <StackPanel Margin="4,4,4,4" Grid.Column="2" Grid.Row="1">
        <TextBlock Height="Auto" Width="Auto" Text="Data to Send:"
         TextWrapping="Wrap" Margin="2,2,2,2"/>
        <TextBox Height="24" Width="Auto" Text="" TextWrapping="Wrap"
         Margin="2,2,2,2" x:Name="DataToSend"/>
      </StackPanel>
      <Button x:Name="RequestDataButton" Height="Auto" Margin="4,4,4,0"
       Click="RequestDataButton_Click" Grid.Column="1" Grid.Row="2"
       VerticalAlignment="Top" Content="Request Data" />
      <StackPanel Margin="0,4,8,4" Grid.Column="2" Grid.Row="2">
        <TextBlock Height="Auto" Margin="2,2,2,2" Width="Auto"
         Text="Received Data:" TextWrapping="Wrap"/>
        <TextBox Height="24" Margin="2,2,2,2" Width="Auto"
         Text="" TextWrapping="Wrap" x:Name="ReceivedData"/>
        <TextBlock Height="16" Width="101"
          Text="Requested Data:" TextWrapping="Wrap"/>
        <TextBox Height="24" Width="Auto"
          Text="" TextWrapping="Wrap" x:Name="RequestedData"/>
      </StackPanel>

      <TextBlock HorizontalAlignment="Left" Margin="4,0,0,4" Width="102"
       Grid.Column="1" Text="TextBlock" TextWrapping="Wrap"
       d:LayoutOverrides="HorizontalAlignment" x:Name="ControlID"/>
    </Grid>
</UserControl>
```

Listing 6-17. *Recipe 6-7's MainPage.xaml.cs File*

```
using System;
using System.Windows;
using System.Windows.Browser;
using System.Windows.Controls;

namespace Ch06_BrowserIntegration.Recipe6_7
{
  public partial class MainPage : UserControl
  {
    private string _partnerControlID;
    public MainPage()
    {
      InitializeComponent();
      Loaded += new RoutedEventHandler(Page_Loaded);
    }

    void Page_Loaded(object sender, RoutedEventArgs e)
    {
      //Make scriptable type available to JavaScript
      //Enable call to ReceiveData from JavaScript
      HtmlPage.RegisterScriptableObject("MainPage", this);
      //Get the ID of the Silverlight Plug-in Control Parent
      string parentId = HtmlPage.Plugin.Parent.Id;
      //Get the ID of the Silverlight Plug-in Control
      ControlID.Text = HtmlPage.Plugin.Id;
      //Obtain a reference to the DOM
      HtmlDocument doc = HtmlPage.Document;
      //Set height and width on parent div so
      //that the control displays properly
      doc.GetElementById(parentId).
              SetStyleAttribute("width", this.Width.ToString());
      doc.GetElementById(parentId).
                SetStyleAttribute("height", this.Height.ToString());
      //Get passed parameter for partner control
      string initParams =
        HtmlPage.Plugin.GetProperty("initParams").ToString();
      string[] paramsArray = initParams.Split(';');
      string[] KeyValue = paramsArray[0].Split('=');
      _partnerControlID = KeyValue[1];
    }
```

```csharp
[ScriptableMember]
public void ReceiveData(object receivedData)
{
  ReceivedData.Text = (string)receivedData;
}

[ScriptableMember]
public string RequestData()
{
  if (DateTime.Now.Millisecond < 500)
    return "RequestedData" + DateTime.Now.ToString();
  else
    return null;
}

private void SendDataButton_Click(object sender, RoutedEventArgs e)
{
  object[] args = new object[1];
  args[0] = DataToSend.Text ;
  HtmlPage.Window.Invoke(_partnerControlID + "DoReceive",args);
}

private void RequestDataButton_Click(object sender, RoutedEventArgs e)
{
  string str = (string)HtmlPage.Window.
    Invoke(_partnerControlID + "RequestData");
  if (str != null)
    RequestedData.Text = str;
  else
    RequestedData.Text = "no data";
}
  }
}
```

6-8. Embedding Silverlight Within a Windows Gadget

Problem

You want to build a gadget for the Windows Sidebar that includes the Silverlight 3 plug-in control for both Windows Vista and Windows 7.

Solution

The Windows Sidebar hosts gadgets that are based on an HTML and JavaScript programming model. As such, gadgets can host ActiveX controls such as the Silverlight plug-in.

How It Works

Windows Sidebar gadgets are meant to be visually appealing and focused on performing a single task well, such as tracking stock quotes, tracking system resource utilization, reporting internal training status, and so forth. Given the ability to create rich user interfaces in Silverlight that you host in a web page, it is a very interesting scenario to host Silverlight in a Windows Sidebar gadget.

■**Note**   Windows Sidebar gadgets that include Silverlight 3 can only be hosted in 32-bit Sidebar process.

Windows Sidebar gadgets generally have small user interfaces in order to fit in the Sidebar. MSDN has sizing guidelines of 130 pixels when docked, which includes 5 pixels of drop shadow—2 pixels on the left, and 3 pixels on the right.

Gadgets can be detached from the Windows Sidebar. In Windows 7, gadgets are free floating by default. When detached or floating, the recommended size is 400 pixels by 400 pixels. Gadgets can have an options dialog box with a client area of 278 pixels wide and no more than 400 pixels high. We use these guidelines to create a Silverlight 3 gadget interface. For more information on Windows Sidebar gadgets interface guidelines, see

http://msdn.microsoft.com/en-us/library/aa974179.aspx

Now that we have covered the basics on the UI for gadgets, here are the three basic steps to create a Windows Sidebar gadget:

1.   Create a development folder for all of the gadget files.

2.   Add the HTML pages, CSS, and JavaScript files to the development folder.

3.   Create a manifest file, and add it to the development folder.

For the first step, we create a web site project named Silverlight3RecipesGadget in the file system under the Code\Ch06_BrowserIntegration folder in the sample code. We remove the App_Data folder, Default.aspx file, and web.config file from the project, since we don't need them.

For the second step, we add three HTML files named DockedUndockedView.html, FlyoutView.html, and SettingsView.html, as well as three folders: a js folder for JavaScript files, a css folder for CSS files, and a ClientBin folder for the Silverlight .xap file. We add Silverlight.js to our project in the js folder and create placeholder JavaScript and CSS files in their respective folders. We obtain Silverlight.js from this folder in the files system:

```
%ProgramFiles%\Microsoft SDKs\Silverlight\v2.0\Tools
```

Figure 6-10 shows the initial layout of our Silverlight gadget web project in the Visual Studio Solution Explorer tool window.

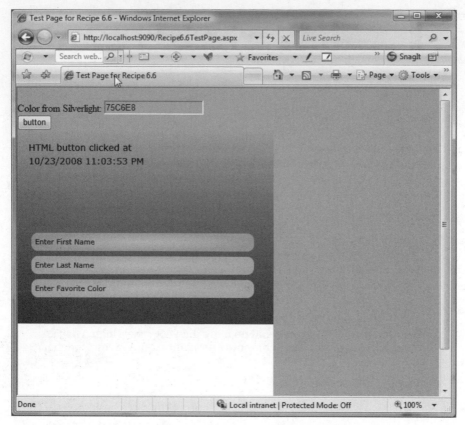

Figure 6-10. *Recipe 6-8's initial Silverlight gadget web project layout*

We also go to the project properties for the Silverlight3Silverlight3RecipesGadget project, and add the "6-8 Embed Silverlight within a Vista Gadget" project to the Silverlight tab. We do not create test pages in the Add Silverlight Application wizard, because we don't need them in this project. Completing the wizard will automatically copy the output from our Silverlight application to the ClientBin folder for the gadget each time the application is compiled.

For the third step, we add an XML file to the web project and name it Gadget.xml. This file defines the startup HMTL page, title, authors, and so on for the gadget. For more information about the format of Gadget.xml, see

```
http://msdn.microsoft.com/en-gb/library/bb508509(VS.85).aspx
```

Essentially, you code gadgets as you would code HTML files. The gadget runs in an Internet Explorer window that doesn't have any of the browser chrome. You can manipulate the DOM, make Ajax calls, and access system resources.

There are several views available for a gadget: docked, undocked, flyout, and settings. Figure 6-11 shows the different views available for a gadget.

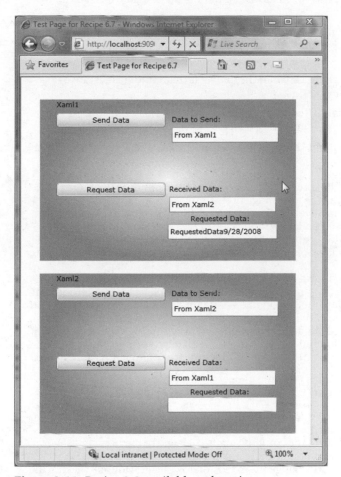

Figure 6-11. *Recipe 6-8 available gadget views*

As we mentioned in the previous paragraph, gadgets consists of HTML pages. Our gadget has the following HMTL pages to provide all of the views listed in Figure 6-13:

- `DockedUndockedView.html`: Displays the docked and undocked views for the gadget and defines the startup HTML view specified in the `Gadget.xml` manifest

- `FlyoutView.html`: Displays the flyout view for the gadget

- `SettingsView.html`: Displays the settings view for the gadget

In general, when you first create a Silverlight application, it includes an `Application` object named App located in the `Application.xaml` file and a single `UserControl` object named Page located in `MainPage.xaml`. The Page `UserControl` is defined as the startup UI and configured as the `App.RootVisual` for the `Application` object in the `Application_Startup` method located in `App.xaml.cs`.

For our Silverlight 3 gadget, we made it our goal to handle all of the UI views shown in Figure 6-13 with the same Silverlight application. We do this by including additional Silverlight `UserControl` objects to handle the various views:

- `DockedView.xaml`: Displays the Silverlight UI when the gadget is in a docked state and serves as the startup view in `DockedUndockedView.html` (originally the Page `UserControl` that we just renamed to `DockedView`)

- `UndockedView.xaml`: Displays the Silverlight UI when the gadget is in an undocked state or floating on the Windows Vista desktop

- `FlyoutView.xaml`: Displays the Silverlight UI when the gadget displays the flyout view in `FlyoutView.html`

- `SettingsView.xaml`: Displays the Silverlight UI when the gadget displays the settings view in `SettingsView.html`

The UI connection point between the hosting HTML pages and corresponding `UserControl` objects is the Silverlight plug-in installation. We take advantage of the initialization parameter functionality on the Silverlight plug-in to tell the Silverlight application which `UserControl` to display.

The gadget development model is based on HTML and `JavaScript`. The programming connection point between gadget programmability and the Silverlight application is the HTML Bridge functionality that enables Silverlight to access `JavaScript` methods as well as enable JavaScript to access managed code methods.

When a user manipulates a gadget to show the flyout view, undock the gadget, or display settings, the gadget API fires JavaScript events. Our approach is to have the JavaScript stub method that receives the gadget API event call the appropriate method in the Silverlight application to update the UI, save settings, and so forth. This puts most of the actual application logic into the Silverlight application, which is where we want it so that we can take advantage of the managed programming model.

There are additional options and considerations such as multilanguage support involved in developing a gadget that we do not cover here. Refer to the MSDN documentation to learn more about building a Windows Vista Sidebar gadget:

`http://msdn.microsoft.com/en-us/library/bb456468.aspx`

The final step is packaging up the gadget, which is simple: just zip up the contents and changing the `.zip` extension `.gadget`. For our example, we navigate to the `Code\Ch06_BrowserIntegration\Silverlight3Silverlight3Recipes` folder, select all of the contents, right-click one of the files, and select Send To ➤ Compressed (zipped) Folder. It will want to name it one of the files or folders with a `.zip` extension. Simply rename it to whatever you like but change the extension to `.gadget`. Double-clicking the `.gadget` file results in the UI shown in Figure 6-12.

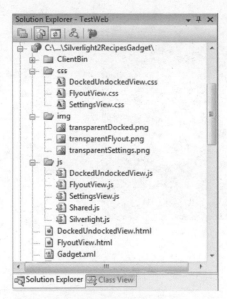

Figure 6-12. *Installing the Silverlight 3 recipes gadget*

Gadgets can also be deployed as a .cab file, which can be signed to avoid the prompt shown in Figure 6-11, but once you click the Install button shown in Figure 6-12 the gadget will display in the Windows Sidebar.

■**Note** When testing a new gadget, you can delete the installation files from this location: `%userprofile%\`
`AppData\Local\Microsoft\Windows Sidebar\Gadgets`.

While automated debugging code running in the Windows Sidebar is not available, you can still attach the debugger to the sidebar and step through breakpoints for both the Silverlight and JavaScript code. When debugging, deploy the gadget with a debug build of the Silverlight application, package it in a ZIP file, and change the extension to .gadget. Once the gadget is installed, attach the debugger using the Visual Studio 2008 Debug ➤ Attach to Process dialog box, as shown in Figure 6-13.

You can enable script debugging in Visual Studio for gadgets as well by following the steps here:

`http://msdn.microsoft.com/en-us/library/bb456467(VS.85).aspx`

We recommend that you take advantage of Silverlight and JavaScript debugging support to speed development. When we tried both JavaScript and Silverlight debugging with breakpoints in the Silverlight code and JavaScript code, JavaScript debugging worked fine, but breakpoints set in Silverlight were not hit. Disabling JavaScript debugging in Internet Explorer and restarting the Windows Sidebar allowed Silverlight breakpoints to function as expected.

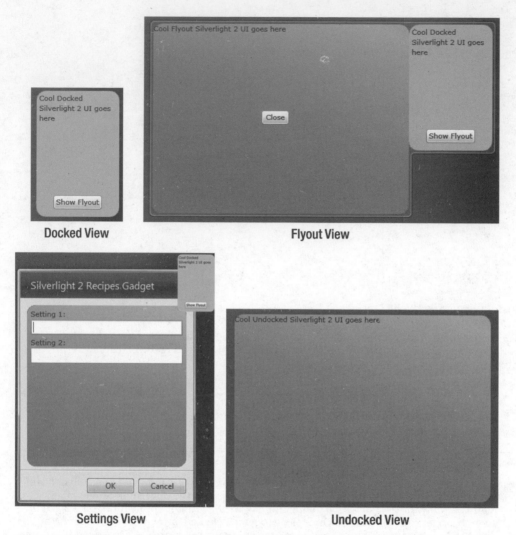

Figure 6-13. *The Visual Studio 2008 Attach to Process dialog box*

The sample code for this recipe is meant to be template gadget to help you get started with developing your own gadgets. The Silverlight UI portions are simply placeholders for building a more useful gadget, but using this recipe as a template will greatly speed gadget development.

To assist with getting started building gadgets with Silverlight 3, a separate solution is included with the source code contained in SLforGadgetSolution.zip located in the \Code\ Ch06_BrowserIntegration folder. This solution contains a bare-bones implementation of the Silverlight project with docking and undocking, flyout menus, and settings support in a simple two-project Visual Studio solution.

The Code

Since we use the same Silverlight application or .xap file for all of the gadget project web pages, we need a method to load the correct view into the Silverlight application depending on the .html page hosting the Silverlight application as described in this recipe's "How It Works" section. We take advantage of the initParams parameter available on the Silverlight plug-in control, which we first demonstrated in recipe 6-7. For example, in the DockedUndockedView.html page, we have this value configured or the Silverlight plug-in control:

```
<param name ="initParams" value="View=DockedUndocked" />
```

The three HTML pages named DockedUndockedView.html, FlyoutView.html, and SettingsView.html all follow this pattern. Listing 6-18 shows the source code for DockedUndockedView.html.

Listing 6-18. *DockedUndockedView.html File*

```
<html xmlns="http://www.w3.org/1999/xhtml">
<head>
  <title>Silverlight 3 Recipes</title>
  <link href="css/DockedUndockedView.css" rel="stylesheet" type="text/css" />
  <script language="javascript" type="text/javascript"
  src="/js/Silverlight.js"></script>
  <script language="javascript" type="text/javascript"
  src="/js/Shared.js"></script>
  <script language="javascript" type="text/javascript"
  src="/js/DockedUndockedView.js"></script>

</head>
<body onload="loadGadget();">
  <div id="errorLocation" style="font-size: small; color: Gray;">
  </div>
  <div id="silverlightControlHost">
    <object data="data:application/x-silverlight-2,"
      type="application/x-silverlight-2"
      width="100%" height="100%" id="XamlGadget">
      <param name="source"
        value="x-gadget:///ClientBin/Ch06_BrowserIntegration.Recipe6_8.xap" />
      <param name="onerror" value="onSilverlightError" />
      <param name="minRuntimeVersion" value="2.0.31005.0" />
      <param name="autoUpgrade" value="true" />
      <param name="enableHtmlAccess" value="true" />
      <param name="windowless" value="true" />
      <param name="background" value="transparent" />
      <param name="initParams" value="View=DockedUndocked" />
      <param name="onload" value="onSilverlightLoad" />
      <a href="http://go.microsoft.com/fwlink/?LinkID= 124807"
      style="text-decoration: none;">
```

```
          <img src="http://go.microsoft.com/fwlink/?LinkId=108181"
          alt="Get Microsoft Silverlight" style="border-style: none" />
        </a>
    </object>
    <g:background src="/img/transparentDocked.png"
     mce_src="/img/transparentDocked.png"
     id="transparentBackground" style="width: 130px;
     height: 200px; z-index: -1" />
  </div>
</body>
</html>
```

The HTML page in Listing 6-18 pulls in three JavaScript files: Silverlight.js, Shared.js, and DockedUndocked.js. We pull in Silverlight.js in case we need it. Shared.js has a common onSilverlightLoad handler for all three pages that sets focus to the gadget in HTML. We cover DockedUndocked.js next.

For the gadget UI, we wanted to have rounded corners for all views. Listing 6-19 shows the XAML for DockedView.xaml, which is the UserControl displayed when the gadget is docked.

Listing 6-19. *DockedView.xaml File*

```
<UserControl x:Class="Ch06_BrowserIntegration.Recipe6_8.DockedView"
    xmlns="http://schemas.microsoft.com/winfx/2006/xaml/presentation"
    xmlns:x="http://schemas.microsoft.com/winfx/2006/xaml"
    Width="130" Height="200" Background="#00FFFFFF"
    HorizontalAlignment="Left" VerticalAlignment="Top">
  <Grid Background="#00FFFFFF" >
    <Border CornerRadius="15,15,15,15">
      <Border.Background>
        <LinearGradientBrush EndPoint="-0.227,0.337"
        StartPoint="1.227,0.663">
          <GradientStop Color="#FFB9D4C6" Offset="0.397"/>
          <GradientStop Color="#FF65E8A5" Offset="1"/>
          <GradientStop Color="#FF65E8A5"/>
          <GradientStop Color="#FFB9D4C6" Offset="0.554"/>
          <GradientStop Color="#FFB9D4C6" Offset="0.482"/>
        </LinearGradientBrush>
      </Border.Background>
      <Grid x:Name="LayoutRoot" Margin="4" Background="{x:Null}">
        <TextBlock Text="Cool Docked Silverlight 3 UI goes here"
          TextWrapping="Wrap"/>
      </Grid>
    </Border>
  </Grid>
</UserControl>
```

In Listing 6-19, you can see that we set the UserControl and outer Grid control to a transparent background. We also ensure that the Silverlight plug-in in the HTML page is configured with a transparent background. Even after setting CornerRadius to 15 for all corners, a white background was visible at the rounded corners in the UI. We followed these steps to allow a transparent background at the corners.

We created a transparent .png using Paint.NET, but you can use your favorite drawing tool to create it. In Paint.NET we created a new 130-pixel-wide by 200-pixel-high image for the docked dimensions of the gadget. We next chose Layers ~TMS Layer Properties and set Opacity to 0. We then saved the image to the img folder as transparentdocked.png.

The gadget JavaScript API provides additional functionality, such as setting the gadget background with the g:background tag. We added this HTML to DockedUndockedView.html file inside the <div> hosting the Silverlight control to configure the background:

```
<g:background src="/img/transparentDocked.png"mce_
src="/img/transparentDocked.png"
id="transparentBackground" style="width:130px;height:200px;z-index:-1"/>
```

This code results in the rounded corners being transparent; however, a slight magenta color can be seen at the corners. This is an artifact of having two transparent objects overlapping within Internet Explorer, which is the rendering engine in the Windows Vista Sidebar.

An additional step is required when displaying the docked or undocked view, because they are both hosted in the same HTML page, DockedUndockedView.html. To handle this, we wire up events in DockedUndockedView.js, shown in Listing 6-21.

Each page has a loadGadget event hooked into the HTML body tag's onload event. loadGadget is the same name for all three HTML pages, but each one does something different specific to the view. Listing 6-20 shows DockedUndockedView.js.

Listing 6-20. *DockedUndockedView.js File*

```
function loadGadget() {
    System.Gadget.onDock = dockStateChanged;
    System.Gadget.onUndock = dockStateChanged;

    System.Gadget.Flyout.file = "FlyoutView.html";
    System.Gadget.settingsUI = "SettingsView.html";
}

function dockStateChanged() {
    //change size depending on state
    if (System.Gadget.docked) {
        document.body.style.width = "130px";
        document.body.style.height = "200px";
        document.getElementById("XamlGadget").Content.GadgetApp.DockGadget(true);
    }
    else {
        document.body.style.width = "400px";
        document.body.style.height = "290px";
        document.getElementById("XamlGadget").Content.GadgetApp.DockGadget(false);
    }
}
```

In `loadGadget` for the Docked/Undocked view, we assign the event handler `dockStateChanged` to the gadget events `onDock` and `onUndock`. When this JavaScript event handler fires, it sets the dimensions on the `<body>` tag to fit the UI and then switches between the Silverlight docked or undocked UI via the HTML Bridge with this call:

```
document.getElementById("XamlGadget").Content.GadgetApp.DockGadget(false);
```

To allow the UI to change, we need to take an additional step to switch between the `DockedView.xaml` and `UndockedView.xaml` `UserControl` objects depending on the gadget's current state of being docked or undocked. Here is the typical `Application_Startup` method for a Silverlight application:

```
private void Application_Startup(object sender, StartupEventArgs e)
{
  this.RootVisual = new MainPage();
}
```

For our Silverlight application, we have additional logic in `GadgetApp.xaml.cs` to choose which `UserControl` to configure for `Application.RootVisual`. In our `Application_Startup`, we first determine which view is requested by obtaining the initialization parameters specified in the hosting HTML page:

```
//Get passed parameter to choose the view.
string initParams =
   HtmlPage.Plugin.GetProperty("initParams").ToString();
string[] paramsArray = initParams.Split(';');
string[] KeyValue = paramsArray[0].Split('=');
```

We next use the value for `KeyValue[1]` in a switch statement to select which view to display. We cannot simply switch the value configured on `Application.RootVisual` as it will not work. We set an empty `Grid` as `RootVisual` and then add the necessary `UserControl` as a child to the `Grid` configured as `RootVisual`.

```
switch (KeyValue[1])
{                  //For DockedUndocked, we set Grid as root
                   //so that we can switch user controls later
                   //at runtime for docked and undocked states.
  case "DockedUndocked": _rootControl = new Grid();
                   this.RootVisual = _rootControl;
                   _dockedView = new DockedView();
                   _rootControl.Children.Clear();
                   _rootControl.Children.Add(_dockedView); break;
  case "Flyout":  this.RootVisual = new FlyoutView(); break;
  case "Settings": this.RootVisual = new SettingsView(); break;
}
```

Since the docked and undocked views are hosted in the same HTML page, `DockedUndockedView.html`, we need to take additional steps so that we can switch the UI depending on whether the gadget is docked or floating. We first declare three private reference variables at the top of the `GadgetApp` Application instance:

```
//Use this as root control so that the user controls
//can be switched from docked to undocked
private Grid _rootControl;
//Hold references to Docked and Undocked Views
private DockedView _dockedView ;
private UndockedView _unDockedView ;
```

We configure `Application.RootVisual` to point to a Grid control referenced by `_rootControl` and add the `DockedView` and `UndockedView` instances as the child to the root `Grid` control depending on the docked or undocked state. Listing 6-21 shows the full source code for `GadgetApp.xaml.cs`.

Listing 6-21. *GadgetApp.xaml.cs File*

```csharp
using System;
using System.Windows;
using System.Windows.Browser;
using System.Windows.Controls;

namespace Ch06_BrowserIntegration.Recipe6_8
{
  public partial class GadgetApp : Application
  {
    //Use this as root control so that the user controls
    //can be switched from docked or undocked
    private Grid _rootControl;
    //Hold references to Docked and Undocked Views
    private DockedView _dockedView;
    private UndockedView _unDockedView;

    public GadgetApp()
    {
      this.Startup += this.Application_Startup;
      this.Exit += this.Application_Exit;
      this.UnhandledException += this.Application_UnhandledException;

      InitializeComponent();
    }

    private void Application_Startup(object sender, StartupEventArgs e)
    {
      //Get passed parameter for partner control
      string initParams =
        HtmlPage.Plugin.GetProperty("initParams").ToString();
      string[] paramsArray = initParams.Split(';');
      string[] KeyValue = paramsArray[0].Split('=');
```

```csharp
            switch (KeyValue[1])
            {                       //For DockedUndocked, we set Grid as root
              //so that we can switch user controls later
              //at runtime for docked and undocked states.
              case "DockedUndocked": _rootControl = new Grid();
                this.RootVisual = _rootControl;
                _dockedView = new DockedView();
                _rootControl.Children.Clear();
                _rootControl.Children.Add(_dockedView); break;
              case "Flyout": this.RootVisual = new FlyoutView(); break;
              case "Settings": this.RootVisual = new SettingsView(); break;
            }
            //Make GadgetApp instance available so that script
            //can call DockGadget method from JavaScript
            HtmlPage.RegisterScriptableObject("GadgetApp", this);
        }

        private void Application_Exit(object sender, EventArgs e)
        {

        }

        private void Application_UnhandledException(object sender,
        ApplicationUnhandledExceptionEventArgs e)
        {
          if (!System.Diagnostics.Debugger.IsAttached)
          {
            e.Handled = true;
            Deployment.Current.Dispatcher.BeginInvoke(
              delegate { ReportErrorToDOM(e); });
          }
        }

        private void ReportErrorToDOM(ApplicationUnhandledExceptionEventArgs e)
        {
          try
          {
            string errorMsg = e.ExceptionObject.Message +
                              e.ExceptionObject.StackTrace;
            errorMsg = errorMsg.Replace('"', '\'').Replace("\r\n", @"\n");

            System.Windows.Browser.HtmlPage.Window.Eval(
            "throw new Error(\"Unhandled Error in Silverlight 3 Application " +
            errorMsg + "\");");
          }
```

```
      catch (Exception)
      {
      }
  }

  [ScriptableMember]
  public void DockGadget(Boolean state)
  {
    switch (state)
    {
      case true: _rootControl.Children.Clear();
        _rootControl.Children.Add(_dockedView); break;
      //First time undocking, create undocked view
      case false: if (null == _unDockedView)
          _unDockedView = new UndockedView();
        //Switch to undocked view when gadget undocked
        _rootControl.Children.Clear();
        _rootControl.Children.Add(_unDockedView); break;
    }
  }
 }
}
```

The DockGadget method in Listing 6-21 is located in GadgetApp.xaml.cs and called by the JavaScript code to switch from the docked to undocked view for the Silverlight application. If true is passed in from JavaScript, the DockGadget method clears the children on the rootControl and adds the saved dockedView instance as the child control to the root Grid. If false is passed in, the UndockedView is created and a reference saved and added as the child control of the root Grid.

Setting the enableHtmlAccess parameter on the Silverlight plug-in to true and calling the below line of code in Application_Startup in GadgetApp.xaml.cs makes the ScriptableMember GadgetApp.DockGadget method available in the JavaScript code:

```
HtmlPage.RegisterScriptableObject("GadgetApp", this);
```

There is a button in the DockedView UI that, when clicked, shows the flyout using this line of code that calls the gadget API:

```
HtmlPage.Window.Eval(@"System.Gadget.Flyout.show = true;");
```

For the flyout view, a simple button closes the flyout when clicked, using this line of code that calls into the gadget API:

```
HtmlPage.Window.Eval(@"System.Gadget.Flyout.show = false;");
```

We don't list the code for FlyoutView and UndockedView, since they are mostly placeholders for content that expands when a user hovers over a particular element or clicks a button; they just provide more information.

The additional core gadget functionalities we implement are saving and retrieving settings for the gadget in the SettingsView UserControl. These gadget functions include the ability to persist settings for the gadget. As an example, the Weather Gadget included with Windows Vista has a setting that allows a user to pick location for weather information. In JavaScript, these are the two methods to read and write settings:

```
System.Gadget.Settings.Read(key);
System.Gadget.Settings.Write(key,value);
```

For our Silverlight 3 gadget, we try to execute as much of the application as possible within Silverlight 3 in the SettingsView control, but we still need code in JavaScript to wire up the Silverlight code with the gadget functionality. As an example, the previous settings' API functions are called from the SettingsView.xaml UserControl code in the LoadGadgetSettings and SaveGadgetSettings methods. Listings 6-22 and 6-23 show the code for the SettingsView UserControl.

Listing 6-22. *SettingsView.xaml File*

```xml
<UserControl x:Class="Ch06_BrowserIntegration.Recipe6_8.SettingsView"
    xmlns="http://schemas.microsoft.com/winfx/2006/xaml/presentation"
    xmlns:x="http://schemas.microsoft.com/winfx/2006/xaml"
    Width="250" Height="250">
  <Grid >
    <Border CornerRadius="15,15,15,15">
      <Border.Background>
        <LinearGradientBrush EndPoint="0.5,1" StartPoint="1.164,-1.028">
          <GradientStop Color="#FF808080"/>
          <GradientStop Color="#FF808080" Offset="1"/>
          <GradientStop Color="#FF96D7A8" Offset="0.50400000810623169"/>
        </LinearGradientBrush>
      </Border.Background>
      <Grid x:Name="LayoutRoot"  Margin="4">
        <StackPanel Margin="0">
          <TextBlock Margin="2,2,2,0" Text="Setting 1:" TextWrapping="Wrap"/>
          <TextBox x:Name="Setting1" Margin="2,0,2,2" TextWrapping="Wrap"/>
          <TextBlock Text="Setting 2:" Margin="2,2,2,0" TextWrapping="Wrap"/>
          <TextBox x:Name="Setting2" Margin="2,0,2,2" TextWrapping="Wrap"/>
        </StackPanel>
      </Grid>
    </Border>
  </Grid>
</UserControl>
```

Listing 6-23. *SettingsView.xaml.cs File*

```csharp
using System;
using System.Windows.Browser;
using System.Windows.Controls;

namespace Ch06_BrowserIntegration.Recipe6_8
{
  public partial class SettingsView : UserControl
  {
    public SettingsView()
    {
      InitializeComponent();
      HtmlPage.RegisterScriptableObject("SettingsView", this);
      //Load settings for gadget
      LoadGadgetSettings();
    }

    private void LoadGadgetSettings()
    {
      try
      {
        //Textbox control name is also Setting name in this example.
        Setting1.Text = (HtmlPage.Window.Eval("System.Gadget.Settings") as
        ScriptObject).Invoke("read", Setting1.Name) as string;
        Setting2.Text = (HtmlPage.Window.Eval("System.Gadget.Settings") as
        ScriptObject).Invoke("read", Setting2.Name) as string;
      }
      catch (Exception err)
      {
        //do something with exception here
      }
    }

    [ScriptableMember]
    public void SaveGadgetSettings()
    {
      try
      {
        (HtmlPage.Window.Eval("System.Gadget.Settings") as ScriptObject).
         Invoke("write", Setting1.Name, Setting1.Text);
        (HtmlPage.Window.Eval("System.Gadget.Settings") as ScriptObject).
         Invoke("write", Setting2.Name, Setting2.Text);
      }
```

```
    catch (Exception err)
    {
      //do something with exception here
    }
  }
 }
}
```

The LoadGadgetSettings and SaveGadgetSettings methods are called from JavaScript events located in SettingsView.js that are wired up in Listing 6-24.

Listing 6-24. *SettingsView.js File*

```
function loadSettingsView()
{
    System.Gadget.onSettingsClosed = settingsViewClosed;
    System.Gadget.onSettingsClosing = settingsViewClosing;
}

function settingsViewClosed(event) {
}

function settingsViewClosing(event) {
    document.getElementById("XamlGadget").Content.SettingsView.SaveGadgetSettings();
    if (event.closeAction == event.Action.commit)
    {
        //call Method to save settings in the SettingsView UserControl
        document.getElementById("XamlGadget").
        Content.SettingsView.SaveGadgetSettings();
    }
    // Allow the Settings dialog to close.
    event.cancel = false;
}
```

The JavaScript function loadSettingsView is called when the <body> tag loads in SettingsView.html. This function wires up two JavaScript events to onSettingsClosed and onSettingsClosing. The settingsViewClosed JavaScript event is not used in our code, but we leave it here as a placeholder. The settingsViewClosing JavaScript makes the call into the SettingsView Silverlight UserControl in this line of code:

```
document.getElementById("XamlGadget").Content.SettingsView.SaveGadgetSettings();
```

This pattern of implementing the logic in Silverlight but wiring up the events in JavaScript is the approach we take to implement the gadget functionality code as much as possible.

The last file we show is the XML file, the manifest file for our gadget shown in Listing 6-25.

Listing 6-25. *Gadget.xml File*

```xml
<?xml version="1.0" encoding="utf-8" ?>
<gadget>
  <name>Silverlight 3 Recipes Gadget</name>
  <namespace>Ch06_BrowserIntegration</namespace>
  <version>1.0</version>
  <author name="Rob Cameron and Jit Ghosh">
  </author>
  <copyright>2008</copyright>
  <description>Testing Silverlight in a Gadget</description>
  <icons>
  </icons>
  <hosts>
    <host name="sidebar">
      <base type="HTML" apiVersion="1.0.0"
            src="DockedUndockedView.html" />
      <permissions>full</permissions>
      <platform minPlatformVersion="1.0" />
    </host>
  </hosts>
</gadget>
```

■**Note** If you're using Notepad or some other text editor to create the file, be sure to save the manifest file as Gadget.XML with encoding as UTF-8; otherwise, it will not be recognized as a valid gadget.

6-9. Embed Silverlight in an Internet Explorer 8 Web Slice

Problem

You need to host Silverlight 3 content in an Internet Explorer 8 Web Slice.

Solution

Internet Explorer 8 (IE8) Web Slices are based on an HTML and JavaScript programming model. As such, IE8 Web Slices can host ActiveX controls, such as the Silverlight plug-in.

How It Works

In Silverlight 2, an ASP.NET server control could be used to host Silverlight within the ASP.NET framework. This control does not ship in Silverlight 3.

An IE8 Web Slice is a new browser feature that allows web site users to subscribe to a portion of a web page. Web Slices are based on the hAtom and hSlice microformats. It is very easy to create a web slice in an existing web page by simply annotating the HTML with class names for title, entry content as well as other properties. For more information regarding Web Slices, here is the Web Slices link on MSDN:

http://msdn.microsoft.com/en-us/library/cc956158(VS.85).aspx

The Code

In order to create our web slice, we first reduce the test pages to just the code necessary to create a web slice. Listing 6-6 has the source code for the .html page. The .aspx page is very similar (see Listing 6-26).

Listing 6-26. *Recipe 6-9's Test Page .html File*

```
<!DOCTYPE html PUBLIC "-//W3C//DTD XHTML 1.0 Transitional//EN"
"http://www.w3.org/TR/xhtml1/DTD/xhtml1-transitional.dtd">
<html xmlns="http://www.w3.org/1999/xhtml">
<head>
  <title>Test Page for Recipe 6.9</title>

</head>
<body>
  <form id="form1" runat="server" style="height: 100%">
  <div id="Recipe6.9WebSlice" class=hslice><!--Web Slice class -->
    <H3 class=entry-title>Recipe6.9 WebSlice Title</H3> <!--Web Slice Title class -->
      <a rel="entry-content" href=
        "http://localhost:9090/Recipe6.9WebSlice.aspx" style="display:none;"></a>
  </div>
  </form>
</body>
</html>
```

You can certainly put more content into this page, but we reduce it down to just what is necessary to demonstrate a Web Slice. Our updated test pages do two things: identify the Web Slice content and bootstrap installation with the help of IE8. Essentially, a Web Slice is a container HTML control, such as a <div>, with has a particular class attribute applied to it. In our case, the <div> with the id of Recipe6.9WebSlice has the class value of hslice on it to identify that it is a Web Slice container. You can add a title to the Web Slice by assigning an HTML element the class value of entry-title, which we do on an <h3> tag. The text contained in the HTML element with the entry-title class is also the text that is used to represent the title of the Web Slice in IE8's Favorites bar. Configuring these classes in HTML causes IE to display the Install a Web Slice button when the user mouses over the <div> tag, as shown in Figure 6-14.

Figure 6-14. *The Add a Web Slice Button and Dialog*

When you move the mouse over the Web Slice <div>, the green button appears over the <div> text. When you click the green button it displays the Add a Web Slice dialog box. This adds the Web Slice to the Favorites section in IE8, as shown in Figure 6-15.

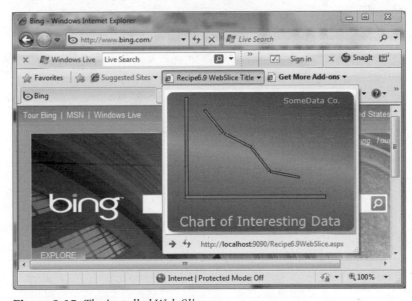

Figure 6-15. *The installed Web Slice*

After installation, the web user can navigate to any web site and still be able to bring up the Web Slice by clicking the link in the Favorites section of IE8. In our case, the Web Slice displays a fictitious graph for a fictitious company, but you can display anything in a Web Slice that you can create in Silverlight.

So far, we have not explained where, exactly, the Silverlight content is loaded from? As we noted previously, the `<a>` tag in Listing 6-26 is part of the Web Slice, which in our case points to a file named `Recipe6.9WebSlice.aspx`:

```
<a rel="entry-content" style="display:none;"
href="http://localhost:9090/Recipe6.9WebSlice.aspx" ></a>
```

We first tried putting the Silverlight `<object>` tag directly in the same page as the test page by adding the entry-content class to a `<div>` where the Silverlight control is instantiated, but that did not work. We note this as background in case you wish to build a Web Slice that does not use Silverlight and want to keep the Web Slice content in the same page.

Listing 6-27 has the code for `Recipe6.9WebSlice.aspx`.

Listing 6-27. *Recipe 6-9's Web Slice .aspx File*

```
<%@ Page Language="C#" AutoEventWireup="true" %>
<!DOCTYPE html PUBLIC "-//W3C//DTD XHTML 1.0 Transitional//EN"
 "http://www.w3.org/TR/xhtml1/DTD/xhtml1-transitional.dtd">
<html xmlns="http://www.w3.org/1999/xhtml">
<head runat="server">
  <title>Test Page for Recipe 6.9</title>
  <style type="text/css">
    html, body
    {
      height: 100%;
      width: 100%;
    }
    body
    {
      padding: 0;
      margin: 0;
    }
    #silverlightControlHost
    {
      height: 100%;
      width: 100%;
      text-align: center;
    }
  </style>
```

```
<script type="text/javascript" src="Silverlight.js"></script>

<script type="text/javascript">
  function onSilverlightError(sender, args) {
    var appSource = "";
    if (sender != null && sender != 0) {
      appSource = sender.getHost().Source;
    }

    var errorType = args.ErrorType;
    var iErrorCode = args.ErrorCode;

    if (errorType == "ImageError" || errorType == "MediaError") {
      return;
    }

    var errMsg = "Unhandled Error in Silverlight Application " + appSource + "\n";

    errMsg += "Code: " + iErrorCode + "     \n";
    errMsg += "Category: " + errorType + "        \n";
    errMsg += "Message: " + args.ErrorMessage + "       \n";

    if (errorType == "ParserError") {
      errMsg += "File: " + args.xamlFile + "      \n";
      errMsg += "Line: " + args.lineNumber + "      \n";
      errMsg += "Position: " + args.charPosition + "       \n";
    }
    else if (errorType == "RuntimeError") {
      if (args.lineNumber != 0) {
        errMsg += "Line: " + args.lineNumber + "      \n";
        errMsg += "Position: " + args.charPosition + "       \n";
      }
      errMsg += "MethodName: " + args.methodName + "       \n";
    }

    throw new Error(errMsg);
  }
</script>

</head>
```

```
<body>
  <form id="form1" runat="server" style="height:100%; width:100%">
  <div id="silverlightControlHost">
    <object data="data:application/x-silverlight-2," type=
            "application/x-silverlight-2"
      width="100%" height="100%">
      <param name="source" value=
              "ClientBin/Ch06_BrowserIntegration.Recipe6_9.xap" />
      <param name="onError" value="onSilverlightError" />
      <param name="background" value="white" />
      <param name="minRuntimeVersion" value="3.0.40613.0" />
      <param name="autoUpgrade" value="true" />
      <a href="http://go.microsoft.com/fwlink/?LinkID=149156&v=3.0.40613.0"
        style="text-decoration: none">
        <img src="http://go.microsoft.com/fwlink/?LinkId=108181"
          alt="Get Microsoft Silverlight" style="border-style: none" />
      </a>
    </object>
    <iframe id="_sl_historyFrame" style="visibility: hidden; height:
      0px; width: 0px; border: 0px"></iframe>
  </div>
  </form>
</body>
</html>
```

This page has some minor modifications related to styles that differ from the typical test page; these deviations prevent scroll bars from appearing when the Web Slice preview is displayed in the IE8 Favorites toolbar. We added style="height:100%; width:100%"> to the form page. We also added the same values to the CSS style for #silverlightControlHost and for the <html> and <body> tags, and we removed the overflow: auto; attribute. This results in the nice clean Web Slice display shown in Figure 6-15.

6-10. Take Advantage of the Navigation Framework

Problem

You want to add navigation to your Silverlight application including support for the browser Back and Forward buttons and URI mapping, and you want the ability to interact with the browser history journal. You would like to have custom URI mappings as well as being able to programmatically navigate to Silverlight pages using query parameters.

Solution

Take advantage of the Navigation Framework built into Silverlight 3 with the new Silverlight Navigation Application project template.

How It Works

In Silverlight 2, providing an application that easily navigated between XAML pages was difficult for developers. In Silverlight 3, Microsoft introduced the Navigation Framework and the new Silverlight Navigation Application project template that allows users to easily navigate between pages. This application template provides support for the browser Back and Forward buttons, as well as providing the user with the ability to bookmark a page in a Silverlight application.

When you create a new application with the Silverlight Navigation Application template, more than the usual user interface is created. Figure 6-16 shows the initial project layout.

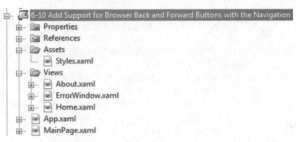

Figure 6-16. *The Silverlight Navigation Application initial project layout*

The additional user interface capabilities help to demonstrate how to plug into the framework to speed adoption. You can, of course, completely change the user interface to suite your needs and still take advantage of the navigation framework.

In Figure 6-16, you see the familiar App.xaml and MainPage.xaml files. In this project template, MainPage.xaml acts as a container for the views listed in the Views folder. The Assets folder is a convenient place to locate additional styles and other resources that are part of an application.

When you run the initial application without making changes, you see the application shown in Figure 6-17.

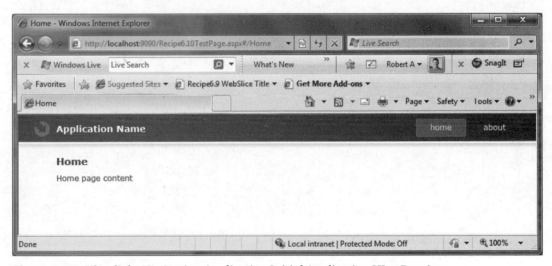

Figure 6-17. *Silverlight Navigation Application Initial Application UI at Runtime*

We take a wide screenshot in order to display the full URL, which as this:

`http://localhost:9090/Recipe6.10TestPage.aspx#/Home`

We next click the "about" button to shift the application to the "about" view located at `/Views/About.xaml` in the project setup files, resulting in a similar display as in Figure 6-17 but with the text "About page content" and the following URL:

`http://localhost:9090/Recipe6.10TestPage.aspx#/About`

Each page results in a navigation entry in the browser history as you would expect However, with the Silverlight Navigation Application template, it is possible to bookmark the "about" view directly by adding the URL `http://localhost:9090/Recipe6.10TestPage.aspx#/About` to the favorites in the web browser or as a shortcut.

The `System.Windows.Controls.Navigation` namespace includes the key controls that provide the navigation application functionality, specifically the `Frame` and `Page` classes.

The `UserControl` class is the type for the `MainPage` object when the Navigation Application template creates a new project. However, the project contains a `Frame` object named `ContentFrame` by default. The `Frame` class acts as a host for the views that are part of a Navigation Application project. The individual view objects inherit from the `System.Windows.Controls.Page` class. The `Page` class is very similar to the `UserControl` class but adds the capability to be hosted in a `Frame` object. The `Page` class also adds the `Title` property, which is set as the title of the page in the web browser as shown in Figure 6-17 above "home" in the browser title bar caption.

The `Frame` class integrates with the browser history by default via the `JournalOwnership` property, which can take one of three values:

- `Automatic`: Whether or not this `Frame` will create and use its own journal depends on its parent. If the parent or browser allows it, the navigation will be recorded in the browser journal.

- `OwnsJournal`: The `Frame` maintains its own journal.

- `UsesParentJournal`: The `Frame` object uses the journal of the next available navigation host up the XAML content tree, if one exists. Otherwise, navigation history is not maintained for the `Frame` object.

Figure 6-18 shows the browser journaling after navigating several times between the home and about page.

Figure 6-10. *Silverlight Navigation Application project browser journaling integration*

The Code

For this recipe, we add a couple of views by right-clicking the View folder, selecting ~TRA New Item, and then selecting Page in the list. We name the new view items ItemList and ItemDetails. We want to make the new Page object available in the UI, so we add two new HyperlinkButton objects to the LinksStackPanel object:

```
<HyperlinkButton x:Name="Link2" Style="{StaticResource LinkStyle}"
    NavigateUri="/ItemList" TargetName="ContentFrame" Content="item list"/>
<Rectangle x:Name="Divider2" Style="{StaticResource DividerStyle}"/>
<HyperlinkButton x:Name="Link3" Style="{StaticResource LinkStyle}"
    NavigateUri="/ItemDetails" TargetName="ContentFrame" Content="item details"/>
```

The important property is NavigateUri, where you set the value to the XAML page name without the .xaml extension. Content is the title for the hyperlink when displayed in the UI. This results in UI shown in Figure 6-19.

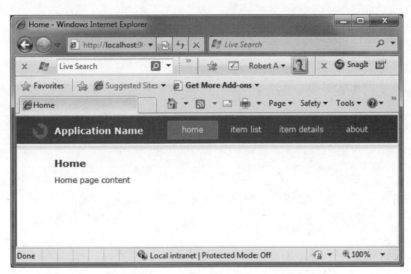

Figure 6-19. *The updated UI with additional menu items*

You can navigate to the new pages just as before, and the navigation will be journaled in the browser history.

You probably noticed that the application is fairly well styled when compared to the normal Silverlight Application template. This helps you visualize the application right away. Conveniently, all of the styles are defined separately in a ResourceDictionary in App.xaml under the Assets project folder:

```
<ResourceDictionary Source="Assets/Styles.xaml"/>
```

This centralizes the styles location for easy editing. It is important to note that the default application layout is not mandatory. For example, you can change the navigation to the left and stack the buttons vertically in a Microsoft Outlook type of layout.

We have not covered yet how to create custom URI mappings or how to pass query parameters when navigating programmatically in code. When the recipe application is initially loaded, the following URL loads:

```
http://localhost:9090/Recipe6.10TestPage.html#/Home
```

The portion of the URL after the hash, /Home, is mapped to the Home.Xaml page by markup located in MainPage.xaml, shown in Listing 6-28, for the Frame.UriMapper object.

Listing 6-28. *Recipe 6-10's Main Page .xaml File*

```
<UserControl
    x:Class="Ch06_BrowserIntegration.Recipe6_2.MainPage"
    xmlns="http://schemas.microsoft.com/winfx/2006/xaml/presentation"
    xmlns:x="http://schemas.microsoft.com/winfx/2006/xaml"
    xmlns:navigation=
      "clr-namespace:System.Windows.Controls;
       assembly=System.Windows.Controls.Navigation"
    xmlns:uriMapper=
    "clr-namespace:System.Windows.Navigation;
     assembly=System.Windows.Controls.Navigation"
    xmlns:d="http://schemas.microsoft.com/expression/blend/2008"
    xmlns:mc="http://schemas.openxmlformats.org/markup-compatibility/2006"
    mc:Ignorable="d" d:DesignWidth="640" d:DesignHeight="480">

  <Grid x:Name="LayoutRoot" Style="{StaticResource LayoutRootGridStyle}">
    <Border x:Name="ContentBorder" Style="{StaticResource ContentBorderStyle}">
      <navigation:Frame x:Name="ContentFrame"
        Style="{StaticResource ContentFrameStyle}"
        Source="/Home" Navigated="ContentFrame_Navigated"
        NavigationFailed="ContentFrame_NavigationFailed">
        <navigation:Frame.UriMapper>
          <uriMapper:UriMapper>
            <uriMapper:UriMapping Uri="/ItemDetails/{lastName}"
                      MappedUri="/Views/ItemDetails.xaml?lastName={lastName}"/>
            <uriMapper:UriMapping Uri="" MappedUri="/Views/Home.xaml"/>
            <uriMapper:UriMapping Uri="/{pageName}"
                      MappedUri="/Views/{pageName}.xaml"/>
            <uriMapper:UriMapping Uri="foo" MappedUri="/Views/About.xaml"/>
          </uriMapper:UriMapper>
        </navigation:Frame.UriMapper>
      </navigation:Frame>
    </Border>
```

```xml
<Grid x:Name="NavigationGrid" Style="{StaticResource NavigationGridStyle}">
    <Border x:Name="BrandingBorder" Style="{StaticResource BrandingBorderStyle}">
        <StackPanel x:Name="BrandingStackPanel"
                    Style="{StaticResource BrandingStackPanelStyle}">
            <ContentControl Style="{StaticResource LogoIcon}"/>
            <TextBlock x:Name="ApplicationNameTextBlock"
                Style="{StaticResource ApplicationNameStyle}" Text="Application Name"/>
        </StackPanel>
    </Border>
    <Border x:Name="LinksBorder" Style="{StaticResource LinksBorderStyle}">
        <StackPanel x:Name="LinksStackPanel"
                    Style="{StaticResource LinksStackPanelStyle}">
            <HyperlinkButton x:Name="Link1" Style="{StaticResource LinkStyle}"
                    NavigateUri="/Home" TargetName="ContentFrame" Content="home"/>
            <Rectangle x:Name="Divider1" Style="{StaticResource DividerStyle}"/>
            <HyperlinkButton x:Name="Link2" Style="{StaticResource LinkStyle}"
                    NavigateUri="/ItemList"
                    TargetName="ContentFrame" Content="item list"/>
            <Rectangle x:Name="Divider2" Style="{StaticResource DividerStyle}"/>
            <HyperlinkButton x:Name="Link3" Style="{StaticResource LinkStyle}"
                    NavigateUri="/ItemDetails" TargetName="ContentFrame"
                    Content="item details"/>
            <Rectangle x:Name="Divider3" Style="{StaticResource DividerStyle}"/>
            <HyperlinkButton x:Name="Link4" Style="{StaticResource LinkStyle}"
                    NavigateUri="/About" TargetName="ContentFrame"
                    Content="about"/>
        </StackPanel>
    </Border>
    </Grid>
  </Grid>
</UserControl>
```

Find the UriMapper object in the listing, and you will see this automatically generated UriMapping.

```xml
<uriMapper:UriMapping Uri="/{pageName}"
MappedUri="/Views/{pageName}.xaml"/>
```

The {pageName} value is a substitution variable such that when /Home is passed in as a URI, the Home is translated to load /Views/Home.xaml as the Silverlight Page object to load in the Frame. There is another URI mapping for this URL:

```
http://localhost:9090/Recipe6.10TestPage.html#foo
```

If you change /Home to foo and run the page, About.xaml will load. This URI mapping makes it happen:

```
<uriMapper:UriMapping Uri="foo" MappedUri="/Views/About.xaml"/>
```

Here we do not append a slash (/) to the front so foo is appended directly at the end of the URL right after the hash to load the mapped Uri. Note that the full URL with #foo at the end can be bookmarked, and the bookmark will load the application with the About.xaml page displayed.

The last bit of code we need to cover allows you programmatically navigate from one page to another page within a Silverlight Navigation Application project. We mentioned previously that we added two pages named ItemList.xaml and ItemDetails.xaml as view items for our application. The ItemList view contains a simple DataGrid pointing to sample automatically data generated in Expression Blend 3, which we covered in Chapter 2. The ItemDetails view contains a text box where we will display the passed in query string value containing the fictitious last name generated in the sample data. We don't include the XAML listings for these files, because the action is in the code-behind files shown in Listings 6-29 and 6-30.

Listing 6-29. *Recipe 6-10's ItemList.Xaml.cs Code File*

```
using System;
using System.Windows.Controls;
using System.Windows.Navigation;
using Expression.Blend.SampleData.SampleDataSource;

namespace Ch06_BrowserIntegration.Recipe6_2.Views
{
  public partial class ItemList : Page
  {
    public ItemList()
    {
      InitializeComponent();
    }

    // Executes when the user navigates to this page.
    protected override void OnNavigatedTo(NavigationEventArgs e)
    {
    }

    private void DataGrid_SelectionChanged(object sender,
      SelectionChangedEventArgs e)
    {
      //test foo
      //this.NavigationService.Navigate(
      //  new Uri("foo",UriKind.Relative))
```

```
      // Navigate without parameters
      // this.NavigationService.Navigate(
      //   new Uri(String.Format("/ItemDetails"),
      //   UriKind.Relative));

      //Navigate with parameters
      string lastName = ((Item)itemsDataGrid.SelectedItem).LastName;
      this.NavigationService.Navigate(
        new Uri(String.Format("/ItemDetails/{0}", lastName.ToString()),
        UriKind.Relative));
    }
  }
}
```

Listing 6-30. *Recipe 6-10's ItemDetails.Xaml.cs Code File*

```
using System.Windows.Controls;
using System.Windows.Navigation;

namespace Ch06_BrowserIntegration.Recipe6_2.Views
{
  public partial class ItemDetails : Page
  {
    public ItemDetails()
    {
      InitializeComponent();
    }

    // Executes when the user navigates to this page.
    protected override void OnNavigatedTo(NavigationEventArgs e)
    {
      if (this.NavigationContext.QueryString.ContainsKey("lastName"))
      itemDetails.Text = "'lastName' query parameter equals "+
        this.NavigationContext.QueryString["lastName"];
    }

  }
}
```

In Listing 6-30, for `ItemList`, which contains a `DataGrid`, the `DataGrid_SelectionChanged` event fires when an item is selected. This event programmatically navigates to the `ItemDetails` page with this code:

```
string lastName = ((Item)itemsDataGrid.SelectedItem).LastName;
this.NavigationService.Navigate(
new Uri(String.Format("/ItemDetails/{0}", lastName.ToString()),
UriKind.Relative));
```

To comply with the URI template in `MainPage.xaml`, we append the query parameter, the `LastName` field from the selected record, at the end of the URI, which replaces the {0} in the URI string. The `UriMapper` in `MainPage.xaml` loads the `ItemDetails` view with the passed in `LastName` value as a query parameter like this:

```
/Views/ItemDetails.xaml?lastName="passedInLastName"
```

In the `ItemDetails.xaml.cs` file's `OnNavigatedTo` event handler, we process the query string with this code:

```
if (this.NavigationContext.QueryString.ContainsKey("lastName"))
itemDetails.Text = "'lastName' query parameter equals "+
  this.NavigationContext.QueryString["lastName"];
```

This code results in this UI as shown in Figure 6-20.

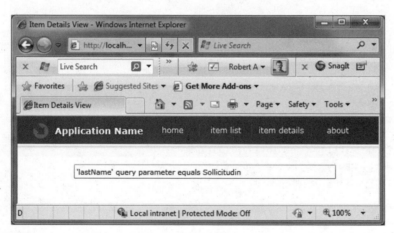

Figure 6-20. *UI Showing Captured Query Parameters*

The functionality we just covered allows developers to pass parameters or state between navigation Page objects for a more unified UI. However, if you look at Figure 6-22 closely, you'll notice that the "item details" button is not highlighted as expected, as it is when you manually click between tabs. The issue is the default URI comparison logic in MainPage.xaml.cs:

```
if (hb.NavigateUri.ToString().Equals(e.Uri.ToString()))
```

When we programmatically navigate between tabs, we append parameters to Uri, which is the Uri value on e.Uri in the ContentFrame_Navigated event in MainPage.xaml.cs. When this value is compared to the configured NavigateUri on all of the navigation Hyperlink buttons, the comparison will fail. We changed the logic to perform this check instead:

```
if (e.Uri.ToString().Contains(hb.NavigateUri.ToString()))
```

With this update, the URI that is being navigated to is checked to see if it contains the configured NavigateUri of any of the Hyperlink buttons. If the check passes, the highlighted state is set on the hyperlink, as shown in Figure 6-21.

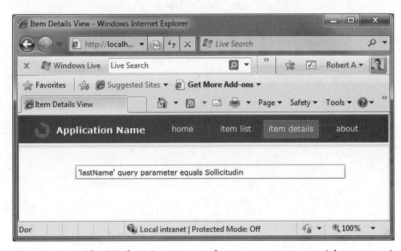

Figure 6-21. *The UI showing captured query parameters with correct visual state*

597

CHAPTER 7

■ ■ ■

Networking and Web Service Integration

In modern, well-architected, loosely coupled systems, a common practice is to expose application processing logic and server-resident data as a set of services. The term *service* is used fairly generically in this context—a service can be anything that has a known endpoint accessible over a standard web protocol like HTTP, offering information exchange capabilities using a standard format like SOAP, plain XML, or JavaScript Object Notation (JSON).

For a server-side UI framework like ASP.NET or a desktop application built using .NET, you can use the full power of the .NET Framework's web service stack to consume these services from the presentation layer of your application.

In the same vein, if you are developing Silverlight-based user experiences, you will often need to consume these services directly from your client-side Silverlight code. The Silverlight .NET libraries include networking APIs that allow you to do just that. The Silverlight network programming stack lets you take advantage of the following high-level features:

- Communicate over HTTP or HTTPS with web services

- Seamlessly integrate with Windows Communication Foundation–based services

- Exchange plain old XML (POX) or JSON-formatted data to communicate with services

- Enable TCP-based communication through TCP sockets

- Respond to network availability state changes from locally installed applications

- Enable local communication between multiple Silverlight applications on the same web page

Note that Silverlight only supports communication with WS-I Basic Profile 1.1–compliant endpoints for SOAP 1.1 over HTTP(S) style message exchange.

Some of the more modern web service standards, such as the WS-* family of protocols, offer a standardized way of enabling advanced distributed computing features in a service-oriented architecture (SOA). Most of these standards are meant for complex SOAs where many services interact with one another across various server platform implementations. Some examples are

- Reliable message delivery using WS-ReliableMessaging

- Atomic transactions across services using WS-AtomicTransactions

- Advanced distributed, cross-platform security mechanisms using WS-Security that go beyond the traditional point-to-point Secure Sockets Layer (SSL) usage

These standards are typically implemented in a layered fashion on top of the basic SOAP standard mentioned earlier, and any client framework enabled for these standards needs client-side implementation. A full implementation of these standards, however, would have meant a significant increase in the size of the runtime and libraries that the Silverlight plug-in contains. To keep a small footprint and provide the efficient, responsive, cross-platform user experience of Silverlight, a decision was made to not support the WS-* standards at this point.

Also of note is the increased use of Representational State Transfer (REST)-styled services in Web 2.0–type web applications, which seems to be a continuing trend moving forward. REST is a way of accessing resources over HTTP, where every resource thus accessible is identifiable with a URI. RESTful services typically use either plain XML or other lightweight formats like JSON to exchange messages over HTTP; operations on such services are equivalent to either acquiring or sending such resources to specified endpoints. These techniques are well supported in Silverlight, as you will see in this chapter.

■Note In the recipes, we have chosen to use Windows Communication Foundation (WCF) to implement the HTTP-based services. As needed, we highlight the specific WCF-related requirements for the services to be usable by Silverlight, but a detailed treatment of WCF is beyond the scope of this book. We also use LINQ and LINQ to XML queries in several of the recipes in this chapter. For more details about WCF, LINQ, and LINQ to XML, refer to the appropriate documentation in the MSDN library at `http://msdn.microsoft.com/en-us/library/default.aspx`. You can also refer to *Pro LINQ: Language Integrated Query in C# 2008* (Apress, 2007) and *Pro WCF: Practical Microsoft SOA Implementation* (Apress, 2007) for in-depth treatments.

A Quick Word about the Samples

The WCF web services in the sample code for this chapter are created as file-system web projects. This is to avoid a dependency on Microsoft Internet Information Services (IIS) and to ensure that you can run all the code samples on your machine without needing IIS. However, keep in mind that we did this purely to reduce the effort in getting the book samples up and running after they are downloaded. For all practical purposes, you should consider a state-of-the-art, industry-leading web application server like IIS for your mission-critical sites and services, whether in a development, test, or production environment.

Also note that file-system web projects are debugged using a development web server built into Visual Studio. When you are in debug mode, Visual Studio takes care of starting up the necessary services. However, if you are running the client from outside Visual Studio or browsing to the test page from inside Visual Studio, the services and development web server are not started automatically. The best way to start them manually is to browse to your `.svc` page for the service project from within the Visual Studio Solution Explorer.

In addition, the Visual Studio development web server randomly picks a port for applications. This is not desirable, especially for web services, because you need to specify the URI for the service in your client code or configuration. You can instruct Visual Studio to always use a fixed port on a per-project basis, from the project's Debug properties page. We have done so in the sample projects already. Take care not to specify the same port on services that need to run together.

7-1. Consuming a WCF Service

Problem

Your Silverlight application needs to communicate with a WCF service.

Solution

Add a reference to the WCF service to your Silverlight application, and use the generated proxy classes to invoke the service.

How It Works

From the context menu of the Silverlight project in Solution Explorer, select Add Service Reference. This brings up the dialog shown in Figure 7-1.

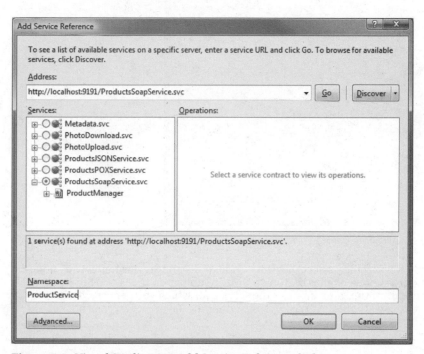

Figure 7-1. *Visual Studio 2008 Add Service Reference dialog*

You have the option of entering the URL of the service endpoint or, if the service project is part of your solution, of clicking Discover to list those services. After the service(s) are listed, select the appropriate service and click OK to add a reference to the service to your application, which generates a set of proxy classes. You can change the namespace in which the generated proxy lives by changing the default namespace specified by the dialog.

Additionally, you also have the option to further customize the generated proxy by clicking the Advanced button. This brings up the dialog shown in Figure 7-2, where you can specify, among other options, the collection types to be used by the proxy to express data collections and dictionaries being exchanged with the service.

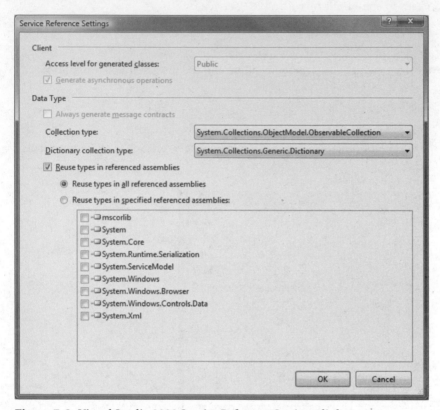

Figure 7-2. *Visual Studio 2008 Service Reference Settings dialog*

To display the generated proxy files, select the proxy node under the Service References node in your project tree, and then click the Show All Files button on the top toolbar on the Visual Studio Solution Explorer. The proxy node has the same name as the service for which you generated the proxy. You can find the generated proxy code in the Reference.cs file under the Reference.svcmap node in the project, as shown in Figure 7-3.

Figure 7-3. *Visual Studio 2008 generated service proxy*

Invoking a Service Operation

Assuming a service named `ProductManager` exists, `Reference.cs` contains a client proxy class for the service named `ProductManagerClient`. It also contains the data-contract types exposed by the service.

Silverlight uses an asynchronous invoke pattern—all web-service invocations are offloaded to a background thread from the local thread pool, and control is returned instantly to the executing Silverlight code. The proxy-generation mechanism implements this by exposing an *xxx*Async() method and *xxx*Completed event pair on the client proxy, where *xxx* is an operation on the service. To invoke the service operation from your Silverlight code, you execute the *xxx*Async() method and handle the *xxx*Completed event, in which you can extract the results returned by the service call from the event arguments. Note that although the service-invocation code executes on a background thread, the framework switches context to the main UI thread before invoking the completion event handler so that you do not have to worry about thread safety in your implementation of the handler.

Listing 7-1 shows such a pair from the generated proxy code for a service operation named `GetProductHeaders`.

Listing 7-1. *Generated Proxy Code for a Service Operation*

```
public event System.EventHandler<GetProductHeadersCompletedEventArgs>
GetProductHeadersCompleted;

public partial class GetProductHeadersCompletedEventArgs :
    System.ComponentModel.AsyncCompletedEventArgs
{
```

```
private object[] results;

  public GetProductHeadersCompletedEventArgs(object[] results,
      Exception exception, bool cancelled, object userState) :
      base(exception, cancelled, userState)
  {
    this.results = results;
  }

  public List<ProductHeader> Result
  {
    get
    {
      base.RaiseExceptionIfNecessary();
      return ((System.Collections.Generic.List<ProductHeader>)(this.results[0]));
    }
  }
}

public void GetProductDetailAsync(ushort ProductId) {
          this.GetProductDetailAsync(ProductId, null);
  }
```

Note the custom event argument type named GetProductHeadersCompletedEventArgs in Listing 7-1. Silverlight creates one of these for every unique operation in your service. Each exposes a Result property as shown, which is strongly typed (in this case, to a List<ProductHeader>) to help you avoid any casting or conversion in retrieving the result of the service call.

Configuring a WCF Service for Silverlight

As we indicated in the introduction to this chapter, Silverlight requires a SOAP/HTTP-based service to be WS-I Basic Profile 1.1 compliant. In WCF terms, that means using BasicHttpBinding on the service endpoint. Listing 7-2 shows a sample configuration section of a service that uses BasicHttpBinding.

Listing 7-2. *WCF Service Configuration in web.config*

```
<system.serviceModel>
    <bindings>
      <basicHttpBinding>
        <binding name="LargeMessage_basicHttpBinding"
                maxReceivedMessageSize="1048576" />
      </basicHttpBinding>
    </bindings>
```

```
  <serviceHostingEnvironment aspNetCompatibilityEnabled="True"/>
  <services>
    <service behaviorConfiguration="ServiceBehavior"
        name="Ch07_Networking.Recipe7_1.ProductsDataSoapService.ProductManager">
      <endpoint address="" binding="basicHttpBinding"
      bindingConfiguration="LargeMessage_basicHttpBinding"
      contract=
"Ch07_Networking.Recipe7_1.ProductsDataSoapService.IProductManager" />
      <endpoint address="mex" binding="mexHttpBinding"
                contract="IMetadataExchange" />
    </service>
  </services>
  <behaviors>
    <serviceBehaviors>
      <behavior name="ServiceBehavior">
        <serviceMetadata httpGetEnabled="true" />
        <serviceDebug includeExceptionDetailInFaults="false" />
      </behavior>
    </serviceBehaviors>
  </behaviors>
</system.serviceModel>
```

The additional endpoint utilizing `mexHttpBinding` is required to expose service-contract metadata, which is needed for the client proxy generation described earlier in this section. Note the setting of the `maxReceivedMessageSize` property on the binding to about 1 MB (defined in bytes). This increases it from its default value of about 65 KB, because we anticipate the messages in the code sample to be larger than that limit.

Also note that similar configuration settings are needed on the Silverlight client to initialize the proxy and consume the service. When you generate the proxy, this is automatically generated for you and stored in a file called `ServiceReferences.ClientConfig`. This file is packaged into the resulting `.xap` file for your Silverlight application, and the settings are automatically read in when you instantiate a service proxy.

The Code

The code sample for this recipe builds a simple master-detail style UI over product inventory data exposed by a WCF service. Listing 7-3 shows the service contract for the WCF service.

Listing 7-3. *Service Contract for the Service in ServiceContract.cs*

```
using System.Collections.Generic;
using System.ServiceModel;

namespace Ch07_Networking.Recipe7_1.ProductsDataSoapService
{
  [ServiceContract]
  public interface IProductManager
```

```
  {
    [OperationContract]
    List<ProductHeader> GetProductHeaders();
    [OperationContract]
    void UpdateProductHeaders(List<ProductHeader> Updates);

    [OperationContract]
    ProductDetail GetProductDetail(ushort ProductId);

    [OperationContract]
    void UpdateProductDetail(ProductDetail Update);
  }
}
```

A service contract models the external interface that the service exposes to the world. You can represent the service contract in a common language runtime (CLR) programming language of your choice (C# in this case) as shown here. The contract itself is an interface, with the operations defined as method signatures in the interface. The attribution of the interface with ServiceContractAttribute, and that of the operations with OperationContractAttribute, indicates to the WCF runtime that this interface is representative of a service contract. When you try to generate a proxy (or model it by hand) using Visual Studio, the Web Service Definition Language (WSDL) that is returned by the service and used to model the proxy also maps to this service contract.

The service contract in Listing 7-3 is implemented as an interface named IProductManager, allows retrieval of a collection of all ProductHeader objects through GetProductHeaders(), and accepts batched ProductHeader changes through UpdateProductHeaders(). It also lets you retrieve ProductDetail using GetProductDetail() for a specific product, in addition to allowing updates to ProductDetail information for a product using UpdateProductDetail() in a similar fashion.

Listing 7-4 shows the data contracts used in the service.

Listing 7-4. *Data Contracts for the Service in DataContracts.cs*

```
namespace Ch07_Networking.Recipe7_1.ProductsDataSoapService
{
  [DataContract]
  public partial class ProductHeader
  {
    private ushort? productIdField;
    private decimal? listPriceField;
    private string nameField;
    private string sellEndDateField;
    private string sellStartDateField;

    [DataMember]
    public ushort? ProductId
    {
      get { return this.productIdField; }
      set { this.productIdField = value; }
    }
```

```csharp
    [DataMember]
    public decimal? ListPrice
    {
      get { return this.listPriceField; }
      set { this.listPriceField = value; }
    }
    [DataMember]
    public string Name
    {
      get { return this.nameField; }
      set { this.nameField = value; }
    }
    [DataMember]
    public string SellEndDate
    {
      get { return this.sellEndDateField; }
      set { this.sellEndDateField = value; }
    }
    [DataMember]
    public string SellStartDate
    {
      get { return this.sellStartDateField; }
      set { this.sellStartDateField = value; }
    }
}


[DataContract]
public partial class ProductDetail
{

  private ushort? productIdField;
  private string classField;
  private string colorField;
  private byte? daysToManufactureField;
  private string discontinuedDateField;
  private string finishedGoodsFlagField;
  private string makeFlagField;
  private string productLineField;
  private string productNumberField;
  private ushort? reorderPointField;
  private ushort? safetyStockLevelField;
```

```csharp
        private string sizeField;
        private decimal? standardCostField;
        private string styleField;
        private string weightField;

        [DataMember]
        public ushort? ProductId
        {
          get { return this.productIdField; }
          set { this.productIdField = value; }
        }
        [DataMember]
        public string Class
        {
          get { return this.classField; }
          set { this.classField = value; }
        }
        [DataMember]
        public string Color
        {
          get { return this.colorField; }
          set { this.colorField = value; }
        }
        [DataMember]
        public byte? DaysToManufacture
        {
          get { return this.daysToManufactureField; }
          set { this.daysToManufactureField = value; }
        }
        [DataMember]
        public string DiscontinuedDate
        {
          get { return this.discontinuedDateField; }
          set { this.discontinuedDateField = value; }
        }
        [DataMember]
        public string FinishedGoodsFlag
        {
          get { return this.finishedGoodsFlagField; }
          set { this.finishedGoodsFlagField = value; }
        }
```

```csharp
[DataMember]
public string MakeFlag
{
  get { return this.makeFlagField; }
  set { this.makeFlagField = value; }
}
[DataMember]
public string ProductLine
{
  get { return this.productLineField; }
  set { this.productLineField = value; }
}
[DataMember]
public string ProductNumber
{
  get { return this.productNumberField; }
  set { this.productNumberField = value; }
}
[DataMember]
public ushort? ReorderPoint
{
  get { return this.reorderPointField; }
  set { this.reorderPointField = value; }
}
[DataMember]
public ushort? SafetyStockLevel
{
  get { return this.safetyStockLevelField; }
  set { this.safetyStockLevelField = value; }
}
[DataMember]
public string Size
{
  get { return this.sizeField; }
  set { this.sizeField = value; }
}
[DataMember]
public decimal? StandardCost
{
  get { return this.standardCostField; }
  set { this.standardCostField = value; }
}
```

```
    [DataMember]
    public string Style
    {
      get { return this.styleField; }
      set { this.styleField = value; }
    }
    [DataMember]
    public string Weight
    {
      get { return this.weightField; }
      set { this.weightField = value; }
    }
  }
}
```

Any custom CLR type that you define in your application and use in your service operations needs to be explicitly known to the WCF runtime. This is so that it can be serialized to/deserialized from the wire format (SOAP/JSON, and so on) to your application code format (CLR type). To provide this information to WCF, you must designate these types as data contracts. The DataContractAttribute is applied to the type, and each property member that you may want to expose is decorated with the DataMemberAttribute. Leaving a property undecorated does not serialize it, and neither is it included in the generated proxy code.

In this case, you define data contracts for the ProductHeader and the ProductDetail types that you use in the service contract. Note that WCF inherently knows how to serialize framework types such as primitive types and collections. Therefore, you do not need specific contracts for them.

Listing 7-5 shows the full implementation of the service in the ProductManager class, implementing the service contract IProductManager.

Listing 7-5. *Service Implementation in ProductManager.cs*

```
using System;
using System.Collections.Generic;
using System.IO;
using System.Linq;
using System.ServiceModel.Activation;
using System.Web;
using System.Xml.Linq;

namespace Ch07_Networking.Recipe7_1.ProductsDataSoapService
{
  [AspNetCompatibilityRequirements(
    RequirementsMode = AspNetCompatibilityRequirementsMode.Required)]
  public class ProductManager : IProductManager
  {
    public List<ProductHeader> GetProductHeaders()
```

```
{
  //open the local XML data file for products
  StreamReader stmrdrProductData = new StreamReader(
    new FileStream(HttpContext.Current.Request.MapPath(
      "App_Data/XML/Products.xml"), FileMode.Open));
  //create a Linq To XML Xdocument and load the data
  XDocument xDocProducts = XDocument.Load(stmrdrProductData);
  //close the stream
  stmrdrProductData.Close();
  //transform the XML data to a collection of ProductHeader
  //using a Linq To XML query
  IEnumerable<ProductHeader> ProductData =
   from elemProduct in xDocProducts.Root.Elements()
   select new ProductHeader
   {
     Name = elemProduct.Attribute("Name") != null ?
      elemProduct.Attribute("Name").Value : null,
     ListPrice = elemProduct.Attribute("ListPrice") != null ?
                 new decimal?(Convert.ToDecimal(
                   elemProduct.Attribute("ListPrice").Value))
                : null,
     ProductId = elemProduct.Attribute("ProductId") != null ?
                 new ushort?(Convert.ToUInt16(
                   elemProduct.Attribute("ProductId").Value)) :
                 null,
     SellEndDate = elemProduct.Attribute("SellEndDate") != null ?
      elemProduct.Attribute("SellEndDate").Value : null,
     SellStartDate = elemProduct.Attribute("SellStartDate") != null ?
      elemProduct.Attribute("SellStartDate").Value : null
   };
  //return a List<ProductHeader>
  return ProductData.ToList();
}

public void UpdateProductHeaders(List<ProductHeader> Updates)
{
  //open the local data file and load into an XDocument
  StreamReader stmrdrProductData = new StreamReader(
    new FileStream(HttpContext.Current.Request.MapPath(
      "App_Data/XML/Products.xml"), FileMode.Open));
  XDocument xDocProducts = XDocument.Load(stmrdrProductData);
  stmrdrProductData.Close();
```

```csharp
      //for each of the ProductHeader instances
      foreach (ProductHeader Prod in Updates)
      {
        //find the corresponding XElement in the loaded XDocument
        XElement elemTarget =
         (from elemProduct in xDocProducts.Root.Elements()
          where Convert.ToUInt16(elemProduct.Attribute("ProductId").Value)
          == Prod.ProductId
          select elemProduct).ToList()[0];
        //and updates the attributes with the changes
        if (elemTarget.Attribute("Name") != null)
          elemTarget.Attribute("Name").SetValue(Prod.Name);
        if (elemTarget.Attribute("ListPrice") != null
              && Prod.ListPrice.HasValue)
          elemTarget.Attribute("ListPrice").SetValue(Prod.ListPrice);
        if (elemTarget.Attribute("SellEndDate") != null)
          elemTarget.Attribute("SellEndDate").SetValue(Prod.SellEndDate);
        if (elemTarget.Attribute("SellStartDate") != null)
          elemTarget.Attribute("SellStartDate").SetValue(Prod.SellStartDate);
      }
      //save the XDocument with the changes back to the data file
      StreamWriter stmwrtrProductData = new StreamWriter(
        new FileStream(HttpContext.Current.Request.MapPath(
          "App_Data/XML/Products.xml"), FileMode.Truncate));
      xDocProducts.Save(stmwrtrProductData);
      stmwrtrProductData.Close();

    }

    public ProductDetail GetProductDetail(ushort ProductId)
    {
      StreamReader stmrdrProductData = new StreamReader(
        new FileStream(
          HttpContext.Current.Request.MapPath("App_Data/XML/Products.xml"),
          FileMode.Open));

      XDocument xDocProducts = XDocument.Load(stmrdrProductData);
      stmrdrProductData.Close();

      IEnumerable<ProductDetail> ProductData =
        from elemProduct in xDocProducts.Root.Elements()
        where elemProduct.Attribute("ProductId").Value == ProductId.ToString()
        select new ProductDetail
        {
```

```
        Class = elemProduct.Attribute("Class") != null ?
            elemProduct.Attribute("Class").Value : null,
        Color = elemProduct.Attribute("Color") != null ?
            elemProduct.Attribute("Color").Value : null,
        DaysToManufacture = elemProduct.Attribute("DaysToManufacture") != null ?
            new byte?(
                Convert.ToByte(elemProduct.Attribute("DaysToManufacture").Value))
                : null,
        DiscontinuedDate = elemProduct.Attribute("DiscontinuedDate") != null ?
            elemProduct.Attribute("DiscontinuedDate").Value : null,
        FinishedGoodsFlag = elemProduct.Attribute("FinishedGoodsFlag") != null ?
            elemProduct.Attribute("FinishedGoodsFlag").Value : null,

        MakeFlag = elemProduct.Attribute("MakeFlag") != null ?
            elemProduct.Attribute("MakeFlag").Value : null,
        ProductId = elemProduct.Attribute("ProductId") != null ?
            new ushort?(
                Convert.ToUInt16(elemProduct.Attribute("ProductId").Value))
                : null,
        ProductLine = elemProduct.Attribute("ProductLine") != null ?
            elemProduct.Attribute("ProductLine").Value : null,
        ProductNumber = elemProduct.Attribute("ProductNumber") != null ?
            elemProduct.Attribute("ProductNumber").Value : null,
        ReorderPoint = elemProduct.Attribute("ReorderPoint") != null ?
            new ushort?(
                Convert.ToUInt16(elemProduct.Attribute("ReorderPoint").Value))
                : null,
        SafetyStockLevel = elemProduct.Attribute("SafetyStockLevel") != null ?
            new ushort?(
                Convert.ToUInt16(elemProduct.Attribute("SafetyStockLevel").Value))
                : null,
        StandardCost = elemProduct.Attribute("StandardCost") != null ?
            new decimal?(Convert.ToDecimal(
                elemProduct.Attribute("StandardCost").Value))
                : null,
        Style = elemProduct.Attribute("Style") != null ?
            elemProduct.Attribute("Style").Value : null

    };

    return ProductData.ToList()[0];
}
```

```csharp
public void UpdateProductDetail(ProductDetail Update)
{
  StreamReader stmrdrProductData = new StreamReader(
    new FileStream(
      HttpContext.Current.Request.MapPath("App_Data/XML/Products.xml"),
      FileMode.Open));
  XDocument xDocProducts = XDocument.Load(stmrdrProductData);
  stmrdrProductData.Close();

  XElement elemTarget =
    (from elemProduct in xDocProducts.Root.Elements()
      where Convert.ToUInt16(elemProduct.Attribute("ProductId").Value)
      == Update.ProductId
      select elemProduct).ToList()[0];

  if (elemTarget.Attribute("Class") != null)
    elemTarget.Attribute("Class").SetValue(Update.Class);
  if (elemTarget.Attribute("Color") != null)
    elemTarget.Attribute("Color").SetValue(Update.Color);
  if (elemTarget.Attribute("DaysToManufacture") != null
    && Update.DaysToManufacture.HasValue)
    elemTarget.Attribute("DaysToManufacture").
      SetValue(Update.DaysToManufacture);
  if (elemTarget.Attribute("DiscontinuedDate") != null)
    elemTarget.Attribute("DiscontinuedDate").
      SetValue(Update.DiscontinuedDate);
  if (elemTarget.Attribute("FinishedGoodsFlag") != null)
    elemTarget.Attribute("FinishedGoodsFlag").
      SetValue(Update.FinishedGoodsFlag);
  if (elemTarget.Attribute("MakeFlag") != null)
    elemTarget.Attribute("MakeFlag").
      SetValue(Update.MakeFlag);
  if (elemTarget.Attribute("ProductLine") != null)
    elemTarget.Attribute("ProductLine").
      SetValue(Update.ProductLine);
  if (elemTarget.Attribute("ProductNumber") != null)
    elemTarget.Attribute("ProductNumber").
      SetValue(Update.ProductNumber);
  if (elemTarget.Attribute("ReorderPoint") != null
    && Update.ReorderPoint.HasValue)
    elemTarget.Attribute("ReorderPoint").
      SetValue(Update.ReorderPoint);
```

```
    if (elemTarget.Attribute("SafetyStockLevel") != null
      && Update.SafetyStockLevel.HasValue)
      elemTarget.Attribute("SafetyStockLevel").
        SetValue(Update.SafetyStockLevel);
    if (elemTarget.Attribute("StandardCost") != null
      && Update.StandardCost.HasValue)
      elemTarget.Attribute("StandardCost").
        SetValue(Update.StandardCost);
    if (elemTarget.Attribute("Style") != null)
      elemTarget.Attribute("Style").
        SetValue(Update.Style);

    StreamWriter stmwrtrProductData =
      new StreamWriter(
        new FileStream(
          HttpContext.Current.Request.MapPath("App_Data/XML/Products.xml"),
          FileMode.Truncate));

    xDocProducts.Save(stmwrtrProductData);
    stmwrtrProductData.Close();
  }
 }
}
```

We discuss the operations for handling product headers briefly. The ones to handle product details are implemented in a similar fashion and should be easy to follow.

All the data for this service is stored in a local data file named Products.xml. In the GetProductHeaders() method, you open the file and read the XML data into an XDocument instance. A LINQ query is used to navigate the XDocument and transform the XML data into a collection of ProductHeader instances. In UpdateProductHeaders(), the XElement instance corresponding to each product is updated with the changes in the ProductHeader instance, and the changes are saved to the same data file.

Note the use of the AspNetCompatibilityRequirementsAttribute setting on the service class, indicating that support to be required. This is because to get to the data files on the file system, you map the incoming HTTP request to a server path in the code. And the HttpContext type that makes the current request available to you is available only if ASP.NET support is enabled this way. This setting needs the corresponding configuration setting

```
<serviceHostingEnvironment aspNetCompatibilityEnabled="True"/>
```

already shown in Listing 7-2.

Figure 7-4 shows the Silverlight application's UI, and Listing 7-6 lists the XAML for the page.

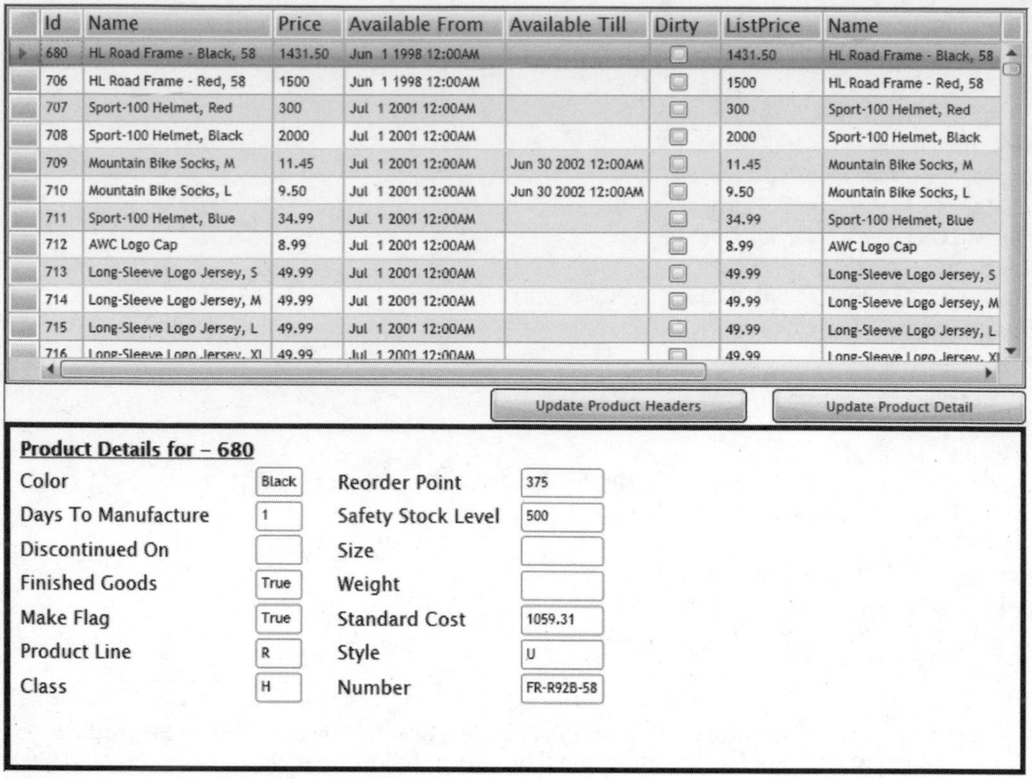

Id	Name	Price	Available From	Available Till	Dirty	ListPrice	Name
680	HL Road Frame - Black, 58	1431.50	Jun 1 1998 12:00AM		☐	1431.50	HL Road Frame - Black, 58
706	HL Road Frame - Red, 58	1500	Jun 1 1998 12:00AM		☐	1500	HL Road Frame - Red, 58
707	Sport-100 Helmet, Red	300	Jul 1 2001 12:00AM		☐	300	Sport-100 Helmet, Red
708	Sport-100 Helmet, Black	2000	Jul 1 2001 12:00AM		☐	2000	Sport-100 Helmet, Black
709	Mountain Bike Socks, M	11.45	Jul 1 2001 12:00AM	Jun 30 2002 12:00AM	☐	11.45	Mountain Bike Socks, M
710	Mountain Bike Socks, L	9.50	Jul 1 2001 12:00AM	Jun 30 2002 12:00AM	☐	9.50	Mountain Bike Socks, L
711	Sport-100 Helmet, Blue	34.99	Jul 1 2001 12:00AM		☐	34.99	Sport-100 Helmet, Blue
712	AWC Logo Cap	8.99	Jul 1 2001 12:00AM		☐	8.99	AWC Logo Cap
713	Long-Sleeve Logo Jersey, S	49.99	Jul 1 2001 12:00AM		☐	49.99	Long-Sleeve Logo Jersey, S
714	Long-Sleeve Logo Jersey, M	49.99	Jul 1 2001 12:00AM		☐	49.99	Long-Sleeve Logo Jersey, M
715	Long-Sleeve Logo Jersey, L	49.99	Jul 1 2001 12:00AM		☐	49.99	Long-Sleeve Logo Jersey, L
716	Long-Sleeve Logo Jersey, Xl	49.99	Jul 1 2001 12:00AM		☐	49.99	Long-Sleeve Logo Jersey, Xl

[Update Product Headers]   [Update Product Detail]

Product Details for – 680

Color	Black	Reorder Point	375
Days To Manufacture	1	Safety Stock Level	500
Discontinued On		Size	
Finished Goods	True	Weight	
Make Flag	True	Standard Cost	1059.31
Product Line	R	Style	U
Class	H	Number	FR-R92B-58

Figure 7-4. *The UI consuming Products data from a WCF service*

Listing 7-6. *XAML for the Page in MainPage.xaml*

```
<UserControl x:Class="Ch07_Networking.Recipe7_1.ProductsDataViewer.MainPage"
  xmlns="http://schemas.microsoft.com/winfx/2006/xaml/presentation"
  xmlns:x="http://schemas.microsoft.com/winfx/2006/xaml"
  xmlns:DataControls=
    "clr-namespace:System.Windows.Controls;assembly=System.Windows.Controls.Data"
  Width="800" Height="600">

  <Grid x:Name="LayoutRoot" Background="White">
    <Grid.RowDefinitions>
      <RowDefinition Height="50*" />
      <RowDefinition Height="5*" />
      <RowDefinition Height="45*" />
    </Grid.RowDefinitions>
```

```xml
<!-- Top Data Grid -->
<DataControls:DataGrid
  HorizontalAlignment="Stretch"
  VerticalAlignment="Stretch"
  x:Name="ProductHeaderDataGrid"
  Grid.Row="0"
  SelectionChanged="ProductHeaderDataGrid_SelectionChanged"
  CurrentCellChanged="ProductHeaderDataGrid_CurrentCellChanged"
  BeginningEdit="ProductHeaderDataGrid_BeginningEdit">
  <DataControls:DataGrid.Columns>
    <DataControls:DataGridTextColumn
      Header="Id"
      Binding="{Binding ProductId}" />
    <DataControls:DataGridTextColumn
      Header="Name"
      Binding="{Binding Name, Mode=TwoWay}" />
    <DataControls:DataGridTextColumn
      Header="Price"
      Binding="{Binding ListPrice, Mode=TwoWay}" />
    <DataControls:DataGridTextColumn
      Header="Available From"
      Binding="{Binding SellStartDate, Mode=TwoWay}" />
    <DataControls:DataGridTextColumn
      Header="Available Till"
      Binding="{Binding SellEndDate, Mode=TwoWay}" />
  </DataControls:DataGrid.Columns>
</DataControls:DataGrid>
<!-- Butons -->
<StackPanel Orientation="Horizontal"
            HorizontalAlignment="Right"
            VerticalAlignment="Center" Grid.Row ="1">
  <Button x:Name="Btn_SendHeaderUpdates" Content="Update Product Headers"
       Width="200" Click="Click_Btn_SendHeaderUpdates" Margin="0,0,20,0"/>
  <Button x:Name="Btn_SendDetailUpdates" Content="Update Product Detail"
       Width="200" Click="Click_Btn_SendDetailUpdate"/>
</StackPanel>
<Rectangle Stroke="Black" StrokeThickness="4" Grid.Row="2" />
<!-- Data entry form -->
<Grid Grid.Row="2" x:Name="ProductDetailsGrid" Margin="10,10,10,10">
  <Grid.RowDefinitions>
    <RowDefinition Height="Auto" />
    <RowDefinition Height="Auto"/>
    <RowDefinition Height="Auto"/>
    <RowDefinition Height="Auto"/>
    <RowDefinition Height="Auto"/>
```

```xml
    <RowDefinition Height="Auto"/>
    <RowDefinition Height="Auto"/>
    <RowDefinition Height="Auto"/>
</Grid.RowDefinitions>
<Grid.ColumnDefinitions>
    <ColumnDefinition Width="Auto"/>
    <ColumnDefinition Width="Auto"/>
    <ColumnDefinition Width="Auto"/>
    <ColumnDefinition Width="Auto"/>
</Grid.ColumnDefinitions>
<StackPanel Orientation="Horizontal"
            Grid.Row="0"
            HorizontalAlignment="Left"
            VerticalAlignment="Top"
            Margin="2,0,0,0">
    <TextBlock Text="Product Details for - "
               FontWeight="Bold"
               TextDecorations="Underline"/>
    <TextBlock Text="{Binding ProductId}"
               FontWeight="Bold"
               TextDecorations="Underline"/>
</StackPanel>
<TextBlock Text="Color" Grid.Row="1" Grid.Column="0"
           Margin="2,2,15,2" />
<TextBlock Text="Days To Manufacture" Grid.Row="2" Grid.Column="0"
           Margin="2,2,15,2" />
<TextBlock Text="Discontinued On" Grid.Row="3" Grid.Column="0"
           Margin="2,2,15,2" />
<TextBlock Text="Finished Goods" Grid.Row="4" Grid.Column="0"
           Margin="2,2,15,2" />
<TextBlock Text="Make Flag" Grid.Row="5" Grid.Column="0"
           Margin="2,2,15,2" />
<TextBlock Text="Product Line" Grid.Row="6" Grid.Column="0"
           Margin="2,2,15,2" />
<TextBlock Text="Class" Grid.Row="7" Grid.Column="0"
           Margin="2,2,15,2"/>
<TextBlock Text="Reorder Point" Grid.Row="1" Grid.Column="2"
           Margin="2,2,15,2" />
<TextBlock Text="Safety Stock Level" Grid.Row="2" Grid.Column="2"
           Margin="2,2,15,2" />
<TextBlock Text="Size" Grid.Row="3" Grid.Column="2"
           Margin="2,2,15,2" />
<TextBlock Text="Weight" Grid.Row="4" Grid.Column="2"
           Margin="2,2,15,2" />
```

```xml
        <TextBlock Text="Standard Cost" Grid.Row="5" Grid.Column="2"
                Margin="2,2,15,2" />
        <TextBlock Text="Style" Grid.Row="6" Grid.Column="2"
                Margin="2,2,15,2" />
        <TextBlock Text="Number" Grid.Row="7" Grid.Column="2"
                Margin="2,2,15,2" />
        <TextBox Text="{Binding Color,Mode=TwoWay}"
                Grid.Row="1" Grid.Column="1" Margin="2,2,25,2" />
        <TextBox Text="{Binding DaysToManufacture,Mode=TwoWay}"
                Grid.Row="2" Grid.Column="1" Margin="2,2,25,2" />
        <TextBox Text="{Binding DiscontinuedDate,Mode=TwoWay}"
                Grid.Row="3" Grid.Column="1" Margin="2,2,25,2" />
        <TextBox Text="{Binding FinishedGoodsFlag,Mode=TwoWay}"
                Grid.Row="4" Grid.Column="1" Margin="2,2,25,2" />
        <TextBox Text="{Binding MakeFlag,Mode=TwoWay}"
                Grid.Row="5" Grid.Column="1" Margin="2,2,25,2" />
        <TextBox Text="{Binding ProductLine,Mode=TwoWay}"
                Grid.Row="6" Grid.Column="1" Margin="2,2,25,2" />
        <TextBox Text="{Binding Class,Mode=TwoWay}"
                Grid.Row="7" Grid.Column="1" Margin="2,2,25,2"/>
        <TextBox Text="{Binding ReorderPoint,Mode=TwoWay}"
                Grid.Row="1" Grid.Column="3" Margin="2,2,25,2" />
        <TextBox Text="{Binding SafetyStockLevel,Mode=TwoWay}"
                Grid.Row="2" Grid.Column="3" Margin="2,2,25,2" />
        <TextBox Text="{Binding Size,Mode=TwoWay}"
                Grid.Row="3" Grid.Column="3" Margin="2,2,25,2" />
        <TextBox Text="{Binding Weight,Mode=TwoWay}"
                Grid.Row="4" Grid.Column="3" Margin="2,2,25,2" />
        <TextBox Text="{Binding StandardCost,Mode=TwoWay}"
                Grid.Row="5" Grid.Column="3" Margin="2,2,25,2" />
        <TextBox Text="{Binding Style,Mode=TwoWay}"
                Grid.Row="6" Grid.Column="3" Margin="2,2,25,2" />
        <TextBox Text="{Binding ProductNumber,Mode=TwoWay}"
                Grid.Row="7" Grid.Column="3" Margin="2,2,25,2" />
      </Grid>
    </Grid>
</UserControl>
```

The preceding XAML uses a DataGrid named ProductHeaderDataGrid to display the ProductHeader properties. For each selected ProductHeader, to display the related details in a master-detail fashion, you further bind the ProductDetail properties to controls in a Grid named ProductDetailsGrid. ProductDetailsGrid uses TextBlocks for labels and appropriately bound TextBoxes for property values, to create a data-entry form for the bound ProductDetail.

You also include two Buttons inside a StackPanel to provide the user with a way to submit updates to ProductHeaders or a ProductDetail.

Listing 7-7 shows the code-behind for the MainPage.

Listing 7-7. *Code-Behind for MainPage in MainPage.xaml.cs*

```
using System;
using System.Collections.Generic;
using System.Linq;
using System.Windows;
using System.Windows.Controls;
using Ch07_Networking.Recipe7_1.ProductsDataViewer.ProductsDataSoapService;

namespace Ch07_Networking.Recipe7_1.ProductsDataViewer
{
  public partial class MainPage : UserControl
  {
    ProductsDataSoapService.ProductManagerClient client = null;
    bool InEdit = false;
    public MainPage()
    {
      InitializeComponent();
      //create a new instance of the proxy
      client = new ProductsDataSoapService.ProductManagerClient();
      //add a handler for the GetProductHeadersCompleted event
      client.GetProductHeadersCompleted +=
        new EventHandler<GetProductHeadersCompletedEventArgs>(
          client_GetProductHeadersCompleted);
      //add a handler for the UpdateProductHeadersCompleted event
      client.UpdateProductHeadersCompleted +=
        new EventHandler<System.ComponentModel.AsyncCompletedEventArgs>(
          client_UpdateProductHeadersCompleted);
      //add a handler for GetProductDetailCompleted
      client.GetProductDetailCompleted +=
        new EventHandler<GetProductDetailCompletedEventArgs>(
          client_GetProductDetailCompleted);
      //invoke the GetProductHeaders() service operation
      client.GetProductHeadersAsync();
    }

    void ProductHeaderDataGrid_SelectionChanged(object sender, EventArgs e)
    {
      if (ProductHeaderDataGrid.SelectedItem != null)
        //invoke the GetProductDetails() service operation,
        //using the ProductId of the currently selected ProductHeader
        client.GetProductDetailAsync(
          (ProductHeaderDataGrid.SelectedItem as
          ProductsDataSoapService.ProductHeader).ProductId.Value);
    }
```

```
void client_GetProductDetailCompleted(object sender,
  GetProductDetailCompletedEventArgs e)
{
  //set the datacontext of the containing grid
  ProductDetailsGrid.DataContext = e.Result;
}
void client_UpdateProductHeadersCompleted(object sender,
  System.ComponentModel.AsyncCompletedEventArgs e)
{
  client.GetProductHeadersAsync();
}

void client_GetProductHeadersCompleted(object sender,
  GetProductHeadersCompletedEventArgs e)
{
  //bind the data of form List<ProductHeader> to the ProductHeaderDataGrid
  ProductHeaderDataGrid.ItemsSource = e.Result;
}

void ProductHeaderDataGrid_CurrentCellChanged(object sender,
  EventArgs e)
{
  //changing the dirty flag on a cell edit for the ProductHeader data grid
  if (InEdit && (sender as DataGrid).SelectedItem != null)
  {
    ((sender as DataGrid).SelectedItem as ProductHeader).Dirty = true;
    InEdit = false;
  }
}
private void ProductHeaderDataGrid_BeginningEdit(object sender,
 DataGridBeginningEditEventArgs e)
{
  InEdit = true;
}

void Click_Btn_SendHeaderUpdates(object Sender, RoutedEventArgs e)
{
  //get all the header items
  List<ProductHeader> AllItems =
    ProductHeaderDataGrid.ItemsSource as List<ProductHeader>;
```

621

```
        //use LINQ to filter out the ones with their dirty flag set to true
        List<ProductHeader> UpdateList =
            new List<ProductHeader>
            (
                from Prod in AllItems
                where Prod.Dirty == true
                select Prod
            );
        //send in the updates
        client.UpdateProductHeadersAsync(UpdateList);
    }

    void Click_Btn_SendDetailUpdate(object Sender, RoutedEventArgs e)
    {
        //send the ProductDetail update
        client.UpdateProductDetailAsync(ProductDetailsGrid.DataContext as
            ProductsDataSoapService.ProductDetail);
    }



    }
}
```

To fetch and bind the initial `ProductHeader` data, in the constructor of the `MainPage`, you create an instance of the `ProductService.ProductManagerClient` type, which is the proxy class created by adding the service reference to the Silverlight project. You then invoke the `GetProductHeaders()` operation on the service. Handle the `GetProductHeadersCompleted` event, and, in it, bind the data to the `DataGrid`. The data is made available to you in the `Results` property of the `GetProductHeadersCompletedEventArgs` type.

Handle the row-selection change for the `DataGrid` in `ProductHeaderDataGrid_SelectionChanged()`, and fetch and bind the appropriate product details information similarly.

To reduce the amount of data sent in updates, you send only the data that has changed. As shown in Listing 7-8, you extend the partial class for the `ProductHeader` data contract to include a `Dirty` flag so that you can track only the `ProductHeader` instances that have changed.

Listing 7-8. *Extension to ProductHeader Type to Include a Dirty Flag*

```
namespace Ch07_Networking.Recipe7_1.ProductsDataViewer.ProductsDataSoapService
{
    public partial class ProductHeader
    {
        //dirty flag
        public bool Dirty { get; set; }
    }
}
```

Referring back to Listing 7-7, you see that to use the `Dirty` flag appropriately, you handle the `BeginningEdit` event on the `ProductHeaderDataGrid`. This event is raised whenever the user starts to edit a cell. In the handler, you set a flag named `InEdit` to indicate that an edit process has started. You also handle the `CurrentCellChanged` event, which is raised whenever the user navigates away from a cell to another one. In this handler, you see if the cell was in edit mode by checking the `InEdit` flag. If it was, you get the current `ProductHeader` data item from the `SelectedItem` property of the `DataGrid` and set its `Dirty` flag appropriately.

You handle the `Click` event of the button `Btn_SendHeaderUpdates` to submit the `ProductHeader` updates. Using a LINQ query on the currently bound collection of `ProductHeaders`, you filter out the changed data based on the `Dirty` flag, and you pass on the changed data set via `UpdateProductHeadersAsync()`. To update a `ProductDetail`, pass on the currently bound `ProductDetail` instance to `UpdateProductDetailAsync()`.

7-2. Exchanging XML Messages over HTTP

Problem

Your Silverlight application needs to exchange plain old XML (POX) messages with an HTTP endpoint.

Solution

Use the `HttpWebRequest`/`HttpWebResponse` pair of types in `System.Net` to exchange POX messages with an HTTP endpoint.

How It Works

POX-style message exchange can be an attractive alternative to the more structured SOAP-based message exchange. It does not impose any of the specific format requirements of SOAP, and there is much more freedom regarding how messages are structured. Consequently, it requires fewer infrastructural requirements, benefits from more implementation options, and can be consumed by almost any XML-aware runtime environment.

The downside of such loose-format messaging, however, is that very often, client frameworks do not have the luxury of tool-based assistance like Visual Studio's service proxy-generation features. Also, client APIs that consume such services are somewhat lower level—in most cases, they implement some sort of request/response mechanism over HTTP, with support for HTTP-related features, like choice of verbs or Multipurpose Internet Mail Extensions (MIME) types.

Using HttpWebRequest/HttpWebResponse in Silverlight

The `HttpWebRequest`/`HttpWebResponse` types implement an API that allows Silverlight clients to send requests and receive responses from HTTP endpoints in an asynchronous fashion.

`HttpWebRequest` and `HttpWebResponse` are abstract classes and hence are not directly constructable. To use the API, you start by invoking the static `Create()` method on the `HttpWebRequest` type, supplying the URL of the endpoint you wish to interact with. What is returned to you is an instance of `WebRequest`—the base class for `HttpWebRequest`. You have the option of setting the desired HTTP verb to use through the `HttpWebRequest.Method` property—`HttpWebRequest` supports GET and POST. The default value of the `Method` property on a newly created web request is GET. You really only need to set it if you are going to use POST.

You also have the option of setting the MIME type using the `ContentType` property.

Using GET

The GET verb is typically used to request a web resource from an endpoint. The request is represented as the URI of the resource, with optional additional query string parameters. You invoke a GET request using the `BeginGetResponse()` method on the `WebRequest` instance. Pass a delegate of the form `AsyncResult` around a handler that you implement. This handler gets called back when the async request operation completes. In the handler, call `EndGetResponse()` to access any response information returned in the form of a `WebResponse` instance. You can then call `WebResponse.GetResponseStream()` to access the returned content.

Using POST

If you need to submit content back to an HTTP endpoint for processing, and you want to include the data in the body of the request, you must use the POST verb. To POST content, you need to write the content to be posted into the request stream. To do this, first call `BeginGetRequestStream()`, again passing in an `AsyncResult` delegate. In the handler, call `EndGetRequestStream()` to acquire a stream to the request's body, and write the content you intend to POST to that stream. Then, call `BeginGetResponse()` using the same pattern outlined earlier.

Handling Asynchronous Invocation

The methods discussed here follow an asynchronous invocation pattern. The `BeginGetResponse()` and `BeginGetRequestStream()` methods dispatch the execution to a randomly allocated background thread, returning control to your main application thread right away. The `AsyncResult` handlers that you pass in as callbacks are invoked on these background threads. If you want to access any parts of your object model created on the main thread—such as the controls on the page or any types that you instantiate elsewhere in your code—from one of these handlers, you cannot do it in the normal fashion, because doing so causes a cross-thread access violation. You need to first switch context to the thread that owns the object you are trying to access. To do this, you must use a type called `Dispatcher`.

   The `Dispatcher` type is designed to manage work items for a specific thread. More specifically, in this context, a `Dispatcher` exposes methods that allow you to execute a piece of code in the context of the thread that owns the `Dispatcher`. The `DependencyObject` type, and hence all derived types, exposes a `Dispatcher` instance, which is associated with the thread that creates the type. One of the easiest instances you can get hold of is exposed on the `Page` itself.

   To use the `Dispatcher`, use the static `BeginInvoke()` function, passing in a delegate to the method that you want to execute on the `Dispatcher`'s thread, regardless of which thread it is called from. `Dispatcher` ensures a proper thread-context switch to execute the targeted method on its owning thread. For instance, if you want to access some element on the `Page` from a background thread, you use the `Page`'s `Dispatcher` as described.

■**Note** Although we chose POX messages as the first example of demonstrating this API, the types are a general-purpose means of HTTP communication from Silverlight. You can exchange other kinds of information over HTTP using these as well. We show you another example using JSON in Recipe 7-3.

Configuring WCF to Use Non-SOAP Endpoints

Although the Silverlight techniques demonstrated in this API can be used with any HTTP endpoint that accepts and responds with POX messages, we have chosen to implement the POX/HTTP endpoint using WCF.

WCF by default uses SOAP-based message exchange, but it also enables a web programming model that allows non-SOAP endpoints over HTTP to be exposed from WCF services. This allows REST-style services to use formats like POX or JSON to exchange messages with clients.

To enable web-style, URI-based invocation of operations on these services, apply one of the WebGetAttribute or WebInvokeAttribute types, found in System.ServiceModel.Web, to the operations. The WebGetAttribute mandates use of the HTTP GET verb to acquire a resource; hence the only way to pass in parameters to such an operation is through query string parameters on the client that are mapped by the WCF runtime to parameters in the operation. As an example, here is the declaration of a GET-style operation:

```
[OperationContract]
[WebGet()]
Information GetSomeInformation(int Param);
```

You can invoke this operation by sending an HTTP GET request to an URI endpoint, formatted like so:

```
http://someserver/someservice.svc/GetSomeInformation?Param=50
```

WebInvokeAttribute defaults to the use of the POST verb but can also be specified to accept the PUT or DELETE verb. If you are using POST, the message body is expected to be in the POST body content, whereas you can continue to use query-string style parameters with a verb like PUT. However, keep in mind that Silverlight only allows the use of POST, not PUT or DELETE.

In addition to using these attributes to decorate your WCF operations, you also need to specify the appropriate binding and behavior. To use POX messaging over HTTP, you must use WebHttpBinding for the endpoint. Here is a snippet from a WCF config file that shows this:

```
<endpoint address="" binding="webHttpBinding" contract="IProductManager" />
```

The Code

The code sample for this recipe reuses the example used in Recipe 7-1. To illustrate the concept, change the WCF service to use POX messages over HTTP, and implement the client using the HttpWebRequest/HttpWebResponse API.

Listing 7-9 shows the service contract for the WCF service adapted for POX exchange over HTTP.

Listing 7-9. *Service Contract for the POX Service in ServiceContract.cs*

```
using System.ServiceModel;
using System.ServiceModel.Web;
using System.Xml;

namespace Ch07_Networking.Recipe7_2.ProductsDataPOXService
{
  [ServiceContract]
  public interface IProductManager
  {
    [OperationContract]
    [XmlSerializerFormat()]
```

```
    [WebGet()]
    XmlDocument GetProductHeaders();

    [OperationContract]
    [XmlSerializerFormat()]
    [WebInvoke()]
    void UpdateProductHeaders(XmlDocument Updates);

    [OperationContract]
    [XmlSerializerFormat()]
    [WebGet()]
    XmlDocument GetProductDetail(ushort ProductId);

    [OperationContract]
    [XmlSerializerFormat()]
    [WebInvoke()]
    void UpdateProductDetail(XmlDocument Update);
  }
}
```

POX messages are just blocks of well-formed XML. Consequently, you use the
System.Xml.XmlDocument type to represent the messages being exchanged. Because XmlDocument does not
have the WCF DataContractAttribute applied to it, WCF cannot use the default data-contract
serialization to serialize these messages. So, you also apply
System.ServiceModel.XmlSerializerFormatAttribute() to the service operations to use XML
serialization.

Listing 7-10 shows the implementation of the GetProductHeaders() and the
UpdateProductHeaders() operations.

Listing 7-10. *Service Implementation for POX Service in ProductManager.cs*

```
using System.IO;
using System.Linq;
using System.ServiceModel.Activation;
using System.Web;
using System.Xml;
using System.Xml.Linq;

namespace Ch07_Networking.Recipe7_2.ProductsDataPOXService
{
  [AspNetCompatibilityRequirements(
    RequirementsMode = AspNetCompatibilityRequirementsMode.Required)]
  public class ProductManager : IProductManager
  {
```

```csharp
public XmlDocument GetProductHeaders()
{
  //open the local data file
  StreamReader stmrdrProductData =
    new StreamReader(
      new FileStream(
        HttpContext.Current.Request.MapPath("App_Data/XML/Products.xml"),
        FileMode.Open));
  //create and load an XmlDocument
  XmlDocument xDoc = new XmlDocument();
  xDoc.LoadXml(stmrdrProductData.ReadToEnd());
  stmrdrProductData.Close();

  //return the document
  HttpContext.Current.Response.Cache.SetCacheability(HttpCacheability.NoCache);
  return xDoc;
}

public void UpdateProductHeaders(XmlDocument Updates)
{
  //load the XmlDocument containing the updates into a LINQ XDocument
  XDocument xDocProductUpdates = XDocument.Parse(Updates.OuterXml);
  //load the local data file
  StreamReader stmrdrProductData =
    new StreamReader(
      new FileStream(
        HttpContext.Current.Request.MapPath("App_Data/XML/Products.xml"),
        FileMode.Open));
  XDocument xDocProducts = XDocument.Load(stmrdrProductData);
  stmrdrProductData.Close();
  //for each of the updated records, find the matching record in the local data
  //using a LINQ query
  //and update the appropriate fields
  foreach (XElement elemProdUpdate in xDocProductUpdates.Root.Elements())
  {
    XElement elemTarget =
      (from elemProduct in xDocProducts.Root.Elements()
        where elemProduct.Attribute("ProductId").Value ==
        elemProdUpdate.Attribute("ProductId").Value
        select elemProduct).ToList()[0];
    if (elemTarget.Attribute("Name") != null)
      elemTarget.Attribute("Name").
        SetValue(elemProdUpdate.Attribute("Name").Value);
```

```
      if (elemTarget.Attribute("ListPrice") != null)
        elemTarget.Attribute("ListPrice").
          SetValue(elemProdUpdate.Attribute("ListPrice").Value);
      if (elemTarget.Attribute("SellEndDate") != null)
        elemTarget.Attribute("SellEndDate").
          SetValue(elemProdUpdate.Attribute("SellEndDate").Value);
      if (elemTarget.Attribute("SellStartDate") != null)
        elemTarget.Attribute("SellStartDate").
          SetValue(elemProdUpdate.Attribute("SellStartDate").Value);
    }
    //save the changes
    StreamWriter stmwrtrProductData =
      new StreamWriter(
        new FileStream(
          HttpContext.Current.Request.MapPath("App_Data/XML/Products.xml"),
          FileMode.Truncate));
    xDocProducts.Save(stmwrtrProductData);
    stmwrtrProductData.Close();
  }

  public XmlDocument GetProductDetail(ushort ProductId)
  {
    StreamReader stmrdrProductData =
      new StreamReader(
        new FileStream(
          HttpContext.Current.Request.MapPath("App_Data/XML/Products.xml"),
          FileMode.Open));
    XDocument xDocProducts = XDocument.Load(stmrdrProductData);
    XDocument xDocProdDetail = new XDocument(
      (from xElem in xDocProducts.Root.Elements()
        where xElem.Attribute("ProductId").Value == ProductId.ToString()
        select xElem).ToList()[0]);

    XmlDocument xDoc = new XmlDocument();
    xDoc.LoadXml(xDocProdDetail.ToString());
    stmrdrProductData.Close();

    HttpContext.Current.Response.Cache.SetCacheability(HttpCacheability.NoCache);
    return xDoc;
  }
  public void UpdateProductDetail(XmlDocument Update)
  {
    XDocument xDocProductUpdates = XDocument.Parse(Update.OuterXml);
    XElement elemProdUpdate = xDocProductUpdates.Root;
```

```
StreamReader stmrdrProductData =
  new StreamReader(
    new FileStream(
      HttpContext.Current.Request.MapPath("App_Data/XML/Products.xml"),
      FileMode.Open));

XDocument xDocProducts = XDocument.Load(stmrdrProductData);
stmrdrProductData.Close();

XElement elemTarget =
  (from elemProduct in xDocProducts.Root.Elements()
   where elemProduct.Attribute("ProductId").Value ==
   elemProdUpdate.Attribute("ProductId").Value
   select elemProduct).ToList()[0];

if (elemTarget.Attribute("Class") != null)
  elemTarget.Attribute("Class").
    SetValue(elemProdUpdate.Attribute("Class").Value);
if (elemTarget.Attribute("Color") != null)
  elemTarget.Attribute("Color").
    SetValue(elemProdUpdate.Attribute("Color").Value);
if (elemTarget.Attribute("DaysToManufacture") != null)
  elemTarget.Attribute("DaysToManufacture").
    SetValue(elemProdUpdate.Attribute("DaysToManufacture").Value);
if (elemTarget.Attribute("DiscontinuedDate") != null)
  elemTarget.Attribute("DiscontinuedDate").
    SetValue(elemProdUpdate.Attribute("DiscontinuedDate").Value);
if (elemTarget.Attribute("FinishedGoodsFlag") != null)
  elemTarget.Attribute("FinishedGoodsFlag").
    SetValue(elemProdUpdate.Attribute("FinishedGoodsFlag").Value);
if (elemTarget.Attribute("MakeFlag") != null)
  elemTarget.Attribute("MakeFlag").
    SetValue(elemProdUpdate.Attribute("MakeFlag").Value);
if (elemTarget.Attribute("ProductLine") != null)
  elemTarget.Attribute("ProductLine").
    SetValue(elemProdUpdate.Attribute("ProductLine").Value);
if (elemTarget.Attribute("ProductNumber") != null)
  elemTarget.Attribute("ProductNumber").
    SetValue(elemProdUpdate.Attribute("ProductNumber").Value);
if (elemTarget.Attribute("ReorderPoint") != null)
  elemTarget.Attribute("ReorderPoint").
    SetValue(elemProdUpdate.Attribute("ReorderPoint").Value);
if (elemTarget.Attribute("SafetyStockLevel") != null)
  elemTarget.Attribute("SafetyStockLevel").
    SetValue(elemProdUpdate.Attribute("SafetyStockLevel").Value);
```

```
      if (elemTarget.Attribute("StandardCost") != null)
        elemTarget.Attribute("StandardCost").
          SetValue(elemProdUpdate.Attribute("StandardCost").Value);
      if (elemTarget.Attribute("Style") != null)
        elemTarget.Attribute("Style").
          SetValue(elemProdUpdate.Attribute("Style").Value);

      StreamWriter stmwrtrProductData = new StreamWriter(new FileStream(HttpContext.
Current.Request.MapPath("App_Data/XML/Products.xml"), FileMode.Truncate));
      xDocProducts.Save(stmwrtrProductData);
      stmwrtrProductData.Close();
    }
  }
}
```

Because GetProductHeaders() returns a POX message, you open the local data file, load the XML content into an XmlDocument instance, and return the XmlDocument instance. The XmlSerializerFormatAttribute on the operation ensures that the XML content is formatted as it is on the wire.

In UpdateProductHeaders(), you receive the updates as a POX message. You parse the content of the message and load it into an instance of the XDocument type so that it can participate in a LINQ to XML query. You use the query to find the matching records in the local XML data, also loaded in an XDocument, and copy over the updates before you save the local data back to its file store.

The GetProductDetail() and UpdateProductDetail() methods follow the same implementation pattern.

Note the call to SetCacheability() to set the cache policy to NoCache before you return data from the GetProductHeaders() and GetProductDetail() methods. The Silverlight network stack relies on the browser's network stack, and the default behavior has the browser look for the data requested in its own cache first. Setting this in the server response causes the browser to never cache the returned data, so that every time the client calls the service operation, the operation is invoked and current data is returned. This is important for data that can be changed between requests, as in this case with the update operations. For purely lookup data that seldom changes, you may want to leave the browser cache on, and possibly stipulate an expiration. You can refer to more information about controlling the browser-caching policy from the server on MSDN at http://msdn.microsoft.com/en-us/library/system.web.httpresponse.cache.aspx.

Now, let's look at the client code in the code-behind class. Because the complete code listing is repetitive between the product header– and product detail–related functionality, we list only the code pertaining to the acquiring and updating product headers. You can access the book's sample code to get the full implementation.

Listing 7-11 shows the product header–related functionality.

Listing 7-11. *Partial Listing of the Code-Behind in MainPage.xaml.cs*

```
using System;
using System.Collections.Generic;
using System.IO;
using System.Linq;
using System.Net;
using System.Windows;
```

```csharp
using System.Windows.Controls;
using System.Xml.Linq;
namespace Ch07_Networking.Recipe7_2.POXProductsDataViewer
{
  public partial class MainPage : UserControl
  {
    private const string ServiceUri =
        "http://localhost:9292/ProductsPOXService.svc";
    bool InEdit = false;

    public MainPage()
    {
      InitializeComponent();

      RequestProductHeaders();
    }


    private List<ProductHeader> DeserializeProductHeaders(string HeaderXml)
    {
      //load into a LINQ to XML Xdocument
      XDocument xDocProducts = XDocument.Parse(HeaderXml);
      //for each Product Xelement, project a new ProductHeader
      List<ProductHeader> ProductList =
        (from elemProduct in xDocProducts.Root.Elements()
         select new ProductHeader
         {
           Name = elemProduct.Attribute("Name") != null ?
             elemProduct.Attribute("Name").Value : null,
           ListPrice = elemProduct.Attribute("ListPrice") != null ?
             new decimal?(
               Convert.ToDecimal(elemProduct.Attribute("ListPrice").
               Value)) : null,
           ProductId = elemProduct.Attribute("ProductId") != null ?
             new ushort?(Convert.ToUInt16(elemProduct.Attribute("ProductId").
               Value)) : null,
           SellEndDate = elemProduct.Attribute("SellEndDate") != null ?
             elemProduct.Attribute("SellEndDate").Value : null,
           SellStartDate = elemProduct.Attribute("SellStartDate") != null ?
             elemProduct.Attribute("SellStartDate").Value : null

         }).ToList();
      //return the list
      return ProductList;
    }
```

```
    private void RequestProductHeaders()
    {
      //create and initialize an HttpWebRequest
      WebRequest webReq = HttpWebRequest.Create(
        new Uri(string.Format("{0}/GetProductHeaders", ServiceUri)));

      //GET a response, passing in OnProductHeadersReceived
      //as the completion callback, and the WebRequest as state
      webReq.BeginGetResponse(
        new AsyncCallback(OnProductHeadersReceived), webReq);
    }

    private void OnProductHeadersReceived(IAsyncResult target)
    {
      //reacquire the WebRequest from the passed in state
      WebRequest webReq = target.AsyncState as WebRequest;
      //get the WebResponse
      WebResponse webResp = webReq.EndGetResponse(target);

      //get the response stream, and wrap in a StreamReader for reading as text
      StreamReader stmReader = new StreamReader(webResp.GetResponseStream());
      //read the incoming POX into a string
      string ProductHeadersXml = stmReader.ReadToEnd();
      stmReader.Close();

      //use the Dispatcher to switch context to the main thread
      //deserialize the POX into a Product Header collection,
//and bind to the DataGrid
      Dispatcher.BeginInvoke(new Action(delegate
      {
        ProductHeaderDataGrid.ItemsSource =
          DeserializeProductHeaders(ProductHeadersXml);
      }), null);

    }
    private void UpdateProductHeaders()
    {
      //create and initialize an HttpWebRequest
      WebRequest webReq = HttpWebRequest.Create(
        new Uri(string.Format("{0}/UpdateProductHeaders", ServiceUri)));
      //set the VERB to POST
      webReq.Method = "POST";
      //set the MIME type to send POX
      webReq.ContentType = "text/xml";
```

```csharp
  //begin acquiring the request stream
  webReq.BeginGetRequestStream(
    new AsyncCallback(OnProdHdrUpdReqStreamAcquired), webReq);
}

private void OnProdHdrUpdReqStreamAcquired(IAsyncResult target)
{
  //get the passed in  WebRequest
  HttpWebRequest webReq = target.AsyncState as HttpWebRequest;
  //get the request stream, wrap in a writer
  StreamWriter stmUpdates =
    new StreamWriter(webReq.EndGetRequestStream(target));
  Dispatcher.BeginInvoke(new Action(delegate
    {
      //select all the updated records
      List<ProductHeader> AllItems =
        ProductHeaderDataGrid.ItemsSource as List<ProductHeader>;
      List<ProductHeader> UpdateList = new List<ProductHeader>
                              (
                                from Prod in AllItems
                                where Prod.Dirty == true
                                select Prod
                              );

      //use LINQ to XML to transform to XML
      XElement Products = new XElement("Products",
        from Prod in UpdateList
        select new XElement("Product",
            new XAttribute("Name", Prod.Name),
            new XAttribute("ListPrice", Prod.ListPrice),
            new XAttribute("ProductId", Prod.ProductId),
            new XAttribute("SellEndDate", Prod.SellEndDate),
            new XAttribute("SellStartDate", Prod.SellStartDate)));

      //write the XML into the request stream
      Products.Save(stmUpdates);
      stmUpdates.Close();
      //start acquiring the response
      webReq.BeginGetResponse(
        new AsyncCallback(OnProdHdrsUpdateCompleted), webReq);
    }));

}
```

```
private void OnProdHdrsUpdateCompleted(IAsyncResult target)
{
  HttpWebRequest webResp = target.AsyncState as HttpWebRequest;
  HttpWebResponse resp =
    webResp.EndGetResponse(target) as HttpWebResponse;
  //if response is OK, refresh the grid to
  //show that the changes actually happened on the server

  if (resp.StatusCode == HttpStatusCode.OK)
    RequestProductHeaders();
}
void ProductHeaderDataGrid_SelectionChanged(object sender, EventArgs e)
{
  if (ProductHeaderDataGrid.SelectedItem != null)
  {

    //invoke the GetProductDetails() service operation,
    //using the ProductId of the currently selected ProductHeader
    RequestProductDetail(
      (ProductHeaderDataGrid.SelectedItem
      as ProductHeader).ProductId.Value);
  }
}
void ProductHeaderDataGrid_CurrentCellChanged(object sender,
 EventArgs e)
    {
      //changing the dirty flag on a cell edit for the ProductHeader data grid
      if (InEdit && (sender as DataGrid).SelectedItem != null)
      {
        ((sender as DataGrid).SelectedItem as ProductHeader).Dirty = true;
        InEdit = false;
      }
    }
private void ProductHeaderDataGrid_BeginningEdit(object sender,
 DataGridBeginningEditEventArgs e)
{
  InEdit = true;
}

void Click_Btn_SendHeaderUpdates(object Sender, RoutedEventArgs e)
{
  UpdateProductHeaders();
}
```

```
    void Click_Btn_SendDetailUpdate(object Sender, RoutedEventArgs e)
    {
       UpdateProductDetail();
    }


    //Product detail functionality omitted -
    //please refer to sample code for full listing
  }
}
```

In the RequestProductHeaders() method, you create the HttpWebRequest and submit it asynchronously using BeginGetResponse(). Note the passing of the WebRequest instance as the state parameter to BeginGetResponse(). On completion of the async call, when the supplied callback handler OnProductHeadersReceived() is called back, you need access to the WebRequest instance in order to complete the call by calling EndGetResponse() on it. Passing it in as the state parameter provides access to it in a thread-safe way, inside the handler executing on a background thread.

In OnProductHeadersReceived(), you obtain the WebRequest from the IAsyncResult.AsyncState parameter and then obtain the WebResponse using the EndGetResponse() method on the WebRequest. Open the response stream using WebResponse.GetResponseStream(), read the POX message from that stream, and bind the data to the ProductHeaderDataGrid after deserializing it into a suitable collection of ProductHeaders using DeserializeProductHeaders(). DeserializeProductHeaders() uses a LINQ to XML query to transform the POX message to an instance of List<ProductHeader>.

To send updates back to the service, you use the UpdateProductHeaders() method. Set the Method property of the request to POST, with the MIME type appropriately set to text/XML. Then, asynchronously acquire the request stream with a call to BeginGetRequestStream().

When BeginGetRequestStream() is completed, the OnProdHdrUpdReqStreamAcquired() callback occurs on a background thread. In the handler, switch thread context back to the main thread using Dispatcher.Invoke(). In the delegate passed to Invoke(), filter out the updated records and transform the records to XML using LINQ to XML, and then serialize the resulting XML to the request stream. After closing the stream, submit the POST calling BeginGetResponse(). After the POST completes, you have the ability to check the StatusCode property to decide on your course of action. If the code is HttpStatusCode.OK, refresh the data from the server by calling RequestProductDetail() again. The only other possible value is HttpStatusCode.NotFound, which indicates a problem with the service call and can be used to display a suitable error message.

Also shown in Listing 7-11 is the handling of the dirty flag, row edits, and button-click handlers for submitting updates, which remain the same as in Recipe 7-1 and hence are not discussed here.

The UI for this sample, and therefore the XAML, remain exactly the same as in Recipe 7-1.

7-3. Using JSON Serialization over HTTP

Problem

Your Silverlight application needs to exchange JavaScript Object Notation (JSON) messages with an HTTP endpoint.

Solution

Use the HttpWebRequest/HttpWebResponse pair of types to exchange JSON messages with the HTTP endpoint. Use DataContractJsonSerializer to serialize/deserialize JSON data.

How It Works

The techniques used in this recipe are largely similar to the ones in Recipe 7-2, so we will highlight the differences.

JSON

JSON is a very lightweight format that can be applied to data exchanged on the wire between computers. JSON is textual, like XML, and is based on a subset of the JavaScript programming language, borrowing those portions of the JavaScript syntax that are needed to represent data structures and collections. JSON has gained a lot of popularity of late as a serialization format of choice, especially for Ajax web applications, where objects and collections need to be serialized to and from JavaScript code. For more on the format specification, and a more detailed introduction, visit http://www.json.org.

Listing 7-12 shows the JSON serialized representation of an instance of the ProductDetail class (which we use in the past recipes and continue to use here), for ProductId of value 680.

Listing 7-12. *JSON Representation of a ProductDetail Instance*

```
{"Class":"H",
"Color":"Black",
"DaysToManufacture":1,
"DiscontinuedDate":"",
"FinishedGoodsFlag":"True",
"MakeFlag":"True",
"ProductId":680,
"ProductLine":"R ",
"ProductNumber":"FR-R92B-58",
"ReorderPoint":375,
"SafetyStockLevel":500,
"Size":null,
"StandardCost":1059.31,
"Style":"U ",
"Weight":null}
```

It is easy to note that the serialized format does not contain any details about the actual CLR type or even the data types of the properties being serialized—it is a collection of named properties and their values. It is the job of an appropriate JSON serializer on both ends of the wire to take this textual format and convert it into an instance of a class.

Part of JSON's popularity is based on the fact that it is much more compact than XML in most cases—although both are textual, JSON is less verbose. However, JSON has some disadvantages as well. It was designed to be a serialization format and therefore is not meant to be used in a stand-alone way. In other words, the serialized textual format shown earlier is not much use until you turn it back into an object. XML, on the other hand, enjoys facilities that can be used to operate on the XML itself, such as XPath, XQuery, XSL transformations, and LINQ to XML, whereby the serialized XML can be useful to you without having to be deserialized into an object structure.

If you must choose formats, and you have control on both ends of the wire, JSON is preferable if you never intend to operate directly on the serialized form; XML is preferable otherwise. If you do not have control on both ends, then the choice may already be made for you.

Using the DataContractJsonSerializer Type

Silverlight provides the DataContractJsonSerializer type in System.Runtime.Serialization.Json. It lets you serialize or deserialize JSON data to and from CLR types decorated with the DataContract attribute.

To use DataContractSerializer, create a new instance of it, and initialize it with the type of the CLR object you want to serialize:

```
DataContractJsonSerializer jsonSer = new
  DataContractJsonSerializer(typeof(List<ProductHeader>));
```

To deserialize some JSON data, pass in a reference to the stream containing the JSON data to the ReadObject() method, and cast the returned object to the desired type:

```
List<ProductHeader> productList =
jsonSer.ReadObject(jsonStream ) as List<ProductHeader>;
```

DataContractJsonSerializer supports object trees with nested objects, and ReadObject() returns to you the object at the root of the tree.

To serialize objects to JSON, use the WriteObject() method, passing in a destination stream, and the root object in the object tree that you want serialized:

```
jsonSer.WriteObject(jsonStream,rootObject);
```

Configuring WCF to Use JSON

We continue to use the WCF service from the previous recipes, but let's configure it this time to use JSON formatting on the messages exchanged.

WebGetAttribute and WebInvokeAttribute expose two properties that let you control this formatting: RequestFormat and ResponseFormat. Both properties are of type WebMessageFormat, which is an enum. You need to set RequestFormat to WebMessageFormat.Json to enable the service to accept JSON-formatted requests; set ResponseFormat identically to send JSON-formatted responses from the service.

You must also configure your WCF service endpoint to specify the use of a JSON serializer. To do this, you apply a custom behavior to the endpoint. Define a behavior named ScriptBehavior; the webHttp element in it enforces the use of JSON:

```
<endpointBehaviors>
  <behavior name="ScriptBehavior">
    <webHttp/>
  </behavior>
</endpointBehaviors>
```

You can apply the behavior to an endpoint as shown here:

```
<endpoint address="" behaviorConfiguration="ScriptBehavior" binding="webHttpBinding"
      contract="IProductManager" />
```

The Code

The code for this sample is virtually identical to that from Recipe 7-2. Listing 7-13 shows the service contract modified to use JSON.

637

Listing 7-13. *Service Contract Modified for JSON in ServiceContract.cs*

```csharp
using System.Collections.Generic;
using System.ServiceModel;
using System.ServiceModel.Web;

namespace Ch07_Networking.Recipe7_3.ProductsDataJSONService
{
  [ServiceContract]
  public interface IProductManager
  {
    [OperationContract]
    [WebGet(ResponseFormat = WebMessageFormat.Json)]
    List<ProductHeader> GetProductHeaders();

    [OperationContract]
    [WebInvoke(RequestFormat = WebMessageFormat.Json)]
    void UpdateProductHeaders(List<ProductHeader> Updates);

    [OperationContract]
    [WebGet(ResponseFormat = WebMessageFormat.Json)]
    ProductDetail GetProductDetail(ushort ProductId);

    [OperationContract]
    [WebInvoke(RequestFormat = WebMessageFormat.Json)]
    void UpdateProductDetail(ProductDetail Update);
  }
}
```

You specify the RequestFormat and the ResponseFormat properties of the WebGet and WebInvoke attributes to use JSON. In this case, in the methods GetProductHeaders() and GetProductDetail(), you only need to specify ResponseFormat, because the query is performed using a GET. In case of the update methods, you do not expect a response back from the POST, so only the RequestFormat is set to use JSON; thus the data sent to the service is formatted appropriately. However, when using POST, you may encounter scenarios where you are both sending and receiving data, in which case you need to specify both properties in WebInvokeAttribute.

Because almost all of the code-behind for the MainPage in this sample is identical to that in Recipe 7-2, we highlight the differences in Listing 7-14. The only real difference is in the way you serialize and deserialize the messages.

Listing 7-14. *Code-Behind for JSON Serialization and Deserialization in MainPage.xaml.cs*

```
private List<ProductHeader> DeserializeProductHeaders(Stream HeaderJson)
{
    //create and initialize a new DataContractJsonSerializer
    DataContractJsonSerializer jsonSer =
      new DataContractJsonSerializer(typeof(List<ProductHeader>));
    //Deserialize - root object returned and cast
    List<ProductHeader> ProductList =
      jsonSer.ReadObject(HeaderJson) as List<ProductHeader>;
    return ProductList;
}
private void OnProdHdrUpdReqStreamAcquired(IAsyncResult target)
{
  HttpWebRequest webReq = target.AsyncState as HttpWebRequest;
  Stream stmUpdates = webReq.EndGetRequestStream(target);
  Dispatcher.BeginInvoke(new Action(delegate
    {
      List<ProductHeader> AllItems =
        ProductHeaderDataGrid.ItemsSource as List<ProductHeader>;

      List<ProductHeader> UpdateList =
        new List<ProductHeader>
        (
          from Prod in AllItems
          where Prod.Dirty == true
          select Prod
        );
      //create and initialize a DataContractJsonSerializer
      DataContractJsonSerializer jsonSer =
        new DataContractJsonSerializer(typeof(List<ProductHeader>));
      //write object tree out to the stream
      jsonSer.WriteObject(stmUpdates, UpdateList);
      stmUpdates.Close();

      webReq.BeginGetResponse(
        new AsyncCallback(OnProductHeadersUpdateCompleted), webReq);
    }));
}
```

```
private ProductDetail DeserializeProductDetails(Stream DetailJson)
{

    DataContractJsonSerializer jsonSer =
      new DataContractJsonSerializer(typeof(ProductDetail));
    ProductDetail Detail =
      jsonSer.ReadObject(DetailJson) as ProductDetail;
    return Detail;
}
private void OnProductDetailUpdateRequestStreamAcquired(IAsyncResult target)
{
  HttpWebRequest webReq =
    (target.AsyncState as object[])[0] as HttpWebRequest;
  Stream stmUpdates = webReq.EndGetRequestStream(target);


  ProductDetail Detail =
    (target.AsyncState as object[])[1] as ProductDetail;

  DataContractJsonSerializer jsonSer =
    new DataContractJsonSerializer(typeof(ProductDetail));
  jsonSer.WriteObject(stmUpdates, Detail);
  stmUpdates.Close();
  webReq.BeginGetResponse(
new AsyncCallback(OnProductDetailsUpdateCompleted), webReq);
}
```

The DeserializeProductHeaders() method uses a DataContractJsonSerializer to deserialize JSON data from a stream to a List<ProductHeader>. You create a new instance of DataContractJsonSerializer, passing in the targeted CLR type. You then call the ReadObject() method, passing in the stream containing the serialized object tree. This deserializes the object and returns it to you as an Object, which you must cast appropriately. Note that if an object tree is serialized into the stream, on deserialization the entire tree is reconstructed, and the root object of the tree is returned to you.

In OnProdHdrUpdReqStreamAcquired(), you switch to the main thread using Dispatcher.Invoke(). Prior to sending an update to a ProductHeader, you serialize a List<ProductHeader> containing the updates to a stream as JSON. After you filter out the collection of ProductHeaders containing the updates using LINQ, you again use a newly constructed DataContractJsonSerializer instance, this time initializing it with the type of List<ProductHeader>. You then call the WriteObject() method on it, passing in the target stream and the List<ProductHeader> instance containing the updates that you want to serialize.

DeserializeProductDetails() and OnProductDetailUpdateRequestStreamAcquired() are implemented following the same pattern and should be self-explanatory.

Note that `DataContractJsonSerializer` needs the data types that are serialized to be declared as `DataContracts`, as in Recipe 7-1. Consequently, the data model used is identical to that in Recipe 7-1.

Also note that while sending POST requests that contain JSON-formatted data, you must set the MIME type appropriately by setting the `ContentType` property on the request to the string "application/json" like so:

```
WebRequest webReq = HttpWebRequest.Create
  (new Uri(string.Format("{0}/UpdateProductHeaders",ServiceUri)));
webReq.Method = "POST";
webReq.ContentType = "application/json";
```

The rest of the application, including its UI logic and the remainder of the code-behind, is identical to Recipe 7-2.

7-4. Accessing Resources over HTTP

Problem

You need to access resources located at a remote HTTP endpoint from your Silverlight application. You may need to read from or write to remote streams or have to download/upload resources over HTTP.

Solution

Use the `WebClient` API to read from or write to remote resources, or download or upload resources.

How It Works

The `WebClient` type has a convenient collection of methods that let you access resources over HTTP. You can use the `WebClient` class in two basic modes: uploading/downloading resources as strings and reading from or writing to streams, both over HTTP.

Downloading/Uploading Resources

You can use the `DownloadStringAsync()` method to asynchronously download any resource over HTTP as the long as the resource is (or can be converted to) a string. `DownloadStringAsync()` accepts a URI to the resource and raises the `DownloadStringProgressChanged` event to report download progress. Download completion is signaled when the `DownloadStringCompleted` event is raised. The `DownloadStringCompletedEventArgs.Result` property exposes the downloaded string resource.

The `UploadStringAsync()` method similarly accepts the upload endpoint URI. It also accepts the string resource to upload and reports completion by raising the `UploadStringCompleted` event.

Both methods accept a user-supplied state object, which is made available in the progress change and the completion event handlers through the UserState property on the DownloadProgressChangedEventArgs, DownloadStringCompletedEventArgs, or UploadStringCompletedeventArgs parameter.

Reading/Writing Remote Streams

The OpenReadAsync() method accepts a remote HTTP URI and attempts to download the resource and make it available as a locally readable stream. Download progress is reported using the DownloadProgressChanged event, as we mentioned earlier. The completion of the asynchronous read is signaled by the runtime by raising the OpenReadCompleted event. In the handler for OpenReadCompleted, the OpenReadCompletedEventArgs.Result property exposes the resource stream.

The OpenWriteAsync() method behaves slightly differently. Before it tries to access the remote resource, it raises the OpenWriteCompleted event synchronously. In the handler for this event, you are expected to write to the OpenWriteCompletedEventArgs.Result stream the data you want to save to the remote resource. After this stream is written and closed, and the handler returns, the runtime attempts to asynchronously send the data to the remote endpoint.

WebClient and HTTP Endpoints

In previous recipes, we outline the use of the HttpWebRequest/HttpWebResponse APIs with POX- or JSON-enabled web services. Although the WebClient API is primarily meant for accessing remote resources, its DownloadStringAsync() and UploadStringAsync() APIs can be effectively used for similar web-service communication as well, where POX or JSON messages formatted as strings are exchanged using this API set. Additionally, WebClient can work with other HTTP endpoints such as ASP.NET web pages. The code samples use a mix of WCF services and ASP.NET pages to illustrate this.

Canceling Long-Running Operations

Depending on the size of the resource being accessed, the available network bandwidth, and similar factors, download operations can be long-running, and it is desirable to provide application users with a way to cancel an operation should they choose to do so. The WebClient type exposes a property called IsBusy, which when true indicates that the WebClient instance is currently performing a background operation. Calling CancelAsync() on a WebClient instance attempts to cancel any such running operation. Note that because the operation is on a background thread, if CancelAsync() succeeds, the completion handler is invoked on the main thread, just as it would be on a successful completion. In the andler, you can check the Cancelled property on the event argument parameter to see if the operation was canceled or if it was a normal completion.

We show the use of all these in the following sample for this recipe.

The Code

The sample used here implements a simple photo-management application. The UI for the application is shown in Figure 7-5.

Figure 7-5. *The photo-management application UI*

The application downloads a ZIP file on start and displays image thumbnails contained in the ZIP. When you select a specific thumbnail, the full-resolution image is downloaded. Additional custom metadata can be associated with the image and saved to the server. Clicking the Upload button allows the user to select and upload a locally available JPEG image file.

The back-end functionality is divided into three sets of operations related to metadata management, photo downloads, and photo uploads, and is implemented across two WCF services and a pair of ASP.NET pages.

Listing 7-15 shows the service and data contracts for the various services.

Listing 7-15. *Service and Data Contracts for the WCF Services in Contracts.cs*

```
using System;
using System.Collections.Generic;
using System.IO;
using System.Runtime.Serialization;
using System.ServiceModel;
using System.ServiceModel.Web;
```

```csharp
namespace Ch07_Networking.Recipe7_4.PhotoService
{
  [ServiceContract]
  public interface IPhotoDownload
  {
    [OperationContract]
    [WebGet()]
    //get the zip file containing the thumbnails
    Stream GetThumbs();

    [OperationContract]
    [WebGet(UriTemplate = "Photos?Name={PhotoName}")]
    //get a full resolution image
    byte[] GetPhoto(string PhotoName);
  }

  [ServiceContract]
  public interface IMetadata
  {
    [OperationContract]
    [WebGet(ResponseFormat = WebMessageFormat.Json)]
    //get the names of all the JPEG images available for download
    List<string> GetPhotoFileNames();

    [OperationContract]
    [WebGet(UriTemplate = "PhotoMetadata?Id={PhotoId}",
ResponseFormat = WebMessageFormat.Json)]
    //get the metadata for a specific image
    PhotoMetaData GetPhotoMetaData(string PhotoId);

  }

  [DataContract]
  public class PhotoMetaData
  {
    [DataMember]
    public string Id { get; set; }
    [DataMember]
    public string Name { get; set; }
    [DataMember]
    public string Description { get; set; }
    [DataMember]
    public string Location { get; set; }
```

```
    [DataMember]
    public int? Rating { get; set; }
    [DataMember]
    public DateTime? DateTaken { get; set; }
  }
}
```

The sample code for this recipe contains the full implementation of two WCF services, `Metadata.svc` and `PhotoDownload.svc`, that implement the `IMetadata` and `IPhotoDownload` contracts respectively, as shown in Listing 7-15. They handle the tasks of downloading metadata and photos. Because the implementation of the WCF services is similar in structure to the implementations described in previous recipes in this chapter, we do not discuss it here. You are encouraged to look at the sample code for this book.

Listing 7-16 shows the code-behind for `MetadataUpload.aspx`. The page markup contains nothing of relevance because the page does not render anything; it is used purely as an endpoint to which some data is posted by a `WebClient` instance.

Listing 7-16. *MetadataUpload.aspx Page Code-Behind in MetadataUpload.aspx.cs*

```csharp
using System;
using System.Collections.Generic;
using System.Linq;
using System.Runtime.Serialization.Json;

namespace Ch07_Networking.Recipe7_4.PhotoService
{
  public partial class MetadataUpload : System.Web.UI.Page
  {
    protected void Page_Load(object sender, EventArgs e)
    {
      if (Request.HttpMethod == "POST")
      {
        DataContractJsonSerializer jsonSer =
          new DataContractJsonSerializer(typeof(PhotoMetaData));
        SetPhotoMetaData(
          jsonSer.ReadObject(Request.InputStream) as PhotoMetaData);
        Response.SuppressContent = true;
      }
    }

    public void SetPhotoMetaData(PhotoMetaData MetaData)
    {
      PhotoStoreDataContext dcPhoto = new PhotoStoreDataContext();
      List<PhotoData> pds = (from pd in dcPhoto.PhotoDatas
                             where pd.PhotoId == MetaData.Id
                             select pd).ToList();
      if (pds.Count == 0)
```

645

```
      {
        dcPhoto.PhotoDatas.InsertOnSubmit(new PhotoData {
          PhotoId = MetaData.Id, Name = MetaData.Name,
          Location = MetaData.Location, DateTaken = MetaData.DateTaken,
          Description = MetaData.Description, Rating = MetaData.Rating });
      }
      else
      {
        pds[0].Name = MetaData.Name;
        pds[0].DateTaken = MetaData.DateTaken;
        pds[0].Description = MetaData.Description;
        pds[0].Location = MetaData.Location;
        pds[0].Rating = MetaData.Rating;
      }
      dcPhoto.SubmitChanges();
    }
  }
}
```

As you can see in Listing 7-16, you check for an incoming POST request in the Page_Load handler of the ASPX page and deserialize the JSON stream into a PhotoMetadata object. You then pass the PhotoMetadata instance to SetPhotoMetadata(), which uses LINQ to SQL to update the database. Before you return from the Page_Load handler, you set Response.SuppressContent to true. This makes sure there is no HTML markup response from the page, because you need none.

Listing 7-17 shows the implementation of PhotoUpload.aspx, which is structured in a similar fashion.

Listing 7-17. *PhotoUpload.aspx Code-Behind in PhotoUpload.aspx.cs*

```
using System;
using System.IO;
using System.Web;

namespace Ch07_Networking.Recipe7_4.PhotoService
{
  public partial class PhotoUpload1 : System.Web.UI.Page
  {
    protected void Page_Load(object sender, EventArgs e)
    {
      if (Request.HttpMethod == "POST")
      {
        AddPhoto(Request.InputStream);
        Response.SuppressContent = true;
      }
    }
```

```csharp
public void AddPhoto(Stream PhotoStream)
{
  //get the file name for the photo
  string PhotoName =
    HttpContext.Current.Request.Headers["Image-Name"];
  if (PhotoName == null) return;
  //open a file stream to store the photo
  FileStream fs = new FileStream(
    HttpContext.Current.Request.MapPath
    (string.Format("APP_DATA/Photos/{0}", PhotoName)),
    FileMode.Create, FileAccess.Write);
  //read and store
  BinaryReader br = new BinaryReader(PhotoStream);
  BinaryWriter bw = new BinaryWriter(fs);

  int ChunkSize = 1024 * 1024;
  byte[] Chunk = null;
  do
  {
    Chunk = br.ReadBytes(ChunkSize);
    bw.Write(Chunk);
    bw.Flush();
  } while (Chunk.Length == ChunkSize);

  br.Close();
  bw.Close();
  }
 }
}
```

Note that the images and the ZIP file containing the thumbnails are stored on the server file system, under the App_Data folder of the ASP.NET web application hosting the WCF services. The metadata for each image, however, is stored in a SQL Server database. For the samples, we use SQL Server 2008 Express version, which you can download for free from http://www.microsoft.com/express/sql/download/default.aspx. When you install the product, take care to name the server SQLEXPRESS. This is the default name that the SQL 2008 installer uses, and so does the code sample. If you change it, visit the web.config files for the web service project named "7.4 PhotoService" in the sample code for this recipe, and change the database-connection strings to reflect your chosen server name. The following snippet shows the configuration entry in web.config:

```xml
<connectionStrings>
 <add name="SLBook_recipe_7_4_dbConnectionString"
 connectionString="Data Source=.\SQLEXPRESS;Initial Catalog=Recipe_7_4_db;
Integrated Security=True" providerName="System.Data.SqlClient"/>
</connectionStrings>
```

After SQL 2008 is installed, you need to create a database named Recipe_4_7_db and run the Recipe_7_4_db.sql file included with the sample code to create the necessary data model. We also include a database backup file named Recipe_4_7_db.bak, which you can restore into your SQL 2008 instance in lieu of creating the database and running the queries yourself.

Listing 7-18 shows some of the data types used in the client application.

Listing 7-18. *Data Types Used in the Client Application in DataTypes.cs*

```
using System;
using System.ComponentModel;
using System.Runtime.Serialization;
using System.Windows;
using System.Windows.Media.Imaging;

namespace Ch07_Networking.Recipe7_4.PhotoClient
{
  public class WrappedImage : INotifyPropertyChanged
  {
    //bound to the thumbnail
    public BitmapImage Small { get; set; }
    //bound to the full res image
    public BitmapImage Large { get; set; }
    //Metadata
    private PhotoMetaData _Info = null;
    public PhotoMetaData Info
    {
      get { return _Info; }
      set
      {
        _Info = value;
        if (PropertyChanged != null)
          PropertyChanged(this, new PropertyChangedEventArgs("Info"));
      }
    }
    //Download Progress
    private double _PercentProgress;
    public double PercentProgress
    {
      get { return _PercentProgress; }
      set
      {
        _PercentProgress = value;
        if (PropertyChanged != null)
          PropertyChanged(this, new PropertyChangedEventArgs("PercentProgress"));
      }
    }
```

```
//show the progress bar
private Visibility _ProgressVisible = Visibility.Collapsed;
public Visibility ProgressVisible
{
  get { return _ProgressVisible; }
  set
  {
    _ProgressVisible = value;
    if (PropertyChanged != null)
      PropertyChanged(this, new PropertyChangedEventArgs("ProgressVisible"));
  }
}
//parts removed for brevity

//download completed - show the image
private Visibility _ImageVisible = Visibility.Collapsed;
public Visibility ImageVisible
{
  get { return _ImageVisible; }
  set
  {
    _ImageVisible = value;
    if (PropertyChanged != null)
      PropertyChanged(this, new PropertyChangedEventArgs("ImageVisible"));
  }
}
//name of the thumbnail file
private string _ThumbName;
public string ThumbName
{
  get { return _ThumbName; }
  set
  {
    _ThumbName = value;
    if (PropertyChanged != null)
      PropertyChanged(this, new PropertyChangedEventArgs("ThumbName"));
  }
}
//name of the image file
private string _FileName;
public string FileName
```

```
    {
      get { return _FileName; }
      set
      {
        _FileName = value;
        if (PropertyChanged != null)
          PropertyChanged(this, new PropertyChangedEventArgs("FileName"));
      }
    }

    public event
      PropertyChangedEventHandler PropertyChanged;

}
[DataContract]
public class PhotoMetaData : INotifyPropertyChanged
{
    //a unique Id for the image file - the file name
    private string _Id;
    [DataMember]
    public string Id
    {
      get { return _Id; }
      set
      {
        _Id = value;
        if (PropertyChanged != null)
          PropertyChanged(this, new PropertyChangedEventArgs("Id"));
      }
    }
    //a user supplied friendly name
    private string _Name;
    [DataMember]
    public string Name
    {
      get { return _Name; }
      set
      {
        _Name = value;
        if (PropertyChanged != null)
          PropertyChanged(this, new PropertyChangedEventArgs("Name"));
      }
    }
```

```
private string _Description;
[DataMember]
public string Description
{
  get { return _Description; }
  set
  {
    _Description = value;
    if (PropertyChanged != null)
      PropertyChanged(this, new PropertyChangedEventArgs("Description"));
  }
}
private string _Location;
[DataMember]
public string Location
{
  get { return _Location; }
  set
  {
    _Location = value;
    if (PropertyChanged != null)
      PropertyChanged(this, new PropertyChangedEventArgs("Location"));
  }
}
private int? _Rating;
[DataMember]
public int? Rating
{
  get { return _Rating; }
  set
  {
    _Rating = value;
    if (PropertyChanged != null)
      PropertyChanged(this, new PropertyChangedEventArgs("Rating"));
  }
}
private DateTime? _DateTaken;
[DataMember]
public DateTime? DateTaken
```

```
      {
        get { return _DateTaken; }
        set
        {
          _DateTaken = value;
          if (PropertyChanged != null)
            PropertyChanged(this, new PropertyChangedEventArgs("DateTaken"));
        }
      }

      public event PropertyChangedEventHandler PropertyChanged;

    }
}
```

The WrappedImage type, as shown in Listing 7-18, is used to wrap an image and its metadata. It implements INotifyPropertyChange to facilitate data binding to XAML elements in the UI. For more about data binding and property-change notifications, refer to Chapter 4. The WrappedImage type contains individual BitmapImage instances for the thumbnail and the high-resolution image, and a few other properties that relate to download-progress reporting and visibility of different parts of the UI.

Also shown is the PhotoMetadata data-contract type used to transfer metadata to and from the WCF services. The difference between the client implementation of PhotoMetadata shown here and the one used in the service shown in Listing 7-15 is that you add property-change notification code to each property in the client-side implementation.

Listing 7-19 shows the XAML for MainPage. The XAML for this page is fairly extensive, so we discuss only pertinent portions briefly.

Listing 7-19. *XAML for MainPage in MainPage.xaml.cs*

```
<UserControl x:Class="Ch07_Networking.Recipe7_4.PhotoClient.MainPage"
  xmlns="http://schemas.microsoft.com/winfx/2006/xaml/presentation"
  xmlns:x="http://schemas.microsoft.com/winfx/2006/xaml"
  FontFamily="Trebuchet MS" FontSize="11"
  Width="800" Height="700"
  xmlns:Controls
  ="clr-namespace:System.Windows.Controls;assembly=System.Windows.Controls"
  xmlns:vsm="clr-namespace:System.Windows;assembly=System.Windows">
  <UserControl.Resources>

    <DataTemplate x:Key="dtProgressMessage">
      <StackPanel Orientation="Horizontal">
        <TextBlock Text="Processing" Margin="0,0,5,0" Foreground="Red"/>
        <TextBlock Text="{Binding}" Margin="0,0,2,0" Foreground="Red"/>
        <TextBlock Text="%" Foreground="Red"/>
      </StackPanel>
    </DataTemplate>
```

```xml
<DataTemplate x:Key="dtThumbnail">
  <Grid>
    <Image Width="100" Height="75"
           Source="{Binding '', Mode=OneWay, Path=Small}"
           Stretch="Fill" Margin="5,5,5,5"/>
  </Grid>
</DataTemplate>

<DataTemplate x:Key="dtLargePhoto">
  <Grid VerticalAlignment="Top" HorizontalAlignment="Stretch" Height="Auto">
    <Grid.RowDefinitions>
      <RowDefinition Height="0.8*"/>
      <RowDefinition Height="0.2*"/>
    </Grid.RowDefinitions>
    <Image  HorizontalAlignment="Stretch"
            VerticalAlignment="Stretch"
            Source="{Binding '', Mode=OneWay, Path=Large}"
            Stretch="Uniform" Grid.Row="0"
            Margin="0,0,0,0"
            Visibility="{Binding Mode=OneWay, Path=ImageVisible}"/>
    <CheckBox Content="{Binding '',Mode=OneWay, Path=FileName}"
              Grid.Row="1" HorizontalAlignment="Center"
              VerticalAlignment="Center"
              Foreground="Black"
              Margin="0,0,0,0" FontSize="16" FontWeight="Bold"
              x:Name="btnMeta" Checked="btnMeta_Checked"
              Unchecked="btnMeta_Unchecked" />
    <ProgressBar
      Maximum="100" Minimum="100" Width="290" Foreground="Red" Height="30"
      Value="{Binding Mode=OneWay, Path=PercentProgress}"
      Visibility="{Binding Mode=OneWay, Path=ProgressVisible}"
      HorizontalAlignment="Center" VerticalAlignment="Center"/>
  </Grid>
</DataTemplate>

<DataTemplate x:Key="dtPhotoMetaData">
  <Grid>
    <Grid.RowDefinitions>
      <RowDefinition Height="0.15*"/>
      <RowDefinition Height="0.15*"/>
      <RowDefinition Height="0.15*"/>
      <RowDefinition Height="0.15*"/>
      <RowDefinition Height="0.15*"/>
```

```xml
        <RowDefinition Height="0.15*"/>
        <RowDefinition Height="0.10*"/>
      </Grid.RowDefinitions>
      <Grid.ColumnDefinitions>
        <ColumnDefinition Width="0.5*" />
        <ColumnDefinition Width="0.5*" />
      </Grid.ColumnDefinitions>
      <TextBlock Grid.Row="0" Grid.Column="0"
                 Grid.ColumnSpan="2" Text="Edit Metadata"
                 HorizontalAlignment="Center"
                 VerticalAlignment="Center" Margin="3,3,3,3"/>
      <TextBlock Grid.Row="1" Grid.Column="0"
                 Text="Name:" Margin="3,3,3,3" />
      <TextBlock Grid.Row="2" Grid.Column="0"
                 Text="Description:" Margin="3,3,3,3" />
      <TextBlock Grid.Row="3" Grid.Column="0"
                 Text="Location:" Margin="3,3,3,3" />
      <TextBlock Grid.Row="4" Grid.Column="0"
                 Text="Rating:" Margin="3,3,3,3" />
      <TextBlock Grid.Row="5" Grid.Column="0"
                 Text="Date Taken:" Margin="3,3,3,3" />
      <TextBox Grid.Row="1" Grid.Column="1"
               Text="{Binding Mode=TwoWay,Path=Info.Name}"
               Width="275" Margin="3,3,3,3" />
      <TextBox Grid.Row="2" Grid.Column="1"
               Text="{Binding Mode=TwoWay,Path=Info.Description}"
               Width="275" Margin="3,3,3,3" TextWrapping="Wrap"
               AcceptsReturn="True" />
      <TextBox Grid.Row="3" Grid.Column="1"
               Text="{Binding Mode=TwoWay,Path=Info.Location}"
               Width="275" Margin="3,3,3,3" TextWrapping="Wrap"
               AcceptsReturn="True" />
      <TextBox Grid.Row="4" Grid.Column="1"
               Text="{Binding Mode=TwoWay,Path=Info.Rating}"
               Width="275" Margin="3,3,3,3" />
      <Controls:DatePicker Grid.Row="5" Grid.Column="1"
                  SelectedDate="{Binding Mode=TwoWay,Path=Info.DateTaken}"
                  Width="275" Margin="3,3,3,3"/>
      <Button Content="Save Changes" x:Name="btnSaveMetaData"
              Grid.Row="6" Grid.ColumnSpan="2" HorizontalAlignment="Center"
              VerticalAlignment="Center" Height="30" Width="100"
              Margin="10,10,10,10" Click="btnSaveMetaData_Click"/>
    </Grid>
</DataTemplate>
```

```xml
<ControlTemplate x:Key="ctThumbnailListBoxItem" TargetType="ListBoxItem">
  <Grid>
    <vsm:VisualStateManager.VisualStateGroups>
      <vsm:VisualStateGroup x:Name="CommonStates">
        <vsm:VisualState x:Name="Normal">
          <Storyboard/>
        </vsm:VisualState>
        <vsm:VisualState x:Name="MouseOver">
          <Storyboard>
            <ColorAnimationUsingKeyFrames
              BeginTime="00:00:00"
              Duration="00:00:00.0010000"
              Storyboard.TargetName="brdrHover"
              Storyboard.TargetProperty=
              "(Border.BorderBrush).(SolidColorBrush.Color)">
              <SplineColorKeyFrame
                KeyTime="00:00:00" Value="#FF0748BD"/>
            </ColorAnimationUsingKeyFrames>
          </Storyboard>
        </vsm:VisualState>
      </vsm:VisualStateGroup>
      <vsm:VisualStateGroup x:Name="SelectionStates">
        <vsm:VisualState x:Name="Unselected"/>
        <vsm:VisualState x:Name="Selected">
          <Storyboard>
            <ColorAnimationUsingKeyFrames
              BeginTime="00:00:00"
              Duration="00:00:00.0010000"
              Storyboard.TargetName="brdrSelect"
              Storyboard.TargetProperty=
              "(Border.Background).(SolidColorBrush.Color)">
              <SplineColorKeyFrame
                KeyTime="00:00:00" Value="#FF0748BD"/>
            </ColorAnimationUsingKeyFrames>
          </Storyboard>
        </vsm:VisualState>
        <vsm:VisualState x:Name="SelectedUnfocused"/>
      </vsm:VisualStateGroup>
      <vsm:VisualStateGroup x:Name="FocusStates">
        <vsm:VisualState x:Name="Unfocused"/>
        <vsm:VisualState x:Name="Focused"/>
      </vsm:VisualStateGroup>
    </vsm:VisualStateManager.VisualStateGroups>
```

```xml
        <Border HorizontalAlignment="Stretch"
                VerticalAlignment="Stretch"
                x:Name="brdrHover" BorderBrush="#FF000000"
                BorderThickness="5" CornerRadius="3,3,3,3"
                Margin="3,3,3,3" >
          <Border  CornerRadius="3,3,3,3" Padding="7,7,7,7"
                  Background="Transparent">
            <Border x:Name="brdrSelect" Background="#FF9AE1F5"
                    CornerRadius="3,3,3,3" Padding="3,3,3,3"  >
              <ContentPresenter
                Content="{TemplateBinding Content}"
                ContentTemplate="{TemplateBinding ContentTemplate}"
                HorizontalAlignment="Left"
                 />
            </Border>
          </Border>
        </Border>
      </Grid>
    </ControlTemplate>
    <Style x:Key="styleThumbnailListBoxItem" TargetType="ListBoxItem">
      <Setter Property="IsEnabled" Value="true" />
      <Setter Property="Foreground" Value="#FF000000" />
      <Setter Property="HorizontalContentAlignment" Value="Left" />
      <Setter Property="VerticalContentAlignment" Value="Top" />
      <Setter Property="FontSize" Value="12" />
      <Setter Property="Background" Value="White" />
      <Setter Property="Padding" Value="2,0,0,0" />
      <Setter Property="Template" Value="{StaticResource ctThumbnailListBoxItem}"/>
    </Style>
  </UserControl.Resources>

  <Grid Background="BurlyWood">
s   <Grid.ColumnDefinitions>
      <ColumnDefinition Width="*"/>
      <ColumnDefinition Width="Auto"/>
    </Grid.ColumnDefinitions>
    <Grid.RowDefinitions>
      <RowDefinition Height="150"/>
      <RowDefinition Height="*"/>
      <RowDefinition Height="Auto"/>
    </Grid.RowDefinitions>
```

```xml
<ListBox HorizontalAlignment="Stretch"
         Margin="5,5,5,5"
         Width="Auto"
         SelectionChanged="lbxThumbs_SelectionChanged"
         ItemTemplate="{StaticResource dtThumbnail}"
         x:Name="lbxThumbs"
         ItemContainerStyle="{StaticResource styleThumbnailListBoxItem}"
         Grid.ColumnSpan="2" Visibility="Collapsed">
  <ListBox.ItemsPanel>
    <ItemsPanelTemplate>
      <StackPanel Orientation="Horizontal"/>
    </ItemsPanelTemplate>
  </ListBox.ItemsPanel>
</ListBox>
<StackPanel x:Name="visualThumbZipDownload" Margin="0,20,0,0">
  <ProgressBar
    Maximum="100" Minimum="0" Height="30" Foreground="Red"
    Width="290" x:Name="pbarThumbZipDownload"
    Visibility="Visible" HorizontalAlignment="Center"
    VerticalAlignment="Center"/>
  <Button x:Name="btnZipDownloadCancel"
          Content="Cancel"
          Click="btnZipDownloadCancel_Click"
          HorizontalAlignment="Center" Width="125" />
</StackPanel>

<ContentControl x:Name="contentctlLargeImage"
                HorizontalAlignment="Stretch"
                VerticalAlignment="Stretch"
                Grid.Row="1" Margin="8,8,8,8"
                ContentTemplate="{StaticResource dtLargePhoto}"
                Grid.RowSpan="1"/>
<ContentControl x:Name="contentctlImageInfo"
                HorizontalAlignment="Stretch"
                VerticalAlignment="Stretch"
                Grid.Row="1" Grid.Column="1"
                Margin="8,0,8,0"
                ContentTemplate="{StaticResource dtPhotoMetaData}"
                Grid.RowSpan="1" Visibility="Collapsed"/>
<Grid HorizontalAlignment="Stretch" Margin="8,8,8,8"
      VerticalAlignment="Stretch" Grid.Row="2">
  <Grid.ColumnDefinitions>
    <ColumnDefinition Width="0.5*"/>
    <ColumnDefinition Width="0.5*"/>
  </Grid.ColumnDefinitions>
```

```
        <Button HorizontalAlignment="Right"
                VerticalAlignment="Stretch" Content="Previous"
                Margin="8,0,8,0"   Height="32.11" x:Name="btnPrevious"
                Width="99.936"
                Click="btnPrev_Click"/>
        <Button Margin="8,0,8,0" VerticalAlignment="Stretch"
                Content="Next" HorizontalAlignment="Left"
                Height="31.11" x:Name="btnNext"
                Grid.Column="1" Width="99.936"
                Click="btnNext_Click"/>
        <Button HorizontalAlignment="Left" Margin="0,0,0,0"
                Width="100" Content="Upload" x:Name="btnUpload"
                Click="btnUpload_Click"/>
      </Grid>
    </Grid>
</UserControl>
```

The main UI is made up of a ListBox named lbxThumbs and two ContentControls named contentctlLargeImage and contentctlImageInfo. A ProgressBar control is also used on MainPage, as well as Buttons for image navigation (btnPrevious and btnNext), a Button to cancel the thumbnail ZIP download (btnZipDownloadCancel), and a Button to upload a local image to the server (btnUpload).

You apply a custom Panel to the ListBox lbxThumbs to change its orientation to display the thumbnail items horizontally from left to right. You also apply a custom control template to each ListBoxItem, using the ItemContainerStyle property of the ListBox, to change the default look and feel of a ListBoxItem. Custom Panels and ControlTemplates are discussed in more detail in Chapter 5.

The dtLargePhoto data template is used to display a selected image and is made up of an Image control, a CheckBox control that can be used to toggle the visibility of the image's metadata, and a ProgressBar that displays the download progress of an image. The Image is bound to the Large property on the WrappedImage type. dtLargePhoto is applied to the ContentControl contentctlLargeImage in the main UI, using its ContentTemplate property.

The dtPhotoMetaData data template creates a data-entry form for image metadata. It has edit controls data-bound to properties in the PhotoMetadata data contract and is applied to the ContentControl contentctlImageInfo in the main UI again, with initial Visibility of the ContentControl set to Collapsed.

The dtThumbnail data template is applied to the ListBox lbxThumbnails through its ItemTemplate property. dtThumbnail also contains an Image control, bound to WrappedImage.Small.

Now, let's look at how the WebClient is used in this MainPage's code-behind to access resources and interact with web services. Listing 7-20 shows the code-behind for MainPage.

Listing 7-20. *Code-Behind for the PhotoClient Application Page in MainPage.xaml.cs*

```
using System;
using System.Collections.Generic;
using System.Collections.ObjectModel;
using System.IO;
using System.Net;
using System.Runtime.Serialization.Json;
using System.Text;
using System.Windows;
```

```csharp
using System.Windows.Controls;
using System.Windows.Media.Imaging;
using System.Windows.Resources;
using System.Xml.Linq;

namespace Ch07_Networking.Recipe7_4.PhotoClient
{
  public partial class Page : UserControl
  {

    private const string MetadataDownloadUri =
      "http://localhost:9494/MetaData.svc";
    private const string MetadataUploadUri =
      "http://localhost:9494/MetaDataUpload.aspx";
    private const string PhotoDownloadUri =
      "http://localhost:9494/PhotoDownload.svc";
    private const string PhotoUploadUri =
      "http://localhost:9494/PhotoUpload.aspx";

    ObservableCollection<WrappedImage> ImageSources =
      new ObservableCollection<WrappedImage>();
    WebClient wcThumbZip = new WebClient();
    public Page()
    {
      InitializeComponent();
      lbxThumbs.ItemsSource = ImageSources;
      contentctlLargeImage.Content = new WrappedImage();
      GetImageNames();
    }

    private void GetImageNames()
    {
      //create a WebClient
      WebClient wcImageNames = new WebClient();
      //attach a handler to the OpenReadCompleted event
      wcImageNames.OpenReadCompleted +=
        new OpenReadCompletedEventHandler(
          delegate(object sender, OpenReadCompletedEventArgs e)
          {
            //initialize a JSON Serializer
            DataContractJsonSerializer jsonSer =
              new DataContractJsonSerializer(typeof(List<string>));
```

```
            //deserialize the returned Stream to a List<string>
            List<string> FileNames =
              jsonSer.ReadObject(e.Result) as List<string>;
            //start loading the thumbnails
            LoadThumbNails(FileNames);
         });
      //Start reading the remote resource as a stream
      wcImageNames.OpenReadAsync(
        new Uri(string.Format("{0}/GetPhotoFileNames", MetadataDownloadUri)));


}

private void LoadThumbNails(List<string> ImageFileNames)
{
   wcThumbZip.OpenReadCompleted +=
     new OpenReadCompletedEventHandler(wcThumbZip_OpenReadCompleted);
   wcThumbZip.DownloadProgressChanged +=
     new DownloadProgressChangedEventHandler
       (
         delegate(object Sender, DownloadProgressChangedEventArgs e)
         {
           //set the progress bar value to the reported progress percentage
           pbarThumbZipDownload.Value = e.ProgressPercentage;
         }
       );
   //start reading the thumbnails zip file as a stream,
   //pass in the ImageFileNames List<string> as user state
   wcThumbZip.OpenReadAsync(
     new Uri(
       string.Format("{0}/GetThumbs", PhotoDownloadUri)), ImageFileNames);
}

void wcThumbZip_OpenReadCompleted(object sender,
   OpenReadCompletedEventArgs e)
{
   //if operation was cancelled, return.
   if (e.Cancelled) return;
   //grab the passed in user state from
   //e.UserState, and cast it appropriately
   List<string> FileNames = e.UserState as List<string>;
   //create a StreamResourceInfo wrapping the returned stream,
   //with content type set to .PNG
   StreamResourceInfo resInfo = new StreamResourceInfo(e.Result, "image/png");
   //for each file name
   for (int i = 0; i < FileNames.Count; i++)
```

```
    {
      //create and initialize a WrappedImage instance
      WrappedImage wi =
        new WrappedImage
        {
          Small = new BitmapImage(),
          Large = null,
          FileName = FileNames[i] + ".jpg",
          ThumbName = FileNames[i] + ".png"
        };
      try
      {
        //Read the thumbnail image from the returned stream (the zip file)
        Stream ThumbStream = Application.GetResourceStream(
          resInfo, new Uri(wi.ThumbName, UriKind.Relative)).Stream;
        //and save it in the WrappedImage instance
        wi.Small.SetSource(ThumbStream);
        //and bind it to the thumbnail listbox
        ImageSources.Add(wi);
      }
      catch
      {
      }
    }
    //hide the progress bar and show the ListBox
    visualThumbZipDownload.Visibility = Visibility.Collapsed;
    lbxThumbs.Visibility = Visibility.Visible;
}
private void btnZipDownloadCancel_Click(object sender, RoutedEventArgs e)
{
    //if downloading thumbnail zip , issue an async request to cancel
    if (wcThumbZip != null && wcThumbZip.IsBusy)
      wcThumbZip.CancelAsync();
}


//thumbnail selection changed
private void lbxThumbs_SelectionChanged(object sender,
    SelectionChangedEventArgs e)
{
    //get the WrappedImage bound to the selected item
    WrappedImage wi = (e.AddedItems[0] as WrappedImage);
    //bind it to the large image display, as well to the metadata display
    contentctlLargeImage.Content = wi;
    contentctlImageInfo.Content = wi;
```

```csharp
      //if the large image has not been downloaded
      if (wi.Large == null)
      {
        //display the progress bar and hid the large image control
        wi.ProgressVisible = Visibility.Visible;
        wi.ImageVisible = Visibility.Collapsed;
        //initialize the BitmapImage for the large image
        wi.Large = new BitmapImage();
        //new web client
        WebClient wcLargePhoto = new WebClient();
        //progress change handler
        wcLargePhoto.DownloadProgressChanged +=
          new DownloadProgressChangedEventHandler(
            delegate(object Sender, DownloadProgressChangedEventArgs e1)
            {
              //update value bound to progress bar
              wi.PercentProgress = e1.ProgressPercentage;
            });
        //completion handler
        wcLargePhoto.DownloadStringCompleted +=
          new DownloadStringCompletedEventHandler(
            wcLargePhoto_DownloadStringCompleted);
        //download image bytes as a string, pass
        //in WrappedImage instance as user supplied state
        wcLargePhoto.DownloadStringAsync(
          new Uri(string.Format("{0}/Photos?Name={1}",
            PhotoDownloadUri, wi.FileName)), wi);
      }
    }
    //large image download completed
    void wcLargePhoto_DownloadStringCompleted(object sender,
      DownloadStringCompletedEventArgs e)
    {
      //get the WrappedImage instance from user supplied state
      WrappedImage wi = (e.UserState as WrappedImage);
      //parse XML formatted response string into an XDocument
      XDocument xDoc = XDocument.Parse(e.Result);
      //grab the root, and decode the default base64
      //representation into the image bytes
      byte[] Buff = Convert.FromBase64String((string)xDoc.Root);
      //wrap in a memory stream, and
      MemoryStream ms = new MemoryStream(Buff);
      wi.Large.SetSource(ms);
      wi.ProgressVisible = Visibility.Collapsed;
```

```
    wi.ImageVisible = Visibility.Visible;
    GetPhotoMetadata(wi);
}

private void btnPrev_Click(object sender, RoutedEventArgs e)
{
    if (lbxThumbs.SelectedIndex == 0) return;
    lbxThumbs.SelectedIndex = lbxThumbs.SelectedIndex - 1;
}

private void btnNext_Click(object sender, RoutedEventArgs e)
{
    if (lbxThumbs.SelectedIndex == lbxThumbs.Items.Count - 1) return;
    lbxThumbs.SelectedIndex = lbxThumbs.SelectedIndex + 1;
}

private void btnMeta_Checked(object sender, RoutedEventArgs e)
{
    contentctlImageInfo.Visibility = Visibility.Visible;
}

private void btnMeta_Unchecked(object sender, RoutedEventArgs e)
{
    contentctlImageInfo.Visibility = Visibility.Collapsed;
}

private void GetPhotoMetadata(WrappedImage wi)
{

    WebClient wcMetadataDownload = new WebClient();
    wcMetadataDownload.DownloadStringCompleted +=
      new DownloadStringCompletedEventHandler(
        delegate(object sender, DownloadStringCompletedEventArgs e)
        {
          DataContractJsonSerializer JsonSer =
            new DataContractJsonSerializer(typeof(PhotoMetaData));
          //decode UTF8 string to byte[], wrap in a memory string and
          //deserialize to PhotoMetadata using DatacontractJsonSerializer
          PhotoMetaData pmd = JsonSer.ReadObject(
            new MemoryStream(new UTF8Encoding().GetBytes(e.Result)))
            as PhotoMetaData;
          //data bind
          (e.UserState as WrappedImage).Info = pmd;
        });
```

```csharp
  wcMetadataDownload.DownloadStringAsync(
    new Uri(string.Format("{0}/PhotoMetadata?Id={1}",
      MetadataDownloadUri,
      wi.FileName)), wi);
}

private void btnSaveMetaData_Click(object sender, RoutedEventArgs e)
{
  SetPhotoMetadata(contentctlImageInfo.Content as WrappedImage);
}
//upload metadata
private void SetPhotoMetadata(WrappedImage wi)
{
  //new WebClient
  WebClient wcMetadataUpload = new WebClient();
  //serialize the metadata as JSON
  DataContractJsonSerializer JsonSer =
    new DataContractJsonSerializer(typeof(PhotoMetaData));
  MemoryStream ms = new MemoryStream();
  JsonSer.WriteObject(ms, wi.Info);
  //convert serialized form to a string
  string SerOutput = new UTF8Encoding().
    GetString(ms.GetBuffer(), 0, (int)ms.Length);
  ms.Close();
  //upload string
  wcMetadataUpload.UploadStringAsync(
    new Uri(MetadataUploadUri), "POST",
   SerOutput);
}


//upload local image file
private void btnUpload_Click(object sender, RoutedEventArgs e)
{
  //open a file dialog and allow the user to select local image files
  OpenFileDialog ofd = new OpenFileDialog();
  ofd.Filter = "JPEG Images|*.jpg;*.jpeg";
  ofd.Multiselect = true;
  if (ofd.ShowDialog() == false) return;
  //for each selected file
  foreach (FileInfo fdfi in ofd.Files)
```

```
    {
      //new web client
      WebClient wcPhotoUpload = new WebClient();
      //content type
      //wcPhotoUpload.Headers["Content-Type"] = "image/jpeg";
      //name of the file as a custom property in header
      wcPhotoUpload.Headers["Image-Name"] = fdfi.Name;
      wcPhotoUpload.OpenWriteCompleted +=
        new OpenWriteCompletedEventHandler(wcPhotoUpload_OpenWriteCompleted);
      //upload image file - pass in the image file stream as user supplied state
      wcPhotoUpload.OpenWriteAsync(new Uri(PhotoUploadUri),
        "POST", fdfi.OpenRead());
    }
  }

  void wcPhotoUpload_OpenWriteCompleted(object sender,
OpenWriteCompletedEventArgs e)
  {
    //get the image file stream from the user supplied state
    Stream imageStream = e.UserState as Stream;
    //write the image file out to the upload stream available in e.Result
    int ChunkSize = 1024 * 1024;
    int ReadCount = 0;
    byte[] Buff = new byte[ChunkSize];
    do
    {
      ReadCount = imageStream.Read(Buff, 0, ChunkSize);
      e.Result.Write(Buff, 0, ReadCount);
    } while (ReadCount == ChunkSize);
    //close upload stream and return - framework will upload in the background
    e.Result.Close();
  }
 }
}
```

The GetImageNames() method uses WebClient.OpenReadAsync() to acquire a list of names for all the image files available to you for download. In the operation contract for IMetaData. GetPhotoFileNames() in Listing 7-15, notice that the response format is specified as JSON. In the WebClient.OpenReadCompleted event handler (implemented using the C# anonymous delegate feature), you use the DataContractJsonSerializer to deserialize content from the returned stream into a List<string> of the file names. You then call the LoadThumbnails() method, passing in the list of file names.

The LoadThumbnails() method uses the WebClient.OpenReadAsync() method again to start downloading the thumbnail ZIP file. In the WebClient.DownloadProgressChanged event handler, the ProgressBar control pbarThumbZipDownload is updated with the percentage of progress. In case of a long download, a Cancel button is provided. You handle the cancellation in btnZipDownloadCancel_Click(), where you check to see if the WebClient is currently downloading using the IsBusy property, and if so issue a cancellation request. The UI for thumbnail ZIP download and cancellation is shown in Figure 7-6.

Figure 7-6. *Thumbnail ZIP download*

The OpenReadCompleted handler wcThumbZip_OpenReadCompleted() first checks to see if the operation was canceled. If not, the file name list is retrieved from the user state, and each thumbnail is retrieved from the ZIP file using the Application.GetResourceStream() method. This method can read individual streams compressed inside a ZIP, as long as the correct content type (in this case, image/png) is provided using the StreamResourceInfo type parameter. The returned stream from GetResourceStream() is the thumbnail file, which is data-bound to the UI via a new instance of a WrappedImage. You create the WrappedImage, initialize its Small property to the thumbnail image, set its FileName and ThumbName properties, and then add it to the ImageSources collection. The ImageSources collection was already bound to lbxThumbs as its ItemsSource in the constructor of the page.

Now, let's look at downloading the full image and its metadata. In the SelectionChanged handler lbxThumbs_SelectionChanged() for the thumbnails ListBox, you acquire the WrappedImage instance bound to the current thumbnail and bind it to the ContentControl contentctlLargeImage as well. You then determine whether the image corresponding to that thumbnail has been downloaded already by checking the WrappedImage.Large property for null. If it is null, you use the DownloadStringAsync() method to download the image. The operation contract of the IPhotoDownload.GetPhoto() in Listing 7-15 shows you that the image is being returned from the service as an array of bytes, but the default WCF DataContractSerializer knows how to serialize the byte[] to a Base64-encoded string. The message returned from GetPhoto() in the completion handler wcLargePhoto_DownloadStringCompleted() is an XML fragment, containing only one element: the Base64-encoded string representing the image. You access the result as an XDocument instance, parsing it using the XDocument.Parse() method. You then decode the root of this XDocument instance back to an array of bytes. You wrap it into a temporary memory stream, set it as the source for the BitmapImage bound to the large image control, and proceed to fetch the metadata.

The PhotoMetadata is returned from the service formatted as JSON. The GetPhotoMetadata() method also uses DownloadStringAsync() to acquire the metadata, decodes the downloaded string from its UTF8 string form to the constituent byte array, deserializes the byte array using the DataContractJsonSerializer, and then binds the resulting PhotoMetadata instance to the metadata UI through the WrappedImage.Info property.

In the SetPhotoMetadata() method, the PhotoMetadata instance is serialized to JSON and then encoded to a UTF8 string, which is then uploaded using the UploadStringAsync() method. Note that the upload uses the MetadataUpload.aspx page as the endpoint. This code sample does not handle the upload-completion event, but you can do so to check for any upload errors.

The last piece of this solution is the image-upload logic. In the click handler btnUpload_Click() for the Upload button, you use the OpenFileDialog to allow the user to select one or more local image files. You can learn more about the OpenFileDialog class in Chapter 2. Each image file is then uploaded using OpenWriteAsync(). Note that the "Content-Type" HTTP header is set to the image/jpeg MIME type to ensure proper encoding. Also note the use of the custom header property Image-Name to upload the name of the image file. As shown in Listing 7-17, this is extracted and used in the code-behind of the PhotoUpload.aspx page to name the image file on the server, after it has been uploaded.

As we mentioned earlier, OpenWriteAsync() immediately calls the completion handler wcPhotoUpload_OpenWriteCompleted(), where you write the image file to the upload stream made available through the OpenWriteCompletedEventArgs.Result property. When the stream is closed and the handler returns, the framework uploads the file asynchronously.

■**Note** You may have noticed the absence of any upload-progress notification handlers. Silverlight does not supply any upload=progress notifications, although future versions may.

7-5. Using Sockets to Communicate over TCP

Problem

You need a Silverlight application to communicate with server side applications using TCP sockets.

Solution

Use the `System.Net.Sockets.Socket` type and related types to connect and exchange data with a server-side TCP socket.

How It Works

Silverlight supports socket communication through the `System.Net.Sockets.Socket` type. This class exposes an API to connect to a TCP endpoint at a specified IP address/port combination, send data to that endpoint, and receive data from that endpoint.

However, the Socket type in Silverlight is slightly different from the equivalent type in the desktop and server versions of the .NET Framework; it supports only the client behavior and has no server abilities. In other words, unlike the desktop or the server version, the Silverlight version does not expose the ability to go into a listen mode and accept incoming connections. Therefore, although Silverlight applications can easily use TCP sockets to exchange data with server applications, a Silverlight application cannot act as a socket-based server.

The Sockets API in Silverlight

All socket functionality in Silverlight works asynchronously, thus avoiding any blocking calls that would prevent the main thread from blocking execution while waiting for any such call completion. This is in line with other networking and web services APIs that you have studied in earlier recipes in this chapter. However, the design pattern for the Socket's asynchronous APIs is somewhat different from the previously discussed Begin-End pattern, as you see in a moment.

The life of a socket connection begins by creating a new instance of a Socket and calling the `ConnectAsync()` method on the socket instance. The call to `ConnectAsync()` is nonblocking and returns immediately. To be notified on completion of the connection process, you can attach a handler to the `Completed` event of the `SocketAsyncEventArgs` parameter, which then is called back by the runtime. The following code excerpt shows a sample of this:

```
//create a new socket
Socket ClientSocket = new Socket(AddressFamily.InterNetwork,
                        SocketType.Stream,
                        ProtocolType.Tcp);
```

```
//create a new SocketEventArgs
SocketAsyncEventArgs sockEvtArgs = new SocketAsyncEventArgs {
  RemoteEndPoint = new IPEndPoint(IPAddress.Parse("192.168.0.10"), 4502),
  UserToken = MyData };
//connect a completion handler
sockEvtArgs.Completed += new EventHandler<SocketAsyncEventArgs>(
    delegate(object sender, SocketAsyncEventArgs e)
    {
      if (e.SocketError == SocketError.Success)
      {

        //connection succeeded - do something
      }
    });
//connect asynchronously
ClientSocket.ConnectAsync(sockEvtArgs);
```

As you can see, the Socket construction parameters let you specify the following:

- The type of addressing scheme used between IPv4 or IPv6 (which also enables IPv4) using the AddressFamily enumeration. To specify an IPv4 addressing scheme, use AddressFamily.InterNetwork; for IPv6, use AddressFamily.InterNetworkV6.

- The SocketType (the only available value is Stream).

- The ProtocolType (the only supported protocol is TCP).

Alternatively, you can set all the enumeration values to unspecified, and the values are inferred at runtime.

The endpoint being connected to is specified as the RemoteEndPoint property of the SocketEventArgs parameter. You can set it to an instance of IPEndPoint if you know the exact IP address or that of a DnsEndPoint if you have a hostname and want the DNS system to translate it to an IP address for you. Additionally, you need to supply the port. You can also supply any user state in the UserToken parameter.

When the connection is made, the Completed event handler is called, and further information is made available to you through the SocketAsyncEventArgs instance passed into the handler. The SocketError property gives you a success status or the type of error that was encountered, and the UserToken parameter can be used to extract any supplied user state.

There is a static version of ConnectAsync(), which behaves similarly. Because you do not explicitly create a Socket instance to use the static version, a connected Socket instance is made available to you through the ConnectSocket property on the SocketEventArgs instance in the Completed handler.

After you are connected, you can begin sending and receiving data. To send data, you can use the SendAsync() method. The data to be sent must be represented as a byte[] and can be copied to the SocketAsynceventArgs.Buffer using the SetBuffer() method, as shown here:

```
SocketAsyncEventArgs sockEvtArgsSend = new SocketAsyncEventArgs();
sockEvtArgsSend.SetBuffer(MyData, 0, MyData.Length);
sockEvtArgsSend.Completed +=
  new EventHandler<SocketAsyncEventArgs>(SendRequest_Completed);
ClientSocket.SendAsync(sockEvtArgsSend);
```

Receiving data uses a similar implementation. To receive data, you allocate a byte[ ] and assign it using the SocketAsyncEventargs.SetBuffer() method as the receiving buffer, followed by a call to ReceiveAsync(). Note that the Silverlight socket implementation gives you no indication when you are about to receive data from a remote endpoint; nor can you poll the socket from time to time. Consequently, when the call to ReceiveAsync() returns in the Completed handler, you may want to execute the code to receive again, thus keeping your client socket in a continuous receive mode. The following code snippet shows such an arrangement:

```
private void ReceiveMessage()
{
  //allocate memory
  byte[] ReceiveBuffer = new Byte[1024];
  SocketAsyncEventArgs sockEvtArgsReceive = new SocketAsyncEventArgs();
  //set the receive buffer
  sockEvtArgsReceive.SetBuffer(ReceiveBuffer, 0, 1024);
  sockEvtArgsReceive.Completed +=
    new EventHandler<SocketAsyncEventArgs>(Receive_Completed);
  //receive
  ClientSocket.ReceiveAsync(sockEvtArgsReceive);
}
void Receive_Completed(object sender, SocketAsyncEventArgs e)
{
  if (e.SocketError == SocketError.Success)
  {
    //switch context
    ParentPage.Dispatcher.BeginInvoke(new Action(delegate
    {
      //access the received data
      byte[] Message = new byte[e.BytesTransferred];
      Array.Copy(e.Buffer, 0, Message, 0, e.BytesTransferred);
      //do something to process the received message

      //keep receiving
      ReceiveMessage();
    }));
  }
}
```

■**Note** The Completed handlers are called on a background thread, necessitating a context switch using Dispatcher, before you can invoke code running on the main UI thread. For more about Dispatcher, refer to Recipe 7-2 in this chapter or to Chapter 2.

Cross-Domain Policy and Port Requirements

Silverlight applications using sockets have to satisfy cross-domain policy requirements to access remote socket servers. Cross-domain policies for both HTTP and TCP communications are discussed in greater detail in Recipe 7-6. There is also a restriction on the range of ports that a Silverlight client can connect to—the port must be within the inclusive range of 4502 to 4534.

The Code

The code sample for this recipe builds a simple one-to-one chat application that consists of a server program that acts as the listener and the gateway for exchanging text-based messages between Silverlight clients.

Running the Sample Code

To start the whole environment, you must first start up the sockets server and the policy server. Both of these are console programs and can be started either from the command line or from inside Visual Studio if you intend to start them in debug mode. The sockets server, which is named ChatBroker.exe, accepts one parameter on the command line: the port number you want it to listen on. Ensure that this is within the allowed port range of 4502 to 4534, inclusive. If you are debugging this from within Visual Studio, you can specify the parameter in your project's Debug properties page. The policy server is called PolicyServer.exe and does not need any startup parameters.

When you have the server instances up and running, you can then start (either in debug mode or by browsing to the page) the client. Figure 7-7 shows the various states of the Silverlight client.

Figure 7-7. *Various states of the Silverlight chat client*

You can specify the IP address and the port at which the sockets server is listening, as well as a name that you want to use in the conversation. After the user logs in, the client displays a list of all other participants currently connected to the server. You can click a participant and start a conversation. To simulate multiple participants, open multiple instances of the client and log in with multiple names.

The Client

The Silverlight client communicates with the server program using TCP sockets. The messages exchanged by the Silverlight client and the server program are expressed as data contracts, and you use JSON as the serialization format. You further convert the JSON-formatted messages to byte arrays before you can use them with sockets.

The applicable data contracts are shown in Listing 7-21.

Listing 7-21. *Data Contracts to Represent Various Messages in MessageTypes.cs*

```csharp
using System.Collections.Generic;
using System.IO;
using System.Runtime.Serialization;
using System.Runtime.Serialization.Json;

[DataContract]
[KnownType(typeof(ConnectionDisconnectionRequest))]
[KnownType(typeof(ConnectionReply))]
[KnownType(typeof(ConnectionDisconnectionNotification))]
[KnownType(typeof(TextMessage))]
[KnownType(typeof(ChatEndNotification))]
// a wrapper message that contains the actual message,
// facilitating easy serialization and deserialization
public class MessageWrapper
{
  [DataMember]
  public object Message { get; set; }

  //Deserialize a byte[] into a MessageWrapper
  public static MessageWrapper DeserializeMessage(byte[] Message)
  {
    MemoryStream ms = new MemoryStream(Message);
    DataContractJsonSerializer dcSer =
      new DataContractJsonSerializer(typeof(MessageWrapper));
    MessageWrapper mw = dcSer.ReadObject(ms) as MessageWrapper;
    return mw;
  }
  //serialize a MessageWrapper into a MemoryStream
  public static MemoryStream SerializeMessage(MessageWrapper Message)
```

```csharp
    {
      MemoryStream ms = new MemoryStream();
      DataContractJsonSerializer dcSer =
        new DataContractJsonSerializer(typeof(MessageWrapper));
      dcSer.WriteObject(ms, Message);
      return ms;
    }
}

//a request from a client to the server for either a connection or a disconnection
[DataContract]
public class ConnectionDisconnectionRequest
{
  [DataMember]
  public string From { get; set; }
  [DataMember]
  public bool Connect { get; set; }

}
//a reply from the server on successful connection
[DataContract]
public class ConnectionReply
{
  [DataMember]
  public List<string> Participants;
}
//a broadcast style notification to all connected clients about a
//specific client's connection/disconnection activity
[DataContract]
public class ConnectionDisconnectionNotification
{
  [DataMember]
  public string Participant { get; set; }
  [DataMember]
  public bool Connect { get; set; }
}
//a notification from a client to the server that it has ended a chat
[DataContract]
public class ChatEndNotification
{
  [DataMember]
  public string From { get; set; }
  [DataMember]
  public string To { get; set; }
}
```

```
//a chat message
[DataContract]
public class TextMessage
{
  [DataMember]
  public string From { get; set; }
  [DataMember]
  public string To { get; set; }
  [DataMember]
  public string Body { get; set; }
}
```

You use `DataContractJsonSerializer` to serialize and deserialize the message types shown in Listing 7-21. For more details about JSON serialization and `DataContractJsonSerializer`, refer to Recipe 7-3.

Because you have to deserialize from a `byte[]` to a CLR type on receiving a message, you face the challenge of not knowing the actual type information to pass on to `DataContractJsonSerializer`. To resolve this problem, you introduce a wrapper type named `MessageWrapper`, as shown in Listing 7-19, with a `Body` property of type `object` that contains the instance of the specific message you want to send. All messages are wrapped in this type before they are serialized to be sent out through the socket.

The `KnownTypeAttributes` applied to `MessageWrapper` ensures that the serializer uses the correct CLR type for the contained message while serializing the `MessageWrapper` instance to JSON, even though the `Body` property is of type `object`. It also allows you to specify `typeof(MessageWrapper)` as the parameter to the `DataContractJsonSerializer` instance for deserialization, ensuring that the correct type is used to deserialize the contained message. You define two static methods, `DeserializeMessage()` and `SerializeMessage()`, on the `MessageWrapper` type that encapsulates this logic.

Before you move into the sockets code, let's quickly look at the XAML UI. Listing 7-22 lists the XAML for `MainPage`.

Listing 7-22. *XAML for the Chat Client Page in MainPage.xaml*

```xml
<UserControl x:Class="Ch07_Networking.Recipe7_5.ChatClient.MainPage"
    xmlns="http://schemas.microsoft.com/winfx/2006/xaml/presentation"
    xmlns:x="http://schemas.microsoft.com/winfx/2006/xaml"
    Width="308" Height="550"
    xmlns:d="http://schemas.microsoft.com/expression/blend/2008"
    xmlns:mc="http://schemas.openxmlformats.org/markup-compatibility/2006"
    mc:Ignorable="d"
    xmlns:vsm="clr-namespace:System.Windows;assembly=System.Windows">
  <UserControl.Resources>
    <ControlTemplate x:Key="ctTalkButton" TargetType="Button">
      <Grid>
        <Image Source="SpeechMicHS.png"/>
      </Grid>
    </ControlTemplate>
```

```xml
<DataTemplate x:Key="dtConversation">
  <Grid Width="Auto" Height="Auto">
    <Grid.RowDefinitions>
      <RowDefinition Height="0.191*"/>
      <RowDefinition Height="0.809*"/>
    </Grid.RowDefinitions>
    <TextBlock Text="{Binding From}"
               TextWrapping="Wrap"
               HorizontalAlignment="Left"
               VerticalAlignment="Top"
               Foreground="#FF1C2E7C"/>
    <TextBlock Text="{Binding Body}"
               TextWrapping="Wrap"
               HorizontalAlignment="Stretch"
               VerticalAlignment="Top"
               d:LayoutOverrides="VerticalAlignment"
               Grid.Row="1"
               Margin="8,8,8,8"
               FontSize="12"
               FontFamily="Georgia"
               FontWeight="Normal"/>
  </Grid>
</DataTemplate>
<ControlTemplate x:Key="ct_lbxConversationItem" TargetType="ListBoxItem">
  <Grid Background="{TemplateBinding Background}">
    <Grid.RowDefinitions>
      <RowDefinition Height="*"/>
      <RowDefinition Height="Auto"/>
    </Grid.RowDefinitions>
    <ContentPresenter
      HorizontalContentAlignment="{TemplateBinding HorizontalContentAlignment}"
      Padding="{TemplateBinding Padding}"
      VerticalContentAlignment="{TemplateBinding VerticalContentAlignment}"
      HorizontalAlignment="Stretch" Content="{TemplateBinding Content}"
      ContentTemplate="{TemplateBinding ContentTemplate}"
      TextAlignment="{TemplateBinding TextAlignment}"
      TextDecorations="{TemplateBinding TextDecorations}"
      TextWrapping="Wrap"/>
  </Grid>
</ControlTemplate>
<Style x:Key="style_lbxitemConversation" TargetType="ListBoxItem">
  <Setter Property="IsEnabled" Value="true"/>
  <Setter Property="Foreground" Value="#FF000000"/>
  <Setter Property="HorizontalContentAlignment" Value="Left"/>
  <Setter Property="VerticalContentAlignment" Value="Top"/>
```

```xml
        <Setter Property="Cursor" Value="Arrow"/>
        <Setter Property="TextAlignment" Value="Left"/>
        <Setter Property="TextWrapping" Value="Wrap"/>
        <Setter Property="FontSize" Value="12"/>
        <Setter Property="Background" Value="White"/>
        <Setter Property="Padding" Value="2,0,0,0"/>
        <Setter Property="Template"
                Value="{StaticResource ct_lbxConversationItem}"/>
    </Style>

</UserControl.Resources>
<Grid x:Name="LayoutRoot" Background="White">
    <Grid.RowDefinitions>
        <RowDefinition Height="Auto"/>
        <RowDefinition Height="Auto"/>
        <RowDefinition Height="Auto"/>
    </Grid.RowDefinitions>
    <Border Padding="4,4,4,4" BorderBrush="Black"
            Background="LightBlue" BorderThickness="4"
            Grid.RowSpan="3"/>
    <Grid Visibility="Visible" x:Name="viewLogin" Width="300" Height="550">
        <Grid.RowDefinitions>
            <RowDefinition Height="0.364*"/>
            <RowDefinition Height="0.086*"/>
            <RowDefinition Height="0.1*"/>
            <RowDefinition Height="0.1*"/>
            <RowDefinition Height="0.35*"/>
        </Grid.RowDefinitions>
        <Grid.ColumnDefinitions>
            <ColumnDefinition Width="0.3*"/>
            <ColumnDefinition Width="0.43*"/>
            <ColumnDefinition Width="0.27*"/>
        </Grid.ColumnDefinitions>
        <TextBlock Text="IP" Grid.Row="0" Grid.Column="1" VerticalAlignment="Bottom"
                   HorizontalAlignment="Center" Margin="0,0,0,3" FontFamily="Arial"
                   FontSize="12" />
        <TextBlock Text="Port" Grid.Row="0" Grid.Column="2"
                   VerticalAlignment="Bottom"
                   HorizontalAlignment="Center" Margin="0,0,0,3"
                   FontFamily="Arial" FontSize="12" />
        <TextBlock Text="Server :" Grid.Row="1" Grid.Column="0"
                   VerticalAlignment="Center" HorizontalAlignment="Left"
                   Margin="0,0,0,0" Width="82" FontSize="12"
                   FontFamily="Arial" TextAlignment="Right" />
```

```xml
            <TextBlock Text="Your Name :" Grid.Row="2" Grid.Column="0"
                    VerticalAlignment="Center"
                    HorizontalAlignment="Left"
                    Margin="0,0,0,0"  Width="82" FontSize="12"
                    FontFamily="Arial" TextAlignment="Right" />
            <TextBox FontSize="16" x:Name="tbxIPAddress"
                    Text="{Binding IP, Mode=TwoWay}"
                    HorizontalContentAlignment="Center" HorizontalAlignment="Stretch"
                    Grid.Row="1" Grid.Column="1"  Margin="4,0,4,0"
                    VerticalAlignment="Center" TextWrapping="NoWrap"
                    VerticalScrollBarVisibility="Disabled" Height="25" />
            <TextBox FontSize="16" x:Name="tbxPort" Text="{Binding Port, Mode=TwoWay}"
                    HorizontalContentAlignment="Center" Width="Auto"
                    HorizontalAlignment="Stretch" Grid.Row="1" Grid.Column="2"
                    Margin="4,0,4,0" VerticalAlignment="Center" TextWrapping="NoWrap"
                    VerticalScrollBarVisibility="Disabled" Height="25" />
            <TextBox FontSize="16" x:Name="tbxParticipantName" Text
                    ="{Binding Me, Mode=TwoWay}"
                    HorizontalContentAlignment="Center" Width="Auto"
                    HorizontalAlignment="Stretch" Grid.Row="2" Grid.Column="1"
                    Grid.ColumnSpan="2"  Margin="4,0,4,0" VerticalAlignment="Center"
                    TextWrapping="NoWrap" VerticalScrollBarVisibility="Disabled"
                    Height="25" />
            <HyperlinkButton FontFamily="Arial" FontSize="16"
                        HorizontalAlignment="Center" Margin="0,8,0,0"
                        x:Name="btnJoin" VerticalAlignment="Top" Grid.Row="3"
                        Grid.Column="1" Grid.ColumnSpan="1"
                        Content="Click here to join" Click="btnJoin_Click"/>
        </Grid>
        <Grid HorizontalAlignment="Stretch" VerticalAlignment="Stretch"
                Grid.Row="1" Visibility="Collapsed"
                x:Name="viewParticipants" Width="300" Height="550">
        <Grid.RowDefinitions>
            <RowDefinition Height="0.1*"/>
            <RowDefinition Height="0.9*"/>
        </Grid.RowDefinitions>
        <ListBox HorizontalAlignment="Stretch" Margin="8,8,8,8"
                VerticalAlignment="Stretch" Grid.Row="1"
                x:Name="lbxParticipants"
                ItemsSource="{Binding Participants, Mode=TwoWay}">
```

```xml
    <ListBox.ItemTemplate>
      <DataTemplate>
        <Grid VerticalAlignment="Stretch" HorizontalAlignment="Stretch">
          <Grid.ColumnDefinitions>
            <ColumnDefinition Width="0.854*"/>
            <ColumnDefinition Width="0.146*"/>
          </Grid.ColumnDefinitions>
          <TextBlock FontSize="12" Text="{Binding}" TextAlignment="Left"
                     TextWrapping="Wrap" HorizontalAlignment="Stretch"
                     Margin="5,5,5,5" VerticalAlignment="Stretch"/>
          <Button Template="{StaticResource ctTalkButton}"
                  HorizontalAlignment="Right" Margin="8,8,8,8"
                  Grid.Column="1" Content="Button" Click="btnTalk_Click"
                  Tag="{Binding}"/>
        </Grid>
      </DataTemplate>
    </ListBox.ItemTemplate>
  </ListBox>
  <HyperlinkButton HorizontalAlignment="Right" VerticalAlignment="Center"
                   Content="Click to Logoff" Margin="8,8,8,8" FontSize="14"
                   x:Name="btnLogoff" Click="btnLogoff_Click" />
</Grid>
<Grid HorizontalAlignment="Stretch" VerticalAlignment="Stretch" Grid.Row="2"
      Visibility="Collapsed" x:Name="viewChat" Width="300" Height="550">
  <Grid.RowDefinitions>
    <RowDefinition Height="0.053*"/>
    <RowDefinition Height="0.607*"/>
    <RowDefinition Height="0.284*"/>
    <RowDefinition Height="0.056*"/>
  </Grid.RowDefinitions>
  <ListBox HorizontalAlignment="Stretch" VerticalAlignment="Stretch"
           Margin="8,8,8,8" x:Name="lbxConversation" Grid.Row="1"
           ItemTemplate="{StaticResource dtConversation}"
           ItemsSource="{Binding Conversation, Mode=TwoWay}"
           ItemContainerStyle="{StaticResource style_lbxitemConversation}"/>
  <TextBox HorizontalAlignment="Stretch" VerticalAlignment="Stretch"
           Text="{Binding MessageBody, Mode=TwoWay}" TextWrapping="Wrap"
           Grid.Row="2" Margin="8,8,8,8" VerticalScrollBarVisibility="Auto"
           FontFamily="Courier New" Foreground="#FF0B356A"
           x:Name="tbxMessage"/>
  <HyperlinkButton HorizontalAlignment="Center" VerticalAlignment="Center"
                   Content="Click to Send" Grid.Row="3"
                   Margin="0,0,0,0" FontSize="14" x:Name="btnSend"
                   Click="btnSend_Click"/>
```

677

```
      <HyperlinkButton FontSize="14" HorizontalAlignment="Right" Margin="0,0,8,8"
                       x:Name="btnEndChat" VerticalAlignment="Stretch"
                       Content="End Chat" Click="btnEndChat_Click"/>
    </Grid>
  </Grid>
</UserControl>
```

The XAML is pretty simple. The UI is broken into three views, contained in three corresponding Grids: viewLogin, viewParticipants, and viewChat.

viewLogin exposes the login UI, made up of TextBoxes to accept the IP address, the server port, and the participant name. The fields are bound to properties on the ClientConnectionManager class, which we discuss momentarily. It also contains a HyperlinkButton, which when clicked initiates the login process.

viewParticipants contains a ListBox named lbxParticipants that displays the currently joined participants, except for the participant logged in through this client instance. lbxParticipants is bound to the ClientConnectionManager.Participants property. The data template for each item consists of a TextBlock showing the participant name, and a custom templated Button displaying an icon, which when clicked initiates a conversation with the corresponding participant. Another HyperlinkButton lets the user log off.

viewChat contains a ListBox named lbxConversation that displays the conversation history, bound to the ClientConnectionManager.Conversation property, and a TextBox that lets the user type in a message, bound to ClientConnectionManager.MessageBody. It also contains two more HyperlinkButtons, to send a message and to end a chat.

viewParticipants and viewChat are initially hidden and are made visible depending on the state of the application.

Let's now look at the code-behind for MainPage in Listing 7-23.

Listing 7-23. *Code-Behind for the MainPage in MainPage.xaml.cs*

```
using System.Windows;
using System.Windows.Controls;

namespace Ch07_Networking.Recipe7_5.ChatClient
{
  public partial class MainPage : UserControl
  {
    public ClientConnectionManager ConnManager { get; set; }

    public MainPage()
    {
      InitializeComponent();
      //initialize the ClientConnectionManager
      ConnManager = new ClientConnectionManager { ParentPage = this };
      //set the data context to the ClientConnetionManager
      LayoutRoot.DataContext = ConnManager;
    }
```

```csharp
    private void btnJoin_Click(object sender, RoutedEventArgs e)
    {
      ConnManager.Join();
    }
    private void btnLogoff_Click(object sender, RoutedEventArgs e)
    {
      ConnManager.Disconnect();
    }

    private void btnTalk_Click(object sender, RoutedEventArgs e)
    {
      //get the participant name from the Button.Tag
      //which was bound to the name at data binding
      ConnManager.TalkingTo = (sender as Button).Tag as string;
      ShowChatView();
    }

    private void btnSend_Click(object sender, RoutedEventArgs e)
    {
      ConnManager.SendTextMessage();
    }

    private void btnEndChat_Click(object sender, RoutedEventArgs e)
    {
      ConnManager.SendChatEnd();
    }
    internal void ShowParticipantsView()
    {
      viewParticipants.Visibility = Visibility.Visible;
      viewLogin.Visibility = Visibility.Collapsed;
      viewChat.Visibility = Visibility.Collapsed;
    }
    internal void ShowChatView()
    {
      viewParticipants.Visibility = Visibility.Collapsed;
      viewLogin.Visibility = Visibility.Collapsed;
      viewChat.Visibility = Visibility.Visible;
    }
    internal void ShowLoginView()
    {
      viewParticipants.Visibility = Visibility.Collapsed;
      viewLogin.Visibility = Visibility.Visible;
      viewChat.Visibility = Visibility.Collapsed;
    }
  }
}
```

The MainPage onstructor creates a new instance of the ClientConnectionManager named ConnManager, initializing its ParentPage property with this Page instance. This is done so that in the ClientConnectionManager implementation, you have access to MainPage and its UI elements to effect various state changes. You also set the DataContext of the topmost Grid named LayoutRoot to ConnManager so that all the bindings to various properties of ClientConnectionManager that you saw in the XAML can be put into effect.

The various Button click handlers are self-explanatory; corresponding functions in the ClientConnectionManager are invoked from them. The ShowLoginView(), ShowParticipantsView(), and ShowChatView() methods toggle between views and are used from within the ClientConnectionManager, as you see next.

We have encapsulated all the client-side sockets–based communication and message processing in ClientConnectionManager. Listing 7-24 shows the ClientConnectionManager class.

Listing 7-24. *ClientConnectionManager in ConnectionManager.cs*

```
using System;
using System.Collections.Generic;
using System.Collections.ObjectModel;
using System.ComponentModel;
using System.IO;
using System.Net;
using System.Net.Sockets;

namespace Ch07_Networking.Recipe7_5.ChatClient
{
  public class ClientConnectionManager : INotifyPropertyChanged
  {
    public event PropertyChangedEventHandler PropertyChanged;

    //create a new socket
    Socket ClientSocket = new Socket(AddressFamily.InterNetwork,
      SocketType.Stream, ProtocolType.Tcp);
    //reference to the parent page
    public Page ParentPage { get; set; }
    //participants collection
    private ObservableCollection<string> _Participants;
    public ObservableCollection<string> Participants
    {
      get { return _Participants; }
      set
      {
        _Participants = value;
        if (PropertyChanged != null)
          PropertyChanged(this, new PropertyChangedEventArgs("Participants"));
      }
    }
```

```
//collection of all messages exchanged in a particular conversation
private ObservableCollection<TextMessage> _Conversation;
public ObservableCollection<TextMessage> Conversation
{
  get { return _Conversation; }
  set
  {
    _Conversation = value;
    if (PropertyChanged != null)
      PropertyChanged(this, new PropertyChangedEventArgs("Conversation"));
  }
}
//IP Address of the server connected to
private string _IP;
public string IP
{
  get { return _IP; }
  set
  {
    _IP = value;
    if (PropertyChanged != null)
      PropertyChanged(this, new PropertyChangedEventArgs("IP"));
  }
}
//Port connected to
private string _Port;
public string Port
{
  get { return _Port; }
  set
  {
    _Port = value;
    if (PropertyChanged != null)
      PropertyChanged(this, new PropertyChangedEventArgs("Port"));
  }
}
//name of the person logged in
private string _Me;
public string Me
{
  get { return _Me; }
  set
  {
    _Me = value;
    if (PropertyChanged != null)
```

```
        PropertyChanged(this, new PropertyChangedEventArgs("Me"));

    }
  }
  //the other person in a conversation
  private string _TalkingTo;
  public string TalkingTo
  {
    get { return _TalkingTo; }
    set
    {
      _TalkingTo = value;
      if (PropertyChanged != null)
        PropertyChanged(this, new PropertyChangedEventArgs("TalkingTo"));
    }
  }
  //the body of a conversation message
  private string _MessageBody;
  public string MessageBody
  {
    get { return _MessageBody; }
    set
    {
      _MessageBody = value;
      if (PropertyChanged != null)
        PropertyChanged(this, new PropertyChangedEventArgs("MessageBody"));
    }
  }
  //buffer used to receive messages
  private const int RECEIVEBUFFERSIZE = 10 * 1024;
  private byte[] ReceiveBuffer = new Byte[RECEIVEBUFFERSIZE];
  //constructor
  public ClientConnectionManager()
  {
    //initialize the collections
    Participants = new ObservableCollection<string>();
    Conversation = new ObservableCollection<TextMessage>();
  }
  //called when the login button is clicked
  public void Join()
  {
    //create a new SocketEventArgs, specify the remote endpoint details
    SocketAsyncEventArgs sockEvtArgs =
      new SocketAsyncEventArgs
      {
```

```
      RemoteEndPoint = new IPEndPoint(IPAddress.Parse(IP),
        Convert.ToInt32(Port)),
      UserToken = Me
    };
  //connect a completion handler
  sockEvtArgs.Completed +=
    new EventHandler<SocketAsyncEventArgs>(Connection_Completed);
  //connect asynchronously
  ClientSocket.ConnectAsync(sockEvtArgs);

}
//connection completion handler
void Connection_Completed(object sender, SocketAsyncEventArgs e)
{
  //connected successfully, send a
  //ConnectionDisconnectionRequest with Connect=true
  if (e.SocketError == SocketError.Success)
  {
    SocketAsyncEventArgs sockEvtArgs =
      new SocketAsyncEventArgs { UserToken = e.UserToken };
    //serialize a new ConnectionDisconnectionMessage into a MemoryStream
    MemoryStream SerializedStream =
      MessageWrapper.SerializeMessage(
      new MessageWrapper
      {
        Message = new ConnectionDisconnectionRequest
        {
          From = e.UserToken as string,
          Connect = true
        }
      });
    //set buffer to the contents of the memorystream
    sockEvtArgs.SetBuffer(SerializedStream.GetBuffer(),
      0, (int)SerializedStream.Length);
    sockEvtArgs.Completed +=
      new EventHandler<SocketAsyncEventArgs>(ConnectionRequestSend_Completed);
    //send
    ClientSocket.SendAsync(sockEvtArgs);
  }
}
//ConnectionDisconnectionRequest send completion handler
void ConnectionRequestSend_Completed(object sender, SocketAsyncEventArgs e)
{
  //sent successfully
  if (e.SocketError == SocketError.Success)
```

```
    {
      //start receiving messages
      ReceiveMessage();
      //switch context
      ParentPage.Dispatcher.BeginInvoke(new Action(delegate
      {
        //switch view to participants
        ParentPage.ShowParticipantsView();
      }));
    }
  }
  //receive a message
  private void ReceiveMessage()
  {
    SocketAsyncEventArgs sockEvtArgsReceive = new SocketAsyncEventArgs();
    sockEvtArgsReceive.SetBuffer(ReceiveBuffer, 0, RECEIVEBUFFERSIZE);
    sockEvtArgsReceive.Completed +=
      new EventHandler<SocketAsyncEventArgs>(Receive_Completed);
    ClientSocket.ReceiveAsync(sockEvtArgsReceive);
  }
  //receive completion handler
  void Receive_Completed(object sender, SocketAsyncEventArgs e)
  {
    if (e.SocketError == SocketError.Success)
    {
      ParentPage.Dispatcher.BeginInvoke(new Action(delegate
      {
        //copy the message to a temporary buffer - this is
        //because we reuse the same buffer for all SocketAsyncEventArgs,
        //and message lengths may vary
        byte[] Message = new byte[e.BytesTransferred];
        Array.Copy(e.Buffer, 0, Message, 0, e.BytesTransferred);
        //process the message
        ProcessMessage(Message);
        //keep receiving
        ReceiveMessage();
      }));
    }
  }
  //process a message
  internal void ProcessMessage(byte[] Message)
  {
    //deserialize the message into the wrapper
    MessageWrapper mw = MessageWrapper.DeserializeMessage(Message);
    //check type of the contained message
```

```
//correct type resolution is ensured through the
//usage of KnownTypeAttribute on the MessageWrapper
//data contract declaration
if (mw.Message is TextMessage)
{
  //receiving a text message from someone -
  //switch to chat view if not there already
  ParentPage.ShowChatView();
  //remember the other party in the conversation
  if (this.TalkingTo == null)
    this.TalkingTo = (mw.Message as TextMessage).From;
  //data bind the text of the message
  Conversation.Add(mw.Message as TextMessage);
}
//someone has ended an ongoing chat
else if (mw.Message is ChatEndNotification)
{
  //reset
  this.TalkingTo = null;
  //reset
  Conversation.Clear();
  //go back to participants list
  ParentPage.ShowParticipantsView();
}
//server has sent a reply to your connection request
else if (mw.Message is ConnectionReply)
{
  //reset
  Participants.Clear();
  //get the list of the other participants
  List<string> ReplyList = (mw.Message as ConnectionReply).Participants;
  //data bind
  foreach (string s in ReplyList)
    Participants.Add(s);

}
//someone has connected or disconnected
else if (mw.Message is ConnectionDisconnectionNotification)
{
  ConnectionDisconnectionNotification notif =
    mw.Message as ConnectionDisconnectionNotification;
```

```csharp
      //if it is a connection
      if (notif.Connect)
        //add to participants list
        Participants.Add(notif.Participant);
      else
      {
        //remove from participants list
        Participants.Remove(notif.Participant);
        //if you were in a conversation with this person,
        //go back to the participants view
        if (notif.Participant == TalkingTo)
        {
          ParentPage.ShowParticipantsView();
        }
      }
    }
  }
}
//send a text message
internal void SendTextMessage()
{
  //package the From, To and Text of the message
  //into a TextMessage, and then into a wrapper
  MessageWrapper mwSend =
    new MessageWrapper
    {
      Message = new TextMessage {
        From = Me, To = TalkingTo, Body = MessageBody }
    };
  //serialize
  MemoryStream SerializedStream = MessageWrapper.SerializeMessage(mwSend);
  SocketAsyncEventArgs sockEvtArgsSend =
    new SocketAsyncEventArgs { UserToken = mwSend.Message };
  //grab the byte[] and set the buffer
  sockEvtArgsSend.SetBuffer(
    SerializedStream.GetBuffer(), 0, (int)SerializedStream.Length);
  //attach handler
  sockEvtArgsSend.Completed +=
    new EventHandler<SocketAsyncEventArgs>(SendTextMessage_Completed);
  //send
  ClientSocket.SendAsync(sockEvtArgsSend);
}
//send completed
void SendTextMessage_Completed(object sender, SocketAsyncEventArgs e)
{
```

```
    //success
    if (e.SocketError == SocketError.Success)
    {
      //switch context
      ParentPage.Dispatcher.BeginInvoke(new Action(delegate
      {
        //send was successful, add message to ongoing conversation
        Conversation.Add(e.UserToken as TextMessage);
        //reset edit box
        MessageBody = "";
      }));
    }
  }
  //disconnect
  internal void Disconnect()
  {
    SocketAsyncEventArgs sockEvtArgs = new SocketAsyncEventArgs();
    //package a ConnectionDisconnectionRequest with Connect=false
    MemoryStream SerializedStream =
      MessageWrapper.SerializeMessage(
      new MessageWrapper
      {
        Message = new ConnectionDisconnectionRequest
        {
          From = Me,
          Connect = false
        }
      });
    sockEvtArgs.SetBuffer(
      SerializedStream.GetBuffer(), 0, (int)SerializedStream.Length);
    sockEvtArgs.Completed +=
      new EventHandler<SocketAsyncEventArgs>(DisconnectRequest_Completed);
    ClientSocket.SendAsync(sockEvtArgs);
  }
  //disconnect completed
  void DisconnectRequest_Completed(object sender, SocketAsyncEventArgs e)
  {
    //success
    if (e.SocketError == SocketError.Success)
    {
      //reset my identity
      this.Me = null;
      //clear all participants
      Participants.Clear();
```

```
        //show login screen
        ParentPage.ShowLoginView();
      }
    }
    //end a chat
    internal void SendChatEnd()
    {
      MessageWrapper mwSend =
        new MessageWrapper
        {
          Message = new ChatEndNotification { From = Me, To = TalkingTo }
        };
      MemoryStream SerializedStream =
        MessageWrapper.SerializeMessage(mwSend);
      SocketAsyncEventArgs sockEvtArgsSend =
        new SocketAsyncEventArgs { UserToken = mwSend.Message };
      sockEvtArgsSend.SetBuffer(
        SerializedStream.GetBuffer(), 0, (int)SerializedStream.Length);
      sockEvtArgsSend.Completed +=
        new EventHandler<SocketAsyncEventArgs>(SendChatEnd_Completed);
      ClientSocket.SendAsync(sockEvtArgsSend);
    }
    //chat ended
    void SendChatEnd_Completed(object sender, SocketAsyncEventArgs e)
    {
      //success
      if (e.SocketError == SocketError.Success)
      {
        //switch context
        ParentPage.Dispatcher.BeginInvoke(new Action(delegate
        {
          //reset identity of the other participant
          this.TalkingTo = null;
          //clear the conversation
          Conversation.Clear();
          //switch back to the participants view
          ParentPage.ShowParticipantsView();
        }));
      }
    }
  }
}
```

As discussed before, ClientConnectionManager is used as the datasource for most of the data bound to the XAML for the client UI, and therefore implements INotifyPropertyChanged; the appropriate property setters raise PropertyChanged events.

After the user specifies the IP address, a port, and a participant name in the initial login screen, you establish a connection to the server. To do this, you call the Join() method, which uses the Socket.ConnectAsync() method to establish the server connection. You specify the details of the remote endpoint (IP address and port) in the SocketeventArgs parameter. You also specify Connection_Completed() as the completion handler for ConnectAsync().

When a successful socket connection is established, in Connection_Completed() you send the first application-specific message of type ConnectionDisconnectionRequest to the server, with the ConnectionDisconnectionRequest.Connect property set to True, to indicate a request for connection. You wrap the message in an instance of the MessageWrapper type, serialize it to a MemoryStream, and use the MemoryStream contents to fill the send buffer. Attach ConnectionRequestSend_Completed() as the completion handler, and then call SendAsync() to send the request.

When the send request returns, ConnectionRequestSend_Completed() is invoked; you check for a successful send by checking the SocketAsyncEventArgs.SocketError property. In the event of a successful operation, this property is set to SocketError.Success; a plethora of other values indicate different error conditions. On a successful send, you prepare the client for receiving a message back from the server by calling ReceiveMessage(). You also switch the client UI to display the view with the list of participants by calling ShowParticipantsView() on the Page.

In ReceiveMessage(), you use a preallocated buffer to receive all your messages. You call Socket.ReceiveAsync() to start receiving messages, after attaching the Receive_Completed() completion handler. When a message is successfully retrieved, you copy it out of the message buffer into a temporary one before you process the message and take appropriate action. Note that you call ReceiveMessage() again as soon as you complete processing the previous message, to keep the socket in a constant receive mode and not miss any incoming messages—albeit on a background thread because of the asynchronous nature of ReceiveAsync().

The ProcessMessage() method is central to the client-side message processing. Incoming messages are deserialized from byte[] to MessageWrapper instances by calling MessageWrapper.DeserializeMessage(), as shown in Listing 7-19. The type of the contained message in MessageWrapper.Body is used to determine the action taken.

The first message a client receives is the server's acknowledgment of the connection, in the form of a ConnectionReply message. The ConnectionReply.Participants collection contains the names of all the other participants logged in; you bind that collection to the participants ListBox on the UI and switch the view by calling ShowParticipantsView() on the page.

For incoming TextMessage instances, if the client is not already in chat mode, you switch the UI appropriately by calling ShowChatView() and then display the message by adding it to the Conversations collection bound to the ListBox used to display a conversation. You also set the ClientConnectionManager.TalkingTo property to the name of the participant from whom you are receiving the message, as indicated by the TextMessage.From property.

Clients can also receive a couple of other types of messages. When you receive a ChatEndNotification, you reset the TalkingTo property, clear the conversation ListBox, and switch to the participants view. For a ConnectionDisconnectionNotification, if the Connect property is True (indicating that a new participant is connecting), you add the participant to the bound Participants property; otherwise, you remove them, and switch views if you were currently in conversation with the disconnecting participant.

The ClientConnectionManager class also implements various methods for sending different types of messages from the client. All of these methods follow the same pattern demonstrated when you sent the first ConnectionDisconnectionRequest earlier: you create and initialize a new message instance of the appropriate message type, serialize it using MessageWrapper.SerializeMessage(), and then send it using Socket.SendAsync().

The Chat Server

The chat server is implemented as a console program. The functionality is divided into two primary classes: ConnectionListener, which accepts incoming client connections, hands them over to a ServerConnectionManager instance, and continues to listen for more connections; and ServerConnectionManager, which manages and processes messages for each connected client and then routes messages between clients.

Listing 7-25 shows the ConnectionListener class that you use in the server program to listen and accept incoming connections from clients.

Listing 7-25. *ConnectionListener Class in ConnectionListener.cs*

```
using System;
using System.Net;
using System.Net.Sockets;

namespace Ch07_Networking.Recipe7_5.ChatBroker
{
  internal class ConnectionListener
  {
    //the socket used for listening to incoming connections
    Socket ListenerSocket { get; set; }
    SocketAsyncEventArgs sockEvtArgs = null;
    //new server connection manager
    ServerConnectionManager ConnManager = new ServerConnectionManager();
    //run the connection listener
    internal void Run(int Port)
    {
      //create a new IP endpoint at the specific port,
      //and on any available IP address
      IPEndPoint ListenerEndPoint = new IPEndPoint(IPAddress.Any, Port);
      //create the listener socket
      ListenerSocket = new Socket(AddressFamily.InterNetwork,
        SocketType.Stream, ProtocolType.Tcp);
      //bind to the endpoint
      ListenerSocket.Bind(ListenerEndPoint);
      //listen with a backlog of 20
      ListenerSocket.Listen(20);
      Console.WriteLine("Waiting for incoming connection ...");
      //start accepting connections
      AcceptIncoming();
    }
```

```
    //accept incoming connections
    internal void AcceptIncoming()
    {
      //pass in the server connection manager
      sockEvtArgs = new SocketAsyncEventArgs { UserToken = ConnManager };
      sockEvtArgs.Completed += new EventHandler<SocketAsyncEventArgs>(
          delegate(object Sender, SocketAsyncEventArgs e)
          {
            Console.WriteLine("Accepted connection..." +
              "Assigning to Connection Manager...." +
              "Waiting for more connections...");
            //pass the connected socket to the server connection manager
            ConnManager.Manage(e.AcceptSocket);
            //keep listening
            AcceptIncoming();
          });
      //accept an incoming connection
      ListenerSocket.AcceptAsync(sockEvtArgs);
    }
  }
}
```

The ConnectionListener class is instantiated and launched by calling its Run() method from the server program's Main() method. In Run(), you create an IPEndpoint using the port number passed in as a command-line argument. Specifying IPAddress.Any as the IPAddress parameter allows the listener to listen on all available IP addresses on the machine, which is especially handy on machines that have multiple active network connections. You then bind the socket to the endpoint and start listening by calling Socket.Listen(). The parameter to Listen() specifies the size of the backlog of incoming connections that the runtime maintains for you while you process them one at a time. Finally, you call AcceptIncoming().

The AcceptIncoming() method uses Socket.AcceptAsync() on the listener socket to asynchronously accept an incoming connection. In the Completed handler of SocketAsyncEventArgs, the connected client socket is available in the SocketAsyncEventArgs.AcceptSocket property. You pass this socket on to an instance of the ServerConnectionManager type through its Manage() method. You then continue to accept more incoming connections.

The ServerConnectionManager type is used to manage all connected client sockets. You also define a Participant type to represent a specific connected client and its communications. Listing 7-26 shows the code for these two classes.

Listing 7-26. *Implementation for ServerConnectionManager and Participant types in MessageProcessing.cs*

```
using System;
using System.Collections.Generic;
using System.IO;
using System.Linq;
using System.Net.Sockets;
using System.Threading;
```

```csharp
namespace Ch07_Networking.Recipe7_5.ChatBroker
{
  internal class ServerConnectionManager
  {

    //list of participants
    private List<Participant> _Participants = new List<Participant>();
    internal List<Participant> Participants
    {
      get { return _Participants; }
    }
    //accept and manage a client socket
    internal void Manage(Socket socket)
    {
      //create a new Participant around the client socket
      Participant p = new Participant { ClientSocket = socket, Parent = this };
      //add it to the list
      _Participants.Add(p);
      //start up the participant
      p.StartUp();
    }
    //broadcast a message from a participant to all other participants
    internal void Broadcast(string From, MessageWrapper Message)
    {
      //get a list of all participants other than the one sending the message
      List<Participant> targets = (from p in Participants
                                   where p.Name != From
                                   select p).ToList();
      //iterate and add to the Send queue for each
      foreach (Participant p in targets)
      {
        lock (p.QueueSyncRoot)
        {
          p.SendQueue.Enqueue(Message);
        }
      }
    }
    //send a message to a specific participant
    internal void Send(string To, MessageWrapper Message)
    {
      //get the Participant from the list
      Participant target = (from p in Participants
                            where p.Name == To
                            select p).ToList()[0];
```

```
      //add to the send queue for the participant
      lock (target.QueueSyncRoot)
      {
        target.SendQueue.Enqueue(Message);
      }
    }
}

internal class Participant
{
  //lock target
  internal object QueueSyncRoot = new object();
  //name as specified at the client
  internal string Name { get; set; }
  //the connected client socket
  internal Socket ClientSocket { get; set; }
  //a reference back to the ServerConnectionManager instance
  internal ServerConnectionManager Parent { get; set; }
  //are we currently receiving a message from this participant?
  bool Receiving = false;
  //are we currently sending a message to this participant?
  bool Sending = false;
  //a queue to hold messages being sent to this participant
  private Queue<MessageWrapper> _SendQueue = new Queue<MessageWrapper>();
  internal Queue<MessageWrapper> SendQueue
  {
    get { return _SendQueue; }
    set { _SendQueue = value; }
  }
  //check to see if there are messages in the queue
  private int HasMessage()
  {
    lock (QueueSyncRoot)
    {
      return SendQueue.Count;
    }
  }
  //start the participant up
  internal void StartUp()
  {
    //create the receiver thread
    Thread thdParticipantReceiver = new Thread(new ThreadStart(
      //thread start delegate
        delegate
        {
```

```
          //loop while the socket is valid
          while (ClientSocket != null)
          {
            //if there is no data available OR
            //we are currently receiving, continue
            if (ClientSocket.Available <= 0 || Receiving) continue;
            //set receiving to true
            Receiving = true;
            //begin to receive the next message
            ReceiveMessage();
          }
       }));
    //set thread to background
    thdParticipantReceiver.IsBackground = true;
    //start receiver thread
    thdParticipantReceiver.Start();
    //create the sender thread
    Thread thdParticipantSender = new Thread(new ThreadStart(
      //thread start delegate
        delegate
        {
          //loop while the socket is valid
          while (ClientSocket != null)
          {
            //if there are no messages to be sent OR
            //we are currently sending, continue
            if (HasMessage() == 0 || Sending) continue;
            //set sending to true
            Sending = true;
            //begin sending
            SendMessage();
          }
       }));
    //set thread to background
    thdParticipantSender.IsBackground = true;
    //start sender thread
    thdParticipantSender.Start();
}
//receive a message
private void ReceiveMessage()
{
  SocketAsyncEventArgs sockEvtArgs = new SocketAsyncEventArgs();
  //allocate a buffer as large as the available data
  sockEvtArgs.SetBuffer(
    new byte[ClientSocket.Available], 0, ClientSocket.Available);
```

```
    sockEvtArgs.Completed += new EventHandler<SocketAsyncEventArgs>(
      //completion handler
        delegate(object sender, SocketAsyncEventArgs e)
        {
          //process the message
          ProcessMessage(e.Buffer);
          //done receiving, thread loop will look for next
          Receiving = false;
        });
    //start receiving
    ClientSocket.ReceiveAsync(sockEvtArgs);
}
internal void ProcessMessage(byte[] Message)
{
    //deserialize message
    MessageWrapper mw = MessageWrapper.DeserializeMessage(Message);
    //if text message
    if (mw.Message is TextMessage)
    {
      //send it to the target participant
      Parent.Send((mw.Message as TextMessage).To, mw);
    }
    //if it is a ConnectionDisconnectionRequest
    else if (mw.Message is ConnectionDisconnectionRequest)
    {
      ConnectionDisconnectionRequest connDisconnReq =
        mw.Message as ConnectionDisconnectionRequest;
      //if connecting
      if (connDisconnReq.Connect)
      {
        this.Name = connDisconnReq.From;
        //broadcast to everyone else
        Parent.Broadcast(this.Name, new MessageWrapper
        {
          Message = new ConnectionDisconnectionNotification
          {
            Participant = this.Name,
            Connect = true
          }
        });
        //send the list of all participants other than
        //the one connecting to the connecting client
        Parent.Send(this.Name, new MessageWrapper
```

```
        {
          Message = new ConnectionReply
          {
            Participants =
            (from part in Parent.Participants
             where part.Name != this.Name
             select part.Name).ToList()
          }
        });
      }
      else //disconnecting
      {
        //remove from the participants list
        Parent.Participants.Remove(this);
        //close socket
        this.ClientSocket.Close();
        //reset
        this.ClientSocket = null;
        //broadcast to everyone else
        Parent.Broadcast(this.Name, new MessageWrapper
        {
          Message = new ConnectionDisconnectionNotification
          {
            Participant = this.Name,
            Connect = false
          }
        });
      }
    }
    //chat end
    else if (mw.Message is ChatEndNotification)
    {
      //send it to the other participant
      Parent.Send((mw.Message as ChatEndNotification).To, mw);
    }
  }
  //send a message
  private void SendMessage()
  {
    MessageWrapper mw = null;
    //dequeue a message from the send queue
    lock (QueueSyncRoot)
    {
      mw = SendQueue.Dequeue();
    }
```

```
  SocketAsyncEventArgs sockEvtArgs =
    new SocketAsyncEventArgs { UserToken = mw };
  //serialize and pack into the send buffer
  MemoryStream SerializedMessage =
    MessageWrapper.SerializeMessage(mw);
  sockEvtArgs.SetBuffer(
    SerializedMessage.GetBuffer(), 0, (int)SerializedMessage.Length);
  sockEvtArgs.Completed += new EventHandler<SocketAsyncEventArgs>(
    //completion handler
      delegate(object sender, SocketAsyncEventArgs e)
      {
        //not sending anymore
        Sending = false;
      });
  //begin send
  ClientSocket.SendAsync(sockEvtArgs);
    }
  }
}
```

An instance of a `Participant` is created and stored in a list when the `ServerConnectionManager` receives a connected client socket through the `Manage()` method. The `Participant.Startup()` method starts two background threads—one each for receiving and sending messages, each of which continue as long as the client socket for that `Participant` is valid.

The receive thread calls the `ReceiveMessage()` method, provided that there is data to be read (as determined by the `Socket.Available` property) and that the `Receiving` boolean flag is set to `false`. The flag is set to `true` prior to calling `ReceiveMessage()` and is reset after `ReceiveMessage()` returns so that the socket is always ready to receive the next message as soon as it arrives.

`ReceiveMessage()` uses the `ProcessMessage()` method to process and act on a received message. `ProcessMessage()` is structured similarly to the one in the Silverlight client in that it deserializes a message and looks at the type of the contained `Body` property to determine the course of action. For messages that are intended to be delivered to other participants, `ProcessMessage` delivers it to that participant either through `ServerConnectionManager.Broadcast()` (which delivers a message to all participants except for the one sending it) or by `ServerConnectionManager.Send()` (which delivers it to a single targeted participant). Delivery of a message in this case is achieved by adding the message to a send queue of type `Queue<MessageWrapper>` defined in each participant.

The send thread continuously checks the `Sending` flag (used similarly to the `Receiving` flag) and the presence of messages in the queue of the owning participant using `Participant.HasMessage()`. When a message is found, `SendMessage()` is called, which then serializes the message and sends it out through the participant's socket.

The Policy Server

The policy server is similarly implemented as a console program that listens on all available IP addresses, bound to a well-known port 943. Listing 7-27 shows the code for the policy server.

Listing 7-27. *Implementation for the PolicyServer type in PolicyListener.cs*

```csharp
using System;
using System.IO;
using System.Net;
using System.Net.Sockets;
using System.Text;

namespace Ch07_Networking.Recipe7_5.PolicyServer
{

  internal class PolicyListener
  {
    Socket ListenerSocket { get; set; }
    SocketAsyncEventArgs sockEvtArgs = null;
    //valid policy request string
    public static string ValidPolicyRequest = "<policy-file-request/>";

    public PolicyListener()
    {
      //bind to all available addresses and port 943
      IPEndPoint ListenerEndPoint =
        new IPEndPoint(IPAddress.Any, 943);
      ListenerSocket =
        new Socket(AddressFamily.InterNetwork, SocketType.Stream, ProtocolType.Tcp);
      ListenerSocket.Bind(ListenerEndPoint);
      ListenerSocket.Listen(20);
    }
    internal void ListenForPolicyRequest()
    {
      sockEvtArgs = new SocketAsyncEventArgs();
      sockEvtArgs.Completed += new EventHandler<SocketAsyncEventArgs>(
          delegate(object Sender, SocketAsyncEventArgs e)
          {
            //process this request
            ReadPolicyRequest(e.AcceptSocket);
            //go back to listening
            ListenForPolicyRequest();
          });
      ListenerSocket.AcceptAsync(sockEvtArgs);
    }
```

```csharp
    private bool ReadPolicyRequest(Socket ClientSocket)
    {
      SocketAsyncEventArgs sockEvtArgs =
        new SocketAsyncEventArgs { UserToken = ClientSocket };
      sockEvtArgs.SetBuffer(
        new byte[ValidPolicyRequest.Length], 0, ValidPolicyRequest.Length);
      sockEvtArgs.Completed += new EventHandler<SocketAsyncEventArgs>(
          delegate(object Sender, SocketAsyncEventArgs e)
          {
            if (e.SocketError == SocketError.Success)
            {
              //get policy request string
              string PolicyRequest = new UTF8Encoding().
                GetString(e.Buffer, 0, e.BytesTransferred);
              //check for valid format
              if (PolicyRequest.CompareTo(ValidPolicyRequest) == 0)
                //valid request-send policy
                SendPolicy(e.UserToken as Socket);
            }
          });
      return ClientSocket.ReceiveAsync(sockEvtArgs);
    }
    private void SendPolicy(Socket ClientSocket)
    {
      //read the policy file
      FileStream fs = new FileStream("clientaccesspolicy.xml", FileMode.Open);
      byte[] PolicyBuffer = new byte[(int)fs.Length];
      fs.Read(PolicyBuffer, 0, (int)fs.Length);
      fs.Close();

      SocketAsyncEventArgs sockEvtArgs =
        new SocketAsyncEventArgs { UserToken = ClientSocket };
      //send the policy
      sockEvtArgs.SetBuffer(PolicyBuffer, 0, PolicyBuffer.Length);
      sockEvtArgs.Completed += new EventHandler<SocketAsyncEventArgs>(
          delegate(object Sender, SocketAsyncEventArgs e)
          {
            //close this connection
            if (e.SocketError == SocketError.Success)
              (e.UserToken as Socket).Close();
          });
      ClientSocket.SendAsync(sockEvtArgs);
    }
  }
}
```

After a connection request is accepted by the policy server, it attempts to receive a policy request from the client and checks it for validity by comparing it to the string literal `<policy-file-request/>`. If valid, the policy file is read into memory and sent back to the client through the connected client socket. When the send is completed, the socket connection is closed, and the policy server keeps listening for more policy requests.

7-6. Enabling Cross-Domain Access

Problem

You need your Silverlight client to access resources or services in a domain different from the one from which it originated.

Solution

Create an appropriate cross-domain policy on the target domain.

How It Works

Attacks where malicious code may make unauthorized calls to a remote services domain or flood the network with a large number of calls to effect denial of service are common threats on the Internet. To prevent this, Silverlight requires an explicit opt-in for a target remote domain to allow a Silverlight application to access network resources in that domain. The domain from which the Silverlight application is served is also called the *site of origin*, and a *remote domain* is any network location other than the site of origin.

This opt-in is implemented by way of a policy file that is downloaded by the Silverlight runtime and evaluated for access permissions. The policy file is defined in an XML syntax and must be named `clientaccesspolicy.xml`.

For HTTP-based communication (which includes the WebClient and the other HTTP communication classes, as well as the Silverlight WCF client proxy implementation), the owner of the target domain needs to place such a policy file at the root of the target site. When your Silverlight application makes the first HTTP request to the target domain in question, the Silverlight runtime tries to download the policy file from the site's root. If the download is successful, the runtime then evaluates the policy settings in the file to determine whether appropriate access has been granted to the resources being requested by the client application. On successful evaluation and the presence of appropriate permissions, the application is allowed to continue with the network call. Otherwise, the network call fails. Figure 7-8 shows the sequence of calls for cross-domain access over HTTP.

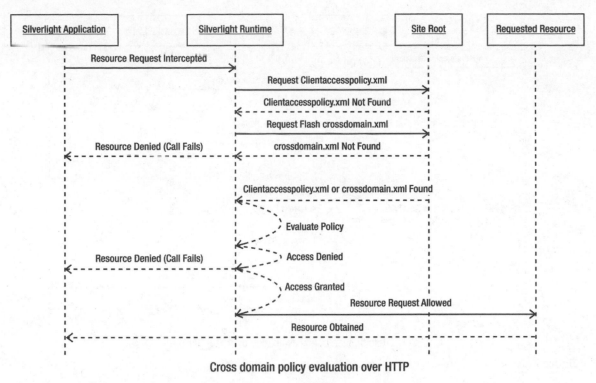

Figure 7-8. *Call sequence for cross-domain access over HTTP*

Also note that Silverlight supports the Flash cross-domain access policy format as well. In the previous scenario, if a clientaccesspolicy.xml is not found, the runtime tries to download a Flash policy file named crossdomain.xml and base resource access on policy specified there.

For sockets-based communication, a similar policy file is used, but there are a few more details. For Silverlight applications using sockets, the cross-domain policy requirements apply to both cross-domain calls as well as those back to the site of origin. On the first attempt to open a connection to a TCP endpoint from a Silverlight application, the runtime attempts to open another TCP connection to the target server (cross-domain or site of origin) at port 943. If this connection succeeds, the runtime then tries to download the policy file over this connection. If the download succeeds, the connection is closed and the downloaded policy file is used for the rest of the session. Figure 7-9 shows the sequence of calls for cross-domain access over TCP sockets.

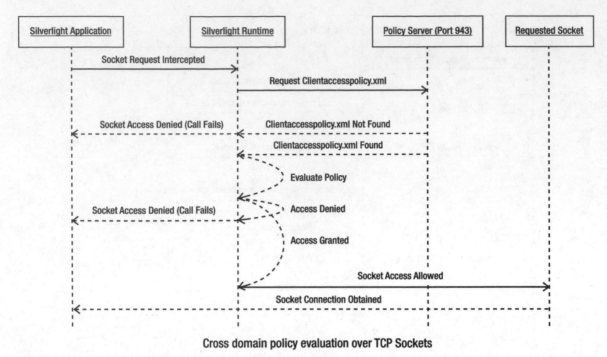

Figure 7-9. *Call sequence for cross-domain access over TCP sockets*

All of this happens behind the scenes as far as your Silverlight code is concerned, so no specific design or code consideration is necessary on the client side for either your HTTP or sockets-based code. However, if you are also implementing the sockets-based server, you need to implement a listener on port 943 and be prepared to serve the policy file when the request comes in. The request is in the form of a special string constant of the value <policy-file-request/>.

The Code

Listing 7-28 shows a sample policy file for HTTP resource access.

Listing 7-28. *Sample clientaccesspolicy.xml for HTTP Access*

```xml
<?xml version="1.0" encoding="utf-8"?>
<access-policy>
  <cross-domain-access>
    <policy>
      <allow-from http-request-headers="MyHeader, X-API-*">
        <domain uri="http://subdomain1.mydomain.com"/>
        <domain uri="http://subdomain2.mydomain.com"/>
        <domain uri="http://mydomain.com:8181"/>
      </allow-from>
```

```
      <grant-to>
        <resource path="/images "/>
        <resource path="/services" include-subpaths="True"/>
      </grant-to>
    </policy>
  </cross-domain-access>
</access-policy>
```

Multiple domain entries can be used to specify specific subdomains on a root domain or nonstandard HTTP ports that are allowed to be accessed. If your domain does not have subdomains or nonstandard ports, or if you want to grant access to the entire domain regardless, include one domain entry as shown here:

```
<allow-from>
  <domain uri="*"/>
</allow-from>
```

Each resource entry specifies a resource for which access permission is granted, with the path property containing the root relative path to the resource. The optional include-subpaths defaults to False and can be left out. If you want to grant access to subpaths for a specific path as well, set include-subpaths to True, as shown in Listing 7-28. Specifying one resource entry with the path value set to / and include-subpaths set to True allows full access to all resources in the site, as shown here:

```
<grant-to>
  <resource path="/" include-subpaths="True"/>
</grant-to>
```

The optional http-request-headers attribute on the allow-from element can be a comma-separated list of allowed HTTP request headers, where you can use an asterisk (*) as a part of a header name to indicate a wildcard. You can also replace the entire list and use the * wildcard to allow all possible headers. If the attribute is left out, no HTTP headers are allowed.

Listing 7-29 shows a clientaccesspolicy.xml file for sockets-based access.

Listing 7-29. *Sample clientaccesspolicy.xml for Sockets-Based Access*

```
<?xml version="1.0" encoding ="utf-8"?>
<access-policy>
  <cross-domain-access>
    <policy>
      <allow-from>
        <domain uri="*" />
      </allow-from>
      <grant-to>
        <socket-resource port="4502-4534" protocol="tcp" />
      </grant-to>
    </policy>
  </cross-domain-access>
</access-policy>
```

The difference here is in the use of the socket-resource element. The socket-resource element has two attributes. The port attribute can be used to specify the range of ports allowed, where the range has to be within 4502–4534. The protocol attribute allows tcp as the only possible value in this version of Silverlight. They are both required attributes.

For complete details on the policy syntax, refer to the related MSDN documentation at http://msdn.microsoft.com/en-us/library/cc645032(VS.95).aspx.

7-7.

Problem

You need a Silverlight application to be locally installed on your desktop. You also need the application to support execution with or without an available network connection.

Solution

Use the local installation support provided by Silverlight 3 to enable the user to locally install the application. Use the network availability API in Silverlight 3 to adapt your application logic to handle execution in an offline mode.

How It Works

In the default deployment model for Silvefrlight, an application is delivered through the Silverlight plug-in embedded in a web page and consequently accessed through the user's choice of browser. In this scenario, the user must be connected to the web site that serves up the application.

Silverlight 3 extends that deployment model and introduces support for installing a Silverlight application on your local desktop. After the application is installed, you can use your platform's traditional mechanism for launching an application (for example, double-clicking an icon on the Start menu or desktop in Windows) to launch and run the application. This model of local installation is also commonly known as the Out Of Browser (OOB) activation model for a Silverlight application.

In the process, you are no longer required to navigate to the application's source web site or open a browser window; nor do you have to be connected to a network. The application runs in its own window like any other native desktop installed application, providing the standard control mechanisms for that host window (Close, Minimize, Maximize, and so on).

Preparing the Application

The first step in enabling local installation for a Silverlight application is to supply the necessary installation settings in the Silverlight application manifest. Bring up the Project Properties page in Visual Studio for the Silverlight project, and you see an "Enable running application out of the browser" check box (see Figure 7-10).

Check that option, and then click the Out-of-Browser Settings button to open the Out-of-Browser Settings dialog for the project (see Figure 7-11).

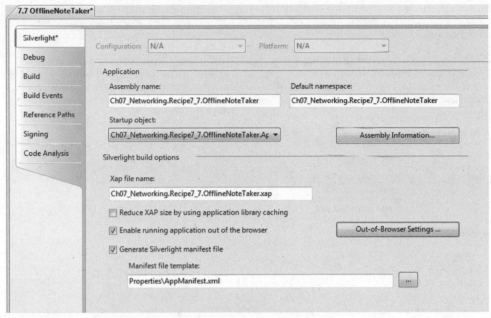

Figure 7-10. *Enabling out-of-browser activation in Visual Studio*

Figure 7-11. *Out-of-Browser Settings dialog*

The "Shortcut name" field provides a user-friendly name for the application when it's installed on the desktop, and the "Download description" field provides a more detailed description. The Use GPU Acceleration check box specifies whether the locally installed application uses GPU acceleration (if available).

The installation process also requires that you provide four images, with square dimensions of 16, 32, 48 and 128 pixels each. These must be in PNG image format and must be included in the project with the Content setting specified for each image in Visual Studio. To select the appropriate image, click the adjoining Browse button to select from images included in your project, as shown in Figure 7-12.

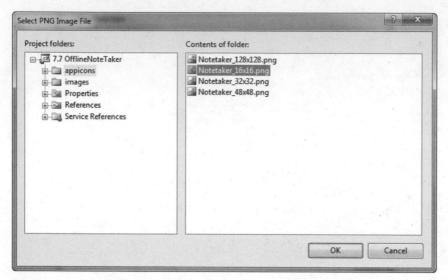

Figure 7-12. *Selecting out-of-browser icons*

You also specify the initial Width, Height, and the Window Title of the host window within which the locally installed application launches. Note that these setting are the initial launch settings only, and the application always launches in a host window of these dimensions. Although the user can resize the host window when the application launches, Silverlight 3 has no facility to remember those settings across launches; nor can you programmatically control these dimensions.

The settings specified in this process are stored as XML in a file named OutOfBrowserSettings.xml under the Properties folder in your Silverlight project. Listing 7-30 shows the contents of a sample OutOfBrowserSettings.xml file.

Listing 7-30. *Sample OutOfBrowserSettings.xml File*

```
<OutOfBrowserSettings ShortName="Offline NoteTaker" EnableGPUAcceleration="False"
                 ShowInstallMenuItem="True">
  <OutOfBrowserSettings.Blurb>Offline NoteTaker on your desktop;
  at home, at work or on the go.</OutOfBrowserSettings.Blurb>
  <OutOfBrowserSettings.WindowSettings>
    <WindowSettings Title="Offline NoteTaker" Height="595" Width="916" />
  </OutOfBrowserSettings.WindowSettings>
```

```
<OutOfBrowserSettings.Icons>
  <Icon Size="16,16">appicons/Notetaker_16x16.png</Icon>
  <Icon Size="32,32">appicons/Notetaker_32x32.png</Icon>
  <Icon Size="48,48">appicons/Notetaker_48x48.png</Icon>
  <Icon Size="128,128">appicons/Notetaker_128x128.png</Icon>
</OutOfBrowserSettings.Icons>
</OutOfBrowserSettings>
```

Installing the Application

If the installation settings are applied properly, you can bring up the Silverlight context menu on the application running in the browser. You see an option to locally install the application, as shown in Figure 7-13.

Figure 7-13. *Local installation menu option in the Silverlight context menu*

Selecting this option opens an installation options dialog. Figure 7-14 shows a sample.

Figure 7-14. *Installation options dialog for local installation of a Silverlight application*

Note the portions marked in bold in the dialog. The title provided in the application identity settings in the application manifest is used to identify the application, and the web URI (http://localhost in Figure 7-14, to indicate that the application is being delivered from the local web server) indicates the application's site of origin. The icon used in this dialog is the 128 x 128 pixel image provided in the application manifest.

After the application is installed, you can launch it directly from either the Start menu icon or the desktop shortcut added during the installation process.

To remove a locally installed application, you need to run the application, either locally or in-browser by visiting the application web site, and bring up the Silverlight context menu. When the application is installed locally, the context menu offers an option to remove the application from your machine (see Figure 7-15).

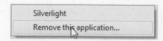

Figure 7-15. *Context menu option for local application removal*

Customizing the Installation Flow

The default mechanism of installing a Silverlight application through the context menu option may not always be a desirable choice. You may want to display a more visually appealing and slightly more obvious way of indicating to the user that the application can be locally installed. You may also want to have additional application logic tied to the process of the local installation. The `System.Windows.Application` class exposes some new APIs to help control programmatic installation.

With the appropriate installation settings present in the application manifest as described earlier, invoking the static method `Application.Install()` from your application code has the same effect as invoking the context menu option for local installation.

The `Application.InstallState` property also gives you the current install state of the application. It is of the enumeration type `System.Windows.InstallState` and can have the following values:

- `NotInstalled`: The current application has not been locally installed on the machine.

- `Installing`: Either `Application.Install()` has been invoked or the user selected the install option from the context menu, and the application is about to be locally installed.

- `Installed`: The currently running application is installed on the machine.

- `InstallFailed`: An attempt to install the application was made, but the attempt failed.

The `ApplicationInstallStateChanged` event is raised whenever the value of `Application.InstallState` changes from one state to another in this list.

Note that the `NotInstalled` and `Installed` states are not necessarily indicative of the current application being run in or out of browser. For instance, if you install an application locally but navigate to the same application again on the same machine and load it in-browser from its site of origin, the `InstallState` of the in-browser application instance reports Installed. To know if your application is being launched locally or in-browser, rely on the `Application.IsRunningOutOfBrowser` static property of type `Boolean`; it returns `true` when the application is running locally and `false` when it is in-browser.

One obvious use of these APIs is to display different UIs to the user depending on the current install state. As an example, see the XAML in Listings 7-31 and 7-32.

Listing 7-31. *OnlinePage.xaml*

```
<UserControl x:Class="Ch07_Networking.Recipe7_7.OfflineNoteTaker.OnlinePage"
    xmlns="http://schemas.microsoft.com/winfx/2006/xaml/presentation"
    xmlns:x="http://schemas.microsoft.com/winfx/2006/xaml"
    Width="400" Height="300">
    <Grid x:Name="LayoutRoot" Background="White">
```

```xml
    <Grid.RowDefinitions>
      <RowDefinition Height="Auto" />
      <RowDefinition Height="Auto" />
    </Grid.RowDefinitions>
      <TextBlock Text="I am running in-browser" Grid.Row="0"/>
    <Button x:Name="btnInstall" Grid.Row="1"
            Content="Install Application"
            Height="50"
            Width="150"
            Click="btnInstall_Click"/>
  </Grid>
</UserControl>
```

Listing 7-32. *LocalPage.xaml*

```xml
<UserControl x:Class="Ch07_Networking.Recipe7_7.OfflineNoteTaker.LocalPage"
             xmlns="http://schemas.microsoft.com/winfx/2006/xaml/presentation"
             xmlns:x="http://schemas.microsoft.com/winfx/2006/xaml"
             Width="400"
             Height="300">
  <Grid x:Name="LayoutRoot"
        Background="White">
    <TextBlock Text="I am running locally"/>
  </Grid>
</UserControl>
```

Listing 7-31 shows a XAML page named OnlinePage.xaml that you want to display when the application is running in-browser. Listing 7-32 shows LocalPage.xaml, which you want the same application to display when running locally.

To detach the application, write some code as shown here in the Click handler of the Button named btnInstall in Listing 7-31:

```csharp
private void btnInstall_Click(object sender, RoutedEventArgs e)
{
  if(Application.Current.InstallState == InstallState.NotInstalled)
    Application.Current.Install();
}
```

You check Application.InstallState; if it indicates that the code is currently running in-browser, you invoke the Install() method to locally install the application.

You also make an additional check in the Application.StartUp event handler and load the appropriate page:

```csharp
private void Application_Startup(object sender, StartupEventArgs e)
{
  if (Application.Current.IsRunningOutOfBrowser)
  this.RootVisual = new LocalPage();
```

```
  else
    this.RootVisual = new OnlinePage();
}
```

Figure 7-16 shows the in-browser and locally installed versions of such an application.

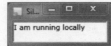

Figure 7-16. *A simple application UI running in-browser and locally installed*

We look at using the InstallState property and installation customization in more detail in this recipe's code sample.

Sensing Network Availability

When you are running a locally installed application, you may want to add application logic that allows the application to behave reasonably well in the absence of network connectivity.

Silverlight 3 adds support in the framework for sensing network connectivity. As network state changes during the lifetime of your application, you can handle the static NetworkAddressChanged event in the System.Net.NetworkInformation.NetworkChange class, to receive network-change notifications from the runtime. This event is raised any time any one of your computer's existing network interfaces goes through a network address change.

However, not all such notifications indicate unavailability of a network connection; they may indicate a transition from one valid network address to another. To determine if a valid network connection is available, in the event handler of the NetworkAddressChanged event (and anywhere else in your code), you can invoke the static GetIsNetworkAvailable() method in the System.Net. NetworkInformation.NetworkInterface class. This method returns true if a valid network connection is available or false if not.

Updating Locally Installed Applications

The new local installation deployment model also adds support for application-initiated self updates for application code. The related API lets you check for updates to the application code at the site of origin and asynchronously download the changes.

The Application.CheckAndDownloadUpdateAsync() method checks for any updates to the application code at the site of origin. If it finds updated code, the updated bits are downloaded to the local machine's application cache asynchronously. The Application.CheckAndDownloadUpdateCompleted event is raised when the download process completes or if the check reveals no changes. The CheckAndDownloadUpdatedCompletedEventArgs. UpdateAvailable property is set to true if updates were downloaded or false if no updates were available. To apply the updates, the user needs to restart the application.

Listing 7-33 shows a possible use of the application-update feature.

Listing 7-33. *Code to Update an Application with Changes*

```
private void Application_Startup(object sender, StartupEventArgs e)
{
  if(Application.Current.InstallState == InstallState.Installed
    && Application.Current.IsRunningOutOfBrowser &&
    NetworkInterface.GetIsNetworkAvailable())
  {
    Application.Current.CheckAndDownloadUpdateCompleted+=
      new CheckAndDownloadUpdateCompletedEventHandler((s,args)=>
    {
      if (args.UpdateAvailable)
      {
        MessageBox.Show("New updates are available for this application." +
          "Please restart the application to apply updates.","Update Status",
          MessageBoxButton.OK);
        this.RootVisual = new CheckUpdatePage();
      }
      else
        this.RootVisual = new MainPage();
    });
    Application.Current.CheckAndDownloadUpdateAsync();

  }
  else
    this.RootVisual = new MainPage();
}
```

As shown in Listing 7-33, you check to see if the application is running from a locally installed version out of the browser and has network connectivity. If so, you proceed to invoke CheckAndDownloadUpdatesAsync(). In the CheckAndDownloadUpdateCompleted handler, you check to see if updates are available. If there are updates, you display an appropriate message and use a different root visual to prevent the main application from running without the updates being applied.

Note that whether you want to enforce the download of an available update depends on application logic specified as shown in Listing 7-33. Should you choose to, you can let the user continue without applying the update, as long as your application can function as an older version without causing any errors.

The Code

The code sample for this recipe builds a simple note-taking application that allows the user to take notes that have a title and a body, and stores them on the server categorized by the date the note was taken. The application can also be installed locally; the user can operate the locally installed application even when disconnected from the network, by providing a local note store. The user can then synchronize the local note store with the server when network connectivity is restored.

Figure 7-17 shows the application running in-browser.

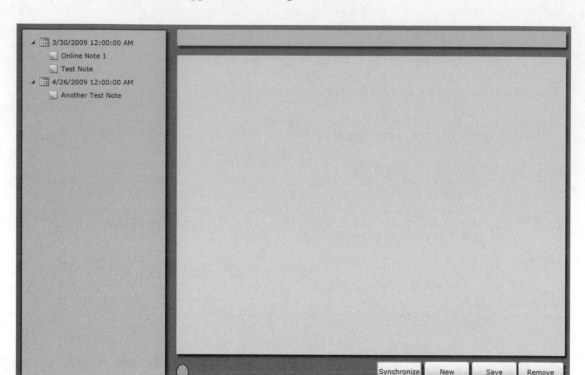

Figure 7-17. *NoteTaker application running in-browser*

The application displays the currently stored notes in a TreeView control, with the top-level nodes displaying the dates containing individual nodes for each note stored on that date. The user can use the buttons on the UI (from left to right) to, respectively, install the application locally, to synchronize any notes stored offline with the server version of notes data, create a new note, save a note, or remove a selected note. (Note that when you run the application locally installed, the install button is not displayed.) The small Ellipse to the left of the buttons is colored green to indicate network availability and red otherwise.

Figure 7-18 shows the application running from a locally installed state. The ellipse at the bottom of the window shows network availability (green when available, red when not).

A WCF service acts as the datasource for the application. The WCF service uses the file system to store notes. Each note file is named with the unique ID of the note and is stored in a folder named after the date the note was created, along with other notes that have the same creation date. We do not go through the details of the service implementation in this recipe, but you are encouraged to look at the sample code, as well as Recipe 7.1, for more details of WCF integration with Silverlight.

Figure 7-18. *NoteTaker application running locally installed with and without network connectivity*

Listing 7-34 shows the service contract definition as well as the data contract that defines the Note type.

Listing 7-34. *Service and Data Contracts for the Note Manager WCF Service in INoteManager.cs*

```
namespace Ch07_Networking.Recipe7_7.NoteManagerService
{
  [ServiceContract]
  public interface INoteManager
  {
    //Get all the dates for which we have notes stored
    [OperationContract]
    List<DateTime> GetDates();
    //Get all the notes for a specific date
    [OperationContract]
    List<Note> GetNotesForDate(DateTime ForDate);
```

```csharp
    //Add a note to the note store
    [OperationContract]
    void AddNote(Note note);

    //Remove a note from the note store
    [OperationContract]
    void RemoveNote(DateTime ForDate, string NoteID);
}

[DataContract]
public class Note
{
    //Unique ID for the note
    [DataMember]
    public string NoteID { get; set; }
    //When was the note created or last modified ?
    [DataMember]
    public DateTime LastModified { get; set; }
    //When was the note last synchronized ?
    [DataMember]
    public DateTime? LastSynchronized { get; set; }
    //Note title
    [DataMember]
    public string Title { get; set; }
    //Note body
    [DataMember]
    public string Body { get; set; }
}
}
```

Let's look at the UI of the application in XAML before we discuss the code. Listing 7-35 shows the XAML for MainPage.xaml.

Listing 7-35. *XAML for the NoteTaker Application UI in MainPage.xaml*

```xml
<UserControl xmlns="http://schemas.microsoft.com/winfx/2006/xaml/presentation"
            xmlns:x="http://schemas.microsoft.com/winfx/2006/xaml"
            xmlns:d="http://schemas.microsoft.com/expression/blend/2008"
            xmlns:mc="http://schemas.openxmlformats.org/markup-compatibility/2006"
            xmlns:controls=
        "clr-namespace:System.Windows.Controls;assembly=System.Windows.Controls"
            x:Class="Ch07_Networking.Recipe7_7.OfflineNoteTaker.MainPage"
            mc:Ignorable="d"
            xmlns:local="clr-namespace:Ch07_Networking.Recipe7_7.OfflineNoteTaker"
            xmlns:windows=
```

```xml
        "clr-namespace:System.Windows;assembly=System.Windows.Controls"
            DataContext="{Binding RelativeSource={RelativeSource Self}}">
<UserControl.Resources>

   <windows:HierarchicalDataTemplate x:Key="dtNoteItem">
     <Grid>
       <Grid.ColumnDefinitions>
         <ColumnDefinition Width="Auto" />
         <ColumnDefinition Width="Auto" />
       </Grid.ColumnDefinitions>
       <Image
  Source="/Ch07_Networking.Recipe7_7.OfflineNoteTaker;component/images/Note.png"
             Width="16"
             Height="16" />
       <TextBlock Text="{Binding Path=Title}" Grid.Column="1"
             HorizontalAlignment="Left" VerticalAlignment="Center"
                 Margin="5,0,0,0"/>
     </Grid>
   </windows:HierarchicalDataTemplate>


   <windows:HierarchicalDataTemplate
       ItemsSource="{Binding Path=Notes, Mode=OneWay}"
                               ItemTemplate="{StaticResource dtNoteItem}"
                               x:Key="dtDateItem">

   <Grid>
     <Grid.ColumnDefinitions>
       <ColumnDefinition Width="Auto" />
       <ColumnDefinition Width="Auto" />
     </Grid.ColumnDefinitions>
     <Image
  Source="/Ch07_Networking.Recipe7_7.OfflineNoteTaker;component/images/Date.png"
             Width="16"
             Height="16" />
     <TextBlock Text="{Binding Path=Date}"
                 Grid.Column="1"
                 HorizontalAlignment="Left"
                 VerticalAlignment="Center"
                 Margin="5,0,0,0" />
   </Grid>
   </windows:HierarchicalDataTemplate>

   <local:BoolToVisibilityConverter x:Key="REF_BoolToVisibilityConverter" />
</UserControl.Resources>
```

```
<Grid x:Name="LayoutRoot"
    Height="595"
    Width="916"
    Background="#FF737373">

<Grid.RowDefinitions>
  <RowDefinition Height="0.93*" />
  <RowDefinition Height="0.07*" />
</Grid.RowDefinitions>
<Grid.ColumnDefinitions>
  <ColumnDefinition Width="0.281*" />
  <ColumnDefinition Width="0.214*" />
  <ColumnDefinition Width="0.505*" />
</Grid.ColumnDefinitions>

<Grid Margin="0,0,8,5" HorizontalAlignment="Right"
      Grid.Row="2"
      Grid.Column="2">
  <Grid.ColumnDefinitions>
    <ColumnDefinition Width="Auto" />
    <ColumnDefinition Width="Auto" />
    <ColumnDefinition Width="Auto" />
    <ColumnDefinition Width="Auto" />
    <ColumnDefinition Width="Auto" />
  </Grid.ColumnDefinitions>
  <Button x:Name="btnInstall"
        Click="btnInstall_Click"
        Content="Install"
        Visibility="{Binding
    Converter={StaticResource REF_BoolToVisibilityConverter},
    ConverterParameter=reverse, Mode=OneWay, Path=Installed}"
        Margin="2,2,2,2"
        VerticalAlignment="Stretch"
        Grid.Column="0"
        HorizontalAlignment="Stretch"
        Width="75"
        Background="#FF092946">
    <Button.Effect>
      <DropShadowEffect />
    </Button.Effect>
  </Button>
```

```xml
<Button x:Name="btnSynchronize"
        Click="btnSynchronize_Click"
        Content="Synchronize"
        Visibility="{Binding
  Converter={StaticResource REF_BoolToVisibilityConverter},
  Mode=OneWay, Path=NetworkOn}"
        HorizontalAlignment="Stretch"
        Margin="2,2,2,2"
        VerticalAlignment="Stretch"
        Grid.Column="1"
        Width="75"
        Background="#FF092946">
  <Button.Effect>
    <DropShadowEffect />
  </Button.Effect>
</Button>
<Button Margin="2,2,2,2"
        Content="New"
        d:LayoutOverrides="Height"
        x:Name="btnNew"
        Click="btnNew_Click"
        Grid.Column="2"
        VerticalAlignment="Stretch"
        HorizontalAlignment="Stretch"
        Width="75"
        Background="#FF092946">
  <Button.Effect>
    <DropShadowEffect />
  </Button.Effect>
</Button>
<Button Margin="2,2,0,2"
        Content="Save"
        d:LayoutOverrides="Height"
        x:Name="btnSave"
        Click="btnSave_Click"
        Grid.Column="3"
        VerticalAlignment="Stretch"
        HorizontalAlignment="Stretch"
        Width="75"
        Background="#FF092946">
  <Button.Effect>
    <DropShadowEffect />
  </Button.Effect>
</Button>
```

```xml
        <Button x:Name="btnRemove"
                Click="btnRemove_Click"
                Content="Remove"
                HorizontalAlignment="Stretch"
                Margin="2,2,2,2"
                VerticalAlignment="Stretch"
                Grid.Column="4"
                Width="75"
                Background="#FF092946">
          <Button.Effect>
            <DropShadowEffect />
          </Button.Effect>
        </Button>
      </Grid>

      <Grid Grid.Column="1"
            Grid.Row="0"
            Grid.ColumnSpan="2">
        <Grid.RowDefinitions>
          <RowDefinition Height="0.077*" />
          <RowDefinition Height="0.923*" />
        </Grid.RowDefinitions>
        <TextBox Margin="8,8,8,8"
                 Text="{Binding Path=CurrentNote.Title, Mode=TwoWay}"
                 TextWrapping="NoWrap"
                 d:LayoutOverrides="Height"
                 Grid.ColumnSpan="1"
                 Background="#FFCDCDCD"
                 BorderBrush="#FF000000"
                 BorderThickness="0,0,0,0"
                 FontWeight="Bold"
                 MaxLength="150"
                 FontSize="12">
          <TextBox.Effect>
            <DropShadowEffect />
          </TextBox.Effect>
        </TextBox>
        <TextBox Margin="8,8,8,8"
                 Grid.Row="1"
                 Text="{Binding Path=CurrentNote.Body, Mode=TwoWay}"
                 TextWrapping="Wrap"
                 Background="#FFFFFC00"
                 BorderBrush="#FF000000"
                 BorderThickness="0,0,0,0"
                 AcceptsReturn="True"
                 FontSize="12">
```

```
    <TextBox.Effect>
      <DropShadowEffect />
    </TextBox.Effect>
  </TextBox>
</Grid>

<controls:TreeView Margin="8,8,8,8"
                   Grid.RowSpan="3"
                   x:Name="NotesTree"
                   ItemsSource="{Binding Path=NotesByDate, Mode=OneWay}"
                   ItemTemplate="{StaticResource dtDateItem}"
                   Background="#FFCDCDCD">
  <controls:TreeView.Effect>
    <DropShadowEffect />
  </controls:TreeView.Effect>
</controls:TreeView>

<Grid Margin="8,8,8,8" HorizontalAlignment="Left"
      Grid.Column="1"
      Grid.Row="1">

  <Ellipse x:Name="signNoNetwork"
           Fill="#FFFF0000"
           Stroke="#FF000000"
           Grid.Column="0"
           Visibility="{Binding Path=NetworkOn,Mode=OneWay,
   Converter={StaticResource REF_BoolToVisibilityConverter},
   ConverterParameter='reverse'}"
           Width="20"
           HorizontalAlignment="Right" />
  <Ellipse x:Name="signNetworkOn"
           Fill="#FF75FF00"
           Stroke="#FF000000"
           Grid.Column="0"
           Visibility="{Binding Path=NetworkOn,Mode=OneWay,
   Converter={StaticResource REF_BoolToVisibilityConverter}}"
           HorizontalAlignment="Right"
           Width="20" />
  </Grid>

  </Grid>
</UserControl>
```

The first thing to note in the XAML in Listing 7-35 is that the DataContext for the top level
UserControl is bound to the MainPage code-behind class using the RelativeSource.Self enumerated value.
This allows the rest of the UI to bind to properties defined directly on the MainPage class, without having to

resort to defining separate data-class types for the most part. For more details about RelativeSource binding, refer to Chapter 4.

The TreeView control instance named NotesTree displays currently stored notes. NotesTree. ItemsSource is bound to a property named NotesByDate of type ObservableCollection<TreeNodeData>, where TreeNodeData is a data class representing a top-level item in the TreeView. Listing 7-36 shows the TreeNodeData class.

Listing 7-36. *TreeNodeData Data Class in MainPage.xaml.cs*

```
//Represents a top level node (Date) in the tree view
//with children nodes (Note)
public class TreeNodeData : INotifyPropertyChanged
{
  public event PropertyChangedEventHandler PropertyChanged;

  private DateTime _Date = default(DateTime);

  public DateTime Date
  {
    get
    {
      return _Date;
    }

    set
    {
      if (value != _Date)
      {
        _Date = value;
        if (PropertyChanged != null)
          PropertyChanged(this, new PropertyChangedEventArgs("Date"));
      }

    }
  }


  private ObservableCollection<Note> _Notes =
    default(ObservableCollection<Note>);

  public ObservableCollection<Note> Notes
  {
    get
    {
      return _Notes;
    }
```

```
    set
    {
      if (value != _Notes)
      {
        _Notes = value;
        if (PropertyChanged != null)
          PropertyChanged(this, new PropertyChangedEventArgs("Notes"));
      }

    }
  }
}
```

Note that the `TreeNodeData` class is hierarchical in nature, in that each instance contains a `Date` property that defines the data at that level and a `Notes` property of type `ObservableCollection <Note>` that defines the data collection for the sublevel. Referring back to Listing 7-35, note the use of the `HierarchicalDataTemplate` type to define the UI for the top-level nodes of `NotesTree`.

A `HierarchicalDataTemplate` is an extension of the data-template type meant to be used with hierarchical data sets such as the ones defined by a collection of `TreeNodeData` instances. It provides for data-template chaining that lets you define data template for multiple levels of a hierarchical data set. In addition to binding a data item to a `HierarchicalDataTemplate`, you can set the `ItemTemplate` and `ItemsSource` properties of the template. The `HierarchicalDataTemplate` then applies the data template in the `ItemTemplate` property to each element in the collection bound to the `ItemsSource`.

In the example, `dtDateItem` is a `HierarchicalDataTemplate` containing the necessary XAML to display the dates as the top-level nodes; it is bound to `TreeNodeData`, defined in Listing 7-36. The `ItemTemplate` property on `dtDateItem` is set to use the `dtNoteItem` data template, whereas its `ItemsSource` is bound to the `TreeNodeData.Notes` property. This causes every `Note` instance in the `Notes` collection to use the `dtNoteItem` data template and be displayed as children to the corresponding date item in the `TreeView`.

Note that there is no system-enforced limit on this kind of chaining. Unlike in the example, if you need more levels in the hierarchy and you have a data structure that supports such nesting, you can use additional `HierarchicalDataTemplates` as children. When you reach a level at which you no longer need children items, you can resort to a simple `DataTemplate`.

The rest of the XAML is self-explanatory. The buttons on the UI serve different functions that we look at a moment when we explore the code-behind. The `tbxTitle` and `tbxBody` TextBoxes are bound to the Title and the Body properties of the `CurrentNote` property of the `MainPage` class, and the `signNoNetwork` and `signNetworkOn` ellipses are colored red and green and are both bound to the `MainPage.NetworkOn` property to be made visible conditionally depending on the value of the `NetworkOn` property. A `ValueConverter` converts bool to the `Visibility` type for these bindings.

Before we look at the main application code-behind, let's cover one more aspect of the sample. Because the application is designed to work seamlessly even in the absence of a network connection, it needs an interface to store and retrieve note data from local storage when the WCF service cannot be reached. To facilitate that, you create a class called `LocalNoteManagerClient`, shown in Listing 7-37. This class mirrors the service contract used on the WCF service, but it implements all the note data-management functionality using the isolated storage feature in Silverlight. To learn more about isolated storage, see Chapter 3.

Listing 7-37. *LocalNoteManagerClient Class for Local Note Management*

```
//Manages notes on the local client using Isolated Storage as the backing store
public class LocalNoteManagerClient
{
  #region INoteManager Members

  //gets all the dates
  public List<DateTime> GetDates()
  {
    IsolatedStorageFile AppStore =
      IsolatedStorageFile.GetUserStoreForApplication();
    //get all the existing folders - each folder represents a date
    //for which notes exist
    string[] val = AppStore.GetDirectoryNames();
    return AppStore.GetDirectoryNames().
      Select((sz) => DateTime.Parse(sz.Replace("_","/"))).ToList();


  }


  //gets all the notes stored in local storage for a specific date
  public ObservableCollection<Note> GetNotesForDate(DateTime ForDate)
  {
    ObservableCollection<Note> RetVal = new ObservableCollection<Note>();
    IsolatedStorageFile AppStore =
      IsolatedStorageFile.GetUserStoreForApplication();
    //get the folder corresponding to this date
    string DirPath = ForDate.ToShortDateString().Replace("/", "_");
    //if folder exists
    if (AppStore.DirectoryExists(DirPath))
    {
      //get all the files
      string[] FileNames = AppStore.
        GetFileNames(System.IO.Path.Combine(DirPath, "*.note"));

      foreach (string FileName in FileNames)
      {
        //open a file
        IsolatedStorageFileStream fs = AppStore.
          OpenFile(System.IO.Path.Combine(DirPath, FileName), FileMode.Open);
```

```
      //deserialize
      DataContractJsonSerializer serNote =
        new DataContractJsonSerializer(typeof(Note));
      //add to returned collection
      RetVal.Add(serNote.ReadObject(fs) as Note);
      //close file
      fs.Close();
    }
  }
  //return collection
  return RetVal;
}


//adds a note to local storage
public void AddNote(Note note)
{
  IsolatedStorageFile AppStore =
    IsolatedStorageFile.GetUserStoreForApplication();
  string DirPath = note.LastModified.ToShortDateString().Replace("/", "_");
  //if a directory for the note date does not exist - create one
  if (AppStore.DirectoryExists(DirPath) == false)
    AppStore.CreateDirectory(DirPath);


  string FilePath = string.Format("{0}\\{1}",
    DirPath, note.NoteID + ".note");

 //create file, serialize and store
    IsolatedStorageFileStream fs = AppStore.
      OpenFile(FilePath, FileMode.Create);
    DataContractJsonSerializer serNote =
      new DataContractJsonSerializer(typeof(Note));
    serNote.WriteObject(fs, note);
    fs.Close();
}


//removes a note from local storage
public void RemoveNote(DateTime ForDate, string NoteID)
{
  IsolatedStorageFile AppStore =
    IsolatedStorageFile.GetUserStoreForApplication();
  string FilePath = string.Format("{0}\\{1}",
    ForDate.ToShortDateString().Replace("/", "_"), NoteID + ".note") ;
```

```
    if (AppStore.FileExists(FilePath))
      AppStore.DeleteFile(FilePath);


  }

  #endregion
}
```

Now, let's look at the main application functionality, most of which is in the MainPage.xaml.cs code-behind class. Listing 7-38 shows the MainPage class.

Listing 7-38. *MainPage.xaml.cs Code-Behind Class for the Offline NoteTaker*

```
public partial class MainPage : UserControl, INotifyPropertyChanged
{
  public event PropertyChangedEventHandler PropertyChanged;
  //initialize to a blank note
  private Note _CurrentNote = new Note()
  {
    NoteID = Guid.NewGuid().ToString(), LastModified = DateTime.Now
  };
  //Tracks the currently selected/displayed note
  public Note CurrentNote
  {
    get
    {
      return _CurrentNote;
    }

    set
    {
      if (value != _CurrentNote)
      {
        _CurrentNote = value;
        if (PropertyChanged != null)
          PropertyChanged(this, new PropertyChangedEventArgs("CurrentNote"));
      }
    }
  }


  private ObservableCollection<TreeNodeData> _NotesByDate =
    default(ObservableCollection<TreeNodeData>);
  //Collection of TreeNodeData that binds to the TreeView to display saved notes
  public ObservableCollection<TreeNodeData> NotesByDate
```

```
{
  get
  {
    //initialize to a blank collection
    if (_NotesByDate == null)
      _NotesByDate = new ObservableCollection<TreeNodeData>();
    return _NotesByDate;
  }

  set
  {
    if (value != _NotesByDate)
    {
      _NotesByDate = value;
      if (PropertyChanged != null)
        PropertyChanged(this, new PropertyChangedEventArgs("NotesByDate"));
    }

  }
}
//Indicates if the app is running offline - used to bind to XAML
public bool Installed
{
  get
  {
    return Application.Current.InstallState == InstallState.Installed;
  }
}
//Indicates if network connectivity is available - used to bind to XAML
public bool NetworkOn
{
  get
  {
    return NetworkInterface.GetIsNetworkAvailable();
  }

}


public MainPage()
{
  InitializeComponent();
```

```csharp
    //listen for network connection/disconnection events
    NetworkChange.NetworkAddressChanged +=
        new NetworkAddressChangedEventHandler((s, a) =>
    {
        //update XAML bound property
        if (PropertyChanged != null)
            PropertyChanged(this, new PropertyChangedEventArgs("NetworkOn"));
        //refresh the treeview to display remote/local notes appropriately
        RefreshNotesView();
    });

    //Refresh notes treeview
    RefreshNotesView();

    //handle selection change in the notes treeview
    NotesTree.SelectedItemChanged +=
        new RoutedPropertyChangedEventHandler<object>((s, a) =>
    {
        if (a.NewValue is Note)
        {
            //set the CurrentNote property to the currently selected note
            CurrentNote = a.NewValue as Note;
        }
    });
}

//take the application offline
private void btnInstall_Click(object sender, RoutedEventArgs e)
{
    Application.Current.Install();
}

private void RefreshNotesView()
{
    //clear current bound collection
    NotesByDate.Clear();
    //reinitialize the CurrentNote
    CurrentNote = new Note()
    {
        NoteID = Guid.NewGuid().ToString(),
        LastModified = DateTime.Now
    };
```

```
//if we have network connectivity
if (NetworkOn)
{
  //use the WCF proxy
  NoteManagerClient client = new NoteManagerClient();
  //handle getting all the dates asynchronously
  client.GetDatesCompleted +=
    new EventHandler<GetDatesCompletedEventArgs>((sender, args) =>
  {

    foreach (DateTime dt in args.Result)
    {
      //create another instance of the WCF proxy
      NoteManagerClient client1 = new NoteManagerClient();
      //handle getting the notes for a date asynchronously
      client1.GetNotesForDateCompleted +=
        new EventHandler<GetNotesForDateCompletedEventArgs>((s, a) =>
      {
        //create a node for the date and add the notes to it
        NotesByDate.Add(
          new TreeNodeData()
          {
            Date = (DateTime)a.UserState,
            Notes = a.Result
          });
      });
      //get all the notes on the server for a specific date
      //pass in the date as user state
      client1.GetNotesForDateAsync(dt, dt);
    }
  });
  //get all the dates for which we have notes on the server
  client.GetDatesAsync();
}
else
{
  //create a client for local note management
  LocalNoteManagerClient client = new LocalNoteManagerClient();
  //Get all the dates
  List<DateTime> dates = client.GetDates();
  foreach (DateTime dt in dates)
  {
    //get the notes for that date
    ObservableCollection<Note> notesForDate = client.GetNotesForDate(dt);
```

```
        //add to the treeview
        NotesByDate.Add(
          new TreeNodeData()
          {
            Date = dt,
            Notes = notesForDate
          });
      }

    }
  }

  //handle the Save button
  private void btnSave_Click(object sender, RoutedEventArgs e)
  {
    if (NetworkOn)
    {
      //use the WCF proxy
      NoteManagerClient client = new NoteManagerClient();
      client.AddNoteCompleted +=
        new EventHandler<AsyncCompletedEventArgs>((s, a) =>
        {
          //refresh the treeview
          RefreshNotesView();
        });
      //add the new/updated note to the server
      client.AddNoteAsync(CurrentNote);
    }
    else
    {
      //use the local note manager
      LocalNoteManagerClient client = new LocalNoteManagerClient();
      //add the note
      client.AddNote(CurrentNote);
      //refresh the tree view
      RefreshNotesView();
    }

  }
```

```
//handle the New Button
private void btnNew_Click(object sender, RoutedEventArgs e)
{
  //reinitialize the CurrentNote
  CurrentNote = new Note()
  {
    NoteID = Guid.NewGuid().ToString(),
    LastModified = DateTime.Now
  };
}
//handle Remove button
private void btnRemove_Click(object sender, RoutedEventArgs e)
{
  //a valid existing note has to be selected
  if (CurrentNote == null ||
    NotesByDate.SelectMany((tnd)=>tnd.Notes).
    Where((nt)=>nt == CurrentNote).Count() > 0)

    return;

  if (NetworkOn)
  {
    //use the WCF proxy
    NoteManagerClient remoteClient = new NoteManagerClient();
    remoteClient.RemoveNoteCompleted +=
      new EventHandler<AsyncCompletedEventArgs>((s, a) =>
      {
        //refresh tree view
        RefreshNotesView();
      });
    //remove the note
    remoteClient.RemoveNoteAsync(CurrentNote.LastModified, CurrentNote.NoteID);
  }
  else
  {
    //use the local client
    LocalNoteManagerClient localClient = new LocalNoteManagerClient();
    //remove note
    localClient.RemoveNote(CurrentNote.LastModified, CurrentNote.NoteID);
    //refresh tree view
    RefreshNotesView();
  }

}
```

```
//handle Synchronize button
private void btnSynchronize_Click(object sender, RoutedEventArgs e)
{
  SynchronizeOfflineStore();
}
private void SynchronizeOfflineStore()
{
  LocalNoteManagerClient localClient = new LocalNoteManagerClient();


  //Notes that are on the server with LastModifiedDate <= LastSynchronizedDate
  //but are missing on the client, must have been deleted on the client
  List<Note> NotesDeletedOnClient =
    NotesByDate.SelectMany((tnd) => tnd.Notes).Distinct().
            Where((nt) => nt.LastSynchronized >= nt.LastModified).
            Except(localClient.GetDates().
        SelectMany((dt) => localClient.GetNotesForDate(dt)).
        Distinct()).ToList();
  //remove the deleted notes from the server
  foreach (Note nt in NotesDeletedOnClient)
  {
    NoteManagerClient remoteClient = new NoteManagerClient();
    remoteClient.RemoveNoteAsync(nt.LastModified, nt.NoteID);
  }
  //Notes that are on the client with LastModifiedDate <= LastSynchronizedDate
  //but are missing on the server, must have been deleted on the server
  List<Note> NotesDeletedOnServer =
    localClient.GetDates().
        SelectMany((dt) => localClient.GetNotesForDate(dt)).Distinct().
        Where((nt)=>nt.LastSynchronized >= nt.LastModified).Except(
    NotesByDate.SelectMany((tnd) => tnd.Notes).Distinct()).ToList();
  //remove the deleted notes from the client
  foreach (Note nt in NotesDeletedOnServer)
    localClient.RemoveNote(nt.LastModified, nt.NoteID);


  //get all the notes on the server that have not been synchronized with the
  //client. Since we are online, the notes represented in NotesByDate
  //constitute the server state
  List<Note> NotesOutOfSyncOnServer =
        NotesByDate.SelectMany((tnd) => tnd.Notes).Distinct().
            Where((nt) => nt.LastSynchronized == null ||
                nt.LastSynchronized < nt.LastModified).ToList();
```

```
//add the server side notes to the client
foreach (Note nt in NotesOutOfSyncOnServer)
{
  //set appropriate timestamps
  nt.LastSynchronized = DateTime.Now;
  nt.LastModified = nt.LastSynchronized.Value;
  localClient.AddNote(nt);
}

//get all the notes on the client that have not been synchronized with the
//server.
List<Note> NotesOutOfSyncOnClient =
      localClient.GetDates().
      SelectMany((dt) => localClient.GetNotesForDate(dt)).Distinct().
        Where((nt) => nt.LastSynchronized == null ||
          nt.LastSynchronized < nt.LastModified).ToList();

//add the client side notes to the server
foreach (Note nt in NotesOutOfSyncOnClient)
{
  NoteManagerClient remoteClient = new NoteManagerClient();
  //timestamps
  nt.LastSynchronized = DateTime.Now;
  nt.LastModified = nt.LastSynchronized.Value;
  remoteClient.AddNoteAsync(nt);
}
//refresh
RefreshNotesView();

  }
}
```

The MainPage class defines a few properties that are noteworthy. The NotesByDate property of type ObservableCollection<TreeNodeData> defines the entire note collection at any point in time, and the CurrentNote property defines the currently selected note in the UI. The Installed property wraps around Application.InstallState and returns true if its value is InstallState.Installed. The NetworkOn property wraps a call to NetworkInterface.GetIsNetworkAvailable() to indicate network availability.

You use the RefreshNotesView() method to load any existing notes in the constructor of the page. As shown in the definition of RefreshNotesView() in Listing 7-38, the NetworkOn property determines network availability. If a network connection is available, you use the WCF service proxy to access the note data and populate the NotesByDate collection, which in turn displays the data in the NotesTree TreeView. In the absence of a network connection, you use the LocalNoteManagerClient class to access the data from local storage and use it similarly.

■**Note** To create a network-unavailable state in your system, the easiest option is to turn of your network adapter. If you have multiple adapters on and connected, make sure you turn all of them off.

In the constructor, you also handle a few events. You attach a handler to the `NetworkChange.NetworkAddressChanged` event; in the event of a network state change, you update the UI by raising the `PropertyChanged` event and invoke `RefreshNotesView()` again to acquire the note data from the appropriate storage location. You also handle the `SelectedItemChanged` event on the `NotesTree` `TreeView` control to set the value of the `CurrentNote` property to the currently selected note.

The handlers for the `Click` events on `btnSave`, `btnRemove`, `btnNew`, and `btnInstall` are straightforward. In each of the first three handlers, you again use either the WCF service or local storage, depending on the state of network availability. And `btnInstall_Click()` is a simple wrapper to an invocation of `Application.Install()` that takes you through the local installation process, as described in the previous section.

The last piece of this recipe is the data-synchronization logic. Before we delve into it, note that this is merely a sample and the synchronization logic demonstrated here is implemented from scratch. If you are building a sizeable application, you should investigate other scalable and robust data-synchronization frameworks like the Microsoft Sync Framework. You can find more information about the Sync Framework at `http://msdn.microsoft.com/en-us/sync/default.aspx`.

The synchronization logic in this sample is invoked through handling the `Click` event of the `btnSynchronize` button on the UI and is encapsulated in the `SynchronizeOfflineStore()` method. Because the `Visibility` property of `btnSynchronize` is tied to network availability through a binding to the `NetworkOn` property, you are assured that this code is invoked only when the network is available.

The synchronization logic in `SynchronizeOfflineStore()` is straightforward. You first use the `LastModifiedDate` and `LastSynchronizedDate` properties on the `Note` instances to look for notes that have been deleted on one side of storage but still exist on the other side. The logic is simple: if a note exists on one side and has been synchronized more recently than it has been modified, but it does not exist on the other side, then it must have been deleted from the side on which it does not exist. You then delete that note from the side on which it currently exists.

Next, you look for notes on either side with a modification date more recent than the last synchronization date. These notes have been either added or updated, and the changes have not been synchronized. You invoke `AddNote()` on the appropriate storage service contract for these notes. The implementation of `AddNote()` on the WCF service and on `LocalNoteManagerClient` always creates a new note. If the data synchronization required an update of a note with partial changes to its data on one side, the complete note file is written again, but in effect it provides the desired result.

This takes care of propagating all the changes bidirectionally. On completion of this method, both data stores are synchronized.

7-8. Exchanging Data Between Silverlight Applications

Problem

You have two or more separate Silverlight applications composing parts of your overall web page, and you need these applications to exchange data with each other.

Solution

Use the local connection feature in Silverlight 3 to enable communication channels between these applications and facilitate cross-application data exchange.

How It Works

The local-connection feature in Silverlight 3 enables you to establish communication channels between two or more Silverlight applications on the same web page.

Receiver Registration

In this mode of communication, an application can act as a sender, a receiver or both. To register itself with the communication system as a receiver, the application has to provide a unique identity, using which messages are directed to it. This identity is a combination of a receiver name (expressed using a string literal) and the application's web domain name, and needs to yield a unique identifier within the scope of the containing page.

To register itself as a receiver, the application can create an instance of the LocalMessageReceiver class in System.Windows.Messaging, passing in the receiver name as shown here:

```
LocalMessageReceiver ThisReceiver = new LocalMessageReceiver("ThisReceiverName");
```

Using this version of the constructor registers the receiver name as unique in its originating domain—other receivers in the page can have the same receiver name, as long as they belong to different domains. Registering in this fashion also allows the receiver to receive messages only from those senders on the page that originate from the same domain as the receiver.

The local-connection API offers granular control over the message receiving heuristics. An overloaded constructor for the LocalMessageReceiver class is made available with the following signature:

```
public LocalMessageReceiver(string receiverName,
    ReceiverNameScope nameScope, IEnumerable<string> allowedSenderDomains);
```

The ReceiverNameScope enumeration used in the second parameter has two possible values. ReceiverNameScope.Domain has the same effect as the previous constructor, requiring that the receiver name be unique within all receivers on the page originating from the same domain. However, ReceiverNameScope.Global requires that the receiver name be unique across all receivers on the page, regardless of their originating domain name.

The third parameter, allowedSenderDomains, enables extending the list of sender domains from which the receiver can receive messages beyond the receiver's originating domain. Setting it to LocalMessageReceiver.AnyDomain allows the receiver to receive messages from any sender on the page, regardless of the sender's originating domain. You can also set allowedSenderDomains to a selective list of the domains from which you want to allow message receipt. The following code snippet shows a receiver being registered as unique across all receiver domains on the page, with the abilty to receive messages from senders in two specific domains (http://www.microsoft.com and http://www.silverlight.net):

```
LocalMessageReceiver ThisReceiver =
    new LocalMessageReceiver("ThisReceiverName",
      ReceiverNameScope.Global, new List<string>{ "http://www.microsoft.com",
        "http://www.silverlight.net"});
```

Receiving Messages

When a receiver has been registered, you need to attach a handler to the `LocalMessageReceiver`. `MessageReceived` event to receive messages and then call the `LocalMessageReceiver.Listen()` method to start listening for incoming messages asynchronously. Here is an example:

```
ThisReceiver.MessageReceived +=
  new EventHandler<MessageReceivedEventArgs>((s, e) =>
  {
    string Msg = e.Message;

    //do something with the received message
    ...
    //optionally send a response message
    string ResponseMessage = PrepareResponseMessage();
    e.Response = ResponseMessage;

  });
ThisReceiver.Listen();
```

The `MessageReceivedEventArgs.Message` property contains the string message that was sent. When your code has processed the message, you can also send a response message back to the sender, in the `MessageReceivedEventArgs.Response` property. The response message follows the same rules as any other local connection message: it must be a string that is less than 1 MB in size. We talk more about the `Response` property in a bit.

Sending Messages

A sender application has no explicit registration process. To send messages to a receiver, you must construct an instance of `System.Windows.Messaging.LocalMessageSender` as shown here, passing in the receiver name and the receiver domain as parameters:

```
LocalMessageSender ThisSender =
  new LocalMessageSender("SomeReceiver","http://localhost");
```

You can also pass the value `LocalMessageSender.Global` as the second parameter. In that case, the system attempts to deliver the message to all receivers with the specified name on the page, regardless of what domain they belong to.

Local-connection messages are always sent asynchronously using the `LocalMessageSender.SendAsync()` method, as show here:

```
string MyMessage;
//create a message here
ThisSender.SendAsync(MyMessage);
```

As you can see, the message being sent is of type `String`. In the current version of Silverlight, only string messages less than 1 MB can be sent and received using the local-connection system. This may seem limiting initially. But consider that you can express any Silverlight data structure in either JSON or XML strings using the Silverlight-supplied serialization mechanisms like data-contract serialization or LINQ to XML XDocument serialization. With that in mind, this approach allows you to build fairly effective and rich data-exchange scenarios.

After the message has been sent, or an attempt to do so fails, the LocalMessageSender.SendCompleted event is raised by the runtime. You need to handle the event to do any error handling or response processing, as shown here:

```
ThisSender.SendCompleted +=
  new EventHandler<SendCompletedEventArgs>((s, e) =>
  {
    if (e.Error != null)
    {
      //we had an error sending the message - do some error reporting here
    }
    else if (e.Response != null)
    {
      //the receiver sent a response - process it here
    }
  });
```

Because the send operation is asynchronous and returns immediately, the local-connection system does not raise a direct exception to the sender if a send operation is unsuccessful. Consequently, in the SendCompleted event handler, you should check the SendCompletedEventArgs.Error property of type Exception for any exception that may be raised in the event of an unsuccessful send attempt. In case of a send-related error, this may be set to an instance of System.Windows.Messaging.SendFailedException.

In the send was successful, the SendCompletedEventArgs.Response may contain a response message, depending on whether the receiver sent a response back.

Request-Response

The Response property is interesting in that it lets you establish a rudimentary request-response correlation using the local connection.

There are no limitations on an application being both a sender and a receiver at the same time. For an application to be both a sender and a receiver, you must perform the appropriate receiver registration and then create both a LocalMessageSender and a LocalMessageReceiver instance, as shown in the previous sections. One way to send responses from a receiver back to a sender would be a role-reversal strategy, where the receiver acts as a sender and the sender acts as a receiver for the response message path. However, because the order of message delivery is not guaranteed in the current implementation, this puts the onus on you to include additional details in the message body, should you need to correlate a sent message with its response.

The Response properties on the MessageReceivedEventArgs and MessageSentEventArgs types let you circumvent that. MessageReceivedEventArgs also contains a Message property and a SenderDomain property, which let the receiver application accurately pair the right response with the incoming message. MessageSentEventArgs also contains Message and Response properties, in addition to information about the receiver that sent the response through the ReceiverDomain and ReceiverName properties. This allows the sender to accurately pair a receiver response with a specific sent message.

The Code

The code sample for this recipe builds on the sample from Recipe 4-4. That recipe has a simple spending analysis application for a family; the expenditures for different categories are maintained in a DataGrid and also graphed in a bar graph as a percentage of the total. The application allows you to change the spending in each category to different values and watch the graph change accordingly. It also lets you drag any bar in the graph using your mouse and watch the corresponding value change in the DataGrid, maintaining the same total.

To adapt that sample to this recipe, you break it into two separate applications. The application named 7.8 HomeExpenseWorksheet encapsulates the DataGrid-based worksheet portion of the sample, whereas the 7.8 HomeExpenseGraph application encapsulates the bar-graph implementation. You then use local-connection-based messaging between the two applications to implement the necessary communication.

Figure 7-19 shows the applications hosted on the same page.

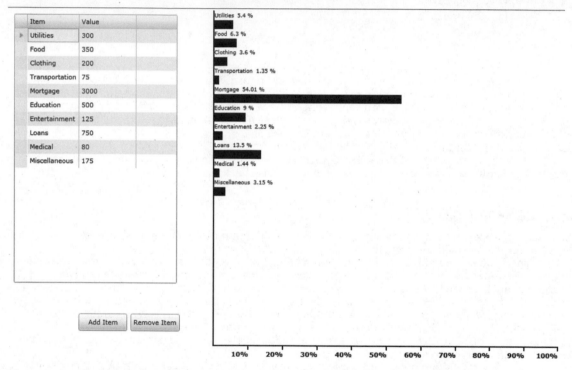

Figure 7-19. *The expense worksheet and the expense graph applications on the same page*

Before we discuss the local-connection-related code changes, let's quickly look at the XAML for the expense worksheet application, shown in Listing 7-39.

Listing 7-39. *XAML for the HomeExpenseWorksheet Application in MainPage.xaml*

```xaml
<UserControl x:Class="Ch07_Networking.Recipe7_8.HomeExpenseWorksheet.MainPage"
            xmlns="http://schemas.microsoft.com/winfx/2006/xaml/presentation"
            xmlns:x="http://schemas.microsoft.com/winfx/2006/xaml"
            xmlns:data=
    "clr-namespace:System.Windows.Controls;assembly=System.Windows.Controls.Data"
            Width="300"
            Height="600">


  <Grid x:Name="LayoutRoot"
        Background="White">
    <Grid.RowDefinitions>
      <RowDefinition Height="0.8*" />
      <RowDefinition Height="0.2*" />
    </Grid.RowDefinitions>
    <data:DataGrid HorizontalAlignment="Stretch"
                   Margin="8,8,8,8"
                   VerticalAlignment="Stretch"
                   HeadersVisibility="All"
                   Grid.Row="0"
                   x:Name="dgSpending"
                   AutoGenerateColumns="False"
                   CellEditEnded="dgSpending_CellEditEnded">
      <data:DataGrid.Columns>
        <data:DataGridTextColumn Header="Item"
                                 Binding="{Binding Item,Mode=TwoWay}" />
        <data:DataGridTextColumn Header="Value"
                                 Width="100"
                                 Binding="{Binding Amount,Mode=TwoWay}" />
      </data:DataGrid.Columns>
    </data:DataGrid>
    <StackPanel Orientation="Horizontal"
                Grid.Row="1"
                HorizontalAlignment="Right">
      <Button x:Name="btnAddItem"
              Margin="3,3,3,3"
              Height="30"
              Width="85"
              Content="Add Item"
              Click="btnAddItem_Click" />
```

```
    <Button x:Name="btnRemoveItem"
            Margin="3,3,3,3"
            Height="30"
            Width="85"
            Content="Remove Item"
            Click="btnRemoveItem_Click" />
   </StackPanel>
  </Grid>
</UserControl>
```

The code in bold in Listing 7-39 shows the only notable changes made to the XAML, as adapted from Recipe 4-4. As you can see, you add two buttons: clicking btnAddItem adds a new row to the DataGrid, and clicking btnRemoveItem removes the currently selected item from the DataGrid. You also attach a handler to the CellEditEnded event of the DataGrid. We cover the details of the implementations of these handlers later in this section.

The XAML for the HomeExpenseGraph application remains largely the same as the comparable part in Recipe 4-4. We do not cover it again here, but we urge you to refer back to the code samples or to Recipe 4-4.

To start with the local-connection implementation, recall that messages are string based. However, strings are cumbersome to work with; so, you define the application messages as a custom CLR type named Message and then resort to serialization to convert Message instances to string representations before sending them. Listing 7-40 shows the Message type.

Listing 7-40. *The Message Custom Type in Messages.cs*

```
using System.Collections.Generic;
using System.IO;
using System.Runtime.Serialization;
using System.Text;

namespace Ch07_Networking.Recipe7_8.SD
{
  public enum MessageType
  {
    ItemRemoved,
    ItemsValueChanged
  }

  [DataContract]
  public class Message
  {
    [DataMember]
    public MessageType MsgType { get; set; }
    [DataMember]
    public List<Spending> Items { get; set; }
```

```
    public static string Serialize(Message Msg)
    {
      DataContractSerializer dcSer = new DataContractSerializer(typeof(Message));
      MemoryStream ms = new MemoryStream();
      dcSer.WriteObject(ms, Msg);
      ms.Flush();
      string RetVal = Encoding.UTF8.GetString(ms.GetBuffer(), 0, (int)ms.Length);
      ms.Close();
      return RetVal;
    }

    public static Message Deserialize(string Msg)
    {
      DataContractSerializer dcSer = new DataContractSerializer(typeof(Message));
      MemoryStream ms = new MemoryStream(Encoding.UTF8.GetBytes(Msg));
      Message RetVal = dcSer.ReadObject(ms) as Message;
      ms.Close();
      return RetVal;
    }
  }
}
```

You handle two kinds of messages in the local connection implementation between the worksheet and the graph applications, as defined in the MessageType enumeration. The MessageType.ItemRemoved value indicates a message that communicates the removal of one or more items; it is sent from the worksheet to the graph only when rows are removed from the worksheet. The MessageType.ItemsValueChanged typed message can be sent in either direction when the values of one or more items change—either in the worksheet for an existing item or a newly added item through user edits, or in the graph when the user drags a bar to resize it.

The Message class contains the MessageType and a list of Items with changed values or a list of Items that were removed. It also defines two static methods that use DataContractSerialization to serialize and deserialize instances of the Message type to and from a string representation. Note that you have the Message class attributed as a DataContract with the Mistyped and Items properties attributed as DataMember.

An individual data item for the application is defined as a class named Spending, and a custom class named SpendingCollection deriving from ObservableCollection<Spending> defines the data collection that initially populates the worksheet and the graph. These classes are not changed much from Recipe 4-4, so we do not cover them in detail. Listing 7-41 shows these classes.

Listing 7-41. *Data Classes in DataClasses.cs*

```
using System.Collections.ObjectModel;
using System.ComponentModel;
using System.Linq;
using System.Runtime.Serialization;
```

```csharp
namespace Ch07_Networking.Recipe7_8.SD
{
  public class SpendingCollection : ObservableCollection<Spending>
  {
    public SpendingCollection()
    {
      this.Add(new Spending
      {
        ParentCollection = this,
        ID = 1,
        Item = "Utilities",
        Amount = 300
      });
      this.Add(new Spending
      {
        ParentCollection = this,
        ID = 2,
        Item = "Food",
        Amount = 350
      });
      this.Add(new Spending
      {
        ParentCollection = this,
        ID = 3,
        Item = "Clothing",
        Amount = 200
      });
      this.Add(new Spending
      {
        ParentCollection = this,
        ID = 4,
        Item = "Transportation",
        Amount = 75
      });
      this.Add(new Spending
      {
        ParentCollection = this,
        ID = 5,
        Item = "Mortgage",
        Amount = 3000
      });
```

```
      this.Add(new Spending
      {
        ParentCollection = this,
        ID = 6,
        Item = "Education",
        Amount = 500
      });
      this.Add(new Spending
      {
        ParentCollection = this,
        ID = 7,
        Item = "Entertainment",
        Amount = 125
      });
      this.Add(new Spending
      {
        ParentCollection = this,
        ID = 8,
        Item = "Loans",
        Amount = 750
      });
      this.Add(new Spending
      {
        ParentCollection = this,
        ID = 9,
        Item = "Medical",
        Amount = 80
      });
      this.Add(new Spending
      {
        ParentCollection = this,
        ID = 10,
        Item = "Miscellaneous",
        Amount = 175
      });
    }

  public double Total
  {
    get
    {
      return this.Sum(spending => spending.Amount);
    }
  }
}
```

```
[DataContract]
public class Spending : INotifyPropertyChanged
{

  public event PropertyChangedEventHandler PropertyChanged;
  internal void RaisePropertyChanged(PropertyChangedEventArgs e)
  {
    if (PropertyChanged != null)
    {
      PropertyChanged(this, e);
    }
  }

  public override int GetHashCode()
  {
    return ID.GetHashCode();
  }

  public override bool Equals(object obj)
  {
    return (obj is Spending) ? this.ID.Equals((obj as Spending).ID) : false;
  }

  SpendingCollection _ParentCollection = null;

  public SpendingCollection ParentCollection
  {
    get { return _ParentCollection; }
    set
    {
      _ParentCollection = value;
      if (ParentCollection != null)
      {
        foreach (Spending sp in ParentCollection)
          sp.RaisePropertyChanged(new PropertyChangedEventArgs("Amount"));
      }
    }
  }

  private int _ID = default(int);
  [DataMember]
  public int ID
  {
    get
```

```
    {
      return _ID;
    }

    set
    {
      if (value != _ID)
      {
        _ID = value;
        if (PropertyChanged != null)
          PropertyChanged(this, new PropertyChangedEventArgs("ID"));
      }
    }
  }
}

private string _Item;
[DataMember]
public string Item
{
  get { return _Item; }
  set
  {
    string OldVal = _Item;
    if (OldVal != value)
    {
      _Item = value;
      RaisePropertyChanged(new PropertyChangedEventArgs("Item"));

    }
  }
}

private double _Amount;
[DataMember]
public double Amount
{
  get { return _Amount; }
  set
  {
    double OldVal = _Amount;
    if (OldVal != value)
    {
      _Amount = value;
```

```
        if (ParentCollection != null)
        {
          foreach (Spending sp in ParentCollection)
            sp.RaisePropertyChanged(new PropertyChangedEventArgs("Amount"));
        }
      }
    }
  }
 }
}
```

The only changes worth noting are the addition of an ID property to the Spending class to uniquely identify it in a collection, and the overrides for GetHashCode() and Equals() to facilitate locating or comparing spending instances based on their IDs. The changes are noted in bold in Listing 7-41.

Now, let's look at the application code. Listing 7-42 lists the code-behind for the worksheet application.

Listing 7-42. *The MainPage Code-Behind in MainPage.xaml.cs for the HomeExpenseWorksheet Application*

```csharp
using System;
using System.Collections.Generic;
using System.Windows;
using System.Windows.Controls;
using System.Windows.Messaging;
using Ch07_Networking.Recipe7_8.SD;

namespace Ch07_Networking.Recipe7_8.HomeExpenseWorksheet
{
  public partial class MainPage : UserControl
  {
    //data source
    SpendingCollection SpendingList = new SpendingCollection();
    //create a sender
    LocalMessageSender WorksheetSender =
      new LocalMessageSender("SpendingGraph",
        LocalMessageSender.Global);
    //create a receiver
    LocalMessageReceiver WorksheetReceiver =
      new LocalMessageReceiver("SpendingWorksheet",
        ReceiverNameScope.Global, LocalMessageReceiver.AnyDomain);

    public MainPage()
    {
      InitializeComponent();
```

```csharp
//bind data
dgSpending.ItemsSource = SpendingList;

//handle message receipt
WorksheetReceiver.MessageReceived+=
    new EventHandler<MessageReceivedEventArgs>((s,e) =>
{
    //deserialize message
    Message Msg = Message.Deserialize(e.Message);
    //if item value changed
    if (Msg.MsgType == MessageType.ItemsValueChanged)
    {
        //for each item for which value has changed
        foreach (Spending sp in Msg.Items)
        {
            //find the corrsponding item in the data source and replace value
            SpendingList[SpendingList.IndexOf(sp)] = sp;
        }
    }
});

//handle send completion
WorksheetSender.SendCompleted +=
    new EventHandler<SendCompletedEventArgs>((s, e) =>
{
    //if error
    if (e.Error != null)
    {
        //we had an error sending the message - do some error reporting here
    }
    //if there was a response
    else if (e.Response != null)
    {
        //the receiver sent a response - process it here
    }
});

//start listening for incoming messages
WorksheetReceiver.Listen();
}
```

```
    //handle add row button click
    private void btnAddItem_Click(object sender, RoutedEventArgs e)
    {
      //add a new Spending instance to the data source
      SpendingList.Add(new Spending() { ParentCollection = SpendingList });
    }

    //handle a cell edit
    private void dgSpending_CellEditEnded(object sender,
      DataGridCellEditEndedEventArgs e)
    {
      //send a message
      WorksheetSender.SendAsync(Message.Serialize(
        new Message()
        {
          //message type - Item value changed
          MsgType = MessageType.ItemsValueChanged,
          //the changed Spending instance
          Items = new List<Spending> { e.Row.DataContext as Spending }
        }));
    }

    //remove the selected item
    private void btnRemoveItem_Click(object sender, RoutedEventArgs e)
    {
      //if there is a selected row
      if (dgSpending.SelectedItem != null)
      {
        //get the corresponding Spending instance
        Spending target = dgSpending.SelectedItem as Spending;
        //remove it from the data source
        SpendingList.Remove(target);
        //send a message
        WorksheetSender.SendAsync(Message.Serialize(
        new Message()
        {
          //message type - Item Removed
          MsgType = MessageType.ItemRemoved,
          //the item that was removed
          Items = new List<Spending> { target }
        }));
      }
    }
  }
}
```

As you can see, you start by creating a `LocalMessageSender` and a `LocalMessageReceiver` instance, respectively, named `WorksheetSender` and `WorksheetReceiver`, as members of the code-behind class. `WorksheetSender` is created to let you send messages to a receiver named `SpendingGraph`, which is globally unique across all receivers on the page. `WorksheetReceiver` registers this application as a receiver named `SpendingWorksheet`, again with a global namescope, and prepared to receive incoming messages from senders in any domain.

During construction, you attach handlers to `WorksheetReceiver.MessageReceived` and `WorksheetSender.SendCompleted`. In the `MessageReceived` handler, you deserialize the incoming message and then process it. You only handle messages of type `MessageType.ItemsValueChanged`, because these are the only types of messages the HomeExpenseGraph application can generate. As a part of the processing, if you do receive `Spending` instances that have changed, you replace them accordingly in the expense worksheet datasource. In the `SendCompleted` handler, you show a skeletal set of statements for handling error conditions and response messages—we leave it as an exercise for you to implement error handling and response correlation as needed.

In the `Click` event handler for the `Button` named `btnAddItem`, you add a new `Spending` item to the datasource. However, you do not immediately send a message to the HomeExpenseGraph application, because the `Spending` item still does not have any meaningful data. Instead, you use the `CellEditEnded` event handler to send item-change notifications. In that handler, you construct a new `Message` instance with the changed `Spending` item as the only item in the `Message.Items` collection, and you set the `MsgType` property to `MessageType.ItemsValueChanged`. You then serialize the message and send it through the `WorksheetSender.SendAsync()` method.

In the `Click` handler for `btnRemoveItem`, you first remove the `Spending` instance bound to the selected `DataGrid` row from the datasource collection. Then, you use the same approach to serialize and send a `Message` instance, with the `MsgType` property set to `MessageType.ItemRemoved`.

Let's look at the HomeExpenseGraph application. Listing 7-43 shows the code-behind for the `MainPage` in that application.

Listing 7-43. *The MainPage Code-Behind in MainPage.xaml.cs for the HomeExpenseGraph Application*

```
using System;
using System.Collections.Generic;
using System.Windows;
using System.Windows.Controls;
using System.Windows.Input;
using System.Windows.Messaging;
using System.Windows.Shapes;
using Ch07_Networking.Recipe7_8.SD;

namespace Ch07_Networking.Recipe7_8.HomeExpenseGraph
{
  public partial class MainPage : UserControl
  {
    //variables to enable mouse interaction
    private bool MouseLeftBtnDown = false;
    private bool Dragging = false;
    Point PreviousPos;
    //data source
    SpendingCollection SpendingList = null;
```

```
//create a sender
LocalMessageSender GraphSender =
  new LocalMessageSender("SpendingWorksheet",
    LocalMessageSender.Global);
//create a receiver
LocalMessageReceiver GraphReceiver =
 new LocalMessageReceiver("SpendingGraph",
   ReceiverNameScope.Global, LocalMessageReceiver.AnyDomain);

public MainPage()
{
  InitializeComponent();

  SpendingList = this.Resources["REF_SpendingList"] as SpendingCollection;
  //handle property changed for each Spending - this is used to send item
  //value changed messages
  foreach (Spending sp in SpendingList)
  {
    sp.PropertyChanged +=
      new System.ComponentModel.
        PropertyChangedEventHandler(Spending_PropertyChanged);
  }
  //handle message receipts
  GraphReceiver.MessageReceived +=
    new EventHandler<MessageReceivedEventArgs>((s, e) =>
  {
    //deserialize message
    Message Msg = Message.Deserialize(e.Message);
    //if value changed
    if (Msg.MsgType == MessageType.ItemsValueChanged)
    {
      //for each changed Spending instance
      foreach (Spending sp in Msg.Items)
      {
        //if it exists
        if (SpendingList.Contains(sp))
        {
          //replace it with the changed one
          SpendingList[SpendingList.IndexOf(sp)] = sp;
        }
        else
        {
          //add the new one
          SpendingList.Add(sp);
        }
```

```
          //handle property changed
          sp.PropertyChanged +=
            new System.ComponentModel.
              PropertyChangedEventHandler(Spending_PropertyChanged);
          //force a recalc of the bars in the graph
          sp.ParentCollection = SpendingList;
        }
      }
      //item removed
      else if (Msg.MsgType == MessageType.ItemRemoved)
      {
        foreach (Spending sp in Msg.Items)
        {
          //unhook the event handler
          SpendingList[SpendingList.IndexOf(sp)].PropertyChanged
            -= Spending_PropertyChanged;
          //remove from data source
          SpendingList.Remove(sp);
        }
        //force a recalc of the bars in the graph
        if (SpendingList.Count > 0)
          SpendingList[0].ParentCollection = SpendingList;

      }
    });

    //start listening for incoming messages
    GraphReceiver.Listen();
}
void Spending_PropertyChanged(object sender,
    System.ComponentModel.PropertyChangedEventArgs e)
{
    //send a message
    GraphSender.SendAsync(
      Message.Serialize(
          new Message
          {
            //changed item
            Items = new List<Spending> { sender as Spending },
            //message type - item value changed
            MsgType = MessageType.ItemsValueChanged
          }));

}
```

```csharp
        private void Rectangle_MouseMove(object sender, MouseEventArgs e)
        {
          if (MouseLeftBtnDown)
          {
            Rectangle rect = (Rectangle)sender;
            if (Dragging == false)
            {
              Dragging = true;
              rect.CaptureMouse();
            }

            Point CurrentPos = e.GetPosition(sender as Rectangle);
            double Moved = CurrentPos.X - PreviousPos.X;
            if (rect.Width + Moved >= 0)
            {
              rect.Width += Moved;
            }
            PreviousPos = CurrentPos;
          }
        }

        private void Rectangle_MouseLeftButtonDown(object sender,
          MouseButtonEventArgs e)
        {
          MouseLeftBtnDown = true;
          PreviousPos = e.GetPosition(sender as Rectangle);
        }

        private void Rectangle_MouseLeftButtonUp(object sender,
          MouseButtonEventArgs e)
        {
          Rectangle rect = (Rectangle)sender;
          if (Dragging)
          {
            Dragging = false;
            rect.ReleaseMouseCapture();
          }
          MouseLeftBtnDown = false;
        }
      }
    }
```

As before, this application needs to both send and receive messages. As shown in Listing 7-43, you create instances of LocalMessageSender and LocalMessageReceiver such that this application can receive messages from the worksheet application and send messages to it as well.

In the constructor, after the datasource is bound, you handle the `PropertyChanged` event for each item in the collection. The `PropertyChanged` event is raised whenever the user drags a bar within the graph; and if you look at the handler for the `PropertyChanged` event, note that you send a message to the other application indicating thus action.

You also handle the `MessageReceived` event as before. In the handler, you handle messages of both types—where item values are changed and where items are removed.

If an item value changes, you check to see if the item that changed already exists or was newly created in the worksheet application and does not exist in the datasource for this application. In it is an existing item, you replace it with the changed item; and if it is a new item, you add it to the collection. You also attach a handler to the `Spending` item so that you can track changes to it in this application. Finally, you set the `Spending.ParentCollection` property to the datasource to which it was added to in which it was replaced. If you look at the definition of the `Spending` type in Listing 7-41, you see that this forces a property-change notification for all the items in the datasource. The bar graph displays the spending as percentages of the total, and this causes the bar graph's bar widths to be recalculated based on the new values.

If an item is removed, you first unattach the `PropertyChanged` event handler from the item that was removed and then remove it from the datasource collection. When the removals are complete, you force a similar recalculation of the bar widths based on the new percentages.

The rest of the code handles mouse events to enable user adjustments of the bars and is covered in Recipe 4-4.

CHAPTER 8

■ ■ ■

Integrating Rich Media

If you are a developer at a digital content producer of any kind, you probably have already built or are thinking of building applications that integrate video, audio, or other kinds of digital media with the resulting end-user experience. The ability to integrate rich media into web applications is one of the strongest and most publicized features of Silverlight, and it is the focus of the recipes in this chapter.

Silverlight supports playing Windows Media Video from version 7 through version 9, including the Windows Media implementation of the Society of Motion Picture and Television Engineers (SMPTE) VC-1 high-definition video standard, as well as H.264 encoded media contained in an MP4 container structure, extending video format support to MP4 video as well as other MP4-derived container s such as H.264 encoded QuickTime video.

Silverlight also supports MPEG Layer-3 (or MP3) audio and audio encoded in the Advanced Audio Coding (AAC) format, but it is currently limited to the AAC LC variant for two-channel stereo sound only.

Silverlight supports playing both client-side and server-side playlists. Silverlight supports media acquisition over the HTTP and HTTPS protocols. You can use the Microsoft Media Server (MMS) protocol, Real Time Streaming Protocol (RTSP), or RTSP using TCP (RTSPT) for media access, but Silverlight falls back to using HTTP when it encounters these protocol schemes. Silverlight also supports accessing media through either progressive download or streaming mechanisms.

In this chapter, we discuss recipes that showcase the various media capabilities of Silverlight, especially those of a type named MediaElement that is central to Silverlight-based media integration. Along the way, you will build a video player that evolves incrementally over the recipes to highlight specific features. Although we focus on media-related types, APIs, and techniques, we assume that you are already familiar with the fundamentals of the programming model, XAML-based UI design, data binding, control design, and networking. Consequently, in explaining the code in the recipes in this chapter, we purely focus on the media-related aspects and rely on you to understand the aforementioned concepts wherever they are used. If you have not covered these topics in this book or elsewhere, we advise you to read Chapters 2, 3, 4, 5, and 7, which help you prepare for the recipes in this chapter.

8-1. Adding Video to a Page

Problem

You want to play some video on your page.

Solution

Add a System.Windows.Controls.MediaElement to the page, and use a System.Windows.Media.VideoBrush to render the video.

How It Works

At the heart of enabling rich media in Silverlight applications is an object called MediaElement from the System.Windows.Controls namespace. MediaElement behaves like a datasource for rich media in your application—you place a MediaElement in your XAML and connect your code to the media by specifying an URI for the actual media source. The MediaElement then starts playing the media on your page. MediaElement supports playing both video and audio, in the formats mentioned in the chapter's introduction.

Using MediaElement

MediaElement implements various properties and events to allow fine-grained control of media playback. Here are some examples:

- You can track and control the progress of play and respond to various stages of download and buffering.

- You can set up various properties to control media playback, such as autoplay, volume, muting, and stretching.

- You can respond to embedded timeline markers in the media to take custom actions.

We look at the MediaElement API in more details in the next recipe when we build a complete player.

This code snippet shows the MediaElement being used in XAML:

```
<MediaElement
  Source="http://localhost/SLBook/Ch08_RichMedia/Media/SuperSpeedway.wmv"
  AutoPlay="True" x:Name="medElem" Opacity="0.0"/>
```

The Source property points to the source of the media. In this case the source is pointing directly to a Windows Media Video file that is progressively downloaded over HTTP. The AutoPlay property determines if the media starts playing immediately. When set to True, for progressive download scenarios, the media starts playing almost immediately. In the case of streamed video, the media starts playing when a specified amount is buffered locally. When set to False, the MediaElement.Start() method needs to be invoked to start playing the media. You learn more about progressive download and streaming in later recipes.

VideoBrush

MediaElement renders video by default in a rectangular shape determined by the Height and the Width properties of the MediaElement. However, you may need to implement more complex designs, such as rendering video bounded by a shape like a Rectangle or a control like the Border. Silverlight defines a type called VideoBrush that can be connected to a MediaElement instance and then used to fill a shape or a control in the XAML with video.

This XAML snippet shows an example:

```
<Border CornerRadius="5,5,5,5" HorizontalAlignment="Stretch"
        VerticalAlignment="Stretch" BorderBrush="Black" BorderThickness="3">
  <Border.Background>
    <VideoBrush SourceName="medElem" Stretch="Fill"/>
  </Border.Background>
</Border>
```

This snippet uses a Border to bound the video and uses the VideoBrush to render the video as the Border's background. The SourceName property of the VideoBrush points to the name of the MediaElement to use, and the Stretch property determines how the video is stretched to fill the area being painted with the VideoBrush.

Note that because the MediaElement renders the video itself, using a VideoBrush this way would normally cause the video to be displayed twice on your UI. The traditional approach is to hide the MediaElement's default rendering and choose to use that of the VideoBrush. Because the VideoBrush can be used any place where any other kind of brush can be, this approach gives you more control over where and how to display the video in the overall UI. We show how to hide the MediaElement later in the recipe's code.

If the Stretch property is set to None, the video is set to play, maintaining its original resolution and aspect ratio. This means that, depending on the dimensions of the container control in which the VideoBrush is rendering, the rendered video may be clipped. Figure 8-1 shows a 720p video clip playing in a Border with Height set to 400 and Width also set to 400, and the Stretch property value of the VideoBrush set to None.

Figure 8-1. *720p video playing in 400×400 container with Stretch=None*

As you can see, the video maintains its original resolution of 1280~TMS720 and its original aspect ratio of 16:9 as evident from the cropping.

If the Stretch property is set to Fill, the VideoBrush scales the video to fill the container exactly. The height and width are scaled independently to exactly match the height and the width of the container. This can cause the video to distort because the original aspect ratio is changed to fit the aspect ratio determined by the dimensions of the container. If the container dimensions match the video's aspect ratio, you can avoid this. Figure 8-2 shows the result of Stretch set to Fill for a 16:9 clip playing inside a 400~TMS400 Border. Note the obvious distortion in the video resulting from the scaling of 16:9 to 1:1.

Figure 8-2. *16:9 clip playing in a 400~TMS400 container with Stretch=Fill*

When Stretch is set to Uniform, the video is scaled to fit completely along both of its dimensions within the container, but the aspect ratio is preserved as well. Unless the dimensions of the container result in an aspect ratio matching that of the video, the video does not completely fill the container along one of the dimensions. Figure 8-3 shows an example. If you compare Figure 8-3 to Figure 8-1, you see that in an attempt to maintain the aspect ratio, the video has expanded beyond the available height of the container; the text visible in Figure 8-1 is no longer visible.

Figure 8-3. *16:9 clip playing in a 400✕400 container with Stretch=Uniform*

The last available setting for Stretch is UniformToFill. When set, this causes the video to scale and completely fill the container, while maintaining the original aspect ratio. The result is that the video gets clipped along one of its dimensions, unless the container is exactly of the same aspect ratio. Figure 8-4 shows an example.

Figure 8-4. *16:9 clip playing in a 400×400 container with Stretch=UniformToFill*

The Code

The code sample for this recipe plays a progressively downloaded 720p video clip. Listing 8-1 shows the XAML.

Listing 8-1. *XAML for the Page Playing the Media*

```
<UserControl x:Class="Ch08_RichMedia.Recipe8_1.MainPage"
    xmlns="http://schemas.microsoft.com/winfx/2006/xaml/presentation"
    xmlns:x="http://schemas.microsoft.com/winfx/2006/xaml"
    Width="400" Height="225">
    <Grid x:Name="LayoutRoot" Background="White">
    <MediaElement
    Source="http://localhost/SLBook/Ch08_RichMedia/Media/Amazon_1080.wmv"
      AutoPlay="True" x:Name="medElem" Opacity="0.0"/>
      <Border HorizontalAlignment="Stretch"
            VerticalAlignment="Stretch" BorderBrush="Black" BorderThickness="3">
        <Border.Background>
          <VideoBrush SourceName="medElem" Stretch="Fill"/>
        </Border.Background>
      </Border>
  </Grid>
</UserControl>
```

The page has a `Width` of 400 and a `Height` of 225, providing an aspect ratio of 16:9. The `Border` stretches to fill the entire page, and the `VideoBrush`'s `Stretch` property is set to `Fill`. This setup preserves the original aspect ratio of the clip.

Note that in order to avoid the video being displayed twice, you set `MediaElement.Opacity` to 0, so that you only see the video being rendered through the `VideoBrush` inside the `Border`.

Figure 8-5 shows the output.

Figure 8-5. *Video playing on a page*

8-2. Creating a Complete Video Player

Problem

You want to develop a video player with the following features:

- Standard play controls like play, pause, and stop

- Seek features like forward and rewind

- Volume control

- A video menu

- Multiple playing videos such as picture-in-picture

- Download and play progress notifications

Solution

Build a UI that provides elements to control these features and utilize the `MediaElement` API to implement the necessary code for the UI function.

How It Works

The `MediaElement` type exposes a rich API that makes it easy to implement most of the listed features in a fairly straightforward way. Let's start by taking a look at parts of this API. We continue to cover this API across some of the other recipes later in this chapter as well.

Acquiring Media

MediaElement can acquire media through both progressive download and streaming methods. All media players have historically supported the download-and-play mechanism of playing media, where the entire media is first downloaded to the client before play can be started. However, this is cumbersome and time consuming, especially for large media files, because the user has to wait to start watching until the download has completed.

With the advancement of storage file-format technologies in most of the modern media file formats, including Windows Media, it is now possible for most types of media to be played almost instantaneously. With this feature, called *progressive download*, a player starts playing the media as soon as the first few seconds of the media are downloaded, while the download continues in the background. Progressive download is carried over HTTP, and any modern web server, including Microsoft Internet Information Services (IIS), can be used as a media server.

Streaming is another technique used to deliver media to a player. Streaming does not require downloading the media file locally, and it is well suited for scenarios involving either live or on-demand broadcasts to a large population of viewers.

This recipe uses progressive download as the media-acquisition technique for the code sample shown later. We discuss streaming in Recipe 8-3.

To have a MediaElement progressively download and play media, you can point the Source property to the HTTP location of the media in XAML, as shown in Recipe 8-1. You can obviously do this in code as well, in scenarios where the URI is possibly only known to you at runtime.

Alternatively. you can use the MediaElement.SetSource() method in your code to specify the media to be played. One overload of SetSource() accepts a System.IO.Stream, which is suited for the scenario where you decide to acquire the media through some other mechanism rather than have the MediaElement handle the download. When you acquire the media file, you can create a Stream around it (using a more concrete type like System.IO.FileStream) and pass it to SetSource().

The second overload of SetSource() accepts an instance of the System.Windows.Media.MediaStreamSource type. The MediaStreamSource type is actually a way to plug a video container file format into Silverlight, for which the MediaElement does not come with a built-in parser. Video container file formats and related specifications are complex topics, and consequently a treatment of MediaStreamSource implementations is outside the scope of this book.

When the Source is set by either mechanism, for progressive download scenarios the MediaElement immediately starts to download the media. The MediaElement.DownloadProgressChanged event is raised repeatedly as the download progresses. The MediaElement.DownloadProgress property reports the download progress as a percentage value (actually a double between 0 and 1 that you can convert to percentage) that you can use to track and report the download progress in the DownloadProgressChanged event handler.

Controlling Media Play

As the media downloads, the MediaElement starts to play the media as soon as enough is available to play the first few frames, provided the MediaElement.AutoPlay property is set to True. If not, you have the option of using MediaElement.Play() in your code to start play. MediaElement also exposes Pause() and Stop(), which you can use to pause and stop a playing media stream. If a media-control function like Play() or Pause() is issued before enough media is downloaded to start playing, the command is internally queued by MediaElement and executed after playing starts.

MediaElement States

As the MediaElement goes through the various states of acquiring and playing media, the MediaElement. CurrentState property of type MediaElementState reflects the current state of the media. Table 8-1 lists the possible values and meanings.

Table 8-1. *Various MediaElementState Values and Their Meanings*

Value	Meaning
Closed	This is the default state of a MediaElement into which no media has been loaded.
Opening	This is the first state that occurs when the MediaElement tries to load a new media source. For a valid source, the MediaElement state moves on to Buffering if MediaElement.AutoPlay is set to True or to Stopped if it is not.
Buffering	This is the state when the MediaElement is buffering content.
Playing	This is the state when the MediaElement is playing media.
Paused	This is the state when currently loaded media has been paused by invoking MediaElement.Pause().
Stopped	This state reflects stopped media and can be achieved by calling MediaElement.Stop() for playing media. This is also the state at the beginning after the media is opened, when MediaElement.AutoPlay is set to False, and at the end when the media has reached its end and the MediaElement.Source has not been changed.

MediaElement raises the CurrentStateChanged event every time a state change happens between the states in Table 8-1. If you need to respond to any of these state changes, check the value of MediaElement.CurrentState in a handler for this event and take appropriate action. MediaElement raises a MediaOpened event after the media has been loaded successfully and is about to play. It also raises MediaFailed for a failure to load and play media, and MediaEnded when the media has finished playing.

Seeking Within the Media

When the media has been opened and the MediaOpened event has been raised, the MediaElement. NaturalDuration property of type System.Windows.Duration provides the total length of the media in time. The time value is contained in the Duration.TimeSpan property. Note that in certain cases like live streams, this value can be TimeSpan.Zero, because there is no way to know the duration of a live stream. We cover this scenario in Recipe 8-3.

The MediaElement.Position property of type TimeSpan determines the position within the media at any given time. Initially, this is set to TimeSpan.Zero. As the MediaElement plays the media, the MediaElement.Position property is updated continuously to reflect the current position. You can set the value of Position to any valid TimeSpan value between TimeSpan.Zero and MediaElement.NaturalDuration.TimeSpan. This positions the MediaElement at that time point in the media accordingly. To rewind, this value would need to be less than the current position, and vice versa for forwarding the media.

Volume

MediaElement.Volume provides the current volume as a double value between 0.0 and 1.0, with the default setting being 0.5. You can set this property to any value in that range to control the volume. The IsMuted property when set to True mutes the audio completely.

The Code

The code sample for this recipe builds a video player utilizing all the features discussed in the previous section, as well as concepts around programming model fundamentals, controls, and networking explored in earlier chapters in the book and mentioned in the introduction to this chapter. Figure 8-6 shows the full player user interface.

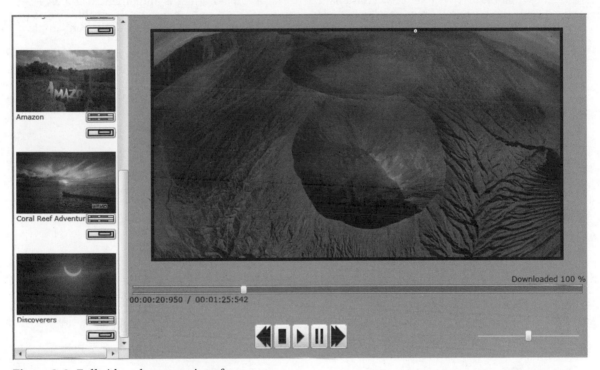

Figure 8-6. *Full video player user interface*

Installing the Sample Code

The sample for this recipe uses progressively downloaded media. To enable this approach, you need to either install or have access to a web server like IIS. The code samples expect all the media to reside under a virtual directory structure <*servername*>/SLBook/Media. We use a locally installed IIS server, and consequently the <*servername*> is localhost. After you create the virtual directory structure, you can acquire the media used in the samples as free downloads from http://www.microsoft.com/windows/windowsmedia/musicandvideo/hdvideo/contentshowcase.aspx. Note that we use the 1080p version of the videos whenever available. The following media files are used in the samples:

- Amazon_1080.wmv

- AdrenalineRush.wmv

- Alexander_Trailer_1080p.wmv

- Amazing_Caves_1080.wmv

- Coral_Reef_Adventure_1080.wmv

- Discoverers_1080.wmv

The sample application acquires the list of available media through a Windows Communication Foundation (WCF) service named MediaLocationProvider.svc, which reads this information from a file named Locations.xml stored in its App_Data folder. We do not discuss the implementation of the MediaLocationProvider WCF service in this chapter. MediaLocationProvider is implemented as a WCF service using the WCF web programming model to return XML data, and we discuss this technique, as well as how to consume it using a WebClient, in Chapter 7. We also encourage you to look at the sample code to review MediaLocationProvider's source.

Listing 8-2 shows a sample Locations.xml.

Listing 8-2. *A Sample locations.xml*

```xml
<?xml version="1.0" encoding="utf-8" ?>
<MediaLocations>
  <MediaLocation>
    <Description>Adrenaline Rush</Description>
    <Uri>http://localhost/SLBook/Ch08_RichMedia/Media/AdrenalineRush.wmv</Uri>
    <ImageUri>
      http://localhost/SLBook/Ch08_RichMedia/Media/AdrenalineRush_Thumb.jpg
    </ImageUri>
  </MediaLocation>
  <MediaLocation>
    <Description>Alexander</Description>
    <Uri>http://localhost/SLBook/Ch08_RichMedia/Media/Alexander_Trailer_1080p.wmv
    </Uri>
    <ImageUri>
    http://localhost/SLBook/Ch08_RichMedia/Media/Alexander_Trailer_1080p_Thumb.jpg
    </ImageUri>
  </MediaLocation>
</MediaLocations>
```

Each <MediaLocation> entry includes three children elements. The <Description> element provides a short description for the media, the <Uri> element points to the actual download location for the media, and the <ImageUri> element points to a JPEG image that represents a thumbnail of the video. You can change the entries in this file to accommodate your own virtual directory structures, server locations, and media files.

The Player Code

Listing 8-3 shows a type named MediaMenuData that maps to an instance of the MediaLocation information shown in Listing 8-2.

Listing 8-3. *MediaMenuData Type Declaration*

```
using System;
using System.ComponentModel;

namespace Ch08_RichMedia.Recipe8_2
{
  public class MediaMenuData : INotifyPropertyChanged
  {
    public event PropertyChangedEventHandler PropertyChanged;
    private object _Description;
    public object Description
    {
      get { return _Description; }
      set
      {
        _Description = value;
        if (PropertyChanged != null)
          PropertyChanged(this, new PropertyChangedEventArgs("Description"));
      }
    }
    private object _MediaPreview;
    public object MediaPreview
    {
      get { return _MediaPreview; }
      set
      {
        _MediaPreview = value;
        if (PropertyChanged != null)
          PropertyChanged(this, new PropertyChangedEventArgs("MediaPreview"));
      }
    }
    private Uri _MediaLocation;
    public Uri MediaLocation
    {
      get { return _MediaLocation; }
      set
      {
        _MediaLocation = value;
```

```
      if (PropertyChanged != null)
      {
        PropertyChanged(this, new PropertyChangedEventArgs("MediaLocation"));
      }
    }
  }
 }
}
```

Let's look at the player user interface next. Listing 8-4 shows the XAML.

Listing 8-4. *XAML for the Player User Interface*

```
<UserControl x:Class="Ch08_RichMedia.Recipe8_2.MainPage"
    xmlns="http://schemas.microsoft.com/winfx/2006/xaml/presentation"
    xmlns:x="http://schemas.microsoft.com/winfx/2006/xaml"
    xmlns:vsm="clr-namespace:System.Windows;assembly=System.Windows"
    xmlns:local="clr-namespace:Ch08_RichMedia.Recipe8_2"
    Width="920" Height="547"
    xmlns:Ch08_RichMedia_Recipe8_2=
"clr-namespace:Ch08_RichMedia.Recipe8_2;assembly=Ch08_RichMedia.Recipe8_2.PlrCntls"
    >
  <UserControl.Resources>
    <!-- Data Template for displaying a media menu item-->
    <DataTemplate x:Key="dtMediaMenuItem">
      <Grid Height="140" Width="160" Margin="0,8,0,8">
        <Grid.RowDefinitions>
          <RowDefinition Height="0.7*" />
          <RowDefinition Height="0.3*" />
        </Grid.RowDefinitions>
        <Grid.ColumnDefinitions>
          <ColumnDefinition Width="0.7*"/>
          <ColumnDefinition Width="0.3*" />
        </Grid.ColumnDefinitions>
        <Image HorizontalAlignment="Stretch"
              VerticalAlignment="Stretch" Stretch="Fill"
              Source="{Binding MediaPreview}" Grid.Row ="0"
              Grid.ColumnSpan="2"/>
        <TextBlock TextAlignment="Left" HorizontalAlignment="Stretch"
              VerticalAlignment="Stretch" Grid.Row="1"
              Text="{Binding Description}" Grid.Column="0"/>
```

```xml
        <Grid Grid.Row="1" Grid.Column="1">
          <Grid.RowDefinitions>
            <RowDefinition Height="0.4*" />
            <RowDefinition Height="0.2*" />
            <RowDefinition Height="0.4*" />
          </Grid.RowDefinitions>
          <Button Grid.Row="0" x:Name="btnPlayFull" Click="PlayFull_Click"
                  Tag="{Binding}" HorizontalAlignment="Center">
            <Button.Content>
              <Path Stretch="Fill" StrokeLineJoin="Round"
                        Stroke="#FF000000"
                        Data="M 120,9.15527e-005L 149.937,
                          9.15527e-005L 149.937,19.9361L 120,
                          19.9361L 120,9.15527e-005 Z M 120,
                          6.04175L 149.812,6.04175M 120,
                          14.0417L 149.937,14.0417M 123.417,
                          0.991364L 131.167,0.991364L 131.167,
                          4.88376L 123.417,4.88376L 123.417,
                          0.991364 Z M 135.125,1.00012L 142.875,
                          1.00012L 142.875,4.89246L 135.125,
                          4.89246L 135.125,1.00012 Z M 123.542,
                          15.035l 131.292,15.035L 131.292,
                          18.9274L 123.542,18.9274L 123.542,
                          15.035 Z M 135.25,15.0438L 143,
                          15.0438L 143,18.9362L 135.25,18.9362L 135.25,
                          15.0438 Z "/>
            </Button.Content>
          </Button>
          <Button Grid.Row="2" x:Name="btnPlayPIP" Click="PlayPIP_Click"
                  Tag="{Binding}" HorizontalAlignment="Center">
            <Button.Content>
              <Path Stretch="Fill" StrokeThickness="2"
                        StrokeLineJoin="Round" Stroke="#FF000000"
                        Data="M 120,39.8333L 149.917,
                          39.8333L 149.917,59.9167L 120,
                          59.9167L 120,39.8333 Z M 132.917,
                          42.8333L 146.667,42.8333L 146.667,
                          52.6667L 132.917,52.6667L 132.917,
                          42.8333 Z "/>
            </Button.Content>
          </Button>
        </Grid>
      </Grid>
    </DataTemplate>
```

```xml
<!--Control template for a media menu item -->
<ControlTemplate x:Key="ctMediaMenuListBoxItem" TargetType="ListBoxItem">
  <Grid>
    <vsm:VisualStateManager.VisualStateGroups>
      <vsm:VisualStateGroup x:Name="SelectionStates">
        <vsm:VisualState x:Name="Unselected"/>
        <vsm:VisualState x:Name="SelectedUnfocused">
          <Storyboard/>
        </vsm:VisualState>
        <vsm:VisualState x:Name="Selected">
          <Storyboard/>
        </vsm:VisualState>
      </vsm:VisualStateGroup>
      <vsm:VisualStateGroup x:Name="FocusStates">
        <vsm:VisualStateGroup.Transitions>
        </vsm:VisualStateGroup.Transitions>
        <vsm:VisualState x:Name="Unfocused"/>
        <vsm:VisualState x:Name="Focused"/>
      </vsm:VisualStateGroup>
      <vsm:VisualStateGroup x:Name="CommonStates">
        <vsm:VisualStateGroup.Transitions>
          <vsm:VisualTransition GeneratedDuration="00:00:00.2000000"
                                To="MouseOver"/>
          <vsm:VisualTransition From="MouseOver"
                                GeneratedDuration="00:00:00.2000000"/>
        </vsm:VisualStateGroup.Transitions>
        <vsm:VisualState x:Name="MouseOver">
          <Storyboard>
            <ColorAnimationUsingKeyFrames BeginTime="00:00:00"
                  Duration="00:00:00.0010000"
                  Storyboard.TargetName="brdrMouseOverIndicator"
                  Storyboard.TargetProperty=
                  "(Border.BorderBrush).(SolidColorBrush.Color)">
              <SplineColorKeyFrame KeyTime="00:00:00" Value="#FF126AB3"/>
            </ColorAnimationUsingKeyFrames>
            <ColorAnimationUsingKeyFrames BeginTime="00:00:00"
                  Duration="00:00:00.0010000"
                  Storyboard.TargetName="brdrMouseOverIndicator"
                  Storyboard.TargetProperty=
                      "(Border.Background).(SolidColorBrush.Color)">
              <SplineColorKeyFrame KeyTime="00:00:00" Value="#FF7FDDE6"/>
            </ColorAnimationUsingKeyFrames>
          </Storyboard>
        </vsm:VisualState>
```

```xml
                <vsm:VisualState x:Name="Normal"/>
              </vsm:VisualStateGroup>
          </vsm:VisualStateManager.VisualStateGroups>
          <Border CornerRadius="2,2,2,2" BorderThickness="3,3,3,3"
                  x:Name="brdrMouseOverIndicator"
                  Background="#007FDDE6" BorderBrush="#00000000">
            <ContentPresenter/>
          </Border>

      </Grid>
    </ControlTemplate>
    <Style x:Key="STYLE_MediaMenuListBoxItem" TargetType="ListBoxItem">
      <Setter Property="Template"
              Value="{StaticResource ctMediaMenuListBoxItem}"/>
    </Style>
</UserControl.Resources>

<!--Player UI -->
<Grid x:Name="LayoutRoot"
      Background="#FFA2A2A2" Height="Auto" Width="Auto">
  <Grid.RowDefinitions>
    <RowDefinition Height="0.752*"/>
    <RowDefinition Height="0.248*"/>
  </Grid.RowDefinitions>
  <Grid.ColumnDefinitions>
    <ColumnDefinition Width="0.2*"/>
    <ColumnDefinition Width="0.8*"/>
  </Grid.ColumnDefinitions>
  <Grid Grid.Row="0" Grid.Column="1">
    <Grid.RowDefinitions>
      <RowDefinition Height="0.05*" />
      <RowDefinition Height="0.9*" />
      <RowDefinition Height="0.05*" />
    </Grid.RowDefinitions>
    <Grid.ColumnDefinitions>
      <ColumnDefinition Width="0.05*"/>
      <ColumnDefinition Width="0.9*"/>
      <ColumnDefinition Width="0.05*"/>
    </Grid.ColumnDefinitions>
    <!--Main Display-->
    <Border x:Name="displayMain"
            VerticalAlignment="Stretch" Grid.Column="1" Grid.Row="1"
            HorizontalAlignment="Stretch" BorderThickness="5,5,5,5"
            BorderBrush="#FF000000" >
```

767

```
      <Border.Background>
        <VideoBrush SourceName="mediaelemMain" Stretch="Fill"
                    x:Name="vidbrushMain" />
      </Border.Background>
    </Border>
    <!--Picture in Picture Display-->
    <Grid Grid.Column="1" Grid.Row="1">
      <Grid.RowDefinitions>
        <RowDefinition Height="0.025*" />
        <RowDefinition Height="0.35*" />
        <RowDefinition Height="0.625*" />
      </Grid.RowDefinitions>
      <Grid.ColumnDefinitions>
        <ColumnDefinition Width="0.635*"/>
        <ColumnDefinition Width="0.35*"/>
        <ColumnDefinition Width="0.015*"/>
      </Grid.ColumnDefinitions>
      <Border Grid.Column="1" Grid.Row="1" HorizontalAlignment="Stretch"
              VerticalAlignment="Stretch"
              MouseLeftButtonUp="displayPIP_MouseLeftButtonUp"
              x:Name="displayPIP" BorderThickness="2,2,2,2"
              BorderBrush="#FF000000" Visibility="Collapsed">
        <Border.Background>
          <VideoBrush SourceName="mediaelemPIP"
                      Stretch="Fill" x:Name="vidbrushPIP"/>
        </Border.Background>
      </Border>
      <Grid HorizontalAlignment="Stretch" Margin="8,8,8,8"
            Grid.RowSpan="1" Grid.Column="1" Grid.Row="1"
            x:Name="buttonsPIP" Visibility="Collapsed" >
        <Grid.RowDefinitions>
          <RowDefinition Height="0.1*"/>
          <RowDefinition Height="0.25*"/>
          <RowDefinition Height="0.1*"/>
          <RowDefinition Height="0.25*"/>
          <RowDefinition Height="0.3*"/>
        </Grid.RowDefinitions>
        <Grid.ColumnDefinitions>
          <ColumnDefinition Width="0.749*"/>
          <ColumnDefinition Width="0.176*"/>
          <ColumnDefinition Width="0.075*"/>
        </Grid.ColumnDefinitions>
```

```
    <Button Margin="0,0,0,0" Grid.RowSpan="1" Grid.Row="1"
            Grid.ColumnSpan="1" Grid.Column="1"
            x:Name="btnClosePIP" Click="btnClosePIP_Click"
             >
      <Button.Content>
        <Path x:Name="Path" Stretch="Fill" StrokeThickness="2"
              StrokeLineJoin="Round" Stroke="#FF000000" Fill="#FFE91111"
              Data="M 110.5,75.7635L 113.209,
              72.9631L 133.396,92.4865L 130.687,95.2869L 110.5,
              75.7635 Z M 130.801,73.4961L 133.393,76.4048L 112.425,
              95.0872L 109.833,92.1785L 130.801,73.4961 Z "/>
      </Button.Content>
    </Button>
    <Button Margin="0,0,0,0" Grid.RowSpan="1" Grid.Row="3"
            Grid.ColumnSpan="1" Grid.Column="1"
            x:Name="btnSwitchPIP" Click="btnSwitchPIP_Click"
             >
      <Button.Content>
        <Path Stretch="Fill" StrokeThickness="2" StrokeLineJoin="Round"
              Stroke="#FF000000" Data="M 120,39.8333L 149.917,
              39.8333L 149.917,59.9167L 120,59.9167L 120,
              39.8333 Z M 132.917,42.8333L 146.667,42.8333L 146.667,
              52.6667L 132.917,52.6667L 132.917,42.8333 Z "/>
      </Button.Content>
    </Button>
  </Grid>
 </Grid>
</Grid>
<Grid Margin="2,2,2,2" VerticalAlignment="Stretch" Grid.Column="1"
      Grid.Row="1" HorizontalAlignment="Stretch">
  <Grid.RowDefinitions>
    <RowDefinition Height="0.5*"/>
    <RowDefinition Height="0.5*"/>
  </Grid.RowDefinitions>
  <Grid.ColumnDefinitions>
    <ColumnDefinition Width="0.75*"/>
    <ColumnDefinition Width="0.25*"/>
  </Grid.ColumnDefinitions>
  <!-- Slider to report and control media progress-->
  <Ch08_RichMedia_Recipe8_2:MediaSlider SourceName="mediaelemMain"
              VerticalAlignment="Top"
              IsEnabled="True"
              x:Name="mediaSlider" Grid.ColumnSpan="2"/>
```

```
    <!--Buttons to control media-->
    <Ch08_RichMedia_Recipe8_2:MediaButtonsPanel Grid.Row="1" Grid.Column="0"
                    SourceName="mediaelemMain"
                    HorizontalAlignment="Center"
                    VerticalAlignment="Center"
                    Width="150" Height="40"
                    x:Name="mediaControl"/>
    <!--Slider to control volume-->
    <Slider x:Name="sliderVolumeControl"  Margin="5,0,5,0" Maximum="1"
            Minimum="0" SmallChange="0.1"
            LargeChange="0.2"  Value="0.5"
            MinWidth="50" Grid.Row="1"
            Grid.Column="1" ValueChanged="sliderVolumeControl_ValueChanged">
    </Slider>
  </Grid>
  <!--Media element for main display-->
  <MediaElement Height="Auto" Margin="0,0,0,0"
                VerticalAlignment="Top" x:Name="mediaelemMain"
                HorizontalAlignment="Left" AutoPlay="True" Opacity="0"/>
  <!--Media element for Picture in Picture display-->
  <MediaElement Height="Auto" Margin="0,0,0,0" VerticalAlignment="Top"
                x:Name="mediaelemPIP" HorizontalAlignment="Left"
                AutoPlay="True" Opacity="0" IsMuted="True" />
  <!--Media Menu-->
  <ListBox Margin="0,0,-2,0" VerticalAlignment="Stretch"
          Grid.RowSpan="2" x:Name="lbxMediaMenu"
          ItemTemplate="{StaticResource dtMediaMenuItem}"
          ItemContainerStyle="{StaticResource STYLE_MediaMenuListBoxItem}"
          >
  </ListBox>
 </Grid>
</UserControl>
```

The ListBox named lbxMediaMenu lists all the media sources available to the player, using the dtMediaMenuItem as the item template. lbxMediaMenu is bound to a collection of MediaMenuData, as shown shortly in the code-behind for the player. dtMediaMenuItem contains an Image control bound to the MediaMenuData.MediaPreview property, a TextBlock bound to the MediaMenuData.Description property, and two buttons named btnPlayFull and btnPlayPIP, each with its Tag property bound to the complete MediaMenuData instance.

The UI contains two MediaElement instances: mediaelemMain and mediaelemPIP. They play two media streams simultaneously, one of which is in a smaller viewing area overlaid in a standard television picture-in-picture style on the main display area. Both are set to AutoPlay, although mediaelemPIP is muted by setting MediaElement.IsMuted to True, to avoid having multiple audio streams getting jumbled together.

The primary display is a Border named displayMain, with its Background set to paint with a VideoBrush named vidbrushMain with mediaelemMain as the source. The secondary or the picture-in-picture (PIP) display is named displayPIP, painted with vidbrushPIP, and sourced from mediaelemPIP.

You also define two additional buttons, named btnClosePIP and btnSwitchPIP—the former closes a PIP display, and the latter switches the videos between the PIP display and the main display. You can use btnPlayFull to play the corresponding media in the main display, although btnPlayPIP plays the media in the PIP window.

The UI also contains two custom controls named mediaSlider and mediaButtons of types MediaSlider and MediaButtonsPanel. MediaSlider represents the slider control below the main display area and encapsulates all the tracking and progress control functionality. MediaButtonsPanel encapsulates the buttons below the media slider that represent play-control functions. We discuss these controls in detail in later sections in this recipe.

Last, the UI contains a Slider control named sliderVolumeControl that is used to control the audio volume for the playing media.

Listing 8-5 shows the code-behind for the player.

Listing 8-5. *Code-Behind for the Complete Player*

```csharp
using System;
using System.Collections.Generic;
using System.Collections.ObjectModel;
using System.Linq;
using System.Net;
using System.Windows;
using System.Windows.Controls;
using System.Windows.Input;
using System.Xml.Linq;

namespace Ch08_RichMedia.Recipe8_2
{
  public partial class MainPage : UserControl
  {
    //change this if you install the services at a different location
    private const string MediaLocatorUri =
      "http://localhost:9191/MediaLocationProvider.svc/GetLocationList";

    private ObservableCollection<MediaMenuData> listMedia =
      new ObservableCollection<MediaMenuData>();

    private MediaElement MainVideo
    {
      get
      {
        return (vidbrushMain.SourceName == "mediaelemMain") ?
        mediaelemMain : mediaelemPIP;
      }
    }
    private MediaElement PIPVideo
    {
      get
```

```csharp
    {
      return (vidbrushPIP.SourceName == "mediaelemMain") ?
      mediaelemMain : mediaelemPIP;
    }
  }

  public MainPage()
  {
    InitializeComponent();
    lbxMediaMenu.ItemsSource = listMedia;
    this.Loaded += new RoutedEventHandler(Page_Loaded);
  }

  void Page_Loaded(object sender, RoutedEventArgs e)
  {
    PopulateMediaMenu();
  }


  private void PopulateMediaMenu()
  {
    WebClient wcMediaLocator = new WebClient();
    wcMediaLocator.DownloadStringCompleted +=
      new DownloadStringCompletedEventHandler(
      delegate(object Sender, DownloadStringCompletedEventArgs e)
      {
        this.Dispatcher.BeginInvoke(new Action(delegate
          {
            XDocument xDoc = XDocument.Parse(e.Result);

            List<MediaMenuData> tempList =
              (from medloc in xDoc.Root.Elements()
                select new MediaMenuData
                {
                  Description = medloc.Element("Description").Value,
                  MediaLocation = new Uri(medloc.Element("Uri").Value),
                  MediaPreview = medloc.Element("ImageUri").Value
                }).ToList();
            foreach (MediaMenuData medloc in tempList)
              listMedia.Add(medloc);
          }));
      });
    wcMediaLocator.DownloadStringAsync(new Uri(MediaLocatorUri));
  }
```

```csharp
private void PlayFull_Click(object sender, RoutedEventArgs e)
{
  MainVideo.Source = ((sender as Button).Tag as MediaMenuData).MediaLocation;
}

private void PlayPIP_Click(object sender, RoutedEventArgs e)
{
  PIPVideo.Source = ((sender as Button).Tag as MediaMenuData).MediaLocation;
  displayPIP.Visibility = Visibility.Visible;
}

private void btnClosePIP_Click(object sender, RoutedEventArgs e)
{
  PIPVideo.Stop();
  buttonsPIP.Visibility = displayPIP.Visibility = Visibility.Collapsed;
}

private void btnSwitchPIP_Click(object sender, RoutedEventArgs e)
{
  if (vidbrushMain.SourceName == "mediaelemMain")
  {
    vidbrushMain.SourceName = "mediaelemPIP";
    vidbrushPIP.SourceName = "mediaelemMain";
    mediaSlider.SourceName = "mediaelemPIP";
    mediaButtons.SourceName = "mediaelemPIP";
    mediaelemMain.IsMuted = true;
    mediaelemPIP.IsMuted = false;
  }
  else
  {
    vidbrushMain.SourceName = "mediaelemMain";
    vidbrushPIP.SourceName = "mediaelemPTP";
    mediaSlider.SourceName = "mediaelemMain";
    mediaButtons.SourceName = "mediaelemMain";
    mediaelemMain.IsMuted = false;
    mediaelemPIP.IsMuted = true;
  }
  MainVideo.Volume = sliderVolumeControl.Value;
}
```

```csharp
    private void displayPIP_MouseLeftButtonUp(object sender,
      MouseButtonEventArgs e)
    {
      if (displayPIP.Visibility == Visibility.Visible)
      {
        buttonsPIP.Visibility =
          (buttonsPIP.Visibility == Visibility.Visible ?
          Visibility.Collapsed : Visibility.Visible);
      }
    }
    private void sliderVolumeControl_ValueChanged(object sender,
      RoutedPropertyChangedEventArgs<double> e)
    {
      if (vidbrushMain != null)
      {
        MainVideo.Volume = e.NewValue;
      }
    }
  }
}
```

The PopulateMediaMenu() method uses the WebClient to invoke the GetLocationList() operation on the MediaLocationProvider service. The GetLocationList() operation returns the contents of the Locations.xml file shown in Listing 8-2; and in the DownloadStringCompleted handler, you parse the XML into a collection of MediaMenuData instances. You then bind the list to lbxMediaMenu, which results in the menu interface shown in Figure 8-6.

The strategy of switching a video between the PIP display and the main display is to swap the MediaElements between the respective VideoBrushes. Because of this, you also create two additional properties named MainVideo and PIPVideo that wrap the access to the MediaElements from code. Within these property getters, you always return the MediaElement associated with the vidbrushMain as MainVideo and the one associated with vidbrushPIP as PIPVideo. This causes any media source or other property settings on MainVideo to always affect the main display and those on PIPVideo to always affect the PIP display.

In PlayFull_Click(), you set the source for MainVideo to the MediaLocation property on the MediaMenuData bound to btnPlayFull.Tag. In PlayPIP_Click(), you perform a similar action using PIPVideo and btnPlayPIP.Tag. Additionally, you make the PIP display visible from its original Collapsed state.

While the PIP display is playing media, the mouse left-button-up handler for the PIP display—displayPIP_MouseLeftButtonUp()—displays the PIP control buttons. Figure 8-7 shows the PIP display with the PIP control buttons visible; the top button closes the PIP window, and the bottom button switches the media with the main display.

Figure 8-7. *Picture-in-picture display with control buttons visible*

In btnClosePIP_Click(), you stop the media by invoking Stop() on PIPVideo and hide the PIP display and the related buttons. In btnSwitchPIP_Click(), you swap the SourceName properties of the respective VideoBrushes to swap the playing media between the displays. You also swap the muted state to play the audio from the main display (remember, the PIP display remains muted), and you swap the SourceName properties on the MediaSlider and the MediaButtonsPanel control instances (which we discuss in the next sections).

You handle the ValueChanged event of sliderVolumeControl, where you set the MainVideo. Volume property to the current value reflected in sliderVolumeControl.

So far, we have not discussed any of the play-control and tracking functionality that is exposed through the MediaElement API. A player such as this needs to utilize such functionality to be useful, and it would typically contain several visual elements that enable that functionality. It is fairly common to have one or more range-style controls to report various progressive activities like the download or the playing of media, which may also aid in seeking through the media. Buttons to play, pause, stop, and so forth are common as well.

You encapsulate some of this functionality inside the MediaSlider and MediaButtonsPanel controls discussed next, to create a clean separation between the player's code shown in Listings 8-4 and 8-5 and these player-control functions. We hope that these controls are reusable enough that you will be able to drop them into your own player projects and reuse them without any major modifications. Finally, because they are custom controls, you do not have to settle for our rather pedestrian design skills and can replace the look and feel of each control with a design that suits your needs while retaining all the functionality.

Note that you can refer to Chapter 5, where we discuss custom control development and custom control templates in detail. In subsequent sections in this chapter, we assume that you are familiar with those control development concepts.

The MediaSlider Custom Control

The MediaSlider custom control encapsulates progress tracking and some of the seeking functionality associated with the player. The MediaSlider is implemented by extending the Slider control that is packaged with the Silverlight framework libraries. You add visual elements to the default template for the Slider control to define the same for MediaSlider. You also further extend the Slider type with custom functionality.

Let's look at the control template first. Note that because the templates for both this control and the next one are defined in the same generic.xaml file, we only list the relevant portions of generic.xaml in each section, not the entire file.

Listing 8-6 shows the control template for MediaSlider.

Listing 8-6. *MediaSlider Control Template*

```
<ControlTemplate TargetType="local:MediaSlider" x:Key="ctMediaSliderDefault">
  <Grid x:Name="Root">
    <Grid.Resources>
      <ControlTemplate x:Key="ctRepeatButton">
        <Grid x:Name="Root" Opacity="0" Background="Transparent"/>
      </ControlTemplate>
    </Grid.Resources>
    <vsm:VisualStateManager.VisualStateGroups>
      <vsm:VisualStateGroup x:Name="CommonStates">
        <vsm:VisualStateGroup.Transitions>
          <vsm:VisualTransition GeneratedDuration="0"/>
        </vsm:VisualStateGroup.Transitions>
        <vsm:VisualState x:Name="Normal"/>
        <vsm:VisualState x:Name="MouseOver"/>
        <vsm:VisualState x:Name="Disabled">
          <Storyboard>
            <DoubleAnimationUsingKeyFrames Storyboard.TargetName="Root"
            Storyboard.TargetProperty="(UIElement.Opacity)">
              <SplineDoubleKeyFrame KeyTime="00:00:00" Value="0.5"/>
            </DoubleAnimationUsingKeyFrames>
          </Storyboard>
        </vsm:VisualState>
      </vsm:VisualStateGroup>
    </vsm:VisualStateManager.VisualStateGroups>
    <Grid>
      <Grid.RowDefinitions>
        <RowDefinition Height="0.33*" />
        <RowDefinition Height="0.34*" />
        <RowDefinition Height="0.33*" />
      </Grid.RowDefinitions>
      <Grid Grid.Row="0" VerticalAlignment="Top"
          HorizontalAlignment="Stretch">
        <Grid.ColumnDefinitions>
          <ColumnDefinition Width="*" />
          <ColumnDefinition Width="Auto" />
        </Grid.ColumnDefinitions>
        <StackPanel Orientation="Horizontal" Grid.Column="1"
                    HorizontalAlignment="Right">
          <TextBlock Text="Downloaded" FontSize="12"
                    Margin="0,0,4,0"/>
          <TextBlock x:Name="textDownloadPercent" FontSize="12"
                    />
        </StackPanel>
      </Grid>
```

```
        <Grid x:Name="HorizontalTemplate" Grid.Row="1" >
          <Grid.ColumnDefinitions>
            <ColumnDefinition Width="Auto" />
            <ColumnDefinition Width="Auto" />
            <ColumnDefinition Width="*" />
          </Grid.ColumnDefinitions>
          <Rectangle Stroke="Black" StrokeThickness="0.5" Fill="#FFE6EFF7"
                     Grid.Column="0" Grid.ColumnSpan="3" Height="14"
                     Margin="5,0,5,0" />
          <Border Height="10" Margin="5,0,5,0" Grid.Column="0"
                  Grid.ColumnSpan="3"
                  x:Name="elemDownloadProgressIndicator"
                  Background="#FF2185D8"
                  HorizontalAlignment="Left" Width="0"  />
          <Border Height="6" Margin="5,0,5,0" Grid.Column="0"
                  Grid.ColumnSpan="3"
                  x:Name="elemPlayProgressIndicator"
                  Background="#FF1CE421"
                  HorizontalAlignment="Left" Width="0"  />
          <RepeatButton x:Name="HorizontalTrackLargeChangeDecreaseRepeatButton"
                        Grid.Column="0"
                        Template="{StaticResource ctRepeatButton}"
                        IsTabStop="False"  />
          <Thumb x:Name="HorizontalThumb" Height="14" Width="11" Grid.Column="1"/>
          <RepeatButton x:Name="HorizontalTrackLargeChangeIncreaseRepeatButton"
                        Grid.Column="2"
                        Template="{StaticResource ctRepeatButton}"
                        IsTabStop="False"  />
        </Grid>
        <Grid Grid.Row="2" VerticalAlignment="Bottom"
              HorizontalAlignment="Stretch">
          <StackPanel x:Name="TotalDuration" Orientation="Horizontal">
            <TextBlock x:Name="textPosition" FontSize="12"/>
            <TextBlock Text=" / " FontSize="12" Margin="3,0,3,0"/>
            <TextBlock x:Name="textDuration" FontSize="12" />
          </StackPanel>
        </Grid>
      </Grid>
    </Grid>
  </Grid>
</ControlTemplate>

<Style TargetType="local:MediaSlider">
  <Setter Property="Template" Value="{StaticResource ctMediaSliderDefault}" />
</Style>
```

If you look at the default control template of the Slider control (one way to do that is to create a copy of the control template in Expression Blend, as we did for the sample in Chapter 5), it is obvious from Listing 8-6 that you use that template as a starting point and make some modifications in creating a control template named ctMediaSliderDefault.

The default Slider control template contains two visual representations: one for when the Slider.Orientation property is set to Orientation.Horizontal and another for when it is set to Orientation.Vertical. These parts are defined within two Grids named HorizontalTemplate and VerticalTemplate. Because you always use the MediaSlider in horizontal orientation, in ctMediaSliderDefault you leave out the VerticalTemplate portion. You can always add it back if you intend to use this control oriented vertically as well. The definition of HorizontalTemplate gives you a good idea of what the vertical counterpart should contain.

Within HorizontalTemplate is a Thumb control named Thumb. As we discuss later, you use the Thumb to report progress by moving it along the slider as media plays. The user can also drag the Thumb along the slider in either direction to seek within the media. Additionally, the two RepeatButton instances, named HorizontalTrackLargeChangeDecreaseRepeatButton and HorizontalTrackLargeChangeIncreaseRepeatButton, form the clickable areas on the slider on the two sides of the Thumb. Clicking causes the Thumb to progress on either side. Because these are RepeatButtons, holding the mouse left button down causes repeated click events to be raised at an interval defined by the RepeatButton.Interval property; this property is set to the number of milliseconds by which you want the click events to be separated. You also add two Border controls, named elemDownloadProgressIndicator and elemPlayProgressIndicator, that progress along the MediaSlider background; the former reports media download progress, and the latter reports play progress and trails the Thumb as it moves along the MediaSlider.

Last, you add a StackPanel named TotalDuration with two TextBlocks in it. The TextBlock named textDuration is set to the total duration of the media after it starts playing, and the one named textPosition reports the media's current position as it plays.

To use the control template, you create a style with the target type set to the control's type and the Template property set to the control template. The style is shown at the end of Listing 8-6. In the control's code, you can see how the style is used. To learn more about control templating and custom controls, refer to Chapter 5.

Listing 8-7 shows the code for the control.

Listing 8-7. *MediaSlider Control Code*

```
using System;
using System.Windows;
using System.Windows.Controls;
using System.Windows.Controls.Primitives;
using System.Windows.Media;
using System.Windows.Threading;

namespace Ch08_RichMedia.Recipe8_2
{
 public class MediaSlider : Slider
  {
    private MediaElement MediaSource;
    private FrameworkElement elemDownloadProgressIndicator;
    private FrameworkElement elemPlayProgressIndicator;
    private FrameworkElement Root;
    private TextBlock textPosition;
```

```csharp
  private TextBlock textDuration;
  private TextBlock textDownloadPercent;
  private Thumb HorizontalThumb;
  private DispatcherTimer disptimerPlayProgressUpdate;

//SourceName dependency property - used to attach
//a Media element to this control
  public static DependencyProperty SourceNameProperty =
    DependencyProperty.Register("SourceName", typeof(string),
    typeof(MediaSlider),
    new PropertyMetadata(new PropertyChangedCallback(OnSourceNameChanged)));
  public string SourceName
  {
    get
    {
      return (string)GetValue(SourceNameProperty);
    }
    set
    {
      SetValue(SourceNameProperty, value);
    }
  }
//SourceName change handler
  private static void OnSourceNameChanged(DependencyObject Source,
    DependencyPropertyChangedEventArgs e)
  {
    MediaSlider thisSlider = Source as MediaSlider;
    if (e.NewValue != null && e.NewValue != e.OldValue
      && thisSlider.Root != null)
    {
      thisSlider.MediaSource =
        thisSlider.Root.FindName(e.NewValue as string) as MediaElement;
      //reinitialize
      thisSlider.InitMediaElementConnections();
    }
  }


  public MediaSlider()
    : base()
  {
    this.DefaultStyleKey = typeof(MediaSlider);
    this.Maximum = 100;
    this.Minimum = 0;
    disptimerPlayProgressUpdate = new DispatcherTimer();
```

```csharp
    disptimerPlayProgressUpdate.Interval = new TimeSpan(0, 0, 0, 0, 50);
    disptimerPlayProgressUpdate.Tick +=
      new EventHandler(PlayProgressUpdate_Tick);
}
public override void OnApplyTemplate()
{
  base.OnApplyTemplate();

  elemDownloadProgressIndicator =
    GetTemplateChild("elemDownloadProgressIndicator") as FrameworkElement;
  elemPlayProgressIndicator =
   GetTemplateChild("elemPlayProgressIndicator") as FrameworkElement;
  HorizontalThumb = GetTemplateChild("HorizontalThumb") as Thumb;
  if (HorizontalThumb != null)
  {
    HorizontalThumb.DragStarted +=
      new DragStartedEventHandler(HorizontalThumb_DragStarted);
    HorizontalThumb.DragCompleted +=
      new DragCompletedEventHandler(HorizontalThumb_DragCompleted);
  }
  textPosition = GetTemplateChild("textPosition") as TextBlock;
  textDuration = GetTemplateChild("textDuration") as TextBlock;
  textDownloadPercent = GetTemplateChild("textDownloadPercent") as TextBlock;

  Root = Helper.FindRoot(this);
  MediaSource = Root.FindName(SourceName) as MediaElement;
  InitMediaElementConnections();
}
//Initialize by wiring up handlers
private void InitMediaElementConnections()
{
  if (MediaSource != null)
  {
    MediaSource.MediaOpened +=
      new RoutedEventHandler(MediaSource_MediaOpened);
    MediaSource.MediaEnded +=
      new RoutedEventHandler(MediaSource_MediaEnded);
    MediaSource.MediaFailed +=
      new EventHandler<ExceptionRoutedEventArgs>(MediaSource_MediaFailed);
    MediaSource.CurrentStateChanged +=
      new RoutedEventHandler(MediaSource_CurrentStateChanged);
    MediaSource.DownloadProgressChanged +=
      new RoutedEventHandler(MediaSource_DownloadProgressChanged);
    MediaSource_CurrentStateChanged(this, new RoutedEventArgs());
  }
}
```

```csharp
    //tick handler for progress timer
    void PlayProgressUpdate_Tick(object sender, EventArgs e)
    {
      this.Value =
        (MediaSource.Position.TotalMilliseconds /
        MediaSource.NaturalDuration.TimeSpan.TotalMilliseconds)
        * (this.Maximum - this.Minimum);

      if (elemPlayProgressIndicator != null)
      {
        elemPlayProgressIndicator.Width =
          (MediaSource.Position.TotalMilliseconds /
          MediaSource.NaturalDuration.TimeSpan.TotalMilliseconds)
          * ActualWidth;
      }
      if (textPosition != null)
        textPosition.Text = string.Format("{0:00}:{1:00}:{2:00}:{3:000}",
          MediaSource.Position.Hours,
          MediaSource.Position.Minutes,
          MediaSource.Position.Seconds,
          MediaSource.Position.Milliseconds);
    }
    //plug into the thumb to pause play while it is being dragged
    void HorizontalThumb_DragStarted(object sender, DragStartedEventArgs e)
    {
      if (MediaSource != null && MediaSource.CurrentState ==
        MediaElementState.Playing)
        MediaSource.Pause();
    }
    void HorizontalThumb_DragCompleted(object sender, DragCompletedEventArgs e)
    {
      if (MediaSource != null)
      {
        MediaSource.Position = new TimeSpan(0,
          0, 0, 0,
          (int)(this.Value *
          MediaSource.NaturalDuration.TimeSpan.TotalMilliseconds /
(this.Maximum - this.Minimum)));
      }
      MediaSource.Play();
    }
```

```
//media element download progress changed
private void MediaSource_DownloadProgressChanged(object sender,
  RoutedEventArgs e)
{
  if (elemDownloadProgressIndicator != null)
  {
    elemDownloadProgressIndicator.Width =
      (MediaSource.DownloadProgress * this.ActualWidth);
    if (textDownloadPercent != null)
      textDownloadPercent.Text = string.Format("{0:##.##} %",
        MediaSource.DownloadProgress * 100);
  }
}
//state changes on the MediaElement
private void MediaSource_CurrentStateChanged(object sender,
  RoutedEventArgs e)
{
  switch (MediaSource.CurrentState)
  {
    case MediaElementState.Playing:
      if (textDuration != null)
        textDuration.Text = string.Format("{0:00}:{1:00}:{2:00}:{3:000}",
          MediaSource.NaturalDuration.TimeSpan.Hours,
          MediaSource.NaturalDuration.TimeSpan.Minutes,
          MediaSource.NaturalDuration.TimeSpan.Seconds,
          MediaSource.NaturalDuration.TimeSpan.Milliseconds);
      if (disptimerPlayProgressUpdate.IsEnabled == false)
      disptimerPlayProgressUpdate.Start();
      break;
    case MediaElementState.Paused:
      if (disptimerPlayProgressUpdate.IsEnabled)
      disptimerPlayProgressUpdate.Stop();
      break;
    case MediaElementState.Stopped:
      if (disptimerPlayProgressUpdate.IsEnabled)
      disptimerPlayProgressUpdate.Stop();
      break;
    case MediaElementState.AcquiringLicense:
    case MediaElementState.Individualizing:
    case MediaElementState.Opening:
    case MediaElementState.Buffering:
    case MediaElementState.Closed:
      break;
```

```
        default:
          break;
      }
    }

  //media ended
   private void MediaSource_MediaEnded(object sender,
     RoutedEventArgs e)
   {
     if (disptimerPlayProgressUpdate.IsEnabled)
     disptimerPlayProgressUpdate.Stop();
   }

  //media failed
   private void MediaSource_MediaFailed(object sender, RoutedEventArgs e)
   {
     disptimerPlayProgressUpdate.Stop();
   }

   void MediaSource_MediaOpened(object sender, RoutedEventArgs e)
   {
     //we do nothing here in this sample
   }
 }
}
```

Note in Listing 8-7 that the MediaSlider directly extends the Slider control type. In the constructor, you set the control's DefaultStyleKey property to the control type. This has the effect of associating the control to the style defined at the end of Listing 8-6 and, consequently, applying the control template referenced through that style to the control. You then initialize the Maximum and Minimum properties to reflect a range from 0 to 100. You can change these defaults by setting a different range where you use the MediaSlider in XAML. You also create and initialize a DispatcherTimer, whose purpose we discuss later in this section.

The MediaSlider defines a dependency property named SourceName, very similar in purpose to the VideoBrush. This property is set to the x:Name of the MediaElement; its intent is to look through the entire XAML starting at the root of the Page within which the MediaSlider is contained, to locate the MediaElement.

The Helper.FindRoot() method shown in Listing 8-8 locates the XAML root. It recursively travels upward in the XAML tree, starting at the MediaSlider, until no more parents are defined.

Listing 8-8. *Code to Locate the Root of a XAML Document*

```
using System.Windows;

namespace Ch08_RichMedia.Recipe8_2
{
  public static class Helper
```

```
    {
      public static FrameworkElement FindRoot(FrameworkElement CurrentLevel)
      {
        FrameworkElement NextParent = null;
        if (CurrentLevel.Parent is FrameworkElement)
          NextParent = FindRoot(CurrentLevel.Parent as FrameworkElement);
        else
          NextParent = CurrentLevel;
        return NextParent;
      }
    }
}
```

In OnApplyTemplate() in Listing 8-7, you first acquire all the named template parts that you are interested in. You then use FindRoot() to locate the page root and store it in MediaSlider.Root. Finally, you use FindName() on the root to locate and store the MediaElement in MediaSlider.MediaSource. After the MediaElement has been located, you invoke InitMediaElementConnections(), in which you add handlers to relevant MediaElement events that you need to handle in the MediaSlider. In the OnSourceNameChanged() property-change handler, you repeat this process for when the MediaSlider is pointed to some other MediaElement during the course of use of the player.

If you refer back to Listing 8-4, note that the SourceName property of the MediaSlider is set to mediaelemMain in the player's XAML. However, if you also refer back to Listing 8-5 and look at the btnSwitchPIP_Click() event handler, notice that when the user switches media from the PIP display to the main display, you switch the MediaSlider.SourceName. This causes the MediaSlider to always reflect the state for the MediaElement currently associated with the main display.

Note that the MediaElement_CurrentStateChanged() handler includes a case label for each permissible state defined in the MediaElementState enumeration. Although you do not need to respond to each of these state transitions to implement this sample, we include them in the code for informational purposes. You can get rid of the fall-through case labels, should you choose to use this code directly.

The first step that a MediaElement performs when trying to load media is to validate and open the media URI. This is signaled by raising the CurrentStateChanged event and by the MediaElement.CurrentState transitioning to MediaElementState.Opening. After the media is successfully opened, the MediaOpened event is raised. In the MediaOpened event handler, you have access to the media's duration through the MediaElement.NaturalDuration property. At this point, the MediaElement begins acquiring the media, and CurrentState moves to Buffering. In the case of progressively downloaded media, as the media downloads, the MediaElement.DownloadProgressChanged event is raised continually as the amount of media downloaded grows, and the resulting download percentage value increases. In the handler named MediaSource_DownloadProgressChanged(), you set the Width of the Border element elemDownloadProgressIndicator by the appropriate percentage of the ActualWidth to reflect download progress. You also report the download percentage through textDownloadPercent. When enough media has been downloaded for play to start, the MediaElement state transitions to Playing. This results in raising the CurrentStateChanged event again. Figure 8-8 shows media still downloading while play has just started.

Figure 8-8. *MediaSlider visual state when media is playing while download continues*

One of the challenges of the MediaElement state transitions is that the state change to Playing is raised only once: right when the media is starting to play. Playing then continues without raising any further notifications until a control event like Stop or Pause causes the MediaElement state to change again. This is for several good reasons, not least of which is performance, because the MediaElement may not perform optimally if it tries to keep raising granular events continuously while it is playing.

However, in order to report progress while the media is playing, you need a mechanism to notify the code at regular intervals. This is where the DispatcherTimer named disptimerPlayProgressUpdate (which is initialized in the constructor) plays its role. In handling the Playing state change in MediaSource_CurrentStateChanged(), you start disptimerPlayProgressUpdate, which raises a tick event every 50 milliseconds. We chose this value fairly randomly; you can either change it to a value that suits your needs or make it a property on the control to allow you to set it. Note that in the same case block, you format and set the value of textDuration to that in MediaSource.NaturalDuration to display the total duration of the clip.

In the Tick handler for disptimerPlayProgressUpdate, named PlayProgressUpdate_Tick(), you move the Thumb by setting its Value to a proportion of the MediaSlider range, matching the ratio of the current Position to the MediaSource.NaturalDuration. You also increase the Width of elemPlayProgressIndicator by the same proportion to trail the Thumb to indicate play progress, and you set textPosition at the lower-left corner of the slider to reflect the current Position value, as shown in Figure 8-8.

If the MediaElement fails to load and play the media, if the media is stopped or paused, and after the play ends, you check disptimerPlayProgressUpdate to see if it is currently ticking (in other words, whether the IsEnabled property is set to True), and stop it if it is.

You also need to enable seeking through the media using the Thumb. To do this, you attach handlers to the Thumb.DragStarted and Thumb.DragCompleted events in OnApplyTemplate(). In the HorizontalThumb_DragStarted() handler, you make sure the media is playing; and if it is, you pause it. This prevents your code in the DispatcherTimer.Tick handler from trying to move the Thumb while the user is dragging it. In HorizontalThumb_DragCompleted(), you set MediaSource.Position by transforming the MediaSlider.Value property back to its corresponding time point in the media's timeline. This causes the media to seek to the newly set position. You then start playing the media again.

One last thing to note is that in InitMediaElementConnections(), you deliberately invoke the MediaElement_CurrentStateChanged() handler. This is for cases where the SourceName changes but the new MediaElement being attached is already playing—that is, someone switched the PIP video with the main video. The MediaElement state change is not going to fire again, so calling the state-change handler once deliberately causes the textDuration to be updated to reflect the change in video sources.

The MediaButtonsPanel Custom Control

The MediaButtonsPanel custom control encapsulates the following play-control functions: play, pause, stop, forward, and rewind. Each function is tied to a Button in the control template. Listing 8-9 shows the control template for MediaButtonsPanel.

Listing 8-9. *Control Template for MediaButtonsPanel Custom Control*

```
<ControlTemplate TargetType="local:MediaButtonsPanel"
                 x:Key="ctMediaButtonsPanelDefault">
  <Grid>
    <Grid.ColumnDefinitions>
      <ColumnDefinition Width="0.2*" />
      <ColumnDefinition Width="0.2*" />
      <ColumnDefinition Width="0.2*" />
```

```
    <ColumnDefinition Width="0.2*" />
    <ColumnDefinition Width="0.2*" />
  </Grid.ColumnDefinitions>
  <RepeatButton Grid.Column="0" x:Name="btnRewind" Margin="0,0,1,0">
    <RepeatButton.Content>
      <Path x:Name="Rewind" Stretch="Fill" StrokeThickness="1"
            StrokeLineJoin="Round" Stroke="#FF000000" Fill="#FF000000"
            Data="M 69.8333,70.0833L 60.5833,
            63.2862L 60.5833,70.0833L 40,
            54.9583L 60.5833,39.8333L 60.5833,
            46.6304L 69.8333,39.8333L 69.8333,
            70.0833 Z "/>
    </RepeatButton.Content>
  </RepeatButton>
  <Button Grid.Column="1" x:Name="btnStop" Margin="1,0,1,0">
    <Button.Content>
      <Path x:Name="Stop" Fill="#FF000000" Stretch="Fill"
            StrokeThickness="0" Margin="5,5,5,5"
            Data="M0,0 L3,0 L3,30.249996 L0,30.249996 z"/>
    </Button.Content>
  </Button>
  <Button Grid.Column="2" x:Name="btnPlay" Margin="1,0,1,0">
    <Button.Content>
      <Path x:Name="Play" Stretch="Fill" StrokeThickness="0"
            Fill="#FF000000" Margin="5,5,5,5"
            Data="M 109.833,14.8944L 79.8333,
            -0.0445251L 79.8333,29.8333L 109.833,
            14.8944 Z "/>
    </Button.Content>
  </Button>
  <Button Grid.Column="3" x:Name="btnPause" Margin="1,0,1,0">
    <Button.Content>
      <Path x:Name="Pause" Stretch="Fill" StrokeThickness="0"
            Fill="#FF000000" Margin="5,5,5,5"
            Data="M 39.8333,0L 50.0833,0L 50.0833,29.8333L 39.8333,
            29.8333L 39.8333,0 Z M 59.8333,0L 69.8333,0L 69.8333,
            29.8333L 59.8333,29.8333L 59.8333,0 Z "/>
    </Button.Content>
  </Button>
  <RepeatButton Grid.Column="4" x:Name="btnForward" Margin="1,0,0,0">
    <RepeatButton.Content>
      <Path x:Name="Forward" Stretch="Fill" StrokeThickness="1"
            StrokeLineJoin="Round" Stroke="#FF000000"
            Fill="#FF000000"
            Data="M 1.27157e-006,39.8334L 9.25,
```

```
            46.6305L 9.25,39.8333L 29.8333,
            54.9583L 9.25,70.0833L 9.25,
            63.2863L 1.27157e-006,
            70.0833L 1.27157e-006,39.8334 Z "/>
      </RepeatButton.Content>
    </RepeatButton>
  </Grid>
</ControlTemplate>

<Style TargetType="local:MediaButtonsPanel">
  <Setter Property="Template"
          Value="{StaticResource ctMediaButtonsPanelDefault}"/>
</Style>
```

Note that although btnStop, btnPause, and btnPlay are Buttons, btnRewind and btnForward are RepeatButtons, with their Delay property set to 75 and Interval property set to 125. This means that when the user presses and holds down either btnRewind or btnForward, Click events are raised repeatedly at an interval of 125 milliseconds, with a delay of 75 milliseconds before repeating starts. This gives the effect of being able to continuously seek through the media either way by holding down these buttons.

Listing 8-10 shows the code for MediaButtonsPanel.

Listing 8-10. *MediaButtonsPanel Control Code*

```
using System;
using System.Windows;
using System.Windows.Controls;
using System.Windows.Controls.Primitives;
using System.Windows.Media;

namespace Ch08_RichMedia.Recipe8_2
{
  public class MediaButtonsPanel : Control
  {
    private MediaElement MediaSource;
    private FrameworkElement Root;
    private ButtonBase btnPlay, btnPause,
      btnStop, btnForward, btnRewind;

    public static DependencyProperty SourceNameProperty =
      DependencyProperty.Register("SourceName", typeof(string),
      typeof(MediaButtonsPanel),
      new PropertyMetadata(new PropertyChangedCallback(OnSourceNameChanged)));
    public string SourceName
    {
      get
```

```csharp
    {
      return (string)GetValue(SourceNameProperty);
    }
    set
    {
      SetValue(SourceNameProperty, value);
    }
  }
  private static void OnSourceNameChanged(DependencyObject Source,
    DependencyPropertyChangedEventArgs e)
  {
    MediaButtonsPanel thisPanel = Source as MediaButtonsPanel;

    if (e.NewValue != e.OldValue && thisPanel.Root != null)
      thisPanel.MediaSource =
        thisPanel.Root.FindName(e.NewValue as string) as MediaElement;
  }

  public MediaButtonsPanel()
  {
    this.DefaultStyleKey = typeof(MediaButtonsPanel);
  }

  public override void OnApplyTemplate()
  {

    btnPlay = GetTemplateChild("btnPlay") as ButtonBase;
    btnPause = GetTemplateChild("btnPause") as ButtonBase;
    btnStop = GetTemplateChild("btnStop") as ButtonBase;
    btnForward = GetTemplateChild("btnForward") as ButtonBase;
    btnRewind = GetTemplateChild("btnRewind") as ButtonBase;
    Root = Helper.FindRoot(this);
    MediaSource = Root.FindName(SourceName) as MediaElement;
    WireButtonEvents();
  }

  private void WireButtonEvents()
  {
    if (btnPlay != null)
      btnPlay.Click += new RoutedEventHandler(btnPlay_Click);
    if (btnPause != null)
      btnPause.Click += new RoutedEventHandler(btnPause_Click);
    if (btnStop != null)
      btnStop.Click += new RoutedEventHandler(btnStop_Click);
```

```
    if (btnForward != null)
      btnForward.Click += new RoutedEventHandler(btnForward_Click);
    if (btnRewind != null)
      btnRewind.Click += new RoutedEventHandler(btnRewind_Click);
  }

  void btnRewind_Click(object sender, RoutedEventArgs e)
  {
    if (MediaSource != null && MediaSource.Position > TimeSpan.Zero)
    {
      MediaSource.Pause();
      //5th of a second
      MediaSource.Position -= new TimeSpan(0, 0, 0, 0,200);
      MediaSource.Play();
    }
  }
  void btnForward_Click(object sender, RoutedEventArgs e)
  {
    if (MediaSource != null &&
      MediaSource.Position <= MediaSource.NaturalDuration.TimeSpan)
    {
      MediaSource.Pause();
      MediaSource.Position += new TimeSpan(0, 0, 0, 0, 200);
      MediaSource.Play();
    }
  }
  void btnStop_Click(object sender, RoutedEventArgs e)
  {
    if (MediaSource != null)
      MediaSource.Stop();
  }
  void btnPause_Click(object sender, RoutedEventArgs e)
  {
    if (MediaSource != null &&
      MediaSource.CurrentState == MediaElementState.Playing)
      MediaSource.Pause();
  }
  void btnPlay_Click(object sender, RoutedEventArgs e)
  {
    if (MediaSource != null &&
      MediaSource.CurrentState != MediaElementState.Playing)
      MediaSource.Play();
  }
 }
}
```

The `MediaButtonsPanel` acquires the `MediaElement` to work on, the same way the `MediaSlider` does—by looking for the `MediaElement` with a name specified through the `SourceName` dependency property.

In `OnApplyTemplate()`, you attach handlers to the `Click` events of the buttons in the template. In `btnStop_Click()`, `btnPause_Click()`, and `btnPlay_Click()`, you invoke the appropriate `MediaElement` methods. In `btnRewind_Click()` and `btnForward_Click()`, you check for some boundary conditions to ensure that the resulting position would be a valid time point within the media's timeline, and then shift the `MediaElement.Position` in the appropriate direction by 200 milliseconds for every click. The sample hard-codes the value of 200, but you can easily make this a dependency property, giving you the ability to control the amount of shift.

8-3. Adding Streaming Media Support

Problem

You need to play streaming video in a Silverlight-based player.

Solution

Set up a media streaming infrastructure, set the `MediaElement` source to use appropriate URIs, and adapt various UI elements on the player to reflect streaming media states.

How It Works

As noted in Recipe 8-2, `MediaElement` can play both progressively downloaded as well as streamed media. You need a streaming media server, such as Windows Server with the Windows Media Services add-on, to stream media. Streaming media servers deliver media actively to the player throughout the duration of the media playing session, without requiring a download of the media file. A player playing streamed media usually plays the bits as they are received, and no copying to the disk is performed.

You can use streaming to broadcast live events over the Internet. In this scenario, the live content is passed from the recording source, such as a camera, directly to an encoder to convert it to the correct digital format. The resulting stream is then received by the streaming media server and broadcast out.

Network Considerations

A streaming media player typically buffers a small amount of content, which allows it to stay slightly ahead of the media stream. When a player starts playing a stream, an initial buffering is conducted before the media can begin playing. In the case of congested networks, where the available network bandwidth may vary over time during the playing session, a network stream may fall behind in continuously supplying content to the player to maintain this read-ahead state. In this case, the player may need to buffer again during the play-out, to gather content to play.

Considering this, when streaming media, you should take the bit rate of the media into consideration. For example, if a piece of media is encoded to require 30 frames of the video to be played per second to result in jitter-free playing, and each frame of video is approximately 34 Kb in size, then the player needs to receive the media at about one Mb per second. When the network between the user and the streaming endpoint frequently falls below the required speed limit, you may see jitter in play-out, where the required frame rate is not being met; or the player may buffer more frequently than expected, resulting in a subpar viewing experience.

Such potential issues with available network bandwidth require that you pay special attention to the settings applied to the video when it is being encoded for streaming, so that the resulting bit-rate requirement of the encoded video is close to the actual network conditions in which it plays. It is common to have multiple encodings done of the same video file at different resulting bit rates, and then have different URIs point to these videos so that players can choose a bit rate suitable to the prevailing network condition.

Silverlight also supports multiple bit rate (MBR) video files. MBR video files are essentially multiple copies of the same video, each fully encoded at a constant bit rate packaged in a single file. When it encounters MBR video, MediaElement chooses the appropriate bit rate suitable for the available bandwidth. MBR files can also work with Silverlight in progressive download scenarios, and Silverlight chooses the highest possible bit rate to play the downloaded video. Do not confuse MBR video with variable bit rate (VBR) video. In VBR video, different parts of the same video stream are encoded at different bit rates to achieve optimal compression of the video. VBR video is not suitable for streaming because it is difficult to determine the network requirements of the video in a predictable fashion throughout the playing session.

A detailed discussion of concepts involved in video encoding and network infrastructure for video streaming is beyond the scope of this book. Here are some excellent resources for a better understanding of topics like video encoding and delivering video over IP networks:

- *Compression for Great Digital Video: Power Tips, Techniques, and Common Sense*, by Ben Waggoner (CMP Books, 2002)

- *Video Over IP: A Practical Guide to Technology and Applications*, by Wes Simpson (Focal Press, 2005)

Windows Media Services

Windows Media Services (WMS) is a streaming media server for Windows Media and is available freely from Microsoft as an add-on to the Windows Server operating system. The samples in this chapter relating to streaming use WMS to set up the streaming backend. We use WMS 2008, available on Windows Server 2008, which enjoys the latest features in Windows Media streaming; but WMS is also available on earlier versions of Windows Server.

Setting Up WMS 2008

After you have Windows Server 2008 installed on your server, you can download WMS 2008 at http://www.microsoft.com/downloads/details.aspx?FamilyID=9ccf6312-723b-4577-be58-7caab2e1c5b7&displaylang=en. You can find full instructions for installing WMS 2008 at http://support.microsoft.com/kb/934518.

When you install WMS on a server that has a web server running and listening on port 80, WMS does not enable the HTTP server control protocol during installation. After you have installed WMS 2008, you need to enable this to let Silverlight work with WMS. To do so, open the Windows Media Services console from Administrative Tools on your Start menu. Navigate to the HTTP server control protocol plug-in, as shown in Figure 8-9.

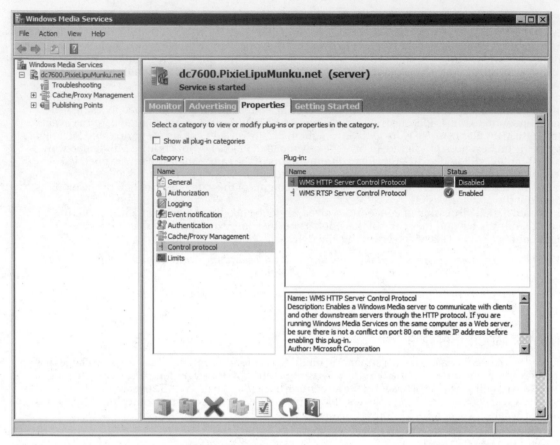

Figure 8-9. *WMS HTTP server control protocol plug-in*

Double-click the protocol entry to bring up the properties sheet. Select "Allow all IP addresses to use this protocol," and then specify a custom port other than 80. Allowing all IP addresses lets the server stream media on all available network interfaces, in case the machine has more than one installed network interface. In Figure 8-10, we have selected port 43000.

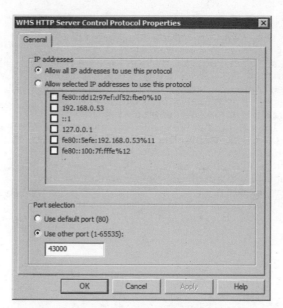

Figure 8-10. *WMS HTTP server control protocol properties*

Right-click the HTTP server control protocol item to bring up its context menu and enable the protocol.

Setting Up Publishing Points

Publishing points define the endpoints of a WMS 2008 installation to which a client connects to receive media. A publishing point can be defined to serve a media file stored on disk, a playlist that defines an ordered collection of media files to be played in sequence, or media that is being acquired real time from a capture device, such as encoder software connected to a camera. The publishing point abstracts the actual source of the media and provides the client with a URL to which the client can connect to start receiving media.

■**Note** We discuss playlists in more detail in Recipe 8-4. We do not discuss live streaming using a capture device in this book. Typically, doing so requires more setup and some knowledge of encoding. To get good-quality live streaming, you need to have high-grade network equipment and broadcast-quality cameras, and we do not assume that you have access to those readily while you are reading the book. If you want to experiment with live streaming from a camera, you can refer to Jit Ghosh's blog entry at http://blogs.msdn.com/jitghosh/archive/2007/11/30/demo-live-streams-in-silverlight.aspx. In that blog entry, the author discusses a basic setup using a commodity webcam and uses Microsoft Expression Encoder and WMS 2008 to set up a basic live streaming scenario with Silverlight as the client front end.

Two kinds of publishing points are possible in WMS: broadcast and on-demand. Either kind can serve media from any of the sources mentioned earlier. Also, multiple publishing points of each types can be defined on a single installation of WMS.

An on-demand publishing point is most often used when you want the user to control the playback and have the ability to pause, rewind, or forward content. Consequently, on-demand publishing points are mostly used with prerecorded video content stored on disk, or with playlists.

Broadcast publishing points create an experience similar to television programs in that the player cannot control playback, and you cannot pause, rewind, or forward content. Also, while streaming from a broadcast publishing point, the MediaElement does not have any information about the duration of the media. These conditions are true even if the broadcast publishing point is being used to stream prerecorded media stored on disk. Broadcast publishing points are mostly used to serve live streams coming directly from encoders or other live sources, like remote servers.

The code sample later in this recipe use one publishing point of each type, but both use disk files as the source of media. Let's look at creating these publishing points.

Right-click the Publishing Points note in the left pane of the WMS management console, and select the Add Publishing Point (Advanced) menu option, as shown in Figure 8-11.

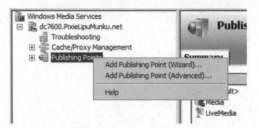

Figure 8-11. *Add Publishing Point context menu*

Choosing that command opens the Add Publishing Point dialog shown in Figure 8-12. Select an on-demand publishing point, provide a name, and select the folder containing the video files. You can also select an individual file for a publishing point or create a playlist. We discuss playlists in greater detail in the next recipe.

Create another publishing point, repeating the same steps, but this time choose a broadcast publishing point, and assign it a different name from the on-demand publishing point. Figure 8-12 shows the choices for the on-demand and broadcast publishing points for this recipe.

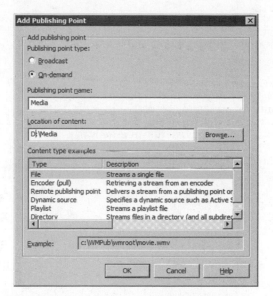 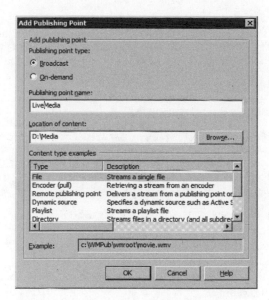

Figure 8-12. *Creating publishing points*

After both publishing points are created, navigate to the Source tab for the broadcast publishing point, and turn on looping by clicking the Loop Directory button, as shown in Figure 8-13. This causes WMS to continuously play all content in the folder in a loop.

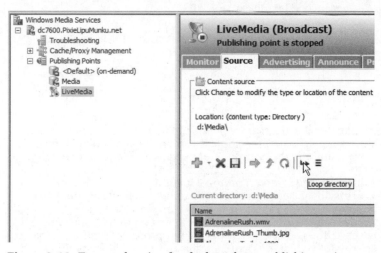

Figure 8-13. *Turn on looping for the broadcast publishing point.*

Then, right-click the broadcast publishing point, and start the publishing point from the context menu.

A detailed discussion of all aspects of WMS setup and operation is beyond the scope of this book. You can refer to the WMS documentation online at http://technet.microsoft.com/en-us/library/cc753790.aspx for a thorough exploration of streaming Windows Media and WMS.

The Code

This sample extends the player you built in Recipe 8-2 to support streaming media features.

The first step is to extend the MediaLocationProvider WCF service to add two more operations, GetOnDemandStreamsList() and GetBroadcastStreamsList(), each of which performs exactly like GetDownloadsList() (defined earlier) but returns different XML. GetOnDemandStreamsList() returns the contents of a file named OnDemandStreams.xml. Listing 8-11 shows a portion of this file.

Listing 8-11. *OnDemandStreams.xml*

```xml
<?xml version="1.0" encoding="utf-8" ?>
<MediaLocations>
  <MediaLocation>
    <Description>Adrenaline Rush</Description>
    <Uri>mms://dc7600:43000/Media/AdrenalineRush.wmv</Uri>
    <ImageUri>
      http://localhost/SLBook/Ch08_RichMedia/Media/AdrenalineRush_Thumb.jpg
    </ImageUri>
  </MediaLocation>
  <MediaLocation>
    <Description>Alexander</Description>
    <Uri>mms://dc7600:43000/Media/Alexander_Trailer_1080p.wmv</Uri>
    <ImageUri>
      http://localhost/SLBook/Ch08_RichMedia/Media/Alexander_Trailer_1080p_Thumb.jpg
    </ImageUri>
  </MediaLocation>
  <!-- more streams here -->
</MediaLocations>
```

As you can see, the <Uri> element for each stream entry points to the media file at the on-demand publishing point on the media server (which in this sample is running on a machine named dc7600 at port 43000). Note that the server name and the port number need to be changed to match your environment for the samples to work.

Also note the use of the mms (Microsoft Media Server) protocol identifier in the first <MediaLocation> entry in Listing 8-11. mms is not an actual protocol but rather a rollover scheme. In Silverlight, the MediaElement only operates over the HTTP protocol. So, whenever an mms protocol identifier is used, the MediaElement automatically rolls over to using HTTP. An additional significance of the protocol identifier is that whenever the MediaElement encounters the mms protocol identifier, it tries to stream the content first. If that is not successful, it then tries a progressive download. If it encounters the HTTP protocol identifier, it tries a progressive download first, followed by an attempt to stream. In both scenarios, you are safe using either protocol identifier. You can find more information about MMS at http://msdn.microsoft.com/en-us/library/cc239490(PROT.10).aspx.

Listing 8-12 shows the BroadcastStreams.xml that is returned by invoking the GetBroadcastStreamsList() operation.

Listing 8-12. *BroadcastStreams.xml*

```xml
<?xml version="1.0" encoding="utf-8" ?>
<MediaLocations>
  <MediaLocation>
    <Description>Random Loop</Description>
    <Uri>http://dc7600:43000/LiveMedia</Uri>
    <ImageUri>
      http://localhost/SLBook/Ch08_RichMedia/Media/AdrenalineRush_Thumb.jpg
    </ImageUri>
  </MediaLocation>
</MediaLocations>
```

Note that the <Uri> element in this case points to the broadcast publishing point that you created without specifying a media file. Recall that because this is a broadcast publishing point, the user has no control over where to begin playing a specific stream and therefore cannot point to a specific file. Because you marked the content to loop, the publishing point, once started, keeps looping the content continuously, and the client joins the stream at the point where it currently is.

Again, we do not list the code for the service operations; we encourage you to refer to Chapter 7 for a better understanding of how Silverlight interacts with WCF services. Check out the sample code for this recipe for the operation implementations.

Changes to the Player

You add a couple more media menus to the player to display the choices for the on-demand and broadcast streams that are returned through the service operations. Listing 8-13 shows the XAML for the player.

Listing 8-13. *XAML for the Streaming Player*

```xml
<UserControl x:Class="Ch08_RichMedia.Recipe8_3.MainPage"
    xmlns="http://schemas.microsoft.com/winfx/2006/xaml/presentation"
    xmlns:x="http://schemas.microsoft.com/winfx/2006/xaml"
    xmlns:vsm="clr-namespace:System.Windows;assembly=System.Windows"
    xmlns:local="clr-namespace:Ch08_RichMedia.Recipe8_3"
    Width="920" Height="547"
    xmlns:Ch08_RichMedia_Recipe8_3=
"clr-namespace:Ch08_RichMedia.Recipe8_3;assembly=Ch08_RichMedia.Recipe8_3.PlrCntls"
    >
  <UserControl.Resources>
    <DataTemplate x:Key="dtMediaMenuItem">
      <Grid Height="140" Width="160" Margin="0,8,0,8">
        <Grid.RowDefinitions>
          <RowDefinition Height="0.7*" />
          <RowDefinition Height="0.3*" />
        </Grid.RowDefinitions>
```

```xml
<Grid.ColumnDefinitions>
  <ColumnDefinition Width="0.7*"/>
  <ColumnDefinition Width="0.3*" />
</Grid.ColumnDefinitions>
<Image HorizontalAlignment="Stretch"
       VerticalAlignment="Stretch" Stretch="Fill"
       Source="{Binding MediaPreview}" Grid.Row ="0"
       Grid.ColumnSpan="2"/>
<TextBlock TextAlignment="Left" HorizontalAlignment="Stretch"
           VerticalAlignment="Stretch" Grid.Row="1"
           Text="{Binding Description}" Grid.Column="0"/>
<Grid Grid.Row="1" Grid.Column="1">
  <Grid.RowDefinitions>
    <RowDefinition Height="0.4*" />
    <RowDefinition Height="0.2*" />
    <RowDefinition Height="0.4*" />
  </Grid.RowDefinitions>
  <Button Grid.Row="0" x:Name="PlayFull" Click="PlayFull_Click"
          Tag="{Binding}" HorizontalAlignment="Center">
    <Button.Content>
      <Path Stretch="Fill" StrokeLineJoin="Round"
                    Stroke="#FF000000"
                    Data="M 120,9.15527e-005L 149.937,
                       9.15527e-005L 149.937,19.9361L 120,
                       19.9361L 120,9.15527e-005 Z M 120,
                       6.04175L 149.812,6.04175M 120,
                       14.0417L 149.937,14.0417M 123.417,
                       0.991364L 131.167,0.991364L 131.167,
                       4.88376L 123.417,4.88376L 123.417,
                       0.991364 Z M 135.125,1.00012L 142.875,
                       1.00012L 142.875,4.89246L 135.125,
                       4.89246L 135.125,1.00012 Z M 123.542,
                       15.035L 131.292,15.035L 131.292,
                       18.9274L 123.542,18.9274L 123.542,
                       15.035 Z M 135.25,15.0438L 143,
                       15.0438L 143,18.9362L 135.25,18.9362L 135.25,
                       15.0438 Z "/>
    </Button.Content>
  </Button>
```

```xml
        <Button Grid.Row="2" x:Name="PlayPIP" Click="PlayPIP_Click"
                Tag="{Binding}" HorizontalAlignment="Center">
          <Button.Content>
            <Path Stretch="Fill" StrokeThickness="2"
                            StrokeLineJoin="Round" Stroke="#FF000000"
                            Data="M 120,39.8333L 149.917,
                            39.8333L 149.917,59.9167L 120,
                            59.9167L 120,39.8333 Z M 132.917,
                            42.8333L 146.667,42.8333L 146.667,
                            52.6667L 132.917,52.6667L 132.917,
                            42.8333 Z "/>
          </Button.Content>
        </Button>
      </Grid>
    </Grid>
  </DataTemplate>
  <ControlTemplate x:Key="ctMediaMenuListBoxItem" TargetType="ListBoxItem">
    <Grid>
      <vsm:VisualStateManager.VisualStateGroups>
        <vsm:VisualStateGroup x:Name="SelectionStates">
          <vsm:VisualState x:Name="Unselected"/>
          <vsm:VisualState x:Name="SelectedUnfocused">
            <Storyboard/>
          </vsm:VisualState>
          <vsm:VisualState x:Name="Selected">
            <Storyboard/>
          </vsm:VisualState>
        </vsm:VisualStateGroup>
        <vsm:VisualStateGroup x:Name="FocusStates">
          <vsm:VisualStateGroup.Transitions>
          </vsm:VisualStateGroup.Transitions>
          <vsm:VisualState x:Name="Unfocused"/>
          <vsm:VisualState x:Name="Focused"/>
        </vsm:VisualStateGroup>
        <vsm:VisualStateGroup x:Name="CommonStates">
          <vsm:VisualStateGroup.Transitions>
            <vsm:VisualTransition
              GeneratedDuration="00:00:00.2000000" To="MouseOver"/>
            <vsm:VisualTransition From="MouseOver"
                                  GeneratedDuration="00:00:00.2000000"/>
          </vsm:VisualStateGroup.Transitions>
```

```
            <vsm:VisualState x:Name="MouseOver">
              <Storyboard>
                <ColorAnimationUsingKeyFrames BeginTime="00:00:00"
                       Duration="00:00:00.0010000"
                       Storyboard.TargetName="brdrMouseOverIndicator"
                       Storyboard.TargetProperty=
                  "(Border.BorderBrush).(SolidColorBrush.Color)">
                  <SplineColorKeyFrame KeyTime="00:00:00" Value="#FF126AB3"/>
                </ColorAnimationUsingKeyFrames>
                <ColorAnimationUsingKeyFrames BeginTime="00:00:00"
                Duration="00:00:00.0010000"
                Storyboard.TargetName="brdrMouseOverIndicator"
                Storyboard.TargetProperty=
"(Border.Background).(SolidColorBrush.Color)">
                  <SplineColorKeyFrame KeyTime="00:00:00" Value="#FF7FDDE6"/>
                </ColorAnimationUsingKeyFrames>
              </Storyboard>
            </vsm:VisualState>
            <vsm:VisualState x:Name="Normal"/>
          </vsm:VisualStateGroup>
        </vsm:VisualStateManager.VisualStateGroups>
        <Border CornerRadius="2,2,2,2" BorderThickness="3,3,3,3"
               x:Name="brdrMouseOverIndicator"
               Background="#007FDDE6" BorderBrush="#00000000">
          <ContentPresenter/>
        </Border>
      </Grid>
    </ControlTemplate>
    <Style x:Key="STYLE_MediaMenuListBoxItem" TargetType="ListBoxItem">
      <Setter Property="Template"
              Value="{StaticResource ctMediaMenuListBoxItem}"/>
    </Style>

    <ControlTemplate x:Key="ctMenuSwitchButton" TargetType="RadioButton">
      <Grid>
        <vsm:VisualStateManager.VisualStateGroups>
          <vsm:VisualStateGroup x:Name="CheckStates">
            <vsm:VisualState x:Name="Unchecked"/>
```

```xml
                <vsm:VisualState x:Name="Checked">
                  <Storyboard>
                    <ColorAnimationUsingKeyFrames BeginTime="00:00:00"
        Duration="00:00:00.0010000"
        Storyboard.TargetName="border"
        Storyboard.TargetProperty="(Border.BorderBrush).(SolidColorBrush.Color)">
                      <SplineColorKeyFrame KeyTime="00:00:00" Value="#FF000000"/>
                    </ColorAnimationUsingKeyFrames>
                    <ColorAnimationUsingKeyFrames BeginTime="00:00:00"
                        Duration="00:00:00.0010000"
                        Storyboard.TargetName="border"
                        Storyboard.TargetProperty=
"(Border.Background).(SolidColorBrush.Color)">
                      <SplineColorKeyFrame KeyTime="00:00:00" Value="#FF3CB1E8"/>
                    </ColorAnimationUsingKeyFrames>
                  </Storyboard>
                </vsm:VisualState>
                <vsm:VisualState x:Name="Indeterminate"/>
              </vsm:VisualStateGroup>
              <vsm:VisualStateGroup x:Name="CommonStates">
                <vsm:VisualState x:Name="Disabled"/>
                <vsm:VisualState x:Name="Normal"/>
                <vsm:VisualState x:Name="MouseOver"/>
                <vsm:VisualState x:Name="Pressed"/>
              </vsm:VisualStateGroup>
              <vsm:VisualStateGroup x:Name="FocusStates">
                <vsm:VisualState x:Name="Focused"/>
                <vsm:VisualState x:Name="Unfocused"/>
              </vsm:VisualStateGroup>
            </vsm:VisualStateManager.VisualStateGroups>
            <Border HorizontalAlignment="Stretch" VerticalAlignment="Stretch"
                    CornerRadius="3,3,0,0" Margin="0,0,0,0"
                    BorderThickness="2,2,2,0" BorderBrush="#FF000000"
                    x:Name="border" Background="#003CB1E8">
              <TextBlock Text="{TemplateBinding Content}"
                    TextWrapping="Wrap" TextAlignment="Center"
                    FontSize="10" FontWeight="Normal"
                    FontFamily="Portable User Interface"
                    VerticalAlignment="Center"/>
            </Border>
          </Grid>
        </ControlTemplate>
      </UserControl.Resources>
```

```
<Grid x:Name="LayoutRoot"
      Background="#FFA2A2A2" Height="Auto" Width="Auto">
  <Grid.RowDefinitions>
    <RowDefinition Height="0.062*"/>
    <RowDefinition Height="0.689*"/>
    <RowDefinition Height="0.249*"/>
  </Grid.RowDefinitions>
  <Grid.ColumnDefinitions>
    <ColumnDefinition Width="0.2*"/>
    <ColumnDefinition Width="0.8*"/>
  </Grid.ColumnDefinitions>
  <MediaElement Height="Auto" Margin="0,0,0,0"
                VerticalAlignment="Top" x:Name="mediaelemMain"
                BufferingTime="0:0:3"
                HorizontalAlignment="Left" AutoPlay="True" Opacity="0"/>
  <MediaElement Height="Auto" Margin="0,0,0,0" VerticalAlignment="Top"
                x:Name="mediaelemPIP" HorizontalAlignment="Left"
                AutoPlay="True" Opacity="0" IsMuted="True"
                BufferingTime="0:0:3"/>

  <Grid Grid.Row="0" Grid.Column="1" Grid.RowSpan="2">
    <Grid.RowDefinitions>
      <RowDefinition Height="0.05*" />
      <RowDefinition Height="0.9*" />
      <RowDefinition Height="0.05*" />
    </Grid.RowDefinitions>
    <Grid.ColumnDefinitions>
      <ColumnDefinition Width="0.05*"/>
      <ColumnDefinition Width="0.9*"/>
      <ColumnDefinition Width="0.05*"/>
    </Grid.ColumnDefinitions>
    <Border x:Name="displayMain"
            VerticalAlignment="Stretch" Grid.Column="1" Grid.Row="1"
            HorizontalAlignment="Stretch" BorderThickness="5,5,5,5"
            BorderBrush="#FF000000" >
      <Border.Background>
        <VideoBrush SourceName="mediaelemMain" Stretch="Fill"
                    x:Name="vidbrushMain" />
      </Border.Background>
    </Border>
```

```
<Grid Grid.Column="1" Grid.Row="1">
  <Grid.RowDefinitions>
    <RowDefinition Height="0.025*" />
    <RowDefinition Height="0.35*" />
    <RowDefinition Height="0.625*" />
  </Grid.RowDefinitions>
  <Grid.ColumnDefinitions>
    <ColumnDefinition Width="0.635*"/>
    <ColumnDefinition Width="0.35*"/>
    <ColumnDefinition Width="0.015*"/>
  </Grid.ColumnDefinitions>
  <Border Grid.Column="1" Grid.Row="1" HorizontalAlignment="Stretch"
          VerticalAlignment="Stretch"
          MouseLeftButtonUp="displayPIP_MouseLeftButtonUp"
          x:Name="displayPIP" BorderThickness="2,2,2,2"
          BorderBrush="#FF000000" Visibility="Collapsed">
    <Border.Background>
      <VideoBrush SourceName="mediaelemPIP"
                  Stretch="Fill" x:Name="vidbrushPIP"/>
    </Border.Background>
  </Border>
  <Grid HorizontalAlignment="Stretch" Margin="8,8,8,8"
        Grid.RowSpan="1" Grid.Column="1" Grid.Row="1"
        x:Name="buttonsPIP" Visibility="Collapsed" >
    <Grid.RowDefinitions>
      <RowDefinition Height="0.1*"/>
      <RowDefinition Height="0.25*"/>
      <RowDefinition Height="0.1*"/>
      <RowDefinition Height="0.25*"/>
      <RowDefinition Height="0.3*"/>
    </Grid.RowDefinitions>
    <Grid.ColumnDefinitions>
      <ColumnDefinition Width="0.749*"/>
      <ColumnDefinition Width="0.176*"/>
      <ColumnDefinition Width="0.075*"/>
    </Grid.ColumnDefinitions>
    <Button Margin="0,0,0,0" Grid.RowSpan="1" Grid.Row="1"
            Grid.ColumnSpan="1" Grid.Column="1"
            x:Name="btnClosePIP" Click="btnClosePIP_Click"
          >
```

```xml
          <Button.Content>
            <Path x:Name="Path" Stretch="Fill" StrokeThickness="2"
                  StrokeLineJoin="Round" Stroke="#FF000000" Fill="#FFE91111"
                  Data="M 110.5,75.7635L 113.209,
                  72.9631L 133.396,92.4865L 130.687,95.2869L 110.5,
                  75.7635 Z M 130.801,73.4961L 133.393,76.4048L 112.425,
                  95.0872L 109.833,92.1785L 130.801,73.4961 Z "/>
          </Button.Content>
        </Button>
        <Button Margin="0,0,0,0" Grid.RowSpan="1" Grid.Row="3"
                Grid.ColumnSpan="1" Grid.Column="1"
                x:Name="btnSwitchPIP" Click="btnSwitchPIP_Click"
                >
          <Button.Content>
            <Path Stretch="Fill" StrokeThickness="2" StrokeLineJoin="Round"
                  Stroke="#FF000000" Data="M 120,39.8333L 149.917,
                  39.8333L 149.917,59.9167L 120,59.9167L 120,
                  39.8333 Z M 132.917,42.8333L 146.667,42.8333L 146.667,
                  52.6667L 132.917,52.6667L 132.917,42.8333 Z "/>
          </Button.Content>
        </Button>
      </Grid>
    </Grid>
  </Grid>
</Grid>
<Grid Margin="2,2,2,2" VerticalAlignment="Stretch" Grid.Column="1"
      Grid.Row="2" HorizontalAlignment="Stretch">
  <Grid.RowDefinitions>
    <RowDefinition Height="0.5*"/>
    <RowDefinition Height="0.5*"/>
  </Grid.RowDefinitions>
  <Grid.ColumnDefinitions>
    <ColumnDefinition Width="0.75*"/>
    <ColumnDefinition Width="0.25*"/>
  </Grid.ColumnDefinitions>
  <Ch08_RichMedia_Recipe8_3:MediaSlider SourceName="mediaelemMain"
                        VerticalAlignment="Top"
                        IsEnabled="True"
                        x:Name="mediaSlider" Grid.ColumnSpan="2"/>
  <Ch08_RichMedia_Recipe8_3:MediaButtonsPanel Grid.Row="1" Grid.Column="0"
                        SourceName="mediaelemMain"
                        HorizontalAlignment="Center"
                        VerticalAlignment="Center"
                        Width="150" Height="40"
                        x:Name="mediaControl"/>
```

```
    <Slider x:Name="sliderVolumeControl"  Margin="5,0,5,0" Maximum="1"
            Minimum="0" SmallChange="0.1"
            LargeChange="0.2"  Value="0.5"
            MinWidth="50" Grid.Row="1"
            Grid.Column="1" ValueChanged="sliderVolumeControl_ValueChanged">
    </Slider>
</Grid>
<Grid Grid.RowSpan="3">
  <Grid.RowDefinitions>
    <RowDefinition Height="Auto" MinHeight="41" />
    <RowDefinition Height="*" />
  </Grid.RowDefinitions>
  <Grid Height="Auto" VerticalAlignment="Stretch">
    <Grid.ColumnDefinitions>
      <ColumnDefinition Width="0.33*"/>
      <ColumnDefinition Width="0.34*"/>
      <ColumnDefinition Width="0.33*"/>
    </Grid.ColumnDefinitions>
    <RadioButton HorizontalAlignment="Stretch" VerticalAlignment="Stretch"
                 Content="Download"
                 Template="{StaticResource ctMenuSwitchButton}"
                 HorizontalContentAlignment="Stretch"
                 VerticalContentAlignment="Stretch"
                 GroupName="MediaMenuChoices"
                 IsChecked="False" x:Name="rbtnDownloadsMenu"
                 Checked="rbtnDownloadsMenu_Checked"/>
    <RadioButton HorizontalAlignment="Stretch" VerticalAlignment="Stretch"
                 Content="On Demand" Grid.Column="1"
                 Template="{StaticResource ctMenuSwitchButton}"
                 HorizontalContentAlignment="Stretch"
                 VerticalContentAlignment="Stretch"
                 GroupName="MediaMenuChoices"
                 IsChecked="True" x:Name="rbtnOnDemandMenu"
                 Checked="rbtnOnDemandMenu_Checked"/>
    <RadioButton HorizontalAlignment="Stretch" VerticalAlignment="Stretch"
                 Content="Broadcast" Grid.Column="2"
                 Template="{StaticResource ctMenuSwitchButton}"
                 HorizontalContentAlignment="Stretch"
                 VerticalContentAlignment="Stretch"
                 GroupName="MediaMenuChoices" x:Name="rbtnBroadcastMenu"
                 Checked="rbtnBroadcastMenu_Checked"/>
  </Grid>
```

```
    <ListBox Margin="0,0,0,0" VerticalAlignment="Stretch"
             x:Name="lbxMediaMenuDownloads"
             ItemTemplate="{StaticResource dtMediaMenuItem}"
             ItemContainerStyle="{StaticResource STYLE_MediaMenuListBoxItem}"
             Grid.RowSpan="1" Grid.Row="1" Background="#FF3CB1E8"
             Visibility="Collapsed"
        />
    <ListBox Margin="0,0,0,0" VerticalAlignment="Stretch"
             x:Name="lbxMediaMenuOnDemandStreams"
             ItemTemplate="{StaticResource dtMediaMenuItem}"
             ItemContainerStyle="{StaticResource STYLE_MediaMenuListBoxItem}"
             Grid.RowSpan="1" Grid.Row="1" Background="#FF3CB1E8"
        />
    <ListBox Margin="0,0,0,0" VerticalAlignment="Stretch"
             x:Name="lbxMediaMenuBroadcastStreams"
             ItemTemplate="{StaticResource dtMediaMenuItem}"
             ItemContainerStyle="{StaticResource STYLE_MediaMenuListBoxItem}"
             Visibility="Collapsed"
             Background="#FF3CB1E8" Grid.RowSpan="1" Grid.Row="1"
        />
  </Grid>
 </Grid>
</UserControl>
```

You implement the two additional menus for on-demand and broadcast content by adding two ListBoxes named lbxMediaMenuOnDemandStreams and lbxMediaMenuBroadcastStreams, as shown in bold in Listing 8-13. You set lbxDownloadsMenu.Visibility and lbxBroadcastMenu.Visibility to Collapsed so that the on-demand list shows up by default. You also add three RadioButton controls—rbtnDownloadsMenu, rbtnOnDemandMenu, and rbtnBroadcastMenu—which switch between the ListBoxes. A custom template named ctMenuSwitchButton is defined and applied to the RadioButtons to make them look more like tabs. Also note the use of the BufferingTime property on the MediaElement. It specifies the minimum content length (in time) that the MediaElement buffers at the start and every time it runs out of content to play.

Figure 8-14 shows the look of the new menu arrangement at startup.

The RadioButtons are also made to belong to the same group by setting a common value for the GroupName property. This means that selecting one will deselect the others automatically. You see the menu-switching in the player code shown in Listing 8-14.

Figure 8-14. *Streaming player menu at startup*

Listing 8-14. *Streaming Player Code-Behind*

```
using System;
using System.Collections.Generic;
using System.Collections.ObjectModel;
using System.Linq;
using System.Net;
using System.Windows;
using System.Windows.Controls;
using System.Windows.Input;
using System.Xml.Linq;

namespace Ch08_RichMedia.Recipe8_3
{
  public partial class Page : UserControl
  {
    private const string DownloadsListUri =
      "http://localhost:9292/MediaLocationProvider.svc/GetDownloadsList";
    private const string OnDemandStreamsListUri =
      "http://localhost:9292/MediaLocationProvider.svc/GetOnDemandStreamsList";
```

```
private const string BroadcastStreamsListUri =
  "http://localhost:9292/MediaLocationProvider.svc/GetBroadcastStreamsList";
private ObservableCollection<MediaMenuData> listDownloads =
  new ObservableCollection<MediaMenuData>();
private ObservableCollection<MediaMenuData> listOnDemandStreams =
 new ObservableCollection<MediaMenuData>();
private ObservableCollection<MediaMenuData> listBroadcastStreams =
 new ObservableCollection<MediaMenuData>();

public Page()
{
  InitializeComponent();
  lbxMediaMenuDownloads.ItemsSource = listDownloads;
  lbxMediaMenuOnDemandStreams.ItemsSource = listOnDemandStreams;
  lbxMediaMenuBroadcastStreams.ItemsSource = listBroadcastStreams;
  this.Loaded += new RoutedEventHandler(Page_Loaded);
}

void Page_Loaded(object sender, RoutedEventArgs e)
{
  PopulateMediaMenu();
}
private MediaElement MainVideo
{
  get
  {
    return (vidbrushMain.SourceName == "mediaelemMain") ?
    mediaelemMain : mediaelemPIP;
  }
}
private MediaElement PIPVideo
{
  get
  {
    return (vidbrushPIP.SourceName == "mediaelemMain") ?
    mediaelemMain : mediaelemPIP;
  }
}

private void PopulateMediaMenu()
{
  WebClient wcDownloads = new WebClient();
  wcDownloads.DownloadStringCompleted +=
    new DownloadStringCompletedEventHandler(ListDownloadCompleted);
  WebClient wcOnDemand = new WebClient();
```

```
      wcOnDemand.DownloadStringCompleted+=
        new DownloadStringCompletedEventHandler(ListDownloadCompleted);
      WebClient wcBroadcast = new WebClient();
      wcBroadcast.DownloadStringCompleted +=
        new DownloadStringCompletedEventHandler(ListDownloadCompleted);

      wcDownloads.DownloadStringAsync(new Uri(DownloadsListUri), listDownloads);
      wcOnDemand.DownloadStringAsync(
new Uri(OnDemandStreamsListUri), listOnDemandStreams);
      wcBroadcast.DownloadStringAsync(
new Uri(BroadcastStreamsListUri), listBroadcastStreams);
    }
    void ListDownloadCompleted(object sender, DownloadStringCompletedEventArgs e)
    {
      this.Dispatcher.BeginInvoke(new Action(delegate
      {
        XDocument xDoc = XDocument.Parse(e.Result);

        List<MediaMenuData> tempList =
          (from medloc in xDoc.Root.Elements()
           select new MediaMenuData
           {
             Description = medloc.Element("Description").Value,
             MediaLocation = new Uri(medloc.Element("Uri").Value),
             MediaPreview = medloc.Element("ImageUri").Value
           }).ToList();

        ObservableCollection<MediaMenuData> target =
(e.UserState as ObservableCollection<MediaMenuData>);
        foreach (MediaMenuData medloc in tempList)
          target.Add(medloc);
      }));
    }

    private void PlayFull_Click(object sender, RoutedEventArgs e)
    {
      MainVideo.Source = ((sender as Button).Tag as MediaMenuData).MediaLocation;
    }

    private void PlayPIP_Click(object sender, RoutedEventArgs e)
    {
      PIPVideo.Source = ((sender as Button).Tag as MediaMenuData).MediaLocation;
      displayPIP.Visibility = Visibility.Visible;
    }
```

```
private void btnClosePIP_Click(object sender, RoutedEventArgs e)
{
  PIPVideo.Stop();
  buttonsPIP.Visibility = displayPIP.Visibility = Visibility.Collapsed;
}

private void btnSwitchPIP_Click(object sender, RoutedEventArgs e)
{
  if (vidbrushMain.SourceName == "mediaelemMain")
  {
    vidbrushMain.SourceName = "mediaelemPIP";
    vidbrushPIP.SourceName = "mediaelemMain";
    mediaSlider.SourceName = "mediaelemPIP";
    mediaControl.SourceName = "mediaelemPIP";
    mediaelemMain.IsMuted = true;
    mediaelemPIP.IsMuted = false;
  }
  else
  {
    vidbrushMain.SourceName = "mediaelemMain";
    vidbrushPIP.SourceName = "mediaelemPIP";
    mediaSlider.SourceName = "mediaelemMain";
    mediaControl.SourceName = "mediaelemMain";
    mediaelemMain.IsMuted = false;
    mediaelemPIP.IsMuted = true;
  }
  MainVideo.Volume = sliderVolumeControl.Value;
}

private void displayPIP_MouseLeftButtonUp(object sender,
  MouseButtonEventArgs e)
{
  if (displayPIP.Visibility == Visibility.Visible)
  {
    buttonsPIP.Visibility =
      (buttonsPIP.Visibility == Visibility.Visible ?
      Visibility.Collapsed : Visibility.Visible);
  }
}
private void sliderVolumeControl_ValueChanged(object sender,
  RoutedPropertyChangedEventArgs<double> e)
{
```

```
    if (vidbrushMain != null)
    {
      MainVideo.Volume = e.NewValue;
    }
  }
  private void rbtnDownloadsMenu_Checked(object sender, RoutedEventArgs e)
  {
    if (lbxMediaMenuBroadcastStreams != null &&
      lbxMediaMenuDownloads != null &&
      lbxMediaMenuOnDemandStreams != null)
    {
      lbxMediaMenuBroadcastStreams.Visibility = Visibility.Collapsed;
      lbxMediaMenuOnDemandStreams.Visibility = Visibility.Collapsed;
      lbxMediaMenuDownloads.Visibility = Visibility.Visible;
    }
  }

  private void rbtnOnDemandMenu_Checked(object sender, RoutedEventArgs e)
  {
    if (lbxMediaMenuBroadcastStreams != null &&
      lbxMediaMenuDownloads != null &&
      lbxMediaMenuOnDemandStreams != null)
    {
      lbxMediaMenuBroadcastStreams.Visibility = Visibility.Collapsed;
      lbxMediaMenuOnDemandStreams.Visibility = Visibility.Visible;
      lbxMediaMenuDownloads.Visibility = Visibility.Collapsed;
    }
  }

  private void rbtnBroadcastMenu_Checked(object sender, RoutedEventArgs e)
  {
    if (lbxMediaMenuBroadcastStreams != null &&
      lbxMediaMenuDownloads != null &&
      lbxMediaMenuOnDemandStreams != null)
    {
      lbxMediaMenuBroadcastStreams.Visibility = Visibility.Visible;
      lbxMediaMenuOnDemandStreams.Visibility = Visibility.Collapsed;
      lbxMediaMenuDownloads.Visibility = Visibility.Collapsed;
    }
  }
}
}
```

You change the `PopulateMediaMenu()` method to add calls to the `GetOnDemandStreamsList()` and `GetBroadcastStreamsList()` service operations, and you bind the results to `lbxMediaMenuOnDemandStreams` and `lbxMediaMenuBroadcastStreams`, respectively. Note that because the underlying schema for the XML returned by all three operations is identical, you use the same handler for handling the `WebClient.DownloadStringAsyncCompleted` event, and the same LINQ to XML–based parsing logic in it. You pass in the appropriate collection bound to the `ListBox` that the returned XML would populate to get the desired results.

You add `Checked` event handlers for the `RadioButtons` where we show only the corresponding `ListBox` and hide the others, as shown in bold in Listing 8-14.

You also make some changes to the `MediaSlider` control. Most of the changes made to this control are to accommodate the various constraints that playback of streaming media may impose in broadcast streams, such as the inability to seek through the media. Listing 8-15 shows the modified XAML for the `MediaSlider` control template.

Listing 8-15. *XAML for the MediaSlider control*

```
<ControlTemplate TargetType="local:MediaSlider" x:Key="ctMediaSliderDefault">
  <Grid x:Name="Root">
    <Grid.Resources>
      <ControlTemplate x:Key="ctRepeatButton">
        <Grid x:Name="Root" Opacity="0" Background="Transparent"/>
      </ControlTemplate>
    </Grid.Resources>
    <vsm:VisualStateManager.VisualStateGroups>
      <vsm:VisualStateGroup x:Name="CommonStates">
        <vsm:VisualStateGroup.Transitions>
          <vsm:VisualTransition GeneratedDuration="0"/>
        </vsm:VisualStateGroup.Transitions>
        <vsm:VisualState x:Name="Normal"/>
        <vsm:VisualState x:Name="MouseOver"/>
        <vsm:VisualState x:Name="Disabled">
          <Storyboard>
            <DoubleAnimationUsingKeyFrames Storyboard.TargetName="Root"
            Storyboard.TargetProperty="(UIElement.Opacity)">
              <SplineDoubleKeyFrame KeyTime="00:00:00" Value="0.5"/>
            </DoubleAnimationUsingKeyFrames>
          </Storyboard>
        </vsm:VisualState>
      </vsm:VisualStateGroup>
      <vsm:VisualStateGroup x:Name="SeekStates">
        <vsm:VisualState x:Name="CannotSeek">
          <Storyboard>
            <ObjectAnimationUsingKeyFrames
              Storyboard.TargetName="HorizontalThumb"
              Storyboard.TargetProperty="Visibility">
```

```xml
            <DiscreteObjectKeyFrame KeyTime="0">
              <DiscreteObjectKeyFrame.Value>
                <Visibility>Collapsed</Visibility>
              </DiscreteObjectKeyFrame.Value>
            </DiscreteObjectKeyFrame>
          </ObjectAnimationUsingKeyFrames>
        </Storyboard>
      </vsm:VisualState>
      <vsm:VisualState x:Name="CanSeek">
        <Storyboard>
          <ObjectAnimationUsingKeyFrames
            Storyboard.TargetName="HorizontalThumb"
            Storyboard.TargetProperty="Visibility">
            <DiscreteObjectKeyFrame KeyTime="0">
              <DiscreteObjectKeyFrame.Value>
                <Visibility>Visible</Visibility>
              </DiscreteObjectKeyFrame.Value>
            </DiscreteObjectKeyFrame>
          </ObjectAnimationUsingKeyFrames>
        </Storyboard>
      </vsm:VisualState>
    </vsm:VisualStateGroup>
      <vsm:VisualStateGroup x:Name="ContentStates">
      <vsm:VisualState x:Name="Buffering">
        <Storyboard>
          <DoubleAnimationUsingKeyFrames BeginTime="00:00:00"
           Duration="00:00:00.0010000"
           Storyboard.TargetName="BufferingProgress"
           Storyboard.TargetProperty="(UIElement.Opacity)">
              <SplineDoubleKeyFrame KeyTime="00:00:00" Value="100"/>
           </DoubleAnimationUsingKeyFrames>
        </Storyboard>
      </vsm:VisualState>
      <vsm:VisualState x:Name="Playing">
        <Storyboard>
          <DoubleAnimationUsingKeyFrames BeginTime="00:00:00"
                Duration="00:00:00.0010000"
                Storyboard.TargetName="BufferingProgress"
                Storyboard.TargetProperty="(UIElement.Opacity)">
              <SplineDoubleKeyFrame KeyTime="00:00:00" Value="0"/>
           </DoubleAnimationUsingKeyFrames>
        </Storyboard>
      </vsm:VisualState>
    </vsm:VisualStateGroup>
```

```xml
    <vsm:VisualStateGroup x:Name="DurationStates">
      <vsm:VisualState x:Name="UnknownDuration">
        <Storyboard>
          <ObjectAnimationUsingKeyFrames Storyboard.TargetName="TotalDuration"
                  Storyboard.TargetProperty="Visibility">
            <DiscreteObjectKeyFrame KeyTime="0">
              <DiscreteObjectKeyFrame.Value>
                <Visibility>Collapsed</Visibility>
              </DiscreteObjectKeyFrame.Value>
            </DiscreteObjectKeyFrame>
          </ObjectAnimationUsingKeyFrames>
          <ObjectAnimationUsingKeyFrames
            Storyboard.TargetName="elemPlayProgressIndicator"
            Storyboard.TargetProperty="Visibility">
            <DiscreteObjectKeyFrame KeyTime="0">
              <DiscreteObjectKeyFrame.Value>
                <Visibility>Collapsed</Visibility>
              </DiscreteObjectKeyFrame.Value>
            </DiscreteObjectKeyFrame>
          </ObjectAnimationUsingKeyFrames>
        </Storyboard>
      </vsm:VisualState>
      <vsm:VisualState x:Name="KnownDuration">
        <Storyboard>
          <ObjectAnimationUsingKeyFrames Storyboard.TargetName="TotalDuration"
                  Storyboard.TargetProperty="Visibility">
            <DiscreteObjectKeyFrame KeyTime="0">
              <DiscreteObjectKeyFrame.Value>
                <Visibility>Visible</Visibility>
              </DiscreteObjectKeyFrame.Value>
            </DiscreteObjectKeyFrame>
          </ObjectAnimationUsingKeyFrames>
          <ObjectAnimationUsingKeyFrames
            Storyboard.TargetName="elemPlayProgressIndicator"
            Storyboard.TargetProperty="Visibility">
            <DiscreteObjectKeyFrame KeyTime="0">
              <DiscreteObjectKeyFrame.Value>
                <Visibility>Visible</Visibility>
              </DiscreteObjectKeyFrame.Value>
            </DiscreteObjectKeyFrame>
          </ObjectAnimationUsingKeyFrames>
        </Storyboard>
      </vsm:VisualState>
    </vsm:VisualStateGroup>
  </vsm:VisualStateManager.VisualStateGroups>
```

```
<Grid>
  <Grid.RowDefinitions>
    <RowDefinition Height="0.33*" />
    <RowDefinition Height="0.34*" />
    <RowDefinition Height="0.33*" />
  </Grid.RowDefinitions>
  <Grid Grid.Row="0" VerticalAlignment="Top" HorizontalAlignment="Stretch">
    <Grid.ColumnDefinitions>
      <ColumnDefinition Width="Auto" />
      <ColumnDefinition Width="*" />
      <ColumnDefinition Width="Auto" />
    </Grid.ColumnDefinitions>
    <StackPanel Orientation="Horizontal" Grid.Column="0"
                HorizontalAlignment="Left"
                x:Name="BufferingProgress" Opacity="0">
      <TextBlock Text="Buffering" FontSize="12"
                Margin="0,0,4,0"/>
      <TextBlock x:Name="textBufferingPercent" FontSize="12"
                />
    </StackPanel>
    <StackPanel Orientation="Horizontal" Grid.Column="2"
                HorizontalAlignment="Right"
                x:Name="DownloadProgress">
      <TextBlock Text="Downloaded" FontSize="12"
                Margin="0,0,4,0"/>
      <TextBlock x:Name="textDownloadPercent" FontSize="12"
                />
    </StackPanel>
  </Grid>
  <Grid x:Name="HorizontalTemplate" Grid.Row="1" >
    <Grid.ColumnDefinitions>
      <ColumnDefinition Width="Auto" />
      <ColumnDefinition Width="Auto" />
      <ColumnDefinition Width="*" />
    </Grid.ColumnDefinitions>
    <Rectangle Stroke="Black" StrokeThickness="0.5" Fill="#FFE6EFF7"
                Grid.Column="0" Grid.ColumnSpan="3" Height="14"
                Margin="5,0,5,0" />
    <Border Height="10" Margin="5,0,5,0" Grid.Column="0" Grid.ColumnSpan="3"
            x:Name="elemDownloadProgressIndicator" Background="#FF2185D8"
            HorizontalAlignment="Left" Width="0"  />
```

```
            <Border Height="6" Margin="5,0,5,0" Grid.Column="0" Grid.ColumnSpan="3"
                    x:Name="elemPlayProgressIndicator" Background="#FF1CE421"
                    HorizontalAlignment="Left" Width="0"  />

            <RepeatButton x:Name="HorizontalTrackLargeChangeDecreaseRepeatButton"
                          Grid.Column="0"
                          Template="{StaticResource ctRepeatButton}"
                          IsTabStop="False"  />
            <Thumb x:Name="HorizontalThumb" Height="14" Width="11" Grid.Column="1"/>
            <RepeatButton x:Name="HorizontalTrackLargeChangeIncreaseRepeatButton"
                          Grid.Column="2"
                          Template="{StaticResource ctRepeatButton}"
                          IsTabStop="False"  />
          </Grid>
          <Grid Grid.Row="2" VerticalAlignment="Bottom"
                HorizontalAlignment="Stretch">
            <StackPanel x:Name="TotalDuration" Orientation="Horizontal"
                        Visibility="Collapsed">
              <TextBlock x:Name="textPosition" FontSize="12"/>
              <TextBlock Text=" / " FontSize="12" Margin="3,0,3,0"/>
              <TextBlock x:Name="textDuration" FontSize="12" />
            </StackPanel>
          </Grid>
        </Grid>
      </Grid>
    </ControlTemplate>

    <Style TargetType="local:MediaSlider">
      <Setter Property="Template" Value="{StaticResource ctMediaSliderDefault}"/>
    </Style>
```

As you can see in Listing 8-15 (indicated in bold), a new TextBlock named textBufferingPercent contained inside a StackPanel named BufferingProgress reports progress when streaming media is buffering.

You also add several visual states to handle certain aspects of streaming media. The SeekStates state group contains two states: CannotSeek, which hides the Thumb to indicate that the media cannot be forwarded or rewound, and CanSeek, which makes the Thumb visible in cases where the media can be forwarded or rewound. The DurationStates group contains KnownDuration, which makes the StackPanel named TotalDuration and its children visible if the total duration of the media is available, and the UnknownDuration state, which hides them when the duration is not known. The ContentStates group contains the Buffering state, which makes the StackPanel named BufferingProgress visible, and the Playing state, which hides the StackPanel. Last is the DownloadStates group, where the NoDownload state hides the DownloadProgressIndicator and the StackPanel named DownloadProgress, whereas the NeedsDownload state does the reverse.

Let's look at the additions to the control code to see how these states are used (see Listing 8-16).

Listing 8-16. *MediaSlider Code with the Changes for Streaming*

```
using System;
using System.Windows;
using System.Windows.Controls;
using System.Windows.Controls.Primitives;
using System.Windows.Media;
using System.Windows.Threading;

namespace Ch08_RichMedia.Recipe8_3
{
  [TemplateVisualState(GroupName="SeekStates",Name="CanSeek")]
  [TemplateVisualState(GroupName = "SeekStates", Name = "CannotSeek")]
  [TemplateVisualState(GroupName = "ContentStates", Name = "Buffering")]
  [TemplateVisualState(GroupName = "ContentStates", Name = "Playing")]
  [TemplateVisualState(GroupName = "DurationStates", Name = "UnknownDuration")]
  [TemplateVisualState(GroupName = "DurationStates", Name = "KnownDuration")]
  public class MediaSlider : Slider
  {
    private MediaElement MediaSource;
    private FrameworkElement elemDownloadProgressIndicator;
    private FrameworkElement elemBufferingProgressIndicator;
    private FrameworkElement elemPlayProgressIndicator;
    private FrameworkElement Root;
    private TextBlock textPosition;
    private TextBlock textDuration;
    private TextBlock textDownloadPercent;
    private TextBlock textBufferingPercent;
    private Thumb HorizontalThumb;
    private DispatcherTimer disptimerPlayProgressUpdate;

    public static DependencyProperty SourceNameProperty =
      DependencyProperty.Register("SourceName", typeof(string),
      typeof(MediaSlider),
      new PropertyMetadata(new PropertyChangedCallback(OnSourceNameChanged)));
    public string SourceName
    {
      get
      {
        return (string)GetValue(SourceNameProperty);
      }
```

```
    set
    {
      SetValue(SourceNameProperty, value);
    }
  }
  private static void OnSourceNameChanged(DependencyObject Source,
    DependencyPropertyChangedEventArgs e)
  {
    MediaSlider thisSlider = Source as MediaSlider;
    if (e.NewValue != null && e.NewValue != e.OldValue
      && thisSlider.Root != null)
    {
      thisSlider.MediaSource =
        thisSlider.Root.FindName(e.NewValue as string) as MediaElement;
      thisSlider.InitMediaElementConnections();
    }
  }

  public MediaSlider()
    : base()
  {
    this.DefaultStyleKey = typeof(MediaSlider);
    this.Maximum = 100;
    this.Minimum = 0;
    disptimerPlayProgressUpdate = new DispatcherTimer();
    disptimerPlayProgressUpdate.Interval = new TimeSpan(0, 0, 0, 0, 50);
    disptimerPlayProgressUpdate.Tick +=
      new EventHandler(PlayProgressUpdate_Tick);
  }
  public override void OnApplyTemplate()
  {
    base.OnApplyTemplate();

    elemDownloadProgressIndicator =
      GetTemplateChild("elemDownloadProgressIndicator") as FrameworkElement;
    elemBufferingProgressIndicator =
      GetTemplateChild("elemBufferingProgressIndicator") as FrameworkElement;
    elemPlayProgressIndicator =
      GetTemplateChild("elemPlayProgressIndicator") as FrameworkElement;
    HorizontalThumb = GetTemplateChild("HorizontalThumb") as Thumb;
```

```
  if (HorizontalThumb != null)
  {
    HorizontalThumb.DragStarted +=
      new DragStartedEventHandler(HorizontalThumb_DragStarted);
    HorizontalThumb.DragCompleted +=
      new DragCompletedEventHandler(HorizontalThumb_DragCompleted);
  }

  textPosition = GetTemplateChild("textPosition") as TextBlock;
  textDuration = GetTemplateChild("textDuration") as TextBlock;
  textDownloadPercent = GetTemplateChild("textDownloadPercent") as TextBlock;
  textBufferingPercent = GetTemplateChild("textBufferingPercent") as TextBlock;
  Root = Helper.FindRoot(this);
  MediaSource = Root.FindName(SourceName) as MediaElement;
  InitMediaElementConnections();
}
private void InitMediaElementConnections()
{
  if (MediaSource != null)
  {
    MediaSource.MediaOpened += new RoutedEventHandler(MediaSource_MediaOpened);
    MediaSource.MediaEnded +=
      new RoutedEventHandler(MediaSource_MediaEnded);
    MediaSource.MediaFailed +=
      new EventHandler<ExceptionRoutedEventArgs>(MediaSource_MediaFailed);
    MediaSource.CurrentStateChanged +=
      new RoutedEventHandler(MediaSource_CurrentStateChanged);
    MediaSource.DownloadProgressChanged +=
      new RoutedEventHandler(MediaSource_DownloadProgressChanged);
    MediaSource.BufferingProgressChanged +=
      new RoutedEventHandler(MediaSource_BufferingProgressChanged);

    MediaSource_CurrentStateChanged(this, new RoutedEventArgs());
  }
}

void PlayProgressUpdate_Tick(object sender, EventArgs e)
{
  if (MediaSource.NaturalDuration.TimeSpan == TimeSpan.Zero)
    return;

  this.Value =
    (MediaSource.Position.TotalMilliseconds /
    MediaSource.NaturalDuration.TimeSpan.TotalMilliseconds)
    * (this.Maximum - this.Minimum);
```

```
    if (elemPlayProgressIndicator != null)
    {
      elemPlayProgressIndicator.Width =
        (MediaSource.Position.TotalMilliseconds /
        MediaSource.NaturalDuration.TimeSpan.TotalMilliseconds)
        * ActualWidth;
    }
    if (textPosition != null)
      textPosition.Text = string.Format("{0:00}:{1:00}:{2:00}:{3:000}",
        MediaSource.Position.Hours,
        MediaSource.Position.Minutes,
        MediaSource.Position.Seconds,
        MediaSource.Position.Milliseconds);
  }
  void HorizontalThumb_DragCompleted(object sender, DragCompletedEventArgs e)
  {
    if (MediaSource != null && MediaSource.CurrentState ==
      MediaElementState.Playing
      && MediaSource.NaturalDuration.TimeSpan != TimeSpan.Zero)
    {
      MediaSource.Position = new TimeSpan(0,
        0, 0, 0,
        (int)(this.Value *
        MediaSource.NaturalDuration.TimeSpan.TotalMilliseconds / 100));
    }
    MediaSource.Play();
  }
  void HorizontalThumb_DragStarted(object sender, DragStartedEventArgs e)
  {
    if(MediaSource != null &&
      MediaSource.CurrentState == MediaElementState.Playing
      && MediaSource.CanPause)
    MediaSource.Pause();
  }

  private void MediaSource_DownloadProgressChanged(object sender,
    RoutedEventArgs e)
  {
    if (elemDownloadProgressIndicator != null)
    {
      elemDownloadProgressIndicator.Width =
        (MediaSource.DownloadProgress * this.ActualWidth);
      if (textDownloadPercent != null)
        textDownloadPercent.Text = string.Format("{0:##.##} %",
```

```
        MediaSource.DownloadProgress * 100);
  }
}
void MediaSource_BufferingProgressChanged(object sender, RoutedEventArgs e)
{
  if (elemDownloadProgressIndicator != null)
  {

    if (textBufferingPercent != null)
      textBufferingPercent.Text = string.Format("{0:##.##} %",
        MediaSource.BufferingProgress * 100);
  }
}
private void MediaSource_CurrentStateChanged(object sender, RoutedEventArgs e)
{
  switch (MediaSource.CurrentState)
  {
    case MediaElementState.Opening:
      VisualStateManager.GoToState(this, "Normal", true);
      break;
    case MediaElementState.Playing:
      RefreshMediaStates();
      if (disptimerPlayProgressUpdate.IsEnabled == false)
        disptimerPlayProgressUpdate.Start();
      break;
    case MediaElementState.Paused:
      if(disptimerPlayProgressUpdate.IsEnabled)
        disptimerPlayProgressUpdate.Stop();
      break;
    case MediaElementState.Stopped:
      if (disptimerPlayProgressUpdate.IsEnabled)
        disptimerPlayProgressUpdate.Stop();
      break;
    case MediaElementState.Buffering:
      VisualStateManager.GoToState(this,"Buffering",true);
      break;
    default:
      break;
  }
}
void MediaSource_MediaOpened(object sender, RoutedEventArgs e)
{
  RefreshMediaStates();
}
```

```
      private void RefreshMediaStates()
      {
        VisualStateManager.GoToState(this,
            (MediaSource.CanSeek) ? "CanSeek" : "CannotSeek", true);
        VisualStateManager.GoToState(this,
          (MediaSource.NaturalDuration.TimeSpan != TimeSpan.Zero) ?
          "KnownDuration" : "UnknownDuration", true);
        VisualStateManager.GoToState(this,
          (MediaSource.DownloadProgress == 1.0) ?
          "NoDownload" : "NeedsDownload", true);
        if (textDuration != null &&
            MediaSource.NaturalDuration.TimeSpan != TimeSpan.Zero)
          textDuration.Text = string.Format("{0:00}:{1:00}:{2:00}:{3:000}",
            MediaSource.NaturalDuration.TimeSpan.Hours,
            MediaSource.NaturalDuration.TimeSpan.Minutes,
            MediaSource.NaturalDuration.TimeSpan.Seconds,
            MediaSource.NaturalDuration.TimeSpan.Milliseconds);
      }
      private void MediaSource_MediaEnded(object sender, RoutedEventArgs e)
      {
        if (disptimerPlayProgressUpdate.IsEnabled)
          disptimerPlayProgressUpdate.Stop();
      }
      private void MediaSource_MediaFailed(object sender, RoutedEventArgs e)
      {
        if(disptimerPlayProgressUpdate.IsEnabled)
          disptimerPlayProgressUpdate.Stop();
      }
    }
  }
}
```

Most of the additions to the MediaSlider code (shown in bold in Listing 8-16) are to make sure you reflect the correct visual state of the slider depending on the state of the media. After the media is opened, in MediaSource_Opened(), you invoke the RefreshMediaStates() method and check to see if the media is seekable, using the value of the CanSeek property, and navigate to the appropriate state in the SeekStates group. If the duration of the media is available, you navigate to the appropriate state in the DurationStates group. You also check to see if MediaSource.DownloadProgress is already at 100 percent (which is the case if the media is being streamed) and navigate to the appropriate state in the DownloadStates group. Finally, you update the textDuration to reflect the duration of the media just opened.

If you refer to the MediaSource_CurrentStateChanged() handler, note that when the media is buffering, you navigate to the Buffering visual state. After the MediaElement starts playing the media, you repeat a call to RefreshMediaStates(). This is to handle cases where the MediaSlider.SourceName gets switched to a MediaElement (consider the PIP scenario again) that is already playing. Then, you navigate to the Playing visual state.

The only other addition here is a BufferingProgressChanged handler that updates textBufferingPercent with the buffering progress. The next few figures show the effects of the various visual state changes.

Figure 8-15 shows the MediaSlider while video is buffering.

Figure 8-15. *Buffering video*

Figure 8-16 shows the MediaSlider while an on-demand video is playing. Note that although the duration is displayed along with the play progress, there is no download progress indication because the media is being streamed. Also note the presence of the Thumb, indicating that although the media is streamed, seeking within it is enabled because of the combination of an on-demand publishing point and disk-based media.

Figure 8-16. *Playing an on-demand stream*

Figure 8-17 shows the MediaSlider while a broadcast video is playing. Note that no play-progress or duration information is displayed. Also note the absence of the Thumb, indicating that the broadcast media does not support seeking.

Figure 8-17. *Playing a broadcast stream*

You make similar changes to the MediaButtonsPanel to reflect appropriate visual states. Listing 8-17 shows the XAML in bold.

Listing 8-17. *XAML for MediaButtonsPanel Control*

```xml
<ControlTemplate TargetType="local:MediaButtonsPanel"
                 x:Key="ctMediaButtonsPanelDefault">
  <Grid>
    <vsm:VisualStateManager.VisualStateGroups>
      <vsm:VisualStateGroup x:Name="CommonStates">
        <vsm:VisualStateGroup.Transitions>
          <vsm:VisualTransition GeneratedDuration="0"/>
        </vsm:VisualStateGroup.Transitions>
        <vsm:VisualState x:Name="Normal"/>
        <vsm:VisualState x:Name="MouseOver"/>
        <vsm:VisualState x:Name="Disabled">
          <Storyboard>
            <DoubleAnimationUsingKeyFrames Storyboard.TargetName="Root"
            Storyboard.TargetProperty="(UIElement.Opacity)">
              <SplineDoubleKeyFrame KeyTime="00:00:00" Value="0.5"/>
            </DoubleAnimationUsingKeyFrames>
          </Storyboard>
        </vsm:VisualState>
      </vsm:VisualStateGroup>
      <vsm:VisualStateGroup x:Name="SeekStates">
        <vsm:VisualState x:Name="CannotSeek">
          <Storyboard>
            <ObjectAnimationUsingKeyFrames
              Storyboard.TargetName="btnRewind"
              Storyboard.TargetProperty="IsEnabled">
              <DiscreteObjectKeyFrame KeyTime="0">
                <DiscreteObjectKeyFrame.Value>
                  <system:Boolean>false</system:Boolean>
                </DiscreteObjectKeyFrame.Value>
              </DiscreteObjectKeyFrame>
            </ObjectAnimationUsingKeyFrames>
            <ObjectAnimationUsingKeyFrames
              Storyboard.TargetName="btnForward"
              Storyboard.TargetProperty="IsEnabled">
              <DiscreteObjectKeyFrame KeyTime="0">
                <DiscreteObjectKeyFrame.Value>
                  <system:Boolean>false</system:Boolean>
                </DiscreteObjectKeyFrame.Value>
              </DiscreteObjectKeyFrame>
            </ObjectAnimationUsingKeyFrames>
          </Storyboard>
        </vsm:VisualState>
```

```xml
<vsm:VisualState x:Name="CanSeek">
  <Storyboard>
    <ObjectAnimationUsingKeyFrames
      Storyboard.TargetName="btnRewind"
      Storyboard.TargetProperty="IsEnabled">
      <DiscreteObjectKeyFrame KeyTime="0">
        <DiscreteObjectKeyFrame.Value>
          <system:Boolean>True</system:Boolean>
        </DiscreteObjectKeyFrame.Value>
      </DiscreteObjectKeyFrame>
    </ObjectAnimationUsingKeyFrames>
    <ObjectAnimationUsingKeyFrames
      Storyboard.TargetName="btnForward"
      Storyboard.TargetProperty="IsEnabled">
      <DiscreteObjectKeyFrame KeyTime="0">
        <DiscreteObjectKeyFrame.Value>
          <Visibility>True</Visibility>
        </DiscreteObjectKeyFrame.Value>
      </DiscreteObjectKeyFrame>
    </ObjectAnimationUsingKeyFrames>
  </Storyboard>
</vsm:VisualState>
</vsm:VisualStateGroup>
<vsm:VisualStateGroup x:Name="PauseStates">
  <vsm:VisualState x:Name="CannotPause">
    <Storyboard>
      <ObjectAnimationUsingKeyFrames
        Storyboard.TargetName="btnPause"
        Storyboard.TargetProperty="IsEnabled">
        <DiscreteObjectKeyFrame KeyTime="0">
          <DiscreteObjectKeyFrame.Value>
            <system:Boolean>false</system:Boolean>
          </DiscreteObjectKeyFrame.Value>
        </DiscreteObjectKeyFrame>
      </ObjectAnimationUsingKeyFrames>
    </Storyboard>
  </vsm:VisualState>
  <vsm:VisualState x:Name="CanPause">
    <Storyboard>
      <ObjectAnimationUsingKeyFrames
        Storyboard.TargetName="btnPause"
        Storyboard.TargetProperty="IsEnabled">
```

```xml
              <DiscreteObjectKeyFrame KeyTime="0">
                <DiscreteObjectKeyFrame.Value>
                  <system:Boolean>True</system:Boolean>
                </DiscreteObjectKeyFrame.Value>
              </DiscreteObjectKeyFrame>
            </ObjectAnimationUsingKeyFrames>
          </Storyboard>
        </vsm:VisualState>
      </vsm:VisualStateGroup>
    </vsm:VisualStateManager.VisualStateGroups>

    <Grid.ColumnDefinitions>
      <ColumnDefinition Width="0.2*" />
      <ColumnDefinition Width="0.2*" />
      <ColumnDefinition Width="0.2*" />
      <ColumnDefinition Width="0.2*" />
      <ColumnDefinition Width="0.2*" />
    </Grid.ColumnDefinitions>
    <RepeatButton Grid.Column="0" x:Name="btnRewind" Margin="0,0,1,0">
      <RepeatButton.Content>
        <Path x:Name="Rewind" Stretch="Fill" StrokeThickness="1"
            StrokeLineJoin="Round" Stroke="#FF000000" Fill="#FF000000"
            Data="M 69.8333,70.0833L 60.5833,
            63.2862L 60.5833,70.0833L 40,
            54.9583L 60.5833,39.8333L 60.5833,
            46.6304L 69.8333,39.8333L 69.8333,
            70.0833 Z "/>
      </RepeatButton.Content>
    </RepeatButton>
    <Button Grid.Column="1" x:Name="btnStop" Margin="1,0,1,0">
      <Button.Content>
        <Path x:Name="Stop" Fill="#FF000000" Stretch="Fill"
            StrokeThickness="0" Margin="5,5,5,5"
            Data="M0,0 L3,0 L3,30.249996 L0,30.249996 z"/>
      </Button.Content>
    </Button>
    <Button Grid.Column="2" x:Name="btnPlay" Margin="1,0,1,0">
      <Button.Content>
        <Path x:Name="Play" Stretch="Fill" StrokeThickness="0"
            Fill="#FF000000" Margin="5,5,5,5"
            Data="M 109.833,14.8944L 79.8333,
            -0.0445251L 79.8333,29.8333L 109.833,
            14.8944 Z "/>
      </Button.Content>
    </Button>
```

```
    <Button Grid.Column="3" x:Name="btnPause" Margin="1,0,1,0">
      <Button.Content>
        <Path x:Name="Pause" Stretch="Fill" StrokeThickness="0"
              Fill="#FF000000" Margin="5,5,5,5"
              Data="M 39.8333,0L 50.0833,0L 50.0833,29.8333L 39.8333,
              29.8333L 39.8333,0 Z M 59.8333,0L 69.8333,0L 69.8333,
              29.8333L 59.8333,29.8333L 59.8333,0 Z "/>
      </Button.Content>
    </Button>
    <RepeatButton Grid.Column="4" x:Name="btnForward" Margin="1,0,0,0">
      <RepeatButton.Content>
        <Path x:Name="Forward" Stretch="Fill" StrokeThickness="1"
              StrokeLineJoin="Round" Stroke="#FF000000"
              Fill="#FF000000"
              Data="M 1.27157e-006,39.8334L 9.25,
              46.6305L 9.25,39.8333L 29.8333,
              54.9583L 9.25,70.0833L 9.25,
              63.2863L 1.27157e-006,
              70.0833L 1.27157e-006,39.8334 Z "/>
      </RepeatButton.Content>
    </RepeatButton>
  </Grid>
</ControlTemplate>

<Style TargetType="local:MediaButtonsPanel">
  <Setter Property="Template"
          Value="{StaticResource ctMediaButtonsPanelDefault}"/>
</Style>
```

      You add the SeekStates group as before, containing the CanSeek and CannotSeek visual states. For the CannotSeek state, you disable btnRewind and btnForward by setting the IsEnabled property on the buttons to false; for the CanSeek state, you do the reverse. You also add two new visual states— CannotPause and CanPause—in a state group named PauseStates, where you act on btnPause based on the value of the MediaElement.CanPause property. The code to navigate to the states, designed in a similar way to the MediaSlider, is shown in Listing 8-18 in bold.

Listing 8-18. *MediaButtonsPanel Control Code*

```
using System;
using System.Windows;
using System.Windows.Controls;
using System.Windows.Controls.Primitives;
using System.Windows.Media;
```

```
namespace Ch08_RichMedia.Recipe8_3
{
  [TemplateVisualState(GroupName = "SeekStates", Name = "CanSeek")]
  [TemplateVisualState(GroupName = "SeekStates", Name = "CannotSeek")]
  [TemplateVisualState(GroupName = "PauseStates", Name = "CanPause")]
  [TemplateVisualState(GroupName = "PauseStates", Name = "CannotPause")]
  public class MediaButtonsPanel : Control
  {

    private MediaElement MediaSource;
    private FrameworkElement Root;
    private ButtonBase btnPlay, btnPause, btnStop, btnForward, btnRewind;

    public static DependencyProperty SourceNameProperty =
      DependencyProperty.Register("SourceName", typeof(string),
      typeof(MediaButtonsPanel),
      new PropertyMetadata(new PropertyChangedCallback(OnSourceNameChanged)));
    public string SourceName
    {
      get
      {
        return (string)GetValue(SourceNameProperty);
      }
      set
      {
        SetValue(SourceNameProperty, value);
      }
    }
    private static void OnSourceNameChanged(DependencyObject Source,
      DependencyPropertyChangedEventArgs e)
    {
      MediaButtonsPanel thisPanel = Source as MediaButtonsPanel;

      if (e.NewValue != e.OldValue && thisPanel.Root != null)
      {
        thisPanel.MediaSource =
thisPanel.Root.FindName(e.NewValue as string) as MediaElement;
        thisPanel.InitMediaElementConnections();
      }
    }
    public MediaButtonsPanel()
    {
      this.DefaultStyleKey = typeof(MediaButtonsPanel);
    }
```

```csharp
public override void OnApplyTemplate()
{

  btnPlay = GetTemplateChild("btnPlay") as ButtonBase;
  btnPause = GetTemplateChild("btnPause") as ButtonBase;
  btnStop = GetTemplateChild("btnStop") as ButtonBase;
  btnForward = GetTemplateChild("btnForward") as ButtonBase;
  btnRewind = GetTemplateChild("btnRewind") as ButtonBase;
  Root = Helper.FindRoot(this);
  MediaSource = Root.FindName(SourceName) as MediaElement;
  InitMediaElementConnections();
  WireButtonEvents();
}
private void WireButtonEvents()
{
  if (btnPlay != null)
    btnPlay.Click += new RoutedEventHandler(btnPlay_Click);
  if (btnPause != null)
    btnPause.Click += new RoutedEventHandler(btnPause_Click);
  if (btnStop != null)
    btnStop.Click += new RoutedEventHandler(btnStop_Click);
  if (btnForward != null)
    btnForward.Click += new RoutedEventHandler(btnForward_Click);
  if (btnRewind != null)
    btnRewind.Click += new RoutedEventHandler(btnRewind_Click);
}


void btnRewind_Click(object sender, RoutedEventArgs e)
{
  if (MediaSource != null && MediaSource.Position > TimeSpan.Zero)
  {
    MediaSource.Pause();
    //5th of a second
    MediaSource.Position -= new TimeSpan(0, 0, 0, 0, 200);
    MediaSource.Play();
  }
}
void btnForward_Click(object sender, RoutedEventArgs e)
{
  if (MediaSource != null && MediaSource.Position
    <= MediaSource.NaturalDuration.TimeSpan)
```

```
    {
      MediaSource.Pause();
      MediaSource.Position += new TimeSpan(0, 0, 0, 0, 200);
      MediaSource.Play();
    }
  }
  void btnStop_Click(object sender, RoutedEventArgs e)
  {
    if (MediaSource != null)
      MediaSource.Stop();
  }
  void btnPause_Click(object sender, RoutedEventArgs e)
  {
    if (MediaSource != null &&
      MediaSource.CurrentState == MediaElementState.Playing)
      MediaSource.Pause();
  }
  void btnPlay_Click(object sender, RoutedEventArgs e)
  {
    if (MediaSource != null &&
      MediaSource.CurrentState != MediaElementState.Playing)
      MediaSource.Play();
  }

  private void InitMediaElementConnections()
  {
    if (MediaSource != null)
    {
      MediaSource.MediaOpened +=
        new RoutedEventHandler(MediaSource_MediaOpened);
      MediaSource.CurrentStateChanged +=
        new RoutedEventHandler(MediaSource_CurrentStateChanged);

      MediaSource_CurrentStateChanged(this, new RoutedEventArgs());
    }
  }
  private void MediaSource_CurrentStateChanged(object sender, RoutedEventArgs e)
  {
    switch (MediaSource.CurrentState)
    {
      case MediaElementState.Playing:
        VisualStateManager.GoToState(this,
    (MediaSource.CanSeek == false) ? "CannotSeek" : "CanSeek", true);
        VisualStateManager.GoToState(this,
```

```
           (MediaSource.CanPause == false) ? "CannotPause" : "CanPause", true);
             break;
          default:
             break;
        }
      }

      private void MediaSource_MediaOpened(object sender, RoutedEventArgs e)
      {
        VisualStateManager.GoToState(this,
        (MediaSource.CanSeek == false) ? "CannotSeek" : "CanSeek", true);
        VisualStateManager.GoToState(this,
        (MediaSource.CanPause == false) ? "CannotPause" : "CanPause", true);
      }
    }
}
```

Once again, you check for the `MediaElement.CanSeek` and `MediaElement.CanPause` properties to navigate to the appropriate visual states, and you do it both in `MediaOpened` and when the `Playing` state is reached in the `CurrentStateChanged` handler.

Figures 8-16 and 8-17 earlier in this recipe show you the resulting button states. In Figure 8-17, where a broadcast stream is playing, and seeking or pausing is not possible, the corresponding buttons are disabled.

8-4. Using Playlists to Package Media

Problem

You are looking for a way to combine a group of media files to be played as one unit in some ordered fashion.

Solution

Create either a server-side or a client-side playlist, depending on your needs, and have the `MediaElement` play the playlist.

How It Works

Playlists are a convenient way to group media sources to be played as one unit. When the `MediaElement` plays a playlist, the user experience is seamless, and it seems as though a single source of media is playing from start to end. You can use playlists to create a broadcast program–like experience where you play a sequence of media in a certain order, with other media files (such as advertisements) interspersed within specific parts of the program.

Silverlight supports two kinds of playlists: client-side playlists (CSPL) and server-side playlists (SSPL). Both CSPL and SSPL are represented as XML documents with specific schemas, which means they are textual and can easily be created using any text or XML editor.

Server-Side Playlists

An SSPL is not directly served to a player but is associated with a WMS publishing point (refer to Recipe 8-3 for more on WMS). Both broadcast and on-demand publishing points in WMS can specify an SSPL as the source of media. Listing 8-19 shows a sample SSPL.

Listing 8-19. *Sample Server-Side Playlist*

```
<?wsx version="1.0" encoding="utf-8"?>
<smil>
  <media src="D:\Media\Amazon_1080.wmv" begin="0s" dur="15s"/>
  <seq>
    <media src="D:\Media\Coral_Reef_Adventure_1080.wmv" dur="20s"/>
    <media src="D:\Media\Discoverers_1080.wmv" begin="prev.begin+10s" dur="30s"/>
    <switch>
      <media src="D:\Media\AdrenalineRush.wmv" dur="15s"/>
      <media src="D:\Media\Alexander_Trailer_1080p.wmv" dur="15s"/>
    </switch>
  </seq>
  <media src="D:\Media\Discoverers_1080.wmv" begin="70s" dur="45s"/>
</smil>
```

The SSPL syntax is based on the Synchronized Multimedia Integration Language (SMIL) 2.0 specification. You can find more information about SMIL at the World Wide Web Consortium (W3C) web site at http://www.w3.org/TR/REC-smil/. Every SSPL document is defined with a root element, <smil>. The <media> element specifies a particular media source to be played, and the dur attribute specifies a duration for the media to play; it can be equal to or less than the total duration of the media. The begin attribute specifies the time when the media starts to play relative to its parent time container. So, media specified in the last entry in the previous listing starts playing as soon as 70 seconds have passed from the beginning of the playlist. This happens even if it does not allow enough time for the previous entries to complete playing their full duration. The second entry in the <seq> element starts playing 10 seconds after the previous element in the same sequence starts playing, even if the previous one has not finished playing.

The <seq> element plays all media items it contains in order. The <switch> element provides a series of alternative sources if one fails. In the sample, everything in the <seq> element plays in order; if the first media source in the <switch> element succeeds in playing, the second one never plays.

The SSPL syntax is extensive and contains many attributes to control the behavior of the media. Coverage of the full SSPL syntax is beyond the scope of this book, but you can refer to http://msdn.microsoft.com/en-us/library/ms752512(VS.85).aspx for a complete reference of all SSPL elements and attributes.

WMS includes an SSPL editor that you can invoke from within the WMS console to create or edit a playlist. To associate an SSPL, select the publishing point, navigate to the Source property tab, and click the View Playlist Editor button, as shown in Figure 8-18.

After the editor is opened, you can create the SSPL by adding the desired children nodes in the tree pane at left and specifying the appropriate attribute values in the grid at right. The context menus for each element type provide options for adding the various possible children elements. When you are done, you can save the SSPL to a desired location. Figure 8-19 shows the Playlist Editor in action. You can learn more about the editor at http://technet.microsoft.com/en-us/library/cc725750.aspx.

Figure 8-18. *Opening the Playlist Editor*

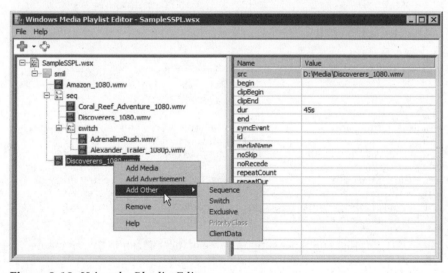

Figure 8-19. *Using the Playlist Editor*

Client-Side Playlists

CSPLs are defined as Windows Media metafiles that Windows Media Player can enumerate and play. A CSPL in spirit is essentially just like an SSPL in that it too defines grouping of media sources to be played together as one unit. However, the CSPL follows a different syntax from the SSPL. Also, a CSPL is not associated with a streaming media service like WMS; it has no relation to streaming, other than the fact that media sources inside a CSPL can point to streaming media sources. Listing 8-20 shows a sample CSPL.

Listing 8-20. *Sample Client-Side Playlist*

```
<asx version="3.0">
  <Title>SampleCSPL</Title>
  <Entry>
    <Duration value = "00:00:10" />
    <Title>Amazon_1080</Title>
    <Ref href = "mms://dc7600:43000/Media/Amazon_1080.wmv"/>
  </Entry>
  <Entry>
    <Title>AdrenalineRush</Title>
    <Ref href = "mms://dc7600:43000/Media/AdrenalineRush.wmv"/>
  </Entry>
  <Entry>
    <Duration value = "00:00:10" />
    <Title>Alexander_Trailer_1080p</Title>
    <Ref href = "mms://dc7600:43000/Media/Alexander_Trailer_1080p.wmv"/>
  </Entry>
  <Entry>
    <Duration value = "00:00:10" />
    <Title>Amazing_Caves_1080</Title>
    <Ref href = "mms://dc7600:43000/Media/Amazing_Caves_1080.wmv"/>
  </Entry>
</asx>
```

Every CSPL document is defined within an `<asx>` element. Each `<Entry>` element can contain a `<Ref>` element pointing to the source of the media; in Listing 8-20, these elements all point back to the WMS on-demand publishing point as defined in Recipe 8-3. You can also define a `<Duration>` element for each `<Entry>` that specifies what duration the media source plays for before the next media source starts playing, no matter what the total length of the media source is. In Listing 8-20, the first entry plays for 10 seconds before making way for the second entry, which plays for its full length, and so on.

Full coverage of CSPL syntax is also beyond the scope of this book, but you can find complete coverage in the Windows Media Metafile reference at http://msdn.microsoft.com/en-us/library/dd564670(VS.85).aspx.

It is important to note that Silverlight does not support some of the SSPL and CSPL elements and attributes. Refer to http://msdn.microsoft.com/en-us/library/cc189080(VS.95).aspx to find out more about the unsupported features.

The Code

This code sample adds an SSPL and a CSPL to the mix of media that you then play through the player developed in Recipes 8-2 and 8-3.

Figure 8-20 shows the new items added to the menus that enable you to test the features.

Figure 8-20. *Items added to the On Demand (left) and Broadcast (right) menus*

To play the SSPL, you create two new publishing points named SSPLBroadcast of type broadcast and SSPLOnDemand of type on-demand in the WMS installation. You then associate the SSPL document shown in Listing 8-19 with each of these publishing points. The SSPL document is named SampleSSPL.wsx and is included with the sample code. You create two publishing points in order to observe the behavior of the MediaElement while playing an SSPL using the two different publishing point types. You then modify the OnDemandStreams.xml file and the BroadcastStreams.xml file to include an entry to the two respective publishing points. Recall from the earlier recipes that these files are used by the MediaLocationProvider WCF service to provide the content of the menus in the player.

To play the CSPL, you add one more entry to the OnDemandStreams.xml that has the <Uri> element pointing to the SampleCSPL.asx file, as shown in Listing 8-20.

Listing 8-21 shows all the entries in the two files.

Listing 8-21. *New Entries in BroadcastStreams.xml and OnDemandStreams.xml*

```
<!--BroadcastStreams.xml entry-->
<MediaLocation>
  <Description>SSPL Broadcast</Description>
  <Uri>mms://dc7600:43000/SSPLBroadcast</Uri>
  <ImageUri>
    http://localhost/SLBook/Ch08_RichMedia/Media/AdrenalineRush_Thumb.jpg
  </ImageUri>
</MediaLocation>

<!--OnDemandStreams.xml entries-->
<MediaLocation>
  <Description>SSPL On Demand</Description>
  <Uri>mms://dc7600:43000/SSPLOnDemand</Uri>
  <ImageUri>
    http://localhost/SLBook/Ch08_RichMedia/Media/AdrenalineRush_Thumb.jpg
  </ImageUri>
</MediaLocation>
<MediaLocation>
  <Description>CSPL</Description>
  <Uri>http://localhost:9393/SampleCSPL.ASX</Uri>
  <ImageUri>
    http://localhost/SLBook/Ch08_RichMedia/Media/Amazon_1080_Thumb.jpg
  </ImageUri>
</MediaLocation>
```

These entries cause three new menu items to appear in the player menus: two called SSPL On Demand and CSPL in the On Demand menu, and the third called SSPL Broadcast in the Broadcast menu. This is shown in Figure 8-20.

If you play SSPL On Demand, the seek Buttons are disabled and the Thumb is missing. This is because the MediaElement does not allow seeking (MediaElement.CanSeek is false) even when the SSPL is being served through an on-demand publishing point. This, as you may recall, is different from your experience in Recipe 8-3, when you played individual media files through an on-demand publishing point. However, the Pause button is enabled, because a playing SSPL can be paused as long as it is being served through an on-demand publishing point (MediaElement.CanPause is set to true).

You can also observe the timing behavior specified through the dur and begin attributes in Listing 8-19 by following the progress and duration counters displayed along with the slider. Note that although the timing behavior forces certain media sources to stop and make way for the next element before they play their entire duration, the MediaElement.NaturalDuration always reports the total duration of each media source as it is loaded in the course of playing the SSPL.

Also note that as the SSPL is played by the MediaElement, state transitions are reported for certain states for each media source. The MediaElement.Opened event is raised every time the SSPL moves to a new source. The MediaElement.CurrentStateChanged event is also raised when the source is buffering or starts playing. This allows the player code from Recipe 8-3 to update various media information such as duration, as well as track play progress and buffering progress for every source change within the SSPL. The MediaElement.Ended event, however, is raised only once: when the entire SSPL is finished playing.

When you play the SSPL Broadcast menu item, you see the same broadcast publishing point experience as in Recipe 8-3—that is, seeking and pausing are disabled, and no duration information is exposed.

Finally, when you play the CSPL item, seeking is available, and the Thumb and the seek Buttons are usable. Also notice the effect of the <Duration> elements. While playing a CSPL entry with a duration set to a time different from the total duration of the referenced media source, the MediaElement reports the duration value from the CSPL rather than the actual total duration. So, for the first element in Listing 8-20, the duration reported is 10 seconds, even though the actual duration of the media source is a little over a minute.

8-5. Using Markers to Display Timed Content

Problem

You want to display some timed content, such as a closed caption, subtitles, or a commercial, at certain points while your media is playing.

Solution

Add markers to the video either through preencoding or at runtime, and respond to MediaElement events to display your content when markers are reached.

How It Works

A *marker* is a piece of metadata associated with a specific time point in a media's timeline. A Windows media file may contain many such markers, and this collection of markers is stored along with the actual media inside the file. While the media is playing, a player like the MediaElement can raise notification events every time a marker is reached, and you can respond to these events in your code to perform a timed task corresponding to that marker's time point.

Markers are useful in many scenarios. Captions or advertisements specific to the content's current context may be displayed at specific time points. You might devise a chapter system by introducing a marker at the beginning of the chapters and allowing the user to seek to the time point defined by the marker to simulate chapter navigation. Markers can also be used to overlay near real-time data, such as a game commentary, over live content.

You can introduce markers into the media either by encoding them using an encoder like Expression Encoder or programmatically at the start of play, provided the playing environment supports such a feature. Let's look at these options.

Encoding Markers Using Expression Encoder 3

Full coverage of Expression Encoder 3 is beyond the scope of the book, and we encourage you to download the trial version and try the different features. You can download a trial version from http://www.microsoft.com/expression/products/Overview.aspx?key=encoder.

After you import a media file into Expression Encoder, you can navigate to the Metadata tab to add markers to the content. To add a marker, move the thumb along the media timeline to the time point where you want to add the marker, and then click the Add button in the Markers pane. Doing so adds a marker with its Time property set to the time point you selected using the Thumb and its Value property set to a blank string. You can provide a meaningful text value to the marker in the Value property if you decide to have application logic dependent on it, as shown later in the sample. When you have added all the markers you need, the Markers pane looks something like Figure 8-21.

Figure 8-21. *Expression Encoder Markers pane with markers added*

Note that the Key Frame check box is checked by default for each marker. This causes a keyframe to be generated at the time point for each marker, resulting in a much faster seek to that marker if needed. You can uncheck the Key Frame check box for markers for which you do not want to generate keyframes. Checking the Thumbnail check box causes Expression Encoder to generate a thumbnail of the video frame at the marker, which may come in handy in scenarios like a chaptering system.

If the media is already encoded to a profile of your choice, you can set the Video encoding profile in the Encode tab to Source, as shown in Figure 8-22. This causes Expression Encoder to add the markers to the media when you click the Encode button, without going through a full encode again, and makes the process a lot faster. A *profile* is a set of predetermined values around the various parameters you can control on the media during the encoding process.

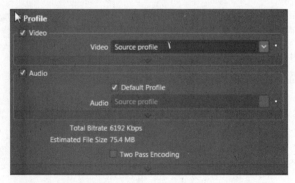

Figure 8-22. *Expression Encoder video profile set to match the source profile*

MediaElement and Markers

When you use a Windows Media file containing markers as a source to a `MediaElement`, the `MediaElement` reads all the markers in the file and stores them in the `MediaElement.Markers` collection, which is of type `System.Windows.Media.TimelineMarkerCollection`. You can access this collection after the media has been successfully opened in the `MediaOpened` event handler and afterward.

Each marker is represented by an instance of the `System.Windows.Media.TimelineMarker` class. The `TimelineMarker.Time` property is of type `TimeSpan` and represents the marker's time point. The `TimelineMarker.`
`Text` property contains the marker's optional text value, which can be user defined. In the case of markers encoded in the video, if you recall the Expression Encoder example in the previous section, this property reflects the values entered in the Value column in the Markers pane. The `TimelineMarker.Type` property can also be any user-defined string and can be used to categorize markers into sets corresponding to a specific usage.

After the media starts playing, as each marker's time point is reached, the `MediaElement` raises the `MarkerReached` event. In the handler for the event, the `Marker` property on `System.Windows.Media.`
`TimelineMarkerRoutedEventArgs` provides access to the `TimelineMarker` instance that causes the `MediaElement` to raise the event.

In addition to markers introduced in the media during encoding, you can add markers to media at runtime. You achieve this by creating and initializing new instances of the `TimelineMarker` type and adding them to the `MediaElement.Markers` collection before the media starts playing. These markers are temporary and are not stored in the media, but are discarded after a new media file is loaded into the `MediaElement`. Apart from that, their behavior is identical to markers contained in the media file, and the `MarkerReached` event is raised for both kinds the same way.

The Code

The code sample for this recipe shows the use of markers encoded into the media file as well as temporary markers added on the client. You enable two scenarios in this sample: a captioning system and overlaid commercials. In the former scenario, animated and context-specific text captions are overlaid on the video at specific time points; for this, you use file-encoded markers. In the latter scenario, a small commercial-like video is overlaid on the main video at regular intervals; for this, you use client-created markers.

You implement all this in the player you have been developing in the previous few recipes.

Figure 8-23 shows both scenarios at work in the player. The caption is the white text near the upper-right corner of the display, and the small Silverlight logo is actually a small video playing near the lower-right corner.

Let's look at the captioning system first. The captions are implemented as independent snippets of XAML defined in an XML file named `Captions.xml`, keyed by a specific marker value. Listing 8-22 shows an abridged `Captions.xml` file.

Figure 8-23. *Overlaid caption and Silverlight commercial*

Listing 8-22. *Captions.xml sample*

```xml
<?xml version="1.0" encoding="utf-8" ?>
<Medias>
  <Media
    Id="http://localhost/SLBook/Ch08_RichMedia/Media/Amazon_1080_WithMarkers.wmv">
    <Marker Value="FirstMarker">
      <![CDATA[
      <Canvas  xmlns="http://schemas.microsoft.com/winfx/2006/xaml/presentation"
    xmlns:x="http://schemas.microsoft.com/winfx/2006/xaml" Height="Auto"
    HorizontalAlignment="Stretch" Margin="0,0,0,0"
    VerticalAlignment="Stretch" Width="Auto"
    Grid.Column="1" Grid.Row="1" x:Name="overlay">
```

```xml
<Canvas.Resources>
<Storyboard x:Name="STBD_AnimateCaption">
  <DoubleAnimationUsingKeyFrames BeginTime="00:00:00"
  Storyboard.TargetName="textBlock"
  Storyboard.TargetProperty="(UIElement.Opacity)">
    <LinearDoubleKeyFrame KeyTime="00:00:01" Value="1"/>
    <LinearDoubleKeyFrame KeyTime="00:00:04" Value="1"/>
    <SplineDoubleKeyFrame KeyTime="00:00:05" Value="0"/>
  </DoubleAnimationUsingKeyFrames>
  <DoubleAnimationUsingKeyFrames BeginTime="00:00:00"
  Storyboard.TargetName="textBlock"
  Storyboard.TargetProperty="(Canvas.Left)">
    <SplineDoubleKeyFrame KeyTime="00:00:01" Value="375"/>
    <SplineDoubleKeyFrame KeyTime="00:00:02" Value="375"/>
    <SplineDoubleKeyFrame KeyTime="00:00:03" Value="375"/>
    <SplineDoubleKeyFrame KeyTime="00:00:04" Value="375"/>
    <SplineDoubleKeyFrame KeyTime="00:00:05" Value="0"/>
  </DoubleAnimationUsingKeyFrames>
  <DoubleAnimationUsingKeyFrames BeginTime="00:00:00"
  Storyboard.TargetName="textBlock"
  Storyboard.TargetProperty="(Canvas.Top)">
    <SplineDoubleKeyFrame KeyTime="00:00:01" Value="35"/>
    <SplineDoubleKeyFrame KeyTime="00:00:02" Value="35"/>
    <SplineDoubleKeyFrame KeyTime="00:00:03" Value="35"/>
    <SplineDoubleKeyFrame KeyTime="00:00:04" Value="35"/>
    <SplineDoubleKeyFrame KeyTime="00:00:05" Value="0"/>
  </DoubleAnimationUsingKeyFrames>
</Storyboard>
</Canvas.Resources>
<TextBlock x:Name="textBlock"
Opacity="0" FontFamily="Portable User Interface" FontSize="24"
FontWeight="Bold" Foreground="#FFFFFDFD" Text="Beautiful Sunset"
TextAlignment="Right" TextWrapping="Wrap" HorizontalAlignment="Left"
VerticalAlignment="Top"/>
  </Canvas>]]>
  </Marker>
  <Marker Value="SecondMarker">
    <![CDATA[<Canvas Height="Auto"
    xmlns="http://schemas.microsoft.com/winfx/2006/xaml/presentation"
    xmlns:x="http://schemas.microsoft.com/winfx/2006/xaml"
    HorizontalAlignment="Stretch" Margin="0,0,0,0"
    VerticalAlignment="Stretch" Width="Auto"
    Grid.Column="1" Grid.Row="1" x:Name="overlay">
```

```
    <Canvas.Resources>
      <Storyboard x:Name="STBD_AnimateCaption">
        <DoubleAnimationUsingKeyFrames BeginTime="00:00:00"
        Storyboard.TargetName="textBlock"
        Storyboard.TargetProperty="(UIElement.Opacity)">
          <LinearDoubleKeyFrame KeyTime="00:00:01" Value="1"/>
          <LinearDoubleKeyFrame KeyTime="00:00:04" Value="1"/>
          <SplineDoubleKeyFrame KeyTime="00:00:05" Value="0"/>
        </DoubleAnimationUsingKeyFrames>
        <DoubleAnimationUsingKeyFrames BeginTime="00:00:00"
        Storyboard.TargetName="textBlock"
        Storyboard.TargetProperty="(Canvas.Left)">
          <SplineDoubleKeyFrame KeyTime="00:00:01" Value="375"/>
          <SplineDoubleKeyFrame KeyTime="00:00:02" Value="375"/>
          <SplineDoubleKeyFrame KeyTime="00:00:03" Value="375"/>
          <SplineDoubleKeyFrame KeyTime="00:00:04" Value="375"/>
          <SplineDoubleKeyFrame KeyTime="00:00:05" Value="0"/>
        </DoubleAnimationUsingKeyFrames>
        <DoubleAnimationUsingKeyFrames BeginTime="00:00:00"
        Storyboard.TargetName="textBlock" S
        Storyboard.TargetProperty="(Canvas.Top)">
          <SplineDoubleKeyFrame KeyTime="00:00:01" Value="35"/>
          <SplineDoubleKeyFrame KeyTime="00:00:02" Value="35"/>
          <SplineDoubleKeyFrame KeyTime="00:00:03" Value="35"/>
          <SplineDoubleKeyFrame KeyTime="00:00:04" Value="35"/>
          <SplineDoubleKeyFrame KeyTime="00:00:05" Value="0"/>
        </DoubleAnimationUsingKeyFrames>
      </Storyboard>
    </Canvas.Resources>
    <TextBlock x:Name="textBlock" Opacity="0"
    FontFamily="Portable User Interface" FontSize="24"
    FontWeight="Bold" Foreground="#FFFFFDFD" Text="Is that a leopard ?"
    TextAlignment="Right" TextWrapping="Wrap" HorizontalAlignment="Left"
    VerticalAlignment="Top"/>
</Canvas>]]>
    </Marker>
  </Media>
</Medias>
```

The root element `<Medias>` is expected to have multiple `<Media>` elements, each uniquely identified by its Id attribute set to the media URI. Each `<Media>` element in turn can have many `<Marker>` elements with a Value attribute set to the marker value, and a CDATA section containing the XAML snippet to be used for that marker. Note that you stipulate that each XAML snippet has at least one Storyboard defined, named STBD_AnimateCaption; you use it later in the code. Also note that the TextBlock at the end of the XAML snippet has the caption text set on the Text property.

■**Note** Several industry standards are defined for including captions and subtitles in digital media for both television and broadband delivery mechanisms. You can look at the Synchronized Multimedia Integration Language (SMIL) specification at `http://www.w3.org/TR/REC-smil/` or the Synchronized Accessible Media Interchange (SAMI) specification at `http://msdn.microsoft.com/en-us/library/dd562301(VS.85).aspx`. The schema outlined here is not aligned with an industry standard by any means. If this mechanism works for you as is, we are happy that you have benefited. However, if your goal is to create a production-ready captioning system, we also encourage you to look at some of the industry standards and possibly combine them with the knowledge gained here to achieve your goals with Silverlight.

You also encode the media file (in the sample `Amazon_1080.wmv` file) with markers placed at appropriate time points, with their `Value` properties set to match the `Value` attributes of the `<Marker>` elements in the `Captions.xml` file (we discussed the Expression Encoder–based encoding process briefly in the previous section). To have this file available to the player to play, you place the encoded file for progressive download in the same location as the other progressively downloaded media files from Recipe 8-2, and add a new entry to the `Downloads.xml` file. To see how this works, refer back to Recipe 8-2.

You define a new operation named `GetCaptionsForMedia()` on the `MediaLocationProvider` WCF service that you have been using since Recipe 8-2. `GetCaptionsForMedia()` accepts the Media URI and returns the complete XML for the corresponding `<Media>` element. You also use a `UriTemplate` in the operation contract to map the operation to the format `<service address>`/Captions?MediaId={*MediaUri*}, where *MediaUri* is the URI of the media you are trying to download and play.

We do not list `GetCaptionsForMedia()`, and you are encouraged to look at Chapter 7 for more about WCF services and the sample code for the implementation.

The player XAML from the previous recipes undergoes a few minor changes. We list the player XAML in Listing 8-23, but we left out the Resources section for brevity and because there are no changes to it.

Listing 8-23. *Modified XAML for the Marker-Enabled Player*

```
<UserControl x:Class="Ch08_RichMedia.Recipe8_5.Page"
    xmlns="http://schemas.microsoft.com/winfx/2006/xaml/presentation"
    xmlns:x="http://schemas.microsoft.com/winfx/2006/xaml"
    xmlns:vsm="clr-namespace:System.Windows;assembly=System.Windows"
    xmlns:local="clr-namespace:Ch08_RichMedia.Recipe8_5"
    Width="920" Height="547"
    xmlns:Ch08_RichMedia_Recipe8_4-
"clr-namespace:Ch08_RichMedia.Recipe8_5;assembly=Ch08_RichMedia.Recipe8_5.PlrCntls"
 >
  <!-- Resources section deliberately left out -->

  <Grid x:Name="LayoutRoot"
        Background="#FFA2A2A2" Height="Auto" Width="Auto">
    <Grid.RowDefinitions>
      <RowDefinition Height="0.062*"/>
      <RowDefinition Height="0.649*"/>
      <RowDefinition Height="0*"/>
      <RowDefinition Height="0.289*"/>
    </Grid.RowDefinitions>
```

```
<Grid.ColumnDefinitions>
  <ColumnDefinition Width="0.2*"/>
  <ColumnDefinition Width="0.8*"/>
</Grid.ColumnDefinitions>
<MediaElement Height="Auto" Margin="0,0,0,0"
              VerticalAlignment="Top" x:Name="mediaelemMain"
              BufferingTime="0:0:3"
              HorizontalAlignment="Left" AutoPlay="True" Opacity="0"/>
<MediaElement Height="Auto" Margin="0,0,0,0" VerticalAlignment="Top"
              x:Name="mediaelemPIP" HorizontalAlignment="Left"
              AutoPlay="True" Opacity="0" IsMuted="True"
              BufferingTime="0:0:3"/>
<Grid Grid.Row="0" Grid.Column="1" Grid.RowSpan="2" Margin="0,0,0,1">
  <Grid.RowDefinitions>
    <RowDefinition Height="0.018*" />
    <RowDefinition Height="0.961*" />
    <RowDefinition Height="0.021*" />
  </Grid.RowDefinitions>
  <Grid.ColumnDefinitions>
    <ColumnDefinition Width="0.05*"/>
    <ColumnDefinition Width="0.9*"/>
    <ColumnDefinition Width="0.05*"/>
  </Grid.ColumnDefinitions>
  <Border x:Name="displayMain"
          VerticalAlignment="Stretch" Grid.Column="1" Grid.Row="1"
          HorizontalAlignment="Stretch" BorderThickness="5,5,5,5"
          BorderBrush="#FF000000" Margin="0,0,0,0" >
    <Border.Background>
      <VideoBrush SourceName="mediaelemMain" Stretch="Fill"
                  x:Name="vidbrushMain" />
    </Border.Background>
    <Grid HorizontalAlignment="Right" MaxHeight="135" MaxWidth="240"
          Grid.Column="1" Grid.Row="1" Opacity="0.5"
          x:Name="adContainer" VerticalAlignment="Bottom">
    </Grid>
  </Border>
  <Grid VerticalAlignment="Stretch" Grid.Column="1" Grid.Row="1"
        HorizontalAlignment="Stretch" x:Name="CaptionContainer"
        Margin="0,0,0,0" />
  <Grid Grid.Column="1" Grid.Row="1" Margin="0,0,0,0">
    <Grid.RowDefinitions>
      <RowDefinition Height="0.025*" />
      <RowDefinition Height="0.35*" />
      <RowDefinition Height="0.625*" />
    </Grid.RowDefinitions>
```

```
        <Grid.ColumnDefinitions>
          <ColumnDefinition Width="0.635*"/>
          <ColumnDefinition Width="0.35*"/>
          <ColumnDefinition Width="0.015*"/>
        </Grid.ColumnDefinitions>
        <Border Grid.Column="1" Grid.Row="1" HorizontalAlignment="Stretch"
                VerticalAlignment="Stretch"
                MouseLeftButtonUp="displayPIP_MouseLeftButtonUp"
                x:Name="displayPIP" BorderThickness="2,2,2,2"
                BorderBrush="#FF000000" Visibility="Collapsed">
          <Border.Background>
            <VideoBrush SourceName="mediaelemPIP"
                        Stretch="Fill" x:Name="vidbrushPIP"/>
          </Border.Background>
        </Border>
        <Grid HorizontalAlignment="Stretch" Margin="8,8,8,8"
              Grid.RowSpan="1" Grid.Column="1" Grid.Row="1"
              x:Name="buttonsPIP" Visibility="Collapsed" >
          <Grid.RowDefinitions>
            <RowDefinition Height="0.1*"/>
            <RowDefinition Height="0.25*"/>
            <RowDefinition Height="0.1*"/>
            <RowDefinition Height="0.25*"/>
            <RowDefinition Height="0.3*"/>
          </Grid.RowDefinitions>
          <Grid.ColumnDefinitions>
            <ColumnDefinition Width="0.749*"/>
            <ColumnDefinition Width="0.176*"/>
            <ColumnDefinition Width="0.075*"/>
          </Grid.ColumnDefinitions>
          <Button Margin="0,0,0,0" Grid.RowSpan="1" Grid.Row="1"
                  Grid.ColumnSpan="1" Grid.Column="1"
                  x:Name="btnClosePIP" Click="btnClosePIP_Click"
                  >
            <Path x:Name="Path" Stretch="Fill" StrokeThickness="2"
StrokeLineJoin="Round" Stroke="#FF000000" Fill="#FFE91111"
Data="M 110.5,75.7635L 113.209,
                72.9631L 133.396,92.4865L 130.687,95.2869L 110.5,
                75.7635 Z M 130.801,73.4961L 133.393,76.4048L 112.425,
                95.0872L 109.833,92.1785L 130.801,73.4961 Z "/>
          </Button>
          <Button Margin="0,0,0,0" Grid.RowSpan="1" Grid.Row="3"
                  Grid.ColumnSpan="1" Grid.Column="1"
                  x:Name="btnSwitchPIP" Click="btnSwitchPIP_Click"
                  >
```

```
            <Path Stretch="Fill" StrokeThickness="2" StrokeLineJoin="Round"
Stroke="#FF000000" Data="M 120,39.8333L 149.917,
                39.8333L 149.917,59.9167L 120,59.9167L 120,
                39.8333 Z M 132.917,42.8333L 146.667,42.8333L 146.667,
                52.6667L 132.917,52.6667L 132.917,42.8333 Z "/>
        </Button>
      </Grid>
    </Grid>
  </Grid>
  <Grid Margin="2,-1,2,0" VerticalAlignment="Stretch" Grid.Column="1"
      Grid.Row="2" HorizontalAlignment="Stretch" Grid.RowSpan="2">
    <Grid.RowDefinitions>
      <RowDefinition Height="0.341*"/>
      <RowDefinition Height="0.341*"/>
    </Grid.RowDefinitions>
    <Grid.ColumnDefinitions>
      <ColumnDefinition Width="0.75*"/>
      <ColumnDefinition Width="0.25*"/>
    </Grid.ColumnDefinitions>
    <Ch08_RichMedia_Recipe8_4:MediaSlider SourceName="mediaelemMain"
                        VerticalAlignment="Stretch"
                        IsEnabled="True"
                        x:Name="mediaSlider" Grid.ColumnSpan="2"
                        Margin="0,0,0,0" Grid.Row="0" />
    <Ch08_RichMedia_Recipe8_4:MediaButtonsPanel Grid.Row="2" Grid.Column="0"
                        SourceName="mediaelemMain"
                        HorizontalAlignment="Center"
                        VerticalAlignment="Center"
                        Width="150" Height="40"
                        x:Name="mediaControl"/>
    <Slider x:Name="sliderVolumeControl"  Margin="5,12,5,0" Maximum="1"
            Minimum="0" SmallChange="0.1"
            LargeChange="0.2"  Value="0.5"
            MinWidth="50" Grid.Row="2"
            Grid.Column="1" ValueChanged="sliderVolumeControl_ValueChanged"/>
  </Grid>
  <Grid Grid.RowSpan="4">
    <Grid.RowDefinitions>
      <RowDefinition Height="Auto" MinHeight="41" />
      <RowDefinition Height="*" />
    </Grid.RowDefinitions>
```

```xml
        <Grid Height="Auto" VerticalAlignment="Stretch">
          <Grid.ColumnDefinitions>
            <ColumnDefinition Width="0.33*"/>
            <ColumnDefinition Width="0.34*"/>
            <ColumnDefinition Width="0.33*"/>
          </Grid.ColumnDefinitions>

<RadioButton HorizontalAlignment="Stretch" VerticalAlignment="Stretch"
          Content="Download"
          Template="{StaticResource ctMenuSwitchButton}"
                HorizontalContentAlignment="Stretch"
                VerticalContentAlignment="Stretch"
                GroupName="MediaMenuChoices"
                IsChecked="True" x:Name="rbtnDownloadsMenu"
                Checked="rbtnDownloadsMenu_Checked"/>
    <RadioButton HorizontalAlignment="Stretch" VerticalAlignment="Stretch"
                Content="On Demand" Grid.Column="1"
                Template="{StaticResource ctMenuSwitchButton}"
                HorizontalContentAlignment="Stretch"
                VerticalContentAlignment="Stretch"
                GroupName="MediaMenuChoices"
                IsChecked="False" x:Name="rbtnOnDemandMenu"
                Checked="rbtnOnDemandMenu_Checked"/>
    <RadioButton HorizontalAlignment="Stretch" VerticalAlignment="Stretch"
                Content="Broadcast" Grid.Column="2"
                Template="{StaticResource ctMenuSwitchButton}"
                HorizontalContentAlignment="Stretch"
                VerticalContentAlignment="Stretch" IsChecked="False"
                GroupName="MediaMenuChoices" x:Name="rbtnBroadcastMenu"
                Checked="rbtnBroadcastMenu_Checked"/>
    </Grid>
    <ListBox Margin="0,0,0,0" VerticalAlignment="Stretch"
                x:Name="lbxMediaMenuDownloads"
                ItemTemplate="{StaticResource dtMediaMenuItem}"
                ItemContainerStyle="{StaticResource STYLE_MediaMenuListBoxItem}"
                Grid.RowSpan="1" Grid.Row="1" Background="#FF3CB1E8"/>
    <ListBox Margin="0,0,0,0" VerticalAlignment="Stretch"
                x:Name="lbxMediaMenuOnDemandStreams"
                ItemTemplate="{StaticResource dtMediaMenuItem}"
                ItemContainerStyle="{StaticResource STYLE_MediaMenuListBoxItem}"
                Grid.RowSpan="1" Grid.Row="1" Background="#FF3CB1E8" Visibility="Collapsed"
            />
```

```
        <ListBox Margin="0,0,0,0" VerticalAlignment="Stretch"
                  x:Name="lbxMediaMenuBroadcastStreams"
                  ItemTemplate="{StaticResource dtMediaMenuItem}"
                  ItemContainerStyle="{StaticResource STYLE_MediaMenuListBoxItem}"
                  Visibility="Collapsed"
                  Background="#FF3CB1E8" Grid.RowSpan="1" Grid.Row="1"
        />
    </Grid>
  </Grid>
</UserControl>
```

The only change in the XAML that pertains to the captioning system is the addition of a Grid named CaptionContainer, overlaid on top of the Border that serves as the main display; this change is shown in bold in Listing 8-23.

Listing 8-24 shows the modifications to the player's code-behind. Again, because major portions of the player's code do not change from previous recipes, we have left out some of the unchanged portions. You are encouraged to look at the previous recipe for the full player listing.

Listing 8-24. *Modifications to the Player Code for Marker Support*

```csharp
using System;
using System.Collections.Generic;
using System.Collections.ObjectModel;
using System.Linq;
using System.Net;
using System.Windows;
using System.Windows.Controls;
using System.Windows.Input;
using System.Windows.Markup;
using System.Windows.Media;
using System.Windows.Media.Animation;
using System.Windows.Threading;
using System.Xml.Linq;

namespace Ch08_RichMedia.Recipe8_5
{
  public partial class Page : UserControl
  {
    private const string DownloadsListUri =
      "http://localhost:9494/MediaLocationProvider.svc/GetDownloadsList";
    private const string OnDemandStreamsListUri =
      "http://localhost:9494/MediaLocationProvider.svc/GetOnDemandStreamsList";
    private const string BroadcastStreamsListUri =
      "http://localhost:9494/MediaLocationProvider.svc/GetBroadcastStreamsList";
    private const string CaptionsListUri =
     "http://localhost:9494/MediaLocationProvider.svc/Captions?MediaId={0}";
```

```
    private const string CommercialsListUri =
      "http://localhost:9494/MediaLocationProvider.svc/Commercial?Marker={0}";

    private Dictionary<string, string> dictCaptions = null;

    DispatcherTimer timerAdManager = null;

    void Page_Loaded(object sender, RoutedEventArgs e)
    {
      PopulateMediaMenu();

      //handle marker reached for the main display
      MainVideo.MarkerReached +=
        new System.Windows.Media.TimelineMarkerRoutedEventHandler
(MainVideo_MarkerReached);
      //handle both media_opened events
      MainVideo.MediaOpened += new RoutedEventHandler(MainVideo_MediaOpened);
      PIPVideo.MediaOpened += new RoutedEventHandler(PIPVideo_MediaOpened);
      //set up a timer to manage commercials
      timerAdManager = new DispatcherTimer();
      timerAdManager.Interval = new TimeSpan(0, 0, 15);
      timerAdManager.Tick += new EventHandler(delegate(object timer, EventArgs args)
      {
        //clear
        if (adContainer.Children.Count > 0)
          adContainer.Children.Clear();
        //stop timer
        if ((timer as DispatcherTimer).IsEnabled)
          (timer as DispatcherTimer).Stop();
      });
    }

    void PIPVideo_MediaOpened(object sender, RoutedEventArgs e)
    {
      //we will never display commercials in the PIP,
      //but it might get switched with the main - hence this
      AttachClientMarkers(PIPVideo);
    }

    void MainVideo_MediaOpened(object sender, RoutedEventArgs e)
    {
      //attach the client markers for commercials demo
      AttachClientMarkers(MainVideo);
    }
```

849

```
    private void AttachClientMarkers(MediaElement medElem)
    {
      TimeSpan ts = TimeSpan.Zero;
      if (medElem.NaturalDuration.TimeSpan != TimeSpan.Zero)
      {
        int Ctr = 0;
        while (ts <= medElem.NaturalDuration.TimeSpan)
        {
          //Text = unique name, Time 5,40, 75, ...
          medElem.Markers.Add(new TimelineMarker
          {
            Text = "ClientMarker" + (++Ctr).ToString(),
            Time = ts + new TimeSpan(0, 0, 5),
            Type = "SLMovie"
          });
          ts += new TimeSpan(0, 0, 30);
        }
      }
    }


    void MainVideo_MarkerReached(object sender,
      System.Windows.Media.TimelineMarkerRoutedEventArgs e)
    {
      //Captions markers coming from encoded video
      if (dictCaptions != null && dictCaptions.Count > 0
        && dictCaptions.ContainsKey(e.Marker.Text))
      {
        //clear if we got here before the previous animation completed
        if (CaptionContainer.Children.Count > 0)
          CaptionContainer.Children.Clear();
        // get the caption XAML
        FrameworkElement fe = XamlReader.Load(dictCaptions[e.Marker.Text])
          as FrameworkElement;
        //add
        CaptionContainer.Children.Add(fe);
        //get the animation
        Storyboard stbd = fe.Resources["STBD_AnimateCaption"] as Storyboard;
        stbd.Completed +=
          new EventHandler(delegate(object anim, EventArgs args)
          {
            //clear on animation completion
            if (CaptionContainer.Children.Count > 0)
              CaptionContainer.Children.Clear();
          });
```

```
      //run animation
      stbd.Begin();
    }
    //commercial marker
    else if (e.Marker.Type == "SLMovie")
    {
      WebClient wcCommercial = new WebClient();
      wcCommercial.DownloadStringCompleted +=
        new DownloadStringCompletedEventHandler(
          delegate(object wc, DownloadStringCompletedEventArgs args)
          {
            if (args.Result == null || args.Result == string.Empty) return;
            if (adContainer.Children.Count > 0)
              adContainer.Children.Clear();
            //parse
            XDocument xDoc = XDocument.Parse(args.Result);
            //add
            adContainer.Children.Add(XamlReader.Load((
              (XCData)xDoc.Root.DescendantNodes().ToList()[0]).Value)
              as FrameworkElement);
            //start timer
            timerAdManager.Start();

          });
      //get commercial for this marker type
      wcCommercial.DownloadStringAsync(
        new Uri(string.Format(CommercialsListUri, e.Marker.Type)));
    }
  }
}
private void PlayFull_Click(object sender, RoutedEventArgs e)
{
  //get the animations
  Uri mediaUri = ((sender as Button).Tag as MediaMenuData).MediaLocation;
  WebClient wcAnimations = new WebClient();
  wcAnimations.DownloadStringCompleted +=
    new DownloadStringCompletedEventHandler(
      wcAnimations_DownloadStringCompleted);
  //pass in the mediaelement and the source URI
  wcAnimations.DownloadStringAsync(
    new Uri(string.Format(CaptionsListUri, mediaUri.AbsoluteUri)),
    new object[] { MainVideo, mediaUri });

}
```

```
void wcAnimations_DownloadStringCompleted(object sender,
  DownloadStringCompletedEventArgs e)
{
  if (e.Result != null && e.Result != string.Empty)
  {
    //parse
    XDocument xDoc = XDocument.Parse(e.Result);
    //get each animation
    var AnimationUnits = from marker in xDoc.Root.Elements()
                         select new
                         {
                           key = marker.Attribute("Value").Value,
                           XamlFragment = ((XCData)marker.DescendantNodes().
                           ToList()[0]).Value
                         };

    dictCaptions = new Dictionary<string, string>();
    //store in dictionary
    foreach (var marker in AnimationUnits)
      dictCaptions.Add(marker.key, marker.XamlFragment);
  }
  //start playing the media
  ((e.UserState as object[])[0] as MediaElement).Source =
    ((e.UserState as object[])[1] as Uri);
}

// REST OF THE CODE OMITTED FOR BREVITY -
//PLEASE LOOK AT RECIPE 8-4 FOR FULL LISTING
  }
}
```

Whenever a user tries to play a media file, you use a WebClient to invoke the GetCaptionsForMedia() WCF service operation. In the DownloadStringCompleted handler, you check to see if any caption definitions were returned. If there is a valid return from the operation, you perform a LINQ query on the returned XML to extract a collection of the marker values and corresponding XAML fragments. You then save each XAML entry representing a caption into a Dictionary named dictCaptions, keyed with the marker value for later access. After this is done, you start playing the media by setting MediaElement.Source.

As the media plays and markers are reached, you handle the MarkerReached event, using the MainVideo_MarkerReached() event handler. Let's look at the if block of the if-else statement in the handler. If the TimelineMarker being reached has a Text property value that corresponds to a key in dictCaptions, you first clear the CaptionContainer. You then load the XAML fragment using XamlReader.Load(). You can find more about XamlReader in Chapter 2. When the XAML is loaded, you cast it to a FrameworkElement and add it to CaptionContainer. Using the FrameworkElement base type allows you to use any FrameworkElement derivative in the XAML fragment, and not just a Canvas as it was defined in the XAML fragment. You then acquire the Storyboard named STBD_AnimateCaption from the FrameworkElement.Resources collection and start it. In the Storyboard.Completed handler, you clear the CaptionContainer after the animation completes.

> **Note** The clearing of the CaptionContainer at the beginning of the if block is for cases where a marker may be reached even before the animation for the previous one has completed.

Also note that the XAML fragments loaded using XamlReader.Load() are evaluated by the XAML parser for validity. Because they are not evaluated in the context of a containing XAML document, they need to be valid on their own. Consequently, if you are cutting and pasting from a containing document, be sure to add the necessary namespace declarations to the top-level element in the fragment to make it independently valid and thus avoid loading exceptions.

Now, let's look at the second part of this sample. For the simulated commercials, you create a similarly structured data file named Commercials.xml. Listing 8-25 shows a sample.

Listing 8-25. *Commercials.xml Sample*

```
<?xml version="1.0" encoding="utf-8" ?>
<Commercials>
  <Marker Type="SLMovie">
    <![CDATA[<Grid
    xmlns="http://schemas.microsoft.com/winfx/2006/xaml/presentation"
    xmlns:x="http://schemas.microsoft.com/winfx/2006/xaml">
          <MediaElement  x:Name="medElem" Opacity="0.0" AutoPlay="true"
          Source="mms://localhost/SLBook/Ch08_RichMedia/Media/sl.wmv"
          HorizontalAlignment="Left" VerticalAlignment="Top" />
          <Border>
          <Border.Background>
            <VideoBrush Stretch="Fill" SourceName="medElem"/>
          </Border.Background>
          </Border>
        </Grid>]]>
  </Marker>
</Commercials>
```

Each commercial is tied to a marker type (derived from the TimelineMarker.Type property discussed earlier). Within each <Marker> element, you again have an XAML snippet defining the commercial. The previous sample includes another MediaElement in the snippet that points to a small Silverlight logo animation captured in a Windows media file. The sl.wmv file used here is a part of the Expression Encoder installation and can be found in the StockContent folder under the Expression Encoder installation root. But you can replace this with any .wmv file or, for that matter, any other XAML snippet.

You also define another WCF service operation named GetCommercial() and apply another UriTemplate to use the Uri format <*serviceaddress*>/Commercial?Marker={*MarkerType*}. GetCommercial() accepts a marker type string and returns the XML for the matching <*Marker*> element. Again, we encourage you to look at the sample code for the service operation details.

Refer back to Listing 8-23, and notice one more addition to the player XAML: another Grid named adContainer, this time contained in the Border serving as the main display. You set adContainer at opacity 0.5 and align it with the lower-right corner of the containing Border.

Referring back to the code in Listing 8-24, notice that you attach handlers to the `MediaOpened` event for both the PIP and the main `MediaElements` in the `Page_Loaded()` handler. In both those handlers, you invoke `AttachClientMarkers()` to attach a set of client-side markers to the media right after it opens. Although you always display the commercial in the main display only, you attach the markers to both, because in previous recipes you enabled the user to switch media elements between displays using the PIP feature.

In `AttachClientMarkers()`, you look at the total duration of the media file; create a new `TimelineMarker` at 30-second intervals, starting the first one at 5 seconds into the media; and add each to the `MediaElement.Markers` collection. You set the `TimelineMarker.Type` property to the string "SLMovie", which matches the entry in Listing 8-25. Note that you use a counter to generate a unique `Text` property for each `TimelineMarker`—the `MediaElement` requires that client markers have unique `Text` values. Whenever a piece of media starts playing, the `MarkerReached` event is raised for each client-side `TimelineMarker` as well.

Next, let's look at the `else` block of the `MainVideo_MarkerReached()` method, which is where you handle the client-side markers. After you verify that the `TimelineMarker.Type` property value matches the string "SLMovie", you use another `WebClient` to invoke the `GetCaption()` service operation. You parse the returned XAML into a `FrameworkElement` and add it to the `adContainer` Grid. Using the XAML fragment from the sample in Listing 8-25, this causes the `MediaElement` named `medElem` to download and play the `sl.wmv` file within the bounds of `adContainer`. You also start a `DispatcherTimer` named `timerAdManager` right after you add the XAML fragment. You have already created `timerAdManager` intervals in the `Page_Loaded()` handler and initialized `timerAdManager` to tick at 15-second intervals. In the `Tick` event handler for `timerAdManager`, you clear the `adContainer` and stop the timer, thus causing the commercial to play for its entire duration or 15 seconds, whichever comes first.

8-6. Displaying and Seeking Using SMPTE Timecodes

Problem

You want to display the time elapsed in the SMPTE timecode format when a video is playing. You also want the user to be able to specify a time in the SMPTE timecode format and have the video seek to that time point.

Solution

Use the `TimeCode` class and the `SmpteFrameRate` enumeration available as a part of the Expression Encoder templates to enable timecode handling in your code.

How It Works

Digital video is a collection of *frames*, where each frame is essentially a discrete bitmap. Video players achieve the illusion of a smoothly moving image by displaying these frames sequentially at a certain speed.

Frame Rate

The speed at which frames are displayed is typically measured in the number of frames displayed per second (fps) and is commonly known as the *frame rate* of a video.

Several different frame rates are used for video around the world. Some of the more common ones are as follows:

- 24 fps: Typically used for movie making

- 25 fps: Used in the PAL Television standards in large parts of Europe and Latin America

- 29.97 fps: Used in the NTSC Television standards in North America

- 30 fps: Used in the HDTV standard

Timecodes

A common way to refer to a specific time point in a video is to use a combination of standard time units and frame count. This mechanism has been formalized by the SMPTE and is commonly referred to as an SMPTE timecode or more formally as the SMPTE 12M specification.

An SMPTE timecode is a way to label each frame in a video with time information for that frame. Using the SMPTE timecode standard, each frame is labeled using the *hh:mm:ss:ff* format, where *ff* is the frame number for that frame within the second immediately following the time specified by the *hh:mm:ss* portion of the timecode.

As an example, consider a video that has been recorded at a frame rate of 25 fps—that is, in the video, a unique frame occurs every 40 milliseconds. The two-thousand-twelfth frame in that video is labeled 00:01:20:12. If you calculate backward, you see that 1 minute and 20 seconds (80 seconds) yields 2,000 frames at 25 fps, and hence 00:01:20:12 denotes the two-thousand-twelfth frame in the video.

Timecodes are typically imprinted into the source video at the time of recording. Consequently, if you are using the source material as is, you may expect the timecodes to be contiguous. However, this is not always the case. Often, video can be edited such that segments of video from different source materials, or disjoint segments from the same source material, are stitched together to form another video. In certain cases, the editor may choose to retain the original SMPTE timecodes from the sources into the resulting video, in which case the resulting video ends up with disjoint ranges of SMPTE timecodes.

We touch on some very basic information about timecoding here. For a somewhat detailed treatment of SMPTE timecodes, you can refer to http://en.wikipedia.org/wiki/SMPTE_timecode. For the detailed 12M timecode specifications, visit the SMPTE at http://www.smpte.org.

Timecodes and Silverlight

The SMPTE timecoding mechanism is very helpful for performing frame-accurate operations on a video, such as seeking to a specific frame within the video or being able to edit the video to the accuracy of specific frames. Consequently, you may need to both display and act on SMPTE timecodes in your Silverlight application.

Calculating the timecode is relatively easy as long as you know the frame rate of the video. If the video clip you are dealing with does not come with any preexisting timecode ranges, you can calculate the timecode at any time point by converting the fractional seconds in the MediaElement.Position property into a number of frames based on the frame rate, and then attaching that to the end of a string that contains the whole number of hours, minutes, and seconds at that time point formatted in the timecode format as discussed in the previous section. In this case, the timecode is extrapolated from the absolute time within the video.

On the other hand, if the video clip is associated with a range of timecodes, you can perform the same extrapolation and then offset the resulting *hh:mm:ss:ff* value with the starting timecode for the range in which that timecode falls.

But you do not have to do this on your own. If you install the Microsoft Expression Encoder tool, it installs a suite of Silverlight player templates that you can use from within Encoder to automatically generate Silverlight players for the video you encode. These templates can typically be found in the *<expression encoder install folder>*/Templates folder. Using your favorite search mechanism, search for two files named Timecode.cs and SmpteFrameRate.cs within the Templates folder. Multiple instances of each result from you're the search, because these classes are included with each template. Copy one instance of each class into your project, and you are ready to deal with SMPTE timecodes on the client.

Before we look at these classes, it is important to note that Silverlight has no built-in mechanism to extract the frame rate of the video your application is handling. Given that the frame rate is required to extrapolate the timecodes, you must devise an alternative mechanism to supply the frame rate of the video to the Silverlight code. Most enterprise content and asset-management systems have a mechanism to extract the frame rate of videos that are stored, and they store that information externally as part of the associated metadata. One option is to build a web service so that the frame rate can be sent to the client for the video concerned.

The SmpteFrameRate.cs file contains an enumeration named SmpteFrameRate that captures all the well-known frame-rate values as distinct members of the enumeration.

The TimeCode.cs file contains a class called TimeCode that can handle the lion's share of the work when it comes to translating from absolute time values to SMPTE timecodes and vice versa, as well as parsing timecodes, accessing different parts of the timecode, validating frame rates, and a lot more.. Discussing the entire API exposed by the TimeCode type is not our intent, but we encourage you to take a good look at it.

For the purpose of building a sample, we look at four methods on the TimeCode class. The TimeCode.ParseFramerate() static method accepts a frame rate as a double value and returns one of the SmpteFrameRate enumerated values, including SmpteFrameRate.Unknown, if the frame rate is not one of the recognizable frame rates listed in the enumeration. You use a TimeCode constructor that accepts a formatted timecode string and an SmpteFrameRate enumerated value to construct a TimeCode instance. You also use the TimeCode.FromTicks() static method, which accepts time measured in CPU ticks and a SmpteFrameRate enumerated value and returns a TimeCode instance. Last, you use the TimeCode.ValidateSmpte12MTimeCode() static method, which accepts a string value and validates it to ensure that it is in the correct timecode format.

The Code

The code sample in this chapter extends the player you built in Recipe 8-2 to include SMPTE timecode support. The extended player displays the SMPTE timecode as the video plays and lets the user seek to any portion of the video by typing in a valid timecode.

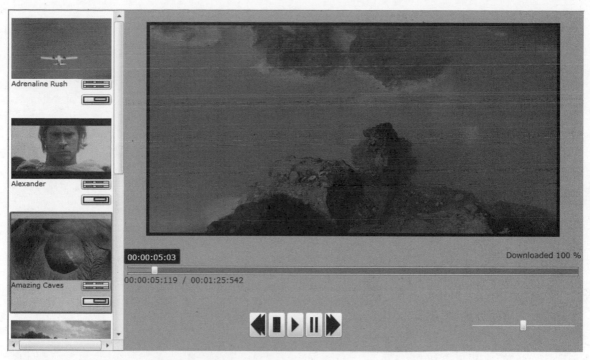

Figure 8-24. *Video Player with SMPTE timecode support*

Figure 8-24 shows the player interface with the SMPTE timecode displayed in a TextBox above the slider in white over a black background. The user can pause the video and then type a valid timecode in the same TextBox to seek to that timecode within the video.

Because you extend the code from Recipe 8-2, we only highlight the changes here. Please refer back to Recipe 8-2 for more details about the rest of the player. Listing 8-26 shows the control template for the Ch08_RichMedia.Recipe8_6.MediaSlider control that is used to display the slider on the player.

Listing 8-26. *Control Template for MediaSlider control*

```
<ControlTemplate TargetType="local:MediaSlider"
                 x:Key="ctMediaSliderDefault">
  <Grid x:Name="Root">
    <Grid.Resources>
      <ControlTemplate x:Key="ctRepeatButton">
        <Grid x:Name="Root"
              Opacity="0"
              Background="Transparent" />
      </ControlTemplate>
    </Grid.Resources>
```

```xml
<vsm:VisualStateManager.VisualStateGroups>
  <vsm:VisualStateGroup x:Name="CommonStates">
    <vsm:VisualStateGroup.Transitions>
      <vsm:VisualTransition GeneratedDuration="0" />
    </vsm:VisualStateGroup.Transitions>
    <vsm:VisualState x:Name="Normal" />
    <vsm:VisualState x:Name="MouseOver" />
    <vsm:VisualState x:Name="Disabled">
      <Storyboard>
        <DoubleAnimationUsingKeyFrames
          Storyboard.TargetName="Root"
          Storyboard.TargetProperty="(UIElement.Opacity)">
          <SplineDoubleKeyFrame KeyTime="00:00:00"
                                Value="0.5" />
        </DoubleAnimationUsingKeyFrames>
      </Storyboard>
    </vsm:VisualState>
  </vsm:VisualStateGroup>
</vsm:VisualStateManager.VisualStateGroups>
<Grid>
  <Grid.RowDefinitions>
    <RowDefinition Height="0.33*" />
    <RowDefinition Height="0.34*" />
    <RowDefinition Height="0.33*" />
  </Grid.RowDefinitions>
  <Grid Grid.Row="0"
        VerticalAlignment="Top"
        HorizontalAlignment="Stretch">
    <Grid.ColumnDefinitions>
      <ColumnDefinition Width="*" />
      <ColumnDefinition Width="Auto" />
    </Grid.ColumnDefinitions>
    <TextBox x:Name="tbxSMPTETimeCode"
            Background="Black"
            Foreground="White"
            Text="{Binding SMPTETimeCode,
      RelativeSource={RelativeSource TemplatedParent},
      Mode=TwoWay, ValidatesOnExceptions=true, NotifyOnValidationError=true}"
            BorderBrush="Blue"
            BorderThickness="2"
            Grid.Column="0"
            HorizontalAlignment="Left"
            Margin="0,0,0,3"
            FontSize="12" />
```

```
    <StackPanel Orientation="Horizontal"
                Grid.Column="1"
                HorizontalAlignment="Right">
      <TextBlock Text="Downloaded"
                 FontSize="12"
                 Margin="0,0,4,0" />
      <TextBlock x:Name="textDownloadPercent"
                 FontSize="12" />
    </StackPanel>
  </Grid>
  <Grid x:Name="HorizontalTemplate"
        Grid.Row="1">
    <Grid.ColumnDefinitions>
      <ColumnDefinition Width="Auto" />
      <ColumnDefinition Width="Auto" />
      <ColumnDefinition Width="*" />
    </Grid.ColumnDefinitions>
    <Rectangle Stroke="Black"
               StrokeThickness="0.5"
               Fill="#FFE6EFF7"
               Grid.Column="0"
               Grid.ColumnSpan="3"
               Height="14"
               Margin="5,0,5,0" />
    <Border Height="10"
            Margin="5,0,5,0"
            Grid.Column="0"
            Grid.ColumnSpan="3"
            x:Name="elemDownloadProgressIndicator"
            Background="#FF2185D8"
            HorizontalAlignment="Left"
            Width="0" />
    <Border Height="6"
            Margin="5,0,5,0"
            Grid.Column="0"
            Grid.ColumnSpan="3"
            x:Name="elemPlayProgressIndicator"
            Background="#FF1CE421"
            HorizontalAlignment="Left"
            Width="0" />
    <RepeatButton x:Name="HorizontalTrackLargeChangeDecreaseRepeatButton"
                  Grid.Column="0"
                  Template="{StaticResource ctRepeatButton}"
                  IsTabStop="False" />
```

```
            <Thumb x:Name="HorizontalThumb"
                   Height="14"
                   Width="11"
                   Grid.Column="1" />
            <RepeatButton x:Name="HorizontalTrackLargeChangeIncreaseRepeatButton"
                          Grid.Column="2"
                          Template="{StaticResource ctRepeatButton}"
                          IsTabStop="False" />
          </Grid>
          <Grid Grid.Row="2"
                VerticalAlignment="Bottom"
                HorizontalAlignment="Stretch">
            <StackPanel x:Name="TotalDuration"
                        Orientation="Horizontal">
              <TextBlock x:Name="textPosition"
                         FontSize="12" />
              <TextBlock Text=" / "
                         FontSize="12"
                         Margin="3,0,3,0" />
              <TextBlock x:Name="textDuration"
                         FontSize="12" />
            </StackPanel>
          </Grid>
        </Grid>
      </Grid>
</ControlTemplate>
```

The only change in the code in Listing 8-26 is the addition of a TextBox named tbxSMPTETimeCode that is used to display the timecode as well let the user edit it to navigate to a specific timecode within the video. As you can see, the Text property on tbxSMPTETimeCode is bound in a TwoWay mode to a property named SMPTETimeCode on the MediaSlider control. Also note that tbxSMPTETimeCode is enabled for data-binding validation. For more about binding validation, refer to the recipes in Chapter 4. Listing 8-27 shows the code for the MediaSlider control.

Listing 8-27. *Code for the MediaSlider control*

```
using System;
using System.Windows;
using System.Windows.Controls;
using System.Windows.Controls.Primitives;
using System.Windows.Media;
using System.Windows.Threading;
using System.ComponentModel;
```

```
namespace Ch08_RichMedia.Recipe8_6
{
  public class MediaSlider : Slider, INotifyPropertyChanged
  {
    private MediaElement MediaSource;
    private FrameworkElement elemDownloadProgressIndicator;
    private FrameworkElement elemPlayProgressIndicator;
    private FrameworkElement Root;
    private TextBlock textPosition;
    private TextBlock textDuration;
    private TextBlock textDownloadPercent;
    private Thumb HorizontalThumb;
    private DispatcherTimer disptimerPlayProgressUpdate;

    //SourceName dependency property - used to attach
    //a Media element to this control
    public static DependencyProperty SourceNameProperty =
      DependencyProperty.Register("SourceName", typeof(string),
      typeof(MediaSlider),
      new PropertyMetadata(new PropertyChangedCallback(OnSourceNameChanged)));
    public string SourceName
    {
      get
      {
        return (string)GetValue(SourceNameProperty);
      }
      set
      {
        SetValue(SourceNameProperty, value);
      }
    }
    //SourceName change handler
    private static void OnSourceNameChanged(DependencyObject Source,
      DependencyPropertyChangedEventArgs e)
    {
      MediaSlider thisSlider = Source as MediaSlider;
      if (e.NewValue != null && e.NewValue != e.OldValue
        && thisSlider.Root != null)
      {
        thisSlider.MediaSource =
          thisSlider.Root.FindName(e.NewValue as string) as MediaElement;
        //reinitialize
        thisSlider.InitMediaElementConnections();
      }
    }
```

```
private double _FrameRate = 24;
public double FrameRate
{
  get
  {
    return _FrameRate;
  }

  set
  {
    if (TimeCode.ParseFrameRate(value) == SmpteFrameRate.Unknown)
      throw new Exception("Unknown Framerate");
    if (value != _FrameRate)
    {
      _FrameRate = value;
      if (disptimerPlayProgressUpdate.IsEnabled)
      {
        disptimerPlayProgressUpdate.Stop();
        disptimerPlayProgressUpdate.Interval =
          TimeSpan.FromSeconds(1 / FrameRate);
        disptimerPlayProgressUpdate.Start();
      }
      else
        disptimerPlayProgressUpdate.Interval =
          TimeSpan.FromSeconds(1 / FrameRate);

      if (PropertyChanged != null) PropertyChanged(this,
        new PropertyChangedEventArgs("FrameRate"));
    }

  }
}

private string _SMPTETimeCode = "00:00:00:00";
public string SMPTETimeCode
{
  get
  {
    return _SMPTETimeCode;
  }
```

```
  set
  {
    if (TimeCode.ValidateSmpte12MTimeCode(value) == false)
    {
      throw new
        Exception("Invalid time code. Time code format must be hh:mm:ss:ff");
    }
    if (value != _SMPTETimeCode)
    {
      _SMPTETimeCode = value;
      if (PropertyChanged != null) PropertyChanged(this,
        new PropertyChangedEventArgs("SMPTETimeCode"));
    }

  }
}

public MediaSlider()
  : base()
{
  this.DefaultStyleKey = typeof(MediaSlider);
  this.Maximum = 100;
  this.Minimum = 0;
  disptimerPlayProgressUpdate = new DispatcherTimer();
  disptimerPlayProgressUpdate.Interval = TimeSpan.FromSeconds(1 / FrameRate);
  disptimerPlayProgressUpdate.Tick +=
    new EventHandler(PlayProgressUpdate_Tick);
}
public override void OnApplyTemplate()
{
  base.OnApplyTemplate();

  elemDownloadProgressIndicator =
    GetTemplateChild("elemDownloadProgressIndicator") as FrameworkElement;
  elemPlayProgressIndicator =
   GetTemplateChild("elemPlayProgressIndicator") as FrameworkElement;
  HorizontalThumb = GetTemplateChild("HorizontalThumb") as Thumb;
  if (HorizontalThumb != null)
  {
    HorizontalThumb.DragStarted +=
      new DragStartedEventHandler(HorizontalThumb_DragStarted);
    HorizontalThumb.DragCompleted +=
      new DragCompletedEventHandler(HorizontalThumb_DragCompleted);
  }
```

```
    textPosition = GetTemplateChild("textPosition") as TextBlock;
    textDuration = GetTemplateChild("textDuration") as TextBlock;
    textDownloadPercent = GetTemplateChild("textDownloadPercent") as TextBlock;

    this.PropertyChanged +=
        new PropertyChangedEventHandler(MediaSlider_PropertyChanged);


    Root = Helper.FindRoot(this);
    MediaSource = Root.FindName(SourceName) as MediaElement;
    InitMediaElementConnections();
}

void MediaSlider_PropertyChanged(object sender, PropertyChangedEventArgs e)
{
    if (e.PropertyName == "SMPTETimeCode" &&
        MediaSource.CurrentState == MediaElementState.Paused)
    {
        MediaSource.Position = TimeSpan.FromSeconds(
            new TimeCode(SMPTETimeCode,
                TimeCode.ParseFrameRate(FrameRate)).Duration);
        this.Value =
(MediaSource.Position.TotalMilliseconds /
MediaSource.NaturalDuration.TimeSpan.TotalMilliseconds)
* (this.Maximum - this.Minimum);
    }
}
//Initialize by wiring up handlers
private void InitMediaElementConnections()
{
    if (MediaSource != null)
    {
        MediaSource.MediaOpened +=
            new RoutedEventHandler(MediaSource_MediaOpened);
        MediaSource.MediaEnded +=
            new RoutedEventHandler(MediaSource_MediaEnded);
        MediaSource.MediaFailed +=
            new EventHandler<ExceptionRoutedEventArgs>(MediaSource_MediaFailed);
        MediaSource.CurrentStateChanged +=
            new RoutedEventHandler(MediaSource_CurrentStateChanged);
        MediaSource.DownloadProgressChanged +=
            new RoutedEventHandler(MediaSource_DownloadProgressChanged);
```

```
    MediaSource_CurrentStateChanged(this, new RoutedEventArgs());
  }
}


//tick handler for progress timer
void PlayProgressUpdate_Tick(object sender, EventArgs e)
{
  this.Value =
    (MediaSource.Position.TotalMilliseconds /
    MediaSource.NaturalDuration.TimeSpan.TotalMilliseconds)
    * (this.Maximum - this.Minimum);

  if (elemPlayProgressIndicator != null)
  {
    elemPlayProgressIndicator.Width =
      (MediaSource.Position.TotalMilliseconds /
      MediaSource.NaturalDuration.TimeSpan.TotalMilliseconds)
      * ActualWidth;
  }
  if (textPosition != null)
    textPosition.Text = string.Format("{0:00}:{1:00}:{2:00}:{3:000}",
      MediaSource.Position.Hours,
      MediaSource.Position.Minutes,
      MediaSource.Position.Seconds,
      MediaSource.Position.Milliseconds);


  SMPTETimeCode = TimeCode.FromTicks(MediaSource.Position.Ticks,
    TimeCode.ParseFrameRate(FrameRate)).ToString();

}
//plug into the thumb to pause play while it is being dragged
void HorizontalThumb_DragStarted(object sender, DragStartedEventArgs e)
{
  if (MediaSource != null && MediaSource.CurrentState ==
    MediaElementState.Playing)
    MediaSource.Pause();
}
void HorizontalThumb_DragCompleted(object sender, DragCompletedEventArgs e)
{
  if (MediaSource != null)
  {
    MediaSource.Position = new TimeSpan(0,
      0, 0, 0,
```

```
        (int)(this.Value *
        MediaSource.NaturalDuration.TimeSpan.TotalMilliseconds /
        (this.Maximum - this.Minimum)));
    }
    MediaSource.Play();
}

//media element download progress changed
private void MediaSource_DownloadProgressChanged(object sender,
  RoutedEventArgs e)
{
  if (elemDownloadProgressIndicator != null)
  {
    elemDownloadProgressIndicator.Width =
      (MediaSource.DownloadProgress * this.ActualWidth);
    if (textDownloadPercent != null)
      textDownloadPercent.Text = string.Format("{0:##.##} %",
        MediaSource.DownloadProgress * 100);
  }
}
//state changes on the MediaElement
private void MediaSource_CurrentStateChanged(object sender,
  RoutedEventArgs e)
{
  switch (MediaSource.CurrentState)
  {
    case MediaElementState.Playing:
      if (textDuration != null)
        textDuration.Text = string.Format("{0:00}:{1:00}:{2:00}:{3:000}",
          MediaSource.NaturalDuration.TimeSpan.Hours,
          MediaSource.NaturalDuration.TimeSpan.Minutes,
          MediaSource.NaturalDuration.TimeSpan.Seconds,
          MediaSource.NaturalDuration.TimeSpan.Milliseconds);
      if (disptimerPlayProgressUpdate.IsEnabled == false)
        disptimerPlayProgressUpdate.Start();
      break;
    case MediaElementState.Paused:
      if (disptimerPlayProgressUpdate.IsEnabled)
        disptimerPlayProgressUpdate.Stop();
      break;
    case MediaElementState.Stopped:
      if (disptimerPlayProgressUpdate.IsEnabled)
        disptimerPlayProgressUpdate.Stop();
      break;
```

```
      case MediaElementState.AcquiringLicense:
      case MediaElementState.Individualizing:
      case MediaElementState.Opening:
      case MediaElementState.Buffering:
      case MediaElementState.Closed:
        break;

      default:
        break;
    }
  }

  //media ended
  private void MediaSource_MediaEnded(object sender,
    RoutedEventArgs e)
  {
    if (disptimerPlayProgressUpdate.IsEnabled)
      disptimerPlayProgressUpdate.Stop();
  }

  //media failed
  private void MediaSource_MediaFailed(object sender, RoutedEventArgs e)
  {
    disptimerPlayProgressUpdate.Stop();
  }

  void MediaSource_MediaOpened(object sender, RoutedEventArgs e)
  {
    //we do nothing here in this sample
  }

  #region INotifyPropertyChanged Members

  public event PropertyChangedEventHandler PropertyChanged;

  #endregion
  }
}
```

As you can see in Listing 8-27, you add two properties, FrameRate and SMPTETimeCode, to the MediaSlider control. Both properties are enabled for change notification.

The FrameRate property defaults to 24. In the property setter for the FrameRate property, you use TimeCode.ParseFrameRate() to check whether the FrameRate is one of the known frame rates and throw an exception if not. As we mentioned earlier in this recipe, Silverlight has no built-in mechanism to extract frame rates. So, in the sample, this always defaults to 24. However, if you devise another mechanism to acquire the frame rate of the video (maybe from a content-management back end that can supply the frame rate through a web service), you can set this property to some other value.

The `SMPTETimeCode` property defaults to a string representing the timecode at the start of the video. It is bound to `tbxSMPTETimeCode` in the XAML to display the timecode. Because that binding is TwoWay, it can also accept user edits. In the property setter, you validate any user input to make sure it is in the valid timecode format using the `TimeCode.ValidateSmpte12MTimeCode()` static method. If the format is invalid, you raise an exception, which is then displayed as a validation error using the binding validation mechanism.

Recall from Recipe 8-2 that the sample uses a `DispatcherTimer` named `PlayProgressUpdate` to raise `DispatcherTime.Tick` events at regular intervals while the video is playing. `PlayProgressUpdate_Tick()` handles the Tick event and changes `Slider.Value` to cause the slider thumb to move. You now set the `PlayProgressUpdate.Interval` property to the duration of a single frame, so that the Tick even fires at each frame interval. You do this once initially in the `MediaSlider` constructor as well as in the property setter of the `FrameRate` property.

In the `PlayProgressUpdate_Tick()` handler method, you update the `SMPTETimeCode` property to the current timecode using the `TimeCode.FromTicks()` static function; this function accepts the current `MediaElement.Position` as CPU ticks and the current frame rate, and returns a `TimeCode` instance. You convert this to a string before you set the property. Because `SMPTETimeCode` is bound to `tbxSMPTETimeCode`, this updates the UI with the timecode as the video plays.

You also handle the `PropertyChanged` event of the `MediaSlider` control. Because the `SMPTETimeCode` property is TwoWay bound to `tbxSMPTETimeCode`, the `PropertyChanged` event on the control is fired when the user edits the value in `tbxSMPTETimeCode`, causing a change in value to `MediaSlider`. `SMPTETimeCode`. In the `MediaSlider_PropertyChanged()` handler, you ensure that you are handling the correct property change. You also make sure the media is currently paused. You then set the position of the media to the user-supplied timecode. To do so, you construct a new `TimeCode` instance, using a constructor that accepts a string-formatted timecode value that you get from `MediaSlider` `SMPTETimeCode`, and the current frame rate parsed into a `SmpteFrameRate` enumerated value. When you have the new `TimeCode` instance, you construct a `TimeSpan` from the `TimeCode.Duration` property, which reflects the total number of whole and fractional seconds in that timecode, and use that to set the current position of the media.

8-7. Building a Managed Decoder for Silverlight

Problem

You want to use Silverlight to play a media file whose storage format and/or encoding scheme is not supported by Silverlight directly.

Solution

Use the managed decoder extensibility mechanism in Silverlight to create a custom `MediaStreamSource` that can parse and decode the custom media file format.

How It Works

The internal structure of a digital media file can be broadly broken up into two parts: metadata and essence.

Metadata is information about the media contained in the file. For example, for a video file, metadata may include information like the aspect ratio of the video, the frame rate, the bit rate, the duration, the author, copyright information, and so on. For an audio file, it may include the bit rate, the artist, album information, and such.

The *essence* is the actual media content, which is also stored inside the container file. Because in most cases an unchanged digital representation of video and audio content is very large, a compression process is used to reduce the size of the essence before it is stored it in the container.

The process of compressing the media to reduce its size and packaging it into a container file along with the correct metadata is generally referred to as *encoding*. The process of parsing the container file to extract the metadata elements and then decompressing the essence to enable play out is called *decoding*. Typically, the ability to encode/decode a specific metadata structure and compression format is packaged together in a single piece of software commonly known as a *codec*.

Silverlight, Containers, and Codecs

Silverlight supports the Microsoft Advanced Systems Format (ASF) and the MP4 File Format (also known as the MPEG-4 File Format version 2) file container structures. Windows Media Video (.wmv) and Windows Media Audio (.wma) files follow the ASF file container structures and can be consumed by Silverlight, and so can MP4 and QuickTime (.mov) files that are common variants of the MP4 container structure.

Silverlight supports decoding essence that is encoded using the Windows Media VC-1 or H.264 (or its equivalents in MPEG-4 part 10 and the MPEG-4 Advanced Video Codec) compression standards. Silverlight also supports decompressing Windows Media Audio as well as the Advanced Audio Coding (AAC) encoded audio streams for up to two-channel stereo.

With this support out of the box, Silverlight can play a wide gamut of media file types. However, occasionally you may come across a scenario where Silverlight does not support the file-container structure or the compression standard used (or both). This recipe deals with an extensibility mechanism built into Silverlight that allows you to implement the file-parsing and/or decompression mechanism yourself for formats that are not supported by Silverlight out of the box.

The default behavior of the Silverlight MediaElement type is such that you point MediaElement. Source to the URL of a media stream or file; that is all you need to do prepare the MediaElement to begin consuming the media. As long as the container structure (Windows Media ASF or MP4) and the codec (VC-1 or H.264) are supported natively, MediaElement parses the container file and decodes the media automatically. MediaElement also exposes two overloads of a method named SetSource(), one of which accepts a Stream. If you have direct access to the media stream, you can use this overload of SetSource() to achieve the same effect as setting MediaElement.Source property.

This recipe uses the second overload of the MediaElement.SetSource() method, which accepts an instance of type System.Windows.Media.MediaStreamSource. The MediaStreamSource type is the extensibility mechanism that lets you build your own managed decoder and plug it into the Silverlight media pipeline. We look at the MediaStreamSource API in more details in the next section.

It is important to note that authoring parsers for media file containers or decompression logic for various compression schemes is a specialized task; a lot of care and very skillful engineering are required, to produce something that meets the bar for performance and quality. Not doing it properly can result in low-performing and, in some cases, faulty processing of media. Our goal in this recipe is not to make you an expert in doing either task, but rather to familiarize you with the API for the related extensibility mechanism in Silverlight. If you take advantage of this facility to integrate a natively unsupported media format into your Silverlight code, we advise you to research the compression and container structure specifications for that format rigorously and apply best-of-breed engineering resources to building the parsing and the decompression logic.

MediaStreamSource

System.Windows.Media.MediaStreamSource is an abstract class that expresses the interaction between the MediaElement and a managed decoder in an abstract API. It lets you create your own concrete type by inheriting from MediaStreamSource and providing implementations for the abstract API to inject custom media decoding logic into the Silverlight media pipeline. When you call MediaElement.SetSource() and pass in an instance of your concrete MediaStreamSource implementation, MediaElement interacts with your code to consume the media.

The MediaStreamSource API is designed to be asynchronous so as to not block the UI thread on calls coming in through the MediaElement. As a result, every abstract method that you implement in your inherited class has a Report<*methodname*>Completed() method defined in the MediaStreamSource base class. The goal is to return from the implementation of your method as quickly as possible to stop holding up the UI, and then, when you are ready with the results of the requested operation, to call the Report<*methodname*>Completed() method to signal the completion of the operation to the MediaElement. This allows you to spin up asynchronous operations on separate threads from within your MediaStreamSource-derived class and process long-running operations in a nonblocking fashion.

As an example, consider the MediaStreamSource.OpenMediaAsync() method. The following snippet shows a possible skeletal implementation:

```
protected override void OpenMediaAsync()
{
  //spin up a thread to process
  Thread thdOpen = new Thread(new ThreadStart(() =>
    {
      //process the request - may take some time
      //when done
      ReportOpenMediaCompleted(..,..);
    }));
  thdOpen.Start();
  //return to MediaElement right away - no blocking
  return;

}
```

You create a thread and start it, and then return from the call right away. But in the thread's processing logic, after you are ready with the results of the operation, you call ReportOpenMediaCompleted() to signal back to the MediaElement that you are finished.

This is an important point to keep in mind. No hard and fast rule dictates what has to be done asynchronously and what does not. In the previous snippet, you might have done all the processing in the call in a blocking fashion and then signal completion before you returned, broken up the processing between the blocking call and the separate thread in some fashion, or done it entirely in an asynchronous fashion as the snippet shows in this case. You make that decision based on the scenario for which you are implementing the MediaStreamSource. For instance, if your implementation of an operation involves a network download of content, it is best done in an asynchronous fashion; where as if it involves reading information locally from the disk, an asynchronous operation may be overkill. The API is designed to let you do everything asynchronously—use your best judgment to decide the course to take on a case-by-case basis.

The MediaStreamSource API covers the following basic interactions driven by the MediaElement: opening and initializing media, acquiring media samples to play, seeking within the media, switching media streams when there are multiple streams (such as video and audio), diagnostics, and cleanup. Let's look at some of these interactions and the related API.

Initializing the Media Stream

When you pass in an instance of your MediaStreamSource-derived class into MediaElement.SetSource() method, the MediaElement invokes your implementation of the MediaStreamSource.OpenMediaAsync() function. The OpenMediaAsync() function implementation is your opportunity to initialize your media and make it ready for consumption, as well as to pass metadata information about your media to the

MediaElement so that it can prepare itself for consuming the media. The logic you implement varies from implementation to implementation, depending on how your media is accessed, how the container format is parsed, and how you extract or otherwise obtain metadata information about the media.

However you choose to implement that functionality, note that logically, the media initialization is complete only after your code calls MediaStreamSource.ReportOpenMediaCompleted(). As we noted while discussing the asynchronous nature of the MediaStreamSource API, you can return from OpenMediaAsync() and then call ReportOpenMediaCompleted() asynchronously from elsewhere in your MediaStreamSource implementation; or you can call it synchronously from your OpenMediaAsync() implementation.

It is worth looking at the information that is expected to be passed in as parameters to ReportOpenMediaCompleted(). These parameters are the mechanism through which you need to pass metadata about the media from your MediaStreamSource implementation to the MediaElement The method signature for ReportOpenMediaCompleted() is as follows:

```
void ReportOpenMediaCompleted(
  IDictionary<MediaSourceAttributesKeys, string> mediaSourceAttributes,
  IEnumerable<MediaStreamDescription> availableMediaStreams);
```

The first parameter is a dictionary of attributes for the overall media source that you are exposing to the MediaElement and appropriate values for each of these attributes. If you look at the System.Windows.Media.MediaSourceAttributesKeys enumeration, you find the following enumerated values:

- MediaSourceAttributesKeys.CanSeek: Use this as a key in the mediaSourceAttributes parameter, to pass in either the string "true" or the string "false" depending on whether you allow seeking through the media in your MediaStreamSource implementation.

- MediaSourceAttributesKeys.Duration: Use this to pass in the total duration of the media. Note that the duration is specified as ticks formatted as a string, where one tick is a unit of time measured as 100 nanoseconds.

- MediaSourceAttributesKeys.DRMHeader: This consists of digital rights management (DRM) header information for right-protected content.

The second parameter, availableMediaStreams, is a collection of System.Windows.Media.MediaStreamDescription instances. Note that your media source may contain more than one media stream. For example, a media file that represents a video clip may include one video stream along with one or more audio streams, with each audio stream representing an audio track for the video in a different language. For each of these streams that you want the MediaElement to play, you must describe the stream using an instance of the MediaStreamDescription added to the availableMediaStreams parameter to ReportOpenMediaCompleted(). The MediaStreamDescription type is as shown here:

```
public class MediaStreamDescription
{

  // Methods
  public MediaStreamDescription(MediaStreamType type,
    IDictionary<MediaStreamAttributeKeys, string> mediaStreamAttributes);

  // Properties
  public IDictionary<MediaStreamAttributeKeys, string> MediaAttributes { get; }
  public int StreamId { get; }
  public MediaStreamType Type { get; }
}
```

As you can see, the first parameter to the `MediaStreamDescription` constructor describes the type of stream you are describing and is of type `System.Windows.Media.MediaStreamType`, which has the following values: `Video`, `Audio`, and `Script`. The second parameter is a dictionary of attributes applicable to the stream you are describing, and the corresponding values formatted as strings. The `MediaStreamAttributeKeys` enumeration has the following values:

- `MediaStreamAttributeKeys.CodecPrivateData`: What you pass in here depends on the codec you expect Silverlight to use to decode your samples. For the `CodecPrivateData` values for the various codecs that come out of box with Silverlight (such as VC-1 and AAC), refer to the Silverlight documentation. On the other hand, if you are handling the decoding of the samples yourself in your `MediaStreamSource` code, or if the samples are not compressed, you can safely ignore this attribute.

- `MediaStreamAttributeKeys.VideoFourCC`: This is the four-character code for video stream types that Silverlight expects, should you choose to use one of the Silverlight-supplied codecs to decode the video, or if you are passing uncompressed samples to Silverlight. Some common examples of FourCC codes acceptable to Silverlight are "RGBA" for uncompressed video that is color coded using the 32-bit four-channel (Red, Green, Blue, Alpha) scheme, "YV12" for uncompressed YCrCb-coded video, "WVC1" for VC-1–encoded video, and "H264" for H.264-encoded video. For a full list of the supported `VideoFourCC` codes, refer to the Silverlight documentation.

- `MediaStreamAttributeKeys.Width`: This is the original `Width` of a frame of the video.

- `MediaStreamAttributeKeys.Height`: This is the original `Height` of a frame of the video.

Note that the last three of these attributes are applicable only when you are describing a video stream. Also note that the `MediaStreamDescription.StreamId` property exposes a zero-based identifier for your stream. The `MediaElement` expects the video stream (if you are exposing video and not just audio) to be at index 0 and the audio streams to be arranged starting at index 1 after that. In the `MediaStreamSource` implementation, you must be aware of this convention and add the `MediaStreamDescription` for your video first. You can then add the audio tracks in the order in which you want them to be made available when a developer accesses a specific audio stream using the `MediaElement.AudioStreamIndex` property.

Sampling

In digital media processing, you can think of a sample as a discrete collection of bytes at any specific time point along the timeline over which the media plays. If you think of digital video as a collection of discrete frames, a sample for that video stream at a time point is the bitmap that represents the frame at that time point.

When you are finished passing all the necessary metadata attributes, the `MediaElement` begins playing your media. The process of playing your media involves the `MediaElement` asking for samples of the media from your `MediaStreamSource`-derived class through the `GetSampleAsync()` method. The `MediaElement` passes the stream for which it is requesting samples using a parameter of the `MediaStreamType` enumerated type to the `GetSampleAsync()` method. Consequently, if you receive `MediaStreamType.Video`, the `MediaElement` is expecting the next sample for the video stream; `MediaStreamType.Audio` indicates that you need to return the next sample in the audio stream.

As before, the API supports asynchronous completion. The sample request from the `MediaElement` can be completed by calling `MediaStreamSource.ReportGetSampleCompleted()`, either synchronously before returning from `GetSampleAsync()` or from somewhere else in your `MediaStreamSource` code in an asynchronous fashion.

`MediaStreamSource.ReportGetSampleCompleted()` accepts one parameter of type `MediaStreamSample`. The following snippet shows the constructor for the `MediaStreamSample` type:

```
public MediaStreamSample(MediaStreamDescription mediaStreamDescription,
  Stream stream, long offset, long count, long timestamp,
  IDictionary<MediaSampleAttributeKeys, string> attributes);
```

As you can see, the first parameter is of type `MediaStreamDescription`. This parameter must match the `MediaStreamDescription` you constructed and returned in `ReportOpenMediaCompleted()` for the stream concerned. It does not have to be the same instance (it could be), but the `MediaStreamDescription.Type` property and the `MediaStreamDescription.MediaAttributes` collection property need to return the same values as were reported by you when the media was initialized. The parameter named stream of type `Stream` points to the actual data stream for the media you are sampling, the `offset` parameter indicates the byte offset in that stream where the `MediaElement` should begin reading the sample, the `count` parameter indicates the byte length of the sample, and the `timestamp` parameter is an optional timestamp for the sample in ticks.

The last parameter, `attributes`, is a dictionary of string-formatted attribute values for the specific sample, keyed by the values in the `System.Windows.Media.MediaSampleAttributeKeys` enumerated type. The `MediaSampleAttributeKeys` enumerated type has the following values defined:

- `MediaSampleAttributeKeys.KeyFrameFlag`: If the sample you are returning represents a keyframe, then this can be set to true.

- `MediaSampleAttributeKeys.DRMInitializationVector`: This is the set of values required to decrypt a DRM-encrypted sample.

- `MediaSampleAttributeKeys.FrameWidth`: This is the width in pixels of the frame the sample represents. It applies to video samples only.

- `MediaSampleAttributeKeys.FrameHeight`: This is the height in pixels of the frame the sample represents. This applies to video samples only.

Based on the length of time it takes your code to extract and return the next sample, you may or may not choose to report progress. `MediaStreamSource.ReportGetSampleProgress()` lets you report the progress of your sample extraction effort to the `MediaElement`. The only parameter to `ReportGetSampleProgress()` is a double named `bufferingProgress`, which represents the percentage of the work done. This is ultimately exposed by the `MediaElement.BufferingProgress` property that you can display in the UI.

Stream Switching

Note that the `MediaElement.AudioStreamIndex` property lets you write code that switches the index among multiple audio tracks (if present). The `MediaStreamSource.SwitchMediaStreamAsync()` method allows you to respond to this in your `MediaStreamSource`. When a stream is switched in the `MediaElement`, it calls your implementation of `SwitchMediaStreamAsync()`, passing in the `MediaStreamDescription` instance corresponding to the stream to which the switch was made. This gives you an opportunity to perform any kind of initialization/preparation work that may be required before the next sampling request for this stream comes through. As usual, you can use `ReportSwitchMediaStreamCompleted()` to asynchronously (or synchronously) notify the `MediaElement` when you are ready with the switch, by passing the `MediaStreamDescription` of the stream you switched to.

Seeking

If your `MediaStreamSource` implementation can support seeking within the media source you are handling, you may have indicated this by passing a string value of "true" keyed with `MediaSourceAttributesKeys.CanSeek`, as discussed earlier. In those cases, the `MediaElement` calls your implementation of the MediaStreamSource.SeekAsync() method, passing in a single parameter named seekToTime that contains the time point to which the user desires to seek, defined in ticks.

When your MediaStreamSource has positioned the media source at the requested time point, it can report completion by calling MediaStreamSource.ReportSeekCompleted(), passing in the same time value. This causes the MediaElement to resume sampling.

The Code

As we have mentioned, the purpose of this recipe and the sample code is not to make you an expert in authoring codecs but to make you familiar with the related MediaStreamSource extensibility mechanism in Silverlight. Keeping that in mind, the sample we discuss here may seem trivial from a decoder complexity perspective. But if you possess the codec-authoring skill set, we hope this recipe offers you some help in using that knowledge to build Silverlight managed decoders.

Armed with what you have learned so far, let's look at building a relatively simple sample. The sample for this recipe has two parts. In the first part, you build a simple Silverlight component that records screenshots of a Silverlight application at a specific frame rate. The component uses the System.Windows.Media.Imaging.WriteableBitmap class to record the screenshots by capturing the root visual in the application's visual tree; it saves the bitmaps into a file on disk. For more information about WriteableBitmap, refer to Chapter 3.

In the second part, you build a custom MediaStreamSource that reads this file and plays your recording as a video through a MediaElement. In an effort to keep the sample simple, we do not tackle audio streams in this sample—the result is a silent movie of the recorded screen shots.

The Recorder

The recorder component is implemented as a class named ScreenRecorder in a project named ScreenRecorderLib, as shown in Listing 8-28.

Listing 8-28. *Code for the ScreenRecorder Class*

```
using System;
using System.Collections.Generic;
using System.ComponentModel;
using System.IO;
using System.Linq;
using System.Runtime.Serialization;
using System.Threading;
using System.Windows;
using System.Windows.Media;
using System.Windows.Media.Imaging;
using System.Windows.Threading;

namespace Ch08_RichMedia.Recipe8_7
{
  public class ScreenRecorder
  {
    private DispatcherTimer snapshotTimer = new DispatcherTimer();
```

```
List<WriteableBitmap> Buffer1 = new List<WriteableBitmap>();
List<WriteableBitmap> Buffer2 = new List<WriteableBitmap>();
List<WriteableBitmap> CurrentBuffer = null;
List<WriteableBitmap> FlushBuffer = null;
private long TotalFrameCounter = 0;
private long FlushCounter = 0;
private double RenderHeight;
private double RenderWidth;
private object WriterLock = new Object();
private MediaInfo Info = new MediaInfo();
private Transform BitmapTransform = null;
private int FrameRate = default(int);

private Stream _TempFile = null;

public Stream TempFile
{
  get { return _TempFile; }
  set { _TempFile = value; }
}

private UIElement _RecordingRoot = default(UIElement);
public UIElement RecordingRoot
{
  get
  {
    if (_RecordingRoot == null)
      _RecordingRoot = Application.Current.RootVisual;
    return _RecordingRoot;
  }

  set
  {
    _RecordingRoot = value;
  }
}

private double _FrameHeight = 180;
public double FrameHeight
{
  get
  {
    return _FrameHeight;
  }
```

```csharp
    set
    {
      _FrameHeight = value;
    }
  }

  private double _FrameWidth = 320;
  public double FrameWidth
  {
    get
    {
      return _FrameWidth;
    }

    set
    {
      _FrameWidth = value;
    }
  }

  public ScreenRecorder(int FrameRate)
  {
    this.FrameRate = FrameRate;
    snapshotTimer.Interval = new TimeSpan(1000*10000/FrameRate);
    snapshotTimer.Tick += new EventHandler(snapshotTimer_Tick);
  }

  public void Start()
  {
    CurrentBuffer = Buffer1;
    snapshotTimer.Start();

    if (TempFile != null)
    {
      byte[] MediaInfoSizePlaceHolder = BitConverter.GetBytes(Int32.MaxValue);
      TempFile.Write(MediaInfoSizePlaceHolder, 0,
        MediaInfoSizePlaceHolder.Length);
    }
  }

  public void Stop()
  {
    if (snapshotTimer != null && snapshotTimer.IsEnabled) snapshotTimer.Stop();
    if (TempFile != null)
    {
```

```
    lock (WriterLock)
    {
      TempFile.Flush();

      MediaInfo Info = new MediaInfo { FrameCount = TotalFrameCounter,
        FrameHeight = this.FrameHeight, FrameWidth = this.FrameWidth,
        FrameRate = this.FrameRate };
      DataContractSerializer ser =
        new DataContractSerializer(typeof(MediaInfo));
      MemoryStream ms = new MemoryStream();
      ser.WriteObject(ms, Info);
      ms.Flush();
      Byte[] Buff = ms.GetBuffer();
      TempFile.Write(Buff, 0, Buff.Length);
      TempFile.Seek(0L, SeekOrigin.Begin);
      Byte[] BuffLength = BitConverter.GetBytes(Buff.Length);
      TempFile.Write(BuffLength, 0, BuffLength.Length);
      TempFile.Close();
    }
  }
}

void snapshotTimer_Tick(object sender, EventArgs e)
{

  if (FlushCounter + 1 > FrameRate && Monitor.TryEnter(WriterLock))
  {
    TotalFrameCounter += FlushCounter;
    FlipBackBuffer();
    Monitor.Exit(WriterLock);
  }
  else
    FlushCounter++;

  if (RenderHeight == 0 || RenderWidth == 0)
  {
    RenderWidth = (int)RecordingRoot.RenderSize.Width;
    RenderHeight = (int)RecordingRoot.RenderSize.Height;
    if (RenderHeight != 0 && RenderWidth != 0)
      BitmapTransform = new ScaleTransform() { CenterX = 0, CenterY = 0,
        ScaleY = FrameHeight / RenderHeight,
        ScaleX = FrameWidth / RenderWidth };
  }
```

```
    if (RenderHeight != 0 && RenderWidth != 0)
    {
        WriteableBitmap capture =
          new WriteableBitmap(RecordingRoot, BitmapTransform);
        CurrentBuffer.Add(capture);
    }
}

private void FlipBackBuffer()
{

  CurrentBuffer = (CurrentBuffer == Buffer1) ? Buffer2 : Buffer1;
  FlushBuffer = (FlushBuffer == Buffer1) ? Buffer2 : Buffer1;
  CurrentBuffer.Clear();
  FlushCounter = 0;
  if (TempFile != null)
  {
    BackgroundWorker bwFlusher = new BackgroundWorker();
    bwFlusher.DoWork += new DoWorkEventHandler(bwFlusher_DoWork);
    bwFlusher.RunWorkerAsync(FlushBuffer);
  }
  return;
}

void bwFlusher_DoWork(object sender, DoWorkEventArgs e)
{
  lock (WriterLock)
  {
    List<WriteableBitmap> Buffer = e.Argument as List<WriteableBitmap>;
    byte[] Flattened = null;
    int PixelCount = (int)FrameHeight * (int)FrameWidth;
    for (int i = 0; i < Buffer.Count; i++)
    {
      Flattened = Buffer[i].Pixels.
        SelectMany((p) => BitConverter.GetBytes(p)).ToArray();
      TempFile.Write(Flattened, 0, Flattened.Length);
    }
    TempFile.Flush();
    Buffer.Clear();
  }
}
```

```
public class MediaInfo
{
  public int FrameRate { get; set; }
  public double FrameHeight { get; set; }
  public double FrameWidth { get; set; }
  public long FrameCount { get; set; }
}

}
```

The RecordingRoot property indicates the UIElement that is being recorded, and FrameHeight and FrameWidth indicate the Height and Width of each frame you want to record; the latter two are set to 180 and 320 by default. You expect the application using the Recorder to pass in an open stream through the TempFile property, to which the frames and related metadata are recorded; it can also optionally set the desired FrameHeight and FrameWidth before invoking the ScreenRecorder.Start() method.

In the ScreenRecorder constructor in Listing 8-28, you pass in a parameter named FrameRate that is the time interval in ticks at which individual frames are to be recorded. You then initialize a DispatcherTimer instance named snapshotTimer to raise its Tick event at the interval set by the FrameRate parameter.

Also note the class named MediaInfo at the end of the listing. This class captures necessary metadata like the frame rate, the width and height of individual frames, and the total number of frames recorded. A serialized instance of this class is stored in the recorded file for later use in the MediaStreamSource.

The ScreenRecorder class uses two memory buffers to manage the act of capturing screenshots and writing the screenshot data to the application supplied stream. These buffers are represented as two List<WriteableBitmap> typed variables named Buffer1 and Buffer2, respectively. The assumption is that writing the buffered bitmaps down to the stream may be a long-running process due to various IO bottlenecks, and you do not want to block the UI thread and hence the process of recording while saving the screenshots to the disk-based file. Hence the ScreenRecorder implementation attempts to perform the stream IO asynchronously while the application continues to use the recorder to keep recording bitmaps at the specified interval. The two-buffer arrangement helps in this process, because you can use one buffer to keep the recording going while the other buffer is emptied into the stream. You see how this works out as we dig further into the code in Listing 8-28.

The process of recording starts when the application using the ScreenRecorder instance calls the Start() method. You set the CurrentBuffer variable to Buffer1 and start the timer. You also write an 8-byte array named MediaInfoSizePlaceHolder in the code, at the beginning of the stream. The content of the byte array is long enough to hold a 32 bit integer and is set to System.Int32.MaxValue initially. But the content is not import, because it is overwritten later—the purpose of this byte array is the important thing to understand.

When the ScreenRecorder.Start() is called, you do not yet know all the metadata that is serialized into the file in the form an instance of the MediaInfo class, because you can only know the total frame count at the end of the recording process. As a result, that data is written at the tail end of the file, after all the screenshots have been saved and the recording has ended. However, as you see later, you must read and deserialize that information in the MediaStreamSource before you can begin processing the file for media consumption. To aid in that process, you need to know the size of that metadata block up front. The 8-byte array you just wrote saves space at the beginning of the file where you write the size of the metadata block when you save it, measured as an integral number of bytes.

To understand this better, look at a diagram of the file layout shown in Figure 8-25.

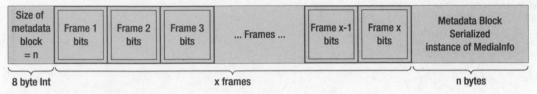

Figure 8-25. *Layout of the file in which the screen recordings are stored*

Now, let's look at what happens when the timer begins raising its Tick events at the specified intervals. In the handler method snapshotTimer_Tick() in Listing 8-28, you first check the value of a variable named FlushCounter. FlushCounter helps you define an interval at which you save the snapshots in the current buffer to disk. In the current implementation, that point is when you have recorded 1 second of content—that is, when the value of FlushCounter equals that of ScreenRecorder.FrameRate.

If FlushCounter is less than FrameRate (you do not have enough data buffered to write to disk yet), you increment FlushCounter by 1 and take the next snapshot. To ensure that the snapshot is taken at the specified FrameHeight and FrameWidth, you must make sure you appropriately shrink or stretch the snapshot to match those dimensions, no matter what the height and width of the RecordingRoot UIElement are. You do that by creating a ScaleTransform, where the scale is set to match the ratio of the original dimensions of the RecordingRoot to the specified dimensions through the FrameHeight and FrameWidth properties. The ScaleTransform is stored in a field named BitmapTransform for subsequent use. You then create and store the WriteableBitmap snapshot of the RecordingRoot, with the ScaleTransform applied to it, into the CurrentBuffer buffer.

If FlushCounter has a value greater than or equal to FrameRate, you first attempt to start the process of saving the current buffer to disk. Because you are dependent on a timer to fire this logic at regular intervals, you must be extra careful here and ensure that you never cause two overlapping attempts to write data to the disk at the same time. To prevent that from happening, you try to acquire a lock before you attempt the disk write, and you proceed only if you can acquire the lock. If you cannot acquire the lock, you take the snapshot as usual. If you do acquire the lock, you accumulate the number of frames snapped between the last save and this one in a variable named TotalFrameCounter and then invoke the FlipBackBuffer() method.

Inside FlipBackBuffer(), you switch the buffer values (Buffer1 and Buffer2) between the buffer variables CurrentBuffer and FlushBuffer, such that the buffer you were using prior to this point to take snapshots is now pointed to by FlushBuffer. You also reset CurrentBuffer and FlushCounter.

Depending on the value of FrameRate and how large the snapshots are, the process of writing to disk can take some time. So, you use the BackgroundWorker class to delegate the work of writing the buffer to disk to a background thread. After delegation, the FlipBackBuffer() method returns immediately to the UI thread, and you take more snapshots as described earlier.

The actual work of saving to disk is done in the BackgroundWorker.DoWork event handler, bwFlusher_DoWork(). Here, you flatten each WriteableBitmap in the FlushBuffer to a byte array, join them to make one contiguous but larger byte array, and write the whole thing to the application-supplied stream available through the TempFile property. After it is written, this buffer is cleared. Note that because you are on a background thread, to prevent concurrent access, you take the same lock as described earlier before you attempt the write.

The consuming application explicitly stops the recording process by invoking the
ScreenRecorder.Stop() method. In stopping the recording process, you first stop the timer. You then
create a new instance of the MediaInfo type and set the FrameCount, FrameWidth, FrameHeight, and
FrameRate properties accordingly. You finally serialize the MediaInfo instance, convert it to a byte array,
and write it out to the tail end of the file. You also write the size of the byte array to the placeholder you
saved at the beginning of the file. At this point, the recording session is complete, and you have a file
with a custom video format and metadata ready for you to consume.

Before you see how to consume this file, let's take a quick look at how the ScreenRecorder
component is used from an application. This sample borrows the code for Recipe 4-7 and extends it to
use the ScreenRecorder. Because most of the code is similar to that in Recipe 4-7, we only highlight the
additions to support recording. This code is found in a project named ScreenRecordingSource in the
associated code sample.

The only change you make to the XAML for the application is to add a CheckBox named
cbxRecord. You handle the Checked and Unchecked events of cbxRecord in the code-behind to start and
stop the recording, respectively. After the CheckBox is checked and recording starts, you can interact with
the UI any way you wish, to generate the custom video file. Make sure you spend at least a minute or so
between the beginning and end of recording, to generate content you can use to test the
MediaStreamSource. Listing 8-29 shows the Checked and Unchecked event handlers in the code-behind for
the MainPage in the application.

Listing 8-29. *Starting and Stopping Recording from an Application Using the ScreenRecorder Class*

```
cbxRecord.Checked += new RoutedEventHandler((s, e) =>
{
  SaveFileDialog sfd = new SaveFileDialog();
  bool? Ret = sfd.ShowDialog();
  if (Ret != null && Ret.Value == true)
  {
    Recorder.TempFile = sfd.OpenFile();
    Recorder.Start();
  }
});

cbxRecord.Unchecked += new RoutedEventHandler((s, e) =>
{
  Recorder.Stop();
});
```

In handling the Checked event, you first create and show a SaveFileDialog instance, to allow the
user to pick a file to save the recording to. SaveFileDialog is covered in more detail in Chapter 2. You
then open the file and set the Recorder.TempFile property to the file stream, assuming that Recorder is
an instance of the ScreenRecorder type that you created earlier in the MainPage code-behind. Finally, you
begin recording by invoking the Recorder.Start() method. In the Unchecked event handler, you invoke
Recorder.Stop(). Figure 8-26 shows the application UI with the Record check box checked.

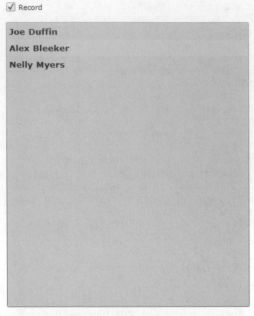

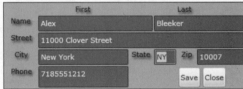

Figure 8-26. *Application user interface with Record turned on*

The Custom MediaStreamSource

Now that you have seen how to create the custom video file, let's look at the `MediaStreamSource`
implementation. Listing 8-30 shows the code for the implementation in a class named
`BitmapToVideoMediaStreamSource` in a project named `BitmapToVideoMSS`.

Listing 8-30. *Custom MediaStreamSource Implementation*

```
using System;
using System.Collections.Generic;
using System.IO;
using System.Linq;
using System.Runtime.Serialization;
using System.Windows.Media;
using System.Threading;
```

```
namespace Ch08_RichMedia.Recipe8_7
{
  public class BitmapToVideoMediaStreamSource : MediaStreamSource
  {
    public Stream MediaStream { get; set; }
    internal MediaInfo mediaInfo { get; set; }

    Dictionary<MediaStreamAttributeKeys, string> mediaStreamAttributes =
      new Dictionary<MediaStreamAttributeKeys, string>();

    Dictionary<MediaSourceAttributesKeys, string> mediaSourceAttributes =
      new Dictionary<MediaSourceAttributesKeys, string>();

    List<MediaStreamDescription> mediaStreamDescriptions = new
      List<MediaStreamDescription>();

    Dictionary<MediaSampleAttributeKeys, string> mediaSampleAttributes =
      new Dictionary<MediaSampleAttributeKeys, string>();

    private long lastFrame = 0;
    private long FrameSize = 0;
    private double FrameDuration = 0;
    private int HdrSizeByteLength = BitConverter.GetBytes(Int32.MaxValue).Length;
    private int HdrByteLength = 0;

    private BitmapToVideoMediaStreamSource()
    {
    }

    public BitmapToVideoMediaStreamSource(Stream media)
    {
      this.MediaStream = media;
      ParseMediaStream(MediaStream);
    }

    private void ParseMediaStream(Stream MediaStream)
    {
      //read the size of the MediaInfo header information
      MediaStream.Seek(0L, SeekOrigin.Begin);

      Byte[] HdrSizeBuff = new Byte[HdrSizeByteLength];
      MediaStream.Read(HdrSizeBuff, 0, HdrSizeByteLength);
      HdrByteLength = BitConverter.ToInt32(HdrSizeBuff, 0);
      Byte[] MediaInfoBuff = new Byte[HdrByteLength];
```

```
    MediaStream.Seek(MediaStream.Length - HdrByteLength, SeekOrigin.Begin);
    MediaStream.Read(MediaInfoBuff, 0, HdrByteLength);
    byte[] TrimmedBuff = MediaInfoBuff.Reverse().SkipWhile((b) =>
      Convert.ToInt32(b) == 0).Reverse().ToArray();
    MemoryStream ms = new MemoryStream(TrimmedBuff);
    DataContractSerializer ser = new DataContractSerializer(typeof(MediaInfo));
    mediaInfo = ser.ReadObject(ms) as MediaInfo;
}

protected override void CloseMedia()
{
    MediaStream.Close();
}

protected override void GetDiagnosticAsync(MediaStreamSourceDiagnosticKind
    diagnosticKind)
{

}

protected override void GetSampleAsync(MediaStreamType mediaStreamType)
{
    if (lastFrame > mediaInfo.FrameCount)
    {
        MediaStreamDescription msd =
            new MediaStreamDescription(MediaStreamType.Video, mediaStreamAttributes);
        MediaStreamSample mediaSample =
            new MediaStreamSample(msd, null, 0, 0, 0, mediaSampleAttributes);
    }
    else
    {
        MediaStreamDescription msd =
            new MediaStreamDescription(MediaStreamType.Video, mediaStreamAttributes);
        MediaStreamSample mediaSample =
            new MediaStreamSample(msd, MediaStream, (lastFrame * FrameSize) +
                HdrSizeByteLength, FrameSize,
                (long)(lastFrame * FrameDuration), mediaSampleAttributes);
        lastFrame++;
        ReportGetSampleCompleted(mediaSample);
    }

}
```

```
    protected override void OpenMediaAsync()
    {
      lastFrame = 0;
      FrameSize = (long)(mediaInfo.FrameHeight * mediaInfo.FrameWidth * 4);
      FrameDuration = TimeSpan.FromMilliseconds(1000 / mediaInfo.FrameRate).Ticks;

      mediaSourceAttributes.Add(MediaSourceAttributesKeys.CanSeek, true.ToString());
      mediaSourceAttributes.Add(MediaSourceAttributesKeys.Duration,
        ((long)(mediaInfo.FrameCount * FrameDuration)).ToString());
      mediaStreamAttributes.Add(MediaStreamAttributeKeys.Height,
        mediaInfo.FrameHeight.ToString());
      mediaStreamAttributes.Add(MediaStreamAttributeKeys.Width,
        mediaInfo.FrameWidth.ToString());
      mediaStreamAttributes.Add(MediaStreamAttributeKeys.CodecPrivateData, "");
      mediaStreamAttributes.Add(MediaStreamAttributeKeys.VideoFourCC, "RGBA");

      mediaStreamDescriptions.Add(new MediaStreamDescription(MediaStreamType.Video,
        mediaStreamAttributes));

      mediaSampleAttributes.Add(MediaSampleAttributeKeys.FrameHeight,
        mediaInfo.FrameHeight.ToString());
      mediaSampleAttributes.Add(MediaSampleAttributeKeys.FrameWidth,
        mediaInfo.FrameWidth.ToString());

      MediaStream.Seek(HdrSizeByteLength, SeekOrigin.Begin);
      ReportOpenMediaCompleted(mediaSourceAttributes, mediaStreamDescriptions);

    }

    protected override void SeekAsync(long seekToTime)
    {
      //find the corresponding frame
      lastFrame = (long)(mediaInfo.FrameRate *
        TimeSpan.FromTicks(seekToTime).TotalSeconds) + HdrSizeByteLength;
      this.ReportSeekCompleted(seekToTime);
    }

    protected override void SwitchMediaStreamAsync(MediaStreamDescription
      mediaStreamDescription)
    {

    }

  }

}
```

The first thing to note in Listing 8-30 is that you prevent the use of the default constructor for the derived class by marking it private; instead, you create a constructor that accepts a Stream. This Stream represents an open stream to the video file that this MediaStreamSource implementation is supposed to parse and decode, and the expectation is that the consuming application passes that in when constructing the MediaStreamSource for the first time. You then save the Stream in a member variable for future access and also invoke the ParseMediaStream() method to parse the metadata.

Recall from Figure 8-25 that the video file format includes the size of the metadata block at the beginning of the file and the actual metadata block at the end of the file, with the recorded frames in between. In ParseMediaStream(), you first read the length of the metadata block. You then seek into the file to position the file pointer at the beginning of the metadata block and read the number of bytes from the tail end of the file as specified by the size information you just retrieved. You trim the byte array for any null byte entries at the tail and then deserialize it into an instance of the MediaInfo class at the end of Listing 8-28. You now have the metadata handy.

Next, the MediaElement invokes the OpenMediaAsync() method, which is where you initialize the media and return the necessary metadata to prime the MediaElement for play. You begin by calculating the frame size in bytes. To do so, you multiply the FrameHeight and the FrameWidth from the MediaInfo metadata instance to get the number of pixels; then, you multiply the product further by 4, because each pixel is a 4-byte structure with 1 byte for the Red, Blue, and Green color channels respectively and the last byte for the alpha or transparency channel. You store the frame size in the FrameSize variable. You also calculate the duration of a frame in ticks from MediaInfo.FrameRate and store the result in the FrameDuration variable. The lastFrame variable keeps track of the last frame consumed by the MediaElement and is initialize to 0. Then, you populate the various metadata structures that you need to return to the MediaElement.

You have declared the mediaSourceAttributes variable of type Dictionary<*MediaSourceattributesKeys,string*> to be the container for the media source metadata. You populate this by setting MediaSourceAttributesKeys.CanSeek to "true" to enable seeking and setting MediaSourceAttributesKeys.Duration to the total duration of the clip; you derive that value from the product of FrameCount and FrameDuration.

You also populate the mediaStreamAttributes variable of type Dictionary <*MediaStreamAttributeKeys,string*>. You include MediaStreamAttributeKeys.Height and MediaStreamAttributeKeys.Width and set them to the FrameHeight and FrameWidth, respectively. You also set MediaStreamAttributeKeys.CodecPrivateData to a blank string and MediaStreamAttributeKeys. VideoFourCC to "RGBA". The four-character code indicates to the MediaElement that the frames are RGBA-style bitmaps and do not need any further decoding—hence the blank string value for CodecPrivateData. You then add a new MediaStreamDescription instance to the variable mediaStreamDescriptions, with the stream type set to MediaStreamType.Video and the attributes set to the just-initialized mediaStreamAttributes.

Note that you have only one media stream description entry, because you have only one stream: the video. If you had additional streams, such as audio and script streams, you would have to add a description entry and related attributes for each of those streams.

You also initialize the mediaSampleAttributes dictionary to set the FrameHeight and FrameWidth respectively, although you do not need this variable until later. You finally complete this method by calling ReportOpenMediaCompleted() and passing in the media source attributes and media stream descriptions. Note that you call this method synchronously; but as discussed earlier, if the initialization process lasts longer than this process takes, you can easily return from OpenMediaAsync sooner and complete this task on a background thread.

At this point, the MediaElement begins calling GetSampleAsync() repeatedly to get samples to play. GetSampleAsync() receives the MediaStreamType for the stream for which samples are being requested, as a parameter.

You first check to see if you are at the end of the file by comparing the lastFrame variable with MediaInfo.FrameCount. If frames remain to be sampled (lastFrame is currently not greater than MediaInfo.FrameCount), you attempt to create a new instance of the MediaStreamSample class to represent the sample. The following snippet shows the MediaStreamSample constructor:

```
public MediaStreamSample(MediaStreamDescription mediaStreamDescription,
  Stream stream, long offset, long count, long timestamp,
  IDictionary<MediaSampleAttributeKeys, string> attributes)
```

The MediaStreamSample constructor accepts a MediaStreamDescription instance as its first parameter. Recall that in the implementation of OpenMediaAsync(), you returned instances of MediaStreamDescription to the MediaElement for each stream you handled. The MediaStreamDescription instance that you supply to the MediaStreamSample constructor here must match the stream description values used earlier for the same stream. As you can see in Listing 8-30, you use the same MediaStreamType and stream attributes dictionary in constructing this MediaStreamDescription instance that you used previously in OpenMediaAsync.

For the second parameter, stream, you pass in the actual media stream. The third parameter, offset, is the byte offset into the stream where the MediaElement can begin reading this frame. As you can in Listing 8-30, you derive this as the product of lastFrame and FrameSize: the total byte size of all the frames that have been read so far, further offset by the header size used to store the metadata block size at the beginning of the file.

The fourth parameter, count, is number of bytes to be read to extract the frame—that is, the value of the FrameSize variable. The fifth parameter is an optional timestamp that you can associate with the sample; you pass in the starting point of this frame in time ticks calculated as the product of frames read so far in lastFrame and FrameDuration. The sixth and last parameter is the mediaSampleAttributes dictionary that you prepopulated in the OpenMediaAsync() method while initializing the media.

You then increment lastFrame and call ReportGetSampleCompleted, passing in the newly constructed MediaStreamSample instance.

If you have read all the available frames, you return a MediaStreamSample with the Stream set to null, causing the MediaElement to stop sampling and signaling the end of media.

You also support seeking through an implementation of the MediaStreamSource.SeekAsync() method. SeekAsync() receives the time to which the user wants to seek as a parameter, with the value measured in ticks. In SeekAsync(), you set the lastFrame variable to the frame at that time point (offset again by the header block size) and let the MediaElement resume sampling.

The last part of this sample is a Silverlight player application in a project named RecordedContentPlayout that uses the custom MediaStreamSource to play recorded content. Listing 8-31 shows the XAML for the application's MainPage.

Listing 8-31. *XAML for the Player Application's MainPage*

```
<UserControl x:Class="Ch08_RichMedia.Recipe8_7.MainPage"
 xmlns="http://schemas.microsoft.com/winfx/2006/xaml/presentation"
 xmlns:x="http://schemas.microsoft.com/winfx/2006/xaml"
 xmlns:mc="http://schemas.openxmlformats.org/markup-compatibility/2006"
 Height="850"
 Width="500">
    <Grid x:Name="LayoutRoot"
          Margin="0,0,0,18">
        <Grid.RowDefinitions>
            <RowDefinition Height="*" />
            <RowDefinition Height="Auto" />
            <RowDefinition Height="Auto" />
        </Grid.RowDefinitions>
```

```xml
            <Border BorderBrush="Black" Grid.Row="0"
                    BorderThickness="2"
                    Height="650"
                    Width="400">
                <MediaElement x:Name="me"
                                BufferingTime="00:00:00"
                                AutoPlay="False"
                                Stretch="Fill" />
            </Border>
            <StackPanel Orientation="Horizontal"
                        Grid.Row="2">
                <Button x:Name="btnPlay"
                        Content="Play"
                        Click="btnPlay_Click"
                        Height="35"
                        Width="50"
                        Margin="108,8,0,11"
                        HorizontalAlignment="Left" />
                <Button x:Name="btnPause"
                        Content="Pause"
                        Click="btnPause_Click"
                        Height="35"
                        Width="50"
                        HorizontalAlignment="Right"
                        Margin="0,8,125,11" />
                </StackPanel>
            <Slider x:Name="sliderSeek"
                    Margin="24,8,21,0"
                    Grid.Row="1"
                    VerticalAlignment="Top"
                    Maximum="100"
                    ValueChanged="sliderSeek_ValueChanged" />
        </Grid>
</UserControl>
```

The XAML in Listing 8-31 creates a simple page with one MediaElement, a Slider control for showing progress and seeking, and two buttons: Play and Pause. Listing 8-32 shows the code-behind for the page.

Listing 8-32. *Code-Behind for Player Using Custom MediaStreamSource*

```
using System;
using System.IO;
using System.Linq;
using System.Windows;
using System.Windows.Controls;
using System.Windows.Controls.Primitives;
using System.Windows.Media;
using System.Windows.Threading;

namespace Ch08_RichMedia.Recipe8_7
{


  public partial class MainPage : UserControl
  {

    private DispatcherTimer sliderTimer = new DispatcherTimer();
    private Thumb SliderThumb = null;
    public MainPage()
    {

      InitializeComponent();

      me.MediaFailed += new EventHandler<ExceptionRoutedEventArgs>(me_MediaFailed);
      me.MediaOpened += new RoutedEventHandler(me_MediaOpened);
      me.CurrentStateChanged += new RoutedEventHandler(me_CurrentStateChanged);
      sliderTimer.Interval = TimeSpan.FromMilliseconds(100);
      sliderTimer.Tick += new EventHandler(sliderTimer_Tick);

    }


    private void HandleSliderThumbDrag()
    {
      if (SliderThumb == null)
      {
        SliderThumb = VisualTreeHelper.FindElementsInHostCoordinates(
          sliderSeek.TransformToVisual(Application.Current.RootVisual).
          TransformBounds(new Rect(0, 0, sliderSeek.ActualWidth,
            sliderSeek.ActualHeight))
          , sliderSeek).Where((uie) => uie is Thumb).FirstOrDefault() as Thumb;
```

```
      SliderThumb.DragStarted += new DragStartedEventHandler((s, args) =>
      {
        if (me.CurrentState == MediaElementState.Playing)
        {
          me.Pause();
        }
      });
    }
  }
  void me_CurrentStateChanged(object sender, RoutedEventArgs e)
  {
    switch (me.CurrentState)
    {
      case MediaElementState.Playing:
        sliderTimer.Start();
        break;
      default:
        sliderTimer.Stop();
        break;

    }
  }


  void me_MediaOpened(object sender, RoutedEventArgs e)
  {
    HandleSliderThumbDrag();
    me.Play();
  }

  void sliderTimer_Tick(object sender, EventArgs e)
  {
    sliderSeek.Value = me.Position.TotalMilliseconds * 100
      / me.NaturalDuration.TimeSpan.TotalMilliseconds;
  }

  void me_MediaFailed(object sender, ExceptionRoutedEventArgs e)
  {
    System.Diagnostics.Debug.WriteLine("{0} - {1}",e.ErrorException.Message,
      e.ErrorException.StackTrace);
  }
```

```
    private void btnPlay_Click(object sender, RoutedEventArgs e)
    {
      if (me.CurrentState == MediaElementState.Paused)
        me.Play();
      else
      {
        OpenFileDialog ofd = new OpenFileDialog() { Multiselect = false };
        if (ofd.ShowDialog() == true)
        {
          FileStream filestream = ofd.File.OpenRead();
          BitmapToVideoMediaStreamSource mss =
            new BitmapToVideoMediaStreamSource(filestream);
          me.SetSource(mss);
        }
      }


    }
    private void sliderSeek_ValueChanged(object sender,
      RoutedPropertyChangedEventArgs<double> e)
    {
      if (me.CurrentState == MediaElementState.Paused)
      {
        me.Position = TimeSpan.FromTicks((long)e.NewValue *
          me.NaturalDuration.TimeSpan.Ticks  / 100);
      }
    }

    private void btnPause_Click(object sender, RoutedEventArgs e)
    {
      me.Pause();
    }
  }
}
```

The code in Listing 8-32 is very similar to players built in earlier samples in this chapter. The only difference is the way you initialize the MediaElement. In the Click handler method named btnPlay_Click() for the Button btnPlay, you use the OpenFileDialog type to ask the user the name of a disk-based file to be played. Keep in mind that this must be a file that has been recorded using the Recorder component discussed previously. After the file is opened, you create a new instance of the BitmapToVideoMediaStreamSource type, passing in the stream; and then invoke SetSource() on the MediaElement, passing in the custom MediaStreamSource instance. Figure 8-27 shows the player playing a recording using the custom MediaStreamSource.

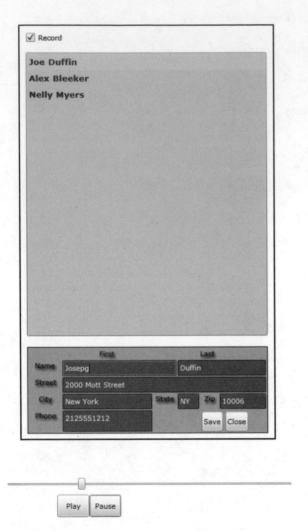

Figure 8-27. *Player using BitmaptoVideoMediaStreamSource*

CHAPTER 9

■ ■ ■

Building LOB Applications

Many prominent web sites have published Silverlight 1 and Silverlight 2 applications that are media focused as a result of Silverlight's strong client-side media capabilities, such as HD video coupled with a Windows Media Services back end. Many other sites also publish interactive content beyond video; but for corporate development support of traditional Create, Read, Update, and Delete or CRUD applications, as well as data-driven rich Internet applications, you need a strong control set with rich data support.

Silverlight 1 is limited to a JavaScript development model with graphics primitives that can be built up to provide controls. Silverlight 2 continues to support the JavaScript development model but also adds a rich control set with the .NET Framework for Silverlight. This has been further enhanced with the Silverlight Toolkit published on CodePlex, which is available here:

http://www.codeplex.com/Silverlight

Silverlight 3 introduces additional controls outlined in Chapter 1. In addition, Silverlight 3 introduced the new Silverlight Navigation Application project template, which provides a great starter application for a line-of-business (LOB) application. We covered the Silverlight Navigation Application basics in Chapter 6 because it also provides great integration with the browser history and support for direct page links.

When you think LOB applications, you automatically think *n*-tier development. We discussed Silverlight's strong network service capabilities in Chapter 7. A framework that was introduced at Mix 09 in beta that we have not covered yet is Microsoft .NET Rich Internet Applications (RIA) Services.

■**Note** RIA Services is available as a Community Technology Preview (CTP) when Silverlight 3 released. However, based on user feedback, Microsoft has removed production restrictions typical with a CTP. You are free to use RIA Services in applications, but it does not have the typical official "go live" support license. You can find more information here: http://timheuer.com/blog/archive/2009/06/09/ria-services-roadmap-updated.aspx.

You can download the Microsoft .NET RIA Services July 2009 Preview here:

http://www.microsoft.com/downloads/details.aspx?FamilyID=76bb3a07-3846-4564-b0c3-27972bcaabce&displaylang=en

Data is easily accessible on the server in ASP.NET and easy to display on the presentation layer with Silverlight 3. However, the effort required to implement data flow between tiers with change tracking and validation is not trivial.

RIA Services builds on the capabilities covered in Chapter 7 to provide a framework that enables you to rapidly build Silverlight LOB *n*-tier applications. The challenge with *n*-tier applications is flowing data across application tiers with support for edits, validation, and so on. RIA Services provides a bridge between Silverlight 3's rich presentation-tier capabilities and ASP.NET's powerful middle-tier capabilities on the server, including support for ASP.NET authentication and user settings management.

You create classes in the middle-tier web application that inherit from the `System.Web.DomainServices.DomainService` base class to define a set of operations on resources such as an ADO.NET Entity Model or other resources such as a user registration service. Classes on the middle tier have the `EnableClientAccess` attribute, where desired and .NET RIA Services automatically generate the corresponding client-side code into the presentation tier (the Silverlight application). At this point, you can code against the generated client-side code without worrying about tracking and packaging up changes, and so forth, to pass back to the middle tier. .NET RIA Services manages this for you. Recipe 9-1 provides a detailed overview of the new project template and .NET RIA Services; we recommend starting there if you are new to .NET RIA Services.

We have one other item to mention regarding LOB applications and the Bing Maps Silverlight control, which you can download here:

`https://connect.microsoft.com/silverlightmapcontrolctp?wa=wsignin1.0`

We do not provide a recipe that demonstrates the Bing Maps Silverlight control and how to integrate it into a LOB application because the control has not been updated since the Mix '09 release and by the time this book released it should be significantly different. Rob Cameron maintains a couple up-to-date of web casts at his blog that cover how to work with the Bing Maps Silverlight Control: `http://blogs.msdn.com/RobCamer`.

9-1. Creating a LOB Application Framework

Problem

You need to create a Silverlight LOB application with application navigation, authentication, user settings, and error handling.

Solution

Take advantage of Microsoft .NET RIA Services and the Silverlight Business Application template to build the foundation of a LOB application.

How It Works

In Silverlight 2, you had to write a lot of custom code to build a robust LOB application. With Silverlight 3 and .NET RIA Services, you can take advantage of powerful built-in functionality to build a LOB application framework.

When you install .NET RIA Services, it adds a new project template called Silverlight Business Application. The Silverlight Business Application template is built on the Silverlight 3 Navigation Application template, which includes support for page navigation. The Business Application template with page navigation facilitates a UI that includes different data forms or views on the data with a basic menu system.

The Business Application template includes support for .NET RIA Services by default. The application template also includes starter application services for user authentication and user profile services. You can create additional services that integrate data, as we demonstrate in Recipe 9-2.

The Code

Although you make some additions to the generated code that we highlight in this recipe, there are no code files other than the default code generated by the Silverlight Business Application project template. We cover the generated code in detail for this recipe as a baseline for the recipes in the rest of this chapter. Also, because the Silverlight Business Application template is based on the Silverlight Navigation Application Project, which we cover in Recipe 6-10, we do not go into detail about the page navigation and other functionality brought in by that application template.

The Silverlight Business Application template defines the RIA link between the Silverlight application and the web application. You can verify this by looking at the Silverlight application properties shown in Figure 9-1.

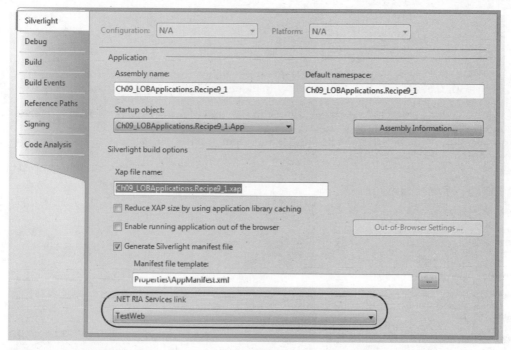

Figure 9-1. *Silverlight application properties with the RIA link property highlighted*

When the RIA link is established, any domain services created in the TestWeb web application are made available within the Silverlight project via the code-generation functionality built into the .NET RIA Services framework. Figure 9-2 shows the Solution Explorer tool window for Recipe 9-1 with hidden files and folders displayed and all folders expanded.

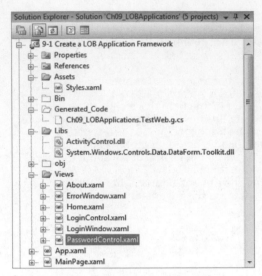

Figure 9-2. *Recipe 9-1 project contents*

You see the typical project layout for the Silverlight Navigation template with the Assets and Views folders along with App.xaml and MainPage.xaml. With hidden folders displayed, you also see a folder named Generated_Code with a generated code file named Ch09_LOBApplications.TestWeb.g.cs. This code file is brought in via .NET RIA Services code generation and is tied to the TestWeb web project, which is also where the file gets its default name.

Before we go through the rest of the Recipe 9-1 Silverlight application, we need to cover the TestWeb project contents (see Figure 9-3).

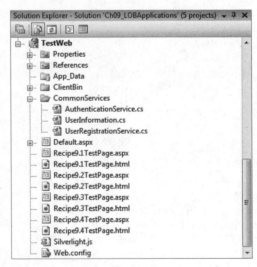

Figure 9-3. *TestWeb web project contents*

You see the standard contents for a web project that includes the output from a linked Silverlight application. The Silverlight Business Application project template adds a new folder named `CommonServices` with three code files: `AuthenticationService.cs`, `UserInformation.cs`, and `UserRegistrationService.cs`. These three code files contain starter-service functionality typical in a LOB application for authentication, user profile information management, and user registration.

The `AuthenticationService.cs` file represents a simple domain service for authentication in an RIA Services application. It is a based on an item template that you can add to an existing Silverlight application as shown in Figure 9-4.

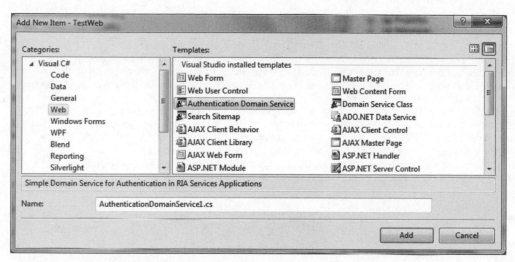

Figure 9-4. *Adding a new Authentication Domain Service item to a project*

This item template includes two class instances based on classes provided by the .NET RIA framework in the `System.Web.Ria.ApplicationServices` namespace: `AuthenticationBase` and `UserBase`. They implement a basic contract for authentication via a domain service. Listing 9-1 has the code for `AuthenticationService.cs`.

Listing 9-1. *The AuthenticationService Code File*

```
using System.Web.Ria;
using System.Web.Ria.ApplicationServices;

namespace Ch09_LOBApplications.TestWeb.CommonServices
{
  [EnableClientAccess]
  public class AuthenticationService : AuthenticationBase<User>
  {
  }
```

```
public class User : UserBase
{
  // NOTE: Profile properties can be added for
  // use in Silverlight application.
  // To enable profiles, edit the appropriate section
  // of web.config file.

  // public string MyProfileProperty { get; set; }
}
}
```

Notice the [EnableClientAccess] attribute on the AuthenticationService class declaration. This tells the RIA Services code generator that this class should be published to the Silverlight application. You can mark any class you desire with the EnableClientAccess attribute to make the class available on the client-side in the Silverlight application as well.

The UserInformation.cs code file contains a simple data class for storing and passing user information between tiers. The UserRegistrationService.cs code file contains an automatically generated domain service that makes ASP.NET forms authentication available in a Silverlight application. These three automatically generated code files (AuthenticationService.cs, UserInformation.cs, and UserRegistrationService.cs) provide excellent starter functionality for building an LOB application.

We now jump back to the Silverlight application with the source code for App.xaml, shown in Listing 9-2.

Listing 9-2. *The App.xaml File*

```xml
<Application
  x:Class="Ch09_LOBApplications.Recipe9_1.App"
  xmlns="http://schemas.microsoft.com/winfx/2006/xaml/presentation"
  xmlns:x="http://schemas.microsoft.com/winfx/2006/xaml"
  xmlns:app="clr-namespace:Ch09_LOBApplications.Recipe9_1"
  xmlns:appsvc="clr-namespace:System.Windows.Ria.ApplicationServices;
                assembly=System.Windows.Ria">
  <Application.Resources>
    <ResourceDictionary>
      <ResourceDictionary.MergedDictionaries>
        <ResourceDictionary Source="Assets/Styles.xaml"/>
      </ResourceDictionary.MergedDictionaries>
    </ResourceDictionary>
  </Application.Resources>
  <Application.ApplicationLifetimeObjects>
    <app:RiaContext>
      <app:RiaContext.Authentication>
        <appsvc:FormsAuthentication/>
        <!--<appsvc:WindowsAuthentication/>-->
      </app:RiaContext.Authentication>
    </app:RiaContext>
  </Application.ApplicationLifetimeObjects>
</Application>
```

You can see that authentication defaults to ASP.NET forms authentication; however, you can uncomment WindowsAuthentication if you prefer that authentication method or use a custom authentication mechanism.

By default, the Business Application template adds an instance of RiaContext to App.xaml by first importing the namespace in this line of code:

```
xmlns:app="clr-namespace:Ch09_LOBApplications.Recipe9_1"
```

The RiaContext class is made available to the Silverlight application by the .NET RIA framework through code generation in the file Ch09_LOBApplications.TestWeb.g.cs in this declaration:

```
namespace Ch09_LOBApplications.Recipe9_1
{
...
public sealed partial class RiaContext :
System.Windows.Ria.RiaContextBase
```

As you can see in Listing 9-2, an instance of the RiaContext class is added to the ApplicationLifetimeObjects collection. The other xmlns declaration imports the System.Windows.Ria.ApplicationServices namespace, which provides access to the RiaContext.Authentication object where you can configure either FormsAuthentication or WindowsAuthentication for the Silverlight application. The option you choose must correspond with the authentication configured for the web project in the Web.config file. For the default application template, this line sets the authentication mode to Forms:

```
<authentication mode="Forms"/>
```

In App.xaml.cs the current and only instance of the RiaContext class is added to the application's resource dictionary with this line of code in Application_Startup:

```
this.Resources.Add("RiaContext", RiaContext.Current);
```

In MainPage.xaml, there is no code related to the Business Application template beyond the expected code for the Navigation Application template. In MainPage.xaml.cs, two additional lines of code are related to authentication in the constructor for MainPage:

```
this.loginContainer.Child = new LoginControl();
RiaContext.Current.Authentication.LoadUser();
```

As shown in Figure 9-2, the Silverlight Business Application template adds three additional XAML assets to the forms included in the default navigation application project template: LoginControl.xaml, LoginWindow.xaml, and PasswordControl.xaml.

LoginControl.xaml contains a custom control named LoginControl that inherits from the UserControl base class. Figure 9-5 shows the starting UI for the Business Application template with the LoginControl custom control circled.

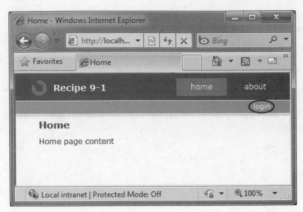

Figure 9-5. *Business Application template UI with the LoginControl highlighted*

Clicking Login in the UI displays the XAML form shown in Figure 9-6.

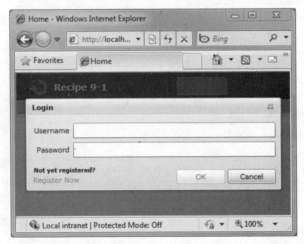

Figure 9-6. *LoginWindow.xaml at runtime after clicking Login in the application*

LoginWindow.xaml contains an instance a ChildWindow class built to provide a Login UI. The Username and Password XAML elements have event handlers assigned to their TextChanged and PasswordChanged events, respectively, in LoginWindow.xaml as part of the default Business Application template. Event handlers are also assigned to the Cancel and OK Button Click events. Listing 9-3 shows the LoginWindow class code-behind file.

Listing 9-3. *The LoginWindow.cs Class File*

```
using System;
using System.Windows;
using System.Windows.Controls;
using System.ComponentModel;
using System.Windows.Ria.ApplicationServices;
using System.Windows.Ria.Data;
using Ch09_LOBApplications.TestWeb.CommonServices;
using System.Windows.Data;
using System.Windows.Ria;

namespace Ch09_LOBApplications.Recipe9_1
{
  public partial class LoginWindow : ChildWindow
  {
    private AuthenticationService _authService = RiaContext.Current.Authentication;
    private AuthenticationOperation _authOp;

    private UserInformation _userInformation = new UserInformation();
    private UserRegistrationContext _registration = new UserRegistrationContext();
    private SubmitOperation _regOp;

    public LoginWindow()
    {
      InitializeComponent();
      this.loginButton.IsEnabled = false;

      this._registration.UserInformations.Add(this._userInformation);
      this.registerForm.CurrentItem = this._userInformation;
    }

    protected override void OnClosing(CancelEventArgs e)
    {

      if (_regOp != null && _regOp.CanCancel)
      {
        _regOp.Cancel();
      }
```

```csharp
    if (_authOp != null && _authOp.CanCancel)
    {
      _authOp.Cancel();
    }

    base.OnClosing(e);
}


private void CancelButton_Click(object sender, RoutedEventArgs e)
{
  this.DialogResult = false;
}

private void LoginButton_Click(object sender, RoutedEventArgs e)
{
  SetEditableState(false);
  _authOp = _authService.Login(this.loginUserNameBox.Text,
      this.loginPasswordBox.Password);
  _authOp.Completed += LoginOperation_Completed;
}


private void LoginOperation_Completed(object sender, EventArgs e)
{
  LoginOperation loginOp = (LoginOperation)sender;

  if (loginOp.LoginSuccess)
  {
    this.DialogResult = true;
    _authOp = null;
  }
  else
  {
    if (loginOp.HasError)
    {
      SetEditableState(true, true);
      new ErrorWindow(loginOp.Error.Message).Show();
    }
```

```
        else
        {
          SetEditableState(true, true);
          new ErrorWindow("Login failed. Please verify user
                  name and password and try again.").Show();
        }
      }
    }

private void RegisterButton_Click(object sender, RoutedEventArgs e)
{
  SetEditableState(false);

  if (this.registerForm.ValidateItem() && this.registerForm.CommitEdit())
  {
    _regOp = _registration.SubmitChanges();
    _regOp.Completed += RegistrationOperation_Completed;
  }
  else
  {
    SetEditableState(true);
  }
}

private void RegistrationOperation_Completed(object sender, EventArgs e)
{
  SubmitOperation asyncResult = (SubmitOperation)sender;

  if (asyncResult.HasError)
  {
    new ErrorWindow(asyncResult.Error.Message).Show();
    SetEditableState(true, true);
  }
  else if (!asyncResult.IsCanceled)
  {
    _authOp = RiaContext.Current.Authentication.Login(
            this._userInformation.UserName, this._userInformation.Password);
    _authOp.Completed += LoginOperation_Completed;
  }

  _regOp = null;
}
```

```csharp
private void RegisterNow_Click(object sender, RoutedEventArgs e)
{
  VisualStateManager.GoToState(this, "GoToNothingTransition", true);
  VisualStateManager.GoToState(this, "GoToRegisterTransition", true);
  ToRegister.Begin();
  this.Title = "Register";
}


private void LoginUserNameBox_TextChanged(object sender,
    TextChangedEventArgs e)
{
  SetLoginButtonEnabled();
}

private void LoginPasswordBox_PasswordChanged(object sender, RoutedEventArgs e)
{
  SetLoginButtonEnabled();
}

private void SetLoginButtonEnabled()
{
  this.loginButton.IsEnabled = (this.loginUserNameBox.Text.Length != 0) &&
                               (this.loginPasswordBox.Password.Length != 0);
}

private void SetEditableState(bool enabled)
{
  SetEditableState(enabled, false);
}

private void SetEditableState(bool enabled, bool setRegisterFormEditState)
{

  activity.IsActive = !enabled;


  if (this.loginPanel.Visibility == Visibility.Collapsed)
  {
    this.registerForm.IsEnabled = enabled;
    this.registerButton.IsEnabled = enabled;
    this.backToLogin.IsEnabled = enabled;
```

```
      if (enabled && setRegisterFormEditState)
      {
        this.registerForm.BeginEdit();
      }
    }
    else
    {
      this.loginButton.IsEnabled = enabled;
      this.loginUserNameBox.IsEnabled = enabled;
      this.loginPasswordBox.IsEnabled = enabled;
      this.registerNow.IsEnabled = enabled;
      this.loginUserNameBox.Focus();
    }

  }

  private void BackToLogin_Click(object sender, RoutedEventArgs e)
  {
    VisualStateManager.GoToState(this, "GoToNothingTransition", true);
    VisualStateManager.GoToState(this, "GoToLoginTransition", true);
    ToLogin.Begin();
    this.Title = "Login";
  }

 }
}
```

The LoginWindow form ties in to the RIA Services framework with these declarations:

```
private AuthenticationService _authService =
    RiaContext.Current.Authentication;
private UserInformation _userInformation = new UserInformation();
private UserRegistrationContext _registration =
    new UserRegistrationContext();
```

The first line of code obtains a reference to the current authentication configuration, which is configured to Forms in App.xaml as part of the default Business Application template.

The other two lines of code obtain references to classes defined on the middle tier with the EnableClientAccess attribute so that they are available in Ch09_LOBApplications.TestWeb.g.cs. Actual login occurs in the LoginButton_Click event handler in Listing 9-3, in this code:

```
_authOp = _authService.Login(this.loginUserNameBox.Text,
        this.loginPasswordBox.Password);
 authOp.Completed += LoginOperation_Completed;
```

New users can click the Registration button to configure the registration UI. Registration occurs in RegisterButton_Click:

```
if (this.registerForm.ValidateItem() && this.registerForm.CommitEdit())
{
  _regOp = _registration.SubmitChanges();
  _regOp.Completed += RegistrationOperation_Completed;
}
else
{
  SetEditableState(true);
}
```

The remaining code configures the UI based on the user interaction and displays a UI to enable new user registration. The other folder in the Business Application project template is Libs, which contains ActivtyControl.dll and System.Windows.Controls.Data.DataForm.Toolkit.dll. These assemblies provide access to the Activity and DataForm custom controls that are part of the Silverlight Toolkit, which is available here as of this writing:

http://www.codeplex.com/Silverlight

The Activity custom control can wrap a combination of controls, databinding its IsActive property to the IsBusy attribute of a DomainDataSource object. The other assembly in the Libs folder is System.Windows.Controls.Data.DataForm.Toolkit.dll. Adding a reference to this assembly makes the DataForm control available to your application, which enables rapid development of data forms. We cover the Activity and DataForm controls in more detail in Recipe 9-3, but we wanted to fully explain the Business Application template as part of this recipe.

9-2. Adding Data to a LOB Application

Problem

You need to access data on a server from a Silverlight LOB application.

Solution

Take advantage of Microsoft .NET RIA Services and the DomainDataSource control to easily make data available to a Silverlight application.

How It Works

Although application services such as authentication, registration, and profile support that the default Business Application template provides are very useful, .NET RIA Services are all about easily providing data to a Silverlight application.

.NET RIA Services includes the DomainService and WebDataService classes for the middle tier as well as the DomainDataSource control for the presentation tier to manage data flow in the application.

For the middle-tier functionality, the DomainService class was part of the original beta available at the Mix 09 conference. Since the MIX conference, Microsoft has received a lot of feedback regarding implementing .NET RIA Services on top of ADO.NET Data Services. Incorporating ADO.NET Data Services as the underlying protocol is part of the plan as of this writing for future .NET RIA Services releases.

The WebDataService class is available via the Domain ADO.NET Data Service project item template. Because the work around ADO.NET Data Services is in its early stages, we do not focus on that option for this book; but we wanted to provide background about the planned approach for .NET RIA Services. Instead, we focus on using the DomainService in this recipe because it is much more complete in terms of features such as support for validation, and so on; and in reality, the only difference is that the WebDataService uses the ADO.NET Data Services functionality as the underlying network protocol.

To create a DomainService instance, you first create an ADO.NET Entity Model in the web application project.

■**Note** You can also use LINQ to SQL in place of the Entity Framework or a custom object-relational mapping (O/RM) tool with a custom DomainService implementation.

The ADO.NET Entity Model represents the data layer for the application. Step through the wizard, selecting the tables, views, and so on that you wish to make available to the Silverlight application.

■**Note** Be sure to build the project after you add the ADO.NET Entity Model so that the model is available in the project for the next step.

You can create an empty domain service, or you can create a DomainService instance based on an ADO.NET Entity Model instance. After you define your DomainService instance, it is made available to the Silverlight application via code generation.

The Code

To get started, right-click the TestWeb web project to bring up the context menu, and choose Add ➤ New Folder to create a folder named Data Model to hold your model. Next, right-click the Data Model project folder to bring up the context menu, and choose Add ➤ New Item to open the Add New Item dialog. Click Data to filter the item list, and select the ADO.NET Entity Data Model class. Name it NorthWindModel because you are working with the NorthWind database, and click Add. Click Next to generate a model based on a database, click New Connection to create a connection to the NorthWind database, accept the default name of NorthWindEntities, and click Next. Select the Categories, Products, and Suppliers tables, and click Finish to generate the model.

Next, right-click the TestWeb web project to bring up the context menu, and choose Add ➤ New Folder to create a folder named Domain Services to hold your domain service. Right-click the Domain Services project folder to bring up the context menu, and choose Add ➤ New Item to open the Add New Item dialog. Click Web to filter the item list, and select the Domain Service Class project item. Name it NorthWindDomainService, because you are working with the NorthWindModel ADO.NET Entity Model, and click Add. Figure 9-7 shows the Add New Domain Service Class dialog.

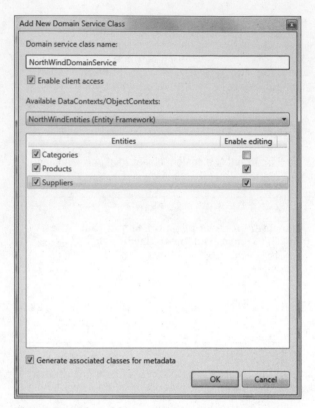

Figure 9-7. *The Add New Domain Service Class dialog*

By default, the wizard detects the NorthWindEntities object and populates the Entities list with the available tables. Select all three, but only enable editing on Products and Suppliers. Also check the "Generate associated classes for metadata" check box so that you can add validation and other functionality in later recipes. Then, click OK.

The result is that two new class files named NorthWindDomainService.cs and NorthWindDomainService.metadata.cs are added to the project. We cover the metadata code file in a later recipe; Listing 9-4 shows the generated domain service code.

Listing 9-4. *The NorthWindDomainService.cs Class File*

```
namespace Ch09_LOBApplications.TestWeb.Domain_Services
{
  using System;
  using System.Collections.Generic;
  using System.ComponentModel;
  using System.ComponentModel.DataAnnotations;
  using System.Linq;
  using System.Web.Ria;
  using System.Web.Ria.Data;
```

```
using System.Web.DomainServices;
using System.Data;
using System.Web.DomainServices.LinqToEntities;
using Ch09_LOBApplications.TestWeb.Data_Model;


// Implements application logic using the NorthWindEntities context.
// TODO: Add your application logic to these methods or in additional methods.
[EnableClientAccess()]
public class NorthWindDomainService :
          LinqToEntitiesDomainService<NorthWindEntities>
{

  // TODO: Consider
  // 1. Adding parameters to this method and constraining
  // returned results, and/or
  // 2. Adding query methods taking different parameters.
  public IQueryable<Categories> GetCategories()
  {
    return this.Context.Categories;
  }

  public void InsertCategories(Categories categories)
  {
    this.Context.AddToCategories(categories);
  }

  public void UpdateCategories(Categories currentCategories)
  {
    this.Context.AttachAsModified(currentCategories,
      this.ChangeSet.GetOriginal(currentCategories));
  }

  public void DeleteCategories(Categories categories)
  {
    if ((categories.EntityState == EntityState.Detached))
    {
      this.Context.Attach(categories);
    }
    this.Context.DeleteObject(categories);
  }

  // TODO: Consider
  // 1. Adding parameters to this method and constraining returned
  // results, and/or
```

```
    // 2. Adding query methods taking different parameters.
    public IQueryable<Products> GetProducts()
    {
      return this.Context.Products;
    }

    // TODO: Consider
    // 1. Adding parameters to this method and constraining returned
    // results, and/or
    // 2. Adding query methods taking different parameters.
    public IQueryable<Suppliers> GetSuppliers()
    {
      return this.Context.Suppliers;
    }

    public void InsertSuppliers(Suppliers suppliers)
    {
      this.Context.AddToSuppliers(suppliers);
    }

    public void UpdateSuppliers(Suppliers currentSuppliers)
    {
      this.Context.AttachAsModified(currentSuppliers,
        this.ChangeSet.GetOriginal(currentSuppliers));
    }

    public void DeleteSuppliers(Suppliers suppliers)
    {
      if ((suppliers.EntityState == EntityState.Detached))
      {
        this.Context.Attach(suppliers);
      }
      this.Context.DeleteObject(suppliers);
    }
  }
}
```

The generated TODO comments provide excellent hints about how you may want to modify the generated class. The generated class file shown in Figure 9-4 can be modified as desired, such as adding methods to constrain returned results, adding a method that takes a parameter to return a subset of results, and so on. As an example, the class by default generates a GetProducts method that does not take any parameters and returns all of the products.

Let's add another method to the `NorthWindDomainService` class that takes a string and returns all products that starts with that particular string. Here is the new method:

```
public IQueryable<Products> GetProductsThatStartWith(string startsWith)
{
  var p = from product in this.Context.Products
          where product.ProductName.StartsWith(startsWith)
          select product;

  return p;
}
```

With a little bit of LINQ code, it is easy to create a handy method that lets a user type in a partial name or just a letter to find a product. When you build the solution, you can check the generated code file Ch09_LOBApplications.TestWeb.g.cs in the Recipe 9-2 Silverlight project to see that in addition to the default RiaContext object that provides access to application services as covered in Recipe 9-1, you now have to additional namespaces brought into the code file. Ch09_LOBApplications.TestWeb.Data_Model and Ch09_LOBApplications.TestWeb.Domain_Services correspond to the work you just did in the TestWeb web project, providing client-side access to the entity model and the domain service, respectively.

You first modify the Home.xaml page by removing all the content in the ContentStackPanel object and replacing it with two ListBox objects: one named ProductsListBox with a basic ItemTemplate and the other named ProductsListBoxManualLoad without a template, as shown in Listing 9-5.

Listing 9-5. *The Recipe 9-2 Home.Xaml File*

```
<navigation:Page
  x:Class="Ch09_LOBApplications.Recipe9_2.Home"
  xmlns:dataControls="clr-namespace:System.Windows.Controls;assembly=
          System.Windows.Controls.Data.DataForm.Toolkit"
  xmlns:input="clr-namespace:System.Windows.Controls;assembly=
          System.Windows.Controls.Input"
  xmlns:data="clr-namespace:System.Windows.Controls;assembly=
          System.Windows.Controls.Data"
  xmlns="http://schemas.microsoft.com/winfx/2006/xaml/presentation"
  xmlns:x="http://schemas.microsoft.com/winfx/2006/xaml"
  xmlns:d="http://schemas.microsoft.com/expression/blend/2008"
  xmlns:mc="http://schemas.openxmlformats.org/markup-compatibility/2006"
  xmlns:navigation="clr-namespace:System.Windows.Controls;assembly=
          System.Windows.Controls.Navigation"
  xmlns:navControls="clr-namespace:System.Windows.Controls;assembly=
          System.Windows.Controls.Navigation"
  mc:Ignorable="d" d:DesignWidth="640" d:DesignHeight="480"
  Title="Home"
  NavigationCacheMode="Enabled"
  Style="{StaticResource PageStyle}">
```

```xml
<navControls:Page.Resources>
  <DataTemplate x:Key="ProductsTemplate">
    <Grid>
      <StackPanel  HorizontalAlignment="Left" VerticalAlignment="Top" >
        <TextBlock HorizontalAlignment="Left"
                   Text="Product Name:" TextWrapping="Wrap" Margin="2"/>
        <TextBlock HorizontalAlignment="Left"
                   Text="{Binding ProductName}" TextWrapping="Wrap" Margin="2"/>
      </StackPanel>
    </Grid>
  </DataTemplate>
</navControls:Page.Resources>

<Grid x:Name="LayoutRoot">
  <ScrollViewer x:Name="PageScrollViewer"
                Style="{StaticResource PageScrollViewerStyle}" >
    <StackPanel x:Name="ContentStackPanel" Margin="8"
                Style="{StaticResource ContentStackPanelStyle}">
<ListBox x:Name="ProductsListBox" Margin="8" Height="150"
                ItemTemplate="{StaticResource ProductsTemplate}"/>
      <ListBox x:Name="ProductsListBoxManualLoad"
                Margin="8" Height="150"/>
    </StackPanel>
  </ScrollViewer>
</Grid>
</navigation:Page>
```

To populate the ListBox control named ProductsListBox, you add code to the Home.xaml.cs code-behind file. First, you bring in the domain service and the data model from the middle tier—now available to the presentation tier in the Ch09_LOBApplications.TestWeb.g.cs generated code file, as shown in Listing 9-6—with these two using statements:

```csharp
using Ch09_LOBApplications.TestWeb.Domain_Services;
using Ch09_LOBApplications.TestWeb.Data_Model;
```

Listing 9-6. *The Recipe 9-2 Home.Xaml.cs Code File*

```csharp
using System;
using System.Windows.Controls;
using System.Windows.Navigation;
using System.Windows.Ria.Data;
using Ch09_LOBApplications.TestWeb.Data_Model;
using Ch09_LOBApplications.TestWeb.Domain_Services;
```

```
namespace Ch09_LOBApplications.Recipe9_2
{
  public partial class Home : Page
  {
    NorthWindDomainContext NorthWindDC = new NorthWindDomainContext();
    LoadOperation<Products> productsLoadOperation;

    public Home()
    {
      InitializeComponent();

      NorthWindDomainContext NorthWindDC = new NorthWindDomainContext();
      ProductsListBox.ItemsSource = NorthWindDC.Products;

      EntityQuery<Products> productQuery =
              NorthWindDC.GetProductsQuery();

      productsLoadOperation = NorthWindDC.Load(productQuery);
      productsLoadOperation.Completed +=
            new EventHandler(productsLoadOperation_Completed);
    }

    void productsLoadOperation_Completed(object sender, EventArgs e)
    {
      LoadOperation<Products> productsLoadResult =
        (LoadOperation<Products>)sender;

      foreach (Products product in productsLoadResult.Entities)
      {
        ProductsListBoxManualLoad.Items.Add(product.ProductName + " " +
                                    String.Format("{0:c}",product.UnitPrice));
      }
    }

    // Executes when the user navigates to this page.
    protected override void OnNavigatedTo(NavigationEventArgs e)
    {
    }
  }
}
```

When you are working with .NET RIA Services, you must always have a context to work with, whether it is the RiaContext for application-level services or a domain data context to work with domain service data. In this case, it is NorthWindDomainContext. For this application, you declare an instance of NorthWindDomainContext and name it NorthWindDC.

In the home page constructor, you configure the `ProductsListBox.ItemsSource` to databind to `NorthWindDC.Products` data, although it is currently empty.

You declare an `EntityQuery` containing `Products` and assign the `NorthWindDC.GetProductsQuery()` value to it. To load `ProductsListBox`, you can call `NorthWindDC.Load(productQuery)` without capturing the return value; the `Products` collection is loaded, and the items appear in the `ProductsListBox` control in the UI.

You capture the return value, assign it to a `LoadOperation<Products>` object named `productsLoadOperation`, and wire up its `Completed` event to a handler where you step through the results and manually load the data into `ProductsListBoxManualLoad`. Figure 9-8 shows the output.

It is common to share custom classes not generated by a tool as helper classes to support application logic between application tiers. To identify a class as shared between the middle tier and presentation tier, create a .NET class as you normally would in the middle tier, but name the class `classname.shared.cs`. The `.shared.cs` part of the filename is recognized by the code generator as a file that should be copied over to the client tier. This provides a simple way to share a class between tiers in the solution.

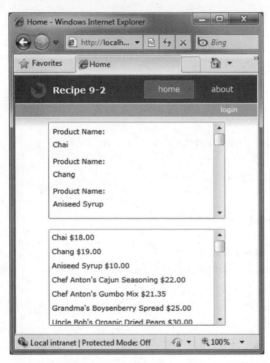

Figure 9-8. *Products loaded into the two ListBox objects*

To demonstrate, add a new folder to the middle-tier `TestWeb` project named `Shared Classes`. Next, add a class called `ProductsHelper.Shared.cs` to the folder, and compile the solution. The class file `ProductsHelper.Shared.cs` appears in the `Generated_Code` folder in a subfolder named `Shared Classes` in the Silverlight application.

As you can see, you can code against the client-side generated code file to access services from the middle tier without issue. You can also share classes between the middle tier and presentation tier. We demonstrate this to help remove some of the mystery around how .NET RIA Services works; in addition, there may be scenarios in which you wish to access data via code. However, in the subsequent recipes, we take things up a notch and incorporate the rich data controls that permit powerful databinding with little or no custom code.

9-3. Adding Advanced LOB Data Access with Data-Form Support

Problem

You need to enhance data access to provide a grid view and editable a data form in the UI.

Solution

Take advantage of the Microsoft .NET RIA Services `DomainDataSource` and `DataForm` objects to quickly create a useful data-editing UI.

How It Works

In Recipe 9-2, we cover how to provide access to data via a `DomainService` class, including how to code against the API. In this recipe, we focus on a more XAML-oriented approach to provide access to data in a Silverlight application.

When you install .NET RIA Services, it adds the `DomainDataSource` control to the Toolbox. The control is located in the `System.Windows.Controls` namespace in the `System.Windows.Ria.Controls` assembly.

The `DomainDataSource` control is the bridge that allows XAML elements to databind to data provided by a domain service without your having to write any code. As an example, in Silverlight 3 you can databind the `ItemsSource` of a `DataGrid` or `ListBox` control to the `Data` property of a `DomainDataSource` control to make that data available.

The `DomainDataSource` control links to the domain service on the middle tier via the code generated into the Silverlight project at compile time in the hidden code file (`Ch09_LOBApplications.TestWeb.g.cs` in the sample code) located in the `Generated_Code` folder in the Silverlight application. The generated code file contains a `DomainContext` instance that is set on the `DomainDataSource` control's `DomainContext` property in order to connect the `DomainDataSource` to the domain service in the middle tier.

The `DataGrid` control is a very popular control for LOB application as a way for users to quickly review available data. However, the `DataGrid` is not always the best control to perform edits from a usability standpoint.

The Silverlight Toolkit includes a `DataForm` control that makes it easy to build a more user-friendly edit form. The Silverlight Business Application template includes a copy of the `System.Windows.Controls.Data.DataForm.Toolkit.dll` assembly in the `Libs` directory, so you can easily take advantage of the `DataForm` control. If you create a new project without using the Silverlight Business Application template, you can download the Silverlight Toolkit from CodePlex to get a copy of the `System.Windows.Controls.Data.DataForm.Toolkit.dll` assembly directly:

```
http://www.codeplex.com/Silverlight
```

This recipe's code demonstrates how to databind in XAML and take advantage of the `DataForm` control. We do not go through the entire process of adding an ADO.NET Entity Framework item and a `DomainService` to the middle tier. Instead, we take advantage of the `DomainService` created in Recipe 6-2. For more information about how to configure the middle tier, refer to Recipe 6-2.

The Code

For this recipe, you modify the project template, changing the `Home` page to a `Page` named `ListBoxPage` where you demonstrate the simple case of databinding in XAML to a `DomainDataSource` control. You also add another `Page` named `Products`, where you demonstrate databinding in XAML as well as the `DataForm` control. You update `MainPage.xaml` so that the navigation works properly. Refer to Recipe 6-10 for more information about the Silverlight Navigation Application project template.

In the `ListBoxPage.xaml` file, you replace the content with a `ListBox`. Drag a `DomainDataSource` control from the Toolbox in Visual Studio, place it just above the `ListBox`, and name it `ProductsDDS`. Set the `QueryName` property to `GetProducts`, because that operation corresponds to the `GetProductsQuery` method in the code-generated file that retrieves the `Products` data by default. You also need to set the `DomainDataSource.DomainContext` property to `NorthWindDomainContext`, also found in the generated code file. To configure the `DomainContext` property, import the namespace by adding an `xmlns` namespace import on the `Page`:

```
xmlns:NWDDS="clr-namespace:
Ch09_LOBApplications.TestWeb.Domain_Services"
```

Here is a snippet from the full code of `ListBoxPage.xaml` in Listing 9-6 that shows the `DomainDataSource` configuration with the `DomainContext` configured. You also set `AutoLoad` to `True` so that the `DomainDataSource` loads the data automatically as needed by a control:

```
<riaControls:DomainDataSource x:Name="ProductsDDS" AutoLoad="True"
                              QueryName="GetProducts" >
  <riaControls:DomainDataSource.DomainContext>
    <NWDDS:NorthWindDomainContext/>
  </riaControls:DomainDataSource.DomainContext>
</riaControls:DomainDataSource>
```

As a seasoned Silverlight developer, you may begin to configure the `DataContext` instead. This can lead to some frustration as you try to figure out what you did wrong, so be alert.

Listing 9-6. *The Recipe 9-3 ListBoxPage.Xaml File*

```
<navigation:Page xmlns:riaControls="clr-namespace:
System.Windows.Controls;assembly=System.Windows.Ria.Controls"
  x:Class="Ch09_LOBApplications.Recipe9_3.ListBoxPage"
  xmlns:dataControls="clr-namespace:System.Windows.Controls;
      assembly=System.Windows.Controls.Data.DataForm.Toolkit"
  xmlns:input="clr-namespace:System.Windows.Controls;
      assembly=System.Windows.Controls.Input"
  xmlns:data="clr-namespace:System.Windows.Controls;
      assembly=System.Windows.Controls.Data"
```

```xml
        xmlns="http://schemas.microsoft.com/winfx/2006/xaml/presentation"
        xmlns:x="http://schemas.microsoft.com/winfx/2006/xaml"
        xmlns:d="http://schemas.microsoft.com/expression/blend/2008"
        xmlns:mc="http://schemas.openxmlformats.org/markup-compatibility/2006"
        xmlns:navigation="clr-namespace:System.Windows.Controls;
            assembly=System.Windows.Controls.Navigation"
        xmlns:navControls="clr-namespace:System.Windows.Controls;
            assembly=System.Windows.Controls.Navigation"
        xmlns:NWDDS="clr-namespace:
            Ch09_LOBApplications.TestWeb.Domain_Services"
        xmlns:NWDM="clr-namespace:
            Ch09_LOBApplications.TestWeb.Data_Model"
        mc:Ignorable="d" d:DesignWidth="640" d:DesignHeight="480"
        Title="Recipe 9.3"  NavigationCacheMode="Enabled"
        Style="{StaticResource PageStyle}">
        <navControls:Page.Resources>
          <DataTemplate x:Key="ProductsTemplate">
            <Grid>
              <StackPanel  HorizontalAlignment="Left" VerticalAlignment="Top" >
                <TextBlock HorizontalAlignment="Left"
                           Text="Product Name:" TextWrapping="Wrap" Margin="2"/>
                <TextBlock HorizontalAlignment="Left"
                           Text="{Binding ProductName}" TextWrapping="Wrap" Margin="2"/>
              </StackPanel>
            </Grid>
          </DataTemplate>
        </navControls:Page.Resources>

        <Grid x:Name="LayoutRoot">
          <ScrollViewer x:Name="PageScrollViewer"
                        Style="{StaticResource PageScrollViewerStyle}" >
            <StackPanel x:Name="ContentStackPanel" Margin="8"
                        Style="{StaticResource ContentStackPanelStyle}">
              <riaControls:DomainDataSource x:Name="ProductsDDS" AutoLoad="True"
                                            QueryName="GetProducts" >
                <riaControls:DomainDataSource.DomainContext>
                  <NWDDS:NorthWindDomainContext/>
                </riaControls:DomainDataSource.DomainContext>
              </riaControls:DomainDataSource>
              <ListBox x:Name="ProductsListBox" Margin="8" Height="150"
                   ItemTemplate="{StaticResource ProductsTemplate}"
                   ItemsSource="{Binding Data, ElementName=ProductsDDS, Mode=OneWay}"/>
            </StackPanel>
          </ScrollViewer>
        </Grid>
</navigation:Page>
```

The rest of the code configures the ListBox with a data template to display the data. Figure 9-9 shows the UI. Note that no C# code is needed in the code-behind to make this work.

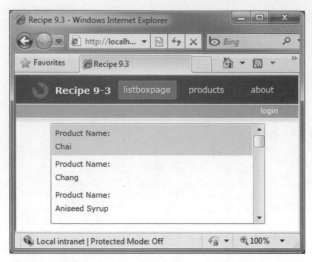

Figure 9-9. *Products loaded into the ListBox via a DomainDataSource*

For the Products Page, you create a UI that lets you scroll through the products data in a DataGrid. The user can select a product in the DataGrid and edit the record in a DataForm below the UI. You also implement the DataPager. None of this functionality requires any C# code. It is all done in XAML, although you do write some code for custom functionality and to submit changes to the database.

Begin by grabbing the DomainDataSource and its configuration from the ListBoxPage. Also copy the appropriate xmlns namespaces to gain access to the client-side domain service code as well as the RIA controls. Next, drag the DataGrid, DataForm, and DataPager controls from the Toolbox to Visual Studio to set things up.

You now databind the DataGrid and DataPager to the ProductsDDS.Data property, just as you did in ListBoxPage.xaml. The DataPager does not have an ItemsSource property. Instead, you use the DataPager.
Source property. Also set PageSize to 5, and make the DataGrid read-only.

Configure the DataForm, setting the Header value to "Product Details", setting AutoCommit to True, and forcing the vertical scrollbar to be visible. The most interesting setting is the DataForm.CurrentItem property that is databound to the ProductsGrid SelectedItem property:

```
CurrentItem="{Binding SelectedItem,ElementName=ProductsGrid}"
```

The work so far results in a functional UI, as shown in Figure 9-10.

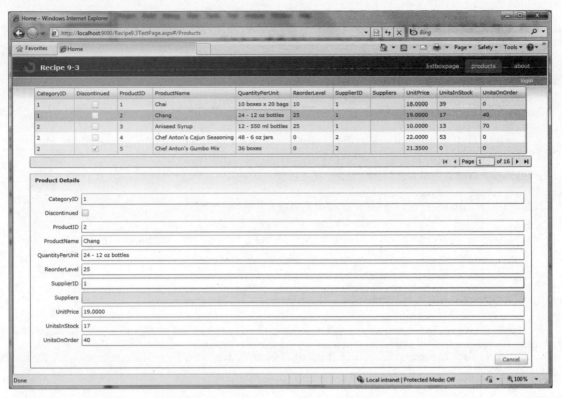

Figure 9-10. *The in-progress ProductsPage UI*

The UI lets you page through the data in the DataGrid as well as edit in the DataForm with AutoCommit equal to True. To make edits permanent in the database, you need a bit more UI. Add two buttons: one to submit changes to the server, and the other as a quick way to mark a product as discontinued. Here is the code to submit changes:

```
private void submitButton_Click(object sender, RoutedEventArgs e)
{
  if (!ProductsDDS.IsBusy && ProductsDDS.HasChanges)
  {
    ProductsDataForm.CommitEdit();
    ProductsDDS.SubmitChanges();
  }
  else
    MessageBox.Show("Please click Save or Cancel before submitting.",
      "Operation In Progress", MessageBoxButton.OK);
}
```

As you can see, the DomainDataSource named ProducsDDS is the center of the action. You next add SortDescriptors to the DommainDataSource to sort the data on the ProductName column in ascending order. The following XAML is nested within the DomainDataSource element declaration in the XAML:

```
<riaControls:DomainDataSource.SortDescriptors>
  <riaData:SortDescriptor PropertyPath="ProductName"
   Direction="Ascending" />
</riaControls:DomainDataSource.SortDescriptors>
```

The last bit of XAML you add to the DomainDataSource implements filtering by nesting FilterDescriptor XAML within the DomainDataSource element:

```
<riaControls:DomainDataSource.FilterDescriptors>
  <riaData:FilterDescriptorCollection>
    <riaData:FilterDescriptor PropertyPath="ReorderLevel"
                              Operator="IsLessThanOrEqualTo">
      <riaData:ControlParameter ControlName="ReorderLevelText"  PropertyName="Text"
                              RefreshEventName="TextChanged" />
    </riaData:FilterDescriptor>
  </riaData:FilterDescriptorCollection>
</riaControls:DomainDataSource.FilterDescriptors>
```

The FilterDescriptor takes a control name and an event to signal when to refresh the filter on the identified column. In this example, you filter on the ReorderLevel column and signal on the TextChanged event for the ReorderLevelText TextBox. Listings 9-7 and 9-8 show the complete code for the ProductsPage view.

Listing 9-7. *The Recipe 9-3 ProductsPage.Xaml File*

```
<navigation:Page
  x:Class="Ch09_LOBApplications.Recipe9_3.ProductsPage"
  xmlns:dataControls="clr-namespace:System.Windows.Controls;
    assembly=System.Windows.Controls.Data.DataForm.Toolkit"
  xmlns:input="clr-namespace:System.Windows.Controls;
    assembly=System.Windows.Controls.Input"
  xmlns:data="clr-namespace:System.Windows.Controls;
    assembly=System.Windows.Controls.Data"
  xmlns="http://schemas.microsoft.com/winfx/2006/xaml/presentation"
  xmlns:x="http://schemas.microsoft.com/winfx/2006/xaml"
  xmlns:d="http://schemas.microsoft.com/expression/blend/2008"
  xmlns:mc="http://schemas.openxmlformats.org/markup-compatibility/2006"
```

```
xmlns:navigation="clr-namespace:System.Windows.Controls;
  assembly=System.Windows.Controls.Navigation"
xmlns:navControls="clr-namespace:System.Windows.Controls;
  assembly=System.Windows.Controls.Navigation"
xmlns:NWDDS="clr-namespace:Ch09_LOBApplications.TestWeb.Domain_Services"
xmlns:riaData="clr-namespace:System.Windows.Data;
assembly-System.Windows.Ria.Controls"
xmlns:riaControls="clr-namespace:System.Windows.Controls;
assembly=System.Windows.Ria.Controls"
mc:Ignorable="d" d:DesignWidth="640" d:DesignHeight="480"
Title="Home"
NavigationCacheMode="Enabled"
Style="{StaticResource PageStyle}">
<Grid x:Name="LayoutRoot">
  <ScrollViewer x:Name="PageScrollViewer"
                Style="{StaticResource PageScrollViewerStyle}" >
    <StackPanel x:Name="ContentStackPanel" Margin="0,12,0,0"
                Style="{StaticResource ContentStackPanelStyle}">
      <TextBlock Text="Products Manager" MinWidth="400" Margin="2"
          HorizontalAlignment="Left" Style="{StaticResource HeaderTextStyle}"/>
      <StackPanel Orientation="Horizontal" HorizontalAlignment="Right" Margin="2">
        <TextBlock VerticalAlignment="Center"
                Text="Reorder Level Less Than:" Margin="2"/>
        <TextBox  x:Name="ReorderLevelText" Width="30" FontSize="11" Margin="2"/>
      </StackPanel>

      <riaControls:DomainDataSource x:Name="ProductsDDS" AutoLoad="True"
                                    QueryName="GetProducts" >
        <riaControls:DomainDataSource.DomainContext>
          <NWDDS:NorthWindDomainContext/>
        </riaControls:DomainDataSource.DomainContext>
        <riaControls:DomainDataSource.SortDescriptors>
          <riaData:SortDescriptor PropertyPath="ProductName"
                                  Direction="Ascending" />
        </riaControls:DomainDataSource.SortDescriptors>
        <riaControls:DomainDataSource.FilterDescriptors>
          <riaData:FilterDescriptorCollection>
            <riaData:FilterDescriptor PropertyPath="ReorderLevel"
                                      Operator="IsLessThanOrEqualTo">
              <riaData:ControlParameter ControlName="ReorderLevelText"
                  PropertyName="Text" RefreshEventName="TextChanged" />
            </riaData:FilterDescriptor>
          </riaData:FilterDescriptorCollection>
        </riaControls:DomainDataSource.FilterDescriptors>
      </riaControls:DomainDataSource>
```

```
        <data:DataGrid x:Name="ProductsGrid" Margin="10,10,10,4" IsReadOnly="True"
                     ItemsSource="{Binding Data, ElementName=ProductsDDS}"
                     Height="Auto" MinHeight="100" />
        <data:DataPager Source="{Binding Data, ElementName=ProductsDDS}"
                     PageSize="5"/>
        <StackPanel Orientation="Horizontal" HorizontalAlignment="Right"
                 Margin="0,12,0,0">
          <Button x:Name="submitButton" Width="75" Height="23"  Content="Submit"
              Margin="4,0,0,0" Click="submitButton_Click"/>
          <Button x:Name="DiscontinueProduct" Width="115" Height="23"
              Content="Discontinue Product"  Margin="4,0,0,0"
                Click="DiscontinueProduct_Click" />
        </StackPanel>
        <dataControls:DataForm x:Name="ProductsDataForm" Header="Product Details"
                            Margin="0,12,0,0"
          AutoCommit="True" ScrollViewer.VerticalScrollBarVisibility="Visible"
          CurrentItem="{Binding SelectedItem,ElementName=ProductsGrid}" >
        </dataControls:DataForm>
      </StackPanel>
    </ScrollViewer>
  </Grid>
</navigation:Page>
```

Listing 9-8. *The Recipe 9-3 ProductsPage.xaml.cs Code File*

```
using System.Windows;
using System.Windows.Controls;
using System.Windows.Navigation;
using Ch09_LOBApplications.TestWeb.Data_Model;

namespace Ch09_LOBApplications.Recipe9_3
{
  public partial class ProductsPage : Page
  {
    public ProductsPage()
    {
      InitializeComponent();
    }
```

```
// Executes when the user navigates to this page.
protected override void OnNavigatedTo(NavigationEventArgs e)
{
}

private void submitButton_Click(object sender, RoutedEventArgs e)
{
  if (!ProductsDDS.IsBusy && ProductsDDS.HasChanges)
  {
    ProductsDataForm.CommitEdit();
    ProductsDDS.SubmitChanges();
  }
  else
    MessageBox.Show("Please click Save or Cancel before submitting.",
      "Operation In Progress", MessageBoxButton.OK);
}
private void DiscontinueProduct_Click(object sender, RoutedEventArgs e)
{
  Products discontinuedProduct =
    (Products)(ProductsGrid.SelectedItem);
  if (null != discontinuedProduct)
  {
    discontinuedProduct.Discontinued = true;
    ProductsDataForm.CommitEdit();
  }
  if (!ProductsDDS.IsBusy)
    ProductsDDS.SubmitChanges();
  else
    MessageBox.Show("A change submit operation is in progress",
      "Operation In Progress", MessageBoxButton.OK);
}
}
}
```

Figure 9-11 shows the final UI with the filter in the upper-right corner of the page.

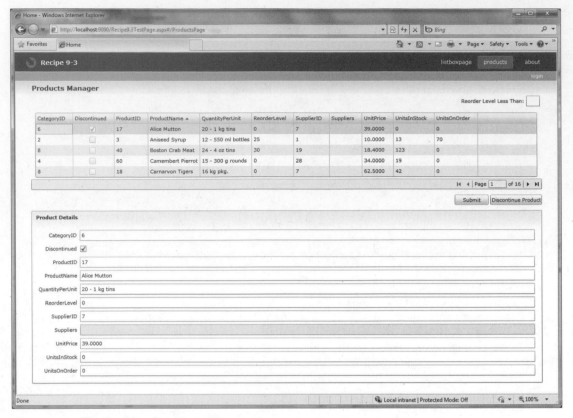

Figure 9-11. *The final ProductsPage UI*

9-4. Adding Support for Data Validation

Problem

You need to add data validation to a LOB application.

Solution

Take advantage of Microsoft .NET RIA Services extensibility by adding validation attributes or a metadata class to support data validation.

How It Works

Validation is a very important component of LOB applications and ensures accurate data input by end users. Validation can be performed in all tiers of an application, from validating with stored procedures in the database, to the middle tier in web service logic, to the presentation layer using built-in Silverlight control functionality or custom code.

There are good reasons to apply validation at all three levels in an *n*-tier application, depending on your circumstances and requirements.

.NET RIA Services provides support for validation in two ways: validation attributes and a metadata class. Here is a list of validation attributes in the System.ComponentModel.DataAnnotations namespace:

- CustomValidationAttribute
- DataTypeAttribute
- RangeAttribute
- RegularExpressionAttribute
- RequiredAttribute
- StringLengthAttribute

When you apply validation attributes to server-side entities in the domain service, the .NET RIA Services code generation propagates the validation attributes to the client-side entity representation when the solution is compiled. The generated entities on the client-side enforce validation in the property setter methods at runtime. The validation attributes are useful when you are creating shared classes in the middle tier that the code-generation system propagates to the client-side as well as when you are creating custom entities not using a tool.

For entity types that are code-generated either via LINQ to SQL or the ADO.NET Entity Framework OR/M tools, you should use a metadata class to define validation attributes. In Figure 9-7, the "Generate associated classes for metadata" is checked. This is the step that creates a new domain service to generate a metadata class template with the domain service class. You may have noticed two files in the Domain Services folder: one is the domain service, and the other is the metadata class named NorthWindDomainService.metadata.cs. We demonstrate how to configure the metadata class in this recipe.

The Code

You used the ADO.NET Entity Framework Wizard to generate the model for the domain service in Recipe 9-2. When you look at the generated code in the hidden folder Generated_Code in the code file Ch09_LOBApplications.TestWeb.g.cs for Recipe 9-4, you see validation attributes automatically applied to the generated code, such as RequiredAttribute and RegularExpressionAttribute on several fields.

Because the code is automatically generated, you should not add additional attributes directly on the model or in the generated code. Instead, configure the associated metadata class—in this case, the NorthWindDomainService.metadata.cs code file. Listing 9-9 shows the default file contents with spaces and extra lines removed but otherwise unmodified.

Listing 9-9. *The Recipe 9-4 ProductsPage.xaml.cs Code File*

```
#pragma warning disable 649 // disable compiler warnings about unassigned fields
namespace Ch09_LOBApplications.TestWeb.Data_Model
{
  using System;
  using System.Collections.Generic;
  using System.ComponentModel;
  using System.ComponentModel.DataAnnotations;
```

```csharp
using System.Linq;
using System.Web.Ria;
using System.Web.Ria.Data;
using System.Web.DomainServices;
using System.Data;
using System.Data.Objects.DataClasses;

// The MetadataTypeAttribute identifies ProductsMetadata as the class
// that carries additional metadata for the Products class.
[MetadataTypeAttribute(typeof(Products.ProductsMetadata))]
public partial class Products
{
  // This class allows you to attach custom attributes to properties
  // of the Products class.
  //
  // For example, the following marks the Xyz property as a
  // required field and specifies the format for valid values:
  //     [Required]
  //     [RegularExpression("[A-Z][A-Za-z0-9]*")]
  //     [StringLength(32)]
  //     public string Xyz;
  internal sealed class ProductsMetadata
  {
    // Metadata classes are not meant to be instantiated.
    private ProductsMetadata()
    {
    }
    public Categories Categories;
    public bool Discontinued;
    public EntityState EntityState;
    public int ProductID;
    public string ProductName;
    public string QuantityPerUnit;
    public Nullable<short> ReorderLevel;
    public Suppliers Suppliers;
    public Nullable<Decimal> UnitPrice;
    public Nullable<short> UnitsInStock;
    public Nullable<short> UnitsOnOrder;
  }
}
```

```csharp
    // The MetadataTypeAttribute identifies SuppliersMetadata as the class
    // that carries additional metadata for the Suppliers class.
    [MetadataTypeAttribute(typeof(Suppliers.SuppliersMetadata))]
    public partial class Suppliers
    {
      // This class allows you to attach custom attributes to properties
      // of the Suppliers class.
      //
      // For example, the following marks the Xyz property as a
      // required field and specifies the format for valid values:
      //      [Required]
      //      [RegularExpression("[A-Z][A-Za-z0-9]*")]
      //      [StringLength(32)]
      //      public string Xyz;
      internal sealed class SuppliersMetadata
      {
        // Metadata classes are not meant to be instantiated.
        private SuppliersMetadata()
        {
        }
        public string Address;
        public string City;
        public string CompanyName;
        public string ContactName;
        public string ContactTitle;
        public string Country;
        public EntityState EntityState;
        public string Fax;
        public string HomePage;
        public Nullable<double> Latitude;
        public string LatLong;
        public Nullable<double> Longitude;
        public string Phone;
        public string PostalCode;
        public EntityCollection<Products> Products;
        public string Region;
        public int SupplierID;
      }
    }
}
#pragma warning restore 649  // re-enable compiler warnings about unassigned fields
```

The default contents of the metadata class have partial classes that correspond to the properties on all the entities defined in the associated domain service. The partial classes each contain an internal sealed class with the same name as the class but with Metadata appended to the end. As an example, the

SuppliersMetadata class allows you to attach custom attributes such as validation attributes to the Suppliers class. You now apply validation attributes to the metadata class to test the functionality.

The Suppliers class has a HomePage property. You want to apply a RegularExpressionAttribute to the HomePage property to validate that a proper URL is entered. You find the HomePage public field on the SuppliersMetadata class and apply the attribute:

```
[RegularExpression(@"^http\://
[a-zA-Z0-9\-\.]+\.[a-zA-Z]{2,3}(/\S*)?$")]
public string HomePage;
```

The attribute is in the Regular Expression Library, which is a handy site for regular expressions:

```
http://regexlib.com/Search.aspx?k=url&c=-1&m=-1&ps=20
```

Create a page that is a copy of what you developed in Recipe 9-3—essentially, a DataGrid listing suppliers and a DataForm for editing. Run the sample code, and enter an invalid URL to test validation. The result is shown in Figure 9-12.

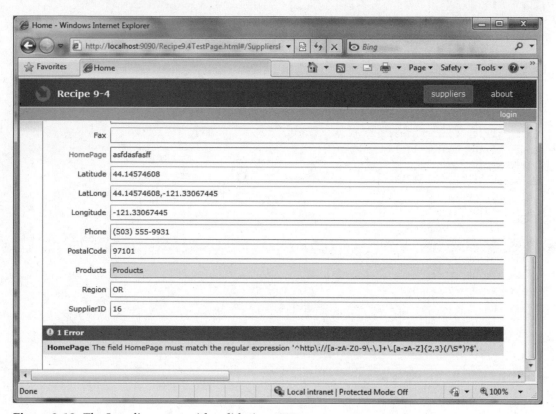

Figure 9-12. *The Suppliers page with validation errors*

The error is displayed as part of the DataForm control at the bottom. If you enter a correct URL such as http://www.apress.com, the error message is removed. The error isn't the friendliest message, so change RegularExpressionAttribute to this:

```
[RegularExpression(@"^http\://[a zA-ZO-9\-\.]+\.[a-zA-
Z]{2,3}(/\S*)?$",
ErrorMessage="Invalid URL. Please correct")]
public string HomePage;
```

Figure 9-13 shows the improved UI with a more useful message.

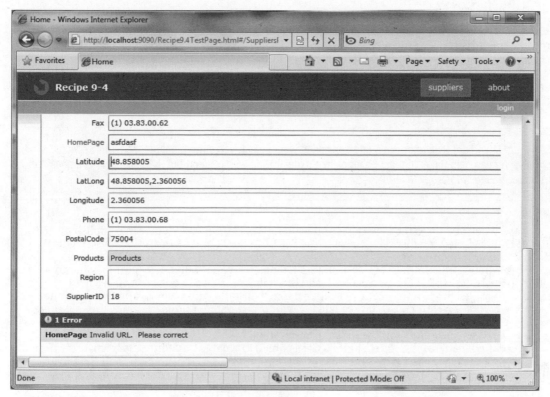

Figure 9-13. *The Suppliers page with validation errors and an improved message*

9-5. Adding .NET RIA Services to an Existing Application

Problem

You have an existing Silverlight application to which you want to add support for .NET RIA Services.

Solution

Establish a .NET RIA link between the Silverlight application and a web project in the solution.

How It Works

You may have an existing Silverlight 2 application in which you wish to take advantage of .NET RIA Services. In this case, open the project in Visual Studio and step through the Visual Studio Conversion Wizard; the solution opens in Visual Studio as a Silverlight 3 application. If the Silverlight 2 solution includes a folder-based web project, you must add a web application project and move the web site into the new web application project.

■**Note** If the Silverlight 2 solution uses a folder-based web project, you cannot enable .NET RIA Services. In Silverlight 3, you can host Silverlight applications in a folder-based web project, but .NET RIA Services does not support folder-based web projects.

Now, when you go to the Silverlight application project properties, you can establish the .NET RIA Services link by selecting the web project in the .NET RIA Services Link drop-down list. Figure 9-14 shows the configuration option.

At this point, the RIA link is established such that after you rebuild the solution, you can select the option in Solution Explorer to view all files, and then click the Refresh button. You see a Generated_Code folder containing a code file with a name that starts with the web application name, followed by a .g.cs file to indicate that the code file is auto-generated. In this example, the web project name is SilverlightApplication7.Web, so the code file in the Generated_Code directory is named WebApplication7.Web.g.cs after you compile the application.

The default generated code includes a class named RiaContext that inherits from System.Windows.Ria.RiaContextBase. This class makes application services and types on the server available for consumption in the Silverlight application.

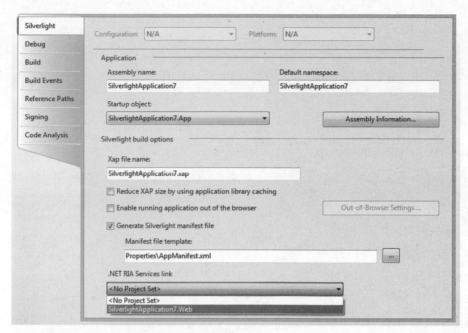

Figure 9-14. *The Enable .NET RIA Services option*

The Code

For this recipe, you do not write any additional Silverlight code. It demonstrates how simple it is to enable .NET RIA Services for an existing application. However, we list the generated code for this recipe because it represents the minimalist implementation of .NET RIA Services (see Listing 9-10). In order to have a minimal representation, we generated this project outside the main solution to demonstrate what it would contain. Otherwise, if you enable the RIA link for Recipe 9.5, you receive all available domain services and application services.

Listing 9-10. *The Recipe 9-5 Generated Code, Ch09_LOBApplications.TestWeh.g.cs Code File*

```
using System;
using System.Collections.Generic;
using System.ComponentModel;
using System.ComponentModel.DataAnnotations;
using System.Linq;
using System.Web.Ria.Data;
using System.Windows.Ria.Data;
```

```
/// <summary>
/// Context for the RIA application.
/// </summary>
/// <remarks>
/// This context extends the base to make application services and types available
/// for consumption from code and xaml.
/// </remarks>
public sealed partial class RiaContext : System.Windows.Ria.RiaContextBase
{
    #region Extensibility Method Definitions
    /// <summary>
    /// This method is invoked from the constructor once initialization is complete
    ///nd can be used for further object setup.
    /// </summary>
    partial void OnCreated();
    #endregion

    /// <summary>
    /// Initializes a new instance of the RiaContext class.
    /// </summary>
    public RiaContext()
    {
        this.OnCreated();
    }

    /// <summary>
    /// Gets the context that is registered as a lifetime object with
    /// the current application.</summary>
    /// <exception cref="InvalidOperationException"> is thrown if there is no
    /// current application, no contexts have been added, or more than one
    /// context has been added.
    /// </exception>
    /// <seealso cref="Application.ApplicationLifetimeObjects"/>
    public new static RiaContext Current
    {
        get
        {
            return ((RiaContext)(System.Windows.Ria.RiaContextBase.Current));
        }
    }
}
```

9-6. Using the .NET RIA Services Class Library to Isolate Services

Problem

You want to be able to control which domain services a set of Silverlight applications can access.

Solution

Do not use the RIA link between the Silverlight applications and the web project. Instead, place domain services into separate Microsoft .NET RIA Services class library projects, and only add references to the libraries that the Silverlight application requires.

How It Works

When a Silverlight application has an RIA link with a web project, all services and types declared in the web project as well as all domain services referenced within the web project are made available via the RIA link in the code-generated file to all associated Silverlight applications that take advantage of .NET RIA Services.

■**Note**   .NET RIA Services is still as a CTP as of the RTM of Silverlight 3. This behavior may change in a future version of .NET RIA Services as it progress toward release.

The RIA link is very convenient and may be all that an application requires in order to easily bring services and types to the Silverlight application. However, as an example, if you have an application with an internally facing version and an externally facing version, and it consists of common services as well as services unique to the internal and external applications, you may not want to use the RIA link. Instead, you can put services into a separate project created using the .NET RIA Services Class Library project template.

Note that in the version of .NET RIA Services available when Silverlight 3 RTW'd, removing the RIA link in the project options by setting .NET RIA Services Link to "no project set" also removes the built-in support for application services such as authentication and user profile settings created as part of the Business Application template. This may change as .NET RIA Services progresses toward release.

The Code

You begin with the Silverlight Navigation Application template for this recipe. Do not check the check box to enable .NET RIA Services when you create the project, because you want to use a .NET RIA Services class library instead. To put it another way, there isn't an RIA link between the Silverlight project and the web project—you do not find a hidden Generated_Code folder with a generated code file when you build the solution.

Right-click the solution, select Add ➤ New Project, click the Silverlight folder if it is not already selected, and choose .NET RIA Services class library. Enter the name Recipe9_6.DomainService1, and then click OK. A Solution folder is created that contains two new projects. Repeat this step, but name the .NET RIA Services class library Recipe9_6.DomainService2. Figure 9-15 shows the project layout.

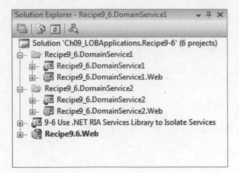

Figure 9-15. *Solution Explorer and the .NET RIA Services class libraries*

This project layout may seem strange at first. What is strange is that you select a project template to create a single project, but you end up creating two projects organized in a Solution folder to keep the two class libraries together within the Solution structure.

Next, follow the steps in Recipe 9-2 to create a domain service in Recipe9_6.DomainService1.Web and Recipe9_6.DomainService2.Web. Point DomainService1 at the NorthWind database and DomainService2 at the Pubs database. Figure 9-16 shows the project layout.

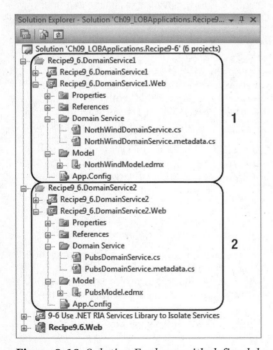

Figure 9-16. *Solution Explorer with defined domain services*

Now, go back to the Recipe9.6.Web web project, and add a reference to the following projects:

Recipe9_6.DomainService1.Web

Recipe9_6.DomainService2.Web

By adding the reference to these two projects, you make it possible for the Recipe9.6.Web web project to make these services available to Silverlight clients. You have to perform one additional step. Notice in these two projects that an App.Config file is generated. You need to manually transfer these settings to the web.config file for the Recipe9.6.Web web project in order for the services to be available. Listing 9-11 shows the contents of DomainService1's App.Config file.

Listing 9-11. *The Recipe 9-6 DomainService1 App.Config File*

```
<?xml version="1.0" encoding="utf-8"?>
<configuration>
  <connectionStrings>
    <add name="NorthwindEntities" connectionString="metadata=
res://*/Model.NorthWindModel.csdl|res://*/Model.NorthWindModel.ssdl|
res://*/Model.NorthWindModel.msl;provider=System.Data.SqlClient;
provider connection string=&quot;Data Source=.\SqlExpress;
Initial Catalog=Northwind;Integrated
Security=True;MultipleActiveResultSets=True&quot;"
providerName="System.Data.EntityClient" />
  </connectionStrings>
  <system.web>
    <httpHandlers>
      <add path="DataService.axd" verb="GET,POST" type=
      "System.Web.Ria.DataServiceFactory, System.Web.Ria,
 Version=2.0.0.0, Culture=neutral, PublicKeyToken=31BF3856AD364E35"
        validate="false" />
    </httpHandlers>
  </system.web>
</configuration>
```

Essentially, you have to copy over the connection string for each project into the web project's web.config file because the httpHandler is already present. If you build the solution, no generated code is brought into the Recipe9-6 Silverlight application because there is no RIA link.

If you establish an RIA link between the Silverlight application and the web project, both DomainService1 (NorthWind) and DomainService2 (Pubs) are available in a generated code file just as before. You cannot choose to have one or the other, so every Silverlight application gains access to all the available domain services. Without the RIA link, you can bring in one or both services selectively for any Silverlight application by adding a reference to either the Recipe9_6.DomainService1 or the Recipe9_6.DomainService2 Silverlight project.

If you reference both domain services and build, you still do not see a Generated_Code folder directly in the Recipe9-6 Silverlight project. However, you have full access to both domain services. How is that possible? The answer is the RIA link between the two projects for each .NET RIA Services class library. As an example, right-click Recipe9_6.DomainService1, and view its properties as shown in Figure 9-17.

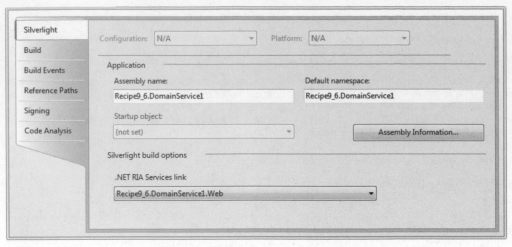

Figure 9-17. *RIA link established between class libraries*

As you can see, the two class libraries generated from the .NET RIA Services Class Library item template have a .NET RIA Services link between them. Therefore, when you add a reference to the Silverlight class projects in your Recipe9-6 Silverlight application, you gain access to the generated code in each project. Figure 9-18 shows the generated code.

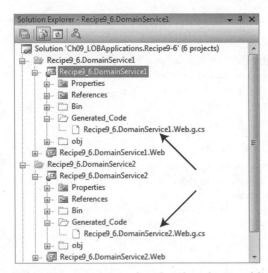

Figure 9-18. *Generated Code Files After Establishing the Ria Link*

Index

▪NUMERICS

3-D effects, adding to UI elements, 223–235

3-D graphics, 4

3-D matrixes, 224

▪A

AcceptIncoming() method, 691

Add CLR Object Data Source dialog, 36

Add New Domain Service Class dialog, 908

Add Service Reference dialog, 601

Add Silverlight Application wizard, 9, 16, 568

AddressFamily enumeration, 668

ADO.NET Entity Framework model, 8, 907, 925

Advanced Audio Coding (AAC), 4, 753

Advanced Encryption Standard (AES), 4

AdventureWorks Online Transaction Processing (OLTP) database, 360

AdventureWorks WCF service, 434

AJAX Library, Microsoft, 543–544

Angle property (RotateTransform), 198

animations, 4

    adding keyframes to create, 24

    bouncing ball example, 181–183

    creating, in Expression Blend, 23–24

    creating dynamic user interfaces with, 173–176

    creating for cartoons/games, 197–201

    improving, with custom easing functions, 247–254

    keyframe, 174

    maximizing performance of, 243–245

    reverting to original, 24

    of UI elements with keyframes, 181–186

App object, 570

App.xaml file, 10–12, 589

Appication.UnhandledException event, 74

application data

    binding to UI, 275–283

    classes, 277–280, 293–300, 311–315, 332–337

application design, prototype, 272–273

application interactivity, reusing, 270–272

Application Lifecycle Management (ALM), 27

application services, creating, 105–110

application themes, 4

Application.ApplicationLifetimeObjects collection, 105

Application.CheckAndDownloadUpdateAsync() method, 710

Application.Install() method, 708

Application.InstallState property, 708

ApplicationInstallStateChanged event, 708

applications. See line-of-business (LOB) applications; Silverlight applications

ArcSegment object, 159, 162

Arrange pass, 136

ArrangeOverride() Method, 440, 441, 447

ASF (Advanced Systems Format), 869
ASP.NET framework
    hosting Silverlight in, 520–521, 584
ASP.NET Silverlight control, 48
ASP.NET Web Application Project, 10
ASP.NET Web Site, 10
AspNetCompatibilityRequirementsAttribu
    te, 615
ASPX page markup (TestWeb project), 14
Assembly.GetManifestResource method,
    96
Assembly.GetManifestResourceStream
    method, 96
Asset Library (Expression Blend), 21
Asset Library toolbar, 144, 152, 155
asx element (CSPL), 834
asynchronous invocation patterns, 624
AsyncResult handlers, 624
Attach to Process dialog box (Visual Studio
    2008), 571
AuthenticationService class, 898
AuthenticationService.cs, 897
automatic layout, 144
AutoPlay property, 754
AutoUpgrade parameter, 517

■B

BackEase, 247
Background property, 97, 144, 168, 517
background threads
    executing work on, 75–85
    updating UI from, 85–89
    worker threads, 75– 76
BackgroundWorker class, 75, 86
BackgroundWorker object, 75–76
BandedSwirlEffect class, 257–258
BasedOn attribute, 361
BasicHttpBinding, 604
BeginGetResponse() method, 635
BeginInvoke() method, 624
*Beginning Silverlight 2: From Novice to
    Professional* (Apress), 117
behaviors
    applying, 270

defined, 270
Expression Blend support for, 270
reuse application interactivity with,
    270–272
Bezier curves, 162, 181, 183
BezierSegment object, 162
binding. *See* data binding
binding expressions, 276
Binding markup extension, 275
binding validiation errors, customizing UI
    for, 492–507
Binding.RelativeSource property, 323
Binding.UpdateSourceTrigger property,
    347
Binding.ValidatesOnExceptions property,
    331
BindingExpression.UpdateSource() method,
    347–348
BindingMode setting, 283
bindings, template, 367–368
BindingValidationError event, 331, 346
Bing Maps for Enterprise Silverlight
    control, 5, 7–8, 894
bit rates, 790
Bitmap API, 4
bitmap caching, 4, 243–245
BitmapImage object, 98
bitmaps, dynamic creation of, 235–242
BitmapSource object, 235
BlurEffect, 256
BoolToVisibilityConverter class, 343
Border control, 168
Border elements, 386
borders, applying to elements, 167–172
BounceEase, 247
bouncing ball animation, 181
bound data, validating input for, 331–346
broadcast publishing points, 794
broadcast stream, playing, 823
BroadcastStreams.xml, 796–797, 835–837
browser caching policy, 630
browser control (Silverlight)
    embedding Silverlight within Windows
        Sidebar, 567–583
    hosting Silverlight 3 in ASP.NET, 520

hosting Silverlight 3 in HTML, 515–518
implementing full-screen UI, 528–533
setting focus for keyboard input, 521–522
browser history journal, 588
browser support, 5
BrowserInformation class, 538
brush editor, 122
brush resources, 123
Brush Transform tool, 125–126
brushes
converting to resources, 94
gradient, 124
btnDropDown_Click() method, 397
btnOpenCustomFile_Click event handler, 242
btnSaveCustomFile_Click event handler, 242
buffering video, 823
built-in easing functions, 247
Business Application template, 895–897, 899, 905–906
Button elements, 532
Button server control, ASP.NET, 551
Button_Click event, 45
ButtonImportFile_Click event handler, 242
buttons
radio button with complex content, 369
sample style targeting a button, 362–363

■C

C# 2008 language, 69
caching
bitmap, 4, 243–245
policy, browser, 630
CancelAsync() method, 642
CancelCellEdit() method, 419–420
CancellationPending property (BackgroundWorker object), 75
Canvas layout control, 132–133
defined, 133
positioning UI elements with, 132–136
Captions.xml sample, 839–843

cartoons, creating animations for, 197–201
CategoryAttribute, 508–509
CellEditingTemplate property, 412–414
cells, applying custom templates to DataGrid, 412–418
CellTemplate property, 412–414
change notifications
for bound data, 291–308
for collection types, 293
for noncollection types, 291
chat application (sockets)
chat server, 690
ClientConnectionManager, 680–689
code-behind for page, 678–680
ConnectionListener class, 690–691
data contracts for messages, 671–673
PolicyServer type, 697–700
running sample code, 670–671
ServerConnectionManager and Participant types, 691–697
XAML for chat client page, 673–678
CheckAndDownloadUpdatesAsync() method, 711
Chiron.exe tool, 102, 104
CircleEase, 247
Circles, forming, 146
Class Library project, Silverlight 3, 8
classes
adding custom to Silverlight applications, 32–38
adding to projects, 32
application data, 277–280
graphic primitive, 117–118
isolated storage, 55
clientaccesspolicy.xml, for HTTP access, 702–704
ClientConnectionManager class (chat application), 680–689
clients, persisting data on, 54–61
client-side playlists (CSPL), 834
Clip property, Image control, 160–161
codecs, 869
code-generation functionality, 895
CodePlex, 893

collection types, change notification for, 293

ColorNameToBrushConverter class, 418

colors and gradients, 121–128

columns
creating, 140, 142
sizing, 141
types, creating custom for DataGrid, 418–424

Combine menu options, 149–150

Commercials.xml sample, 853–854

Community Technology Preview (CTP), 5, 893

composite user control, creating, 425–436

Compression for Great Digital Video: Power Tips, Techniques, and Common Sense (CMP Books), 791

ConnectAsync() method, 667–668

Connection_Completed()method, 689

ConnectionListener class (chat application), 690–691

ConnectionRequestSend_Completed() method, 689

content model controls, 368-370

content, providing scrollable for layouts, 165–166

ContentPresenter control, 370

ContentStates group, 816

control handles, drawing using, 157

control skinning, 4

controls. *See also* custom controls; use controls; *specific controls*
adding custom to Silverlight applications, 39–41
applying custom templates to DataGrid cells, 412–418
content model, 368–370
controlling scroll behavior in ScrollView, 482–492
creating composite user control, 425–436
creating custom column types for DataGrids, 418–424
creating custom controls, 453–469

creating custom layout container, 439–452

custom, for Expression Blend, 507–512

customizing binding validation UI, 492–507

customizing default ListBoxItem UI, 381–390

customizing styles and applying to, 360–364

data binding, 35

defining custom visual state in custom control, 470–482

displaying information in pop-ups, 390–402

displaying row details in DataGrids, 402–412

locating, 42–47

overview, 359

presenter, 368–370

property attributes, 508–509

ready-to-use, 4

replacing default UI of, 364–381

types of, 425

visual state management, 370–375

WCF service as data source for recipes, 360

<ControlTemplate> tag, 364

Convert to Path option, 153

Convert() method, 418

ConvertBack() method, 310, 418

ConvertFrom() method, 424

converting values during data binding, 309–321

copy and paste, for animations, 24

CornerRadius property, 168

Create Data Binding dialog, 36

CreateFromXaml() method, 47–48

cross-application data exchange, 733–751

cross-domain access, enabling
clientaccesspolicy.xml for HTTP access, 700–704

cross-domain policy requirements, 670

cross-thread invocations, 75

CubicEase, 247

curves

Bezier, 162, 181, 183
  creating, with Line tool, 155
custom classes, adding to Silverlight
      applications, 32–38
custom controls, 425
  adding to Silverlight applications, 39–
      41
  basics, 425
  creating, 453–469
  defining custom visual state in, 470–482
  designer-unsafe, 510
  for Expression Blend, 507–512
  sample data for, 511
  structure, 453–454
custom easing functions, 248–254
custom layout container, creating, 439–452
custom visual state, defining in custom
      control, 470–482
CustomImageSource type, 449–451

■D
data
  adding to LOB applications, 906–915
  bound, validating input for, 331–346
  design-time, in Expression Blend, 259–
      269
  exchanging between multiple plug-ins,
      560–562
  exchanging between Silverlight
      applications, 732–751
  persisting, on client, 54–61
  pushing, 561
data binding, 35
  across elements, 323–330
  binding application data to UI, 275-283
  change notifications for bound data,
      291–308
  controlling updates, 347–357
  converting values during, 309–321
  creating in code, 282–283
  defined, 275
  dependency properties and, 427–428
  RelativeSource, 456
  using data templates, 283–290

validating input for bound data, 331–
      346
data contracts
  for WCF web services, 606–610, 643–645
  to represent messages (chat
      application), 671–673
data initialization example, 286–287
Data panel, Expression Blend, 260–267
data source, associating the, 276
data support, 5
data types
  in client application (photo
      management), 648–652
  single menu item, 393–394
data validation, adding to LOB application,
      924–929
data-bound page example, 282
DataContext property, 38, 916
DataContexts, 276, 281
DataContractJsonSerializer type, 637, 673
data-editing UI, 915–924
DataForm control, 7, 915–924
DataGrid, 311, 915
  applying custom templates to cells,
      412–418
  Color column, 418
  creating custom column types for, 418–
      424
  displaying row details in, 402–412
DataGridBoundColumn class, 418
DataGridCheckBoxColumn class, 412, 419
DataGridColumn types, 412
DataGridDateColumn Class, 420–423
DataGridDateTimeConverter Class, 423–
      424
DataGridTemplateColumn class, 412
DataGridTextColumn class, 412, 419
DataTemplate
  applied to ItemTemplate of ListBox,
      290
  binding with, 283–290
  in ContentControl, 290
  declaring, 284–285
  defining (example), 287–290
  using, 285

deadlocks, 75
debugger, 346
debugging, Silverlight and JavaScript, 571
decoding, 869
Deep Zoom Composer, 7
Define New Object Data Source dialog, 36
DELETE verb, 625
denial of service (DOS) attacks, 700
dependency properties, 276, 428–430
    defined, 134
    dependency property system, 43, 117
DependencyObject class, 43, 159, 227, 624
DependencyObject.GetValue() method,
        430
DependencyProperty.Register() method,
        429
DependencyPropertyChangedEventArgs,
        430
DescriptionAttribute, 509
DeserializeMessage() method, 673
DeserializeProductHeaders() method, 635,
        640
design prototypes, 272–273
DesignerProperties static class, 510
designers, 17–19
design-time data, working with in
        Expression Blend, 259–269
developer/designer workflow, 17–20
development/designer environment, 6–7
Dictionary collections, 90
Digital Rights Management (DRM), 4
Direct Selection tool, 144, 153, 155
DirectX SDK, 255
Dirty flags, 623
discrete interpolation method, 181
Dispatcher class, 85
Dispatcher type, 624
Divideoption (Combine menu), 150
DockedUndockedView files (Sidebar
        gadget), 567–569, 573–577
DockedView.xaml file, 570, 574–575
DockGadget method, 579
docking, 133
dockStateChanged event handler, 576

document.getElementById method, 48,
        538
DomainContext property, 916
DomainDataSource control, 906, 915, 918–
        920
DomainService class, 906, 915
DoReceive JavaScript functions, 561
downloading
    resources, 641–642
    Ruby, 102
DownloadStringAsync() method, 641, 666
drawing
    with geometries (Expression Blend),
        159–163
    with paths (Expression Blend), 152–158
    with shapes (Expression Blend), 146–152
    within web browsers, 216–219
drop shadows, 255
DropShadowEffect, 256
Duration element (CSPL), 834
dynamic 3-D transformations, 230–231
Dynamic Language Runtime SDK
        (Silverlight), 101–102
dynamic user interfaces
    creating with animations, 173–176
dynamically loading XAML
    from JavaScript, 47–49
    from managed code, 52–53

■E
easing functions, 247–254
    built-in, 247
    custom, 248–254
EasingFunctionBase, 247
EditorBrowsableAttribute, 509, 510
Effect property, 255
ElasticEase, 247
elements
    applying borders to, 167–172
    binding across, 323–330
Ellipse objects, 146
EllipseGeometry, 159
embedded resources, managing
    Silverlight applications, 96–98

enableCacheVisualation parameter, 243
EnableClientAccess attribute, 898, 905
enableFramerateCounter parameter, 517
enableGPUAcceleration parameter, 244
enableHtmlAccess parameter, 517, 579
encoding, 869
encoding markers with Expression
    Encoder, 837–838
EnterSound behavior, 271
Entry element (CSPL), 834
error information, retrieving, 331
events, adding in Visual Studio 2008, 25–27
exceptions
    catching with background thread, 76
    managing unhandled, 74
Exclude Overlap(Combine menu), 150
Expander custom control (example), 471–
    482
ExponentialEase, 247
Expression Blend 3, 6, 13, 18
    brush editor, 125
    control behavior in, 507–512
    creating resource dictionaries in, 112–
    113
    creating UI in, 20–27
    Data panel, 260–267
    designer support in, 18–19
    designing control templates with, 365–
    367
    drawing with geometries, 159–163
    drawing with paths, 152–158
    drawing with shapes, 146–152
    EastingFunction tab, 248
    features, 21–22
    importing from Adobe Photoshop and
    Illustrator, 19
    installing, 7
    navigating, 21
    opening Silverlight application in, 20
    resources support in, 92–94
    Resources tab, 93
    Sketchflow, 20
    time line recording mode, 23
    visual editing tools, 122
    working with colors and gradients in,
    121–128
    working with design-time data in, 259–
    269
Expression Blend Asset Library toolbar, 137
Expression Design
    Export dialog box, 120
    importing from, 118–120
    UI, 118
Expression Encoder, encoding markers
    with, 837–838
Expression Gallery, 4
Extensible Application Markup Language.
    See XAML

■F
family spending chart (example), 311
FileIndex property, 62
files
    opening local from Silverlight
    applications, 61–63
    saving, anywhere on system, 114–115
Fill property, 159
FilterDescriptor, 920
FilterIndex property, 61
FindElementsInHostCoordinates()
    method, 483
FindName method, 42–48, 515–516
Firefox, 2
floating-point values, 193
FlyoutView.html, 567–569
FlyoutView.xaml, 570
font rendering, 4
fooGetData method (JavaScript), 538
Foreground property, 97, 128
Form class, 132
FormatDecimal namespace, 226
Frame class, 590
frame rate, 854
FrameRate property, 867
frames, 854
frames displayed per second (fps), 854
FrameworkElement class, 117, 361

FrameworkElement.GetBindingExpression() method, 348
FrameworkElement.SetBinding() method, 275, 419
full-screen mode, Silverlight implementing, 528–533
with uniform scale applied, 532
without resizing content, 529
FullScreenChanged event, 531

■G

gadget development model, 570
gadget JavaScript API, 575
Gadget.xml file, 582–583
GadgetApp.xaml.cs file, 577–580
gadgets, Vista Sidebar. *See* Vista Sidebar gadget
GenerateEditingElement() Method, 419–424
GenerateElement() method, 419–422
generic.xaml file, 453
geometry objects, drawing with (Expression Blend), 159–163
GeometryGroup, 159–160
GET verb, 624
GetBindingExpression() method, 348
GetColor() method, 539
GetData() method, 412, 469
getElementById() method, 49, 547
GetImageNames() method, 665
GetLocationList() method, 774
GetManifestResourceNames() method, 451
GetManifestResourceStream() method, 394, 451
GetProductDetail() method, 606, 630
GetProductHeaders() method, 615, 630
GetProductPageAsync() method, 437
GetProductsAsync() method, 412
GetProductsCountAsync() method, 437
GetResourceStream() method, 666
GetSampleAsync() method, 886
GetTemplateChild() method, 454–455
GetUserStoreForApplication() method, 55

Global Offset X value, 230
Global Offset Y value, 230
GPU acceleration, 243
gradient brushes, 123–124
GradientBrush, 123
gradients and colors, 121–128, 144
graphic primitive classes, 117–118
Grid control, 48, 133, 140–144
Grid.ColumnSpan, 140
Grid.RowSpan, 140
Gridobject, 133
GridSplitter control, 141
Group Into menu (Expression Blend), 156

■H

handwriting recognition, 216
Hard Rock Cafe, 7
hardware acceleration, 243–245
Height property, 143
HierarchicalDataTemplate, 721
High Level Shading Language (HLSL), 255
HLSL pixel shaders, 255
hosting Silverlight 3
in ASP.NET, 520
in HTML on all platforms, 515–518
HTML Bridge, 537, 547, 560
HTML test page file, 518
HtmlDocument class, 538
HtmlDocument object, 537
HtmlElement class, 538
HtmlPage class, 538
HtmlPage object, 537
HtmlPage.Window.Invoke() method, 560
HtmlUtility class, 538
HtmlWindow class, 538
HTTP (Hypertext Transfer Protocol)
accessing resources over, 641–666
cross-domain access and, 700
exchanging messages with HTTP endpoints, 635–636
exchanging XML (POX) messages over, 623
WebClient and HTTP endpoints, 642

HttpWebRequest/HttpWebResponse
    types, 623–625, 635
HyperlinkButton objects, 591
IApplicationLifetimeAware interface, 105–
    106
IApplicationService interfacc, 105–106
IEasingFunction interface, 247

■I

iframe, 15
Image control
    Clip property, 160–161
    nested, 97
ImageBrush, 126–127
images
    bitmap, dynamic creation of, 235–242
    UI with image selected, 97
ImagesCollection type, 449–451
ImageUri property setter, 394
importing, from Expression Design, 118–
    120
inheritance, style, 361
InitData() function, 437
initialization parameters, 110, 561
InitializeComponent() method, 12, 427
initParams parameter, 517, 573
InkPresenter control, 216–219
INotifyCollectionChanged interface, 293
INotifyPropertyChanged sample
    implementation, 292–293
installation and update control, 32
Intellisense, attached properties in, 134
interactivity, reusing across UI clements
    and applications, 270–272
Internet applications, rich, 4–5
Internet Explorer 8 Web Slice, embedding
    Silverlight in, 583–588
Internet Information Services (IIS), 600
Intersect option (Combine menu), 149
InvalidateMeasure() method, 447
invocation patterns, asynchronous, 624
InvokedFromHtmlButtonClick() method,
    549
invoking WCF web services, 601–604

IronPython, programming SilverLight
    with, 101–105
IronRuby, programming SilverLight with,
    101–105
IsBusy property, 642
IsMuted property, 761
isolated storage, 54–61
IsolatedStorage file system, 66
IsolatedStorageFile object, 55
IsolatedStorageFile.IncreaseQuotaTo()
    method, 55
IsolatedStorageFileStream class, 55
IsolatedStorageSettings class, 55
ItemContainerStyle (ListBox), 98, 381
ItemSource property (ListBox), 34
ItemsPanelTemplate definition, 449–451
ItemsSource properties, 390
IValueConverter interface, 310

■J

JavaScript
    calling managed code methods from,
        546–560
    development model, 893
    dynamically loading XAML from, 47–49
    method, calling from managed code,
        537–545
JavaScript Object Notation (JSON), 31
    configuring WCF to use, 637
    DataContractJsonSerializer type, 637
    defined, 636
    exchanging messages with HTTP
        endpoints, 635–636
    representation of ProductDetail
        instance, 636
    serialization and deserialization code-
        behind, 638–641
    service contract modified for, 637–638
Join() method, 689
JScript, programming SilvcrLight with,
    101–105

■K

keyboard input

capturing, 209–213
setting Silverlight control focus for, 521–522
Keyboard.Modifiers property, 210
KeyDown event handlers, 209–210
KeyEventArgs, 209
keyframes, 174
adding to create animations, 24
animating UI elements with, 181–186
creating, 24
KeySpline Bezier curve, 182–183
KeySpline property, 181
KeyUp event handlers, 209–210

■ L

Language-Integrated Query (LINQ). *See* LINQ
large projects, managing resources in, 111–114
layout container, creating custom, 439–452
layout system, 133–136, 141, 144
LayoutRoot, 235
layouts, scrollable content for, 165–166
LbxItemRoot_MouseEnter() method, 397
Line tool, 152–155
linear gradient example, 125
linear interpolation method, 181
LinearGradientBrush, 92
LineGeometry, 159
line-of-business (LOB) applications, 5, 17
adding .NET RIA Services to, 930–931
adding data to, 906–915
adding data validation to, 924–929
building, 893–936
controlling access to domain services in, 933–936
creating framework, 894–906
enhanced data access, 915–924
LinksStackPanel object, 591
LINQ
accessing XML data with, 69–71
queries, 852
LINQ to XML
documentation, 600

parsing XML data with, 66
Linux, running Silverlight 3 on, 29
ListBox control, 97
DataContext property, 38
ItemSource property, 34
page hosting, 451–452, 461–464
page populating photo, 465–469
using WrapPanel for layout, 448–449
ListBoxItem
control template, 381–386
UI, customizing default, 381–390
Load Form Data button, 56
Load() method, 52
LoadComponent() method, 428
Loaded event, 174–175
loadGadget event, 575
LoadGadgetSettings() method, 582
LoadingRowDetails event, 402, 412
LoadThumbnails() method, 665
LOB applications. *See* line-of-business (LOB) applications
local files, opening from Silverlight application, 61–63
local installation support, 704–732
local: prefix, 277
local-connection feature, 733–751
locally installed applications, 710
LocalMessageReceiver class, 733
LocalMessageReceiver.Listen() method, 734
LocalMessageSender.SendAsync() method, 734
Locations.xml, 762
LoginControl.xaml, 899
long-running operations, canceling, 642

■ M

Mac, running Silverlight 3 on, 28
MacDonald, Matthew, 359
MainPage.xaml, 10–13, 25, 27, 33, 589
Make Clipping Path option, 153
Make Compound Path option, 153
Make Control function, 151
Make Into UserControl dialog, 151

Manage() method, 697
managed code
    calling JavaScript method from, 537–545
    dynamically loading XAML from, 52–53
    method, calling from JavaScript, 546–560
    setting web page background color from, 549
managed decoder, building, 868–892
manifest file, 14
ManualResetEvent class, 75
Margin property, 136, 140
marker-enabled player XAML, 843–848
markers
    defined, 837
    encoding with Expression Encoder, 837–838
    MediaElement and, 839
    player code modification to support, 848–853
markup extensions, 276
Matrix3D class, 223
Matrix3DProjection class, 223
matrixes, 3-D, 224
MatrixTransform class, 192
maxFramerate parameter, 517
MBR (multiple bit rate) video files, 791
Measure pass, 136
Measure() method, 446
MeasureOverride() method, 440, 446–447
media element (SSPL), 832
media files
    adding markers to, 837–854
    building managed decoder for, 868–892
    internal structure of, 868
    sampling, 872–873
    starting and stopping recording, 881
    types supported by Silverlight, 869
    using playlists to package, 831–837
media menus, adding to video player, 797–806
media play, controlling, 759
media streams
    initializing, 870–872

stream switching, 873
media support, 3
MediaButtonsPanel control, 771
    code, 787–790, 827–831
    control template for, 785–787
    XAML code, 823–827
MediaElement, 128
    acquiring media with, 759
    basics, 754
    default behavior of, 869
    markers and, 839
    states, 760
MediaElement.SetSource() method, 869
MediaLocationProvider.svc, 762
MediaMenuData type, 763–771
MediaSlider control, 771, 857, 860, 867
    code, 778–783
    code with streaming changes, 816–823
    custom, 775–778
    template, 775–778
    XAML code, 812–816
MediaSlider_PropertyChanged() handler, 868
MediaStreamAttributeKeys enumeration, 872
McdiaStreamSource 869–870, 882, 886, 887
memory buffers, 879
menus, data type for single menu item, 393–394
merged resource dictionaries, 111–114
MergedDictionaries, 91
messages
    receiving, 734
    sending, 734–735
metadata, 868
MetadataUpload.aspx (photo management), 645–646
mexHttpBinding, 605
Microsoft .NET RIA Services. See .NET RIA Services

Microsoft Advanced Systems Format (ASF), 869
Microsoft AJAX Library, 543–544

Microsoft Developer Network (MSDN) Premium subscriber, 7
Microsoft Internet Information Services (IIS), 600
Microsoft Media Server (MMS) protocol, 753
minRuntimeVersion parameter, 517
mms protocol identifier, 796
mobile devices, 2
Mode property, 291, 305
Moonlight plug-in (Linux), 1, 29
motion blur, 255
MouseEnter/MouseLeave animations, 175
MouseLeftButtonDown event, 217–218
MouseLeftButtonUp event, 217
MouseMove event, 217
MP4 File Format, 869
MPEG-4 File Format version 2, 869
MSDN library, 600
multi-animation storyboard, 185
Multipurpose Internet Mail Extensions (MIME) types, 623
Multiselect property (OpenFileDialog class), 61–62

■N

namescope, XAML, 43
namespaces
    available in Silverlight, 3
    importing, 33, 39
Navigation Application template, 224
Navigation Framework, 588–597
nested containers, 144
nested Image control, 97
.NET Framework, 2, 31
.NET libraries, Silverlight, 691–697
.NET RIA Services, 5
    adding data to LOB applications using, 906–915
    adding to Silverlight applications, 930–931
    building LOB applications with, 894–906
    code-generation functionality, 895

data validation support in, 925–929
installing, 7–8
isolating services using, 933–936
network availability
    API, 704–732
    detecting, 710
network resources, accessing, 700
NetworkAddressChanged event, 710
networking APIs, 599
networks, streaming video and, 790–791
New Silverlight Application dialog, 9
noncollection types, change notification for, 291
Notepad, 6
NoteTaker application, 711–732
notifications for bound data, 291–308
NotifyCollectionChangedEventArgs, 300

■O

Object class, 117
<object> tags, 14–15, 515–518
Objects and Timeline window, 182
objects, transforming, 191–193
offline mode, 704–732
OnApplyTemplate() method, 454–455, 460, 473, 511
on-demand publishing points, 794
on-demand stream, playing, 823
OnDemandStreams.xml, 796, 835–837
onLoad parameter, 517
OnProdHdrUpdReqStreamAcquired() method, 640
OnProductHeadersReceived() method, 635
onSilverlightError function, 516
onSilverlightLoad event, 49
OnWebRequestCompleted JavaScript method, 545
OpacityMask, 123
OpenFileDialog class, 61–62
OpenMediaAsync() method, 870, 886
OpenRead() method, 63
OpenReadAsync() method, 642
OpenReadCompleted handler, 666
OpenText() method, 63

OpenWriteAsync() method, 642, 666
OperationContractAttribute, 606
Organization class file, 36–38
Orientation property, 139, 447
out-of-browser experience, 5
Out-of-Browser Settings dialog, 704–706

■P

Padding property, 136, 140
Page UserControl object, 570
PagedProductsGrid user control example,
    430–437
Paint.NET, 575
Panel class, 132
param tags, 517
parameters, initialization, 561
Participant types (chat application), 691–
    697
Path Context menu suboptions, 153
Path Mini-Language, 154–156, 159, 162
Path objects, 146
    adding node to existing, 158
    closing, 158
    defaulting to Path Mini-Language
        syntax, 163
    drawing with, 152–158
    with GeometryGroup, 160
    shaped as a ring via Combine, 151
PathGeometry object, 159, 162
Pen tool, 152–158
Pencil tool, 152, 158
persisting data, on client, 54–61
perspective transforms feature, 223–235
photo management application
    code-behind for, 658–666
    data types in client application, 648–
        652
    MetadataUpload.aspx, 645–646
    page XAML, 652–658
    PhotoUpload.aspx, 646–648
    user interface, 643
PhotoMetadata data-contract type, 652
PhotoUpload.aspx (photo management),
    646–648

PIP display, 774
Pixel Shader, 4, 254–259
Pixel Shader Effects library, 257
PixelShaderConstantCallback method, 257
plain old XML (POX), 31. *See also* POX
    service
PlaneProjection class, 224
platform key codes, 209
Playlist Editor, opening, 832
playlists, to package media
    BroadcastStreams.xml, new entries in,
        835–837
    client-side playlists (CSPL), 834
    OnDemandStreams.xml, new entries
        in, 835–837
    overviewG, 831
    Playlist Editor, opening, 832
    server-side playlists (SSPL), 832
PlayProgressUpdate_Tick() handler
    method, 868
PlayReady Content Protection, 4
PlaySoundAction behavior, 271
plug-ins, exchanging data between
    multiple, 560–562
PointAnimation, 176
PolicyServer type (chat application), 697–
    700
PopulateMediaMenu() method, 774
Popup type, 390
    content creation, 392
    creating and initializing, 390
    positioning, 391–392
pop-ups, displaying information in, 390–
    402
port requirements, 670
POST verb, 624
PowerEase, 247
POX service
    code-behind listing, 630–635
    contract for, 625–626
    service implementation for, 626–635
PrepareCellForEdit() Method, 419–420
presentation framework, 31
presenter controls, 368-370

Pro LINQ: Language Integrated Query in C# 2008 (Apress), 69, 600
Pro Silverlight 2 in C# 2008 (Apress), 359
Pro WCF: Practical Microsoft SOA Implementation (Apress), 600
ProcessMessage() method, 689, 697
ProductHeader objects, 606
ProductHeaderDataGrid, 619
ProductHeaderDataGrid_SelectionChanged() method, 622
ProgressBar control (example), 456–469
ProgressChanged event, 75
progressive download, 759
Projection property, UIElement base class, 223
Projects tab (Expression Blend), 23
properties
    control, 508–509
    customizing control, 360-364
    dependency, 276, 428–430
property updates, controlling, 347–357
prototype application design, 272–273
publishing points, setting up (WMS), 793–796
PUT verb, 625

■Q

QuadraticEase, 247
QuarticEase, 247
QuinticEase, 247

■R

radial gradient example, 126
radientBrush, 121
radio button control
    with complex content, 369
    template, 375–379
radioactive ball animation, 210
RadiusX value, 147
RadiusY value, 147
Rattz, Joseph C., 69
ReadFormData_Click event, 56
Real Time Streaming Protocol (RTSP), 753
ReceiveAsync() method, 669

ReceiveMessage() method, 689, 697
receiver registration, 733
Record Keyframe button (Expression Blend), 24
rectangle objects, 127, 139, 146
Rectangle tool, 137, 146
Rectangle_MouseMove() method, 321
ReduceScaleTransform, 532
RefreshNotesView() method, 731
RegisterScriptableObject() method, 547
RelativeSource property, 323-324, 456
Release Clipping Path option, 153
Release Compound Path option, 153
remote domain, 700
remote streams, reading/writing, 642
rendering capabilities, enhanced, 4
RenderTransform property, 461
ReportOpenMediaCompleted() method, 871, 873, 886
ReportProgress method, 75
Representational State Transfer (REST) services, 31, 600
RequestData() method, 561
RequestFormat property, 637
RequestProductHeaders() method, 635
request-response, 735
resizing capabilities, 144
resizing UI, 530
resource dictionaries, 3, 91, 112–113
resource keys, 111
resource referencing, 429
ResourceDictionary objects, 90, 111
ResourceDictionary.MergedDictionaries XAMP element, 112
ResourceNames (ListBox control), 97
resources
    accessing over HTTP, 641–666
    defined at StackPanel level, 95
    defining, in order of dependency, 92
    downloading/uploading, 641–642
    embedded, managing, 96–98
    Expression Blend 3 support for, 92–94
    long-running operations, canceling, 642
    managing XAML, 90–95

managing, in large projects, 111–114
remote streams, reading/writing, 642
uploading, 641–642
WebClient and HTTP endpoints, 642
Response property, 735
ResponseFormat property, 637
RetrieveXmlCompleted callback method, 87
Rich Internet Applications (RIA) Services, 5, 893–894
RotateTransform class, 191–192, 197–198, 460
rotation, applying, 224
RotationY parameter, 230
RotationZ parameter, 230
RotatorDemoControl class, 328, 330
rounded corners
applying to controls, 167
for TextBox control, 170–171
RoutedEvents, 175
RowDetailsTemplate property, 402, 407
RowDetailsVisibilityChanged event, 402
RowDetailsVisibilityMode property, 402
rows
creating, 140, 142
displaying details in DataGrid, 402–412
sizing, 141
RTSP using TCP (RTSPT), 753
Ruby, downloading, 102

■S
SAMI (Synchronized Accessible Media Interchange) specification, 843
Save Form Data button, 56
SaveFileDialog object, 114–115, 242
SaveFormData_Click event, 56
SaveGadgetSettings() method, 582
ScaleTransform class, 191–193, 197, 529
SCCOL namespace, 40
ScreenRecorder class, 874, 879, 881
scriptable methods, 545
ScriptableMember attribute, 546
ScriptableMethodAttribute, 560
ScriptableType attribute, 546

scriptKey parameter, 547
ScriptManager control, 543, 548
scrollable content, for layouts, 165–166
ScrollBar.ValueChanged events, 482
ScrollBars, 482, 492
ScrollViewer control, 154, 482–492
search engine optimization (SEO), 5
Search text box (Expression Blend), 21
SeekAsync() method, 887
Selection tool, 144
SelectionChanged handler, 308
SendAsync() method, 668
sender parameter, 209
seq element (SSPL), 832
SerializeMessage() method, 673
server.bat batch command, 104
ServerConnectionManager (chat application), 690–697
server-side playlists (SSPL), 832
service contracts
modified for JSON, 637–638
for POX service (example), 625–626
for WCF web services, 605, 606, 643–645
service operations, invoking, 601–604
Service Reference Settings dialog, 602
ServiceContractAttribute, 606
service-oriented architecture (SOA), 599
ServiceReferences.ClientConfig file, 605
SetBinding() method, 275, 282, 419
SetBookXMLData() method, 545
SetStyleAttribute() method, 549
SetSubMenuPosition() method, 397
SettingsView.html, 567, 569
SettingsView.js, 582
SettingsView.xaml, 570, 580
SetTopMenuPosition() method, 397
ShaderEffect base class, 257
shaders, 4
Shape objects, 123
shapes
combining, 147–149
drawing with (Expression Blend), 146–152
Shapes namespace, 117
ShowDialog method, 62–63

Silverlight 2, 3
Silverlight 3. *See also* Silverlight
    applications
  browser control, 515–533
  Class Library project, 8
  configuring WCF web services for, 604–
    605
  creating new application, 8–17
  developer/designer workflow, 17–20
  Dynamic Language Runtime SDK, 101–
    102
  embedding in Internet Explorer 8 Web
    Slice, 583–588
  embedding in Vista Sidebar gadget,
    567–583
  enhancements in, 3–5, 32
    browser support, 5
    data support, 5
    Internet applications, 4–5
    line-of-business, 4–5
    media, 3
    out-of-browser capabilities, 5
    rendering capabilities, 4
  Expression Blend 3, creating UI in, 20–
    27
  hosting in ASP.NET, 520
  hosting in HTML on all platforms, 515–
    518
  initial project layout, 10
  installation, 2
  installation/update control, 32
  installing services and controls, 7–8
  introduction to, 1–6
  layout system, 133–136, 141, 144
  namespaces available in, 3
  .NET framework for, 31
  .NET libraries, 599, 691–697
  parameters, 517
  presentation framework, 31
  RecipesGadget project, 567–568
  running on Linux, 29
  running on Mac, 28
  setting up development/designer
    environment, 6–7

Team Foundation Server (TFS),
    accessing projects from, 27–28
  transforms in, 192
  WPF and, 6
Silverlight Application template, 9
Silverlight applications
  accessing XML data with LINQ, 69–71
  accessing XML data with XmlReader,
    66–69
  adding .NET RIA Services to, 930–931
  adding custom classes to, 32–38
  adding custom controls to, 39–41
  controlling access to domain services
    in, 933–936
  creating application services for, 105–
    110
  embedded resources, managing, 96–98
  exchanging data between, 732–751
  executing work on background threads
    with updates, 75–85
  installation, customizing, 708
  local installation of, 704–732
  managing unhandled exceptions in, 74
  mechanics of, 31–32
  navigation features, 588–597
  opening local files from, 61–63
  updating UI from background threads,
    85–89
Silverlight Applications tab, 15–17
Silverlight Business Application template,
    894, 897, 899
Silverlight Navigation Application project
    template, 9, 588–597, 893
Silverlight Toolkit, installing, 7, 8
Simple Object Access Protocol SOAP, 31
  configuring WCF for non-SOAP
    endpoints, 624–625
  vs. POX-style message exchange, 623
SimpleControl, 40–41
  .xaml file, 41
SineEase, 247
site of origin, 700
SketchFlow, 20, 272–273
SkewTransform class, 191–193, 197
Slider control, 775

sliderVolumeControl, 771
SMIL (Synchronized Multimedia
    Integration Language) 2.0
    specification, 832
Smooth Streaming, 3
SMPTE timecode format, 854–868
SMPTE VC-1 high-definition video
    standard, 753
SmpteFrameRate enumeration, 854
SMPTETimeCode property, 868
SOAP. *See* Simple Objec Access Protocol
socket-resource element, 704
sockets, TCP
    API in Silverlight, 667–669
    to communicate over TCP, 667
sockets-based communication, 701
SolidColorBrush, 121–123
source control, accessing, 27–28
source properties, 275
Source property (media), 754
sourcePropertyPath, 276
special effects, visual, 254–259
splashScreenSource parameter, 517
SQL Server 2008 Express, 360, 647
StackPanels, 44, 133
    positioning UI elements with, 136–139
    resource defined at, 95
star sizing, 141
StartService() method, 105
Static3DTransform XAML file, 226, 229
StaticResource extension, 91, 144, 175, 277
StatusEllipse_MouseLeftButtonDown
    event, 78
Storyboard class, 174
storyboards
    defined, 21
    multi-animation, 185
streaming video. *See also* video
    adding media menus to player, 797–806
    adding support for, 790–831
    BroadcastStreams.xml, 796–797
    buffering video, 823
    defined, 759
    maximizing performance of, 243–245

MediaButtonsPanel Control code, 823–
    831
MediaSlider code with streaming
    changes, 816–823
MediaSlider control XAML, 812–816
network considerations, 790–791
OnDemandStreams.xml, 796
overview, 790
playing broadcast stream, 823
playing on-demand stream, 823
publishing points, setting up (WMS),
    793–796
streaming player code-behind, 806–812
streaming player XAML, 797–806
Windows Media Services (WMS), 791–
    793
StreamReader class, 63
streams, remote, 642
Stretch property, 755
Stroke property, 159
stroke, defined, 216
Style dependency property, 361
styles, 98
    customizing and applying to controls,
        360–364
    defined, 360
    inheritance, 361
    scoping, 361
stylus, 216
Subtract option (Combine menu), 149
switch element (SSPL), 832
Symbian, 2
SynchronizeOfflineStore() method, 732
System.ComponentModel.BackgroundWor
    ker class, 75
System.IO.IsolatedStorage namespace, 55
System.Linq namespace, 69
System.Net.Sockets.Socket type, 667
System.Runtime.Serialization.Json, 637
System.Threading namespace, 86
System.Threading.Thread classes, 75
System.Web.UI.SilverlightControls.Silverli
    ght control, 14
System.Windows.Browser namespace, 537

System.Windows.Browser namespace
    classes, 538
System.Windows.Controls namespace, 359,
    425, 754
System.Windows.Controls.ContentControl
    type, 369
System.Windows.Controls.Panel abstract
    class, 440
System.Windows.Data.Binding type, 275
System.Windows.Data.IValueConverter,
    309
System.Windows.Markup namespace, 52
System.Windows.Media.MediaStreamSour
    ce class, 869–870
System.Windows.VisualStateManager
    type, 471
System.Xml namespace, 66, 69

■T

tablet computers, 216
target properties, 275
TargetName, 174
TargetProperty, 174
targetPropertyName, 276
TCP (Transmission Control Protocol), 667
TCP sockets, 667–669
Team Foundation Client, 7
Team Foundation Server (TFS), 20, 27–28
template bindings, 367–370
TemplateBinding, 456
TemplatedParent, 324, 456
templates, 9. *See also specific templates*
    applying custom, to DataGrid cells,
        412–418
    binding with data templates, 283–290
    control, 364–368
TemplateVisualStateAttribute, 470–471
TestWeb web project, 14
text animation, 4
TextBlock objects, 133–136
TextBox control
    applying borders to, 168–169
    brushes available for, 123
    rounded corners for, 170–171

TFS (Team Foundation Server). *See* Team
    Foundation Server (TFS)
threads, background
    executing work on, 75–85
    updating UI from, 85–89
TimeCode class, 854
TimeCode.FromTicks() method, 856
TimeCode.ParseFramerate() method, 856
TimeCode.ValidateSmpte12MTimeCode()
    method, 856
timecodes
    overview, 855
    Silverlight and, 855–856
timed content, displaying with markers
    Captions.xml sample, 839–843
    Commercials.xml sample, 853–854
    encoding markers with Expression
        Encoder, 837–838
    marker-enabled player XAML, 843–848
    MediaElement and markers, 839
    overview, 837
    player code modification for marker
        support, 848–853
TimelineMarker class, 839
Tooltips, validation error, 493–497
Transform classes, 192
TransformGroup objects, 192–193
transforming objects, 191–193
transforms
    dynamic 3-D, 230–231
    in Silverlight 3, 192
    perspective, 223–235
TransformToVisual() method, 392, 492
TranslateTransform class, 191–193
TreeNodeData Data Class, 720
triggers, 174–175, 270
TwoWay binding, 331
type converters, 91
TypeConverter class, 321, 423

■U

UI elements
    adding 3-D effects to, 223–235
    animating with keyframes, 181–186

manipulating to produce visual effects, 191–193
positioning with Canvas object, 132–136
positioning with Grid panel, 140–144
positioning with StackPanels, 136–139
UIElement class, 43, 52, 117, 209, 223, 255
UndockcdView.xaml, 570
unhandled exceptions, 74
Unite option, 148, 154
UnloadingRowDetails event, 402
Update Data button, 539
UpdateProductDetail() method, 630
UpdateProductHeaders() method, 606, 615, 630, 635
updates
    controlling in data binding, 347–357
    UI, from background threads, 85–89
UpdateSource() method, 348
UpdateSourceTrigger attribute, 347
uploading resources, 641–642
UploadStringAsync() method, 641
UriMapper object, 593
<UserControl> tag, 32, 43
user controls
    adding, 426
    basics, 425
    creating composite, 425–436
    loading XAML for, 427–428
    PagedProductsGrid user control, 430–434
    structure, 426–427
    test page hosting user control, 437–439
    Visual Studio-generated startup code for, 427–428
user experience, enhanced, 4
user interface (UI), 6
    binding application data to, 275–283
    creating, in Expression Blend 3, 20–27
    customizing binding validation for, 492–507
    data entry UI example (XAML), 300–305
    data-editing, 915–924
    development workflow, 20
    dynamic, creating with animations, 173–176

implementing full-screen, 528–533
photo management application, 643
pop-ups in, 390
replacing default (controls), 364–381
UI consuming products data from web services, 615–623
updating from background threads, 85–89
using shapes to draw, 146–152
working with design-time data, 259–269
UserControl class, 570, 590
using statements, 32–33

V
validating input for bound data, 331–346
validation errors
    notification of, 331
    summary of, 332
    tooltip, 493–497
ValidationSummary control, 332, 343, 492, 497–498, 502–506
validationToolTip, 496
ValidationTooltipTemplate, 492
value conversion, implementing, 310, 319–321
value converters, 418
values, converting during data binding, 309–321
VBR (variable bit rate) video, 791
vector-graphic primitives, 146, 152
video. *See also* streaming video
    adding markers to, 837–854
    adding to pages, 753–758
    displaying elapsed time in, 854–868
    frame rate of, 854
    frames, 854
    sampling, 872–873
    seeking specific time point in, 854–868
    starting and stopping recording, 881
    stream switching, 873
Video Over IP: A Practical Guide to Technology and Applications (Focal Press), 791
video player, creating

acquiring media with MediaElement, 759

controlling media play, 759

installing sample code, 761–762

MediaButtonsPanel control code, 785–790

MediaElement states, 760

MediaMenuData type declaration, 763–771

MediaSlider control code, 775–783

overview, 758

player code, 763

player code-behind, 771–775

user interface XAML, 764

volume, 761

VideoBrush, 127–128, 754–755

Visibility property (controls), 309

Vista Sidebar gadget, embedding Silverlight in, 567–583

visual effects

manipulating UI elements to produce, 191–193

pixel shader, 254–259

visual state management (controls), 370–375

Visual State Manager (VSM), 370

visual states, 470–482, 816

Visual Studio 2008

Add Service Reference dialog, 601

adding events in, 25–27

Attach to Process dialog box, 572

generated service proxy, 602

installing, 7

Service Pack 1, 6

service reference settings dialog, 602

Silverlight 3 designer, 17

Visual Studio Conversion Wizard, 930

Visual Studio debugger, 346

VisualStateManager class, 374

VisualStateManager.GoToState() method, 470–471

VisualTreeHelper class, 483

VisualTreeHelper.FindElementsInHostCo ordinates() method, 492

volume, video player, 761

<vsm:VisualState> element, 374–375

■W

Waggoner, Ben, 791

WCF (Windows Communication Foundation) services, 216, 360

adding references to invoke, 601–604

as data source for recipes, 360

configuring for non-SOAP endpoints, 624–625

configuring for Silverlight, 604–605

configuring to use JSON, 637

consuming, 601–623

data contracts for, 606–610

documentation, 600

in sample code, 600

service and data contracts for, 605–606, 643–645

service implementation, 610–615

UI consuming products data from, 615–623

Web Service Definition Language (WSDL), 606

web services, 599–600

web sites, for downloading

Dynamic Language Runtime SDK (Silverlight), 101

Expression Blend 3 SP1, 7

Expression Encoder, 837

Microsoft AJAX Library, 544

Moonlight plug-in (Linux), 29

Ruby, 102

Silverlight 3 plug-in, 28

SQL Server 2008 Express, 360, 647

WMS 2008, 791

web sites, for further information

animation classes in code, 186

CSPL syntax, 834

dependency properties, 134

Expression Blend 3 SP1 training, 27

Expression Blend tutorial and training, 119

Grid object configuration options, 142

GridSplitter control, 141

handwriting recognition processing, 216

Hard Rock Cafe, 7

installing WMS 2008, 791

JSON, 636

Macintosh-specific platform key codes, 209

Moonlight project, 1

MSDN library, 600, 630

OpacityMask, 123

RoutedEvents, 175

SAMI, 843

Silverlight documentation, 359

Silverlight Tools for Visual Studio 2008, 7

SMIL, 832, 843

SSPL syntax, 832

streaming from cameras, 793

transformation matrix format, 192

unsupported features in SSPL and CSPL, 834

WCF documentation, 600

Windows Media Metafile reference, 834

Windows-specific platform key codes, 209

WMS documentation, 796

WebClient API, 641–642

WebClient.OpenReadCompleted event handler, 110

WebDataService class, 906

WebGetAttribute/WebInvokeAttribute types, 625, 637

WebHttpBinding, 625

WebRequest class, 86

Width property, 143

Windows 7 Sidebar gadget, embedding Silverlight in, 567–583

Windows Communication Foundation (WCF). *See* WCF (Windows Communication Foundation) services.

Windows Forms applications, 132

Windows Media Audio (.wma) files, 869

Windows Media Metafile reference, 834

Windows Media Services (WMS), 791–793

Windows Media Video (.wmv) files, 753, 869

Windows Mobile, 2

Windows Presentation Foundation (WPF), 4, 77, 133

Windows Sidebar, embedding Silverlight within, 567–583

WMS HTTP server control protocol plug-in, 791

worker_DoWork member() function, 75

worker_ProgressChanged event handler, 77

worker_RunWorkerCompleted event handler, 77

WPF Futures CodePlex project, 255

WrapPanel implementation, 441–452

WrappedImage type, 652

WriteableBitmap object, 235–242

WriteObject() method, 640

■X, Y, Z

XAML (Extensible Application Markup Language)

browser applications (XBAPs), 6

custom classes and, 33

data entry UI example, 300

defined, 118

design advantages of, 18–19

documents, coad to locate root of, 783–785

dynamically loading from JavaScript, 47–49

dynamically loading from managed code, 52–53

elements, binding across, 323–330

loading for user control, 427–428

managing resources, 90–95

namescopes, 43

XAML browser applications (XBAPs), 6

XAML Silverlight Canvas, 132–136

XamlReader object, 52

XamlReader.Load() method, 52

XAP file, 10

x:Class attribute, 38, 427

x:Key attribute, 92

xC:Name property, 43
XDocument class, 70
XDocument.Load (XmlReader), 70
XDocument.Parse() method, 666
XmalXapResolver, 66
XML (Extensible Markup Language)
    exchanging XML (POX) messages over
        HTTP, 623
    XmlDocument type, 626
    XmlSerializerFormatAttribute()method,
        626

XML data
    accessing with LINQ, 69–71
    accessing with XmlReader, 66–69
XmlDocument class, 70
xmlns namespace import statement, 33
XmlReader class, 66–69
XmlReaderSettings class, 66
XmlUrlResolver class, 66
XmlXapResolver class, 66, 67, 7